HISTORY OF THE WORLD IN PHOTOGRAPHS

HISTORY OF THE WORLD IN PHOTOGRAPHS

gettyimages®

Black Dog & Leventhal Publishers
New York

Published by Black Dog & Leventhal Publishers, Inc.
151 West 19th Street
New York, NY 10011

Distributed by
Workman Publishing Company
225 Varick Street
New York, NY 10014

Manufactured in Singapore

Cover design by Elizabeth Driesbach

ISBN-13: 978-1-57912-583-7
h g f e d c b a

Paperback bookclucb ISBN-13: 978-1-6037-6-089-8
h g f e d c b a

This book was created in association with Endeavour London Ltd.
info@endeavourlondon.com

endeavour

Right: Senator John F. Kennedy is given a rousing ovation during his presidential campaign.

Previous page: A U.S. Army cinematographer filming a U.S. Nieuport 28 biplane taking off during the summer counter-offensive.

KENNEDY

CONTENTS

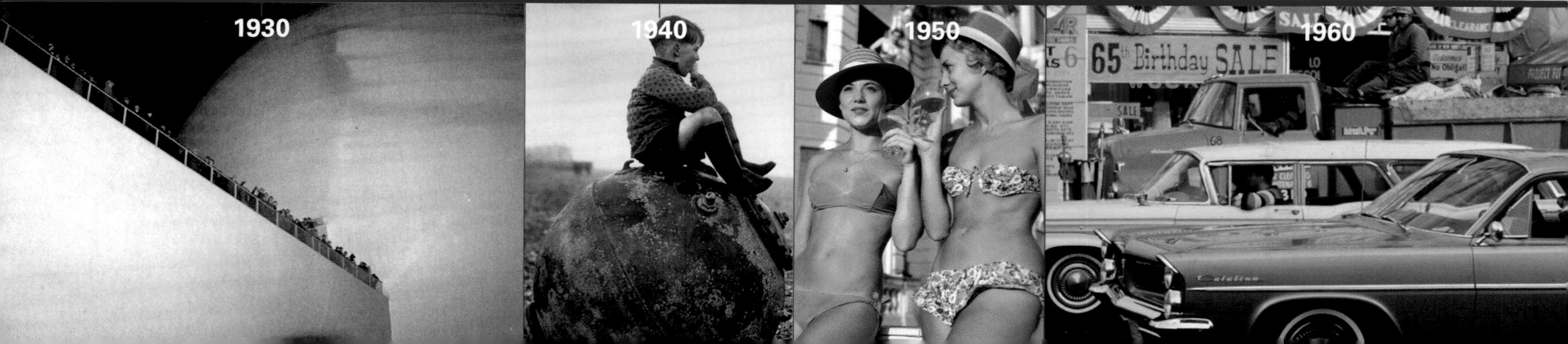

1890
1900
1910
1920

1970
1980
1990
2000

This is an authoritative, comprehensive history reference book to the 150+ years of the camera era, beginning in 1850 when photography transformed how the world is recorded. The book's two major ingredients are a timeline of events, compiled by the editors of the *Encyclopædia Britannica*, and pictures from the unrivaled Getty Images collection.

The timeline's 6,000 entries, running across the top and bottom of each page, describe the developments and happenings throughout the world, year by year. Each entry has a keyword or phrase highlighted in bold type, together with a symbol representing science, medicine, and technology [ ]; business and commerce [$]; history and politics [ ]; the arts [ ]; daily life and society [ ]; or religion, philosophy, and education [ ]. These symbols and keywords allow the reader to quickly identify and categorize the subject of each entry.

Across the middle of each spread are numerous pictures, illustrating some of the most important and visually arresting entries. Each picture is keyed into its entry by a number in red, and each one is captioned in depth, with information adding to that already given in the corresponding timeline entry. On about 150 of the 260+ spreads there is also a mini-essay, usually derived from *Encyclopædia Britannica* sources, expanding on one of the entries on that spread and illustrated with at least one picture.

In addition, *History of the World in Photographs* includes a specially prepared CD-ROM with nearly 20,000 images, including all the photographs in the book itself, extensively supported by uniquely designed keyword search software. Using the search-and-retrieval tools, readers can find images by subject, by period, by picture attributes, mood, nationality, location, and countless other categories. Lists and folders can be assembled and customized according to the interests of the user. By accessing the special portals on the *History of the World* CD-ROM, users are invited to browse online among millions more Getty Images as well as facts and articles from *Encyclopædia Britannica*. Although the software provides enhanced features for the PC user, most but not all features of the software are available to Macintosh users.

Here is a compilation that will guide anyone eager to find his or her way into history. It is an invaluable resource for students in introductory history courses in grade school, high school, or college.

The statue of Vladimir Ilyich Lenin is dismantled in Vilnius, the capital of Lithuania, because the government banned the Communist Party, August 23, 1991.

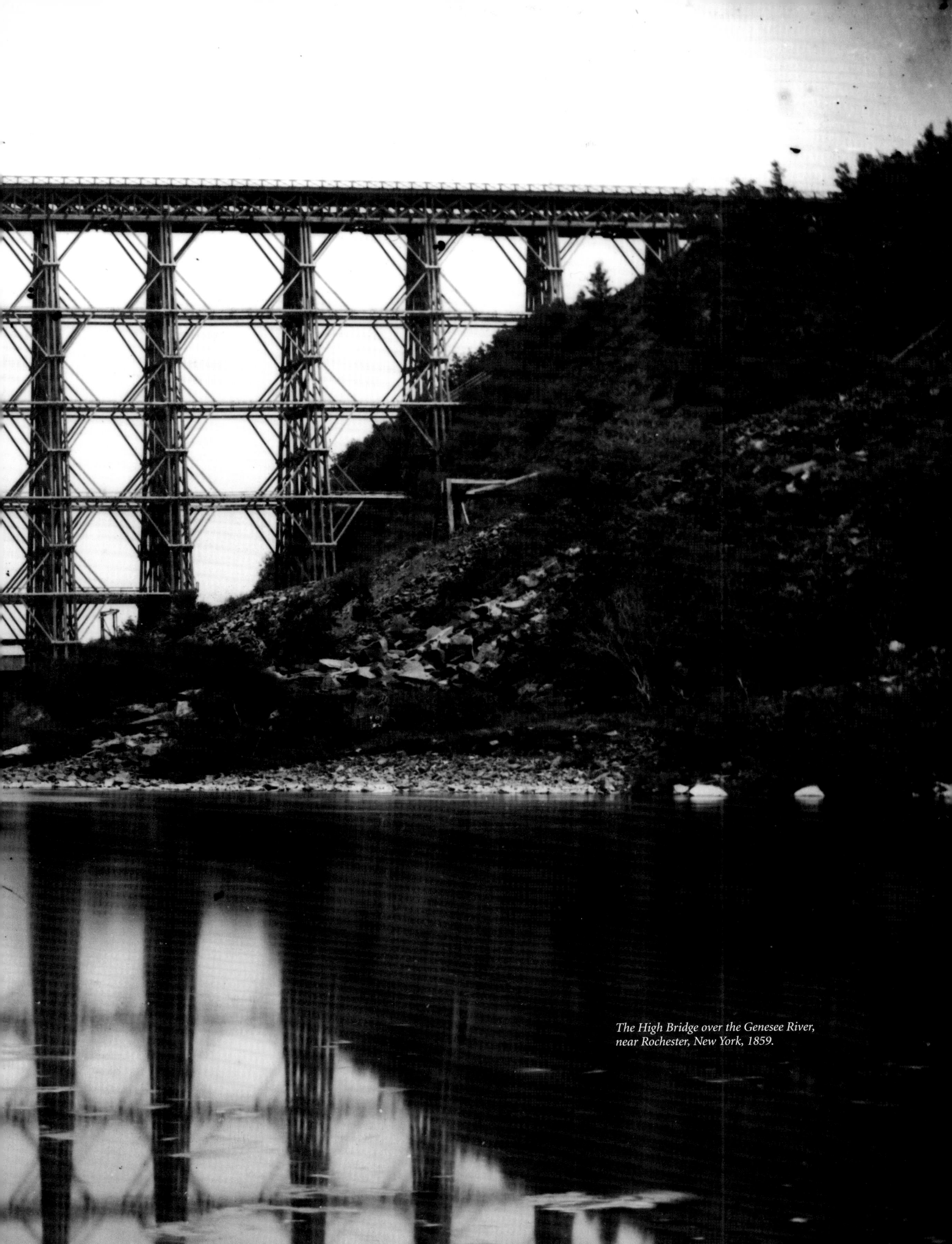

The High Bridge over the Genesee River, near Rochester, New York, 1859.

1850

1850
A second U.S. **Fugitive Slave Act** (the first was in 1793) is enacted to ensure that runaway slaves are returned to their owners. This harsh law only encourages the Abolition movement.

1850
A series of measures, called the **Compromise of 1850**, is passed by the U.S. Congress in an effort to settle several outstanding slavery issues and to avert the threat of dissolution of the Union.

1850
Alfred Tennyson publishes "In Memoriam," an elegy on the death of his friend Arthur Hallam; its great success with both reviewers and the public wins him the friendship of Queen Victoria and helps bring about his appointment as poet laureate.

 [1]

1850
American novelist **Nathaniel Hawthorne** completes his moralistic masterpiece, *The Scarlet Letter*, demonstrating his mastery of the allegorical and symbolic tale.

 [2]

1850
British chemist **John Mercer** is granted a patent for the mercerization process for cotton fabrics, giving them increased tensile strength, greater absorptive properties, and, usually, a high degree of luster.

1850
Elizabeth Barrett Browning publishes *Sonnets from the Portuguese*, now considered an early feminist text.

TAIPING REBELLION

China implodes

The rebellion, which caused an estimated 20 million deaths, was led by Hong Xiuquan (1814–64) who, having failed the civil service examination, proclaimed himself the son of God and believed that he was sent to reform China. Feng Yunshan, a friend of Hong, formed a new religious group, the God Worshippers' Society (Bai Shangdi hui), among the poor peasants of Guangxi. In 1847, Hong joined the God Worshippers, and three years later led them in rebellion. On January 1, 1851, Hong proclaimed his new dynasty, the Taiping Tianguo (Heavenly Kingdom of Great Peace), and assumed the title of Tianwang, or Heavenly King.

His slogan—to share property in common—attracted many peasants, workers, and miners. The Taiping recruited soldiers (above) who eventually numbered over a million. Sweeping north through the Yangtze River Valley, they captured Nanjing in 1853.

The rebellion was later weakened by internal rivalries that led to the assassination of several leaders. Some of the surviving generals fled for their lives, taking their troops with them, thus undermining Hong's position.

In 1860, an attempt by the Taipings to take Shanghai was stopped by the Western-trained "Ever-Victorious Army" under General Charles Gordon. The Taipings' anti-Confucianism alienated the gentry, who united under Zeng Guofan, a Chinese official of the Manchu government. In July 1862, Zeng's forces surrounded Nanjing, and the city fell in July 1864. Hong committed suicide. Taiping resistance continued in other parts of the country until 1868.

[2] *Nathaniel Hawthorne. In 1851 he will publish* The House of the Seven Gables *before coming to England as the U.S. Consul in Liverpool in 1853.*

[4] *Amelia Bloomer is an advocate of women's rights and of temperance in her own magazine. She no longer promotes bloomers once the crinoline comes in, c. 1859, since that, she feels, allows an equivalent freedom of movement.*

[6] *The improvident Mr. Micawber, one of Dickens's great comic creations, modelled in part on his father, walks down the street with David Copperfield.*

1850
Jean-François Millet monumentalizes farmwork in *The Sower*, in which an anonymous and timeless figure sweeps across the canvas. Millet specializes in paintings of peasant life.

1850
Jump rope, or skip rope, becomes popular with school children, especially in England and Germany.

1850
Levi Strauss begins selling dry goods to California miners and develops denim jeans for them.

 [5]

1850
London hat-making firm **Thomas Bowler** introduces the hard shellacked bowler (derby) hat, which will become a classic look for businessmen.

 [6]

1850
One of the most famous of all the British Victorian novelists, Charles Dickens, publishes the autobiographical **David Copperfield**. He quickly follows with *Bleak House* (1853) and *Hard Times* (1854).

 [7]

1850
Policeman **Allan Pinkerton** organizes a private detective agency that specializes in railway theft cases. The Pinkerton National Detective Agency becomes one of the most famous organizations of its kind.

1850
Failed gold prospector **Domingo Ghirardelli**, an Italian who arrived in California from Peru in 1849, opens a tent store in Stockton to sell supplies and confectionery to miners; in 1852 his business will become the Ghirardelli Chocolate Company.

1850
Flogging is banned as a punishment in the U.S. Navy.

1850
Great Britain becomes the first sizeable country in the world in which more than half of the **population** lives in cities.

1850
The Taiping Rebellion breaks out in China. Led by a quasi-Christian group, it attracts many hungry peasants, workers, and miners with its propaganda against the foreign Manchu rulers. Its ranks swell to more than 1,000,000 disciplined yet fanatical soldiers.

1850
Harriet Tubman guides members of her family to freedom via the Underground Railroad. Helping more than 300 slaves to escape, she comes to be known as the "Moses of her people."
 [3]

1850
In an effort to give women freedom of movement, **Amelia Jenks Bloomer** invents a "rational dress," which includes a jacket, skirt, and the now-famous loose trousers or bloomers.
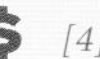  [4]

[3] Harriet Tubman. During the Civil War she is to work for the Union Army as cook or nurse, and then as an armed scout or spy.

[9] This is the carte de visite photograph that Sojourner Truth sells copies of to raise funds for her causes. The motto under it reads: "I sell the Shadow to Support the Substance."

[5] The bowler originates from a request for a hat that can be worn by gamekeepers on the estate of Lord Leicester to protect them from attack by poachers or blows from low branches.

[1] Alfred Tennyson. "In Memoriam" combines the magical evocation of landscape with reassurance for those beset by religious doubts.

[7] During the Civil War, Pinkerton sets up the Union Intelligence Service, which foils an attempted assassination of President Lincoln and organizes espionage. His agency's notorious activities against labor unions grow after 1865.

[8] Courbet was masterly in his portrayal of everyday life, of beautiful women both nude and clothed, and of landscape. His formidable and rebellious personality is clear in this photograph.

 [8]
1850
Realism, an artistic movement begun in the arts by French painter **Gustave Courbet**, reaches French literature, influencing the work of Balzac, Flaubert, and the brothers Goncourt.

1850
Searching for the lost John Franklin expedition of 1845, Irish explorer **Robert John Le Mesurier McClure** becomes the first to traverse the Northwest Passage, a Canadian Arctic waterway connecting the Atlantic and Pacific oceans.

 [9]
1850
Speaking on behalf of the Abolitionist movement, former slave **Sojourner Truth** travels throughout the American Midwest, developing a reputation for personal magnetism and drawing large crowds.

1850
The **Chesapeake and Ohio Canal**, begun in 1828, reaches Cumberland, Maryland, after which further construction is abandoned, owing to competition from the Erie Canal.

1850
The **Clayton-Bulwer Treaty** provides that the United States and Great Britain will jointly control and protect the canal that they expect soon to be built across the Isthmus of Panama.

1850
The first national convention of the U.S. women's movement is held in Worcester, Massachusetts, organized by **Lucy Stone** and a group of prominent Eastern suffragists.

1850-1851

1850
The game of **mah-jongg** originates in China. It will become a fad in England, the United States, and Australia in the mid-1920s.

1850
The **first undersea cable** is laid beneath the English Channel, bringing almost instantaneous telegraphic communication between Europe and Britain.

1850
Xianfeng, seventh emperor of China's Qing dynasty, ascends the throne. During his reign, China will be beset internally by the Taiping Rebellion (1850–64) and externally by conflicts with encroaching European powers.

1850
Two-thirds elective legislatures are established in Victoria, South Australia, and Tasmania. The population in **Australia** is rapidly increasing: the immigrant population was 50,000 in 1825, but in 1851 it will be about 450,000.

 [1]

1850
World's total use of inanimate energy surpasses one billion megawatts for the first time. The main source is **coal**, used in steam engines.

1850
Harper's New Monthly Magazine begins publication in New York City; it is the first U.S. magazine to introduce the extensive use of woodcut illustrations. It is still being published.

[1] A white settler with his wife and aborigine servants in what is thought to be the first photograph ever taken in Australia.

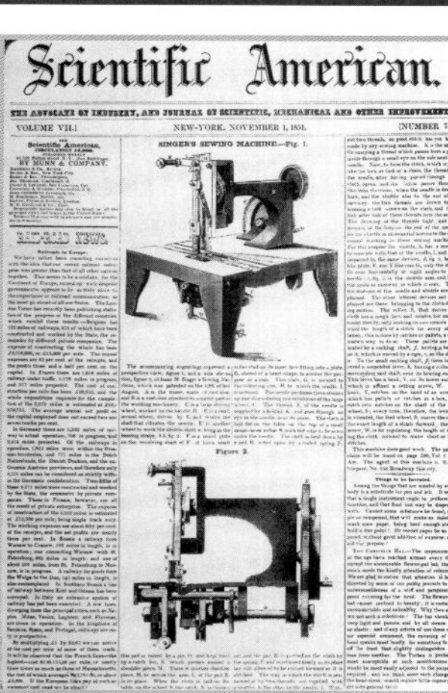

Scientific American.

[7] Singer's sewing machine: his success will be built on reaching agreement with rival claimants to the technology and on his machine being suited to home use.

[6] Melville, a comparatively successful writer before his whaling adventure Moby-Dick, *ironically begins to sink into obscurity after it appears.*

[4] Jenny Lind has already conquered the continent and had a huge success in England. She is to give away to charity much of the $250,000 that she will earn in the U.S.

[5] A group of slaves sits on the steps of the Florida Club, sometime during the 1850s. A white girl stands aloof and half withdrawn behind the post.

 [4]

September 1850
Swedish soprano **Jenny Lind** embarks on a two-year American tour organized by showman P.T. Barnum, who has created such excitement around "the Swedish nightingale" that 40,000 people gather to welcome her.

September 9, 1850
California is admitted to the United States as the 31st state, its population swelled by 80,000 Forty-Niners after gold was discovered at Sutter's Mill in 1848. At the same time, the Texas, New Mexico, and Utah territories are organized.

November 29, 1850
Prussia and Austria sign the **Punctation of Olmütz**, an agreement regulating the two powers' relations.

 [5]

June and November 1850
At the **Nashville Convention**, a two-session meeting of proslavery Southerners in the United States, delegates from nine Southern states discuss unity in the face of Northern moves toward abolishing slavery.

 [6]

1851
American author Herman Melville publishes **Moby-Dick**, his masterpiece and one of the most influential novels in American literature.

 [7]

1851
American **Isaac Singer** founds I. M. Singer & Company, which by 1860 is the world's largest sewing machine manufacturer.

March 18, 1850
The American Express Company is formed through the consolidation of three companies active in the express transport of goods, valuables, and currency between New York City and Buffalo, New York, and points in the Midwest.

April 4, 1850
With a population totaling about 1,600, **Los Angeles** is incorporated as an American city.

July 1850
Harvard Observatory takes the first photograph of a star, Vega.

July 9, 1850
Twelfth U.S. President Zachary Taylor dies only 16 months after taking office. He is succeeded by **Millard Fillmore** on July 10.

 [2]

August 20, 1850
The first performance of German composer Richard Wagner's **Lohengrin** is given at Weimar, Germany, conducted by Franz Liszt.

 [3]

August 31, 1850
King Kamehameha III officially declares Honolulu a city and the capital of his kingdom.

[8] *This heroic depiction owes more than a little to the various versions of* Napoleon Crossing the Alps *painted in France around 1800. Washington and Napoleon are depicted confronting the elements as much as their human foes.*

[3] *Lohengrin, knight of the Holy Grail, son of Parsifal, an identity that, once revealed, means the end of his love affair with the opera's heroine, Elsa.*

[2] *An election poster for Zachary Taylor.*

[10] *It is well known that the earth rotates, but Foucault's 28-kilogram weight on the end of a 67-meter wire suspended from the top of the Pantheon dome offers the first dynamic proof.*

[9] *Archer's is the dominant photographic process from 1851 until the 1870s and the invention of gelatine emulsion. Glass plates have to be exposed while still wet with liquid collodion.*

1851
Britain repeals its **window tax**, which had been in force since 1696.

1851
Construction on the **Erie Railroad** reaches Lake Erie, completing the first rail connection between New York City and the Great Lakes.

 [8]

1851
Emanuel Gottlieb Leutze paints **Washington Crossing the Delaware**, which will become one of the most popular and widely reproduced images of an American historical event.

 [9]

1851
English photographer **Frederick Scott Archer** invents the wet collodion photographic process. Unlike daguerreotypes, which are printed on metal, the images on collodion plates can be reproduced on paper.

 [10]

1851
French physicist Jean-Bernard-Léon **Foucault's pendulum** demonstrations inside the Panthéon in Paris illustrate the diurnal rotation of the earth.

1851
German scientist **Hermann von Helmholtz** invents the ophthalmoscope to study the structure and function of the eye and the condition of retinal blood vessels.

1851-1852

1851
Gold is discovered in the **Ballarat and Bendigo** regions of Victoria, Australia. Nuggets weighing hundreds of pounds are found.

1851
Heinrich Daniel Ruhmkorff, a German mechanic, develops an induction coil, or **spark coil**. An improved version will later evolve into the alternating-current transformer.

1851
In the Oregon Territory, American settlers arrive at **Alki Point**; the settlement will be laid out as a town and named **Seattle** in 1853.

1851
Jacob Fussell opens the first wholesale **ice-cream** business in Baltimore, Maryland.

1851
Joseph Paxton's **Crystal Palace**, the first modern exhibition building, is a spectacular construction of cast iron and glass and a symbol of Victorian ingenuity.

1851
Mexican general and statesman **Mariano Arista**, who had led Mexican forces against U.S. general Zachary Taylor in the Mexican-American War, is appointed president of Mexico.

THE GREAT EXHIBITION

The Great Exhibition of Works of Industry of all Nations, held in London's Hyde Park

In 1851 Britain was the workshop of the world and the main influence on the industrialization of other nations. The Great Exhibition of 1851 in London symbolized this economic supremacy. It was unparalleled in magnitude and magnificence. The exhibition was housed in a huge glass and iron building called by a journalist—with a touch of romance—"the Crystal Palace." The success of the exhibition was political as much as economic. The objects on display came from all parts of the world, including India and the countries with recent white settlements, such as Australia and New Zealand, that constituted the new British empire. One popular attraction was a colossal plaster head (below left), a symbol of Bavaria. Many of the visitors who flocked to London came from European cities.

The Crystal Palace (left) was the brainchild of Prince Albert, consort of Queen Victoria, and was realized by Joseph Paxton (the Duke of Devonshire's gardener). It resembled, on a great scale, Paxton's greenhouse at Chatsworth and occupied an area of 18 acres (7 hectares) in London's Hyde Park. Its length was 1,848 feet (563 m), and its width in the broadest part was 408 feet (124 m). There were about 14,000 exhibitors (below). The Great Exhibition was opened by Queen Victoria on May 1, 1851, and it remained open until October 11, by which time it had attracted more than six million visitors. After the exhibition had closed, the buildings were dismantled and moved to south London, where they were re-erected in the suburb that now bears its name.

[2]
1851
Under Commodore John C. Stevens, the *America* wins a yachting competition against 14 British vessels. The victor's prize cup is for all subsequent contests known as the **America's Cup**.

March 11, 1851
The opera **Rigoletto**, by Giuseppe Verdi, premieres at Teatro La Fenice in Venice.

May 1, 1851
The Great Exhibition of 1851 opens at the Crystal Palace in London. Prince Albert, husband of Queen Victoria and president of the Royal Society of Arts, has called the exhibition to focus attention on technologies and manufacturing.

June 2, 1851
Maine, under the leadership of politician and temperance advocate **Neal Dow**, passes the first U.S. state law prohibiting the manufacture and sale of liquor.

July 28, 1851
A **total solar eclipse** is captured for the first time on a daguerreotype at Königsberg, Prussia (now Kaliningrad, Russia).

 *[3]*
December 2, 1851
A coup d'état led by **Louis-Napoléon**, president of France and the nephew of Napoleon I, leads to the end of the Second Republic and the establishment of the Second Empire, with Louis-Napoléon taking the name Napoleon III.

1851
Nearly 46,000 cases of famine-caused **blindness** are reported in Ireland, an increase over approximately 14,000 cases in 1849.

1851
Reuters News Service is started in England by German entrepreneur **Paul Julius Reuter** as a telegraph office near the London Stock Exchange.

 [1]

1851
The **Amalgamated Society of Engineers**, which will eventually become one of Britain's leading trade unions, is formed through a merger of several craft unions.

1851
The **first international chess tournament** is held in London. Adolf Anderssen, a German schoolteacher, wins the London tournament and with it recognition as unofficial champion.

1851
The Flying Cloud, a classic clipper ship built by Canadian-born shipbuilder Donald McKay at his shipyard at East Boston, Massachusetts, makes the voyage from New York City to San Francisco in a record 89 days.

1851
The New York Times begins publication. It will become the most highly regarded newspaper in the United States.

[1] A few years earlier Reuter used pigeons to carry stock-market information from Brussels to Aachen, the only gap in the telegraph between Paris and Berlin.

[2] The original yacht America. *The cup named after her is the oldest trophy in international sport still competed for. It will remain in the United States until 1983, when the* Australia II *wins it.*

[4] Alexandre Dumas is to be one of the three leading French dramatists in the later part of the 19th century, but greater fame went to his father, author of The Three Musketeers *and* The Count of Monte Cristo.

[3] Napoléon III with his wife, Eugenie, whom he married in 1853, and their son, the prince imperial, who will be killed by the Zulus when fighting with the British Army in 1879.

[5] A melodramatic poster for a stage version of Uncle Tom's Cabin.

December 24, 1851
A serious fire at the **Library of Congress** in Washington, D.C., destroys two-thirds of the books in the collection acquired from Thomas Jefferson in 1815.

 [4]

1852
Alexandre Dumas produces a stage version of his novel **La Dame aux camelias**, known in English as *Camille*. Giuseppe Verdi will later base his opera *La traviata* on this play.

 [5]

1852
American novelist Harriet Beecher Stowe publishes **Uncle Tom's Cabin**; *or, Life Among the Lowly*. The novel helps turn American public opinion against slavery.

1852
Arthur Wellesley, the **duke of Wellington**, dies. He served as a British army commander during the Napoleonic Wars and as prime minister of Great Britain from 1828 to 1830.

1852
Brazilian, Uruguayan, and Argentinian troops overthrow the Argentinian dictator **Juan Manuel de Rosas**. Argentina holds a constitutional convention later that year.

1852
The second **Anglo-Burmese war** begins. The first war lasted from 1824 to 1826. After the second war, the British control the southern part of Burma (now Myanmar). They annex the northern part of the country in 1886.

1852-1853

1852
Charles Tufts founds **Tufts College** in Massachusetts. It will become Tufts University in 1955.

1852
Cholera breaks out in India, spreading rapidly through Persia (present-day Iran) to Europe, the United States, Africa, and then the rest of the world.

1852
French physicist Jean-Bernard-Léon Foucault invents the **gyroscope**.

1852
Friedrich Froebel, a German educator who developed the kindergarten in the 1830s, dies. He was one of the most influential education reformers of the 19th century.

1852
One of England's great parliamentary orators, Edward Smith-Stanley, 14th earl of **Derby**, begins the first of his three terms (1852, 1858–59, 1866–68) as Conservative prime minister.

 [1]

1852
German-born U.S. civil engineer John Roebling erects the first wire-rope suspension bridge over **Niagara Falls**. It serves as a model for later suspension bridges, including Roebling's Brooklyn Bridge (opened 1883).

[2]

THE HOUSES OF PARLIAMENT

The current British parliament buildings were opened in 1852.

There had been a royal palace on the north bank of the Thames River since the 11th century, but the original structure was abandoned after it was severely damaged by fire in 1512. One surviving part, St. Stephen's Chapel, was used from around 1550 for meetings of the House of Commons; the Lords used another apartment of the palace. A fire in 1834 destroyed the whole palace except the historic Westminster Hall, the Jewel Tower, the cloisters, and the crypt of St. Stephen's Chapel.

Sir Charles Barry, assisted by Augustus Welby Northmore Pugin, designed the present buildings in the Gothic Revival style. Construction began in 1837, the cornerstone was laid in 1840, it was opened in 1852, and work was finished in 1860. The House of Lords is an ornate chamber 97 feet (29.5 m) in length; the Commons is 70 feet (21 m) long. The southwestern Victoria Tower is 336 feet (102 m) high. St. Stephen's Tower, 320 feet (97.5 m) in height and contains the famous tower clock Big Ben. The Houses of Parliament were designated a UNESCO World Heritage site in 1987.

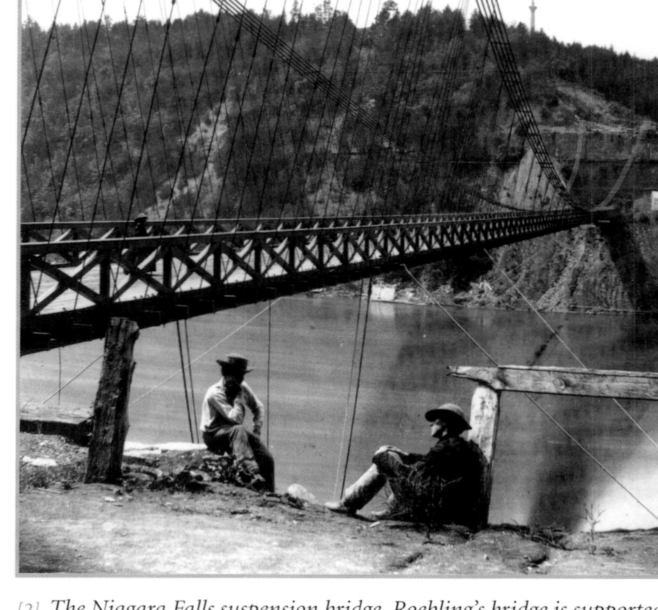

[2] The Niagara Falls suspension bridge. Roebling's bridge is supported by cables. Earlier suspension bridges had been supported by chains. This one will collapse in 1864 because stabilizing guy wires have been removed to avoid a build-up of ice.

[3] A man of integrity, honor, and peace, Aberdeen still leads his country into its first major war since 1815.

[6] This type of airship is called a "dirigible" by the French, since it can be "directed" or controlled and is not completely at the mercy of the winds.

1852
The British recognize the independence of the **Transvaal** region of southern Africa. The Transvaal will later become the South African Republic.

 [6]

1852
The first successful airship, which incorporates a steam-driven propeller, is built by **Henri Giffard** of France.

1852
The United Kingdom passes the Constitution Act granting **New Zealand** self-government.

1852
The **Wells Fargo** company is founded. Henry Wells, William Fargo, and other investors found the company to handle the banking and shipping business prompted by the California Gold Rush, which began in 1848.

1852
U.S. statesman Henry Clay, called the **Great Compromiser**, dies.

1852
The new Houses of Parliament open in London.

1852
Henry and Clement Studebaker found a blacksmith and wagon shop in Indiana. Other brothers later join the Studebaker company, which becomes the world's largest producer of horse-drawn vehicles and a leader in automobile manufacturing.

1852
George Hamilton-Gordon, 4th earl of **Aberdeen**, becomes the British prime minister. His coalition government will involve Great Britain in the Crimean War against Russia (1853–56).

 [3]

1852
Peter Mark Roget, an English physician and philologist, publishes his first **Thesaurus of English Words and Phrases**.

1852
Russian author **Ivan Turgenev** publishes *A Sportsman's Sketches.* The short-story collection brings him lasting fame. Many of the sketches are drawn from his experience, of the life of the manorial, serf-owning Russian gentry.

[4]

1852
Russian novelist **Nikolay Gogol** dies. His novel *Myortvye dushi* (*Dead Souls*) and short story "Shinel" ("The Overcoat") are considered the foundations of the great 19th-century tradition of Russian realism.

 [5]

1852
The American Pharmaceutical Association is founded as the first nationwide trade association in the U.S.

[4] Turgenev's book, A Sportsman's Sketches, *is credited with helping to bring about the abolition of serfdom in Russia. Of his later books, perhaps the most famous is* Fathers and Sons.

[1] As well as keeping the Conservative Party alive during a period of eclipse, Derby leads a princely existence in Lancashire, where he will do much to relieve the unemployed British cotton workers during the American Civil War.

[5] Gogol is best remembered today for his comedy The Government Inspector *(1836), which holds bureaucracy up to ridicule.*

[8] One of Hausmann's new boulevards in Paris; his comprehensive plans beautified the city while also making it easier to control with troops and artillery.

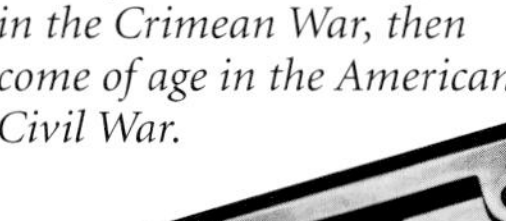

[7] The Colt revolver will be used by some British officers in the Crimean War, then come of age in the American Civil War.

1853
American chef **George Crum** invents the potato chip in Saratoga Springs, New York.

 [7]

1853
American entrepreneur **Samuel Colt** opens an armory to produce his revolver, which he patented in 1836; his manufacturing innovations will revolutionize the production of small arms.

1853
American horticulturist **Ephraim Bull** develops the concord grape.

 [8]

1853
Baron **Georges-Eugène Haussmann** becomes prefect of the Seine département, Paris, and (until 1870) directs a variety of projects that transform the city, adding boulevards, sewers, and monuments.

1853
Brazil bans the importation of African slaves. Brazil imported 40 percent of the 11 million slaves taken from Africa, more than any other nation.

1853
Ferdinand V. Hayden begins a 30-year survey of the western U.S., contributing to the foundation of the U.S. Geological Survey and helping to create Yellowstone National Park.

1853

1853
German furniture maker **Michael Thonet** and his sons set up a corporation for the manufacture of bentwood chairs.

 [1]

1853
Influential art critic **John Ruskin** publishes the third and final volume of *The Stones of Venice*, a history of Venetian architecture. He insists that art and architecture are the direct expression of the social conditions in which they were produced.

 [2]

1853
Italian composer Giuseppe Verdi writes his classic **La Traviata** ("The Fallen Woman"). He is the leading figure in 19th-century opera, writing such great works as *Aida* (1871) and *Otello* (1887).

 [3]

1853
Kong Chow Temple, the first Buddhist temple in the United States, is opened in San Francisco, California.

1853
Mountaineering grows in popularity among European and British gentlemen. Among other things, the sport is lauded for its intellectual value, as many of its leaders are scientists or artists.

  [4]

1853
Nanjing, China, is captured and renamed Tianjing ("Heavenly Capital") by forces of Hong Xiuquan, leader of the **Taiping Rebellion**, one of the greatest civil wars in world history.

[1] *A Thonet rocking chair, its elegant, sinuous lines anticipating the art nouveau style of around 1900.*

[7] *A double-decker viaduct carrying the Semmering Railway across an Alpine valley.*

[2] *John Ruskin, a hugely influential art and architectural critic, social reformer, and moralist.*

[3] *Giuseppe Verdi. No other composer communicated so directly, for so long, and to such a huge audience.*

[4] *Across a glacier: a mixed party of alpinists makes few concessions to the terrain in their costume.*

1853
The first major American railroad, the **New York Central,** is formed in 1853 from the consolidation of 10 rail lines between Albany and Buffalo, New York.

1853
The first railroad begins operations in **India**. The line, which starts at Bombay, will link Calcutta, Madras, and Nagpur by 1856.

1853
The **hollow hypodermic needle** is invented by French surgeon Charles Gabriel Pravaz. It is first used in the treatment of disease in the same year by Scottish physician Alexander Wood.

1853
The **Indian telegraph system** opens, facilitating British administrative and military control of the colony.

1853
The **Mount Vernon Hotel**, in Cape May, New Jersey, is the world's first hotel to offer guests their own private baths.

 [7]

1853
The **Semmering Railway**, with service between Vienna and Trieste through the Alps, opens; it holds the record as the highest public railway on its completion.

1853
New York City is authorized by the state to purchase land in the heart of the city in order to create a pastoral retreat for citizens; the public land later becomes known as **Central Park**.

 [5]

1853
Polish pharmacist Ignacy Lukasiewicz invents the **kerosene lamp**.

1853
Queen Victoria delivers her eighth child under **chloroform**. Her approval and recommendation of it popularizes use of the anesthetic.

1853
John Rae learns that members of the **Franklin expedition** of 1845 perished from exposure and starvation while surveying Boothia Peninsula in the Arctic. Rae is among the first explorers to adopt Eskimo survival practices.

1853
Scottish missionary-doctor David Livingstone embarks on a series of treks through southern and central Africa, tracing the course of the Zambezi River and naming **Victoria Falls**.

 [6]

1853
Swedish inventor J. E. Lundström patents the **safety match**.

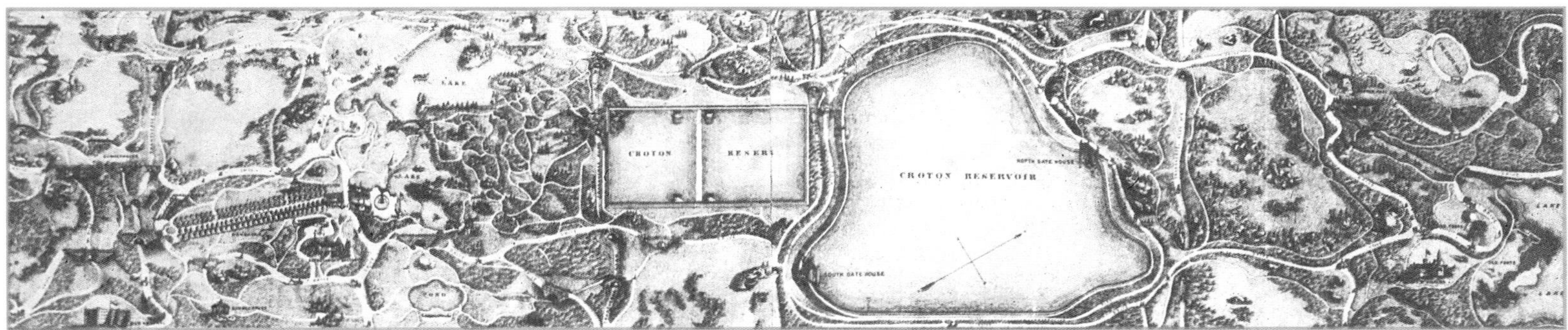

[5] Central Park in New York, at 843 acres, is twice the size of Monaco. Crosstown traffic is hidden from view in cuttings.

THE FIRST RAILROAD IN INDIA

The dawn of the Steam Age on the subcontinent

A rail system in India was first proposed in 1832, but no action was taken at the time because of concerns about the difficulties of the terrain, the weather, and wild animals and the possibility of sabotage along the proposed route between Madras and Bangalore.

Ten years later, however, when a new plan was presented to the East India Company by British civil engineer Charles Blacker Vignoles, Governor-general Lord Hardinge took the view that a rail system was desirable from political and military viewpoints, and that construction should begin as soon as possible regardless of all other reservations.

By 1845, two companies had been formed: the East Indian Railway Company, operating from Calcutta, and the Great Indian Peninsula Railway, operating from Bombay. The first train in India ran the 21 miles (34 km) from Bombay to Thana on April 16, 1853. By the 1860s (as the photograph above shows), railways were well established.

[8] Donald McKay, the great Boston clipper-ship builder.

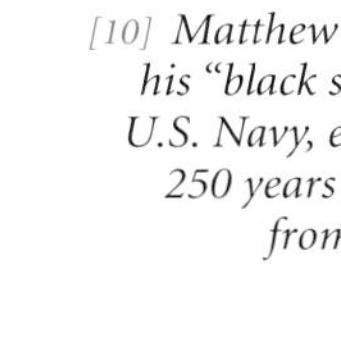

[10] Matthew Perry, with his "black ships" of the U.S. Navy, ends Japan's 250 years of isolation from the world.

[9] Franklin Pierce, U.S. president until 1857, by which time his reputation will have been much damaged by the divisive effect of several of his decisions.

[6] Victoria Falls, where the Zambezi River drops 400 feet, was named by David Livingstone in 1855.

1853
The **University of Melbourne** is founded in Australia.

 [8]

1853
The world's largest sailing ship, the *Great Republic*, is launched by Canadian-born American shipbuilder **Donald McKay**. The ship draws 4,555 tons and uses a 15-horsepower engine to handle the sails.

 [3]

January 19, 1853
Giuseppe Verdi's opera **Il trovatore** premieres in Rome.

 [9]

March 4, 1853
Franklin Pierce is inaugurated as 14th president of the United States. His vice president is William Rufus de Vane King.

April 1853
Antonio López de Santa Anna returns from exile and assumes the Mexican presidency, only to be overthrown and banished once more in 1855.

 [10]

July 8, 1853
With two frigates and two sailing vessels, **Matthew Perry** enters the fortified harbor of Uraga to force Japan to enter into trade and diplomatic relations with the West.

1853-1854

July 14, 1853
The first **World's Fair** in the United States opens in New York City; the Crystal Palace Exposition venue is based on the 1851 London Great Exhibition.

October 16, 1853
Turkey declares war on Russia, which has demanded protection over the Orthodox subjects of the Ottoman sultan. This begins the Crimean War.

December 30, 1853
The **Gadsden Purchase** transfers to the United States nearly 30,000 square miles (78,000 square km) of northern Mexican territory, now southern Arizona and southern New Mexico, in exchange for $10 million.

1854
American chemist Benjamin Silliman performs the first fractional distillation of **petroleum**.

 [1]

1854
American machinist Daniel Halliday invents **a windmill for pumping water** and other uses. His windmill will be widely used throughout the American prairie states.

1854
An outbreak of cholera in London kills some 10,000 people; physician **John Snow** traces one outbreak to a single water pump, proving that the disease is waterborne.

[5] Wheatstone (left, with his friend Charles Chevalier) is also the inventor of the concertina, harmonica, and stereoscope. And in 1837 he took out the first patent for an electric telegraph.

[3] George Boole. The discoverer of Boolean algebra is a self-taught Irishman, teaching at Queen's College in Cork.

[1] Halliday's windmill is a success because its introduction coincides with a cheap iron water-pump becoming available. The Sears Roebuck catalog will advertise the machinery for $15 and the tower for $25.

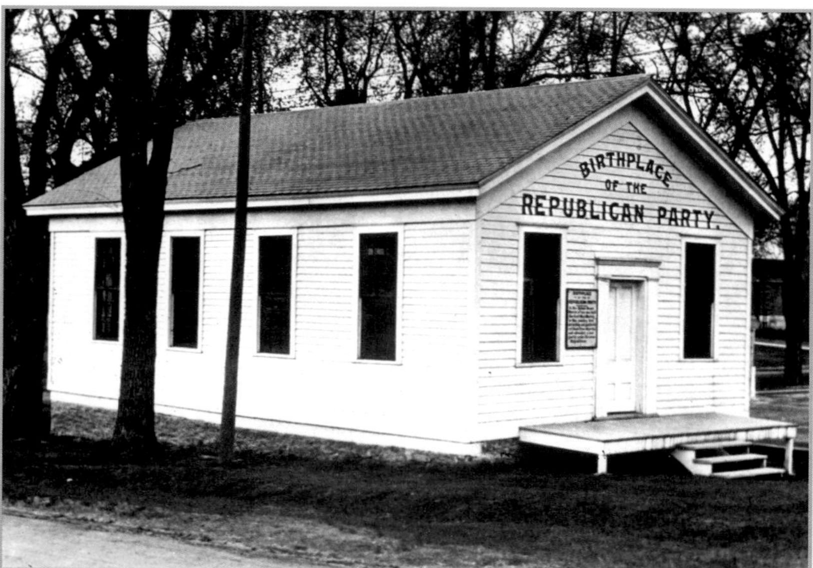

[7] A wooden building in Ripon, Wisconsin, is claimed as the birthplace of the Republican Party, a child of the antislavery movement.

 [4]

1854
English nursing pioneer **Florence Nightingale** arrives in Constantinople during the Crimean War and takes charge of nursing in the military hospital; her experiences with the war will lead to major advances in health care.

1854
English tobacco merchant **Philip Morris** begins making cigarettes.

 [5]

1854
Englishman Sir Charles Wheatstone invents the **Playfair cipher**, which will be used by British forces in the second Boer War and in World War I.

1854
Paris-educated **Sa'id Pasha** succeeds Abbas I as Ottoman viceroy (khedive) of Egypt. His administrative policies foster the development of individual landownership and reduce the influence of the sheikhs (village headmen).

1854
French scientist Henri Sainte-Claire Deville devises the first commercial method for producing aluminum; at the time, **aluminum** is considered more valuable than gold.

1854
French telegraphist **Charles Bourseul** publishes the basic concept of using electricity to transmit speech, for which he is sometimes credited with inventing the telephone.

1854
Austrian monk **Gregor Mendel** begins his experiments to trace the transmission of hereditary characteristics in successive generations of hybrid progeny—using garden peas—so laying the mathematical foundation of the science of genetics.

[2]

1854
Britain and France declare war on Russia. Most of the fighting will take place in the **Crimean peninsula**.

1854
British naturalist **Alfred Russel Wallace** begins an eight-year expedition gathering Malaysian and Moluccan animals and plants, formulating a theory of natural selection later published simultaneously with Charles Darwin's.

1854
Canadian Abraham Gesner invents a process for extracting **kerosene** from coal.

1854
The Catholic University of Ireland (later named University College) is founded in Dublin.

1854
English mathematician **George Boole** publishes *An Investigation on the Laws of Thought, on Which Are Founded the Mathematical Theories of Logic and Probabilities.* Boolean logic will become the basis for computer computations.

[3]

THE CRIMEAN WAR

Inconclusive East-West conflict fought near the northern coast of the Black Sea

The Crimean War—which broke out in October 1853—was fought between Russia and an alliance between Britain (some of whose dragoons are shown in Roger Fenton's photograph, above, drinking with French Zouaves), the Ottoman Empire, France, and Sardinia-Piedmont.

The conflict had several causes, but the flashpoint came when Russia demanded the right to exercise protection over the Orthodox subjects of the Ottoman sultan. In September 1854 the allies landed troops in Russian Crimea and besieged Sevastopol. Major battles were fought at the Alma River on September 20, at Balaklava on October 25, and at Inkerman on November 5. Finally, on September 11, 1855, three days after a successful French assault on the Malakhov, a major strongpoint in the Russian defenses, the Russians evacuated Sevastopol. After Austria threatened to join the allies, Russia accepted defeat on February 1, 1856. The peace was formalized at the Congress of Paris (February 25–March 30).

The war was managed and commanded poorly by both sides. One of the most notorious misadventures was the disastrous British Charge of the Light Brigade at Balaklava. Disease accounted for many of the approximately 250,000 men lost by each side. The war did not settle the relations of the powers in Eastern Europe, but it did alert Tsar Alexander II to the need to modernize Russia.

[2] Genetics pioneer Gregor Mendel taught physics while also cultivating and testing 29,000 pea plants at his Augustinian monastery in Austrian Silesia (now the Czech Republic).

[6] Much of Thoreau's work, published after his death in 1862, is from the journals that he regularly keeps at Walden Pond in Concord, Massachusetts.

[4] Florence Nightingale, the Lady with the Lamp, is not merely a nursing pioneer but a very able administrator and formidable politician, which helps her push through her reforms.

1854
German scientist Heinrich Ernst Beyrich identifies the **Oligocene Period** in archaeology.

[6]

1854
Henry David Thoreau publishes *Walden.* His reflections on man and nature, which help spur the conservation movement, draw on Romantic philosophy and New England Transcendentalism.

1854
French diplomat Ferdinand de Lesseps receives an Act of Concession from the viceroy of Egypt, Sa'id Pasha, to construct **a canal across the Isthmus of Suez**.

1854
The Australian newspaper **The Age** is founded in Melbourne.

1854
The first graduates of the **U.S. Naval Academy** are commissioned.

[7]

1854
The first meeting of the **Republican Party**, one of the two major U.S. political parties, takes place in Jackson, Michigan.

1854-1855

1854
Theodor Mommsen publishes the first three volumes of his masterwork, *Römische Geschichte* (*The History of Rome*). He will be awarded the Nobel Prize for Literature in 1902.

 [1]

1854
The Polish inventor Ignacy Lukasiewicz drills the **world's first oil well** in Poland.

1854
The **Ostend Manifesto**, written by American diplomats in Europe, advocates acquiring Cuba by purchase or force from Spain. The northern states react strongly. They suspect an attempt to extend slavery and the South's power in Congress.

1854
William Armstrong, an English hydraulic engineer, designs an entirely new type of artillery weapon, a breech-loading gun with an internally rifled barrel. It is soon adopted by the British army and navy.

 [2]

February 23, 1854
Under the Bloemfontein Convention, the British relinquish their sovereignty over the area in southern Africa between the Orange and Vaal rivers, and Boer settlers form the independent **Orange Free State**.

March 1, 1854
The **City of Glasgow** departs from Liverpool, England, en route to Philadelphia, Pennsylvania. It never arrives, and its nearly 500 passengers are presumed to have gone down with the ship somewhere in the Atlantic.

[2] Armstrong guns and ammunition on display in London in 1862.

[5] A horse-powered windlass, also called a whim-wham, in the Australian gold fields is the only means for raising and lowering "diggers" and ore. Reaction to harsh working conditions eventually will result in the introduction of full white-male suffrage.

[1] Theodor Mommsen's History *is of the Roman Republic only, ending with Julius Caesar. He dipicted the period in an authoritative manor with an unparrelled knowledge of nonliterary sources, such as coins and Latin inscriptions.*

[4] Obeying misunderstood orders, the Light Brigade charge the Russian guns at the end of the "Valley of Death."

December 8, 1854
Pope Pius IX declares that the doctrine of the **Immaculate Conception** is to be firmly believed by all Catholics. It holds that Mary, the mother of Jesus, was preserved free from original sin from the first instant of her conception.

1855
A 49-mile (79-km) transcontinental railroad, the **Panama-Colón line**, is completed by a U.S. company. It provides an overland route between the Atlantic and Pacific oceans and drastically cuts shipping times.

1855
A group is established in Britain to provide access to safe housing, skill development, and Bible study for the many women who have migrated to towns; it will later be called the **Young Women's Christian Association** (YWCA).

1855
Anglo-American inventor David Hughes takes out a patent on his **type-printing telegraph** instrument. Its success is immediate, and in some places it continues in use until the 1930s.

 [6]

1855
Anthony Trollope publishes *The Warden*, the first of his Barsetshire novels, a series that excels in memorable characters and exudes the atmosphere of the cathedral community and the landed aristocracy.

1855
Britain and Siam (now Thailand) agree to the **Bowring Treaty.** It achieves commercial and political aims that earlier British missions failed to gain and opens up Siam to Western influence and trade.

March 31, 1854
"Commodore" **Matthew Perry**, who has appeared in Edo (modern Tokyo) Bay in a show of force with nine ships, concludes the first trading treaty between the U.S. and Japan. Japan is soon forced to sign similar treaties with other Western nations.

May 30, 1854
The **Kansas-Nebraska Act** critically affirms the concept of popular sovereignty (in which the residents decide whether a territory will permit slavery) over the congressional edict banning the expansion of slavery.

June 5, 1854
Canada and the United States sign the **Elgin-Marcy Reciprocity Treaty**, which establishes fairer trade relations between the two countries.

June 30, 1854
The French and British land troops in Russian Crimea, on the north shore of the Black Sea, and begin a year-long siege of the Russian fortress of **Sevastopol**.

 [3]

October 25, 1854
James Thomas Brudenell, 7th earl of Cardigan, leads the **Charge of the Light Brigade** of British cavalry against the Russians in the Battle of Balaklava, during the Crimean War—an incident immortalized in a poem by Alfred Tennyson.

 [4]

December 3, 1854
After hastily constructing a fortification and barricading themselves inside, aggrieved miners ("diggers") working in the **Eureka Goldfield** in Victoria, Australia, open fire on government forces surrounding the stockade.

  [5]

[3] The landlocked harbor of Balaklava filled with vessels supplying the British and French forces in the Crimea. Until a railway is built in 1855, linking it to the distant encampments, it is a dreadful bottleneck.

[6] Anthony Trollope in a splendid pair of check "sponge-bag" trousers. Hugely productive, he excels in depicting the households of Victorian clergy, politicians of every rank, the workings of society, the hunting field, and women. His unadorned style can hide the acuity of his perceptions.

RICHARD BURTON

English scholar-explorer and Orientalist

Expelled from Oxford in 1842, Richard Burton (left) went to India as an army officer. There he disguised himself as a Muslim and wrote detailed reports of merchant bazaars and urban brothels. He then traveled to Arabia, again disguised as a Muslim, and became the first non-Muslim European to penetrate the forbidden holy cities; he recounted his adventures in *Pilgrimage to El-Medinah and Mecca* (1855–56). In 1857 and 1858, he led an expedition with John Hanning Speke in search of the source of the Nile River.

Burton's later travels resulted in a total of 43 accounts of such subjects as Mormons, West African peoples, the Brazilian highlands, Iceland, and Etruscan Bologna. He learned 25 languages and numerous dialects; among his 30 volumes of translations were ancient Eastern manuals on the art of love, and he larded his famous *Arabian Nights* translation with ethnological footnotes and daring essays that won him many enemies in Victorian society. After his death, his wife, Isabel, burned his 40 years of diaries and journals, fearing a scandal if they became public.

1855
British chemist Alexander Parkes invents **Parkesine**, a flexible, durable material made of castor oil and chloroform that is a forerunner of the first plastic, celluloid.

1855
British explorer Richard Burton publishes **Pilgrimage to El-Medinah and Mecca**, a great adventure narrative that will also become a classic commentary on Muslim life and manners, especially on the annual pilgrimage.

1855
Dry cleaning is invented by Jean Baptiste Jolly, the owner of a French dye company. He discovers that a fabric appears clean after kerosene is spilled on it.

1855
English sociologist and philosopher **Herbert Spencer** publishes the first part of *The Principles of Psychology*, the first volume of *The Synthetic Philosophy*, covering biology, psychology, morality, and sociology.

1855
In the wake of immigration following the gold rushes, Australian provincial parliaments adopt "**white Australia**" immigration policies excluding Chinese immigrants.

1855
John Mercer Langston, a former slave, is elected clerk of Brownhelm Township in Ohio. He is the first black person to win an elective political office in the United States.

1855-1856

1855
Joseph Medill and five partners buy the **Chicago Tribune**, to promulgate his Free-Soil and Abolitionist views. It is one of the most influential early supporters of Abraham Lincoln.

1855
Men and Women, English poet **Robert Browning's** most memorable volume of poetry, is published while he is living in Italy.

 [1]

1855
Milwaukee entrepreneur Frederick Miller buys the abandoned Best Brothers brewery. After his death in 1888, his company will be reorganized and renamed Frederick **Miller Brewing Company**.

1855
Piedmont-Sardinia and Sweden join Britain and France in alliance against Russia in the **Crimean War**.

1855
Publisher **Frank Leslie** begins publishing *Frank Leslie's Illustrated Newspaper*; its circulation will soon soar to 100,000, and it will become one of the leading illustrated publications of the day.

1855
The **Barbizon School** of French naturalist landscape painters is established. Its leaders are Théodore Rousseau and Jean-François Millet, who settled in the village of Barbizon.

 [2]

[2] Woman Grazing Her Cow by Jean-Francois Millet. His focus on peasant life, as here, sets him apart from the rest of the school.

[1] Robert Browning's book contains two of his most renowned dramatic monologues, where he recreates the rhythms of speech: "Fra Lippo Lippi" and "Bishop Blougram's Apology."

[5] Tsar Alexander II, seated, with other members of his family. He is eventually assassinated in 1881.

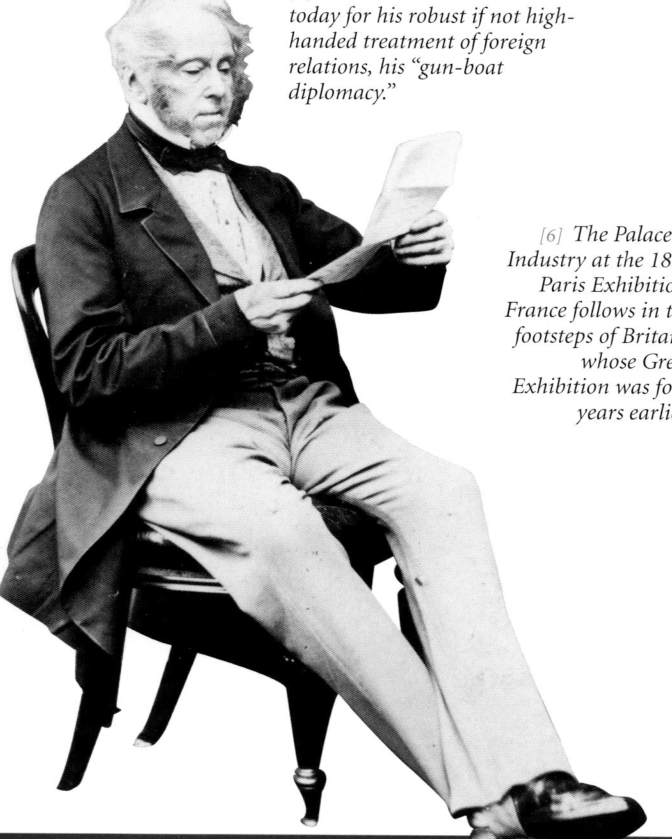

[3] Palmerston is remembered today for his robust if not high-handed treatment of foreign relations, his "gun-boat diplomacy."

[6] The Palace of Industry at the 1855 Paris Exhibition. France follows in the footsteps of Britain, whose Great Exhibition was four years earlier.

 [3]

1855
The Whig-Liberal statesman Henry John Temple, 3rd Viscount **Palmerston**, becomes prime minister of Great Britain after many years as foreign secretary.

 [4]

1855
Walt Whitman, arguably the most influential American poet and "grandfather" of Modernism, publishes *Leaves of Grass*. It will go through many revisions and editions and be periodically condemned as immoral.

January 23, 1855
The first bridge across the **Mississippi River** opens at the town that will soon be incorporated as Minneapolis, Minnesota.

 [5]

February 1855
Tsar Alexander II of Russia, who will later institute a series of domestic reforms, including the emancipation of the serfs (1861), ascends to the throne.

April 1855
Elmira Female College, in New York, is the first women's college to offer a program of study as rigorous as those offered at men's colleges. The word "female" will be removed in 1856. It becomes coeducational in 1969.

 [6]

May 15, 1855
The Paris Exposition (Universal Exposition of the Products of Agriculture, Industry, and the Fine Arts) opens. More than five million people will attend the exposition, which will remain open until November 15.

1855
The community of **Amana** is founded in Iowa by about 1,200 members of the communal Ebenezer Society from New York. In addition to advocating communal property and opposing military service, it opposes taking oaths, amusement, and a paid ministry.

1855
The Parker House hotel opens in Boston; it will become famous for the Parker House dinner roll, invented in its kitchens.

1855
The Pennsylvania Rock Oil Company is founded in New York. Several years later, a minor stockholder, **Edwin Drake**, will lease land at Titusville from the company and strike oil in 1859.

1855
The racket sport of **squash** is developed at the English public school Harrow.

1855
The reference work **Familiar Quotations** is published by Boston bookseller John Bartlett. The book will go through nine editions in his lifetime and appear in a centennial edition, the 13th, in 1955.

1855
The **screwdriver** comes into popular use after advances in precision machining make the manufacture of screws easier.

PHOTOGRAPHING THE WAR

The conflict in the Crimea was the first ever to be recorded on film; the trailblazing cameraman was Roger Fenton.

Roger Fenton's pictures of the Crimean War were the first extensive photographic documents of a war. Fenton (1819–69) studied painting and then law. Following a trip in 1851 to Paris, which he probably visited with the photographer Gustave Le Gray, he returned to England and was inspired to pursue photography. In the winter of 1855 his government connections as the founder (1853) and first honorary secretary of the Royal Photographic Society helped him gain an appointment as official photographer of the Crimean War. He was sent to provide visual evidence to counter the caustic written reports dispatched by William Howard Russell, war correspondent for *The Times* of London, criticizing military mismanagement and the inadequate, unsanitary living conditions of the soldiers. Fenton and his assistant, Marcus Sparling, arrived in Russia on the ship *Hecla* and set up their darkroom in a wagon (left above). Despite the difficulties of developing wet-collodion plates with impure water, in high temperatures, and under enemy fire, during his four-month stay Fenton produced 360 photographs. As an agent of the government, however, Fenton portrayed only the "acceptable" parts of the conflict. By then other photographers were in the Crimea, including the Italian-born Briton Felice Beato (c. 1830–1904) who took the picture (below left) of French troops celebrating after capturing the Malakoff redoubt. Even the disastrous charge of the Light Brigade—so movingly recounted by Alfred Tennyson's poem of the same name—was depicted as glorious. Although little of the real action or agony of war was shown, the images were nevertheless a historic landmark as the first to depict the more mundane aspects of modern warfare.

Upon Fenton's return to England, his war images were successfully exhibited in London and Paris, and wood engravings of the particularly notable photographs were printed in the *Illustrated London News.*

[7] *Castle Garden is the immigrant's gateway to the U.S. until it is replaced by Ellis Island.*

[4] *Walt Whitman. His specifically American idiom and subject matter and his distillation of his Civil War experiences win him a particular place in the country's pantheon.*

June 18, 1855
The "Soo" canal and locks open at **Sault Ste. Marie**, on the St. Mary's River in Michigan. The engineering marvel bypasses the river's rapids, which connect Lake Superior and Lake Huron, making it a boon to Great Lakes shipping.

June 29, 1855
The Daily Telegraph begins publication. It will become London's first penny paper and remains one of Britain's three biggest quality newspapers, along with *The Times* and *The Guardian*.

[7]
August 3, 1855
New York City opens its immigration station at **Castle Garden** (also known as Castle Clinton), at the southern tip of Manhattan Island; it will be the point of entry for more than eight million immigrants before Ellis Island opens in 1892.

September 11, 1855
The **Siege of Sevastopol** ends after British and French troops finally capture the main naval base of the Russian Black Sea fleet during the Crimean War.

November 23, 1855
Mexico passes the **Ley Juárez**, which abolishes special courts for the clergy and military. The law has been promoted by justice minister Benito Juárez, who wishes to eliminate the remnants of colonialism.

1856
The kingdom of Oudh, capital **Lucknow**, in India, is annexed by the British.

1856

1856
Balmoral Castle, a private residence of the British sovereign, is completed on the right bank of the River Dee, Aberdeenshire, Scotland. It is a modern granite building designed in Scottish baronial style.

 [1]

1856
Bavarian Lothar von Faber contracts for exclusive control of all **graphite** being mined in Siberia, for his pencil manufacturing operation.

1856
British chemist William Perkin receives a patent for aniline dye, known as **aniline purple**, Tyrian purple, or mauve; it is the first important synthetic dye used in clothing and consumer goods.

1856
British soldiers returning from the Crimea introduce **Turkish cigarettes**, which they learned to smoke during the war, to Great Britain.

1856
Canada's Legislative Council is changed from an appointed to an elected body.

1856
Cixi, while still a low-ranking concubine of the Xianfeng emperor of China, bears his only son. She will become of one of the most powerful women in the history of China.

[1] Balmoral Castle. Queen Victoria will publish her Leaves from a Highland Journal *describing her life there. Much of its furnishing is carried out in tartan.*

[8] "For Valour." The Victoria Cross, until 1942 made from the metal of guns captured at Sevastopol in 1855.

[3] Elizabeth Barrett Browning with her son, Pen. The message of Aurora Leigh *is that a woman cannot be fulfilled through her art alone.*

[6] Abdul Abdülmecid

[4] Henry Englehard Steinway

 [6]

1856
Ottoman sultan **Abdülmecid** I issues a reform edict known as the Hatt-i Hümayun. It proclaims the equality of all citizens under the law and grants civil and political rights to Christians.

1856
Parliament founds the **National Portrait Gallery** to house portraits of Britons who have made notable contributions to the nation's history since Tudor times.

1856
Quarrymen unearth humanlike fossilized remains in the Neander valley, or **Neanderthal**, in Germany. Some believe the bones represent an archaic and extinct human form, while others say they belong to an abnormal modern human.

1856
The **Declaration of Paris** establishes international maritime law in time of war, specifically abolishing privateering and defining the terms of neutral flags and goods and blockades.

1856
The first **kindergarten** in the United States opens in Watertown, Wisconsin. Its founder is Margarethe Meyer Schurz, a German immigrant who studied with Friedrich Froebel, the creator of the kindergarten concept.

1856
The first railway bridge is constructed across the **Mississippi River** at Rock Island, Illinois.

1856
Credit Suisse (Schweizerische Kreditanstalt) is founded in Zurich, establishing the modern Swiss banking system.

1856
English inventor **Henry Bessemer** patents a converter that introduces cold air into molten iron to produce steel in larger quantities at lower cost than previously was possible.

[2]

1856
English poet **Elizabeth Barrett Browning** publishes her epic-verse novel, *Aurora Leigh*.

[3]

1856
German-born instrument-maker Henry Engelhard Steinway produces the first **Steinway** grand piano, in his shop in New York. The Steinway will become one of the most prized grand pianos.

 [4]

1856
Great Britain allows the formation of **limited-liability corporations**: the loss that an owner (shareholder) of a business firm may incur is limited to the amount of capital he invests in it and does not extend to his personal assets.

1856
London's **Buckingham Palace**, the residence of Queen Victoria, gets an addition—a new south wing with a ballroom that is the largest room in England.

 [5]

STEEL PRODUCTION

The development of an economic method of making steel in large quantities transformed world industry.

Bulk steel production was made possible by Henry Bessemer in 1855, when he obtained British patents for a pneumatic steelmaking process. (A similar process is said to have been used in the United States by William Kelly in 1851, but it was not patented until 1857.) Bessemer used a pear-shaped vessel (above) lined with ganister, a refractory material containing silica, into which air was blown from the bottom through a charge of molten pig iron. Bessemer realized that the subsequent oxidation of the silicon and carbon in the iron would release heat and that, if a large enough vessel were used, the heat generated would more than offset the heat lost. A temperature of 1,650°C (3,000°F) could thus be obtained in a blowing time of 15 minutes with a charge weight of half a ton.

Bessemer's process could convert only a pig iron low in phosphorus and sulfur. (These elements could have been removed by adding a flux such as lime, but the slag produced would have degraded the lining of Bessemer's converter.) While there were good supplies of low-phosphorus iron ores in Britain and the United States, they were more expensive than phosphorus-rich ores.

[5] Buckingham Palace's ballroom. The east front, the palace's public face, will not take its familiar present form until 1913.

[7] An artist's impression of the Illinois Central in its 1890s heyday, with a globe in the background emphasizing the importance of the railway's network.

[2] Henry Bessemer, whose method of steelmaking enables temperatures high enough to eliminate impurities. Steel can become a metal of mass production for the first time.

1856
The French publishing house **Larousse** produces its *Dictionnaire de la langue française*.

 [7]

1856
The **Illinois Central**, reaching from Chicago to Cairo, Illinois, becomes the longest railway in the United States. At the line's completion the company is awarded 2.5 million acres (1,011,750 hectares) of land.

1856
The Second Opium War breaks out in China; France soon joins Britain in the conflict. **The Opium Wars** arose from China's attempts to suppress the opium trade. British traders had been illegally exporting opium to China.

 [8]

1856
The Victoria Cross, the highest decoration for valor in the British armed forces, is instituted by Queen Victoria at the request of her consort, Prince Albert. The first medals are awarded during the Crimean War.

1856
The **Western Union** Telegraph Company is chartered. It is an amalgamation of several independent telegraph lines and will become the largest provider of telegraphic services in the United States.

1856
In Egypt **Theodor Bilharz** identifies the parasites that cause schistosomiasis (or bilharzia), a group of chronic disorders caused by small, parasitic flatworms or blood flukes; it is second only to malaria among parasitic infections.

1856-1857

1856
Warwick, Rhode Island, textile manufacturers Benjamin and Robert Knight christen their products with the brand name **Fruit of the Loom**.

1856
William Walker, an American adventurer who had been invited to assist a revolutionary faction, makes himself president of Nicaragua, a key transport link between the Atlantic and Pacific oceans.

March 30, 1856
The Treaty of Paris ends the Crimean War. The war was managed and commanded very poorly on both sides. Disease accounted for a disproportionate number of the approximately 250,000 men lost by each side.

April 1856
Actress **Ellen Terry** begins her long and legendary career, making her stage debut in London at the age of nine. She plays the role of Mamillius in Shakespeare's *The Winter's Tale*.

May 21, 1856
A mob of proslavery sympathizers sack Lawrence, Kansas, which is part of the **Underground Railroad**.

May 22, 1856
Congressman **Preston S. Brooks** of South Carolina invades the U.S. Senate and viciously beats Senator Charles Sumner with a cane. Sumner had two days previously railed against the Kansas-Nebraska Act extending slavery.

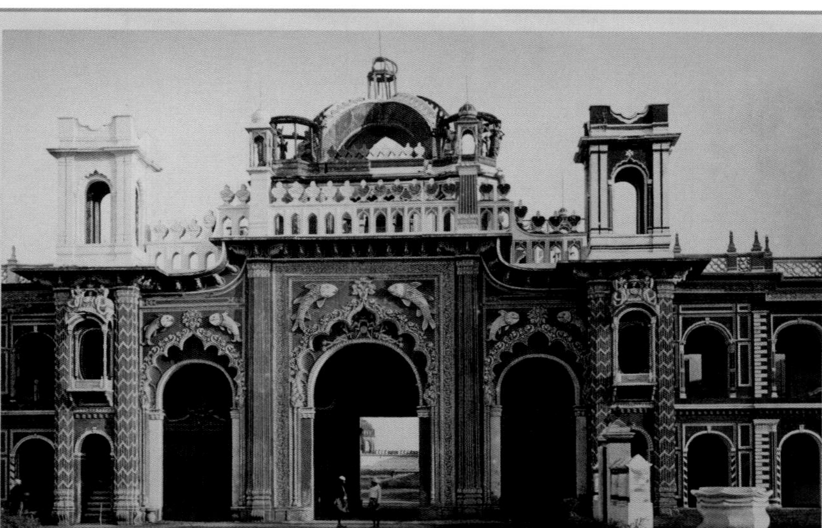

LUCKNOW

The Indian city is renowned for its distinguished 18th- and 19th-century buildings.

Lucknow contains many notable examples of architecture in a wide range of styles, most of which were constructed during the late 18th and first half of the 19th century. The best-preserved monument is the Residency, which was completed in 1800 and defended by British troops during the 1857 mutiny. The Great Imambara (1784) is a single-storied structure where Shi'ite Muslims assemble during the month of Muharram. Completed in 1784, the Rumi Darwaza, or Turkish Gate, was modeled after the Sublime Porte (Bab-iHümayun) in Istanbul. The great gateway of the Kaiserbagh Palace (left) was built in 1850 by Nawab Wajid Ali Shah. The stucco fish decorating the arch are symbols of the nawabs who ruled Lucknow.

The British abandoned Lucknow for a period during the Indian Mutiny after relieving the besieged garrison, but they returned in 1858 and drove out the mutineers.

[2] The actor Charles Keane with the young Ellen Terry, dressed for their parts in The Winter's Tale.

[1] The Congress of Paris meets to end the Crimean War. The independence of Turkey is to be respected, the Black Sea is to be neutral, and large parts of present-day Romania are handed back to Turkey by Russia.

1857
Frederic Edwin Church paints *Niagara*, one of the most important canvases of this American Romantic landscape painter, who was one of the most prominent members of the Hudson River School.

1857
French poet **Charles Baudelaire** is brought to trial for "offenses against religious morals" resulting from his recently published collection of verse, *Les Fleurs du mal* (*The Flowers of Evil*).

1857
French realist **Gustave Flaubert** publishes his enduring novel, *Madame Bovary*, which leads to a trial on charges of the novel's alleged immorality because of its sympathetic depiction of an adulteress.

1857
Friction between the Mormons and the federal judiciary leads President James Buchanan to replace **Brigham Young** as governor of the territory of Utah, and an army is sent to establish the primacy of federal rule in the territory.

1857
In a building designed by Napoleon Le Brun and Gustavus Runge, the **Philadelphia Academy of Music** opens.

1857
In Boston the **Atlantic Monthly** begins publication under the editorship of James Russell Lowell. It will be known for a long line of distinguished editors and authors, including Ralph Waldo Emerson, Henry Wadsworth Longfellow, and Oliver Wendell Holmes.

May 24-25, 1856
Militant abolitionist **John Brown** leads a nighttime raid on a proslavery settlement at Pottawatomie Creek, Kansas, in which five men are hacked to death. The raid is in retaliation for the sacking of Lawrence, Kansas.

August 10, 1856
A devastating hurricane strikes the vulnerable city of **New Orleans** and the Louisiana coast, causing severe damage. Lafcadio Hearn's 1889 novel *Chita* will tell the story.

1857
Gail Borden's **condensed milk** begins commercial production. Purity crusades and the distribution of samples lead to its widespread adoption. Based on skim milk with no additives, the product will contribute to rickets in many American children.

1857
A New Orleans **yellow fever epidemic** takes more than 7,000 lives. "Bring out your dead," cry the death-cart pushers.

1857
Bethlehem Steel is founded in Pennsylvania.

1857
British game laws are eased. For many years poachers had been punished with a seven-year sentence in Australia.

[6] Dred Scott is denied his freedom by the Supreme Court, and his case heightens tension between the states.

[5] Brigham Young, second from the left, with some Mormon colleagues.

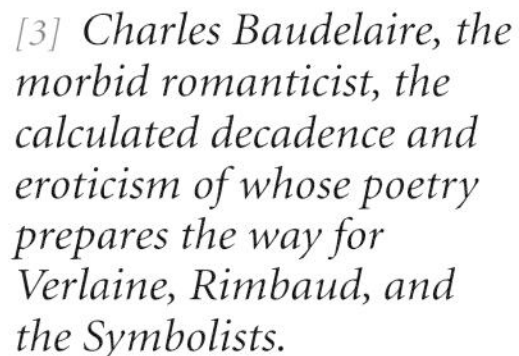

[3] Charles Baudelaire, the morbid romanticist, the calculated decadence and eroticism of whose poetry prepares the way for Verlaine, Rimbaud, and the Symbolists.

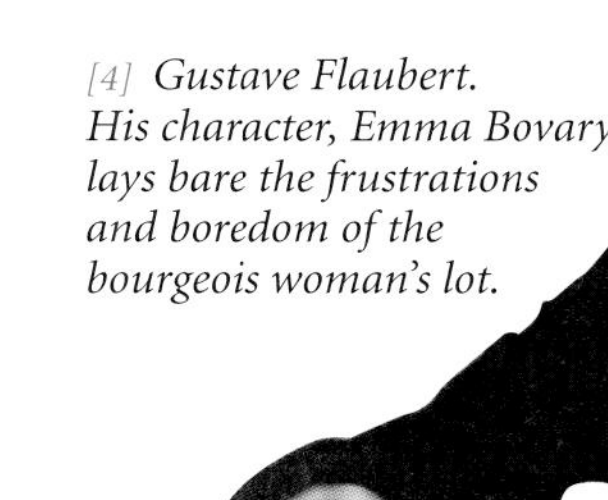

[4] Gustave Flaubert. His character, Emma Bovary, lays bare the frustrations and boredom of the bourgeois woman's lot.

[7] Elijah Otis, whose elevator design incorporates shaft-mounted ratchets to prevent cars from falling.

[6]
1857
In the **Dred Scott** decision, the U.S. Supreme Court rules that residing in a U.S. territory does not make a slave a free man, as only a state can bar slavery. African Americans had "no rights which any white man was bound to respect."

[7]
1857
Inventor Elijah Graves Otis installs the first **safety elevator** for passenger service in the store of E. V. Haughwout & Company in New York City. His invention makes high-rise buildings a practical possibility.

1857
Jean-François Millet, a French painter renowned for his peasant subjects, paints **The Gleaners**, one of his best-known works.

1857
London's rampant child prostitution and venereal disease spur a reform campaign by the **Englishwoman's Review**.

1857
A new liberal constitution, prescribes that **Mexico** be a representative, democratic, republican country, and calls for sweeping reforms. Reactions from religious and military conservatives soon lead to civil war.

1857
New York and St. Louis are connected by rail, a feat greeted by national celebration.

1857-1858

1857
North Carolina farmer Hinton Rowan Helper publishes ***The Impending Crisis of the South***, arguing that slavery is unprofitable for slave owners and ruinous for small farmers who do not own slaves.

1857
Paul C. Morphy wins the American chess championship at the first American Chess Congress. The American Chess Association is formed during the competition.

1857
Queen Victoria selects **Ottawa** as the site to be the capital of Canada.

1857
The firm **Currier & Ives** is founded by Nathaniel Currier, who set up a print publishing company in New York City in 1834, and James Merritt Ives. Their lithographic prints will be among the most popular wall hangings in 19th-century America.

 [1]

1857
The Matrimonial Causes Act is passed in Britain, establishing alimony payments for the first time.

1857
The Michigan State College of Agriculture (later **Michigan State University**) opens. This institution will be the first of many in the United States to offer practical and scientific studies in agriculture.

[2] *President James Buchanan with his cabinet. He is the only president never to marry. It is under him that the country disintegrates over the slavery question.*

[3] *English-born Elizabeth Blackwell, the first woman doctor in the United States. After 1869, when she returns to England, she becomes the first female physician and doctor on the United Kingdom Medical Register.*

[4] *The marriage of Queen Victoria's eldest daughter, Vicky, to Frederick, the future emperor of Germany.*

[1] *A typical Currier & Ives print, based on a George Catlin drawing of Native Americans performing a bear dance.*

1857
Tuberculosis, not at this time considered contagious, is the largest single cause of death in American cities. U.S. urban death rates are the highest in the world.

1857
Venice is connected to the Italian mainland—and thus to other European cities—with the opening of the Milan-Venice railway.

 [2]

March 4, 1857
Democrat **James Buchanan** is inaugurated as the 15th president of the United States. His vice president is John C. Breckinridge.

March 8, 1857
Hundreds of **women workers** in New York City's garment and textile factories stage a strike against low wages, long working hours, and inhumane work conditions.

March 21, 1857
An earthquake hits **Tokyo**, killing more than 100,000 people.

May 1, 1857
Nicaragua's head, **William Walker**, surrenders to the U.S. Navy. Walker—to aid several ambitious Vanderbilt employees in return for payment—has seized transportation properties belonging to Cornelius Vanderbilt.

1857
The **Pennsylvania Railroad** completes its consolidation of the route from Philadelphia to Pittsburgh. To eliminate competition, the railway company also buys up the state's main canal system.

1857
The popular winter song "**Jingle Bells**" is written by American James Pierpont.

1857
The **Indian Mutiny** against the British administration breaks out in India among native soldiers who believe they are being asked to violate religious restrictions; the mutiny is characterized by ferocity on both sides.

1857
The South African Republic is formed in the **Transvaal**, with the capital at Pretoria and with Martinus Pretorius, eldest son of the Great Trek leader Andries Pretorius, as president.

1857
The **University of California** is founded in Oakland. It will grow into one of the world's great university systems.

1857
Tom Brown's School Days, by Thomas Hughes, is published. The book's success—nearly 50 editions by 1890—will help create an enduring image of the British public school and popularize the doctrine of "muscular Christianity."

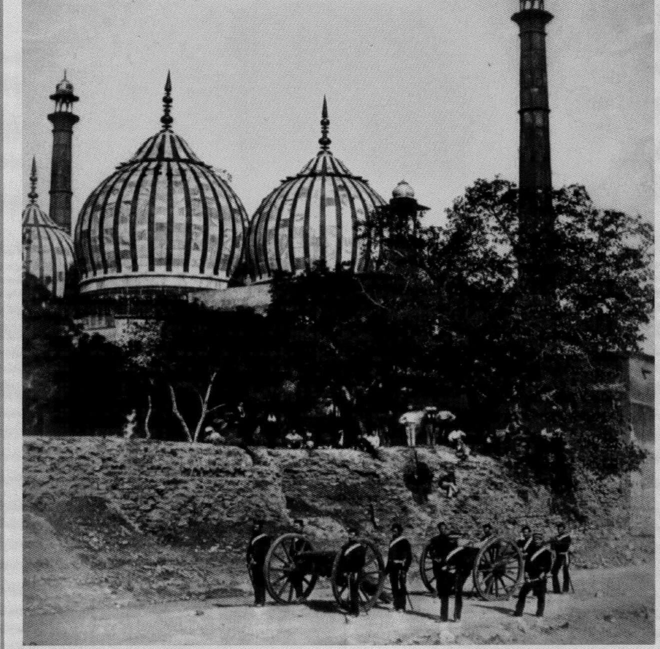

INDIAN MUTINY

Widespread but ultimately unsuccessful revolt against British rule in India

The Indian Mutiny was begun by Indian troops (sepoys) in the service of the British East India Company. It began in Meerut and then spread to Delhi, Agra, Cawnpore, and Lucknow.

The pretext for revolt was the introduction of the new Enfield rifle; to load it, the sepoys had to bite off the ends of the cartridges that were thought to have been lubricated with a mixture of pigs' and cows' lard, which both Muslims and Hindus were forbidden to touch by religious stricture. Late in April 1857, sepoy troopers at Meerut refused the cartridges; they were sentenced to long prison terms and immediately thrown into jail. This punishment incensed their comrades, who rose on May 10, shot their British officers, and marched to Delhi (the photograph below left shows British guns outside the city's Khynabee Gate). The local sepoy garrison joined the Meerut men, and by nightfall the aged Mughal emperor Bahadur Shah II had been nominally restored to power.

The mutiny then spread throughout northern India, although some sections of Indian society, like the Sikh irregulars (above left), remained loyal to the British. British operations to suppress the uprising were divided into three parts. First came the desperate struggles at Delhi, Cawnpore, and Lucknow during the summer; then the operations around Lucknow in the winter of 1857–58 directed by Sir Colin Campbell; and finally the "mopping up" campaigns of Sir Hugh Rose in early 1858. Peace was officially declared on July 8, 1858.

One of the most distressing features of the mutiny was the ferocity that accompanied it. The mutineers commonly shot their British officers on rising and were responsible for massacres at Delhi, Cawnpore, and elsewhere, but in the end the reprisals far outweighed the original excesses. Hundreds of sepoys were blown apart by cannons in a frenzy of British vengeance (though some British officers did protest the bloodshed).

The immediate result of the mutiny was a general clean-up of the Indian administration. The East India Company was abolished, and India was brought under direct rule from Britain. India's administrative and financial structures were modernized, along with its army. The Indian Mutiny also led to the introduction of government by consultation rather than decree. The Legislative Council of 1853 had contained only Europeans, but the council of 1861 was given an Indian-nominated element.

Finally, there was the effect of the mutiny on the people of India themselves. Traditional society had made its protest against the incoming alien influences, and it had failed; the princes and other natural leaders had either held themselves aloof from the mutiny or had proved for the most part incompetent. From this time all serious hope of a revival of the past or an exclusion of the West diminished. The traditional structure of Indian society began to break down and was eventually superseded by a westernized class system, from which emerged a strong middle class with a heightened sense of Indian nationalism.

[3]
May 12, 1857
Physician **Elizabeth Blackwell** and two other women open the New York Infirmary for Women and Children, which will be run entirely by women. Blackwell had previously been denied the opportunity to practice medicine.

June 27, 1857
Scientific American magazine predicts that whale oil is not a feasible long-term source of light. Supplies are dwindling, and increasing literacy spurs demand.

1858
A gold rush transforms a fur-trapping outpost into a prosperous and dynamic society that is proclaimed the **Colony of British Columbia**.

[4]
1858
A **wedding tradition** begins: Britain's Princess Royal and Prussia's Prince Frederick have marches from both Mendelssohn's *A Midsummer Night's Dream* and Wagner's *Lohengrin* at their wedding.

1858
American inventor John L. Mason invents the reusable glass **canning jar** with a reusable, screw-on lid for the home canning of produce.

1858
American inventor Joseph Rechendorfer patents a combination **pencil and eraser**.

1858

1858
Big Ben, the clock in the tower of Westminster Palace in London, begins chiming its famous tune.
 [1]

1858
Central Park in New York is opened for public use. Designed by pioneering landscape architects Frederick Law Olmsted and Calvert Vaux, it will be completed in 1863, but its remote location means that New Yorkers will not use it in large numbers for many years.

1858
Cornelius ("Commodore") Vanderbilt sells his shipping business and begins amassing railroad stock, eventually creating the first railway to serve the New York to Chicago route and building Grand Central Station in New York.

1858
Cotton flour and feed bags begin to replace barrels when St. Louis bag maker Judson Moss Bemis promises that his machine-sewn bags will not tear. By 1874, the business will manufacture 20,000 bags a day.

1858
English dressmaker **Charles Worth** establishes haute couture in Paris. He is the first to prepare and show a collection in advance, the first man to become prominent in the field of fashion, and the first to use young girls as models. His designs are copied and distributed worldwide.
 [2]

1858
Exploring the tributaries of the Mekong River, French naturalist Henri Mouhot becomes the first Westerner to encounter the ruins of **Angkor**, capital of the ancient Khmer civilization of Cambodia.
 [3]

THE *GREAT EASTERN* LAUNCH

The prototype of the modern ocean liner

Designed by British engineers Isambard Kingdom Brunel and John Scott Russell (seen above, second from right and far left) for the Eastern Navigation Company to carry cargo and passengers between England and India, the *Great Eastern* was by far the largest ship in the world at the time of its launching (1858), displacing 32,160 tons and measuring 692 feet (211 m) overall. It had a projected speed of 14.5 knots (27 km per hour) and alternate methods of propulsion: two paddle engines, a single screw engine, and sails rigged on six masts.

Before launching, the *Great Eastern* passed to the Great Ship Company, which put it on a New York trade route. The huge cargo holds never were filled to capacity, and in 1864, after years of deficit operation, the ship was sold to the Great Eastern Steamship Company, which used it as a cable vessel until 1874; it was during this time that it laid the first successful transatlantic telegraph cable. Cable laying was interrupted in 1867, when it made a voyage from Liverpool to New York to attract American visitors to the Paris Exhibition.

[1] Big Ben is actually the name of the main bell in the chime of bells at the Houses of Parliament; it is seen here being tested before installation.

[5] James Stephens learned revolutionary ways during years of exile in France. Failure of the Fenian uprising in Ireland in 1867 will show that his claims of support are unrealistic.

[2] Charles Worth, the first dressmaker to dictate to his customers what they should wear. The patronage of the Empress Eugenie will bring him fame.

[6] John Speke, who later is the first European to see Lake Victoria and rightly guesses that it is the source of the White Nile. Richard Burton, too ill to accompany him, disputes the claim.

1858
The Caribbean island of **Grenada** produces its first crop of nutmeg and mace. It will become the world's leading producer of these spices.

1858
The city of Boston begins filling in **Back Bay**. Much of the modern downtown will be built on the new land created by the project.

1858
The first edition of *Anatomy of the Human Body*, by British physician **Henry Gray**, is published. The work will become known as *Gray's Anatomy*, a standard medical textbook through the 20th century.

1858
The **Great Eastern**, for several decades the largest ship afloat, is launched on the Thames .

1858
The first mechanical **refrigerator** is made by French inventor P. A. Carré. It cools by means of a compression engine that uses liquid ammonia. In 1862 it will be used to make ice at the London Exposition.

 [7]
1858
The first steam-driven farm **tractors** are used.

1858
France begins military action in **Indochina** to secure commercial and religious interests in the region.

1858
French composer **Jacques Offenbach** produces the operetta *Orpheus in the Underworld.* His light burlesque French comic operas become one of the most characteristic artistic products of the period.

1858
German chemist **August Kekule von Stradonitz** publishes the second of his two articles establishing a structural theory of organic composition, demonstrating the role of carbon atoms in organic molecules.

1858
In *Die Cellular Pathologie*, German physician **Rudolf Virchow** proposes that the cell is the locus of pathology. His work makes humoral and environmental theories of disease obsolete.

1858
James Stephens founds the Irish Republican Brotherhood a secret society active chiefly in Ireland, the United States, and Britain. The name derives from the Fianna Eireann, the legendary band of Irish warriors led by Finn MacCool.
[5]

1858
Searching for the source of the Nile, English explorers Richard Burton and John Speke locate **Lake Tanganyika**.
 [6]

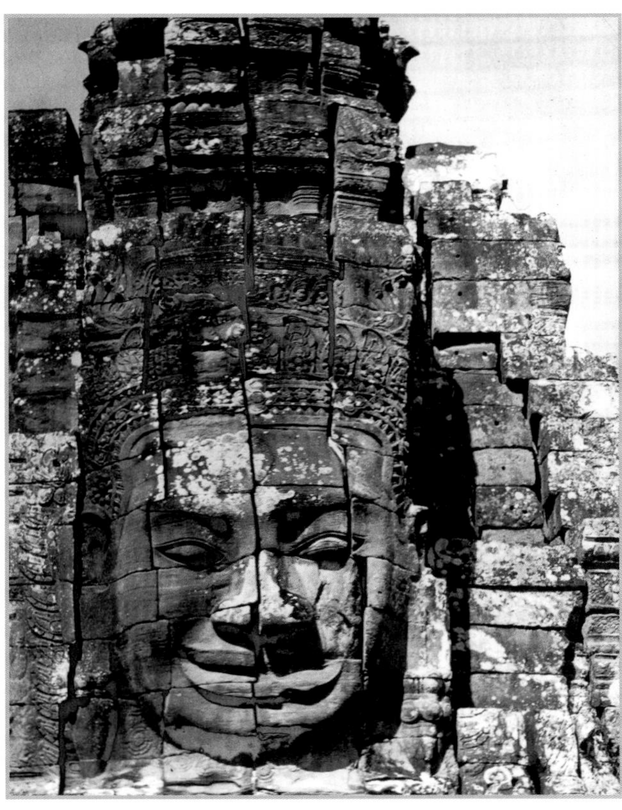

[3] *One of the many huge enigmatic faces on the temple of Bayon, close to the central temple at Angkor, thought to date from around A.D. 1200.*

[7] *Fowler's steam plow in action. The traction engine remains stationary, and the plow is pulled back and forth on a cable running between the "tractor" and the windlass (right).*

[4] *This elegantly crinolined lady and her Chinese charges, pupils at a missionary school in Shanghai, are testimony to the growing penetration of China by the West.*

[8] *Execution of rebels during the Indian Mutiny. Many rebels are simply lynched, without even summary justice, in reprisal for the murder of British women and children.*

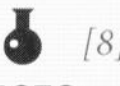 [8]
1858
The **Indian Mutiny** ends. Its aftereffects have far-reaching consequences for Indian society and government. The East India Company is abolished in favor of direct rule by the British government.

1858
The infant **Tokugawa Iemochi** is chosen as the next shogun of Japan after the death of Tokugawa Iesada.

1858
The **mint julep** originates in Virginia. The drink at first contains brandy, sugar, limestone water, crushed ice, and mint; eventually bourbon whiskey will commonly be used in place of the brandy.

1858
The term **"monkey wrench"** comes into use to describe a popular type of adjustable wrench invented by Charles Moncky.

 [4]
1858
The **Treaties of Tianjin** (Tientsin) require China to open additional ports, allow foreign envoys to reside in Beijing, allow foreigners to travel throughout the country, and allow Christian missionaries to work in any location.

1858
Work on *A New English Dictionary on Historical Principles* begins. This radical work, based on actual usage, will become the basis of the **Oxford English Dictionary**.

1858-1859

January 14, 1858
Bombs explode in an assassination attempt on France's **Napoleon III** and his wife. Ten are dead and 150 injured, but the targets are unharmed.

 [1]

February 11–July 16, 1858
Bernadette Soubirous, of Lourdes, France, has a series of visions of the **Virgin Mary**. Lourdes becomes a place of pilgrimage; a spring in a grotto is declared to have miraculous qualities.

 [2]

May 11, 1858
Minnesota is admitted to the United States as the 32nd state.

July 6, 1858
American shoemaker **Lyman Reed Blake** patents a shoemaking machine, permitting the production of low-cost shoes. The machine will be promoted by Gordon McKay and become known as the McKay machine.

July 29, 1858
U.S. politician and diplomat **Townsend Harris**, the first Western consul to reside in Japan, persuades that country to sign the Harris Treaty, an agreement securing commercial and diplomatic privileges for the United States in Japan.

August 21–October 15, 1858
A series of seven debates take place between incumbent Democratic senator Stephen A. Douglas and Republican challenger **Abraham Lincoln** during the 1858 Illinois senatorial campaign, largely concerning the issue of slavery extension into the territories.

 [3]

[3] A beardless Lincoln moves closer to the White House as he debates publicly in Illinois.

[1] Felice Orsini, the Italian revolutionary executed for his attempt on the life of Napoleon III.

[2] Bernadette Soubirous kneels in prayer before a statue of the Virgin Mary. Bernadette will soon become a nun.

[4] The first Macy's Store, on Sixth Avenue's "Ladies' Mile" in New York.

 [7]

1859
British philosopher and social critic **John Stuart Mill** publishes his classic treatise attacking tyranny, *On Liberty*.

 [8]

1859
Charles Darwin's **On the Origin of Species** proposes the theory of evolution by natural selection and posits links between humans and lower animals, stirring great controversy among those who believe in the literal truth of Genesis.

1859
Daniel Decatur Emmett composes the song "**Dixie**"; this tune will become popular as a marching song of the Confederate Army during the American Civil War and will often be considered the Confederate anthem.

1859
Jules Léotard performs his first flying trapeze act.

1859
English translator **Edward FitzGerald** publishes his version of the 12th-century Persian poem *The Rubáiyát of Omar Khayyám*.

 [9]

1859
Napoleon III and Francis Joseph I meet at Villafranca, concluding a preliminary peace agreement ending the **Franco-Piedmontese war** against Austria; it marks the beginning of Italy's unification under Piedmontese leadership.

October 27, 1858
American merchant Rowland Hussey Macy opens a New York store, **R. H. Macy Company**. The chain becomes identified with a logo based on the red star tattooed on Macy's arm.

 [4]

December 17, 1858
Ottoman statesman and diplomat **Mustafa Resid Pasa** dies. He was instrumental in carrying out Westernizing reforms in the Ottoman Empire, including the abolition of the slave trade.

1859
American inventor Ezra Warner invents the **can opener**, a rather dangerous implement with a point to pierce the can, which nonetheless is an improvement over the hammer and chisel commonly used.

1859
American tailor **Ebenezer Butterick** develops paper patterns to be used for the home sewing of clothing.

 [5]

1859
Belgian inventor Jean-Joseph-Étienne Lenoir designs the first commercially successful **internal-combustion engine**, based on the horizontal steam engine and using coal gas as fuel.

1859
British author **George Eliot** (née Mary Ann Evans) produces her first major novel, *Adam Bede*.

 [6]

THE RED HOUSE

Custom-built English rural home in which was hatched an artistic revolution

The Red House (above) was built in Bexleyheath, Kent, in countryside on the southeastern outskirts of London, England, for William Morris (1834–96), a designer, craftsman, poet, and early socialist. His designs for furniture, fabrics, stained glass, wallpaper, and other decorative arts were heavily influenced by his view of the Middle Ages and generated the Arts and Crafts Movement, which revolutionized Victorian taste.

Morris lived there from 1860 to 1865, during one of his most productive periods. The design of the building, with its light, space and natural, gently detailed materials was part of the movement's manifesto. The Red House was highly influential, setting a new architectural agenda for the middle classes on both sides of the Atlantic.

[7] *J. S. Mill with his stepdaughter Helen Taylor. This striking image serves as a reminder that Mill is a pioneering champion of women's rights.*

[5] *A dress being fitted at home. Butterick patterns will be graded in different sizes, unlike previous patterns, which have had to be adjusted to fit.*

[10] *Drake's oil well at Titusville, Pennsylvania. Its owner wears a top hat. Oil has been struck 69 feet down.*

[6] *The arresting appearance of George Eliot, for some the greatest of women novelists.*

[8] *The beetling brow of Charles Darwin, behind which the most revolutionary idea of the 19th century has been incubating.*

[9] *The emperors of France and Austria conclude peace. Napoleon III, conspiratorial as always, has failed to inform his Piedmontese ally.*

1859
French physicist Gaston Planté produces the first **electric storage battery**, or accumulator, in improved form; his invention will be widely used in automobiles.

1859
German physicist Gustav Robert Kirchhoff and chemist Robert Bunsen discover the principles of **spectrum analysis**.

1859
Philip Webb designs the Red House, Kent, England. The first house of the **Arts and Crafts Movement**, the Red House was built for one of the movement's leaders, William Morris.

 [10]

1859
The first productive oil well in the United States is drilled by former railway conductor **Edwin Laurentine Drake**.

1859
The Great Atlantic & Pacific Tea Company, Inc., opens its first store in New York City, beginning the modern **chain store** merchandizing concept.

1859
Thomas Austin introduces **English rabbits** to Australia as game to hunt. In the absence of disease and predators, the rabbit population grows to half a billion within a century and causes widespread environmental devastation.

1859

1859
Whale oil for illumination begins to become obsolete with the onset of the oil industry in Pennsylvania.

February 14, 1859
Oregon is admitted to the United States as the 33rd state.

June 1859
A rich lode of silver is discovered in Nevada, named for **Henry Comstock**, part-owner of the property on which it is found. The prospectors it draws swell the territory's population, as Virginia City, Washoe, and other mining boomtowns quickly arise.

 [1]

June 30, 1859
Jean-François Gravelet, known as **Blondin**, crosses Niagara Falls on a tightrope 335 meters (1,100 feet) long and 49 meters (160 feet) above the water.

July 5, 1859
Captain N. C. Brooks lands on the **Midway Islands** in the central Pacific Ocean and claims the territory for the United States.

October 16, 1859
Abolitionist **John Brown** leads a raid on the federal arsenal at Harpers Ferry, Virginia, hoping that escaped slaves will join an "army of emancipation" to liberate fellow slaves. Brown will be convicted of murder, slave insurrection, and treason.

 [2]

[1] *The Gould and Curry Mine Mill, where silver is extracted from Comstock Lode ore, in Virginia City.*

[2] *John Brown. Two of his sons are killed at Harpers Ferry, while he is wounded, captured, and then tried and executed.*

BLONDIN, THE TIGHTROPE WALKER

Spectacular stuntman whose death-defying feats captured the world's imagination

Blondin was a French tightrope walker and acrobat who owed his celebrity and fortune to his feat of crossing Niagara Falls on a tightrope 1,100 feet (335 m) long, 160 feet (49 m) above the water.

The son of a tightrope walker, Blondin was born Jean-François Gravelet in 1824. When he was five years old, he was sent to the École de Gymnase at Lyon, and after six months' training as an acrobat, he made his first public appearance as "the Little Wonder." On his first visit to the United States, he appeared in New York as part of the American circus impresario P. T. Barnum's Greatest Show on Earth. He crossed Niagara Falls (below) a number of times, first in 1859, and always with different theatrical variations: blindfolded, in a sack, trundling a wheelbarrow (below left), on stilts, carrying a man on his back (left), and sitting down midway to cook an omelette.

These feats established Blondin's reputation, and he became a highly paid performer whose name on any bill was guaranteed to draw big crowds. In 1861 he appeared in London at the Crystal Palace, turning somersaults on stilts on a rope stretched across the central transept, 170 feet (52 m) from the ground. He reputedly earned £100 for each of these performances, an astonishingly high fee for the time. British novelist Charles Dickens wrote: "Half of London is here eager for some dreadful accident."

Blondin kept working into his seventies and gave his final performance at Belfast in 1896. He died in England a year later.

A Union infantryman poses during the American Civil War.

1860

1860
A decade of strife begins as Maoris and white settlers battle over land in **New Zealand**.

 [1]

1860
American adventurer **William Walker** lands in Honduras, where he is taken prisoner by the British Navy, then turned over to Honduran authorities, who execute him.

1860
B. T. Henry, chief gun designer of Oliver Fisher Winchester's New Haven Arms Company, patents the **Henry lever-action repeating rifle**, which will be widely used in the coming Civil War.

1860
Britain and France conclude a **treaty of reciprocity** to increase trade between the two countries, despite opposition by the French public.

1860
Taku forts in China are taken during the Second Opium War.

 [2]

1860
British chemist Fredrick Walton invents **linoleum** as a durable, inexpensive floor covering.

[1] A former British soldier, wearing his campaign medal, outside his home in New Zealand, c.1860, with his family. He lives at Taranaki on North Island.

[3] The Chinese emperor's summer palace near Beijing is looted and burned by French and British soldiers in 1860 at the end of the Second Opium War.

[6] Major Albert Myer (with two rows of buttons) surrounded by officers of the U.S. Signal Corps in training at Georgetown.

[5] Starving slaves rescued from a slave ship off the African coast.

[7] Prince Michael is a member of the Obrenovic family, whose feud with the rival House of Karadjordje dominates Serbian politics until the murder of the last Obrenovic in 1903.

[2] The scene at one of the Taku forts guarding the river leading up to Beijing, very soon after it has been taken by French and British forces in 1860. Chinese corpses are strewn around, the first-ever war dead to be photographed.

1860
Hawaii's population is less than half what it was in 1850, as the native population succumbs to diseases imported from abroad.

1860
Henry Varnum Poor begins an investment information service that is the precursor of *Standard and Poor's Index*.

 [5]

1860
In defiance of international law, the **Clotilda**, the last ship bearing Africans taken as slaves, smuggles its cargo into Alabama.

 [6]

1860
Major Albert J. Myer is appointed the first officer of the U.S. Signal Corps; he has invented a method of signaling by "wig-wag": two flags by day or two torches by night signify letters. He also founds the U.S. Weather Bureau.

1860
Manuelito leads a force of 1,000 **Navajos**, whose livestock has been shot by soldiers, in an attack on Fort Defiance in the New Mexico Territory.

 [7]

1860
Michael III ascends to the throne of **Serbia**; he will institute the rule of law and attempt to found a Balkan federation aimed against the Ottoman Empire.

1860
British colonists in Natal in southern Africa import **Indian workers** as indentured laborers to work on sugar plantations.

1860
Cotton makes up more than half the total value of U.S. exports.

1860
Elizabeth Peabody founds the first English-language preschool in the United States.

1860
British and French troops occupy Beijing and burn the emperor's **summer palace**.

1860
French architect Charles Garnier begins work on the **Paris Opera House**. Crowning a great new boulevard, the opulently sumptuous opera house is designed as a place to both see and be seen.

1860
French lithographer and painter **Honoré Daumier** paints his *Third-Class Carriage*. It sympathetically portrays ordinary people in an introspective mood.

COTTON

The wealth of the antebellum United States was founded on production of the crop.

On the eve of the Civil War, cotton was the United States' most economically important natural resource. The international trading price was high, and America was the world's largest supplier. The most productive states were in the South, where the fields were tended and the crops gathered in by vast numbers of African slaves (left). In Alabama, for example, nearly half the population was black—435,000 out of a total of 964,000. Without forced labor, the cotton industry in the South would have been unsustainable, and so it was a matter of grave concern to plantation-owning white Southerners when the the frontrunner in the 1860 presidential campaign became Abraham Lincoln, whom they regarded as a dyed-in-the-wool abolitionist and described disparagingly as "the Black Republican." Cotton production was thus one of the most important causes of the war between the states.

[9] Florence Nightingale with a group of nurses from various London hospitals at the home of her brother-in-law, Sir Harry Verney (standing, back row), at Claydon in Buckinghamshire.

[4] The Paris Opera House, a lavish display of statuary, marble of every shade, murals, splendiferous foyers, and the grandest of staircases.

[8] Mississippi River steamboats moored at New Orleans in the 1860s.

1860
More than 1,000 steamboats carry freight and passengers on the **Mississippi River**, more than double the amount of 1840.

1860
Movement toward the **unification of Italy** proceeds as plebiscites in Tuscany, Parma, Modena, and Romagna favor union with Piedmont.

1860
Nicholas Petrovic comes to the throne of **Montenegro** as Nicholas I after the assassination of his uncle Danilo.

1860
Nursing pioneer **Florence Nightingale** establishes the Nightingale School for Nurses, the world's first school for nurses, at St. Thomas's Hospital in London.

1860
Swiss art and cultural historian **Jacob Burckhardt** publishes *The Civilization of the Renaissance in Italy*, deftly analyzing the daily life of Renaissance Italy, its political climate, and thought.

1860
The **dime novel** makes its debut with *Maleska: The Indian Wife of a White Hunter* by Anne S. W. Stephens. Its publishers will release hundreds more, including the exploits of Deadwood Dick and Nick Carter.

1860-1861

1860
The first **British Open** golf tournament is played at Prestwick, Scotland.
 [1]

1860
The first **expedition to cross Australia** from south to north sets out from Melbourne, led by Robert O'Hara Burke; it will reach the Gulf of Carpentaria in February 1861.
 [2]

1860
The first **Melbourne Cup** race is run over a 3,200-meter distance at Flemington Race Course and is won by Archer, a horse from Nowra, New South Wales.

1860
The **first world heavyweight boxing championship** in fought in England, with U.S. champion John C. Heenan facing British champion Tom Sayers. The brutal bout continues for 42 rounds.

1860
Vladivostok is founded in extreme southeastern Russia as a military outpost on the Sea of Japan.

1860
Wilkie Collins publishes *The Woman in White*, regarded as the first English mystery novel.
 [3]

[3] *A poster for Wilkie Collins's own stage adaptation of* The Woman in White *in 1871.*

[2] *Robert Burke with one of the camels used on his tragic journey. While he and William John Wills die in 1861 at Coopers Creek, a third member of the party, John King, survives.*

[6] *An envelope bearing the Pony Express postmark and dated October 24, 1860; posted in San Francisco, its destination is New York. Within a few years the railways will have driven the service out of business.*

[1] *"Old" Tom Morris tees off at Prestwick in 1860. He and his son, "Young" Tom, will win the Open in 1867 and 1868 respectively, the only father-son pair so to do.*

[4] *What J. H. Kellogg's enterprise will lead to: Corn Flakes, the most famous cereal of all, advertised here for the first time in 1906.*

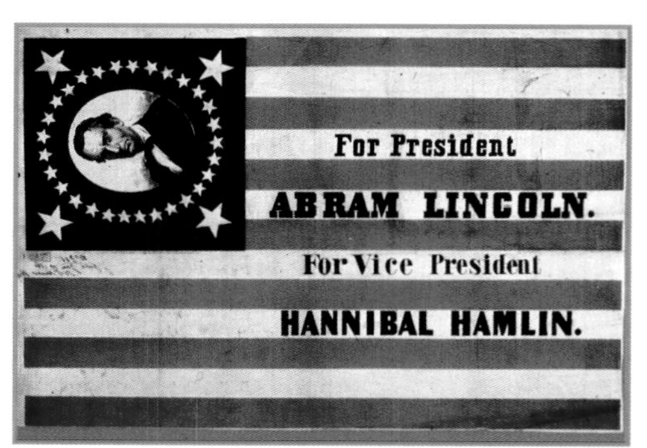

[8] *A flag produced for Lincoln's presidential campaign.*

September 7, 1860
Garibaldi's republican forces enter **Naples** on the Italian mainland.

October 3, 1860
In a decisive battle at the **Volturno River**, Garibaldi effectively ends control of Naples by Francis II; in a plebiscite October 21–22 Francis will be deposed, and the south of Italy will be united with the north under Victor Emmanuel.

 [8]
November 6, 1860
Abraham Lincoln is elected 16th president of the United States. His vice presidents are Hannibal Hamlin (1861–65) and Andrew Johnson (1865).

December 1860
Félix María Zuloaga **Trillo** becomes Mexican president for the third time.

December 20, 1860
South Carolina is the first state to secede from union with the United States and is soon joined by Alabama, Florida, Georgia, Louisiana, Mississippi, and Texas.

1861
A U.S. entrepreneur with a checkered past, **Henry Meiggs** is contracted to complete a railroad between Santiago and Valparaiso in Chile.

c. 1860
Increased global demand for **coffee** leads to the clearing of large parts of the Brazilian Atlantic forest. The growth of railroad lines allows planters to move deep into the forest.

c. 1860
J. H. Kellogg and C. W. Post develop processed **breakfast cereal** as a health food in Battle Creek, Michigan.

 [4]

c. 1860
Louis Pasteur discovers the principles of the process of heating foods to kill microorganisms. It is called **pasteurization** in his honor.

c. 1860
The **minstrel show**—a group of black-faced white performers whose material caricatures the singing and dancing of slaves—reaches the height of its popularity. Minstrel troupes composed of black performers will be formed after the Civil War.

 [5]

April 3, 1860
The **Pony Express** begins mail delivery by continuous horse-and-rider relays between St. Joseph, Missouri, and Sacramento, California. The route is approximately 1,800 miles (2,900 km) long, has 157 stations, and requires about 10 days to cover.

 [6]

May 11, 1860
Giuseppe **Garibaldi** reaches Marsala in Sicily with his 1,000 Redshirt guerrillas and in the name of Victor Emmanuel, king of Sardinia-Piedmont, proclaims himself dictator, liberating the island from the Bourbon king of Naples.

 [7]

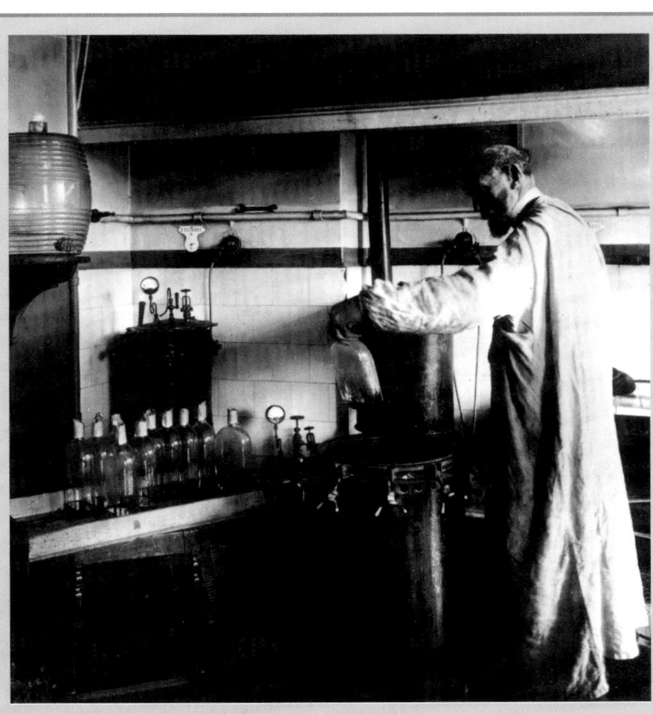

LOUIS PASTEUR

French chemist who found a cure for rabies

After spending the early part of his career researching the effects of polarized light on chemical compounds, in 1857 Louis Pasteur (above) became director of scientific studies at the École Normale Supérieure in Paris. His studies of fermentation of alcohol and milk (souring) showed that yeast could reproduce without free oxygen (the Pasteur effect); he deduced that fermentation and food spoilage were due to the activity of microorganisms and could be prevented by excluding or destroying them.

Pasteur's work overturned the concept of spontaneous generation (life arising from nonliving matter) and led to heat pasteurization, which allowed vinegar, wine, and beer to be produced and transported without spoiling. He saved the French silk industry with his work on silkworm diseases. In 1881 he perfected a way to isolate and weaken germs, and he went on to develop vaccines against anthrax in sheep and cholera in chickens, following Edward Jenner's example. He turned his attention to researching rabies, and in 1885 he saved the life of a boy bitten by a rabid dog by inoculating the child with a weakened virus.

[5] Charles H. King, "the master banjoist of the universe," famous for his "masterpiece of banjo music, 'Home, Sweet Home.'" To reassure his white audience, there is a picture of him without makeup on the sole of his huge shoe.

[9] Sultan Abdulaziz, an enthusiast for ram fights and camel wrestling, will fall under the influence of the Russians in the 1870s and be deposed before killing himself.

[7] Garibaldi, every inch the heroic patriotic leader, in one of the colorful outfits that do so much for his image.

 [9]

1861
Abdülaziz becomes Ottoman sultan and begins a course of modernization.

1861
Albert Bierstadt paints *Laramie Peak*, the first of his grandiose scenes of the Rockies, the Grand Canyon, and Yosemite Valley that extend the Hudson River School of monumental landscape painting to the American West.

1861
An escalating series of incidents pits the U.S. Army against the **Apache** tribes of Arizona, led by Cochise and Mangas Colorado.

1861
Bavarian **John Eberhard Faber** launches an American branch of the family business by establishing a pencil factory in New York City.

1861
Britain establishes a protectorate over the **Bahrain** Islands in the Persian Gulf.

1861
British physicist **James Clerk Maxwell** begins his formulation of an electromagnetic theory that will lay the foundation for 20th-century physics.

1861
Charles Digby Harrod takes over his father's grocery store and begins to turn it into what will be the greatest department store in England.

 [1]

1861
Count Agoston Haraszthy brings cuttings of 300 varieties of wine grapes to California at the request of the state legislature, thus inaugurating the **California wine industry**.

1861
Detective **Allan Pinkerton** thwarts a plot to assassinate President-elect Abraham Lincoln as he passes though Baltimore on his way to be inaugurated.

 [2]

1861
Estonian physician, folklorist, and poet **F. Reinhold Kreutzwald** compiles the Estonian national epic poem *Kalevipoeg* (*The Son of Kalevi*).

1861
Frederick William IV, king of Prussia from 1840, dies at Sanssouci Palace.

 [3]

1861
French microbiologist **Louis Pasteur** publishes a paper refuting the widely held theory of the spontaneous generation of bacteria.

MONTE CARLO

The opening of a casino in Monaco turned the state into a playground for the rich.

The world's second smallest nation (after the Vatican City), Monaco is a principality situated northeast of Nice on the French Riviera. In 1856 Charles III of Monaco granted a charter allowing a joint-stock company to build a casino, which opened in 1861. The district around it became known as Monte Carlo, in honor of the crown prince, the Italian version of whose name was Carlo. Monaco was soon one of Europe's most popular tourist destinations, as well as a luxurious playground for the world's wealthy, who flocked to the gaming tables in palatial surroundings (left) to play a wide range of card and dice games, including blackjack (*vingt-et-un*) and roulette.

The Monte Carlo casino complex also includes the Grand Théâtre de Monte Carlo, an opera and ballet house, and the headquarters of the Ballets de Monte Carlo. Monaco also hosts an annual Formula 1 Grand Prix, which passes outside the casino.

[7] Queen Victoria, wearing the newly fashionable crinoline, with Prince Albert shortly before he dies of typhoid brought on by Windsor Castle's inadequate drains.

[1] Harrods, not the pinky-orange palace of today, but a medley of terrace houses run together. Its success began with serving visitors to the nearby Great Exhibition in 1851.

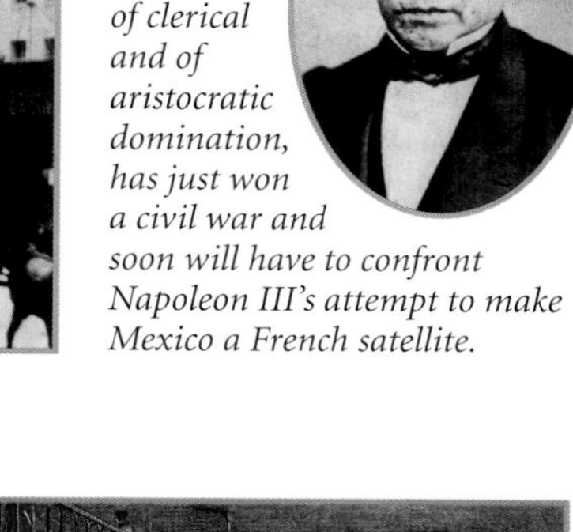

[8] Juarez, opponent of clerical and of aristocratic domination, has just won a civil war and soon will have to confront Napoleon III's attempt to make Mexico a French satellite.

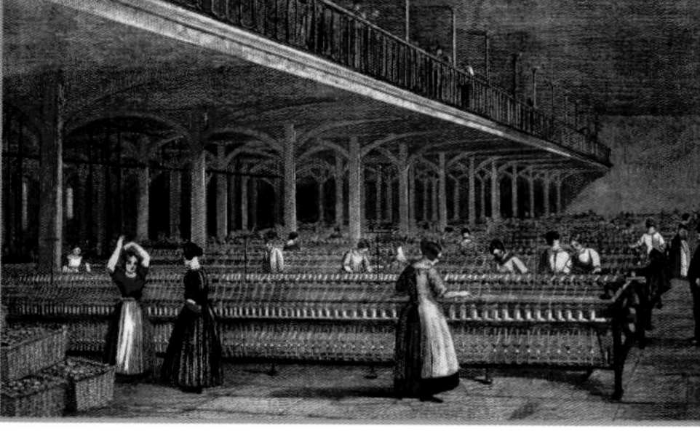

[9] A typical Victorian cotton mill, the machinery largely minded by "mill girls."

[3] Frederick William survived the revolutions that swept Europe in 1848 and had the measure of Bismarck: "Only to be used when bayonets are fixed." After his death, there will be three wars in nine years.

 [7]

1861
Queen Victoria's beloved consort, **Prince Albert**, dies of typhoid fever at the age of 42. She will wear black in mourning for him for the rest of her life.

 [8]

1861
Reformer **Benito Juárez** is elected president of Mexico.

1861
Taking advantage of the increased popularity of gambling, the **casino at Monte Carlo** opens. Casinos become popular destinations for wealthy tourists in the mid-19th century.

 [9]

1861
Textile mills in Lancashire, England, are forced to close when the Union blockade of Southern ports cuts off their supply of raw cotton; mass unemployment results.

 [10]

1861
The Arts and Crafts Movement in England gains influence. Led by **William Morris**, the movement seeks to recapture the spirit and workmanship of medieval design and production.

1861
The **Colorado**, **Nevada**, and **Dakota** territories are formed.

1861
French surgeon and anthropologist **Paul Broca** announces that the seat of articulate speech is localized to the left frontal region of the brain, a region since known as the convolution of Broca.

1861
Frenchmen Pierre Michaux and his son, Ernest, invent the **velocipede**, the first pedal-powered bicycle.

 [4]

1861
Gilbert and Frank Van Camp of Indianapolis secure a contact to provide **canned pork and beans** for the Union army; their product proves to be popular, eventually making the brand the market leader.

1861
Mrs. Beeton publishes her *Book of Household Management*, one of the best-selling cookbooks in history, which is, in addition, an exhaustive guide to running a proper Victorian home.

 [5]

1861
The seven states already seceded from the Union are joined by Arkansas, North Carolina, Tennessee, and Virginia to form the **Confederate States of America**. Mississippi senator Jefferson Davis is chosen president.

 [6]

1861
Prolific German-born English engineer and inventor William Siemens patents the **open-hearth furnace process for steelmaking**.

[4] A velocipede adapted for the ice, with two blades instead of the small rear wheel. The projecting cross-piece in front is to rest the feet on when freewheeling.

[5] A supper for 16, as envisaged in Mrs. Beeton's book.

[10] An interior at Kelmscott, the 17th-century Oxfordshire house lived in by William Morris and his family. Its uncluttered simplicity, by mid-Victorian standards, is a foretaste of what the Arts and Crafts Movement will aim at.

[11] Macaulay once thought his history would start in 1688 and finish in 1830, but it only just reaches the 1700s.

[6] Jefferson Davis, first and last Confederate president.

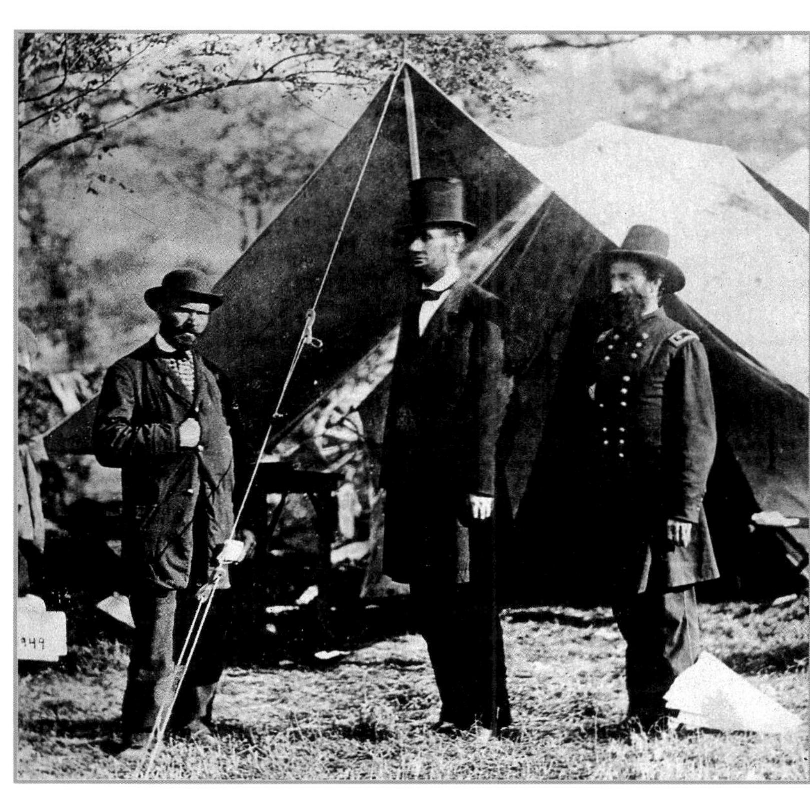

[2] Lincoln with two Pinkerton detectives at Antietam in 1862.

1861
The **Congressional Medal of Honor**, the foremost U.S. military decoration, is instituted by Congress for the navy (and in 1862 for the army) for "conspicuous gallantry and intrepidity at the risk of life, above and beyond the call of duty."

1861
President Abraham Lincoln calls for 75,000 militiamen to serve for three months. He proclaims a **naval blockade of the Confederate states**. The Confederate government has previously authorized a call for 100,000 soldiers, soon increased to 400,000.

1861
The **Trent Affair** causes hostility between the U.S. and Britain when a U.S. ship seizes two Confederates from the ship that is bound for Europe.

1861
The U.S. Congress levies an **income tax** to pay for the war effort; any income higher than $800 is taxed.

1861
The Vatican begins publication of **L'Osservatore Romano**, one of the most influential newspapers in Italy and the de facto voice of the Holy See.

 [11]

1861
Thomas Babbington Macaulay's fifth and final volume of his *History of England* is published posthumously, securing his place as one of the founders of what has been called the Whig interpretation of history.

1861-1862

1861
Tongzhi ascends the throne of China at the age of six. During his reign, a short revitalization of the beleaguered Qing government will occur.

1861
Tsar Alexander II's Edict of Emancipation emancipates the serfs of Russia, but the terms ensure that they will remain paupers.

1861
U.S. locksmith **Linus Yale** patents the pin-tumbler lock that opens with a flat key.

1861
Union general George B. McClellan is placed in command of what is to become the Army of the Potomac, charged with the defense of the capital and destruction of the enemy's forces in northern and eastern Virginia.

1861
Western Union opens a **transcontinental telegraph** line between San Francisco (thus Telegraph Hill) and New York City. This development is the death knell for the Pony Express.

1861
William I, the future kaiser (emperor) of Germany, succeeds to the throne of Prussia.

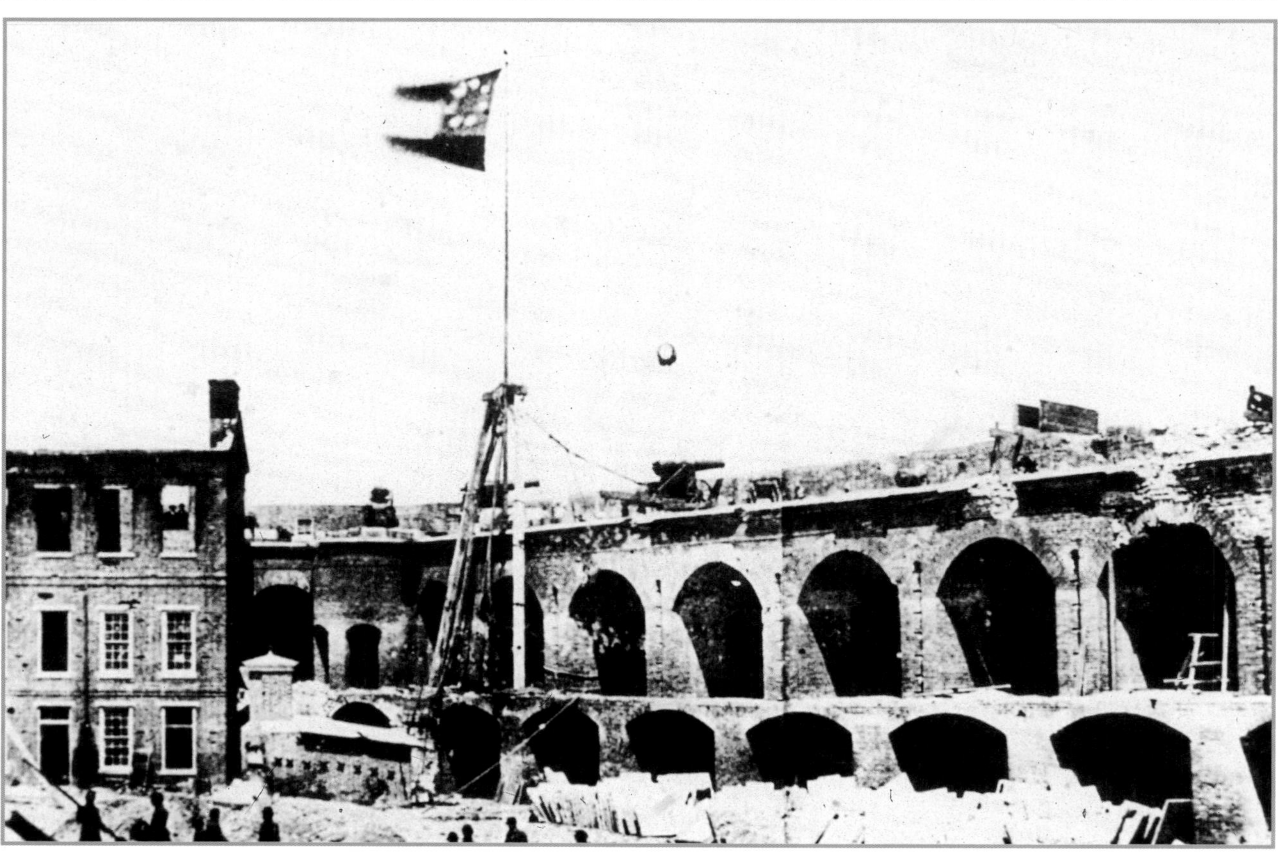

[3] *A Confederate flag flies over a battered Fort Sumter.*

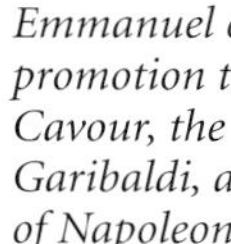

[2] *Previously the king of Sardinia-Piedmont, Victor Emmanuel owes his promotion to the statesman Cavour, the soldier Garibaldi, and the schemes of Napoleon III.*

[4] *Confederate soldiers look down on the railroad junction at Manassas in 1862. The junction's strategic position is the reason why the two battles of Bull Run are fought there.*

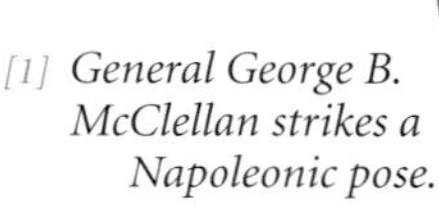

[1] *General George B. McClellan strikes a Napoleonic pose.*

September 17, 1861
The forces of Buenos Aires province, commanded by Governor Bartolomé Mitre, defeat those of the Argentine Confederation, led by Justo José de Urquiza, at the **Battle of Pavón**.

October 24, 1861
The first **transcontinental telegram** is sent via the telegraph in the United States.

1862
The London International Exhibition attempts to repeat the success of the 1851 exhibition.

1862
Unemployment in Lancashire cotton-manufacturing districts grows.

1862
American Richard J. Gatling invents the crank-operated, multibarrel **Gatling gun**, the first practical machine gun.

1862
Belize is proclaimed a British colony under the name **British Honduras**.

1861
Yale University becomes the first American university to award doctoral degrees.

January 28, 1861
Kansas is admitted to the United States as the 34th state.

March 17, 1861
Victor Emmanuel is proclaimed the first king of a united Italy, comprising Lombardy, Piedmont, Parma, Modena, Lucca, Romagna, Tuscany, and the two Sicilies. Rome, however, is held by Napoleon III.

 [2]

April 12, 1861
After a bloodless bombardment, Robert Anderson and about 85 soldiers surrender **Fort Sumter** in the harbor of Charleston, South Carolina, to some 5,500 besieging Confederate troops under General P. G. T. Beauregard. The U.S. Civil War has begun.

[3]

July 21, 1861
At Manassas, Virginia, the Union troops of General Irvin McDowell are routed by those of Confederate generals P. G. T. Beauregard and Joseph E. Johnson in the **First Battle of Bull Run**.

 [4]

September 9, 1861
Sally Louisa Tompkins is commissioned a cavalry captain; she is the only woman to be commissioned in the Confederate army.

[7] A homesteading family with their covered wagon, on the way to claim their 160 acres.

[6] An elaborately set up shot of Glaisher and Coxwell in the basket of their balloon, with a stout anchor or grappling iron and rope attached to the side.

[5] A Gatling gun, its cylindrical magazine protruding above its barrels.

[8] Victor Hugo will be able to return to France in 1870, on the fall of Napoleon III and the ending of the Second Empire.

TRANSCONTINENTAL RAILWAYS

An ambitious project begins to join eastern and western America.

Preliminary work had already begun on a railroad link between the Atlantic and Pacific coasts when two Pacific Railway Acts (1862, 1864) provided the federal aid that turned the dream into reality.

The first act granted rights-of-way to the Union Pacific Railroad to build westward from Omaha, Nebraska, and to the Central Pacific Railroad to build eastward from Sacramento, California. The second act doubled the size of the land grants adjacent to the rights-of-way and allowed the railroads to sell bonds to raise more money. Congressional investigations later showed that some railroad owners had illegally profited from the railway acts.

Union Pacific crews (left) surveyed and laid 1,087 miles (1,749 km) of track across the Missouri River, through Nebraska, Colorado, Wyoming, and Utah, where they connected with their Central Pacific counterparts at Promontory Summit. The line was one of the greatest engineering feats of the 19th century.

1862
British explorer John Speke is the first European to explore Lake Victoria and locate the **source of the Nile**.

 [6]

1862
British meteorologist James Glaisher and aeronaut James Henry Coxwell explore the **upper atmosphere** in hot-air balloons, reaching heights of seven miles above the earth.

 [7]

1862
With the **Homestead Act**, 160 acres in the West, Midwest, and Great Plains can go virtually free to anyone who is either 21 or head of a family, a citizen or person who had filed for citizenship, and who will cultivate the land for five years.

1862
Congress creates the U.S. **Department of Agriculture**.

1862
Construction begins on two U.S. railroads, the **Central Pacific**, building east from Sacramento, California, and the **Union Pacific**, building west from Omaha, Nebraska. The Central Pacific recruits Chinese workmen to construct its railroad.

 [8]

1862
In exile, **Victor Hugo** writes *Les Miserables*, the story of the convict Jean Valjean, a victim of society imprisoned for 19 years for stealing a loaf of bread, and the obsessive detective Javert, who hounds him.

1862

1862
Leo Tolstoy writes his masterpiece, *War and Peace*, set against the background of Russia's involvement in the Napoleonic Wars.

 [1]

1862
Major General Ulysses S. Grant garners the first significant victories for the Union at the battles of **Fort Henry** on the Tennessee River and **Fort Donelson** on the Cumberland River.

1862
Musicologist Ludwig, Ritter von **Köchel**, compiles the most complete chronological catalog of Wolfgang Amadeus Mozart's works, which are identified almost universally by the letter *K* (for Köchel).

1862
Otto of Wittelsbach, who was chosen king of Greece by the Great Powers at the conference of London in May 1832, is deposed by a coup d'état and replaced by a prince of the Danish Glücksburg family, who reigns as **King George I of the Hellenes**.

1862
Otto von Bismarck is appointed prime minister and foreign minster of Prussia. He states that "it is not by means of speeches and majority resolutions that the great issues of the day will be decided. . . but by **blood and iron**."

1862
Petko Rachev Slaveykov translates the Bible, reestablishing the **Bulgarian vernacular** as a medium for literature.

[4] Johnny Clem, a Union drummer boy who becomes a hero after the Battle of Shiloh.

[1] A group of Russian writers: Tolstoy, in uniform, stands immediately behind Ivan Turgenev.

[2] Christina Rossetti with her brother, the Pre-Raphaelite poet and painter Dante Gabriel Rossetti.

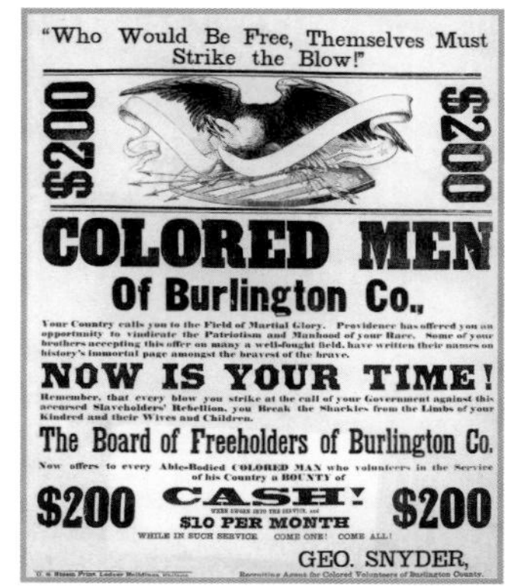

[5] An 1863 recruiting poster offering black men in Burlington County, New Jersey, $200 if they will join the Union army.

[3] The Monitor *after the battle, its gun turret armor bearing scars from Confederate hits.*

1862
The principalities of Moldavia and Walachia are united under the rule of Alexandru Cuza as **Romania**; Cuza sets about a program of reforms, though the area is still under the control of the Ottoman sultan.

1862
The **Treaty of Saigon** gives France Saigon and three southern provinces of Cochinchina, the opening of three ports, freedom to conduct missionary activity, a vague protectorate over Vietnam's foreign relations, and a large cash indemnity.

c. 1862
John B. Stetson designs the ten-gallon hat that will become an icon of the American West. He will open a hat-making company in 1865 in Philadelphia, and his most famous model will be "the Boss of the Plains."

 [3]

March 9, 1862
The Union ship *Monitor* engages the Confederacy's *Virginia* (formerly *Merrimack*) in history's first duel between **ironclad warships**, marking the beginning of a new era of naval warfare.

April 4, 1862
Union forces under George B. McClellan begin the unsuccessful **Peninsular Campaign** to capture the Confederate capital of Richmond, Virginia.

 [4]

April 6–7, 1862
The **Battle of Shiloh** (Pittsburgh Landing), is fought in southwestern Tennessee, resulting in a victory for the North under General Ulysses S. Grant and 10,000 casualties on either side.

1862
Russian novelist and short-story writer **Ivan Turgenev** writes his greatest novel, *Fathers and Sons*, which illustrates, with remarkable balance and profundity, the issues that divide the generations.

 [1]

1862
The Atlantic Monthly publishes Julia Ward Howe's "**Battle Hymn of the Republic**," to be set to an old folk tune also used for "John Brown's Body." Written during a visit to a camp in 1861, it becomes the semiofficial song of the Union.

1862
The bugle call "**Taps**" is composed by Union general Daniel Adams Butterfield. It is first played as the signal for lights out at the end of the day, then adopted as the farewell at military funerals.

1862
The Civil War is carried to the Southwest as Albuquerque and Santa Fe are taken by the Confederates, but at the **Battle of La Glorieta**, they are routed and forced to retreat into Texas.

1862
The **Morrill Act** grants each U.S. state 30,000 acres of federal land for each of its members of Congress, to be sold to finance schools to teach "agriculture and the mechanic arts." Many state engineering colleges are founded in the act's wake.

1862
The Pre-Raphaelite poet **Christina Rossetti** publishes *Goblin Market and Other Poems.*

 [2]

THE AMERICAN CIVIL WAR

Conflict during which 11 Southern states attempt unsuccessfully to secede from the Union

It arose out of disputes over the issues of slavery, trade and tariffs, and the doctrine of states' rights. In the 1840s and '50s, Northern opposition to slavery in the Western territories caused the Southern states to fear that existing slaveholdings, which formed the economic base of the South, were also in danger. By the 1850s, abolitionism was growing in the North, and when the antislavery Republican Abraham Lincoln was elected president in 1860, the Southern states seceded to protect what they saw as their right to keep slaves. They were organized as the Confederate States of America under Jefferson Davis.

The war began in Charleston, South Carolina, when Confederate artillery fired on Fort Sumter on April 12, 1861. Both sides quickly raised armies. In July 1861, 30,000 Union troops (above, and below at their base at Yorktown, Virginia) marched toward the Confederate capital at Richmond, Virginia, but were stopped by Confederate forces in the Battle of Bull Run and forced to retreat to Washington, D.C. The defeat shocked the Union, which called for 500,000 more recruits. The war's first major campaign began in February 1862, when Union troops under Ulysses S. Grant captured Confederate forts in western Tennessee. Union victories at the battles of Shiloh and New Orleans followed. In the East, Robert E. Lee won several Confederate victories in the Seven Days' Battles and, after defeat at Antietam, in the Battle of Fredericksburg (December 1862). After the Confederate victory at Chancellorsville, Lee invaded the North and engaged Union forces at Gettysburg. The war's turning point in the West occurred in July 1863 with Grant's success in the Vicksburg Campaign, which brought the entire Mississippi River under Union control. Grant's command was expanded after the Union defeat at Chickamauga, and in March 1864 Lincoln gave him supreme command of the Union armies. Grant began a strategy of attrition and, despite heavy Union casualties at the battles of the Wilderness and Spotsylvania, surrounded Lee's troops in Petersburg, Virginia. Meanwhile, William T. Sherman captured Atlanta in September, set out on a march through Georgia, and captured Savannah. Grant captured Richmond on April 3, 1865, and accepted Lee's surrender on April 9 at Appomattox Court House. On April 26 Sherman received the surrender of Joseph Johnston, thereby ending the war. The mortality rates of the war were staggering—620,000 deaths out of 2.4 million soldiers.

April 25, 1862
Union naval forces under Captain David Farragut seize **New Orleans**, a vital port, which is subsequently occupied by Benjamin F. Butler's army.

May 5, 1862
A battle at Puebla, between the Mexican army and the forces sent by Napoleon III to establish a French satellite state in Mexico,. ends in a Mexican victory, celebrated as **Cinco de Mayo** (Fifth of May).

June 27, 1862
During the **first Battle of Cold Harbor**, Confederate general Robert E. Lee attacks Union troops, driving them back in disorder and forcing them to withdraw to the south side of the Chickahominy River.

 [5]

July 1862
The Union's First Carolina regiment enlists **black troops**, including former slaves.

August 29–30, 1862
At the **second Battle of Bull Run**, a Confederate army of more than 56,000 men under General Robert E. Lee forces the retreat of the Union force of 70,000 troops under Major General John Pope.

September 1862
U.S. President Abraham Lincoln calls on the Confederate States to return to the Union or have their slaves declared free men. When none return he issues the **Emancipation Proclamation** on January 1, 1863.

1862-1863

September 17, 1862
The **Battle of Antietam**, a decisive engagement in the American Civil War, halts the Confederate advance on Maryland and one of the greatest Confederate threats to Washington, D.C.
 [1]

October 3, 1862
The **Battle of Corinth** begins; it will end in a decisive Union victory over Confederate forces in northeastern Mississippi.

November 1862
President Lincoln relieves General George B. McClellan of his post as head of the Army of the Potomac in favor of **General Ambrose Everett Burnside**.
[2]

December 13, 1862
Confederate forces under General Robert E. Lee crush the Union army of General Ambrose E. Burnside at the **Battle of Fredericksburg** in Virginia, immeasurably strengthening the Confederate cause.
 [3]

December 26, 1862
A **Sioux uprising** culminates in a mass hanging at Mankato, Minnesota, when 38 Sioux are executed for having massacred white settlers. President Abraham Lincoln reduces the number from more than 300 sentenced to death.
 [4]

1863
A first attempt to establish general principles to govern the **international postal service** is made at an international conference in Paris.

[1] Antietam: the aftermath of the bloodiest day in American history. The dead await burial in front of Dunker Church.

[2] Lincoln looks toward McClellan when visiting his headquarters at Antietam. Lincoln will relieve him of his command in November 1862.

[3] General Burnside's photograph makes clear why he will lend a reversal of his name to a certain sort of facial hair.

[3] General Robert E. Lee, one of the greatest strategists of any age.

[4] The public execution of 38 Sioux during the Sioux uprising.

[6] Chancellor of the Exchequer William Gladstone (closest to the camera) takes a trial trip on the London Underground's first line, the Metropolitan, which runs from Paddington Station to the city.

1863
German chemist Joseph Willbrand synthesizes the explosive **TNT (trinitrotoluene)**.

1863
Insurgent nationalists in Poland call on the peoples of **Poland, Lithuania, and Rus (Ukraine)** to rise against foreign domination and emancipate the peasants; they appeal for support from the Jews ("Poles of Mosaic faith").

1863
Isma'il Pasha becomes viceroy of Egypt under Ottoman rule; his administrative policies, notably the accumulation of an enormous foreign debt, will be instrumental in leading to British occupation of Egypt.

1863
James L. Plimpton of Medford, Massachusetts, designs the first modern four-wheel roller skate, leading to an explosion in the popularity of **roller-skating**.

1863
John D. Rockefeller builds his first oil refinery, near Cleveland, Ohio, seeing the immense commercial potential in the rapidly expanding oil business.

 [6]
1863
London's Underground, the world's first subway system, opens and transports 9.5 million passengers in its first year of operation.

1863
Archduke Maximilian of Austria accepts the throne of Mexico. He believes that the people have voted him their king; in fact, the offer is a scheme between conservative Mexicans, opposed to the liberal Juárez government, and emperor Napoleon III.

1863
British writer **Charles Kingsley** publishes his didactic children's fantasy *The Water-Babies*, combining Kingsley's concern for sanitary reform with his interest in natural history and the theory of evolution.

1863
Cambodia becomes a French protectorate.

1863
Christian IX succeeds Frederick VII as king of Denmark at the height of a crisis over **Schleswig-Holstein**, long a bone of contention between Denmark and Prussia.

1863
French archaeologist Charles Champoiseau discovers fragments of a marble statue at Samothrace in Greece; the statue, known as **The Winged Victory**, will be exhibited at the Louvre in Paris as one of its treasures.

1863
Georges Bizet's opera *The Pearl Fishers* has its first performance in Paris.

THE FOOTBALL ASSOCIATION ESTABLISHED

The foundation of the FA brought order to football and gave it one of its names—"soccer" is a contraction of "association."

The Football Association (FA), the ruling body for English football (soccer), was founded in 1863 to codify and regulate a game that was already popular throughout the country, especially in private schools such as Harrow (one of whose teams of the period is pictured above).

The FA controls every aspect of the organized game, both amateur and professional, and is responsible for national competitions, including the Challenge Cup series that culminates in the traditional Cup Final at Wembley.

The FA helped organize Scottish, Welsh, and Irish associations in the late 1800s to supervise the game in those countries. It later joined the Fédération Internationale de Football Association (FIFA) to formulate rules of international competition.

In the early 21st century, the FA represented about 37,000 clubs and millions of players. Its activities include producing instructional materials for coaches, players, and referees, advising foreign football organizations, approving rules and regulations of English leagues, and serving as a court for those charged with having broken such rules. The FA headquarters are in London.

[8] Swiss humanitarian Henri Dunant is inspired to found the Red Cross after seeing the horrors on the battlefield of Solferino in 1859, when the French fought the Austrians in Italy.

[5] The Reverend Charles Kingsley and his wife outside his study at Eversley Rectory in Hampshire.

[7] Tom Thumb and Lavinia Warren's wedding photograph.

1863
Dictator Francisco Solano López embroils his nation in the **Paraguayan War** (also known as the War of the Triple Alliance). Paraguay will be nearly destroyed by the two powerful states of Brazil and Argentina, in alliance with Uruguay.

1863
Showman P.T. Barnum promotes the wedding of two of his attractions, **Tom Thumb** (Charles Stratton), who stands 2 feet 9 inches, and Lavinia Warren (Mercy Bunn), who stands 2 feet 8 inches.

1863
Source **Perrier** begins bottling carbonated mineral water in Vergeze, in the south of France.

[8]

1863
Henri Dunant founds the International Committee for the Relief of the Wounded (now International Committee of the **Red Cross**), and in 1864 the first national societies and the first Geneva Convention come into being.

1863
The first major U.S. horseracing track opens at **Saratoga Springs**, New York.

1863
The **Football Association** is established in England, and a uniform set of football (soccer) rules is set down.

1863-1864

1863
A **scarlet fever** epidemic in England kills more than 30,000.

1863
The **Ruby Valley Treaty** allows the building of railroads across Native American land in the Nevada Territory; the land reserved for the tribes is mostly desert.

1863
The **Salon des Refusés** is held in Paris, by order of Napoleon III, for those works rejected by the jury of the official Salon. Among the exhibitors now and years to come are Paul Cézanne, Camille Pissarro, James McNeill Whistler, and Édouard Manet.

 [1]

1863
The Singer Manufacturing Company sells its **sewing machines** on the installment plan, allowing buyers to pay $5 per month for the $100 machine, setting a precedent that will have a profound effect on consumer sales in modern society.

 [2]

1863
The territory of **Idaho** is separated from the Washington Territory, and the **Arizona** Territory is separated from the New Mexico Territory.

1863
The U.S. Congress establishes the **National Academy of Sciences** to serve as an official adviser to the government in all matters of science and technology.

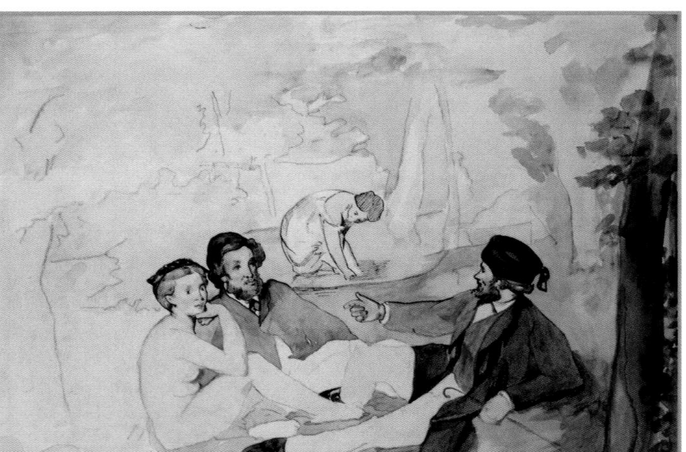

[1] *A study for Manet's picture* Dejeuner sur l'Herbe *so shocks Parisians when it is displayed at the Salon des Refusés that the exhibition is closed.*

[5] *Prussian troops in front of a windmill in Schleswig-Holstein that has been much damaged by their artillery.*

[3] *Union General Hooker looking the part. He will resign after his defeat at Chancellorsville.*

[4] *A siege cannon at Vicksburg.*

[2] *An elegant English girl operates a treadle sewing machine. The harp in the background seems to imply that this accomplishment is on a par with fashionable music making.*

July 2–3, 1863
In a three-day battle at **Gettysburg**, Pennsylvania, the Union Army stops the advance of the Confederates, but the toll is high—23,000 casualties for the North and 20,000 for the South.

 [4]

July 4, 1863
General Ulysses S. Grant captures the Confederate stronghold of **Vicksburg**, Mississippi. This, with the victory at Gettysburg, greatly heartens the North and marks the turning point of the war.

August 21, 1863
Quantrill's Raiders (among them Jesse James, age 15), a Confederate force led by Captain William C. Quantrill, raid Lawrence, Kansas, sacking and burning the town and killing 180 men, women, and children.

October 3, 1863
President Abraham Lincoln declares the first **Thanksgiving Day**; Sarah Josepha Hale, editor of *Godey's Ladies' Book*, has been campaigning for a national Thanksgiving Day observance.

November 19, 1863
At the dedication of a national cemetery at Gettysburg, Lincoln delivers his famous **address**: "this nation, under God, shall have a new birth of freedom. . . and government of the people, by the people, for the people, shall not perish from the earth."

November 19–20, 1863
The **Battle of Chickamauga** in Georgia is won by the Confederates under General Braxton Bragg, but with heavy casualties.

1863
Three days of **rioting** to protest the drafting of soldiers to fight in the U.S. Civil War leave 1,000 people dead in New York City.

1863
Venezuela becomes the first country to **abolish capital punishment** for all crimes, including serious offenses against the state (e.g., treason and military offenses in time of war).

January 2, 1863
The **Battle of Stones River** in Tennessee comes to an end; it has been a bloody but indecisive struggle.

February–April 1863
Cities throughout the South fall to the inexorable **Union armies**. Columbia, South Carolina, falls on February 17; Charleston, besieged from the sea, on February 18; Fayetteville, North Carolina, on March 11; Petersburg and Richmond, Virginia, on April 3.

May 1–4, 1863
Confederate forces defeat the Union army of General Joseph Hooker at the Battle of Chancellorsville, Virginia, but suffer the loss of **Thomas J. ("Stonewall") Jackson**, who will die of wounds sustained in the battle.

June 2, 1863
West Virginia is admitted to the United States as the 35th state, created from antislavery counties of Virginia.

GETTYSBURG

A momentous and pivotal battle of the American Civil War ends in heavy defeat for the Confederate side.

After defeating the Union forces of General Joseph Hooker at Chancellorsville, Virginia, in May, Confederate General Robert E. Lee decided to invade the North in hopes of further discouraging the enemy and possibly inducing European countries to recognize the Confederacy. His invasion army numbered 75,000 troops. When he learned that the Union Army of the Potomac had a new commander, General George G. Meade, Lee ordered General R. S. Ewell to move to Cashtown or Gettysburg. However, the commander of Meade's advance cavalry, General John Buford, recognized the strategic importance of Gettysburg as a road center and was prepared to hold this site until reinforcements arrived.

The first day of battle, July 1, 1863, was notable for the Union troops' use of newly issued Spencer repeating carbines and for heavy casualties on both sides; some dead soldiers of the 24th Michigan Infantry are shown above left.

On the second day there were numerous attacks and counterattacks as each army attempted to gain control of such locations as Little Round Top, Cemetery Hill, Devil's Den, the Wheatfield, and the Peach Orchard.

On the third day Lee was determined to attack. Some 15,000 Confederate troops assaulted Cemetery Ridge, held by about 10,000 Union infantrymen. The Southern spearhead broke through and penetrated the ridge but could do no more. Critically weakened by artillery during their approach, formations hopelessly tangled, lacking reinforcement, and under savage attack from three sides, the Southerners retreated, leaving 19 battle flags and hundreds of prisoners. On July 4 Lee waited to meet an attack that never came. That night, taking advantage of a heavy rain, he started retreating toward Virginia. His defeat stemmed from overconfidence in his troops, Ewell's inability to fill the boots of General Thomas J. "Stonewall" Jackson, and faulty reconnaissance. Though Meade has been criticized for not destroying the enemy by a vigorous pursuit, he had stopped the Confederate invasion and won a critical three-day battle.

Losses were among the war's heaviest: of 88,000 Northern troops, casualties numbered about 23,000; out of 75,000 Southerners, more than 20,000. Dedication of the national cemetery at the site in November 1863 was the occasion of President Abraham Lincoln's Gettysburg Address (below left).

November 24–25, 1863
Union forces succeed in routing Confederates at **Chattanooga** on the Tennessee River, a vital railroad junction for the Confederacy.

December 2, 1863
Freedom, a bronze statue 19.5 feet high by Thomas Crawford, is installed on top of the cupola on the dome of the **Capitol building in Washington, D.C.**, completing the structure that was begun in 1793.

1864
The Schleswig-Holstein War between Denmark and Austria-Prussia begins. Prussian leader Otto von Bismarck's first move in his European power-play.

1864
Alexandru Cuza abolishes serfdom in **Romania**.

1864
American songwriter Stephen Foster, alcoholic and debt-ridden, writes "**Beautiful Dreamer**" shortly before dying in obscurity.

1864
Bellevue Hospital Medical College opens in New York City; the hospital had been founded in 1736.

1864

1864
British astronomer William Huggins determines spectroscopically that some nebulae are gaseous. His work provides one of the foundations for the new discipline of **astrophysics**.

 [1]

1864
Camille Corot, a member of the French Barbizon group, which practices on-the-spot study of nature and effects of light, paints *Souvenir de Mortefontaine*.

 [2]

1864
Clara Barton is appointed superintendent of nurses for the Union's Army of the James; she has been aiding soldiers since the beginning of the war, sometimes passing through the battle lines to distribute supplies, search for the missing, and nurse the wounded.

 [3]

1864
Former slave **Samuel Crowther**, the first African to be ordained by the Anglican Church Missionary Society, is consecrated bishop of the Niger Territory.

1864
George Perkins Marsh publishes *Man and Nature*. This **classic of conservation** laments the damage perpetrated by human action in the Mediterranean world and the United States.

1864
John Henry Newman, who led the Oxford Movement in the Church of England and later will become a cardinal-deacon in the Roman Catholic Church, publishes *Apologia pro Vita Sua*, a history of the evolution of his religious opinions.

  [4]

[1] Sir William Huggins in old age, in his academic robes.

[2] Corot fully set up for plein-air painting.

[3] Nurses of the Michigan Soldiers' Relief Society outside a Union field hospital, where a field kitchen is in action.

[5] Samuel Baker, the archetypal white hunter, poses with a rhino head to one side and a buffalo skull to the other.

[6] Kit Carson, mountain man, trapper, army scout, and associate of John C. Fremont in the opening up of the Oregon Trail and encroachment on Mexican California.

[4] Cardinal Newman not long before his death.

1864
Regional Canadian leaders agree to establish a general federal union, uniting the provinces.

 [5]

1864
Samuel White Baker, traveling with his future wife, Florence von Sass, reaches Lake Albert on the border of the present-day Democratic Republic of the Congo and Uganda and determines the lake to be a source of the Nile River.

 [6]

1864
U.S. Army colonel **Kit Carson**, after Navajo crops, homes, livestock, and equipment are destroyed, has 8,000 Navajos confined to the Bosque Redondo, an arid, alkaline piece of land south of Santa Fe.

March 10, 1864
The **Red River Campaign** begins in the American Civil War. It is an unsuccessful Union effort to seize control of the important cotton-growing states of Louisiana, Arkansas, and Texas.

 [7]

April 12, 1864
Confederates under General Nathan B. Forrest capture **Fort Pillow** in Tennessee and kill all the black troops within; some are burned or buried alive. More than 300 black people, including women and children, are slain after the fort surrenders.

May 5–7, 1864
General Ulysses S. Grant meets a Confederate army under General Robert E. Lee in Virginia in the **Wilderness**, and after two days, moves on to another frustrating battle at **Spottsylvania Court House**.

1864
Kojong, 26th monarch of the Choson (Yi) dynasty and the last to effectively rule **Korea**, begins his reign, with his father, Taewon-gun, as regent.

1864
The Montana Territory is formed from a portion of the Idaho Territory.

1864
Nanjing is retaken by the Chinese government. More than 20 million peasants have lost their lives in the **Taiping Rebellion**.

1864
Pope Pius IX issues the encyclical *Syllabus Errorum*, condemning liberalism, socialism, and rationalism, and stigmatizing the view that "the Roman Pontiff can and should reconcile himself to and agree with progress, liberalism, and modern civilization."

1864
President Abraham Lincoln is reelected to a second term, defeating the Democratic challenger, General George B. McClellan.

1864
Prolific British novelist **Anthony Trollope** publishes *Can You Forgive Her?*, the first novel in his Palliser series.

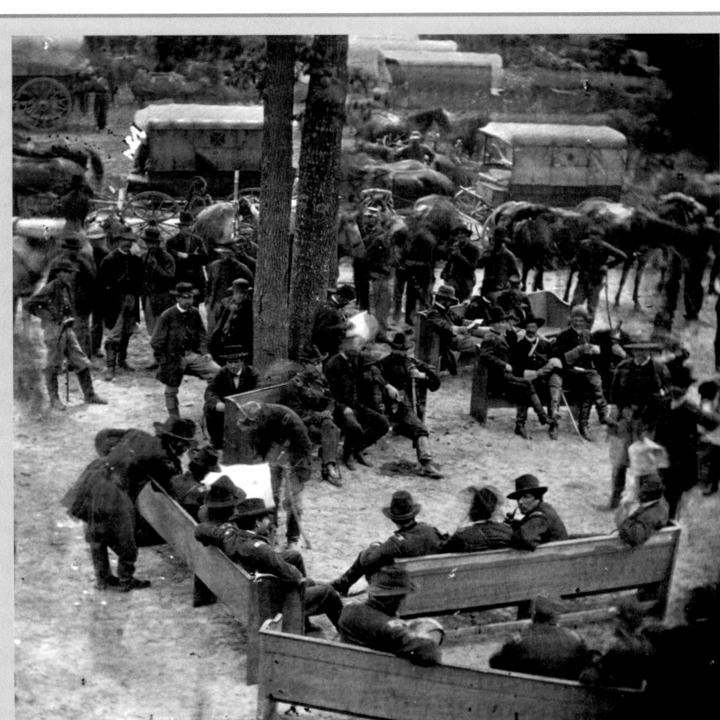

GRANT IN THE WILDERNESS

Beginning of the Union's overland campaign

In March 1864, President Abraham Lincoln appointed Ulysses S. Grant lieutenant general and commander of the Union Army. Grant took control of the Army of the Potomac and sought to move his army against Confederate General Robert E. Lee in northern Virginia. In May, Grant led 115,000 of his men into the Wilderness, a woodland 10 miles (16 km) west of Fredericksburg, Virginia.

Lee then sent in his own troops, hoping that the wild terrain would reduce the effectiveness of the Union's superior artillery and cavalry. The two sides confronted each other on May 5. Two days of bitter, indecisive combat ensued. Finally, Grant pulled away from the Wilderness battlefield and moved southeastward to the crossroads point of Spotsylvania Court House. The Confederates got there first. In savage action (May 18–19), including hand-to-hand fighting at the famous "Bloody Angle," Grant, although gaining a little ground, was essentially thrown back. He had lost 18,399 men at Spotsylvania. Lee's combined losses at the Wilderness and Spotsylvania were an estimated 17,250. In the photograph General Grant (left), leaning on one of the pews dragged out of nearby Massaponax Church, looks over General George G. Meade's shoulder at a map, on May 21.

[7] The Fort Pillow

[8] A Mathew Brady photograph of Union admiral David Farragut.

June 3, 1864
Considered one of the worst Northern defeats of the American Civil War, the **second Battle of Cold Harbor** (Virginia) begins. It will result in the loss of about 7,000 Union soldiers.

 *[8]*

August 5, 1864
Union ships led by Admiral David Farragut succeed in closing **Mobile Bay** to Confederate blockade runners. During the battle he exhorts his men, "Damn the torpedoes: full speed ahead!"

September 1, 1864
The Charlottetown Conference, the first of a series of meetings that ultimately lead to the formation of the **Dominion of Canada**, convenes at Charlottetown, Prince Edward Island.

September 2, 1864
Union forces occupy **Atlanta**, Georgia, a key depot, the site of Southern war industries, and the keystone of Confederate rail transportation east of the Mississippi River.

September 4, 1864
John Hunt Morgan, the Confederate guerrilla leader of **Morgan's Raiders**, is killed by Union troops.

October 19, 1864
Confederate soldiers based in Canada cross into **St. Albans**, **Vermont**, and rob three banks in order to agitate the Union during the American Civil War.

1864-1865

October 31, 1864
Nevada is admitted to the United States as the 36th state.

November 15, 1864
Union general William Tecumseh Sherman commences his **great march to the sea**, laying waste to Georgia.
 [1]

November 29, 1864
Twelve hundred U.S. troops attack a surrendered, partially disarmed **Cheyenne** Indian camp in southeastern Colorado Territory; 150 to 500 Indians are massacred, including many women and children.
 [2]

December 1864
Salmon P. Chase is appointed sixth chief justice of the U.S. Supreme Court by President Abraham Lincoln. He will serve from 1864 to 1873.
 [3]

December 21, 1864
General William Tecumseh Sherman's Union army captures the important Confederate port city of **Savannah,** Georgia.

1865
G. E. Street wins the competition to build **London Law Courts**.

[1] Atlanta, Georgia: what Sherman left behind him in his march to the sea.

[9] Lord John Russell. Queen Victoria says he would be better company if he had a third subject, for he is interested in nothing except the Constitution of 1688 and himself.

[3] Salmon P. Chase. In the 1850s he was the great champion of antislavery in the Senate, then the first Republican governor of Ohio, before becoming Lincoln's invaluable secretary of the treasury.

[6] Mary Edwards Walker, wearing her Medal of Honor.

[7] Mathew Brady's buggy turned into a mobile darkroom, which the troops christen his "whatisit wagon."

[5] One of Sir John Tenniel's famous illustrations for Alice's Adventures in Wonderland.

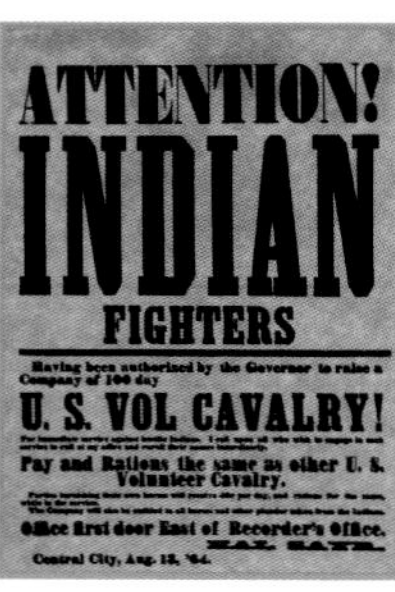

[2] A 1864 recruiting poster for cavalry to fight Indians in Colorado.

1865
Chicago retailer Potter Palmer takes as partners **Marshall Field** and Levi Zeigler Leiter and begins to build what will become one of the premier department stores in the U.S.

1865
In Great Britain, **river pollution** reaches such proportions that a royal commission is appointed to look into the matter. Part of its report is written with River Calder water instead of ink.

 [5]
1865
Lewis Carroll's unique, multileveled novel *Alice's Adventures in Wonderland* marks a transition from an emphasis on moral training to pleasure in children's literature.

 [6]
1865
Mary Edwards Walker, thought to have been the only woman surgeon formally engaged for field duty during the American Civil War, is awarded the Medal of Honor for her services to the Union army.

 [7]
1865
Mathew Brady, Timothy O'Sullivan, and **Alexander Gardner** record the horrors and destruction of the American Civil War in photographs.

 [8]
1865
Scottish physician Joseph Lister begins developing techniques for **antiseptic surgery**, including the sterilization of instruments. His innovations result in vastly lower surgical mortality rates.

1865
In London's **Hyde Park, riots** break out over the right to vote.

1865
Former slaves riot in Jamaica, and the chief magistrate and 18 others of European ancestry are killed. Governor **Edward John Eyre** declares martial law; 430 men and women are shot or hung, 600 men and women are flogged, and more than 1,000 homes destroyed.

[4]

1865
Adolphus Busch goes into the brewing business with his father-in-law, Eberhard Anheuser, in St. Louis; by 1901 the **Anheuser-Busch** company will be the largest brewer in the United States.

1865
Americans **Francis Asbury Pratt** and **Amos Whitney** form a company that pioneers the use of interchangeable parts in manufacturing and will develop innovations in machine tools and the standardization of gauges.

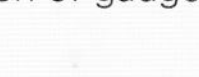

1865
Édouard Manet's painting *Olympia* causes a scandal (as had his *Déjeuner sur l'herbe* in 1863).

1865
Bon Marché, located in Paris, develops into the world's first true department store.

[4] Before losing his reputation in Jamaica, Edward John Eyre made a name for himself exploring the Australian interior, showing desert to stretch west and north and the best land to be to the east.

[10] A mother beds down her child in a Pullman sleeper.

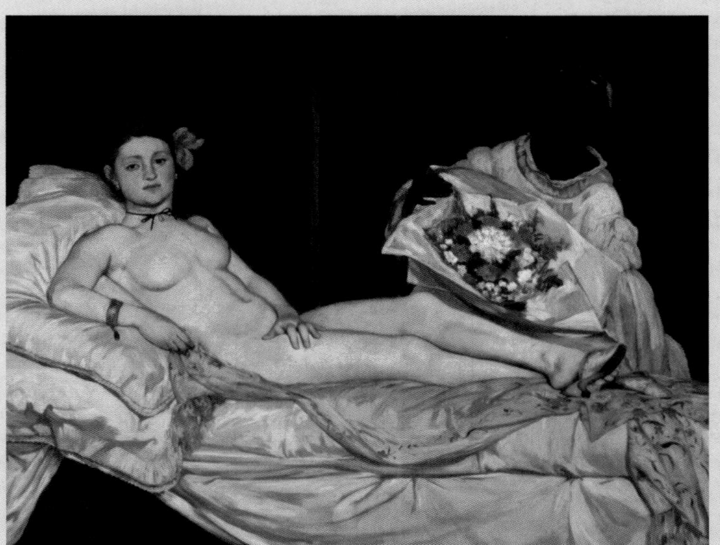

MANET'S *OLYMPIA*

This painting caused a scandal when it was first unveiled and left the artist under a cloud of controversy for the rest of his life.

The French painter Éduoard Manet (1832–83) broke new ground by defying traditional techniques of representation and by choosing subjects from the events and circumstances of his own time. His paintings aroused the hostility of critics and the enthusiasm of the young painters who later formed the nucleus of the Impressionist group.

At the Paris Salon of 1865, his painting *Olympia* (above), created two years earlier, caused a great scandal that adversely affected his subsequent career. The painting's reclining female nude gazes brazenly at the viewer and is depicted in a harsh, brilliant light that obliterates interior modeling and turns her into an almost two-dimensional figure. However, what sparked controversy was not the nudity, but various symbolic details in the canvas—most tellingly, the little black cat—that indicated that the subject was a prostitute.

This contemporary odalisque was denounced as indecent by critics and the public alike. Although Manet had deliberately broken with artistic tradition, he was devasted by the reaction to his work, and he wrote to his friend, the French poet Charles Baudelaire, "They are raining insults on me. Someone must be wrong." The critical resistance to Manet's work did not abate until near the end of his career; it was not until the 20th century that his reputation was secured by art historians and critics.

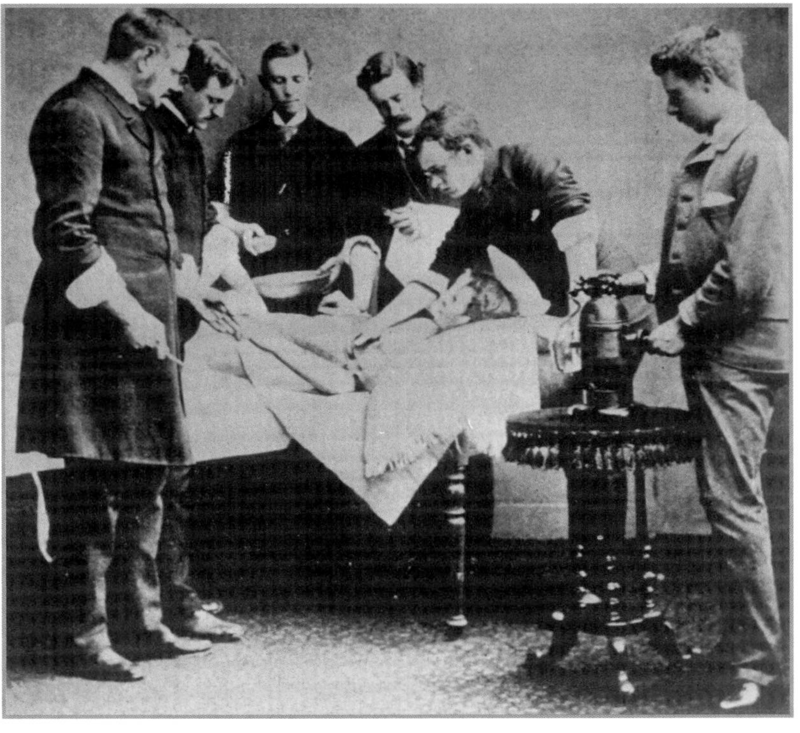

[8] A carbolic antiseptic spray in use during an operation.

[9]

1865
Lord John Russell, who led the fight for passage of the Reform Bill of 1832, is appointed prime minister of Great Britain for the second time. His efforts at further reforms are frustrated. Instead the Tory Benjamin Disraeli will bring them in.

1865
The defeated South decries the arrival of **carpetbaggers**, politicians or financial adventurers accused of going to the South to use the newly enfranchised freedmen as a means of obtaining office or profit.

[10]

1865
The first real **Pullman railway sleeping car**, the "Pioneer," appears. It contains folding upper berths and seat cushions that can be extended to make lower berths.

1865
The first U.S. **train robbery** occurs near North Bend, Ohio.

1865
The **Massachusetts Institute of Technology**, chartered in 1861, holds its first classes in Boston. MIT moves to Cambridge in 1916.

1865
The Nation, a weekly liberal journal of opinion, begins publication in New York, with Edwin L. Godkin as editor. *The Nation* is an eloquent and increasingly influential voice against Reconstruction excesses and graft and corruption in government.

1865

1865
The **Union Stock Yards** open in Chicago, as railroads replace Mississippi River traffic as the chief means of shipping. Pens are built to hold 10,000 cattle and 100,000 hogs.

1865
The **University of Zürich** is the first European university to admit women.

1865
Trading of **wheat futures** begins at the Chicago Board of Trade, an association of grain merchants that had been established in 1848.

1865
Vassar College for women opens in Poughkeepsie, New York, endowed by brewer Matthew Vassar. It is dedicated to providing women with the high caliber of education previously available only to men.

 [1]

1865
William Gilbert Grace of England plays his first match of first-class cricket. He becomes the greatest cricketer of the Victorian era, with 54,896 runs and 2,876 wickets in a 44-year career.

 [2]

1865
Fyodor Dostoyevsky begins writing *Crime and Punishment*, the story of the intellectual Raskolnikov, who kills an old woman. Dostoyevsky specializes in the analysis of pathological states of mind and in the exploration of difficult, destructive emotions.

 [3]

[1] A member of the Laurel and Abanakis Base Ball Club at Vassar College.

[2] The bearded W. G. Grace with the rest of his cricket team.

[3] Dostoyevsky will survive a mock execution and four years in a penal settlement.

[5] John Wilkes Booth

[6] Richard Wagner. He has just won the patronage of King Ludwig II of Bavaria, without whose unlimited financial backing Wagner's huge musical ambitions could never be fulfilled.

[5] The execution of Booth's four co-conspirators.

April 15, 1865
President Abraham Lincoln dies. Andrew Johnson becomes the 17th president of the United States as the country is thrown into mourning. Johnson will have no vice president.

 [5]

April 26, 1865
Assassin John Wilkes Booth is shot—either by himself or by federal troops—in a barn in Virginia. Authorities will also round up a number of other individuals. **Four are hanged** and others receive long prison terms.

May 10, 1865
Jefferson Davis, president of the Confederacy, is captured by Union troops near Irwinville, Georgia.

May 26, 1865
A large holdout group of Confederates surrenders, and the port of **Galveston**, Texas, yields to the Union army on June 2, ending the last Confederate holdouts of the Civil War.

 [6]

June 10, 1865
Tristan und Isolde, the earliest example of what **Richard Wagner** called "music drama," is first performed in Munich, Germany.

June 19, 1865
News of the Emancipation Proclamation reaches the slaves of Galveston, Texas. The day will be celebrated thereafter as **Juneteenth** by the black community.

c. 1865
The game of shinty is played by British soldiers stationed in Canada. Not long after, it evolves into the modern game of **ice hockey**.

February 3, 1865
In a personal meeting with Confederate representatives, President **Abraham Lincoln** offers liberal pardons in exchange for the South's quitting the Civil War, with reunion as a precondition of peace. His offer is rejected.

March 2, 1865
Confederate forces under General Jubal A. Early suffer a decisive defeat that ends Southern resistance in the **Shenandoah Valley** in Virginia.

April 9, 1865
Robert E. Lee surrenders to Ulysses S. Grant at **Appomattox Court House**, Virginia, ending the American Civil War. The cost of the war is staggering, but of the almost 618,000 dead, only a third died in battle—the rest succumbed to disease.

 [4]

April 14, 1865
While watching a play at Ford's Theatre in Washington, D.C., President Abraham Lincoln is shot and mortally wounded by **John Wilkes Booth**, a rabid advocate of slavery with ties to the South. Booth cries "Sic semper tyrannus!" ("Thus always to tyrants!").

April 14, 1865
Assassin John Wilkes Booth's co-conspirators make an unsuccessful attempt on the life of Secretary of State **William Seward**.

MOUNTAINEERING—A NEW SPORT

Climbing the Alps and beyond

Mountaineering for sport began when a young Genevese scientist, Horace-Bénédict de Saussure, on a first visit to Chamonix in 1760, viewed Mont Blanc (at 15,771 feet the tallest peak in Europe). He offered prize money for the first ascent of Mont Blanc, but it was not until 1786, more than 25 years later, that his money was claimed by a Chamonix doctor, Michel-Gabriel Paccard, and his porter, Jacques Balmat. A year later de Saussure himself climbed to the summit of Mont Blanc. After 1850, groups of British climbers with Swiss, Italian, or French guides scaled one after another of the high peaks of Switzerland. A landmark climb in the growth of the sport was the spectacular first ascent of the Matterhorn (14,692 feet) on July 14, 1865, by a party led by an English illustrator, Edward Whymper (left). But tragedy struck on the way down when four of the seven-man party fell to their deaths. The rope linking them to the survivors snapped, though there were unproven accusations that it was cut. Whymper described this ascent and his previous nine unsuccessful attempts on the mountain in his classic book *Scrambles Amongst the Alps* (1871).

By 1870 all of the principal Alpine summits had been scaled, and climbers began to seek new and more difficult routes on peaks that had already been ascended. As the few remaining minor peaks of the Alps were overcome, by the end of the 19th century climbers turned their attention to the Andes of South America, the North American Rockies, the Caucasus, Africa's peaks, and finally the Himalayas, Pamirs, and the Hindu Kush. Aconcagua (22,831 feet), the highest peak of the Andes, was first climbed in 1897, and the Grand Teton (13,747 feet) in the Rocky Mountains was ascended in 1898. The Italian duke of the Abruzzi in 1897 made the first ascent of Mount St. Elias (18,009 feet) on the border of Alaska and Canada, and in 1906 successfully climbed Margherita in the Ruwenzori Group (16,795 feet) in East Africa. In 1913 an American, Hudson Stuck, ascended Alaska's Mount McKinley (20,320 feet), the highest peak in North America.

[4] Appomattox Court House, where the Civil War ends.

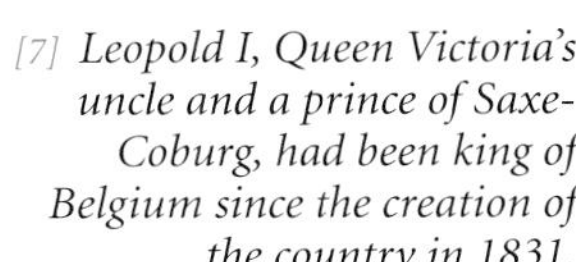

[7] Leopold I, Queen Victoria's uncle and a prince of Saxe-Coburg, had been king of Belgium since the creation of the country in 1831.

June 23, 1865
The Cherokee chief and Confederate general **Stand Watie** surrenders at the close of the American Civil War; he is one of the last Confederate commanders to do so.

July 5, 1865
The **U.S. Secret Service** begins operation under the auspices of the Treasury Department to aid in the prevention of counterfeiting.

July 14, 1865
The summit of the **Matterhorn** is reached from the Swiss side by the British climber Edward Whymper. Three days later it is scaled from the Italian side by a party of Italians, led by guide Giovanni Antonio Carrel.

November 10, 1865
Captain Henry Wirz, the commandant of the **Andersonville prison camp** for Union soldiers, where 13,000 have died of disease and malnutrition, is hanged; he is the only person in the U.S. to have been executed for war crimes.

 [7]

December 10, 1865
Leopold I, the first king of the Belgians, dies and is succeeded by his son, Leopold II, who will become notorious for his ruthless exploitation of the Belgian Congo colony.

December 17, 1865
The first performance of Franz **Schubert's Unfinished Symphony**, written in 1822, is given in the Great Redoutensaal of the Vienna Hofburg.

1865-1867

December 18, 1865
The **Thirteenth Amendment** to the U.S. Constitution, outlawing slavery, officially enters into force, having been ratified by the requisite states on December 6.

December 29, 1865
Abolitionist crusader **William Lloyd Garrison** publishes the last issue of *The Liberator*.

 [1]

1866
After several years' effort, the first permanent **transatlantic telegraph cable** is laid, linking America and Europe.

 [2]

1866
Alexandru Cuza is driven into exile, and Charles of Hohenzollern-Sigmaringen becomes king of Romania, ruling as **Carol I**.

 [3]

1866
George W. McGill of New York develops the first successful **stapler**.

1866
German philosopher-zoologist Ernst Haeckel coins the word "**ecology**" to mean the science of the relations between living things and their external world.

 [4]

[1] William Lloyd Garrison, the "archpriest of abolition."

[3] Romania, formed from the Danubian principalities of Wallachia and Moldavia, will move from autonomy within Turkey to full independence under King Carol in 1877.

[6] Alfred Nobel, a year or two before he is awarded his dynamite patent.

[5] An early Ku Klux Klan initiation ceremony, or mock lynching, before the Klan's adoption of the plain white sheet as its costume of choice.

[2] The Great Eastern, *for many years the largest ship in the world, comes into her own by laying a third transatlantic cable. Two earlier cables did not work.*

[4] Ernst Haeckel (seated) with a friend in Italy, surrounded by the accoutrements of the natural historian, including a starfish, crab, and piece of coral.

[5]

1866
The **Ku Klux Klan** becomes a vehicle for Southern white underground resistance to radical Reconstruction. The Klan seeks restoration of white supremacy through the violent intimidation of blacks.

$

1866
The **National Labor Union** is organized in Baltimore, Maryland, seeking to improve working conditions through legislative reform rather than collective bargaining. It will attract 500,000 members before it is disbanded in 1873.

1866
The U.S. Congress passes a **civil rights act**, over President Andrew Johnson's veto, to ensure that former slaves are allowed full citizenship rights. It also says that all persons born in the United States are U.S. citizens.

1866
The U.S. Supreme Court rules, in **Ex parte Milligan**, that the federal government cannot establish military courts to try civilians, except where civil courts are no longer functioning in an actual theater of war.

1866
Through the terms of the treaty of Vienna, Italy obtains **Venetia** from Austria.

1866
Tokugawa Keiki becomes shogun of Japan as Tokugawa Yoshinobu; he will be the **last shogun** to hold power.

1866
Henri Nestlé develops a milk-based baby food and begins marketing it from Vevey, Switzerland.

1866
Henry Burgh of New York founds the American **Society for the Prevention of Cruelty to Animals** (based on Britain's example) and convinces the New York state legislature to pass an anticruelty law.

1866
Richard Norman Shaw, one of England's most versatile and talented domestic architects, designs Leyswood, Sussex. The project marks the transfer of small-scale domestic design to the large country house.

1866
Rioters in **New Orleans** kill 35 black citizens and wound more than 100. The event is influential in focusing public opinion in the North on the necessity of taking firmer measures to govern the South during the Reconstruction.

1866
Sixteen clipper ships take part in the **Great Tea Race** from Fuzhou (Foochow), China, to England. After 99 days at sea, the winning ships arrive at the London Docks within hours of each other.

1866
Sondre Nordheim wins the first known **ski-jumping** competition. The contest is held in his hometown of Telemark, Norway.

CLIPPER SHIPS

Elegant sailing vessels that significantly reduced ocean voyage times

Apparently starting from the small, swift coastal packet known as the Baltimore clipper, the true clipper evolved first in American and later in British shipyards. In its ultimate form it was a long, slim, graceful vessel with a projecting bow, a radically streamlined hull, and an exceptionally large spread of sail on three tall masts. Most clippers were produced in American and British shipyards, but several other nations also built them, including France and the Netherlands.

Renowned for its beauty, the clipper was the classic sailing ship of the 19th century. Clippers were generally narrow, which restricted their load-carrying capacity, but any shortcomings in that area were more than compensated by their speed through the water. Clippers achieved several firsts: the *Flying Cloud*, launched in 1851, made the voyage from New York City to San Francisco in a record 89 days, and the *James Baines* set the transatlantic sailing record of 12 days 6 hours from Boston to Liverpool, England. The *Lightning* set the all-time record for a single day's sail, covering 436 nautical miles in 24 hours. The *Sovereign of the Seas* (below left, in the port of Antwerp), is reputed to have sailed 3,736 miles (6,000 km) in 12 days. The *Lightning* and the *James Baines* (both launched in 1854 or 1855), as well as the *Flying Cloud* and the *Sovereign of the Seas*, were all built by Donald McKay, a Canadian-born shipbuilder, at his shipyard at East Boston, Massachusetts.

The emphasis on speed came partly from the desire to bring the first tea of the season back from China, partly from the competition with the overland route across North America to the California goldfields. The prime clipper sailings were between New York and San Francisco around Cape Horn during the Gold Rush. However, clippers made their mark in many other parts of the world, especially on trade routes between Britain and its colonies in the Far East (the photograph left above shows vessels of this type in London's East India Docks). The Dutch were also leading clipper users on the route to Java; their most famous vessel was the *Telanak*, which was built in 1859.

Although clippers are most commonly associated with the tea trade, they also carried high-quality wool from Australia, passengers—the clippers were the immediate precursors of the luxury steam liners—and spices, which were low in volume and high in profit.

1866
Wilhelm Steinitz of Prague defeats Adolf Anderssen for the **first world chess championship**. Steinitz remains champion for nearly 30 years.

June 9, 1866
Prussian troops invade Holstein and, a few days later, Austria, which is supported by the smaller states of Saxony, Hesse-Kassel, and Hanover. The conflict has been fomented by Otto von Bismarck.

July 3, 1866
Prussia defeats Austria at the **Battle of Koeniggratz**, thanks to the timely arrival of reinforcements and being equipped with new rifles that can be reloaded quicker than the Austrians'.

August 23, 1866
War between **Austria** and **Prussia** is concluded; Schleswig-Holstein is given to Prussia, which also annexes Hanover, Hesse-Kassel, Nassau, and Frankfurt outright, moving toward the unification of Germany under Prussia.

1867
Irish **Fenian** attacks in England.

 *[6]*

1867
Alfred Nobel, Swedish chemist and engineer, is awarded a patent for dynamite. Nobel later will endow the Nobel Prizes, among the world's most prestigious awards for notable achievements.

1867
American physician John Bobbs performs the first successful **gallstone operation**.

1867
Brooklyn pitcher William Cummings invents the **curveball pitch**.

1867
Refrigerated railway cars allow long-distance transport of perishables such as meat and dairy products. They also permit expanded ranching and pastoralism in the U.S., Canada, and Argentina.

1867
French inventor Georges Leclanché designs the first practical **dry cell battery**.

1867
Geologist **John Wesley Powell** begins exploration of the Green and Colorado rivers and the Rocky Mountains. Later he directs federal surveys of western lands in the public domain and encourages the government to initiate land-utilization projects.

1867
German chemist August Wilhelm von Hoffmann discovers **formaldehyde**, which is used as a disinfectant and preservative.

JOHN WESLEY POWELL

American geologist and ethnologist who published the first classification of American Indian languages and was the first director of the U.S. Bureau of Ethnology

After fighting in the American Civil War, John Wesley Powell (1834–1902) joined Illinois Wesleyan University as professor of geology. In 1867 he became a lecturer at Illinois Normal College (now Illinois State University at Normal) and began a series of journies to the Rocky Mountains and on the Colorado and Green rivers. The photograph above shows him setting off on one of his trips.

From 1871 to 1879, Powell directed a federal geologic and geographic survey of western lands in the public domain and encouraged the government to initiate land-utilization projects. During this period, he published three major works. In the first of these he originated and formalized a number of concepts that became part of the standard working vocabulary of geology. He then developed the first comprehensive classification of American Indian languages—the photograph at left shows him in conversation with a Paluti Indian in southern Utah. Powell's third important publication—a report on the lands of the arid region of the United States—is regarded as a landmark in conservation literature.

When the U.S. Bureau of Ethnology of the Smithsonian Institution was established in 1879, Powell became its first director and remained with it until his death in 1902. Continuing the study of Indian ethnology and languages, he published the first complete and still-authoritative classification and distribution map of 58 language stocks of the United States and Canada (1891). Powell also served as director of the U.S. Geological Survey (1881–92), working extensively on the mapping of water sources and advancing irrigation projects.

1867
Portugal becomes the first European country to abolish the **death penalty**.

 [4]

1867
The first American **elevated railway** begins operation in New York City.

1867
The first **Belmont Stakes** is run; it becomes part of what will be known as the U.S. Triple Crown of horse racing

 [5]

1867
The first ship passes through the **Suez Canal**, though the canal will not officially open until 1869.

1867
The first **stock ticker**, which prints transactions on a long ribbon of paper, is developed by Edward A. Calahan, chief telegrapher for Western Union in New York, New York. The New York Stock Exchange is one of the first customers.

 [6]

1867
The **Queensberry Rules** for boxing are written by John Graham Chambers of the British Amateur Athletic Club, and published under the sponsorship of John Sholto Douglas, 9th marquess of Queensberry.

1867
German economist **Karl Marx** publishes the first volume of *Das Kapital*, which advocates workers' control of the means of production.
 [1]

1867
Howard University is founded in Washington, D.C., for African American students.

1867
In the United Kingdom, the **Second Reform Act**, largely the work of the Tory Benjamin Disraeli, gives the right to vote to many workingmen in the towns and cities, doubling the number of eligible voters.
 [2]

1867
Johann Strauss, Jr., composes his most famous waltz, *An der schönen blauen Donau* (*On the Beautiful Blue Danube*), the main theme of which becomes one of the best-known melodies in 19th-century music.

1867
Oliver Kelley, a former field investigator for the U.S. Department of Agriculture, founds the **Granger movement**, a farm organization that will become a major economic and political movement.

1867
Paris World's Fair hosts 50,000 exhibitors and nearly 10 million visitors.
 [3]

[1] *Karl Marx, the father of Communism, is German-born but permanently exiled in England.*

[5] *Part of the workforce building the Suez Canal.*

[3] *The pavilions of different exhibiting countries at the Paris World's Fair.*

[4] *The Third Avenue "El" snakes its way through lower Manhattan, contrasting with the rigging of the sailing ships*

[6] *The Marquess of Queensberry's only other claim to fame is as the persecutor of Oscar Wilde in the 1890s.*

[2] *Benjamin Disraeli, under whom the British Conservative Party first comes into its own, thanks to his realization that many of the newly enfranchised will vote for it, not the Liberals.*

[7] *A ticket admitting General Sherman to the impeachment trial of President Johnson in the Senate.*

1867
The United States acquires the **Midway Islands** in the Pacific.

1867
The use of concrete in architecture increases with the development of **reinforced concrete**. Embedded with metal, it displays great tensile strength.

February 8, 1867
The Ausgleich ("Compromise") establishes the **dual monarchy of Austria-Hungary**.

March 1, 1867
Nebraska is admitted to the United States as the 37th state.

March 2, 1867
Over U.S. president Andrew Johnson's veto, radical Republicans in Congress pass the **Tenure of Office Act**, forbidding the president to remove civil officers without senatorial consent.

 [7]
March 2, 1867
The first **Reconstruction Act** is passed by the U.S. Congress. The second will be passed on March 23, and the third in July. Attempts by President Andrew Johnson to veto the bills will contribute to the calls for his impeachment.

1867-1868

March 2, 1867
The U.S. Congress establishes the first **Department of Education**, which will be demoted to the Office of Education the following year.

March 29, 1867
The British North America Act unites Nova Scotia, New Brunswick, and Canada as one dominion under the name of Canada.

June 8, 1867
Francis Joseph is crowned king of Hungary.

 [1]

June 19, 1867
Maximilian, the emperor of Mexico, is executed by a firing squad.

 [2]

July 1, 1867
Sir John Alexander Macdonald, a conservative, becomes the first prime minister of the Dominion of Canada (1867–73; 1878–91). He will lead the country through its period of early growth.

July 1, 1867
The **Dominion of Canada** is formed, an event subsequently celebrated as an annual Canadian holiday (its current name, Canada Day, was adopted in 1982).

  [3]

[2] Maximilian's Mexican adventure, initiated by France, ends ignominiously, except for the inspiration it affords Edouard Manet for his painting. The real firing squad can be seen in the photograph below.

[1] Francis Joseph's Austrian Empire is transformed into the Dual Monarchy of Austria-Hungary, a compromise that it is hoped will satisfy the national aspirations of the latter.

[5] Louisa May Alcott. A prolific writer in many genres besides children's books, she has over 300 titles to her name by her death.

[3] The parties involved in the formation of the Dominion of Canada meet in London to frame the enabling act.

[6] Domingo Faustino Sarmiento has the distinction of being the first civilian president of Argentina.

[4] The $7,200,000 check that buys Alaska for the United States.

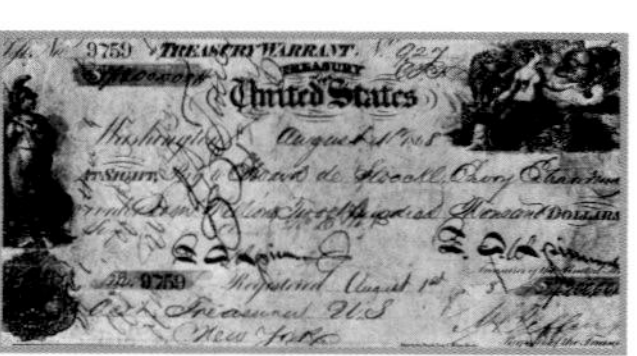

1868
English metallurgist Robert F. Mushet invents **tungsten steel**, which is much harder than earlier steel alloys.

1868
French astronomer **Pierre Janssen** and English amateur astronomer **Joseph Lockyer** independently discover the characteristic absorption line for helium in the sun's spectrum during a total eclipse.

1868
German doctor Karl August Wunderlich's *Body Temperature and Disease* popularizes the practice of using **thermometers** to determine the body temperature of patients.

1868
In England, a new legal definition says **obscene material** is marked by a tendency "to deprave and corrupt those whose minds are open to such immoral influences and into whose hands a publication of this sort may fall."

1868
Public executions, once attended by large crowds, are banned in England.

1868
Russian novelist **Fyodor Dostoyevsky** publishes *The Idiot*. The work's hero, Prince Myshkin, is perfectly generous and so innocent as to be regarded as an idiot; however, he is also gifted with profound psychological insight.

October 18, 1867
After much opposition, a deal negotiated by U.S. Secretary of State William Seward for the U.S. purchase of the Russian colony of **Alaska** (Seward's Folly) is approved, and the U.S. flag is flown over the capital, Sitka.

 *[4]*

1868
Britain invades **Abyssinia/Ethiopia**, and Emperor Theodore is defeated.

1868
American inventor Christopher Latham Sholes, building on the work of earlier engineers, patents the first modern **typewriter**. It is sold in 1873 as the Remington typewriter.

1868
American inventor William Davis patents the **refrigerated railroad car**.

1868
Based on her recollections of her own childhood, **Louisa May Alcott's** *Little Women* traces the differing personalities and fortunes of four sisters as they emerge from childhood. It will be followed by *Little Men* in 1871.

 *[5]*

1868
Domingo Faustino Sarmiento is elected president of **Argentina** and immediately begins to apply his liberal ideals—his belief in democratic principles and civil liberties and his opposition to dictatorial regimes in any form.

 *[6]*

ABYSSINIA

The British topple the ruler of Ethiopia to demonstrate their power in Africa.

The 1868 British Expedition to Abyssinia was a punitive raid against Emperor Tewodros II of Ethiopia, a capable but capricious ruler who had taken offense at Queen Victoria's failure to answer his letters. He made his displeasure known by imprisoning several missionaries (below left) and two representatives of the British government.

The British decided on military intervention and ordered the preparation of an invasion force, which eventually consisted of 13,000 soldiers (British and Indian), 26,000 camp followers, and more than 40,000 animals, including elephants. The expedition set sail from Bombay in a fleet of 280 steam and sailing ships. The advance guard of engineers landed at Zula on the Red Sea coast. By the first week of December 1867, a railway into the interior of the country was under construction, and two piers had been built.

It then took British forces three months to make their way over 400 miles of mountainous terrain to the capital, Magdela. They faced little opposition en route, partly because many of the indigenous people were indifferent to Tewodros's fate. The decisive military encounter took place outside the emperor's fortress on April 13, 1868. Over 700 of Tewodros's men were killed and approximately twice as many wounded in just two hours; British casualties were only 20 wounded, with only two of them subsequently dying from their wounds. A few days later, the hostages were released. Tewodros committed suicide to avoid capture, leaving an orphaned son, Dejatch Alamayou (photographed holding a doll, above left, by Julia Margaret Cameron), who was sent to be educated in England, where Queen Victoria took an interest in him. He had no aptitude for book learning while he was at Rugby School, but was allowed to enter the Royal Military Academy at Sandhurst without taking an exam. His unhappy time there ended when he caught pleurisy and died in 1879, at age 19.

Following Tewodros's defeat, the victorious British general, Sir Robert Napier, allowed his troops to loot and burn Magdela, including its churches, as a punitive measure before withdrawing. On the way out of Ethiopia, the British gave substantial supplies and armaments to one of the local leaders who had helped them, Ras Kassai, and with his newfound power, Kassai later became emperor.

The British expedition brought home large quantities of treasure, numerous valuable manuscripts, and many religious items, which today can be seen in various museums and libraries in Europe, as well as in private collections. The manuscripts ignited Western interest in Ethiopic studies, but their removal provoked lasting resentment in their country of origin. A few of the items were subsequently returned to Ethiopia. The most important of these was the crown of Tewodros II, which King George V personally presented to the future emperor Haile Selassie on his visit to England in 1925.

1868
Shinto becomes the official religion of Japan. It is focused on imperial household ceremonies and public Shinto shrines and is founded on the ancient precedent of *saisei itchi*, the unity of religion and government, in which the emperor is considered a divinity.

1868
The British **Trades Union Congress** is founded. It will help establish the Labour Party at the turn of the 20th century.

1868
The first edition of the **World Almanac** is published by the *New York World* newspaper.

1868
The first recorded **bicycle race** is held in Paris.

1868
The **Fourteenth Amendment** of the U.S. Constitution is ratified, guaranteeing all people equal protection under the law.

1868
French archaeologist Édouard Lartet discovers **Cro-Magnon** skeletal remains in a cave near Périgueux, France.

1868-1869

1868
The **Meiji Restoration** returns power to the emperor of Japan from the Tokogawa shogunate and marks the entrance of Japan into the modern world. Edo is renamed Tokyo.

 [1]

1868
The United States begins affixing **tax stamps** on cigarette packages.

1868
William Ewart Gladstone of the Liberal Party is appointed to the first of his four terms (1868–74, 1880–85, 1886, 1892–94) as prime minister of Great Britain.

 [2]

February 24, 1868
The U.S. House of Representatives votes 126 to 47 to impeach **President Andrew Johnson**, whose lenient Reconstruction policies regarding the South after the Civil War have angered radical Republicans in Congress.

May 16, 1868
The first of two key votes is held in the Senate **impeachment trial** of U.S. president Andrew Johnson, who is ultimately acquitted of all charges.

May 22, 1868
A gang makes off with almost $100,000 from a train near Marshfield, Indiana, in what quickly becomes known as the **Great Train Robbery**.

THE SUEZ CANAL

An artificial waterway is completed between the Mediterranean Sea and the Red Sea.

The first feasibility study for the Suez Canal was undertaken during the French occupation of Egypt (1798–1801). J. M. Le Père, Napoleon's chief lines-of-communication engineer, erroneously calculated that the level of the Red Sea was 33 feet (10 m) above that of the Mediterranean and, therefore, that locks would be needed. Considering the adverse conditions under which the French surveyors worked and the prevailing belief in the disparity of levels of the two seas, the error was excusable, and Le Père's conclusion was uncritically accepted by a succession of subsequent authors of canal projects. Studies for a canal were made again in 1834 and in 1846. In 1854 Ferdinand de Lesseps received an act of concession from the viceroy (khedive) of Egypt, Sa'id Pasha, to construct a canal, and in 1856 a second act conferred on the Suez Canal Company (Compagnie Universelle du Canal Maritime de Suez) the right to operate a maritime canal for 99 years after completion of the work. Construction began in 1859 and took 10 years instead of the six that had been envisaged; climatic difficulties, a cholera epidemic in 1865, and early labor troubles all slowed down operations. An initial project cut a small canal (the Al-Isma'iliyah) from the delta along the Wadi Tumelat and a southern branch (now called the Al-Suways al-Hulwah Canal; the combined canals were formerly called the Sweet Water Canal) to Suez and a northern canal (Al-Abbasiyah Canal) to Port Said. The Al-Abbasiyah supplied drinking water in an otherwise arid area and was completed in 1863.

At first, digging was done by hand with picks and baskets, and peasants were drafted as forced labor. Later, dredgers and steam shovels operated by European laborers took over, and, as dredging proved cheaper than dry excavation, the terrain was artificially flooded and dredged wherever possible. Other than in the few areas where rock strata were met, the entire canal was driven through sand or alluvium.

In August 1869 the waterway was completed, and it was officially opened with an elaborate ceremony (above left) on November 17. Among the first distinguished visitors was the Prince of Wales (below left, seated, holding a cane). The future King Edward VII led a delegation on behalf of the British government, which was interested in the canal for strategic, political, and commercial reasons.

October 18, 1868
La Prensa is published in Buenos Aires, Argentina; it soon becomes the most-read newspaper in South America.

1869
After 10 years of construction, the **Suez Canal** is opened, linking the Mediterranean with the Red Sea and dramatically reducing sailing times from Europe to Asia. The project has been headed by Ferdinand de Lesseps.

1869
American inventor George Westinghouse patents the **railroad air brake**. Westinghouse later becomes the leading advocate of alternating current for power systems in the U.S.

1869
American shipping and railroad magnate **Cornelius Vanderbilt** achieves a monopoly by consolidating the Hudson River and the New York Central railroads. Later he can offer the first rail service from New York to Chicago.

1869
At New Brunswick, New Jersey, the College of New Jersey (later renamed Princeton University) and Rutgers College play the **first intercollegiate football game**.

1869
Charles Gounod's *Faust*, his most famous opera, is first performed in Paris.

May 30, 1868
Memorial Day is first celebrated in the U.S. in commemoration of the soldiers who died in the Civil War.

June 10, 1868
Prince Michael III of Serbia is assassinated, derailing the Balkan League's plans for a coordinated rebellion against the Ottomans and destroying the league.

July 14, 1868
American Alvin Fellows patents a **tape measure**.

August 11, 1868
Thaddeus Stevens, U.S. congressman and architect of radical Reconstruction following the Civil War, dies in Washington, D.C. He battled for freedmen's rights and insisted on stern requirements for readmission of Southern states into the Union.

August 13, 1868
A 9.0-magnitude earthquake hits off the Pacific coast of Peru and generates a **tsunami** that kills thousands of people in Peru and Ecuador; the tsunami travels as far away as New Zealand.

September 23, 1868
A small group of Puerto Rican radicals committed to independence attempts an uprising, **El Grito de Lares**; the revolt is crushed by the Spanish.

[1] The old Japan about to vanish: a samurai warrior in elaborate armor and silks, his fabulous helmet beside him, with bows and arrows behind.

[3] Thaddeus Stevens: "Have not loyal blacks quite as good a right to choose rulers and make laws as rebel whites?"

[4] Cigar-smoking, bloomer-wearing, hen-pecking—here is the new breed of women, according to this caricaturist, ready to vote for Susan Sharp-Tongue.

[2] A caricature of Gladstone by Ape (Carlo Pelligrini). The accompanying profile suggests that "were he a worse man, he would be a better statesman."

[5] The bogus Cardiff Giant comes to the surface, only a year after he was buried by the hoaxers.

1869
Elizabeth Cady Stanton and Susan B. Anthony found the **National Woman Suffrage Association** (NWSA) to campaign for the right of American women to vote.

1869
German physician Paul Langerhans first describes the islets of **Langerhans**, irregularly shaped patches of endocrine tissue located within the pancreas of most vertebrates.

1869
In the United States, the **Prohibition Party** is founded to campaign for legislation to prohibit the manufacture and sale of intoxicating liquors.

1869
Margarine is developed by French chemist Hippolyte Mège-Mouriès. He is awarded a prize offered by Napoleon III for a satisfactory butter substitute.

1869
Russian chemist Dmitry Ivanovich **Mendeleyev** pronounces the periodic law of elements, one of the basic laws of modern chemistry.

1869
The Cardiff Giant, a hoax perpetrated by George Hall (or Hull) of Binghamton, New York, is "discovered" by well diggers. The statue is alleged to be a 10-foot-tall, petrified prehistoric man.

1869

1869
The **Cutty Sark**, a three-masted British clipper ship, is launched at Dumbarton, Scotland. The vessel will serve in the English-Chinese tea trade and later in the Australian wool trade.
$ [1]

1869
The **H.J. Heinz Company**, a major U.S. manufacturer of processed foods, is founded in 1869 by Henry John Heinz. He will become known as the "Pickle King."

1869
The **Pillsbury Company**, a U.S. flour and bakery products firm, originates when Charles A. Pillsbury buys a share in a Minneapolis flour mill.
$

1869
The process for manufacturing **celluloid** is developed by U.S. inventor John Wesley Hyatt.

1869
The Staatsoper, or **Vienna State Opera**, opens in Vienna. It will be one of the world's leading opera houses, known especially for performances of works by Richard Wagner, Wolfgang Amadeus Mozart, and Richard Strauss.
 [2]

1869
Wyoming is the first U.S. state to give women the right to vote.

[1] The Cutty Sark is launched in the year that the Suez Canal opens; ironically, the canal is suited to steamships and so means the end for the tea clippers.

[2] The Vienna Opera will be badly damaged by bombing in 1945, losing its stage and auditorium. Two of its legendary general directors are Gustav Mahler around 1900 and Herbert von Karajan around 1960.

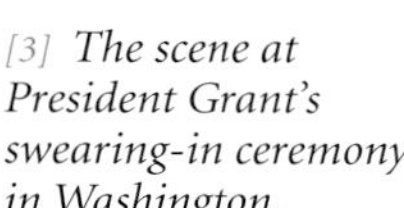

[3] The scene at President Grant's swearing-in ceremony in Washington.

[4] A golden spike is driven into the rail, and the two locomotives are christened in champagne to celebrate completion of the transcontinental railroad line.

[5] Panic reigns on the floor of the New York Stock Exchange on Black Friday, 1869.

1860s
Robert Chesebrough, a chemist from Brooklyn, New York, begins working with "rod wax," a byproduct of oil drilling in Pennsylvania. He develops it into a skin-care product marketed as **Vaseline**.

 [3]
March 4, 1869
Politically inexperienced Civil War hero **Ulysses S. Grant** enters the White House as 18th president of the United States; at age 46, he is the youngest man theretofore elected president.

 [4]
May 10, 1869
At Promontory, Utah, a golden spike is driven to mark the completion of the **first transcontinental railroad** in the U.S. The 1,800 miles of track link the Central Pacific and Union Pacific railroads.

July 3, 1869
The **Mount Washington Cog Railway** makes its first ascent to the summit of Mount Washington in New Hampshire. The railway is based on designs by inventor Sylvester Marsh.

September 1, 1869
The first **daily weather bulletin** is posted by Cleveland Abbe, an American meteorologist who will lead the development of the U.S. Weather Bureau (later renamed the National Weather Service).

 [5]
September 24, 1869
Plummeting gold prices lead to a **financial panic**, when President Ulysses S. Grant, after learning of an attempt by Jay Gould and James Fisk to drive up the gold market, orders $4 million of government gold to be sold on the market.

Head of the Statue of Liberty on display in Paris, 1878.

1870

1870
Borrowing the phrase "**Go west, young man**," New York newspaper publisher Horace Greeley writes an editorial in favor of Western expansion. The town of Greeley, Colorado, is later named for him.

 [1]

1870
F.A.O. Schwarz opens a modest toy shop in New York City. By 1908 it becomes a mammoth store offering 16,000 items.

1870
Italian troops breach the walls at Porta Pia and enter Rome. Refusing to accept Italy's occupation of the city, **Pius IX** withdraws and declares himself a prisoner in the Vatican palace, a position that his successors will maintain until 1929.

 [2]

1870
French opera and ballet composer Léo Delibes writes **Coppélia**. It is choreographed by Arthur Saint-Léon, the French dancer, choreographer, violinist, and inventor of a method of dance notation.

1870
Henry Clay Frick begins building and operating coke ovens in Pennsylvania. As chairman of Carnegie Brothers and Company (appointed 1889), he will help build the world's largest coke and steel operations.

1870
Hiram R. Revels of Mississippi takes the former seat of Jefferson Davis in the U.S. Senate, becoming the only African American in the U.S. Congress and the first elected to the Senate.

  [3]

[1] Horace Greeley's New York Tribune *is the most important American newspaper from the 1840s to the 1870s, taking an antislavery stance and appealing to a respectable and thoughtful audience. Karl Marx is one of its foreign correspondents in the 1850s.*

[2] For twenty years "Pio Nono's" position in Rome has been secured by French troops. With his temporal powers fast waning, the pope has compensated by claiming enlarged spiritual authority, culminating in the declaration of papal infallibility.

[3] Hiram R. Revels is a minister and preacher who helped raise two black regiments in the Civil War and who was present at the Battle of Vicksburg. He impresses the Senate with his speeches and his dignified and studious bearing.

U.S. IMMIGRATION

Millions of people move to the United States to escape poverty and oppression in their native lands.

Beginning in about 1870, millions of immigrants began arriving in the United States. The new wave was caused partly by poor conditions in the immigrants' native countries and partly by increasing U.S. prosperity after the Civil War. During the 1870s and 1880s, most of the immigrants came from Germany, Ireland, and England, although there were also significant numbers from Scandinavia—the photograph (left) shows Norwegians sailing to America on the steamship *Hero*.

Chinese immigration, which started during the 1849 Calfornia Gold Rush, continued. Some of the Chinese worked for a time and returned home with whatever savings they had accumulated, but others stayed on in low-paying industrial jobs or opened businesses such as restaurants, laundries, and other personal-service operations.

The influx of European immigrants increased competition for menial jobs, and the Chinese suffered in consequence. There were anti-Chinese riots, and in 1882 Congress passed the Chinese Exclusion Act, which virtually ended Chinese immigration for nearly a century.

1870
The census shows that the **foreign-born population** in the U.S. has increased by more than 3,300,000 since the first U.S. census in 1850, spurred in great measure by the Homestead Act of 1862.

1870
U.S. inventor Margaret Knight retools a bag-folding machine to allow for the production of **square-bottomed bags**. A prolific inventor, Knight receives some 27 patents.

 [7]

c. 1870
Plein-air painting, in which oil paintings of landscapes are executed in the field, begins to attract the attention of critics following the work of Claude Monet.

 [8]

c. 1870
Portuguese visitors introduce the machada to Hawaii. It is adapted by the Hawaiians and renamed the **ukulele**, Hawaiian for "flea."

c. 1870
The **gymkhana**, an athletics and equestrian exhibition, spreads from India to England. It is one of several sports or sporting events that migrate between England and its imperial possessions.

c. 1870
The **pari-mutuel** system of wagering on horse races is introduced in France by businessman Pierre Oller.

1870
Isabella II, queen of Spain, abdicates in favor of her eldest surviving son, the future Alfonso XII. She will return to Spain for a time after Alfonso's accession but will be unsuccessful in influencing political affairs.

 [4]

1870
Italian chemist and toxicologist Francesco Selmi coins the term **ptomaine poisoning** to identify acute gastrointestinal illness resulting from the consumption of foods containing one or more representatives of three main groups of harmful agents.

1870
John D. Rockefeller and a few associates incorporate the Standard Oil Company (Ohio). By 1872, it controls nearly all the refineries in Cleveland, and by 1882 it will have a near monopoly on the oil business in the United States.

 [5]

1870
Joseph Hayne Rainey is the first African American elected to the U.S. House of Representatives. This congressman from South Carolina will enjoy the longest tenure of any African American during Reconstruction.

 [6]

1870
Manitoba becomes Canada's fifth province when the area that had been the Red River Settlement is admitted to the confederation.

1870
Norwegian poet, novelist, and playwright Bjørnstjerne Martinius Bjørnson publishes his epic poem, **Arnljot Gelline**.

[4] Isabella II with her son, Alfonso XII. She had already been exiled during the revolution of 1868, which was inspired in large part by her political meddling and her manipulation by corrupt courtiers and favorites.

[5] Standard Oil's monopolistic tentacles stretch out in every direction to grasp all manner of business.

[8] "Hawaiian Music Girls": the two in front hold ukuleles.

[6] Joseph Hayne Rainey, a barber until the end of the Civil War, will be re-elected to Congress four times, serving until March 1879.

[7] An ambitious French plein-air painter tackles a very large canvas, around which a protective shelter has been rigged.

[9] The Democrat donkey's first appearance, kicking the recently deceased secretary for war, E. M. Stanton, in Thomas Nast's cartoon.

c. 1870
Thomas Adams invents modern **chewing gum**.

 [9]

January 15, 1870
The **donkey** appears as a symbol of the U.S. Democratic Party in a Thomas Nast cartoon.

February 3, 1870
The **Fifteenth Amendment** to the U.S. Constitution is ratified, guaranteeing citizens the right to vote regardless of race. It is intended to ensure, with the Fourteenth Amendment, the civil rights of former slaves.

February 23, 1870
Mississippi is readmitted to the United States following the American Civil War.

March 1, 1870
Paraguayan dictator **Francisco Solano López**, responsible for the Paraguayan War, in which Paraguay was nearly destroyed by Brazil, Argentina, and Uruguay, is killed.

March 31, 1870
Thomas Peterson-Mundy of Perth Amboy, New Jersey, becomes the first African American to vote under the Fifteenth Amendment to the U.S. Constitution.

1870-1871

June 9, 1870
English writer **Charles Dickens,** generally considered the greatest Victorian novelist, dies at Gad's Hill near Chatham, Kent.

 [1]

June 21, 1870
The **Tianjin Massacre**—a violent outbreak of Chinese xenophobic sentiment toward Westerners—erupts.

July 2, 1870
The doctrine of **papal infallibility**, whereby the pope is presumed free from error when he teaches definitively that a doctrine concerning faith or morals is to be believed by the whole church, is approved during the First Vatican Council.

July 19, 1870
The French emperor, Napoleon III, declares war on Prussia, beginning the **Franco-German War**.

September 1, 1870
The French army suffers a decisive defeat at the **Battle of Sedan** in the Franco-German War.

 [2]

September 4, 1870
Napoleon III, who ruled France first as president (1850–52) and then as emperor (1852–70), is deposed and the Third Republic is proclaimed.

 [3]

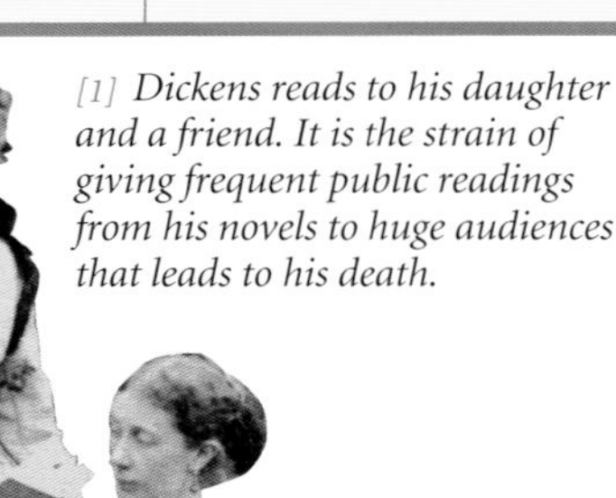

[1] Dickens reads to his daughter and a friend. It is the strain of giving frequent public readings from his novels to huge audiences that leads to his death.

[2] Prussians stand in front of French artillery captured at Sedan.

[3] Napoleon III and his empress, Eugenie, in exile after his deposition.

[8] The profile of Whistler's mother is one of the most striking profiles in art, against a very carefully calculated background.

[7] Heinrich Schliemann's wife, Sophie, decked out in what he claimed were "the jewels of Helen of Troy."

[6] George Eliot in about 1868.

 [6]

1871
George Eliot begins publication of **Middlemarch**, considered by many to be the best novel written during the Victorian era.

 [7]

1871
German pioneer archaeologist **Heinrich Schliemann** begins the excavation of what he believes (correctly) to be the ancient city of Troy in Anatolia. His discovery helps establish the modern field of archaeology.

 [8]

1871
James McNeill Whistler begins what will become his best-known painting, *Arrangement in Grey and Black No. 1: The Artist's Mother*. Completed in 1872, "Whistler's Mother" shows the influence of Japanese art.

1871
Smith College, a liberal arts college for women in Massachusetts, is established through the bequest of heiress Sophia Smith. The first women's college basketball game will be played there in 1893.

1871
The **burakumin**, an outcast or "untouchable" Japanese minority, is abolished. Nonetheless, vast numbers of burakumin continue to live in ghettolike communities throughout Japan.

1871
The era of modern photography begins when the technology for **dry-plate photography** is developed by English physician Richard Leach Maddox. Dry plates coated with gelatin containing silver salts are mass-produced.

October 17, 1870
French republican statesman **Léon Gambetta** escapes Paris in a hot-air balloon. Establishing himself at Tours, he helps direct the defense of France as the Franco-German War continues.

 [4]

1871
Albert Jones develops **corrugated cardboard** for use in packaging.

1871
American paleontologist Othniel Charles Marsh and a team of researchers discover the first remains of a **pterodactyl** (a flying reptile) found in the United States. Marsh will be credited with the discovery of more than 1,000 fossil vertebrates and the description of at least 500 more.

1871
Brigham Young, religious leader, second president of the Mormon church, and colonizer who significantly influenced the development of the American West, is tried for polygamy. He is not convicted.

1871
British labor unions receive their legal foundation in the **Trade-Union Act** of 1871.

1871
French writer **Émile Zola** publishes the first novel in his 20-volume series *Les Rougon-Macquart*. Zola is considered the founder of the artistic movement known as naturalism. Books in the series include *Nana* (1880) and *Germinal* (1885).

 [5]

[4] Gambetta proclaims the Third Republic after the deposition of Napoleon III. A balloon, similar to the one in which he will escape Paris, is readied in Montmartre for a flight over the lines of the Germans besieging Paris.

[11] H. M. Stanley poses in the clothes he wore when meeting Livingstone. His boy-servant, Kalula, stands beside him.

[5] Emile Zola, at the height of his powers, in the mid-1870s.

[12] William I, king of Prussia and the first kaiser, or emperor, of Germany (1871–1888).

[10] The Tuileries Palace is burned as a symbol of monarchy during the Commune, the world's first socialist government, formed in Paris in March after the Prussian victory over the French.

[9] The Royal Albert Hall, now a much-loved London institution, famous for the promenade concerts of classical music held there every summer and broadcast by the BBC.

[13] A parade of Prussian horse artillery and infantry in the Champs Elysees in Paris, celebrating their victory over the French.

1871
The **National Rifle Association** of America is founded under the leadership of former Union general Ambrose Burnside.

 [9]

1871
The **Royal Albert Hall** of Arts and Sciences, a concert hall in the City of Westminster, London, opens. It seats more than 5,000 but will hold a record audience of 9,000 in 1906 for a gramophone (phonograph) concert.

 [10]

1871
The **Tuileries Palace**, the French royal residence adjacent to the Louvre in Paris, is destroyed by arson.

 [11]

1871
While tracing the source of the Nile, explorer and missionary **David Livingstone** meets journalist Henry Morton Stanley on his publicity jaunt to search for the "lost" missionary, who had not been heard from for several years.

 [12]

January 18, 1871
The **German Empire**, forged as a result of diplomacy rather than an outpouring of popular nationalist feeling, is founded in the aftermath of three successful wars by the North German state of Prussia.

 [13]

January 28, 1871
The French capital, **Paris**, falls following a four-month siege during the Franco-German War.

1871-1872

March 18, 1871
The **Commune of Paris**, an insurrection of Parisians against the French government, begins, lasting until May 28.

 [1]

March 21, 1871
Otto von Bismarck, prime minister of Prussia (1862–73, 1873–90), who will succeed in preserving peace in Europe for about two decades, becomes the first chancellor of the German Empire.

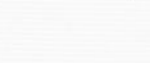

May 13, 1871
With the **Law of Guarantees**, the Italian government attempts to settle the question of its relationship with the pope, who had been deprived of his lands in the process of Italian national unification.

May 21, 1871
The Commune of Paris is attacked by troops of the French national government under Adolphe Thiers, beginning a period of violence known as **Bloody Week**.

June 27, 1871
First minted in 1869, the **yen** is adopted as Japan's official monetary unit when the government suspends the exchange of clan notes, money issued by feudal lords, which had circulated since the 16th century.

August 30, 1871
French statesman, journalist, and historian **Adolphe Thiers** is elected the first president (1871–73) of the Third Republic.

 [2]

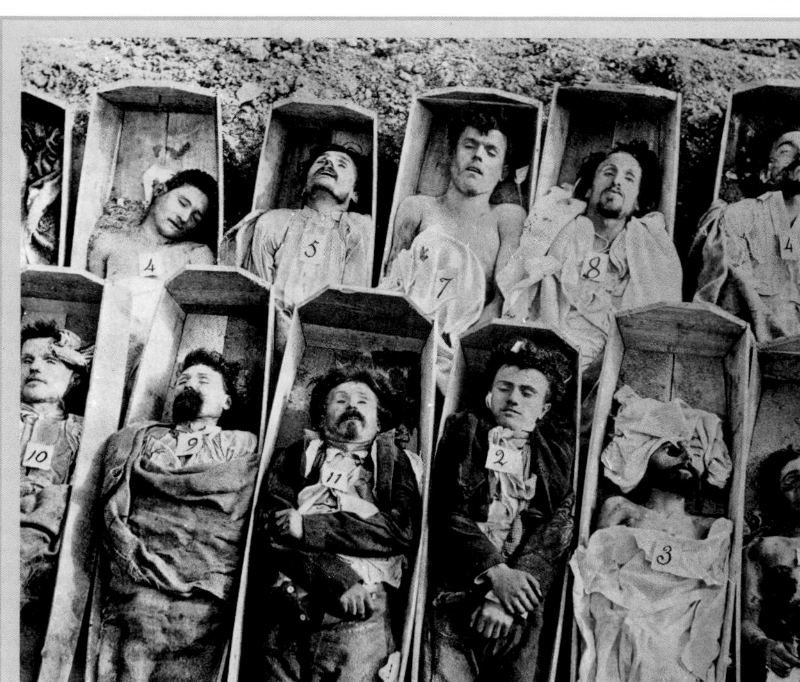

THE PARIS COMMUNE

Insurrection against the French government in the wake of France's defeat by Germany and the end of its Second Empire

The republican Parisians feared that the National Assembly would restore the monarchy. On March 26, municipal elections in the French capital brought victory for the revolutionaries, who formed the Commune government. This included three main groups: the so-called Jacobins, who wanted the Paris Commune to control the whole revolution; the Proudhonists, socialists who supported a federation of communes throughout the country; and the Blanquistes, socialists who demanded violent action.

With the quick suppression of communes at Lyon, Saint-Étienne, Marseille, and Toulouse, the Commune of Paris alone faced the opposition of the Versailles government. On May 21, government troops entered an undefended section of Paris. During *la semaine sanglante*, or "the bloody week," that followed, the regular troops crushed the opposition of the Communards, who in their defense set up barricades in the streets and burned public buildings. About 20,000 insurrectionists were killed (left), along with about 750 government troops.

[1] The column in the Place Vendome in Paris, demolished by the Communards, egged on by the artist Gustave Courbet. Erected by Napoleon I, seen sculpted in classical Roman costume here. The column's fall symbolized the Communards' hatred of autocracy.

[5] Sarah Bernhardt, daringly dressed in trousers and jackets, as if she were a sculptor, poses beside a bust of herself.

[4] A typical frontier town, with raised boardwalks, saloons, stores, a "mammoth sleeping palace," and a "grand opera."

[6] Karl Weyprecht exhorts his fellow officer Julius von Payer and their men during their Arctic expedition: "We shall never retreat."

 [4]

1872
Dodge City, Kansas, which will become a notorious U.S. frontier town, is settled with the arrival of the Santa Fe Railway.

1872
Frank Furness designs the **Pennsylvania Academy of Fine Arts** in Philadelphia. The polychromed, eclectic museum and art school is one of the masterpieces of this unique American architect.

 [5]

1872
French actress **Sarah Bernhardt** returns to the the Comédie-Française in Paris, where she will become the greatest French actress of the later 19th century and one of the best-known figures in the history of the stage.

 [6]

1872
Austrian Arctic explorer Karl Weyprecht locates **Franz Josef Land** after his ship is caught in polar ice and drifts for more than a year. Weyprecht will become an advocate of international polar research.

1872
German naturalist and botanist Ferdinand Cohn becomes the director of the Institute of Plant Physiology at the University of Breslau. He will be considered one of the founders of **bacteriology**.

1872
H. H. Richardson designs **Trinity Church**, which establishes his popularity as an architect in Boston. With its large bulk and massive tower, the building exemplifies the Romanesque style that Richardson favors.

October 8, 1871
Fire breaks out on Chicago's West Side (supposedly when a cow kicks over a lantern), starting a blaze that claims about 300 lives and causes $200 million in damage. Roughly one-third of the city lies in ruins, and nearly 100,000 people are homeless.

 [3]

October 8, 1871
Winds whip up Wisconsin forest fires that had been burning for several days, and flames destroy hundreds of square miles of forest and farmland. The town of **Peshtigo** is burned to the ground, and about 800 people are killed; the total number of deaths reaches some 1,200.

1872
A small rubber factory, Società Italiana **Pirelli**, is founded in Milan by Giovanni Battista Pirelli. It will produce insulated telegraph cables, bicycle and automobile tires, cables, and transmission belts.

1872
An **income tax** enacted during the American Civil War (1862) is rescinded.

1872
Charlotte E. Ray is the first African American woman lawyer in the United States. She is the first woman admitted to the bar in the District of Columbia.

1872
The **viceroy of India**, Lord Mayo, is murdered by a Muslim fanatic.

[2] Adolphe Thiers. After leading the parliamentary opposition to Napoleon III, he heads the provisional government that ushers in the Third Republic.

[7] King Oscar II of Sweden. It is during his reign that Norway gains its independence from Sweden.

[3] Chicago in the aftermath of the great fire.

[9] Civilian scientific staff aboard HMS Challenger. *The figure on the far right is accompanied by his parrot.*

[8] Oil wells at the developed Baku oilfield.

 [7]

1872
In Sweden, **Oscar II** succeeds his brother, becoming king of Sweden (1872–1907) and of Norway (1872–1905).

 [8]

1872
In the Russian Empire, commercial oil exploitation begins on the Abseron Peninsula near **Baku**.

1872
Polyvinyl chloride (PVC) is first prepared by German chemist Eugen Baumann.

1872
The Boston Daily Globe is founded in Boston, Massachusetts. Eventually known as the **Boston Globe**, it will become the city's largest papers and one of the most influential newspapers in the United States.

 [9]

1872
The British ship ***Challenger*** begins nearly four years of data gathering on oceanic temperature, life, currents, and the depths and contours of the ocean basins. Its survey of deep-sea life is the first systematic scientific one.

1872
The first **mail-order catalog** is issued by Aaron Montgomery Ward. It is a single sheet listing about 150 items.

1872-1873

1872
The first U.S. national park, **Yellowstone**, is established. Its opening reflects the growing power of preservationist thinking and is soon followed by the establishment of parks around the world.
 [1]

1872
The **first railroad in Japan**, built by British engineers, opens between Tokyo and Yokohama.
 [2]

1872
The International Bible Students Association is founded in 1872 in Pittsburgh by Charles Taze Russell; it is a forerunner of the **Jehovah's Witnesses**.

1872
The **Western Electric Manufacturing Company** is incorporated in Chicago. It will manufacture the world's first commercial typewriters and incandescent lamps.

November 28, 1872
German scientist and traveler Wilhelm Reiss becomes the first climber to reach the top of **Cotopaxi**, the world's highest active volcano, in Ecuador.

1873
American physicist Josiah Willard Gibbs begins publishing his work on thermodynamics and statistical mechanics that eventually helps establish the field of **physical chemistry**.

[1] Harry Yount, the first park ranger of Yellowstone National Park.

[2] Japan's first railroad. The arrangement of the locomotive's wheels has defeated the artist.

[3] Everybody's idealized image of a Canadian Mountie.

[5] Jesse James in the early 1870s.

[6] The Union Jack is hoisted for the first time at a ceremony at Port Moresby.

1873
German musicologist Philipp Spitta publishes the first volume of his monumental two-volume study of **J. S. Bach**. In 1885 he cofounds the first scholarly journal of musicology.

1873
Germany adopts a new coinage known as the gold mark. The **mark** replaces the taler and the guilder.

 [5]
1873
Jesse James and the James Younger gang pull off the first successful train robbery in the American West.

1873
Margarine is patented in the United States and is no longer allowed to be sold as butter in Europe.

 [6]
1873
Port Moresby, the capital of Papua New Guinea, is founded by British captain John Moresby.

1873
Prince Edward Island joins the Canadian Confederation, becoming the seventh Canadian province.

1873
American shipping and railroad magnate **Cornelius Vanderbilt** offers the first rail service from New York to Chicago.

1873
Barbed wire is introduced at the DeKalb County Fair in Illinois by local farmer Henry Rose.

1873
The Bellevue Hospital School of Nursing is established in New York City. It is the first nursing school to use the Nightingale model to train nurses.

1873
Canada's federal police force, the Northwest Mounted Rifles, is founded. The name is later changed to the **Royal Canadian Mounted Police** (RCMP), or Mounties.

 [3]

1873
English physician **William Budd** publishes *Typhoid Fever,* a compilation of his studies of typhoid in which he establishes that the disease is contagious.

 [4]

1873
George S. Boutwell steps down from his position as secretary of the treasury to become a U.S. senator. Boutwell will become the leading Radical Republican during the Reconstruction Era.

[4] William Budd, who won fame in 1866 by stamping out cholera in Bristol.

[7] James Clerk Maxwell, whose work paves the way for wireless telegraphy and radio. He also studies gases, optics, and color sensation.

SAN FRANCISCO CABLE CARS

In most of the places that had cable cars, the systems were soon replaced by electric trams; in San Francisco, however, they remain a symbol of the city.

The cable car, the invention of Andrew Hallidie, was introduced in San Francisco (above) on Sacramento and Clay streets in 1873. The cars were drawn by an endless cable running in a slot between the rails and passing over a steam-driven shaft in the powerhouse. The system was well adapted for operation on steep hills and reached its most extensive use in San Francisco and Seattle. The cars operated more smoothly than did early electric cars, but they could run only at a constant speed; broken or jammed cable tied up all the cars on the line. Beginning about 1900, most cable trackage was replaced by electric cars, but the Seattle lines lasted until the 1930s. At the start of the 21st century, San Francisco had the world's only remaining cable-car system. The current network, part of the San Francisco Municipal Railway, consists of two lines between the downtown area near Union Square and Fisherman's Wharf, and a third line along California Street. Each cable is 1 inch (2.5 cm) in diameter and driven by a 510 horsepower (380 kW) electric motor at a constant speed of 9.5 miles per hour (15.3 km/h).

Early streetcars were either horse-drawn or powered by storage batteries that were expensive and inefficient. In 1834 Thomas Davenport, a blacksmith from Brandon, Vermont, built a small battery-powered electric motor and used it to operate a small car on a short section of track. In 1860 an American, G. F. Train, opened three lines in London and one line in Birkenhead. Other such systems, called tramways in Britain, were established at Salford in 1862 and at Liverpool in 1865. The invention of the dynamo (generator) allowed transmitted power to be applied to streetcar lines by means of overhead electrified wires, and these electrified streetcars subsequently proliferated throughout Britain, Europe, and the United States.

1873
Professional bookmaking makes its first appearance at American horse tracks.

 [7]

1873
Scottish physicist **James Clerk Maxwell** publishes his *Treatise on Electricity and Magnetism*, in which he describes his theory of electromagnetism and establishes himself among the great scientists of history.

1873
The black, polled beef cattle, for many years known as **Aberdeen Angus**, originating in northeastern Scotland, are introduced into the United States.

1873
The **Coors Brewing Company** is established by Adolph Coors and Joseph Schueler in Golden, Colorado.

1873
The Employment of Females Act is passed in **New Zealand**. It is the first act to attempt to establish work hours, sanitation standards, and holidays for factory workers in New Zealand.

1873
The **first cable car** is introduced in San Francisco.

1873-1874

1873
The first European to visit **Ayers Rock**, a giant monolith in Australia's Northwest Territory, is explorer William Gosse. He names the rock after South Australian premier Sir Henry Ayers.

1873
The Japanese government implements land and tax reform as part of the **Meiji Restoration reforms**, another step in bringing about the modernization and westernization of Japan.

1873
Several tribunals are joined to create the English **Court of Appeal and High Court of Justice**: a first modern attempt to reduce the clutter and inefficiency of courts that have jurisdiction throughout England and Wales.

1873
The **Modoc War** comes to an end.

1873
The Panic of 1873, which began with financial crises in Vienna in June and in New York City in September, marks the end of the long-term expansion of the world economy that had begun in the late 1840s.

 [1]

1873
The **Slaughterhouse Cases** result in a landmark U.S. Supreme Court decision that limits the protection of the privileges and immunities clause of the Fourteenth Amendment to the U.S. Constitution.

THE MODOC WAR

Native American uprising against resettlement

The U.S. government pressed the Modoc and Klamath tribes to relinquish most of their territory in the south of the Cascade mountain range and move to a reservation around Upper Klamath Lake. The land was traditionally Klamath, and that tribe treated the Modoc as intruders; the U.S. government, moreover, failed in its obligations to supply rations to the Modoc. In 1870 an insurgent band of Modocs under Kintpuash, a subchief known to the American military as Captain Jack, left the reservation. Federal efforts to induce this group's return precipitated the Modoc War of 1872–73, in which about 80 warriors and their families retreated to the California Lava Beds, where they mounted an effective resistance. After the murder of Brigadier General Edward Canby in 1873, U.S. troops pursued the war more vigorously. Captain Jack surrendered and was hanged. His followers were removed to the Indian Territory (Oklahoma). Donald McKay (standing third from left, above), a Native American scout who captured Captain Jack, became famous through images such as this one, and later became a star of Wild West shows.

[1] The doors of the New York Stock Exchange have to be closed during the 1873 financial panic.

[4] Marshal Mac-Mahon. A monarchist at heart, he will fail in his attempt to place an Orleanist prince on the French throne.

[5] The sultan of Zanzibar with courtiers a few years after he has been forced to end the open slave trade in his country.

1873
Woodward's Garden, the first aquarium on America's West Coast, opens in San Francisco. Sixteen tanks made of one-inch-thick glass house saltwater and freshwater fishes.

c. 1873
The Indian court game of poona is introduced to England at the country estate of **Badminton**. The game's name is soon changed to that of the estate.

February 1873
The **first Spanish republic** is proclaimed by the Cortes Parliament following the abdication of King Amadeo.

April 1873
The English White Star Liner **Atlantic**, carrying 957 passengers, runs aground off the coast of Halifax, Nova Scotia. An estimated 545 people die in the disaster.

May 1873
The first running of the **Preakness Stakes** takes place at Pimlico Race Course in Baltimore, Maryland.

 [4]

May 24, 1873
Marie-Edme-Patrice-Maurice, count de **Mac-Mahon**, marshal of France, is elected president of the Third French Republic.

1873
The **Timber Culture Act** is passed by the U.S. Congress. The act states that anyone who plants 2.5 acres of trees and cares for them for eight years can receive in return 40 acres of land at no cost.

1873
The U.S. Congress passes the **Comstock Act**, which criminalizes the publication, distribution, and possession of information about or devices or medications for unlawful abortion or contraception.

1873
The U.S. industrialist and philanthropist **Henry Clay Frick** acquires extensive coal deposits following the Panic of 1873 and uses them to supply Pittsburgh with the coke required for its steel and iron industries. By 1879, at the age of 30, Frick will be a millionaire.

 [2]

1873
The **U.S. Mint** becomes part of the Department of the Treasury in Washington, D.C. Prior to this, the mint had functioned in Philadelphia as a self-governing agency for nearly 74 years.

1873
The **University of the Cape of Good Hope** is founded. The name will be changed to the University of South Africa (UNISA) in 1916.

1873
Timothy O'Sullivan's monumental photograph *Canyon de Chelly*, depicting majestic rock forms in the American Southwest, embraces a new subject matter and composition style.

 [3]

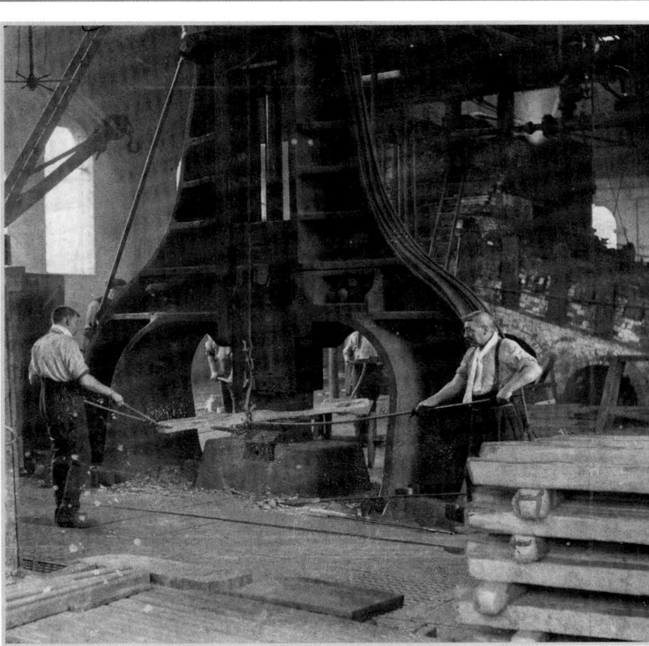

[2] *A large forging hammer is used in a Pittsburgh steel plant.*

[3] *Sullivan's photograph of the Canyon de Chelly in Arizona. Note the three tiny tents at the bottom left.*

[6] *Paul Verlaine. He and Rimbaud have been wandering around France, Belgium, and England since 1871.*

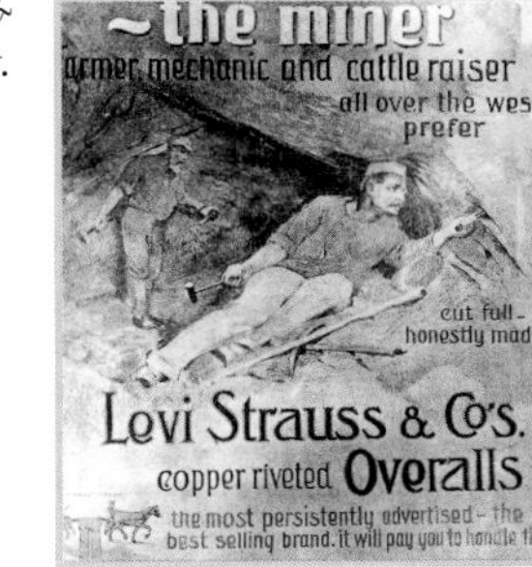

[8] *A Levi Strauss & Co. advertisement.*

[7] *A toast is shared to celebrate the end of the second Ashanti War in West Africa (Ghana). It will be followed by two more wars.*

[9] *The painting from which the name Impressionist came:* Impression, Soleil Levant *(*Sun Rising*) by Claude Monet.*

 [5]

June 1873
The sultan of Zanzibar, pressured by the British government, closes the public slave trade in **Zanzibar**.

 [6]

July 10, 1873
French poet **Paul Verlaine**, known as the leader of the Symbolists and founder of the Decadents, shoots and wounds young French poet Arthur Rimbaud. Verlaine will serve two years in jail for his crime.

November 7, 1873
Scottish-born politician **Alexander Mackenzie** becomes the first Liberal prime minister of Canada (1873–78).

 [7]

1874
British General Wolseley wins the second **Ashanti War** in West Africa.

 [8]

1874
Levi Strauss & Co. starts using copper rivets to strengthen its work clothes.

 [9]

1874
A journalist reviewing a show by Monet, Renoir, Pisarro, and others dismisses them as **Impressionists**, drawing on the name of an 1872 painting by Monet. The group adopts the epithet as its name.

1874

1874
Belgian-born American inventor Charles Joseph Van Depoele demonstrates the feasibility of **electrical traction**.

1874
Benjamin Disraeli, prime minister for nine months in 1868, starts his second term (1874–80). He provides the Conservative Party with a twofold policy of Tory democracy and imperialism.

 [1]

1874
Composer **Johann Strauss** the Younger, famous for his Viennese waltzes and operettas, completes *Die Fledermaus*, which becomes a historically classic example of a Viennese operetta.

[2]

1874
DDT is synthesized by German chemist Othmar Zeidler. First used as an insecticide in 1939, its effects as an environmental toxin will lead most countries to ban the substance in the 1970s.

1874
Following negotiations and an offer of unconditional cessation, **Fiji** becomes a British crown colony.

 [3]

1874
George Edmund Street begins work on the **Law Courts, London**. The last major monument of the English Gothic revival, this building, by a master of Victorian Gothic, fits into the streetscape despite its bulk.

 [4]

[1] Benjamin Disraeli, standing left, poses with friends at his home, Hughenden Manor. His secretary, Montagu Corry, lies in front.

[4] The new Law Courts in the Strand in London, on the left. The statue of a winged dragon in the distance marks the western boundary of the City of London and the start of Fleet Street.

[2] Two of the lead singers in an 1894 production of Die Fledermaus *(*The Bat*). One of the title creatures can be seen decorating the heroine's hair.*

[3] A Fijian couple are introduced to Britannia by Benjamin Disraeli after the British colonization of the islands.

[7] The few survivors of the Cospatrick*, as the ship that will rescue them comes into sight.*

1874
The **Bronx** towns of Morrisania, West Farms, and Kingsbridge are annexed by Manhattan. Additional land from the Bronx will be added in 1898, creating the modern New York borough.

1874
The *Encyclopedia of Wit and Wisdom* is published by American humorist **Josh Billings**.

1874
The first game of **baseball** played outside the United States takes place in England. The Athletics beat the Bostons, scoring five runs in the 10th inning to win.

1874
The first **Hutterites**, members of the Hutterian Brethren from Austria and South Germany, migrate to the United States and settle first in South Dakota.

1874
The **ice cream soda** is invented in Philadelphia, the center of ice-cream making in the United States.

 [7]

1874
The immigrant ship **Cospatrick** catches fire and sinks off the coast of Auckland, New Zealand, with a loss of more than 450 lives.

1874
Gold is discovered in the **Black Hills of South Dakota**, foretelling disaster for the Western Sioux Indians, whose rights to the region, which they regard as sacred, were guaranteed by the Second Treaty of Fort Laramie in 1868.

1874
H. J. Lawson of England designs the first **chain-driven bicycle**.

 [5]

1874
Joseph Glidden of DeKalb, Illinois, develops machinery for the efficient production of **barbed wire**. By 1890, fenced pastureland will have virtually replaced the open range in the western United States.

1874
P.T. Barnum's Hippodrome opens in New York City. It is later renamed **Madison Square Garden**.

 [6]

1874
The R.H. Macy Company in New York City is the first department store to set up a Christmas window display of its dolls. These window displays contribute to Macy's popularity and are a tradition that the store will continue.

1874
Robert Wood Johnson begins to manufacture antiseptic bandages and wound dressings; with his brother, he founds the company **Johnson & Johnson**.

[5] *King Edward VII's daughter, Princess Louise, with her husband, the duke of Fife, and their early models of chain-driven bicycles.*

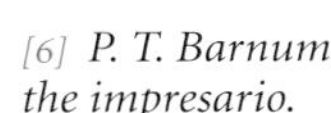

[6] *P. T. Barnum, the impresario.*

[8] *The Republican elephant, with Uncle Sam on board, tramples the Democratic tiger in 1876.*

GOLD IN SOUTH DAKOTA

Gold strikes bring a rush of fortune-seekers to a previously remote area of northwestern North America.

The search for gold in the Black Hills in the early 1870s attracted non-Indians to the western part of the Dakota Territory, despite the recognition of Indian ownership by federal treaties. In 1877 the Indians were forced by Congress to accept a reduction of their reservation and to cede the Black Hills to the federal government. Rapid City emerged as the main gateway city to the region. Freight and stage lines connected the mining population with the East until railroads entered west-river provinces early in the 20th century.

At one location, near Rockerville, South Dakota, gold panners (above) extracted $350,000 worth of the metal between 1876 and 1878. Such strikes were not exceptional. As news of the finds spread, there was a gold rush and a flood of settlers into the east-river region, swelling its population from about 80,000 to 325,000 between 1878 and 1887. This rapid expansion led to calls for the division of the territory at the 46th parallel and separate statehood for the southern half. In the north and in Congress a single state was favored. The southern section held constitutional conventions in 1883 and 1885; at the latter, the state of Dakota was established. Dual statehood based on a division below the 46th parallel received congressional approval in 1889, and both North and South Dakota were admitted to the Union simultaneously. However, the manner in which the region was incorporated into the United States caused lasting friction between Indians and settlers.

1874
The London School of Medicine for Women is founded by British physician **Sophia Jex-Blake**.

1874
The Philadelphia Zoological Gardens is the **first zoo** to open in the United States. It contains an animal inventory of several hundred native and exotic specimens.

 [8]

1874
The Republican Party's symbol, the **elephant**, appears in a cartoon in *Harper's Weekly*. The elephant has been used in several earlier drawings by Thomas Nast in association with the party.

1874
The **Social Democratic Workingmen's Party** is formed in North America. The group works toward holding a congress to unite itself with the International Association of Social Democrats and other groups.

1874
The Treaty of Bern, forming the **General Postal Union**, is signed in Bern, Switzerland.

1874
The **University of Adelaide** is founded in South Australia.

1874-1875

1874
The Woman's Christian Temperance Union (WCTU) is founded in Cleveland, Ohio, in response to the "Woman's Crusade," a series of temperance demonstrations.

 [1]

January 13, 1874
Unemployed workers assemble, intending to march on New York City Hall. The New York police attack them the next morning, injuring hundreds of protestors.

January 19, 1874
Morrison Remick Waite is appointed seventh chief justice of the U.S. Supreme Court by President Ulysses S. Grant. He will serve from 1874 to 1888.

July 1, 1874
The **first kidnapping for ransom** occurs in the United States, when four-year-old Charles Ross is taken and held for $20,000 ransom.

July 29, 1874
Major Walter Clopton Wingfield takes out a patent on his **portable tennis court**. He originally calls the game sphairistike, but it is soon called lawn tennis.

 [2]

August 1874
In New Haven, Connecticut, Harry S. Parmalee invents the first **sprinkler system** that is useful for fire protection.

[1] Women temperance crusaders pray outside a New York tavern.

[2] Early lady tennis players stand either side of the net. Their long skirts are a considerable restraint on their freedom of movement, but women have played tennis from the first.

[6] Carmen lies dead at the end of the opera, stabbed by her lover Don José, whom she has spurned.

[7] Charles Parnell, ironically, a Protestant landlord who speaks with an English accent and owns 4,000 acres in County Wicklow.

[8] Mary Baker Eddy. Her First Church of Christ, Scientist will be located in Lynn, Massachusetts.

 [6]

1875
Georges Bizet's great opera **Carmen** is first performed in Paris, based on a story by Prosper Mérimée. The realism of the work, which causes a scandal, inaugurates a new chapter in the history of opera.

1875
German explorer Karl Weyprecht proposes international cooperation in collecting scientific data during **Arctic** studies. His proposal leads to the first International Polar Year (1882–83), when Arctic stations pool their data.

 [7]

1875
Irish nationalist **Charles Stewart Parnell** becomes a member of the British Parliament (1875–91) and later leads the struggle for Irish Home Rule.

1875
Japan seizes the **Kuril Islands** from Russia. The islands will be ceded to the Soviet Union as part of the Yalta agreements in 1945.

1875
Lycopene is isolated from tomatoes.

 [8]

1875
Mary Baker Eddy publishes her major work, *Science and Health*, outlining the basic tenets of **Christian Science**.

1875
American dentist George F. Green patents the **first electric dental drill** designed to saw, file, and polish teeth. [3]

1875
American Realist painter **Thomas Eakins** paints his masterpiece, *The Gross Clinic*. The painting demonstrates his command of human anatomy, but its subject meets with disfavor among contemporaries.

1875
Successful industrialist **Andrew Carnegie** opens his first steel plant, the J. Edgar Thomson Steel Works, in Braddock, Pennsylvania. [4]

1875
At Churchill Downs in Louisville, Kentucky, Aristides wins the inaugural **Kentucky Derby**. The Derby becomes the most prestigious horse race in the United States.

1875
Englishman Matthew Webb becomes the first person known to have swum across the **English Channel**, from Dover to Calais. [5]

1875
French scientist **Paul-Jean Coulier** discovers that dust particles in the atmosphere play a fundamental role in atmospheric condensation and cloud formation.

[3] The horrors of early dentistry. A tooth is extracted while the customer's head is held steady with the aid of a towel.

[4] Andrew Carnegie. He has laid the foundations of his fortune by investing in oil and sleeping cars.

[5] Matthew Webb, a merchant navy captain, takes 21 hours to swim the English Channel.

[10] A woman sits beside a workbench laden with fireworks that she is making by hand.

[9] Three homeless children get what shelter they can on Mulberry Street in New York.

 [9]

1875
New York becomes the first U.S. state to legislate protection for children. It serves as a model for other states, all of which begin to legislate statutes designating **child abuse** as a criminal offense.

1875
The **Whiskey Ring**, a group of whiskey distillers who had conspired to defraud the U.S. government of taxes, disbands. A secret investigation exposed the ring, resulting in 238 indictments and 110 convictions.

1875
The **20-cent piece** is introduced and closely resembles the quarter. Produced primarily as a result of silver-mining interests in the American West, it is quickly deemed useless, and its production canceled in 1876.

 [10]

1875
The Explosives Act of 1875 is implemented in the United Kingdom, providing a measure of control over the manufacture, importation, storage, and sale of **fireworks**.

1875
The first private telegraph line is installed in India by the **Indian Telegraph** Department.

1875
The first recorded public **indoor ice hockey** game, with rules largely borrowed from field hockey, takes place in Montreal's Victoria Skating Rink between two teams of McGill University students.

1875-1876

1875
The **first recorded shutout in professional baseball** history occurs when Chicago beats St. Louis.

1875
The **Ottoman Empire** enters into a crisis following the success of Tanzimat reformers. Centralization removes the checks on the power of the sultan. The crisis will last until 1878.

1875
The **Palace Hotel in San Francisco** is completed. It is comprises seven stories and 755 rooms. It will be destroyed in the 1906 San Francisco earthquake.

1875
The **Resumption Act** attempts to resolve the struggle between "soft money" forces, who advocate continued use of Civil War greenbacks, and their "hard money" opponents, who want to redeem paper money and resume a specie currency.

1875
The Sale of Food and Drugs Law in Britain prevents the sale of **adulterated foods**.

1875
The **Sons of the American Revolution** (SAR) is instituted. It will be chartered by the U.S. Congress in 1906.

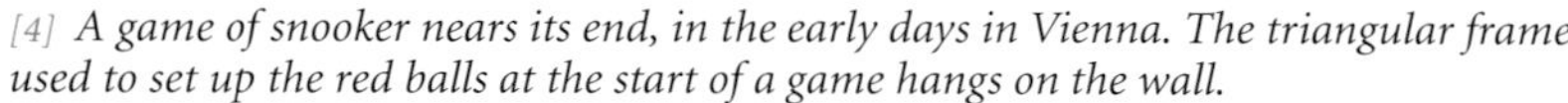

[4] *A game of snooker nears its end, in the early days in Vienna. The triangular frame used to set up the red balls at the start of a game hangs on the wall.*

[1] *The Palace Hotel on Market Street in San Francisco.*

[2] *One of the first greenbacks: a dollar bill issued by the Union in 1862.*

[7] *The empress dowager of China, Cixi, notorious for her ruthlessness and cruelty.*

February 25, 1875
At the death of China's emperor, empress dowager Cixi's four-year-old nephew (whom she adopted) becomes the Guangxu emperor. Empress dowagers Cixi and Ci'an, and later **Cixi** alone, are regents.

March 1, 1875
Republicans in the U.S. Congress pass the last of the **Force Acts**, which protect the constitutional rights of blacks during the Reconstruction.

March 15, 1875
Pope Pius IX appoints John McCloskey **the first American cardinal** of the Roman Catholic Church.

May 20, 1875
The **International Bureau of Weights and Measures**, an organization founded to unify the world's systems of measurement, is established in Paris.

June 14, 1875
German astronomer Heinrich Louis d'Arrest dies. While a student, he hastened the discovery of **Neptune** by suggesting comparison of the sky with a new star chart. The planet was found the same night.

1876
A route to the East is established for Los Angeles and San Francisco as the **Southern Pacific Railroad** reaches Los Angeles.

1875
The **Westminster Kennel Club** is formed in New York City. Its first annual dog show will be held two years later.

1875
The opera *Trial By Jury* establishes the popularity of **W. S. Gilbert and Arthur Sullivan**. Their collaboration later yields such "Savoy Operas" as *H.M.S. Pinafore* (1878), *Pirates of Penzance* (1879), and *The Mikado* (1885).

 [3]

c.1875
British soldier Sir Neville Francis Fitzgerald Chamberlain invents the billiards game of **snooker**, a variation of pool.

 [4]

January 5, 1875
The **Paris Opera House**, designed by Charles Garnier, opens. The building, considered one of the masterpieces of the Second Empire style, was begun in 1861.

 [5]

February 1875
The **Red River War** comes to an end as the Southern Plains Indians surrender to military authorities at Fort Sill in Oklahoma. After relentless pursuit by the U.S. Army, the Indians, exhausted and trapped, can no longer fight.

 [6]

February 22, 1875
French painter **Camille Corot** dies in Paris. His landscape paintings are noted for their technical freedom and clear color, as well as their inspiration for Impressionists.

[3] Arthur Sullivan, the best-known English musician of his day, is a brilliant musical parodist and pasticheur.

[5] The splendiferous frontage of the Paris Opera House, redolent of the Second Empire but completed in the Third Republic.

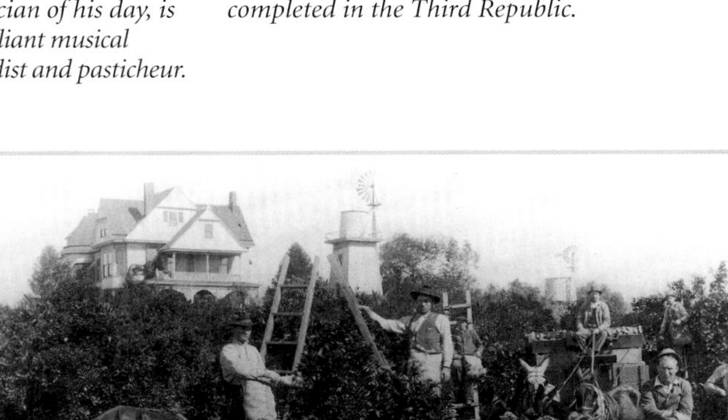

[9] Gathering the citrus harvest in a California orange grove.

[8] Bell's telephone in operation.

[6] Comanche leader Quanah Parker with one of his eight wives after his surrender at Fort Sill. His mother was a white captive, Cynthia Ann Parker.

1876
American architect Henry Hobson Richardson completes the Walter **Sherman House** in Newport, Rhode Island.

 [8]

1876
American inventor Alexander Graham Bell patents the **telephone**.

1876
American librarian Melvil Dewey publishes the **Dewey Decimal Classification**.

1876
Belgian king Leopold II creates the Association Internationale du Congo to explore Africa.

 [9]

1876
California fruit reaches the Mississippi Valley by train car for the first time.

1876
China's Shansi province and India's Deccan Plateau experience **severe droughts**, which kill wheat fields.

1876-1877

1876
Compositional effects owing much to both Japanese prints and an interest in ballet movement and dress are central to the works of French painter **Edgar Degas**, such as his *Prima Ballerina.*

1876
Corriere della Sera becomes a morning daily newspaper and eventually one of Italy's leading papers.

1876
Edvard Grieg, a founder of the Norwegian nationalist school of music, writes the incidental music for Henrik Ibsen's *Peer Gynt*, first performed in Christiana (later Oslo).

1876
John Wanamaker converts an abandoned railroad depot in Philadelphia into a multipurpose clothing and specialties store called **Wanamaker's**, catering to an upscale market. Among his innovations is the price tag, which gives a set price for an item.

1876
Julius Wolff establishes the first successful **sardine cannery** in the United States.

1876
Mark Twain publishes *The Adventures of Tom Sawyer*, a classic of American children's literature and an evocation of 19th-century small-town life. He begins *The Adventures of Huckleberry Finn* the same year.

 [1]

[1] *Mark Twain draws on his own youth in Hannibal, Missouri, on the Mississippi River, when writing his books.*

[6] *The disembodied arm and torch of the Statue of Liberty is exhibited in Philadelphia. The statue will not be completed until 1886.*

[2] *Nikolaus A. Otto*

[7] *Sitting Bull, chief of the Dakota Sioux (near right). After escaping to Canada, he will surrender in 1881 and then tour with Buffalo Bill's Wild West show. Colonel Custer's arrogance is very evident in this photograph (far right).*

[5] *Harry Wright organized, managed, and played for the Cincinnati Red Stockings, the first all-professional baseball team.*

[5]
1876
The **National League of Professional Baseball Clubs** is established. The rival American League will be founded in 1900.

 [6]
1876
The **Philadelphia Centennial Exposition** is held in celebration of the 100th anniversary of the Declaration of Independence.

1876
The Sherwin-Williams Company develops **ready-to-apply** paint.

1876
The **U.S. Coast Guard Academy**, an institution of higher learning for the training of commissioned officers for the U.S. Coast Guard, is founded by act of Congress.

May 10, 1876
The **Eli Lilly Company**, which specializes in pharmaceutical products, is founded in Indianapolis.

 [7]
June 25, 1876
Lieutenant Colonel George Armstrong Custer's seventh Cavalry attacks an encampment of Indians led by Sitting Bull near the **Little Bighorn** River in Montana. Of the more than 200 cavalrymen, not one lives to tell the story.

1876
Nikolaus A. Otto builds an **internal-combustion engine** utilizing the four-stroke cycle (four strokes of the piston for each ignition).

1876
Ontario is linked with the Maritime Provinces by **Canada's Intercolonial Railway**.

1876
Pierre-Auguste Renoir applies Impressionist techniques to the crowd in *Le Moulin de la galette*, which depicts pleasures of urban life.

1876
Porfirio Díaz defeats the forces of the Mexican government at the Battle of Tecoac.

1876
Architect **Richard Norman Shaw** begins work on **Bedford Park**, the earliest garden suburb, outside London.

1876
Stenotype, a system of **machine shorthand**, is first used in courtroom reporting.

[3] Renoir summons up a delectable Paris, recovered from the Franco-Prussian War and the Commune, in this view of the dancers at an open-air place of entertainment.

[4] Richard Norman Shaw. With Bedford Park, he has moved on from his early Gothic style to a happy, mixed, picturesque "Queen Anne" style.

[9] The Wagnerites' mecca: the Festspielhaus at Bayreuth in Bavaria, photographed about 1920.

[10] Frank James in 1915.

[8] Wild Bill Hickok: a Union sharpshooter and scout in the Civil War and then a Kansas marshal who killed several desperadoes.

SAMURAI UPRISING

Attempt by Japanese warriors to restore feudal rule

Emperor Meiji's attempts to westernize Japan were opposed by conservatives, particularly former members of the samurai (left), the warrior class that had been disbanded in 1871. On January 29, 1877, disciples of Saigo Takamori, a leading clansman and one of Meiji's main critics, attacked the Kagoshima arsenal and navy yard. The action turned into a full-scale uprising, and on February 15 the rebels set out for Tokyo. Government forces blocked their advance at Kumamoto, and war ensued for the next six months. By May Saigo was on the defensive; during the summer he suffered a series of disastrous defeats, and by September the situation was hopeless. With a few hundred men, he returned to Kagoshima to make his last stand. On September 24, 1877, the government troops launched the final attack; Saigo was critically wounded, and, as he had previously arranged, one of his faithful lieutenants took his life by beheading him. Of the 40,000 troops he had led in February, only some 200 remained to surrender. Losses on both sides were estimated at approximately 12,000 dead and 20,000 wounded.

August 1, 1876
Colorado is admitted to the United States as the 38th state.

August 2, 1876
Wild Bill Hickok is murdered in Deadwood, South Dakota, while playing poker. His cards—a pair of black aces and a pair of black eights plus an unknown fifth card—become known as the dead man's hand.

August 13-17, 1876
Richard Wagner's great cycle of four operas, *The Ring of the Nibelung*, receives its triumphant first complete performance in the new Festspielhaus at Bayreuth, Germany.

September 7, 1876
The **Younger Brothers**, a group of American outlaws, are captured following an unsuccessful bank robbery in Northfield, Minnesota. Jesse and Frank James escape.

December 23, 1876
The first comprehensive constitution of the **Ottoman Empire** goes into effect, giving the sultan full executive power.

1877
A **samurai uprising** led by Saigo Takamori takes place in Japan.

1877
Arthur Kennedy, Queensland governor, approves a measure that will drastically cut **Chinese immigration to Australia**.

1877
Chicago meat-packer Gustavus Franklin Swift sends the first shipment of beef to Boston in a **refrigerated railcar** designed to prevent spoilage.

1877
Chief Joseph of the **Nez Percé** tries to flee to Canada with some of his tribe to avoid being placed on a reservation. He is finally surrounded and says, "Hear me, my chiefs; my heart is sick and sad. From where the sun now stands, I will fight no more forever."

 [1]

1877
Cholera sweeps through Japan, where more than 150,000 cases and 90,000 deaths are recorded between 1877 and 1879.

1877
Famine in Bengal, India, kills 4 million.

1877
German botanist **Wilhelm Pfeffer** devises a semipermeable membrane that he uses to study osmosis.

[1] Chief Joseph of the Nez Percé

[6] Rutherford B. Hayes, who reached the rank of major-general in the Civil War.

[2] Robert Koch, whose work leads to the identification of many of the great killer diseases.

[5] H. M. Stanley, mapper of the Congo River

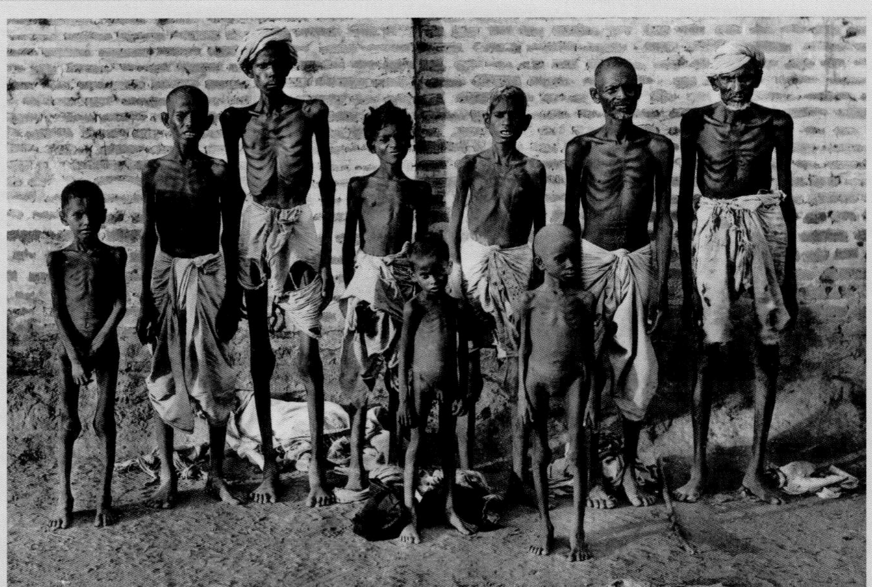

INDIAN FAMINE

Drought and political machinations cause the death of millions.

From October 1875 to October 1877, four successive monsoons failed to bring their full supply of rain. The prolonged drought affected the whole of southern India, particularly its grain production. Although at the time India had a net surplus of rice and wheat, the inhabitants were unable to benefit because the viceroy, Lord Lytton, misguidedly believed that "more food will reach the famine-stricken districts if private enterprise is left to itself . . . than if it were paralysed by government competition." He wanted as much of the food as possible to be shipped to Britain, which had itself suffered a poor harvest in 1876. As the food left the country, the Indian farmers were left destitute, and there was a famine throughout the Deccan plateau. Some of the victims are shown above.

Traders used India's new railroad system to transport the grain to wherever it would fetch the highest prices, rather than to the places it was most urgently needed to relieve starvation. This policy was bolstered by British legislation. The Anti-Charitable Contributions Act of 1877 prohibited "at the pain of imprisonment private relief donations that potentially interfered with the market fixing of grain prices." At the height of the crisis, the British army in India pressed for immediate payment of tax arrears accumulated since the start of the dry period. Some victims of the famine sought the only remedy they could—working in the parched fields in return for subsistence rations—but they were too weak and the earth was too dry for them to have any significant effect.

The British government estimated that 5.5 million died in the famine; some historians have put the total at more than 7 million.

 [5]

1877
Journalist-turned-explorer **Henry Morton Stanley** descends the Congo River to its mouth, charting its course and dubbing its 220 miles of rapids and cataracts Livingstone Falls.

1877
Jules Simon, French political leader, philosopher, and theorist of the French Radical Party, resigns as premier.

1877
Leo Tolstoy, Russian author, master of realistic fiction, and one of the world's greatest novelists, completes *Anna Karenina*.

1877
Patrick Manson, a British pioneer in tropical medicine, shows in China how insects can carry disease and how the embryos of the *Filaria* worm, which can cause elephantiasis, are transmitted by the mosquito.

1877
Peter Ilich Tchaikovsky's *Swan Lake* is first performed in Moscow. Tchaikovsky is regarded as the leading Russian composer of the late 19th century, particularly for his classical ballets.

1877
Rutherford B. Hayes of the Republican Party serves as the 19th president of the United States from 1877 to 1881. His vice president is William A. Wheeler.

1877
German physician **Robert Koch** publishes an important paper on the investigation, preservation, and photographing of bacteria.

 [2]

1877
German urologist Max Nitze develops the **cystoscope**, an instrument for viewing the bladder.

1877
In San Francisco 25 **Chinatown** wash houses are burned by a mob angry that Chinese laborers are willing to work for low wages.

 [3]

1877
A strike by **railroad workers** spreads across the United States.

 [4]

1877
John D. Rockefeller, founder of the Standard Oil Company, strengthens his oil-rail monopoly by signing a contract with the Pennsylvania Railroad.

1877
Johns Hopkins University begins the **first American university press**, as the *American Journal of Mathematics* begins publication.

[7] The Mirror of Venus *by Sir Edward Burne-Jones (above), who is normally categorized as one of the second generation of Pre-Raphaelite painters but could just as well be called an early Symbolist. Something of his otherworldliness can be detected in his photograph (left).*

[3] *A street scene in San Francisco's Chinatown.*

[8] *One of the illustrations in an early edition of* Black Beauty.

[4] *The burned-out shell of a locomotive roundhouse in Pittsburgh, set on fire by striking railroad workers.*

1877
Several members of the **Molly Maguires**, a secret group of coal miners who attacked U.S. coal company officials, are executed. The original Molly Maguires may have been a violent secret society in Ireland during the potato famine.

 [7]

1877
Sir Edward Burne-Jones, one of the last major painters inspired by the Pre-Raphaelite ideal, establishes his reputation at an exhibit featuring *The Beguiling of Merlin* and *The Mirror of Venus*.

 [8]

1877
The children's classic **Black Beauty**, by English author Anna Sewell, is published. One of her goals was "to induce kindness, sympathy, and an understanding treatment of horses."

1877
The **Farm Journal**, which will become one of the leading farm magazines in the United States, begins publication in Philadelphia.

1877
The first **Bell telephone** is sold.

1877
The first **housing project** opens in Brooklyn, New York.

1877-1878

1877
Henry Ossian Flipper becomes the first black person to graduate from **West Point** Military Academy.
[1]

1877
The first **Wimbledon tennis championship** is held on one of the croquet lawns of the All England Croquet and Lawn Tennis Club. The competition is still played on natural grass.
[2]

1877
The **Japanese Red Cross Society** is founded, with its headquarters located in Tokyo.

1877
The last federal troops leave the South, thus ending **Reconstruction** and undermining protections for former slaves. African Americans will not achieve true equality under the law until the 1960s.

1877
The **Quaker Oats** trademark is registered by Henry Parsons Crowell (1855–1944), an Ohio milling company owner.
 [3]

1877
The U.S. Entomological Commission, created to control **grasshoppers**, is established by Congress.

CLEOPATRA'S NEEDLE

Ancient stone monoliths transported from Egypt to Britain and the United States to cement relations between the countries

In the 19th century the government of Egypt divided a pair of obelisks, giving one to Great Britain and the other, later, to the United States. One now stands on the Thames embankment in London (the photograph shows it being erected in its new home), and the other stands in Central Park, New York City. Although known as Cleopatra's Needles, they were dedicated at Heliopolis by Thutmose III about 1500 BC and bear inscriptions to him and to Ramses II (c. 1304–c. 1237 BC). Carved from the typical red granite of the region, they stand 69 feet 6 inches (21.2 m) high, have a rectangular base that is 7 feet 9 inches by 7 feet 8 inches (2.36 by 2.33 m), and weigh 180 tons. The quarrying and erection of these pillars is a measure of the mechanical genius and the almost unlimited manpower available to the ancient Egyptians.

The British were given their obelisk in 1819 to commemorate Nelson's victory at the 1798 Battle of the Nile. It was not until 1877 that it was transported from Alexandria to London by sea. On the voyage the cigar-shaped vessel carrying it almost capsized in a storm in the Bay of Biscay. The vessel was saved and repaired and then completed its journey.

The American needle was offered to the United States in 1869 by Isma'il Pasha, the Ottoman viceroy of Egypt, who was keen to cultivate U.S. trade through the Suez Canal. It arrived in New York in 1880. The British needle reached London thanks to the philanthropist Sir Erasmus Wilson, while the American obelisk reached Central Park thanks to financial support from tycoon William Henry Vanderbilt.

[7] *Osman Pasha, commander of the Ottoman army, defends the Bulgarian town of Plevna from the Russians.*

[2] *An early game of tennis at Wimbledon.*

[3] *In this early Quaker Oats advertisement, the Quaker grasps a box of oats and a certificate of purity.*

 [7]
April 24, 1877
War breaks out between **Russia and the Ottoman Empire** at the conclusion of the Serbo-Turkish War, resulting in independence for Serbia and Montenegro.

September 5, 1877
The Sioux Indian chief **Crazy Horse**, a leader of the Sioux resistance to the invasion of America's northern Great Plains by whites, dies during a scuffle with soldiers trying to imprison him.

September 24, 1877
Saigo Takamori, a hero of the Meiji Restoration, is killed after reluctantly leading a rebellion against the Meiji government.

December 6, 1877
The Washington Post, a morning daily newspaper published in Washington, D.C., begins publication.

1878
Cleopatra's Needle (ancient Egyptian obelisk) is erected on Thames embankment.

 [8]
1878
HMS Pinafore by W. S. Gilbert and Arthur Sullivan premieres.

1877
The **University of Tokyo** is founded as the first Japanese institution of higher learning based on a Western model.

1877
Thomas Edison patents the **phonograph**. By making it possible to record musical performances, it transforms the music industry.

1877
Wisconsin cheese maker John Jossi invents **brick cheese**.

January 4, 1877
American shipping and railroad magnate **Cornelius Vanderbilt** dies, leaving a personal fortune of more than $100,000,000.

March 2, 1877
The **Electoral Commission**, established to resolve the disputed election of 1876, decides in favor of Republican Rutherford B. Hayes, who is duly inaugurated president despite losing the popular vote to Democrat Samuel Tilden.

April 12, 1877
The **South African Republic** surrenders its independence to Britain in return for protection from the Zulus.

[1] *Henry Ossian Flipper.*

[5] *Cornelius Vanderbilt, said to be "ruthless, gruff, uneducated, and uncultured."*

[6] *Men accused of voter fraud in the Hayes-Tilden presidential election of 1876 are taken into custody.*

[4] *Thomas Edison with his phonograph.*

[8] *The famous comic songwriter and actor George Grossmith in the role of Sir Joseph Porter, the over-promoted civil servant who ends up as "the ruler of the Queen's navee" in* HMS Pinafore.

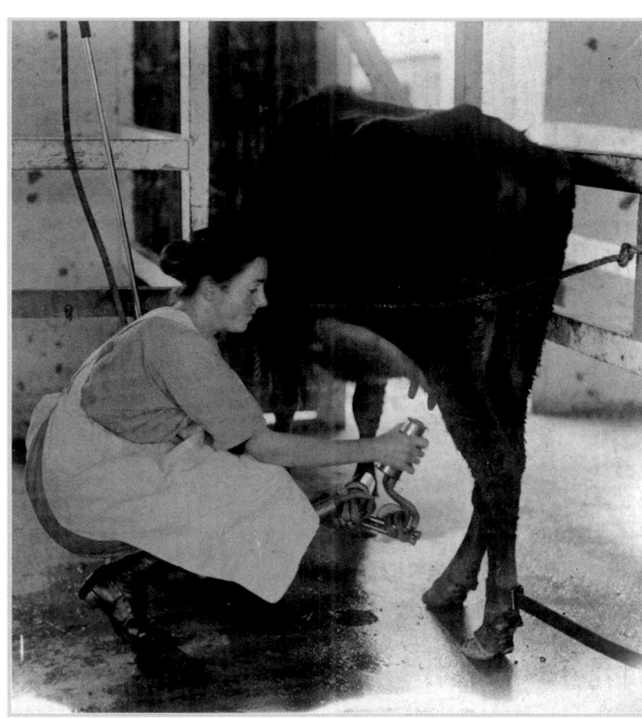

[9] *A dairy maid, in an inappropriate pair of boots, attaches a milking machine to a cow's udder.*

1878
A **shift key** system, allowing for upper- and lowercase letters, is added to the Remington typewriter, improving on the 1876 model.

1878
A **yellow fever** outbreak along the U.S. Gulf Coast results in the loss of approximately 14,000 lives.

1878
Albert Durant introduces a machine invented by L. O. Colvin, and the first commercial **milking machines** are produced in New York.

1878
Aletta Jacobs opens the world's first **birth-control clinic** at Amsterdam.

1878
American inventor **Thomas Alva Edison** founds the Edison Electric Light Company.

1878
American newspaper publisher **Adolph Simon Ochs** buys a controlling interest in the *Chattanooga Times,* which he will develop into one of the leading newspapers in the South.

1878

1878
American painter and craftsman **Louis Comfort Tiffany** establishes a factory that will produce his famous Favrile glass.

 [1]

1878
For the first time since 1858, the **Democrats** gain control of both houses of Congress in the congressional elections.

1878
Anglo-American inventor David E. Hughes develops the **carbon microphone**, which is important to the development of telephony. Hughes's microphone is the forerunner of the various carbon microphones now in use.

1878
French painter **Pierre-Auguste Renoir** completes his masterpiece *Mme Charpentier and Her Children.*

 [2]

1878
Henry Tate, London's sugar magnate, introduces the first sugar cubes created at the Silvertown Refinery. He will endow the **Tate Gallery** in London.

1878
Martha Jane Canary, better known as **Calamity Jane**, nurses the ill as a smallpox epidemic hits Deadwood, South Dakota.

 [3]

1870-1879

[1] Louis Comfort Tiffany, c. 1910, 30 or more years after he began manufacturing his opalescent glass.

[2] Renoir in the 1880s.

[3] Calamity Jane in fringed buckskin frontiersman's dress, armed with revolver and rifle, and looking fully up to her jobs as scout, Pony Express rider, gold prospector and drover. She will be buried in Deadwood in 1903.

[7] The Congress of Berlin, which manages to stem the tide of Russian advance in the Balkans. Disraeli stands, with the help of a stick, on the left. Bismarck shakes hands in the middle.

1878
The first **Easter egg roll** is held on the White House lawn, hosted by President Rutherford B. Hayes and his wife, Lucy.

1878
The first U.S. **pathology laboratory** is opened at Bellevue Hospital by New York physician William Henry Welch.

1878
In the name of conservation, the **Indian Forest Act** appropriates 100,000 square miles of forest to the state in the British colony of India.

1878
The **Musée de l'Homme**, a museum and library of ethnography and anthropology, is founded in Paris.

1878
The New Haven Telephone Company issues the first **telephone directory**; it contains 50 subscribers.

1878
The **Pulkovo Observatory**, an astronomical observatory founded in 1839 near St. Petersburg, Russia, builds what will be, for the next 10 years, the world's largest refractor, measuring 30 inches.

1878
Paul Cézanne withdraws from the Impressionists, marking the beginnings of Postimpressionism. The movement will flourish in the 1880s.

 [4]

1878
Sir Henry Irving, one of the most famous of English actors, becomes the manager of the Lyceum Theatre in London and will continue in this position for the next 21 years.

 [5]

1878
The American **Evangelical Lutheran Church** is formally organized as a synod in Neenah, Wisconsin, under the name Danish Evangelical Lutheran Church in America.

1878
The **cream separator**, used in dairy processing, is invented by Swedish engineer Carl Gustaf Patrik de Laval.

1878
The first **Berlitz school of languages** is established at Providence, Rhode Island, by German-born teacher Maximilian Berlitz. He discovers that students learn most in a setting of "total immersion" in another language.

 [6]

1878
Treaty of San Stefano, a peace settlement imposed on the Ottoman government by Russia at the conclusion of the Russo-Turkish War of 1877–78, is signed.

[4] A self-portrait by Paul Cezanne, painted in 1885-86. His search is for the structure within nature, beyond the fleeting impression implanted on its surface by light.

[10] Sam Bass, Wild West outlaw

[5] Henry Irving as Mathias in the great Victorian melodrama The Bells, *the role by which he established his reputation in the 1870s.*

[8] William Booth, c. 1900. The Salvation Army is a name much better suited to the worldwide spread of his organization.

[6] The Berlitz language school on Madison Square in New York.

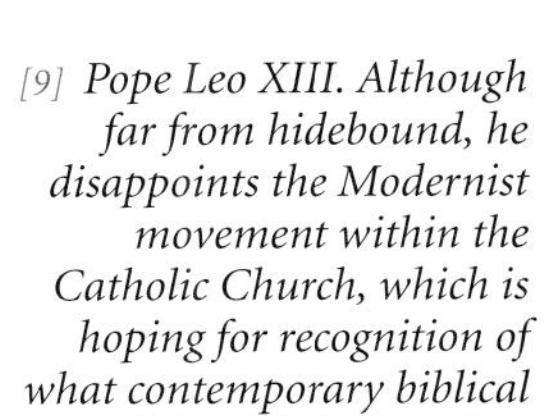

[9] Pope Leo XIII. Although far from hidebound, he disappoints the Modernist movement within the Catholic Church, which is hoping for recognition of what contemporary biblical scholarship has to offer.

 [7]

1878
The **Treaty of Berlin** is signed, revising the earlier Treaty of San Stefano that set the terms that ended the Russo-Turkish War.

 [8]

1878
William Booth changes the name of his evangelical ministry in the East End of London, founded in 1865, to the **Salvation Army**. His mission is to feed and house the poor.

January 11, 1878
Milk is delivered for the first time in **glass bottles** in New York City.

February 7, 1878
Pope Pius IX dies. His pontificate (1846–78) was the longest in history and was marked by a transition from moderate political liberalism to conservatism.

 [9]

February 20, 1878
Pope Leo XIII takes office. He will assume more conciliatory positions toward civil governments, take care that the church not oppose scientific progress, and stay aware of the pastoral and social needs of the times.

 [10]

July 21, 1878
American Western outlaw **Sam Bass**, who led a career robbing trains and stagecoaches, is gunned down by Texas rangers.

1878-1879

November 21, 1878
Lord Lytton, the viceroy of India, launches the **second Afghan War**.

1879
Siemens tries out the first **electric train** in Germany. [1]

1879
Thomas Edison produces lamps with carbon filaments in evacuated glass bulbs. Although Sir Joseph Swan invented a similar **bulb** in 1878, Edison receives the major credit because of his development of the power lines and other equipment.

1879
Armour & Company introduces canning in its meatpacking practices. This technique, along with refrigeration, will make Chicago the meatpacking capital of the world.

1879
Frank Woolworth founds his first five-cent stores in Utica, New York, and Lancaster, Pennsylvania; he soon raises the ceiling price to 10 cents.

1879
Racehorse **Kincsem**, a filly bred in Hungary of English stock, is retired with a record of 54 victories in 54 races. It still stands as the best unbeaten record in Thoroughbred racing history.

[3] Sir Louis Cavagnari, the British envoy en route to Kabul in Afghanistan, sits cross-legged and surrounded by Afghans forming his escort.

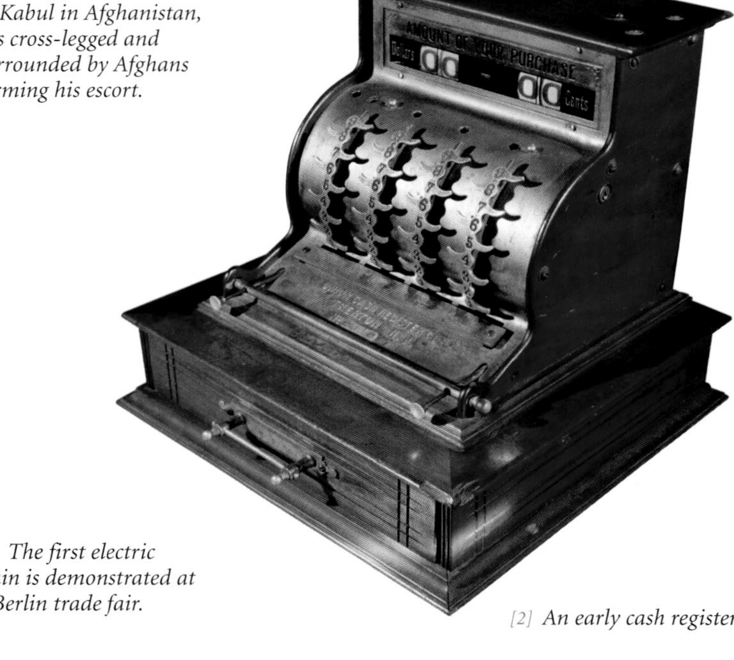

[2] An early cash register

[1] The first electric train is demonstrated at a Berlin trade fair.

[4] An Irish landlord's wife practices with a revolver in case she has to defend herself from any violence stirred up by Land League activity.

[5] Henrik Ibsen, Norwegian champion of the new realist drama.

[6] Searching for bodies after the collapse of the railway bridge across the Tay in Scotland.

February 14, 1879
The **War of the Pacific** begins when Chilean forces occupy the Bolivian city of Antofagasta. After four years of fighting, Chile will defeat Bolivia and its ally, Peru, and claim the nitrate-rich Atacama Desert.

February 15, 1879
U.S. president Rutherford B. Hayes signs into law a bill that allows **women attorneys** to argue cases before the Supreme Court.

March 1879
The **Ryukyu Islands** are formally annexed by Japan, creating the Okinawa prefecture.

April 3, 1879
Sofia, liberated from the Ottoman Empire by Russian troops, is named the capital of Bulgaria.

May 1879
The International Congress of Geographical Sciences meets in Paris and assigns to Suez Canal architect **Ferdinand de Lesseps** the design and construction of a canal across the Isthmus of Panama.

May 26, 1879 [3]
The Treaty of Gandamak is signed, establishing a British diplomatic presence in the Afghan capital of **Kabul**. Less than four months later, the British envoy and his escort will be killed, and, in response, the British will garrison the city.

1879
Saccharin is discovered at Johns Hopkins University by chemist Ira Remsen and visiting student Constantin Fahlberg. Their investigation of the oxidation of o-toluenesulfonamide yields a sweet-tasting compound that becomes the first artificial sweetener.

1879
The **cash register** is invented by saloonkeeper James Ritty; it is nicknamed the "Incorruptible Cashier."

 [2]

1879
The first **artificially frozen ice skating rink** in the United States is opened at New York's Madison Square Garden.

January 1, 1879
The United States resumes specie payment—the exchange of paper money or bank notes for **gold**—for the first time since the Civil War.

January 12, 1879
The Zulu War begins this week in 1879, as the British seek control over Zululand in eastern South Africa. Despite initial setbacks, British forces are victorious over the Zulu army after six months of fighting.

January 30, 1879
Jules Grévy is elected president of France.

THE ZULU WAR

Decisive six-month war in eastern South Africa, resulting in a British victory over the Zulu

In 1877, the British annexed the Boer republic of Transvaal, an event that fostered a drive to federate the southern African white colonies and to destroy the autonomy of the independent southern African kingdoms. The British took over preexisting Boer claims to parts of western Zululand, and in early 1878, Sir Theophilus Shepstone, the Transvaal administrator, and Sir Bartle Frere, the high commissioner of the Cape, accused the Zulu and their king, Cetshwayo (left below), of unwillingness to work in the British colonies near Zululand. They also alleged that the Zulu posed a military threat to the colony of Natal. Cetshwayo was depicted as a despot barely able to hold back his warriors. As British intentions became clear, Cetshwayo, eager to avoid any hint of provocation, withdrew his army behind the border.

In December 1878, Frere issued an ultimatum that was designed to be impossible for Cetshwayo to satisfy: the Zulu were, among other things, to dismantle their "military system" within 30 days. As expected, the ultimatum was not met, and in January 1879 the British attacked Zululand with support from Africans from Natal (left above). Although seasonal rains impeded travel and the tall grasses of Zululand blocked their view, the invaders advanced without taking normal precautions (such as scouts and sentries).

Sensing an opportunity, the Zulu army attacked on January 22 and 23, 1879. At Isandhlwana, the British failed to defend their encampment, leading to the obliteration of an imperial force of about 1,700 men by more than 20,000 Zulu, who advanced unnoticed. Though the Zulu lost 3,000 to 4,000 men, their unscathed rear guard advanced on the British base at nearby Rorke's Drift, which was, however, forewarned by the few survivors of Isandhlwana and was well fortified. Just over 120 men fended off the Zulu attack with minimal losses. The subsequent Battle of Kambula (March 28 and 29, 1879), in which the Zulu lost more than 2,000 men, was a decisive British victory.

Later, British reinforcements arrived, and Cetshwayo fled. The British met a setback in April with the unsolicited arrival of a French prince, Napoleon III's son, in search of adventure. He joined a British expedition, underestimated the enemy, and was killed in a surprise attack in May. His death was an embarrassment for the British. Their victories continued nevertheless.

The British later reached Ulundi (the capital of Zululand), seizing and burning it in July; this was followed by Cetshwayo's capture in August and his subsequent exile to Cape Town. Zululand was annexed to Natal in 1887.

July 8, 1879
The ill-fated U.S. Navy **Arctic expedition** under George Washington De Long sets sail. The party will spend more than two years stuck in the polar ice pack before most succumb to starvation or the elements.

August 4, 1879
Pope Leo XIII issues the encyclical *Aeterni Patris*, making Thomism the dominant philosophical viewpoint in Roman Catholicism.

 [4]

October 1879
Michael Davitt forms the **Irish Land League** to work for reform of Ireland's landlord system under British rule.

October 7, 1879
Germany and Austria-Hungary conclude the **Dual Alliance**, a defensive treaty that will remain in effect through World War I.

 [5]

December 21, 1879
Henrik Ibsen's masterpiece, *A Doll's House*, premieres at the Royal Theatre in Copenhagen, Denmark.

 [6]

December 28, 1879
The **Tay Bridge**, which spans an inlet of the North Sea near Dundee, Scotland, collapses in a storm, killing 75.

1880-1889

Fishing boats setting sail from Whitby in Yorkshire, England, 1880.

1880-1881

1880
British occupy **Kabul** in the second Afghan War

1880
American James A. Bonsack receives the first patent for a **cigarette-making machine**, paving the way for the mass production of cigarettes and the growth of the industry.

1880
American mining magnate **George Hearst** acquires the struggling *San Francisco Examiner* for political purposes. His son, William Randolph, will take control of the paper in 1887 and eventually establish a media empire.

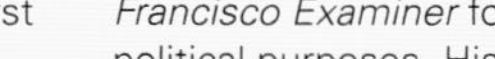

1880
French sculptor **Auguste Rodin** completes his most famous piece—*Le Penseur* (*The Thinker*).

 [1]

1880
German research chemist **Adolph von Baeyer** synthesizes the blue dye indigo and will formulate its structure in 1883. He will be awarded the Nobel Prize for Chemistry in 1905.

1880
New York's theater district along **Broadway** is illuminated with electric lights, an improvement that will lead to the street being dubbed "the Great White Way."

SECOND AFGHAN WAR

Dangerous meddling by the British in Afghanistan to counter the Russians

British Prime Minister Benjamin Disraeli and his secretary of state for India, Robert Salisbury, pressed the government of India to pursue an interventionist line with the Afghan government to counter a feared Russian encroachment. Lord Lytton, the viceroy, was more than eager to act as his prime minister desired, and, soon after he reached Calcutta, he notified Afghanistan's emir, Shir'Ali, that he was sending a "mission" to Kabul. When the emir refused to grant Lytton permission to enter Afghanistan, the viceroy declaimed that Afghanistan was but "an earthen pipkin between two metal pots." He did not, however, take action against the kingdom until 1878, when Russia's General Stolyetov was admitted to Kabul and Lytton's envoy, Sir Neville Chamberlain, was turned back at the border by Afghan troops.

The viceroy decided to crush his neighboring "pipkin" and launched the second Afghan War on November 21, 1878, with a British invasion. Shir'Ali fled the country, dying in exile early in 1879. The British army occupied Kabul (above), and a treaty was signed at Gandamak on May 26, 1879, with the former emir's son, Ya'qub Khan. Ya'qub Khan promised, in exchange for British protection, to admit to his court a British resident who would direct Afghan foreign relations, but the resident, Sir Louis Cavagnari, was assassinated on September 3, 1879, two months after he arrived. This led to further fighting. British troops trudged back over the passes to Kabul, under the command of General Sir Frederick Roberts. After much fighting, including the defeat of a British detachment at Maiwand in July 1880, Roberts fought a decisive action at Kandahar in September. British control of Afghan foreign relations was re-established, but the idea of a British resident was abandoned.

[1] *Rodin's* Le Penseur, *conceived originally as part of his giant commission, "The Gates of Hell", still unfinished in 1900.*

[2] *Cologne Cathedral. Its most famous relics are the remains of the three kings, or magi, who visited the infant Christ: Caspar, Melchior, and Balthazar.*

[3] *Captain Boycott adopts a comically melodramatic pose in the studio, some years before he is to meet real opposition from Irish tenants.*

April 19, 1880
At the Battle of Ahmed Khel during the second Afghan War, a reporter for *The Times* of London **telephones his report** into his paper's office, the first time a war correspondent has filed a story in this way.

 [2]

August 14, 1880
Originally started in 1248, construction of the cathedral (Kölner Dom) in **Cologne**, Germany—the largest Gothic church in northern Europe and the city's major landmark—is finally completed.

 [3]

September 1880
Irish tenant farmers demand lower rents in the wake of reduced harvests and refuse to deal with agents of British estate manager **Charles Boycott**. His name becomes synonymous with collective ostracism.

[4]

October 1880
Joe Juneau and Richard Harris discover gold on the shores of the Gastineau Channel in Alaska. The campsite they establish will become the city of **Juneau**.

 [5]

October 1, 1880
John Philip Sousa becomes leader of the U.S. Marine Corps band. The Marine band will be raised to the highest standard of performance, and Sousa will earn the nickname "the March King" for his compositions.

October 5, 1880
American inventor Alonzo Cross receives a patent for the **ballpoint pen**, but a practical commercial model will not appear for another half-century.

1880
Railcar baron **George Pullman** purchases 4,000 acres of land just south of Chicago and establishes an experimental, company-owned town that bears his name.

1880
Swiss author Johanna Spyri publishes **Heidi**, the story of an orphan girl whose pluck is admired by all; the book will become a children's classic.

1880
The **Chicago School of Architecture** emerges. The members of this influential group develop the modern skyscraper and contribute to the development of modernism.

1880
The first shipment of **frozen meat** from Australia arrives in Britain on the ship *Strathleven*.

c. 1880
Cities in North and South America and Europe begin to establish **electric railways** and subways.

c. 1880
The Greek board game of Halma is invented. In a slightly altered form, it is marketed in the United States as **Chinese checkers** in the 1930s.

[4] *Panning for gold in Alaska.*

[5] *Sousa with the Marine Corps band.*

[6] *Sarah Bernhardt in one of the publicity photographs taken for her American tour.*

[7] *Ned Kelly wearing his famous bullet-proof helmet.*

November 6, 1880
French physician **Alphonse Laveran** discovers the parasite that causes malaria in humans. He will receive the Nobel Prize for Physiology or Medicine for his work in 1907.

[6]
November 8, 1880
French stage actress **Sarah Bernhardt** makes her New York City debut at the head of her first international tour.

[7]
November 11, 1880
Australian outlaw **Ned Kelly** is hanged in a Melbourne jail after being convicted of a series of robberies and murders.

1881
American novelist **Henry James** completes the first of his three writing periods with the distinctively international novel *The Portrait of a Lady*.

1881
James A. Garfield of the Republican Party serves as the 20th president of the United States from March 4 to his death on September 19, 1881. His vice president is Chester A. Arthur.

1881
Chicago architects Dankmar Adler and Louis Sullivan form the partnership of **Adler and Sullivan**. The firm will produce some of the most important buildings of the century and will train Frank Lloyd Wright.

1881-1882

1881
Clara Barton establishes the American branch of the **Red Cross** and becomes its first president.

 [1]

1881
Coney Island amusement park, with its 3.5-mile boardwalk, becomes a popular New York City tourist attraction. The area also includes sideshows, museums, and orchestra halls.

 [2]

1881
Helen Hunt Jackson publishes *A Century of Dishonor*, a profound condemnation of the treatment of **Native Americans** by the United States.

 [3]

1881
Impresario Tony Pastor opens his Fourteenth Street Theatre in New York City, advertised as "the first specialty and **vaudeville theatre** of America, catering to polite tastes, aiming to amuse, and fully up to current times and topics."

July 2, 1881
U.S. President **James Garfield** is shot, after only four months in office, by Charles J. Guiteau, a disappointed office seeker with messianic visions. Garfield will eventually die of blood poisoning on September 19.

 [4]

1881
Marshall Field introduces into his Chicago department store many revolutionary merchandising concepts. Placing strong emphasis on total customer service, his store is a complete shopping world.

[1] Clara Barton. Active during the Civil War, distributing medical supplies and visiting some of the worst battlefields, she was asked by Lincoln to head the search for missing Union soldiers.

[3] Helen Hunt Jackson: poet, novelist, champion of the Native American. She is particularly associated with the "Mission Indians" of southern California.

[2] Early days at Coney Island: camel rides and a Ferris wheel.

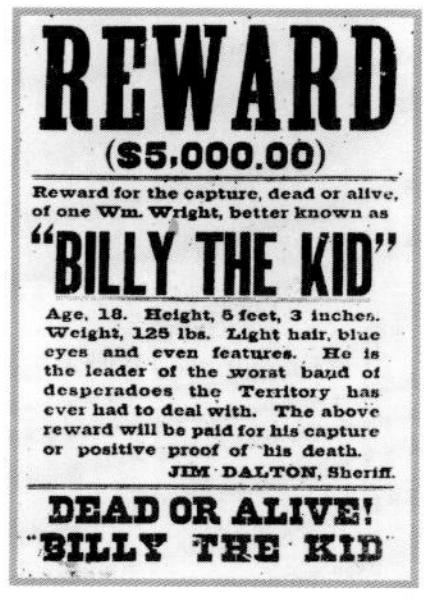

[9] A poster advertising a $5,000 reward for Billy the Kid, dead or alive, issued some time before his death.

[8] Booker T. Washington, who rises from slavery to start the first college for black teachers and then becomes a spokesman for all black Americans.

[11] The small urn containing the ashes of cricket stumps and bails presented by some Melbourne ladies to the captain of the English cricket team. It will become the trophy played for in the test matches between Australia and England.

[4] The madman Charles Guiteau, President Garfield's assassin.

 [8]

July 4, 1881
Tuskegee Institute is founded in Alabama, with Booker T. Washington as the school's first president.

 [9]

July 14, 1881
Billy the Kid, one of the most notorious gunfighters of the American West, who is reputed to have killed at least 27 men, is shot and killed at about age 21 by Sheriff Pat Garrett.

 [10]

October 26, 1881
In Tombstone, Arizona, a gang led by Ike Clanton engages the Earp brothers (Virgil, Wyatt, and Morgan) and Doc Holliday in a gunfight at the **O.K. Corral**. Three of the Clanton gang are killed. Ike and another escape.

 [11]

1882
England plays Australia for **the Ashes** cricket trophy for the first time.

1882
Irish secretary Lord Frederick Cavendish and his assistant are murdered in **Phoenix Park** in Dublin.

1882
American educator **F. J. Child** publishes *The English and Scottish Popular Ballads*, the greatest collection of early ballads (anonymous narrative songs) ever compiled.

1881
Robert Louis Stevenson writes *Treasure Island*, a fast-paced adventure tale. His later works include *A Child's Garden of Verses*, *Kidnapped*, and the horror classic *The Strange Case of Dr. Jekyll and Mr. Hyde*.

 [5]

1881
The Academic Festival Overture of **Johannes Brahms** is first performed at the University of Breslau, Germany.

1881
Theodor Billroth, head of a surgical clinic in Vienna and the founder of modern abdominal surgery, performs the first successful operation to remove part of the stomach to treat cancer.

 [6]

February 19, 1881
Kansas becomes the first U.S. state to include the **prohibition** of alcoholic beverages in its state constitution.

March 13, 1881
Russian Emperor **Alexander III**, a strong supporter of Russian nationalism, ascends to the throne after the assassination of his father, Alexander II.

 [7]

1881
Chester A. Arthur of the Republican Party takes office as the 21st president of the United States. He will serve until 1885. He has no vice president.

[5] *Robert Louis Stevenson, one of Scotland's greatest literary figures.*

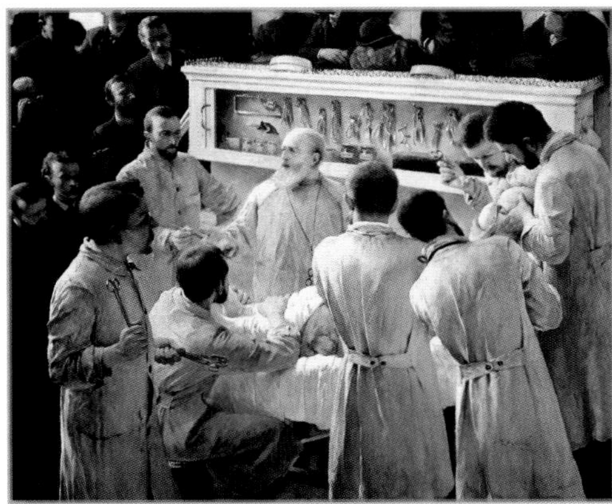

[6] *Theodor Billroth lectures as he operates at the General Hospital in Vienna, a painting by A. F. Seligmann.*

[10] *The bodies of the three members of the Clanton gang shot at the O.K. Corral.*

[7] *The bearded Tsar Alexander III and his family. At the outset of his reign, he makes clear that he has no intention of weakening his autocratic powers or bringing in liberal measures.*

[12] *The Masonic Temple in Chicago. Its first nine floors contain shops, with offices above. It will remain the city's highest building until the 1920s.*

[13] *Manet's slightly melancholy barmaid, with a bowl of tangerines and bottles of beer, rosé, champagne, and crème de menthe in front of her.*

 [12]

1882
Chicago's new 10- and 12-story buildings attract the term **skyscraper**, formerly used for large horses, tall hats, and fly balls in baseball.

 [13]

1882
Édouard Manet paints *A Bar at the Folies-Bergère*, his final masterpiece before his death in 1883.

1882
Geophysicist Karl Weyprecht instigates the first **International Polar Year**, which rejects nationalistic geographic exploration in favor of systematic coordinated observations from stations set up by 10 countries.

1882
German composer **Richard Wagner**, one of the most influential and controversial figures in 19th-century music, completes his last work, *Parsifal*.

1882
German musicologist **Hugo Riemann** publishes his classic *Musiklexikon*. Riemann's work on musical harmony will lay the foundations for modern music theory.

1882
German physician Robert Koch, known for advancing the germ theory of disease, isolates the tubercle bacillus, the cause of **tuberculosis**. He isolates the cholera bacillus the following year.

1882

1882
German psychophysiologist William T. Preyer publishes *Die seele des kindes* (*The Mind of the Child*), a milestone in the early history of **child psychology**.

1882
In Tokyo, Kano Jigoro establishes the first school of **judo**, which comes to be known as the Kodokan School.

1882
Manganese steel is invented by English metallurgist Sir Robert Abbott Hadfield. It is prized for its toughness.

1882
The **electric iron** is patented by Henry W. Seely of New York, New York.

1882
The use of **refrigerated ships** encourages ranching in regions remote from big markets, such as New Zealand, Australia, and Argentina.

1882
The **Western Electric Company** is granted the contract to supply telephone equipment to the American Bell Telephone Company, which will procure a majority interest in Western Electric.

[1] Longfellow: his verses, such as "Paul Revere's Ride" and "Hiawatha," go some way to establishing an American mythology.

[2] Jumbo is transported along Broadway, with horses pulling and another elephant pushing.

[3] Italian and Swiss workmen meet as the last rock is broken through in the St. Gotthard tunnel.

[4] British soldiers pose by the Sphinx at the time of the Battle of Tall al-Kabir.

 [2]
April 10, 1882
Jumbo the elephant makes his North American debut at Madison Square Garden in New York as part of Barnum & Bailey's circus.

May 6, 1882
The **Chinese Exclusion Act**, a result of rising racial tension in the American West, is enacted. It bars all Chinese immigration to the United States for 10-year period; it will not be repealed until 1943.

May 20, 1882
Germany, Austria-Hungary, and Italy secretly form the **Triple Alliance**, a treaty organization that provides for mutual protection against attacks by other European powers. The alliance lasts until Italy enters World War I.

 [3]
May 20, 1882
The **St. Gotthard tunnel** railway opens. Connecting Luzern, Switzerland, with Milan, Italy, it is the first high-capacity railway tunnel through the Alps.

June 6, 1882
A cyclone in the Arabian Sea makes landfall near **Bombay**, India. An estimated 100,000 people are killed.

July 5, 1882
The **Eritrean port of Assab** is taken over by Italy. Assab will become the seat of Italy's Eritrean colony in 1890.

January 2, 1882
The Standard Oil Company and affiliated companies that are engaged in producing, refining, and marketing oil are combined in the **Standard Oil Trust** to circumvent existing antimonopoly laws.

February 16, 1882
An explosion at the **Trimdon Grange Colliery** near Durham, England, kills 74 coal miners.

March 6, 1882
Milan IV of the Obrenovic dynasty in Serbia proclaims himself king and declares the principality of **Serbia** a kingdom.

March 14, 1882
U.S. president Chester A. Arthur signs the Edmunds Act into law, making **polygamy** punishable by five years imprisonment and a $500 fine.

March 24, 1882
American poet **Henry Wadsworth Longfellow** dies in Cambridge, Massachusetts. One of the favorite poets of the 19th century, his notable works include *The Song of Hiawatha* (1855) and *The Courtship of Miles Standish* (1858).

 *[1]*

April 3, 1882
American outlaw and bank robber **Jesse James** is killed in St. Joseph, Missouri, with a gunshot to the back of the head, by fellow gang member Robert Ford. He shoots James to claim the $10,000 reward.

THE ASSASSINATION OF JESSE JAMES

The most notorious outlaw of the age is shot dead in cold blood by a bounty-hunting member of his own gang.

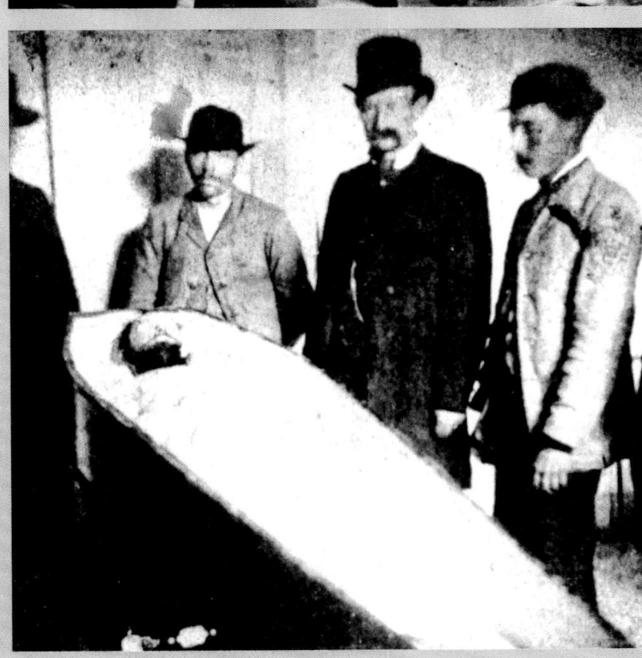

Jesse James and his older brother, Frank, became famous for a series of robberies that came to typify the hazards of the 19th-century frontier.

Reared on a Missouri farm, Jesse and Frank shared their family's sympathy with the Southern cause when the American Civil War broke out (1861). Frank joined William C. Quantrill's Confederate guerrillas, becoming friends with Cole Younger, a fellow member. Jesse followed suit by joining "Bloody" Bill Anderson's guerrilla band. At the end of the war, the bands surrendered, but Jesse was reportedly shot and severely wounded by Union soldiers while under a flag of truce. He and Frank, joined by eight other men, then began their outlaw career by robbing a bank in Liberty, Missouri, on February 13, 1866. During the same year, Cole Younger joined the gang, with the other Younger brothers following his lead one by one during the next few years. The James gang robbed banks from Iowa to Alabama and Texas and began holding up trains in 1873. The bandits also preyed upon stagecoaches, stores, and individuals. Throughout their long career and afterward, their exploits were seized upon by writers who exaggerated and romanticized their deeds to meet Eastern readers' demands for bloody Western tales of derring-do. To the Missouri Ozark people, Jesse James emerged as a romantic figure, hounded into a life of crime by authorities who never forgave his allegiance to the South. Jesse and Frank did, in fact, always seek to justify their banditry on grounds of persecution.

On September 7, 1876, the James gang was nearly destroyed while trying to rob the First National Bank at Northfield, Minnesota. Of the eight bandits only the James brothers escaped death or capture. After gathering a new gang in 1879, the James brothers resumed robbing, and in 1881 Missouri governor Thomas T. Crittenden offered a $10,000 reward for their capture, dead or alive. While living at St. Joseph under the pseudonym of Thomas Howard, the unarmed Jesse was adjusting a picture on the wall in his home when he was shot in the back of the head and instantly killed by Robert Ford (left above), a gang member, who claimed the reward. A group of people later posed for a photograph beside the gangster's coffin (left below); one of them is his brother (second left).

A few months later, Frank James gave himself up. He was tried for murder in Missouri and found not guilty, tried for robbery in Alabama and found not guilty, and finally tried for armed robbery in Missouri and again released. A free man, he retired to a quiet life on his family's farm, dying in 1915 in the room in which he was born.

Robert Ford received part of the reward money (the rest was given to various law-enforcement officers). He then moved to Colorado, where he was shot dead on June 8, 1892. His killer, Edward Capehart O'Kelley, was sentenced to life in prison, but he was released in 1902 because of a medical condition.

August 1882
Ellison Hatfield is killed by three sons of Randall McCoy, sparking the deadliest phase of the **Hatfield-McCoy feud** and making their names notorious in the United States in the 1880s and '90s.

August 20, 1882
Pyotr Tchaikovsky's **1812 Overture**, commemorating Russia's victory over Napoleon, has its first performance in Moscow.

September 4, 1882
Thomas **Edison's Electric Illuminating Company** provides electric power and light to a one-square-mile area in lower Manhattan.

September 5, 1882
The first **Labor Day parade** is held in New York City in honor of the American worker.

 *[4]*

September 13, 1882
British forces under Sir Garnet Wolseley defeat the Egyptians at the **Battle of Tall al-Kabir**.

September 25, 1882
The first **baseball double-header**, which gives fans the chance to see two games for the price of one admission, is played between the Worcester Brown Stockings and the Providence Grays.

1882-1884

December 6, 1882
Venus transits across the face of the sun. This allows the calculation of the astronomical unit (AU), which is the distance between the earth and sun.

1883
Sir Evelyn Baring begins his rule in Egypt, although his title is merely that of consul general. He will stand down in 1907. [1]

1883
Al-Mahdi begins to threaten Khartoum, capital of the Sudan, which will be defended by an Egyptian garrison under the British General Charles George ("Chinese") Gordon. [2]

1883
The first fully automatic **machine gun** is developed by American engineer and inventor Hiram Maxim while he is residing in England. The Maxim will be in large part responsible for the epithet "the machine-gun war" for World War I. [3]

1883
French explorer and colonial administrator **Pierre Savorgnan de Brazza** founds the city of Brazzaville on the north bank of the Congo River. Brazzaville will become the capital of French Equatorial Africa and later of the Republic of Congo. [4]

1883
Germany introduces the first general **social insurance** program. Austria (1888), Italy (1893), and Sweden and the Netherlands (1901) soon adopt their own social security programs.

[1] Baring, later Lord Cromer, rules in the interests of Britain, the many other countries to which Egypt is indebted, and the Egyptian peasants whose standard of living is considerably raised.

[2] Al-Mahdi, regarded as a messiah by his Muslim followers, seeks to end the rule of Egypt over the Sudan.

[3] In the Maxim gun the recoil energy from the firing of one round is used to load and fire the next round in the belt of ammunition.

[7] In his earlier career Cody was a scout and a Pony Express rider.

[4] De Brazza, who benefits from an attractive character and physique, is, in fact, Italian by birth, though in the employ of the French.

[8] Paul Kruger's Afrikaners, or Boers, have regained their independence by defeating Britain in the first Boer War in 1881.

[7]
1883
Buffalo Bill Cody's Wild West show opens. It will become a very successful spectacle of sharpshooting, trick horsemanship, and historical reenactments. In 1887, Queen Victoria will see the show three times.

January 16, 1883
The Pendleton Civil Service Act establishes the **Civil Service Commission** in the United States.

January 19, 1883
In the North Sea the German steamer **Cimbria** collides with the British steamer **Sultan** and sinks, killing 340.

February 16, 1883
The Ladies Home Journal, a U.S. monthly magazine and trendsetter among women's periodicals, is founded as a supplement to the *Tribune and Farmer*. *The Ladies Home Journal* will begin independent publication in 1884.

March 3, 1883
The Navy Act authorizes the commissioning of the first **steel vessels** for the U.S. Navy.

[8]
April 16, 1883
Paul Kruger is elected president of the Transvaal. He is credited as the builder of the Afrikaner nation. He will remain in office until his flight to Europe in 1900 after the outbreak of the second South African (Boer) War.

1883
Indonesian volcano **Krakatoa** erupts catastrophically. Explosions are heard 2,200 miles away. Krakatoa throws into the air nearly 5 cubic miles of rock fragments, and ash falls over an area of 300,000 square miles.

 [5]

1883
The Brooklyn Bridge, designed by John and Washington Roebling, opens after 14 years of construction. The bridge is hailed as one of the masterworks of 19th-century engineering; its beauty inspires poets and artists.

1883
The **Fabian Society**, one of the earliest socialist organizations, is founded in London. Fabians believe in evolutionary socialism rather than revolution and use public meetings and lectures, research, and publishing to educate the public.

1883
The **Metropolitan Opera** Association opens in New York City with a performance of Charles Gounod's *Faust*.

1883
The **Orient Express**, a luxury passenger train, makes its inaugural run from Paris to Constantinople. It boasts Oriental rugs, velvet draperies, mahogany paneling, deep armchairs covered in soft Spanish leather, and fine cuisine.

 [6]

1883
The United States **National Horse Show** is held for the first time, at the original Madison Square Garden in New York City.

THE BROOKLYN BRIDGE OPENS

The suspension bridge spans New York's East River.

The bridge linking Brooklyn to Manhattan Island was the first to use steel for cable wire, and during its construction explosives were used inside a pneumatic caisson for the first time.

The masterwork of John Augustus Roebling, the Brooklyn Bridge (left) was built (1869–83) in the face of immense difficulties. Roebling died as a result of an accident at the outset, and his son, Washington Roebling, taking over as chief engineer, suffered a crippling attack of decompression sickness during the founding of the New York pier (1872). Confined to his apartment in Columbia Heights, he continued to direct operations, observing with field glasses and sending messages to the site by his wife. At least 20 workers were killed during construction, and many more suffered decompression sickness.

The Brooklyn Bridge's 1,595-foot (486-m) main span was the longest in the world until the completion of the Firth of Forth cantilever bridge in Scotland in 1890. Its deck, supported by four cables, carries both automobile and pedestrian traffic. A distinctive feature is the broad promenade above the roadway.

The bridge's opening day (May 24, 1883) was marked by much celebration, and the building of it came to represent a landmark in technological achievement for a generation. It inspired poets, notably Walt Whitman, Hart Crane, and Marianne Moore, and photographers and painters, including Joseph Stella, John Marin, and Berenice Abbott.

[5] Krakatoa, located in the Sunda Strait between Java and Sumatra, where some 36,000 perish from the tsunami the volcano's eruption causes.

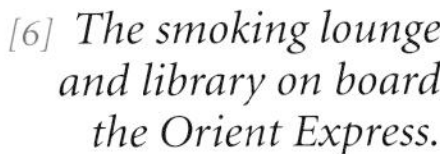

[6] The smoking lounge and library on board the Orient Express.

May 26, 1883
Abdelkader, amir of Mascara (from 1832), dies in Damascus, Syria. A military and religious leader, he founded the Algerian state and led the Algerians in their struggle against French domination between 1840 and 1846.

May 31, 1883
French forces bombard the port of Tamatave, Madagascar, to begin the first **Franco-Merina War**. French marines land to assert control over the northern part of Madagascar.

October 15, 1883
The U.S. Supreme Court proclaims the Civil Rights Act of 1875 unconstitutional. This ruling creates the conditions for **racial segregation** in private-sector enterprises, which will continue until the mid-20th century.

October 20, 1883
The Treaty of Ancon is signed by Chile, Peru, and Bolivia to end the **War of the Pacific**. Peru turns over to Chile full possession of the province of Tarapacá.

November 26, 1883
African American evangelist and reformer **Sojourner Truth** (Isabella Van Wagener) dies. She applied her religious fervor to the abolitionist and women's rights movements.

1884
A plan formulated by Canadian Sandford Fleming for defining **24 time zones** is adopted. It creates a standard framework for worldwide timekeeping.

1884

1884
American physician and health-food pioneer **John Harvey Kellogg** applies for a patent for flaked cereal. The production of cornflakes will occur under the direction of his brother, William.

1884
Chrome tanning, a process designed to create leather from animal hides using chromium, is first patented in the United States by Augustus Schultz.

1884
British photographer **Eadweard Muybridge** photographs sequences of human and animal movement in *Figure Hopping* and other photo series. The photographs form a visual compendium for the use of artists and scientists.

 [1]

1884
English engineer Charles Algernon Parsons invents the **steam turbine** engine, passing steam through rotors to achieve high-speed rotary motion.

1884
German bacteriologist Friedrich Loeffler codiscovers the **diphtheria bacillus**. Building on this work, he articulates the principles of disease causation later known as "Koch's postulates."

1884
Lewis E. Waterman receives a patent for his **fountain pen**. The modern fountain pen takes its shape in the late 1800s, as various inventors work to improve it.

 [2]

[2] *An advertisement for Waterman's fountain pens.*

[1] *Until such sequences as these, artists have painted horses at full gallop with hind legs both stretched out to the rear and forelegs both out in front. The sequence also proves that at one point, all four legs are off the ground.*

[5] Bathers at Asnières *by Georges Seurat, the first important Neo-Impressionist work. It begins to demonstrate his strict ideas about composition and his technique of divisionism (or pointillism)—applying paint in dots and commas so as to achieve bright secondary colors and more accurate shadowed areas.*

[6] *Maud Watson: a long way from Martina Navratilova and the Williams sisters.*

[5]
1884
The **Neo-Impressionists** are formed, a group devoted to precise and scientific methods of painting, in contrast to the apparently spontaneous style of the Impressionists.

1884
The southeastern quadrant of New Guinea is established as a British protectorate, which it will remain until 1906. Thereafter, Australia will govern the area until **Papua New Guinea** becomes independent in 1973.

 [6]
1884
Wimbledon holds its first women's singles tennis championship; Maud Watson is the first winner.

February 1, 1884
The first of 10 volumes of the **Oxford English Dictionary** are published in London. The final volume will not be published until April 19, 1928.

February 8, 1884
Geologist, geographer, and educator **Arnold Henry Guyot** dies. His meteorological observations led to the founding of the U.S. Weather Bureau. The guyot, a flat-topped volcanic peak rising from the ocean floor, is named after him.

February 19, 1884
An outbreak of **tornadoes** striking the southeastern United States kills an estimated 800 people from Mississippi through North Carolina.

1884
Manon, an opera by **Jules Massenet** and widely considered to be his masterpiece, premieres in Paris. Marked by sensuous melody and skilled personification, it uses leading themes and motifs to identify and characterize protagonists and emotions.

 [3]

1884
The artificial fiber **rayon** is patented by French chemist Hilaire Bernigaud, count of Chardonnet. He will introduce products made of rayon during the Paris Exposition of 1889.

1884
The **Dow Jones Averages**, which will become one of the most commonly used indicators of general trends in the prices of stocks and bonds in the United States, publishes its first report in the *Customers Afternoon Letter*.

1884
The English engineer **Frederick Henry Royce** establishes F. H. Royce and Company to manufacture dynamos, electric motors, and electric cranes. He will join with Charles Stewart Rolls to form Rolls-Royce Ltd. in 1906.

 [4]

1884
The era of the modern **roller coaster** begins when La Marcus Thompson, the "Father of the Gravity Ride," opens a 600-foot switchback railway at Coney Island.

1884
The **National Society for the Prevention of Cruelty to Children** is incorporated in Great Britain and helps to promote children's rights.

[3] *Marie Roze as Manon Lescaut, the ill-fated heroine of Massenet's opera. Puccini also composes a notable opera based on the story in 1893.*

[9] *A McCormick reaper in the midwestern U.S. This model will be superseded by one that binds the cut wheat into sheaves automatically. There will then be no need for someone to stand at the back of the machine to rake off the cut wheat and for others to then tie the sheaves.*

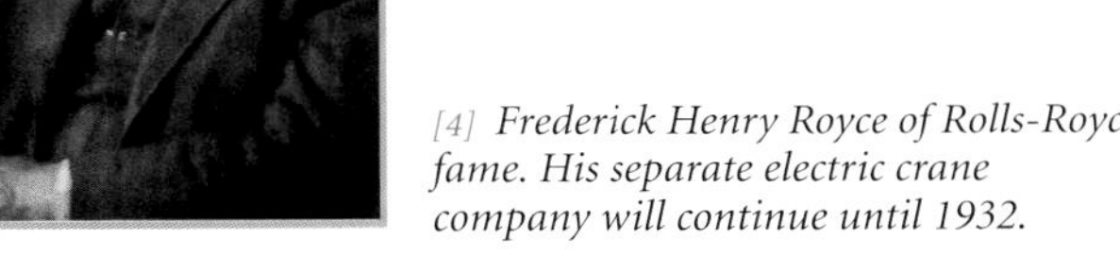

[4] *Frederick Henry Royce of Rolls-Royce fame. His separate electric crane company will continue until 1932.*

[7] *Making a call in the early days.*

[8] *Judah P. Benjamin, one of the most prominent Jewish figures in 19th-century America.*

[10] *A poster for Ringling brothers' circus menagerie includes an inset, top left, of the five brothers.*

February 27, 1884
Paul Kruger, president of the **Transvaal**, the South African Republic, signs a treaty in London that disavows British authority over the Transvaal.

March 12, 1884
The first state college for women in the United States, the **Mississippi University for Women**, is founded in Columbus by the Mississippi state legislature.

 [7]

March 27, 1884
The first **long-distance telephone call** using copper wire in transmission connects Boston and New York. Limited commercial service between the cities will begin later in the year.

 [8]

May 6, 1884
Prominent American lawyer **Judah P. Benjamin** dies in Paris. He became the first professing Jew elected to the U.S. Senate (1852; reelected 1858) and held high offices in the Confederate government, including minister of war.

 [9]

May 13, 1884
American industrialist and inventor **Cyrus Hall McCormick** dies in Chicago. McCormick is generally credited with the development (from 1831) of the mechanical reaper.

 [10]

May 19, 1884
The **Ringling brothers** open a small circus in Baraboo, Wisconsin. By the early 20th century, they will have transformed it into the Ringling Bros. and Barnum & Bailey Circus, the leading American circus.

1884-1885

August 9, 1884
La France, the world's **first true dirigible**, makes its maiden voyage. French army captains Charles Renard and Arthur Krebs produce an airship that can be steered in any direction irrespective of wind.

 [1]

November 15, 1884
The **Berlin West Africa Conference** opens, in which the major European nations meet to decide all questions of colonial expansion in the Congo River basin of Central Africa.

December 1884
Conservative Mexican statesman José de la Cruz **Porfirio Díaz** becomes president of Mexico for the second time.

1885
American architect William Le Baron Jenney's 10-story Home Insurance Company Building in Chicago is the first skyscraper to use **steel-girder construction**, the secret behind construction of truly tall buildings.

1885
Anti-immigration sentiments explode during riots in Tacoma, Washington, and Rock Springs, Wyoming. Dozens of Chinese laborers are killed during the riots, and hundreds are driven from their homes.

1885
Austrian chemist and engineer Carl Auer von Welsbach invents the **gas mantle**, which is still widely used in kerosene and other lanterns.

[1] A postcard advertises Liebig's meat extract with the help of the new wonder—steerable airships.

[9] The Marshall Field Warehouse Store in Chicago.

[8] Cleveland will be re-elected in 1893 as 24th president.

[5] Carl Benz founded his firm in 1883 to build stationary engines, two years before he drives his three-wheeler through the streets of Munich.

[6] Daimler's prototype motorcycle.

[7] Hertz shows that electromagnetic waves can be reflected, refracted, and polarized, and he measures their length and velocity.

1885
German cytologist and physician Theodor Heinrich Boveri begins to study **chromosomes**. His work will eventually prove that chromosomes are separate, continuous entities within the nucleus of a cell.

[5]
1885
German designer Karl Benz builds the first practical **automobile powered by an internal-combustion engine**. Inventors around the world are experimenting with various aspects of automotive design.

[6]
1885
German mechanical engineers Gottlieb Daimler and Wilhelm Maybach install gasoline engines on a bicycle, creating what is considered the world's first **motorcycle**.

[7]
1885
German physicist Heinrich Rudolph Hertz begins generating and propagating **artificial electromagnetic waves**. This work is the start of research on radio broadcasting.

1885
Adolf Neuendorff directs musicians of the Boston Symphony Orchestra in their first "Promenade" concert. Soon to be known as the **Boston Pops**, these concerts feature lighter classical music in café settings.

 [8]
1885
Grover Cleveland of the Democratic Party takes office as the 22nd president of the United States. He will serve until 1889. His vice president is Thomas A. Hendricks.

1885
Austrian firearms designer Ferdinand von Mannlicher develops the **cartridge clip**, a device that loads a rifle's box magazine in one motion. The clip will be almost universally adopted for automatic-feeding pistols and rifles.

1885
Canada creates its first **national park at Banff**, Alberta, in the spectacularly scenic Front Ranges of the Rocky Mountains.

 [2]

1885
Conservative politician Robert Cecil, 3rd marquess of **Salisbury**, begins the first of his three terms (1885–86, 1886–92, 1895–1902) as the British prime minister, presiding over a wide expansion of Great Britain's colonial empire.

 [3]

1885
Consumer magazine **Good Housekeeping** is founded. Its investigations expose contamination in America's food supplies and help to spur the creation of the Pure Food and Drug Act.

1885
English scientist Francis Galton establishes that human **fingerprints** are unique and proposes the first system for classifying fingerprints.

 [4]

1885
For the first time in a century, the U.S. Post Office doubles the rate for **first-class mail**. Postage for each letter now costs two cents.

[2] *Moraine Lake, in the Rockies of Banff National Park, Canada.*

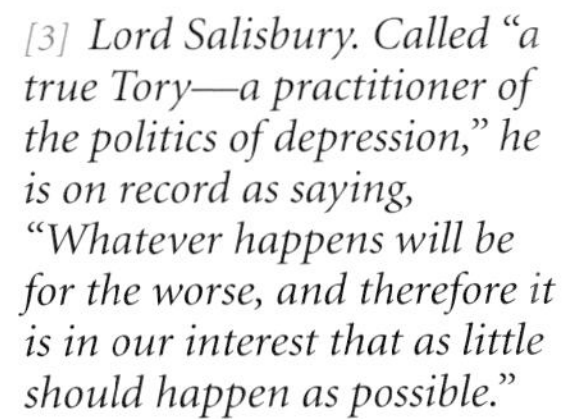

[3] *Lord Salisbury. Called "a true Tory—a practitioner of the politics of depression," he is on record as saying, "Whatever happens will be for the worse, and therefore it is in our interest that as little should happen as possible."*

[4] *Francis Galton, influenced by his cousin Charles Darwin, is interested in heredity, which leads him to pioneer the study of eugenics, soon to be used by racists for their own ends.*

[11] *A later German caricature of Leopold II, surrounded by the severed heads of Congolese, victims of the forced labor policy in the rubber plantations there.*

[10] *Students and faculty members at Bryn Mawr College in 1886. The figure standing on the right in the doorway is the young Woodrow Wilson.*

1885
Gungunhana is crowned king of the **last great independent Bantu kingdom**, Gaza, in what is now Mozambique. He plays the European powers against one another, but is conquered by the Portuguese in 1895.

[9]

1885
H. H. Richardson designs the **Marshall Field Warehouse Store**, Chicago. Richardson, a master of the Romanesque, fills an entire Chicago block with powerful but subtly articulated masonry.

1885
Hamburg, Germany, hosts the first international **speed skating competition**.

[10]

1885
Joseph Taylor, a member of the Society of Friends (Quakers), founds **Bryn Mawr College**, the first institution of higher learning in the United States to offer graduate instruction to women.

 [11]

1885
King **Leopold II** of Belgium becomes sovereign of the Congo Free State. By the end of his brutal rule (1908), the population of the country will have declined from some 20 million to 8 million.

1885
Leland and Jane Stanford found **Stanford University** in Palo Alto, California, in memory of their son, Leland Stanford, Jr.

1885-1886

1885
Leo Daft, an English-born American engineer, establishes the first **electric trolleybus** line in Baltimore, Maryland.

1885
Mark Twain publishes *The Adventures of Huckleberry Finn*, a novel in the voice of the title character, a youth who wrestles with moral and personal implications of life in a society built upon slavery.

 [1]

1885
Samuel David Ferguson becomes the first African American member of the Episcopal Church's House of Bishops.

1885
Serbian-American engineer **Nikola Tesla** sells the patent rights to his alternating-current technology to George Westinghouse.

 [2]

1885
The Criminal Law Amendment Act of Great Britain is passed; its vague wording, making **gross indecencies** punishable as a misdemeanor, is later interpreted to apply to consensual same-sex acts between male adults.

1885
Lever Brothers of Great Britain begins selling wrapped **bars of soap** made from animal and vegetable fats; it also pioneers aggressive marketing.

 [3]

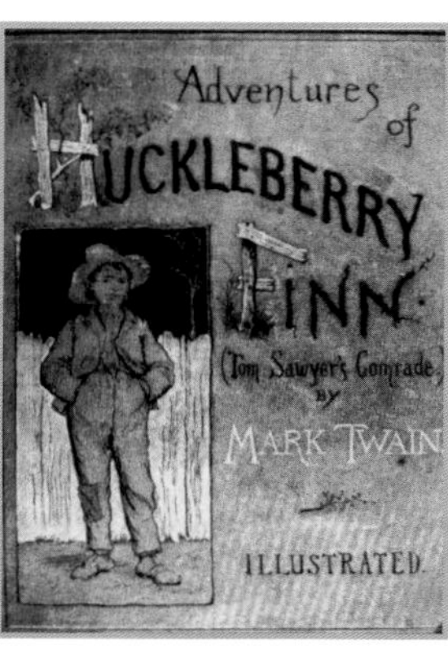

[1] The cover of the first edition of The Adventures of Huckleberry Finn, *one of the greatest American novels.*

[2] Nikola Tesla lecturing in France.

[3] An example of Lever Brothers' forceful pictorial advertising for one of its soaps.

[4] Gordon, as messianic as his opponent the Mahdi, is in large part responsible for his own death because he has ignored specific instructions to evacuate the Sudan. Known as Chinese Gordon, he earned the nickname putting down the Taiping rebels for the Qing Dynasty in the 1860s.

[5] The state funeral afforded to Victor Hugo, a hugely important figure for French republicans.

March 26, 1885
The second clash of the **Riel Rebellion** takes place in Duck Lake, Saskatchewan. Louis Riel is a leader of the Metis (persons of both European and Indian descent).

May 15, 1885
Louis Riel surrenders after leading two rebellions against the Canadian government in response to its efforts to assume the territorial rights of the Hudson's Bay Company in northwestern Canada. He is later hanged for treason.

 [5]

May 22, 1885
French poet, novelist, and dramatist **Victor Hugo** dies in Paris.

September 18, 1885
Bulgarian nationalists in **Eastern Rumelia** mount a coup and declare the province's unification with Bulgaria, leading to the Serbo-Bulgarian War.

 [6]

November 14, 1885
The **Serbo-Bulgarian War** begins when Serbian king Milan Obrenovic IV declares war on Bulgaria.

November 15, 1885
St. Joseph Mukasa, one of the **martyrs of Uganda**, is beheaded by order of Mwanga, kabaka (ruler) of Buganda.

1885
The psychologically intense paintings of Edvard Munch, Vincent van Gogh, and James Ensor signal the beginnings of **Expressionism**.

1885
The **safety bicycle** is popularized by the Rover Safety model, manufactured by British designer John K. Starley. It is a significant advance over earlier, more dangerous models and the prototype of all modern bicycles.

1885
The **Santa Fe Railway** Company reaches the Los Angeles basin, and the **Northern Pacific Railway** Company reaches Puget Sound, forever changing the American West by opening southern California and the Pacific Northwest.

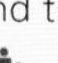

1885
Using newly developed vaccination procedures, French scientist Louis Pasteur saves the life of a boy stricken with **rabies**. Serum treatment of rabies will be introduced in 1899.

c. 1885
Tin Pan Alley—28th Street between Fifth Avenue and Broadway in New York City—becomes the center of popular music publishing.

January 26, 1885
British general **Charles Gordon** and other defenders of Khartoum are killed by Sudanese rebels.

 [4]

THE IRON HORSE

Railway lines spread out rapidly across all parts of North America.

The completion in 1869 of the first line between the Atlantic and Pacific coasts was a historic event that overshadowed the frenzy of railway construction occurring elsewhere the continent.

One of the fastest growing systems was the Santa Fe Railway, one of whose trains is shown crossing the Canyon Diablo viaduct (left above). Chartered in Kansas as the Atchison and Topeka Railroad Company in 1859, it later exercised great influence on the settlement of the southwestern United States. It was renamed the Atchison, Topeka and Santa Fe Railroad in 1863. Its founder was Cyrus K. Holliday, a Topeka lawyer and business promoter, who sought to build a railroad along the Santa Fe Trail, a 19th-century trading route that ran from Independence, Missouri, to Santa Fe, New Mexico. The railroad's main line to the Colorado state line was completed in 1872, and the network was further expanded in the 1880s and early 1890s to reach about 9,000 miles (14,480 km).

In Canada, a second transcontinental main line—the Canadian Pacific from Montreal to Port Moody, British Columbia (a Vancouver suburb)—was completed in 1885. The photograph (left below) shows the final spike being driven in at Craigellachie, British Columbia. The company later absorbed other railroads, including several in the United States, and also operated paddle wheelers and steamships on interior waterways and an ocean shipping fleet.

THE GRAPHIC
AN ILLUSTRATED WEEKLY NEWSPAPER
SATURDAY, DECEMBER 26, 1885

[6] Serbians read a list of war casualties posted in Belgrade.

[7] The sort of scene that Gladstone's Irish Home Rule bill seeks to banish: a battering ram employed in County Clare to break into a house so its tenants can be evicted for non-payment of rent. A squad of police is in attendance.

December 1885
The first **Indian National Congress** convenes. From the 1920s, it will be led by Mohandas Gandhi, whose nonviolent civil-disobedience strategy will lead to India's independence from Great Britain in 1947.

 [7]

1886
British prime minister William E. Gladstone's bill for **Irish Home Rule** is passed.

1886
A **decade-long drought begins in the American West**, causing humans and livestock to starve. Blizzards will finish off many of the surviving cattle, and the losses will effectively end America's cowboy era.

1886
Acetanilide, a synthetic-organic compound that is a precursor to acetaminophen, is introduced as an **alternative to aspirin**.

1886
Dankmar Adler and Louis Sullivan win the commission to design the **Auditorium Building, Chicago**. The building presages modern multiuse structures and signals Sullivan's professional maturity.

1886
Dutch physician Christiaan Eijkman travels to Java to investigate **beriberi**, a tropical disease that he discovers is caused by poor diet. This leads to the **discovery of vitamins**, for which he will win a Nobel Prize.

1886

1886
England and the United States play the **first international polo match**.

1886
French painter **Georges Seurat** completes *Sunday Afternoon on the Island of La Grande Jatte*. In this and other works he develops his pointillist technique, based on study of color, light, and vision.

1886
German chemist Clemens Winkler discovers **germanium** (Ge), an element that will become crucial in the manufacture of semiconductors, transistors, rectifiers, and photocells.

1886
German chemist Viktor Meyer creates a process for the reliable synthesis of **mustard gas**, one of the first weapons of mass destruction. It will be used to terrible effect on the battlefields of World War I.

1886
Great Bend, Kansas, hosts the first major **greyhound races** in the United States.

1886
The U.S. Supreme Court establishes that **corporations are "persons"** within the meaning of the Fourteenth Amendment, extending to them the rights of due process and equal protection.

[1] The British-born Samuel Gompers, no friend of socialism.

[2] The Linotype machine, which will end the laborious, letter-by-letter setting of type by hand. Its large keyboard is clearly visible.

[3] San Francisco cable streetcars, with a peak-capped driver and conductor.

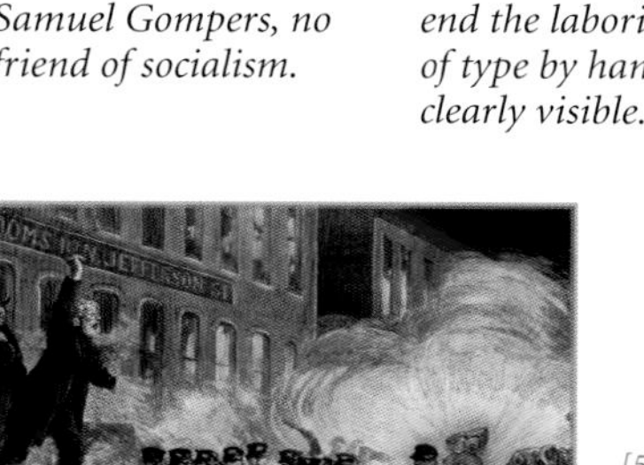

[5] The moment when a protestor's bomb explodes during the Chicago riot. The police respond with indiscriminate gunfire.

[4] Geronimo, on the right, with some of his tribe.

1886
The **dishwasher** is designed by Josephine Cochrane, a Chicago socialite. It is initially used by restaurants and hotels. The first home dishwasher will be introduced in 1949.

1886
The **Berne Convention** is signed, to protect copyright. Signatories agree to provide automatic protection for works first published in other countries of the Berne union and for unpublished works whose authors are citizens or residents.

1886
Tobacco heir Griswold Lorillard wears a short dinner jacket with satin lapels to a high-society ball at the Tuxedo Park Country Club northwest of New York. The **tuxedo** quickly supplements white tie and tails for evening wear.

1886
British physician David Bruce isolates and identifies the bacteria that causes **brucellosis**, a potentially fatal disease of humans and domestic animals.

 [5]

May 4, 1886
Violence between police and labor protesters erupts in the **Haymarket Riot** in Chicago, dramatizing the labor movement's struggle for recognition in the United States.

May 15, 1886
American poet **Emily Dickinson** dies in Amherst, Massachusetts.

1886
Johannesburg, one of the youngest of the world's major cities, is founded in South Africa following the discovery of gold.

1886
John S. Pemberton of Atlanta, Georgia, concocts the formula for a "tonic," which is named **Coca-Cola**.

1886
Labor leader **Samuel Gompers** becomes the first president of the American Federation of Labor. He will shift the primary goal of American unionism toward the "bread and butter" issues of wages, benefits, hours, and working conditions.

[1]

1886
Ottmar Mergenthaler's first **Linotype machines** are put into work setting the type for the *New York Tribune*; they soon set the standard for mechanical typesetting.

 [2]

1886
Streetcar workers strike in New York and San Francisco. They eventually gain a 12-hour workday (down from 14 hours), a 30-minute lunch break, and a wage of between $2.00 and $2.50 per day.

 [3]

1886
The Apache leader **Geronimo** surrenders to General Nelson A. Miles at a conference in Skeleton Canyon in Arizona.

 [4]

[7] The Hungarian Franz Liszt seated at the piano.

THE STATUE OF LIBERTY

Symbol of republican freedom

The colossal statue (left, under construction) on Liberty Island in the Upper New York Bay, commemorates the friendship of the peoples of the United States and France. Standing 305 feet (93 m) high including its pedestal, it represents a woman holding a torch in her raised right hand and a tablet bearing the adoption date of the Declaration of Independence (July 4, 1776) in her left. The torch, which measures 29 feet (8.8 m) from the flame tip to the bottom of the handle, is accessible via a 42-foot (12.8-m) service ladder inside the arm. An elevator carries visitors to the observation deck in the pedestal, which may also be reached by stairway, and a spiral staircase leads to an observation platform in the figure's crown.

A French historian, Edouard de Laboulaye, made the proposal for the statue. Funds were contributed by the French people, and work began in France in 1875 under sculptor Frédéric-Auguste Bartholdi. The statue was made of copper sheets, hammered into shape by hand and assembled over a framework of four gigantic steel supports, designed by Eugène-Emmanuel Viollet-le-Duc and Alexandre-Gustave Eiffel. In 1885 the completed statue, 151 feet 1 inch (46 m) high and weighing 225 tons, was disassembled and shipped to New York City. The pedestal, designed by American architect Richard Morris Hunt, was completed later. The statue, mounted on its pedestal, was dedicated by President Grover Cleveland on October 28, 1886.

[6] Frances Folsom. Cleveland has been her guardian for ten years.

[8] A locomotive derailed by the South Carolina earthquake.

May 23, 1886
Leopold von Ranke, a leading German historian of the 19th century, dies. His scholarly method and pioneering historical seminars have had a great influence on Western historiography.

[6]

June 2, 1886
Frances Folsom, age 21, marries U.S. president Grover Cleveland in the White House and becomes the youngest first lady in American history.

July 18, 1886
Portuguese poet **Cesário Verde** dies of tuberculosis. Verde had revived Portuguese poetry by introducing colloquial language and by exploring its capacity for expression. He dealt extensively with urban themes.

[7]

July 19, 1886
Franz Liszt, the greatest piano virtuoso of his time and who radically extended composition for the instrument, plays the piano for the last time at a concert in Luxembourg.

[8]

August 31, 1886
An **earthquake in Charleston, South Carolina**, leaves 100 dead and damages hundreds of buildings. At 7.6 on the Richter scale, its shockwaves are felt as far away as Chicago and Cuba.

October 28, 1886
The **Statue of Liberty**, a gift from the people of France to the people of the United States on the occasion of America's 100th anniversary in 1876, is officially dedicated by U.S. president Grover Cleveland.

1887

1887
Bloody Sunday riot by unemployed and Socialists takes place in Trafalgar Square, London.

 [1]

1887
A treaty grants the United States the exclusive use of **Pearl Harbor** in Hawaii.

1887
American newspaper scion James Gordon Bennett, Jr., founds the *Paris Herald, a* daily newspaper published in Paris. It will become the **International Herald Tribune**, the staple source of English-language news for American expatriates.

1887
American physicists Albert Michelson and Edward Morley disprove the existence of a luminiferous ether and establish that the **speed of light** is a constant.

1887
An **earthquake** on the French Riviera kills some 2,000 people.

1887
Charles Follen McKim, of McKim, Mead, and White, designs the **Boston Public Library**. One of the best examples of 19th-century American Neoclassicism, it signals the firm's shift from residential to institutional design.

VICTORIA'S GOLDEN JUBILEE

Marking 50 glorious years on the throne of England

On June 20, 1887, the first of two consecutive days marked out for celebrations, Queen Victoria took breakfast in the grounds of Windsor Castle near the mausoleum she had had built for her beloved husband, Prince Albert, who died in 1861.

She then boarded the specially decorated royal train, which took her up the main line of Brunel's Great Western Railway to London. Onlookers thronged the trackside all along the way. From Paddington Station, she was driven to Buckingham Palace in time to prepare for a sumptuous banquet in the evening. Fifty foreign kings and princes, along with the heads of Britain's overseas colonies and dominions, attended the feast. The widowed queen was escorted for the evening by Christian IX, King of Denmark. On her other side at the table sat King George I of Greece, whom Victoria knew as Willy. After dinner, the guests adjourned to the ballroom, where a band played.

On the second day of festivities, Queen Victoria traveled in an open landau, drawn by six cream-colored horses, to Westminster Abbey (left). Her coach was followed by several Indian princes in ceremonial dress and the Indian cavalry. Vast crowds lined the streets; in the words of Mark Twain, they "stretched to the limit of sight in both directions."

The queen then returned to Buckingham Palace, but she did not disappear for long from public view. She reemerged on the balcony to acknowledge the acclaim of the thousands who lined the mall and Constitution Hill below. Later, she returned to the royal ballroom to distribute special commemorative brooches to her family. In the evening, she changed into a splendid gown, embroidered with silver roses, thistles, and shamrocks, for another banquet. Afterwards she received a long procession of diplomats and Indian princes. She was then wheeled in her chair to sit and watch a fireworks display in the palace gardens.

On a personal level, the Golden Jubilee was an important morale-booster for Victoria, who since being widowed had found state occasions burdensome. She was particularly gratified by the warmth of the reception she received from her subjects.

$

1887
Richard W. Sears' R.W. Sears Watch Company publishes its first mail-order catalog. With Alvah C. Roebuck, he will form **Sears**, **Roebuck** and Company in 1893.

1887
Scottish chemists John S. MacArthur, Robert W. Forrest, and William Forrest invent the **cyanide process**, a method of extracting silver and gold from their ores.

 [3]

1887
Scottish writer Arthur Conan Doyle publishes *A Study in Scarlet*, introducing the immortal detectives **Sherlock Holmes** and Dr. Watson.

 [4]

1887
The **Boone & Crockett Club** is founded by Theodore Roosevelt and others. It will promote conservationist legislation and hunter's ethics, one of the few organizations to do so from a politically conservative position.

1887
The British celebrate **Queen Victoria's Golden Jubilee**, the 50th year of her reign.

 [5]

1887
The **Canadian Pacific Railway** completes its main line, running from Montreal to Port Moody (a Vancouver suburb), British Columbia.

1887
Denver, Colorado, plays host to the first **rodeo** competition. Like many sports, rodeo is a formalized version of practical activities: riding and roping are essential skills for ranchers.

 [2]

1887
Dr. Joseph J. Kinyoun directs the first "laboratory of hygiene" within the U.S. Marine Hospital Service. Devoted to the study of infectious disease, the laboratory will become the **National Institutes of Health**.

1887
German scientist Adolf Fick invents the **contact lens**. Made of glass, it cannot be worn long but does correct irregular astigmatism.

1887
Hungarian explorer Count Sámuel Teleki and Austrian naval officer Ludwig von Höhnel set out from Pangani (now in Tanzania) and traverse Kenya to the southern end of Ethiopia, climbing **Mt. Kilimanjaro and Mt. Kenya** on the way.

1887
Lloyd's of London writes its first non-marine insurance policy. It was established in the 18th century to insure ships' cargoes.

1887
Polish oculist L. L. Zamenhof invents **Esperanto**, which he intends for use as an international second language.

[1] Policemen battle with protestors near Trafalgar Square in November.

[3] The cerebral Sherlock Holmes, in his trademark deerstalker hat, explains a deduction to the stolid Dr. Watson during a train journey. One of Sidney Paget's original illustrations from the Strand *magazine.*

[2] Bonnie McCarroll parts company with her bucking bronco at an Oregon rodeo in the early 1900s.

[4] Theodore Roosevelt shows of his affinity with nature, taking a ride—or a swim—aboard a moose.

[5] A rudimentary third-class sleeping car with drop-down beds, on the Canadian Pacific Railway.

1887
The famous aphorism "Power tends to corrupt, and absolute power corrupts absolutely" is penned by John Emerich Edward Dalberg, **Lord Acton**, in a letter to Bishop Mandell Creighton.

1887
The first **Groundhog Day** celebration takes place, in Punxsutawney, Pennsylvania

1887
The **Pasteur Institute** is founded in France. Its scientists will battle infectious diseases all over the world, saving millions of lives by developing vaccines and other treatments.

1887
The **Tokyo Electric Light Company** builds a generating station with a 25-kilowatt capacity to provide power for the city.

1887
The U.S. Congress passes the **Interstate Commerce Act**, an early attempt to regulate trade monopolies. The law sets rules for the railroads moving cargo and establishes a commission to enforce the law.

1887
The **worst flood in history**, on the Yellow River of China, inundates some 50,000 square miles and kills more than 900,000 people.

1887-1888

1887
William Grant's **Glenfiddich** Distillery produces its first single-malt scotch.

1887
Zululand, in South Africa, is made a British crown colony.

February 8, 1887
The United States passes the **Dawes General Allotment Act**, providing for the distribution of American Indian reservation land among individual tribesmen.

  [1]

June 18, 1887
Russia and Germany sign the **Reinsurance Treaty**. Each party will remain neutral if the other becomes involved in a war with a third great power, except if Germany attacks France or Russia attacks Austria.

December 3, 1887
Sadi Carnot, engineer turned statesman, is elected president of France. He will be assassinated by an Italian anarchist in 1894.

 [2]

1888
Vincent Van Gogh moves from Paris to Arles in the South of France, where he starts painting a stream of electrifying works using color "more arbitrarily so as to express myself more forcibly" and employing brushwork of the utmost vigor.

 [3]

[1] *Members of the Crow tribe under armed guard while their land is being taken over by white settlers in 1887. The Dawes Act does nothing to correct basic injustices such as this.*

[3] Starry Night Over the Rhone, *painted by Van Gogh in Arles after he moves there from Paris in February 1888.*

[2] *President Carnot of France. Perhaps his most valuable contribution is to stand in the way of the right-wing dictatorial ambitions of General Boulanger in the next two years.*

[7] *The Ponce de Leon Hotel in St Augustine, Florida.*

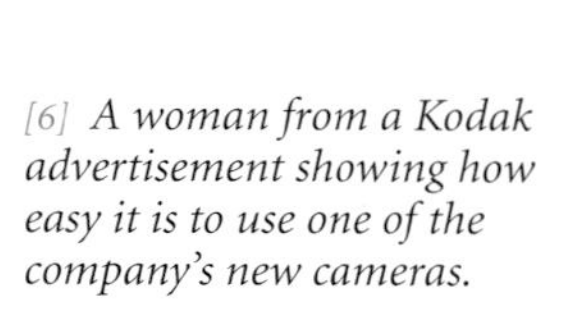

[6] *A woman from a Kodak advertisement showing how easy it is to use one of the company's new cameras.*

1888
French chemist Henry-Louis Le Chatelier develops the Le Chatelier principle, or **Law of Equilibrium**, making it possible to predict the effect a change of conditions will have on a chemical reaction.

 [6]

1888
George Eastman creates the **Kodak**, the first portable camera. Through the Kodak and other film and camera products, Eastman revolutionizes amateur photography.

1888
Golf becomes an organized sport in the United States with the opening of the St. Andrews Golf Club in Yonkers, New York.

 [7]

1888
Henry Flagler opens the **Ponce de Leon Hotel** in St. Augustine, Florida. A Spanish Renaissance building, it is the first to be constructed entirely of poured concrete.

1888
Ernest L. Thayer publishes "**Casey at the Bat**," which closes with the line, "But there is no joy in Mudville—mighty Casey has struck out." De Wolf Hopper immediately popularizes the poem by reading it during his comedy acts.

1888
In Sudbury, Ontario, a **nickel-smelting** complex opens. It is destined to be one of the greatest single sources of air pollution and acid rain in North America.

1888
American chemist Charles Martin Hall, discoverer of the electrolytic method of producing aluminum, founds the Pittsburgh Reduction Company to make and market **commercial aluminum**.

1888
Belgian woodcarver Pierre Degeyter sets the words of Parisian transport worker Eugène Pottier to music, publishing the "**L'Internationale**"—from 1918 to 1944, the national anthem of the Soviet Union.

1888
Belgian-born American inventor Charles Joseph Van Depoele patents the carbon commutator brush, a technology that **stabilizes the voltage of electric current**.

1888
Cecil Rhodes incorporates **De Beers** Consolidated Mining, Ltd. in southern Africa. It will become the world's largest producer and distributor of diamonds.

 [4]

1888
Dissatisfied with commercially available writing instruments, American teacher George Safford Parker founds the **Parker Pen Company**.

1888
Former Thomas Edison employee Frank Sprague installs the first successful **electric trolley system**, in Richmond, Virginia. The new transportation system will soon be adopted by hundreds of other cities.

  [5]

[4] Sorting rough diamonds in Kimberley, South Africa.

[5] An electric trolley (tram) in Richmond, Virginia.

[9] John Boyd Dunlop holds the first bicycle to be fitted with pneumatic tires.

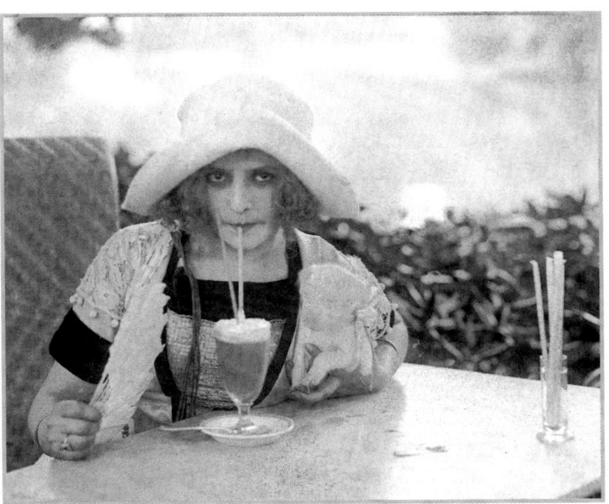

[8] A French woman keeps herself and her puppy cool with a hand fan, while sucking a cold drink through one of the new paper straws.

[10] Richard Burton in the 1880s, his days as an African explorer over.

 [8]

1888
Marvin Stone of Washington, D.C., patents a method for manufacturing the **paper drinking straw**. His spiral-wound process becomes the standard for manufacturing paper-tube products such as bobbins, insulators, and cores.

1888
Melville Weston Fuller is appointed eighth chief justice of the U.S. Supreme Court by President Grover Cleveland. He will serve until 1910.

1888
Rinderpest, a lethal cattle disease, breaks out in Ethiopia and spreads throughout eastern and southern Africa. By 1900 it kills up to 95 percent of cattle and devastates pastoral societies.

 [9]

1888
Scottish veterinarian John Boyd Dunlop creates the **pneumatic tire**.

1888
Sholem Aleichem revitalizes Yiddish writing by editing *Di Yidishe Folksbibliotek* (*The Jewish Popular Library*) in Kiev.

 [10]

1888
Richard Burton publishes the final volume of the **Arabian Nights**. His translations are praised for their robustness and honesty, but also attacked as "an appalling collection of degrading customs and statistics of vice."

1888-1889

1888
Sir Thomas Francis Wade, diplomat and sinologist who developed the famous **Wade-Giles system** of romanizing the Chinese language, is elected Cambridge's first professor of Chinese.

1888
The **Amateur Athletic Union** of the United States is founded for the purpose of preserving "sport for sport's sake."

1888
The factories of W. Duke, Sons & produce 745 million cigarettes. "Cigarette wars" between the top producers will soon follow, and Washington Duke will become president of the conglomerate **American Tobacco Company**.

 [1]

1888
The first **Foster's lager** is brewed in Australia.

1888
The **International Council of Women** is founded by Susan B. Anthony, May Wright Sewell, and Frances Willard, among others. Its goal is to promote health, peace, equality, and education around the world, especially for women.

 [2]

1888
The major maritime powers sign the Convention of Constantinople, agreeing that the **Suez Canal** should be open to ships of all countries in peace and war. It also forbids acts of hostility in the canal and fortifications on its banks. Great Britain signs it only in 1904.

[1] *A saucy cigarette card for the Virginia Brights brand, one card of a set of nine. Enticing smokers to collect these cards is a way of keeping them loyal to a particular brand.*

[5] *The Washington Monument in the process of construction.*

[2] *Women vote in a local municipal election in Boston in December 1888. Their only opportunity to vote at this time is in certain city elections.*

[4] *The year of the three kaisers: William I (top) dies and is succeeded by his sick son Frederick III (left). On Frederick's death his son, William II, (right) comes to the throne. The German Empire will end in 1918 before the fourth generation, Prince Frederick William (bottom), can inherit.*

[9] *Nellie Bly. The year before her world trip, she found fame by pretending to be mad so she could expose the barbaric conditions in a New York women's lunatic asylum.*

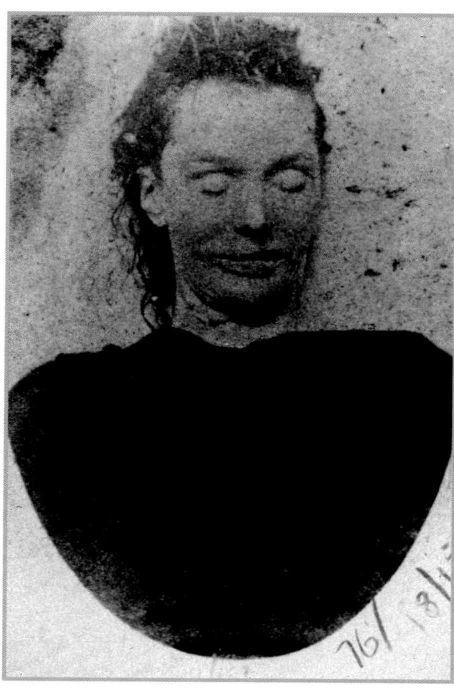

[6] *The corpse of one of the five prostitutes killed by Jack the Ripper.*

 [4]

March 9, 1888
Frederick III, an invalid, becomes emperor of Germany (1888).

May 13, 1888
Brazil frees its last slaves; previous actions in 1871 and 1885 had freed all children of slaves and all slaves older than 60, respectively.

June 15, 1888
William II, who will be known for his frequently militaristic manner as well as for his vacillating policies, becomes emperor of Germany (1888–1918).

 [5]

October 9, 1888
Built between 1848 and 1884 and dedicated in 1885, the **Washington Monument**—a marble-faced granite obelisk that honors the first U.S. president, George Washington—opens to the public in Washington, D.C.

November 6, 1888
Benjamin Harrison is elected U.S. president by an electoral majority despite losing the popular vote by more than 90,000 to his opponent, Grover Cleveland.

 [6]

November 10, 1888
Jack the Ripper's infamous killing spree in the Whitechapel district of London's East End comes to an end.

1888
The **Marine Biological Laboratory at Woods Hole**, Massachusetts, a major center for biological and oceanographic research, is founded.

1888
The **National Geographic Society** begins publication of *National Geographic*, a monthly magazine.

1888
The **revolving door** is invented by Theophilus von Kannel of Philadelphia.

1888
The Sheridan brothers found the ***Financial Times***, a London daily newspaper. Printed as a broadsheet on distinctive pink paper, the *Financial Times* is the only paper in England providing full daily reports on the London Stock Exchange and world markets.

1888
The **world's worst hailstorm** occurs at Moradabad, India, killing nearly 250 people.

March 1888
After a very mild winter, a **three-day blizzard** sweeps the American Northeast, dumping more than 20 inches of snow that accumulates in drifts up to 20 feet high. Some 200 ships are lost or severely damaged, and hundreds of people die from exposure.

 [3]

[7] *General Boulanger. A figurehead for those Frenchman seeking revenge on the Germans, he reveals his feet of clay when confronted with his chance to take power.*

[3] *The aftermath of the great blizzard in New York.*

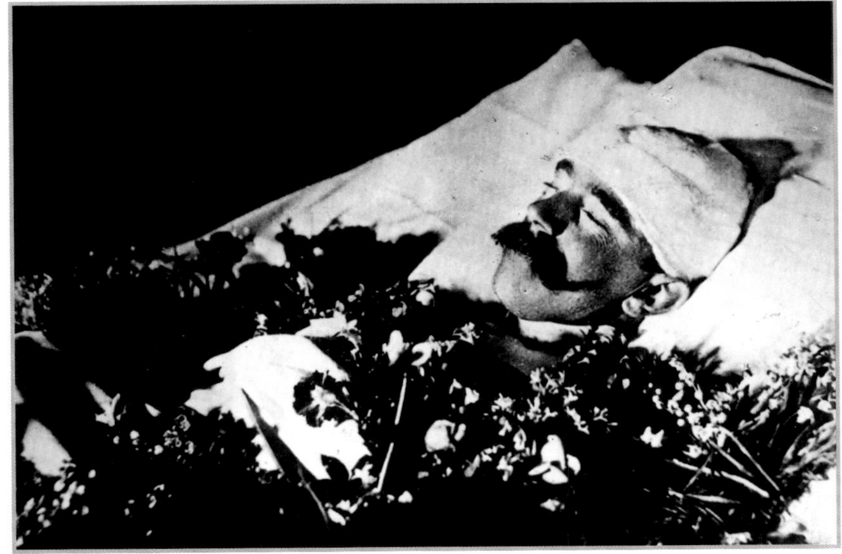

[8] *Crown Prince Rudolf lies in state after committing suicide, together with his lover, Marie von Vetsera (left), at his hunting lodge in Mayerling.*

[10] *Andrew Carnegie, a ruthless employer, a great philanthropist.*

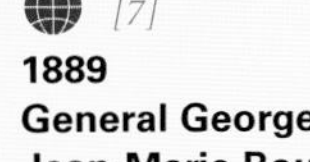

1889
General Georges-Ernest-Jean-Marie Boulanger fails at an attempt to stage a revanchist coup in France.

 [8]

1889
Heir to the Austro-Hungarian throne, **Crown Prince Rudolf**, commits suicide.

 [9]

1889
American journalist **Nellie Bly** sets off around the world to beat the fictional record of Phileas Fogg, hero of Jules Verne's romance *Around the World in Eighty Days*. She completes her journey in 72 days, 6 hours, 11 minutes.

$ [10]

1889
Andrew Carnegie's vast holdings are consolidated into the **Carnegie Steel Company**, a limited partnership that henceforth will dominate the American steel industry.

1889
Barnard College opens as a women's college adjacent to Columbia University, New York.

1889
Benjamin Harrison of the Republican Party takes office as the 23rd president of the United States. He will serve until 1893. His vice president is Levi Parons Morton.

1889
Chemist Herbert Henry Dow finds a new, less expensive process for producing **bromine**, which is used in medicine and photography. He will eventually form the Dow Chemical Company.

1889
Daniel Burnham and John W. Root design the 16-story **Monadnock Building**, Chicago. It is the tallest building supported by its exterior walls rather than an internal iron or steel framework.

[1]

1889
Ebenezer Howard publishes *Tomorrow: A Peaceful Path to Social Reform*, an influential book that lays the intellectual groundwork for the English **Garden City movement**.

1889
Edward W. Bok becomes editor of the *Ladies' Home Journal*.

1889
Fundamentalist evangelist Dwight Lyman Moody founds the **Chicago Bible Institute** (now the Moody Bible Institute).

 [2]

1889
Future president **Theodore Roosevelt** battles corruption as a member of the U.S. Civil Service Commission.

[1] *The Monadnock Building, Chicago, on the left.*

[2] *A bearded and capped Dwight Moody with a group of orphans at one of his Chicago missions, some years before founding the Chicago Bible Institute.*

THE MOULIN ROUGE

The Paris dance hall becomes world famous for its can-can cabaret.

The Moulin Rouge (above) was opened on the Boulevard de Clichy in Pigalle, one of Paris's most notorious red-light districts. Primarily a dance hall, the special attraction was a nightly cabaret interlude in which female dancers performed the can-can on stage. This dance was already well-established among the French working classes, but the girls of the Moulin Rouge transformed it into a titillating and controversial spectacle in which they hoisted their skirts and kicked their legs up so that the audience could see their petticoats.

The Moulin Rouge soon became one of the city's main attractions. Its reputation was based on lasciviousness, and the management was constantly looking for ways to remain in the headlines. That was how the club became one of the first mainstream venues to present striptease, the original conceit of which was that a woman took her clothes off while trying to find a flea on her body.

Naturally, acts of this kind outraged some people, but most were intrigued, and many foreigners came to Paris specifically to spend an evening at the Moulin Rouge. Over the years, the bill began to feature a much wider range of entertainment, and it soon became the venue that all the stars of variety and music halls most wanted to play.

The world of the Moulin Rouge in its heyday was immortalized in the graphic art of Henri de Toulouse-Lautrec (1864–1901, see 1891). The theater has since remained one of the top items on the tourist trail, and even visitors who do not take in a show generally make a point of seeing the exterior of the building, which is one of the most distinctive landmarks of Paris.

1889
The first **Pan-American Conference** is held in Washington, D.C., and all Latin American countries except Santo Domingo are in attendance.

1889
The **Harlem Opera House**, built by Oscar Hammerstein, opens on 125th Street in New York City.

1889
The **jukebox** is invented by Louis Glass of San Francisco.

1889
The **Moulin Rouge**, one of the earliest and most famous cabarets, opens in Paris. The cabaret will later be transplanted to Germany and the U.S., where it becomes a venue for popular music.

 [6]

1889
The Paris Exhibition features two cast iron masterpieces that show the transformation of engineering to art: Gustave Eiffel's 100-meter-tall **Eiffel Tower** and Ferdinand Dutert and Victor Contamin's **Palais des Machines**.

1889
The Pearl Milling Company brings out **Aunt Jemima pancake flour**, the first prepared food mix to be sold commercially in the United States.

1889
Hull House, one of the first social settlements in North America, is founded in Chicago by Jane Addams and Ellen Gates Starr. It offers a wide variety of social and educational services to the city. Addams will win the Nobel Prize for Peace in 1931.
 [3]

1889
Menilek of Shewa becomes emperor of Ethiopia.

1889
Sir John Fowler and Sir Benjamin Baker complete the **Forth Bridge** in Scotland.
 [4]

1889
The Demarest building in midtown Manhattan installs the world's **first electric elevators**.
 [5]

1889
The first **electric trolley (tram) in Europe** begins service at Northfleet, Kent, England.

1889
The first **juvenile court** is established in Chicago. Its originators consider it futile and unjust to punish a child for wrongdoing, preferring rehabilitation instead.

[3] Jane Addams. Hull House offers among its facilities a night school, kindergarten, kitchen, art gallery, coffee house, gymnasium, swimming pool, music school, and library.

[4] The Forth Bridge carries the railway northwards from Edinburgh across a wide arm of the sea, the Firth of Forth. It is given huge strength by its cantilever-steel construction so as to avoid another disaster like the Tay Bridge collapse.

[7] The Renshaw brothers. They win the Wimbledon doubles seven times, while William wins seven singles titles and Ernest one. They roll their sleeves up but still wear ties.

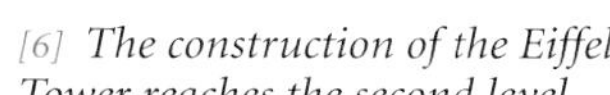

[6] The construction of the Eiffel Tower reaches the second level.

[5] An early Otis electric elevator.

[7]
1889
William Renshaw, who, along with his brother Ernest, is credited with transforming tennis into a spectator sport, wins the men's singles title at Wimbledon for the seventh time.

1889
Yamagata Aritomo, Japanese soldier and statesman, becomes the first prime minister of Japan to serve (1889–91; 1898–1900) under the parliamentary regime. He will exert a strong militaristic influence.

c. 1889
American astronomer George Ellery Hale invents the **spectroheliograph**, a device for photographing the sun at precise wavelengths. He later founds both the Yerkes and Mount Wilson observatories.

c. 1889
The Gilded Age, a period of gross materialism and blatant political corruption in the United States, will begin to weaken by the end of the 19th century.

January 10, 1889
France makes the **Ivory Coast** a protectorate.

February 11, 1889
The first written **Japanese constitution** gives power to the emperor only if the Imperial Diet approves his measures.

1889

March 6, 1889
Serbian king **Milan Obrenovic IV** abdicates after 21 years.

April 22, 1889
At noon, by U.S. federal decree, white settlers are allowed into Indian Territory, sparking a land rush involving tens of thousands in what becomes the **Oklahoma Territory**. Settlers who arrive before the official start are called "sooners."

May 1, 1889
May Day—traditionally a celebration of the return of spring, marked by dancing around a maypole—is first observed as a labor holiday, designated as such by the International Socialist Congress.

May 27, 1889
The American petrochemical corporation South Penn Oil Company, later **Pennzoil Company**, is founded in Pennsylvania.

May 31, 1889
The South Fork Dam on the Conemaugh River in Pennsylvania collapses after heavy rains; a wall of water 30 feet high smashes into **Johnstown**, sweeping away most of the northern half of the city, killing 2,209 people and destroying 1,600 homes.

June 1889
"Wealth," by Andrew Carnegie, appears in the *North American Review*, outlining the **Gospel of Wealth:** a man who accumulates great wealth has a duty to improve of mankind through philanthropy. A "man who dies rich dies disgraced."

[1] Settler wagons stretch as far as the eye can see across the plains.

[3] The aftermath of the Johnstown flood. An uprooted tree impales a house thrown on its side.

[4] The Savoy Hotel's river frontage, looking over the Thames. The Impressionist Claude Monet, intent on capturing the ever-changing mist and light effects on the river, will regularly stay at the hotel so he can paint in one of its rooms.

[2] Dancing round the maypole at Oxford, New York, evidence of the revival of interest in the old traditions associated with May Day in Britain and America.

July 8, 1889
John L. Sullivan beats Jake Kilrain in 75 rounds to defend his title in the last heavyweight championship bout held under **London Prize Ring rules**.

July 8, 1889
Journalist Charles Henry Dow publishes the first issue of **The Wall Street Journal**.

August 6, 1889
The luxurious **Savoy Hotel**, managed by César Ritz, opens in London. Ritz will go on to open the Ritz Hotel in Paris.

August 20, 1889
Labor activists close the entire Port of London in the **London Dock Strike**.

November 1889
Four states are admitted to the United States: **North Dakota** on November 2 (39th), **South Dakota** on November 2 (40th), **Montana** on November 8 (41st), and **Washington** on November 11 (42nd).

November 15, 1889
Emperor Pedro II of Brazil is forced to abdicate by a group of military officers led by Manuel Deodoro da Fonseca.

An Indian prince, the Nawab of Junagad, c.1890.

1890

1890
Britain swaps **Heligoland for Uganda** with Germany.

1890
Baring's Bank crashes in the city of London.

1890
A financial crisis leads to a political one in **Argentina**, when a revolt over the inaction of President Miguel Juárez Celman leads to his resignation. Vice President Carlos Pellegrini then takes office.

1890
Alfred Thayer Mahan's *The Influence of Sea Power Upon History, 1660–1783* is published. The book will provide a strong impetus for increasing the power of the U.S. Navy.

1890
American architect Louis Sullivan completes work on the **Wainwright Building** in St. Louis, Missouri.

1890
American **bison**, some 50 million strong in 1865, are reduced to less than one million by the demand for meat and hides and by the U.S. Army's strategy of destroying the "Indians' commissary."

 [1]

[1] Passengers on the Kansas-Pacific Railroad get some sport shooting bison in the 1870s. The driver has obligingly stopped the train to help them aim better. This is killing for its own sake.

[5] William II with Bismarck outside his home, Friedrichsruhe. Without Bismarck's restraining influence, the kaiser will contribute greatly to German bellicosity.

[4] Elizabeth Robins, the actress who first portrayed the character Hedda Gabler on the London stage.

[7] A formidable group of the Daughters of the American Revolution in New York.

1890
John Nicolay and John M. Hay publish **Abraham Lincoln: A History**, which will become a quintessential biography of the 16th president.

 [4]

1890
Norwegian playwright Henrik Ibsen produces his puzzling, uniquely satirical play **Hedda Gabler**.

 [5]

1890
Otto von **Bismarck** resigns as prime minister of Prussia.

[6]

1890
Poems by **Emily Dickinson**, a posthumous collection edited by Mabel Loomis Todd and T. W. Higginson, is published. The enterprise of publishing Dickinson's 1,775 poems continues until 1955.

 [7]

1890
The **Daughters of the American Revolution** (DAR) is founded. Membership is limited to direct lineal descendants of soldiers or others of the Revolutionary period who aided the cause of independence.

1890
The **Imperial Diet of Japan**, which from 1947 will be called just the Diet, convenes its first session.

1890
Dutch geologist Eugene Dubois discovers bone fragments of a **prehistoric human** ancestor on the island of Java. He calls the remains "upright ape-man," to indicate an intermediate phase in the evolution from simian ancestors.

1890
German bacteriologist Emil von Behring produces the first immunization for **diphtheria**. The following year he will win the Nobel Prize for his work on the use of serum therapy to treat diphtheria.

1890
German medical researcher Emil von Behring and Japanese bacteriologist Kitasato Shibasaburo announce that blood serum from animals exposed to **tetanus** bacillus has antitoxin properties.

1890
Herman Hollerith invents a card tabulation machine for handling the 1890 U.S. census. His Tabulating Machine Company will merge in 1924 with the Computing-Tabulating-Recording Company to form IBM.

 [2]

1890
Illustrator Charles Dana Gibson sees his **Gibson girl** drawings appear for the first time in *Life* magazine. Modeled after his wife, the Gibson girl will begin to delineate the American ideal of femininity at the turn of the century.

 [3]

1890
John J. McLaughlin begins manufacturing **Canada Dry** ginger ale in a Toronto plant and marketing it as a mixer for juice and other flavored drinks.

[8] The arbitration committee trying to find a settlement to end the strike on the New York Central Railroad.

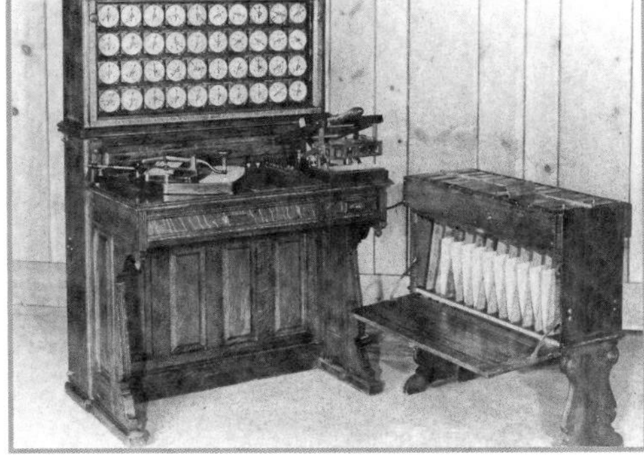

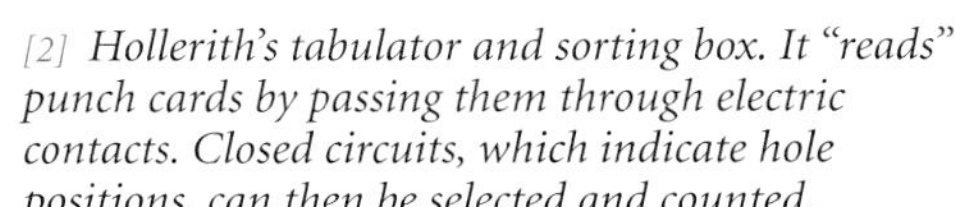

[2] Hollerith's tabulator and sorting box. It "reads" punch cards by passing them through electric contacts. Closed circuits, which indicate hole positions, can then be selected and counted.

[3] Two typical Gibson girls draw an admiring look in London.

[6] A detail of a daguerreotype taken of Emily Dickinson in 1848, the only known picture of this famously reclusive poet. By the time of her death in 1886, only seven of her poems had been published. Intrusive and insensitive editing will delay full appreciation of her originality.

[9] A Mormon husband with his wives and children.

 [8]

1890
The **Knights of Labor** go on strike against the New York Central Railroad.

 [9]

1890
The Mormon Church officially bans the practice of **polygamy**.

1890
The **Sherman Antitrust Act** becomes law; it is the first legislation enacted by the United States Congress to curb concentrations of power that interfere with trade and reduce economic competition.

1890
The state of Mississippi begins to enact **measures to restrict voting by African Americans**. Such methods as a poll tax, literacy tests, and a grandfather clause will pave the way for other Southern states to follow.

1890
The **University of Chicago** is founded. It will become one of the world's leading research institutions.

1890
The **Weather Bureau** is created within the U.S. Department of Agriculture.

1890-1891

1890
The **Yosemite** area in California's Sierra Nevada is designated a national park, largely through the efforts of naturalist John Muir. It contains Bridalveil Falls and the granite monolith El Capitan.
 [1]

1890
U.S. newspaper reporter and social reformer Jacob Riis publishes **How the Other Half Lives**, a realistic and powerful photographic record of the lives of slum dwellers in New York City. [2]

1890
William Stewart Halsted introduces the use of **rubber gloves** in surgery, at Johns Hopkins Hospital, Baltimore, Maryland.

c. 1890
American inventor Thomas A. Edison and his French counterparts, Auguste and Louis Lumière, introduce the first **motion pictures**.
 [3]

c. 1890
Amid controversy, many areas in the United States begin to pass laws to ensure that **milk is pasteurized**.

c. 1890
Entrepreneur Joseph Newton Pew forms the Sun Oil Company by consolidating his oil-producing holdings in Ohio, Illinois, West Virginia, and Texas and begins marketing his products under the name **Sunoco**.

[1] *William Henry Jackson photographs Yosemite Falls from Glacier Point.*

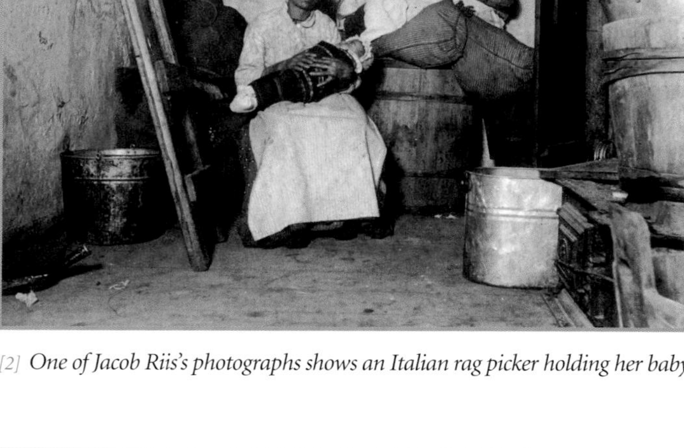

[2] *One of Jacob Riis's photographs shows an Italian rag picker holding her baby.*

[3] *Edison's "Black Maria," the first motion picture studio, built next to his laboratory.*

[6] *Miners outside a Cripple Creek real estate office, which, judging by the pole on the right, doubles up as a barbershop.*

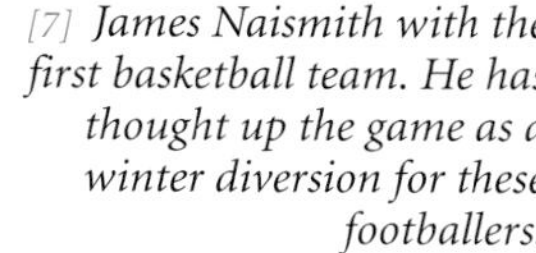

[7] *James Naismith with the first basketball team. He has thought up the game as a winter diversion for these footballers.*

c.1890
The **blues** develops in the American Deep South. While its origins are obscure, the genre has an immense impact on popular music in the 20th century, particularly in the United States and England.

March 20, 1890
Leo von Caprivi, a distinguished soldier, becomes imperial chancellor of Germany (1890–94).

June 27, 1890
Canadian-born American boxer **George Dixon** becomes the first black man to win a world boxing championship when he knocks out Nunc Wallace of England in the 18th round of the bantamweight championship.

July 1890
Two states are admitted to the United States: **Idaho** on July 3 as the 43rd state and **Wyoming** on July 10 as the 44th.

August 6, 1890
At Auburn State Prison in New York, William Kemmler becomes the first prisoner to be put to death by **electrocution**. According to Kemmler's doctors, the execution is botched, and there is "extensive charring" of the body.

November 29, 1890
The first **Army-Navy football** game is played at West Point, New York, marking the first occurrence of the annual event between West Point and Annapolis.

c. 1890
Germany begins a speedy advance toward **industrial maturity** and will witness a doubling of the number of workers in machine building, as well as a huge expansion in the number of factories in Berlin and the Ruhr.

 [4]

c. 1890
Social smoking by men becomes much more common in the United States, although it is still uncommon for women.

c. 1890
The **boll weevil**, a cotton pest, enters the U.S. from Mexico and becomes the scourge of cotton planters in the South. It is estimated that between three and five million bales of cotton are destroyed annually by this pest.

 [5]

c. 1890
The population of **Los Angeles**, California, continues to skyrocket, reaching almost 50,000.

c. 1890
The **rise of labor unions** in New South Wales and Queensland, Australia, mirrors that within many other countries including the United States, Great Britain, and Russia.

c. 1890
The **two-step**, a popular ballroom dance, comes into fashion in the United States and replaces older dances like the polka and the galop.

[4] *German factory girls sorting amber collected from the beaches of the Baltic coast before the stones are turned into jewelry.*

WOUNDED KNEE

The final defeat of the North American Indian

In an attempt to escape the harsh conditions of their reservation at Pine Ridge, the Teton Sioux began performing the Ghost Dance, a rite that they believed would make the white man disappear. The federal army subdued the Ghost Dance movement, but Chief Sitting Bull (left) was killed while being arrested (December 15). A few hundred Sioux then went into hiding in the Badlands but surrendered near Wounded Knee Creek on the night of December 28. The next morning, as some of the Indians grappled with a rifle, a shot was fired at the U.S. troopers, one of whom fell. The soldiers responded with machine guns from close range and massacred the poorly armed Indians. Fleeing Indians were pursued, and some were killed miles from the camp; 144 of them were buried in a communal grave (below). About 30 soldiers were killed.

[5] *Picking cotton near Savannah, Georgia.*

December 15, 1890
The Teton Sioux Indian chief **Sitting Bull** is killed by U.S. troops on the Grand River in South Dakota.

December 29, 1890
More than 200 Sioux men, women, and children are massacred by U.S. troops in what has been called the Battle of **Wounded Knee**, an episode that concluded the conquest of the North American Indian.

 [6]

1891
A massive gold rush begins in Cripple Creek on the slopes of **Pikes Peak** in Colorado. The tiny settlement will quickly become a boomtown and one of the largest gold producers in the world.

1891
A presidential proclamation opens a further 900,000 acres of Native American land in the **Oklahoma Territory** to white settlers.

1891
A public health act passed in Britain requires butchers to publicly state their record of **selling tainted meat** to their customers.

 [7]

1891
At the International Young Men's Christian Association Training School in Springfield, Massachusetts, physical education teacher James Naismith invents the game of **basketball**.

1891

1891
Charles Cruft books his first dog show under his name in London. The shows will be held yearly, under the auspices of the Kennel Club after 1948. The show moves to Birmingham in 1991.

 [1]

1891
Entrepreneur Henry O. Havemeyer reopens his New York-based Sugar Refineries Company as the **American Sugar Refining Company** in New Jersey to avoid antitrust laws.

1891
Factory workers in Germany win the right to negotiate with their employers.

1891
French painter **Claude Monet** produces repeated studies of the same motif in series, changing canvases with the light or as his interest shifts. These series are frequently exhibited in groups—for example, his groups of haystacks (1891) and of Rouen cathedral (1894).

 [2]

1891
French painter **Paul Gauguin** moves to Tahiti. There he paints Pacific scenes in a flat, brightly colored style he developed in France.

 [3]

1891
Henri de Toulouse-Lautrec creates his first poster, *Moulin Rouge—La Goulue*, one of 30 that document the bohemian life of the cafés, cabarets, entertainers, and artists of the Montmartre area of Paris.

 [4]

[1] *Entrants for Crufts Dog Show queue outside with their owners in the 1900s. The Cross sisters on the left are famous for their Pekinese.*

[4] *Henri de Toulouse-Lautrec with Tremolada, the proprietor of the Moulin Rouge, in front of a poster advertising this dance hall and cabaret.*

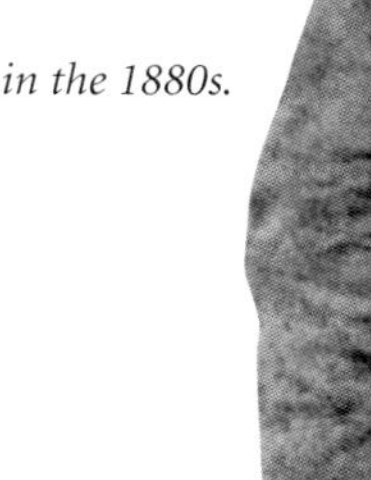

[2] *Claude Monet in the 1880s.*

[3] *Paul Gauguin in front of one of his Tahitian paintings.*

[7] *One of Hubert Herkomer's illustrations for* Tess. *She looks up from her work to see Alec d'Urberville watching her.*

1891
The English physician George Redmayne Murray successfully treats myxedema (the common form of **hypothyroidism**) with an extract of the thyroid gland.

1891
The **escalator** is designed by New York inventor Jesse W. Reno, who refers to his invention as an "endless conveyor."

1891
The first **cafeteria** is established at the YWCA in Kansas City, Missouri, to provide low-cost meals for working women.

1891
Thomas A. Edison and William K. L. Dickson invent the **motion-picture camera**.

[7]
1891
Thomas Hardy publishes **Tess of the d'Urbervilles**, which profoundly questions society's sexual mores by its compassionate portrayal of a heroine who is seduced, and perhaps raped, by the son of her employer.

1891
Throop University, which will be renamed the **California Institute of Technology**, is founded as a school for arts and crafts in Pasadena, California.

1891
Nikola Pasic becomes prime minister of **Serbia**. In the 20th century he will become one of the founders of Yugoslavia.

1891
Pope Leo XIII issues the encyclical **Rerum Novarum**, thereby instructing employers to improve the lives of their workers.

1891
Provident Hospital in Chicago is founded as the first interracial hospital in the United States. It includes a nursing school open to African American women.

1891
Scottish physician **Leander Starr Jameson** becomes administrator of the British South Africa Company's territories.

 [5]

1891
The **American Express** Company begins marketing its travelers' checks, which protect a traveler against theft or loss.

 [6]

1891
The Chicago Orchestra, later renamed the **Chicago Symphony Orchestra**, is founded by German-American conductor Theodore Thomas.

[5] Leander Starr Jameson, the instrument of Cecil Rhodes's expansionist ambitions in Africa.

[9] An immigrant family just arrived at Ellis Island from Eastern Europe. The father has perhaps come ahead of them to get a job and find a place to live.

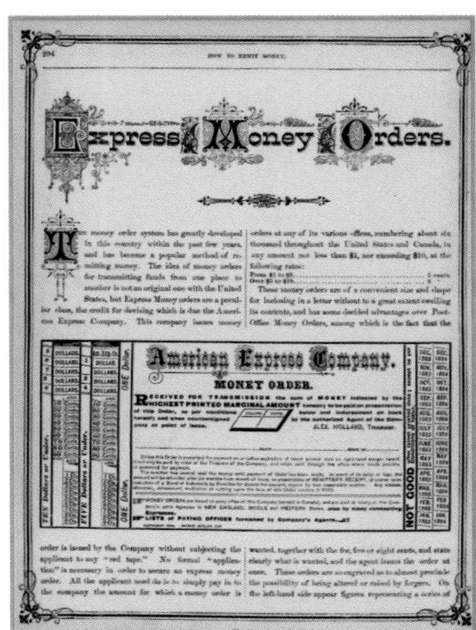

Express Money Orders.

American Express Company.

MONEY ORDER.

[6] An early American Express money order.

[8] Walter Camp, "Father of American Football."

[10] A street scene in Chile.

 [8]

1891
Yale University football coach **Walter Camp** writes the first book about the sport, introducing rule changes and clarifying the differences between rugby and American football.

c. 1891
Due to widespread crop failure, many **Russians face starvation**. Rural peasants conduct food raids in local towns, and U.S. president William Henry Harrison responds by shipping flour to Russia.

 [9]

c. 1891
Immigration to the United States continues at a strong pace. Earlier immigrants had come mainly from northern and western Europe. Now they are from southern and eastern Europe as well as the Middle East.

c. 1891
In the United States **manufactured goods** begin to compete with agricultural products for the highest percentage of exports, signaling a future decrease in agricultural production.

c. 1891
Many **Kansas farmers** go bankrupt, causing a mass exodus back East.

 [10]

c. 1891
Strikes in factories, saltpeter mines, and public utilities begin in **Chile** due to the expansion of industry and the growth of the working class.

1891-1892

January 20, 1891
King David Kalakaua of **Hawaii** dies. He is succeeded by his sister, Queen Liliuokalani.
[1]

March 14, 1891
In **New Orleans** a mob breaks into a city jail and lynches 11 Italians just acquitted of murder.

May 1891
Carnegie Hall, located at Seventh Avenue and 57th Street in New York City, opens, with Pyotr Ilyich Tchaikovsky serving as guest conductor during opening week.

[2]

May 1, 1891
Two die and more are injured when **troops fire on striking workers** at the Sans Pareille factory in Fourmies, France.

June 16, 1891
Lawyer and statesman Sir John Abbott, a conservative, becomes prime minister of **Canada** (1891–92).

September 28, 1891
American author **Herman Melville** dies in New York City in obscurity. At the end of the 1840s, he had been among the most celebrated of American writers, yet his death brings about a single obituary notice.

[3]

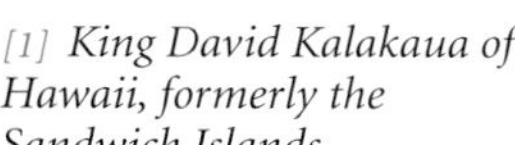
[1] King David Kalakaua of Hawaii, formerly the Sandwich Islands.

[2] Carnegie Hall, one of the fruits of Andrew Carnegie's philanthropy.

[3] Herman Melville. Many of his journals, as well as the unfinished Billy Budd, *will be published after his death.*

[7] Ellis Island, the gateway to the promised land for over 20 million immigrants, off Manhattan.

[8] Sir Arthur Conan Doyle and his first wife on their particular bicycle made for two.

1892
British chemist and physicist James Dewar uses vacuum-jacketed vessels for the storage of low-temperature liquid gases. The principle of the Dewar flask will become the basis for the common **Thermos**.

1892
Chicago businessman William Wrigley, Jr., begins selling **chewing gum**.

[7]
1892
Ellis Island begins to serve as the major immigration station to the United States. During the next three decades, an estimated 17 million immigrants will pass through its doors.

1892
English businessman Marcus Samuel opens **Shell Oil**, later Royal Dutch/Shell, and thereby breaks the monopoly held by Standard Oil in the Far East.

1892
English scholar H. A. Giles publishes his **Chinese-English dictionary**, which firmly establishes his Wade-Giles system for the romanization of Chinese languages.

[8]
1892
English songwriter Harry Dacre popularizes the song "**Daisy Bell**" ("**A Bicycle Built for Two**").

October 18, 1891
In New York City's Madison Square Garden, the first international **six-day bicycle race** is won by "Plugger Bill" Martin.

1892
"**After the Ball**," written by Charles K. Harris, becomes a popular song in the United States and will continue in popularity after the World's Columbian Exposition held in Chicago the following year.

1892
African American journalist Ida B. Wells-Barnett begins her campaign against **lynching**. Her newspaper offices are burned, and she is driven out of Memphis.

[4]

1892
American feminist writer Charlotte Perkins Gilman writes her infamous short story of postpartum "fog" and helplessness, **The Yellow Wall Paper**.

 [5]

1892
American **Mary Cassatt** paints *The Bath*. Influenced by Japanese prints, it evokes the intimacy of mother and child in a flat, bold style.

 [6]

1892
Bernhard Laurits Frederik Bang, a Danish veterinarian, discovers a way to rid dairy herds of **tuberculosis**.

[6] The Bath *by Mary Cassatt. Living in Paris since 1868, she was asked by Degas to exhibit her work with the Impressionists, which she did from 1879 until 1886. She acts as their ambassador in America.*

[4] *Ida Wells-Barnett. Her editorials, written in her paper, the* Memphis Free Speech, *after the murder of three black businessmen, lead to its offices being burned.*

[5] *Charlotte Perkins Gilman. She draws on her experiences of a nervous breakdown during her first marriage when writing her story.*

[10] *Gottlieb Daimler. His carburetor follows on his "motor vehicle" and motor bicycle of 1886.*

[9] *One of Panhard and Levassor's front-engined automobiles is exhibited in England.*

1892
Francis Bellamy, assistant editor of the *Youth's Companion*, writes the **Pledge of Allegiance**.

1892
Frank Lloyd Wright assists Louis Sullivan in designing the Charnley house in Chicago, believed to be one of Wright's earliest houses.

[9]
1892
French automobile engineers René Panhard and Émile Levassor begin selling their invention: the first vehicle with an internal-combustion **engine mounted at the front** of the chassis rather than under the driver's seat.

1892
French colonel Alfred-Amédée Dodds defeats native uprisings in the western Africa region of **Dahomey** to establish it as a French protectorate.

 [10]

1892
German mechanical engineer Gottlieb Daimler invents a **carburetor** that mixes vaporized fuel with air to create a combustible gas.

1892
In Italy the **minimum age a girl can legally marry** is raised to 12.

1892-1893

1892
In **South Africa** the first trains begin running between Johannesburg and Cape Town.

1892
In the first championship fight with padded gloves and the Marquess of **Queensberry rules**, Jim Corbett defeats champion John L. Sullivan for the heavyweight crown.

1892
Iowa blacksmith John Froehlich builds the first farm vehicle powered by a gasoline engine. Mass-produced **gasoline tractors** signal the beginning of fossil-fuel agriculture and the declining importance of animal power on farms.

1892
John Muir and associates found the **Sierra Club**, the most powerful and influential American conservation organization for most of the 20th century. [3]

1892
Lizzie Borden is acquitted of killing her parents. The incident is immortalized in the quatrain: **"**Lizzie Borden took an axe/And gave her mother forty whacks;/And when she saw what she had done/She gave her father forty-one."

1892
Mary Baker Eddy reorganizes her Lynn, Massachusetts, church as the **First Church of Christ, Scientist**, in Boston.

[2] *An early gasoline tractor goes through its paces pulling a load of wheat sheaves.*

[3] *John Muir, champion of the American wilderness.*

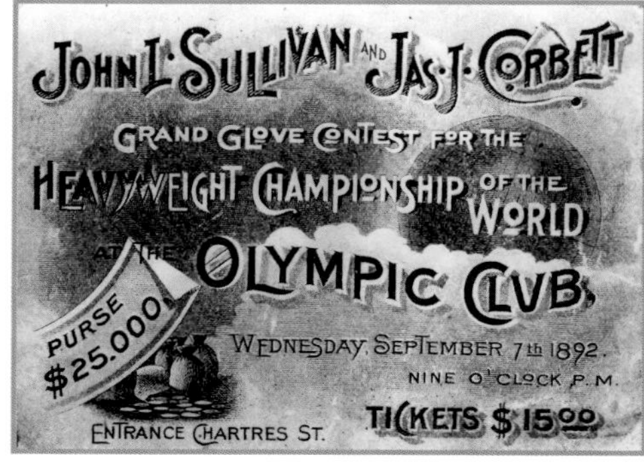

[1] *A poster for the Corbett-Sullivan fight.*

[7] *A caricature of the Egyptian Khedive Tawfiq.*

[8] *One of the banks in Coffeyville, Kansas, targeted by the Dalton Gang.*

c. 1892
Cholera is brought to the United States by German passengers arriving on the *Moravia.*

c. 1892
The Populist, or **People's, Party** is founded as a coalition of agrarian reformers in the Midwest and South to advocate for a wide range of economic and political legislation.

January 7, 1892
Khedive Muhammad Tawfiq Pasha of **Egypt** dies after ruling for 12 years as a powerless leader under the British occupation.

October 5, 1892
The notorious **Dalton Gang**, a band of outlaws from Kansas, is met with lethal gunfire from local townspeople when it attempts to rob two banks in Coffeyville, Kansas. Three of the four members of the gang are killed.

October 15, 1892
A presidential proclamation opens the **Crow Indian reservation in Montana** to settlers.

October 18, 1892
Telephone service begins between New York and Chicago.

1892
Rudolf Diesel of Germany receives a patent for an efficient heavy-oil engine. The **Diesel engine** is eventually used extensively in trucks and locomotives.

1892
The **Coca-Cola Company** is founded. By the late 20th century, its sweet, carbonated drink is one of the world's best-selling beverages and a cultural institution in the United States.

 [4]

1892
The **General Electric Company** is created by the merger of Edison General Electric and Thomson-Houston.

 [5]

1892
The Ohio Supreme Court rules against John D. Rockefeller's **Standard Oil** Trust under the provisions of the 1890 Sherman Act but is ultimately unable to remove his control of the company's finances.

1892
The Reformed Churches in the **Netherlands** are organized by a merger of the Christian Reformed Church and a group of Reformed churches that are followers of Abraham Kuyper, a Dutch theologian and statesman.

1892
Workers go on strike at the **Homestead, Pennsylvania, steel mill** owned by Andrew Carnegie and are suppressed by Pinkerton guards called in to subdue them.

 [6]

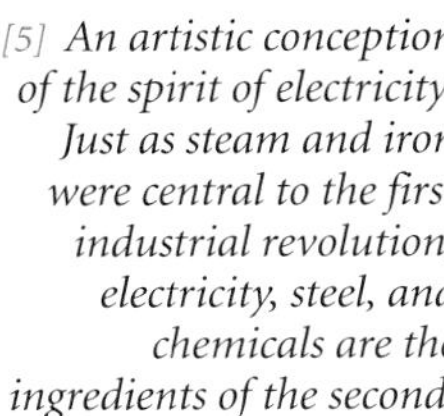

[4] *An early Coca-Cola promotional aid: a bookmark featuring the American opera singer Lillian Nordica.*

[5] *An artistic conception of the spirit of electricity. Just as steam and iron were central to the first industrial revolution, electricity, steel, and chemicals are the ingredients of the second.*

[6] *The Homestead Steel Works*

[9] *A cathedral starts to grow: St. John the Divine, Manhattan.*

[10] *The first Ferris wheel, at the World's Columbian Exposition in Chicago.*

December 5, 1892
Jurist and statesman Sir John Sparrow David Thompson, a conservative, is elected prime minister of **Canada** (1892–94).

December 17, 1892
Pyotr Ilyich Tchaikovsky's ballet **The Nutcracker** is first presented at the Mariinsky Theatre in St. Petersburg.

 [9]

December 27, 1892
The cornerstone is laid for the Protestant Episcopal Cathedral of **St. John the Divine** in upper Manhattan.

1893
William E. Gladstone's **Irish Home Rule Bill** is defeated.

 [10]

1893
Washington Gale Ferris's creation, the world's first **Ferris wheel**, opens on the Midway at the World's Columbian Exposition in Chicago; the wheel is 250 feet in diameter and has 36 cars that can seat 40 people each.

1893
Patty Smith Hill and her sister Mildred Hill cowrite *Song Stories for the Kindergarten*, a collection that includes "Good Morning to All," which will become the melody for "**Happy Birthday**."

1893

1893
The **World's Columbian Exposition is held in Chicago**. The designers, headed by Daniel Burnham, established Neoclassicism as the dominant style for American public architecture.

 [1]

1893
Belgians Henry van de Velde and Victor Horta originate the **art nouveau** style, based on graceful, organic forms.

 [2]

1893
Côte d'Ivoire (**Ivory Coast**) is established as a French colony in Africa.

1893
English traveler and naturalist **Mary Kingsley**, disregarding the conventions of her time, explores West Africa, along the way collecting beetles and freshwater fishes for the British Museum.

 [3]

1893
France, developing a colonial presence in Southeast Asia, makes **Laos** a protectorate and will control the country by 1895.

1893
French Guiana is established as a French colony in South America.

[3] Mary Kingsley, niece of Charles Kingsley. When describing falling into an animal trap lined with spikes in the African jungle, she writes of "the blessings of a good thick skirt." She will die of fever nursing Boer prisoners in South Africa in 1900.

[1] Visitors at the World's Columbian Exposition in Chicago. There is not much Neoclassicism to be seen, but there is a hot-air balloon instead.

[5] Eugene Sandow, who is one of the attractions at the World's Columbian Exposition in Chicago.

[6] The 250-feet-high walls of the Corinth Ship Canal.

[5]
1893
The American **Florenz Ziegfeld** begins his show-business career managing the strongman Eugene Sandow. He will bring the theatrical revue to spectacular heights under the slogan "Glorifying the American Girl."

1893
The **Art Institute of Chicago** (founded in 1879 as the Chicago Academy of Fine Arts), moves into a classical Beaux-Arts building on Michigan Avenue.

 [6]

1893
The **Corinth Ship Canal** opens, linking the Gulf of Corinth and the Gulf of Athens. This 3.9-mile deep-water canal had been envisioned by the emperor Nero in the first century A.D.

1893
The first **electric toaster** is developed in England by the Crompton Company. Charles P. Strite, an employee of a Minnesota manufacturing plant, patents the pop-up toaster in 1921. It becomes known as "the Toastmaster."

1893
The first **souvenir picture postcards** are issued, at the World's Columbian Exhibition in Chicago and are sold at a cost of one cent.

1893
The **Independent Labour Party** is formed in Britain. In 1906 it will take the name Labour Party and will become one of Britain's two leading political parties.

1893
German-born U.S. engineer Charles Steinmetz presents at the International Electrical Congress a method of calculation that will allow engineers to devise applications for **alternating electric current**.

1893
Grover Cleveland of the Democratic Party becomes the 24th president of the United States. He will serve until 1897. His vice president is Adlai E. Stevenson.

1893
Lillian D. Wald and Mary M. Brewster found the Henry Street Settlement House on Manhattan's Lower East Side. It will become the home of the first **visiting nurse** organization.

1893
New Zealand is the first nation to grant women the right to vote.

1893
Norwegian explorer-oceanographer **Fridtjof Nansen** departs in the specially designed ship *Fram* to drift in pack ice across the polar basin. In 1895 he leaves the ship to sledge farther north than previous explorers before returning to Norway.

 *[4]*

1893
Norwegian Expressionist **Edvard Munch** paints his most arresting image, *The Cry* (also known as *The Scream*), which reverberates in an abstracted landscape.

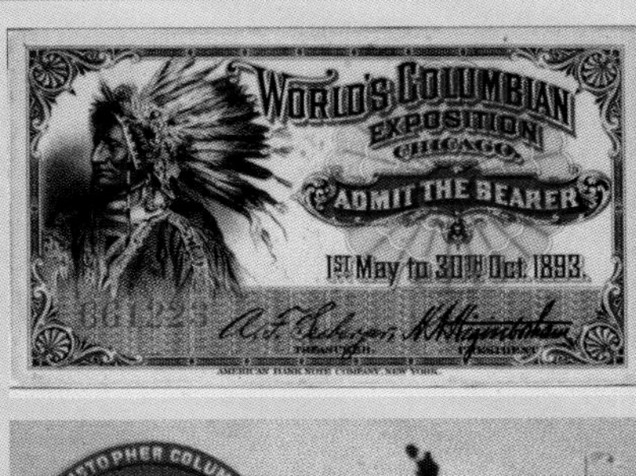

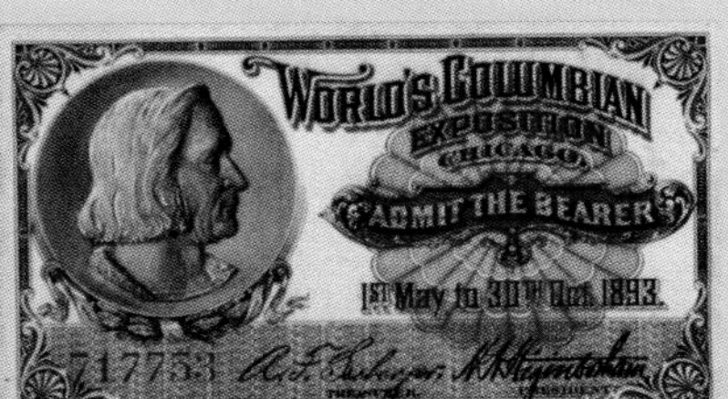

THE CHICAGO EXPOSITION

Event held to celebrate the 400th anniversary of Christopher Columbus's discovery of America

Chicago was chosen to stage the exposition over several competing cities in part because it was a railroad center and in part because it offered a guarantee of $10,000,000 to the federal organizers.

The World's Columbian Exposition was spread over 686 acres (278 hectares) along the city's south lakefront area. The chief planner was the Chicago architect Daniel H. Burnham; Charles B. Atwood was designer in chief, and Frederick Law Olmsted was entrusted with landscaping. The exposition's new buildings had impressive classical facades with a uniform cornice height of 60 feet (18.25 m). The plaster palace fronts bore little functional relationship to the exhibition halls inside, but the grandeur of the "White City," electrically lighted at night, temporarily led to a resurgent interest in Classical architecture. Behind the calm, pillared facades and Classical porticoes, the visitor found unexpected excitement and novelty. The Ferris wheel (invented by W. G. Ferris, a Pittsburgh engineer) and a dazzling new wonder—electricity—were presented for the first time in America. The first souvenir picture postcards (above) also appeared here. Nearly 26 million visitors attended the exposition.

[4] Fridtjof Nansen on skis. It is at this time that skiing is brought to Switzerland from its original home in Norway.

[2] The staircase and elevator doors in the Majolika House in Vienna—an exuberant example of art nouveau metalwork.

1893
The prototype of a slide fastener is exhibited by Whitcomb L. Judson at the World's Columbian Exposition in Chicago; it is later renamed the **zipper**.

1893
The U.S. **Migratory Bird Protection Act** puts an end to the uncontrolled hunting of migratory birds for meat and feathers, which has drastically reduced bird populations, especially of waterfowl, and driven some species to extinction.

1893
At the World's Columbian Exposition in Chicago, Fred and Louis Rueckheim sell a blend of popcorn, peanuts, and molasses that later comes to be called **Cracker Jack**. The buyer could mail in a coupon found in every box to claim a prize.

1893
Congressman Thomas E. Watson pushes through legislation for the **Rural Free Delivery** system, extending mail service to farms throughout the U.S. Shop owners fear competition from mail order, but the system begins in 1896.

1893
William Wrigley, Jr., introduces **Juicy Fruit** chewing gum, which will become the leading brand in the United States.

c. 1893
Henry O. Tanner, a student of Thomas Eakins and the first prominent African-American painter, paints *The Banjo Lesson*. Its suffused, soft interior light gives its figures an understated intimacy.

1893-1894

January 17, 1893
Acting for sugar interests, a committee led by Sanford Ballard Dole deposes **Hawaiian queen Liliuokalani** and installs a provisional government with Dole as president.

 [1]

February 9, 1893
Giuseppe Verdi's last opera, **Falstaff** (libretto by Arrigo Boito, derived largely from Shakespeare's *Merry Wives of Windsor* and *Henry IV*), is first performed at Milan's La Scala Theatre.

June 30, 1893
The **Excelsior Diamond**—which, weighing 995 carats, is the largest uncut diamond ever found to that time—is discovered in the De Beers mine at Jagersfontein, Orange Free State.

July 1, 1893
San Francisco Bay City Club opens a **wooden track for bicycle racing**, the first in the United States.

July 9, 1893
Chicago surgeon Daniel Hale Williams performs, without anesthesia, the first successful **open-heart surgery**.

July 11, 1893
Kokichi Mikimoto, a Japanese entrepreneur, obtains the first **cultured pearl** five years after starting his pearl farm.

 [2]

[1] Liliuokalani, last queen of Hawaii.

[6] George du Maurier, whose novel lends its name to the soft felt Trilby hat, as worn by the heroine, as well as coining the term "Svengali."

[2] Kokichi Mikimoto, the cultivator of pearls, with many strings of them behind him.

[5] Lord Rosebery succumbs to the pressures of the premiership, lasting less than a year in office. Outside politics, he wins the Derby three times.

[7] A 1948 version of the Wild West: cowboys from a nearby ranch try their luck on slot machines in the fledgling city of Las Vegas.

1894
American educator John Dewey founds the first Laboratory School in Chicago. It helps to establish the University of Chicago as a leading center of **social science research**.

1894
American surgeon Charles McBurney develops innovative diagnostic and surgical techniques for the treatment of **appendicitis**.

 [5]

1894
Archibald Philip Primrose, 5th earl of **Rosebery**, becomes prime minister of Great Britain as the leader of the Liberal Party.

 [6]

1894
British caricaturist and novelist George du Maurier publishes **Trilby**, in which the malevolent hypnotist Svengali appears. The name will become a term for a person who with evil intent tries to get others to do his bidding.

 [7]

1894
Charles August Fey builds the first modern **slot machine**. He will build the first three-reel slot machine with automatic cash payouts and one designed with horseshoes and bells as well as playing-card suitmarks on the reels.

1894
James Hennegan and W. H. Donaldson begin publishing *Billboard Advertising*. They later introduce sections focusing on theater (1901) and film (1907), transforming the paper into the show-business weekly **Billboard**.

July 31, 1893
Henry Perky obtains a U.S. patent on **shredded wheat** cereal.

November 6, 1893
Pyotr Ilyich **Tchaikovsky** dies in St. Petersburg, Russia, in a cholera epidemic, days after conducting the premiere of his *Symphony No. 6* (*Pathétique*), which will become one of his most celebrated works.

 [3]

1894
Death duties are introduced in Britain.

1894
A well drilled for water begins spouting oil in Corsicana, Texas, opening the first major **oil field west of the Mississippi** River.

1894
Bernard Berenson publishes his first book, *The Venetian Painters of the Renaissance*. His discriminating eye, exceptional memory, perceptive intelligence, and learning make his opinion sought by major collectors and museums.

 [4]

1894
American composer Charles B. Lawlor and lyricist James W. Blake write "**The Sidewalks of New York**" ("East side, west side, all around the town...").

[8] *Aubrey Beardsley in a photograph almost as arresting as his brilliantly decadent illustrations, which combine strength and delicacy of line with refined yet blatant sexuality.*

[9] *Emanuel Lasker. He will hold the world chess title until defeated by Capablanca in 1921.*

[3] *Tchaikovsky, Russia's greatest composer of the 19th century.*

[4] *Bernard Berenson in 1887, the precocious Harvard scholar from Lithuania, patronized by the legendary collector Isabella Stewart Gardner.*

[10] *An early Marks & Spencer "bazaar," or store, in Holloway, London.*

 [8]

1894
English graphic artist **Aubrey Beardsley** illustrates Oscar Wilde's play *Salomé* with grotesque end-of-the-century elegance.

 [9]

1894
German chess master Emanuel Lasker defeats Wilhelm Steinitz for the **world chess title**, which he will hold until 1921.

1894
German graphic artist and sculptor **Käthe Kollwitz** publishes her first important print, *Weaver's Revolt*. With boldly accentuated forms, she is an eloquent advocate for victims of social injustice, war, and inhumanity.

1894
Offshore oil-drilling is pioneered in Californian waters. Subsequent undersea drilling in the North Sea, Gulf of Mexico, and elsewhere proves a source of oil and oil pollution.

 [10]

1894
Polish-born merchant Michael Marks and his financial backer, Thomas Spencer, open the Penny Bazaar, which will evolve into **Marks & Spencer**, Britain's largest retailer, in 1922.

1894
Radcliffe College for Women opens in Cambridge, Massachusetts. Named for Anne Radcliffe, the first woman to donate money to Harvard University, the college will eventually merge with Harvard.

1894-1895

1894
Ralston Purina is founded as the Robinson-Danforth Commission Company when St. Louis, Missouri, feed merchants George Robinson and William H. Danforth produce a new feed from corn and oats.

1894
Swiss bacteriologist Alexandre Yersin and Japanese bacteriologist Kitasato Shibasaburo independently discover the causative organism of the **bubonic plague** during an outbreak in China.

1894
The **Andes** Mountains, in South America, are crossed by rail for the first time.

 [1]

1894
The German parliament building (the **Reichstag**), designed by Paul Wallot, opens in Berlin.

 [2]

1894
The **International Olympic Committee** is formed in Paris.

1894
The **Stanley Cup**, the oldest trophy that can be won by professional athletes in North America, is awarded for the first time, to the Montreal Amateur Athletic Association; it will become the property of the National Hockey League in 1926.

[1] *The Andes form a spectacular backdrop to Viscas Bridge.*

[6] *Women playing volleyball.*

[2] *The Reichstag, an ostentatious architectural gesture by Europe's newest empire.*

[4] *The last tsar with Tsarina Alexandra, one of Queen Victoria's many granddaughters. Nicholas's aunt, also Alexandra, is the wife of Queen Victoria's eldest son, the Prince of Wales.*

[3] *Troops guard rolling stock from strikers in Chicago.*

[7] *A cast of Rodin's* The Burghers of Calais *in front of the Victoria Tower at the Houses of Parliament in Westminster.*

February 3, 1894
The **first American steel ship**, the *Dirigo*, is launched from Bath, Maine.

June 28, 1894
The U.S. Congress declares the first Monday of September to be **Labor Day**, a holiday to honor the American worker.

 [3]

July 20, 1894
The **Pullman Strike**, a widespread railroad strike in the United States, ends shortly after President Grover Cleveland orders federal troops to Chicago.

September 10, 1894
The **United Daughters of the Confederacy**, an American women's patriotic society, is founded in Nashville, Tennessee.

October 29, 1894
Chlodwig Karl Viktor **Hohenlohe-Schillingsfürst** becomes Prussian prime minister and imperial chancellor of Germany (1894–1900).

November 1, 1894
Nicholas II succeeds his father, Alexander III, as tsar of Russia.

1894
The **Tonghak Revolt** by peasants and followers of the Korean apocalyptic antiforeign Tonghak (Ch'ondogyo) religion against the Choson (Yi) government is violently suppressed.

1894
Tower Bridge in London opens. This movable bridge spans the River Thames between the Greater London boroughs of Tower Hamlets and Southwark. It is a distinct landmark that aesthetically complements the Tower of London.

1894
The U.S. Congress establishes the **Bureau of Immigration** in a time of massive immigration from Asia, Central Europe, and Latin America. Anti-immigrant measures are rampant in the United States.

1894
The **U.S. Open golf tournament** begins in Yonkers, New York.

1894
The world's last **bubonic plague** pandemic, originating in China, strikes the ports of Canton and Hong Kong, from which it spreads to India in 1898.

1894
William Ramsay, a British physical chemist, discovers **argon**, an inert gas. He will later find three others (neon, krypton, and xenon) and show that they (with helium and radon) form an entire family of new elements, the **noble gases**.

THE OPENING OF TOWER BRIDGE

Unique structure that marks the entrance to the Pool of London

Tower Bridge is a double-leaf bascule (drawbridge) type that spans the River Thames in central London. It is a distinct landmark that aesthetically complements the nearby Tower of London, which is visible in the right background of the photograph above.

For many years, the British capital had needed at least one more river crossing to cope with north-south road traffic, but none had been built because all the plans submitted would have restricted the size of ships that could pass under it to the Pool of London docks at the city's very center.

Finally, two architects—Horace Jones and John Wolfe Barry—came up with the perfect solution: a bridge that could be raised to allow the largest vessels to pass through. After eight years' construction, the bridge—the first in the British capital to the east of London Bridge—was completed in 1894. It provides an opening 250 feet (76 m) wide. Its twin towers rise 200 feet (61 m) above the Thames. Between the towers stretch a pair of glass-covered walkways that are popular among tourists. The walkways were originally designed to allow pedestrians to cross even while the bridge was raised, but they became hangouts for prostitutes and thieves and so were closed from 1909 to 1982. Tower Bridge was operated by hydraulic pumps driven by steam until 1976, when electric motors were put into operation; the steam-power system is still kept (in good repair) as a tourist display. Because the Pool of London is no longer used as a dock, however, the leaves are now seldom raised.

[5] Dreyfus stands in court to hear his sentence for allegedly passing documents to the Germans.

[8] Oscar Wilde poses with Lord Alfred Douglas, with whom he is infatuated. A week or two after Wilde's play has opened, Douglas's father, the Marquess of Queensberry (see 1867), will accuse Wilde of sodomy. This leads to his imprisonment.

 [4]
November 26, 1894
Nicholas II, the last tsar of Russia, marries **Alexandra** (originally Alix, princess of Hesse-Darmstadt).

December 21, 1894
Publisher and political leader **Sir Mackenzie Bowell**, a conservative, becomes prime minister of Canada (1894–96).

 [5]
December 22, 1894
On the basis of specious evidence and anti-Semitism, French army officer **Alfred Dreyfus** is sentenced to life in prison for treason, sparking a controversy that divides France for 12 years.

 [6]
1895
American William G. Morgan invents **volleyball** for the benefit of those who find the new game of basketball too taxing. Morgan initially calls the game "mintonette."

 [7]
1895
Auguste Rodin's monumental bronze sculpture group, *Les Bourgeois de Calais* (**The Burghers of Calais**), is dedicated. The burghers gave themselves as hostages to King Edward III of England in 1347.

 [8]
1895
British playwright **Oscar Wilde's** famous comedy, *The Importance of Being Earnest*, has its premiere in London.

1895-1896

1895
German physicist Wilhelm Conrad Röntgen discovers **X-rays**. The discovery soon revolutionizes physics, medical diagnosis, and engineering.

 [1]

1895
In Britain the **National Trust** is founded to safeguard the nation's architectural and landscape heritage against destruction.

1895
Fashionable Beaux-Arts architect Richard Morris Hunt completes **the Breakers, in Newport, Rhode Island**, for Cornelius Vanderbilt. This mansion-sized summer "cottage" is a testament to the splendid opulence of the Gilded Age.

 [2]

1895
French psychologist **Alfred Binet** founds the journal *L'Année Psychologique*. He also founds a laboratory for research in childhood education, beginning a long and influential career in the field.

1895
Indian-born English writer Rudyard Kipling finishes his multileveled **Jungle Books**; he will become the first English author to receive the Nobel Prize for Literature (1907).

 [3]

1895
King C. Gillette, American inventor and entrepreneur, develops the **safety razor** with disposable blades, which replace conventional straight razors.

 [4]

[2] The Breakers in Newport, Rhode Island.

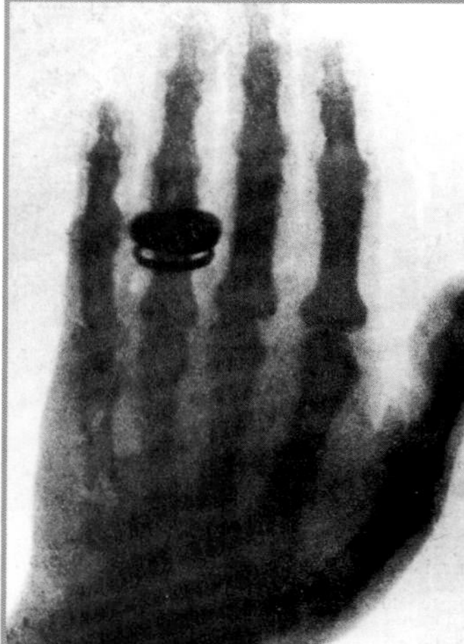

[1] An X-ray of Röntgen's wife's hand, complete with a ring on one finger.

[3] Rudyard Kipling also delights children with his Just So Stories *and* Puck of Pook's Hill, *while adults relish his stories of India and elsewhere, and his poetry.*

Le Petit Journal
SUPPLÉMENT ILLUSTRÉ
DIMANCHE 24 MARS 1895
MANIFESTATION PATRIOTIQUE

[8] French troops leave for the invasion of Madagascar.

[4] A packet of Gillette disposable double-edged razor blades for use with Gillette's safety razor.

[10] The start of the 100-yard sprint race, before the days of starting blocks, at the first Olympic Games.

 [9]

December 29, 1895
Leander Starr Jameson launches an abortive raid into the Transvaal to overthrow the Boer government of Paul Kruger.

1896
A **major earthquake** hits Japan, killing more than 20,000 people.

1896
Colgate Ribbon Dental Cream, the first **toothpaste in a tube**, is marketed in the United States.

1896
Dow Jones & Company, founded by Charles Henry Dow and Edward D. Jones, begins computing a daily industrials average, using a list of 12 stocks and dividing their total price by 12.

 [10]

1896
Due largely to the efforts of Pierre, baron de Coubertin, the first modern **Olympic Games** are held in Athens; 280 men from 13 countries participate.

1896
English bacteriologist and immunologist Almroth Edward Wright develops an **antityphoid immunization**.

1895
Playwright and author **Oscar Wilde** is sentenced to two years at hard labor for homosexual activities.

1895
The **first automobile race in the United States** takes place on Thanksgiving Day. The course runs from Chicago to Evanston, Illinois, and is won by a car driving an average of 7.5 miles per hour.

1895
The island of **Taiwan** and the Pescadores are ceded to Japan in the Treaty of Shimonoseki that ends the first Sino-Japanese War.

 [5]

January 15, 1895
Félix Faure is elected president of France; his presidency will be marked by diplomatic conflicts with England, rapprochement with Russia, and the continuing problem of the Dreyfus Affair.

 [6]

April 11, 1895
Cuban patriot José Julián Martí lands in **Cuba** at the head of an invading force whose goal is to win independence from Spain.

September 30, 1895
French troops occupy Antananarivo, **Madagascar**, after the refusal of Rainilaiarivony, the prime minister, to submit to French suzerainty.

[5] Victorious Japanese troops with a triumphal arch that they have erected near Seoul in Korea to celebrate their victory over the Chinese. Korea theoretically becomes independent as a result of the victory but in fact will be increasingly dominated by the Japanese.

[7] José Julián Martí. He dies in a skirmish with the Spanish in Cuba.

[9] Leander Starr Jameson (fourth from the left), surrounded by some of those who took part in his raid. They are on their way back to England to stand trial with him. He will serve a prison sentence but then return to South Africa as premier of Cape Colony after the Boer War.

[11] Thomas Hardy's last novel shocks many late Victorians with its frank treatment of sex. It is called "Jude the Obscene," and some booksellers wrap their copies in brown paper bags.

[6] Félix Faure. The son of a tanner, he took to the pomp and circumstance of the presidency with ease, but is to achieve notoriety after his unedifying death in the arms of his mistress, Madame Steinheil, in 1899.

[12] Guglielmo Marconi comes to England and is introduced to the post office's chief engineer. He demonstrates his equipment on Salisbury Plain and across the Bristol Channel.

1896
English writer Thomas Hardy's period as a novelist ends with the publication of his greatest, darkest work, **Jude the Obscure**.

1896
In Budapest, a 2.5-mile (4-km) **electric subway** opens. It is the first subway on the European continent.

1896
In *Plessy v. Ferguson* the U.S. Supreme Court permits **racial segregation** in "separate but equal" public facilities. The *Plessy* decision will stand until 1954.

1896
Inspired in part by the work of Wilhelm Röntgen the previous year, French physicist Henri Becquerel discovers **radioactivity**.

1896
Italian engineer **Guglielmo Marconi** files the first of his patents for a wireless radio system.

1896
Johns Hopkins Medical School opens in Baltimore, Maryland. The women who raise a good part of the funding insist that men and women be admitted equally.

1896

1896
Polish novelist Henryk Sienkiewicz, winner of the Nobel Prize for Literature in 1905, publishes **Quo Vadis?**

1896
Otto Lilienthal dies in one of the many gliders he has constructed, based on his study of bird wings, and then successfully flown.

 [1]

1896
Nicaraguan poet, journalist, and diplomat **Rubén Darío** publishes *Prosas profanas y otros poemas* (*Profane Hymns and Other Poems*). This continues the stylistic trends of his earlier work but also shows the influence of contemporary French Symbolist poets.

1896
Lancashire Steam Motor Company is founded. It will be renamed **Leyland Motors** in 1907 and will eventually become the British Leyland Motor Corporation, responsible for creating Mini Cooper and M.G. cars.

 [2]

1896
Swedish scientist Svante Arrhenius describes the physics of the atmosphere's **greenhouse effect**, whereby solar energy is trapped on earth. He also predicts global warming.

1896
The city of **Miami**, Florida, is incorporated.

 [3]

[1] Otto Lilienthal soars off a hillside, his body dangling below one of his elegant gliders.

[2] An early Leyland Motors Royal Mail truck.

[6] An advertisement illustrating a movie show using Edison's Vitascope.

[5] Emperor Menilek II under a ceremonial umbrella with his wife, Taitu.

[3] Flagler Street in downtown Miami, circa 1900.

January 4, 1896
Utah is admitted to the United States as the 45th state.

February 1896
The infant son of **Ferdinand**, prince (1887–1908) and first king (1908–18) of modern Bulgaria, is received into the Orthodox church, strengthening Ferdinand's powers.

February 16, 1896
Richard Felton Outcault's drawing of an urchin appears in the *New York World*. Dubbed the "Yellow Kid," it will give rise to a press war that will result in the expression "**yellow journalism**" being used to describe sensational publishing.

 [5]

March 1, 1896
The Ethiopian army of Emperor **Menilek II** wins a decisive victory against the Italian army at Adwa, Ethiopia.

 [6]

April 1896
At Koster and Bial's Music Hall in New York City, **Thomas Edison's Vitascope** is given its first public demonstration. It will bring film projection to the United States in a format that lasts for several years.

April 29, 1896
American harness racehorse (Standardbred) **Dan Patch** is foaled in Indiana; a nearly legendary horse in his time, in 1905 he will establish a world pacing record of 1:55 1/4 that endures for 33 years. He will never lose a race.

1896
The College of New Jersey, founded in 1746, is renamed **Princeton University**.

1896
The religious social-welfare organization **Volunteers of America** is founded in New York City.

1896
Theodor Herzl publishes *The Jewish State*. Although Herzl will die long before Israel's birth, he is an indefatigable organizer, propagandist, and diplomat helping make Zionism into a political movement of worldwide significance.

[4]

1896
Tom Brown's tramps Weary Willie and Tired Tim are the first characters to appear regularly in **British comic strips**.

1896
Victor Horta designs the Maison du Peuple, Brussels. In this pioneering modernist design, native brick and stone architecture is combined with iron to serve the socialist cause.

1896
William Randolph Hearst publishes the first **weekly color comic-strip supplement** in the *Morning Journal*.

[9] William Jennings Bryan addresses a crowd at a whistle stop on his presidential election campaign.

[4] Theodor Herzl at home in Vienna with his children.

[8] Samuel Pierpont Langley, metaphorically wearing his astrophysicist hat, stands beside his bolometer for measuring the distribution of heat in the spectrum of the sun.

[10] Bleak conditions on the way to the Klondike gold fields, with tiny figures struggling up snowy slopes in the background.

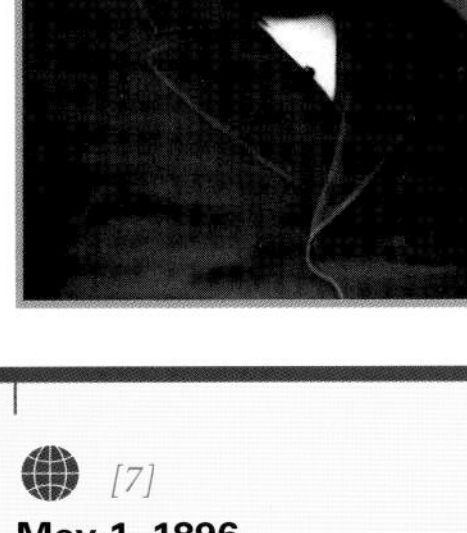

[7] Sir Charles Tupper. The successful completion of the Canadian Pacific Railway owes much to him.

[7]
May 1, 1896
Sir Charles Tupper, a conservative who will be responsible for the legislation making Nova Scotia a province of Canada in 1867, becomes Canadian prime minister (1896).

[8]
May 6, 1896
A **steam-powered model aircraft**, created by American astrophysicist and aeronautical pioneer Samuel Pierpont Langley, flies some 3,000 feet (some 900 m) over the Potomac River.

 [9]
July 8, 1896
William Jennings Bryan delivers his famous Cross of Gold speech at the Democratic National Convention in Chicago, so electrifying delegates that they nominate the 36-year-old Bryan as their candidate for president.

July 11, 1896
Wilfrid Laurier, a member of the Liberal Party who will be known for his attempts to define the role of French Canada in the federal state and to define Canada's relations to Great Britain, becomes prime minister (1896–1911).

August 6, 1896
The French parliament votes to annex **Madagascar** as a French colony.

 [10]
August 17, 1896
George Washington Carmack unearths gold in Bonanza Creek, a tributary of the **Klondike** River in the Yukon Territory, Canada, setting off a gold rush into the Klondike valley.

1896-1897

August 18, 1896
According to lore, more than 200 outlaws from regional gangs gather at Brown's Hole in the American West, where Butch Cassidy proposes a Train Robbers' Syndicate, the **Wild Bunch**.

 [1]

December 30, 1896
Philippine nationalist **José Rizal** is publicly executed, enraging and uniting Filipinos.

1897
A steam turbine developed by Charles Algernon Parsons helps the **Turbinia** reach a speed of more than 34 knots. It is the first use of a steam turbine for marine propulsion.

 [2]

1897
Aboard the *Belgica*, Belgian naval officer Adrien de Gerlache explores the west coast of the **Antarctic peninsula**, inaugurating a new wave of scientific polar exploration and inadvertently wintering in the Bellingshausen Sea.

1897
Alice McLellan Birney and Phoebe Apperson Hearst found the (U.S.) National Congress of Mothers, later called the **Parent-Teacher Association** (PTA). Membership is later broadened to include teachers, fathers, and other citizens.

 [3]

1897
American bandmaster John Philip Sousa composes the military march "**The Stars and Stripes Forever**."

[1] *The Wild Bunch: left to right (standing) William Carver, Harvey "Kid Curry" Logan; (seated) Harry "Sundance Kid" Langbaugh, Ben "the Tall Texan" Kilpatrick, Robert LeRoy "Butch Cassidy" Parker.*

[2] *The* Turbinia, *her bows well out of the water and clear of the bow wave, leaves an impressive wake behind her, all indicating the speed at which she is travelling.*

[3] *Phoebe Hearst. As well as the PTA, she has also given birth, in 1863, to the legendary newspaper tycoon William Randolph Hearst.*

1890-1899

[5] *Amsterdam Stock Exchange (left).*

[6] *The Tate Gallery on Millbank beside the Thames. It now houses British art up to the modern period.*

[7] *An early image of Santa Claus and his reindeer.*

1897
General Foods Corporation begins selling the breakfast cereal **Grape Nuts**.

1897
Rudolph Dirks creates the **Katzenjammer Kids**, the first fully developed form of the newspaper comic strip: it uses speech balloons, has a continuous cast of characters, and is divided into small regular panels.

 [5]

1897
Architect Hendrik Petrus Berlage begins work on the **Amsterdam Stock Exchange**, one of the most influential buildings of the early 20th century.

 [6]

1897
In London the **Tate Gallery**, designed by Sidney Smith, is opened to the public.

 [7]

1897
In the pages of the *New York Sun*, editor Francis Church informs eight-year-old Virginia O'Hanlon that, "**Yes, Virginia, there is a Santa Claus**."

1897
In **Zanzibar** the legal status of slavery is abolished.

1897
At the **Ashio Copper Mine** in central Japan, air and water pollution motivate a series of peasant protests, including marches on Tokyo.

1897
Britain's **Royal Automobile Club** (RAC) is formed.

1897
British army surgeon Ronald Ross discovers the **malarial parasite** carried by the *Anopheles* mosquito. This work advances antimalarial campaigns and wins Ross the Nobel Prize for Medicine in 1902.

 [4]

1897
British physicist J. J. Thomson helps revolutionize the knowledge of atomic structure by his discovery of the **electron**. He will receive the Nobel Prize for Physics in 1906.

1897
Construction of the first practical **subway line** in the United States is completed. Built in Boston, it is 1.5 miles (2.4 km) long and uses trolley streetcars, or tramcars.

1897
French artist **Henri Rousseau**, considered the archetype of the modern naive artist, completes *The Sleeping Gypsy*. It is the most important of his later paintings.

DIAMOND JUBILEE

Britain and the Empire mark 60 years of the Victorian age.

Queen Victoria's Diamond Jubilee—which, at the instigation of Colonial Secretary Joseph Chamberlain, had been declared a festival of the British Empire—was marked by many commemorative events. Nevertheless, the occasion was in general less lavishly celebrated than the Golden Jubilee had been, mainly because the monarch was now much more frail than she had been 10 years previously.

The highlight came on June 22, 1897, 60 years and two days after Victoria succeeded to the British throne on the death of her uncle, William IV. The royal party progressed slowly through the streets of London from Buckingham Palace to St. Paul's Cathedral. The above left photograph shows Her Majesty's carriage passing the Law Courts in the Strand; on horseback (extreme left) is her son, the Prince of Wales, the future King Edward VII.

On arrival at St. Paul's, a short service of thanksgiving was held outside the building, as the queen was too lame to climb the steps to the western doors. Eleven colonial prime ministers were in attendance, together with numerous chosen representatives of the colonial armed forces (left below). Leaving the cathedral, the royal carriage bore the queen via the Mansion House (the official residence of the lord mayor of London), across London Bridge, and through parts of South London, before returning over Westminster Bridge, past the Houses of Parliament, to Buckingham Palace.

In her journal the queen wrote: "No one ever, I believe, has met with such an ovation as was given to me, passing through those 6 miles of streets.... The cheering was quite deafening & every face seemed to be filled with real joy. I was much moved and gratified."

[8] Bram Stoker (left), in his day a very important figure in British theater as manager of the Lyceum Theatre in partnership with Sir Henry Irving. Bela Lugosi (right) plays Count Dracula in the 1931 film version.

[9] A pioneering skier in Switzerland in the 1890s.

[4] Sir Ronald Ross. His years in the Indian Medical Service have steered him towards the problem of malaria.

[8]
1897
Irish-born author Bram Stoker publishes the novel **Dracula**. Count Dracula, its "undead" villain from Transylvania, will become the representative type of vampire, and his story will be retold in countless stage and film adaptations.

1897
Japanese physician Ogata Masanori describes an outbreak of the plague on Formosa as "ratpest" and shows that **rat fleas** carry the plague bacillus, an important discovery in the study of the disease.

1897
Jell-O is invented by Pearle B. Wait and named by his wife, May. The first flavors are strawberry, raspberry, orange, and lemon.

1897
John J. McDermott of New York City wins the first **Boston Marathon** with a time of 2 hours 55 minutes 10 seconds.

[9]
1897
Moravian Matthias Zdarsky publishes the **first ski instruction manual**, *Die alpine Lilienfelder Skifahrtechnik*. The book helps define and popularize the sport of Alpine skiing.

1897
Queen Victoria celebrates her **Diamond Jubilee**, commemorating 60 years as Great Britain's queen.

1897-1898

1897
The Argonaut, designed by American inventor Simon Lake, is the first **submarine** to operate extensively in open water.

1897
The **Croquet Association**, which governs croquet tournaments in the United Kingdom, is created.

 [1]

1897
The **gold standard** is adopted in Japan, overseen by minister of finance Matsukata Masayoshi, and in Russia, overseen by minister of finance Sergey Yulyevich Witte.

1897
The **Library of Congress** in Washington, D.C., moves to its permanent quarters.

 [2]

1897
The play *Cyrano de Bergerac*, by French dramatist **Edmond Rostand**, is first performed in Paris. It is Rostand's most popular and enduring work.

 [3]

1897
The Scientific-Humanitarian Committee, advocating **rights for homosexuals**, is founded in Berlin. It campaigns for legal reform throughout Germany and in the Netherlands and Austria, developing some 25 local chapters by 1922.

[1] Children playing croquet. Their respect for the rules probably falls short of what the Croquet Association would like.

[3] The famous British actor-manager Sir Charles Wyndham in the title role of the first English production of Cyrano de Bergerac, *his profile allowing us to see the full splendor of Cyrano's famous nose.*

[6] Pierre and Marie Curie on their honeymoon, looking thoroughly at ease with the new rational mode of transport, safety bicycles.

[2] The reading room at the new Library of Congress.

[7] A panorama of greater New York, with the Produce Exchange in the foreground (left), a great many masts and sails along and on the East River, and the Brooklyn Bridge and Brooklyn beyond.

1898
Alfred Cartier and his son Louis establish a jewelry firm of great refinement in Paris. **Cartier** will soon become the most famous jeweler in the world, supplying jewels to European royalty.

1898
Austrian George Luger invents the **Luger pistol**, a semiautomatic German hand weapon. It will become the standard pistol of the German armed forces from 1908 to 1938.

1898
Joshua Slocum of Nova Scotia is the first man in recorded history to sail around the world singlehandedly; he has sailed 46,000 miles (74,000 km) in three years, two months, and two days, in his fishing boat, *Spray*.

1898
Danish engineer Valdemar Poulsen invents the **telegraphone**, a forerunner of the modern magnetic sound recorder.

 [6]

1898
French physicists **Pierre and Marie Curie** discover polonium and radium. They will share the 1903 Nobel Prize for Physics, along with Henri Becquerel.

 [7]

1898
Greater New York is formed when Manhattan is joined with the newly created boroughs of Brooklyn, Queens, Richmond, and the Bronx.

1897
The Yiddish-language newspaper **Forverts** (*Jewish Daily Forward*) is founded in New York City by the Jewish Socialist Press Federation as a civic aid and a unifying device for Jewish immigrants from Europe.

1897
William McKinley of the Republican Party takes office as the 25th president of the United States. He will serve until 1901. His vice presidents are Garret A. Hobart (1897–99) and Theodore Roosevelt (1899–1901).

 [4]

c. 1897
The **progressive education movement** takes form in Europe and the United States. Critical of traditional education's narrow scope and strictness, it seeks to educate the "whole child."

[5]

February 27, 1897
French general Joseph-Simon Gallieni sends the queen of **Madagascar** into exile, an important element of his efforts to pacify and integrate the island into the French colonial empire.

May 20, 1897
During the first Greco-Turkish war, the Greeks—fighting for the annexation of **Crete**—yield to pressures from European powers to withdraw their troops from Crete and accept an armistice on the mainland.

1898
Ahmadu Seku, the second and last ruler of the **Tukulor empire in West Africa**, known for his resistance to the French occupation, dies in northern Nigeria.

THE VIENNA SECESSION

Late 19th-century movement in which young Austrian artists asserted their independence from established Germanic traditions

The development of a distinctly Viennese school of art began in 1897 following the Austrian artists' rejection of the academic style traditionally adopted by the painters of the Künstlerhaus. Led by Gustav Klimt, the Secession movement tangentially involved a number of innovative architects, including Otto Wagner, Adolf Loos, and Josef Hoffmann, who also helped found a cooperative enterprise for crafts and design called the Wiener Werkstätte ("Vienna Workshops"), which produced furniture and design objects.

A later group was formed centering around an exhibition known as the "Kunstschau," from which emerged some of the most distinguished modern Austrian painters, including Oskar Kokoschka, Alfred Kubin, and Egon Schiele.

At the heart of the movement was a desire to develop new modes of expression. This was reflected in the exhibition house (left above), designed by Joseph Maria Olbrich and opened in 1898. Known simply as *die Sezession* (the Secession), the building had over its entrance the epigraph: "To every age its art and to art its freedom."

In their exhibition posters and layouts and illustrations for the Secession magazine, *Ver Sacrum*, members pushed graphic design in uncharted aesthetic directions. Koloman Moser's poster for the 13th Secession exhibition (1902) blends three figures, lettering, and geometric ornament into a modular whole. The work is composed of horizontal, vertical, and circular lines that define flat shapes of red, blue, and white.

The Secessionists modified art nouveau, or Jugendstil as it is known in the German regions, in a classical manner—an example is the façade of the Majolika House by Otto Wagner (left below), which is decorated in a linear pattern sometimes known as whiplash or eel style.

The experiments with pure form begun in the 1890s continued and evolved in the first decade of the 20th century, although Klimt abandoned the movement in 1905 after a disagreement with fellow members about their future direction.

[4] President McKinley with his wife, Ida Saxton McKinley.

[5] One of the manifestations of progressive education: open-air physical exercise or calisthenics for children, here at Crotona Park in the Bronx.

1898
Heroin is introduced as a commercial product by the Bayer Company of Germany. Originally used as a narcotic analgesic, its undesirable side effects are soon found to far outweigh its value as a painkiller, and it will be prohibited.

1898
In the Transvaal republic (South Africa), President Paul Kruger creates the first **game reserve** in response to anxieties about wildlife depletion. It later becomes Kruger National Park.

1898
Joseph Maria Olbrich designs the **Secession Building**, Vienna. Crowned by a giant ball of gilded laurel leaves, the building is home to the Wiener Sezession (Vienna Secession), a center of early modernism.

1898
Otto Wagner, one of the founders of European modern architecture, designs **the Majolika House**, Vienna. Its tiled façade, with a spreading flower pattern, is intended as a model for modern, hygienic housing.

1898
Peking University, one of the oldest and most important institutions of higher learning in China, is founded in Beijing.

1898
Pharmacist Caleb D. Bradham (1866–1934), hoping to duplicate the recent success of Coca-Cola, creates the first **Pepsi-Cola** in New Bern, North Carolina.

1898-1899

1898
Russian physiologist **Ivan Pavlov** begins research that will eventually lead him to develop the concept of the conditioned reflex.

 [1]

1898
The first world championship birling (**logrolling**) competition is held in Omaha, Nebraska.

1898
The German automotive company **Opel AG** is founded when the five Opel brothers begin converting the bicycle and sewing-machine factory of Adam Opel (1837–95) into an automobile complex.

1898
The **Goodyear Tire & Rubber Company** is founded by Charles and Frank Seiberling in Akron, Ohio.

1898
The U.S. Congress passes a joint annexation resolution, the final stamp of U.S. domination over **Hawaii**. This status will be confirmed by the establishment of Hawaii as a territory in 1900.

1898
Theodore Roosevelt organizes the first Volunteer Cavalry, known as the **Rough Riders**, who are sent to fight in Cuba. Their charge (on foot) up Kettle Hill during the Battle of Santiago makes Roosevelt the biggest national hero of the war.

  [2]

[1] Ivan Pavlov, after whom the Pavlovian Reaction is named.

[9] Empress Elizabeth, consort of Emperor Franz-Joseph. Obsessed by her figure, she used to be sewn into her riding habit when foxhunting in Britain.

[2] Teddy Roosevelt (right) with some of his Rough Riders in Cuba.

[7] U.S. troops line an embankment in a swamp in the Philippines near Manila.

[8] British forces inside Khartoum after the Battle of Omdurman.

June 11, 1898
The Guangxu emperor of China issues his first reform decree initiating the **Hundred Days of Reform**, an imperial attempt at renovating the Chinese state and social system.

June 12, 1898
The **Philippines**, under revolutionary leader Emilio Aguinaldo, declares its independence from Spain.

July 25, 1898
U.S. forces under General Nelson A. Miles invade **Puerto Rico** during the Spanish-American War.

 [7]

August 13, 1898
The U.S. Army takes control of the Philippine port of **Manila** during the Spanish-American War.

 [8]

September 2, 1898
Anglo-Egyptian forces under Sir Horatio Herbert Kitchener (later Lord Kitchener) defeat the Sudanese forces of the Mahdist leader 'Abd Allah in the **Battle of Omdurman**.

 [9]

September 10, 1898
Elizabeth, empress consort of Austria, dies in Geneva after being stabbed by Luigi Luccheni, an Italian anarchist.

1898
Trelawny of the "Wells," a play written for the Royal Court Theatre by English dramatist Arthur Wing Pinero, is produced. It portrays theatrical-company life of the 1860s, which is already a vanishing tradition.

 [3]

1898
The Union Carbide Company is founded by Chicago businessmen. It will later be absorbed by the Union Carbide and Carbon Corp., a major contributor to the development of the first atomic bomb.

January 13, 1898
French author Émile Zola publishes an open letter in the newspaper **L'Aurore**, beginning, "J'accuse." It denounces the French general staff for its role in the 1894 treason conviction of Jewish French army officer Alfred Dreyfus.

 [4]

February 15, 1898
An explosion in Havana harbor sinks the **battleship Maine**, killing 260 American seamen and precipitating the Spanish-American War.

 [5]

April 24, 1898
Spain declares war on the United States. Called the **Spanish-American War**, the conflict leads to the end of Spanish colonial rule in the Americas and to the U.S. acquisition of territories in the western Pacific and Latin America.

 [6]

May 1, 1898
The **Battle of Manila Bay** ends in the defeat of the Spanish Pacific fleet by the U.S. Navy, resulting in the fall of the Philippines and contributing to the final U.S. victory in the Spanish-American War.

[3] *The cast of* Trelawny of the "Wells." *The most famous actors here are Gerald Du Maurier, third from the left at the back, Irene Vanbrugh in a tiered skirt, and Dion Boucicault on the right in a dressing gown.*

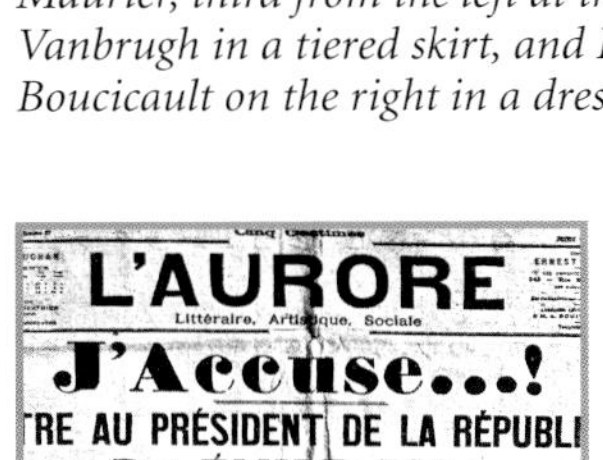

L'AURORE

Littéraire, Artistique, Sociale

J'Accuse...!

RE AU PRÉSIDENT DE LA RÉPUBLI

Par ÉMILE ZOLA

[4] *Zola's letter to President Faure of France. Two days before it is published, Major Esterhazy, who undoubtedly had been spying for the Germans and had incriminated Dreyfus, is tried and acquitted.*

[6] *U.S. Marines and Cuban insurgents (in straw hats) at Guantanamo Bay in Cuba. In the foreground is a Colt Model 1895 machine gun.*

[10] *Kitchener in a tarboosh, or fez, as sirdar or commander of the Egyptian army.*

[5] *A mast and some of the superstructure of the U.S. battleship Maine rises above the water in Havana harbor, Cuba.*

[11] *An advertisement for aspirin made by a French pharmaceutical company, from the magazine* La Vie Parisienne.

 [10]

September 18, 1898
British forces under Sir Horatio Herbert Kitchener confront French forces commanded by Jean-Baptiste Marchand at the disputed fort of **Fashoda** in the Egyptian Sudan.

October 12, 1898
A landmark in labor-union history, a coal-mine riot takes place in Virden, Illinois, when **strikebreakers** are brought in.

October 18, 1898
Puerto Rico is turned over to the United States near the end of the Spanish-American War.

December 10, 1898
Representatives of Spain and the United States sign the **Treaty of Paris**, concluding the Spanish-American War.

1899
A **cholera pandemic** begins. It will last until 1923 and will be especially lethal in India, in Arabia, and along the North African coast.

 [11]

1899
A German chemical and pharmaceutical company, which later adopts the name Bayer AG, develops **aspirin** and markets it as an effective analgesic.

1899

1899
A **hurricane** kills about 3,000 people in Puerto Rico.

1899
African-American composer **Scott Joplin** publishes his "Maple Leaf Rag," which quickly sells one million copies.

 [1]

1899
American economist and social scientist Thorstein Veblen publishes **The Theory of the Leisure Class**, in which he coins the phrase "conspicuous consumption."

 [2]

1899
American novelist **Frank Norris**, the first important naturalist writer in the United States, publishes the novel *McTeague*, the story of a brutal dentist who murders his miserly wife.

1899
American novelist **Kate Chopin** publishes *The Awakening*, a frankly feminist novella of a late-19th-century woman's emotional and sexual "awakening."

1899
American painter **Winslow Homer** reaches the apex of his career with *The Gulf Stream*, in which a man lies inert on the deck of a small shattered sailboat while sharks circle.

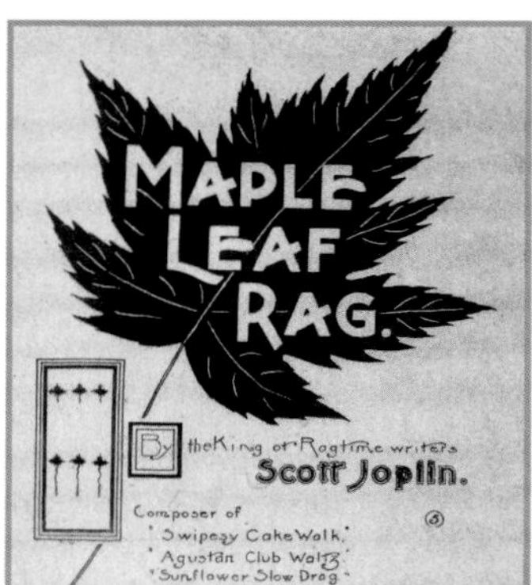

[1] The sheet music cover for the "Maple Leaf Rag" by Scott Joplin, "composer of Swipesey Cake Walk, Augustan Club Waltz, and Sunflower Slow Drag."

[2] Thorstein Veblen argues in his book that extremes of costume, such as the wasp-waist corset here, indicate detachment from any need to live modestly within one's means.

[7] Mt. Rainier viewed from the national park surrounding it.

[8] A big Fiat breaks down, circa 1905. While the chauffeur looks under the hood, the passengers, wearing goggles against the dust, sun themselves.

[6] French minister of war Mercier (left) with, next to him, Colonel Jouart, president of the military court retrying Dreyfus. Its carefully ambiguous verdict: "guilty, but with extenuating circumstances," is crafted to save the face of the army.

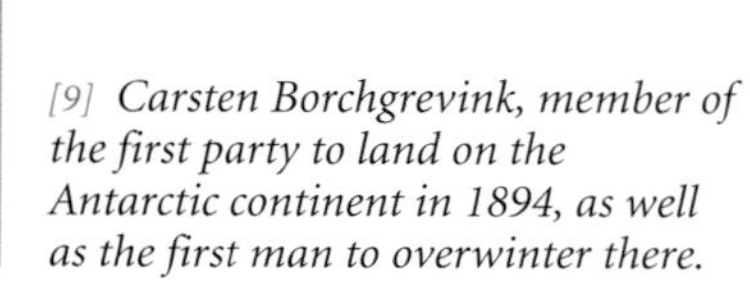

[9] Carsten Borchgrevink, member of the first party to land on the Antarctic continent in 1894, as well as the first man to overwinter there.

 [6]

1899
Jewish French army officer **Alfred Dreyfus** is found guilty by a new court martial but is pardoned by France's president.

1899
Louis Sullivan designs his late-career masterpiece, the Carson Pirie Scott Building, Chicago. Though the steel structural frame is clearly visible, Sullivan adds a masterful cast-iron ornament to the facade.

 [7]

1899
Mt. Rainier National Park is created in Washington state to preserve **Mt. Rainier**, a dormant volcano over 14,000 feet high, and the surrounding area.

1899
Nippon Electric Company is founded with funding from the Western Electric Company of the United States. It is the first Japanese joint venture with a foreign company.

1899
The company that will become **DuPont** is first incorporated. Eight years later it will become the target of a U.S. antitrust suit because of its near-monopoly of the American explosives industry.

1899
The **electric hand torch**, a battery-operated flashlight, is patented in the U.S. by Russian-born inventor Conrad Hubert.

1899
Edward Elgar's *Enigma Variations* receives its first performance, conducted by the Hungarian Hans Richter. It brings Elgar recognition as a leading composer, and it became his most frequently performed composition.

 [3]

1899
English author Rudyard Kipling publishes his poem "**The White Man's Burden**," exhorting the United States to take up its "burden" in colonizing the Philippines.

1899
For the first time, an Arab (Meletios Doumani) rather than a Greek is elected as **patriarch of Antioch** in the Orthodox Catholic Church.

1899
In **Bolivia** the Liberals seize power from the Conservatives in the so-called Federal Revolution.

1899
In Kansas, temperance crusader **Carry Nation** begins her campaign to close saloons; she attacks bars with her hatchet.

 [4]

1899
Jean Sibelius, the leading composer of Scandinavia, writes his tone poem **Finlandia**; his inspiration is the Scandinavian landscape.

 [5]

[3] Edward Elgar's Enigma Variations *are so called because they contain oblique musical allusions to the characters of a number of his friends.*

[5] Jean Sibelius, the embodiment of Finland's cultural identity, both before and after it gains independence from Russia.

[4] Carry Nation, Bible in one hand, hatchet in the other. Since Kansas is a prohibition state, she takes it on herself to smash up saloons there. She gets arrested, fined, imprisoned, shot at, and beaten up for her pains.

THE BIRTH OF RENAULT

What would become the largest automobile company in France

Louis Renault (shown at the wheel of the middle vehicle above) built his first automobile in 1898. Known as the Voiturette, it was a modified De Dion-Bouton cycle, which featured a revolutionary three-speed gearbox.

Renault then joined forces with his older brothers, Fernand and Marcel, to produce a series of small cars and formed the automobile firm Renault Frères ("Renault Brothers"). Renault vehicles attracted much attention by winning numerous road races until Marcel was killed during a Paris-Madrid run in 1903. The firm then withdrew from racing and concentrated on manufacturing road vehicles.

In 1905 Renault introduced the first of two best-selling models that were widely employed as taxicabs. These became famous during World War I (1914–18) when 600 Paris taxis were used to carry soldiers to the first Battle of the Marne. Renault also contributed to the war effort by producing shells, airplane engines, and in 1918 the Renault tank, which was often used as a troop-escort vehicle in the last months of World War I.

Louis Renault continued to increase the productive capacity of his Boulogne-Billancourt works, and after the war he extended his production to include farm equipment, marine and industrial machinery, and diesel motors. In World War II, the factories were brought under German control, and many were heavily damaged by Allied bombings. When Paris was liberated in 1944, the facilities that had not been destroyed were confiscated by the French government, which nationalized the firm.

1899
The first design for a **paper clip** is patented by Norwegian inventor Johan Vaaler. He patents his design in Germany.

1899
The French automobile manufacturer **Renault**, established by Louis Renault and his brothers, Marcel and Fernand, receives its first orders.

 [8]

1899
The Italian automobile manufacturer **Fiat** is founded by Giovanni Agnelli in Turin.

 [9]

1899
The Southern Cross expedition leaves Norwegian-born Australian explorer **Carsten Borchgrevink** at Cape Adare in Antarctica to spend the first winter on the Antarctic continent.

1899
The **United Fruit Company** is founded. It is the result of the merger of the Boston Fruit Company and other companies producing and marketing bananas grown in the Caribbean islands, Central America, and Colombia.

1899
The United States makes its first statement of the **Open Door policy**, aiming for the protection of equal privileges among countries trading with China and in support of Chinese territorial and administrative integrity.

1899

1899
The world's first **children's museum** is established in Brooklyn, New York.

1899
Twenty paper mills in the northeastern United States merge to become the **International Paper Company**.

1899
Viennese psychiatrist Sigmund Freud publishes **The Interpretation of Dreams**, a landmark in the history of psychoanalysis. In it he presents his theory of the Oedipus complex. His writings on child sexuality are among his most controversial.

 [1]

c. 1899
A three-piece **rubber golf ball** is invented by Coburn Haskell, a golfer from Cleveland, Ohio, and Bertram G. Work of the B.F. Goodrich Company. It will revolutionize the game of golf worldwide.

 [2]

c. 1899
The **fin de siècle** begins to draw to a close. The term describes the movement inaugurated by the Decadent poets of France and the Aestheticism of England. Sophistication and escapism are its hallmarks.

February 18, 1899
Émile Loubet is elected president of France. He will contribute both to the break between the French government and the Vatican (1905) and to improved relations with Great Britain.

[1] Sigmund Freud. He advances the idea that dreams are an unconscious representation of repressed desires, often sexual ones.

[3] British soldiers, wearing the new khaki uniforms and pith helmets to protect them from the sun, simulate a bayonet charge in South Africa for the benefit of a press photographer.

[2] French golfer Armaud Massy takes his driver to one of the new rubber golf balls.

[3] Two Boers, a schoolmaster and his pupil, are part of the force besieging Mafeking.

May 1899
George Horace Lorimer becomes editor of **The Saturday Evening Post**. He vastly expands its circulation, publishing Stephen Crane, Theodore Dreiser, and Willa Cather among others; he also hires artist Norman Rockwell.

May 18, 1899
The first **Hague Conference** convenes, seeking to limit armaments. Although it fails in its primary purpose, it does define the conditions of a state of belligerency and other customs relating to war.

June 9, 1899
James Jackson Jeffries knocks out Bob Fitzsimmons to become world heavyweight champion. In 1910 Jeffries, the "Great White Hope," will lose to Jack Johnson, the first black heavyweight champion.

 [3]

October 11, 1899
The **South African (Boer) War** begins between Great Britain and the two Boer (Afrikaner) republics—the South African Republic (Transvaal) and the Orange Free State.

A Nez Perce tribesman and his wife, c.1900.

1900

1900
Colonel Robert Baden-Powell withstands the besieging Boers at **Mafeking**.
[1]

1900
The Exposition Universalle is held in Paris.

1900
The Central Line, London's first **deep underground**, is opened.
 [2]

1900
First British **motor bus** is put into service. Horse buses are soon obsolete.

1900
A major **sleeping sickness** epidemic in east Africa breaks out. Colonial disruptions of land use practices have brought on devastating epidemics and famines in central and east Africa.

1900
American writer L. Frank Baum publishes **The Wizard of Oz**. The book will have many sequels and will be adapted for film. The annual showing of the well-loved film becomes an American TV broadcast tradition.

THE PARIS EXPOSITION

A century in retrospect

Held between April and November, 1900, on a four-part site along the banks of the River Seine, the Exposition Universelle was a review of the great achievements of the 19th century. The 83,000 main exhibits were divided into three main categories—technology, the arts, and education and science. Some 43 nations participated, and the show received more than 50 million visitors. Among the most popular attractions were the "stage sets," made of papier maché and plaster, that promoted industrial products from all over the world.

The most striking of the numerous structures erected for the Exposition was a huge celestial globe (left). Mounted on four stone pillars, it had an outer diameter of 520 feet (160 m). Inside it was another, smaller globe measuring 414 feet (127.5 m) across, and inside that was a library full of valuable and interesting books from the Bibliothèque Nationale de France.

[6] Beatrix Potter, acutely attuned to the animal world and never far removed from an animal, poses, age 15, with her spaniel.

[2] One of the electric locomotives that haul the trains on London's new Central Line. Its cab is arranged so that it can be driven in either direction.

[7] A dapper Puccini poses around 1900.

[1] Crowds celebrate the relief of Mafeking outside Baden-Powell's London home, decorated with his initials.

 [6]
1900
English author **Beatrix Potter** publishes the *Tale of Peter Rabbit*. Potter's charming and well-illustrated stories establish her as one of the most beloved children's writers of the 20th century.

 [7]
1900
Giacomo Puccini's opera **Tosca** premieres in Rome. His other compositions, including *La Bohème* (1896) and *Madama Butterfly* (1904), are among the greatest works in the history of opera.

 [8]
1900
German physicist Max Planck formulates **quantum theory**, sparking a revolution in modern physics continued by Albert Einstein and other physicists. He will be awarded the 1918 Nobel Prize for Physics.

1900
Enrico Caruso makes his La Scala debut in Milan with *La Bohème*. He becomes the most admired Italian operatic tenor of the early 20th century and one of the first musicians to document his voice on gramophone recordings.

1900
British protectorates are set up in **Nigeria**, West Africa.

1900
The Michelin Guide, the first guide to European restaurants, begins publication in Paris.

1900
Antoni Gaudí designs the Villa Bell Esguard, Barcelona. The highly idiosyncratic Gaudí designs buildings that feature sinuous, undulating lines borrowed from nature and complex textured surfaces.

1900
At the **Olympic Games in Paris**, American Ray C. Ewry takes the gold medal in all three standing jumps. Ewry enters eight Olympic jumping events and wins them all during his career.

 [3]

1900
Bubonic plague breaks out in Honolulu, Hawaii, and spreads to San Francisco, California, the first occurrence of the **plague in the United States**.

1900
Chicago authorities reverse the flow of the **Chicago River** through the construction of a canal, causing the waters to flow away from Lake Michigan inland to the Mississippi River. This is considered one of the greatest feats of modern engineering.

 [4]

1900
Yoshioka Yayoi founds **Japan's first medical school for women**.

1900
English archaeologist Arthur John Evans discovers the palace of **Knossos** on Crete.

[5]

[3] Ray C. Ewry doing a standing high jump at the Paris Olympics. He wins this event, as well as the standing long jump and standing triple jump. These events, which did not allow run-ups to jumps, have been long discontinued.

[4] A tugboat pulls a Great Lakes freighter on the Chicago River.

[5] A fresco in the Minoan palace of Knossos. Servants carry wine vessels to the table.

[8] Max Planck, the father of quantum physics.

[9] Some of Hector Guimard's art nouveau metalwork at the entrance to the Bastille Métro station in Paris.

[10] A Boxer rebel armed with nothing more than a split-cane shield and a blade on a pole.

 [9]

1900
Hector Guimard designs the Chatelet Métro Station, Paris. One of the three types of Métro station designed by Guimard, the small glass-and-iron pavilion is distinctive.

1900
Hills Brothers begins selling **vacuum-packed ground coffee**, which signals the end of local coffee-roasting stores throughout the United States until the 1980s.

 [10]

1900
A Chinese secret society called Righteous and Harmonious Fists (Boxers), begins a siege of foreign legations in Beijing. The **Boxer Rebellion** is supported by the Chinese government, hoping to drive out all foreigners

1900
The American League of Professional Baseball Clubs is organized; in 1901 it will become the **American League** (a major league) when it declines to renew a minor league agreement with the National League.

1900
The **British Labour Party** is formed.

1900
The Carnegie Institute of Technology (now **Carnegie Mellon University**) is founded in Pittsburgh, Pennsylvania, by American steel industrialist Andrew Carnegie.

1900
The first **Davis Cup** tennis competition is won by the American team.
 [1]

1900
The United States goes on the **gold standard** for its currency.

1900
The **Trans-Siberian Railway** begins operation between Moscow and Irkutsk, Russia.
 [2]

1900
An anarchist shoots at the **Prince of Wales** when he is on a visit to Belgium.

1900
The **Prairie style** of architecture begins to emerge. Centered in the U.S. Midwest, Prairie-style practitioners create low buildings, anchored to the ground with large chimneys, that appear to be extensions of the land.

1900
U.S. Army Major Walter Reed proves that **yellow fever** is transmitted by mosquitoes.

[1] Dwight Davis, founder of the Davis Cup (right), with Holcombe Ward at Wimbledon in 1901. They have just won the All-Comers' Doubles there.

[7] Field marshal Lord Roberts with members of his staff in South Africa. Once in command, he brings success to Britain's efforts in the Boer War after a series of defeats.

[6] Horses in every direction, as a policeman holds up the traffic outside the Mansion House in the City of London.

[2] The Trans-Siberian Railway, watched by Cossack soldiers as it crosses the steppe.

[3] A stretch of the New River, fed by the Colorado River, runs through the farmland it irrigates.

c. 1900
The first **little magazines**, avant-garde journals of fiction, poetry, and criticism often associated with specific movements, are published in France.

 [6]
c. 1900
Urban use of **horses** peaks. In London about a million tons of horse manure are removed from the city streets annually.

January 29, 1900
Russian revolutionary **Vladimir Lenin** ends three years of exile in Siberia. Following emigration, he begins editing *Iskra* (*The Spark*), a newspaper smuggled into Russia that advocates revolution.

April 30, 1900
Casey Jones, an American railroad engineer and folk hero made famous in song, dies in a train wreck.

 [7]
May 1900
The United Kingdom annexes the **Orange Free State** and the **Transvaal** (South African Republic) following successful battles in the Boer War (South African War).

May 21, 1900
Russia annexes **Manchuria**; growing competition with Japan in the region will lead to the Russo-Japanese War (1904–05).

1900
Water from the **Colorado River** begins to be diverted to California's Imperial Valley, which soon becomes America's major produce grower. [3]

1900
William Carney becomes the first African American to be awarded the Medal of Honor, for heroism in the Civil War.

1900
Women compete in the modern **Olympic Games**. British tennis player Charlotte Cooper wins the first women's gold medal at the Olympics. [4]

c. 1900
Escape artist **Harry Houdini** begins to earn an international reputation for his daring feats.

c. 1900
George Eastman introduces his **Brownie** camera, the first easy-to-use amateur instrument, and photography begins its rise as a popular art. [5]

c. 1900
Hydrogenated solid shortening is developed from cottonseed oil; it replaces liquid oils or animal fats in cooking.

HARRY HOUDINI

Hungarian immigrant wins fame as an escapologist.

Harry Houdini (real name Erik Weisz) earned an international reputation for his daring feats of extrication from shackles, ropes, and handcuffs and from various locked containers ranging from milk cans to coffins to prison cells. In a typical act (left) he was shackled with chains and placed in a box that was locked, roped, and weighted. The box was submerged from a boat, to which he returned after freeing himself underwater. In another outdoor exhibition he allowed himself to be suspended, head down, about 75 feet (23 m) above ground and then freed himself from a straitjacket. These demonstrations were typically watched by many thousands of people. Houdini's uncanny escape abilities depended partly on his great physical strength and agility and partly on his extraordinary skill at manipulating locks. He exhibited his skills in many motion pictures from 1916 to 1923.

[4] Charlotte Cooper. It is hard to believe she could play effectively in that collar.

[8] The first zeppelin on its maiden flight over Lake Constance. Count Zeppelin is at the controls.

[9] King Umberto I of Italy.

[10] Friedrich Nietzsche. Cheap derivatives of his ideas proliferate after 1918 among the Nazis and their like.

[5] The box Brownie camera, "not a toy," as the advertisement points out.

June 14, 1900
Hawaii is annexed by the United States with the status of territory, the resolution of a century of maneuvering for dominance there between France, Great Britain, and the United States.

June 14, 1900
The first international **automobile race** is held, running from Paris to Lyon, France.

 [8]

July 2, 1900
German aviation pioneer Ferdinand von **Zeppelin** launches the first rigid airship (or zeppelin).

 [9]

July 29, 1900
Italian king **Umberto** I is assassinated by anarchist Gaetano Bresci.

August 3, 1900
The **Firestone Tire & Rubber Company** is founded by industrialist Harvey Firestone.

 [10]

August 25, 1900
German Classical scholar, philosopher, and critic of culture **Friedrich Nietzsche** dies. His attempts to unmask the motives underlying Western morality and philosophy affect generations of thinkers and writers.

1900-1901

September 8, 1900
Galveston, Texas, is struck by a hurricane that kills 6,000 to 8,000 people, at the time the worst natural disaster recorded in North America.
[1]

October 17, 1900
Bernhard Bülow becomes Prussian prime minister and imperial chancellor of Germany (1900–09). He will pursue a policy of German aggrandizement.
[2]

November 10, 1900
The first **automobile show** in the United States opens at Madison Square Garden in New York City.

1901
American novelist **Frank Norris**—the first important naturalist writer in the United States—publishes his masterpiece, *The Octopus*, which examines the struggle of California wheat farmers against the powerful railroad monopoly.

1901
Austrian immunologist and pathologist Karl Landsteiner identifies type A, B, and O blood groups on the basis of the antigens on the surface of the red blood cells. **Blood typing** makes transfusion routine. Landsteiner will receive a Nobel Prize in 1930.
 [3]

1901
Based on the findings of U.S. Army pathologist and bacteriologist Walter Reed, whose experiments proved that yellow fever is transmitted by the bite of a mosquito, **insect controls** are instituted in Havana, ridding the area of the disease.

[1] *Galveston: a substantial church destroyed by the hurricane.*

[5] *George Eastman with one of his cameras on board a ship.*

[6] *The pioneer immunologist Emil von Behring, winner of the first Nobel Prize awarded for physiology and medicine.*

[2] *Prince Bernhard von Bülow. "Our place in the sun" is what he demands on behalf of all Germans.*

[3] *Karl Landsteiner*

[7] *Lionel Rothschild's early Mercedes, with a chain drive, a bulb horn, brass headlamps, and wicker basketry.*

1901
New York's Harlem neighborhood begins its rise to prominence following the start of construction of a **Lenox Avenue subway line**, which triggers a real estate boom.

1901
Scottish-born American industrialist Andrew Carnegie, one of the most important philanthropists of his era, gives $5.2 million to open the first branches of the **New York Public Library**.

 [5]
1901
The **Eastman Kodak Company** is incorporated as the successor to a business established in Rochester, New York, in 1880 by camera pioneer George Eastman.

 [6]
1901
The first **Nobel Prizes** are awarded, endowed by Swedish inventor and industrialist Alfred Bernhard Nobel, for achievements in the fields of physics, chemistry, physiology or medicine, literature, and peace.

 [7]
1901
The **Mercedes**, introduced by Gottlieb Daimler, is named for the daughter of Emil Jellinek, Austrian consul at Nice. The consul promises to buy and distribute an entire year's production of the car in return.

1901
The **Platt Amendment** is appended to a U.S. Army appropriations bill, stipulating the conditions for withdrawal of U.S. troops remaining in Cuba since the Spanish-American War.

1901
British inventor Hubert Cecil Booth creates the first successful **vacuum cleaner**. It is powered by a gasoline engine.

 [4]

1901
Edmund Barton, a member of the Protectionist Party, who has guided the Australian federation movement to a successful conclusion, becomes the first prime minister of the resulting commonwealth.

1901
In Australia the debut of **Federation wheat**, a new drought-resistant breed developed by agricultural researcher William Farrer, propels the wheat frontier onto Australia's interior plains.

1901
J. P. Morgan, Elbert H. Gary, Charles M. Schwab, and Andrew Carnegie found **U.S. Steel**, making it the world's first billion-dollar corporation. It constitutes, in its day, the most expensive act of consolidation in American history.

1901
King Camp Gillette raises $5,000 to start a safety-razor company. Gillette's innovative sales strategy—he sells the razors for a loss and makes his profits on the blades—will make the product a success.

1901
New York City streetcars and elevators are converted to **electric power**, but horsecars continue to travel up and down Fifth Avenue.

[4] An early vacuum cleaner, a great improvement on the first model since it is electrically powered.

[8] President Theodore Roosevelt, the picture of confidence as he sails over a fence at the Chevy Chase Club in Washington.

[10] A Texas oil gusher

[9] Booker T. Washington at his foundation, the Tuskegee Institute in Alabama, flanked by Andrew Carnegie (right) and the future President W. H. Taft.

[11] King Edward VII follows Queen Victoria's coffin down the entrance ramp to Paddington Station, where it will go by train for burial at Windsor. Behind him on the white horse is his nephew, the German emperor, William II.

 [8]

1901
Theodore Roosevelt of the Republican Party begins serving as the 26th president of the United States. He will hold office until 1909. His vice president is Charles Warren Fairbanks.

 [9]

1901
Up from Slavery, the autobiography of educator, reformer, and Tuskegee Institute president **Booker T. Washington**, is published.

January 1, 1901
The **Australian Commonwealth** is formed. It establishes a written constitution that outlines the duties of the federal government and the division of powers between it and the states.

 [10]

January 10, 1901
The first major oil field in Texas is discovered near Beaumont. The **Beaumont Field** reportedly contains more oil than all the other fields in the United States combined.

 [11]

January 22, 1901
Queen Victoria of Great Britain dies. By the end of her reign, the longest in English history, she has restored both the dignity and popularity of the British crown and has seen the monarchy take on its modern ceremonial character.

July 24, 1901
American short-story writer **O. Henry** (pseudonym of William Sydney Porter)—whose tales romanticize the commonplace and set a standard for the surprise ending—is released from prison after serving three years for embezzlement.

1901-1902

September 2, 1901
Vice President Theodore Roosevelt sets forth his approach to U.S. foreign policy: "**Speak softly and carry a big stick**," in a speech at the Minnesota State Fair.

September 6, 1901
Republican **William McKinley**, the 25th president of the United States (1897–1901), is shot by Leon Czolgosz, an anarchist, at the Pan-American Exposition in Buffalo, New York.

September 7, 1901
The **Peace of Beijing** ends the Boxer Rebellion. China is obligated to pay indemnities to the world powers suffering losses in the conflict.

September 9, 1901
French artist **Henri de Toulouse-Lautrec** dies. Called at the time "the soul of Montmartre," his lithography posters for its entertainments are the summit of that particular art form.

 [1]

September 14, 1901
U.S. president **William McKinley** dies eight days after being shot.

October 16, 1901
Booker T. Washington—educator, reformer, and president of the Tuskegee Institute—attends a White House dinner given by President Theodore Roosevelt. Outraged whites take reprisals against Southern blacks.

[1] Toulouse-Lautrec at the easel. Diminutive in size because of childhood injuries and addicted to absinthe, he excused his indulgence by saying at least he did not have far to fall when intoxicated.

[7] Joseph Conrad. A Pole by birth, he served some years in the British merchant marines, from which he retired in 1894.

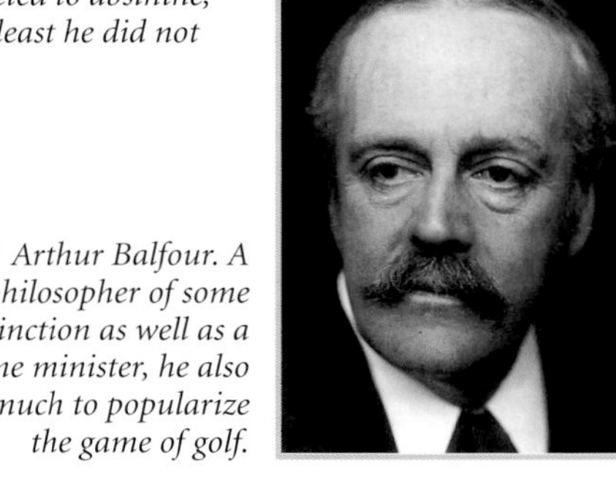

[6] Arthur Balfour. A philosopher of some distinction as well as a prime minister, he also does much to popularize the game of golf.

[2] Santos-Dumont's first attempt to win the Deutsch Prize. Shortly after this picture is taken, his airship crashes into the Trocadéro Restaurant. When he does win the prize, he gives most of the money away.

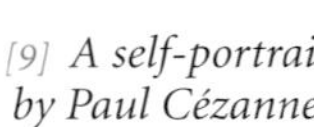

[8] The luxuriously equipped barber shop at the Algonquin Hotel.

[9] A self-portrait by Paul Cézanne.

 [6]

1902
Arthur James Balfour becomes Conservative British prime minister, but is best remembered for the Balfour Declaration he makes as foreign secretary in 1917, expressing official British approval of Zionism.

1902
Animal Crackers are introduced by the National Biscuit Company just before Christmas. The animal-shaped crackers are packaged in a box with a white string, allowing it to be hung on Christmas trees.

 [7]

1902
British author **Joseph Conrad** publishes his best-known story, "The Heart of Darkness." Conrad's works portray individuals faced with nature's indifference, man's malevolence, and their own inner battles with good and evil.

1902
Crayola **crayons** are introduced by Binney & Smith of Easton, Pennsylvania. Edwin Binney develops crayons by adding oil and pigments to the black paraffin and stearic acid marking devices sold by the firm.

1902
Ida Tarbell begins publishing *The History of the Standard Oil Company* in *McClure's Magazine*. Her exposé will contribute to the breakup of the company by Supreme Court order in 1911.

 [8]

1902
New York's **Algonquin Hotel** opens at 59 West 44th Street. It will become famous for the Algonquin Round Table, an informal group of writers known for their witty banter. They meet regularly at the hotel in the 1920s.

October 19, 1901
Brazilian aviation pioneer **Alberto Santos-Dumont** achieves one of the high points of his career by winning the 100,000-franc Deutsch Prize for a 7-mile (11.3-km) flight from the Paris suburb of Saint-Cloud to the Eiffel Tower and back in less than half an hour.

 [2]

October 29, 1901
Anarchist **Leon Czolgosz** is executed for the assassination of U.S. president William McKinley.

 [3]

December 12, 1901
Physicist and inventor Guglielmo Marconi receives the first **transatlantic wireless message** in Newfoundland. An English teacher in Cornwall, England, taps out the letter *S*, and Marconi picks it up across the ocean with a kite antenna.

1902
The White House becomes the official name of the U.S. president's residence in Washington, D.C. It was originally called the President's Palace but was renamed the Executive Mansion in 1810 to avoid connotations of royalty.

 [4]

1902
American inventor Willis Haviland Carrier develops the **air conditioner** to control indoor levels of temperature and humidity.

1902
American photographer **Alfred Stieglitz**, seeking to elevate photography's status as a medium for artistic expression, founds the Photo-Secession group.

 [5]

[3] *Leon Czolgosz, assassin of President McKinley, behind bars before his execution.*

[4] *The White House in the 1900s.*

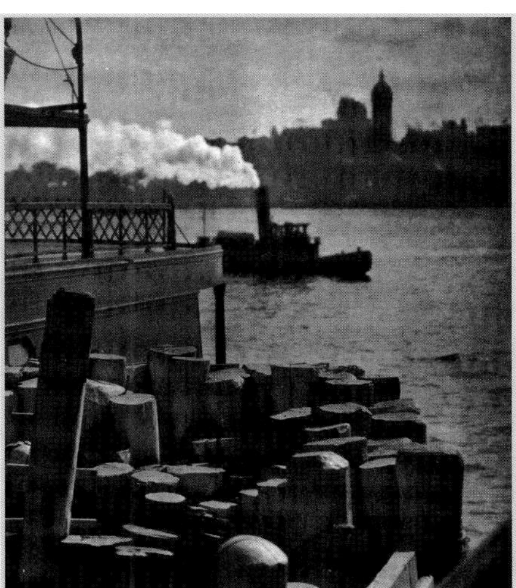

[5] *A memorable Stieglitz image of the East River and lower Manhattan.*

THE FLATIRON BUILDING

The unusually shaped New York skyscraper

Although officially named the Fuller Building, this office block (left) soon became known universally as the Flatiron Building because of its wedgelike shape, which was dictated by its location on a triangular island block at the intersection of 23rd Street, Fifth Avenue, and Broadway. (However, some historians claim that the area was already called the Flatiron District.)

At 285 feet (87 m), the Flatiron Building was never the tallest structure in Manhattan—the Park Row Building, completed in 1899, was 106 feet (32 m) higher—but it was the most distinctive. At its sharp end, it measures only 6.5 feet (2 m) across.

Designed by the architect Daniel Burnham, already well known for work on tall buildings in his native Chicago, this steel-framed terra-cotta and stone-clad skyscraper combined elements of French and Italian Renaissance architecture, which saved the sheer faces of the building from monotony.

The Flatiron Building was part of a bid to create a new business center north of Wall Street. Although that attempt was unsuccessful, the skyscraper fascinated photographers, and it was immortalized in the work of Edward Steichen and Alfred Steiglitz.

 [9]

1902
Paul Cézanne, nearing the end of his life, paints landscapes of the Provençal countryside that restructure the visible world, flatten space, and break objects into colored planes.

1902
Photographs are transmitted by telegraph for the first time by German inventor Arthur Korn.

1902
The **Carnegie Institution of Washington**, D.C., is founded with a $10 million gift from Andrew Carnegie; it concentrates on funding scientific research.

1902
The famous **Flatiron** Fuller Building in New York is completed near Madison Square by Chicago architect Daniel Burnham. The building's triangular shape inspires its nickname; it is one of the tallest buildings of its day.

1902
The first **Rose Bowl** football game is played in Pasadena, California, featuring the University of Michigan and Stanford University. The football game will become an annual event in 1916.

1902
The **Hawaiian Pineapple Company** is founded by James Drummond Dole, whose father is a first cousin of Hawaii's governor, Sanford Dole.

1902-1903

1902
The McCormick Harvesting Company joins with other companies to form the **International Harvester Company**, with Cyrus McCormick's son, Cyrus, Jr., as its first president.
 [1]

1902
The **Times Literary Supplement** is founded as a supplement to *The Sunday Times* of London. Known as the *TLS*, it will set the tone and standards for excellence in the field of literary criticism.

1902
The U.S. Congress passes the Spooner Act, named for its author, Senator John Spooner of Wisconsin, authorizing President Theodore Roosevelt to purchase the assets of a French company and the rights to build the **Panama Canal.**

1902
The U.S. Congress revises the **Chinese Exclusion Act of 1882** to prohibit immigration of Asians from U.S. island territories such as Hawaii and the Philippines and makes the exclusion permanent.

1902
The U.S.'s **Reclamation Act** establishes the bureaucracy (Bureau of Reclamation) that oversees federal dam building and irrigation in the West. Over 600 dams and reservoirs are built, including the Hoover and Grand Coulee dams.

1902
While on a hunting trip, U.S. president Theodore Roosevelt refuses to shoot a tethered bear; toymakers begin to market stuffed toy bears named for him—**teddy bears**.
 [2]

[1] *A McCormick reaper-binder harvesting wheat.*

[3] *Orville Wright flies a biplane glider at Kitty Hawk, North Carolina.*

[7] *A pile of rubble by St. Mark's in Venice, all that is left after the collapse of the campanile. It will be rebuilt.*

[8] *Orville Wright's first powered flight, covering 38.8 yards at 6.8 mph. The secret of the brothers' success is their concentration on control, which they achieve with wing warping, a forward elevator, and a rear rudder.*

[9] *Arnold Schoenberg.* Verklärte Nacht, *his earliest important work, looks back to the world of Brahms, Wagner, and Mahler, but also has hints of his music's atonal future.*

[2] *Theodore Roosevelt in hunting mode, with a Winchester rifle and fringed buckskins.*

 [7]
July 14, 1902
The **Campanile of St. Mark's** Basilica in Venice suddenly collapses, making a fortune for the photographer who captures the event. Work to rebuild it will be completed in 1912.

 [8]
1903
After several years' experimentation and careful study of the work of predecessors, American mechanics **Orville and Wilbur Wright** fly in a heavier-than-air vehicle at Kitty Hawk, North Carolina.

1903
Albert Peter Low commands *Neptune* on the first **Canadian Arctic exploring mission**, employing science to bolster Canadian claims to sovereignty.

1903
Alfred Deakin of the Protectionist Party, later noted for his nonwhite immigration, social welfare, and protection of domestic industry policies, is elected prime minister of Australia. He will later serve two more terms.

 [9]
1903
Arnold Schoenberg's sextet *Verklarte Nacht* has its first performance in Vienna.

1903
Auguste Perret designs an apartment block at 25 rue Franklin, Paris. Perret, a French pioneer in ferro-concrete construction, created the first apartment block designed to be built in concrete.

1902
Wilbur and Orville Wright design and build a successful **biplane glider**. The glider demonstrates that the Wright brothers have solved the key problems blocking the route to heavier-than-air flight.

 [3]

March 26, 1902
At his death, Cecil Rhodes—financier, statesman, empire builder of British South Africa—makes provision in his will to establish the **Rhodes Scholarships** at Oxford University.

 [4]

April 14, 1902
James Cash Penney opens the Golden Rule, a dry goods and clothing shop, in Kemmerer, Wyoming, the progenitor of the J.C. Penney retail chain of stores.

May 8, 1902
Mount Pelée on the island of Martinique erupts, killing approximately 30,000 people, 15 percent of the island's population. So dramatic is this event that this fiery kind of eruption is henceforth called the "pelean-type" eruption of ash and gas.

 [5]

May 31, 1902
The South African War, or **Boer War**, comes to a close with the signing of the Peace of Vereeniging.

 [6]

July 12, 1902
The Australian parliament agrees to **woman suffrage**. Aboriginals, however, continue to be denied citizenship rights under the constitution.

[4] Cecil Rhodes inspects the spot where he will be buried, in the Matopo Hills in Zimbabwe (formerly Southern Rhodesia).

[6] A group of Boer prisoners of war held by the British in India. The front three rows are mere boys.

[11] Louis Renault, founder of Renault Frères and participant in the Paris-Madrid race, arrives at Bordeaux only to be told of his brother's death in the race.

[5] Saint-Pierre in Martinique devastated by the eruption of Mount Pelée.

[10] A still from the film The Great Train Robbery.

[12] The Pittsburgh Pirates baseball team around 1900.

1903
Dutch physiologist Willem Einthoven invents the **electrocardiograph** to measure electrical impulses of the heart.

 [10]

1903
Edwin S. Porter's film **The Great Train Robbery** premieres and is a runaway success.

1903
Florida receives the title to the **Everglades** from the U.S. government.

 [11]

1903
French authorities stop the **Paris-to-Madrid auto race** at Bordeaux because of the large number of accidents.

1903
Henry Ford incorporates the **Ford Motor Company**. His application of assembly-line methods will revolutionize factory production throughout the industrialized world. He envisions the car as the ordinary man's utility rather than the rich man's luxury.

 [12]

1903
In baseball's first **World Series**, the Boston Red Sox of the American League beat the Pittsburgh Pirates of the National League.

1903

1903
Konstantin Tsiokolvsky's article "Exploration of Cosmic Space by Means of Reaction Devices" lays out many of the **principles of spaceflight.**

1903
Mary Anderson of the U.S. invents the **windshield wiper.**

1903
Michael Owens invents the fully automatic **bottle-making machine**, which revolutionizes the glass industry.

1903
Milton Hershey begins construction of a chocolate factory in Derry Church, Pennsylvania. The new town of Hershey will grow up around the factory.

 [1]

1903
New York Giants pitcher **Christy Mathewson** sets a record of 267 strikeouts in a season. This record will stand for nearly 50 years.

 [2]

1903
Norwegian **Roald Amundsen** sets out to navigate the Northwest Passage entirely by sea, on the small sloop *Gjöa.* This accomplishment inspires a lifetime of polar adventuring.

[2] Amundsen on the deck of the Gjoa. *It will not be until October 1905 that his voyage through the Northwest Passage is complete.*

[7] Maurice Garin, first winner of the Tour de France, nicknamed "the Chimney Sweep." Ironically, the race began as a publicity stunt for a magazine about automobiles.

[1] Pitcher Christy Mathewson

[9] Du Bois became, in 1895, the first African American to receive a Ph.D. from Harvard University.

[8] Staff at the Women's Trade Union League headquarters, New York, 1910.

[6] Lenin, leader of the Bolsheviks, about 1900.

 [6]

1903
The Russian Social Democratic Workers Party splits into two factions, the moderate **Mensheviks** and the extremist **Bolsheviks**, led by Vladimir Lenin.

 [7]

1903
The **Tour de France** is established by French cyclist and journalist Henri Desgrange. The three-week race is the world's most prestigious and most difficult bicycle race; it will be run every year except during the world wars.

1903
The **wire coat hanger** is invented by Albert J. Parkhouse in Jackson, Michigan.

 [8]

1903
The **Women's Trade Union League**, the first American national association dedicated to organizing women workers, is founded.

 [9]

1903
W. E. B. Du Bois publishes **The Souls of Black Folk**, which declares that "the problem of the Twentieth Century is the problem of the color-line," and discusses the dual identity of black Americans.

January 2, 1903
President Theodore Roosevelt closes the post office in Indianola, Mississippi, because of the town's refusal to accept the appointment of a **African American postmistress**.

1903
Russia reneges on its promise to Japan to evacuate **Manchuria**. This will lead to the Russo-Japanese war of 1904–05.

1903
Russian playwright Anton Chekhov writes his last play, **The Cherry Orchard**, which is first performed the following year in Moscow.

 [3]

1903
The era of **muckraking journalism** begins with an issue of *McClure's Magazine* that features articles on municipal government, labor, and trusts. The muckrakers expose political and economic corruption.

1903
The first **Harley-Davidson** motorcycle is sold.

 [4]

1903
The first Harmsworth Cup of **motorboat racing** is won by Englishman S. F. Edge.

1903
The **New York Stock Exchange** Building is completed.

 [5]

[4] *The first Harley-Davidson on show during its centenary year, 2003.*

[5] *The New York Stock Exchange, with a hansom cab in the foreground.*

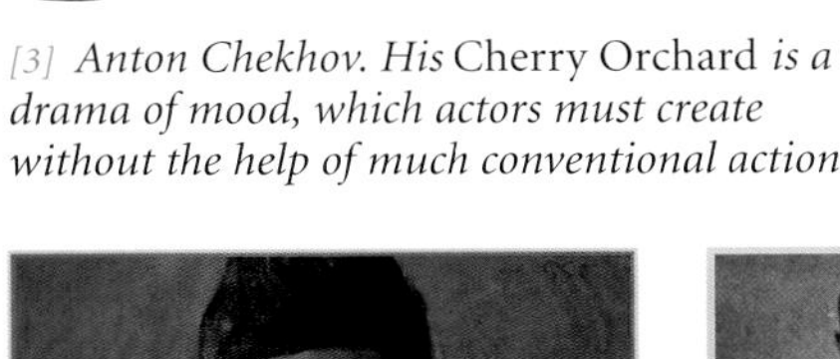

[3] *Anton Chekhov. His* Cherry Orchard *is a drama of mood, which actors must create without the help of much conventional action.*

[10] *Paul Gauguin. His life in the Pacific becomes something of a template for those who believe authenticity, sincerity, and the truth are best found close to nature, to the primitive and the tribal.*

[11] *King Alexander is the last of the Obrenovic line to rule. His mistakes are to suspend the constitution and to be suspected of making his unpopular wife's brother his heir.*

[12] *Barney Oldfield's early feats behind the wheel do much to make both him and Henry Ford household names.*

February 14, 1903
The U.S. **Department of Commerce and Labor** is created.

April 1903
A **pogrom in Kishenev, Russia**, kills 49 Jews, sparking worldwide outcry.

 [10]

May 8, 1903
French painter **Paul Gauguin**, who sought to achieve a "primitive" expression of spiritual and emotional states in his work and who was noted for his artistic experimentation, dies in the Marquesas Islands.

May 23, 1903
Horatio Nelson Jackson and Sewall Crocker leave San Francisco in a 1903 Winton automobile for New York. They arrive on July 26, having become **the first to cross the U.S. by car**.

 [11]

June 10, 1903
Serbian king Alexander I, his wife, Draga, and members of his court are assassinated in a coup d'état.

 [12]

June 15, 1903
American automobile-racing driver Barney Oldfield accomplishes the first **mile-a-minute** performance in a car at Indianapolis, Indiana.

July 4, 1903
President Theodore Roosevelt sends the first message over the **Pacific Cable**, which connects San Francisco with Honolulu and then Manila.

September 1903
Massachusetts issues the first **license plates**.

October 1903
British suffragists Emmeline and Christabel Pankhurst found the **Women's Social and Political Union** to fight for woman suffrage.

 [1]

October 13, 1903
Victor Herbert's operetta **Babes in Toyland** premieres in New York.

November 1, 1903
German historian **Theodor Mommsen**, famous for his masterpiece *The History of Rome,* dies near Berlin.

November 3, 1903
Influenced by Philippe-Jean Bunau-Varilla and U.S. interests, a revolutionary junta proclaims **Panamanian independence** from Colombia.

PANAMA CANAL

Work begins on an artificial waterway across Central America to link the Atlantic and Pacific oceans.

The idea was not a new one. As early as the 16th century, the Spanish—eager to build a shortcut to the west coast of America that avoided Cape Horn—had investigated the feasibility of a canal across the Central American isthmus, but they decided that the climate and the terrain made the project impractical. In 1881 a French company began constructing a canal, but the enterprise collapsed in 1889. Under a 1903 treaty, Panama granted the U.S. the Panama Canal Zone and the rights to build and operate a canal.

Work began in 1904. Where tropical diseases—yellow fever and malaria in particular—had decimated the ranks of French workers, those in charge of the American effort were determined to prevent the same thing from happening again. American medical staff understood how the diseases were transmitted and how they could be controlled, and by 1906 the canal zone was safe for work to resume in earnest.

At times more than 40,000 people were employed on the project. Most were laborers from the West Indian islands of Barbados, Martinique, and Guadeloupe—the photograph (left below) shows some of the 1,500 Barbadians brought in on a single trip aboard the SS *Ancon.* There were also many engineers, administrators, and skilled tradesmen from the United States. Railroads and heavy machinery were critical elements. Most notable was the use of more than 100 steam shovels, many of which were used to dig the Culebra Cut, later called Gaillard Cut after David du Bose Gaillard, the American engineer who supervised its construction until his death in 1913. The unstable nature of the soil and rock in the area of the cut made it one of the most difficult and challenging sections of the entire canal project. Workers, who labored in temperatures of 38°C (100°F) or higher, used rock drills, dynamite, and steam shovels to remove as much as 73 million cubic meters (96 million cubic yards) of earth and rock as they lowered the floor of the excavation to within 12 meters (40 feet) of sea level. Hillsides were subject to unpredictable earth and mud slides, and at times the floor of the excavation was known to rise precipitously simply due to the weight of the hillsides. The well-known Cucaracha slide of 1907 continued for years and poured millions of cubic meters of earth into the canal excavation. The photograph (left above) shows the construction of the Gatún locks, two parallel sets of locks, each consisting of three flights, which raise Pacific-bound ships a total of 84 feet (26 m) to Gatún Lake.

The Panama Canal—51 miles (81 km) long—was opened to traffic on August 15, 1914. It was undoubtedly the greatest engineering feat yet achieved by mankind.

1904
Architect **Albert Kahn** receives his first commission—the new Packard Motor Car factory in Detroit. He will go on to revolutionize factory design and become the father of modern industrial architecture.

 [6]

1904
An ice cream vendor devises the **ice cream cone** at the World's Fair in St. Louis, Missouri.

 [7]

1904
British counsular official **Roger Casement** reveals atrocious cruelty in the exploitation of native labor by white traders in the Congo. These revelations will lead to a major reorganization of Belgian rule there.

1904
Chris Watson is elected the first Labor prime minister of Australia.

1904
Construction begins on the **Panama Canal**.

1904
Cy Young pitches the first perfect game in major league baseball history by not allowing a single opposing player to reach base. Young goes on to win a record 511 games in his career.

November 13, 1903
French painter **Camille Pissarro**, a key figure in the Impressionist movement, dies in Paris.
[2]

November 23, 1903
Italian tenor **Enrico Caruso** makes his New York debut in Verdi's *Rigoletto*.
[3]

December 8, 1903
English sociologist and philosopher **Herbert Spencer**, an early advocate of the theory of evolution and of the preeminence of the individual over society and of science over religion, dies in Brighton.
 [4]

December 19, 1903
The **Williamsburg Bridge** in New York opens and is the first suspension bridge with steel towers.
[5]

December 30, 1903
A fire in **Chicago's Iroquois Theater** kills 602 people.

1904
Blackbirding, the practice of enslaving (often by force and deception) South Pacific islanders on the cotton and sugar plantations of Queensland, Australia, is put to a stop.

[2] Pissarro has always been at the core of Impressionism, admired by and giving back support and inspiration to Renoir, Monet, Degas, and Cézanne.

[3] Nine years into his career, Caruso starts his association with New York's Metropolitan Opera. In 1904 he will start pioneering recorded music.

[6] Young London boys, eating ice cream cones, circa 1905.

[5] The Williamsburg Bridge, across the East River, under construction.

[4] Despite having grown increasingly conservative with age, Herbert Spencer maintains his opposition to imperialism to the end.

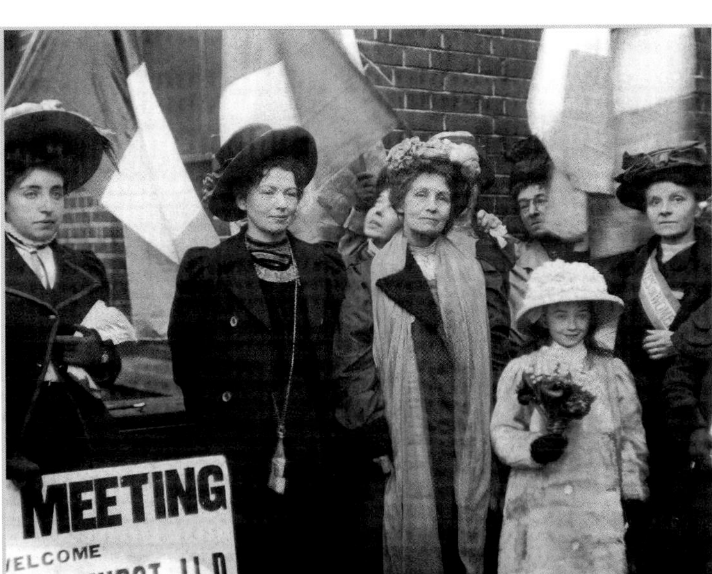

[1] Emmeline Pankhurst and her daughter, Christabel, outside Bow Street Court after their release from their cells in 1908. The lack of interest shown by the British press in women's rights soon forces the WSPU to go militant and use violence in its struggle for the vote.

[7] Roger Casement, from an Ulster Protestant family, will be knighted for his Congo exposé. He will transfer his concern for the exploited back to Ireland in due course.

1904
Dutch physicist Hendrik Lorentz develops the **Lorentz transformations**, a set of equations that are crucial for the theory of relativity.

1904
English chemist Frederic Stanley Kipping pioneers the chemistry of silicones, which are organic derivatives of silicon. **Silicones** find nearly universal applications as synthetic rubber, water repellents, hydraulic fluids, and greases.

1904
English engineer John Fleming, the first professor of electrical engineering in Britain, invents the **vacuum diode**, a key component in radio technology.

1904
Frank Lloyd Wright's **Larkin Building** in Buffalo, New York, is one of his most remarkable, with filtered, conditioned, mechanical ventilation; metal desks, chairs, and files; soundproofing and balanced light.

1904
German physicist Ludwig Prandtl's discovery of the boundary layer leads to an understanding of skin friction drag and of the way **streamlining** reduces the drag of airplane wings and other moving bodies.

1904
Italian immigrant Amadeo Giannini founds the **Bank of Italy** in San Francisco. This bank will later become Bank of America.

1904

1904
Lincoln Steffens's ***The Shame of the Cities***, an investigation of urban political corruption in America, is published.

 [1]

1904
Pneumatic tires appear on automobiles. Tire chains for snowy weather also become available.

 [2]

1904
New York cook Mary Mallon, better known as **Typhoid Mary**, is incarcerated by public health officials when an epidemic of typhoid fever is traced to the homes in which she worked.

1904
McKim, Mead, and White design **Pennsylvania Railway Station**, New York City. Modeled on classical Roman baths, this station is a remarkable gateway to the city and an exemplar of American Neoclassical style.

 [3]

1904
President Theodore Roosevelt introduces the **Roosevelt Corollary to the Monroe Doctrine**, which states that, in cases of flagrant wrongdoing by a Latin American nation, the U.S. can intervene in the internal affairs of that nation.

1904
The Fédération Internationale de Football Association (**FIFA**) is organized as the global governing body of amateur football (soccer).

[1] *Lincoln Steffens. This muckraking journalist calls his autobiography* The Nutcracker.

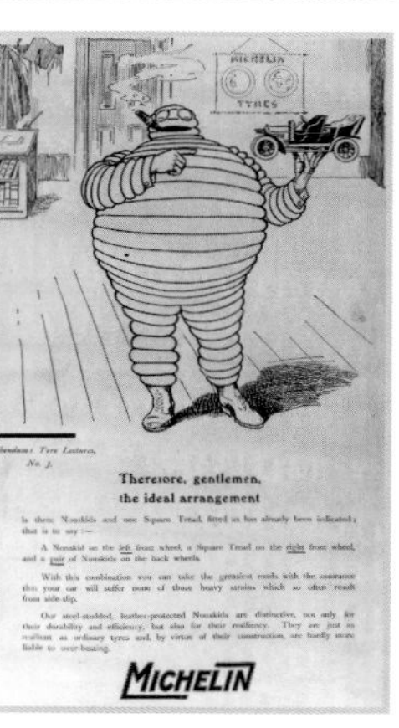

[2] *An advertisement for pneumatic rubber tires featuring the famous Michelin Man. He is promoting the firm's nonskid and square tread tires.*

[4] *Hans Richter in the robes of an honorary doctor of music.*

[3] *Pennsylvania Station. Unforgivably, it will be demolished in the 1960s and its great columns dumped in a New Jersey swamp.*

[5] *Nina Boucicault, the first Peter Pan. She is the daughter of Dion Boucicault (see 1898).*

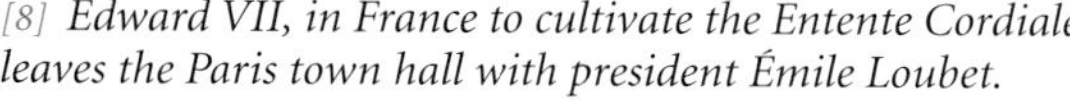

[8] *Edward VII, in France to cultivate the Entente Cordiale, leaves the Paris town hall with president Émile Loubet.*

1904
The **Trans-Siberian Railroad**, stretching from Moscow 5,778 miles east to Vladivostok and beyond, opens up a major resource frontier and encourages timber, mining, and other extractive industries in Siberia.

1904
The world's first **geothermal electricity generation plant** opens in Lardarello, Italy, in Tuscany. Today, steam from wells drilled to depths of hundreds of meters drives the plant's turbine generators.

1904
The young **Pablo Picasso** paints his elegiac *Woman Ironing*, which reveals the depth and distinctive vision of his Blue Period.

1904
Tony Garnier designs his **Cité Industrielle**. Garnier's plan for an entire city, including housing, factories, and offices, was never fully realized but shows the possibilities of modern city planning.

January 1904
The **Union of Liberation**, the first major liberal political group in Russia, is founded in St. Petersburg.

February 1, 1904
Iceland gains home rule from Denmark.

1904
The first race for the Gold Cup, the premier annual **motorboat-racing** prize in the U.S., is held on the Hudson River. C. C. Riotte's *Standard* wins with a heat of 23.6 miles per hour.

1904
The first Vanderbilt Cup **automobile race** is run. Races are an important means of advertising the still-new form of transportation and encourage technological innovation in auto design.

1904
The **London Symphony Orchestra** gives its first concert, conducted by Hans Richter, the first principal conductor, at the Queen's Hall. It is Britain's first independent, self-governing orchestra.

 [4]

1904
The Netherlands wins the **Achinese War**, a long guerilla conflict against the sultanate of Acheh in Sumatra.

1904
The play **Peter Pan**, *the Boy Who Wouldn't Grow Up*, is produced in London. Dramatist James Barrie adds a new character to the mythology of the English-speaking world.

 [5]

1904
The summer **Olympic Games** take place in St. Louis, Missouri, at the same time as the **St. Louis World's Fair**.

 [6]

RUSSO–JAPANESE WAR

Conflict over territorial expansion in East Asia

After Russia leased the strategically important Port Arthur (now Lüshun, China) and expanded into Manchuria (northeastern China), it faced the increasing power of Japan. When Russia reneged on its agreement with Japan to withdraw troops from Manchuria, the Japanese fleet destroyed the Russia naval squadron (left) at Port Arthur, without war having been declared first, and began a siege of the city in February 1904. Japanese land forces cut off the Russian army coming to aid Port Arthur and pushed it back to Mukden (now Shenyang). The reinforced Russian army took the offensive in October, but poor military leadership blunted its effectiveness. In January 1905 the corrupt Russian commander of Port Arthur surrendered the garrison without consulting his officers, despite having adequate stores and ammunition. Heavy fighting around Mukden ended in March 1905 with the withdrawal of Russian troops under Aleksey Kuropatkin. A decisive naval defeat at the Battle of Tsushima brought Russia to the peace table. With the signing of the Treaty of Portsmouth, Russia abandoned its expansionist policy in eastern Asia, and Japan gained effective control of Korea and much of Manchuria.

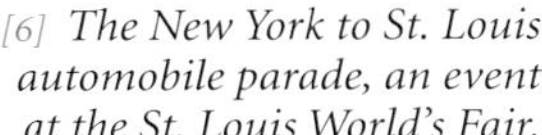
[6] *The New York to St. Louis automobile parade, an event at the St. Louis World's Fair.*

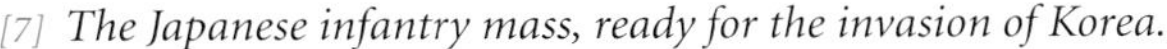
[7] *The Japanese infantry mass, ready for the invasion of Korea.*

February 7, 1904
A fire razes most of **Baltimore's** business district.

February 8, 1904
The **Russo-Japanese War** begins when the main Japanese fleet launches a surprise attack and siege on the Russian naval squadron at Port Arthur in Manchuria.

February 14, 1904
Giacomo Puccini's opera **Madama Butterfly** premieres at La Scala in Milan.

 [7]

March 1904
Japan invades **Korea**.

 [8]

April 8, 1904
The **Entente Cordiale** between England and France paves the way for their diplomatic cooperation against German pressures in the decade preceding World War I.

April 19, 1904
Much of **Toronto's** downtown burns down.

1904-1905

May 1, 1904
Bohemian composer **Antonin Dvorak**, noted for turning folk material into the language of 19th-century Romantic music, dies in Prague.

 [1]

May 26, 1904
Japanese forces cut off the **Port Arthur** garrison from the main body of Russian forces in Manchuria.

June 15, 1904
Over 1,000 people die when the boat **General Slocum** catches fire on a Hudson River excursion.

 [2]

July 14, 1904
Paul Kruger, noted in South African history as the builder of the Afrikaner nation, dies in Switzerland.

July 21, 1904
In Belgium, French driver Louis Rigolly breaks the 100-miles-per-hour barrier with a new speed record of **104 miles per hour**.

August 2, 1904
British forces enter **Lhasa**, the capital of Tibet.

 [3]

[1] *Dvorak's two most famous works, his cello concerto and his ninth, "New World," symphony were composed while he was in New York as director of the National Conservatory of Music.*

[2] *The* General Slocum *burns on the East River.*

[3] *The Younghusband expedition advances into Tibet. Unfounded fear of Russian influence at Lhasa is the excuse for this invasion from British India.*

[8] *Edith Wharton, chronicler of the lives and workings of the New York upper class.*

[6] *A classic Steichen photograph of Paris racegoers.*

[7] *Percival Lowell. One of his abiding interests is in the "canals" on Mars. Pluto will be discovered fourteen years after his death in 1916.*

[9] *George Reid. His time as prime minister is short because the tide of opinion has turned against free trade.*

1905
Alfred Binet and Theodore Simon begin to develop their highly influential scales for the **measurement of intelligence in children**.

 [6]

1905
Alfred Stieglitz opens the Little Galleries of the **Photo-Secession** (later named 291 after its address) to exhibit such photographers as Edward Steichen.

 [7]

1905
American astronomer **Percival Lowell**, with the staff of his observatory, begins a systematic search for a planet beyond Neptune.

 [8]

1905
American novelist, poet, and essayist **Edith Wharton** completes one of her earliest and most enduring novels, *The House of Mirth.*

1905
Decaffeinated coffee is developed under the direction of German coffee merchant Ludwig Roselius, who began experimenting with coffee beans that had been saturated with seawater during transport.

1905
Eighteen players die of injuries during the **college football** season. President Theodore Roosevelt summons representatives from Harvard, Yale, and Princeton to the White House, where he urges them to reform the game.

1900-1909

August 25, 1904
Japan defeats Russia at the battle of Liaoyang. Russian army falls back to **Mukden**.

October 18, 1904
Gustav Mahler's *Symphony No. 5* premieres in Cologne.
[4]

October 27, 1904
The **New York subway** system opens.

November 17, 1904
George M. Cohan's *Little Johnny Jones* opens in New York; songs include "Give My Regards to Broadway" and "Yankee Doodle Boy."

November 30, 1904
The first four cyclists in the second **Tour de France** are disqualified for various infractions, including riding in a car.
 [5]

1905
The last **yellow fever** epidemic in the United States kills more than 450 people in New Orleans. A U.S. Public Health Service anti-mosquito campaign ends the epidemic.

[4] *Mahler's fifth symphony is regarded as the first of his second period, when his work becomes more severe. He writes it while director of the Vienna Opera.*

[11] *Albert Einstein. His papers, written while working in the Swiss Patent Office, are on the nature of light, on Brownian motion (supporting the atomic theory), on the equivalence of matter and energy, and lastly the special theory, reconciling mechanics with electromagnetism.*

[12] *Sun Yat-Sen. He became celebrated in 1896 when he was kidnapped by the staff of the Chinese legation in London but luckily was rescued before he could be spirited away to China and certain death.*

[5] *Henri Cortot, one of the participants in the notorious 1904 Tour de France. Fans threw nails in front of unpopular riders.*

[10] *Claude Debussy. He is the bridge between the later Romantics and the modernist composers. He completed* La Mer *when staying in the unromantic English seaside resort of Eastbourne.*

NEW YORK SUBWAY OPENS

The first line on an urban railway system that becomes the largest of its kind in the world

The first subway in New York City was opened to the public on October 27, 1904, by Democratic mayor George B. McClellan, who was at the controls of the inaugural train. The line was operated by the Interborough Rapid Transit (IRT) Company. It had been formally dedicated the previous year in a ceremony attended by McClellan's predecessor, Seth Low (with long-handled hammer in photograph at left).

The first trains ran between City Hall and 145th Street, but the line was soon extended to the Bronx. The earliest parts of the system were built by the "cut-and-cover" method, in which streets were dug up, tracks laid, and a tunnel built around them, before the road surface was leveled once more. As the network developed, however, more demanding construction methods were required. The tunnels through the bedrock under Harlem and beneath the East River, for example, could be excavated only by powerful drilling machines.

 [9]
1905
George Reid, after directing an economic recovery program, maintaining free trade, and introducing a tax to break up land monopolies as premier of New South Wales, is elected prime minister of Australia.

 [10]
1905
French composer **Claude Debussy**, a seminal force in the music of the 20th century, writes perhaps his best-known work, *La Mer* ("The Sea"), an evocation of the many moods of the waters.

 [11]
1905
In German physicist **Albert Einstein's** "annus mirabilis," he publishes four papers that announce, among other findings, the special theory of relativity.

1905
German surgeon Heinrich Braun introduces **novocaine** for use in dentistry.

 [12]
1905
In Tokyo, **Sun Yat-sen** founds the United League, a revolutionary coalition dedicated to political change in China.

1905
Interviewed in *Plunkitt of Tammany Hall*, New York state senator **George Washington Plunkitt** sums up machine politics by making the distinction between "honest" and "dishonest graft."

1905

1905
Josef Hoffmann designs the **Palais Stoclet** (Stoclet House), Brussels. The massive, elegant house, designed in conjunction with the Wiener Werkstätte, is one of Hoffmann's finest works.
 [1]

1905
Max Weber finishes **The Protestant Ethic and the Spirit of Capitalism**, which holds that the Protestant ethic was an important factor in the early stages of European capitalism.

1905
Norwegians pioneer the exploitation of **whales** in Antarctic waters, the world's richest whaling grounds, bringing most species to the edge of extinction within decades.

1905
Sir Henry Campbell-Bannerman accepts the post of prime minister of Great Britain from King Edward VII. Throughout his term, his popularity unifies his own Liberal Party and the unusually strong cabinet he leads.

1905
The **Chinese system of competitive examinations**, which used knowledge of Confucian texts as a basis for recruiting officials, is abolished.

1905
The **Cullinan Diamond**, the largest gem diamond ever (3,106 carats), is discovered in South Africa.
 [2]

[1] *The Palais Stoclet, although located in Brussels, is really a prime example of the Vienna Secession movement's work.*

[6] *Ty Cobb slides into third base.*

[2] *The colossal Cullinan Diamond in its rough, uncut state.*

[5] *Fifth Avenue from the St Regis. Alvin Langdon Coburn uses the effect of fog to achieve a magical photo-cityscape.*

[7] *The entrance to the Simplon Tunnel with the locomotive pulling the Orient Express about to enter it, circa 1905.*

[9] Joe and Myra Keaton with their son, Buster, a family vaudeville act around 1905. Buster has a handle sewn into the back of his jacket so his parents can slide him across the stage into the audience, who then throw him back.

[8] *Sheet music cover for Irving Berlin's "Alexander's Ragtime Band."*

 [5]
1905
The word "**smog**," an amalgam of "smoke" and "fog," is coined in England. It achieves wide currency only with the photochemical smogs of motorized cities after 1950.

 [6]
1905
Ty Cobb, one of the greatest offensive players in baseball history, begins his professional career with the Detroit Tigers. He will hold long-standing records of 4,191 hits, 2,244 runs scored, and 3,033 games played.

1905
U.S. biologists Nettie Stevens and Edmund Beecher Wilson independently discover that the **X and Y chromosomes** are responsible for the determination of the sex of an individual.

1905
Variety, the newspaper covering all aspects of show business, is founded.

 [7]
1905
The **Simplon Tunnel**, one of the world's longest railroad tunnels, opens, connecting Iselle, Italy, and Brig, Switzerland.

 [8]
c. 1905
Propulsively syncopated **ragtime** is the predominant style of American popular music.

1905
The first **pizzeria** in the United States opens in New York City; pizza, of Neapolitan origin, soon becomes an international favorite.

1905
The German art movement **Die Brücke** ("The Bridge") is founded. It will play a pivotal role in the development of Expressionism.

1905
The **National Audubon Society**, a U.S. organization dedicated to conserving and restoring natural ecosystems, is founded.

1905
The **Nickelodeon** movie theatre opens in Pittsburgh, Pennsylvania, and its name becomes the generic term for the thousands of new movie theaters that will open across the United States.

1905
The **U.S. Forest Service** is established.

1905
The U.S. Supreme Court rules that a state labor law limiting the **number of hours in the work week** violates due process because the "right of contract between the employer and employees" is protected under the Fourteenth Amendment.

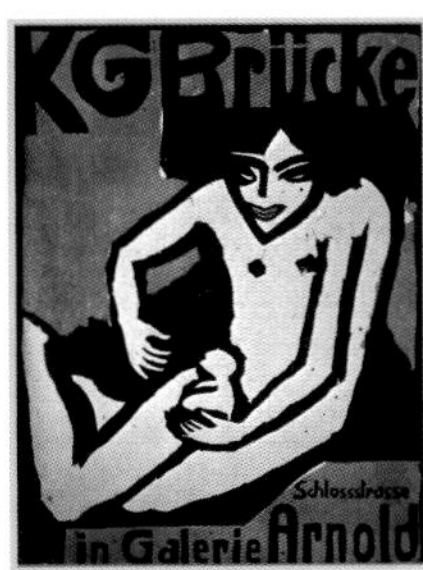

[3] A poster, designed by Ludwig Kirchner, for an exhibition of paintings by members of Die Brücke movement.

[4] A nickelodeon movie theater, entrance five cents (a nickel). The barkers, whose job is to entice in the public, line up outside.

[11] Russian forces prepare to pull out from the burning town of Mukden.

[10] A Japanese battery fires on Port Arthur.

[12] Mata Hari in seductive mode.

c. 1905
Vaudeville is a popular form of light entertainment, consisting of 10 to 15 individual unrelated acts, featuring magicians, acrobats, comedians, trained animals, jugglers, singers, and dancers.

January 2, 1905
The Russians surrender **Port Arthur** (now Lüshun, China) to the Japanese in the Russo-Japanese War.

January 22, 1905
On what was later known as **Bloody Sunday**, Russian workers marching in St. Petersburg are fired on by Russian troops.

February 23, 1905
The first **Rotary Club** is founded by Chicago attorney Paul P. Harris.

March 1905
Japanese forces defeat the Russian army at **Mukden**.

March 13, 1905
Margaretha Geertruida MacLeod begins to dance professionally in Paris. She takes the stage name **Mata Hari**.

1905-1906

March 17, 1905
Eleanor Roosevelt, niece of President Theodore Roosevelt, marries her distant cousin Franklin D. Roosevelt, later U.S. president.

May 5, 1905
The **Chicago Defender**, the most influential African American newspaper during the early and mid-20th century, is founded.

May 13, 1905
Hiram Cronk, the last surviving **veteran of the War of 1812**, dies at the age of 105.

May 29, 1905
The Russian navy is defeated in the **Battle of Tsushima** during the Russo-Japanese War.

 [1]

June 1905
Sailors aboard the Russian **battleship Potemkin** revolt.

 [2]

June 1905
The labor union **Industrial Workers of the World** (IWW, or "Wobblies") is founded in Chicago.

[1] The Russian fleet is annihilated by the Japanese at Tsushima.

[2] Afanasy Matuchenko, in a white shirt, leader of the mutiny aboard the battleship Potemkin.

[5] A much dramatized depiction of a strikers' meeting being raided by the Russian police. Pistols are drawn and incriminating documents burned.

[6] Tsar Nicholas and Tsarina Alexandra in magnificent traditional Russian finery.

[8] Emmy Destinn, the Czech soprano and a famous Salome.

[7] Haakon VII, the king of newly independent Norway, with his wife, Maud, daughter of Edward VII of Britain.

 [5]

October 1905
Most large Russian cities experience a **general strike**.

October 26, 1905
Sweden recognizes Norway's independence.

October 26, 1905
The **St. Petersburg Soviet** (workers' council) is formed during the 1905 Russian Revolution.

 [6]

October 30, 1905
Tsar Nicholas II issues the **October Manifesto**, bringing the end of unlimited autocracy in Russia and ushering in an era of constitutional monarchy.

November 1905
Korea becomes a protectorate of Japan.

 [7]

November 18, 1905
Prince Charles (Carl) of Denmark is elected king of Norway as **Haakon VII**.

June 7, 1905
Norway declares its independence from Sweden.

June 23, 1905
The **Wright brothers' third powered airplane** is the final step in their quest for a practical airplane that can stay aloft for extended periods of time under the complete control of the pilot.

July 11–14, 1905
The **Niagara Movement**, an organization of black intellectuals led by W. E. B. Du Bois and calling for full political, civil, and social rights for black Americans, is founded in Niagara Falls, Ontario.

Autumn 1905
The first public exhibition of paintings by **Les Fauves** ("wild beasts"), who used pure, brilliant color to create a sense of an explosion on the canvas, is held. Les Fauves included Henri Matisse and André Derain.

 [3]

September 1, 1905
Alberta and **Saskatchewan** become the eighth and ninth provinces of Canada.

September 5, 1905
A **peace treaty between Russia and Japan** is signed in Portsmouth, New Hampshire. President Theodore Roosevelt will win the Nobel Prize for Peace in 1906 for mediating the treaty.

 [4]

WRIGHT BROTHERS

U.S. inventors who achieved the first powered, sustained, and controlled airplane flight

Wilbur and Orville Wright first worked in printing-machinery design and later in bicycle manufacturing, which financed their early experiments in airplane design. To test flight control, essential to successful powered flight, they built and flew three biplane gliders (1900–02). Propeller and engine innovations led to their first powered airplane, which Orville flew successfully for 12 seconds and Wilbur later flew for 59 seconds at Kill Devil Hills, North Carolina (near the village of Kitty Hawk), on December 17, 1903.

By October 1905 the brothers could remain aloft for up to 39 minutes at a time, performing circles and other maneuvers. Then, no longer able to hide the extent of their success from the press and concerned that the essential features of their machine would be understood and copied by knowledgeable observers, the Wrights decided to cease flying and remain on the ground until their invention was protected by patents and they had negotiated a contract for its sale.

They established an aircraft company and produced the first planes for the U.S. Army, the Wright Type B (above). Later they demonstrated their planes in Europe and the U.S.; in 1908 Wilbur gave over 100 exhibition flights in France, setting an airborne duration record of 2 hours and 20 minutes.

[3] A view of the Thames Embankment looking towards Charing Cross railway bridge by Les Fauve painter André Derain.

[9] Lily Elsie, who created the role of the Merry Widow on the London stage.

[11] Emma Goldman in later years, about to be deported to Russia in 1919 after a two-year sentence for conspiring against the draft.

[4] President Roosevelt with Russian and Japanese delegates at the peace talks.

[10] Alfred Dreyfus, readmitted to the French army after his official exoneration, and promoted to the rank of major.

 [8]

December 9, 1905
Richard Strauss's opera **Salome** premieres in Dresden.

 [9]

December 28, 1905
Franz Lehár's operetta **The Merry Widow** premieres in Vienna. Lehár created a new style of Viennese operetta, introducing waltz tunes and imitations of the Parisian can-can dances as well as a certain satirical element.

December 30, 1905
Former Idaho governor **Frank Steunenberg** is killed by a bomb outside his home. Three leaders of the Western Federation of Miners labor union will be accused of the crime and acquitted.

 [10]

1906
Alfred Dreyfus is officially exonerated by a military commission.

 [11]

1906
Anarchist **Emma Goldman** begins publishing *Mother Earth* magazine. She will regularly be imprisoned in the U.S. for inciting to riot and distributing birth-control literature.

1906
As Japan's power in **Korea** increases, the Korean emperor sends a secret emissary to the international peace conference at the Hague to urge the great powers to intercede with Japan on behalf of Korea, to no avail.

1906-1907

1906
Bela Bartók and **Zoltán Kodály** publish their first volume of *Hungarian Folk Songs*, sparking a new interest in the ethnomusicology of Central Europe.

 [1]

1906
British biochemist F. G. Hopkins demonstrates the importance of certain amino acids (later called **vitamins**) to nutrition.

1906
Canadian-American engineer Reginald Fessenden broadcasts the **first radio program featuring voice and music**.

1906
Frank Lloyd Wright designs the **Unity Temple**, **Oak Park, Illinois**. One of his most successful designs, the church displays a masterful use of concrete and a simple but powerful arrangement of space.

1906
German medical researchers August von Wassermann, Albert Neisser, and Carl Bruck develop the serum test for **syphilis**, one of the first major applications of immunology to medical diagnosis.

 [2]

1906
German neuropathologist **Alois Alzheimer** describes physical abnormalities in the brain of a patient with severe dementia, establishing a physiological basis of such illnesses (Alzheimer's disease).

[1] A hatless young Bela Bartok listens to Hungarian folk music on an early gramophone.

[8] The Kiss by Gustav Klimt. He is much influenced by Byzantine mosaics and their use of gold.

[3] J. Stuart Blackton (right) in late years with his pioneering color camera.

1900-1909

[5] Gandhi, the young lawyer-activist, in South Africa.

[2] August von Wassermann

[6] Annette Kellerman in a one-piece bathing suit at the start of an attempt to swim the English Channel.

[7] Rainier Maria Rilke. He lives in Paris in the 1900s, working for a time as secretary to the sculptor Auguste Rodin and falling under the spell of Cezanne.

[4] The Romanian Trajan Vuia's monoplane, the first in the world. The best it achieves is a hop, rather than a certifiable flight.

April 18, 1906
A massive earthquake strikes **San Francisco**, followed by fires that burn for four days, destroying four square miles and 25,000 buildings worth about $350 million. About 3,000 die.

April 23, 1906
Russian tsar Nicholas II promulgates the **Fundamental Laws**, which mark the end of unlimited autocracy but fall short of the reforms promised in the October Manifesto.

 [5]

September 1906
At a mass protest meeting at Johannesburg, Indians led by **Mohandas Gandhi** pledge to oppose the racist policies of the South African government through satyagraha ("devotion to truth"), or nonviolent resistance.

September 29, 1906
The United States occupies **Cuba** after the rebellion surrounding the reelection of Tomás Estrada Palma.

 [6]

1907
Australian swimmer Annette Kellerman introduces the **one-piece bathing suit** at a beach near Boston, Massachusetts, but is arrested in the process for indecent exposure.

 [7]

1907
Austrian-Hungarian lyric poet **Rainer Maria Rilke** begins publishing the fruits of his new style of lyric poetry, Ding-Gedicht ("object poem"), in his collection *Neue Gedichte* (*New Poems*).

1906
Hollywood film director J. Stuart Blackton develops **motion-picture animation**.

 [3]

1906
Luther Haws of Berkeley, California, invents the **drinking fountain**.

1906
The **Intercollegiate Athletic Association** is formed and draws up competition rules for football and other intercollegiate sports. Later it becomes the National Collegiate Athletic Association (NCAA).

1906
Upton Sinclair's novel **The Jungle** reveals in stomach-turning detail the insanitary conditions of the Chicago stockyards and meat-packing plants. The Meat Inspection Act is passed the same year, as is the Pure Food and Drug Act.

February 18, 1906
Armand Fallières is elected president of France.

March 18, 1906
The **first monoplane**, constructed by the Romanian inventor Trajan Vuia, makes a flight of 12 meters (40 feet).

 [4]

SAN FRANCISCO EARTHQUAKE

A seismic tremor lasting less than a minute causes the worst natural disaster in U.S. history.

San Francisco lies on the San Andreas Fault, a fracture of the earth's crust that extends for more than 800 miles (1,300 km) from the northern end of the Gulf of California through western California, passing seaward into the Pacific Ocean near the city. Tectonic movement along the fault has long been associated with occasional large earthquakes originating near the surface along its path.

The biggest quake of all in the region occurred on April 18, 1906, at about 5:12 AM, when the San Andreas Fault slipped along a segment about 270 miles (430 km) long, extending from San Juan Bautista in San Benito County to Humboldt County, and from there perhaps out under the sea to an unknown distance. The shaking was felt from Los Angeles in the south to Coos Bay, Oregon, in the north and as far inland as western Nevada. According to modern estimates, the earthquake registered at least 7.5 and perhaps as high as 8.25 on the Richter scale.

The damage was most severe in San Francisco. The photographs shown here give some sense of the quake's destructive power: a crack in a road has partly swallowed a cart (left above) and a wooden building teeters on the point of collapse (left below). Many other towns in California were also hit; they included San Jose, Salinas, and Santa Rosa, 19 miles (30 km) from the line of the fault. The epicenter is now believed to have been beneath the bed of the Pacific Ocean, a little way beyond the Golden Gate.

In central San Francisco the seismic shocks caused the outbreak of a series of small fires—some caused by burning oil lamps that were upset in the quake, some by leaks from fractured gas pipes, and others by uncontrolled campfires lit by those rendered homeless in their makeshift open-air encampments.

The city's firefighters tried their best, but they were unable to cope in the surrounding chaos; to make matters worse, many of the underground water pipes to their hydrants had been breached. Some of their attempts to bring the fire under control—notably their decision to dynamite quake-damaged buildings in an effort to create firebreaks—actually accelerated the spread of the flames. The fires took hold quickly and soon amalgamated into a great conflagration that destroyed 490 city blocks, a total of 25,000 buildings; the fire made over 250,000 homeless and killed between 450 and 700. The total damage was estimated at between $350,000,000 and $400,000,000.

Despite the destruction, the city recovered quickly, and by 1915, it had been almost completely rebuilt. Subsequent geologic studies of the San Francisco disaster led to the detailed formation of the theory that the shaking associated with earthquakes is caused by the elastic rebound of strained faults.

1907
Chemist Eugène Schueller establishes the **L'Oréal perfume company** in France, which will grow into one of the world's largest manufacturers of hair products and cosmetics.

1907
Chicago movie projectionist Donald H. Bell and camera repairman Albert S. Howell establish the **Bell & Howell Company**, a future leader in high-quality equipment for the production and projection of motion pictures.

1907
German animal trainer Carl Hagenbeck opens a **zoo in Hamburg**, Germany, with barless, moated display areas that mimic natural habitats.

1907
Gulf Oil is incorporated. The company's refinery in Port Arthur, Texas, will eventually process oil not only from fields in Texas, Oklahoma, and Louisiana but also from fields in Mexico and Venezuela.

 [8]

1907
Gustav Klimt, leader of Vienna Secession, maximizes the decorative possibilities of fin de siècle sexuality in his elaborate, decadent work *The Kiss*, completed in 1908.

1907
Gustav Mahler completes his monumental *Symphony No. 8 in E Flat Major* for eight soloists, double choir, and orchestra, known as the *Symphony of a Thousand* owing to the large number of performers it requires.

1907

1907
Hermann Muthesius and Henry van de Velde found the **Deutscher Werkbund**. Devoted to applying crafts standards to mass-produced goods, the group has a strong influence on 20th-century architecture.

1907
Maria Montessori opens her Casa dei Bambini (Children's House) in a slum district of Rome. The **Montessori school movement** stresses individual student interests and self-directed learning.

 [1]

1907
Mothercraft is introduced, in New Zealand. The list of 12 essentials: air and sunshine, water, food, clothing, bathing, muscular exercise and sensory stimulation, warmth, regularity, cleanliness, mothering, management, and rest and sleep.

 [2]

1907
Royal Dutch/Shell Group is formed through a merger of Royal Dutch Petroleum of the Hague with Shell Transport and Trading Company of London to become one of the world's largest corporate entities.

 [3]

1907
Swiss psychologist and psychiatrist **Carl Gustav Jung** meets psychoanalyst Sigmund Freud, with whom he will collaborate for some years. Jung eventually comes to dispute Freud's insistence on the sexual bases of neurosis.

 [4]

1907
The **Bloomsbury Group**, a circle of British artists, writers, and critics whose members include Clive and Vanessa Bell, Virginia Woolf, E. M. Forster, Lytton Strachey, and John Maynard Keynes, is formed.

 [5]

[1] *Three young children in sunhats at a Montessori school. "Spontaneous self-development" of the child lies at the center of Montessori's methods.*

[4] *Carl Jung. He draws on dreams, mythology, art, and the religions of the world in his work and sounds a warning against an over-reliance on the rational and scientific.*

[9] *Some girls from the chorus line of the Ziegfeld Follies, about 1915.*

[3] *An advertisement for Shell "motor spirit"—gasoline, or petrol.*

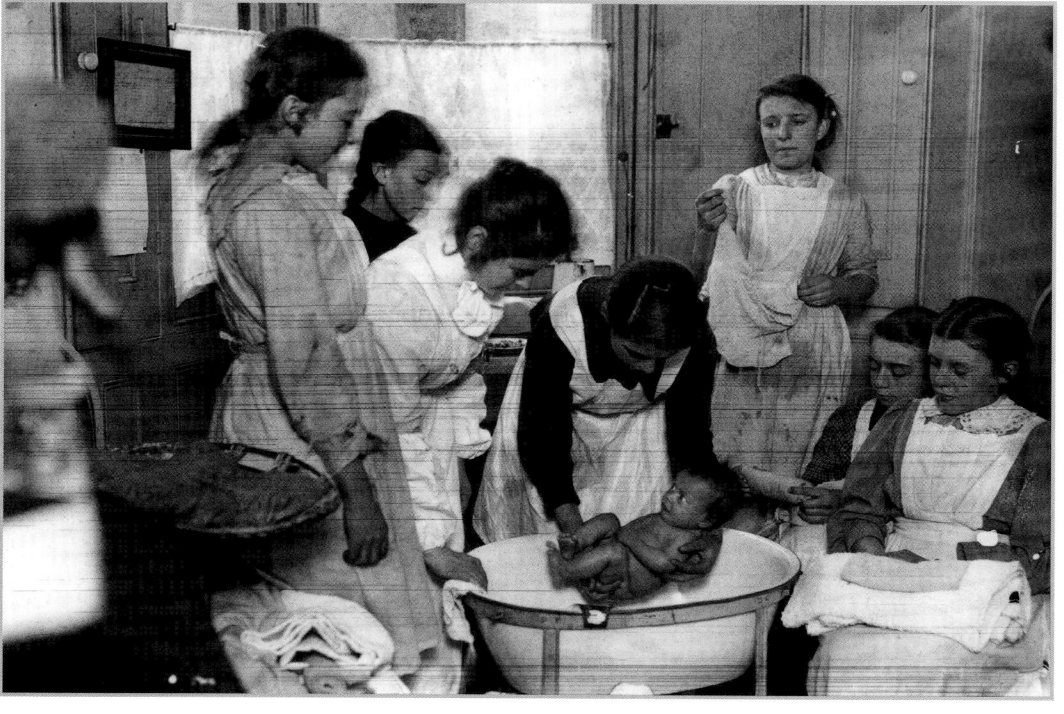

[2] *How to bathe a baby: a Mothercraft lesson at a day nursery in Acton, London.*

[5] *Three key members of the Bloomsbury Group: the biographer and essayist Lytton Strachey, the sisters Vanessa Bell (left) and Virginia Woolf (née Stephen).*

1907
Zoologist Ross Granville Harrison cultivates tadpole tissue, finding that nerve fibers with protoplasmic activity grow from it. This is the foundation of nerve physiology and neurology, and **tissue cultivation** will have many applications.

c. 1907
The death toll from bubonic plague in **India** rises to more than one million.

January 1907
Austria introduces universal, secret, direct suffrage for men.

January 1, 1907
Agrarian reforms in **Russia** end the communal system of landholding, allowing farmers to leave a commune and receive parcels of land, which they will own and operate themselves.

June 10, 1907
The **Franco-Japanese Entente** is signed, providing an "open door" to China for both France and Japan, while guaranteeing protection for those parts of China where Japan has a special interest.

 [9]

July 18, 1907
In New York City **Florenz Ziegfeld** stages *The Follies of 1907*, a revue combining seminudity, pageantry, and comedy. This style of revue will be repeated for 23 more years until the advent of the Great Depression.

1907
The British ship **Lusitania**, the largest ocean liner of the time, makes her maiden voyage. Eight years later the ship will be sunk by a German submarine, contributing indirectly to the entry of the United States into World War I.
 [6]

1907
The first commercially successful **outboard motor** is produced by Norwegian-American inventor Ole Evinrude. Subsequent outboard motors follow his transmission design, which uses a vertical drive shaft with bevel gears (a set of two wheel-like gears).

1907
The Ringling brothers purchase the Barnum & Bailey Circus, making the new **Ringling Bros. and Barnum & Bailey Circus** "the Greatest Show on Earth" and the largest circus in the United States.
 [7]

1907
The **Tourist Trophy motorcycle races** are run for the first time, on the Isle of Man, just off the northwestern coast of England.
 [8]

1907
The **United Press** (UP) is established in direct competition with the Associated Press (AP) and the International News Service (INS).

1907
Women are permitted to stand for election in **Norway**.

[6] *The ill-fated* Lusitania.

[8] *The start of an Isle of Man Tourist Trophy (TT) race in 1911.*

[10] *The Washington National Cathedral.*

[7] *A poster for the combined Ringling Brothers and Barnum & Bailey shows.*

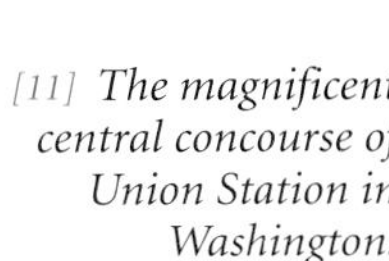
[11] *The magnificent central concourse of Union Station in Washington.*

July 18, 1907
The French occupy **Casablanca**, which will later be made a French protectorate (1912–56) and emerge as the chief port of Morocco.

July 19, 1907
Kojong, **Korea's last ruling king**, in the face of Japanese occupation abdicates the throne after a 43-year reign.

September 10, 1907
The first **Nieman-Marcus** department store, catering to the tastes of the affluent, opens in Dallas, Texas.

 [10]
September 29, 1907
The cornerstone is laid for the **Washington National Cathedral** in Washington, D.C., an English Gothic-style structure designed by English architect George F. Bodley and his American student Henry Vaughan.

October 21, 1907
Franz Lehár's operetta **The Merry Widow** opens in New York City.

 [11]
October 27, 1907
Union Station opens in Washington, D.C. It was designed in the Beaux-Arts style by Chicago architect Daniel Burnham.

1907-1909

November 16, 1907
Oklahoma is admitted to the United States as the 46th state.

1908
Cass Gilbert begins work on the **Woolworth Building**, New York City. Cloaked in a Gothic skin, this skyscraper is nicknamed the "Cathedral of Commerce."

1908
American expatriate poet **Ezra Pound**, often called the "poet's poet" because of his marked influence on 20th-century literature, publishes his first collection, *A lume spento*, in Venice.
 [1]

1908
A two-day **race riot** breaks out in Springfield, Illinois. Almost the entire Illinois state militia is required to quell the frenzy of the white mob, which shoots innocent people, burns homes, loots stores, and mutilates and lynches two elderly blacks.

1908
Charles and Henry Greene design the **Gamble House, Pasadena**. An example of California bungalow style, the Gamble House features natural materials and a design that mixes indoor and outdoor space.

1908
Ford proclaims the birth of the **Model T Ford**. In the 19 years of the Model T's existence, Ford will sell 15,500,000 of the cars in the United States, almost 1,000,000 more in Canada, and 250,000 in Great Britain, amounting to half the world's auto output.
 [2]

[7] Robert Baden-Powell surrounded by boy scouts at a camp, probably shortly after World War I.

[2] A Model T Ford, the "Tin Lizzie," with a top speed of 45 mph. Electric starting only comes in 1919.

[1] Ezra Pound. After his first volume comes out, Pound moves to London and is soon in close association with the poet W. B. Yeats.

[6] The Kiss *by Constantin Brancusi.*

[8] A famous Olympic moment, when the Italian marathon runner Dorando Pietri, on the verge of collapse though leading the field, is helped across the finishing line in London. This is enough to get him disqualified and lose the title.

 [6]
1908
Romanian sculptor **Constantin Brancusi** executes his first truly original work, *The Kiss*, in which the vertical figures of two entwined adolescents form a closed volume with symmetrical lines.

 [7]
1908
The **Boy Scouts** are founded in Great Britain by Lieutenant General Robert Baden-Powell. The movement eventually spreads around the world.

1908
The **drip method of coffee brewing** is developed by Melitta Bentz, who used her children's blotting paper to filter the coffee grounds.

1908
The **Fédération Internationale de Natation Amateur** (FINA) is founded in London to regulate swimming competitions; it is now based in Lausanne, Switzerland.

 [8]
1908
The summer **Olympic Games** take place in London.

 **1908**
U.S. attorney general Charles J. Bonaparte fills the country's need for a federal investigative body by establishing the Bureau of Investigation within the Department of Justice. It will become the **FBI**.

1908
Frank Lloyd Wright designs the **Robie House, Chicago**. The epitome of Wright's Prairie style, this long, low house, built of Roman brick, seems to rise out of the earth.

 [3]

1908
French writer and moralist André Gide cofounds **La Nouvelle Revue Française**, one of the most important literary magazines in pre-World War II France.

1908
Great Britain enacts social-welfare legislation, including the first unemployment insurance.

1908
Jack Johnson defeats Canadian Tommy Burns to become the first African American man to win the world heavyweight boxing championship.

 [4]

1908
Leo Baekeland invents **Bakelite**, the first major thermosetting plastic. The new plastic soon displaces celluloid for nearly all the latter's applications. Plastics relieve pressure on forests, but plastic debris proves to be a durable variety of pollution.

1908
Liberal politician H. H. **Asquith** becomes prime minister of Britain. He is responsible for the Parliament Act of 1911, which limits the power of the House of Lords, and he will lead Britain at the start of World War I.

 [5]

[3] Frank Lloyd Wright's Robie House.

[10] The funeral cortege of Empress Dowager Cixi.

[11] Rows and rows of Kewpie dolls at a fairground in the 1930s.

[4] Jack Johnson works out in the gym.

[9] People stop and stare as Henri Farman flies 16 miles from Chalons to Reims in France.

[5] H. H. Asquith comes to the prime-ministership because of the death of Sir Henry Campbell-Bannerman, the previous Liberal prime minister.

June 30, 1908
An **enormous aerial explosion**, presumably caused by a comet fragment colliding with the earth, flattens approximately 2,000 square km (500,000 acres) of pine forest in central Siberia.

 [9]

October 31, 1908
Henri Farman pilots his Voisin box-kite plane on Europe's first **cross-country flight**, a 16-mile journey.

 [10]

November 15, 1908
Empress dowager Cixi of China dies, and her nephew, the Guangxu emperor, is announced as having died the previous day. Cixi's final decree passes the throne to the emperor's three-year-old nephew.

November 30, 1908
The United States and Japan sign the **Root-Takahira Agreement**, which averts a drift toward possible war through the mutual acknowledgment of certain international policies and spheres of influence in the Pacific.

1909
A group of whites merges with W. E. B. Du Bois's Niagara Movement, forming the **National Association for the Advancement of Colored People (NAACP)**.

 [11]

1909
American illustrator, writer, and businesswoman Rose Cecil O'Neill introduces the **Kewpie doll** in a full-page spread in *Ladies' Home Journal*. The dolls will become a rage in the first part of the 20th century.

1909

1909
American industrialist and philanthropist John D. Rockefeller establishes the Rockefeller Sanitary Commission for the **Eradication of Hookworm Disease**.

1909
American physicist Robert Andrews Millikan's oil-drop experiment yields the first accurate value of **the charge of the electron**. He wins the Nobel Prize for Physics for his work in 1923.

1909
American sociologist-turned-photographer **Lewis Hine** documents the exploitation of child labor in American factories, mills, and other industries in his photo stories "Child Labor in the Carolinas" and "Day Laborers Before Their Time."

1909
American zoologist and geneticist Thomas Hunt Morgan advances a **theory of the gene** based on his study of fruit flies, breaking new ground in research of heredity.

1909
Arnold Schoenberg begins one of the great experiments in modern music when he composes his **first atonal works**, the piano piece *Opus 11, No. 1* and *Five Orchestral Pieces, Opus 16*.

1909
British merchant and yachtsman **Thomas Lipton** begins blending and packaging his tea in New York City.

 [1]

CHILD LABOR

Photographer highlights plight of poor children.

The National Child Labor Committee was formed in 1904 in an attempt to persuade the U.S. Congress to regulate the working conditions of the young. A 1907 report found that there were over two million children under the age of 16 in paid employment in the United States. According to committee activist Jane Addams, that explained why there were "580,000 children between the ages of 10 and 14 years who cannot read or write."

In 1908 the National Child Labor Committee employed Lewis Hine as staff investigator and photographer. Hine traveled the country taking pictures, such as that shown (left) of children working in factories. Hine also lectured on the subject, on one occasion telling an audience: "Perhaps you are weary of child labor pictures. Well, so are the rest of us, but we propose to make you and the whole country so sick and tired of the whole business that when the time for action comes, child labor pictures will be records of the past."

[4] *Selma Lagerlöf. Her children's book,* The Wonderful Adventures of Nils, *is much translated.*

[5] *An 84-year-old from Minsk in Russia, working on a kibbutz in Palestine in 1913, after saving for ten years to finance the trip.*

[6] *The crowd in London's Oxford Street on the day that Selfridge's opens.*

[1] *Sir Thomas Lipton, in white trousers, entertaining Thomas Alva Edison, center left, in a bowler hat, on board one of his yachts.*

1909
Safety glass is patented in France by artist and chemist Édouard Bénédictus. His design uses a sheet of celluloid bonded between two pieces of glass.

 [4]

1909
Selma Lagerlöf is the first woman and also the first Swedish writer to win the Nobel Prize for Literature.

1909
The **Boston Museum of Fine Arts** opens at its new (and present) location on the Fenway in Boston, Massachusetts.

 [5]

1909
The first **kibbutz** is founded at Deganya in Palestine. Others will be created in subsequent years, and by the early 21st century there would be more than 250 kibbutzim in Israel, with a population of over 100,000.

 [6]

1909
Selfridge's department store opens on Oxford Street in London.

1909
The Imperial Cricket Conference is formed by England, South Africa, and Australia. **Cricket** is one of the enduring legacies of the British Empire and is played in Africa, India, and the Caribbean.

1909
Industrial designer **Peter Behrens** begins work on the AEG turbine factory, Berlin. With its powerful massing and curtain glass wall, it is one of the great monuments of modern architecture.

1909
Italian poet Filippo Marinetti publishes his **Futurist Manifesto**. It inspires a circle of Italian writers, artists, and architects with the power of engineering and technology. Futurism becomes an important movement in the arts and literature in Russia as well.

1909
Labor Party member **Andrew Fisher**, who will sponsor important legislation in the fields of social welfare, economic development, labor relations, and defense, is elected to his first term as prime minister of Australia. He will serve until 1915.

1909
On his third attempt to reach the North Pole, **Robert Peary** and his African American associate **Matthew Henson** reach their goal only to return to news that Frederick Cook, later discredited, claims to have preceded them.

 *[2]*

1909
On the *Nimrod* expedition, **Ernest Shackleton** leads a sledging party to within 97 miles of the South Pole and claims Victoria Land Plateau for Britain. Another party from the expedition reaches the magnetic pole.

 *[3]*

1909
Prospector Benny Hollinger discovers a **major gold deposit near Ontario**, which will trigger a gold rush and lead Canada to become the world's third largest gold producer.

[2] Matthew Henson holding a musk calf.

[2] Robert Peary in a splendid suit of furs.

[3] Ernest Shackleton, second from the left, returning from his attempt to reach the South Pole.

[7] The Metropolitan Life Insurance Building and Tower in New York.

[8] A cover by the artist Lovis Corinth for the music to Richard Strauss's opera Elektra, *the one in which he went furthest down the path of dissonance.*

[9] The Queensboro Bridge thrusting out over the East River.

1909
The Japanese begin their occupation of **Korea**, which will span more than 30 years.

1909
The **Laguna Dam**, the first authorized dam on the Colorado River, is completed north of Yuma, Arizona, to irrigate desert land.

 *[7]*

1909
The **Metropolitan Life Insurance Building**, modeled by Napoleon Le Brun after the Campanile of St. Mark's in Venice, is completed in New York City. The structure will reign as the world's tallest for several years.

 *[8]*

1909
The opera **Elektra**, with music by Richard Strauss and libretto by Hugo von Hofmannsthal, debuts at the Königliches Opernhaus in Dresden, Germany.

 *[9]*

1909
The **Queensboro Bridge** across the East River to Manhattan and the **Manhattan Bridge** between Manhattan and Brooklyn open in New York City.

1909
The U.S. House of Representatives and Senate approve the **Sixteenth Amendment** to the Constitution, which will allow Congress to impose an **income tax**.

1909

1909
Vaslav Nijinsky's first ballet performance at the Théâtre du Châtelet takes Paris by storm. His extraordinary virtuosity and dramatic acting make him a genius of the ballet.
 [1]

1909
Walter Reed Army Medical Center is founded in Washington, D.C.

1909
William Howard Taft of the Republican Party becomes the 27th president of the United States. He will serve until 1913. His vice president is James Schoolcraft Sherman.

1909
Working in the Realist tradition, American **George Bellows**, a member of the Ashcan School, paints the gritty boxing scene *Stag at Sharkey's*.

February 20, 1909
Italian author **Filippo Marinetti** coins the term "Futurism" in the Parisian newspaper *Le Figaro*.
 [2]

March 4, 1909
The U.S. Congress passes the **Copyright Act**, giving authors, publishers, and composers exclusive, legally secured right to reproduce, distribute, and perform a literary, musical, dramatic, or artistic work.

[1] Nijinsky in the role of Petruska in 1911.

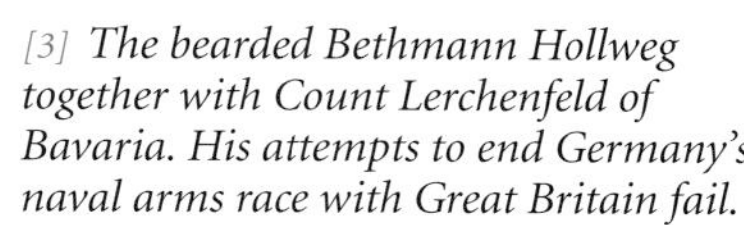

[3] The bearded Bethmann Hollweg together with Count Lerchenfeld of Bavaria. His attempts to end Germany's naval arms race with Great Britain fail.

[5] Ito Hirobumi, four times premier of Japan. As a young man he was one of five Japanese sent to study at University College, London in 1863.

[2] Filippo Marinetti: "Art can be nothing but violence, cruelty and injustice." "The past must be abandoned." "Glorify war—the only hygiene of the world."

[4] Louis Blériot poses by his plane at Dover with his wife the day after his English Channel flight.

1900–1909

April 1909
Turkish Muslim fundamentalists massacre more than **30,000 Armenians** in the city of Adana.

July 1909
Orville and Wilbur Wright sell their military flyer—the **first military airplane**—to the U.S. Army Signal Corps.

 [3]
July 14, 1909
Theobald von **Bethmann Hollweg**, who will successfully prevent the expansion of the Balkan Wars into a major conflict between Austria-Hungary and Russia, becomes imperial chancellor of Germany (1909–17).

 [4]
July 25, 1909
French airplane manufacturer and aviator **Louis Blériot** makes the first flight of an airplane between continental Europe and Great Britain.

 [5]
October 26, 1909
Ito Hirobumi, Japanese elder statesman and premier, is shot in Harbin, China, by An Chung-gun, a member of the Korean independence movement. The assassination will influence Japan's decision to annex **Korea** in 1910.

December 1909
The **Amsterdam News** begins publication in New York City. Selling for two cents per copy, the six-page paper will become the largest nonreligious black weekly in the United States.

U.S. soldiers march in a victory parade, November 1918.

1910

1910
A pair of Nebraskan brothers found a wholesale card company in Kansas City that will later become **Hallmark**, the world's largest producer of greeting cards.

1910
A **trans-Andean railway** linking Chile and Argentina is completed.

1910
Adolf Loos designs the **Steiner House, Vienna**. Undecorated, planar surfaces, punctuated by windows, contribute to the overwhelming simplicity of this building.

 [1]

1910
American inventor Elmer Sperry founds the **Sperry Gyroscope Company**, a major producer of navigational and control systems.

1910
American physician and clinical cardiologist James Bryan Herrick is the first to observe and describe **sickle-cell anemia**.

1910
American Viscose Company, the first successful U.S. producer of **rayon**, is founded.

[1] The Steiner House, Vienna. Modernist simplicity arrives, reacting against the excesses of the Vienna Secession.

[6] Japanese police surrounded by Koreans in their distinctive headgear.

[4] Paul Ehrlich. Sulfa drugs, penicillin, and antibiotics have their origins in the lines of research he established.

[3] Frances Hodgson Burnett. Her story of the bed-ridden boy transformed by the efforts of the young girl is now a classic children's book, filmed more than once.

[5] Glacier National Park

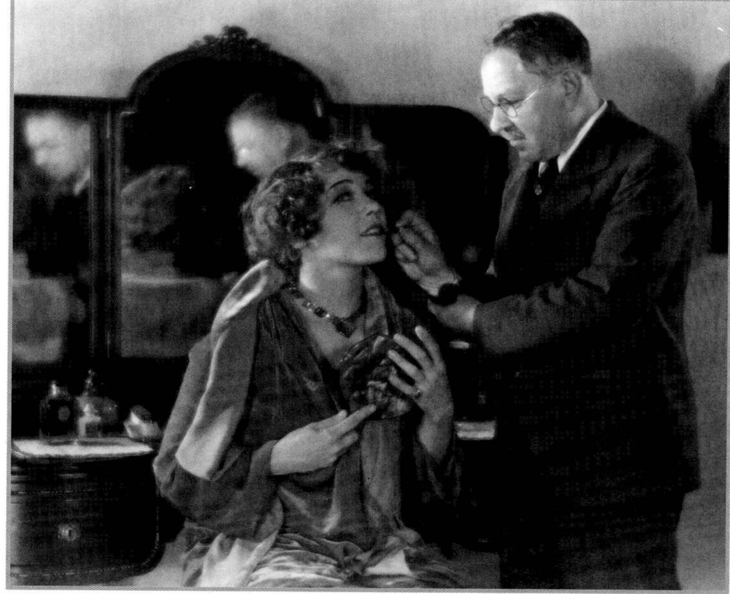

[7] Max Factor applies lipstick to the silent-movie star Louise Fazenda in the 1920s.

 [3]

1910
Frances Hodgson Burnett's novel **The Secret Garden** is published.

1910
French artist and chemist Édouard Bénédictus patents **safety glass**; when struck, safety glass bulges or breaks into tiny, relatively harmless fragments rather than shattering into large, jagged pieces.

 [4]

1910
German medical researcher Paul Ehrlich and his colleague Sahachiro Hata inaugurate **chemotherapy** by showing that the synthetic compound arsphenamine (Salvarsan) is effective against syphilis.

 [5]

1910
Glacier National Park is formed when more than a million acres of Montana land are preserved as wilderness by an act of Congress.

1910
Inspired by a British organization started two years before, Daniel Carter Beard founds the **Boy Scouts of America**.

1910
John Randolph Bray, a newspaper cartoonist, pioneers a "cel" system of **animation** that will become the standard for all future animators.

1910
Antonio Gaudí devotes himself full-time to work on the Templo Expiatorio de la **Familia Sagrada**, **Barcelona**. Gaudí's most ambitious project by far, the massive church will be unfinished at his death in 1926.

 [2]

1910
Botanist Frederick Covine develops a large, nearly seedless **blueberry**, which will revolutionize the market.

1910
Canadian-American Florence Nightingale Graham opens a New York beauty parlor that will expand to become the **Elizabeth Arden** chain of salons.

1910
China abolishes **slavery**.

1910
Driven by demand for imitation sable and sealskin in Paris, trappers in China begin hunting Manchurian marmots; many animals are infected with the **bubonic plague**, which will spread and claim over a million lives in India and China over the next decade.

1910
Edward Douglass White is appointed ninth chief justice of the U.S. Supreme Court by President William Howard Taft. He takes office early the following year and serves until 1921.

[2] *The Sagrada Familia, for many the biggest visual draw in Barcelona. The latest estimate says that it might be completed by 2026.*

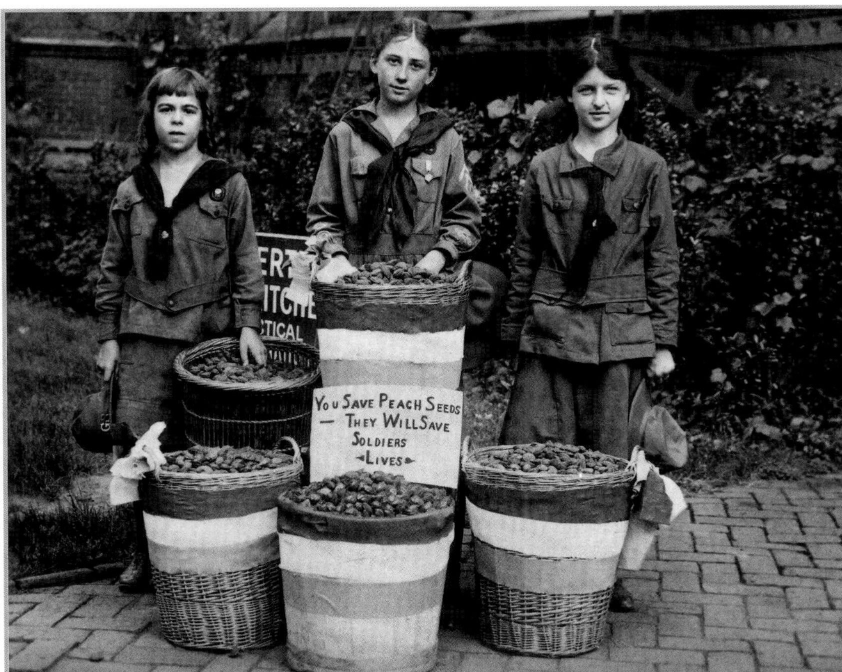

[11] *Three American Girl Guides helping the war effort in 1917–1918 by collecting peach pits or stones, to be ground up and used as filter material in gas masks.*

[9] *Georges Braque in his studio. He and Picasso, under the influence of the big Cezanne retrospective show in 1907, work closely together on cubism, determined to get away from illusion and expose paintings as manmade objects. Their partnership ends when Braque goes off to fight for France in the first World War.*

[8] *Francisco Madero just visible on horseback, surrounded by supporters.*

[10] *A 1913 Wassily Kandinsky abstract,* Composition 7, *is lifted into place.*

 [6]

1910
Korea is annexed by Japan, and Japanese colonial rule in Korea begins.

 [7]

1910
Max Factor devises makeup especially for the needs of actors in black-and-white motion pictures.

 [8]

1910
Mexican revolutionary **Francisco Madero** temporarily unifies various democratic and anti-Díaz forces to become president (1911–13).

 [9]

1910
Pablo Picasso and Georges Braque begin to develop analytical **cubism**, in which structure and mass are reorganized into angular components.

 [10]

1910
Painter **Wassily Kandinsky**, finding his creativity restricted by traditional subjects, begins to experiment with abstract forms in paintings such as *Improvisation XIV*.

 [11]

1910
Robert Baden-Powell founds the **Girl Guides** as a parallel to the Boy Scouts.

1910-1911

1910
The first glass-lined **milk car** begins transport on the Boston & Maine railroad for Whiting Milk Company, based in Boston.

1910
The **Portuguese monarchy**, established in 1143, is ended, and a republic is proclaimed.

1910
The **neon light** is invented by French chemical engineer Georges Claude. His invention finds widespread use in signs and becomes the forerunner of the fluorescent light.

1910
The National Association for the Advancement of Colored People (**NAACP**), created to work for the abolition of segregation and discrimination, to oppose racism, and to ensure African Americans their constitutional rights, is founded in New York. [1]

1910
The **S. S. Mauretania** sets a new transatlantic record, sailing from Cobb to New York in just under five days. [2]

1910
Women in Washington state achieve the **right to vote**.

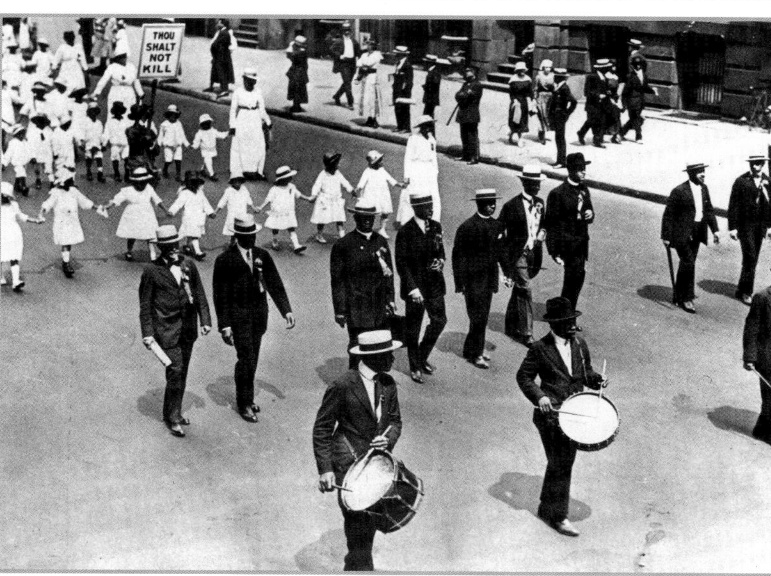

[1] An NAACP march in 1917, protesting against lynch law.

[3] The famous early director Mack Sennett (left) directs a scene on a Hollywood set, circa 1915.

[9] A study for Chagall's painting Over Vitebsk. *Its fantastical subject matter, of a Jewish pedlar flying over the Belarus city, is very typical of Chagall's work.*

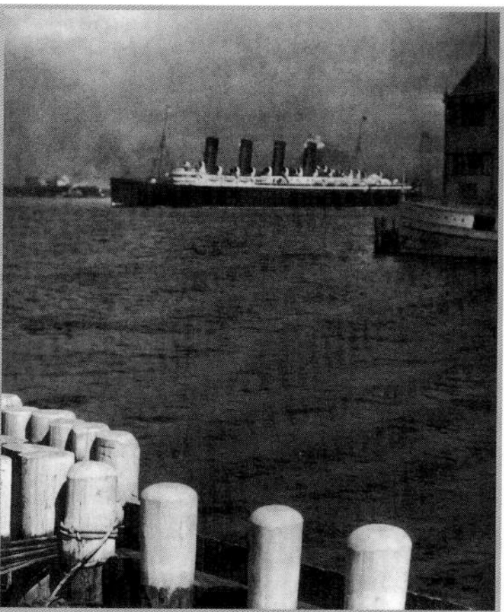

[2] An Alfred Stieglitz photograph of the Mauretania.

[7] King Nicholas of Montenegro is embraced by one of his loyal followers.

[8] Pancho Villa (left) and Emiliano Zapata, Mexican revolutionaries smoking together.

 [7]

August 28, 1910
Montenegro declares itself an independent kingdom.

October 1, 1910
A bomb explodes at the **Los Angeles Times office**, killing 20. Three union radicals, including two brothers, James and John McNamara, will later confess to the crime.

 [8]

November 20, 1910
Francisco Madero launches a revolt in Mexico, inspiring hope in such leaders as Pancho Villa and Emiliano Zapata. Dictator Porfirio Diaz is ousted in 1911.

December 26, 1910
The **London Palladium** opens.

1911
A giant tobacco trust, the **American Tobacco Company**, is dissolved by the U.S. Court of Appeals.

1911
A local revolutionary group in Wuhan, China, unexpectedly manages to overthrow the provincial government. Its success inspires other provincial secessions, leading to the ouster of the 267-year-old **Qing (Ch'ing) Dynasty**.

c. 1910
Hollywood, California, becomes a mecca for motion-picture studios. It has both the temperate climate required for year-round production and a wide range of topography: mountains, valleys, forests, lakes, islands, seacoast, and desert.
[3]

February 20, 1910
Egyptian premier Butrus Ghali is assassinated.

May 6, 1910
King Edward VII dies, and King George V succeeds to the British throne.
[4]

May 31, 1910
Louis Botha forms the first government of the **Union of South Africa**.
[5]

June 19, 1910
Father's Day is observed for the first time in the state of Washington.

June 25, 1910
The Firebird by Igor Stravinsky and Michel Fokine premiers at the Paris Opéra.
[6]

[5] *Louis Botha and his wife outside their house in Pretoria, South Africa.*

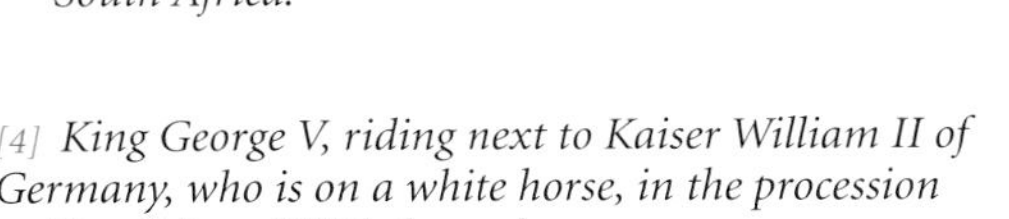

[4] *King George V, riding next to Kaiser William II of Germany, who is on a white horse, in the procession at King Edward VII's funeral.*

[6] *Tamara Karsavina in the title role from the original Ballets Russes production of* The Firebird.

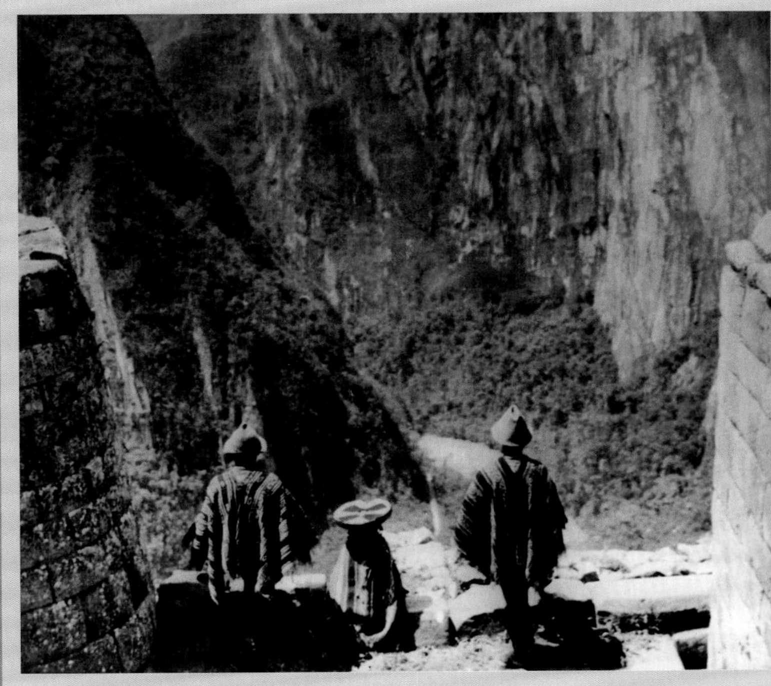

THE DISCOVERY OF MACHU PICCHU

Lost city of the Incas found in the Peruvian mountains by American archaeologist Hiram Bingham

Machu Picchu, the site of ancient Inca ruins located about 50 miles (80 km) northwest of Cuzco, Peru, in the Andes Mountains, was "discovered" in 1911 by the Yale University professor Hiram Bingham, who was led to the site by a local Quechua-speaking resident. It is perched above the Urubamba River valley in a narrow saddle between two sharp peaks. Bingham had been seeking Vilcabamba (Vilcapampa), the "lost city of the Incas," from which the last Inca rulers led a rebellion against Spanish rule until 1572 (the Spaniards had never found it).

The dwellings at Machu Picchu were probably built and occupied from the mid-15th to the early or mid-16th century. Walkways and thousands of steps are carved into underlying rock, connecting the plazas, the residential areas, the terraces, the cemetery, and the major buildings. Its southern, eastern, and western portions are surrounded by dozens of stepped agricultural terraces formerly watered by an aqueduct system. Some of those terraces were still being used by local Indians (left) when Bingham arrived in 1911.

1911
A military coup funded and outfitted by U.S. banana planter Samuel Zemurray overthrows the Honduran government and creates a **banana republic**.

1911
British physicist **Ernest Rutherford** proposes the modern theory of atomic structure, saying it consists of a massive nucleus surrounded by orbiting electrons.

1911
American Benjamin Holt invents a **combine** capable of harvesting, threshing, and cleaning wheat.

1911
American historian and archaeologist Hiram Bingham discovers the ancient Inca city of **Machu Picchu**, Peru.

[9]
1911
Belorussian-born artist **Marc Chagall** moves to Paris and begins producing paintings with characteristic elements: Russian and Jewish themes, floating figures, complex coloration, and a dreamlike atmosphere.

1911
American author **Edith Wharton** publishes *Ethan Frome*.

1911

1911
Charles F. Kettering invents the **electric self-starter** for automobile and truck engines, improving their safety; the mechanism is first introduced on Cadillac vehicles.

1911
Designed by Giuseppe Sucani, the **Victor Emmanuel II monument** in Rome is completed after 28 years of work.

[1]

1911
Former General Motors Corporation head W. C. Durant founds **Chevrolet Motor Company**.

$ [2]

1911
French author Gaston Leroux publishes **The Phantom of the Opera**, which will later achieve fame in various film and stage renditions.

1911
German architect **Peter Behrens** designs the German Embassy, St. Petersburg, Russia. Powerful and brooding forms turn the building into an emblem of the power of modern government.

1911
Henry Ginaca invents for James Dole a **pineapple-shelling-and-coring machine** that revolutionizes the industry by enabling the mass production of canned pineapple.

[1] One part of the enormous Victor Emmanuel II Monument in Rome, known to the locals as "the wedding cake" or "the false teeth."

[5] The New York Public Library flagship building, in the Beaux Arts style. There are now 87 libraries under that name, in Manhattan, the Bronx, and Staten Island.

[2] The prototype Chevrolet automobile, with its designer, Swiss-born Louis Chevrolet, at the wheel.

[3] A typical dreamlike scene by Giorgio de Chirico.

[4] Spectators line the Indianapolis motor-racing track by the finishing line during an early "500" race.

[6] W. C. Handy, the Father of the Blues, though he freely admits to have transcribed them, not invented them.

1911
The *Berline* is built as the first aircraft with an **enclosed passenger cabin**.

1911
The **Black Hand** is founded. It uses terrorist methods to promote the liberation of Serbs outside Serbia from Habsburg or Ottoman rule, and it will assassinate Austrian archduke Francis Ferdinand, precipitating the outbreak of World War I.

1911
The **Carnegie Corporation** of New York, designed to foster education, is founded with a $125 million gift from Scottish-born industrialist and steel tycoon Andrew Carnegie.

1911
The first **Indianapolis 500** auto race is won by Ray Harroun driving a Marmon Wasp.

1911
The main branch of the **New York Public Library** opens in New York City.

1911
W. C. Handy marks the transition from ragtime to **jazz**. With his "Memphis Blues" (1911) and especially his "St. Louis Blues" (1914), he introduces a nostalgic element peculiar to the music of Southern blacks.

1911
The Computing-Tabulating-Recording Company is incorporated. It will take the name **International Business Machines** (IBM) in 1924 under the leadership of Thomas Watson.

1911
Italian painter **Giorgio de Chirico**, founder of the style of metaphysical painting, begins to produce paintings in which classical statues, dark arcades, and small, isolated figures are overpowered by their own shadows and by severe, oppressive architecture.

 [3]

1911
Norwegian explorer Roald Amundsen reaches the **South Pole** on a carefully planned and executed sled-dog journey involving preliminary forays to deposit supplies for his return trip.

1911
Portuguese women gain the **right to vote**.

1911
Publication of the literary magazine *Seito* begins in Tokyo, marking the slow start of the women's liberation movement in **Japan**.

1911
Swiss engineer Jacques E. Brandenberger invents **cellophane**.

AMUNDSEN REACHES THE SOUTH POLE

Norwegian explorer wins race against British rival

Roald Amundsen was one of the greatest figures in the field of polar exploration. The Norwegian was the first to reach the South Pole, the first to make a ship voyage through the Northwest Passage, and one of the first to cross the Arctic by air.

Amundsen had planned for a journey to the North Pole, but after learning that Robert E. Peary had reached that goal, he set off for the South Pole in 1910. When Amundsen left Norway in June, no one but his brother knew that he was heading for the South Pole instead of the North. He sailed directly from the Madeira Islands to the Bay of Whales, Antarctica, along the Ross Sea. The base he set up there was 60 miles (100 km) closer to the pole than the Antarctic base of the English explorer Robert Falcon Scott, who was heading a rival expedition with the same goal. An experienced polar traveler, Amundsen prepared carefully for the coming journey, making a preliminary trip to deposit food supplies along the first part of his route to the pole and back. To transport his supplies, he used sled dogs, while Scott depended on Siberian ponies.

Amundsen set out with 4 companions, 52 dogs, and 4 sledges on October 19, 1911, and, after encountering good weather, arrived at the South Pole on December 14 (left). The explorers recorded scientific data at the pole before beginning the return journey on December 17, and they safely reached their base at the Bay of Whales on January 25, 1912. Scott, in the meantime, had reached the South Pole on January 17, but on a difficult return journey he and all his men perished

[7] Peter Stolypin, hammer of the Russian revolutionaries but champion of the peasants, to whom he saw that land was transferred in increasing quantities.

[8] Lieutenant Eugene Ely takes off in a Curtiss biplane from the flight deck constructed on the battleship Pennsylvania, *after having landed on it, the first-ever such landing.*

1911
The U.S. Supreme Court rules that the **Standard Oil Company of New Jersey**, controlling most of the U.S. petroleum industry, constitutes an undue restraint of trade and orders its dissolution.

1911
U.S. geographer Isaiah Bowman completes **Forest Physiography**, the first detailed geographical study of the United States.

 [7]

1911
Russian premier **Peter Stolypin** is assassinated by a double agent. With his death goes the last best hope of Russia avoiding violent upheaval.

1911
Walter Gropius and **Adolf Meyer** design Faguswerk at Alfeld-an-der-Leine, Germany, a clean, innovative design with large expanses of glass wall.

1911
Women in California gain the **right to vote** through an amendment to the state constitution.

 [8]

January 18, 1911
The first **aircraft landing on a ship's flight deck** is performed by American pilot Eugene Ely on the battleship *Pennsylvania* in San Francisco Bay.

1911-1912

March 25, 1911
A fire at the **Triangle Shirtwaist Company** in New York City kills 146 people, prompting the creation of health and safety legislation.
$ [1]

April 17, 1911
Ellis Island experiences a record influx, receiving 11,745 immigrants in a single day.
[2]

July 7, 1911
The Convention for the Preservation and Protection of **Fur Seals** is concluded by the United States, Japan, Russia, and the United Kingdom.

August 10, 1911
The Parliament Act of 1911 is passed by the British Parliament, depriving the **House of Lords** of its absolute power of veto on legislation.

September 28, 1911
Using the pretext of infringement of Italian interests in the Turkish provinces of **Tripolitana and Cyrenaica** (**Libya**), the Italian government issues an ultimatum to Turkey and declares war the next day.
[3]

October 10, 1911
Robert Laird Borden becomes Canadian prime minister (1911–20). He will play a decisive role—notably by insisting on separate Canadian membership in the League of Nations—in transforming his country from colony into nation.
[4]

[3] *A Turkish mounted military band leads troops off to fight the Italians.*

[1] *In the aftermath of the Triangle Shirtwaist Company fire, people pass along a line of corpses, trying to identify them.*

1910-1919

[2] *Immigrants cheer and wave their hats as the Statue of Liberty emerges from the mist to tell them they have arrived in America.*

[8] *A Fokker DR-1 triplane, as used by the Red Baron, Manfred von Richthofen. This plane belongs to another ace, Heinrich Gontermann, seen standing by it.*

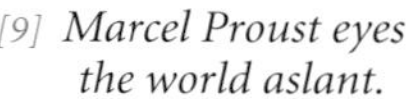

[9] *Marcel Proust eyes the world aslant.*

[7]
1912
British polar explorer Robert Falcon Scott arrives at the **South Pole**, only to find that Roald Amundsen beat him by a month. He and his party perish during their return trek.

1912
British spy agency MI6, responsible for foreign intelligence, is constituted by Commander (later Sir) Mansfield Cumming as part of Britain's attempt to coordinate intelligence activities prior to 1914.

1912
Carl Laemmle, a film exhibitor turned producer, forms **Universal Pictures**, a U.S. motion-picture studio that will become one of the leading producers of film serials in the 1920s and of popular horror films in the 1930s.

[8]
1912
Dutch aircraft manufacturer Anthony **Fokker introduces** the Fokker airplane; during World War I, Fokker will introduce the gear system so that a machine gun can fire through the propeller arc without hitting the blades.

1912
Financed by rubber tycoons, **Brazil's Madeira-Mamoro Railway** is opened after six years of construction.

[9]
1912
French novelist **Marcel Proust** finishes the first draft of his seven-part autobiographical novel, *À la recherche du temps perdu* (*Remembrance of Things Past*).

1912
All federal employees are extended the **eight-hour workday**, while private industry laborers continue to work 10 to 12 hours a day.

1912
American biochemists Elmer McCollum and Marguerite Davis identify in butter and eggs the nutrient that will come to be known as **vitamin A**.

1912
American novelist **Edgar Rice Burroughs** publishes the first of his Tarzan stories about the son of an English nobleman raised by apes in the African jungle.

 [5]

1912
American physician James B. Herrick makes the first diagnosis of a **heart attack** in a living patient, linking a number of symptoms with a myocardial infarction caused by a blood clot.

1912
American woman of letters **Harriet Monroe** begins editing *Poetry* magazine, which makes its reputation publishing avant-garde Modernist poets such as Ezra Pound, D. H. Lawrence, and Hilda Doolittle.

1912
At the Summer Olympics in Stockholm, Native American **Jim Thorpe** wins the pentathlon and decathlon. He goes on to play professional football and baseball.

 [6]

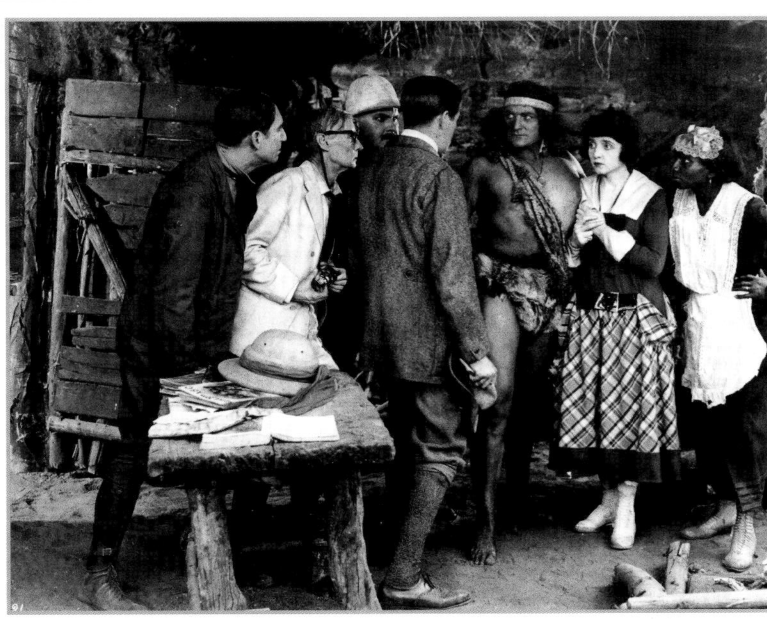

[5] *Elmo Lincoln, the first screen Tarzan, in a scene from the silent movie,* Tarzan of the Apes, *1918. Enid Markey, beside him, is Jane.*

[6] *Jim Thorpe in action in Stockholm, throwing the discus. Within a year he will lose his gold medals because he had accepted payment for coaching at a youth camp.*

[4] *Sir Robert Borden. He must take the credit for transforming his government into a wartime administration, as well as his part in transforming the British Empire into a commonwealth.*

[7] *Captain Scott and his men pulling a sledge in the Antarctic.*

[10] Nude Descending a Staircase, *by Marcel Duchamp.*

1912
German meteorologist and geophysicist Alfred Lothar Wegener proposes his theory of **continental drift**, positing that one large continent he called Pangaea had gradually broken apart into the present continents.

1912
Hull House veteran Julia Lathrop is named chief of the newly created **U.S. Children's Bureau**. The bureau brings progressive ideas and concerns about child welfare to the federal level.

1912
Leon Leonwood Bean, inventor of the Maine hunting shoe, opens a clothing store in partnership with his brother that will lay the foundation of the **L.L. Bean** catalog empire.

 [10]

1912
Marcel Duchamp, echoing futurists and extending analytical cubism to describe movement, represents the human figure as a set of planes in *Nude Descending a Staircase, No. 2.*

1912
Peppermint-flavored **Life Savers** debut. The famous five-flavor roll will not be marketed until 1934.

1912
Polish biochemist Casimir Funk coins the name "**vitamine**" (from *vital amine*) to describe essential growth substances that must be provided in the diet.

1912
Thub-bstan-rgya-mtsho, the **13th Dalai Lama**, re-establishes independent Tibet. He will rule with great personal authority until 1933.

1912
The first **Girl Scout** troop in the United States is formed in 1912 by Juliette Gordon Low of Savannah, Georgia, and follows the pattern set up for the British Girl Guides.

 [1]

1912
The umbrella organization for the **Better Business Bureau** (BBB) system of the United States and Canada is founded to protect consumers against unfair, misleading, or fraudulent advertising and selling practices.

$

1912
The **first minimum wage** in the United States, covering only women, is enacted by the state of Massachusetts. A federal minimum wage will be adopted in 1938, set at 25 cents per hour.

1912
The foreign-owned Turkish Petroleum Company is established to exploit oil discovered near **Kirkuk** in Iraq.

1912
The **International Amateur Athletic Federation** is founded in Stockholm for the purpose of uniting over 160 national track-and-field associations.

 [2]

SINKING OF THE *TITANIC*

Luxury liner in peacetime maritime disaster

On April 14 and 15, 1912, the luxury passenger liner *Titanic* sank en route to New York City from Southampton, England, during its maiden voyage, killing about 1,500 passengers and ship personnel.

The *Titanic* was one of the largest and most luxurious ships in the world. It had a gross registered tonnage of 46,329 tons, and when fully laden the ship displaced (weighed) 66,000 tons. The *Titanic* was 882.5 feet (269 m) long and 92.5 feet (28.2 m) wide at its widest point. It was owned by the White Star Line and designed and built by William Pirrie's Belfast firm Harland and Wolff to service the highly competitive Atlantic Ferry route, which at the time was dominated by the Cunard Line. It had a double-bottomed hull divided into 16 compartments that were presumed to be watertight. Because four of these could be flooded without endangering the liner's buoyancy, the *Titanic* was thought to be unsinkable.

On April 10, 1912, the *Titanic* departed Southampton, England, in a blaze of publicity. Its first stop was Cherbourg, France, where it picked up a large number of first-class passengers. The vessel then called at Queenstown (Cobh) on the east coast of Ireland; most of the people who joined the vessel there had third-class tickets. The ship then set off across the Atlantic on April 12; it was due to get to the United States five days later.

Shortly before midnight on April 14, the ship collided with an iceberg about 400 miles (640 km) south of Newfoundland, and at least five of its watertight compartments toward the bow were ruptured. The first four of these five compartments filled with water, which pulled down the bow of the ship. The *Titanic*'s compartments were not capped at the top, so water from the ruptured forward compartments filled each succeeding compartment aft as the ship's incline brought the bow below the waterline. The ship sank at 2:20 AM on April 15. The *Titanic* had only 1,178 lifeboat spaces for the 2,224 persons aboard, and many of the lifeboats were lowered into the water only partly filled with passengers, thus leaving many people stranded on the sinking ship. The disaster immediately made the front pages (the top left photograph shows a newspaper boy selling copies of the *London Evening News* outside the White Star offices in London on April 16).

Inquiries held in the United States and Great Britain alleged that the Leyland liner *Californian*, which was less than 20 miles (32 km) away all night, could have aided the stricken vessel had its radio operator been on duty and thereby received the *Titanic*'s distress signals. Only the arrival of the Cunard liner *Carpathia* one hour and 20 minutes after the *Titanic* went down prevented further loss of life in the icy waters.

As a result of the disaster, changes were made to maritime law—it was required that every ship have lifeboat space for each person embarked, that lifeboat drills be held during each voyage, and that ships maintain a 24-hour radio watch.

 [3]

c. 1912
The **Chicago literary renaissance**, whose participants include Carl Sandburg, Theodore Dreiser, Vachel Lindsay, and Sherwood Anderson, flourishes in poetry, fiction, and journalism.

January 6, 1912
New Mexico is admitted to the United States as the 47th state.

February 2, 1912
Frederick Rodman Law performs what is considered the **first motion-picture stunt**, parachuting from the Statue of Liberty in New York Harbor.

February 14, 1912
Arizona is admitted to the United States as the 48th state.

March 30, 1912
The Treaty of Fès establishes the French protectorate in **Morocco**.

April 14–15, 1912
The British luxury passenger ship **Titanic** en route to New York City from Southampton, England, on its maiden voyage, strikes an iceberg and sinks, killing about 1,500 passengers and crew members.

1912
The **Qing (Ch'ing) Dynasty** (1644–1911/12), last of the imperial dynasties of China, ends its long rule as the last emperor abdicates.

1912
The South African Native National Congress is founded. It will be renamed **African National Congress** in 1923 and will campaign for voting rights in Cape Province and later to eliminate apartheid.

1912
The use of a **Morse Code SOS** is adopted as the universal call for distress by an International Radio-Telegraph Conference.

1912
The **Whitman's Sampler**, a box of chocolates with an index showing the filling in each candy, is introduced.

1912
U.S. football regulations are developed with the addition of the fourth down, the value of a touchdown increasing from five to six points, the reduction in the size of the football, and the standardization of the football field (360 by 160 feet).

1912
Wild boars are introduced into the United States from Germany.

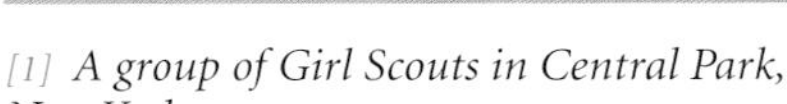
[1] A group of Girl Scouts in Central Park, New York.

[2] Swedish gymnasts in action in the Swedish System Gymnastics event at the 1912 Olympics. The IAAF is forned to decide which sports systems and rules are to be used internationally.

[5] John Schrank. Luckily his shot hits Roosevelt's spectacle case and a folded copy of his speech, before lodging in his chest. Roosevelt insists on making the speech, and the bullet remains in his chest until he dies years later.

[4] Harriet Quimby, theater critic and screenplay writer. In July 1912 she and her passenger fall to their deaths from her new Blériot two-seater.

[3] Theodore Dreiser (left) and Sherwood Anderson, two leading members of the Chicago literary renaissance, who portrayed the contemporary urban scene.

[6] Two Albanian girls in national costume photographed in front of members of a British delegation to the Balkans in 1915.

[7] A recreation of the Piltdown Man based on the bogus skull and jawbone fragments "found" in 1912 in Sussex, England. The skull was modern, the jawbone that of an orangutan.

 [4]
April 16, 1912
American aviator **Harriet Quimby** becomes the first woman to fly across the English Channel, guiding her French Blériot monoplane through heavy overcast from Dover, England, to Hardelot, France.

 [5]
October 14, 1912
Former U.S. president **Theodore Roosevelt** is wounded in an assassination attempt by John Schrank while running for re-election.

November 12, 1912
Spanish Prime Minister **José Canalejas** is assassinated by the anarchist Manuel Pardiñas.

 [6]
November 28, 1912
Albanian national delegates, led by Ismail Qemal, issue the Vlorë proclamation, which declares **Albania's independence**.

 [7]
December 18, 1912
The discovery of fossil remains of **Piltdown Man**, an extinct human species, is announced at a meeting of the Geological Society of London, but the remains are later proved to be a fraud.

1913
A number of Canadian painters working as commercial artists in Toronto meet and form what will become the **Group of Seven**, which will devote itself to the creation of a national style.

1913

1913
A peace treaty is signed in London ending the **first Balkan War** and stripping the Ottoman Empire of most of its European holdings.

1913
American poet **Robert Frost**'s first poetry collection, *A Boy's Will*, is published in London with the support of such Modernist poets as Ezra Pound. *North of Boston* appears the following year.

 [1]

1913
The **metric carat**, equal to 0.200 gram, and the point, equal to 0.01 carat, are adopted by the United States and subsequently by most other countries. The weights of diamonds, rubies, sapphires, emeralds, and other gems will be expressed in carats.

1913
Displacement Law is first formulated, stating that radioactive decay produces daughter atoms whose position in the periodic table of the chemical elements is shifted from that of their parents: two lower for alpha decay and one higher for negative beta decay.

1913
Edwin Lutyens, a designer in New Delhi, India, begins work on the Viceroy's House. The pomp and circumstance of British India are well expressed in this massive building of the new capital.

 [2]

1913
Fifinella is foaled; an English racehorse (Thoroughbred), she will win the Derby in 1916 and two days later the Oaks. She will be the last horse to win both events in one year.

[2] Edwin Lutyens's Viceregal Lodge in New Delhi, the new seat of British-Indian government. The great central dome mounted on a drum is derived from a Buddhist stupa.

[6] The neo-Gothic Woolworth Building, for which Frank Woolworth pays $13,500,000, in cash.

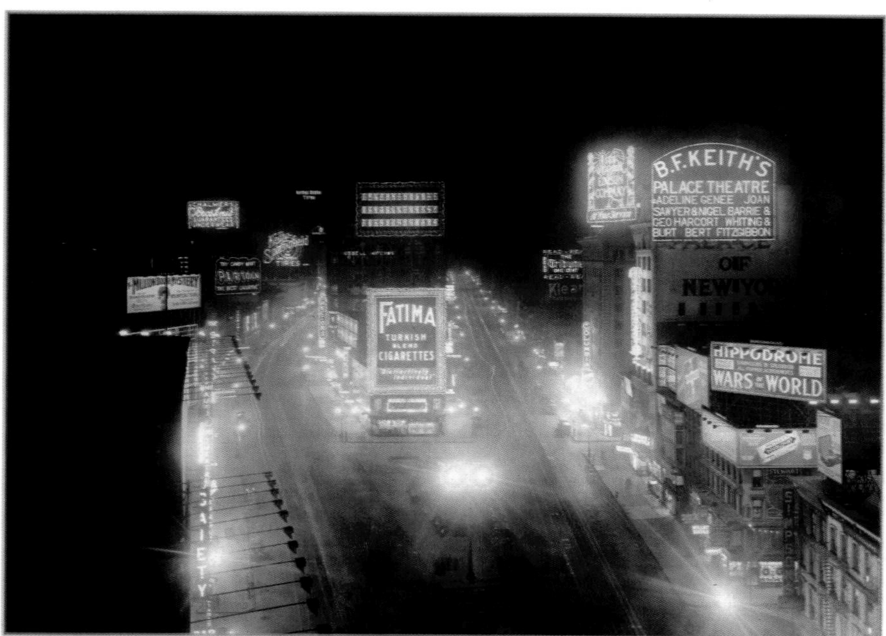

[7] The Palace Theater at night (right) on New York's Times Square.

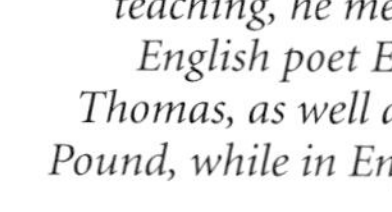

[1] Robert Frost. An unsuccessful farmer in New Hampshire before taking up teaching, he meets the English poet Edward Thomas, as well as Ezra Pound, while in England.

 [6]

1913
The 60-story **Woolworth Building**, designed by architect Cass Gilbert, is completed in New York City. It is the world's tallest building to date.

1913
The American Society for the Control of Cancer, later the **American Cancer Society**, is formed.

1913
The **Armory Show**, an exhibition of avant-garde and other modern European and American art in New York City, shocks critics and the public but inspires a generation of American artists.

1913
The B'Nai B'rith (Sons of the Covenant), the oldest and largest Jewish service organization in the world, establishes the **Anti-Defamation League** to address prejudice and anti-Semitism in America.

1913
The **Federal Reserve System** is created. It acts as a fiscal agent for the U.S. government, is custodian of the reserve accounts of commercial banks, makes loans to commercial banks, and oversees the supply of currency.

1913
The first modern **crossword puzzle** is published in the *New York World*'s Sunday supplement.

1913
German physical chemist Fritz Haber develops the **Haber-Bosch Method** of directly synthesizing ammonia from hydrogen and nitrogen. Ammonia synthesis inaugurates an era of artificial nitrogen fertilizers, improving crop yields.

 [3]

1913
Grand Central Terminal is opened in New York City.

 [4]

1913
In Great Britain, Parliament passes the Temporary Discharge for Ill-Health Act of 1913 (the "Cat and Mouse Act"), providing for **hunger-striking prisoners** to be freed for a time and then reincarcerated upon regaining their health to some extent.

 [5]

1913
Max Berg designs the **Jahrhunderthalle (Centennial Hall), Breslau**, Germany. Made of ferro-concrete, this commemorative hall demonstrates the plasticity and limitless potential of concrete buildings.

1913
Pennsylvania celebrates **Mother's Day** as a state holiday; the day will later receive recognition as a national holiday.

1913
Swiss chemist **Alfred Werner** wins the Nobel Prize for Chemistry for his research into the structure of coordination compounds.

[4] A remarkable photograph by Hal Morey of the interior of Grand Central Terminal in New York transforms it into a temple of transport.

[3] Fritz Haber. As well as fame for synthetic ammonia, he also gains notoriety for his work on chlorine gas used in World War I and his invention of Zyklon B, the gas used in Nazi concentration camps.

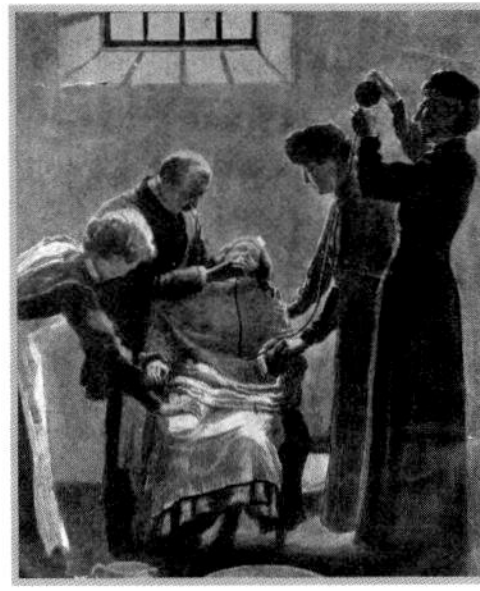

[5] A jailed British suffragette on hunger strike is forcibly fed. It is to avoid scenes like this that the "Cat and Mouse Act" is enacted.

[8] The suffragettes march up Pennsylvania Avenue in Washington D.C. Men slap the marchers, spit at them, and poke them with lit cigars, and a brawl means they are stopped before reaching the White House.

[9] Margaret Sanger. She coins the term "birth control" and argues that each woman should be "absolute mistress of her own body."

1913
The **Food and Drug Administration** is established in the United States.

1913
The opening night of Igor Stravinsky's modern ballet **The Rite of Spring**, in Paris, choreographed by Vaslav Nijinsky, causes a riot. Stravinsky's music is part of the core of 20th-century modernism.

 [7]

1913
The **Palace Theater** opens in New York City.

1913
The Sixteenth Amendment to the Constitution of the United States is ratified, enabling the federal government to levy an **income tax**.

 [8]

1913
Five thousand suffragettes march in Washington behind Alice Paul, founder of the National Woman's Party.

 [9]

1913
U.S. reformer Margaret Sanger publishes *The Woman Rebel*. The magazine provides information about **birth control** in defiance of social and legal proscriptions.

1913-1914

1913
William D. Coolidge of General Electric invents the **X-ray tube**, which will be patented in 1916.

1913
Woodrow Wilson of the Democratic Party becomes the 28th president of the United States. He will serve until 1921. His vice president is Thomas R. Marshall.

 [1]

c. 1913
Shuffleboard is introduced into Florida by Daytona Beach hoteliers Mr. and Mrs. Robert Ball.

 [2]

February 18, 1913
French statesman **Raymond Poincaré**, who as prime minister in 1912 will largely determine the policy that led to France's involvement in World War I, is elected president of France.

 [3]

March 10, 1913
In Toledo, Ohio, William Knox becomes the **first bowler to make a perfect score of 300** in an American Bowling Congress tournament.

April 8, 1913
The Seventeenth Amendment to the U.S. Constitution, providing for the **direct election of U.S. senators**, is ratified.

[1] President Woodrow Wilson at his inauguration, accompanied by his predecessor, William Howard Taft.

[2] Playing shuffleboard on the deck of the liner Lusitania.

1910-1919

[3] President Poincaré (left) greets the visiting King Alfonso XIII of Spain in Paris.

[6] Harry Vardon. In 1900 he won the U.S. Open and was runner-up in 1913, as he will be again in 1920, at age 50.

[7] The first production of Pygmalion. *Mrs. Patrick Campbell, as Eliza Doolittle, cocks a snoot at her father, Alfred the dustman, while Professor Higgins restrains him. The part has been specially written for Campbell, but she is really too old for it.*

[6]
1914
Golfer **Harry Vardon** of England wins his sixth British Open. The Vardon Trophy—awarded annually to the professional with the best scoring average—is named for him.

$
1914
In late July the Montreal, Toronto, Madrid, London, and New York **stock exchanges** all close within a few days of one another.

[7]
1914
Irish playwright **George Bernard Shaw** produces his romantic comedy *Pygmalion* in London. *Pygmalion* will be both filmed (1938), and adapted into an immensely popular musical *My Fair Lady* (1956; motion-picture version, 1964).

1914
Irish-born composer Victor Herbert helps found the **American Society of Composers, Arrangers, and Producers (ASCAP)** to enforce musical copyright.

1914
Italian architect Antonio Sant'Elia designs his vision of the city of the future in **Città Nuova**. Sant'Elia, who never realized a structure, strongly influenced the futurists and later movements.

1914
Large-scale **pasta** production begins in the United States when Italian sources are made unavailable by World War I.

May 26, 1913
The **Actors' Equity Association**, the trade union for American performing artists, is founded.

June 13, 1913
Hudson Stuck and Harry Karstens lead a mountaineering party to the south peak, the true summit of **Mount McKinley**, becoming the first people to ascend North America's highest peak (6,194 meters [20,320 feet]).

 [4]

June 29, 1913
Following a year of war with the Ottoman Empire, members of the victorious Balkan League quarrel over the division of the conquered territories, resulting in the **Second Balkan War**.

 [5]

July 29, 1913
Albania is formally recognized by the major European powers as an independent principality following the issuance of the Vlorë proclamation.

1914
Bruno Taut designs his **Glass Pavilion for the Werkbund Exhibit, Cologne**. Taut's small, crystalline building exemplifies the fascination with glass that characterized Expressionist architecture.

1914
George Washington Carver of the Tuskegee Institute reveals his experiments concerning **peanuts and sweet potatoes**, popularizing alternative crops and aiding the renewal of depleted land in the U.S. South.

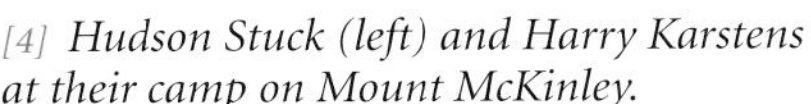

[4] *Hudson Stuck (left) and Harry Karstens at their camp on Mount McKinley.*

[8] *James Joyce, photographed in Zürich during World War I.* Dubliners *portrays the city that he never visited again after 1912.*

[5] *A Bulgarian battery ready to go into action. The battery commander uses a limber to get a better view of the target.*

[9] *A passenger liner, "dressed overall" with flags, is triumphantly towed through the newly opened Panama Canal.*

GEORGE WASHINGTON CARVER

The man who revolutionized Southern farming

Agricultural chemist George Washington Carver (above, in his laboratory) helped to modernize the agriculture of the U.S. South. He developed new products derived from peanuts and soybeans and promoted the planting of these as a way of liberating the South from its dependency on cotton. In 1914, when the boll weevil had almost ruined cotton growers, Carver revealed his experiments to the public, and increasing numbers of the South's farmers began to turn to peanuts, sweet potatoes, and their derivatives for income. Much exhausted land was renewed by the peanut's ability to extract nitrogen from the air and deposit it in the soil, and the South became a major new supplier of products. When Carver became director of agricultural research at the Tuskegee Institute (now Tuskegee University) in Alabama in 1896, the peanut had not even been recognized as a crop, but within the next half century it became one of the six leading crops throughout the United States.

1914
Mohandas **Gandhi** returns to India after more than 20 years in South Africa.

1914
U.S. president Woodrow Wilson declares **Mother's Day** a national holiday.

 [8]

1914
Prolific and gifted Irish writer **James Joyce** publishes his short-story collection *Dubliners*. His short novel *A Portrait of the Artist as a Young Man* will be published in 1916.

1914
Recognizing that a few men could plunge the country into a financial panic, Congress passes the **Clayton Antitrust Act**, closing loopholes left by the Sherman Antitrust Act of 1890.

1914
Seeking a way to prevent cutlery from rusting, Harry Brearley of Sheffield, England, develops the first commercially successful **stainless steel**.

 [9]

1914
The 50-mile (80-km) **Panama Canal**, one of the world's most strategic waterways, is opened, joining the Atlantic and Pacific oceans. Its operation is under control of the United States.

1914-1915

1914
The North American **passenger pigeon** is driven to extinction. Once numbering about five billion, the species is destroyed by commercial hunting after 1865.

 [1]

1914
The **Royal Ontario Museum** opens to the public in Toronto. The ROM will be known for its collections of Chinese and ancient Egyptian art, American ethnology, and Canadian arts and crafts.

1914
The **Sunday Post** begins publication in Glasgow, Scotland. The newspaper will grow to command the readership of 80 percent of all Scots over age 15.

1914
The **trench coat** is designed for British officers in World War I. Fashion designer Coco Chanel will later popularize the style for both men and women.

 [2]

1914
Tinkertoys are created by Charles Pajeau. In the succeeding decades the rugged wooden construction toys become a staple of toy boxes throughout Europe and America.

c. 1914
Andalusian matador **Juan Belmonte** revolutionizes bullfighting by emphasizing graceful capework and exposure to danger over the act of killing.

[1] A museum display of stuffed passenger pigeons.

[3] Henry Ford's moving assembly line, the secret behind the mass production of the Model T. The idea for it is said to have come from the disassembly lines to be seen in the abattoirs of the Chicago stockyards.

[4] The aftermath of the Ludlow Massacre: strikers' temporary shelters burned to the ground after being attacked by company detectives.

[9] French "poilus" march through Paris in August, cheered by the crowd, large bayonets fixed to their rifles.

[11] French soldiers turn a captured machine gun on the Germans at the Battle of the Marne.

[2] One of the very few good things to come out of the Western Front: the design for the trench coat, here interpreted long afterwards by the Burberry company.

[10] A German trench hastily dug in the sandy street of a Belgian seaside town.

August 4, 1914
In response to the German army's invasion of Belgium, on its way to attack France, **Great Britain** declares war on Germany.

July–August, 1914
Russia comes to the support of Serbia, declaring war on Austria-Hungary. **France** aligns with Russia, and Germany with Austria-Hungary.

August 5, 1914
The world's first red and green **traffic lights** are established in Cleveland, Ohio.

 [9]

August 10, 1914
France declares war on Austria-Hungary.

 [10]

August 20, 1914
The **German army captures Brussels**.

August 28, 1914
The first major engagement of the British and German navies during World War I occurs at the **Battle of Helgoland Bight**.

January 5, 1914
Following the great success of the **Model T**, American automobile maker Henry Ford raises his workers' pay from $2.40 to $5.00 a day and reduces the hours of the workday.

 [3]

April 20, 1914
Sit-in strikers at the Rockefeller-controlled Colorado Fuel and Iron Company are fired on by militiamen, resulting in 17 deaths. The **Ludlow Massacre**, as it is termed, is said to have solidified Rockefeller's devotion to humanitarian causes.

 [4]

May 29, 1914
Canadian Pacific's **Empress of Ireland** collides with another ship in the Gulf of St. Lawrence, killing 1,023 people.

 [5]

June 28, 1914
Archduke Francis Ferdinand, heir to the Austro-Hungarian throne, and his consort, Sophie, are assassinated by Gavrilo Princip in **Sarajevo**, Bosnia, precipitating the outbreak of World War I.

 [6]

July 28, 1914
Using the assassination of the Austrian archduke Francis Ferdinand as a pretext to present **Serbia** with an unacceptable ultimatum, Austria-Hungary declares war on the Slavic country.

 [7]

August 3, 1914
Germany declares war on France.

 [8]

[5] Crowds gather for news outside the Canadian Pacific offices in Trafalgar Square, after the Empress of Iceland *sinking.*

[8] German reservists go off to war, still in civilian hats, while small boys wear their spiked helmets.

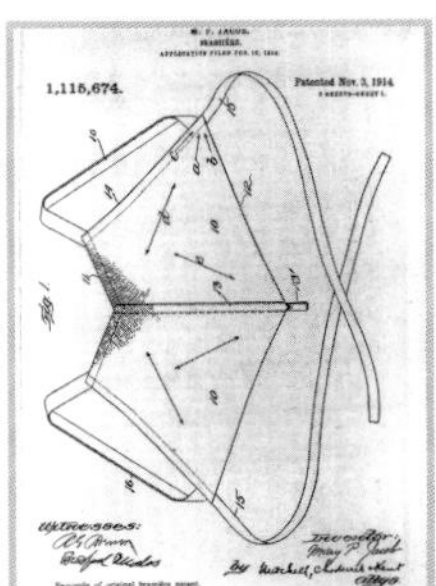

[12] The drawing accompanying the first patent application for a brassiere.

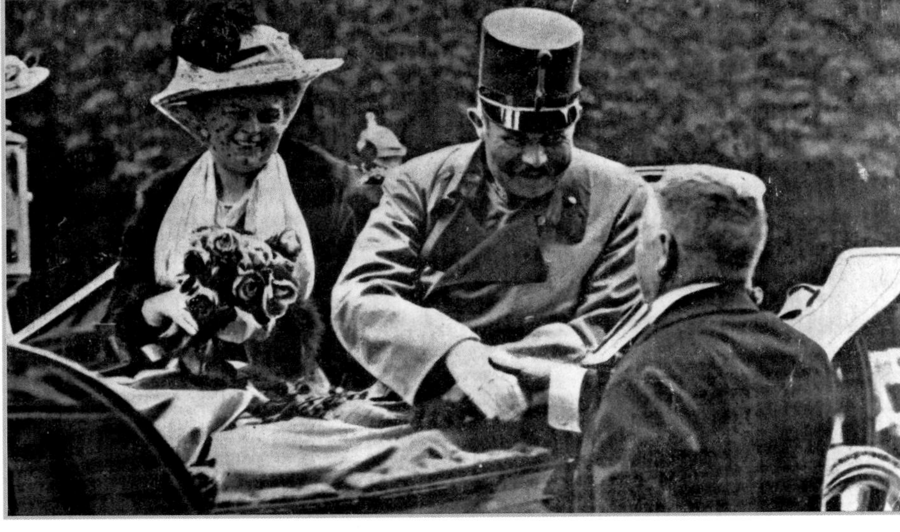

[6] Archduke Franz Ferdinand and his wife on the day they are assassinated. He is married to a Czech and therefore, ironically, sympathetic to the lot of Slavs, like Gavrilo Princip and his accomplices, within the Austro-Hungarian Empire.

[7] A Serbian soldier going off to fight is accompanied to the station by his wife.

[11]

September 6, 1914
French and British forces launch an offensive against advancing Germans in the first **Battle of the Marne** during World War I.

 [12]

November 1914
Mary Phelps Jacob is awarded a patent for the elastic **brassiere**, which will later replace the corset.

November 5, 1914
France and Britain declare war on **Turkey**, widening the conflict.

December 1914
Britain proclaims a protectorate over **Egypt** and deposes Abbas Hilmi II. The British give his uncle, Husayn Kamil, the title of sultan, replacing the old title of khedive.

1915
British author **Ford Madox Ford** publishes his novel *The Good Soldier*, a controversial exploration of Western morals and sexuality.

1915
Corning Glass produces **Pyrex**, a heat- and shock-resistant glass that will be widely used in oven ware and coffeemakers.

1915

1915
Czech novelist **Franz Kafka** publishes his novella *The Metamorphosis*, the story of Gregor Samsa, a man who wakes up one morning to find himself transformed into a beetle.

 [1]

1915
English novelist **D. H. Lawrence** publishes his first modernist novel, *The Rainbow*. The sequel, *Women in Love*, will appear in 1921. They will both be condemned as obscene, as will the notorious *Lady Chatterley's Lover* (1928).

[2]

1915
Ernest H. Shackleton's ship **Endurance** is crushed in the pack ice of the Weddell Sea, thus aborting one of the most ambitious polar expeditions to date.

 [3]

1915
Ford Motor Company produces its one millionth automobile.

 [4]

1915
France outlaws the production of **absinthe**, a flavored, distilled liquor made in part from wormwood and thought to cause hallucinations and psychoses.

 [5]

1915
French physicist Paul Langevin develops **sonar** as a means of detecting submarines.

[1] Franz Kafka in a bowler. Was it from this that he got the idea for the industrial worker's hard hat—an innovation attributed to him—while working for an insurance company?

[2] D. H. Lawrence. His autobiographical novel, Sons and Lovers, *had been published in 1913.*

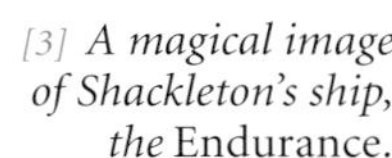

[3] A magical image of Shackleton's ship, the Endurance.

[5] The allure of absinthe: a suggestive poster for one particular brand from the 1900s.

[7] "Big Willie," the second model of tank, with wheels at the back to help it steer and a wire cage on top to deflect bombs and grenades.

[4] An engine is attached to a chassis in the Ford factory.

[8] The cover of a brochure issued by the Ku Klux Klan in Atlanta: "an urgent call to real men from the imperial palace."

 [7]

1915
The first military **tank**, nicknamed "Little Willie," is built in Great Britain by the Admiralty Landships Committee. A second model, called "Big Willie," quickly follows.

1915
The **Fox Film Corporation** is founded by William Fox, a New York City film exhibitor and distributor. It will merge with Twentieth Century Pictures in 1935 to create one of the major American motion-picture studios.

 [8]

1915
The **Ku Klux Klan** is revived. To the old Klan's hostility toward blacks the new Klan—which becomes strong in the Midwest as well as in the South—adds bias against Roman Catholics, Jews, foreigners, and organized labor.

1915
The mass production of **lipstick** begins when American inventor Maurice Levy designs the metal lipstick case.

1915
The **Provincetown Players** begin performing in Provincetown, Massachusetts, founded by a nontheater group of writers and artists for the production of new and experimental plays.

January 18, 1915
Japan delivers the **Twenty-one Demands**, for special privileges in China. The Chinese president, Yuan Shikai, will be forced to accept nearly all the demands, and anti-Japanese feeling in China will greatly increase.

1915
Labor Party member **William Hughes**, who will become a mainstay of national politics for 50 years, is elected prime minister of Australia. He will serve until 1923.

1915
Nearly all U.S. states have laws that ban **brothels** or regulate the profits of **prostitution**. These legislative efforts were encouraged by the federal Mann Act (1910), which prohibited interstate transportation of women for "immoral purposes."

1915
Ottoman Turks, who control part of the traditional land of the **Armenians**, accuse them of siding with the Russians.

1915
Polish-born British anthropologist **Bronislaw Malinowski** begins fieldwork in the Trobriand Islands of New Guinea. His experiences and writings help create the field of social anthropology.

1915
Ruth St. Denis and Ted Shawn found the **Denishawn School of Dancing** and Related Arts, the foremost school of American modern dance.

1915
Silent film "vamp" and one of cinema's first sex symbols **Theda Bara** appears in her first major movie, *A Fool There Was*.

 [6]

THE ARMENIAN MASSACRES

Genocide in the Ottoman Empire

It is estimated that nearly two million Christian Armenians lived in the Ottoman Empire by the late 1880s. The Armenians in the eastern provinces at that time, encouraged by Russia, began promoting Armenian territorial autonomy. At the same time, Abdülhamid II, the sultan of the Ottoman Empire, intent on suppressing all separatist sentiments in the empire, drastically raised taxes on the Armenians and aroused resentment against them among the neighboring Kurds. When the Armenians in Sasun refused to pay the oppressive taxes, Turkish troops and Kurdish tribesmen killed thousands of them and burned their villages (1894).

In the hope of calling attention to their cause, Armenian revolutionaries staged another demonstration two years later: they seized the Ottoman Bank in Istanbul. In the mayhem that followed, more than 50,000 Armenians were killed by mobs of Muslim Turks whose actions were apparently coordinated by government troops.

The last and deadliest of the massacres occurred during World War I (1914–18). Armenians from the Caucasus region of the Russian Empire formed volunteer battalions to help the Russian army against the Turks. Early in 1915 these battalions recruited Turkish Armenians from behind the Turkish lines. In response, the Turkish government ordered the deportation of about 1,750,000 Armenians to Syria and Mesopotamia. In the course of this forced exodus, about 600,000 Armenians died of starvation (above) or were killed by Turkish soldiers and police while en route in the desert. Hundreds of thousands more were forced into exile.

[6] *Theda Bara, born Theodosia Goodman, a pioneering sex symbol. The label "vamp" is short for vampire.*

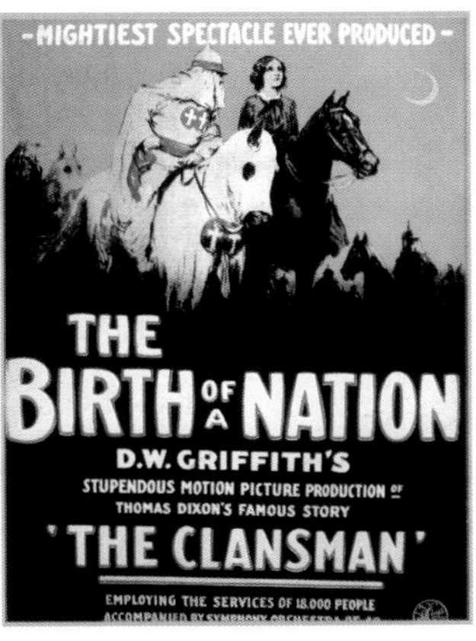

[9] *A poster, featuring a mounted Ku Klux Klansman, for* The Birth of a Nation.

[10] *German sailors on watch from the conning tower of a surfaced U-boat.*

January 25, 1915
The first **transcontinental telephone call** is made between New York and San Francisco.

January 28, 1915
Congress creates the **U.S. Coast Guard** by combining the Revenue Cutter Service with the U.S. Lifesaving Service.

[9]

February 8, 1915
The landmark film **The Birth of a Nation**, by D. W. Griffith, has its premiere at Clune's Auditorium in Los Angeles.

 [10]

February 18, 1915
German forces begin a **U-boat (submarine) blockade** of Britain.

March 18, 1915
Russia, Britain, and France sign the secret **Constantinople Agreement**, on the postwar partition of the Ottoman Empire, never carried out because Russia will become hostile to the Allies after its revolution.

April 1915
The Turkish government initiates the **forced migration of Armenians** to Syria. Of the 1.75 million that will be deported, over 600,000 will die of starvation or at the hands of Turkish soldiers.

1915-1916

April 22, 1915
German forces introduce the systematized use of chemical warfare when they release **chlorine gas** along a 4-mile (6-km) front at the Second Battle of Ypres.

 [1]

April 23, 1915
English poet **Rupert Brooke** dies on the way to Gallipoli, of blood poisoning. He is best known for *1914*, a collection of wartime sonnets.

 [2]

April 25, 1915
The Australian and New Zealand Army Corps (ANZAC) lands at **Gallipoli** in western Turkey. The invasion, involving British and French troops as well, fails because of poor planning and poor leadership.

 [3]

April 26, 1915
Italy agrees to the secret Treaty of London, which commits it to enter World War I against Austria-Hungary within a month. In return the Allies promise Italy extensive territory and money.

May 7, 1915
A German submarine sinks the **Lusitania**, a British ocean liner, indirectly contributing to the entry of the United States into World War I.

May 23, 1915
Italy declares war on Austria-Hungary, entering World War I on the side of the Allies.

[1] German soldiers rely on the wind to carry poison gas towards the enemy. It seems amazing that they are not equipped with gas masks.

[2] Rupert Brooke: "If I should die, think only this of me..."

[6] Douglas Haig in France with Prime Minister David Lloyd George and General Joseph Joffre, the French Commander-in-Chief, in 1916.

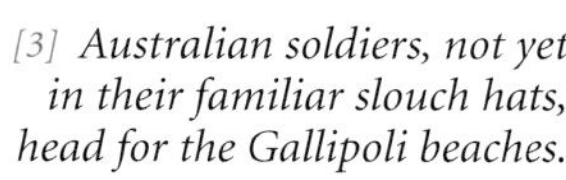

[3] Australian soldiers, not yet in their familiar slouch hats, head for the Gallipoli beaches.

"All the News That's Fit to Print."

The New York Times.

LUSITANIA SUNK BY A SUBMARINE, PROBABLY 1,000 DEAD; TWICE TORPEDOED OFF IRISH COAST; SINKS IN 15 MINUTES; AMERICANS ABOARD INCLUDED VANDERBILT AND FROHMAN; WASHINGTON BELIEVES THAT A GRAVE CRISIS IS AT HAND

THE *LUSITANIA*

British liner sunk by German U-boat

On May 7, 1915, the British ocean liner the *Lusitania* was sunk by a German submarine off the coast of Ireland. The British Admiralty had warned the *Lusitania* to avoid the area and to use the evasive tactic of zigzagging, but the crew ignored these recommendations. Though unarmed, the ship was carrying a cargo of rifle ammunition and shells for the Allies, and the Germans had circulated warnings that the ship would be sunk. The loss of life—1,198 people drowned, including 128 U.S. citizens—outraged public opinion (above, British sailors at a funeral procession in Ireland for the victims). The U.S. protested Germany's action, and Germany limited its submarine campaign against Britain. When Germany renewed unrestricted submarine warfare, the U.S. entered World War I in April 1917.

 [6]

December 17, 1915
Douglas Haig becomes commander-in-chief of the British Expeditionary Force. His strategy of attrition leads to enormous numbers of British casualties but little territorial gain, until an eventual breakthrough in 1918.

1916
A German **potato blight** contributes to the starvation of 700,000 citizens and soldiers over the next two years.

1916
After several years' work, German physicist Albert Einstein publishes his **general theory of relativity**. He will be regarded as the most influential physicist of the 20th century.

1916
American oilman Harry F. Sinclair consolidates his interests into **Sinclair Oil** and Refining (later Sinclair Oil). Within a few years he will become a major independent producer with holdings worldwide.

1916
American poet H. D. (**Hilda Doolittle**) publishes her first volume of verse, *Sea Garden*. It establishes her as an important voice among the radical young Imagist poets.

1916
American reformer Margaret Sanger opens the first **American birth control clinic** in Brooklyn, New York.

May 31, 1915
A German **zeppelin** bombs London and kills seven in the first strategic bombing of a civilian target.

 [4]

July 24, 1915
More than 800 people die when the excursion boat **Eastland** rolls over in the Chicago River.

July 28, 1915
U.S. Marines invade **Haiti** after the assassination of the Haitian prime minister. The Marines will occupy Haiti, and the U.S. government will control the affairs of the nation for the next 19 years.

October 1915
Bulgaria joins World War I on the side of the Central Powers by declaring war on Serbia.

October 12, 1915
English nurse **Edith Cavell** is executed for helping Allied soldiers escape from German-occupied Belgium. She will become a popular heroine as the Allies publicize her death.

 [5]

November 19, 1915
Labor organizer and songwriter **Joe Hill** is executed by Utah state officials and becomes a folk hero in the American labour movement.

[4] *A damaged house in Shoreditch, East London, after a zeppelin raid.*

[7] Intolerance. *Its theme is chosen to counteract the criticism Griffith received about the racism in* The Birth of a Nation. *It tells four parallel stories, employs 3,000 extras, and is a box office flop.*

[9] *Eugene O'Neill. His play is performed by the Provincetown Players in Massachusetts.*

[10] *Jean-Jules Jusserand and his wife. In his lifetime his books on medieval England are also very popular.*

[5] *Edith Cavell with a child sometime before World War I.*

[8] *David Lloyd George inspecting troops at a training camp.*

1916
American timber merchant William E. Boeing founds Aero Products Company shortly after he and U.S. Navy officer Conrad Westervelt develop a single-engine seaplane. The company will be renamed **Boeing Airplane Company** in 1917.

1916
Cai Yuanpei, Chinese educator and revolutionary, is named chancellor of **Peking University**, which under his leadership will play a major role in the development of a new spirit of nationalism and social reform in China.

 [7]

1916
D. W. Griffith directs his second silent film masterpiece, **Intolerance**.

 [8]

1916
David Lloyd George of the Liberal Party succeeds H. H. Asquith as British prime minister and dominates the British political scene in the latter part of World War I.

 [9]

1916
Eugene O'Neill makes his debut as a playwright with *Bound East for Cardiff*. O'Neill goes on to become one of the century's best-known playwrights, winning the Nobel Prize for Literature in 1936.

 [10]

1916
Jean-Jules Jusserand, the French ambassador to Washington, D.C., publishes *With Americans of Past and Present Days*. It will win the **first Pulitzer Prize** for history.

1916

1916
Jeannette Rankin is elected to Congress from Montana; she is the first female member of the U.S. House of Representatives.

 [1]

1916
Lincoln Logs, simple toy sets for building houses and other structures, are popularized by John Lloyd Wright, son of the famous American architect Frank Lloyd Wright.

1916
Psychologist Lewis Madison Terman introduces the term **I.Q. (intelligence quotient)** and creates the first widely used intelligence test.

1916
The American Tobacco Company introduces the cigarette brand **Lucky Strike**. An advertising campaign spearheaded by George Washington Hill and Edward L. Bernays will make it the company's most popular brand.

1916
The Anglican Church begins to oppose the **Braid movement**, led by Garrick (Sokari) Braid. Begun about 1910, it is the first prophet-healing movement in Nigeria and one of the earliest in Africa.

1916
The ash-filled wasteland in southwestern Alaska known as the **Valley of Ten Thousand Smokes** is viewed for the first time. Once a green valley, it was devastated by the violent eruption of Novarupta Volcano in 1912.

EASTER RISING

Militant Irish republicans attempt to win independence from Britain.

On Easter Monday, April 24, 1916, Irish republicans rose up against their British rulers in Dublin. Led by Patrick Pearse and Tom Clarke, some 1,560 Irish Volunteers and 200 members of the Irish Citizen Army seized the Dublin General Post Office and other strategic points in Dublin. After five days of fighting, British troops (above, snipers at the Dublin quays) put down the rebellion, and 15 of its leaders were tried and executed. Though the uprising itself had been unpopular with most of the Irish, the executions caused revulsion against the British authorities. The uprising heralded the end of British power in Ireland.

[2] *French troops under fire at Verdun.*

[3] *Some of Pancho Villa's bandits under guard after their capture by U.S. troops during a punitive raid into Mexico in retaliation for the incident at Columbus.*

January 1, 1916
The first **Rose Bowl football game** is played, between Washington State and Brown universities. The Rose Bowl will go on to become the oldest and most prestigious collegiate bowl game.

 [2]

February 21, 1916
The **Battle of Verdun**, one of the most devastating engagements of World War I, begins, as the French repulse a major German offensive. The 10-month battle results in some one million casualties, half of them fatalities.

 [3]

March 9, 1916
Pancho Villa's men kill more than a dozen in a raid on Columbus, New Mexico.

April 24, 1916
Members of the Irish Volunteers and the Irish Citizen Army seize strategic points in Dublin during the **Easter Rising**, which heralds the end of British power in Ireland.

 [4]

April 29, 1916
About 10,000 British troops surrender to Ottoman Turks at **Al-Kut**, Iraq, following a five-month siege.

 [5]

May 31, 1916
British and German naval fleets meet in the **Battle of Jutland**.

1916
The **Cleveland Museum of Art** opens. It will house one of the finest art collections in the United States.

1916
The **Confederación Sudamericana de Fútbol** (CONMEBOL) is founded. It will serve as the governing body of the sport of football (soccer) in South America.

1916
The **Dada** art movement begins with meetings of a group of minimalist artists at the Cabaret Voltaire in Zürich.

1916
The **estate tax** is reimposed in the United States to help finance mobilization for World War I.

1916
The Summer **Olympic Games** do not take place due to World War I.

c. 1916
The **Great Migration** begins; between 1916 and 1970 some six million African American Southerners migrate to urban centers in the North and West.

[6] Sir Roger Casement, probably handcuffed shortly before his execution for arranging to supply weapons from Germany to the Irish rebels.

[1] Jeanette Rankin. A lifelong pacifist, she votes against U.S. entry into World Wars I and II and will lead a march of 5,000 women in Washington D.C. against the Vietnam War in 1968.

[8] British machine gunners wearing gas masks during the Battle of the Somme.

[5] A battleship fires at the German High Seas Fleet at the Battle of Jutland.

[4] British reinforcements sail up the Tigris to Al-Kut before it surrenders to the Turks.

[7] What a German infantryman sees during a British attack.

June 1916
Sharif Husayn ibn 'Ali of Mecca, with assurance of British support, revolts against the Ottomans. He takes **Mecca** but fails to capture Medina.

July 1, 1916
Coca-Cola introduces its famous contoured bottle to distinguish the soft drink now known as Coca-Cola Classic from imitators.

 [6]

August 3, 1916
Irish-born public servant **Sir Roger Casement** is executed in London for treason. He becomes one of the principal martyrs in the revolt against British rule in Ireland.

September 14, 1916
American philosopher **Josiah Royce** dies. His emphasis on individuality and will, rather than intellect, strongly influences 20th-century philosophy in the United States.

 [7]

September 15, 1916
The **tank** is used for the first time in combat, by the British, during World War I. Of the 32 tanks used in an attack during the Battle of the Somme, nine reach the German lines.

 [8]

November 13, 1916
The costly four-month offensive, largely British, against German positions along the **Somme** River ends.

November 5, 1916
The Central Powers issue the Two Emperors' Manifesto, which proclaims the creation of the **Polish kingdom**, although its status and borders remain undefined.

December 1916
The Indian National Congress and the All-India Muslim League agree to the **Lucknow Pact**, which addresses the structure of India's government and the relations between Hindu and Muslim communities.

December 30, 1916
Grigory Yefimovich **Rasputin** is poisoned by Russian conservatives in an effort to halt his influence over Empress Alexandra and the royal family.

 [1]

1917
American dramatist and poet **Edna St. Vincent Millay** publishes her fresh, romantic first collection of poems, *Renascence and Other Poems.*

1917
Arab forces under the leadership of T. E. Lawrence (**Lawrence of Arabia**) take the port of Aqaba on the Red Sea from the Ottoman Turks.

 [2]

1917
Donald F. Jones devises a breeding technique for hybrids known as the "double cross," maximizing the best traits of four strains of corn. The first **hybrid corn** involving inbred lines to be produced commercially will be sold in 1921.

[1] *Rasputin, who has gained huge influence at the imperial court in Russia because he alone seems able to control the young tsarevich's hemophilia.*

[2] *T. E. Lawrence in Arab costume. Whatever the legends he will allow or encourage to accumulate around him, he remains a remarkable phenomenon.*

[6] *The crew of U-boat U3 pose by its conning tower.*

FEBRUARY REVOLUTION

The end of the Russian monarchy

By 1917 the bond between the tsar and most of the Russian people had been broken. Governmental corruption and inefficiency were rampant. The tsar's reactionary policies, including the occasional dissolution of the Duma (parliament), the chief fruit of the 1905 revolution, had spread dissatisfaction even to moderate elements. The Russian Empire's many ethnic minorities grew increasingly restive under Russian domination.

But it was the government's inefficient participation in World War I that finally provided the challenge the old regime could not meet. Ill equipped and poorly led, Russian armies suffered catastrophic losses in campaign after campaign against German armies. The war showed that Russia was no longer a military match for the nations of central and western Europe, and it disrupted the economy.

In late February riots over the scarcity of food broke out in the capital, Petrograd (formerly St. Petersburg). There were strikes, political gatherings, and rallies (above, demonstrators gathered outside the Winter Palace) throughout the city. When most of the Petrograd garrison joined the revolt, Tsar Nicholas II was forced to abdicate on March 2. When his brother, Grand Duke Michael, refused the throne, more than 300 years of rule by the Romanov dynasty came to an end.

A committee of the Duma appointed a provisional government. This government, intended as an interim stage in the creation of a permanent democratic-parliamentary polity for Russia, was in turn overthrown by the Bolsheviks, who established the Soviet Communist government in October 1917.

 [5]

c. 1917
De Stijl, a Dutch movement in the modern arts and architecture, coalesces around the journal *De Stijl.* Its members include Piet Mondrian, Gerrit Rietveld, and J. J. P. Oud.

January 17, 1917
The United States purchases three of the **Virgin Islands**—St. Thomas, St. John, and St. Croix—from Denmark for $25 million.

 [6]

February 3, 1917
Not yet involved in World War I, the United States breaks off diplomatic relations with Germany after the Germans announce their intention to practice **unrestricted submarine warfare**.

February 5, 1917
Mexico adopts its present constitution.

March 2, 1917
The Jones Act takes effect, designating **Puerto Rico** as a territory of the United States, "organized but unincorporated," and conferring U.S. citizenship collectively on Puerto Ricans.

March 8, 1917
Rioting in St. Petersburg marks the beginning of the **February Revolution** and the first stage of the Russian Revolution.

1917
During the anti-German atmosphere of World War I, the name of the ruling house of the United Kingdom is changed from Saxe-Coburg-Gotha to **Windsor**.

 [3]

1917
Hu Shih, China's foremost liberal during the Nationalist era, sets forth eight tenets of literary reform, his famous **Eight Don'ts**, in the Chinese literary journal *New Youth*, thereby launching the vernacular literature movement in China.

1917
In Great Britain, the Representation of the People Act is passed by the House of Commons in June and by the House of Lords in February 1918. Under this act, all women age 30 or over receive the **right to vote**.

1917
Marcel Duchamp, a member of the Dada movement, challenges the definition of art with his "ready-mades," including *Fountain*, an ordinary urinal he exhibits in an art museum.

 [4]

1917
Moderate **Venustiano Carranza**, who had been revolutionary commander in Mexico, officially assumes the presidency.

1917
President Venustiano Carranza creates the first national park in Mexico, the **Desert of the Lions**, southwest of Mexico City. It occupies a wide expanse of mountains, pine forests, springs, and aqueducts.

[3] *King George V and Queen Mary drive out with their daughter, the Princess Royal, and one of their younger sons in a midshipman's uniform.*

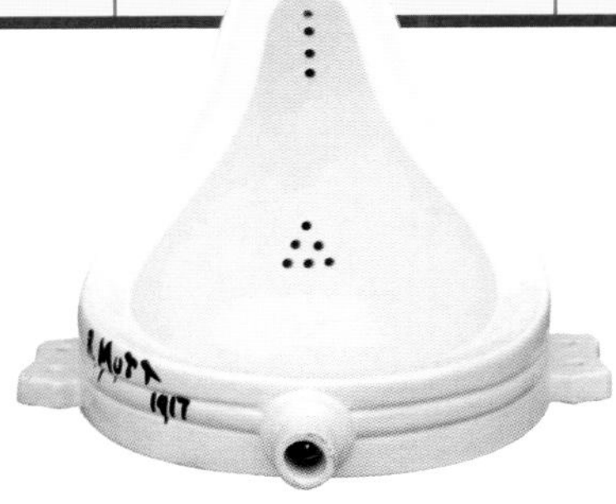

[4] *The beginnings of conceptual art? Marcel Duchamp calls a urinal a sculpture, and so it immediately becomes one.*

[5] Composition IX, opus 18, *by Theo van Doesburg, a member of the De Stijl group and publisher of the journal of the same namme. Another step into abstraction.*

[7] *Tsar Nicholas II with some of his family in confinement after his abdication.*

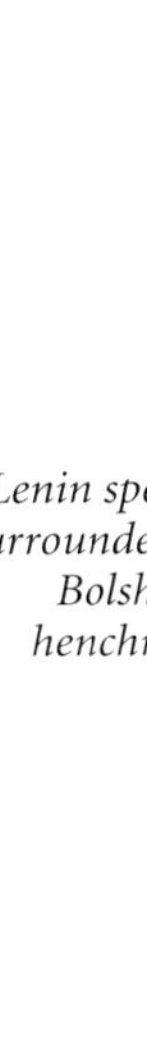

[9] *Lenin speaks, surrounded by Bolshevik henchmen.*

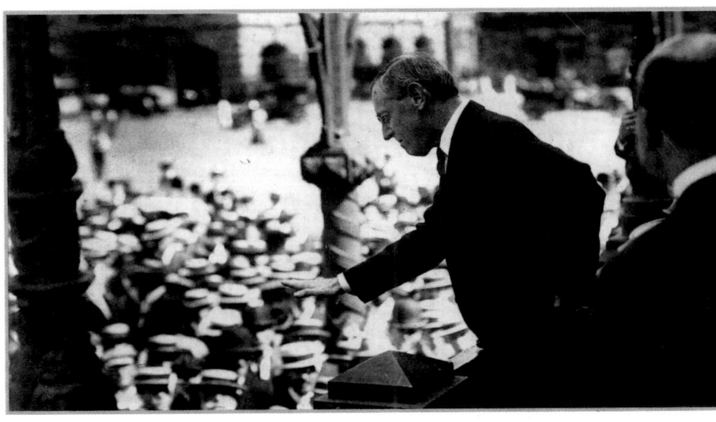

[8] *President Woodrow Wilson speaks.*

March 8, 1917
The U.S. Senate votes to limit **filibusters** by adopting the rule of cloture.

 [7]

March 15, 1917
During the first phase of the Russian Revolution, **Tsar Nicholas II is forced to abdicate**, thus ending the rule of the Romanov dynasty.

March 29, 1917
Man o' War, probably the most famous American racehorse (Thoroughbred), is foaled in Kentucky; he is overwhelmingly voted, in an Associated Press poll taken in 1950, the greatest horse of the first half of the 20th century.

 [8]

April 2, 1917
U.S. president Woodrow Wilson asks Congress for a **declaration of war against Germany**, thereby entering World War I.

 [9]

April 16, 1917
One month after Russia's tsar had been forced to abdicate, Vladimir Ilich **Lenin** ends his 17-year exile and returns to Russia to form a provisional government.

May 13, 1917
At **Fátima** in Portugal, three young peasant children see a woman who identifies herself as the Lady of the Rosary—that is, Mary, the mother of Jesus.

1917-1918

June 27, 1917
Greece declares war on the Central Powers.

July 16, 1917
Georg Michaelis, whose government will prove totally dependent on the military supreme command, becomes imperial chancellor of Germany (1917).

July 20, 1917
The Corfu Declaration is issued, calling for the establishment of a unified **Yugoslav state** following World War I.

July 24, 1917
Dutch-born dancer and courtesan **Mata Hari**, whose name becomes a synonym for the seductive female spy, is accused of spying for Germany, goes on trial, and is subsequently found guilty and shot by a firing squad.

 [1]

August 1917
The British launch the **Passchendaele offensive** to relieve pressure on the French army, where many divisions have mutinied. In November, it ends where it started, after 500,000 Allied and 250,000 German casualties.

 [2]

October 24, 1917
More than 600,000 Italians surrender or retreat at the Battle of **Caporetto** during World War I.

 [3]

[1] Mata Hari, at what looks like a point very close to the end of the dance of the seven veils.

[2] The full horror of Passchendaele: British dead and wounded lie in the mud.

[7] Seattle policemen wearing face masks during the influenza epidemic. It has been estimated that the majority of the world's population caught the infection.

[6] Willa Cather: she draws on her Nebraska prairie upbringing for her novels.

[8] Babe Ruth in the uniform of the Boston Red Sox.

[9] An elegant British woman drops her voting paper in the ballot box.

[10] Siegfried Sassoon. He shows near-suicidal courage on the Western Front before adopting a pacifist stance. The authorities then send him to a psychiatric hospital to avoid having to court martial him.

 [6]

1918
American frontier novelist **Willa Cather** publishes *My Ántonia.*

[7]

1918
A worldwide **influenza pandemic** kills perhaps 30 million people; it is among the most devastating epidemics in human history. Troop movements and demobilizations spread the disease to every continent.

[8]

1918
Babe Ruth wins the first of his dozen American League home-run crowns. The baseball slugger's exploits are so renowned that the term "Ruthian" is coined to describe remarkable feats of batting.

[9]

1918
The **Representation of People Act** is passed in Great Britain, giving the right to vote to all men age 21 or older and to all women age 30 or older.

1918
Edwin H. Armstrong invents the **superheterodyne circuit**, a means of receiving, converting, and greatly amplifying very weak, high-frequency electromagnetic waves, vital for radio, radar, and television reception.

[10]

1918
English poet **Siegfried Sassoon** publishes *Counterattack*, a collection of antiwar poems drawing on his experiences fighting in France.

November 2, 1917
A. J. Balfour, the British foreign secretary, in a letter to the 2nd Baron Rothschild, a leader of British Jewry, issues the **Balfour Declaration**, a statement of British support for "the establishment in Palestine of a national home for the Jewish people."

November 6, 1917
The second phase of the Russian Revolution of 1917 begins as the **Bolsheviks seize power** in Russia.

 [4]

November 20, 1917
For the first time, tanks are used in large numbers, by the British at the **Battle of Cambrai**.

 [5]

December 2, 1917
Georg, Graf von Hertling, a conservative German statesman and philosopher, becomes imperial chancellor for the final year of World War I.

December 6, 1917
Finland declares itself independent of Russia following the Bolshevik Revolution.

December 7, 1917
The United States declares war on the **Austro-Hungarian Empire**.

[4] Red Guards and marines outside St. Isaac's Cathedral in St. Petersburg during the October Revolution.

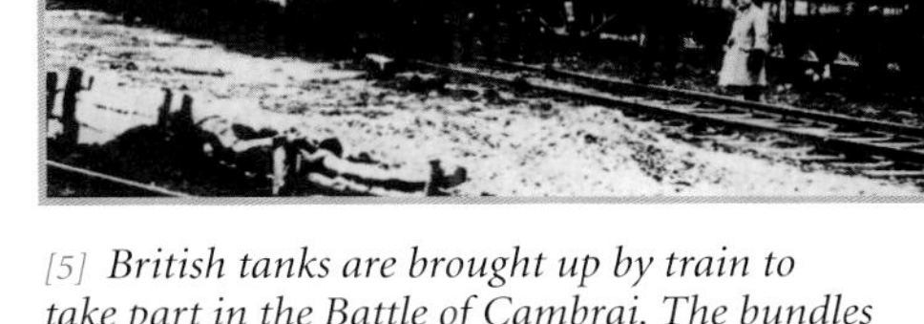

[5] British tanks are brought up by train to take part in the Battle of Cambrai. The bundles of wood can be dropped into trenches ahead of a tank so it does not get stuck.

[3] Italian troops after their defeat by the Austro-Hungarians and Germans at Caporetto in what is now Slovenia.

[11] A political meeting in Moscow's Red Square early in 1918.

1918
In response, in part, to the Russian Revolution and the Easter Rising in Ireland, the U.S. government passes the **Sedition Act**, which forbids citizens from using "disloyal" language about the government, flag, or armed forces.

1918
Lu Xun, China's most famous modern writer, publishes his first short story, *Diary of a Madman*. The first published Western-style story written wholly in vernacular Chinese, it leads to Chinese acceptance of the short-story form.

1918
The last **Carolina parakeet** dies in the Cincinnati Zoo. The only parrot native to the U.S., the birds were decimated by deforestation and extensively hunted by farmers whose crops they destroyed.

1918
The practical and convenient **wristwatch** is popularized for men. Prior to World War I, the pocket watch was the more popular style.

1918
Canada gives women the **right to vote**.

 [11]

1918
The **Russian Civil War** between the royalist "Whites" and Bolshevik "Reds" begins.

1918

January 8, 1918
U.S. president Woodrow Wilson announces his **Fourteen Points**, an outline for peace following World War I.

February 14, 1918
Russia adopts the **Gregorian calendar**, changing February 1 to February 14 and moving the country into line with the rest of Europe.

February 16, 1918
The 20-member Taryba (council) of **Lithuanian delegates** proclaim their country an independent state.

March 3, 1918
The second of two treaties of **Brest-Litovsk** concludes hostilities between the Central Powers and Soviet Russia during World War I.

 [1]

March 19, 1918
The U.S. Congress approves **daylight saving time**, a system for uniformly advancing clocks so as to extend daylight hours during conventional working time (but its unpopularity forces its repeal in 1919).

March 21, 1918
The second Battle of the Somme, or **Spring Offensive**, resulting in a major advance against Allied forces on the Western Front, begins.

[2]

[1] *The Germans and Austro-Hungarians (left) and the Russian Communists (right) sign the Treaty of Brest-Litovsk.*

[2] *German storm troopers advance during the Spring Offensive.*

[8] *An American machine-gun team fighting near Saint-Mihiel in the Argonne.*

[13] *Casualties of war: two French soldiers, blinded, probably by gas, are led along a road shielded from enemy observation by a high screen.*

[7] *Prince Max of Baden and his family. He will announce the abdication of the kaiser without his consent, before standing down himself.*

[9] *Tomás Masaryk (center), the first president of Czechoslovakia.*

1910–1919

September 29, 1918
German Chancellor Georg **von Hertling tenders his resignation** on the day of the Bulgarian armistice and the British attack of the Western Front during World War I.

October 5, 1918
Allied forces break through the **Hindenburg Line**.

[7]

October 5, 1918
Maxmilian, prinz von Baden, becomes imperial chancellor of Germany (1918). His humanitarian reputation makes Emperor William II think him capable of bringing World War I to a quick end.

 [8]

October 8, 1918
Corporal Alvin Cullum York single-handedly captures 132 Germans and kills another 25 during the Meuse-Argonne offensive of World War I.

October 26, 1918
Prussian general Erich **Ludendorff** is forced to resign by Emperor William II on Prince Maximilian's advice, in an effort to establish an armistice agreement.

 [9]

October 28, 1918
Tomás Masaryk, Edvard Benes, and other leaders issue a proclamation announcing the formation of an independent **Czechoslovakian state**.

April 1, 1918
The United Kingdom's **Royal Air Force** is formed.
[3]

April 21, 1918
Manfred, Freiherr (baron) **von Richthofen**, Germany's top flying ace in World War I, is shot down and killed during a battle near Amiens, France.
[4]

May 15, 1918
The first regular **airmail** route in the United States opens between New York City and Washington, D.C.

July 18, 1918
French General Ferdinand **Foch**, at the head of French, British, and U.S. forces, launches a counterstrike that sends the Germans into a hasty retreat during the second Battle of the Marne, the last large German offensive of World War I.
[5]

July 16, 1918
Former Russian tsar **Nicholas II and his family** are executed by Bolsheviks.
[6]

September 27, 1918
British forces attack the **Hindenburg Line** in the final offensive on the Western Front during World War I.

[3] *Number 1 Squadron of the RAF pose in front of their aircraft out in France.*

[5] *French colonial troops from Algeria collect weapons abandoned by or taken from the Germans during the second Battle of the Marne.*

[4] *Manfred von Richthofen sits in his Fokker triplane, talking to a mechanic.*

[11] *Josef Pilsudski. He has fought against Russia until its defeat but then withdraws his support from Germany and Austria-Hungary.*

[6] *Tsar Nicholas II and his children at Ekaterinburg a few days before they are shot.*

[10] *Wilfred Owen, the greatest of the British war poets and a protégé of Siegfried Sassoon.*

[13] *Celebrating the armistice in London's Strand.*

[12] *Marshal Foch, the Allied commander-in-chief (bottom center, with stick) outside his railway carriage at Compiègne, where the armistice is signed.*

 [10]
November 4, 1918
English poet **Wilfred Owen**, author of some of the best poems detailing the experience of combat in World War I, is killed a week before Armistice Day.

November 9, 1918
Friedrich Ebert, a leader of the Social Democrat movement in Germany, who will attempt to unite the country after its defeat by bringing about the Weimar Republic, becomes imperial chancellor for one day.

 [11]
November 10, 1918
Józef Pilsudski, Polish revolutionary and first chief of state of the newly reconstituted Poland, arrives in Warsaw to declare **Poland** an independent state.

 [12]
November 11, 1918
At 5 AM the Allied powers and Germany sign an **armistice** document in the railway carriage of Ferdinand Foch, the commander of the Allied armies, and six hours later World War I comes to an end.

November 12, 1918
After Emperor Charles's abdication, the National Assembly of **Austria** resolves that "German Austria is a democratic republic" and "a component part of the German republic."

 [13]
November 1918
At the **close of World War I**, some 8.5 million soldiers have died as the result of wounds or disease, 21 million are disabled, and 7.7 million more are taken prisoner or missing.

1918-1919

November 13, 1918
Egyptian patriot Sa'd Zaghlul forms **Al-Wafd al-Misri** (Arabic: "Egyptian Delegation"), a nationalist political party that is instrumental in gaining Egyptian independence from Britain.

December 1918
David Lloyd George, at the head of the National Liberal Coalition, wins a landslide victory in the **general election**, promising a land "fit for heroes to live in".

December 4, 1918
U.S. president Woodrow Wilson departs for France to attend the **Paris Peace Conference**, where, following the cessation of hostilities in World War I, the League of Nations is established and the Treaty of Versailles is drafted.

December 30, 1918
The **Spartacus League** is transformed into the Communist Party of Germany at a party congress.

1919
American journalist John Reed's eyewitness account of the Russian Revolution, **Ten Days That Shook the World**, is published.

 [1]

1919
Sherwood Anderson publishes *Winesburg, Ohio*, an account of small-town life in the United States. Its interrelated short sketches and tales are told by a newspaper reporter-narrator who is as emotionally stunted in some ways as the people he describes.

[1] A revolutionary poster from 1919, depicting a Russian sailor.

1910-1919

[5] The Chicago White Sox team in 1919. Shoeless Joe Jackson is in the bottom row, center.

THE UNITED ARTISTS CORPORATION

Hollywood filmmakers form their own company in order to keep creative and financial control.

The United Artists Corporation, a film production and distribution company, was formed on February 5, 1919, by Charlie Chaplin (third left), the comedy star; Mary Pickford (left) and her husband, Douglas Fairbanks (right), the popular film stars; and D. W. Griffith (second left), the director who was a pioneer in the development of camera techniques. They were the leading filmmakers of their day and wanted complete freedom in promoting, exploiting, and marketing their motion pictures. They also wanted to secure for themselves the highest revenues possible. At the time Hollywood producers and distributors were trying to tighten their grip over their stars' salaries and the creative control of films. The four partners received advice and support from the prominent lawyer and Democrat politician William Gibbs McAdoo (son-in-law of President Woodrow Wilson). The company also handled the distribution of high-quality films made by independent producers.

United Artists was the first major production company to be controlled by its artists rather than by businessmen. It also started the trend among studios to act as distributing agencies for films other than those it produced. In the 1920s the United Artists prospered with films starring Charlie Chaplin (including *The Gold Rush*) Gloria Swanson, Norma Talmadge, Buster Keaton, and Rudolph Valentino. The company met the new challenge of sound films in the 1930s with the talents of such producers as Samuel Goldwyn, Howard Hughes, and Alexander Korda.

1919
Robert H. Goddard, the father of modern rocketry, publishes his landmark treatise, **A Method of Reaching Extreme Altitudes**.

1919
New Guinea native peoples, seeing colonial officials bringing supplies, begin forming **cargo cults**, based on the belief that a new age of blessing has arrived.

 [5]

1919
In the **Black Sox Scandal**, the Chicago White Sox are bribed to lose the 1919 World Series. "Say it ain't so, Joe," pleads a young fan to outfielder Shoeless Joe Jackson. They are acquitted for lack of evidence but banned from baseball for life.

1919
The first chapter of **Save the Children** is founded in Great Britain. Established to provide relief to European children, it later grows into an international organization.

1919
The **International Labour Organization** is established as an affiliated agency of the League of Nations. It is now a specialized agency of the United Nations dedicated to improving labor conditions and living standards.

1919
The **Radio Corporation of America (RCA)** is founded.

 [2]

1919
American-born **Lady Nancy Astor** becomes the first female member of the British House of Commons.

 [3]

1919
Arthur Eddington observes the bending of light rays during a total solar eclipse and thus provides the first confirmation of Einstein's theory of general relativity.

1919
Hans Poelzig designs the **Grosses Schauspielhaus, Berlin**. With its stalactite-like forms, the theater's cavernous interior is one of the major monuments of Expressionist architecture.

1919
The U.S. Supreme Court upholds the conviction of an American socialist for distributing antidraft leaflets during wartime, ruling **freedom of expression** may be limited when there exists a "clear and present danger that [it] will bring about the substantive evils."

 [4]

1919
In the United States, the popularity of dog (**greyhound**) racing explodes after the mechanical rabbit is invented by O. P. Smith.

1919
Journalist **H. L. Mencken** publishes *The American Language,* an attempt to bring together examples of American, rather than English, expressions and idioms. In 1945 and 1948 Mencken will publish substantial supplements.

[2] Nancy Astor looking pleased as the results of the election securing her a seat in the House of Commons are announced.

[7] Anton Drexler in Bavarian costume and smoking a traditional pipe.

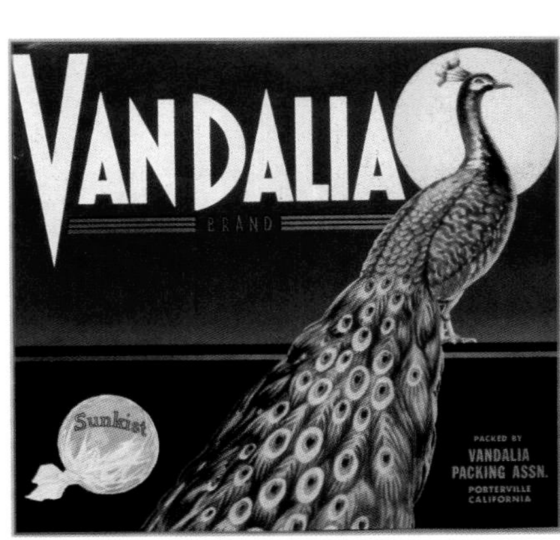

[6] An advertising poster featuring a Sunkist orange.

[3] Arthur Eddington. When told only three people understand relativity, he replies, "Oh, who's the third?"

[4] A mechanical hare or rabbit that makes possible the huge growth in greyhound or dog racing in the U.S. and Britain.

1919
The **United Artists Corporation** is formed. "So the lunatics have taken charge of the asylum," quips Metro Pictures president Richard Rowland.

 [6]

1919
The word "**Sunkist**" is burned into the skin of an orange, becoming the first trademark of a fresh fruit commodity.

1919
U.S. president **Woodrow Wilson** is awarded the Nobel Peace Prize for his promotion of the League of Nations.

1919
Walter Gropius becomes head of the **Bauhaus**, a school of design and art. It trains and inspires a generation of modern architects, while the design and applied arts produced there help define 20th-century culture.

1919
Woman suffrage comes to Germany, Austria, Poland, and Czechoslovakia.

 [7]

January 5, 1919
Anton Drexler founds the **German Workers' Party**, the forerunner of the Nazi Party, in Munich, Germany.

1919

January 1919
In the **Spartacist Uprising** in Berlin, Communists under Rosa Luxemburg and Karl Liebknecht are defeated by far-right Freikorps paramilitares employed by Social Democrat leader Fredrich Eisert.

[1]

January 21, 1919
The **Irish War of Independence** begins when members of the Irish Republican Army kill two policemen in County Tipperary.

[2]

January 29, 1919
The **Prohibition** (Eighteenth) Amendment to the U.S. Constitution is ratified and goes into effect the following year.

 [3]

February 6, 1919
A German constitutional assembly meets to form the **Weimar Republic**.

February 26, 1919
U.S. Congress establishes **Grand Canyon National Park** in northwestern Arizona.

 [4]

April 1919
The Korean provisional government is established in Shanghai by Korean patriots involved in the struggle for Korea's independence from Japan. **Syngman Rhee**, then residing in the U.S., is elected its first president.

[1] *Soldiers who have gone over to the Spartacist ranks pose by a primitive armored car, "firing" at loyalist officers in Berlin Castle.*

[2] *A casualty is carried off in a Dublin street after an incident in which two policemen have been shot and killed, during the struggle for Irish independence.*

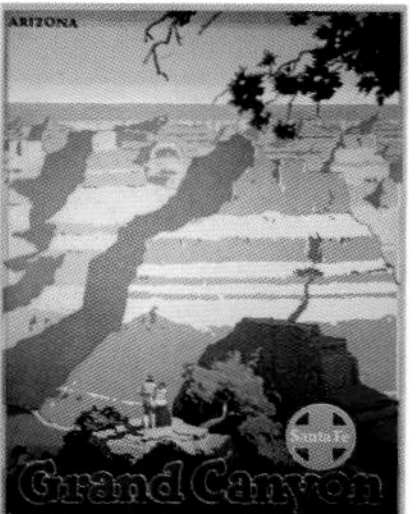

[4] *A railroad poster featuring the spectacular Grand Canyon National Park.*

[7] *Members of the National Guard stand on the streets of Chicago to restore order after the race riot.*

[8] *Gabriele d'Annunzio, man of action and literary figure, dramatist, and airman. His ambitions for Italy are enormous, but his actions and methods are often dubious.*

[3] *Barrels of liquor are smashed and emptied at the start of American Prohibition.*

 [7]

July 27, 1919
The **Chicago race riot** of 1919 is ignited after a young black man is stoned and drowned in Lake Michigan for swimming in an area reserved for whites.

August 1919
Great Britain confirms the independence of **Afghanistan**, under the leadership of Amanullah Khan.

August 11, 1919
The **Weimar constitution** is formally declared, establishing Germany as a republic.

August 14, 1919
Gustav Bauer, an officer who founded the Office Employees Association and is a member of the Social Democratic Party, becomes chancellor of the Weimar Republic (1919–20).

September 10, 1919
Austria and the Allied powers sign the Treaty of Saint-Germain, concluding hostilities.

 [8]

September 12, 1919
Italian nationalist poet **Gabriele d'Annunzio** leads an occupation of the Adriatic port city of Fiume (now Rijeka, Croatia), bringing to the forefront the Fiume question.

April 13, 1919
British troops fire on a crowd of unarmed Indian protesters, killing an estimated 379 people and wounding another 1,200 in what becomes known as the **Massacre of Amritsar**.

April 20, 1919
In an ongoing dispute over the possession of Vilnius, **Polish forces drive out Russia's Red Army**—which had previously ousted the newly established Lithuanian government—and occupies the city.

May 4, 1919
Students in Beijing protest the decision at Versailles that Japan should retain Germany's rights and possessions in Shandong. The name "**May Fourth Movement**" comes to be applied to the whole intellectual revolution in China from 1917 to 1921.

May 19, 1919
Mustafa Kemal lands at Samsun in Anatolia and begins to organize a national Turkish resistance movement against the orders of his superiors, a moment that is often regarded as the beginning of the Turkish War of Independence. [5]

June 1919
John Alcock and Arthur Whitten Brown make the first **transatlantic flight** from Newfoundland to Ireland. [6]

June 28, 1919
The **Treaty of Versailles** is signed at the Palace of Versailles in France, signifying the end of World War I.

THE TREATY OF VERSAILLES

International agreement to conclude World War I

On November 11, 1918, an armistice was signed, ending war in Europe. Following this the peace conference took place at the Palace of Versailles, on the outskirts of Paris, France. On June 1, 1919, the victorious Allied leaders met there; the photograph far left shows British prime minister David Lloyd George (left), French prime minister Georges Clemenceau (middle), and U.S. president Woodrow Wilson (right) arriving. Four weeks later, on June 28, in the Hall of Mirrors at Versailles (top left), the peace treaty was signed. (The bottom left photograph shows French citizens celebrating in a Paris street on the day of the signing).

The treaty was negotiated primarily by the U.S., Britain, and France, without participation by the war's losers. Germany was forced to accept blame for Allied losses and to pay major reparations. Its European territory was reduced by about 10 percent, its overseas possessions were confiscated, and its military establishment was reduced. Although some of the treaty's terms were eased in the 1920s, the bitterness it created helped to foster an environment that led to the growth of Fascism in Italy and the rise of the Nazi Party in Germany. The treaty also established the League of Nations, the International Labour Organization, and the Permanent Court of International Justice (later the International Court of Justice).

[5] *Mustafa Kemal (Kemal Atatürk), his forceful character etched on his features.*

[6] *The adapted Vickers Vimy twin-engined bomber in which Alcock and Brown fly across the Atlantic.*

September 16, 1919
The U.S. Congress grants a national charter to the **American Legion**, an organization of U.S. war veterans.

October 7, 1919
Royal Dutch Airlines (KLM) is founded and will become the world's longest continuously operating airline.

October 28, 1919
The U.S. Congress overrides President Woodrow Wilson's veto and passes **the Volstead Act**, providing enforcement guidelines for **Prohibition**.

November 27, 1919
The **Treaty of Neuilly**, outlining the post–World War I peace terms for **Bulgaria**, is signed between the defeated country and the Allied powers.

Art Deco chorus girls, 1929.

1920

1920
A hair-styling device, the **blow-dryer**, is invented in Racine, Wisconsin.
 [1]

1920
Adolf Hitler formulates the 25-point program that becomes the basis of the **Nazi Party**.

1920
African American participation in professional baseball begins in the United States with the formation of the **Negro National League**. Negro League play is rendered obsolete in the 1940s, when the major leagues are integrated
 [2]

1920
Agatha Christie publishes her first mystery novel, *The Mysterious Affair at Styles*, introducing the cerebral Belgian detective Hercule Poirot.

1920
Big Bill Tilden wins the first of six consecutive U.S. tennis championships. He goes on to win a total of 70 American and international titles.
 [3]

1920
Donald Douglas founds the **Douglas Aircraft Company**.

[7] Eugene V. Debs campaigning for the presidency in a prison uniform. "While there is a lower class, I am in it, and while there is a criminal element I am of it, and while there is a soul in prison, I am not free."

[2] The Chicago American Giants team, a member of the Negro National League.

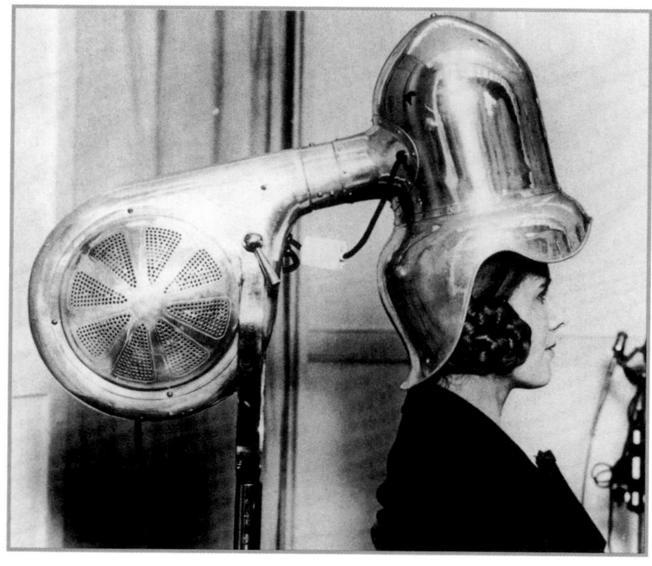

[1] A blow-dryer in a late 1920s hairdressing salon, looking like a helmet from an early science-fiction magazine.

[3] Bill Tilden at Wimbledon: full of grace and poise, he will win 11 Grand Slam men's singles titles.

 [7]
1920
Socialist **Eugene V. Debs** wins 915,000 votes for U.S. president, despite being in prison for having criticized the U.S. government's prosecution of persons charged with violation of the 1917 Espionage Act.

1920
Suzuki Motor Company—one of the leading producers of motorcycles and other lightweight vehicles—is founded.

1920
The **Bolshevik government** recognizes Estonia, Latvia, and Lithuania as independent nations after unsuccessful attempts to absorb them into the U.S.S.R.

1920
The first **Baby Ruth candy bar**, named for President Grover Cleveland's daughter, debuts.

1920
The Juilliard Musical Foundation is incorporated, which will go on to direct the renowned Juilliard School of arts education in New York City.

1920
The legal organization **American Civil Liberties Union** (ACLU) is founded to champion constitutional liberties in the United States.

1920
Edith Wharton publishes **The Age of Innocence**, which wins the Pulitzer Prize for fiction the following year.

1920
English playwright **Noël Coward** produces the first of his popular comedies of manners, *I'll Leave It to You*. His later works include *Bitter Sweet* (1929) and *Private Lives* (1930).

 [4]

1920
John T. Thompson, retired American army officer, patents the Thompson submachine, or "**Tommy**," **gun**.

 [5]

1920
KDKA, **the first commercial U.S. radio station**, begins broadcasting in Pittsburgh, Pennsylvania. It covers the Harding-Cox presidential election returns.

1920
Qantas Airways is founded in Australia. It is the oldest airline in the English-speaking world and will begin opearations in 1922.

1920
Sinclair Lewis's **Main Street** establishes his reputation as a leading American writer. He follows with *Babbitt* (1922) and *Arrowsmith* (1925) and wins the Nobel Prize for Literature in 1930.

 [6]

[4] *Noël Coward with Lilian Braithwaite in his play* The Vortex.

[5] *An early model of the Tommy gun. This one has a conventional magazine, rather than the trademark round version.*

[6] *Sinclair Lewis. It won't take many years for sales of* Main Street *to reach two million.*

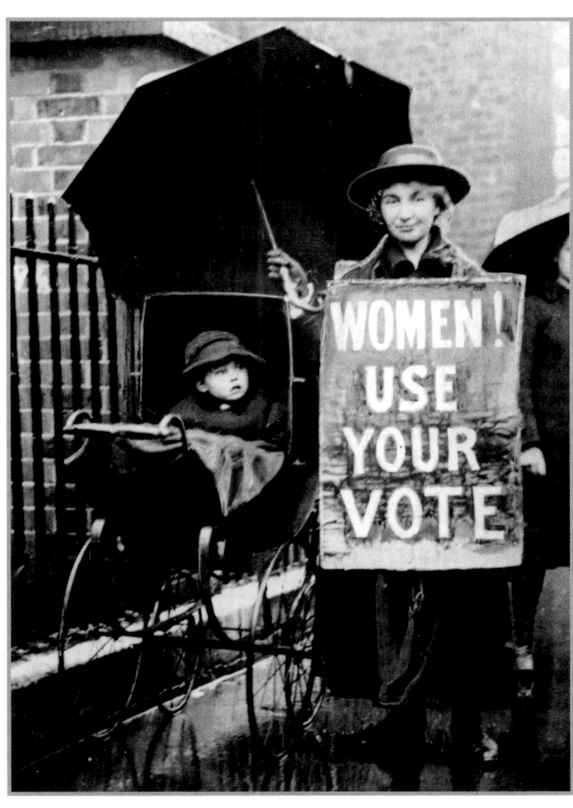

[8] *A campaign urges American women to use their newly granted right.*

[9] *Suzanne Lenglen of France at full stretch during the Antwerp Olympics.*

1920
The **National Football League** is founded in Canton, Ohio, with Jim Thorpe as its first president.

 [8]

1920
The Nineteenth Amendment to the U.S. Constitution is signed into law, giving women the right to vote.

1920
The **Royal Canadian Mounted Police** (RCMP) is established and given responsibility for federal law enforcement in all Canadian provinces and territories.

 [9]

1920
The **Summer Olympic Games** take place in Antwerp, Belgium.

1920
The U.S. becomes a predominantly **urban nation**, as more than half of the population lives in cities.

1920
University of Oxford admits its **first full-degree female students**.

1920

c. 1920
The **Harlem Renaissance** begins. The period will see a flourishing of African American arts, letters, and music.
 [1]

c. 1920
The **Russian Constructivism** movement, inspired by the work of Vladimir Tatlin, emerges with the publication of the *Realist Manifesto* in Moscow.

c. 1920
Young women adopt a new style as **flappers**—they smoke cigarettes, bob their hair, wear short skirts, and reject the idea of being chaperoned. The Jazz Age begins.
 [2]

January 3, 1920
The **Boston Red Sox** sell the rights to Babe Ruth to the New York Yankees for $125,000, the largest amount ever paid for an athlete at the time.

January 10, 1920
The League of Nations is established in Geneva.
 [3]

February 14, 1920
With the establishment of **woman suffrage in the United States**, Carrie Chapman Catt forms the League of Women Voters in Chicago.
 [4]

RUSSIAN CONSTRUCTIVISM

Art and architecture movement

Constructivism was first influenced by Cubism and Futurism and is generally considered to have been initiated in 1913 with the "painting reliefs"—abstract geometric constructions—of Vladimir Tatlin. The expatriate Russian sculptors Antoine Pevsner and Naum Gabo joined Tatlin and his followers in Moscow, and upon publication of their jointly written *Realist Manifesto* in 1920 they became the spokesmen of the movement. It is from the manifesto that the name "Constructivism" was derived; one of the directives that it contained was "to construct" art.

Other important figures associated with Constructivism were Alexander Rodchenko and El Lissitzky (shown at left is Rodchenko's painting *A Picturesque Composition* from 1919). Soviet opposition to the Constructivists' aesthetic radicalism resulted in the group's dispersion. Tatlin and Rodchenko remained in the Soviet Union, the latter turning to photography, but Gabo and Pevsner influenced the Abstract-Creation group in Paris, and later in the 1930s Gabo spread Constructivism to England and in the 1940s to the United States.

[1] James Weldon Johnson, poet, playwright, journalist, diplomat, historian of the Harlem Renaissance, secretary of the NAACP.

1920-1929

[4] A poster issued by the League of Women Voters.

[2] The accoutrements of the flapper: black silk stockings, short skirt, cloche hat, cigarette holder.

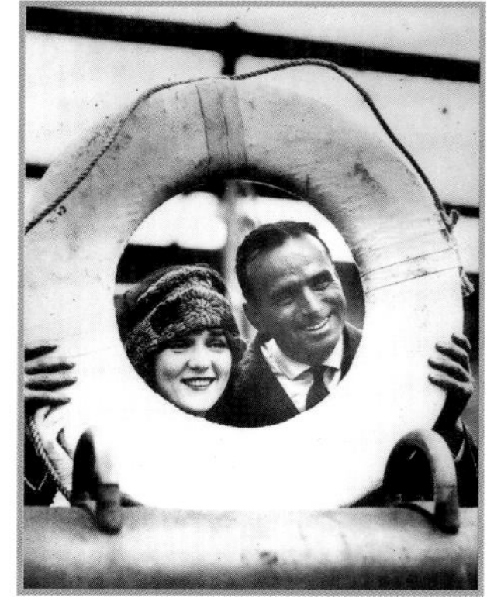

[7] Mary Pickford and Douglas Fairbanks set off on their European honeymoon.

[3] The League of Nations pauses for a photo call during a session in Geneva.

[8] An Irish suspect is searched at pistol point by the Black and Tans. A dead body lies on the ground behind.

 [7]
March 28, 1920
American motion-picture actors **Mary Pickford** and **Douglas Fairbanks** are wed.

May 16, 1920
Joan of Arc, national heroine of France, is canonized as a saint by Pope Benedict XV.

June 4, 1920
The Treaty of Trianon is signed by representatives of Hungary on one side and the Allied powers on the other, concluding World War I.

June 21, 1920
Noted criminal lawyer **Konstantin Fehrenbach**, a member of the Catholic Centre Party, becomes chancellor of the Weimar Republic (1920–21).

 [8]
July 1920
The British government begins employing "**Black and Tan**" auxiliary policemen—named for their khaki and dark green uniforms—who engage in fierce reprisals against the Irish Republican Army.

July 10, 1920
Canadian politician **Arthur Meighen**, who will wage a successful campaign in 1921 against renewal of the Anglo-Japanese alliance, starts the first of two non-consecutive terms as prime minister.

February 18, 1920
Paul Deschanel is elected president of France.

February 29, 1920
A new, democratic constitution is adopted by the national assembly elected by Czech and Slovak leaders, furthering the consolidation of the two states into **Czechoslovakia**.

March 1, 1920
Miklós Horthy is elected regent of Hungary and proceeds to block attempts by King Charles IV to regain his throne, resulting in a "monarchy without a monarch" that comes under German influence in the following years.

[5]

March 13, 1920
Berlin is seized in a **right-wing Putsch** led by Wolfgang Kapp. This attempt to overthrow the newly formed Weimar Republic is undone four days later when a general strike cripples Kapp's authority.

[6]

March 19, 1920
Józef Pilsudski is named marshal of Poland.

March 27, 1920
Hermann Müller, a leader of the Social Democratic Party, becomes chancellor of the Weimar Republic for the first of two coalition governments (1920; 1928–30).

[5] Admiral Horthy parades through Budapest. He has come to power after the short-lived Communist regime of Béla Kun in Hungary has been ended by the intervention of Romanian forces.

[6] A Freikorps armored car, decorated with a skull-and-crossbones, a symbol used by many of these irregular corps. The helmeted man holds the barrel of a flame thrower. It is government moves to disband the Freikorps that have sparked the Kapp Putsch.

[9] Marcus Garvey, promoter of the Back to Africa movement, in which both the Nation of Islam and the Rastafari movement have their roots.

[11] The Cairo Gang, British intelligence agents killed by the Irish Republicans on Bloody Sunday.

[10] Gandhi with his wife, Kasturba. His call for nonviolent resistance follows a massacre at Amritsar in 1919.

July 12, 1920
The independent republic of **Lithuania**, having successfully expelled invading Soviet troops, signs a peace treaty with Russia.

 [9]

August 2, 1920
Marcus Garvey, black leader and founder of the Universal Negro Improvement Association, reaches the height of his power as he presides at an international convention in New York City.

 [10]

September 1920
Mohandas Gandhi organizes India's first large-scale **nonviolent resistance campaign** against British rule, known as the Noncooperation Movement.

September 23, 1920
Alexandre Millerand, who will be noted for his desire to strengthen the power of the president by constitutional revision, is elected president of France.

October 12, 1920
The Russo-Polish War over the possession of the Ukraine ends.

 [11]

November 21, 1920
On **Bloody Sunday**, the Irish Republican Army kill 11 Englishmen suspected of being intelligence agents, and the Black and Tans take revenge, killing 12 and wounding 60 Irish.

1920-1921

1921
A massive **famine** kills more than five million people in the Soviet Union.
 [1]

1921
Agnes McPhail becomes the first female Canadian member of Parliament.

1921
At the Washington Naval Conference, U.S. secretary of state Charles Evans Hughes negotiates the **first effective arms-reduction agreement** in history.

1921
Benton MacKaye, a regional planner for the state of Massachusetts, publishes an article promoting the creation of the **Appalachian Trail**; he will be credited with spearheading the effort to make the proposed hiking path a reality.

1921
British educator A. S. Neill opens **Summerhill**, a revolutionary school designed for self-development.

1921
Canadian physician Frederick Banting and colleagues Charles H. Best and J. J. R. Macleod discover **insulin**. Their discovery transforms the treatment of patients with diabetes.
 [2]

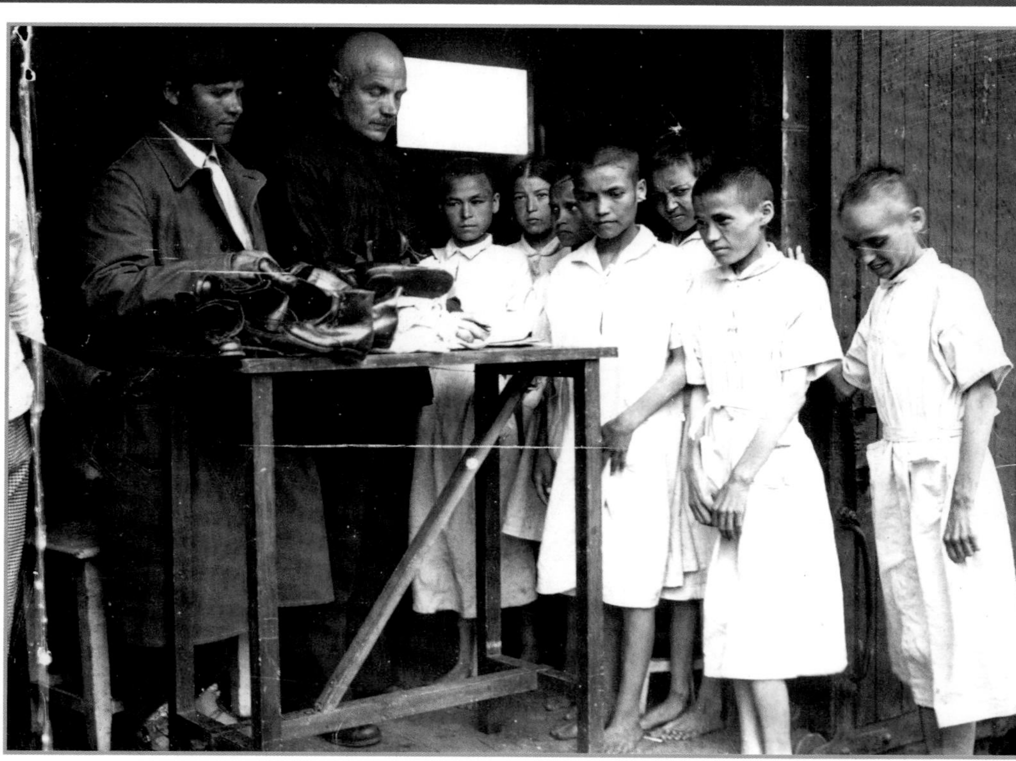

[1] *Children from an area hit by famine are issued with footwear on arrival in Moscow.*

[2] *Banting and Best with one of the diabetic dogs on whom insulin has first been tested.*

1920-1929

[6] *The 1920 proposal for a glass skyscraper, by Mies van der Rohe.*

[7] *Margaret Sanger (front row, right) with other delegates to a birth-control conference in New York.*

[8] *Marie Stopes with her second husband, Humphrey Verdon Roe.*

 [6]
1921
Ludwig Mies van der Rohe proposes a glass skyscraper, Berlin. While unbuilt, this model for the first all-glass skyscraper is symbolic of a new era in architecture.

 [7]
1921
Margaret Sanger and Mary Ware Dennett found the **American Birth Control League**, which later becomes the Planned Parenthood Federation of America

 [8]
1921
Marie Stopes founds the U.K.'s first clinic for contraception. Although her work provokes violent opposition, especially from Roman Catholics, she greatly influences the Church of England's gradual relaxation of its stand.

1921
Norwegian meteorologist Vilhelm Bjerknes develops the idea of warm and cold fronts, a key idea in **modern meteorology** and weather forecasting.

1921
The **adhesive bandage** is developed by Earle Dickson, a cotton buyer for Johnson & Johnson.

1921
The **Betty Crocker** persona is created by the Washburn-Crosby Company (later acquired by General Mills), maker of Gold Medal flour. Betty Crocker will become the epitome of the competent, friendly American homemaker.

1921
Chess champion **Emanuel Lasker** of Germany is defeated by Cuban-born José Raúl Capablanca, ending Lasker's 27-year-reign as world chess champion.

 [3]

1921
Coronary heart disease is now the leading cause of death in the United States.

1921
International powers begin meeting to limit the **naval arms race** and to work out security agreements in the Pacific area. The conference will result, over the next year, in the drafting and signing of several major and minor treaty agreements.

1921
Italian immigrant Simon Rodia begins construction on **Watts Towers** in Los Angeles. The 17 bricolage spires are constructed from broken tiles, dishes, rocks, bottles, and seashells and will become a national historic landmark.

 [4]

1921
Italian-born actor Rudolph Valentino appears in the silent film **The Sheik** and immediately becomes a star, idolized as the "Great Lover" of the 1920s.

 [5]

1921
Langston Hughes, African American poet and a leading interpreter of the black experience in the United States, publishes his first poem, "**The Negro Speaks of Rivers**."

[3] *Lasker (left) plays Capablanca. This particular game ends in a draw.*

[10] *A seal of a bull from Mohenjodaro, a city of the Indus Valley civilization.*

[5] *Rudolph Valentino as the Sheik embraces Agnes Ayers, who seems rather nonplussed.*

[4] *Simon Rodia poses with a portion of his Watts Towers.*

[9] *Sacco and Vanzetti, handcuffed to each other and to a policeman.*

1921
The **First Congress of the Chinese Communist Party** is held in Shanghai, encouraged by the Bolshevik Revolution in Russia.

1921
The first successful **lie detector** is developed by medical student John A. Larson. It measures physiological phenomena such as blood pressure, pulse rate, and respiration as a subject answers questions.

1921
The **Hague Rules**—in maritime law, the international code defining the rights and liabilities of a carrier—are introduced at the International Law Association meeting in Brussels, Belgium. They will be adopted in 1923.

 [9]

1921
The highly controversial trial of **Nicola Sacco** and **Bartolomeo Vanzetti**, two Italian immigrants, concludes with their being convicted of a double murder in Braintree, Massachusetts.

 [10]

1921
The **Indus civilization**—the earliest known urban culture of the Indian subcontinent—is first identified at Harappa in the Punjab (now in Pakistan).

1921
The U.S. **General Accounting Office** (GAO) is created to assist Congress by examining all federal receipts and expenditures.

1921-1922

1921
The U.S. Supreme Court holds in *Truax* v. *Corrigan* that an Arizona **picketing law is unconstitutional**—a victory for organized labor.

1921
Thomas Hitchcock, Jr., leads the **American polo team** that defeats Great Britain in the Westchester Cup. In his storied career, he receives the highest possible rating in 18 of 19 seasons.

 [1]

1921
Thomas Midgley, Jr., recommends the use of tetraethyl **lead in gasoline** to permit higher compression engines. Automobile exhausts begin to disperse lead into the atmosphere and biosphere despite known health risks.

1921
Warren G. Harding of the Republican Party takes office as the 29th president of the United States. He will serve until 1923. His vice president is Calvin Coolidge. Harding will die in office in 1923.

 [2]

1921
William Howard Taft is appointed 10th chief justice of the U.S. Supreme Court by President Warren G. Harding. He will serve from 1921 to 1930.

 [3]

c. 1921
The **suntan** begins to be a sign of affluence and exotic travel, thanks to the influence of designer Coco Chanel. Formerly, sun-browned skin had been associated with outdoor labor.

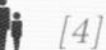 [4]

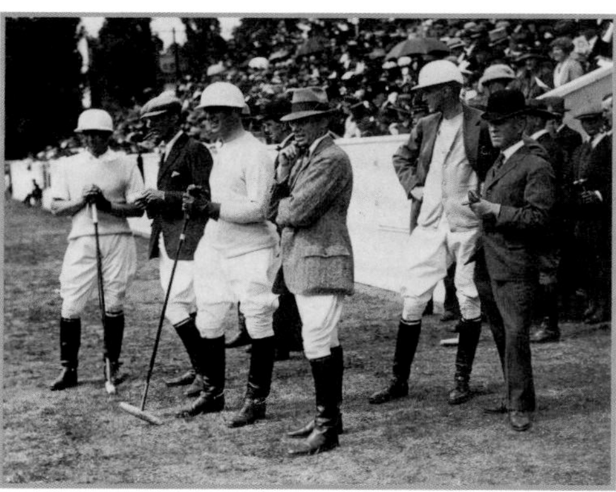

[1] Members of the U.S. polo team.

[2] President Warren Harding outside the White House with his dog, Laddie Boy.

[3] Former president and now chief justice: William Howard Taft.

[8] The coffin of Britain's Unknown Soldier in Boulogne about to be put on a Channel ferry and then taken for burial in Westminster Abbey.

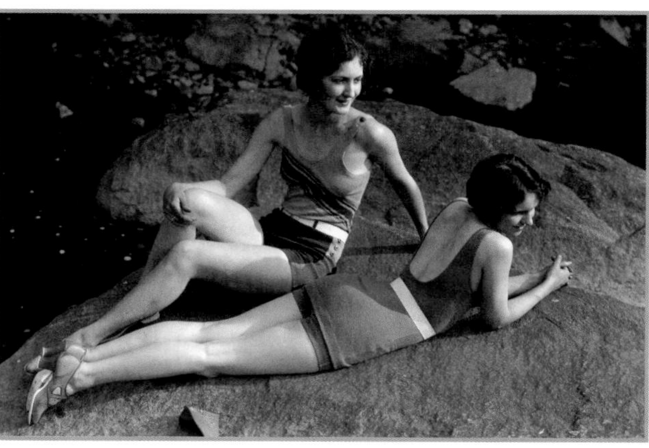

[4] Sunbathing, the new fashion.

[9] Catholics pray outside Downing Street for a successful conclusion to the talks taking place there about an Anglo-Irish settlement. Note the temporary wooden security barrier in the background.

[10] Mackenzie King makes the cover of Time *magazine.*

November 4, 1921
Hara Takashi, prime minister of Japan, is assassinated by a young rightist fanatic.

 [8]

November 11, 1921
The anniversary of the end of World War I, the first Armistice Day is commemorated with the burial of the bodies of **unknown soldiers** in tombs in Paris, in London, and outside Washington, D.C.

 [9]

December 6, 1921
The British government and Irish leaders Arthur Griffith, Michael Collins, and others sign the **Anglo-Irish Treaty**, establishing the Irish Free State as an independent member of the British Commonwealth.

December 13, 1921
The **Four-Power Pact** is signed by the United States, Great Britain, Japan, and France, stipulating that all will be consulted in the event of a controversy between two of them over "any Pacific question."

 [10]

December 29, 1921
William Lyon **Mackenzie King**, a member of the Liberal Party of Canada who will, as prime minister (1921–26; 1926–30; 1935–48), help preserve the unity of the English and French populations, begins his first term.

1922
A **bank-wire system** is established by the U.S. Federal Reserve Board, removing the need for the physical transfer of securities from one city to another and thereby reducing the chance of loss or theft.

January 12, 1921
U.S. federal judge Kenesaw Mountain Landis is elected the first **commissioner of baseball**.

 [5]

February 1921
Reza Khan overthrows the government of Persia (now Iran). He will become Reza Shah Pahlavi and will be the **shah of Iran** (1925–41).

 [6]

March 1921
Sailors at the **Kronshtadt naval base** protest Soviet rule, demanding economic and labor reform and political freedoms. Although the rebellion is crushed, it forces the Communist Party to enact economic reform.

March 1921
The **New Economic Policy** (NEP) is introduced in the Soviet Union. The policy represents a temporary retreat from the government's previous policy of extreme centralization and doctrinaire socialism.

March 8, 1921
Eduardo Dato Iradier, prime minister of Spain, is assassinated by anarchists.

 [7]

May 10, 1921
Joseph Karl Wirth, who will advocate fulfillment of Germany's obligations under the Versailles Treaty and consistently oppose German militarism, becomes chancellor of the Weimar Republic (1921–22).

[5] Kenesaw Mountain Landis throws the ball in to start a baseball game. His first task is to deal with the 1919 Black Sox scandal.

[6] Reza Shah Pahlavi with the future Shah Mohammad Reza on his knee.

[11] Striking miners with wives and children in West Virginia.

[7] Eduardo Dato, assassinated by Catalan anarchists.

TUTANKHAMEN'S TOMB

Howard Carter discovers unparalleled treasures inside the pharoah's tomb.

In 1922 the 5th Earl of Carnarvon, a collector of antiquities, decided to finance one last season of excavations in the Valley of the Kings, in the search for the legendary tomb of Tutankhamen. Howard Carter, a British Egyptologist, supervised excavations. On November 4, 1922, Carter found the first sign of what proved to be Tutankhamen's tomb, but it was not until November 26 that a second sealed doorway was reached, behind which were the treasures. The tomb had escaped the great series of robberies at the end of the 20th dynasty and was preserved intact. Inside his small tomb, the king's mummy lay within a nest of three coffins (left, being examined by Carter). The other rooms were crammed with furniture, statuary, clothes, a chariot, weapons, staffs, and numerous other objects. For the next 10 years Carter supervised the removal of their contents, most of which are now housed in the Egyptian Museum in Cairo.

1922
A **strike by coal miners** in the United States lasts almost six months and severely hampers the country's coal-mining industry.

1922
Arnold Lunn of England introduces **slalom gates** to downhill skiing, thus creating the modern alpine slalom race.

1922
Aviator **Bessie Coleman**, who later refuses to perform before segregated audiences in the South, stages the first public flight by an African American woman.

1922
Awangarda Krakowska, the Polish avant-garde literary movement opposing the lyrical poetry of Poland's most popular contemporary poets, is launched in Kraków.

1922
Better Homes and Gardens is founded, giving fresh impetus to the trend toward "service" by helping both men and women in the running of their homes.

1922
British archaeologist Howard Carter makes one of the richest and most celebrated contributions to Egyptology: the discovery of the largely intact tomb of **King Tutankhamen**.

1922

1922
Walter Rathenau, Germany's outstanding foreign minister, is assassinated by right-wingers.

1922
Germany's stock market fails; hyperinflation takes root and will lead to economic collapse the following year.

$ [1]

1922
In Kansas City, Missouri, the **first unified shopping mall**, Country Club Plaza, is opened by the J.C. Nichols Company.

1922
James Joyce's definitive Modernist masterpiece **Ulysses**, which recounts one day (June 16, 1904) in the lives of Stephen Dedalus, Leopold Bloom, and Molly Bloom, is published in Paris.

 [2]

1922
Le Corbusier proposes his City of Three Million People project. Featuring a series of cruciform skyscrapers in Paris, Le Corbusier's plan has an unfortunately strong influence on modern city planning.

1922
Prince Albert of Monaco dies and is succeeded by his son, **Louis II**.

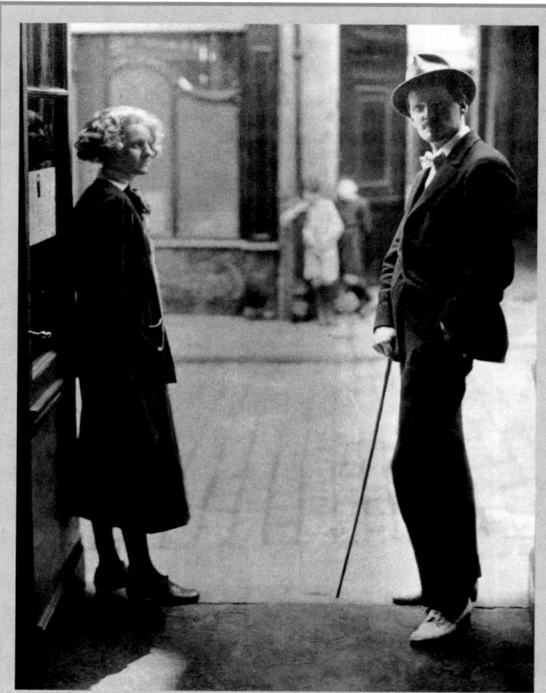

ULYSSES PUBLISHED

Irish writer's masterpiece

In 1920 the Irish novelist James Joyce—at the invitation of Ezra Pound—went to Paris. His novel *Ulysses* was published there on February 2, 1922, by Sylvia Beach (shown above with Joyce), proprietor of a bookshop called "Shakespeare and Company." Joyce had spent seven years writing the book, and initially it was banned in the U.S. and Britain. *Ulysses* is constructed as a modern parallel to Homer's *Odyssey*. All of the action of the novel takes place in Dublin on a single day. The three central characters—Stephen Dedalus, Leopold Bloom, and Molly Bloom—are intended to be modern counterparts of Telemachus, Ulysses, and Penelope. The book embodies a highly experimental use of language and exploration of literary methods such as interior monologue and stream-of-consciousness narrative. It is widely regarded by many as the greatest English-language novel of the 20th century.

[2] Le Corbusier, uncharacteristically frivolous, balances a vase on his head. His brother, the violinist and composer Albert Jeanneret, is beside him and, on the left, the Cubist painter Amédée Ozenfant, with whom Le Corbusier writes two books advocating Purism, a hardline version of Cubism, paying much attention to the idea of the golden section.

[1] A man being arrested in Berlin for a foreign-exchange transaction, made illegal in an attempt to protect the German currency.

[7] James Doolittle in the cockpit.

1920-1929

 [5]

1922
The **Chicago Tribune Tower** competition draws submissions from all over the world and in every conceivable style. The winning design is a Neo-Gothic skyscraper by Raymond Hood and John Mead Howells.

1922
The first commercially successful one- or two-passenger **snowmobile** is built and sold by Joseph-Armand Bombardier of Canada. It becomes a popular recreational vehicle in North America.

1922
The first **Newbery Medal** is awarded. It becomes an annual honor, given to the author of the most distinguished American children's book of the previous year.

1922
The introduction of the **Essex coach**, a no-frills, two-door, closed sedan produced by the Hudson Motor Car Company, reduces the cost of sheltered motoring.

 [6]

1922
The **British Broadcasting Corporation** is founded, the original charter giving it a monopoly covering all phases of broadcasting in Britain. Although ultimately answerable to Parliament, the BBC has virtually complete independence.

 [7]

1922
U.S. Army Air Corps Lieutenant **James Harold Doolittle** flies from Florida to California in less than 22 hours, marking the first time a coast-to-coast flight is completed within a day.

1922
Reader's Digest, a magazine of condensed articles taken from other periodicals, is founded by DeWitt Wallace and his wife, Lila Acheson; it will have one of the largest circulations of any periodical.

1922
Rebecca Ann Latimer Felton becomes the first woman to serve in the U.S. Senate. She serves only two days, in a symbolic gesture, filling the seat of a deceased senator just days before the newly elected senator is to take his seat.

1922
Russian mathematician and physical scientist Aleksandr Aleksandrovich Friedmann is one of the first proponents of a "**big bang**" model for the evolution of the universe.

1922
Sir Leonard Woolley, a British archaeologist, discovers and begins excavation of the ancient Sumerian city of Ur (now in Iraq), greatly advancing knowledge of ancient Mesopotamian civilization.

 [3]

1922
Swiss painter and Bauhaus member **Paul Klee** develops an abstract, artistic language of signs, used in such works as *Twittering Machine*.

1922
"**The Waste Land**," American Modernist poet T. S. Eliot's most famous and most complex poem, is published to a wealth of praise.

 [4]

[5] *The Chicago Tribune Tower, topped by flying buttresses.*

[3] *One of Sir Leonard Woolley's finds from Ur: an inlay of Sumerian war chariots, warriors, and captives, now in the British Museum.*

[6] *Stanton Jeffries, known to his listeners as Uncle Jeff, broadcasts for children in the early days of the BBC.*

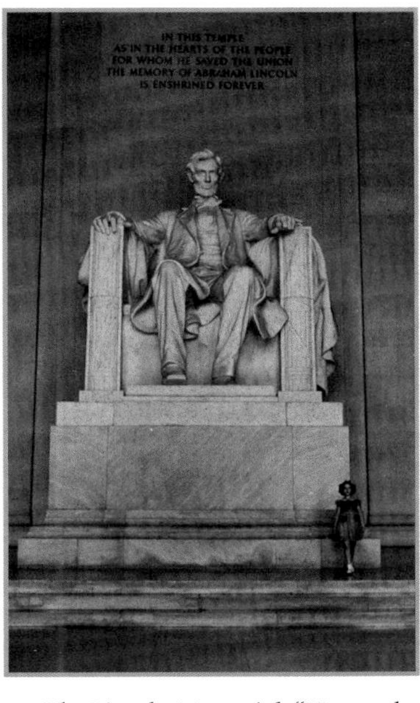

[8] *The Lincoln Memorial: "He saved the Union." Its scale is indicated by the child by the plinth.*

[4] *T. S. Eliot. The huge range of sources Eliot draws on and literary allusions he makes, or quotations he includes, in "The Waste Land" turn it into a happy hunting ground for English literature scholars.*

c. 1922
The Fugitives, a group of distinguished Southern writers under the leadership of John Crowe Ransom, forms at Vanderbilt University in Nashville, Tennessee.

February 28, 1922
Egypt is declared an independent country.

April 7, 1922
U.S. secretary of the interior Albert B. Fall secretly leases federal oil reserves to the Mammoth Oil Company in return for cash gifts in the **Teapot Dome Scandal**.

 [8]

May 30, 1922
The **Lincoln Memorial** is dedicated in Washington, D.C.

July 1922
In response to a fraudulent presidential election, a handful of disgruntled military officers stage a poorly planned and unsuccessful coup in **Rio de Janeiro**.

August 11, 1922
"**Deutschland über Alles**" becomes the national anthem of Germany.

1922-1923

September 27, 1922
In Greece, **King Constantine I abdicates** in favor of his eldest son, who becomes King George II.
[1]

October 24, 1922
Benito Mussolini summons a **march on Rome** and subsequently becomes dictator of Italy.
[2]

November 1, 1922
The Grand National Assembly, at the behest of **Mustafa Kemal** (Atatürk), votes to abolish the sultanate of Turkey.
 [3]

November 22, 1922
German politician and business leader **Wilhelm Carl Josef Cuno**, who is not affiliated with a party, becomes chancellor of the Weimar Republic (1922–23) and serves through the Franco-Belgian invasion of the Ruhr (1923).

December 30, 1922
The Russian and Transcaucasian Soviet Republics and the Ukrainian and Belorussian Soviet Republics combine to form the **Union of Soviet Socialist Republics** in the territory of the former Russian Empire.

1923
Alice Paul, founder of the National Women's Party, drafts the first equal-rights amendment to the Constitution and introduces it into the U.S. Congress; it fails to pass.
 [4]

[1] King Constantine. His abdication is a result of defeat in the Greco-Turkish War (1920–22).

[2] Mussolini, center, leads the march on Rome.

[4] Alice Paul, in 1920, unfurls a banner with thirty-six stars, one for each state that had then voted for a national amendment guaranteeing women the right to vote.

[3] Greeks flee from Smyrna (Izmir) after its capture by Mustafa Kemal's forces. This marks the final defeat of the Greeks by Turkey and the consolidation of Kemal's position within Turkey.

[10] W. B. Yeats with his wife

[9] E. E. Cummings. In choosing to live in Europe, and Paris in particular, he is typical of his generation of American writers.

[11] Jelly Roll Morton (at the piano) and his Red Hot Peppers: "Hello Central, give me Doctor Jazz."

1920-1929

1923
Credit cards are introduced in the United States, issued first by hotels and gas stations. The industry will rapidly expand after World War II.

 [9]
1923
E. E. Cummings publishes his first collection of poetry, *Tulips and Chimneys*.

1923
Representatives of the criminal police forces of 20 countries met in Vienna and formed the **International Criminal Police Commission** (ICPC). The organization was later renamed Interpol.

1923
Ich und Du (*I and Thou*), by German-Jewish religious philosopher Martin Buber, is published; it will become the classic work on **I-Thou theological doctrine**.

 [10]
1923
Irish poet and playwright **William Butler Yeats** is awarded the Nobel Prize for Literature.

 [11]
1923
Jelly Roll Morton, American jazz composer and pianist who pioneered the use of prearranged, semiorchestrated effects in jazz-band performances, makes his recording debut.

1923
American engineer Lee De Forest unveils a working system of **motion pictures with sound**.

 [5]

1923
American lyric poet **William Carlos Williams** publishes his collection of fresh poems and prose statements, *Spring and All*.

1923
Australian Nationalist Party member and diplomat **Stanley Bruce**, who will become his country's leading emissary to Great Britain, becomes prime minister of Australia.

 [6]

1923
Austrian novelist and journalist Felix Salten publishes **Bambi**, a children's classic and adult allegory; it is a sensitively told story of the life of a wild deer.

1923
Bobsledding gains international recognition as a sport. A year later it is included in the program of the first Winter Olympic Games, held in Chamonix, France.

 [7]

1923
Calvin Coolidge of the Republican Party becomes the 30th president of the United States. He will serve until 1929. His vice president is Charles G. Dawes.

[8]

[5] Pioneering the use of sound on film in the Mojave Desert, by Fox Movietone.

[7] The British four-man bobsled in action, in 1924, at Chamonix.

[6] Stanley Bruce, a patrician figure who drives a Rolls-Royce, exploits fears of Communism and militant trade unions, and upholds a white Australia policy.

[13] Margaret Bondfield. She will be the first woman to be a British Cabinet minister.

[12] Walter Gropius (left), the German modernist architect and founder of the Bauhaus, and his wife and Le Corbusier at Les Deux Magots, the famous Paris café.

[8] President Coolidge and his wife try out some skis on the White House lawn.

 [12]

1923
Le Corbusier publishes his influential **Vers une architecture** (*Toward a New Architecture*), a polemic praising the value of functionalist, machine-inspired design.

 [13]

1923
Margaret Bondfield becomes the first woman to serve as chairperson of the Trades Union Congress, the national organization of British trade unions.

1923
Mexican revolutionary and guerrilla fighter **Pancho Villa** is killed by a sniper on his ranch in Chihuahua state.

1923
Opportunity: Journal of Negro Life is first published; editor Charles S. Johnson aims to give voice to black culture, hitherto neglected by mainstream American publishing.

1923
Plato und die sogenannten Pythagoreer (*Plato and the So-called Pythagoreans*), one of German philosopher Erich Frank's principal works, is published

1923
Russian-born U.S. engineer Vladimir Zworykin patents the **iconoscope**, an electronic picture tube that is a key technology for the first television.

1923-1924

1923
The **Dawson Valley Irrigation Project** is inaugurated; it is centered along the Dawson River in eastern Queensland, Australia.

1923
The **Ahiram epitaph** is discovered at Byblos, Phoenicia (now in Lebanon); it is the earliest Phoenician inscription ever found, dating to the 11th century BC.

1923
Stanley Baldwin is appointed British prime minister. He will serve three times between 1923 and 1937. A Conservative, he heads the government during the General Strike of 1926, the Ethiopian crisis of 1935, and the abdication crisis of 1936.

 [1]

1923
The **Hollywood** sign is built in the hills above Los Angeles, California. It originally reads "Hollywoodland," but the four last letters will be dropped after renovation in 1940s, and the entire sign will be rebuilt in 1978.

[2]

1923
The **Milky Way bar** is created, the first of many candies to be introduced by the Mars family; others will also include Snickers and Mars bars.

1923
The **Poetical Works of Dafydd Nanmor** is published, celebrating the works of the 15th-century Welsh poet.

TOKYO EARTHQUAKE

Disaster strikes Japan

A great earthquake struck the Tokyo-Yokohama metropolitan area near noon on September 1, 1923; the photograph shows earthquake and fire damage on Honjokuchu Street and the Kanda District. The death toll from this shock was estimated at more than 140,000. Fifty-four percent of the brick buildings and 10 percent of the reinforced-concrete structures collapsed. Many hundreds of thousands of houses were either shaken down or burned. The shock started a tsunami that reached a height of 12 meters (39.5 feet) at Atami on Sagami Gulf, where it destroyed 155 houses and killed 60 persons.

The only comparable Japanese earthquake in the 20th century was at Kobe on January 16, 1995. About 5,100 people died, and there was much damage and widespread fires in the city.

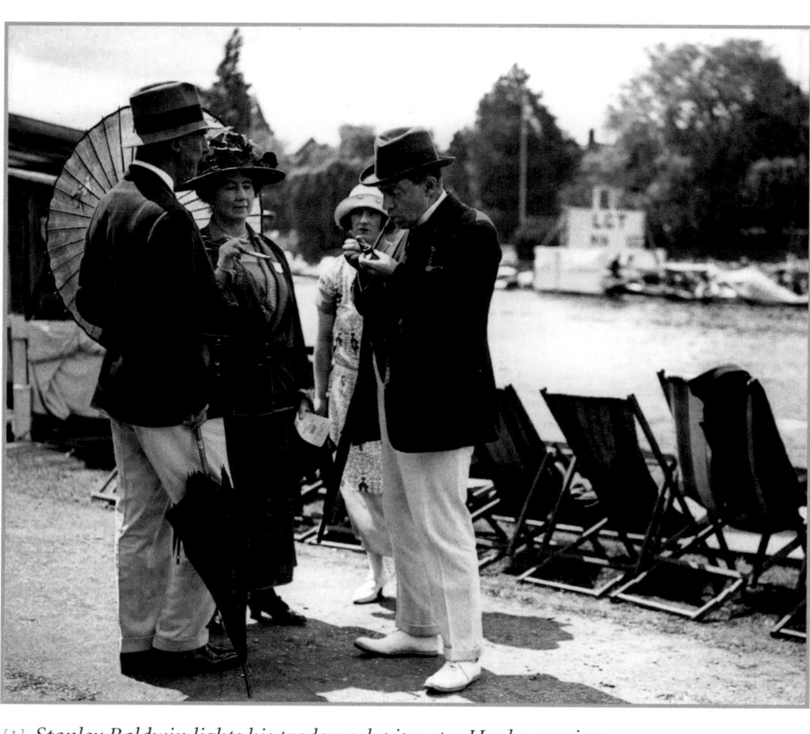

[1] Stanley Baldwin lights his trademark pipe at a Henley rowing regatta. His wife and daughter are with him.

[2] The original version of the Hollywood sign.

[4] Gustav Stresemann, the diminutive but effective German chancellor and the most distinguished politician of the Weimar era.

[3] My Wife and Daughters in the Garden, *painted in 1907 by Joaquin Sorolla.*

June 28, 1923
Prince Devawongse Varoprakar dies; as foreign minister of Siam (now Thailand) from 1885 to 1923, his policies are credited with enabling the kingdom to survive as an independent state.

July 24, 1923
The **Treaty of Lausanne**, the final treaty concluding World War I, is signed at Lausanne, Switzerland.

July 30, 1923
The **Ross Dependency** in Antarctica is claimed by New Zealand.

 [3]

August 10, 1923
Spanish painter **Joaquin Sorolla y Bastida**, whose style is a variant of Impressionism and whose best works, painted in the open air, vividly portray the sunny seacoast of Valencia, dies in 1923.

 [4]

August 13, 1923
Gustav Stresemann, a member of the German People's Party who will be largely responsible for restoring Germany's international status after World War I, becomes chancellor of the Weimar Republic.

September 1, 1923
A great **earthquake** strikes the Tokyo-Yokohama area about noontime, killing more than 140,000 and destroying 54 percent of the brick buildings and 10 percent of the reinforced-concrete structures.

1923
Typography, a significant type specimen book, is published by Pelican Press; it is also an essay on book production.

February 1, 1923
The private army of **Blackshirts** that had helped Benito Mussolini come to power in Italy is officially transformed into a national militia, the Voluntary Fascist Militia for National Security.

March 26, 1923
Sarah Bernhardt, one of the best-known figures in the history of the stage, dies in Paris.

March 3, 1923
The first issue of the American weekly newsmagazine **Time** is published.

May 25, 1923
The United Kingdom grants **autonomy to Transjordan** (now Jordan).

June 9, 1923
The **Bulgarian military** overthrows the government of Prime Minister Aleksandur Stamboliyski; he will be executed on June 14.

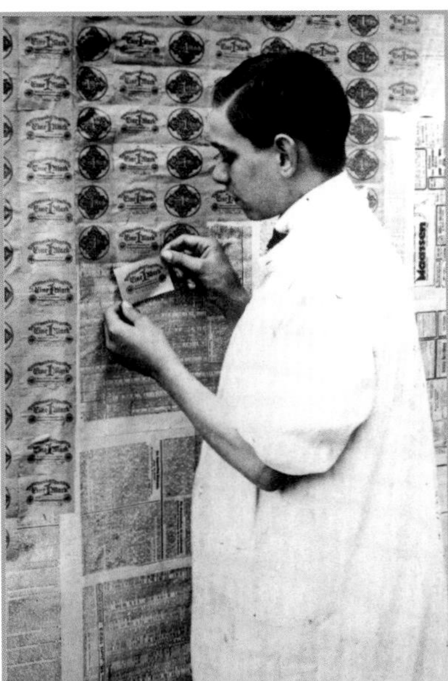

[8] In 1923, it becomes cheaper to decorate a room in Germany with currency than with wallpaper.

[6] Mustafa Kemal in the costume worn by the Janissaries, the Ottoman sultan's elite troops.

[9] Wilhelm Marx leaves a polling station. He will manage to bring stability in 1924 after the hyperinflation of 1923.

[10] Johnny Weissmuller. In 1932 he will star as Tarzan in the first of twelve movies, creating the famous yodelling Tarzan yell.

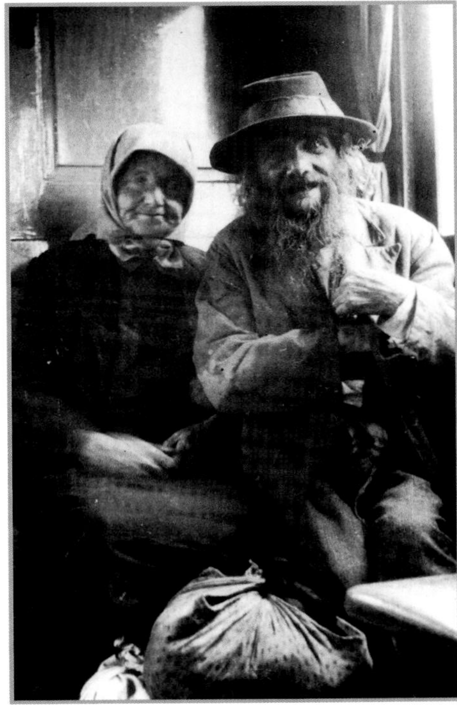

[5] An elderly Jewish couple on their way to the promised land—Palestine.

[7] Adolf Hitler during the Beer Hall Putsch, with Alfred Rosenberg, the Nazi's chief racial theorist, and a Freikorps commander on the right.

 [5]

September 29, 1923
Set in motion by the Balfour Declaration of 1917, the **British mandate** for the establishment of a Jewish homeland in Palestine is finally approved by the Council of the League of Nations and comes into force.

 [6]

October 29, 1923
The Grand National Assembly declares **Turkey** a republic, and Mustafa Kemal is elected as the first president.

 [7]

November 8–9, 1923
Adolf Hitler attempts to start an insurrection in Munich with his **Beer Hall Putsch**; the putsch fails and Hitler will be imprisoned, where he will use the time to write his political manifesto, *Mein Kampf.*

 [8]

November 15, 1923
After rampant **hyperinflation in Germany**—it now takes 4.2 trillion German marks to buy a single American dollar, as compared to 7,260 marks at the beginning of the year—the economy collapses.

 [9]

November 30, 1923
Wilhelm Marx, leader of the Roman Catholic Centre Party, becomes chancellor of the Weimar Republic for the first of two terms (1923–25; 1926–28).

 [10]

1924
At the Summer Olympics in Paris, American swimmer **Johnny Weissmuller** wins the first three of his five Olympic gold medals. He later portrays Tarzan in a series of motion pictures.

1924

1924
Against a University of Michigan football team that has not been beaten in three years, **Red Grange of Illinois** scores on long touchdown runs the first four times he touches the ball.

1924
The Wahabi sultan of Nejd, **Abdul-Aziz Ibn Saud**, conquers the Hejaz and enters Mecca.

1924
A **conveyor belt** is successfully used in an anthracite mine in central Pennsylvania to carry coal to a string of cars at the mine entrance. By the 1960s belts will almost completely replace railcars for intermediate coal haulage.

1924
British novelist and literary critic E. M. Forster publishes his masterpiece, **A Passage to India**.

1924
Chilean expatriate poet **Pablo Neruda** publishes his most widely read poetry collection, *Veinte poemas de amor y una canción desesperada* (*Twenty Love Poems and a Song of Despair*).

1924
French poet André Breton writes **the Surrealist Manifesto**, promoting the role of chance and the unconscious in art and naming one of the most important movements in 20th-century art. [1]

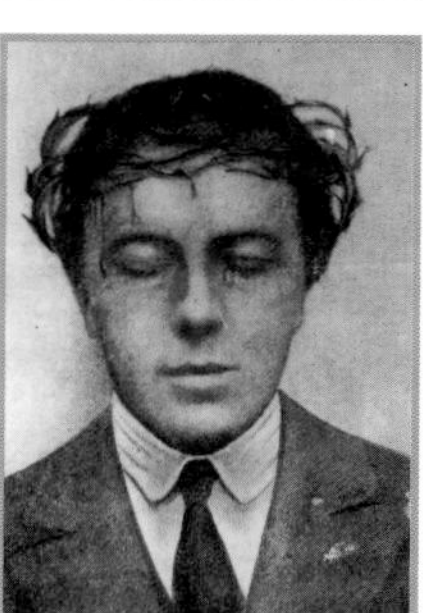

[1] *André Breton, wearing a crown of thorns. Former Dadaist, former orderly in a hospital for shell-shocked soldiers, future communist: for the moment, he seeks to create "pure psychic automatism."*

[7] *Crowds at Lenin's funeral in Red Square, Moscow. An immortalization commission is established to ensure his lasting legacy as a great revolutionary leader.*

Hello Everybody!
MACDONALD
Calling
LABOUR in
POWER
THIS TIME

[6] *A poster for the British 1924 election.*

[8] *Lenin (left), with his successor, Stalin, whom he disliked and would have sidelined if Lenin had not been incapacitated by a series of strokes.*

[9] *Herma Planck-Szabo of Austria winning her figure-skating Olympic gold at Chamonix.*

1924
Self-taught U.S. electrical engineer William P. Lear sells the first successful design for an **automobile radio** to the Motorola Company.

1924
South African physical anthropologist and paleontologist Raymond Dart discovers the first **Australopithecus fossil** in a limestone quarry near Taung, South Africa.

1924
The **first self-winding wristwatch is patented** by English inventor John Harwood.

1924
The first stretch of the **Autostrada**, the national Italian expressway system, is laid from Venice to Turin.

 [6]

1924
With Liberal support, the Labour Party, led by James Ramsay MacDonald, forms **Britain's first Labour government**. His minority administration will be brought down in less than a year.

c. 1924
Frederic Truby King's Mothercraft movement, with its maxim "Breast-fed is Best-fed," brings **breast-feeding** back into the mainstream.

1924
George Gershwin's **Rhapsody in Blue** is first performed, conducted by bandleader Paul Whiteman. The revolutionary work incorporates trademarks of the jazz idiom (blue notes, syncopated rhythms, onomatopoeic instrumental effects) into a symphonic context.

 [2]

1924
German artist Käthe Kollwitz's lithograph "**Nie Wieder Krieg**" ("Never Again War") crowns an oeuvre of graphic work intensely concerned with social justice.

1924
German novelist **Thomas Mann** publishes his great novel *The Magic Mountain.* He wins the Nobel Prize for Literature in 1929.

 [3]

1924
German pilot Hugo Eckener flies the **zeppelin ZR-3** in the first Atlantic airship crossing. He will fly the Graf zeppelin around the world in 1929.

 [4]

1924
John Ford, an American motion-picture director who will become Hollywood's best-known director of Westerns, directs and releases his first high budget "big Western," *The Iron Horse.*

 [5]

1924
Plutarco Elías Calles, founder of the Mexican Partido Nacional Revolucionario (National Revolutionary Party), is elected president of Mexico.

[2] George Gershwin. He asks Ravel for lessons; when Ravel hears how much he earns, he says, "How about you give ME some lessons?"

[3] Thomas Mann with his wife, Katia.

[4] Hugo Eckener with his crew in front of ZR-3, which will become the U.S.S. Los Angeles.

[5] John Ford. He will win four Academy Awards for best director, more than anyone else, and is celebrated for pioneering location shooting, particularly in Utah's Monument Valley.

MUSSOLINI, *IL DUCE*

Italian dictator wins elections

Advocating government by dictatorship, Benito Mussolini (left, with his pet lion, Ras) formed a political group in Italy in 1919 that marked the beginning of Fascism. In 1922 he organized the March on Rome to prevent a socialist-led general strike. After the government fell, he was appointed prime minister. Anxious to demonstrate that he was not merely the leader of Fascism but also the head of a united Italy, he presented to the king a list of ministers, a majority of whom were not members of his party. He made it clear, however, that he intended to govern authoritatively. He obtained full dictatorial powers for a year; and in that year he pushed through a law that enabled the Fascists to cement a majority in the parliament. The elections in 1924, though undoubtedly fraudulent, secured his personal power.

 [7]

January 21, 1924
Vladimir Ilyich Lenin, founder of the Russian Communist Party, dies from a stroke in Gorki, Russia.

 [8]

January 1924
Joseph Stalin begins his efforts to assume power in the U.S.S.R.

February 1, 1924
To stop inflation, Wladyslaw Grabski, prime minister of Poland, introduces a Polish currency, the gold-based **zloty**.

 [9]

February 25, 1924
The first **Winter Olympics** open in Chamonix, France.

April 1924
The Italian Fascist-dominated bloc wins 64 percent and 374 seats in parliamentary elections, signaling the rise of **Benito Mussolini** to power.

April 20, 1924
Finalizing the **dissolution of the Ottoman Empire**, Turkey's Grand National Assembly votes to adopt a full republican constitution, with General Mustafa Kemal becoming the first president of the republic.

1924-1925

May 10, 1924
J. Edgar Hoover is appointed head of the U.S. Federal Bureau of Investigation (FBI), where he will remain until his death in 1972.

 [1]

May 21, 1924
Nathan Leopold, Jr., and Richard Loeb, two Chicago men, kidnap and murder 14-year-old Robert ("Bobbie") Franks. Later they will plead guilty and will be defended by a lawyer Clarence Darrow.

 [2]

June 3, 1924
Franz Kafka dies of tuberculosis. His posthumously published novels—especially *Der Prozess* (1925; *The Trial*) and *Das Schloss* (1926; *The Castle*)—express the anxieties and alienation of 20th-century man.

June 8, 1924
British mountaineers **George Mallory and Andrew Irvine** are last seen climbing Mount Everest in the early afternoon. Whether they reached the summit is one of the most perplexing mysteries of the 20th century.

 [3]

June 13, 1924
Gaston Doumergue enters office as president of France.

August 11, 1924
The **first newsreel of U.S. presidential candidates**, which includes footage of Calvin Coolidge, John W. Davis, and Robert La Follette, is filmed.

[1] *J. Edgar Hoover with a Tommy gun.*

[2] *Leopold and Loeb in court to hear their sentence. Thanks to Darrow's skill, it is for life imprisonment instead of the death penalty.*

[3] *George Mallory climbing in the Alps before World War I.*

[6] *Virginia Woolf, perhaps the most central figure within the Bloomsbury Group, whose letters and diaries are today appreciated as much as her novels.*

[7] *Bix (Bismark) Beiderbecke. He will die young in 1931, a martyr to Prohibition-era bathtub gin.*

[11] *Saturday night at the Grand Ole Opry in the 1930s, and the stage is filled with country-and-western performers.*

[6]
1925
British author Virginia Woolf completes one of her most lyrical, brilliant novels, **Mrs. Dalloway.** *To The Lighthouse* and *Orlando* are published in 1927 and 1928.

$
1925
The Caterpillar Tractor Company is incorporated after the Holt Manufacturing Company merges with another tractor manufacturer, the C.L. Best Tractor Company. **Caterpillar** will become a major American manufacturer.

1925
Charles T. Manley perfects his electric **popcorn machine**, which allows popcorn vendors to move inside movie theaters. Sales of popcorn will often make more money than ticket sales.

1925
Greenwich Mean Time (GMT) is adopted by astronomers so that the astronomical day begins at midnight, the same time as the civil day.

1925
In fashion, the **skirt line** reaches its shortest length of the early 20th century: knee length.

 [7]
1925
Jazz cornetist **Bix Beiderbecke**, an outstanding improviser and composer of the 1920s and the first major white jazz soloist, begins playing with the great black innovators Louis Armstrong, King Oliver, and Jimmy Noone.

October 22, 1924
Ralph Smedley establishes the first **Toastmasters club** in Santa Ana, California, to help people learn to become effective speakers. Toastmasters International will be incorporated under California law in 1932 and have over 10,500 clubs in 90 countries by 2005.

November 26, 1924
After the defeat of the White Russians and the Chinese, the **Mongolian People's Republic** is proclaimed.

November 27, 1924
Macy's holds its first Thanksgiving Day parade in New York City. It will continue this tradition with annual parades full of huge balloons.

1925
American novelist F. Scott Fitzgerald publishes his enduring story of East Egg and West Egg (modeled after Manhattan and Long Island), **The Great Gatsby**.

 [4]

1925
During an Alaskan diphtheria epidemic, a team of mushers battles blizzard conditions and rushes serum from Anchorage to icebound Nome by dogsled. A statue of lead dog **Balto** is erected in Central Park in New York City.

 [5]

1925
Bell Laboratories, a research branch of American Telephone and Telegraph (AT&T), opens. It will become one of the best-known scientific and engineering research laboratories of the 20th century.

[4] F. Scott Fitzgerald with his wife, Zelda, and daughter, Frances, on the liner that has brought them to Europe. Zelda holds a large doll and Fitzgerald has a dog on a lead.

[9] Beau Geste is filmed. The director, Herbert Brenon of Paramount, makes for a confusing image by wearing a Mexican sombrero alongside star Ronald Colman's kepi.

[5] Balto the Alaskan huskie takes shape at the hands of the sculptor Frederick Roth.

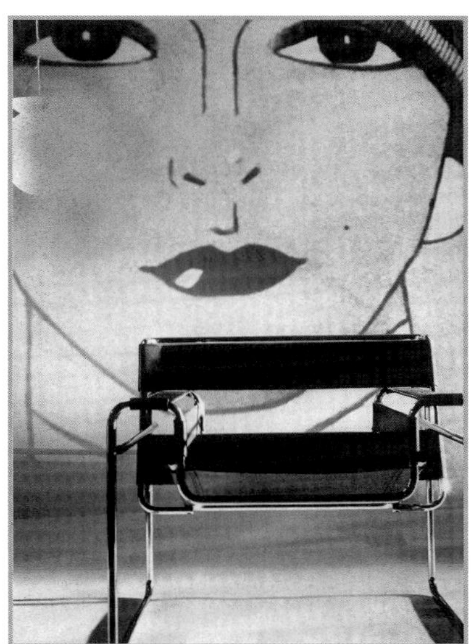

[8] The classic Marcel Breuer chair.

[10] Prajadhipok, king of Siam. Educated in England at Eton and the Royal Military Academy, he will abdicate in 1935 and retire there.

 [8]

1925
Marcel Breuer, inspired by bicycle handlebars, designs an innovative chair with a tubular metal frame; the design is widely imitated.

 [9]

1925
P. C. Wren's **Beau Geste** is published, romanticizing the French Foreign Legion as a haven for criminals, forlorn lovers, and unhappy noblemen serving under assumed names. In reality it is a highly professional army.

 [10]

1925
Prajadhipok, or Rama VII, is crowned the **last absolute king of Siam**, under whose rule the Thai revolution of 1932 will institute a constitutional monarchy.

1925
Richard G. Drew of 3M, a U.S. sandpaper manufacturer, invents the first **masking tape** for use in automobile painting. He will invent the first transparent adhesive tape, known as Scotch tape, in 1930.

 [11]

1925
The **Grand Ole Opry** is founded in Nashville, Tennessee. One of the most important centers for country music performance in the United States, it establishes Nashville as the capital of country music.

1925
The first patent on a design for **water skis** is awarded to Fred Waller of Long Island, New York.

1925-1926

1925
The **Bauhaus**, an architecture, design, and applied arts school, moves to a building in Dessau, Germany, designed by its founder, Walter Gropius.

1925
The **Art Institute of Chicago** acquires superb Impressionist and post–Impressionist paintings as a result of a bequest and a gift, including Seurat's famous *Sunday Afternoon on the Island of La Grande Jatte.*

1925
The **portable metal detector** is invented in the United States by German-born engineer Gerhard Fisher.

1925
Trumpeter **Louis Armstrong** begins creating his most important early works, the Armstrong Hot Five and Hot Seven recordings of 1925–28, on which he emerges as the first great jazz soloist.

[1]

1925
The new **Charleston** dance sweeps the western world at every level of society.

1925
U.S. Army aviation pioneer **Billy Mitchell** is court-martialed for insubordination after publicly accusing the War and Navy departments of "incompetency, criminal negligence, and almost treasonable administration of the national defense."

BAUHAUS

Influential, forward-looking German school of architecture and applied arts

It was founded by Walter Gropius with the ideal of integrating art, craftsmanship, and technology. Realizing that mass production had to be the precondition of successful design in the machine age, its members rejected the Arts and Crafts Movement's emphasis on individually executed luxury objects. The Bauhaus is often associated with a severe but elegant geometric style carried out with great economy of means, though in fact the works produced by its members were richly diverse. Its faculty included Josef Albers, László Moholy-Nagy, Lyonel Feininger, Paul Klee, Vasily Kandinsky, and Marcel Breuer. The school was based in Weimar until 1925, Dessau through 1932 (left, designed by Gropius), and Berlin in its final months, when its last director, Mies van der Rohe, closed the school in anticipation of the Nazis' doing so.

[4] The Shanghai police station where Sikh police under British command open fire in May and kill a number of demonstrators. Shanghai has international enclaves, hence the presence of foreign police.

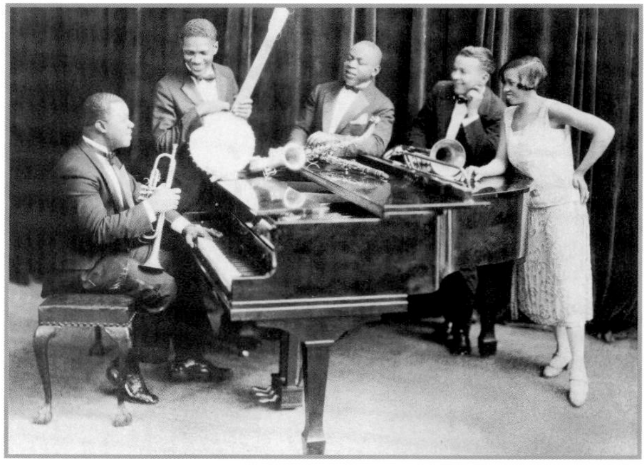

[1] Louis Armstrong's Hot Five: Louis Armstrong holding a trumpet, Johnny St. Cyr with a banjo, Johnny Dodds with a saxophone, Kid Ory with a trombone, and Armstrong's second wife, piano player Lil Hardin.

[6] Clarence Darrow for the defense (left) and William Jennings Bryan for the prosecution try and keep cool in shirt sleeves and with the help of a fan in the Scopes "Monkey Trial."

[5] German actress Camilla Horn in her Chrysler coupé.

 *[4]*
May 30, 1925
In China a series of strikes and demonstrations is precipitated by the **killing of 13 labor demonstrators in Shanghai** by British police. The Chinese Communist Party greatly benefits from the anti-imperialist sentiment.

 *[5]*
June 6, 1925
The automobile manufacturer **Chrysler Corporation** is incorporated.

June 8, 1925
The U.S. Supreme Court holds that through the Fourteenth Amendment's due-process clause the First Amendment's guarantees of **freedom of speech and the press** apply to state governments as well as the federal government.

June 23, 1925
An expedition under **A. H. MacCarthy** and **H. F. Lambert** becomes the first to reach the summit of Mount Logan, the second highest mountain in North America.

 *[6]*
July 10, 1925
The famous **Scopes "Monkey Trial"** begins in Dayton, Tennessee. Scopes is a high-school teacher charged with violating state law by teaching evolutionary theory.

 *[7]*
July 18, 1925
The first volume of **Mein Kampf**, the political manifesto written by Adolf Hitler that becomes the bible of Nazism in Germany's Third Reich, is published. Two years later the second volume appears.

January 5, 1925
Nellie Tayloe Ross assumes office in Wyoming, becoming the **first female governor in the United States**.

January 16, 1925
German statesman **Hans Luther**, not affiliated with a party, who will help bring Germany's disastrous post–World War I inflation under control, becomes chancellor of the Weimar Republic (1925–26).

February 21, 1925
The American weekly magazine **The New Yorker** begins publication under Harold W. Ross.

March 18, 1925
The **Great Tri-State Tornado**, which hits Missouri, Illinois, and Indiana, kills over 600 people and will be widely considered the largest and most damaging tornado in U.S. history.

 [2]

April 10, 1925
The first government led by French premier **Édouard Herriot**, a Radical Party leader who had been put into office by the left-wing coalition Cartel des Gauches, falls.

May 30, 1925
British explorer **Percy Fawcett** is last seen entering the Amazon. He will never be seen again, and his disappearance will become one of the most captivating mysteries in modern exploration.

 [3]

[2] The work of the Tri-State Tornado at West Frankfurt, Illinois.

[9] A. A. Milne (above) and his son, Christopher Robin (top) as a wistful knight-in-armor.

[3] A shadowy picture of Percy Fawcett before he disappeared into the Amazon jungle for the last time. Numerous expeditions will search for him and more than 100 lives will be lost, to no avail.

[8] Traffic disruption at the center of the City of London, by the Royal Exchange and Mansion House, caused by the general strike. No public transport means workers must walk or use bicycles or private automobiles.

[7] A copy of the first edition of Mein Kampf, written by Hitler while in prison serving his sentence for mounting the abortive Beer Hall Putsch.

[10] Sylvia Beach poses outside her bookshop with the new talent, Ernest Hemingway.

December 1, 1925
Germany, France, Belgium, Great Britain, and Italy sign the **Pact of Locarno**, a series of agreements intended to guarantee peace in western Europe.

1926
"**When the Red, Red Robin Comes Bob, Bob, Bobbin' Along**" is a popular song in the United States.

 [8]

1926
A **general strike** in Britain by members of the Trade Union Congress brings the economy to a standstill as workers protest wage cuts.

1926
A **leftist rebellion in Nicaragua** causes the U.S. Marines to intervene. This intervention will later pave the way for the dictatorial regime of the Somozas.

 [9]

1926
A. A. Milne publishes **Winnie-the-Pooh**. The chronicles of Christopher Robin and his toy animals, including Pooh, Tigger, Piglet, and Eeyore, become children's classics.

 [10]

1926
American author Ernest Hemingway publishes **The Sun Also Rises**, a novel about a group of aimless expatriates in France and Spain, who Hemingway characterizes as the postwar "Lost Generation."

1926

1926
American New Critic and Fugitive poet **Allen Tate** writes his most famous poem, "Ode to the Confederate Dead."

1926
American physicist Robert Goddard supervises the flight of the first **liquid-fuel rocket**, in Auburn, Massachusetts. He is later recognized as one of the founders of modern rocketry.

 [1]

1926
American pioneer aviator **Richard Byrd** claims to be the first to fly over the North Pole. His journal, found in 1996, suggests that he did not actually reach it. American explorer **Lincoln Ellsworth** crosses it in a dirigible three days after Richard Byrd's flight.

[2]

1926
Considered variously a realist and an abstract painter, American **Georgia O'Keeffe** focuses on the interior of a flower in *Black Iris III*.

1926
Construction begins on the **Chrysler Building**, New York City. Designed by William Van Alen, this famous art deco skyscraper features ornaments based on stylized car parts.

1926
Gertrude Ederle of New York City becomes the first woman to swim across the English Channel.

 [3]

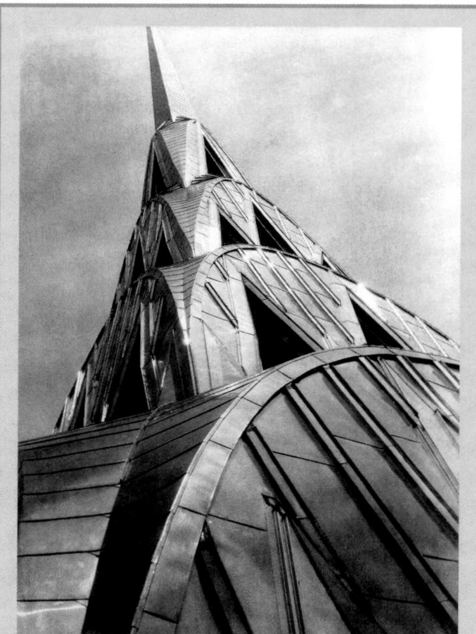

CHRYSLER BUILDING

Art deco comes to New York.

The Chrysler Building was designed by William Van Alen and is often cited as the epitome of the art deco skyscraper. Its sunburst-patterned stainless steel spire (above) remains one of the most striking features of the Manhattan skyline. Built between 1926 and 1930, the Chrysler Building was briefly the tallest in the world, at 1,046 feet (318.8 m). It claimed this honor in November 1929—when the building was topped off with a 180-foot (55-m) spire—and held the record until the Empire State Building opened in 1931. The decorative scheme of the façade and interior is largely geometric; at the request of Walter P. Chrysler, who commissioned the building, stainless steel automobile icons were incorporated in the frieze at the base of the tower and in decorative work on other parts of the building.

[1] *Robert Goddard with his rocket prior to its launch.*

[2] *Commander Richard Byrd takes off to fly to the North Pole.*

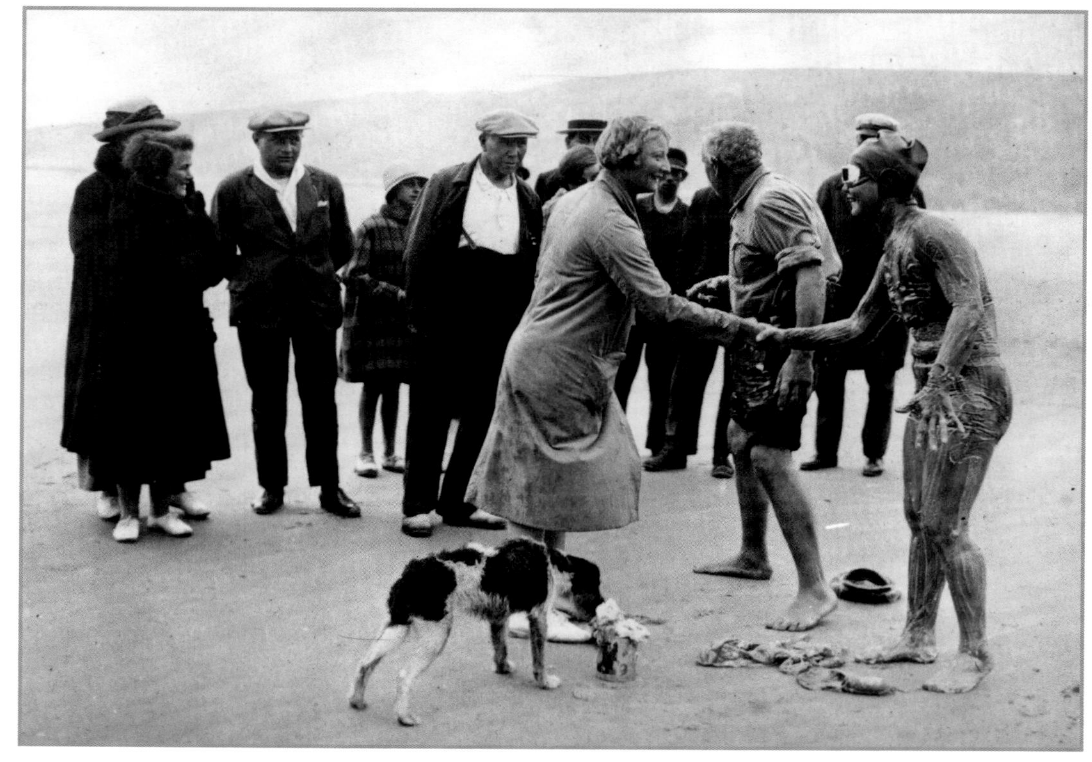

[3] *Well coated in grease, Gertrude Ederle is about to begin her Channel swim.*

1926
The Ford Motor Company announces plans to cut the workday to eight hours and to institute a **five-day work week**.

1926
The **Hambletonian Stake** is held for the first time. The leading horse race for trotters, it is named after the foundation sire of nearly all modern U.S. trotters.

 [5]

1926
The **National Broadcasting Company** (NBC) is formed by the RCA, GE, and Westinghouse. It is the first American company organized solely to operate a radio broadcasting network.

1926
The **Philadelphia-Camden bridge**, stretching 1,750 feet (525 m) across the Delaware River from Pennsylvania to New Jersey, officially opens to the public. It will later be renamed the Benjamin Franklin Bridge.

1926
The **Stanley Cup** becomes the property of the National Hockey League, to be presented annually to the league champion.

1926
U.S. author Watty Piper (Mabel C. Bragg) publishes **The Little Engine That Could**, which will become a time-honored children's classic.

1926
Hungarian-born Bauhaus member **László Moholy-Nagy** experiments with recording images directly on photographic film, producing abstract works called photograms.

1926
Kodak begins to manufacture **16mm movie film**, increasing the portability of movie cameras.

1926
Norwegian inventor Erik Rotheim develops the first **aerosol spray can**.

1926
Publisher Hugo Gernsback founds science-fiction magazine **Amazing Stories**. During the 1930s the magazine helps establish the genre as a serious (albeit popular) form of literature.

 [4]

1926
The **Book-of-the-Month Club** is founded in the United States. In addition to popularizing serious books, it invents the "negative option" form of mail-order sales.

1926
John Logie Baird gives the first successful demonstration of **television** in London.

[4] Cover of the August 1927 edition of Amazing Stories. *It includes tales by H. G. Wells and Julian Huxley.*

[6] Automobiles parked by Nantasket Beach, Massachusetts, July 4, 1925.

[7] Chicago's Union Station, another temple to transport.

[5] Inside the main control room at the AT&T Company, New York, at the moment when the first NBC show goes on the air.

1926
Witty American writer **Dorothy Parker** publishes her first collection of verse, the smash success *Enough Rope*.

 [6]

c. 1926
American **auto ownership** continues to increase rapidly, reaching nearly four times the level of the previous decade.

 [7]

c. 1926
Chicago's **Union Station** opens initially to link passengers to four railroads.

c. 1926
Sarah Lawrence is founded as a college for women in Bronxville, New York. Founder William Lawrence names the school for his wife.

c. 1926
The manufacture and sale of liquor goes on in the United States despite the Twenty-first Amendment. Many blame the varying levels of government support for **Prohibition** in places where it is unpopular.

April 15, 1926
Robertson Aircraft, one of the companies that later develops into American Airlines, flies its **first mail route**, between Chicago and St. Louis, with Charles A. Lindbergh as the pilot.

April 25, 1926
Giacomo Puccini's uncompleted opera **Turandot** is performed posthumously at La Scala under the direction of Arturo Toscanini.

May 12, 1926
Aboard the semirigid airship *Norge*, Norwegian explorer Roald Amundsen, American scientist Lincoln Ellsworth, and Italian engineer Umberto Nobile make the first undisputed **flight over the North Pole**.

May 28, 1926
A bloodless military coup overthrows the parliamentary government of Portugal, bringing **General António Oscar de Fragoso Carmona** to power.

August 23, 1926
American motion-picture actor **Rudolph Valentino**, "the Great Lover," dies suddenly at age 31, prompting widespread public grief from his fans.

 [1]

October 17, 1926
Father Charles Coughlin, a Catholic priest and activist, broadcasts his first program from a Detroit radio station. The Catholic Church will eventually ask him to discontinue the broadcasts due to their racist, often anti-Semitic, content.

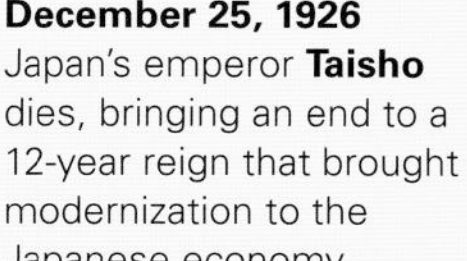

December 25, 1926
Japan's emperor **Taisho** dies, bringing an end to a 12-year reign that brought modernization to the Japanese economy.

FLIGHT OVER THE NORTH POLE

The dirigible Norge *makes the first crossing of the Arctic.*

In 1911 the Norwegian explorer Roald Amundsen had become the first person to reach the South Pole. With funds resulting from his Antarctic adventure, Amundsen established a successful shipping business. He acquired a new ship, the *Maud*, and tried in 1918 to complete his old plan of drifting across the North Pole, but he was forced to abandon this scheme in favor of trying to reach the North Pole by airplane.

In a flight (1925) with the American explorer Lincoln Ellsworth he arrived to within 150 miles (250 km) of the pole. In 1926, with Ellsworth and the Italian aeronautical engineer Umberto Nobile, he passed over the North Pole in a dirigible the *Norge* (left, departing from Kings Bay), crossing from Spitsbergen (now Svalbard), north of Norway, to Alaska. Disputes over the credit for the flight embittered his final years. In 1928 Amundsen lost his life while flying to rescue Nobile from a dirigible crash near Spitsbergen.

[5] *Charles Nungesser with his copilot, François Coli, in front of their plane,* L'Oiseau Blanc, *before taking off in France.*

[6] *Young polio patients at Roosevelt's Georgia Warm Springs Foundation.*

[7] *Hermann Hesse. There will be a great revival of interest in his writings in the counter culture of the 1960s and 1970s.*

[1] *Rudolph Valentino lying in state.*

 [5]

1927
Charles Nungesser, a successful French fighter pilot during World War I, disappears while attempting to cross the Atlantic Ocean by air.

1927
Commercial **transatlantic telephone** service between New York and London begins. The call costs $75 for the first three minutes.

1927
Dorothy Gerber conceives of **canned baby foods**. Production of Gerber baby foods will begin in 1928 at the Gerber family's canning company in Fremont, Michigan.

 [6]

1927
Franklin D. Roosevelt establishes the **Georgia Warm Springs Foundation** as a hospital for patients, like himself, who have poliomyelitis.

1927
German physicist Werner Heisenberg announces his **uncertainty principle**, which holds that it is impossible to know simultaneously both the position and momentum of an elementary particle.

1927
German physicists **H. Geiger and W. Müller** invent the radiation-detecting Geiger counter. The device facilitates laboratory study—and later industrial use—of radioactive materials.

1927
African American poet and editor Countee Cullen edits one of the most important early collections of verse by African Americans, **Caroling Dusk**.

 [2]

1927
Alvar Aalto designs the Viipuri Library, Finland. Aalto creates a building that blends into the wooded landscape and is an important regional adaptation of the International Style.

 [3]

1927
American author **Willa Cather** publishes *Death Comes for the Archbishop*, a novel about pioneering missionaries in the Santa Fe, New Mexico, region.

1927
American inventor Buckminster Fuller displays his **Dymaxion Dwelling Machine**, a six-sided, prefabricated house made of metal and suspended from a tower.

 [4]

1927
August Sander shows 60 photographs of "Man in the Twentieth Century," and two years later he publishes *Antlitz der Zeit* (*Face of Our Time*), the first of a projected sociological, pictorial survey of the class structure of Germany.

1927
Canadian anthropologist **Davison Black** discovers the "Peking man," a prehistoric human ancestor that he will later compare to "Java man," near Beijing, China.

[2] *Countee Cullen. In later years he will teach the young James Baldwin in school.*

[3] *Alvar Aalto's Viipuri Library, completed in 1935 and now in Russia*

[4] *Buckminster Fuller's Dymaxion Dwelling Machine: a later adaptation of the original six-sided one.*

[8] *Leon Trotsky and men of the Red Army in 1925.*

[10] *The Cyclone roller coaster at Coney Island.*

[9] *A Kirkuk, Iraq, oil well.*

 [7]

1927
German writer **Hermann Hesse** publishes his famous novel *Steppenwolf*, which, like his other novels, is strongly influenced by Eastern philosophy. He wins the Nobel Prize for Literature in 1946.

 [8]

1927
Joseph Stalin, continuing to view Leon Trotsky as a political enemy, expels him from the Central Committee of the Communist Party in the Soviet Union.

1927
Kool-Aid, a powdered fruit-flavored drink mix, is developed by American entrepreneur Edwin E. Perkins.

 [9]

1927
Petroleum prospectors discover **oil** near Kirkuk, Iraq, and are amazed that the oil well, Baba Gurgur No. 1, gushes tens of thousands of barrels of oil each day before it is finally capped.

1927
Several **Spanish poets** and writers, including Luis Cernuda and Federico García Lorca, collaborate on a commemorative edition of Luis de Góngora y Argote's poetry. The writers earn the nickname "Generación del 1927."

 [10]

1927
The Cyclone **roller coaster** opens at Coney Island, New York. It will later become a national landmark.

1927-1928

1927
The **Academy of Motion Picture Arts and Sciences** is created by 36 film industry leaders.

1927
The first world championships of **table tennis** are held in London.

1927
The Deutscher Werkbund sponsors the **Weissenhof Siedlung housing exhibition** in Stuttgart, Germany. With entries by Walter Gropius, Le Corbusier, and others, it summarizes the state of modern architecture.

 [1]

1927
Singer **Al Jolson** stars in *The Jazz Singer*, the first feature film with synchronized speech as well as music and sound effects. The picture revolutionizes the motion-picture industry and marks the end of the silent-film era.

[2]

1927
The **Peace Bridge** between Fort Erie, Ontario, and Buffalo, New York, opens as a memorial to 100 years of peaceful relations between the United States and Canada.

1927
The **quartz-crystal clock** is developed by Warren A. Marrison of Bell Laboratories.

[1] The Weissenhof Siedlung housing project. The long block of apartments (right) is by Ludwig Mies van der Rohe. Le Corbusier's house is on the left.

[2] A movie theater shows The Jazz Singer, *with a blow-up of Al Jolson outside.*

[5] Ty Cobb exercises his penetrating gaze.

[6] Gene Tunney (left) and Jack Dempsey.

[4] Charles Lindbergh in front of his plane.

[7] Traffic in the Holland Tunnel.

1920-1929

May 9, 1927
Ceremonies in **Australia** mark the official transfer of the federal parliament from Melbourne to the new capital in Canberra.

 [4]

May 20–21, 1927
In his monoplane *Spirit of St. Louis*, **Charles A. Lindbergh** makes the first nonstop solo transatlantic flight, leaving from Roosevelt Field, Long Island, New York, and arriving at Le Bourget Aerodrome, Paris.

 [5]

July 18, 1927
American baseball player **Ty Cobb** makes his 4,000th career hit.

August 1, 1927
The **Nanchang Uprising** in China gives birth to the Communist People's Liberation Army (PLA), now the unified organization of Chinese land, sea, and air forces and one of the world's largest military forces.

 [6]

September 22, 1927
Gene Tunney successfully defends his world heavyweight boxing title by defeating Jack Dempsey after the controversial "long count" in the seventh round.

 [7]

November 13, 1927
The **Holland Tunnel** opens, connecting Canal Street in Manhattan with Jersey City, New Jersey, thus bringing an alternative to ferry boats.

1927
The **Ryder Cup** match-play golf tournament is held for the first time; it alternates between British and U.S. venues.

 [3]

1927
The U.S. Supreme Court rules in the **Teapot Dome** case that former secretary of the interior Albert B. Fall's leasing of federal oil reserves was fraudulent.

1927
The **U.S. Food and Drug Administration** is formed as a law-enforcement agency to regulate the purity and safety of food, food additives, drugs, chemicals, cosmetics, and household and medical devices.

1927
U.S. president **Calvin Coolidge** announces he will not run for re-election. The next year he will retire to Northampton, Massachusetts, to write his autobiography before his death four years later.

March 26, 1927
The **Mille Miglia**, the famed automobile race across Italy, is inaugurated.

April 7, 1927
The first public demonstration of a one-way **videophone** occurs between Herbert Hoover in Washington, D.C., and officials of the American Telephone & Telegraph Company (AT&T) in New York City.

[3] The British Ryder Cup team sails to America. Businessman Samuel Ryder, founder of the competition, is second from the left.

[9] Walt Disney poses with Mickey Mouse.

[10] Chiang Kai-shek (right) with the ex-playboy and drug addict ruler of Manchuria, Zhang Xueliang, who has recently succeeded his assassinated warlord father. Zhang is doing his best to keep the Japanese out of Manchuria.

[8] Sonja Henie practices at St. Moritz.

1928
The year old United Independent Broadcasters changes its name to the **Columbia Broadcasting System** (CBS). This small radio network will become a dominant broadcasting company by midcentury.

1928
American artist **Charles Demuth**, an exponent of Precisionism, completes the painting *I Saw the Figure 5 in Gold*. It will be particularly influential, in both technique and imagery, on proto-pop artist Jasper Johns.

1928
American automobile manufacturer Chrysler Corporation introduces the **Plymouth** brand to compete with Ford and Chevrolet in the low-priced-car market.

 [8]

1928
At the Winter Olympics in St. Moritz, Switzerland, 15-year-old Norwegian **Sonja Henie** wins the gold medal in figure skating. She will repeat the feat in 1932 and 1936.

 [9]

1928
Cartoonist Walt Disney introduces Mickey Mouse in the animated cartoon "Steamboat Willie." **Mickey Mouse** becomes one of the best-known animated characters on the planet.

 [10]

1928
Chiang Kai-shek, soldier and statesman, becomes head of the Nationalist government in China.

1928

1928
Colgate & Company, best known for its toothpaste, is bought by **Palmolive-Peet Company**, best known for its soap.

1928
Die Dreigroschenoper (*The Threepenny Opera*), a collaboration between playwright **Bertolt Brecht** and composer **Kurt Weill**, opens in Berlin.

 [1]

1928
Distillers Corporation, a Montreal distillery owned by Samuel Bronfman, acquires Joseph E. Seagram & Sons. Renamed **Distillers Corporation-Seagrams Ltd.**, it will become the largest distiller in both Canada and the United States by the 1940s.

1928
During his presidential campaign **Herbert Hoover** says, "We are nearer today to the ideal of the abolition of poverty...than ever before in any land." One year later the United States will start the worst economic collapse in its history.

1928
Early planning begins for what will become **Rockefeller Center** in New York City. John D. Rockefeller, Jr., largely funds the construction project that will create 75,000 jobs at a time of widespread unemployment.

 [2]

1928
English artist and writer **Percy Wyndham Lewis** publishes *The Childermass*, the first of his powerful sequence of politico-theological novels *The Human Age*.

 [3]

[1] *Kurt Weill. His* Threepenny Opera *is a very loose adaptation of the 18th-century* Beggar's Opera.

[3] *Percy Wyndham Lewis*

[2] *The steel frame of another building at the Rockefeller Center goes up.*

1928
Maurice Ravel's orchestral piece **Boléro** (originally a ballet) nearly starts a riot during its debut in Paris. It is reputed to be the world's most frequently played piece of classical music.

1928
Motorola is founded in Chicago by brothers Paul and Joseph Galvin as the Galvin Manufacturing Corporation.

1928
Newark Airport opens in New Jersey. It will become one of the world's busiest airports, serving both Newark and the New York City area.

1928
Otto Frederick Rohwedder invents the bread-slicing machine.

1928
R. R. R. Dhlomo publishes **An African Tragedy**, the first novel in English by a Zulu writer.

 [7]

1928
Scottish bacteriologist **Alexander Fleming** discovers penicillin. The most powerful and versatile antibiotic discovered to date, it will transform medical treatment during and after World War II.

1928
English aviator **Amy Johnson** gains her pilot's license. Her attempt in 1930 to set a record for solo flight from London to Darwin, Australia, will fail but will earn her great popularity as the "Queen of the Air."

1928
Finland's **Paavo Nurmi** wins the 10,000-meter run at the Summer Olympics in Amsterdam, the last of his six individual gold-medal performances over three Olympic Games.

 [4]

1928
The first meeting of the **Congres Internationaux d'Architecture Moderne (CIAM)** is held in La Sarraz, Switzerland, as a forum for the defense of avant-garde architectural values.

1928
Hwange National Park is founded as a game reserve in Rhodesia, what is now northwestern **Zimbabwe**. It will become one of Africa's largest elephant sanctuaries.

 [5]

1928
Irish playwright **George Bernard Shaw**, winner of the Nobel Prize for Literature in 1925, publishes the encyclopedic political tract *The Intelligent Woman's Guide to Socialism and Capitalism.*

 [6]

1928
Jacob Schick, a retired U.S. Army colonel, develops the first **electric razor**. He places it on the market in 1931.

[4] Paavo Nurmi, the Flying Finn, trails Vilho Ritola in the 5,000 meters in Amsterdam.

[5] A slaughtered elephant is cut up for food in Rhodesia.

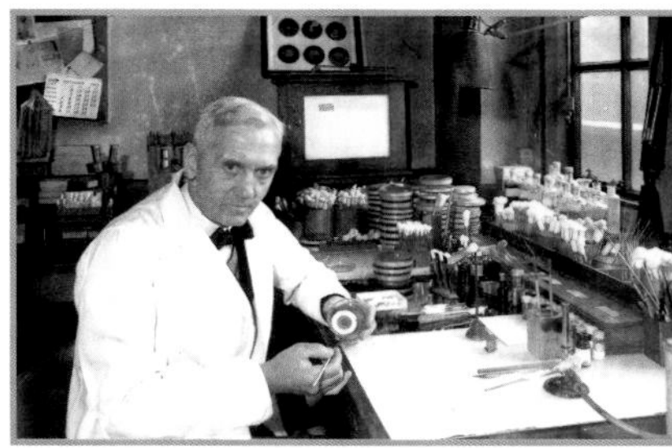

[7] Alexander Fleming in his laboratory at St. Mary's Hospital, Paddington, London, with a penicillin mold in a dish.

[6] George Bernard Shaw warms his hands before the fire.

[8] The Benguela Railway in 2007, after 27 years of civil war in Angola. It is, however, functioning once more, with Chinese help.

1928
Svenska Tändsticks AB, created by Swedish financier Ivar Kreuger, likely controls more than half the **match production** of the world.

1928
Tampa, Florida, is connected by road to Miami via the **Tamiami Trail**, which aids development in both cities.

1928
The **audiotape** is invented by German engineer Fritz Pfleumer.

 [8]

1928
The **Benguela Railway** connects the Belgian Congo with the Angolan port city of Lobito, which soon benefits from increased development.

1928
The first all-talking motion picture, **The Lights of New York**, opens in New York City.

1928
The **voting age for women** is lowered to 21 in the United Kingdom.

1928-1929

1928
Topaze (1928), by French playwright Marcel Paul Pagnol, premieres in Paris. It secures his reputation as a major French playwright and will be adapted for film and the Broadway stage.
 [1]

May 1928
The Academy of Motion Picture Arts and Sciences approves a proposal to present **Academy Awards** of merit in 12 categories, including most outstanding production.
 [2]

May 16, 1928
English translator and critic **Sir Edmund Gosse**, who introduced the plays of Henrik Ibsen to English readers, dies.

July 17, 1928
Mexican president **Álvaro Obregón** dies after being shot by José de León Toral, a Roman Catholic who held Obregón responsible for religious persecutions.
 [3]

August 27, 1928
The **Kellogg-Briand Pact** is signed between France and the United States in a series of peacekeeping efforts after World War I.
 [4]

September 1, 1928
Ahmed Bey Zogu is proclaimed king of Albania. He will rule as **Zog I** until 1939.
 [5]

[1] Marcel Paul Pagnol, who will have a major impact on French film, extolling in particular life in the "Midi," the south of France.

[2] Film star Dolores Del Rio with her husband, Cedric Gibbons, designer of the Oscar statuette, and film director Fritz Lang.

[4] Secretary of State Frank Kellogg signs the Kellogg-Briand Pact. It will later be extended to Russia, Britain, and Germany, condemning "recourse to war for settlement of international differences."

[3] Alvaro Obregon

[7] Popeye the Sailorman

[5] King Zog with his sisters and mother. Before 1928 he had been first prime minister and then president of Albania. He survives 55 assassination attempts.

1929
Clarence Birdseye begins the widespread retail sale of **quick-frozen foods**. His methods of quick freezing transform American food consumption.

1929
Construction on **St. Vitus's Cathedral** in Prague, which had begun in 1344, is completed.

1929
Delta Air Service, a Southern U.S. crop-dusting service, inaugurates **passenger service**. It will become Delta Air Lines in 1945.

 [7]
1929
Elzie Segar introduces the cartoon sailor **Popeye** into his existing newspaper cartoon strip, *Thimble Theatre*.

1929
English writer **Graham Greene** publishes his first novel, *The Man Within*. As well as novels he will write "entertainments," such as *The Confidential Agent* (1939), similar to thrillers but of greater moral complexity and depth.

1929
Enzo Ferrari forms a racing-car team, Scuderia Ferrari, which will remain the official team of the Alfa Romeo Company even after Ferrari himself ceases to drive in races in 1932.

October 10, 1928
A reorganized **National Government of the Republic of China** is established with its capital at Nanjing; the imperial capital Beijing is renamed Beiping, "Northern Peace."

December 1928
Bolivia and Paraguay clash over the **Chaco Boreal**, a disputed wilderness region. Fighting will escalate by 1932 into the Chaco War, which will end in 1935 with 100,000 dead.

1929
American **Avery Brundage** begins his 24-year presidency of the U.S. Olympic Association and Committee. He will also head the International Olympic Committee from 1952 to 1972.

1929
American physicist Ernest Lawrence designs his first **cyclotron**, an instrument for accelerating elementary particles to very high energies.

1929
An ordinary **recession** occurs in the United States over the summer, even as stock prices continue to rise to record-breaking levels.

1929
Belgian **René Magritte** brings a philosophical note to Surrealism in *The Betrayal of Images*. His best-known works explore and blur the line between representation and reality.

[6] Bolivian peasants conscripted to fight in the futile Chaco War.

[9] Thomas Dorsey with his gospel quartet.

[10] A Herbert Hoover campaign button.

[8] Erich Maria Remarque (right) with the German-born Carl Laemmle of Universal Pictures, who directs the famous film of Remarque's novel in 1930.

1929
German indebtedness to foreign investors reaches nearly 15 billion marks, and prices on the **German stock exchanges** plunge late in the year. Both will contribute to Adolf Hitler's ascension to power.

1929
German novelist **Erich Maria Remarque** publishes his classic World War I novel, *All Quiet on the Western Front*. The book is an immediate international success.

1929
German writer **Alfred Döblin** publishes *Berlin Alexanderplatz*, his best-known and most expressionistic novel.

1929
Gospel music, which has its origins in the African American Pentecostal church movement, finds its mature voice in the work of the "Father of Gospel Music," **Thomas Dorsey**, who blends sacred music and blues.

1929
Herbert Hoover of the Republican Party becomes the 31st president of the United States, serving until 1933. His vice president is Charles Curtis.

1929
Margaret Grace Bondfield becomes minister of labour; she is the first British female Cabinet minister.

1929

1929
J. D. Cockcroft and E. T. S. Walton develop the first **particle accelerator**. Using it in 1932, they disintegrate lithium nuclei with protons, the first artificial nuclear reaction not using radioactive substances.

1929
Lincoln Filene leads a merger of William Filene's Sons Company with other department stores in Brooklyn, New York, and Columbus, Ohio, to form the **Federated Department Stores**.

1929
Ludwig Mies van der Rohe designs the **German Pavilion** for the 1929 Barcelona World Fair. The pavilion makes majestic use of luxurious materials and is one of Mies's masterpieces.

 [1]

1929
James Scullin of the Labor Party, who will guide the country through the early years of the Great Depression but will later be plagued by dissension within his own party, becomes prime minister of Australia.

1929
Pan American Airways establishes a 12,000-mile (19,000-km) route linking the United States, Cuba, Haiti, the Dominican Republic, Puerto Rico, Mexico, British Honduras (Belize), Panama, and Colombia.

 [2]

1929
Joseph Stalin's **first Five-Year Plan** collectivizes agriculture and industrializes the Soviet Union. This leads to pollution and famine in the 1930s; as many as 10 million peasants may have perished as a result of his policies.

 [3]

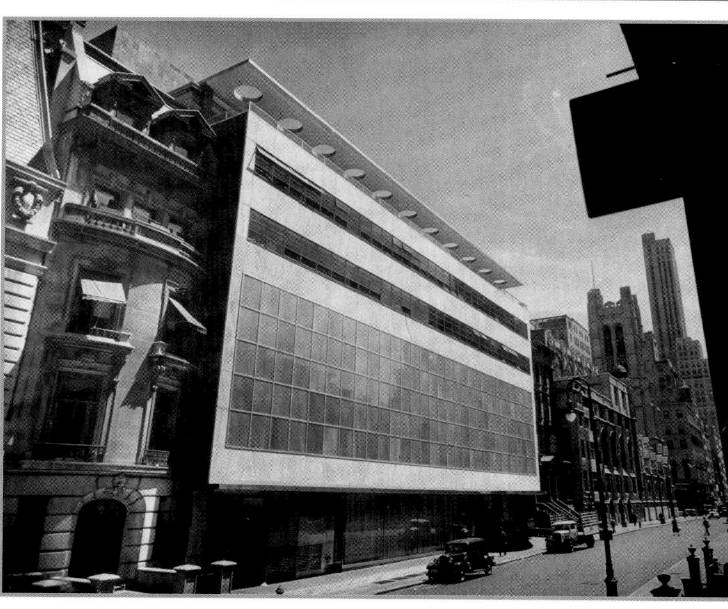

[5] *The MOMA building in New York on its opening day in 1939.*

[3] *Destitute Russian peasants, victims of Stalin's Five-Year Plan.*

[1] *The Barcelona Chair, a classic piece of 20th-century furniture, designed by Mies van der Rohe and Lilly Reich for the German Pavilion at Barcelona. They collaborated on several exhibition design projects in the 1920s and 1930s.*

ST. VALENTINE'S DAY MASSACRE

Gangland killing in Chicago

In 1919 Brooklyn gangster Al Capone had joined Johnny Torrio in Chicago to help run a prostitution ring there. When Torrio was wounded in an assassination attempt and retired (1925), Capone became the city's crime czar, running gambling, prostitution, and bootlegging rackets. He expanded his territory by killing his rivals, most famously in the St. Valentine's Day Massacre, in which members of the George "Bugs" Moran gang were machine-gunned on February 14, 1929.

Disguising themselves as policemen, members of the Al Capone gang entered a garage at 2122 North Clark Street run by members of the Moran gang, lined their opponents up against a wall and shot them in cold blood. The victims included gang members Adam Heyer, Frank Gusenberg, Pete Gusenberg, John May, Al Weinshank, and James Clark, as well as an innocent visitor, Dr. Reinhardt H. Schwimmer. At the time of the killings, Capone was a thousand miles away in Florida. In 1931 Capone was convicted for income-tax evasion and sentenced to 11 years in prison; eventually he served time in the new Alcatraz prison. He was granted an early release from prison in 1939, in part because he suffered from an advanced stage of syphilis, and died a powerless recluse at his Florida estate in 1947.

The St. Valentine's Day Massacre and other gangland killings, frequently portrayed vividly by the mass media throughout the world, came to symbolize the violence of the Prohibition Era in Chicago.

1929
The **Lapua Movement** emerges in Finland. A fascist movement, it will threaten the young state's democratic institutions and for a time dictate government policies.

 [5]

1929
The **Museum of Modern Art** (MOMA), the first major American museum devoted to 20th-century and avant-garde art, is founded in New York City.

1929
Thomas Midgley, Jr., invents **chlorofluorocarbons**, manufactured under the trade name Freon. They are useful as refrigerants but are eventually discovered to damage the earth's stratospheric ozone layer.

1929
Work begins on the **Savoye House** in Poissy, France, the most famous house designed by the Swiss architect Le Corbusier.

February 11, 1929
A committee meets in Paris to devise the **Young Plan**, a revision of the Dawes Plan of 1924, that renegotiated Germany's reparations for World War I.

February 14, 1929
Members of **Al Capone's** gang of bootleggers massacre a rival gang run by George "Bugs" Moran in Chicago. The infamous murders become known as "the St. Valentine's Day Massacre."

1929
The Auburn Automobile Company, headed by American industrialist Errett Lobban Cord, launches the **Cord L-29**, the first widely sold front-wheel-drive car.

1929
The **Chicago Defender**, the most influential African American newspaper during the early and mid-20th century, sells more than 250,000 copies each week.

1929
The **electroencephalograph**, an instrument for measuring and recording brain wave patterns, is developed by Hans Berger of Germany.

1929
The expulsions of Leon Trotsky from the Soviet Union and Nikolay Bukharin from the Politburo help **Joseph Stalin** consolidate his power as head of the Communist Party.

1929
The Jewish Agency, an international body representing the World Zionist Organization, is created by **Chaim Weizmann**, with headquarters in Jerusalem.

 [4]

1929
The Kingdom of Serbs, Croats, and Slovenes is renamed **Yugoslavia**.

[2] *A Pan American plane against the majestic backdrop of 23,089-foot Mount Aconcaqua in the Andes.*

[4] *Chaim Weizmann, one of the most important figures within Zionism.*

[6] *"How many battalions has the pope?" Members of Pope Pius XI's military entourage, c. 1930.*

[7] *Crowds mill about in Wall Street near the Stock Exchange as the Great Crash brings the financial world to its knees.*

February 20, 1929
The U.S. Congress formally accepts the deeds of cession of eastern Samoa, forming **American Samoa**.

 [6]

June 7, 1929
Through the **Lateran Treaty**—signed February 11, 1929, by Benito Mussolini for Italy and by Pietro Gasparri, cardinal secretary of state, for the papacy and ratified this day—Vatican City becomes a sovereign state.

 [7]

October 24, 1929
A record 12,894,650 shares of stock are traded, causing the first day of real panic in the **Crash of 1929**, known as "Black Thursday."

October 29, 1929
Just five days after nearly 13 million shares of U.S. stock were sold in one day in 1929, an additional 16 million shares are sold this day, called "Black Tuesday," further fueling the crisis known as the **Great Depression**.

December 5, 1929
Tajikistan is named a full-fledged member of the Soviet Union. It will undergo a spectacular economic and social transformation.

A line to enter the Perisphere at the New York World's Fair, 1939.

1930

1930
A classsic of German cinema, *Der blaue Engel* (*The Blue Angel*), introduces the sultry leading lady **Marlene Dietrich**. [1]

1930
American astronomer Clyde Tombaugh discovers a body he calls **Pluto**. For many years, it is considered the outermost and smallest planet. In 2006, scientists will decide Pluto actually belongs to a new group of objects called dwarf planets.

1930
American novelist Dashiell Hammett publishes his masterpiece of "hard-boiled" fiction, **The Maltese Falcon**. The film version, starring Humphrey Bogart, becomes a cinema classic. [2]

1930
Charles Evans Hughes is appointed 11th chief justice of the U.S. Supreme Court by President Herbert Hoover. He serves from 1930 to 1941.

1930
DuPont Company chemist Wallace H. Carothers directs research that results in the discovery, in 1931, of **neoprene**, the first wholly synthetic fiber.

1930
Ellen Church is hired as an airline stewardess by United Airlines; she recruits seven other nurses to serve as the first **flight attendants**.

 [3]

[1] Poster for the original German-language version of The Blue Angel.

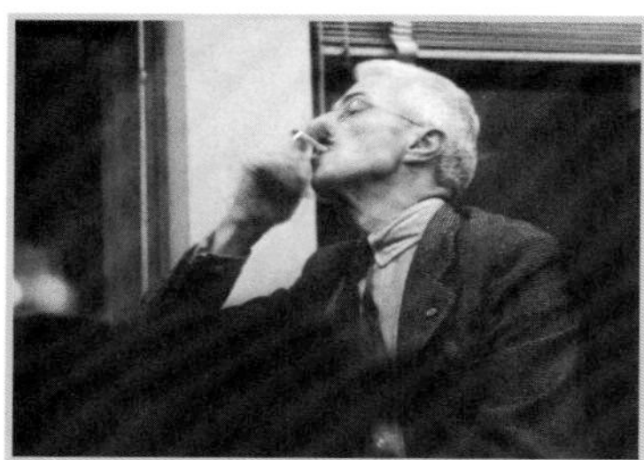

[2] Dashiell Hammett. His years at the Pinkerton Detective Agency provide raw material for his books.

[10] Huddie "Leadbelly" Ledbetter, the blues singer.

[8] The Uruguayan captain (left) shakes hands with the Argentinian captain in the first World Cup final in Montevideo. The referee can't make up his mind whether he is at a football match or going riding.

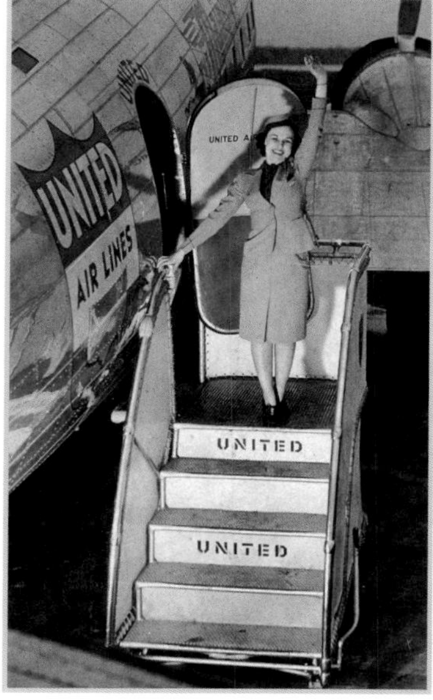

[3] Pretty, vivacious, and capable, the dream stewardess welcomes her passengers aboard.

SALT MARCH

Gandhi starts his nonviolent campaign in India.

At the Calcutta Congress in December 1928 Mohandas Gandhi moved the crucial resolution demanding dominion status from the British government within a year under threat of a nationwide nonviolent campaign for complete independence. In March 1930, he launched the *satyagraha* (nonviolent resistence) against the tax on salt, which affected the poorest section of the community. Gandhi marched (shown here fourth from left) with his supporters from Ahmedabad to the Arabian Sea. On April 25 he arrived at the vilage of Dandi on the coast. The next day he took a lump of salty mud from the shore in a symbolic gesture of defiance against the British. One of the most spectacular and successful campaigns in Gandhi's nonviolent war against the British Raj, the march resulted in the imprisonment of more than 60,000 persons. A year later, after talks with Viceroy Lord Irwin, Gandhi accepted a truce, called off civil disobedience, and agreed to attend the Round Table Conference in London as the sole representative of the Indian National Congress.

1930
The **Radio Flyer Wagon** begins to be mass-produced out of stamped metal. The Radio Flyer red wagon will become one of the most popular toys of all time.

 [8]

1930
Uruguay wins the first World Cup of soccer. Held every four years, the World Cup is one of the most popular and closely followed sporting events on earth.

1930
Wali Farad Muhammad, declaring himself to be a prophet of Allah to African Americans, establishes the **Nation of Islam** in Detroit, while his assistant, Elijah Muhammad, establishes the Nation's second center in Chicago.

1930
Gandhi makes his Salt March, walking to the sea to collect tax-free salt as a symbolic gesture in defiance of British rule in India.

 [9]

1930
The British **R-101 airship** is destroyed in France.

1930s
U.S. medical researcher **Charles Richard Drew** develops the first blood bank, Plasma for Britain, in Great Britain. He will become director of the Red Cross National Blood Donor Service in 1941.

1930
English aviation engineer and pilot **Frank Whittle** is granted the first patent for a turbojet engine.

1930
British aviator **Amy Johnson** flies solo from England to Australia.

 [4]

1930
Irish-born Michael Cullen opens the first **supermarket** in Queens, New York, forever changing the way people shop for food. By emphasizing high-volume items with lower profit margins, his store, King Kullen, invents modern mass merchandising.

$ [5]

1930
Mexican muralist **Diego Rivera** begins a mural for the National Palace, Mexico City. His bold, stylized work and grand themes make him one of the best-known and best-respected Latin-American artists.

 [6]

1930
The **Irish Sweepstakes** is authorized by the Irish government, with profits to aid Irish hospitals. The sweepstakes is replaced in 1987 by a state lottery.

1930
The number of **tractors** in use in the U.S. surpasses one million. By 1950 it will reach four million, and the farm horse will be obsolete in America.

 [7]

[4] Amy Johnson arrives in Darwin, in northern Australia, 19 days after leaving England.

[6] A Diego Rivera mural in the National Palace, Mexico City, shows maize being cultivated and cooked.

[7] A solid-wheeled Ford tractor comes in handy for towing an auto.

[5] An early King Kullen supermarket at Rockville Center, Long Island.

[11] An early General Electric refrigerator.

[9] The R-101 about to leave the mooring mast on its first proper flight, to India. This flight turns out to be its last, since it crashes in France and catches fire, killing 48.

c. 1930
Airplane-assisted migration of the West African mosquito (*Anopheles gambiae*) to Brazil touches off the largest **malaria epidemic** in Brazilian history.

c. 1930
American folk music scholars **Alan Lomax** and **John Lomax**, touring the prisons of the American Deep South and recording folk-song performances for the Library of Congress, discover Huddie "Leadbelly" Ledbetter.

c. 1930
Electric refrigerators begin to replace iceboxes in American kitchens.

January 21, 1930
Great Britain, the United States, France, Italy, and Japan discuss **naval disarmament**, agreeing to regulate submarine warfare and a five-year moratorium on construction of capital ships.

March 11, 1930
William Howard Taft becomes the first U.S. president to be buried in Arlington National Cemetery in Arlington, Virginia.

March 28, 1930
Built as Byzantium about 657 BC, then renamed Constantinople in the 4th century AD after Constantine the Great made the city his capital, the Turkish city of **Istanbul** officially receives its present name.

March 30, 1930
Conservative German statesman **Heinrich Brüning**, a member of the Catholic Centre Party who will hasten the drift toward rightist dictatorship, becomes chancellor.
 [1]

June 17, 1930
The United States imposes the protectionist **Smoot-Hawley Tariff**, raising the average tariff by some 20 percent and making worse an already beleaguered world economy.

July 16, 1930
In the amalgamation of divisions of Western Air Express (founded 1925) and Transcontinental Air Transport (founded 1928), **Trans World Airlines** (TWA) is formed. Later that year it will inaugurate coast-to-coast service in the U.S.
$ [2]

August 7, 1930
Richard Bedford Bennett, leader of the Conservative Party of Canada, becomes prime minister (1930–35). He will work to combat the country's widespread unemployment during the Great Depression.

November 2, 1930
Tafari Makonnen is crowned emperor of Ethiopia, taking the name **Haile Selassie**.
 [3]

November 12, 1930
The first **Round Table Conference**, called by the British government to consider the future constitution of India, opens in London.

THE EMPIRE STATE BUILDING

World's tallest structure completed

In the first half of the 20th century, advancing techniques for large-scale construction produced many spectacular skyscrapers in the United States. The city of New York acquired its characteristic skyline, built upon the exploitation of steel frames and reinforced concrete. Conventional methods of building in brick and masonry had reached the limits of feasibility in the 1800s with office blocks up to 16 stories high, and the future lay with the skeleton frame or cage construction pioneered in the 1880s in Chicago. The vital ingredients for the new tall buildings, or skyscrapers, that followed were abundant cheap steel—for columns, beams, and trusses—and efficient passenger elevators. The availability of these developments and the demand for more and more office space caused the boom in skyscraper building.

One of the most famous buildings of the era is the Empire State Building (left above) in New York City. The Democratic politician and former governor of New York, Alfred E. Smith, and the financier John Jakob Raskob helped oversee the building's construction and management. Over 60,000 tons of Pittsburgh steel, 10 million bricks, and 200,000 cubic feet of Indiana limestone were used in its constuction. It was completed just 410 days after construction commenced and involved over 3,000 workers (left below, a construction worker being hoisted to work with the Chrysler Building in the background). It was officially opened on May 1, 1931, by President Herbert Hoover. However, the building's completion coincided with the start the Great Depression and for many years much of it was unrented.

The steel-framed, 102-story building rises to a height of 1,454 feet (including a television antenna on top) and was the first skyscraper of such great vertical dimension. The strength of its structure was demonstrated in July 1945 when a B-25 bomber crashed into the building, causing only minor damage. It was the highest structure in the world until 1954, and the world's tallest building until 1972 when it was overtaken by the World Trade Center. After the destruction of the World Trade Center in 2001, it again became the tallest building in New York.

[3] Tafari Makonnen of Ethiopia.

[6] Salvador Dali, his moustache echoing his eyebrows.

1931
French author and artist Jean de Brunhoff creates **Babar the Elephant**, one of the most beloved characters in children's literature.

1931
George Howe and William Lescaze design the **Philadelphia Savings Fund Society (PSFS) building** in Philadelphia. The building is the first major work of European-style modernism in America.

1931
Japan and Great Britain abandon the **gold standard** as a mechanism for currency valuation. In 1933 the United States will do the same, as will France, Switzerland, Italy, and Belgium in 1936.

1931
Louis S. B. Leakey begins his search for the earliest human ancestors in Olduvai Gorge in Tanganyika; his discoveries there contribute to the theory that humans originated in Africa some 2.5 million years ago.

 [6]
1931
Spanish painter **Salvador Dalí** creates the Surrealist icon *The Persistence of Memory*, imagining distorted watches in a barren landscape.

1931
The **Empire State Building** is erected in New York City. At a height of 1,250 feet, it is the tallest structure in the world at the time. It will remain the tallest structure until 1954.

1931
American composer Hoagy Carmichael records his hit song "**Stardust**" with Isham Jones. The song had been popular since its publication in 1927 and remains a classic.

1931
American physicist Robert Van de Graaff builds his first electrostatic generator at MIT. The **Van de Graaff generator** becomes one of the most widely used particle accelerators.

1931
American writer **Pearl Buck** publishes *The Good Earth*, the first of her several novels dealing with life in China. She will win the Nobel Prize for Literature in 1938.

1931
The **Great Depression** maintains its grip on the U.S., with bank failures and hunger marches.

1931
Billie Holiday begins singing in Harlem nightclubs, displaying a vivid style that establishes her as the premier jazz singer from the 1930s to the 1950s.
 [4]

1931
English actor **Boris Karloff** gives his most famous performance as the monster in *Frankenstein*, one of Hollywood's first important horror films. The film was adapted from the novel by English author Mary Shelley.
 [5]

[2] A TWA plane over midtown Manhattan.

[4] Billie Holiday sings at the Metropolitan Opera House in 1943.

[7] President Paul Doumer of France. He will die by the hand of a mad White Russian émigré.

[1] German Chancellor Heinrich Brüning after voting for Hindenburg in the 1932 presidential election. He is a believer in enlightened absolutism for a country in the grip of Depression and where Nazis and Communists are fighting in the streets.

[5] Boris Karloff as the monster in the movie of Frankenstein.

[8] Japanese troops march into Manchuria, a rich prize that Japan has been eyeing for many years.

1931
The International Bible Students Association, under the leadership of Joseph Franklin Rutherford, is renamed the **Jehovah's Witnesses**.

February 21, 1931
The first reported **airline hijacking** (skyjacking) occurs in Peru.

March 3, 1931
"The Star-Spangled Banner," written by Francis Scott Key during the War of 1812, is officially adopted as the **national anthem** of the United States by act of Congress.

 [7]
May 13, 1931
Paul Doumer is elected president of France. His term will be cut short by an assassin's bullet.

 [8]
September 18, 1931
In the so-called **Mukden Incident**, the Japanese army in Manchuria use the pretext of an explosion along its railway to occupy Mukden and to increase its control, within three months, to all of Manchuria.

November 7, 1931
Chinese Communists establish a soviet government, the **Jiangxi Soviet,** in Jiangxi province in southeastern China.

1932

1932
The Puddle Family show is broadcast on radio, sponsored by Procter & Gamble; it is soon known as the first soap opera.

1932
Aldous Huxley publishes *Brave New World*, a dystopian novel set in the 25th century that foreshadows the development of *in vitro* fertilization and cloning.

 [1]

1932
American author Laura Ingalls Wilder publishes **The Little House in the Big Woods**, the first of her series of novels based on her life in the frontier Midwest. Their warm, truthful portrayal is of a life made picturesque by its very simplicity.

1932
American aviator **Amelia Earhart** becomes the first woman to fly alone across the Atlantic.

 [2]

1932
At the **Summer Olympics** in Los Angeles, versatile American athlete Babe Didrikson wins medals in the hurdles, javelin competitions, and high jump. She goes on to a spectacular career in golf.

 [3]

1932
British physicist James Chadwick discovers the **neutron**, for which he will win the 1935 Nobel Prize in Physics.

[1] Aldous Huxley, a member of a family at the center of England's intellectual elite. His other novels, such as Antic Hay *and* Point Counter Point, *are good guides to life and opinion in such circles during the 1920s and 1930s.*

[2] Amelia Earhart, still managing to look chic just after landing at Derry in Northern Ireland at the end of her flight.

[3] Babe Didrikson, winner of the women's gold for the javelin.

[7] Hattie Caraway. She will serve 14 years in the Senate, though making no speeches from the floor.

[6] Stalin and various Politburo members surrounded by happy children, in a particularly cloying example of a Socialist Realist painting, by Vasili Svarog.

[8] Medal ceremony for the four-man bobsled at Lake Placid. The U.S. teams come first and second with Germany third.

1932
Ole Kirk Christiansen names his company **Lego**, an abbreviation for Danish words meaning "play well." The plastic Lego building brick will be created in 1949.

 [6]

1932
Socialist realism becomes the official style for literature and art in the Soviet Union, encouraging works of art of impeccable political purity and grinding mediocrity.

1932
Some of American artist Joseph Cornell's constructions of **found objects** are shown in the group exhibition *Surréalisme* at the Julien Levy Gallery in New York City.

 [7]

January 12, 1932
Hattie Ophelia Caraway becomes the first woman elected to the U.S. Senate.

 [8]

February 4, 1932
The United States hosts its first **Winter Olympic Games**, in Lake Placid, New York.

February 22, 1932
The **Purple Heart**, a U.S. military decoration originally instituted by George Washington in 1782 to honor bravery in battle, is revived as an award for those wounded or killed in action against an enemy.

1932
British physicists **John Douglas Cockcroft** and **Ernest Walton** are the first to split the nucleus of an atom, by bombarding lithium and boron nuclei with protons.

 [4]

1932
Concerned about automobile traffic and the difficulty of parking, newspaper publisher Carl C. Magee invents the **parking meter** in Oklahoma City.

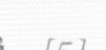 [5]

1932
German researcher Gerhard Domagk announces the discovery of the antibacterial effects of the **sulfonamide Prontosil**, the first synthetic compound to cure general bacterial infections in humans.

1932
Group f.64 is founded in the U.S. by photographers Ansel Adams, Imogen Cunningham, Edward Weston, and Willard Van Dyke. It exalts sharp, detailed, technically virtuosic photographs over soft-focus composition.

1932
Henry-Russell Hitchcock and Philip Johnson introduce the term "**International Style**" into general circulation with their eponymous show at the Museum of Modern Art in New York City.

1932
Joseph Lyons, who helped form the United Australia Party in 1931, becomes prime minister of Australia. During his term in office, he will oversee the nation's economic recovery from the Great Depression and increase defense activity.

[4] Lord Rutherford, director of the Cavendish Laboratory at Cambridge, stands between Walton (left) and Cockcroft.

[10] The Lindbergh baby

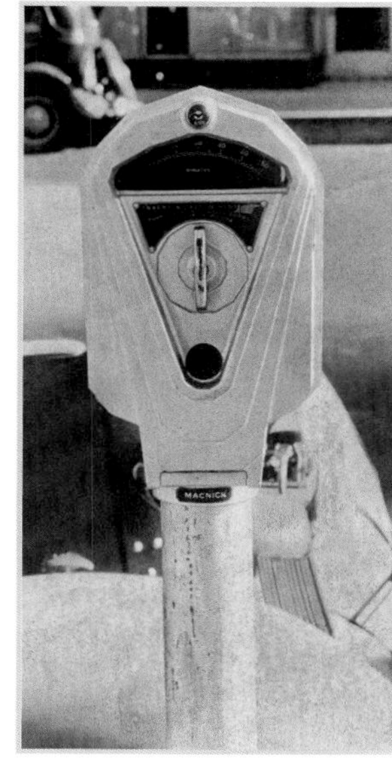

[5] An early wind-up parking meter.

[9] Security men fight with a Ford striker. Police fire into a crowd during the strike, killing four and wounding 100.

[11] Bonus Marchers protesting in Washington: the army, under General Douglas MacArthur, is used to disperse them.

 [9]

March 1932
Violence breaks out during the strike at the **Ford Motor Company** in Dearborn, Michigan.

[10]

March 1, 1932
The infant son of American aviator **Charles A. Lindbergh** is abducted from his home. Bruno Hauptmann is later convicted of the baby's kidnapping and murder.

 [11]

May 1932
Twenty-five thousand war veterans, known as **Bonus Marchers**, trying to get bonuses not due until 1945, descend on Washington.

May 10, 1932
Albert Lebrun is elected the last president of France's Third Republic. He will seek to preserve French unity in the face of internal political dissension and the German military threat during the first years of World War II.

May 15, 1932
Inukai Tsuyoshi, prime minister of Japan, is assassinated by ultranationalist naval officers, ending party participation in the government in the period preceding World War II.

June 1, 1932
German statesman and diplomat **Franz von Papen**, who will play a leading role in dissolving the Weimar Republic, becomes chancellor.

1932-1933

June 3, 1932
U.S. baseball great **Lou Gehrig** hits four consecutive home runs in one game.

June 16, 1932
The **Lausanne Conference**, held to liquidate Germany's payment of reparations to the former Allied and Associated powers of World War I, opens.

June 24, 1932
The **Promoters Revolution**, a bloodless coup, overthrows Prajadhipok, the king of Thailand, ending the absolute monarchy in that country and initiating the Constitutional Era.

July 2, 1932
Franklin D. Roosevelt coins the term "**New Deal**" in his acceptance speech for the Democratic presidential nomination.

September 18, 1932
By royal decree the dual kingdom of the Hejaz and Najd, along with its dependencies, is unified under the name of the **Kingdom of Saudi Arabia**.

November 8, 1932
During the Great Depression, Democrat **Franklin D. Roosevelt** easily defeats incumbent Republican Herbert Hoover to win the presidency of the United States. He will ultimately be elected to a record three more terms.
 [1]

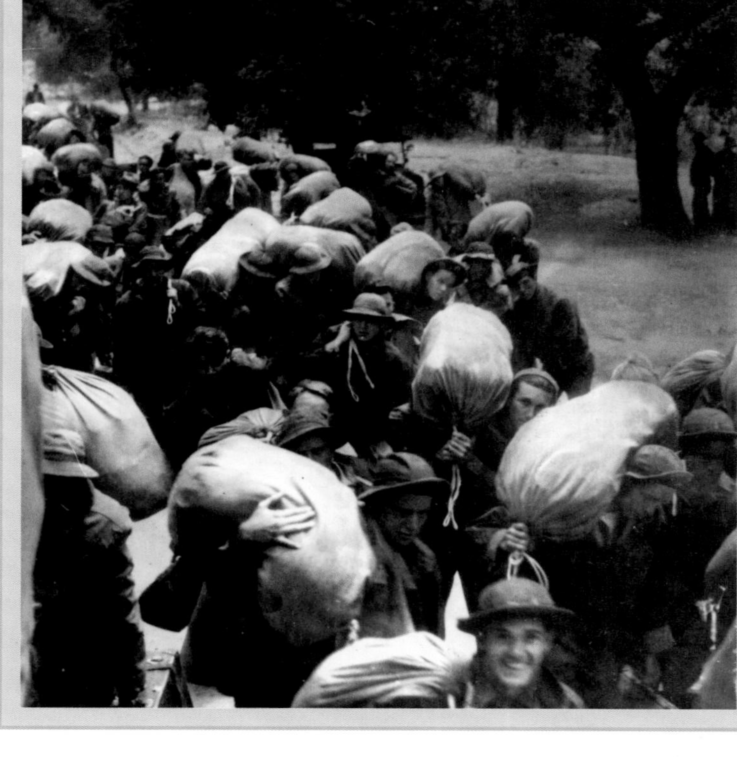

THE NEW DEAL

Roosevelt's measures for economic recovery

When Roosevelt ran for president in 1932, the United States was facing a financial crisis. He needed to act quickly to restore public confidence. The term "New Deal" was taken from his speech accepting the 1932 presidential nomination, in which he promised "a new deal for the American people." New Deal legislation was enacted mainly in the first three months of 1933 (Roosevelt's "hundred days") and established such agencies as the Civil Works Administration and the Civilian Conservation Corps to alleviate unemployment (the photograph shows young men carrying kit bags as they go off to work camps in California), the National Recovery Administration to revive industrial production, the Federal Deposit Insurance Corporation and the Securities and Exchange Commission to regulate financial institutions, the Agricultural Adjustment Administration to support farm production, and the Tennessee Valley Authority to provide public power and flood control.

A second period of legislation (1935–36), often called the Second New Deal, established the National Labor Relations Board, the Works Progress Administration, and the social-security system. Some legislation was declared unconstitutional by the U.S. Supreme Court, and some programs did not accomplish their aims. But many reforms were continued by later administrations and permanently changed the role of government.

[6] The Chicago Bears on the charge in their win over the New York Giants.

[5] Darryl F. Zanuck at ease in front of furniture covered in the skin of a zebra he shot on an African trip.

[4] Berlin policemen line up outside a restaurant being used as a polling station in order to vote in the March 1933 election. In spite of the Nazis' stranglehold on the country, they achieve only a bare majority. It will be the last election in Germany for a long time.

1933
German electrical engineer **Ernst Ruska** invents the electron microscope. The first commercial electron microscope, based on his design, is marketed in 1939.

 [4]
1933
Germany bans all political parties except the **Nazi Party**.

 [5]
1933
Joseph Schenck and Darryl F. Zanuck create **Twentieth Century Pictures** after Zanuck quits as head of production at Warner Brothers.

 [6]
1933
League founder George Halas coaches the **Chicago Bears** to a win over the New York Giants, 23 to 21, in the first National Football League championship game.

1933
Mao Dun, generally considered China's greatest realist novelist during the Nationalist period (1912–49), publishes *Midnight*.

 [7]
1933
Massachusetts Institute of Technology engineer Vannevar Bush and students construct the differential analyzer, a powerful **analog computer.**

December 3, 1932
German army officer **Kurt von Schleicher**, an opponent of Adolf Hitler, becomes the last chancellor of the Weimar Republic.
[2]

December 27, 1932
The **internal passport system**, previously denounced by Vladimir Ilyich Lenin as one of the worst stigmas of tsarist backwardness and despotism, is reinstated in the Soviet Union by Joseph Stalin.

1933
Baseball's first **All-Star Game** is won by the American League over the National League, 4 to 2, at Chicago's Comiskey Park.

1933
Eccentric American writer Gertrude Stein, who completes most of her important works while living in Paris, finishes her first commercial success, **The Autobiography of Alice B. Toklas**.

1933
Frances Perkins is appointed secretary of labor by President Franklin D. Roosevelt, becoming the first woman to serve as a Cabinet member.
 [3]

1933
The **National Industrial Recovery Act** becomes law in the U.S. Its goal is to stimulate business recovery. This law will be struck down by the Supreme Court in 1935.

[1] Roosevelt flanked by his wife and son, whom he holds onto for support, during his campaign for the U.S. presidency.

[2] Chancellor Kurt von Schleicher takes his dachshunds for a walk. He and his wife will be killed by the Nazis during the Night of the Long Knives in 1934.

[3] Frances Perkins. A loyal Roosevelt supporter who gets the labor movement into line behind him.

[7] Vannevar Bush (left) behind his "electrical brain," christened the Integraph, at MIT.

[8] Bartenders at Sloppy Joe's in Chicago pour drinks for patrons, celebrating the end of Prohibition.

[9] King Kong carries Fay Wray above the Manhattan skyline.

 [8]
1933
Prohbition ends after thirteen years.

 [9]
1933
King Kong the most famous monster movie ever, has its premier.

1933
The **Chicago World's Fair** is held to celebrate the city's centennial. The theme is technological innovation.

1933
The **Amateur Softball Association of America** is founded. Five years later, it has the largest membership of any amateur sports organization in the world.

1933
The **Banking Act of 1933** (also known as the Glass-Steagall Act) establishes deposit insurance in the United States and prohibits banks from underwriting or dealing in securities.

1933
The board game **Monopoly** is developed. It quickly becomes one of the most popular games of all time.

1933-1934

1933
The **Children and Young Persons Act** is passed in Great Britain. It sets standards for the rehabilitation of delinquent and neglected children and declares the state's interest in curbing child abuse.

1933
The first pure chemical carcinogen is isolated by British biochemist **Ernest Kennaway**.

1933
The first complete English translation (by Arthur Waley) of **The Tale of Genji** is published. The book was written in Japan in the 1,000s A.D. and is considered the world's first novel. The translation will become a classic of English literature.

1933
The German-American **Bund**, a pro-Nazi, quasi-military group, is organized. It will be active in the years immediately preceding U.S. entry into World War II.

 [1]

1933
The **Museum of Science and Industry** opens in Chicago, endowed by the philanthropist Julius Rosenwald, chairman of Sears, Roebuck, and Company.

1933
The **Tennessee Valley Authority (TVA)** is established by the U.S. Congress and begins an enormous program of building dams, hydroelectric generating stations, and flood-control projects.

 [2]

THE REICHSTAG BURNS

The start of Hitler's dictatorship

The burning of the Reichstag (parliament) building in Berlin, on the night of February 27, 1933 (above) was a key event in the establishment of the Nazi dictatorship. Adolf Hitler had secured the chancellorship after the elections of November 1932, but his Nazi Party had not won an overall majority. Meanwhile, his propaganda minister, Joseph Goebbels, is supposed to have devised the scheme whereby Nazi agents were to start the fire, but the Communists were to be blamed. The accused arsonist was a Dutchman, Marinus van der Lubbe, whom some have claimed was brought to the scene of the crime by Nazi agents. Others have contended that there was no proof of Nazi complicity in the crime, but that Hitler merely capitalized on van der Lubbe's independent act. On February 28, 1933, the day after the fire, Hitler's dictatorship began with a decree "for the Protection of the People and the State," which dispensed with all constitutional protection of political, personal, and property rights.

[1] *A Nazi rally in White Plains, New York, organized by the German-American Bund.*

[2] *The Cherokee Dam, part of the Tennessee Valley Authority project.*

[7] *A Nazi book burning on the Opernplatz in Berlin.*

February 15, 1933
An assassin's bullet meant for the U.S. president-elect, Franklin D. Roosevelt, wounds Mayor **Anton J. Cermak** of Chicago, who dies three weeks later.

February 27, 1933
In Berlin the **Reichstag** (parliament) building catches fire, an event widely believed to have been contrived by the Nazi government to turn public opinion against its opponents.

March 6, 1933
U.S. president Franklin Roosevelt declares a **bank holiday**, closing all banks in the country and permitting their reopening only after their solvency is verified by government inspectors.

 [6]

March 10, 1933
The first concentration camps in Germany are opened, including **Dachau**, where at least 32,000 people will eventually die from disease, malnutrition, physical oppression, or execution.

May 1933
The Agricultural Adjustment Act, an omnibus farm-relief bill, establishes the **Agricultural Adjustment Administration**. It will subsidize producers of basic commodities for cutting their output.

 [7]

May 1933
Un-German books are burned by students and Nazi officials.

1933
The U.S. Hare–Hawes–Cutting Act sets a specific date for **Philippine independence** from the United States. American farmers, who fear competition from Filipino sugar and coconut oils, and Filipino leaders have pressed for it.

1933
Warner Brothers releases two **Busby Berkeley** musicals, *Gold Diggers of 1933* and *Footlight Parade*. Berkeley's dancing-girl extravaganzas are noted for their elaborate sets and innovative camera techniques, revolutionizing the genre of the musical.

 [3]

January 5, 1933
Construction begins on the **Golden Gate Bridge** in San Francisco. The suspension bridge will be celebrated for the magnificence of its setting.

 [4]

January 29, 1933
The fictional character the **Lone Ranger** is introduced on radio station WXYZ in Detroit, Michigan.

 [5]

January 30, 1933
Adolf Hitler, leader of the National Socialist (Nazi) Party, becomes chancellor of Germany. He will establish an absolute dictatorship once in power.

February 6, 1933
The **Twentieth Amendment** to the U.S. Constitution, changing inauguration day for the U.S. president from March 4 to January 20, is ratified.

[3] A scene from Busby Berkeley's Footlight Parade. *At first glance, the dancers' configuration looks like an airplane engine.*

[4] The Golden Gate Bridge under construction.

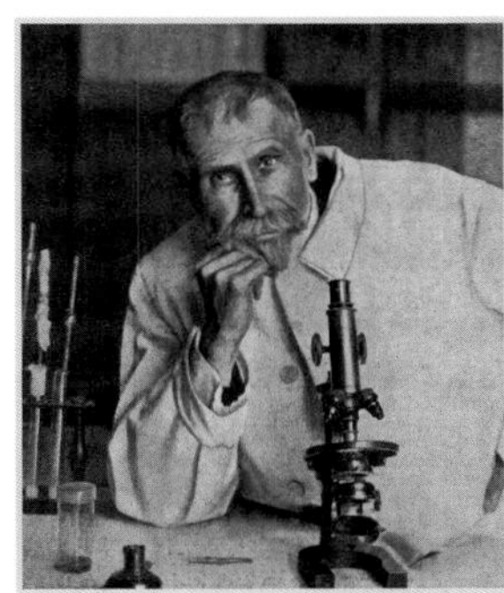

[8] Émile Roux with his weapon against disease: the microscope.

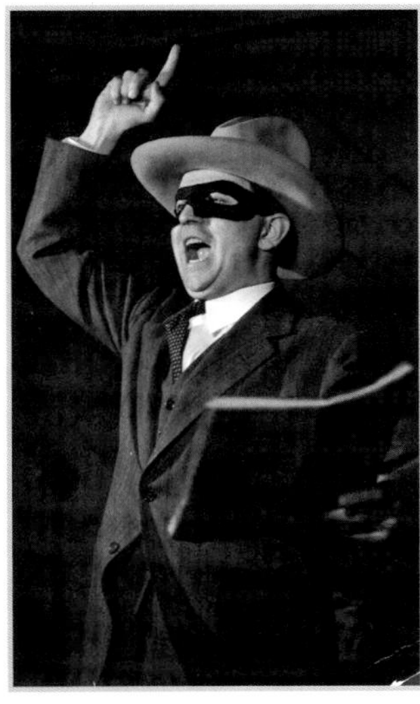

[5] Earl Grosser, the Lone Ranger, forced to broadcast in his character's black mask by the demands of his obsessional young radio audience.

[9] Alcatraz Prison: "the Rock."

[6] Prisoners put to work at one of the new concentration camps at Oranienburg. No secret is made of the camps by the Nazis as the existence of this press photo shows.

[10] A car full of "Okies" (from Oklahoma), refugees from the Dust Bowl, arrive in San Francisco looking for work.

 [8]

November 3, 1933
French bacteriologist **Émile Roux** dies in Paris. He is remembered for his work on diphtheria and tetanus and for his collaboration with Louis Pasteur in the development of vaccines.

 [9]

1934
Alcatraz, the rocky island in San Francisco Bay, begins its first year as a federal prison for some of the most dangerous civilian prisoners.

1934
American scientist **Harold C. Urey** is awarded the Nobel Prize for Chemistry for his discovery of the heavy form of hydrogen known as deuterium.

1934
Australian-born British writer P. L. Travers publishes her first book, **Mary Poppins**, featuring a magical, no-nonsense, but endearing, nanny.

1934
Bombay Talkies, launched by Himansu Rai, spearheads the growth of Indian cinema—called **Bollywood**.

 [10]

1934
The devastation of the **American Dust Bowl** reaches its peak. During this period thousands of farm families are forced to leave the Great Plains after drought and unwise cultivation in the region lead to massive topsoil erosion.

1934

1934
Golf legend **Bobby Jones** helps to initiate the annual Masters Tournament at the Augusta (Georgia) National Golf Club.

 [1]

1934
The **Great Smoky Mountains National Park** is established. It will eventually become America's most visited national park.

1934
Mexico's constitution is amended to extend the presidential term to six years.

1934
Monosodium glutamate (MSG), a substance that is used to intensify the natural flavor of certain foods, is produced commercially in the United States for the first time.

1934
National Action Bloc, the first Moroccan political party, is created to counteract mounting French domination of Morocco and to secure recognition of the equality of Moroccans and Frenchmen under the French protectorate.

1934
Shirley Temple sings her signature "On the Good Ship Lollipop" in the motion picture *Bright Eyes*. The film helps to establish her as one of Hollywood's most popular stars.

 [2]

[4] Clyde Barrow and Bonnie Parker before the law catches up with them.

[5] The Dionne quintuplets sing on air in 1940.

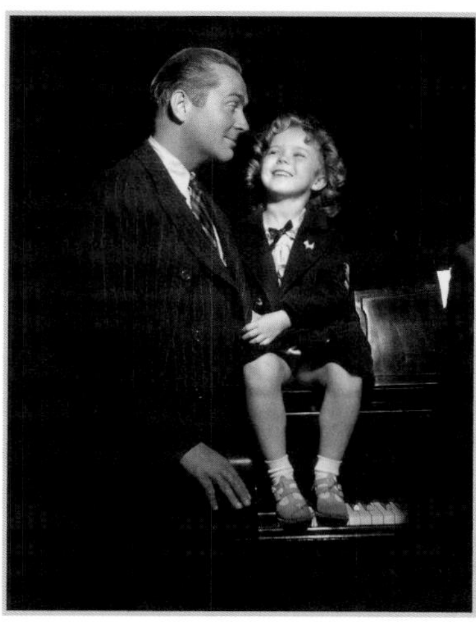

[2] Shirley Temple and her winning smile, with actor James Dunn

[1] Bobby Jones at the end of his swing.

[6] Adolf Hitler at a rally with Ernst Röhm, head of the SA Brownshirts, on his right. Both the army and Hitler himself feel threatened by the million-strong SA, so the army does not object when Hitler sends out the SS to shoot Röhm and other SA commanders on June 30.

February 17, 1934
Albert I, king of the Belgians, who led the Belgian army during World War I and guided his country's postwar recovery, dies from a fall while rock-climbing.

 [4]

May 23, 1934
Bonnie and Clyde, notorious American outlaws, are killed in a police shoot-out near Gibsland, Louisiana.

 [5]

May 28, 1934
The **Dionne quintuplets**, the first set of documented quintuplets to survive, are born near Callander, Ontario, Canada, to Oliva and Elzire Dionne.

June 6, 1934
The **Securities and Exchange Commission (SEC)**—a U.S. regulatory agency—is established.

June 19, 1934
The **Federal Communications Commission** (FCC) is organized in the United States.

 [6]

June 30, 1934
In the **Night of the Long Knives**, Adolf Hitler summarily executes many leading officials of the SA, a Nazi paramilitary group that marched in rallies and carried out violence against opponents.

1934
Switzerland passes the **Swiss Banking Law**, which makes it a criminal offense to divulge information about clients and their accounts without consent.

1934
The **American Ballet Company** is founded in conjunction with the School of American Ballet by Lincoln Kirstein and Edward Warburg, with George Balanchine as artistic director.

 [3]

1934
The United States becomes a member of the **International Labour Organization**. This organization is a specialized agency of the United Nations dedicated to improving labor conditions and living standards throughout the world.

1934
Wallace D. Fard, Mecca-born founder of the **Nation of Islam** (sometimes called Black Muslim) movement in the United States, disappears without a trace.

1934
William Beebe and Otis Barton, inventors of the **bathysphere**, dive in it to a record 3,028 feet (923 m) off Bermuda.

February 9, 1934
The **Balkan Entente** is signed. It is a mutual-defense agreement between Greece, Turkey, Romania, and Yugoslavia intended to guarantee the signatories' territorial integrity and political independence against attack by other Balkan states.

[3] *Two dancers on a window sill at the School of American Ballet.*

[7] *A poster advertising a short newsreel about John Dillinger, Public Enemy Number 1.*

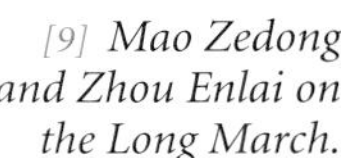

[9] *Mao Zedong and Zhou Enlai on the Long March.*

[10] *Pretty Boy Floyd with friend Beulah Ash. His funeral is the largest ever in Oklahoma history, attended by 20,000 to 40,000 people.*

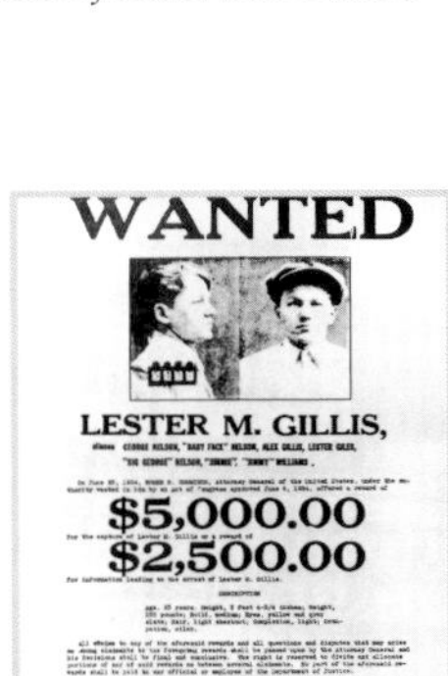

[11] *A "wanted" poster for Baby Face Nelson a.k.a. Lester Gillis, a member of Dillinger's gang.*

[8] *Paul von Hindenburg's body on the way to burial at Tannenberg, where he won his great victory over the Russians in August 1914.*

 [7]

July 22, 1934
John Dillinger, most famous of all U.S. bank robbers, dies. His end comes through a trap set up by the FBI, Indiana police, and Anna Sage, a friend and brothel madam.

 [8]

August 2, 1934
Paul von Hindenburg, president of the Weimar Republic, dies. His presidential terms were wracked by political instability, economic depression, and the rise to power of Adolf Hitler.

September 12, 1934
Estonia, Latvia, and Lithuania sign the Treaty of Understanding and Cooperation, providing for mutual defense mainly against Nazi Germany, which has replaced the Soviet Union as their most likely aggressor.

 [9]

October 15, 1934
Chinese communists begin a journey known as the **Long March** from their base in southeastern China to the town of Yan'an in northwestern China, escaping destruction by Chiang Kai-shek's Nationalist armies.

 [10]

October 22, 1934
Infamous criminal **Charles "Pretty Boy" Floyd** is fatally shot in a field near East Liverpool, Ohio, by FBI agents.

 [11]

November 27, 1934
Baby Face Nelson, American bank robber noted for his vicious killings and youthful looks, is killed in a wild shoot-out with FBI agents.

December 1, 1934
Lázaro Cárdenas, a member of the Partido Nacional Revolucionario (National Revolutionary Party), is elected president of Mexico and instigates a series of reform programs.

December 13, 1934
British astronomer J. P. M. Prentice discovers **Nova Herculis**, one of the brightest novas of the 20th century.

December 13, 1934
Peruvian poet **José Santos Chocano** dies. He is noted for his attempt to synthesize in poetry the history and culture of Latin America.

1935
The **U.S. Revenue Act** of 1935 institutes a progressive tax called a wealth tax that takes as much as 75 percent of the highest incomes. It helps fund New Deal programs.

1935
American composer **Irving Berlin**, famous for such songs as "White Christmas" and "God Bless America," composes his first film musical score for *Top Hat*, starring Fred Astaire and Ginger Rogers.

1935
American singer **Ella Fitzgerald** begins her career with the Chick Webb orchestra. In the 1940s and 1950s she will become one of the best-known female jazz singers.

 [1]

THE *NORMANDIE*

French cruise liner wins the Blue Riband on its maiden voyage.

The *Normandie* was the first large ship to be built according to the 1929 Convention for Safety of Life at Sea and was designed so the forward end of the promenade deck served as a breakwater, permitting it to maintain a high speed even in rough weather. The *Normandie* (above left at Saint-Nazaire shipyard shortly after her launch in 1932) was built by the Compagnie Générale Transatlantique (CGT) and offered seven accommodation classes in a total of 1,975 berths; the crew numbered 1,345. The ship popularized the Moderne, or art deco, design style (below left is the door between the smoking room and grand salon). The bow was designed with the U-shape favored by the designer Vladimir Yourkevitch. Turboelectric propelling machines of 160,000 shaft horsepower allowed a speed of 32.1 knots in trials in 1935. On May 29, 1935, the *Normandie* left Le Havre for New York on her maiden voyage. The ship arrived after just 4 days, 3 hours and 14 minutes to win the Blue Riband from the *Rex*.

To compete with the *Normandie*, in 1930 Cunard built the *Queen Mary*, which was launched in 1934. At 975 feet (297 m), it was Britain's first entry in the 1,000-foot category. The ship was never so elegant as its French rival and was a bit slower, but its luck was much better. The *Normandie* burned at the dock in New York in February 1942 while being refitted as a troopship.

[5] *Robert Watson-Watt experimenting with a kite-assisted radio transmitter.*

[4] *Clifford Odets. The success of his play propels him to Hollywood, in spite of his socialist stance.*

[1] *Ella Fitzgerald with bandleader Chick Webb.*

1935
George Gallup founds the **Gallup Organization**, a polling firm emphasizing objectivity and independence from special interests.

 [4]

1935
Clifford Odets writes **Waiting for Lefty**. The actors and the audience on opening night rise at the end of the play to demonstrate their solidarity with New York City taxi drivers by chanting "Strike! Strike! Strike!"

1935
Japanese neosensualist writer **Kawabata Yasunari** begins work on his novel *Yukiguni* (*Snow Country*). He will win the Nobel Prize for Literature in 1968.

1935
Jay Berwanger of the University of Chicago is the first winner of the **Heisman Trophy**, an annual award that recognizes the finest college football player in the United States.

1935
The new French liner **Normandie** breaks the record time for crossing the Atlantic, and so wins the Blue Riband trophy.

 [5]

1935
Scottish physicist **Robert Watson-Watt** designs first radar (radio detection and ranging) equipment, which detects distant objects through the reflection of radio waves.

1935
Anthropologist Margaret Mead publishes **Sex and Temperament in Three Primitive Societies**, challenging Western assumptions about gender relations.

 [2]

1935
Author Enid Bagnold publishes the novel **National Velvet**, which tells the story of an ambitious 14-year-old girl who rides to victory in Great Britain's Grand National steeplechase on a horse bought for only £10.

1935
Adolf Hitler creates the **Luftwaffe**, the German air force, giving Hermann Goering responsibility for it.

1935
British chemists Eric Fawcett and Reginald Gibson develop **polyethylene** in the lab. The first industrial polyethylene is used during World War II as an insulator for radar cables.

1935
French physicists Frédéric and Irène Joliot-Curie win the Nobel Prize for Chemistry for producing **artificial radioactive elements** by bombarding lighter elements with X-rays.

1935
Gene Autry (with his horse Champion) stars in the movie *Tumbling Tumbleweeds*, building on his radio career as America's first singing cowboy.

 [3]

[6] Malcolm Campbell showing his new Bluebird automobile to the press in England. Later in the year he will set a new land speed record of 276 mph at Daytona Beach in Florida and be the first man to drive an automobile at over 300 mph.

[2] Margaret Mead. Her first book, Coming of Age in Samoa *(1928), claimed adolescents there indulged in casual sex. Now her second claims women are dominant in a certain area of New Guinea. Much discussion continues today about both points.*

[7] A WPA Art Project poster advertising an exhibition— Index of American Design.

[3] Gene Autry sharing a joke with Champion.

 [6]

1935
Malcolm Campbell breaks the land speed record in an automobile called Bluebird.

1935
The Anglo-Persian Oil Company is renamed the **Anglo-Iranian Oil Company**. It will become the British Petroleum Company, also known as BP.

1935
The radio show **Your Hit Parade** is launched. Its theme song is "Happy Days Are Here Again."

1935
The **Richter scale** for measuring earthquake magnitude is developed at California Institute of Technology by Charles Francis Richter and Beno Gutenberg.

1935
The **U.S. Social Security Act** establishes federal pensions in an effort to alleviate the effects of poverty on retired workers, dependent children, the blind, and the disabled.

 [7]

1935
The U.S. Works Progress Administration (WPA) starts the **Federal Art Project** and **Federal Writers' Project**, which supports the work of such writers as Ralph Ellison and Saul Bellow.

1935-1936

1935
The world's first successful commercial airliner, the **DC-3**, is flown. It can seat 21 or 28 passengers or carry 6,000 pounds of cargo.

 [1]

1935
Toyota builds prototypes for its first truck and passenger car. As a division of the Toyoda Automatic Loom Works, it will be incorporated as the Toyota Motor Company in 1937.

1935
Through the **Wagner Act**, the U.S. Congress creates the National Labor Relations Board to determine if an appropriate bargaining unit of employees exists for collective bargaining and to prevent or correct unfair labor practices by employers and unions.

1935
U.K. publisher Allen Lane founds **Penguin Books** to pioneer the publication of paperback books. His belief in a market for high-quality books at low prices helps to create a new reading public and also leads to improved printing and binding techniques.

 [2]

January 2, 1935
The widely publicized trial of **Bruno Hauptmann** begins in New Jersey as he faces charges for kidnapping and murdering the infant son of famed American aviator Charles A. Lindbergh.

 [3]

April 30, 1935
The **Resettlement Administration** is created by U.S. president Franklin D. Roosevelt. As an agency of the Department of Agriculture, it attempts to move farmers from poor lands to more productive areas.

[1] *An American Airlines Douglas DC-3. The plane is also known as the Dakota or the C-47. Over 10,600 will be built in the U.S. alone, and others will be constructed in Russia and Japan under license.*

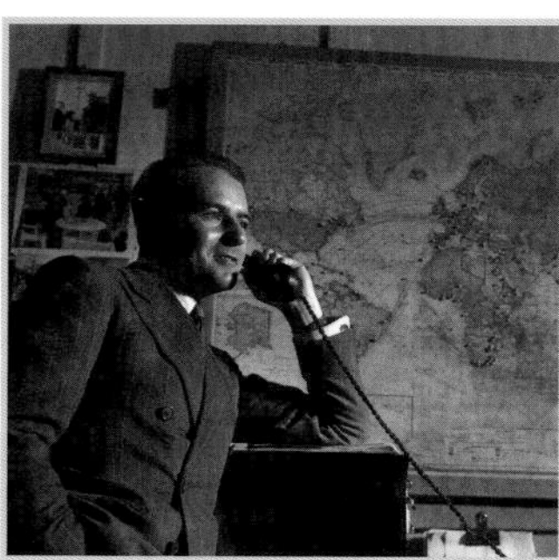

[2] *Allen Lane poses before a map, hinting at the worldwide market that his Penguin paperbacks have found.*

[3] *Bruno Hauptmann on the way to Trenton, New Jersey, where he will be electrocuted for the murder of the Lindbergh baby.*

[6] *Sheet music cover for one of the songs from* Porgy and Bess.

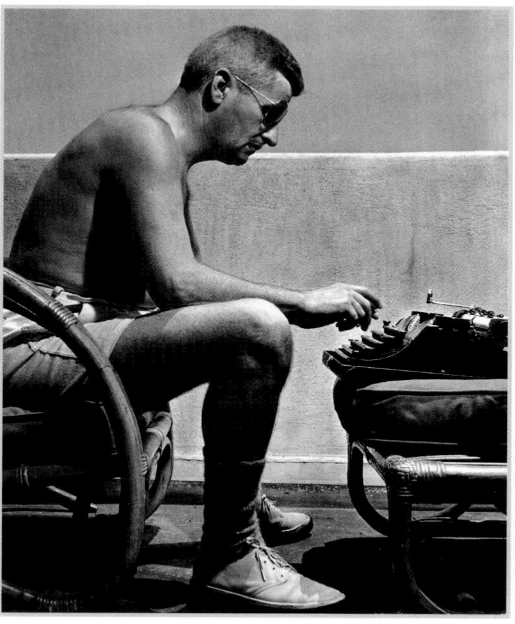

[7] *William Faulkner at work in Hollywood.*

[8] *A Labour Corps march at Nürnberg with some of Speer's specially conceived architecture in the background.*

October 7, 1935
The **U.S. Supreme Court** holds its first session in a new building designed by Cass Gilbert.

 [6]

October 10, 1935
George Gershwin's opera **Porgy and Bess** opens on Broadway.

November 1935
Eight unions announce the formation of the **Committee for Industrial Organization (CIO)**. Two more unions will join later. The CIO builds momentum by organizing the key steel, rubber, and automobile companies.

 [7]

1936
Absalom, Absalom!, Southern novelist William Faulkner's masterpiece, is completed but soon falls out of print. When rediscovered, it will be hailed as the best American novel of the 20th century.

 [8]

1936
Albert Speer designs the **Zeppelinfeld** in Nürnberg, Germany. Speer, favoring Neoclassical architecture, blows its proportions wildly out of scale, creating an overpowering and dehumanizing structure.

1936
Dale Carnegie publishes *How To Win Friends and Influence People*. While hugely popular, it reveals little that is unknown about human psychology but stresses that an individual's attitude is crucial.

May 1935
Alcoholics Anonymous begins with the meeting of two alcoholics attempting to overcome their drinking problems, a New York stockbroker, "Bill W." (William Griffith Wilson), and a surgeon from Akron, Ohio, "Dr. Bob S." (Robert Holbrook Smith).

May 2, 1935
The peasants of **Luzon, Philippines**, rise up in arms against oppressive land tenancy laws.

August 15, 1935
American entertainers **Wiley Post** and **Will Rogers** are killed in a plane crash near Point Barrow, Alaska.

September 12, 1935
American manufacturer, aviator, and motion-picture producer **Howard Hughes** establishes the world's landplane speed record of 352.46 miles per hour in an airplane of his own design.

 [4]

September 15, 1935
The racist **Nürnberg Laws**, aimed at the Jews and designed by Adolf Hitler, are approved by the Nazi Party at a convention in Nürnberg, Germany.

October 3, 1935
Italian forces, under orders from Benito Mussolini, invade **Abyssinia** (Ethiopia) in hopes of building a "new Roman Empire." Ethiopian emperor Haile Selassie orders troop mobilization as a result.

 [5]

[12] Frank Lloyd Wright's Fallingwater.

[9] Dorothea Lange's iconic image.

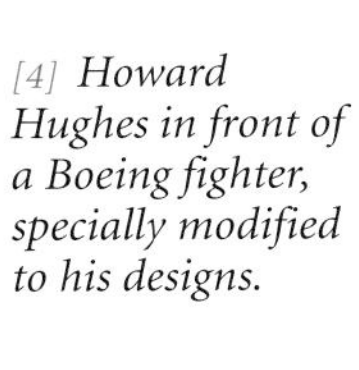

[4] Howard Hughes in front of a Boeing fighter, specially modified to his designs.

[11] Beryl Markham

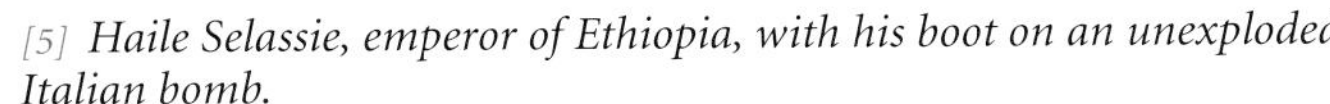

[5] Haile Selassie, emperor of Ethiopia, with his boot on an unexploded Italian bomb.

[10] Boulder Dam on the Nevada-Arizona border, later renamed the Hoover Dam.

 [9]

1936
American photographer **Dorothea Lange** conveys the desperate plight of Dust Bowl refugees in a photograph entitled *Migrant Mother, Nipomo, California.*

 [10]

1936
Boulder Dam, harnessing the Colorado River for electricity production, is completed after six years' work. It is renamed the Hoover Dam in 1947.

1936
British mathematician and logician **Alan Turing** defines a universal computing machine.

 [11]

1936
British pilot **Beryl Markham** is the first person to fly solo across the Atlantic from east to west.

1936
John Maynard Keynes publishes *The General Theory of Employment, Interest and Money*, which advocates a remedy for economic recession based on a government-sponsored policy of full employment.

 [12]

1936
Frank Lloyd Wright designs his masterful **Fallingwater** in Bear Run, Pennsylvania. Designed to be integrated into its landscape, this house is a mature refinement of Wright's ideas on organic architecture.

1936-1937

1936
Unemployed workers from the shipyard town of **Jarrow** on the river Tyne in north-east England march to London.

 [1]

1936
In the Summer Olympics at Berlin, African American athlete **Jesse Owens** silences Adolf Hitler's claims of Aryan supremacy when he wins four gold medals in track and field competitions.

1936
In New York City, publisher Henry Luce launches the weekly picture magazine **Life**. It emphasizes superbly chosen news photographs, photo features, and photo essays on a range of international topics.

[2]

1936
John Reith, director general of the British Broadcasting Corporation (BBC), institutes the world's **first regular television service.** His concept of public-service broadcasting prevails in Great Britain and influences broadcasting in many other countries.

 [3]

1936
Lao She, China's foremost modern humorist, publishes **Camel Xiangzi**, the tragic story of the trials of a rickshaw puller in Beijing. An unauthorized English translation, titled *Rickshaw Boy* (1945), with a happy ending added, becomes a U.S. best seller.

1936
The **Baseball Hall of Fame** is founded at Cooperstown, New York. The first five inductees are Ty Cobb, Walter Johnson, Christy Mathewson, Babe Ruth, and Honus Wagner.

JESSE OWENS

African-American athlete dominates track and field at Berlin Olympics.

In the 1936 Olympics in Berlin, the American athlete Jesse Owens won four gold medals, breaking the world record in the 100-m run (in the middle above after receiving his gold medal; Martinus Osendarp of Holland, on the left, took bronze, and Ralph Metcalfe, on the right, silver), breaking the world record in the 200-m run, running the final segment for the world-record-breaking U.S. 400-m relay team, and breaking the listed world record for the long jump. This remarkable performance by an African American dramatically foiled Adolph Hitler's intention to use the Berlin games to show Aryan racial superiority. For a time, Owens held alone or shared the world records for all sprint distances recognized by the International Amateur Athletic Federation.

[1] *The Jarrow Crusade: unemployed workers march to London to draw attention to their plight.*

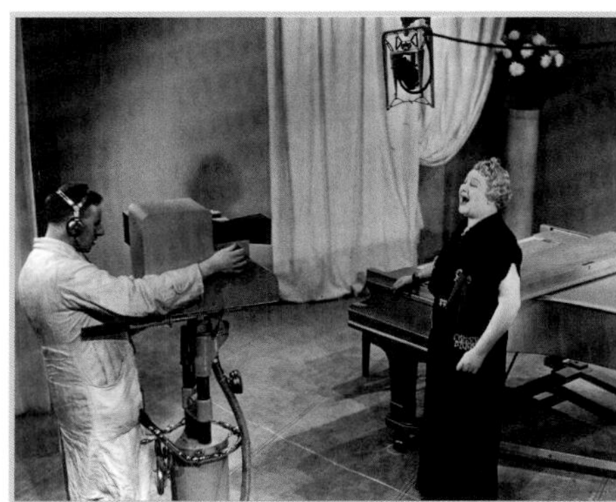

[3] *Sophie Tucker sings for BBC television.*

[6] *Members of the American International Brigade, from Latin America as well as the U.S., get a lecture in Spain.*

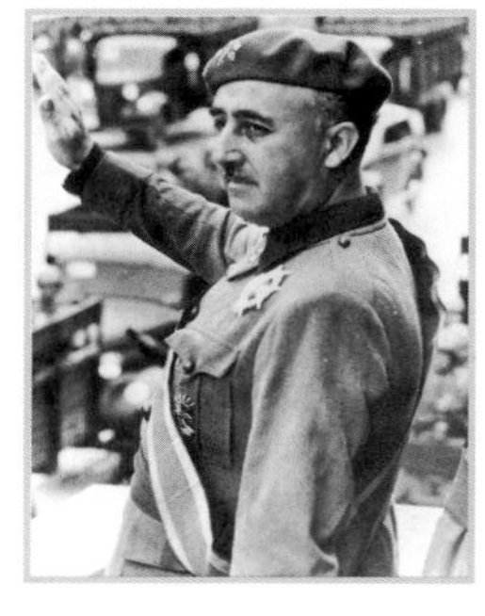

[5] *Franco takes the salute at a parade.*

[5] *Some of Franco's Nationalist troops.*

 [4]
May 27, 1936
The **Queen Mary**, an 80,000-ton British ocean liner, departs on her maiden voyage from Southampton to Cherbourg, France.

 [5]
July 17, 1936
Francisco Franco, at the head of right-wing Nationalist rebel forces, invades Spain and so begins the Spanish Civil War.

August 1936
The first of three widely publicized show trials and a series of closed trials begins in the Soviet Union. As a result of the trials, also known as the **Great Purge**, many prominent Bolsheviks are executed or imprisoned.

August 26, 1936
The **Anglo-Egyptian Treaty** establishes Egypt as a sovereign state after 50 years of British occupation.

 [6]
October 14, 1936
The first group of 500 trainees for the **International Brigades** arrives in Albacete, Spain, to fight in the Spanish Civil War on the Republican side.

October 25, 1936
Germany and Italy establish the **Rome-Berlin Axis**.

1936
The U.S. Bullion Depository, a solid, square, bomb-proof structure with mechanical protective devices, is built at **Fort Knox** in northern Kentucky. It will hold the bulk of the nation's gold reserves.

1936
The Union Pacific Corporation builds the Sun Valley Lodge in Idaho and develops a ski area nearby. The new **ski resort** features the world's first chairlifts, which are based on a conveyer used for loading bananas.

1936
The United Steelworkers, a U.S. labor union, is founded. First known as the **Steel Workers Organizing Committee (SWOC)**, it represents an agreement between the CIO and an older union that had failed to organize steelworkers.

$

February 26, 1936
A group of conservative young military officers in Japan attempt a coup and assassinate Prime Minister **Saito Makoto**; the coup fails, but it furthers militarism and, for Japan, is a step toward World War II.

May 7, 1936
Adolf Hitler's forces reoccupy the **Rhineland** in defiance of treaty terms. France and Britain fail to retaliate.

May 9, 1936
Seven months after invading Ethiopia and driving Emperor Haile Selassie I into exile, Italy annexes **Ethiopia** as part of Italian East Africa.

[2] An early cover of Life *magazine featuring the world's first chairlift at Sun Valley.*

[4] The Queen Mary *leaves Clydebank, Glasgow, in Scotland where she has been built and fitted out.*

[7] Edward VIII with Wallis Simpson (center) on an Adriatic cruise.

[8] Elements from the minotaur legend and the bullring, two of Picasso's abiding obsessions, help make Guernica *a universal image of the effects of 20th-century warfare.*

November 25, 1936
Germany and Japan form the **Anti-Comintern Pact** against the Soviet Union.

[7]
December 11, 1936
Edward VIII, failing to win acceptance for his desire to marry American divorcée Wallis Warfield Simpson, becomes the only British sovereign to voluntarily resign the crown. His abdication is formally approved this day.

December 12–25, 1936
Chinese Nationalist generalissimo **Chiang Kai-shek** is seized in Xi'an by one of his own generals, Zhang Xueliang (see 1927–28), who opposes Chiang's policy of continuing to fight the Chinese communists instead of the Japanese.

1937
African-American author Zora Neale Hurston publishes her masterpiece, **Their Eyes Were Watching God**. The novel goes out of print and will not be rediscovered until the 1970s.

1937
After the German Luftwaffe's Condor Legion bombs the Basque village of Guernica, Spain, Pablo Picasso paints **Guernica**, revealing Cubism's power to express horror and tragedy.

1937
American chemist Wallace H. Carothers heads a research team that invents **nylon**. The successful production of a useful fiber from readily available compounds leads to a rapidly proliferating family of synthetics.

1937

1937
American physicist Chester F. Carlson invents **xerography**, an electrostatic dry-copying process with uses ranging from office copying to reproducing out-of-print books.

1937
American physicist Ernest Lawrence and physician John Lawrence develop neutron therapy to destroy cancers. The first patient to receive **radiation therapy** is their mother, Gunda.

1937
Buchenwald concentration camp opens; it is one of the first and biggest of the Nazi German concentration camps established on German soil.

1937
Danish writer **Isak Dinesen** publishes her autobiographical novel about her life in the African Ngong hills, *Out of Africa.*

1937
Mickey Rooney plays Andy Hardy, the teenage son of a small-town judge, in the movie *A Family Affair.* The idealized Hardy family proves so popular that MGM will feature it in 14 more films over the next nine years.

 [1]

1937
Nazi propagandists stage the **Degenerate Art exhibition** in Munich. The combination of official hostility and the emigration of many artists end Germany's contribution to the modern-art movement.

[5] Palestinian police under British command take Arab suspects off for questioning after the shooting of some police and civilians.

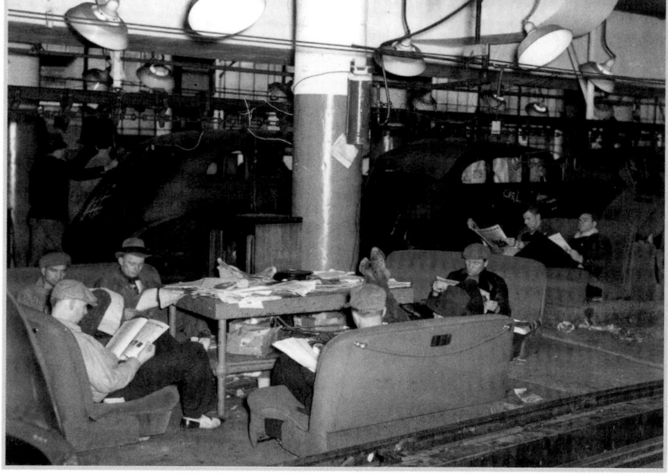

[2] Strikers "sit down" at the General Motors Fisher Body Plant in some comfort, using automobile seats.

[3] Traffic moves across the newly completed Golden Gate Bridge.

[1] Mickey Rooney in Out West with the Hardys.

January 25, 1937
Guiding Light, a **soap opera**, debuts as a radio broadcast; the show will later move to TV and become the longest-running drama in broadcast history.

January 30, 1937
Adolf Hitler repudiates the "war guilt" clause of the Versailles Treaty, demands the return of former German colonies, and declares that **the Reich** is replacing an "era of surprises" with one of international cooperation.

March 6, 1937
The Firestone Tire and Rubber Company closes its Akron (Ohio) plants after receiving a demand for recognition of the United Rubber Workers of America as sole **collective bargaining** agent for its 10,000 workers.

March 18, 1937
Pope Pius XI issues an anti-communist encyclical urging states "to prevent within their territories the ravages of the anti-God campaign."

March 22, 1937
The French liner **Normandie** sets a new eastward, transatlantic crossing record of 4 days, 6 minutes, and 23 seconds for 2,967 miles, from Ambrose Light, in the United States, to Bishop's Rock, in Great Britain.

April 29, 1937
In Germany the Nazi government launches an attack on the Catholic Church, announcing **mass trials** of more than 1,000 priests, monks, and lay brothers on immorality charges.

1937
The **sit-down**—a nonviolent civil disobedience tactic where demonstrators remain seated until forcibly evicted or until their grievances are answered—is first used on a large scale in the U.S. during the United Automobile Workers' strike against General Motors.

 [2]

1937
The **Golden Gate Bridge**, spanning the San Francisco Bay in California, opens.

 [3]

1937
The National Gallery of Art in Washington, D.C., is founded when financier **Andrew Mellon** donates a collection of paintings by European masters and a large sum of money.

 [4]

1937
The nickel-smelting complex at **Norilsk**, in northwest Siberia, opens. The world's single largest source of atmospheric sulphur dioxide, it will emit more of the pollutant in the 1980s than all of Italy.

1937
U.S. Supreme Court Justice **Owen Roberts** makes the famous "switch in time that saved nine," persuaded by Chief Justice Charles Evans Hughes to change his vote on a New Deal minimum-wage case.

1937
Unrest continues in **Palestine** as the Arab population protests at the increasing influx of Jews.

 [5]

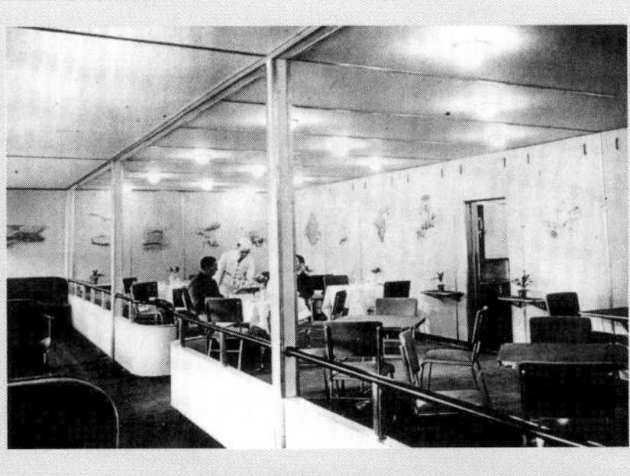

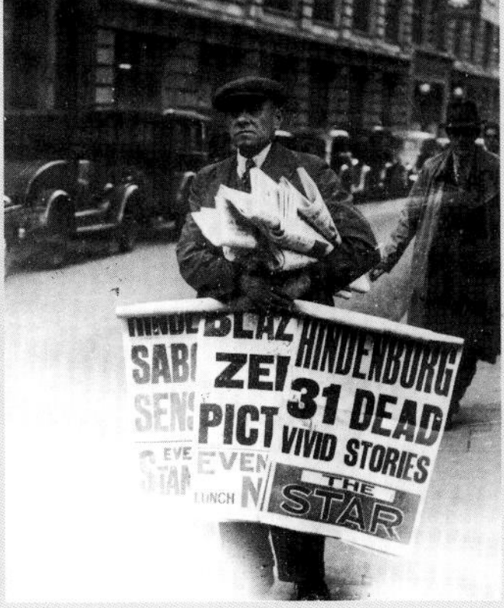

THE *HINDENBURG*

The largest rigid airship burns in a spectacular disaster.

The *Hindenburg* was a 245-meter- (804-foot-) long airship of conventional zeppelin design that was launched at Friedrichshafen, Germany, in March 1936. It had a maximum speed of 135 km (84 miles) per hour and a cruising speed of 126 km (78 miles) per hour. Though it was designed to be filled with helium gas, the airship was filled with highly flammable hydrogen owing to export restrictions by the United States against Nazi Germany. In 1936 the *Hindenburg* inaugurated commercial air service (top left, the dining room) across the North Atlantic by carrying 1,002 passengers on 10 scheduled trips between Germany and the United States .

On May 6, 1937, while landing at Lakehurst, New Jersey, on the first of its scheduled 1937 transatlantic crossings (far left above), the *Hindenburg* burst into flames (far left) and was completely destroyed. Thirty-six of the 97 persons aboard were killed (left, news vendor in Fleet Street, London). The fire was officially attributed to a discharge of atmospheric electricity in the vicinity of a hydrogen gas leak from the airship, though there was speculation that the airship was the victim of an anti-Nazi act of sabotage. The disaster marked the end of the use of rigid airships in commercial air transportation.

[4] The monumental portico of the National Gallery of Art in Washington D.C., the windowless walks to either side clearly stating it is a building in which to hang pictures.

[6] King George VI, with his wife, Queen Elizabeth, and their two daughters, Elizabeth (left) and Margaret, on the balcony outside Buckingham Palace after the Coronation.

May 3, 1937
American author **Margaret Mitchell** receives the Pulitzer Prize for her novel *Gone with the Wind*; the enormously popular story will be made into an Academy Award–winning film in 1939.

May 6, 1937
The **Hindenburg**, the largest rigid airship ever built, bursts into flames in the air over Lakehurst Naval Air Station, New Jersey. Thirty-six of the 97 persons aboard are killed.

 [6]

May 12, 1937
George VI is crowned king of Britain; he actually assumed the throne on December 11, 1936.

May 22, 1937
The Soviet government reports the execution of more than 20 **anti-Stalin conspirators** in Tiflis (now Tbilisi), Georgia.

May 24, 1937
The **Social Security Act** is upheld in three decisions of the U.S. Supreme Court; on the same day, President Franklin D. Roosevelt supports a bill establishing maximum hours and minimum wages and abolishing child labor.

May 25, 1937
Benito Mussolini's Milan newspaper orders **Italian Jews** to support Fascism wholeheartedly or leave the country.

1937-1938

May 28, 1937
Neville Chamberlain, whose name will become identified with the policy of "appeasement" toward Adolf Hitler's Germany in the period immediately preceding World War II, becomes prime minister of Great Britain.

May 31, 1937
German warships bombard **Almeria, Spain**, in reprisal for the Spanish Loyalist bombing of the German battleship *Deutschland* on May 29.

July 2, 1937
During an attempt to fly around the world, **Amelia Earhart** and her navigator, Fred Noonan, vanish over the central Pacific Ocean near the International Date Line; the wreckage of their plane is never found.

July 7, 1937
The **Sino-Japanese War** begins with a minor clash between Japanese and Chinese troops near Beiping (now Beijing) as China resists the expansion of Japanese influence in its territory.

August 21, 1937
The U.S.S.R. and China sign a **nonaggression pact**, the U.S.S.R. quickly beginning to send munitions, military advisers, and hundreds of aircraft with Soviet pilots to fight Japanese forces invading China.

October 3, 1937
A strike of 250,000 U.S. **railway workers** is averted by an agreement that increases the pay of all engine, train, and yard service employees by 44 cents a day.

[1] Amelia Earhart with her navigator, Fred Noonan, in Brazil before they head out over the Pacific Ocean.

[2] A Chinese machine gunner fires at the Japanese early in the Sino-Japanese War.

[5] Don Budge executing a backhand volley with grace and control at Wimbledon.

[6] Nylon stockings: they will be standard women's wear for several decades until the coming of nylon tights.

[7] Joe Louis back in his corner after flooring Max Schmeling, while the referee completes his count of ten.

1938
American **Don Budge** becomes the first amateur lawn player to win tennis's grand slam (Wimbledon, plus the Australian, French, and U.S. opens) in one year.

1938
Daniel Olorunfemi Fagunwa's allegorical novel *Ogboju Ode Ninu Igbo Irunmale* (*The Forest of a Thousand Daemons*) is the first novel published in the Yoruba language (a Niger-Congo language widely spoken in Nigeria).

1938
DuPont begins production of **nylon**. Produced by chemical synthesis from compounds readily available from air, water, and coal or petroleum, it leads to a rapidly proliferating family of synthetics.

1938
French chef Prosper Montagné publishes the **Larousse Gastronomique**, an encyclopedic documentation of the recipes and techniques of classic French cuisine.

1938
Heavyweight champion **Joe Louis** of the United States avenges what had been his only defeat by knocking out German Max Schmeling in the first round.

1938
Hungarian journalist and Surrealist painter **László József Bíró** invents the ballpoint pen. In some countries it is known as the biro.

December 11, 1937
Italy withdraws from the League of Nations.

December 13, 1937
The Japanese Imperial Army seizes Peking, Hankow, and Shanghai before moving on Nanjing, where it perpetrates the **Nanjing Massacre**, in which up to 300,000 Chinese may have been killed.

 [3]

December 29, 1937
The Irish Free State promulgates a new constitution and changes its name to **Eire (Ireland)**.

1938
A mistake in the DuPont laboratory inspires U.S. chemist Roy Plunkett to develop **Teflon**. The polymer becomes a popular nonstick coating for cookware.

1938
Action Comics introduces **Superman**, written by Jerry Siegel and drawn by Joseph Shuster.

 [4]

1938
American companies Corning Glass and Owens-Illinois spin off a joint glass-fiber venture. The new company, Owens-Corning Fiberglas Corporation, becomes a leading manufacturer of **insulation** products.

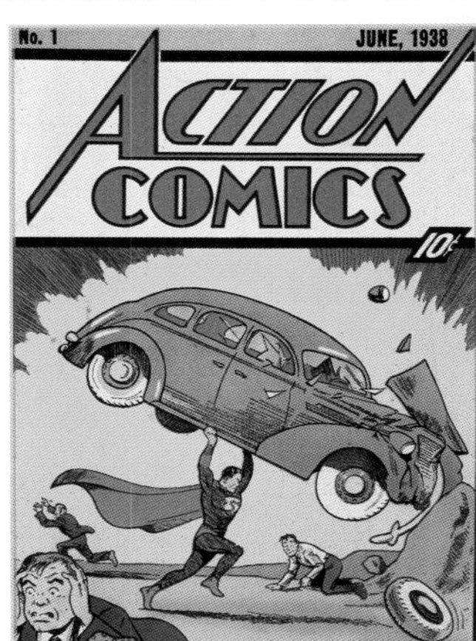

[4] The cover of the first Action comics, introducing Superman to the world.

[9] Sudeten Germans welcome German troops after Czechoslovakia is forced to cede the Sudetenland border area to Germany under the October 1938 Munich Agreement. The motorbike and sidecar are decorated with flowers.

[3] Wreckage in Shanghai after a Japanese bombing.

[10] The coelacanth

[8] The official FIFA poster for the soccer World Cup held in France.

[8]
1938
Italy defeats Hungary in the **World Cup** soccer championship by a score of 4 to 2.

1938
Mount Nyamulagira, a volcano in the Virunga Mountains of the Belgian Congo, erupts with such force that its southwest slope opens and lava reaches Lake Kivu, about 16 miles to the south.

1938
Nazi Germany mounts the **Ritscher expedition** to establish German territorial claims in Antarctica.

1938
Samuel Barber's Adagio for Strings is performed by the NBC Symphony Orchestra under Arturo Toscanini and acquires extraordinary popularity in the United States and Europe.

 [9]

1938
The 3,500,000-strong German minority of the **Sudetenland** in Czechoslovakia demands autonomy; Adolf Hitler champions their cause. Czechoslovakia will cede the Sudetenland to Germany later that year.

 [10]

1938
The **coelacanth**, an archaic marine form believed extinct for more than 60 million years, is discovered to be alive off the east coast of South Africa.

1938-1939

1938
The **U.S. Fair Labor Standards Act** prescribes nationwide compulsory federal regulation of wages and hours. The law establishes the minimum age of employment for children.

1938
Warner Brothers Pictures' cartoon character **Bugs Bunny** makes his debut.

c. 1938
Grandma Moses (Anna Mary Robertson Moses), then in her late 70s, begins painting folk works of rural life in the United States.

January 16, 1938
Benny Goodman's orchestra gives a concert at Carnegie Hall, a high point in his career as "King of Swing." The recording of it has been released several times since and is heralded as one of the greatest albums of live jazz.

February 10, 1938
King Carol of Romania proclaims a corporatist dictatorship in order to counter attempts by the pro-Nazi Iron Guard movement to seize power. He is supported by Armand Calinescu, staunch ally of France and Britain, his minister of the interior and then prime minister.

 *[1]*

February 16, 1938
Austrian chancellor **Kurt von Schuschnigg** admits an Austrian Nazi to his cabinet—the first step in the German overthrow of his government.

 *[2]*

[1] Armand Calinescu. He fights to keep Romania, with its vital oil fields, from slipping into the hands of Germany, which it will if the Iron Guard has its way.

[2] The Austrian Nazi Arthur Seyss-Inquart (center) about to leave Berlin to take up his post as Austrian Minister of the Interior, as demanded by Hitler.

[3] Austrians welcome German forces to Salzburg during the Anschluss.

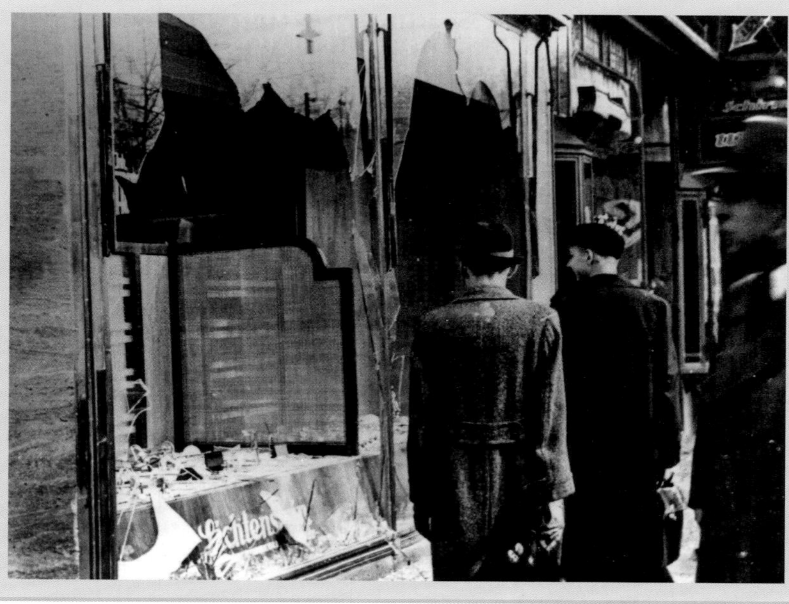

KRISTALLNACHT

Nazi pogrom against German Jews

On the night of November 9–10, 1938, German Nazis attacked Jewish persons and property. The name *Kristallnacht* refers ironically to the litter of broken glass left in the streets afterwards (left). The pretext was the shooting in Paris on November 7 of the German diplomat Ernst vom Rath by a Polish-Jewish student, Herschel Grynszpan. News of Rath's death reached Adolf Hitler on November 9 in Munich, where he was celebrating the anniversary of the abortive 1923 Beer Hall Putsch. There, Minister of Propaganda Joseph Goebbels, after conferring with Hitler, urged violent reprisals staged to appear as "spontaneous demonstrations." The violence left 91 Jews dead and hundreds seriously injured. About 7,500 Jewish businesses were gutted and some 1,000 synagogues burned or damaged. The Gestapo arrested 30,000 Jewish males, offering to release them only if they emigrated and surrendered their wealth.

July 14, 1938
Japan withdraws its invitation to act as host to the 1940 **Olympic Games**; Helsinki, Finland, will be selected as the replacement site.

July 21, 1938
Bolivia and Paraguay sign the **Chaco peace treaty**, which ends an intermittent war between the two nations begun in 1928.

August 1938
Two French cabinet ministers resign following **Premier Eduard Daladier's** declaration that the work week should be lengthened from 40 hours to speed up France's defense program.

August 14, 1938
The **Queen Mary** establishes a new record for eastward crossing of the Atlantic Ocean: 3 days, 20 hours, 42 minutes. Six days before, it had set a new westbound record.

September 1, 1938
Foreign Jews who have entered Italy since 1919 are ordered to emigrate within six months; the next day, the **Italian government** continues its attack on Jews by barring non-Aryan teachers and students from all schools.

September 29, 1938
Poland demands the cession of **Teschen**, a rich region that had been contested and then divided between Poland and Czechoslovakia following World War I.

March 13, 1938
The **Anschluss**, a political union between Austria and Germany, is announced.

 [3]

March 17, 1938
Poland issues an ultimatum to Lithuania in an attempt to settle a territorial dispute over the city of Vilnius.

March 18, 1938
Mexican president Lázaro Cárdenas expropriates all foreign oil interests and establishes **Petróleos Mexicanos (Pemex)** to manage the consolidated industry.

 [4]

March 27, 1938
The University of Chicago shows that the Nazis have dismissed **1,684 educators**. Some 800 have been dismissed for being Jews, Catholics, or "politically unreliable," including Albert Einstein, James Franck, Gustav Hertz, and Fritz Haber.

April 10, 1938
In a controlled plebiscite in **Austria** soon after Adolf Hitler's invasion of the country, 99.7 percent of Austrians approve the Anschluss.

July 1938
Flying a Lockheed 14, American manufacturer, aviator, and motion-picture producer **Howard Hughes** circles the earth in a record 91 hours and 14 minutes. He will land in New York City on July 14.

 [5]

[4] *A coffin, representing the death of foreign control of the Mexican oil industry, is burned in Mexico City.*

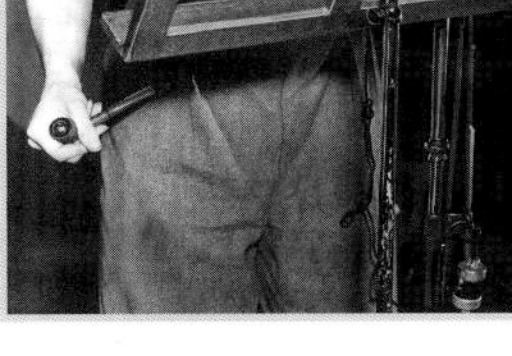

[7] *Orson Welles at the radio microphone.*

[8] *Charlie "Bird" Parker will soon be a leading influence on the emerging bebop style of jazz.*

[6] *The British prime minister, Neville Chamberlain, arrives in England after his flight back from Munich and waves the treaty document which he claims will secure "peace in our time."*

[5] *Howard Hughes flies over the East River in New York City in his Lockheed 14 Super Electra.*

September 29, 1938
The American harness racehorse **Greyhound** establishes a trotting record for one mile in 1:551/4.

 [6]

September 30, 1938
The notorious **Munich Agreement** is reached, by which Britain's Neville Chamberlain and France's Edouard Daladier appease Adolf Hitler's demands over Czechoslovakia in the hope of preventing World War II.

 [7]

October 30, 1938
Orson Welles's radio dramatization of H. G. Wells's **War of the Worlds** causes a national panic as thousands of listeners fear a genuine invasion from Mars.

November 9, 1938
Orchestrated anti-Jewish violence "erupts" throughout the German Reich on **Kristallnacht.** 30,000 Jewish men are sent to concentration camps.

November 15, 1938
A farewell parade is held in Barcelona, Spain, for the volunteers of the **International Brigades** who fought for the Republicans during the Spanish Civil War.

 [8]

1939
Alto saxophonist **Charles Parker** moves to New York, where he plays with Dizzy Gillespie and other jazz notables; he establishes a reputation as the genre's best improvisational player.

1939

1939
American inventor John Atanasoff builds the first special-purpose **electronic computer**.

1939
American **Alexander Calder's** *Lobster Trap and Fish Tail* brings balance and movement to sculpture. Calder, the son and grandson of sculptors, invented the moving sculpture called the mobile (so named by Marcel Duchamp).

1939
New York holds its **World's Fair**. Alvar Alto's sympathetic use of wood in the Finnish pavilion marks a break with the technological fascination so prevalent in modern architecture and the fair itself.

[1]

1939
American novelist **John Steinbeck** publishes *The Grapes of Wrath* (1939), which sums up the bitterness of the Great Depression decade and arouses widespread sympathy for the plight of migratory farm workers.

 [2]

1939
American novelist Raymond Chandler's **The Big Sleep** introduces detective Philip Marlowe and helps establish the hard-boiled detective novel as a serious literary form.

1939
An unusually rich year for **motion pictures** sees the premieres of *Gone With the Wind, The Wizard of Oz, The Rules of the Game, Stagecoach, The Women, Mr. Smith Goes to Washington,* and *Ninotchka*.

 [3]

[1] The New York World's Fair: the poster features the 700-foot-tall Trylon and the Perisphere, entered by an escalator and exited by a curved walkway.

[2] The Grapes of Wrath*: Henry Fonda (center) in a scene from John Ford's screen adaptation of John Steinbeck's novel.*

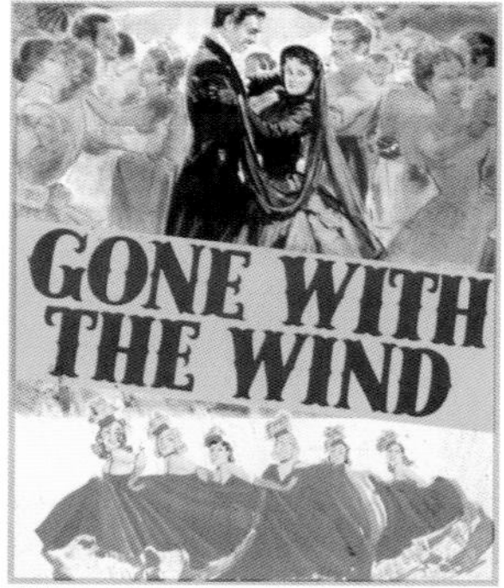

[3] A poster for Gone With the Wind, *with Clark Gable as Rhett Butler and Vivien Leigh as Scarlett O'Hara.*

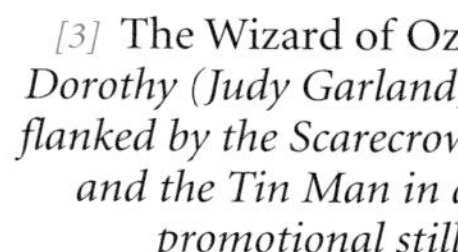

[3] The Wizard of Oz: *Dorothy (Judy Garland) flanked by the Scarecrow and the Tin Man in a promotional still.*

[6] Two early types of helicopter invented by the Russian émigré Igor Sikorsky.

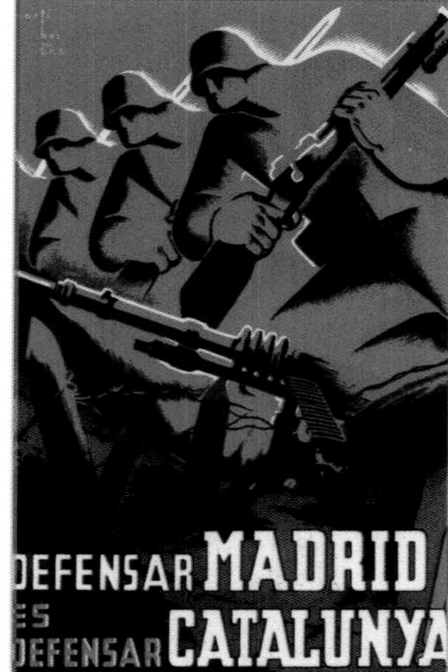

[7] A Spanish Republican poster exhorting its followers to go on defending Madrid because, if it falls to Franco, so will all Catalania to the north.

1939
Reinhard Heydrich becomes head of the Reichssicherheitshauptamt ("Reich Security Central Office"), which is in charge of all security and secret police in Nazi Germany.

1939
Swiss chemist Paul Müller discovers DDT's properties as an insecticide. Initially successful against most insects, **DDT** also damages birds, amphibians, and other animals and by 1970 will be widely restricted.

1939
The first **jet aircraft** flight, by a Heinkel He 178 with an engine designed by Hans Pabst von Ohain, takes place successfully in Germany.

 [6]

1939
The first successful **helicopter** is built by Russian-born U.S. aircraft designer Igor Sikorsky.

1939
The **View-Master**, a modern version of the stereopticon, is introduced at the 1939 New York World's Fair and will be marketed toward specialty camera stores.

1939
Thomas Joseph Mooney, U.S. socialist union organizer and activist convicted of murder in connection with a 1916 San Francisco bomb explosion, is pardoned by the governor of California.

1939
Antarctica's **Queen Maud Land** is claimed by Norway.

1939
Germany initiates the **T4 Program**—for the euthanasia of mentally retarded, physically disabled, and emotionally disturbed Germans who depart from the ideal of Aryan supremacy. Gas chambers and mass crematoria are pioneered.

1939
German painter and art teacher **Hans Hofmann** breaks away from Expressionistic landscapes and still lifes, and develops a totally abstract manner notable for its invention, vigorous brushwork, and saturated color.

1939
Little League is founded in Williamsport, Pennsylvania. It admits girls in 1974. **Little League** teams spread all over the world: its World Series draws on more countries than the professional version.

 [4]

1939
Martinique poet **Aimé Césaire** publishes his *Cahier d'un retour au pays natal* (*Return to My Native Land*), one of the most significant poetry works of the Negritude movement.

1939
New York Yankee **Lou Gehrig**, stricken with amyotrophic lateral sclerosis, retires from baseball having played in 2,130 consecutive games, a record that will stand until 1995. He is inducted into the baseball Hall of Fame the same year.

 [5]

[4] *Little League players in Massachusetts dispute the umpire's decision.*

[8] *Marian Anderson sings, with Lincoln's tacit approval.*

[7] *Madrid has fallen, and former Republican soldiers transfer their allegiance to Franco's Nationalist regime, in a ceremony that involves kissing its flag.*

[5] *Lou Gehrig says farewell at the Yankee Stadium.*

c. 1939
The **Negritude movement**, a searching critique of European colonialism led by African writer Léopold Sédar Senghor and Caribbean writers Aimé Césaire and Léon Damas, begins to flourish in Paris.

 [7]

March 28, 1939
Francisco Franco, leader of the Nationalist forces during the Spanish Civil War, captures the capital city of **Madrid** en route to his overthrow of the democratic Spanish Republic.

April 7, 1939
Earle Page, who as head of the Country Party (1920–39) was a spokesman for the party's goal of rural economic development, is briefly prime minister of Australia.

April 7, 1939
Italian dictator Benito Mussolini makes **Albania** a protectorate of his country, installing Italy's Victor Emmanuel III as king, while Albanian king Zog I goes into exile.

 [8]

April 9, 1939
African American contralto **Marian Anderson** gives a concert at the Lincoln Memorial after the Daughters of the American Revolution refuse to allow her to sing at Constitution Hall.

April 26, 1939
United Australia Party member **Robert Menzies**, who will strengthen military ties with the United States and foster industrial growth and immigration from Europe, is elected to his first term as prime minister of Australia.

April 30, 1939
The National Broadcasting Company (NBC) makes the **first public television broadcast** in the United States, at the New York World's Fair.

May 20, 1939
Pan American Airways' *Yankee Clipper* inaugurates **transatlantic airmail service**, flying from Port Washington, New York, to Lisbon.

May 22, 1939
Adolf Hitler of Germany and Benito Mussolini of Italy sign the **Pact of Steel**, a full military and political alliance between their countries.

August 23, 1939
Germany and the Soviet Union sign a **nonaggression pact** dividing Eastern Europe into German and Soviet spheres of influence.

September 1, 1939
Germany invades **Poland**.

September 3, 1939
Britain, France, Australia, and New Zealand declare war on **Germany**.

GERMANY INVADES POLAND

World War II begins

At 12:40 PM on August 31, 1939, Adolf Hitler ordered hostilities against Poland to start at 4:45 the next morning. The invasion began as ordered (left, motorized German forces invading). The German attack, or *blitzkrieg,* was fast and furious. They used surprise, speed, and enormous firepower to overwhelm the Polish forces. All the German armies made fast progress in fulfilling their parts in a great enveloping maneuver. The Polish defense was already reduced to random efforts by isolated bodies of troops when another blow fell: on September 17, 1939, Soviet forces entered Poland from the east. The next day, the Polish government and high command crossed the Romanian frontier on their way into exile. The Warsaw garrison held out against the Germans until September 28. The last considerable fragment of the Polish army resisted until October 5.

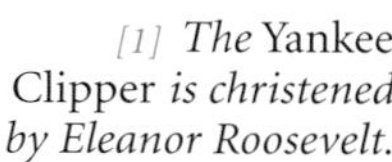

[1] *The* Yankee Clipper *is christened by Eleanor Roosevelt.*

[3] *A newspaper vendor in Trafalgar Square.*

[2] *Hitler and Mussolini during the former's visit to Italy in 1938 when the groundwork for the 1939 Pact of Steel was laid.*

September 17, 1939
The **Soviet army** invades Poland from the east, and the Polish government flees to Romania.

November 30, 1939
After **Finland** refuses to grant the Soviet Union a naval base and other concessions in the fall of 1939, Soviet troops totaling about one million men attack Finland on several fronts, initiating the Russo-Finnish War.

A boy eats an ice cream, sitting on a mine that has been washed up, 1940.

1940
African American novelist **Richard Wright** completes his novel *Native Son.*
 [1]

1940
American poet, historian, and folklorist Carl Sandburg's **Abraham Lincoln: The War Years** wins the Pulitzer Prize for history.
 [2]

1940
American physicists Edwin M. McMillan and Philip H. Abelson, bombarding uranium with neutrons, artificially create the first sample of a **transuranium** element (neptunium).

1940
Ernest Hemingway publishes his most popular novel, *For Whom the Bell Tolls*, loosely based on the author's experiences during the Spanish Civil War. Hemingway will be awarded the 1954 Nobel Prize for Literature.
 [3]

1940
After losing the support of many Conservatives in the House of Commons, British prime minister **Neville Chamberlain** resigns his office and is replaced by Winston Churchill.
 [4]

1940
At his first speech in the House of Commons, Prime Minister **Winston Churchill** faces the coming struggle: "I have nothing to offer but blood, toil, tears and sweat" and commits himself and the nation to all-out war.
 [5]

[1] Richard Wright. His novel is the first big bestseller by a black writer and the first to be chosen by the Book-of-the-Month Club, in spite of the bleak picture it gives.

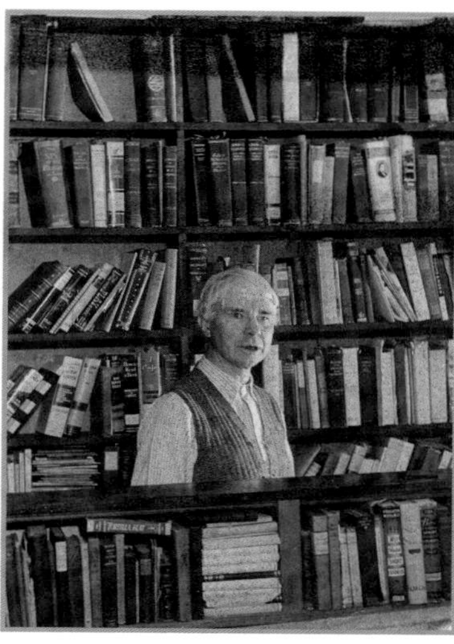
[2] Carl Sandburg, Lincoln's biographer.

[3] Ernest Hemingway (center) in Spain with two other journalists during the Spanish Civil War.

[5] Churchill (center-right, with cane) striding out through the City of London, imparting his own energy and defiance to the Londoners surrounding him.

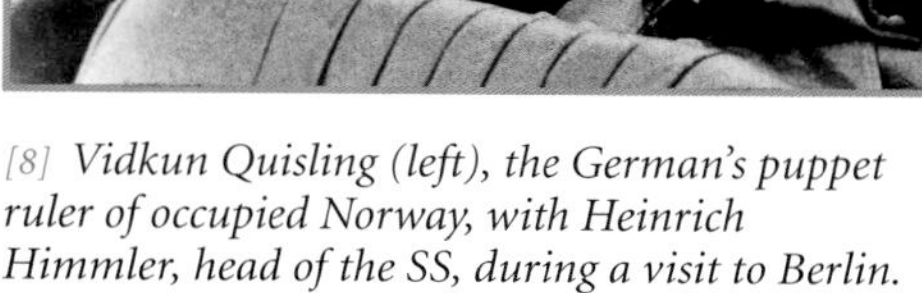
[8] Vidkun Quisling (left), the German's puppet ruler of occupied Norway, with Heinrich Himmler, head of the SS, during a visit to Berlin.

1940
Theodor Seuss Geisel (Dr. Seuss) publishes *Horton Hatches the Egg.* **Dr. Seuss's** whimsical pictures and tongue-twisting rhymes make him a favorite with American parents and children.

1940
Vannevar Bush becomes first head of the American National Defense Research Committee (NDRC), which directs wartime research in radar, medicine, and atomic weapons.

January 14, 1940
The FBI announces the arrest in New York of 18 members of the **Christian Front**, and charges them with "plotting to overthrow the government of the U.S."

February 19, 1940
A **German decree** confiscating all factories, farms, and forest lands in Polish territory incorporated in the Reich goes into effect.

March 1, 1940
Prohibition against the practice of their professions by **Jews** in Italy, except to serve their fellow Jews, goes into effect.

March 12, 1940
Finland agrees to Soviet peace terms, including the cession of western Karelia and the construction of a Soviet naval base on the Hanko Peninsula, to end the **Russo-Finnish War**.

1940
Winston Churchill rallies the nation: "Let us therefore brace ourselves to our duties, and so bear ourselves that if the British Empire and its Commonwealth last for a thousand years, men will still say, 'This was their finest hour.'"

1940
Charlie Chaplin stars in his first full talkie, **The Great Dictator**, a devastating lampoon of Adolf Hitler. It will prove to be the comedian's most profitable film.

 [6]

1940
Former Group f.64 member **Edward Weston** publishes his retrospective *California and the West*. This and other works establish him as one of the century's most important photographers.

1940
Frank Sinatra, a veteran of the Harry James and Tommy Dorsey orchestras, first reaches national prominence as a soloist on the radio program *Your Hit Parade*.

 [7]

1940
Neither the Summer nor the Winter **Olympic Games** take place due to World War II.

1940
St. Louis, Missouri, pioneers the first comprehensive smoke reduction program in any industrial city, sharply reducing smoke, soot, and **air pollution**.

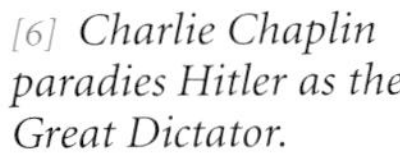

[6] Charlie Chaplin paradies Hitler as the Great Dictator.

[7] Frank Sinatra in the early 1940s.

[11] Belgian refugees take cover in a ditch as German planes threaten to strafe the road they have been on.

[4] Churchill leaves the garden of 10 Downing Street after his first cabinet meeting as prime minister. With him are Kingsley Wood, air minister, on the left, and Anthony Eden, foreign secretary, on the right.

[9] An American destroyer, the Hammann, *at anchor off Hawaii in September with other elements of the U.S. Pacific Fleet.*

[10] A German tank crew talks to infantry on the way through Holland.

March 28, 1940
President Franklin D. Roosevelt signs a bill increasing from two to ten years, imprisonment the maximum penalty for **espionage** against the U.S.

 [8]

April 9, 1940
German troops enter Denmark and Norway. **Norway** declares war on Germany. Although British forces come to its aid, it falls to Germany.

April 18, 1940
A committee of the **Indian National Congress** calls on the people to prepare to pursue a policy of civil disobedience in protest against British control.

 [9]

May 7, 1940
The **American Pacific Fleet** is ordered to remain in Hawaiian waters indefinitely.

 [10]

May 10, 1940
Germany invades **Belgium**, **Luxembourg**, and **the Netherlands**.

 [11]

May 18, 1940
Brussels falls to the invading German army and is subjected to harsh terms of occupation.

1940-1941

May 26, 1940
The British Expeditionary Force and other Allied troops, cut off by the Germans, begin evacuating from **Dunkirk**, France, to England.

 [1]

June 9, 1940
German tank forces under Major General **Erwin Rommel** cross the Seine River in a push to the Atlantic coast of France during World War II.

June 10, 1940
Italy declares war against France and Great Britain, entering World War II.

June 14, 1940
The first transport of Polish political prisoners arrives at **Auschwitz**, which becomes Nazi Germany's largest concentration, extermination, and slave-labor camp, where more than one million people will die.

June 17, 1940
The Soviet Red Army invades **Latvia**, which leads to the incorporation of the country into the U.S.S.R.

June 18, 1940
Broadcasting from London after France fell to the Nazis, French general **Charles de Gaulle** appeals to his compatriots to continue World War II under his leadership.

 [2]

[1] Long lines of British and French troops patiently waiting to be taken off the Dunkirk beaches.

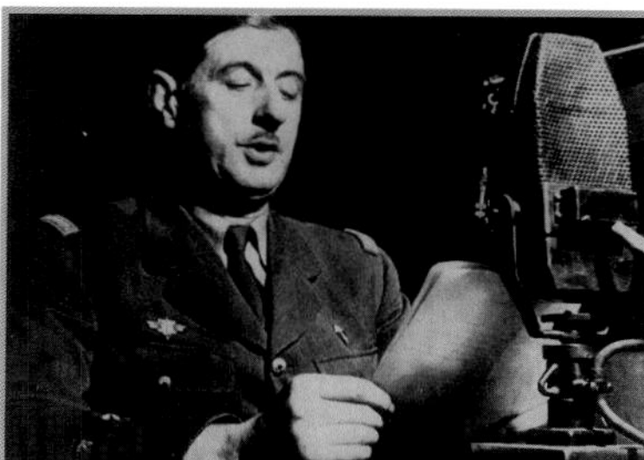

[2] General de Gaulle broadcasts his appeal to Frenchmen to go on fighting under his leadership.

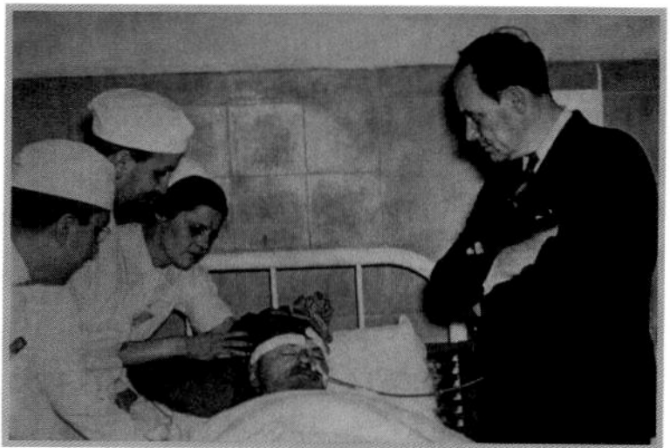

[5] Trotsky in a Mexican hospital, watched by anxious medical attendants as death approaches. His assailant penetrated his skull with an ice pick.

[3] Marshal Pétain (left) meets Hitler in France in October.

[6] German Dornier Z-17 bombers over East London. West Ham Greyhound Stadium shows up clearly between them.

1940-1949

 [5]

August 20, 1940
Leon Trotsky—a leader in Russia's October Revolution in 1917, and later commissar of foreign affairs and of war in the Soviet Union (1917–24)—is assassinated by a Stalinist agent in Mexico.

[6]

September 1940
The **Luftwaffe** stops bombing airfields and starts the bombing of London known as the **Blitz**. This is lucky for the Royal Air Force, which was close to being paralyzed by the attacks on its bases.

September 22, 1940
Jean Decoux, the French governor-general of **Indochina** appointed by the Vichy government after the fall of France, concludes an agreement with the Japanese that permits the stationing of 30,000 Japanese troops in Indochina.

October 24, 1940
The 40-hour workweek goes into effect under the **U.S. Fair Labor Standards Act** of 1938.

October 28, 1940
Seven Italian divisions based in Albania invade **Greece**. Within two weeks, they will be halted and driven back by Greek forces under the command of Alexandros Papagos.

 [7]

November 5, 1940
Franklin D. Roosevelt is elected to an unprecedented third term as president of the United States.

June 22, 1940
The French government under the leadership of Marshal Philippe Pétain, a national hero for his defense of Verdun in 1916, signs an armistice with Germany, thereby creating **Vichy France**, which collaborates with the Germans.

 [3]

July 3, 1940
The **Royal Navy** attacks and destroys the **French fleet** at anchor in Mers-el-Kebir in North Africa, killing 1,147 French sailors. It would not join the British, who could not afford for it to fall to Germany.

 [4]

July 10, 1940
The **Battle of Britain** begins. The German Luftwaffe bombs convoys, airfields, and later civilian targets.

August 1940
Italian forces overrun **British Somaliland** in East Africa.

August 1, 1940
John F. Kennedy's *Why England Slept* is published. It is a critical account of the British military that will become a best seller.

August 3, 1940
Lithuania is "accepted" into the U.S.S.R. following the Soviet occupation of the Baltic states. Estonia is annexed.

THE BATTLE OF BRITAIN

The Luftwaffe fails to destroy the Royal Air Force.

After the fall of France, Germany started a series of air raids against Great Britain in preparation for an invasion ("Operation Sea Lion"). The Battle of Britain was essentially over by mid-September 1940 when the invasion was postponed indefinitely. Although the Royal Air Force was greatly outnumbered (left, British pilots run to their planes), it succeeded in blocking the German air force through superior tactics, advanced air defenses, including radar, and the penetration of German secret codes. The British pilots, fighting closer to their bases, could spend longer in the air, and the Luftwaffe made the tactical error of switching from bombing airfields and radar equipment to bombing London.

[8] The Tacoma Narrows Bridge oscillates shortly before its destruction.

[4] French sailors fighting a fire on board their ship at Mers-el-Kebir.

[7] Franklin D. Roosevelt speaks to 25,000 in Madison Square Gardens, New York, before his sweeping reelection.

[9] The Tuskegee Airmen on parade, being inspected by their commander, Captain Davis.

[8]
November 7, 1940
The **Tacoma Narrows Bridge** connecting the Olympic Peninsula with Tacoma, Washington, breaks up in a wind of about 42 miles per hour.

December 24, 1940
Japan and **Thailand** proclaim a treaty in which each pledges to respect the territorial integrity of the other.

1941
American poet **John Crowe Ransom** publishes his famous book of essays *The New Criticism*, which helps establish the New Criticism school of literary theory.

1941
Australian accountant, politician, and member of the Country Party **Arthur Fadden** becomes prime minister of Australia.

1941
Following considerable protest, the War Department forms the all-black 99th Pursuit Squadron of the U.S. Army Air Corps, later known as the **Tuskegee Airmen**, commanded by Benjamin Oliver Davis, Jr.

1941
German engineer Konrad Zuse builds **Z3**, the first process-controlled computer (which also uses binary representations).

1941

1941
Harlan Fiske Stone is appointed 12th chief justice of the U.S. Supreme Court by President Franklin D. Roosevelt. He will serve from 1941 to 1946.

1941
John Curtin of the Labor Party becomes prime minister of Australia. He will serve during most of World War II.

1941
Les Paul designs the first solid-body **electric guitar**.

1941
Let Us Now Praise Famous Men, with text by James Agee and photographs by Walker Evans, reveals the plight of sharecroppers in Alabama. The lyrical text and riveting images combine to create a book of great power.

 [1]

1941
M&M's Chocolate Candies, with their multicolored candy coating, are introduced.

1941
One major league baseball season sees two magnificent feats: **Ted Williams** bats .406 for the year, and **Joe DiMaggio** sets a record by hitting safely in 56 consecutive games.

 [2]

[1] An Alabama sharecropper with his wife and child, photographed by Walker Evans.

[4] Press photographers and newsreel cameramen are present in strength in the White House as President Roosevelt signs the Lend-Lease Act, an invaluable lifeline thrown to Britain.

[2] Ted Williams (left) of the Boston Red Sox and Joe DiMaggio of the New York Yankees.

[5] Fire engines in Berlin tackle a blaze caused by British bombing.

 [4]

March 11, 1941
The U.S. Congress passes the **Lend-Lease Act**, establishing a system by which the United States aids its World War II allies with war materials, trucks, food, and other raw materials.

April 1941
Konoe Fumimaro, prime minister of Japan (1937–39, 1940–41), devotes all his energy to Japanese–U.S. negotiations, but in 1945 he will be arrested by the occupation army on suspicion of being a war criminal and will later commit suicide.

April 6, 1941
Nazi armies invade **Yugoslavia** and **Greece**.

 [5]

April 9, 1941
British planes bomb the heart of **Berlin**, Germany, damaging the State Opera House and other buildings.

April 13, 1941
Japan concludes a neutrality pact with the Soviet Union in World War II.

April 17, 1941
Yugoslavia surrenders to invading German forces.

1941
Orson Welles releases his masterwork **Citizen Kane**. His innovative narrative techniques and use of photography, dramatic lighting, and music combine to make the film hugely influential. He wrote, directed, produced, and acted in it.

 [3]

1941
Pacifist **Jeannette Rankin** is the only congressperson to vote against United States' entry into World War II.

1941
Willie Mosconi wins the first of 15 pocket billiards championships. Known for his accuracy and fancy shots, he elevates the game to respectability in the United States.

January 6, 1941
U.S. president Franklin D. Roosevelt outlines his **Four Freedoms in his State of the Union** message to Congress.

January 22, 1941
Japan offers to mediate the **Thai-French dispute** over the Indochina border. An armistice will be signed aboard a Japanese cruiser at Saigon, Vietnam, nine days later.

February 4, 1941
The United Service Organizations for National Defense, also known as the **USO**, is chartered. Its mission is to provide social, welfare, and recreational services for members of the U.S. armed forces and their families.

[3] Orson Welles as Citizen Kane, a figure based on William Randolph Hearst.

[7] A poster of an African-American pilot encourages U.S. citizens to buy war bonds.

[8] The remains of the Messerschmidt 110 in which Rudolf Hess flew across the North Sea before bailing out over Scotland.

[6] German paratroopers pass dead British and Greek soldiers during the battle for Crete, in late May.

[9] Survivors, picked up after the sinking of the Bismarck, *are landed in England.*

 [6]

May 1941
All mainland Greece and all the Greek Aegean islands, including **Crete**, fall to invading German army units. Greece's Ionian islands are occupied by Italian forces.

 [7]

May 1, 1941
The sale of U.S. **defense bonds** and stamps is opened to the public.

 [8]

May 10, 1941
Rudolf Hess, who was Adolf Hitler's deputy as party leader, secretly flies to Great Britain on an abortive self-styled mission to negotiate a peace between Britain and Germany.

May 18, 1941
The **Duke of Spoleto**, the cousin of King Victor Emmanuel III, becomes king of Croatia.

May 27, 1941
A 15-minute test **blackout** is staged in Newark, New Jersey.

 [9]

May 27, 1941
The British navy sinks the German battleship **Bismarck**.

June 22, 1941
Germany violates the **German-Soviet Nonaggression Pact** of 1939 and attacks the Soviet Union during World War II.
[1]

June 29, 1941
The **FBI** seizes 29 suspects in the New York area on charges of espionage and conspiracy.
 [2]

August 14, 1941
Winston Churchill and Franklin D. Roosevelt issue the **Atlantic Charter**, a joint declaration that states, among other points, that they desire no territorial changes without the free assent of the peoples concerned.
[3]

August 17, 1941
The U.S. orders a **census** of all foreign-owned property.

September 8, 1941
The prolonged siege of **Leningrad** (St. Petersburg) by German and Finnish armed forces begins. The siege will last 872 days, causing immense hardship, before a successful Soviet offensive drives the Germans from the city's outskirts.
[4]

September 16, 1941
Reza Shah Pahlevi abdicates because of failing health; his son, 21-year-old Mohammed Reza Pahlevi, succeeds to the throne of Iran.

[1] German Panzer units advance farther into Russia, through a burning village that was probably set on fire by its inhabitants before they fled.

[4] "Let's shield Leningrad with out breasts": a Russian propaganda poster.

[2] Spy-ring suspects sit in a Brooklyn court behind members of the FBI.

[3] Churchill and Roosevelt at a Sunday service aboard the battleship Prince of Wales *in Placentia Bay, Newfoundland, while drawing up the Atlantic Charter.*

PEARL HARBOR

Japan launches an attack against the United States.

On December 7, 1941, the Japanese launched a surprise air attack against the U.S. Pacific Fleet at its naval base at Pearl Harbor, southern Oahu Island, Hawaii. The attack temporarily crippled the U.S. fleet and resulted in the United States' entry into World War II.

The first Japanese dive bomber appeared over Pearl Harbor at 7:55 AM. Most of the damage to the battleships was inflicted in the first 30 minutes of the assault. The *Arizona* was completely destroyed, and the *Oklahoma* capsized. The *California*, *Nevada*, and *West Virginia* (left) sank in shallow water. More than 180 aircraft were destroyed. U.S. military casualties totaled more than 3,400, including more than 2,300 killed. However, the three aircraft carriers attached to the Pacific Fleet were not at Pearl Harbor at the time and thus escaped. Of the eight battleships, all but the *Arizona* and *Oklahoma* were eventually repaired and returned to service, and the Japanese failed to destroy the important oil storage facilities on the island

December 7, 1941
Japanese bombers launch a surprise aerial attack on the U.S. naval base at **Pearl Harbor** on the island of Oahu, Hawaii, precipitating the entry of the United States into World War II.

December 8, 1941
The U.S. Congress declares war on **Japan**.

December 10, 1941
Japanese forces land on the island of **Luzon** in the Philippines. The main assault, consisting of the bulk of one division, is made at Lingayen Gulf, 100 miles north-northwest of Manila.

December 10, 1941
Los Angeles, California, is blacked out for three hours.

December 10, 1941
The British battleship *Prince of Wales* and the battle cruiser *Repulse*, sailing from Singapore to cut Japanese communications during the Japanese landings in **Malaya**, are sunk by Japanese aircraft.

December 11, 1941
Adolf Hitler declares that Germany is at war with the United States following the Japanese attacks on the U.S., British, and Dutch positions in the Pacific and in East Asia.

September 28–29, 1941
Nazis kill 33,771 Jews in **Baby Yar**, a ravine on the northern edge of Kiev, Ukraine. Baby Yar becomes the symbol of the first stage of killing during the Holocaust, the work of the Einsatzgruppen (German: "deployment groups")—the mobile killing units. [5]

November 23, 1941
As part of the U.S. war effort, the use of **lead and tin foil** for wrapping cigarettes, candy, and similar products will be prohibited after March 15, 1942.

November 26, 1941
U.S. Secretary of State **Cordell Hull** sends a harsh notice to Japan, calling for a full withdrawal from China and Indochina.

December 1941
The German drive on Moscow, led by **Fedor von Bock**, is halted by extremely cold winter conditions combined with tenacious Soviet armed-forces resistance. [6]

December 6, 1941
Britain declares war on Finland, Hungary, and Romania.

December 7, 1941
Adolf Hitler issues his **Night and Fog Decree**, a secret order for the arrest and execution of "persons endangering German security."

[6] Russian soldiers pull an antitank gun into position near Moscow.

[5] Baby Yar: batches of Jews are lined up on the edge of a pit and then shot in the back of the head with pistols by men of the Einsatzgruppen.

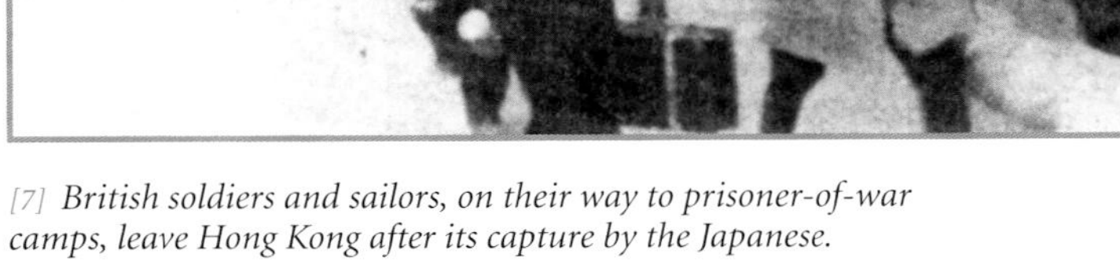

[8] Manhattan Project workers gather on a tower at Los Alamos stacked with 100 tons of TNT to be exploded as part of a fall-out experiment.

[7] British soldiers and sailors, on their way to prisoner-of-war camps, leave Hong Kong after its capture by the Japanese.

December 22, 1941
One hundred thousand Japanese troops land at Gulf of Lingayen for the invasion of **Philippines**.

December 23, 1941
Early in World War II, invading Japanese forces defeat U.S. troops at the **Battle of Wake Island**.

[7]
December 25, 1941
British and Canadian defenders surrender the British outpost of **Hong Kong** to invading Japanese forces.

1942
A team led by Italian-born American physicist **Enrico Fermi** oversees the first self-sustaining nuclear chain reaction (in a squash court under Stagg Field at the University of Chicago).

1942
American painter **Edward Hopper's** *Nighthawks* captures the mood of late-night urban introspection and isolation.

[8]
1942
American research on nuclear fission is organized into the **Manhattan Project**. The project develops and builds the atomic bombs that will be dropped on Hiroshima and Nagasaki in 1945.

1942

1942
Bing Crosby's recording of Irving Berlin's "White Christmas" becomes one of the most popular songs in American history.

 [1]

1942
Brazilian novelist and social critic **Jorge Amado** publishes his classic *Terras do sem fim* (*The Violent Land*), a panoramic novel about plantation life in Bahia.

1942
French writer Albert Camus publishes his first novel, **L'Étranger** (*The Stranger*, or *The Outsider*). He will be awarded the 1957 Nobel Prize for Literature.

 [2]

1942
The basic **autobahn** network is completed in Germany. Featuring limited access and the elimination of cross streets, it is the first national expressway system.

1942
The **guided missile**, a projectile provided with means for altering its direction after leaving its launching device, is developed by German engineer Wernher von Braun.

1942
Thirteen-year-old **Anne Frank**, her family, and four fellow Jews go into hiding in Amsterdam to avoid Nazi persecution. In March 1945 she will die in the Nazi concentration camp at Bergen-Belsen. Her diary of her years in hiding will become a classic.

 [3]

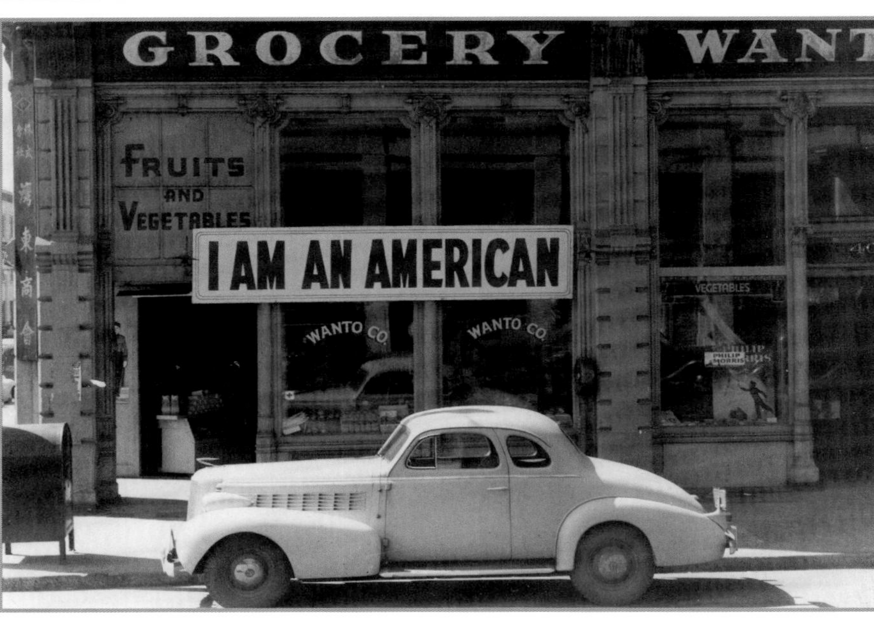

[5] *A store owner of Japanese descent in Oakland, California, hopes to make matters clear the day after the attack on Pearl Harbor.*

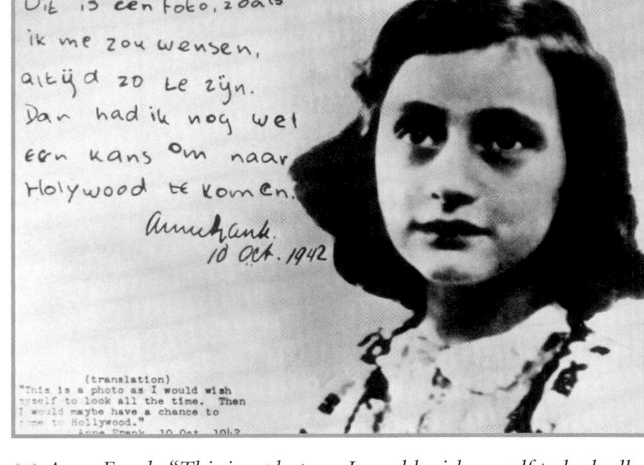

[3] *Anne Frank: "This is a photo as I would wish myself to look all the time. Then I would maybe have a chance to come to Hollywood."*

[2] *French writer Abert Camus, known for his work in leftist causes, as well as for his novels and essays.*

[7] *Douglas MacArthur (in cap, front seat) on a tour of inspection of Australian troops fighting in New Guinea.*

[6] *American soldiers captured on Java.*

 [5]

February 19, 1942
U.S. president Franklin D. Roosevelt signs the executive order allowing the **internment** of Japanese Americans.

February 24, 1942
The **Voice of America** makes its first broadcast, in German, to counter the propaganda of Nazi leaders.

 [6]

February 28, 1942
Japanese troops land on the island of **Java**, which they occupy until 1945.

March 8, 1942
Japanese troops capture **Rangoon**, Burma (Yangôn, Myanmar), during World War II.

March 10, 1942
Metropolitan opera basso **Ezio Pinza** is taken to Ellis Island as an enemy alien by the FBI.

 [7]

March 11, 1942
Allied forces in the Southwest Pacific theater come under the command of U.S. **general Douglas MacArthur** following his tour on the Bataan Peninsula in the Philippines.

January 9, 1942
Joe Louis, in his 20th defense of his world championship heavyweight title, knocks out Buddy Baer in the first round.

January 13, 1942
American industrialist **Henry Ford** patents plastic automobile construction.

January 15, 1942
The U.S. **blacklists** 1,800 companies in the five remaining neutral countries of Europe for doing business with Axis powers.

January 26, 1942
The first **U.S. expeditionary force** to land in Europe during World War II reaches Northern Ireland.

January 31, 1942
The entire **Malayan mainland** falls to Japanese forces when British troops are driven across the Strait of Johore.

February 15, 1942
Singapore surrenders unconditionally to Japan.

 [4]

[1] Bing Crosby wearing a "tin hat," with a group of Hollywood actresses while entertaining U.S. forces.

[8] Japanese troops haul down the American flag on Corregidor.

[4] White flag and Union Jack: at Singapore, British officers lead the surrender of over 130,000 men to the Japanese.

[10] American torpedo bombers fly over a burning Japanese ship at the Battle of Midway.

[9] The Lexington *burns while the destroyer* Hammann *(see May 7, 1940) picks up nearly 500 survivors. The* Hammann *will be sunk at Midway helping another stricken carrier, the* Yorktown.

March 17, 1942
The third U.S. **draft lottery** is held in Washington, D.C.

[8]

May 6, 1942
The American garrison on **Corregidor Island**, under the command of General Jonathan M. Wainwright, surrenders to the Japanese after a 27-day standoff during World War II.

[9]

May 8, 1942
In the **Battle of the Coral Sea**, the USS *Lexington* becomes the first U.S. aircraft carrier to be sunk, but a Japanese invasion force heading for the strategic Port Moresby, New Guinea, is turned back.

May 22, 1942
Mexico enters World War II by declaring war on Germany, Italy, and Japan.

May 30, 1942
During World War II the British **Royal Air Force** dispatches more than 1,000 bombers against Cologne, Germany.

[10]

June 4, 1942
Japan is repulsed by the United States at the **Battle of Midway**.

1942-1943

June 9, 1942
The villagers of **Lidice** are rounded up, most to be massacred in reprisal for the assassination of Reinhard Heydrich, deputy leader of the SS, by Czech underground fighters, in Prague.

June 21, 1942
Tobruk in Libya falls to the German Afrika Korps under Field Marshal **Erwin Rommel**, who then advances to El-Alamein, Egypt.

 [1]

July 13, 1942
FBI agents arrest eight men and six women suspected of helping eight arrested Nazi suspects on trial for sabotage.

August 7, 1942
In the Allies' first major offensive in the Pacific theater during World War II, U.S. Marines land on **Guadalcanal** and capture the airfield from Japan, sparking a battle that lasts some six months.

October 23, 1942
The British, led by Field Marshal **Bernard Montgomery**, launch a successful large-scale assault against the Germans at El-Alamein, Egypt.

 [2]

November 25, 1942
Leslie Groves and **J. Robert Oppenheimer** choose Los Alamos, New Mexico, as the site of Project Y, which develops the first atomic bomb.

[1] Erwin Rommel in the North African desert. The goggles are protection against dust and sand.

[2] Montgomery in his famous beret, on which he wears several badges of regiments under his command.

[5] Crowds outside the Paramount Theater before a Frank Sinatra performance.

[6] The All-American Girls Professional Baseball League, group photo.

[7] Roosevelt (second from left) and Churchill (right) in Casablanca with Generals Giraud (left) and de Gaulle, both contenders for leadership of the French in North Africa.

1940-1949

1943
Engineer Richard James patents the **Slinky toy**. Mass production will begin in 1945.

 [5]

1943
Near-hysteria is generated before Frank Sinatra's appearances at New York's Paramount Theater by throngs of screaming young female fans—known as "**bobby-soxers**."

 [6]

1943
The **All-American Girls Professional Baseball League** is founded by Chicago Cubs owner Philip Wrigley. Between 1943 and its dissolution in 1954, it grows from a stopgap wartime entertainment to a professional showcase.

1943
The **Colossus computer**, generally recognized as the first true computer, is built by the British to break German codes. Alan Turing is part of the Bletchley Park code-breaking team.

January 2, 1943
Representatives of 26 countries at war with the Axis powers sign in Washington a **Declaration of United Nations**, pledging not to make separate armistice or peace and to employ all military resources to win.

 [7]

January 17, 1943
British prime minister Winston Churchill and U.S. president Franklin D. Roosevelt meet at **Casablanca, Morocco**.

November 26, 1942
Set in occupied Morocco during World War II, directed by Michael Curtiz, and starring Humphrey Bogart, Ingrid Bergman, and Paul Henreid, **Casablanca** premiers this day in 1942. It will become one of Hollywood's most revered films.

 [3]

November 27, 1942
The French navy scuttles 73 ships at **Toulon** in order to avoid their seizure by the Germans.

 [4]

December 24, 1942
Admiral François Darlan, a leading figure in Marshal Philippe Pétain's Vichy government, is assassinated in Algiers.

1943
American correspondent **Ernie Pyle** publishes *Here Is Your War*, a collection of dispatches from the front. At his death in 1945, Pyle is the most famous of all World War II correspondents.

1943
American microbiologist Selman Waksman isolates **streptomycin**, the first antibiotic effective against gram-negative bacteria (which cause such diseases as tuberculosis).

1943
Duke Ellington, one of the most successful originators of big-band jazz, composes the suite *Black, Brown and Beige*, a portrayal of African American history combining jazz with classical forms.

[3] Casablanca: Humphrey Bogart drinks with Sydney Greenstreet on this poster, while Ingrid Bergman's alarmingly colored profile is on the right.

[9] Parícutin erupts.

[4] The French fleet destroying itself at Toulon. A photograph of the scene the day after the mass scuttling showing ships ablaze in the harbor.

THE LIBERATION OF STALINGRAD

Germany fails to capture the Soviet city.

During the summer of 1942 the German army advanced to the suburbs of the city of Stalingrad but failed to take the city against a determined defense by the Soviet Red Army, despite repeated attacks by the sixth Army under Friedrich Paulus and part of the fourth Panzer Army under Hermann Hoth. On November 19 the Soviets launched a counterattack in the form of pincer movements north and south of the city, and by November 23, they had encircled the sixth Army and part of the fourth within Stalingrad (above, Soviet troops advancing). A German attempt to relieve Paulus failed in mid-December. Under orders from Adolf Hitler, Paulus continued to fight on, making possible the eventual escape of the beleaguered German forces from the Caucasus. On January 31, 1943, Paulus disobeyed Hitler and surrendered, and on February 2 the last of his remaining 91,000 troops turned themselves over to the Soviets. The Soviets recovered 250,000 German and Romanian corpses in and around Stalingrad. Official Russian military historians estimate that 1,100,000 Soviet soldiers lost their lives in the campaign to defend the city.

[8] The first British tank, a Valentine, enters Tripoli in North Africa, with a bagpiper aboard.

 [8]

January 15, 1943
Tripoli in Libya falls to British general Bernard Montgomery's Eighth Army.

January 18, 1943
To save on the costs of labor and equipment, the United States bans the sale of **presliced bread**.

January 22, 1943
All Japanese resistance in **Papua**, on the island of New Guinea, site of an important Allied base at Port Moresby, ceases.

January 31, 1943
German field marshal **Friedrich Paulus** surrenders to the Soviet Red Army at Stalingrad, his troops surrendering two days later.

February 5, 1943
American middleweight boxer **Jake La Motta**, the "Bronx Bull," hands Sugar Ray Robinson his first defeat.

 [9]

February 20, 1943
The volcano **Parícutin** in Michoacán, Mexico, erupts, eventually burying two villages.

April 5, 1943
German forces in North Africa surrender in **Tunisia**.

April 13, 1943
The **Thomas Jefferson Memorial** is dedicated in East Potomac Park on the south bank of the Tidal Basin in Washington, D.C.

April 19, 1943
The **Warsaw Ghetto Uprising**, an act of resistance by Polish Jews under Nazi occupation, begins this day and is quelled four weeks later, on May 16.

May 1943
Royal Air Force Lancaster bombers of 617 Squadron carry out the **Dambusters' Raid** on the Möhne and Eder dams in Germany.

May 11, 1943
U.S. troops invade **Attu**, one of the Aleutian Islands captured by the Japanese in 1942.

June 25, 1943
The **Smith-Connally Anti-Strike Act** is enacted by the U.S. Congress, giving the president power to seize and operate privately owned war plants when a strike or threat of a strike interferes with war production.

[2] The Möhne Dam, breached in the Dambusters' Raid.

[1] The domed rotunda of the Jefferson Memorial.

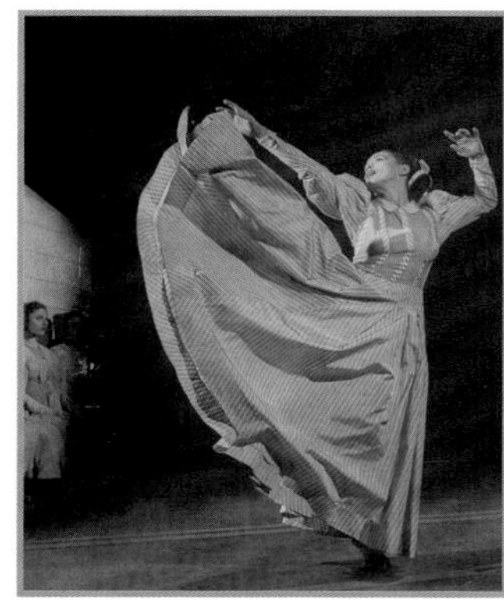

[8] Martha Graham dancing in the premiere performance of Appalachian Spring.

[3] A G.I. suffering from frostbite is put into a Jeep on Attu Island, off Alaska.

WARSAW GHETTO UPRISING

Jews resist the Nazis in Poland.

As part of Adolf Hitler's "final solution" for ridding Europe of Jews, the Nazis established ghettos in areas under German control to confine Jews until they could be executed. The Warsaw ghetto comprised the old Jewish quarter of Warsaw, Poland. By July 1942 the Nazis had herded 500,000 Jews from surrounding areas into the ghetto. Though starvation and disease killed thousands each month, the Nazis began transferring more than 5,000 Jews a day to rural "labor camps" (above, Jewish families being rounded up). When word reached the ghetto in early 1943 that the destination was actually the gas chambers at Treblinka, the newly formed Jewish Fighting Organization (ZOB) attacked the Nazis, killing 50 and causing the deportations to halt.

On April 19 Heinrich Himmler sent 2,000 SS men and army troops to clear the ghetto of its remaining Jews. For four weeks the ZOB and guerrillas fought with pistols and homemade bombs, destroying tanks and killing several hundred Nazis, until their ammunition ran out. Not until May 8 did the Nazis manage to take the ZOB headquarters bunker. Many of the surviving ZOB fighters took their own lives to avoid being captured. The battle raged until May 16, when the SS chief declared, "The Warsaw Ghetto is no more." During the 28 days of the uprising, more than 40,000 Jews were either killed or deported.

November 22–26, 1943
The first **Cairo Conference** is held. Winston Churchill, Franklin D. Roosevelt, and Chiang Kai-shek declare the goal of stripping Japan of the territories it had seized since 1914 and restoring Korea to independence.

December 24, 1943
General **Dwight D. Eisenhower** is appointed supreme commander of the Allied Expeditionary Force in Europe.

1944
Ansel Adams, with characteristic mastery of tonal properties and composition, photographs *Mount Williamson—Clearing Storm*. Adams ranks as the most important landscape photographer of the 20th century.

1944
Appalachian Spring, a ballet by Aaron Copland, is danced for the first time by Martha Graham's company. Copland's work is notable for its use of folk-music melodies.

1944
Aramco (the Arab American Oil Company) is established as a joint venture between a number of American oil companies and the Saudi government.

1944
Argentine writer **Jorge Luis Borges** attracts an international following with his *Ficciones*, a collection of stories that involve the reader in dazzling displays of erudition and imagination.

July 1943
Kursk, the greatest tank battle ever, involving 6,000 tanks, starts. By August, it will be won by Russia.

 [4]

July 22, 1943
Led by U.S. general **George S. Patton**, Allied forces take Palermo, on the northwest corner of Sicily, giving them a strategic foothold from which to invade mainland Italy.

 [5]

August 2, 1943
PT-109, a U.S. Navy torpedo boat under **John F. Kennedy's** command, is sunk by a Japanese destroyer.

 [6]

August 17, 1943
Allied forces land in southern Italy. The **Salerno** landings follow on September 9.

 [7]

September 12, 1943
German commandos effect the escape of **Benito Mussolini** to Munich.

November 28, 1943
The **Tehran Conference**, attended by U.S. president Franklin D. Roosevelt, British prime minister Winston Churchill, and Soviet premier Joseph Stalin, at which Stalin pressed for an invasion of France, opens this day in 1943.

[4] *A German soldier holds his head, a dead comrade beside him, during the Battle of Kursk.*

[5] *Italian troops, surrendering in Sicily.*

[7] *American troops come ashore during the Salerno landings, near Naples.*

[6] *John F. Kennedy (extreme right) with his PT boat crew in the South Pacific.*

[9] *U.S. treasury secretary Henry Morgenthau (left) with Britain's representative, John Maynard Keynes, sometime member of the Bloomsbury Group, at Bretton Woods.*

[10] *Film star Betty Grable shows off the best legs in the business in this famous photograph.*

1944
Austrian-born British economist **Friedrich A. Hayek** publishes *The Road to Serfdom*, a critique of centrally planned economies. It becomes an immediate best seller.

 [9]

1944
Delegates representing 44 countries meet at **Bretton Woods**, New Hampshire, to draft the Articles of Agreement for a proposed International Monetary Fund to promote world trade, investment, and economic growth.

 [10]

1944
Pinups of U.S. film star **Betty Grable** boost Allied morale in the middle years of the war.

1944
Psychologist **Bruno Bettelheim** becomes head of the Sonia Shankman Orthogenic School at the University of Chicago, where he conducts research on autistic and emotionally disturbed children.

1944
The **assault rifle**, a lightweight weapon most effective at a distance of 300 yards, is designed by Hugo Schmeisser of Germany. The design is based on a concept that will dominate infantry weapons henceforth.

1944
The first commercially successful **sunscreen** is developed by U.S. pharmacist Benjamin Green.

1944

1944
German forces hold out on the slopes of **Monte Cassino** and then in the ruins of its monastery, blocking the Allied advance on Rome until May.

 [1]

1944
The first **jet-powered aircraft** are developed in the United States, Britain, and Germany, leading to adoption of jet power in aircraft of many types in succeeding decades.

 [2]

1944
The U.S. Congress passes the Serviceman's Readjustment Act. Better known as the **G.I. Bill of Rights**, it helps make college education accessible to millions of American veterans.

1944
The U.S. Supreme Court rules that the order mandating the internment of **Japanese Americans** in 1942 was constitutional.

1944
The V-2 rocket, designed by German aeronautical engineer **Werner von Braun**, enters service, attacking cities in England. Von Braun and his group defect to the United States in 1945.

 [3]

1944
U.S. Department of War adviser Raphael Lemkin coins the term "**genocide**," derived from the Greek *genos* ("race," "tribe," or "nation") and the Latin *cide* ("killing"), in his work *Axis Rule in Occupied Europe.*

[1] The ruins of the monastery on top of Monte Cassino.

[3] A liquid-fuelled V-2 rocket, called "revenge weapon two," prepared for launching in north Germany. It will be lifted into a vertical position before blast-off.

[7] A German sniper has opened fire in Paris very shortly after its liberation, and a Free French soldier runs to take cover behind a car already sheltering a gendarme and a Resistance fighter armed with a rifle.

[5] G.I.s at Falaise pose by a wrecked German tank at the end of the battle.

[6] Resistance fighters emerge from the ruins of Warsaw after the unsuccessful uprising.

[8] A British tank is covered with jubilant locals as it drives through Brussels, which has been abandoned by the Germans.

July 24, 1944
Soviet forces liberate the **Majdanek** concentration and extermination camp on the outskirts of the city of Lublin, Poland.

 [5]

August 1944
The Falaise Pocket is the culmination of the Normandy campaign when the German Fifth and Seventh Panzer armies are destroyed.

 [6]

August 1, 1944
The Warsaw Uprising, of the Polish Underground, begins against the Germans, but it receives no help from the Russians and is crushed.

August 12, 1944
U.S. naval pilot **Joseph P. Kennedy, Jr.**, son of Joseph P. Kennedy and brother of future president John F. Kennedy, dies in a plane crash while flying on a secret mission during Word War II.

 [7]

August 25, 1944
Some two months after the Allied invasion of Normandy, **Paris is liberated** from German occupiers as the Free French Second Armored Division under General Jacques-Philippe Leclerc enters the city.

 [8]

September 5, 1944
British forces race from the river Seine through northern France to relieve **Brussels** and Belgium.

January 27, 1944
The **Soviet Red Army** ousts German and Finnish forces from Leningrad (St. Petersburg), concluding an 872-day siege.

 [4]

June 6, 1944
Led by U.S. general Dwight D. Eisenhower, an Allied armada of ships, planes, and landing craft and some 156,000 troops begin the invasion of northern France from England—the famous **D-Day** of World War II.

June 15, 1944
U.S. Marines attack **Saipan** in the Mariana Islands.

June 19, 1944
The Japanese Combined Fleet and the U.S. Fifth Fleet engage in a major air-and-sea battle, the **Battle of the Philippine Sea**, which ends the next day with a U.S. victory.

July 17, 1944
German field marshal **Erwin Rommel** is seriously injured when his car is forced off the road by British fighter-bombers.

July 20, 1944
German military leaders attempt to assassinate Adolf Hitler in the **July Plot**.

[4] Two Russian snipers in snow camouflage on the Leningrad front.

[2] The Messerschmidt 262A-1 can reach 530 mph. Although a formidable weapon, it is not produced in numbers. And there is not enough fuel for even those that are in service.

[9] British Guards Armoured Division Sherman tanks, with men of the U.S. 505th Parachute Infantry Regiment on board, on September 19, are about to make the first unsuccessful attempt to take the Nijmegen bridge.

D-DAY LANDINGS

Allied invasion of northern Europe

The largest amphibious landing in history started on on June 6, 1944, in Normandy, France. Also called Operation Overlord, the landing transported 156,000 U.S., British, and Canadian troops across the English Channel in over 5,000 ships and 10,000 planes (top, U.S. reinforcements disembarking). Commanded by General Dwight D. Eisenhower, the Allied forces landed at five beaches on the Normandy coast and soon established lodgement areas, despite stiff German resistance and heavy losses at the code-named Omaha Beach (bottom) and Juno Beach. Though delayed by heavy fighting near Cherbourg and around Caen, the Allied ground troops broke out of the beachheads in mid-July and began a rapid advance across northern France.

September 11, 1944
Winston Churchill and Franklin D. Roosevelt meet in Canada at the **second Quebec Conference**.

 [9]

September 19, 1944
In **Operation Market Garden**, Allies attempt to seize Rhine crossings with large numbers of airborne troops. The bridge over the river Waal at Nijmegen is captured, but the attempt to take the Rhine bridge at Arnhem fails.

October 7, 1944
The **Dumbarton Oaks Conference**, in which the United States, China, the Soviet Union, and the United Kingdom formulate proposals for a world organization that becomes the basis for the United Nations, concludes.

October 14, 1944
German field marshal **Erwin Rommel**, the "Desert Fox," ends his life by drinking poison following the discovery of his connection to a conspiracy to assassinate Adolf Hitler.

October 23, 1944
U.S. forces under the leadership of **Admiral William F. Halsey, Jr.**, commence a decisive air and sea battle against the Japanese on the central Philippine island of Leyte.

November 7, 1944
Franklin D. Roosevelt defeats Thomas E. Dewey and is elected to an unprecedented fourth term as president of the United States.

1944-1945

December 15, 1944
The plane carrying American big band leader and trombonist **Glen Miller** disappears without a trace over the English Channel.

December 16, 1944
German forces attempt to push through Allied lines in the Ardennes, beginning the **Battle of the Bulge**.

1945
American electrical engineer Percy L. Spencer receives a patent for a **microwave oven**, an appliance that cooks food by means of high-frequency electromagnetic waves called microwaves.

1945
Baseball owners choose **Happy Chandler** as commissioner, but later regret it when he overrides their opposition to integrating the major leagues. In 1951 Chandler will fail to win reelection.

1945
British novelist **George Orwell** publishes *Animal Farm*, a political fable based on the story of the Russian Revolution and its betrayal by Joseph Stalin, with its chilling conclusion: "All animals are equal, but some animals are more equal than others."

1945
British sculptor **Henry Moore** begins work on his elmwood *Reclining Figure*, using void as well as mass to suggest the human form.

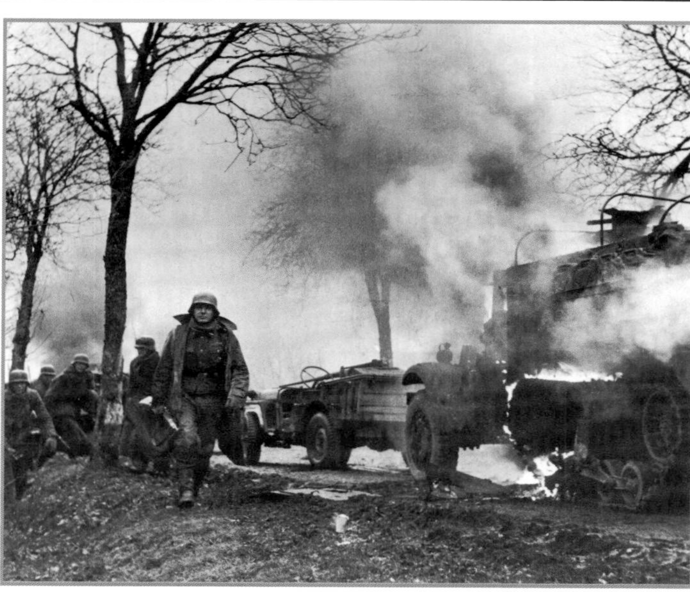

[1] *German soldiers pass a burning American half-track; 19,000 Americans are killed during the Battle of the Bulge.*

[2] *George Orwell fought on the Republican side in the Spanish Civil War.*

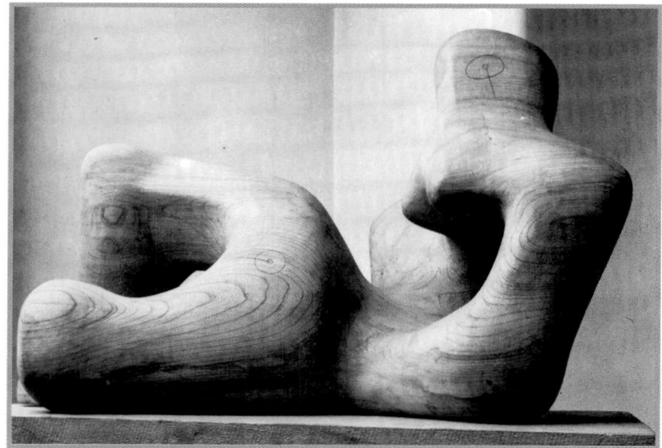

[3] *Henry Moore's monumental elmwood* Reclining Figure.

[8] *A sick Roosevelt between Churchill and Stalin at Yalta.*

[7] *Child inmates of Auschwitz.*

[9] *Unloading supplies on Iwo Jima.*

1945
John H. Johnson founds **Ebony**, the first U.S. mass-market magazine aimed at a black audience.

1945
Sir Gladwyn Jebb of Britain serves as the acting secretary general of the United Nations until 1946.

January 27, 1945
The Nazi concentration camp at **Auschwitz**, Poland, is liberated by Soviet troops.

February 4, 1945
The **Yalta Conference** opens with Franklin D. Roosevelt, Winston Churchill, and Joseph Stalin meeting to plan the final defeat and occupation of Nazi Germany.

February 16, 1945
American paratroopers land on **Corregidor Island** in the Philippines during World War II, and within two weeks they recapture it from the Japanese.

February 19, 1945
U.S. Marines invade **Iwo Jima** to wrest control of the strategically important island from the Japanese, who put up fierce resistance in the ensuing battle.

1945
Byron Nelson wins 18 golf tournaments in one year, including a streak of 11 in a row.

1945
Clement Attlee becomes prime minister of the United Kingdom. In his six-year term, he presides over the establishment of the welfare state, the nationalization of much of British industry, and the granting of independence to India.

 [4]

1945
Shinto is abolished as the official religion of Japan by a decree of the Allied occupation forces; the decree forbids government subsidy and support of Shinto shrines and repudiates the emperor's divinity. The ban is continued in the postwar constitution.

1945
Francis Forde of the Labor Party, who will serve the shortest term in Australian history, becomes prime minister of Australia.

1945
French writers Jean-Paul Sartre and Simone de Beauvoir found **Les Temps modernes**, an influential journal of arts and politics. Sartre will be awarded, but will decline, the Nobel Prize for Literature in 1964.

 [5]

1945
Jackie Robinson becomes the first African American baseball player in the modern major leagues when he joins the Brooklyn Dodgers.

 [6]

[4] Clement Attlee and his wife, Violet, jubilant at Labour Party headquarters just after he wins the election.

[10] The flag is raised on Mount Suribachi, Iwo Jima.

[12] Harry Truman sits in Roosevelt's chair to broadcast to the nation.

[6] Jackie Robinson of the Brooklyn Dodgers.

[5] Jean-Paul Sartre and Simone de Beauvoir, uncrowned king and queen of the Paris literati of the Left: "to oppose Communism is to oppose the proletariat."

[11] The aircraft carrier Bunker Hill, *hit by a Japanese kamikaze plane off Okinawa.*

 [10]

February 23, 1945
Six U.S. servicemen famously raise the **American flag over Mount Suribachi** on the island of Iwo Jima during World War II. A photograph commemorating the event becomes one of the most famous images of the war.

March 9, 1945
The U.S. Army air forces bomb **Tokyo** with napalm, causing fires that destroy a quarter of the city and kill some 80,000 civilians.

March 22, 1945
The **Arab League**, a regional organization of Arab states in the Middle East, is organized in Cairo by Egypt, Syria, Lebanon, Iraq, Transjordan (now Jordan), Saudi Arabia, and Yemen.

March 24, 1945
With the debut of the **Billboard** magazine pop album chart, American pianist and singer Nat King Cole's *King Cole Trio* becomes the first record album to appear at number one.

 [11]

April 1, 1945
U.S. troops land on the Japanese island of **Okinawa** during World War II. It proves to be the longest and bloodiest Pacific campaign for the U.S. since Guadalcanal in 1942.

 [12]

April 12, 1945
Harry S. Truman of the Democratic Party becomes the 33rd president of the United States after the death of Franklin Roosevelt. He will be reelected in 1948, and his vice president will be Alben W. Barkley.

1945-1946

April 28, 1945
Italian dictator **Benito Mussolini**, "Il Duce," who, after a series of military misadventures, becomes unpopular even among his fellow Fascists, is captured while trying to flee Italy and executed.

April 29, 1945
The U.S. Seventh Army liberates tens of thousands of inmates at the Nazi concentration camp in **Dachau**, Germany.

April 30, 1945
German dictator Adolf Hitler and his wife, Eva Braun, whom he has just married, commit suicide in a bunker in Berlin. **Hitler shoots himself** and his wife takes poison. In accordance with his instructions, their bodies are burned.

April–May, 1945
Bitter street fighting continues in **Berlin** until the afternoon of May 2.

May 7, 1945
A German delegation that includes General Alfred Jodl comes to U.S. general Dwight D. Eisenhower's headquarters in Reims, France, and signs the **German surrender** documents.

May 8, 1945
V-E Day marks the end of the war in Europe. The war in the Pacific continues.

HIROSHIMA AND NAGASAKI

The United States drops atomic bombs on Japanese cities.

During World World II, the United States developed atomic bombs under a program called the Manhattan Project. The first atomic bomb to be used in warfare was dropped by the United States on the city of Hiroshima, Japan, on August 6, 1945. The explosion, which had the force of more than 15,000 tons of TNT, instantly and completely devastated 4 square miles (10 square km) of the heart of this city of 343,000 inhabitants. Of this number, 66,000 were killed immediately and 69,000 were injured; more than 67 percent of the city's structures were destroyed or damaged (the photo by Alfred Eisenstaedt shows a mother and child four months after the bomb had exploded). Another atomic bomb was dropped on Nagasaki, Japan, on August 9, 1945, producing a blast equal to 21,000 tons of TNT: 39,000 persons were killed immediately, and 25,000 were injured; about 40 percent of the city's structures were destroyed or seriously damaged. The Japanese initiated surrender negotiations the next day.

[1] The bodies of Mussolini and his mistress, who have been killed by the Italian partisans, are exposed for ridicule in Milan.

[4] General Jodl (center) signs the unconditional surrender.

[3] Russian infantry run past a dead German in Berlin.

August 6, 1945
Hiroshima is the first city in the world to be struck by an atomic bomb, dropped by the B-29 bomber *Enola Gay* of the U.S. Air Force. Estimates of the number killed range upward from 70,000.

August 8, 1945
The United States, the Soviet Union, Great Britain, and France sign the **London Agreement**, which authorizes the Nürnberg trials.

August 9, 1945
The second atomic bomb is dropped, on **Nagasaki**, Japan. Between 60,000 and 80,000 persons are killed.

August 17, 1945
Sukarno declares **Indonesia's independence** from the Netherlands. After the Dutch transfer sovereignty four years later, he serves as the country's first president (1949–67).

August 19, 1945
A commando force formed by **Vo Nguyen Giap**, under Vietnamese nationalist leader Ho Chi Minh, enters the Vietnamese capital of Hanoi.

August 25, 1945
John Birch, an American Baptist missionary and U.S. Army intelligence officer, is killed by Chinese communists, which later inspires the foundation of the **John Birch Society**—a private organization that considers Birch to be the first hero of the Cold War.

June 1, 1945
In a speech, Indonesian nationalist leader **Sukarno** articulates the Pancasila—the Five Principles—that become the founding philosophy of the independent Indonesian state.

June 26, 1945
The **charter of the United Nations** is signed in San Francisco.

 [6]

July 1945
The **Korean peninsula** is divided at the 38th parallel at the Potsdam Conference. Intended to be a temporary division, the line will become the boundary between a U.S.-oriented regime in South Korea and a communist regime in North Korea.

July 16, 1945
The first **atomic bomb** is exploded at the "Trinity Site" 60 miles northwest of Alamogordo, New Mexico.

July 17, 1945
Joseph Stalin, Winston Churchill, and Harry S. Truman meet at the **Potsdam Conference**, the last Allied summit conference of World War II.

July 23, 1945
Philippe Pétain of France goes on trial for treason during World War II.

 [7]

[6] General Smuts, prime minister of South Africa, signs the charter of the United Nations.

[2] Dachau prisoners cheer their liberators.

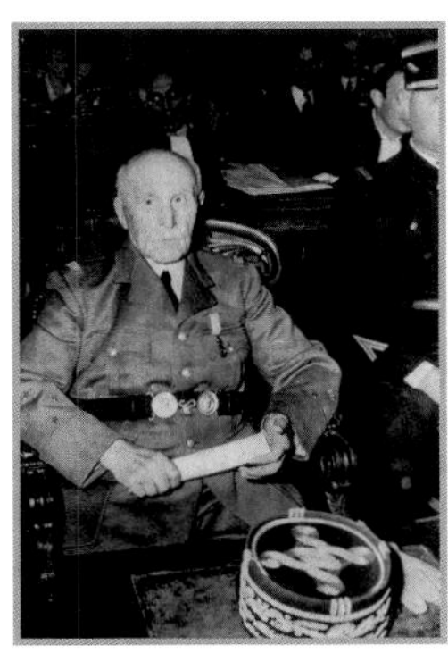

[7] Marshal Pétain. He has been offered asylum by the Swiss but has refused it. His death sentence is commuted to life imprisonment.

[5] A kiss in Times Square, New York, on V-E Day.

[8] The Japanese come to surrender.

September 2, 1945
Ho Chi Minh declares Vietnam independent from France.

 [8]

September 2, 1945
World War II comes to an end as Japanese foreign minister Shigemitsu Mamoru and general Umezu Yoshijiro sign Japan's formal surrender aboard the USS *Missouri*.

September 8, 1945
At the end of World War II, the first U.S. troops enter the Korean peninsula south of the **38th parallel** to receive the Japanese surrender; north of the parallel, Japanese troops surrender to Soviet forces.

October 3, 1945
The **May-Johnson bill**, keeping the atomic bomb a secret and establishing security regulations, is introduced into the U.S. Congress.

October 24, 1945
The charter of the United Nations—the world's premier international organization, established at the end of World War II to maintain **world peace** and friendly relations among nations—enters into force.

1946
American Fugitive poet and prominent Southern novelist **Robert Penn Warren** publishes his classic political novel *All the King's Men*.

1946

1946
American metaphysical "poet of wit" **Elizabeth Bishop** publishes her first collection of verse, *North & South.*

1946
American poet **Robert Lowell's** first major work, *Lord Weary's Castle,* is published; it will win the Pulitzer Prize the next year.

 [1]

1946
Benjamin Spock publishes **Common Sense Book of Baby and Child Care**. The book, which encourages parents to trust their instincts over expert advice, shapes the childhoods of millions of baby boomers.

1946
Carbon-14 dating is developed by Willard F. Libby as a means of determining the age of fossils and archaeological specimens from 500 to 50,000 years old. He will be awarded the 1960 Nobel Prize for Chemistry.

1946
Construction begins on **Levittown**, the archetypal mass suburban housing development, in Long Island, New York.

 [2]

1946
Hungarian-born American mathematician John von Neumann, together with Arthur Burks and Herman Goldstine, writes the paper that defines the modern, or "von Neumann architecture," **computer**.

[1] *Robert Lowell has been a conscientious objector during the war, serving several months in prison.* Lord Weary's Castle *includes the magnificent long poem "The Quaker Graveyard in Nantucket."*

[2] *Aerial view of a Levittown-type development.*

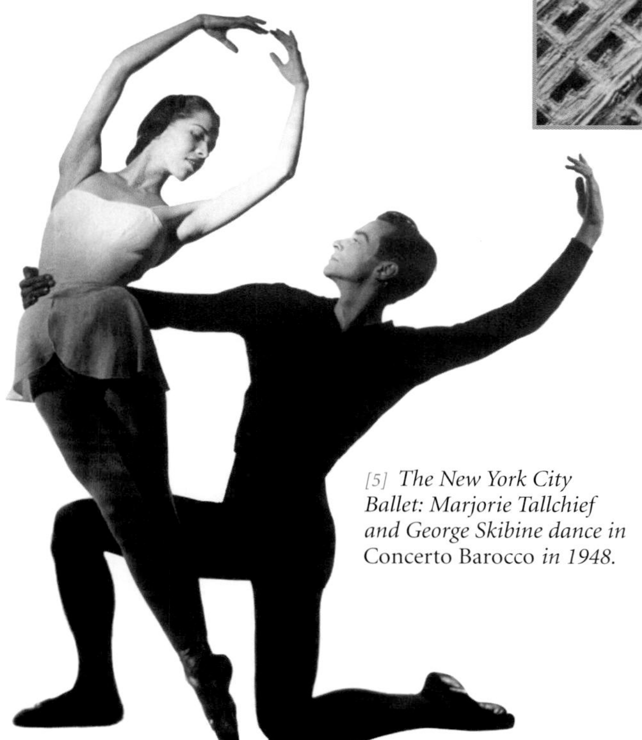

[5] *The New York City Ballet: Marjorie Tallchief and George Skibine dance in* Concerto Barocco *in 1948.*

[8] *The British foreign secretary, Ernest Bevin, with the U.S.S.R. delegate on his right, speaks at the first United Nations General Assembly in London.*

1940-1949

 [5]

1946
The Ballet Society is founded in New York by choreographer George Balanchine and Lincoln Kirstein; its name is changed to the **New York City Ballet** in 1948.

 [6]

1946
The British **National Health Service** under government administration, is established. It will provide free (except for certain minor charges) health coverage to virtually the entire population.

1946
The **five-cent price is abandoned** by dealers throughout the United States shortly after the decontrol of candy prices by the Office of Price Administration.

 [7]

1946
Trygve Lie of Norway becomes the first secretary general of the United Nations, serving until 1952, when he will resign.

1946
Tupperware plastic storage containers debut in department stores, but they will become famous for the home "parties" at which they will be sold.

January 10, 1946
Radar contact with the moon is established by U.S. Army Signal Corps; a signal sent to the moon from a laboratory in Belmar, New Jersey, echoed back to the sending station in 2.4 seconds.

1946
Ludwig Mies van der Rohe begins work on the **Farnsworth House**, Plano, Illinois. An essay at producing a perfect space for dwelling, this house seems to float above the ground.

1946
Mobster **Bugsy Siegel** opens the Flamingo Hotel in Las Vegas, Nevada. The desert city's boom in gambling and entertainment begins.

 [3]

1946
Penicillin-resistant bacteria are detected in London hospitals. Henceforth, pathogens and medical research are locked in a race between human ingenuity and microbial evolution.

1946
Procter & Gamble develops Tide, the first synthetic **laundry detergent**. In 1949, it will introduce Joy, the first synthetic liquid detergent.

1946
Robert Menzies begins his second term as prime minister of Australia.

1946
The all-electronic **ENIAC** (electronic numerical integrator and computer) becomes fully operational; built during World War II to compute artillery range tables, it is first used for hydrogen-bomb calculations after the war.

 [4]

[3] The Flamingo Hotel, Las Vegas, begins to take shape. In front of it is the notorious Meyer Lansky, gangster and friend of Bugsy Siegel.

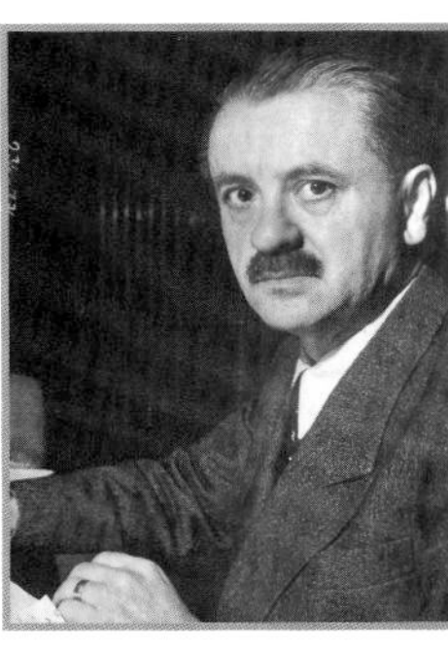

[9] Zoltan Tildy, Hungarian president until the communist seizure of power in 1948.

[4] A basic version of the ENIAC computer being built in England by Dr. Andrew Donald Booth.

[7] Secretary General Trygve Lie at the United Nations. He was foreign minister of the Norwegian government-in-exile during the Second World War. Perhaps his greatest moment comes when he organizes support for the defense of South Korea in 1950.

[6] Two children receive orthopaedic treatment at the Bristol Health Centre, part of the new British National Health Service.

 [8]

January 10, 1946
The first **United Nations General Assembly** meets in London.

January 28, 1946
A six-day state of siege is proclaimed by the Chilean government after **riots in Santiago** between police and demonstrating Chilean union members result in four deaths.

January 31, 1946
Brazilian major general **Eurico Gaspar Dutra**, whose administration will be noted for its restoration of constitutional democracy, is sworn in as president of Brazil.

 [9]

February 1, 1946
Hungary is proclaimed a republic, and Premier Zoltan Tildy is elected president by the new Hungarian national assembly.

March 5, 1946
British prime minister Winston Churchill popularizes the term "**Iron Curtain**"—describing the separation between Soviet and Western nations—in a speech at Fulton, Missouri.

March 9, 1946
Finnish premier **Juho K. Paasikivi**, is elected president of Finland by that country's parliament.

1946-1947

April 3, 1946
The Japanese army general **Homma Masaharu** is executed for forcing the Bataan Death March.

April 12, 1946
Japan's two principal conservative parties—liberal and progressive—win control of **the Diet** in the first general election after end of World War II.

April 29, 1946
Tojo Hideki, prime minister of Japan from 1941 to 1944, is indicted for war crimes and tried with other Japanese wartime leaders before the International Military Tribunal for the Far East. He will be found guilty and hanged.

[1]

May 12, 1946
Parleys end in failure when Hindu and Muslim parties are unable to reach common ground on plans for an independent, unified **India**.

May 26, 1946
Yoshida Shigeru becomes prime minister of Japan, serving for most of the period between 1946 and 1954. He will guide his country back to economic prosperity, setting the course for postwar cooperation with the United States and western Europe.

June 2, 1946
In the aftermath of World War II, the people of **Italy** vote in a referendum to replace the governing monarchy with a republic.

NÜRNBERG TRIALS

Nazi leaders indicted and tried as war criminals.

These were a series of trials held in Nürnberg, Germany, in 1945 and 1946, by the International Military Tribunal. The indictment lodged against the Nazi leaders contained four counts: crimes against peace (the planning, initiating, and waging of wars of aggression in violation of international treaties and agreements), crimes against humanity (exterminations, deportations, and genocide), war crimes (violations of the laws of war), and "a common plan or conspiracy to commit" the criminal acts listed in the first three counts. After 216 court sessions, on October 1, 1946, the verdict for 22 of the original 24 defendants was handed down. Three of the defendants were acquitted. Four were sentenced to terms of imprisonment ranging from 10 to 20 years: Karl Dönitz, Baldur von Schirach, Albert Speer, and Konstantin von Neurath. Three were sentenced to life imprisonment: Rudolf Hess (resting his hands on the bench), Walther Funk, and Erich Raeder. Twelve of the defendants were sentenced to death by hanging. Ten of them—Hans Frank, Wilhelm Frick, Julius Streicher, Alfred Rosenberg, Ernst Kaltenbrunner, Joachim von Ribbentrop (second right), Fritz Sauckel, Alfred Jodl, Wilhelm Keitel (far right), and Arthur Seyss-Inquart—were hanged on October 16, 1946. Martin Bormann was tried and condemned to death in absentia, and Hermann Göring (far left) committed suicide before he could be executed.

[1] *Tojo Hideki on trial for his life.*

[6] *Two members of the Boston Red Sox team shake hands: Rudy York (right) and Bobby Doerr.*

[5] *British soldiers search through the wreckage of the King David Hotel in Jerusalem, hoping to find survivors.*

 [5]

July 22, 1946
The Irgun Zvai Leumi, a violent Jewish right-wing underground movement in Palestine, blows up a wing of the **King David Hotel** in Jerusalem, killing 91 soldiers and civilians.

October 1, 1946
The verdict is handed down on 22 of the original 24 defendants in the Nürnberg trials, a series of trials held after World War II in which the **International Military Tribunal** indicts and tries former Nazi leaders as war criminals.

 [6]

October 15, 1946
The National League champion **St. Louis Cardinals** defeat the American League winner, the Boston Red Sox, 4 to 3, in the seventh and deciding game of the World Series.

 [7]

October 16, 1946
Ten of the twelve defendants sentenced to death at the **Nürnberg trials** of former Nazi leaders are executed.

November 23, 1946
At least 6,000 Vietnamese civilians are killed in a French naval bombardment of the port city of **Haiphong**.

November 28, 1946
Vincent Auriol is elected first president of the Fourth French Republic.

June 6, 1946
Argentina and the Soviet Union resume diplomatic relations after 28-year lapse.

June 6, 1946
Fred M. Vinson is appointed 13th chief justice of the U.S. Supreme Court by President Harry S. Truman. He will serve from 1946 to 1953.

 [2]

June 8, 1946
A breakdown in Dutch-Indonesian negotiations for sovereignty is implied as **President Sukarno** of the Indonesian republic broadcasts an appeal to his followers to mobilize against the Dutch.

 [3]

July 4, 1946
The **Republic of the Philippines** is proclaimed an independent country, with Manuel Roxas as its first president.

July 7, 1946
Mother Frances Xavier Cabrini becomes the first U.S. citizen to be canonized by the Roman Catholic Church.

[4]

July 21, 1946
A revolt in **Bolivia** results in the assassination of President Gualberto Villarroel, whose body is hung from a lamppost in La Paz's public square.

[2] Fred Vinson

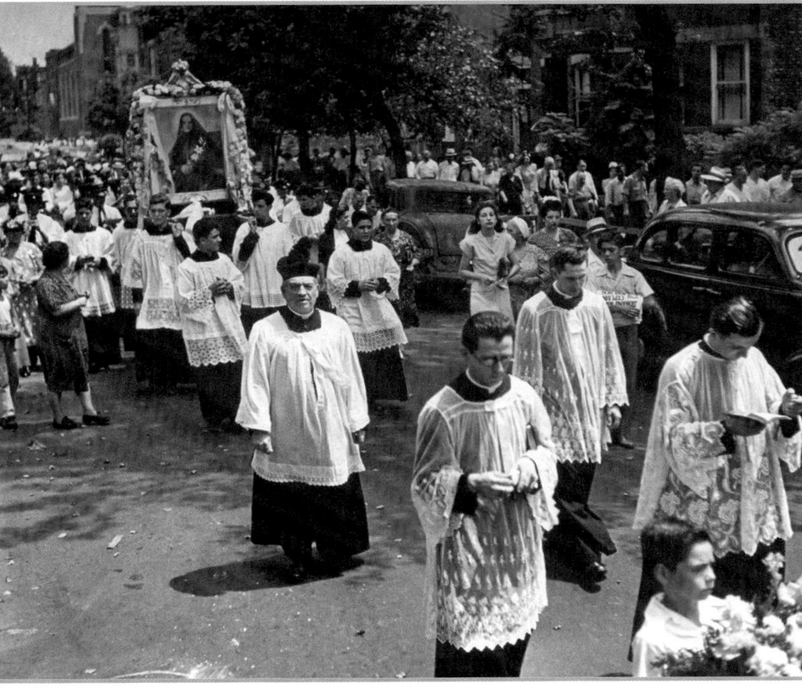

[4] A Roman Catholic procession to celebrate the opening in America of the first church dedicated to Mother Cabrini.

[8] Ho Chi Minh. He has eliminated possible rival Vietnamese leaders against the French so that he is the sole focus of the opposition.

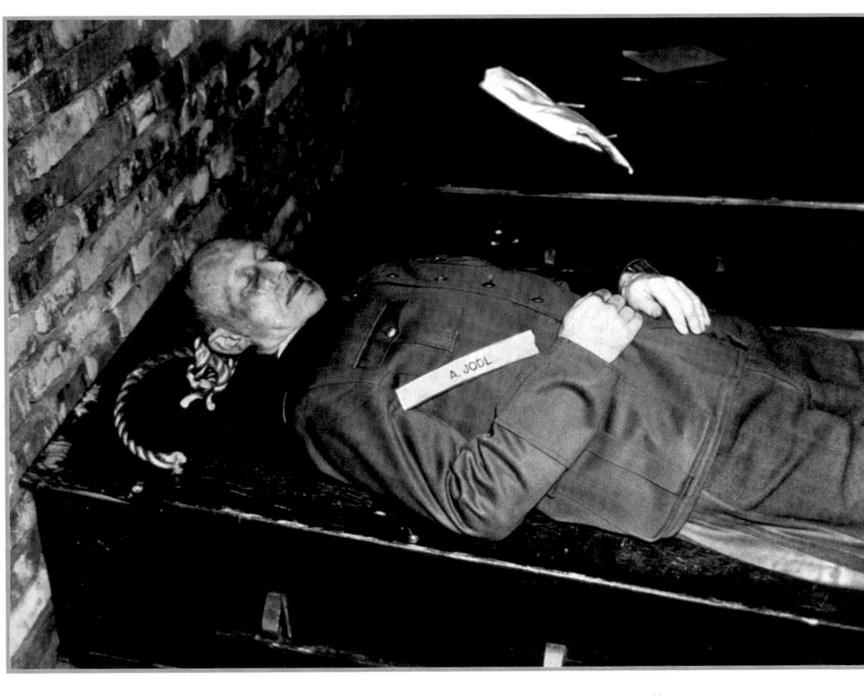

[7] The body of Jodl, chief adviser to Hitler and chief of operations staff, after his execution, at Nürnberg.

[3] President Sukarno. His determination to secure full Indonesian independence from the Dutch has been shown by his willingness to collaborate with the Japanese during their wartime occupation of the country.

[9] French actress Barbara Loage in a bikini she has made herself from one yard of cloth.

December 1, 1946
Partido Revolucionario Institucional (Revolutionary Institutional Party) candidate **Miguel Alemán** is elected president of Mexico and leads the country through a period of economic growth.

December 11, 1946
The **United Nations International Children's Emergency Fund** (UNICEF) is created by the United Nations to provide relief to children in countries devastated by World War II.

December 15, 1946
Siam becomes the 55th member of the United Nations, receiving a unanimous vote in the U.N. General Assembly.

 [8]

December 19, 1946
The Viet Minh, founded by Vietnamese nationalist Ho Chi Minh, begin the **First Indochina War** against France.

1947
Earl W. Flosdorf receives a patent for the process of **freeze-drying** foods and other biological materials.

 [9]

1947
A daring two-piece style of women's bathing suit, the **bikini**, comes into fashion. It is named after a Pacific island on which atomic bomb tests are being conducted.

1947

1947
A mysterious object crashes to earth near **Roswell**, New Mexico; many are convinced it is an extraterrestrial UFO and that the details are being kept secret by the government.

 [1]

1947
A shepherd boy discovers the first of the **Dead Sea Scrolls** in a cave at Khirbat Qumran on the northwestern shore of the Dead Sea; they date from the third to the first century BC. The 15,000 fragments are the remains of 800 to 900 manuscripts.

 [2]

1947
Americans John Bardeen, Walter Brattain, and William Shockley invent the **transistor** at Bell Laboratories. They will win the Nobel Prize for Physics in 1956.

1947
French fashion designer **Christian Dior** introduces the feminine "New Look," with full skirts and tight waists, in marked contrast to practical wartime styles.

1947
Instant photography is developed by Edwin Herbert Land, whose one-step process for developing and printing photographs creates a revolution unparalleled since the advent of roll film. His product is known as the Polaroid Land Camera.

 [3]

1947
Jazz trumpeter and singer **Louis Armstrong**, the most famous and popular jazz musician in the U.S. since the 1930s, forms his All Stars jazz ensemble.

 [4]

THE "NEW LOOK"

French designer conquers fashion world.

Christian Dior, the French fashion designer, dominated world fashion in the decade following World War II. Dior trained for the French diplomatic service, but in the midst of the financial crisis of the 1930s he went to work illustrating fashions for the weekly *Figaro Illustré*. In 1947, backed by a French textile manufacturer, Marcel Boussac, he introduced his revolutionary "New Look," spurring international controversy over the radically lowered hemline. The look featured small shoulders, a natural waistline, and a voluminous skirt (above), a drastic change from the World War II look of padded shoulders and short skirts. The "New Look" was an overnight success.

[1] The Roswell UFO at the local army airfield; it turns out to be part of a radar target.

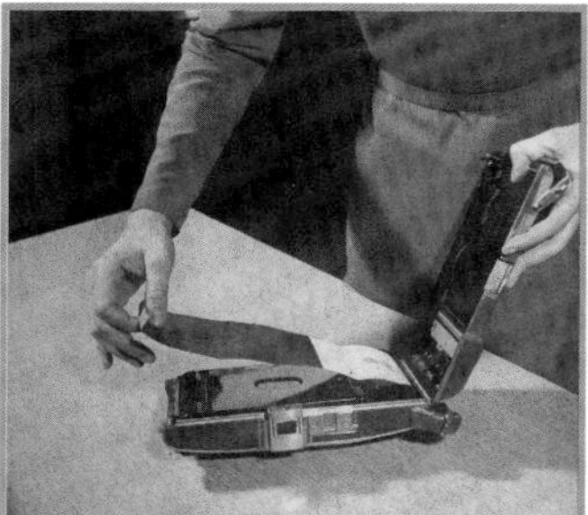

[3] The new Polaroid camera, "producing pictures in a minute."

[4] "Saint Louis Blues": a sheet music cover featuring Louis Armstrong and his All Stars.

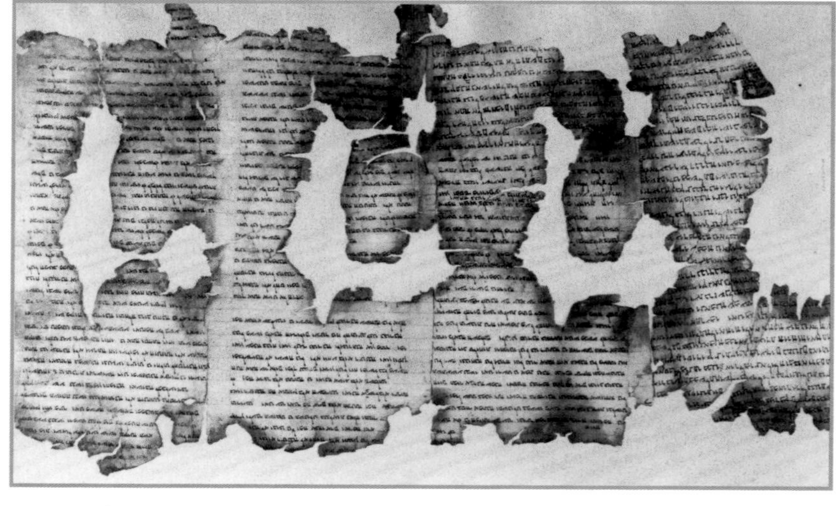

[2] One of the Dead Sea Scrolls: part of the Old Testament book of Isaiah.

January 7, 1947
American president Truman nominates **General George C. Marshall** as secretary of state.

February 5, 1947
Communist **Boleslaw Bierut** is elected president of Poland. He will come to be called the Joseph Stalin of Poland.

March 12, 1947
U.S. president Harry S. Truman articulates what becomes known as the **Truman Doctrine** when he asks Congress to appropriate aid for Greece and Turkey, both of which are facing Communist threats.

April 2, 1947
A proposal to give U.S. sole trusteeship over former mandated **Japanese islands** in the Pacific is unanimously approved by the U.N. security council.

April 20, 1947
Crown Prince Frederik succeeds to the throne of Denmark as **King Frederik IX** upon the death of his father, Christian X.

May 9, 1947
The **World Bank**, in the first loan made under its charter, lends France $250,000,000 for postwar reconstruction purposes.

1947
Lego, a building toy invented in 1932 by Dutch carpenter and toymaker Ole Kirk Christiansen, begins to be manufactured in plastic as well as wood. **Lego** becomes one of the world's most popular toys.

1947
Norwegian ethnologist and adventurer **Thor Heyerdahl** attempts to prove that Easter Island and Hawaii had been settled by ancient people from the Americas by sailing his balsawood raft, the *Kon-Tiki*, westward from Peru.

 [5]

1947
Richard Rodgers and Oscar Hammerstein's **Oklahoma!** opens on Broadway, with choreography by Agnes De Mille. Its songs and dances advance the plot and characterization rather than simply being interludes in the story.

1947
The **Central Intelligence Agency**, the principal foreign intelligence and counterintelligence agency of the U.S. government, is formally established.

1947
The postwar constitution of **Japan** takes effect.

1947
Using fuller's earth, a highly absorbent clay compound, American entrepreneur Edward Lowe develops **cat litter**.

[5] *Thor Heyerdahl with the sail of the* Kon-Tiki *behind him.*

[7] *A threshing machine, part of the Marshall Plan's aid for Europe, at work in Austria, its origins clearly indicated.*

[6] *Ferenc Nagy (center). He and his Smallholders Party try and resist the Communists. He is forced to resign when they kidnap his son.*

[8] *Lord Mountbatten, India's last viceroy, with Muslim leader Jinnah on the right and Congress Leader Nehru on the left. In the background is Lord Ismay, one of the viceroy's advisers.*

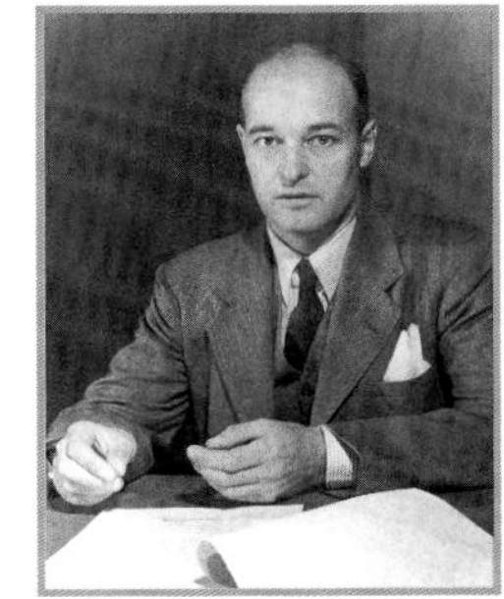

[9] *George Kennan, America's guide through the early Cold War era, though he is increasingly at odds with U.S. policy as it grows more aggressive.*

 [6]

May 31, 1947
Ferenc Nagy is ousted as premier of Hungary while vacationing in Switzerland.

 [7]

June 5, 1947
In an address at Harvard University, U.S. secretary of state George C. Marshall advances the idea of the **Marshall Plan**, a European self-help program to be financed by the United States.

 [8]

June 15, 1947
The British plan for **partitioning India** into Hindu and Muslim states is accepted by the All-India committee of the Congress Party, which, however, rejects independence for princely states.

June 16, 1947
An **American tax bill** calling for cuts in personal income taxes ranging from 19.5 to 30 percent is vetoed by President Harry Truman on grounds that it would probably induce the "very recession we seek to avoid."

June 19, 1947
American Albert Boyd sets the **world speed record** of 623.8 miles per hour flying a P-80R, a U.S. Army jet-propelled plane.

 [9]

July 1947
George F. Kennan, under the signature "X," in an article in *Foreign Affairs* magazine, articulates containment, which will become the basis of U.S. foreign policy toward the Soviet Union.

1947-1948

July 26, 1947
President Harry Truman signs legislation unifying the U.S. armed forces. The legislation creates the **Department of Defense**.

August 15, 1947
Britain's long rule over **India** is formally ended, and the country achieves independence as two separate dominions, India and Pakistan.

August 23, 1947
An army revolt in **Ecuador** leads to the overthrow of President Jose Naria Velasco Ibarra and assumption of power by defense minister Colonel Carlos Mancheno, who proclaimed himself president.

August 23, 1947
The Greek government headed by Premier **Demetrios Maximos** resigns after failing to rally the country to fight against guerrillas.

September 16, 1947
Dr. Oswaldo Aranha of Brazil is elected president of the second regular session of U.N. General Assembly.

October 6, 1947
The National League champion **New York Yankees** defeat the American League winner, the Brooklyn Dodgers, 4 to 3, in the seventh game of the World Series.

[1] *Indians celebrate independence in Calcutta.*

[3] *Hollywood star spectators stand to see better at the House Un-American Activities Committee: from the left, Danny Kaye, June Havoc, Humphrey Bogart. Bogart's wife, Lauren Bacall, sits beside him.*

[2] *Princess Elizabeth and Prince Philip on the Buckingham Palace balcony on their wedding day.*

[5] *Alfred Kinsey (left) with three of his researchers.*

[6] *Bob Mathias (center) with the silver and bronze decathlon medalists, in London.*

1948
Abstract expressionism, a movement that will dominate painting in the 1950s and establish America as the world center for modern art, begins to develop.

1948
Al-Ghawar, the world's largest oilfield, is discovered in Saudi Arabia. Middle East oil strikes lower energy prices and drive a great burst of energy intensification in the Western world.

1948
American researcher Alfred Kinsey publishes **Sexual Behavior in the Human Male**. Released five years later will be *Sexual Behavior in the Human Female*. The works are controversial but recognized as important surveys of sexual behavior.

1948
American researchers announce that **cortisone**, a substance produced by the adrenal gland, has anti-inflammatory properties and can relieve arthritis.

1948
At the **Summer Olympics** in London, American Bob Mathias becomes the youngest track-and-field champion ever, winning the decathlon at age 17. He also triumphs four years later in Helsinki, Finland.

1948
Britain's **Labour government** nationalizes production and distribution of electricity and also the railways.

October 14, 1947
American pilot **Chuck Yeager** breaks the sound barrier, flying an experimental X-1 rocket craft. He sets a world speed record of 1,650 miles per hour in 1953 in an X-1A rocket plane.

November 9, 1947
Bangkok, Thailand, is seized in a coup d'état staged by a **Siamese military** clique headed by Field Marshal Luang Pibul Songgram, announcing the overthrow of Premier Thawan Thamrong Nawasawat's government.

November 20, 1947
Princess Elizabeth, heir to the British throne, and Prince Philip, duke of Edinburgh, are married in London, England.

[2]

November 24, 1947
The Hollywood Ten, a group of motion-picture producers, directors, and screenwriters who appeared before the **House Un-American Activities Committee** in October 1947, are found in contempt of Congress.

 [3]

November 29, 1947
The United Nations General Assembly adopts a resolution (not implemented) calling for the partition of **Palestine** into two separate states—an Arab and a Jewish one—that would retain an economic union.

1948
The Hale reflector telescope, then the world's largest at 200 inches, is dedicated at Palomar Mountain Observatory in California.

 [4]

CHUCK YEAGER

American pilot breaks the sound barrier in the X-1 jet aircraft.

American test pilot and U.S. Air Force officer Chuck Yeager was chosen from several volunteers to test-fly the secret experimental X-1 aircraft, built by the Bell Aircraft Company to test the capabilities of the human pilot and a fixed-wing aircraft against the severe aerodynamic stresses of sonic flight. On October 14, 1947, over Rogers Dry Lake in southern California, he rode the X-1, attached to a B-29 mother ship, to an altitude of 25,000 feet (7,600 m). The X-1 then rocketed separately to 40,000 feet (12,000 m), and Yeager became the first man to break the sound barrier, which was approximately 662 miles (1,066 km) per hour at that altitude (the photo shows Yeager being congratulated by Lawrence D. Bell, president of Bell Aircraft Corporation). The feat was not announced publicly until June 1948.

[7] *American skier Steve Knowlton in the first Olympic downhill competition at St. Moritz.*

[4] *The Mount Palomar Observatory building housing the Hale telescope.*

[8] *Peter Goldmark demonstrates the capability of the LP. Those he holds have on them all the music on the tall stack of 78-rpm records.*

1948
Baby, built at the University of Manchester in England, is the first stored-program digital computer.

1948
Bluegrass as a musical genre is invented by mandolin player Bill Monroe, leader of the Blue Grass Boys, and banjo player Earl Scruggs.

1948
British engineer **Andrew Donald Booth** invents the magnetic drum memory for computers.

 [7]

1948
For the first time, both disciplines of alpine skiing (downhill and slalom) are **Winter Olympic medal events** in the games at St. Moritz, Switzerland.

1948
Holography is developed by Dennis Gabor, a Hungarian-born electrical engineer. He will be awarded the Nobel Prize for Physics in 1971 for his invention.

 [8]

1948
Hungarian-born American engineer Peter Carl Goldmark leads a team that develops the **long-playing (LP) record**, rendering 78-rpm records obsolete. A single LP holds the equivalent of six 78-rpm records.

1948

1948
Kevin Tuohy develops the modern plastic contact lens. The first contact lens, made of glass, had been developed by Adolf Fick in 1887 to correct irregular astigmatism.

1948
MIT mathematician Norbert Wiener publishes **Cybernetics**, a pioneering study of control and communications systems that draws on his research in fire control and neurology.

1948
Norman Mailer publishes *The Naked and the Dead*, hailed immediately as one of the finest American novels to come out of World War II.

1948
Physicists George Gamow and Ralph Alpher elaborate the modern version of the "**big-bang**" model of the origins of the universe.

1948
Senegalese poet **Léopold Sédar Senghor** edits and publishes *Anthology of the New Negro and Madagascan Poetry*, a collection that includes some of the major works of the Negritude movement.

1948
Taking a cue from burrs picked up while hiking, Swiss inventor George de Mestral develops **Velcro**, a fabric fastening tape. Tiny hooks and loops cause the two pieces of material to stick together.

[2] Jews look at the destruction caused by a bomb planted in Jerusalem by Palestinian Arabs in March.

[4] Gandhi's body lies in state before being taken to be burned by the River Jumna.

[5] How the Communists cow opposition in Czechoslovakia: an "action squad" of armed workers marching through Prague.

 [4]
January 30, 1948
Mahatma Gandhi is assassinated by Hindu nationalist Nathuram Godse in Delhi, India.

February 4, 1948
Ceylon (now Sri Lanka) gains independence from Great Britain.

 [5]
February 25, 1948
Communists seize control of the government of **Czechoslovakia**.

April 3, 1948
U.S. president Harry S. Truman signs into law George C. **Marshall's post–World War II plan** to revive the economies of western and southern European countries in order to foster democracy in the region.

April 16, 1948
To restore the economy after World War II, 16 European countries form the **Organisation for European Economic Co-operation** (later the Organisation for Economic Co-operation and Development).

April 30, 1948
The charter of the **Organization of American States** is signed at the conclusion of the Ninth Pan-American Conference held in Bogotá, Colombia. It will promote economic, military, and cultural cooperation.

1948
The design for the **Frisbee** flying disc is patented by Fred Morrison.

 [1]

1948
The United Nations founds the **World Health Organization** to further international cooperation in medicine and public health.

1948
United Nations peacekeepers are first used to observe cease-fires in Kashmir and Palestine. The forces, under the authority of the U.N. Security Council, will win the Nobel Peace Prize in 1988.

1948
Violence between Arabs and Jews continues in the months leading up to **Israel's independence** in May.

 [2]

c. 1948
Jazz performers, most notably alto saxophonist Charlie Parker and trumpeter Dizzy Gillespie, experiment with **bebop**, a fluid improvisational style employing chromatic scales and complex rhythms.

 [3]

January 4, 1948
The Southeast Asian nation of **Burma** (Myanmar) formally gains independence, completing the transfer of power negotiated by Burmese leader Aung San and British prime minister Clement Attlee in 1947.

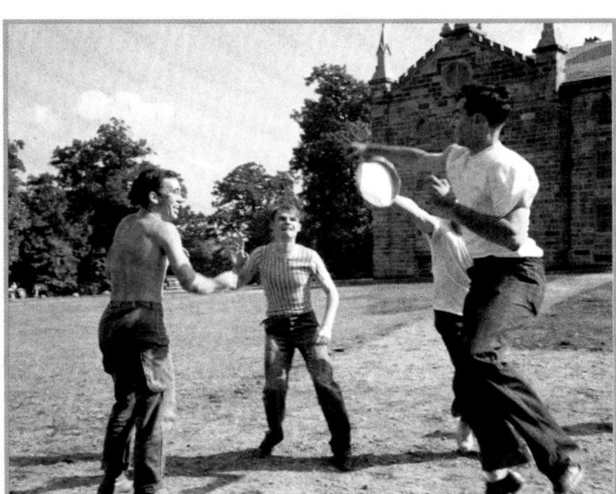

[1] The Frisbee's early days: Kenyon College students play with one.

[3] Dizzy Gillespie, king of the bebop trumpeters.

[6] Young Israelis celebrate their country's declaration of independence in Tel Aviv on May 14.

[7] A crowd of Berliners look up at a U.S. C-47 cargo plane coming in to land at Tempelhof airfield, part of the airlift bringing in supplies from the West.

[8] President Syngman Rhee together with General Douglas MacArthur at a ceremony for the founding of South Korea.

[9] Kim Il Sung, premier of North Korea and founder of its communist dynasty.

May 10, 1948
U.N.-sponsored elections are held in **South Korea** prior to the formation of a republic.

 [6]

May 14, 1948
Israel declares its independence and is quickly recognized by the United States, the Soviet Union, and numerous other countries, fulfilling the Zionist dream of an internationally approved Jewish state.

 [7]

June 24, 1948
The **Berlin Blockade** intensifies when the Soviet Union announces that the Western Allied powers no longer have any rights in Berlin.

July 5, 1948
The U.S. Public Health Service issues a report finding a 32 percent higher death rate among **smokers** in a study of 198,926 veterans.

 [8]

August 15, 1948
The **Republic of Korea** (South Korea) is inaugurated, with Seoul as the capital and Syngman Rhee as the president.

 [9]

August 25, 1948
The **Democratic People's Republic of Korea** (North Korea) is established, with P'yongyang as the capital and Kim Il Sung as the premier.

1948-1949

September 17, 1948
Swedish humanitarian and diplomat **Folke, Count Bernadotte**, is assassinated by Jewish extremists while serving the United Nations as mediator between the Arabs and the Israelis.

 [1]

September 18, 1948
A local communist commander seizes power in Madiun, Indonesia, as part of a rebellion effort against the Sukarno government in an incident known as the **Madiun Affair**.

November 15, 1948
Canadian statesman and jurist **Louis Saint Laurent**, a member of the Liberal Party who will help to maintain Canadian unity and bring about reforms, becomes prime minister (1948–57).

December 1948
The United Nations General Assembly approves the **Genocide Convention**, the first U.S. human rights treaty. It defines genocide as certain acts committed with intent to destroy, in whole or in part, a national, ethnical, racial, or religious group.

December 10, 1948
The General Assembly of the United Nations adopts the **Universal Declaration of Human Rights**.

December 15, 1948
Former U.S. State Department official **Alger Hiss** is indicted on two charges of perjury for lying about his dealings with Whittaker Chambers, who accuses him of membership in a communist espionage ring.

 [2]

[1] Count Folke Bernadotte (left) with U.S. diplomat Ralph Bunche, who will succeed him as U.N. mediator.

[7] Bob Cousy. His career with the Boston Celtics starts at the same time as the NBA, and he carries on as star player and broadcaster for many years. His number 14 jersey still hangs in the rafters of Boston Garden.

[2] Alger Hiss and his wife leave court after he has received a five-year sentence.

[4] Simone de Beauvoir, who founds modern feminism with her book, in which she discusses such then taboo topics as prostitution, abortion, sexual equality, and divorce.

[6] Miles Davis. He comes out from under the shadow of Charlie Parker as a soloist in his own right.

[5] Aaron Siskind: carrying abstract expressionism into photography.

1940-1949

 [4]

1949
French existentialist Simone de Beauvoir publishes **The Second Sex**, a scholarly and passionate plea for the abolition of what she called the myth of the "eternal feminine."

[5]

1949
In *Chicago 1949* and other works, American photographer **Aaron Siskind** pursues abstraction in photographs by taking weathered and marked surfaces as his subjects.

 [6]

1949
Jazz trumpeter **Miles Davis** releases *Birth of the Cool*, which defines the West Coast "cool" style of jazz. His later albums are milestones in modal jazz, jazz rock, and electronic jazz.

1949
Joseph Chifley of the Labor Party, whose ministry will be noted for banking reform and expansion of social services and immigration, becomes prime minister of Australia.

1949
Philip Johnson designs his Glass House, New Canaan, Connecticut. One of Johnson's first works, this building derives from the work of Mies van der Rohe.

 [7]

1949
The National Basketball League and Basketball Association of America merge to form the **National Basketball Association**.

1949
Aldo Leopold's **A Sand County Almanac** is published posthumously; it is one of the most influential American conservation and ecological books of the first half of the 20th century.

1949
American chemist Linus Pauling and colleagues show that **sickle-cell anemia** is a "molecular disease" caused by a single amino acid change in the hemoglobin molecule.

1949
British novelist George Orwell publishes his profoundly anti-Utopian novel **1984**, which examines the dangers of totalitarian rule. It quickly becomes a classic.

 [3]

1949
Eleanor Abbott, a recovering polio victim, creates the board game **Candyland**. It will become one of the most popular children's games of all time.

1949
Finnish-born American architect **Eliel Saarinen** begins work on his late masterpiece, Christ Lutheran Church, in Minneapolis, Minnesota.

1949
Frank Zamboni, owner of an indoor skating rink in California, patents the Model A Zamboni Ice Resurfacer. Future models of the zamboni are used by thousands of ice rinks around the world.

THE ALGER HISS AFFAIR

U.S. government official accused of spying

In 1948, Whittaker Chambers, a newspaper and magazine editor, testified before the House Un-American Activities Committee (HUAC) that Alger Hiss, a U.S. government official, had been a fellow member of a communist spy ring in the 1930s. When Chambers repeated the charge in public, unprotected by congressional immunity, Hiss sued him for slander. In a federal grand-jury investigation of the case, both Chambers and Hiss testified; Hiss was later indicted on two charges of perjury. His first trial (1949) ended with a hung jury; at his second trial (1950) he was found guilty. He was released from jail in 1954, still protesting his innocence. The Hiss case brought national attention to Congressman Richard Nixon, whose hostile questioning of Hiss during the HUAC hearings (far left) did much to establish his reputation as a fervent anticommunist.

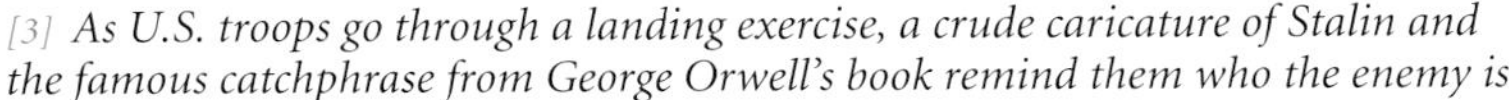
[3] As U.S. troops go through a landing exercise, a crude caricature of Stalin and the famous catchphrase from George Orwell's book remind them who the enemy is.

[8] Chaim Weizmann is sworn in as Israel's first president.

1949
Theoretical physicist Richard Feynman introduces **Feynman diagrams**, which provide a vastly simplified method of calculating elementary-particle reactions.

January 21, 1949
The military regimes established by revolutions in **Venezuela** and **El Salvador** are recognized by the United States.

January 29, 1949
De facto recognition of **Israel** is announced by the British Foreign Office.

February 16, 1949
The first **Knesset** (Hebrew: "Assembly"), the unicameral parliament of Israel and supreme authority of that state, opens in Jerusalem.

 [8]

February 17, 1949
Chaim Weizmann is elected the first president of Israel.

February 25, 1949
General Motors makes its first postwar price cuts on its passenger cars and trucks.

1949

March 2, 1949
The U.S. Air Force **B-50** Superfortress lands at Fort Worth, Texas, completing the first nonstop round-the-world flight.

 [1]

March 8, 1949
The independence of **Vietnam** within the French union is recognized in an exchange of letters between French president Vincent Auriol and Bao Dai, the former emperor of Annam.

March 20, 1949
The **deutsche mark** is made the only legal tender in western sectors of Berlin. It was the prospect of this happening in 1948 that caused Joseph Stalin to begin the Berlin Blockade.

 [2]

March 31, 1949
The British Crown Colony of **Newfoundland** becomes Canada's 10th province.

April 4, 1949
The **North Atlantic Treaty Organization**, a military alliance, is formed by Belgium, Canada, Denmark, France, Iceland, Italy, Luxembourg, the Netherlands, Norway, Portugal, the United Kingdom, and the United States.

[3]

April 14, 1949
Nineteen former Nazi officials and military leaders, the last defendants scheduled for trial, are given prison terms by the U.S. **war-crimes tribunal**.

[1] A B-50 bomber (left) is refuelled in flight.

[2] Reichsmark currency is replaced by the deutsche mark: the first step towards the establishment of a West German state.

[3] Foreign Secretary Ernest Bevin signs up Britain for membership of NATO, watched by Harry Truman under the potted palm, in Washington.

[6] Members of the Ku Klux Klan march through Pell City, Alabama, with their faces uncovered.

[7] Konrad Adenauer, pre-war mayor of Cologne, speaks in Berlin after becoming chancellor.

 [6]

June 28, 1949
Alabama's governor signs a bill, aimed at the **Ku Klux Klan**, making it unlawful to wear hoods or masks in public.

July 18, 1949
The **Kingdom of Laos** is granted independence within the French union by a treaty signed in Paris.

August 12, 1949
An international conference approves four **Geneva conventions**, on the treatment of the wounded and sick combat forces in the field and at sea, the care of prisoners of war, and the protection of civilians during time of war.

August 14, 1949
The government of President Husni al-Zaim of **Syria** is overthrown by a group of army leaders; Zaim is summarily tried and executed.

August 28, 1949
Six U.S. Civil War veterans meet at Indianapolis, Indiana, for the 83rd and last encampment of the **Grand Army of the Republic**.

September 12, 1949
Liberal democratic legislator and author **Theodor Heuss**, the leader of the Free Democratic Party who will help draft a new constitution for postwar West Germany, becomes the country's first president (1949–59).

April 18, 1949
Eire formally becomes the **Republic of Ireland** as a law takes effect that cuts the last link with the United Kingdom.

April 24, 1949
Communist forces occupy the Chinese capital, Nanking (Nanjing), after crossing the Yangtze River virtually unopposed by adherents to the Nationalist government under President **Chiang Kai-shek**.

May 2, 1949
American playwright Arthur Miller's most important work, **Death of a Salesman**, wins the Pulitzer Prize. It is the tragic story of Willy Loman, a small man destroyed by false values that are in large part the values of his society.

 [4]

May 12, 1949
The Soviet Union lifts its blockade of **Berlin**.

 [5]

June 6, 1949
Stock prices on the **New York Stock Exchange** drop to their lowest level since May 1947.

$

June 12, 1949
The **University of California at Berkeley** discloses that it will require all faculty members and administrative officers to take loyalty oaths in order to weed out communists and other agitators.

[4] Director Elia Kazan (left) and Arthur Miller on the set of Death of a Salesman.

[5] The first convoy of trucks arrives in Berlin after the lifting of the blockade.

[10] Russian soldiers on patrol in Leipzig in September, the month before the Soviet occupation zone becomes the German Democratic Republic (East Germany).

[9] Mao Zedong proclaims the founding of the People's Republic of China as he stands on the top of the Gate of Heavenly Peace.

[8] Greek government troops, with British-supplied weapons and American parkas, fight their Communist countrymen.

 [7]

September 14, 1949
Konrad Adenauer, who will work to reconcile his country with its former enemies, especially France, becomes the first chancellor (1949–63) of the Federal Republic of Germany (West Germany).

 [8]

October 1949
The **Greek Civil War**, which has been raging since 1945 as Communist guerrillas try to seize control, ends with their defeat.

 [9]

October 1, 1949
Mao Zedong proclaims the founding of the People's Republic of China on Tiananmen ("Gate of Heavenly Peace") Square in Beijing.

 [10]

October 7, 1949
A constitution goes into effect in the Soviet occupation zone of Germany that forms the country of **East Germany**, which exists alongside West Germany until 1990.

October 7, 1949
Johannes Dieckmann, a member of the Liberal Democratic Party of Germany, becomes president (1949, 1960) of the German Democratic Republic (East Germany).

October 8, 1949
Elpidio Quirino is reelected president of the Republic of the Philippines.

October 8, 1949
France and **Cambodia** sign a treaty confirming Cambodia's status as an independent state within the French union.
 [1]

October 11, 1949
Wilhelm Pieck, a member of the Socialist Unity Party of Germany, becomes president (1949–60) of the German Democratic Republic (East Germany).
 [2]

October 12, 1949
Otto Grotewohl is elected minister-president (premier) of the German Democratic Republic; all the key cabinet posts go to veteran Communists.
 [2]

November 2, 1949
The Netherlands and the Republic of Indonesia sign the **Hague Agreement**, an attempt to end conflict over Indonesia's proclaimed independence.

December 1949
Romania, in return for Israeli government payment, allows **Jews to go to Israel**. Over 100,000 go. Nearly 40,000 are also going to Israel from Bulgaria, and many thousands from Turkey.
 [3]

December 27, 1949
Four years after nationalist revolutionary leader Sukarno declared Indonesia's independence, formal sovereignty over the country is transferred from the Dutch to the United States of **Indonesia**.

[1] King Norodom Sihanouk II of Cambodia in France with the French colonial secretary, Coste-Fleuret.

[2] Wilhelm Pieck (left) and Otto Grotewohl, both veteran Communists. "While everything should look democratic, we must be in control" is their formula for East Germany.

[3] Jewish immigrant families, newly arrived in Israel, look out from temporary tented accommodation.

IMMIGRANTS TO ISRAEL

The Israeli government allows Jews from all of the world to settle in the new country.

In 1947, the UN voted to partition the region of Palestine into separate Jewish and Arab states. Israel's declaration of independence on May 14, 1948, was quickly recognized by the United States, the Soviet Union, and many other governments, fulfilling the Zionist dream of an internationally approved Jewish state. However, Israel was immediately invaded by five Arab states—Egypt, Iraq, Lebanon, Syria, and Transjordan. Israel won the war, and when it secured the final armistice, the new state controlled one-fifth more territory than the original partition plan had specified. During the early years, Israel had to absorb a major influx of immigrants, including several hundred thousand nearly destitute Holocaust survivors and a large influx of Sephardic Jews from Arab states (left, Yemeni Jews at an immigrant camp at Rosh Ha'ayin in 1949), who felt increasingly insecure in their home countries following the Arab defeat in 1948. As a result, the Knesset passed the Law of Return in 1950, granting Jews immediate citizenship.

A glass of wine outside the Carlton Hotel, Cannes, 1958.

1950

1950
American **Jackson Pollock** creates nonrepresentational *Autumn Rhythm* by dripping and pouring paint on the canvas in a technique called action painting.

1950
British mathematician and logician Alan Turing suggests what will become known as the **Turing test** as a measure for artificial intelligence.

1950
British writer C. S. Lewis publishes **The Lion, the Witch and the Wardrobe,** the first of seven tales about the kingdom of Narnia. The Narnia books are exciting, humorous, inventive, and, in the final scenes of *The Last Battle* (1956), moving.

 [1]

1950
General Electric engineer James Wright, in the search for a synthetic substitute for rubber, creates **Silly Putty**.

1950
In an extension of the policy of **apartheid** ("apartness"), two South African laws, the Population Registration Act and the Group Areas Act, define the racial designation of every citizen and strictly enforce the segregation of the races.

 [2]

1950
In the United States the first major gay men's organization, founded in 1950–51, is the **Mattachine Society** (its name reputedly derived from a medieval French society of masked players, Société Mattachine).

[2] *A protest march against apartheid in South Africa in the 1950s. The banners are in the colors of the African National Congress.*

[1] *C. S. Lewis in his rooms at Magdalen College, Oxford, of which he is a Fellow.*

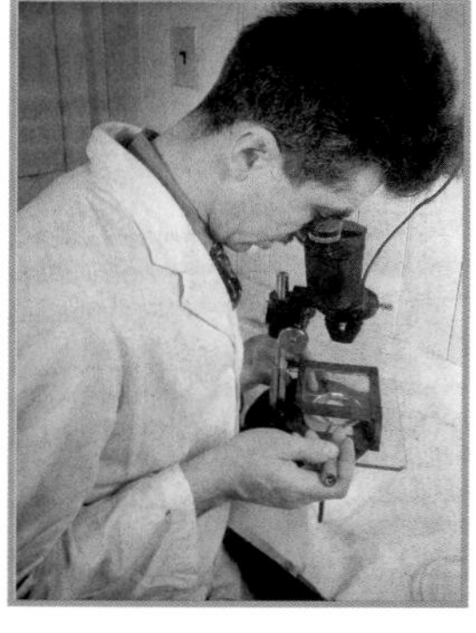

[8] *Gregory Pincus counting unfertilized eggs under a microscope.*

[9] *Striking auto workers outside a Chrysler plant.*

1950s
The **Mr. Potato Head** TV commercial airs, the first ever for a toy, helping Hasbro earn more than $4 million in sales in a few months.

 [8]

early 1950s
Oral contraceptives for women are developed in the U.S. by Gregory Pincus, John Rock, and Min Chueh Chang.

c. 1950
Firm evidence points to tobacco smoking as a cause of **lung cancer** and other serious illnesses. Campaigns to educate consumers begin.

c. 1950
First used on airplanes, **seatbelts** begin to be featured in automobiles.

c. 1950
Jean Piaget develops his theory of cognition in children, which features four stages of development. Piaget's work in child psychology make him one of the central figures in the discipline.

c. 1950
The world's total use of inanimate energy surpasses 20 billion megawatts for the first time, reflecting the rapid expansion of **fossil fuel** use.

1950
Le Corbusier begins work on Notre-Dame-du-Haut, Ronchamp, France. The powerful church, with its sweeping roof, marks a turn to a more plastic and sculptural style for the master architect.

 [3]

1950
Mysterious, reclusive American writer J. D. Salinger publishes his famous coming-of-age novel, **The Catcher in the Rye**.

 [4]

1950
The aged French painter **Henri Matisse** begins to create large-scale, brightly colored gouache "cutouts" in which shape and color juxtapositions take precedence over subject matter.

 [5]

1950
The first of **Willem de Kooning's** "Woman" series hints at representation within the vigorous brushwork of abstract expressionism.

 [6]

1950
Uruguay defeats Brazil in the men's **World Cup soccer** championship by a score of 2 to 1.

1950
The original Broadway production **Guys and Dolls** opens, based on the stories of Damon Runyon.

 [7]

[3] *Le Corbusier's Notre-Dame-du-Haut.*

[4] *The first edition of J. D. Salinger's novel.*

[5] *Henri Matisse in front of a stained glass panel that is entirely in the style of his "cutouts."*

[6] *Willem de Kooning in his studio.*

[7] *Sam Levene, as Nathan Detroit, gets tousled by Vivian Blaine, as Adelaide, with the Hotbox Club girls in the background, in a scene from* Guys and Dolls.

January 6, 1950
Great Britain announces its recognition of the **People's Republic of China**.

 [9]

January 25, 1950
The **United Automobile Workers** call a nationwide strike against the Chrysler Corporatioin to enforce demands for a wage increase or a pension and welfare program.

February 7, 1950
Great Britain and the United States recognize the governments of **Laos** and **Cambodia** and the Vietnamese government headed by Bao Dai in **French Indochina**.

March 3, 1950
The U.S. House of Representatives approves the admission of **Alaska** as a state by a vote of 186 to 146.

March 7, 1950
The U.S. House of Representatives approves a bill granting statehood to **Hawaii** by a vote of 261 to 110.

March 8, 1950
Legislation in East Germany is passed creating the Ministry for State Security, or **Stasi**. The Stasi will become one of the most hated and feared institutions of the East German Communist government.

March 14, 1950
The **FBI's Ten Most Wanted** Fugitives list first appears. Public assistance will facilitate some 150 arrests from the list by the early 21st century.

March 17, 1950
The discovery of a new element, named **californium**, is reported by the University of California, Berkeley.

March 23, 1950
Sophocles Venizélos becomes prime minister of Greece at the head of a Liberal minority cabinet.

April 8, 1950
Jawaharlal Nehru of India concludes the **Delhi Pact** with Liaqat Ali Khan of Pakistan, providing for the safe passage of refugees displaced after the two countries severed relations in December 1949.

 [1]

May 1, 1950
Richard Rodgers and Oscar Hammerstein II win the 1950 Pulitzer Prize for their musical **South Pacific**. It is exceptional for a musical in addressing the subject of racial prejudice.

 [2]

May 14, 1950
The Republican People's Party, in power in **Turkey** since 1923, is overwhelmingly defeated in parliamentary elections by the Democratic Party.

THE KOREAN WAR

The United Nations goes to war for the first time.

The division of Korea into two parts was intended to be an interim measure after World War II but the North became a Soviet client state while the South was backed by the United States. In 1950 North Korea invaded South Korea and U.S. president Harry S. Truman ordered troops to assist South Korea. The U.N. Security Council, minus the absent Soviet delegate, passed a resolution calling for the assistance of all U.N. members in halting the North Koreans. At first North Korean troops drove the South Korean and U.S. forces down to the southern tip of the Korean peninsula, but a brilliant amphibious landing at Inchon (shown above), conceived by General Douglas MacArthur, 200 miles behind the North Korean lines, turned the tide. U.N. troops advanced near the border of North Korea and China. The Chinese then entered the war and drove the U.N. forces back south; the front line stabilized at the 38th parallel. Peace talks began in 1951, and two years later an armistice was signed.

[1] *Jawaharlal Nehru*

[2] South Pacific*: Mary Martin and Ezio Pinza sing "Some Enchanted Evening" in the original Broadway production.*

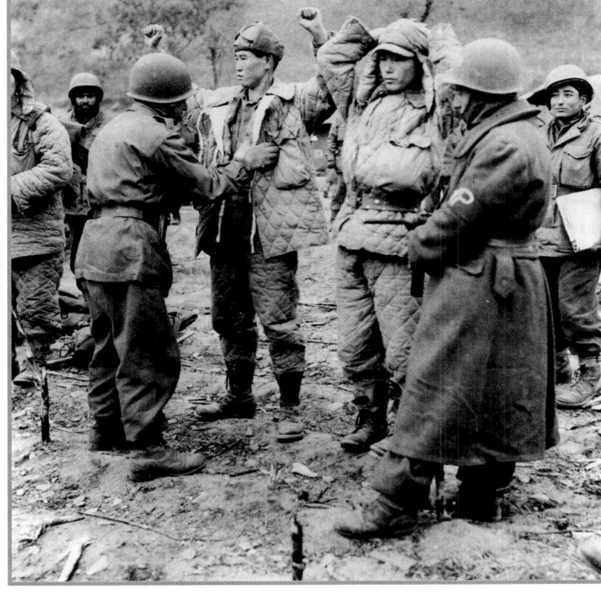

[6] *Chinese prisoners-of-war are searched by Turkish soldiers of the U.N. forces in Korea.*

[7] *Amos, Alvin Childress (center), and Andy, Spencer Williams (left), watch George "Kingfish" Stevens, played by Tim Moore.*

July 5, 1950
The Knesset passes the **Law of Return**, granting Jews the freedom to immigrate to Israel and receive immediate citizenship, but it proves controversial when the question "Who is a Jew?" raises other issues.

July 22, 1950
King Leopold III returns to Belgium after a six-year exile abroad.

September 15, 1950
United Nations troops land at **Inchon**, South Korea, crippling a North Korean invasion.

September 22, 1950
The 1950 Nobel Peace Prize is awarded to **Ralph J. Bunche**, director of the U.N. trusteeship division and former U.N. acting mediator in Palestine.

October 29, 1950
King Gustav V of Sweden, who ascended to the throne in 1907 and was a strong proponent of Swedish neutrality during World War II, dies in Stockholm.

 [6]

November 1950
Chinese troops enter Korea in large numbers; they move along the Yalu River after the Inchon landing by U.N. forces. By the end of 1952, 1.2 million Chinese will be engaged in the Korean War under the command of Peng Dehuai.

May 25, 1950
The **Brooklyn-Battery tunnel**, the longest vehicular tunnel in the United States, is formally opened to traffic in New York City.

 [3]

June 11, 1950
Capping a dramatic recovery from a near-fatal automobile accident, American golfer **Ben Hogan** wins the U.S. Open.

June 24, 1950
A Northwest Airlines plane disappears over Lake Michigan with 58 people aboard; no wreckage is ever found. It is the worst U.S. commercial **airline disaster** to date.

June 25, 1950
North Korean troops launch a full-scale invasion southward across the 38th parallel, beginning the **Korean War**.

 [4]

June 27, 1950
The U.S. Navy and Air Force are ordered into combat in Korea by **President Harry Truman**.

July 1950
The U.N. creates a unified command in Korea with **General Douglas MacArthur** as commander. Sixteen member nations send armed contingents, but the U.S. furnishes the great bulk of the air units, naval forces, supplies, and financing.

 [5]

[4] Koreans flee south with their possessions from the area where the invading North Korean forces are being confronted.

[5] American Colossus: General Douglas MacArthur bellowing orders at U.S. Marines during the Inchon landings in Korea.

[3] The procession of limousines that has driven through the new Brooklyn-Battery tunnel to mark its official opening.

[8] Helen Frankenthaler in her studio, with paintings floor to ceiling.

November 1, 1950
Puerto Rican nationalists, members of the **Armed Forces of National Liberation** (FALN), attempt to assassinate U.S. president Harry S. Truman.

November 2, 1950
Pope Pius XII in a papal bull proclaims the assumption of the Virgin Mary to be a dogma of the Roman Catholic Church.

 [7]

1951
A TV version of the radio show **Amos 'N' Andy** premiers in the U.S. It is the first network series to feature an all-black cast.

1951
After six years of Labour government, Conservative **Winston Churchill** becomes British prime minister for a second time.

 [8]

1951
American abstract expressionist painter **Helen Frankenthaler** stages her first one-woman show. Her work is noted for its brilliant color and lyric style.

1951
American poet and pioneer of "poetic literalism" (an extension of imagism) **Marianne Moore** publishes her *Collected Poems*.

1951

1951
Australian authorities intentionally introduce a Brazilian rabbit disease, **myxomatosis**, in an effort to control the rabbit population.

1951
The **Festival of Britain** is mounted on London's South Bank and in the nearby Battersea Pleasure Gardens. Of its landmark structures like the Skylon and the Dome of Discovery, only the Royal Festival Hall remains today.

 [1]

1951
German-born American political scientist and philosopher **Hannah Arendt** is established as a major political thinker with the publication of the *Origins of Totalitarianism*, which also treated 19th-century anti-Semitism, imperialism, and racism.

1951
Italian-born American composer **Gian Carlo Menotti** is commissioned by NBC to write the first opera for television, *Amahl and the Night Visitors*.

1951
The British **Ferranti** I (Manchester Mark I) is the first computer to go into commercial production.

 [2]

1951
The first UNIVAC (Universal Automatic Computer) is delivered to the U.S. Census Bureau, ushering in the age of "**big iron**."

[1] The edge of the Dome of Discovery at the Festival of Britain. Shaped like one saucer inverted on top of another, it is a striking high-tech design but will be dismantled on the orders of the Conservative government when it regains power.

[2] Two showgirls play a game on the Ferranti computer at the Science Museum in London.

[5] Julius and Ethel Rosenberg in a police van shortly before they are electrocuted.

[6] General Douglas MacArthur addresses the joint session of Congress after his sacking by President Truman. He quotes the World War I song: "Old soldiers never die; they simply fade away."

[7] Mud left behind in the main street of North Topeka, Kansas, after the worst floods in U.S. history.

February 27, 1951
The **Twenty-second Amendment** to the U.S. Constitution, limiting a president to two terms in office, is ratified.

 [5]

March 29, 1951
Julius and **Ethel Rosenberg** are found guilty of espionage and sentenced to death for turning over U.S. military secrets to the Soviet Union. The Rosenbergs are the first American civilians to be executed for espionage.

 [6]

April 11, 1951
President Harry S. Truman relieves **General Douglas MacArthur** of his command in Korea after he threatens to bomb Chinese cities.

April 18, 1951
A treaty is signed in Paris giving effect to the **Schuman plan** to pool western Europe's coal and steel production.

May 24, 1951
In the U.S. nuclear program, the fourth test of **Operation Greenhouse** is conducted, resulting in the first proof-of-principle test of a booster design in nuclear fission.

June 4, 1951
In **Dennis v. United States** the U.S. Supreme Court upholds the convictions of several leaders of the Communist Party for advocating the violent overthrow of the U.S. government, saying that such advocacy created a "clear and present danger" to the country.

1951
The leaders of Belgium, France, Italy, Luxembourg, the Netherlands, and West Germany sign the **Treaty of Paris**, which founds the European Coal and Steel Community. The ECSC will ultimately lead to the European Union.

January 27, 1951
The **U.S. Atomic Energy Commission** sets off an atomic explosion on an air force bombing and gunnery range northwest of Las Vegas, Nevada.

 [3]

February 1, 1951
The U.N. General Assembly adopts, 44 to 7, a U.S. resolution accusing Communist China of aggression in **Korea**.

February 8, 1951
Striking railroad workers return to work after the U.S. Army, acting on orders of President Harry Truman, threatens them with dismissal.

February 16, 1951
Joseph Stalin says that he does not believe world war is inevitable, but that warmongers could make it so; that the U.N. has doomed itself by condemning China's actions in Korea; and that the U.S.S.R. has extensively demobilized.

February 26, 1951
American novelist James Jones publishes **From Here to Eternity**, about the U.S. Army in Hawaii before the 1941 attack on Pearl Harbor.

 [4]

[3] The mushroom cloud forms over Nevada and watching troops.

[9] Iranian women, all in Western dress, march through Teheran in support of the moves to nationalize the oil industry in Iran.

[4] James Jones with his mentor and lover, Lowney Handy. They set up a writers' colony in Marshall, Illinois, funded by Jones's royalties from his novel, and the colony lasts for a few years.

[8] Eva "Evita" Peron campaigns for her husband, Juan Peron, to be reelected as president of Argentina. She is champion of the "descamisados," the shirtless ones—that is, Argentina's poor. She dies the following year.

June 20, 1951
Twenty-one **U.S. Communist Party leaders** are indicted in New York City on charges of conspiring to teach and advocate the overthrow of the U.S. government by force.

 [7]

July 14, 1951
President Harry S. Truman proclaims Kansas and Missouri a disaster area as result of **floods**.

 [8]

August, 1951
President Juan Peron of Argentina stands for re-election and his wife is one of his most powerful electoral weapons, helping him to win.

 [9]

August 22, 1951
Negotiations on the **oil nationalization** issue between the Iranian government, under prime minister Mohammad Mossadegh, and the British mission ends in disagreement.

September 1, 1951
Australia, New Zealand, and the United States sign the **ANZUS Pact**.

September 8, 1951
Japan recognizes the independence of Korea and renounces all rights to Taiwan, the Pescadores, the Kurils, and southern Sakhalin, as well as the Pacific islands earlier mandated to it by the League of Nations.

1951-1952

September 12, 1951
The **Vatican** publishes an encyclical of Pope Pius XII calling upon all Christians to "unite and fight under a single banner" against communism.

October 24, 1951
President Harry S. Truman issues a proclamation formally ending a state of war with Germany pursuant to a congressional resolution to that effect.

December 24, 1951
Independence of new kingdom of **Libya** in northern Africa is proclaimed at Bengasi by King Idris I.

1952
African American novelist Ralph Ellison writes his groundbreaking novel **Invisible Man**.

 [1]

1952
Albert Schweitzer, Alsatian German theologian, philosopher, organist, and mission doctor in Africa, is awarded the 1952 Nobel Peace Prize for his works in behalf of "the Brotherhood of Nations."

 [2]

1952
A mountain of solid **iron ore** is found in the Hammersley Range, Australia. It remains a secret for ten years until a change in the law allows its finder to exploit it.

[1] Ralph Ellison. His novel sees life through the eyes of an anonymous black man in New York.

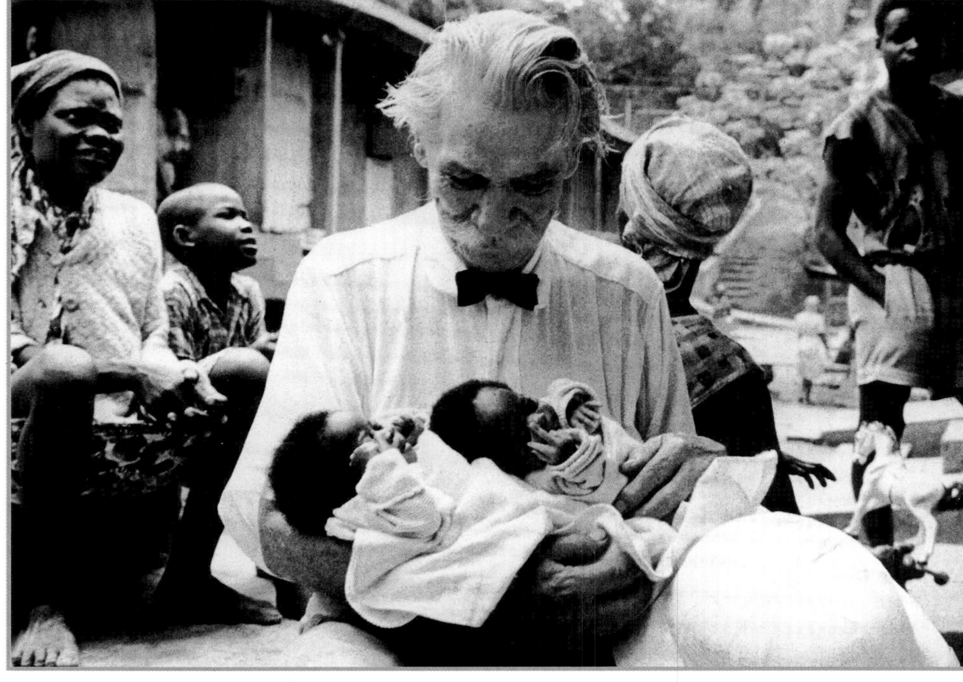

[2] Albert Schweitzer with two babies at his hospital at Lambaréné in French Equatorial Africa.

[6] The Lever House: the first building in New York constructed using the glass-and-steel curtain wall technique.

[7] John Cage. This year he also composes his notorious 4' 33" (four minutes, thirty-three seconds), not the sound of silence but the background noise the audience can hear during that period of time.

[10] Dylan Thomas: a glass seems never to have been far from his lips in his last years. He dies in 1953.

[8] Flannery O'Connor, a Southern Gothic writer with a sardonic sense of humor and a deep Catholic faith.

[6]
1952
Gordon Bunshaft, of Skidmore, Owings & Merrill, designs the **Lever House**, New York City. One of the first modern skyscrapers in New York, the tower of the Lever House seems to float above its base.

1952
British archaeologist Michael Ventris decyphers the **Linear B script**, as used by the Minoan civilization, c.1450 BC.

 [7]
1952
John Cage creates his first "taped" work, *Landscape No. 5*, for a dance by Jean Erdman. Cage becomes one of the most famous postwar American composers.

1952
John Hetrick devises a safety cushion for passenger cars. It becomes the prototype for the **automotive airbag**.

1952
Joseph Woodland develops the **bar code** as a means for entering data into a computer system. It will become a ubiquitous part of routine commercial transactions.

 [8]
1952
Quirky Southern writer **Flannery O'Connor** publishes her comic masterpiece, *Wise Blood*.

1952
An acute **smog** episode in London kills about 4,000 people and serves to mobilize popular and political efforts against urban air pollution.

 [3]

1952
At the Summer Olympics in Helsinki, Finland, **Emil Zátopek** of Czechoslovakia performs the superhuman feat of winning the 5,000- and 10,000-meter races and the marathon.

 [4]

1952
Boxer **Rocky Marciano** becomes heavyweight world champion, unseating Jersey Joe Walcott. Marciano is undefeated until his retirement in 1956; 43 of his 49 professional victories are knockouts.

1952
CERN, a physics research facility located near Geneva, Switzerland, is founded. It grows to become one of the largest and most productive basic research centers in the world.

1952
English playwright Samuel Beckett produces his postmodernist, experimental play **Waiting for Godot**, during which nothing happens.

 [5]

1952
French photographer **Henri Cartier-Bresson** publishes *The Decisive Moment*, embodying his theory that photography can capture the meaning beneath outward appearance in instants of extraordinary clarity.

[3] *Smog swirling round the statue of Eros at Piccadilly Circus in London.*

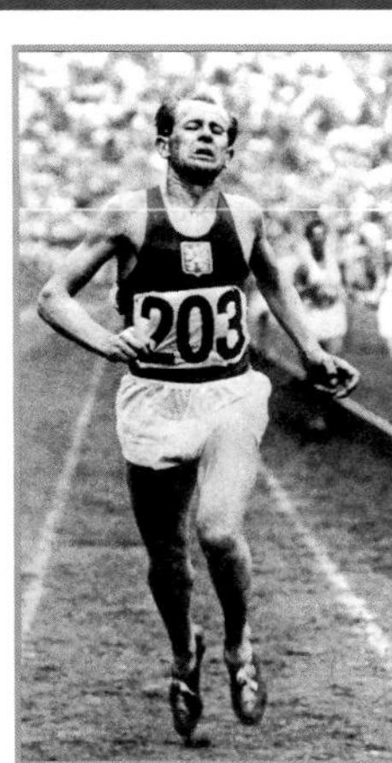

[4] *Emil Zátopek crosses the finishing line to win the marathon at Helsinki.*

ROCKY MARCIANO

Undefeated heavyweight champion of the world

Born Rocco Francis Marchegiano, and known as "the Brockton Blockbuster," Rocky Marciano became world heavyweight boxing champion on September 23, 1952, when he knocked out reigning title holder, Jersey Joe Walcott, in 13 rounds in Philadelphia. A still from their fight, with Walcott avoiding a left from Marciano, is shown above.

Marciano began to box while in the U.S. Army during World War II. He had his first professional fight on March 17, 1947. Knockouts of Rex Layne, Louis, Lee Savold, and Harry "Kid" Matthews earned him a chance to win the championship. Marciano, knocked down by Walcott in the first round, was behind on points when, in the 13th round, he knocked the champion unconscious with a single punch.

Marciano successfully defended the title six times until he retired on April 27, 1956. He was undefeated in 49 professional fights, scoring 43 knockouts. Among his victims were former heavyweight champions Joe Louis and Ezzard Charles.

[5] *The 1953 French production of* Waiting for Godot.

[9] *Eigil Nansen, grandson of the explorer, skis with the Olympic flame at the opening ceremony in Oslo.*

1952
Research by U.S. cardiologist **Paul M. Zoll** leads to the development of the cardiac defibrillator. Zoll's efforts are later concentrated on improving and miniaturizing cardiac pacemakers.

1952
The **Apgar Score System**, developed by American physician Virginia Apgar, is introduced. Based on a point system where a maximum score of 10 is best, it evaluates the condition of newborn babies.

 [9]

1952
The **Winter Olympic Games** take place in Oslo, Norway.

1952
U.S. clergyman Norman Vincent Peale publishes **The Power of Positive Thinking**. It becomes one of the best-selling religious books of its time.

 [10]

1952
Welsh poet **Dylan Thomas** publishes his *Collected Poems*.

c. 1952
Cattle raisers begin to routinely feed **antibiotics to livestock** as a preventive measure.

January 11, 1952
The U.N. General Assembly votes to set up the 12-nation **disarmament commission** consisting of Security Council members and Canada.

January 26, 1952
All of **Egypt** is placed under martial law after mobs wreck many British, U.S., and French business places in Cairo.

February 6, 1952
King George VI of the United Kingdom dies at Sandringham in Norfolk. His daughter, Princess Elizabeth, becomes queen as Elizabeth II.

 [1]

March 3, 1952
The Puerto Rican people overwhelmingly ratify a constitution giving them **self-government** under U.S. control.

April 2, 1952
General Dwight D. Eisenhower states in his first annual report as supreme commander of the Allied powers in Europe, that the **free world** is much better able to defend itself than a year before.

April 28, 1952
The Allied occupation of **Japan** comes to an end, after seven years of rapid social and economic change following the country's surrender in World War II.

 [2]

[1] Queen Elizabeth, now the Queen Mother, is followed by the new Queen Elizabeth II and then Princess Margaret, all in deep mourning as they accompany the coffin of the dead king from Sandringham House to London.

[2] Japanese students urge American forces on their way at a May Day rally.

[5] A rancher demonstrates the size of the cracks in the dried mud of what was once a water hole.

[6] Ernest Hemingway looking not unlike the hero of his Pulitzer Prize–winning novella.

[7] Mau Mau suspects from the Kikuyu tribe, detained in Nairobi.

 [5]

August 7, 1952
Tennessee and Kentucky are designated **drought** disaster areas by President Harry S. Truman.

September 6, 1952
The first Canadian television broadcast is made from Montreal by the **Canadian Broadcasting Corporation** (CBC).

 [6]

September 8, 1952
Ernest Hemingway's *The Old Man and the Sea* is published, a short heroic novel about an old Cuban fisherman who, after an extended struggle, hooks and captures a giant marlin only to have it eaten by voracious sharks during the long voyage home.

October 3, 1952
Britain's first atomic weapon is successfully exploded in the Monte Bello Islands about 50 miles northwest of Australia.

October 22, 1952
Iran formally breaks off diplomatic relations with the United Kingdom.

 [7]

October 30, 1952
More than 500 persons are reported arrested in **Kenya**, as British authorities continue their efforts to curb terrorism by the militant nationalist Mau Mau.

May 1, 1952
The U.S. State Department announces a **ban on travel** by U.S. citizens in the U.S.S.R. and Soviet-controlled countries without specific permission of the U.S. government.

May 28, 1952
French police arrest more than 600 persons, including communist leader **Jacques Duclos**, during communist demonstrations against General Matthew Ridgway's arrival in Paris.

June 1, 1952
Western Berlin residents are barred by Soviet authorities from the Soviet zone of Germany.

June 14, 1952
The keel of the **U.S.S. Nautilus**, the world's first atomic-powered submarine, is laid at Groton, Connecticut, by President Harry S.Truman.

 [3]

July 23, 1952
The Free Officers, a nationalistic military group led by Colonel **Gamal Abdel Nasser**, engineers a coup that overthrows King Farouk I of Egypt, ending the monarchy and bringing Nasser to power.

 [4]

August 5, 1952
Fourteen **California Communist Party** leaders are found guilty by a federal jury of conspiring to teach and advocate the overthrow of the U.S. government by force and violence.

[3] The uncluttered and apparently slim conning tower of the Nautilus.

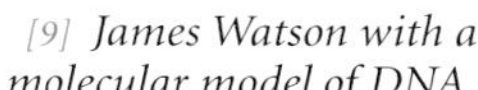

[9] James Watson with a molecular model of DNA.

[8] Dwight D. Eisenhower cheers for victory.

[4] The Free Officers meet in Cairo. Mohammed Naguib is in the chair, Gamal Nasser sits to his right, and Anwar Sadat is two beyond him.

HYDROGEN BOMB

The United States explodes a thermonuclear device hundreds of times more powerful than the atomic bomb.

In September 1951, Los Alamos Scientific Laboratory proposed a test of a new type of bomb based on the Teller–Ulam concept (a two-stage radiation implosion developed by Edward Teller and Stanislaw M. Ulam) for November 1952. Engineering of the device, nicknamed Mike, began in October 1951, but unforeseen difficulties required a major redesign of the experiment in March 1952. The Mike device weighed 82 tons, owing in part to cryogenic (low-temperature) refrigeration equipment necessary to keep the deuterium in liquid form.

This hydrogen bomb was successfully detonated during Operation Ivy at Enewetak atoll in the Marshall Islands in the western Pacific Ocean on November 1, 1952. The explosion produced a great mushroom cloud (above). The bomb yielded an explosion equivalent to 10 million tons (10 megatons) of TNT. Teller subsequently became known in the United States as "the father of the H-bomb."

The event marked the beginning of a new phase in the international arms race. The U.S.S.R. first tested a hydrogen bomb on August 12, 1953, followed by the United Kingdom (May 1957), China (1967), and France (1968). Further proliferation followed, and by the late 1980s there were 40,000 thermonuclear devices stored in the arsenals of the world's nuclear powers.

November 1, 1952
On an atoll of the Marshall Islands, Edward Teller and other American scientists test the first **thermonuclear hydrogen bomb**, its power resulting from an uncontrolled, self-sustaining nuclear chain reaction.

 [8]

November 4, 1952
With the election of **Dwight D. Eisenhower**, Republicans also win control of both houses of Congress by a narrow margin.

December 12, 1952
One hundred sixty-seven Arabs are sentenced to prison by a Moroccan court in **Casablanca** for demonstrating against the French government.

 [9]

1953
American geneticist James D. Watson and British scientist Francis Crick discover that the structure of **DNA** is a double helix.

1953
American science-fiction writer Ray Bradbury completes his most famous novel, **Fahrenheit 451**.

1953
American surgeon John H. Gibbon, Jr., performs the first open-heart surgery with the aid of a **heart-lung machine**.

1953-1954

1953
American writer **Saul Bellow** publishes his acclaimed third novel, *The Adventures of Augie March.* He will win the Nobel Prize for Literature in 1976.

 [1]

1953
Dag Hammarskjöld of Sweden becomes the secretary general of the United Nations. He will serve until he is killed in a plane crash in September 1961.

January 1, 1953
American country and western musician **Hank Williams** dies. Among his best-selling recordings were "Cold, Cold Heart," "Your Cheatin' Heart," and "Hey, Good Lookin'."

 [2]

January 7, 1953
President Harry S. Truman, in his annual State of the Union message to Congress, says that the U.S. had entered a **new age of atomic power** and warned Soviet premier Joseph Stalin that a war provoked by the U.S.S.R. would mean its ruin.

January 20, 1953
Dwight D. Eisenhower of the Republican Party becomes the 34th president of the United States. He will serve until 1961. His vice president is Richard M. Nixon.

January 31–February 5, 1953
North Sea storms and tides flood lowlands of the Netherlands and Belgium and batters the coasts of Great Britain, France, and Germany; 1,794 people die in the Netherlands alone.

 [3]

[2] Hank Williams's death at 29 robs the 20th century of one of its most influential and popular composers and performers.

[9] A single Mormon family from Short Creek, Arizona.

[3] A street in Dortrecht, Holland, flooded by the great North Sea storm-tide combination.

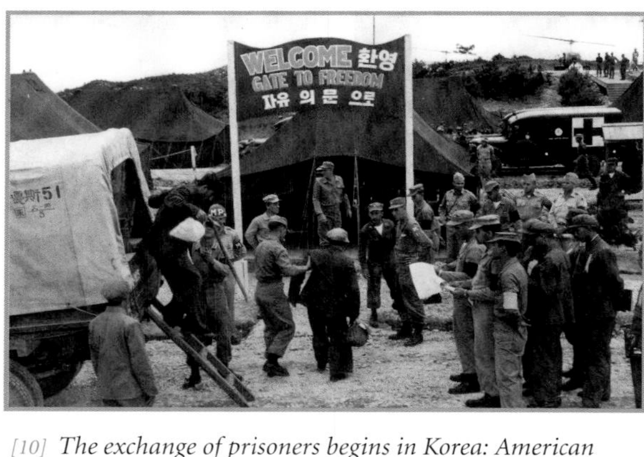

[10] The exchange of prisoners begins in Korea: American prisoners-of-war climb down from a truck and pass through the Welcome Gate at Panmunjom.

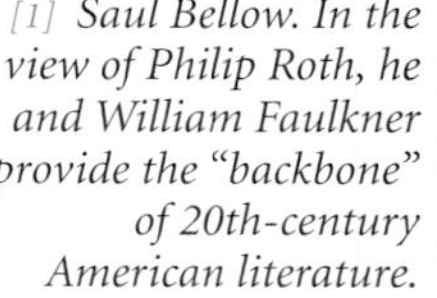

[1] Saul Bellow. In the view of Philip Roth, he and William Faulkner provide the "backbone" of 20th-century American literature.

[8] General Naguib receives the plaudits of the Egyptian people while, a pensive Nasser stands on his right. Naguib will soon be ousted by Nasser and spend 18 years under house arrest.

 [8]

June 18, 1953
The Egyptian council of the revolution proclaims **Egypt** a republic with Mohammed Naguib as the president and premier.

 [9]

July 26, 1953
Virtually the whole adult population of **Short Creek, Arizona**, is arrested in a mass raid aimed at wiping out what is said to be the last remaining center of organized polygamy in the U.S.

July 27, 1953
An armistice halts the Korean War, and the **38th parallel** becomes the boundary between North and South Korea.

July 31, 1953
The FCC reports that, for the first time, **television** has surpassed radio in its revenues.

 [10]

August 5, 1953
Exchange of the first prisoners-of-war begins at **Panmunjom** under Korean armistice terms.

August 8, 1953
Soviet premier G. M. Malenkov tells the Supreme Soviet that the U.S. does not have a monopoly on the **hydrogen bomb**; the U.S.S.R. has a hydrogen bomb as well.

March 5, 1953
Soviet premier **Joseph Stalin** dies in Moscow and is succeeded by Georgy Malenkov.
[4]

March 26, 1953
Mau Mau terrorists massacre about 150 loyal Kikuyu tribesman near Nairobi, Kenya.

May 18, 1953
American aviator **Jacqueline Cochran** becomes the first woman to break the sound barrier.

[5]

May 27, 1953
New Zealand mountaineer Edmund Hillary and his Sherpa partner, Tenzing Norgay, reach the summit of **Mount Everest**. They are the first humans to reach the summit and return.

[6]

June 2, 1953
The 27-year-old daughter of King George VI is crowned **Queen Elizabeth II** of the United Kingdom at Westminster Abbey, having inherited the throne upon her father's death in February 1952.

June 17, 1953
East German workers stage an uprising against their Communist government, only for it to be supressed by Soviet tanks.

[7]

QUEEN ELIZABETH II

Britain enters a new Elizabethan age.

After her coronation on June 2, 1953, the new monarch returned to Buckingham Palace, where she appeared on the balcony to acknowledge public acclaim. Among those with the queen in the photograph (left) are her husband, Prince Philip, the three-year-old Prince Charles, and Princess Anne, aged 18 months.

The coronation of Queen Elizabeth II gave TV in the U.K. its great lift-off: 20 million watched the event from their homes, and 250,000 television sets were produced by British manufacturers during the 1950s.

[6] Edmund Hillary and Tenzing Norgay on the way down after climbing Everest.

[7] The Columbus House in the Potzdamer Platz, East Berlin, burns during the East German workers' insurrection.

[4] Stalin's body lies in state. Soon it will join Lenin's in the Red Square mausoleum, there to be worshipped by the Communist faithful.

[5] Jacqueline Cochran held a female speed record before the war and during it she taught 1,200 women to fly. She will go on breaking records into the 1960s.

August 19, 1953
The **shah** regains power in Iran through a coup organized by the CIA, and the populist leader Mohammed Mossadegh is arrested.

August 26, 1953
French postal services, railways, and municipal services are reported to be operating normally following the termination of a three-week **strike**.

September 30, 1953
Earl Warren is appointed 14th chief justice of the U.S. Supreme Court by President Dwight D. Eisenhower. He will serve from 1953 to 1969.

December 8, 1953
President Dwight D. Eisenhower, in a speech to the **U.N. General Assembly**, calls upon the U.S.S.R. to join the U.S. in contributing part of its economic stockpile to an international pool available for peaceful uses.

1954
American chemist **Linus Pauling** wins the Nobel Prize for Chemistry for his application of quantum theory to molecular bonding. He will win a second Nobel (for Peace) in 1962.

1954
American poet **Wallace Stevens** publishes *The Collected Poems of Wallace Stevens* shortly before his death.

1954

1954
British painter **Francis Bacon** appropriates from Old Masters, adding a distinctively gruesome, distorting vision, in *Head with Sides of Beef.*

1954
Color television broadcasting is launched in the United States.

1954
England's **Roger Bannister** is the first person to run the mile in under four minutes.

[1]

1954
English novelist William Golding publishes his acclaimed **Lord of the Flies**. He will win the Nobel Prize for Literature in 1983.

1954
IBM introduces **FORTRAN**, the first higher-level programming language.

1954
J. R. R. Tolkien publishes the first section of his three-part epic fantasy novel **The Lord of the Rings**. On its publication in paperback in the United States in 1965, it will attain cult status on college campuses. It will sell more than 50 million copies by the year 2000.

 *[2]*

[3] Kingsley Amis. For his book, Britain's first campus novel, Amis draws on his time teaching at the University of Wales in Swansea.

[2] J. R. R. Tolkien in his study. He is a professor of Anglo-Saxon and then of English at Oxford University.

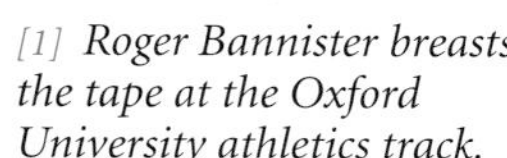

[1] Roger Bannister breasts the tape at the Oxford University athletics track.

[5] Marilyn Monroe and Joe DiMaggio wed: a celebrity pairing to top them all.

[4] A Comet airliner is examined to try and find out why the airliners are crashing.

1954
West Germany defeats Hungary in the men's **World Cup** soccer championship by a score of 3 to 2.

 *[4]*

1954
A series of crashes of British **Comet** jet airliners forces their withdrawal. It turns out there are structural weaknesses in the round windows, caused by the new phenomenon of metal fatigue.

 *[5]*

January 14, 1954
Baseball player **Joe DiMaggio** and actress Marilyn Monroe marry at City Hall in San Francisco.

January 15, 1954
British security forces in Kenya disclose the capture of Waruhiu Itote ("General China"), the second-ranking leader of the **Mau Mau** terrorist group.

January 16, 1954
René Coty is elected president of France.

February 23, 1954
Inoculation of school children with the **polio vaccine**, developed by Jonas E. Salk, begins in Pittsburgh, Pennsylvania.

1954
Kingsley Amis starts his long and distinguished literary career with the publication of one of the best-known works of the Angry Young Men, *Lucky Jim*.

 [3]

1954
Marshmallow Peeps, candies, in the shape of Easter chicks, are debuted by Just Born.

1954
Pianist George Wein organizes the annual **Newport (Rhode Island) Jazz Festival**, the first outdoor music festival devoted entirely to jazz; over the years the annual festival features "a virtual pantheon of jazz immortals."

1954
The **KGB** is established in the Soviet Union to serve as the "sword and shield of the Communist Party." It is both a foreign intelligence and domestic security agency.

1954
The **Soviet "Virgin Lands" program** begins in an effort to plow up 115 million acres of steppe in Russia and Kazakhstan; it constitutes the last major conversion of grassland to arable in world history.

1954
The term "**New Brutalism**" is applied to the more vigorous forms designed by Le Corbusier and other architects in the 1950s.

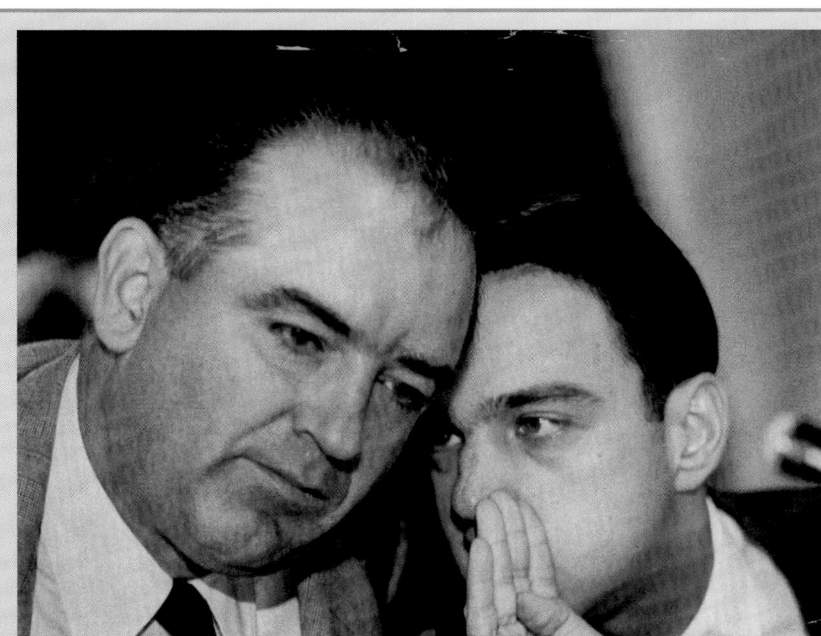

MCCARTHY HUNTS COMMUNISTS

U.S. senator leads sensational witch hunts against supposed "un-American activities"

Joseph McCarthy (in the left of the photograph, with attorney Roy M. Cohn) made headlines in February 1950, when he claimed that 205 communists had infiltrated the State Department. Although he was subsequently unable to produce the name of a single "card-carrying communist" in any government department, he gained popular support for his campaign of accusations by capitalizing on the fears of a nation weary of the Korean War and appalled by communist advances in eastern Europe and China.

McCarthy's increasingly irresponsible attacks came to include President Dwight D. Eisenhower. His influence waned in 1954 as a result of the nationally televised, 36-day hearing on his charges of subversion by U.S. Army officers and civilian officials. This detailed television exposure of his brutal and truculent interrogative tactics discredited him and helped to turn the tide of public opinion against him.

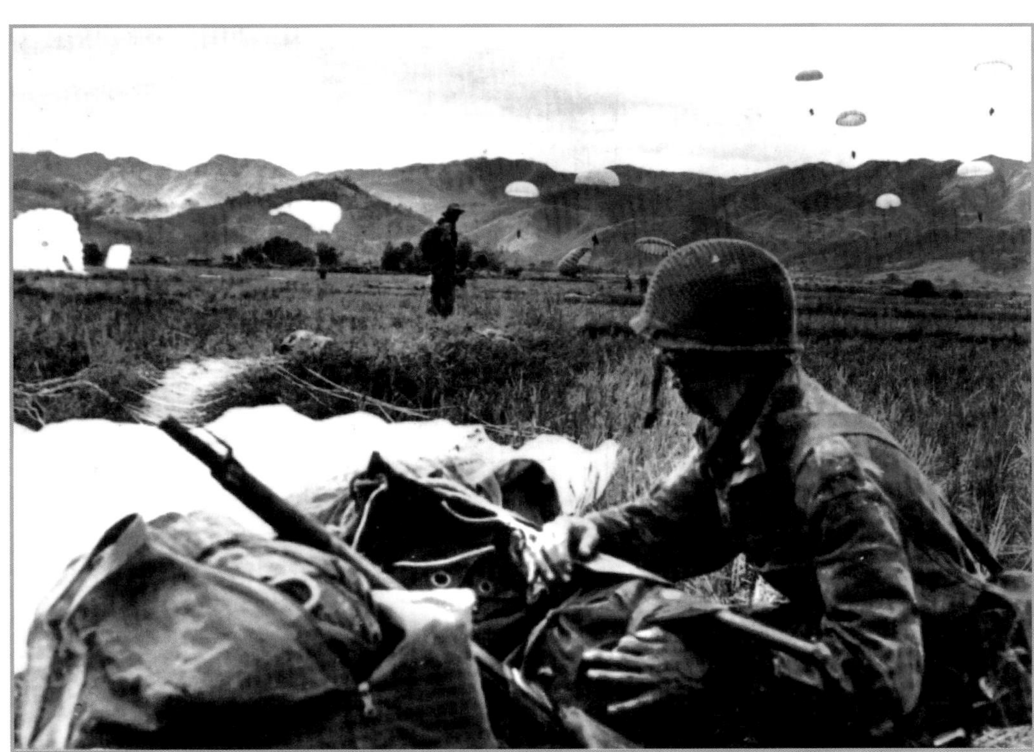

[6] *French paratroopers land at Dien Bien Phu. The hills from which the Viet Minh artillery will prevent their effective resupply by air can be seen in the background.*

[7] *Thurgood Marshall: lawyer and future Supreme Court justice. If any one event marks the start of the Civil Rights movement, it is* Brown v. Board of Education.

March 1, 1954
Five members of the U.S. House of Representatives are shot on the house floor by assailants identified as **Puerto Rican nationalists**.

March 26, 1954
The Soviet government announces that the **German Democratic Republic** has become a sovereign state but adds that Soviet troops will remain there temporarily.

April 1, 1954
The **United States Air Force Academy** is created by an act of Congress and later built in Colorado Springs, Colorado.

April 22, 1954
The U.S. Senate permanent investigations subcommittee begins public hearings on the dispute between its chairman, **Senator Joseph R. McCarthy** and the U.S. Army.

 [6]

May 7, 1954
Viet Minh general Vo Nguyen Giap takes the French by surprise at the **Battle of Dien Bien Phu**, surrounding their base with 40,000 men and employing heavy artillery to capture it during the First Indochina War.

 [7]

May 17, 1954
Thurgood Marshall scores a landmark victory as the U.S. Supreme Court unanimously rules in **Brown v. Board of Education** of Topeka that racial segregation in public schools is unconstitutional.

1954-1955

July 3, 1954
All **food rationing** in Britain ends at midnight with the relinquishment by the food ministry's control over meat and bacon.

 [1]

July 13, 1954
Mexican painter **Frida Kahlo** dies. Her intense, brilliantly colored self-portraits will make her as famous as her husband, muralist Diego Rivera.

 [2]

July 21, 1954
The Geneva Accords effectively divide **Vietnam** at the 17th parallel.

July 22, 1954
North Vietnam's de facto Communist government announces the composition of its cabinet, headed by Ho Chi Minh as premier.

August 31, 1954
The conduct of Senator Joseph R. McCarthy is denounced by Democrats and mildly criticized by Republicans in a report issued by the subcommittee headed by **Senator Karl E. Mundt**.

 [3]

September 27, 1954
The landmark late-evening talk show and variety program **The Tonight Show** premiers (as *Tonight!*), with Steve Allen as host.

 [4]

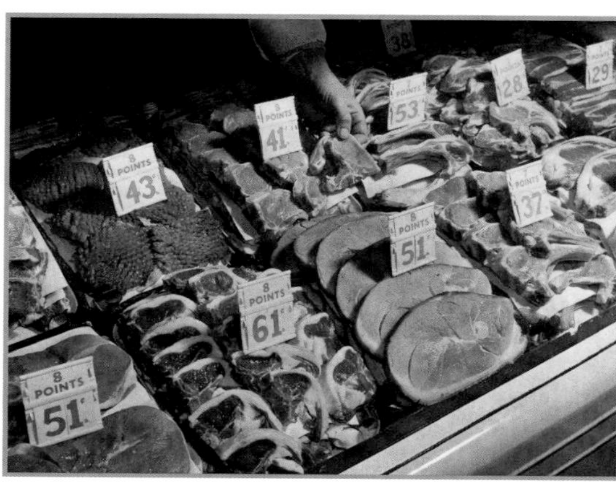

[1] *A British butcher's display in the days of rationing: meat marked with the number of ration coupons (points) per pound weight that would have to be surrendered when buying it, and the "ceiling" price.*

[3] *Senator Joe McCarthy in his famous television confrontation with Ed Murrow in April. Rather than rebut his charges of lying and inaccuracy, McCarthy rambles, calling Murrow, "the cleverest of the jackal pack."*

[4] *Steve Allen, host of the* Tonight Show *(right), wearing a Davy Crockett hat along with singers Eydie Gormé and her husband, Steve Lawrence (standing). The Davy Crockett craze is sweeping America on the back of the Walt Disney film about him.*

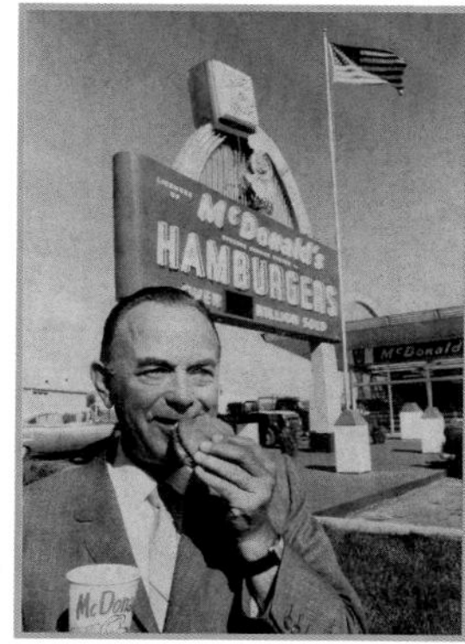

[9] *Ray Kroc eats one of his own McDonald's hamburgers, one of the first billion.*

[7] *Marion Anderson in rehearsal at the Metropolitan Opera.*

[8] The Family of Man *exhibition at MOMA.*

[7]
1955
Marian Anderson is the first African American to perform as a member of the Metropolitan Opera in New York City. Before she begins, as Ulrica in Verdi's *Un ballo in maschera*, she is given a standing ovation.

[8]
1955
Photographer **Edward Steichen** curates the exhibition *The Family of Man* at the Museum of Modern Art in New York City, comprising 503 images from around the world based on the concept of human solidarity.

1955
Quiz shows become popular on American television, drawing large audiences and the backing of parents and educators, who applaud the emphasis on intellectual prowess.

[9]
1955
Ray Kroc opens his first **McDonald's** fast food restaurant, in Des Plaines, Illinois. By the end of 1963, the company will have sold more than one billion hamburgers, an achievement proudly advertised.

1955
RCA engineers invent the first electronic synthesizer. Improved by **Robert Moog** and others in the 1960s and 1970s, electronic instruments will revolutionize modern composition and performance.

[10]
1955
Sir Anthony Eden succeeds Winston Churchill as Conservative prime minister of the United Kingdom. A year later he helps direct an Anglo-French attack on Egypt over the rights to the Suez Canal.

November 3, 1954
Stocks listed on the **New York Stock Exchange** make their largest gains since September 5, 1939.

December 2, 1954
The U.S. Senate votes to censure **Senator Joseph R. McCarthy** for his irresponsible conduct in the investigation of communism in the United States.

1955
The first **wireless remote control** for television is produced. Designed by Robert Adler, it sends signals to the TV via high-frequency sound. The technology will be replaced by infrared technology in the 1980s.

1955
Bell Laboratories introduces the first **transistor computer**.

1955
Disneyland theme park opens in Anaheim, California. It soon becomes a destination for tourists from around the world, helping consolidate Walt Disney's central place in American popular culture.

 *[5]*

1955
Johnny Cash signs with Sun Records. Such songs as "Cry, Cry, Cry," "Hey, Porter," "Folsom Prison Blues," and "I Walk the Line" bring him considerable attention, and by 1957 Cash is the top recording artist in the U.S. country and western field.

 *[6]*

[2] Frida Kahlo. In spite of the apparent self-obsession in her art, it will be several decades before her current fame and reputation begin to build up, thanks to biographies, films, and exhibitions.

[5] The giant teacup ride at Disneyland, California.

[11] George Meany and Walter Reuther clasp hands at the AFL-CIO merger.

[10] At last! Churchill hands over the prime ministership to Anthony Eden, his heir apparent whom he has kept waiting for several years.

[6] Johnny Cash in concert.

[11]
1955
The **AFL-CIO** is formed through the merger of the American Federation of Labor and the Congress of Industrial Organizations. At the time of the merger, the new labor entity includes about one-third of all nonagricultural workers.

1955
The lesbian and women's organization the **Daughters of Bilitis** (named after the Sapphic love poems of Pierre Louÿs, *Chansons de Bilitis*) is founded by Phyllis Lyon and Del Martin in San Francisco.

1955
The Liberal Democratic Party is founded in **Japan**. Except for a brief interlude in the early 1990s, the party will govern for the rest of the century and into the 21st.

1955
The **Mickey Mouse Club** is one of the most popular television shows for children in the U.S., and the signature black cap with mouse ears one of the most widely distributed items in merchandising history.

1955
The **Salk vaccine** for infantile paralysis (poliomyelitis) is made available commercially. It and the Sabin vaccine virtually eliminate what had been one of the most feared childhood diseases.

1955
The world's total **motor vehicle** count surpasses 100 million.

1955

January 1, 1955
José Roman Guizado takes over as president of Panama after the assassination of José Antonio Remón. Guizado will, in turn, be assassinated before the year is out.

 [1]

January 1, 1955
The U.S. Foreign Operations Administration begins supplying direct financial aid to the states of South Vietnam, Cambodia, and Laos in **Indochina**.

 [2]

January 3, 1955
The U.S. State Department declares 27 percent of the U.S. off limits to **Soviet citizens**.

January 5, 1955
The International Bank for Reconstruction and Development announces the explusion of **Czechoslovakia**, its only Eastern European member.

January 8, 1955
The New York state mental-hygiene department reports that **mental patients** have shown improvement after being treated with two new drugs, Thorazine and Reserpin.

January 9, 1955
The U.S. Atomic Energy Commission announces plans to help private industry develop and operate experimental **atomic power plants**.

[1] Panamanian politics: President Guizado (third from the right) with members of his cabinet.

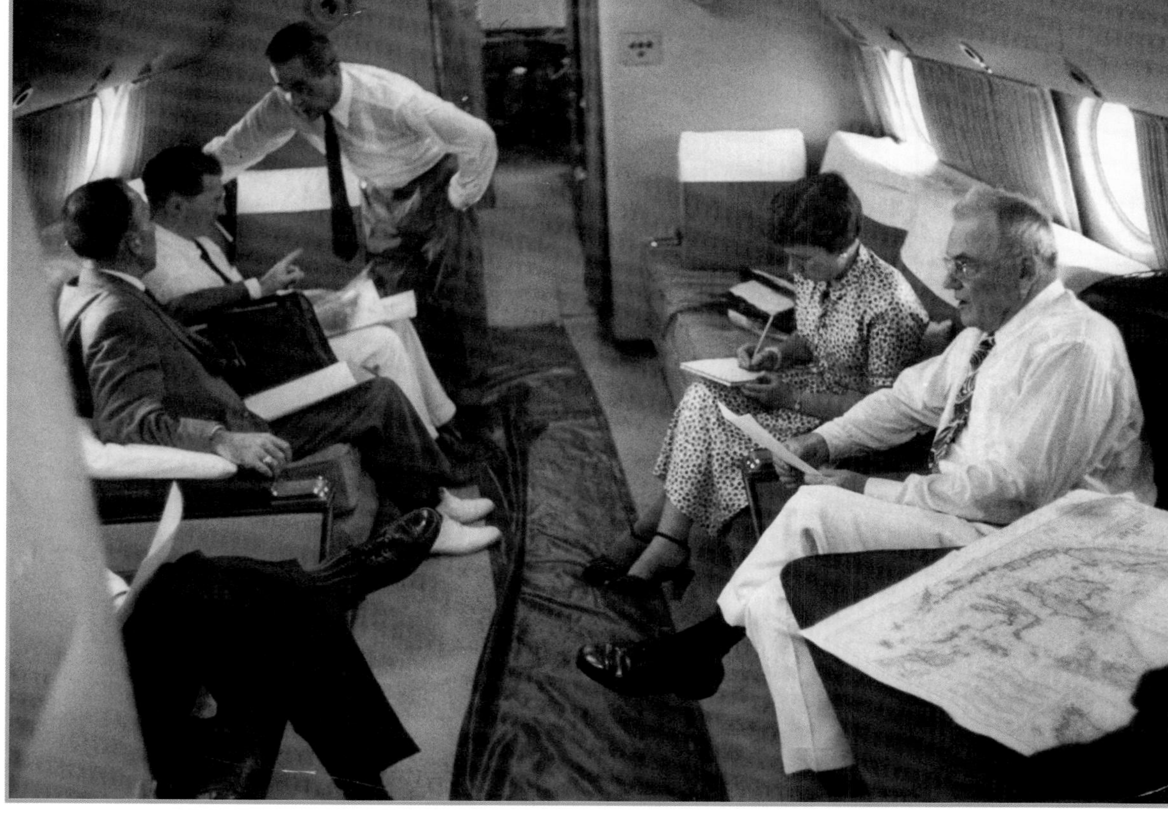

[2] Secretary of State John Foster Dulles and his aides fly to a South East Asia Treaty Organization (SEATO) meeting.

[3] Refugees from the Tachen Islands are covered in DDT powder as a health precaution before landing in Taiwan.

[5] Stirling Moss, the outline of his goggles clearly visible on his dust-covered face, is elated by victory and by the amphetamines he has legally been taking to keep alert during the Mille Miglia race.

February 17, 1955
British minister of defense **Harold Macmillan** announces plans to develop and produce hydrogen bombs.

March 2, 1955
The U.S. Post Office begins withholding delivery to private U.S. subscribers of *Pravda* and *Izvestia*, the leading **Soviet newspapers**.

 [4]

March 30, 1955
The motion picture **On the Waterfront** receives the Oscar as the best picture of 1954; awards for best starring performances go to Marlon Brando and to Grace Kelly for her part in *Rear Window* by Alfred Hitchcock.

April 5, 1955
An attempt to overthrow the Imam Ahmad, the ruler of the Arabian kingdom of **Yemen**, is reported to have failed.

April 30, 1955
The University of California announces the discovery of a new chemical element, number 101, named **mendelevium**.

 [5]

May 1955
British motor-racing driver Stirling Moss becomes world famous with his win in the 1,597-kilometer open-road **Mille Miglia** race in Italy.

January 10, 1955
The Chinese national (Taiwanese) defense ministry states that Communist Chinese planes have carried out a day-long raid on the nationalist-held **Tachen Islands**, 200 miles north of Taiwan.
 [3]

January 19, 1955
U.S. president Dwight D. Eisenhower holds the first-ever **televised presidential press conference**.

January 20, 1955
A state of siege is declared throughout **Guatemala** after an unsuccessful uprising against the government.

January 25, 1955
The **Soviet government** formally terminates the state of war between the U.S.S.R. and Germany that has existed since World War II.

February 15, 1955
The **U.S. Atomic Energy Commission** reveals that the hydrogen bomb tested by the U.S. in the Pacific in 1954 has polluted an area of 7,000 square miles with radioactive materials.

February 16, 1955
General Electric Company discloses that its scientists have created **artificial diamonds** of industrial quality.

[4] *Marlon Brando and Eva Marie Saint in Elia Kazan's* On the Waterfront.

[6] *This quintet beat the rail strike by bringing back into use an 1897 Dunlop quintuplet racing bicycle.*

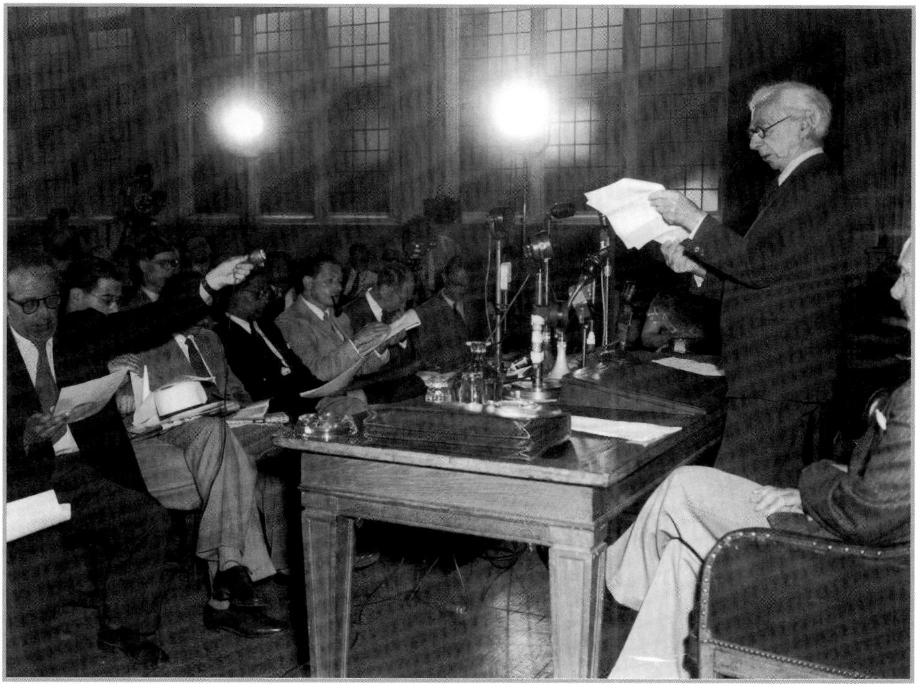

[7] *Bertrand Russell at a press conference he has called to warn of the perils of nuclear war.*

May 3, 1955
Venezuela announces its decision to withdraw from the International Labour Organization.

May 14, 1955
The **Warsaw Pact** is created by the Soviet Union and originally includes Albania, Bulgaria, Czechoslovakia, East Germany, Hungary, Poland, and Romania. Soviet military units will be stationed in these countries.

 [6]
May 31, 1955
A **state of emergency** proclaimed in the United Kingdom because of a nationwide railway strike.

 [7]
July 9, 1955
A declaration is signed by nine distinguished scientists, including Bertrand Russell and Albert Einstein, that calls upon mankind to **renounce war**.

August 8, 1955
An international conference on the **peaceful uses of atomic energy** opens at Geneva, Switzerland, with representatives of 72 nations, including the U.S.S.R., in attendance.

August 12, 1955
German novelist and Nobel Prize winner **Thomas Mann** dies near Zürich, Switzerland.

1955-1956

August 18, 1955
The **Organization of Central American States** opens its first conference in Antigua, Guatemala.

August 23, 1955
A **British twin jet Canberra bomber** flies from London to New York and back in the record time of 14 hours, 21 minutes, 45.4 seconds.

August 27, 1955
Australia's tennis team regains the **Davis Cup** from the U.S. by winning the first three out of five matches.

September 4, 1955
The U.N. announces that both Egypt and Israel have given unconditional agreement to an urgent appeal for enforcement of a general cease-fire in the **Gaza** area.

September 16, 1955
All of **Argentina** is placed under martial law as rebel forces claim control of southern Argentina and Cordoba province.

September 19, 1955
A new **Lebanese government** is formed by Sayed Rashid Karameh to replace that of Sami Solh.

[2] James Dean and a fast car, perhaps the Porsche in which he dies.

[5] Nashua with his trainer, Jim Fitzsimmons.

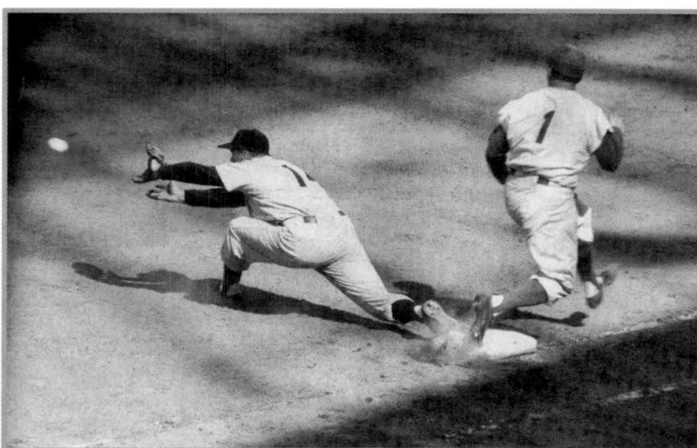

[3] Pee Wee Reese of the Brooklyn Dodgers beats the throw to first baseman Bill "Moose" Skowron of the New York Yankees.

[6] A beardless Allen Ginsberg (center) on a TV show with Norman Mailer (left) and British author Ashley Montagu.

[4] Rosa Parks (center), her victory won, rides in a newly integrated Alabama bus.

[1] Juan Perón speaks from a balcony shortly before his overthrow.

October 26, 1955
A constitutional law of perpetual neutrality in **Austria** is promulgated.

 [4]

December 1, 1955
In Montgomery, Alabama, **Rosa Parks**, refuses to surrender her bus seat to a white passenger and is arrested for violating the city's segregation law. The incident sparks a boycott that eventually leads to the buses being desegregated.

 [5]

December 15, 1955
Nashua, champion U.S. race horse of 1955, is sold for $1,251,200 to a syndicate of bidders. He is the first million-dollar racehorse.

1956
American **Mark Rothko** paints *Orange and Yellow*. In this example of Color Field Painting, rectangles of color with subtle variations and blurred edges are juxtaposed, creating emotional resonance.

1956
American poet **John Berryman** publishes his most successful short poem, *Homage to Mistress Bradstreet*.

 [6]

1956
Beat poet Allen Ginsberg publishes **Howl**, his denunciation of American society and answer to Walt Whitman's *Leaves of Grass*.

September 19, 1955
President Juan Perón of Argentina is overthrown and flees to Paraguay after an army-navy revolt led by democratically inspired officers.
 [1]

September 22, 1955
Oil is discovered for the first time in Israel, near Huleikat, in the Negev region.

September 22, 1955
The United Kingdom's first commercial television program financed by **advertising** is telecast from London.

September 30, 1955
American motion-picture actor **James Dean**, a symbol of the confused, restless, and idealistic youth of the 1950s, dies in an automobile crash in Paso Robles, California.
 [2]

October 4, 1955
The **Brooklyn Dodgers** win their first World Series, defeating the New York Yankees four games to three.
 [3]

October 18, 1955
The discovery of a **new atomic particle**—the anti-proton—is announced at the University of California.

[7] Ella Fitzgerald sings at Mr. Kelly's nightclub.

[8] The TWA Terminal at Idlewyld Airport (now John F. Kennedy International Airport).

HEARTBREAK HOTEL

Elvis Presley tops the U.S. charts for the first time.

After recording five singles on the Sun Records label, Elvis Presley—a blues-influenced pop singer with a high tenor voice—turned over his management to "Colonel" Tom Parker, a country-music hustler who had made stars of Eddy Arnold and Hank Snow. Parker arranged for Presley's song catalog and recording contract to be sold to major New York City–based enterprises, Hill and Range and RCA Victor, respectively. Sun received a total of $35,000; Elvis got $5,000.

Presley (left) began recording at RCA's studios in Nashville, Tennessee, with his original band—guitarist Scotty Moore, bassist Bill Black, and drummer D. J. Fontana—together with several backing musicians. With his flamboyant image, he created a national sensation. "Heartbreak Hotel," recorded in January 1956, spent eight weeks at number 1 on the *Billboard* Hot 100. He had further chart toppers that year with "Don't Be Cruel" and "Love Me Tender." The King had taken over the country.

1956
A collage by British artist **Richard Hamilton**, drawing on popular images and postwar commercialism, marks the beginning of the pop art movement.

1956
Egyptian writer **Naguib Mahfouz** completes his trilogy of historical novels, *The Cairo Trilogy*. In 1988 he will become the first Arabic writer to win the Nobel Prize for Literature.

[7]
1956
Ella Fitzgerald begins to record a 19-volume series of "songbooks," nearly 250 outstanding songs by Richard Rodgers, Cole Porter, George Gershwin, Duke Ellington, Jerome Kern, Irving Berlin, and Johnny Mercer.

1956
Elvis Presley releases "**Heartbreak Hotel**" for RCA. Presley helps popularize rock and roll among white audiences and will be a permanent fixture of American pop culture even after his death in 1977.

[8]
1956
Finnish-born American architect Eero Saarinen begins work on the **Trans World Airlines Terminal**, New York City. The sweeping concrete shape of the terminal is reminiscent of a giant bird.

1956
In Britain the **Clean Air Act**, a response to the London smog of 1952, regulates coal smoke. Oil and gas soon replace coal as the domestic fuel of choice, improving British urban air quality.

1956

1956
Calder Hall, England, the world's first commercial nuclear power plant opens. Optimists imagine electric power will soon be "too cheap to meter."

 [1]

1956
Indian lawyer and government official **Bhimrao Ramji Ambedkar** leads 200,000 fellow "untouchable" Hindus into conversion to Buddhism to escape oppression of the Hindu caste system.

 [2]

1956
Mies van der Rohe begins work on the **Seagram Building**, New York City. The ultimate modernist skyscraper, it features a restrained but sophisticated use of materials.

 [3]

1956
Noah W. and Joseph S. McVicker of Cincinnatti, Ohio, begin selling **Play-Doh**, a pliable, moldable plastic modeling compound.

1956
The **Hundred Flowers Campaign** begins in China, allowing broader freedom of criticism and expression. Its name derives from a historical Chinese saying, "Let a hundred flowers bloom, and a hundred schools of thought contend."

1956
The **Summer Olympic Games** take place in Melbourne, Australia.

 [4]

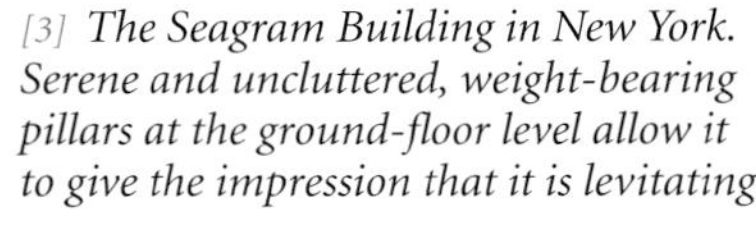

[3] The Seagram Building in New York. Serene and uncluttered, weight-bearing pillars at the ground-floor level allow it to give the impression that it is levitating.

[1] Calder Hall at Windscale, or Sellafield, as it is renamed in 1985, in Cumbria. It will close down in 2003. Until 1964 it is mostly used to produce weapons-grade plutonium.

[4] Soviet gymnast Larissa Latynina on the beam at the Melbourne Olympics. She will win four golds there and three in Rome in 1960.

[7] Martin Luther King, Jr., beside a bus at the end of the Montgomery, Alabama, bus boycott sparked by the action of Rosa Parks.

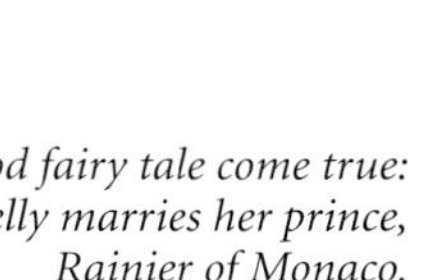

[8] Hollywood fairy tale come true: star Grace Kelly marries her prince, Rainier of Monaco.

March 2, 1956
Morocco proclaims its independence from France, with the sultan Muhammad V forming its first government.

March 21, 1956
Marty receives the Academy of Motion Picture Arts and Sciences award as the best picture of 1955; awards for best actor and best actress go to Ernest Borgnine and Anna Magnani, respectively.

 [7]

March 22, 1956
Martin Luther King, Jr., is convicted in a state court of illegally conspiring to boycott segregated buses in Montgomery, Alabama.

March 23, 1956
Pakistan formally becomes a republic within the British Commonwealth of Nations.

April 14, 1956
An electronic device for recording TV programs on **magnetic tape** for immediate or delayed playback is demonstrated in Chicago.

April 16, 1956
Austria is admitted to membership in the Council of Europe at a meeting of its council of ministers.

1956
The U.S. begins construction of its **interstate highway system**, ending the ascendancy of railroads and reorganizing American landscapes. Costing billions of dollars, it is one of history's largest public works.

1956
John Osborne's play attacking conformity and voicing frustration, **Look Back in Anger**, has its premiere in London, and the literary phenomenon of "the Angry Young Man" is born.

[5]

January 1, 1956
Sudan becomes an independent republic.

January 24, 1956
The governors of Georgia, Mississippi, South Carolina, and Virginia agree to stand together in opposing the U.S. Supreme Court's ruling that voids **racial segregation in public schools**.

 [6]

February 25, 1956
The Twentieth Congress of the Communist Party of the Soviet Union comes to a close after First Secretary **Nikita S. Khrushchev** delivers a secret speech denouncing the late Soviet leader Joseph Stalin.

February 29, 1956
Somalia, a U.N. trust territory (formerly Italian Somaliland), holds its first national elections.

[2] Harijans (untouchables) protest outside a Jain temple in Delhi after they have been refused admission on Gandhi's birthday—he who championed their right to be treated like any other Indians.

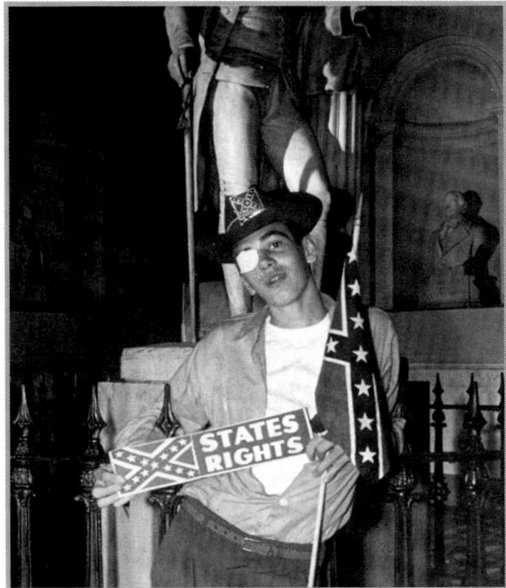

[6] A young Southerner makes clear his allegiance with Confederate flags and the old slogan of states' rights. He has lost an eye earlier, protesting against integration in public schools.

[5] Playwright John Osborne (right) with actor Kenneth Haigh, playing Jimmy Porter in Osborne's play Look Back in Anger, *premiered at the Royal Court Theatre in Sloane Square, London (behind).*

[9] A procession of saffron-robed Buddhist monks files past the Shiva Dagon Pagoda in Burma.

April 17, 1956
The **Cominform**, the international Communist Information Bureau founded in 1947, is disbanded as part of a Soviet program of reconciliation with Yugoslavia.

 [8]

April 19, 1956
American actress Grace Kelly marries Prince Rainier of Monaco, becoming **Princess Grace**.

May 7, 1956
Columbia University announces the 1955 **Pulitzer Prizes**, including one for MacKinlay Kantor for his novel *Andersonville* and one to Frances Goodrich and Albert Hackett for their play *The Diary of Anne Frank*.

May 14, 1956
Pope Pius XII approves using corneas taken from cadavers to restore the sight of blind people.

May 19, 1956
Pope Pius XII condemns **artificial insemination** as immoral and illicit.

 [9]

May 24, 1956
The 2,500th anniversary of **Buddhism** is celebrated in ceremonies throughout India.

1956-1957

June 13, 1956
Britain's 74-year occupation of the **Suez Canal** ends as the last British troops sail for Cyprus from Port Said.

 [1]

July 20, 1956
The U.N. Security Council votes unanimously to recommend the admission of **Morocco** to the U.N.

July 26, 1956
Egyptian president **Gamal Abdel Nasser** seizes control of the Suez Canal and nationalizes it.

 [2]

July 30, 1956
The phrase "**In God we trust**" legally becomes the national motto of the United States.

August 11, 1956
American painter **Jackson Pollock**, a leading exponent of abstract expressionism, whose great fame and serious recognition come from his radical poured, or "drip," technique, dies in an automobile accident.

August 31, 1956
The **Soviet track team** cancels a meet in London because of the arrest by British police of a Soviet female athlete on a shoplifting charge.

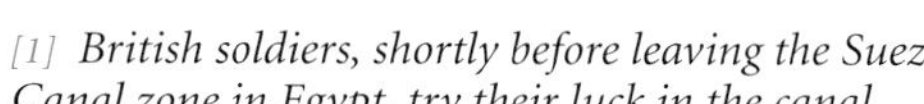

[1] British soldiers, shortly before leaving the Suez Canal zone in Egypt, try their luck in the canal.

[2] President Nasser

[5] The Suez crisis results in a petrol shortage in Britain. A female theatrical fire eater, described as a "stationary engine" to fit in with rationing regulations, collects her alloation here.

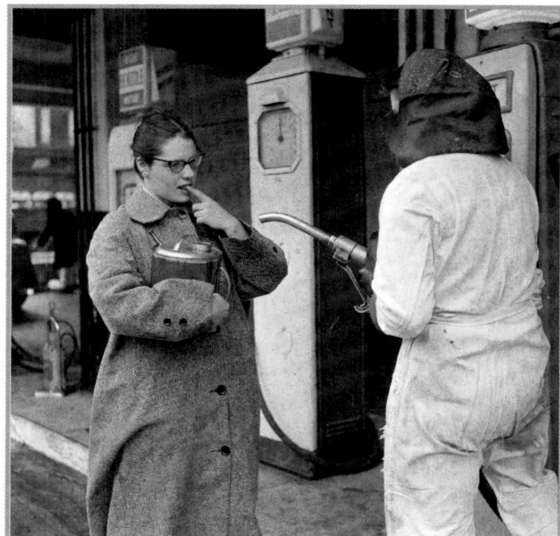

[3] One of the ships sunk at the entrance to the Suez Canal by the Egyptians to block the waterway.

[4] British troops on patrol in Port Said after the Anglo-French invasion in November.

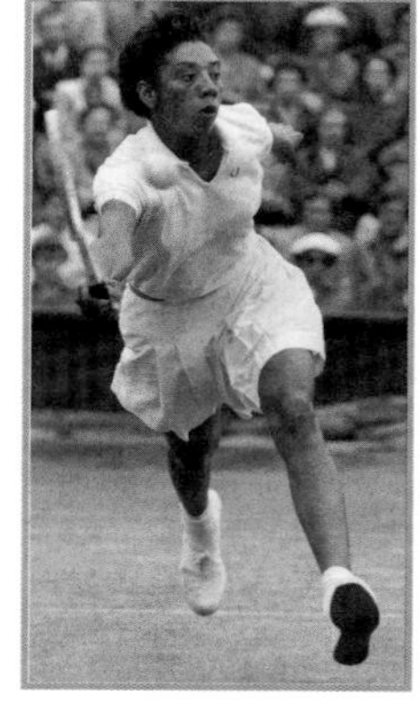

[6] Althea Gibson on her way to her Wimbledon singles title.

November 1, 1956
The 1956 **Nobel Prize** for **Physics** is awarded to William B. Shockley, Walter H. Brattain, and John Bardeen (U.S.); the chemistry prize is awarded to Sir Cyril Hinshelwood (U.K.) and Nikolay N. Semyonov (U.S.S.R.).

November 7, 1956
The **Nobel Peace Prize** committee announces that it has found no worthy recipients for the 1955 and 1956 prizes.

December 10, 1956
The **motion-picture industry** revises and relaxes its code of morals for the first time since its adoption in 1930.

 [5]

December 17, 1956
Gasoline rationing resumes in Britain for the first time since May 1950.

1957
A Soviet nuclear accident occurs at **Kyshtym** in the Ural Mountains. Seventy to eighty tons of radioactive material escape, and 11,000 people are evacuated. The incident remains an official secret until 1989.

 [6]

1957
Althea Gibson is the first African American player to win a Wimbledon singles tennis championship.

September 14, 1956
Egypt takes over full control of the Suez Canal, staffing operations with almost entirely Egyptian personnel after most foreign employees quit.

October 14, 1956
Pope Pius XII, in a radio address, deplores the employment of women in heavy industry.

October 18, 1956
The 1956 Nobel Prize for Medicine is awarded to Dickinson W. Richards and André F. Cournand of Columbia University and Werner Forssmann (West Germany) for their work in **cardiology**.

October 23, 1956
The **Hungarian Revolution** begins with a massive demonstration in Budapest.

 [3]

October 29, 1956
Israel's army seizes the Gaza Strip and attacks Egypt in the **Sinai Peninsula.**

 [4]

November 5, 1956
In collusion with Israel, **French and British** paratroopers and conventional forces invade the Suez Canal zone in Egypt but are then forced to withdraw because of opposition from the United States.

HUNGARIAN REVOLUTION

The people of Hungary rise against Communist rule, but their rebellion is crushed swiftly and brutally by Soviet forces.

Soviet leader Nikita Khrushchev's decision to acknowledge some of the crimes of his predecessor, Joseph Stalin, opened the floodgates of pent-up criticism and resentment against the Communist leaders of Hungary.

Hungarian party leader Mátyás Rákosi was ousted in July 1956 and replaced by Erno Gero. But Gero was unable to contain the rising tide of unrest and discontent, which broke out into active fighting (above left, Hungarian freedom fighters, and right, a colonel in the hated secret police [AVO] being beaten by protestors) late in October, and he appealed for Soviet help. The first phase of the Hungarian Revolution ended in victory for the rebels: Imre Nagy became premier and agreed, in response to popular demands, to establish a multiparty system; on November 1 he declared Hungarian neutrality and appealed to the United Nations. On November 4 the Soviet Union, profiting from the lack of response to Nagy from the Western powers and from the British and French involvement in action against Egypt, invaded Hungary in force and stopped the revolution.

[3] Israeli general Moshe Dayan, with his famous eyepatch, is surrounded by his men in the Sinai.

[7] Kwame Nkrumah, with the Duchess of Kent, at Ghana's independence celebrations in Accra. Ghana was formerly the Gold Coast colony.

[8] Prime Minister Harold Macmillan and his wife, Dorothy, at the Epsom races for the 1957 Derby.

1957
Diane Arbus quits work as a fashion photographer to concentrate on photographing New York City and its people. The unusual and often freakish nature of her subjects proves unsettling for many viewers.

1957
Eero Saarinen begins work near Washington, D.C., on the **Dulles International Airport terminal**, a masterpiece of sculptural design and his most famous building.

 [7]

1957
Ghana becomes the first African colony to gain independence from Great Britain. Its first leader is Prime Minister Kwame Nkrumah.

 [8]

1957
Harold Macmillan of the Conservative Party is appointed British prime minister following the resignation of Sir Anthony Eden.

1957
Hungarian-born French artist Victor Vasarely builds on optical experiments, painting *Vega*, a characteristic work of **Op Art**.

1957
Israel withdraws its forces from the Sinai peninsula and hands the Gaza Strip over to U.N. troops.

1957

1957
Johnny Cash establishes his position as a leading country-music artist with songs such as "Folsom Prison Blues" and "I Walk the Line."

1957
Leonard Bernstein's musical **West Side Story**, based on William Shakespeare's *Romeo and Juliet*, makes its debut in New York. It is choreographed by Jerome Robbins.

 [1]

1957
Monitoring of the atmosphere's carbon dioxide content begins and quickly reveals that **CO2 levels** are rising as a result of fossil-fuel burning and deforestation.

[2]

1957
On the Road, one of the most influential novels of the 20th century, is published by Beat Generation founder and writer Jack Kerouac.

 [3]

1957
The anti-rightist movement begins in China against critics of the government, thus **ending the Hundred Flowers Campaign**.

1957
The International Geophysical Year brings big science to **Antarctica** and inaugurates a geophysical inventory of the continent and oceans and atmosphere surrounding it.

[6] Nixon and Eisenhower at the latter's second inauguration as president.

[2] Chimneys belch smoke into the atmosphere at Halifax, a textile town in Yorkshire, England.

[7] Wladyslaw Gomulka signs an autograph after voting in the Polish elections.

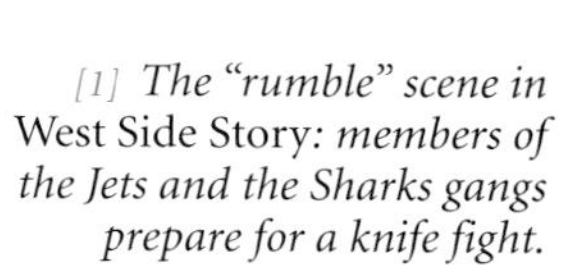

[1] The "rumble" scene in West Side Story*: members of the Jets and the Sharks gangs prepare for a knife fight.*

 [6]

January 20, 1957
President Dwight D. Eisenhower and Vice President Richard M. Nixon take their oaths of office to second terms in a private ceremony at the White House.

[7]

January 20, 1957
The National Unity Front, led by **Wladyslaw Gomulka**, wins an overwhelming victory in Polish parliamentary elections, which gave voters, for the first time in any Communist country, some freedom of choice.

February 9, 1957
The **Soviet Union** becomes the first country to ratify the charter of the International Atomic Energy Agency.

February 14, 1957
The U.S. and Chinese envoys resume talks in Geneva, Switzerland, on the questions of U.S. prisoners held in **China** and on visits by U.S. news reporters to China.

February 20, 1957
The English High Court of Justice invalidates a legacy given by **George Bernard Shaw** for someone to develop a 40-letter alphabet.

February 22, 1957
Queen Elizabeth II bestows the title of prince of the United Kingdom on her husband, **Philip, Duke of Edinburgh**.

1957
The **Wolfenden Report**, a study containing recommendations for laws governing sexual behavior, is published in Great Britain, recommending that private homosexual liaisons between consenting adults be decriminalized. This only happens only in 1967.

c. 1957
Windsurfing originates in the United States, as Californians combine aspects of sailing and surfing on a one-person craft called a sailboard.

 [4]

January 1, 1957
Governor Leroy Collins of Florida orders the suspension of bus service in Tallahassee to prevent violence over racial segregation of passengers.

 [5]

January 12, 1957
Chinese premier **Zhou Enlai**, in a speech in Warsaw, declares that the principal problem of the communist world is avoiding "fundamental conflicts" among its members.

January 15, 1957
The Egyptian government announces the immediate "**Egyptianization**" of all British and French banks and insurance companies in Egypt.

$

January 20, 1957
India's first atomic reactor is inaugurated at Trombay, near Bombay, by Prime Minister Jawaharlal Nehru.

[4] A sailboard in action, this one with a passenger.

[5] A Tallahassee bus emptied by the boycott, which will lead to the suspension of all bus services there.

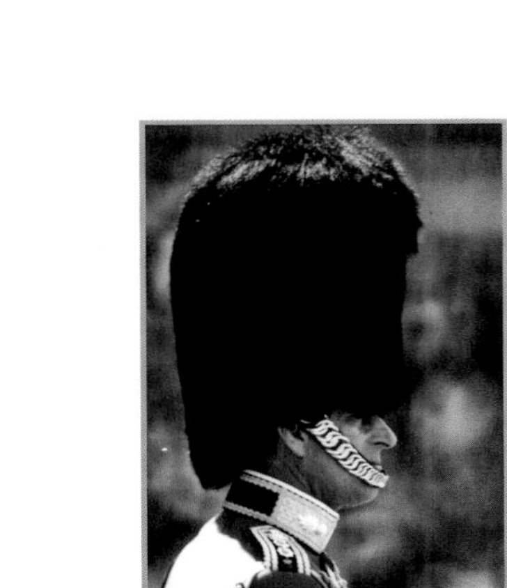

[8] Prince Philip in the uniform of the Grenadier Guards.

[3] Some of the Beat Generation meet up in a café: painter and musician Larry Rivers (left) with Jack Kerouac beside him; poet Allen Ginsberg (right) and musician David Amram picking his teeth. Poet Gregory Corso wears the woolly hat.

[9] Konrad Adenauer (center) signs the Treaty of Rome for Germany.

March 13, 1957
More than 40 people are reported killed in **Havana** in a surprise attempt to overthrow the Cuban government.

 [9]

March 25, 1957
The **Treaty of Rome** is signed, establishing the European Community, the Common Market. and the European Atomic Energy Community.

March 30, 1957
The **USS Sea-wolf**, the second U.S. atomic-powered submarine, is commissioned at Groton, Connecticut.

March 31, 1957
During a conference in Bermuda, the Soviet foreign ministry charges the United States and Britain with choosing "the course of direct preparations for **an atomic war**."

April 3, 1957
A state of siege and a curfew are imposed throughout **Chile** following several days of severe rioting.

April 13, 1957
Normal Saturday mail deliveries are halted and post offices closed by the order of **U.S. postmaster general Arthur E. Summerfield** because of the failure of Congress to appropriate supplemental funds.

1957

April 18, 1957
The **U.S. Atomic Energy Commission** announces that the Soviet Union has set off one of the largest nuclear explosions in that country's current series.

April 19, 1957
The first British ship to pay tolls to the **Egyptian Suez Canal Authority** completes passage through the canal.

April 23, 1957
Ten-year-old **Robert Strom** of New York City wins the record sum of $192,000 on a national TV quiz program.

 [1]

May 6, 1957
Columbia University announces the 1956 Pulitzer Prizes, including a posthumous award to **Eugene O'Neill** for his play *Long Day's Journey into Night* and a prize to George F. Kennan for his historical work *Russia Leaves the War.*

 [2]

May 6, 1957
The U.S. Supreme Court rules in two cases that a license to practice law might not be refused solely on the grounds of past membership in the **Communist Party** or pro-communist sentiments.

May 24, 1957
The U.S. embassy in **Taipei**, Taiwan, is wrecked by anti-U.S. riots that sweep the city.

 [3]

[1] *Robert Strom on the* 64,000 Dollar Question *TV quiz show, an amount he wins three times over. Quiz master Hal March sits on a stool to come down to his level.*

[2] *Eugene O'Neill*

[3] *Wrecked furniture and typewriters from the U.S. embassy in Taipei, Taiwan.*

[6] *Oliver Hardy and Stan Laurel*

July 1957
The **Pugwash Conferences**, a series of meetings by scientists to discuss problems of nuclear weapons and world security, begin at the estate of the American philanthropist Cyrus Eaton in Pugwash, Nova Scotia.

July 1, 1957
The **International Geophysical Year**, 1957–58, opens with scientists and technicians from about 70 countries cooperating in an 18-month study of the Earth and its physical environment.

July 5, 1957
The most powerful **atomic explosion** set off on the North American continent since 1945 is detonated at the atomic-proving grounds at Yucca Flat, Nevada.

July 16, 1957
The U.S. Senate votes 71 to 18 to make the **civil-rights bill** its pending business.

July 19, 1957
The first U.S. rocket with an **atomic warhead** is fired at the Nevada proving grounds.

July 29, 1957
The **International Atomic Energy Agency** is created.

June 2, 1957
The Communist Party's first secretary, **Nikita Khrushchev**, in an interview telecast in the United States, indicates that the Soviet Union is prepared to work toward disarmament by first agreeing to some small steps.

June 4, 1957
The **American Cancer Society**, in a final report to the American Medical Association, reports a high degree of connection between cigarette smoking and deaths from lung cancer.

June 10, 1957
The **U.S. Supreme Court**, by vote of 6 to 2, rules that the military trials of two women who had been convicted of killing their servicemen husbands overseas are unconstitutional.

June 12, 1957
Mayflower II, a replica of the original *Mayflower*, arrives at Provincetown, Massachusetts, 53 days after leaving Plymouth, England.

 [4]

June 21, 1957
John Diefenbaker, leader of the Progressive Conservative Party of Canada is chosen as prime minister. He will be forced to call a replacement election after ministerial resignations over the manufacture of nuclear weapons in Canada.

 [5]

June 24, 1957
The U.S. Supreme Court holds in three decisions that **obscene literature** falls outside of the constitutional guarantees of freedom of speech and of the press.

[4] The *Mayflower* replica in Plymouth, Massachusetts.

[5] *John Diefenbaker is congratulated on becoming prime minister of Canada.*

[7] *The original Sputnik, before its launch.*

LITTLE ROCK

Major U.S. confrontation over desegregation in schools

The city of Little Rock, Arkansas, became the focus of world attention in 1957 over the right of nine black students to attend Central High School there under a gradual desegregation plan adopted by the city school board in accordance with the 1954 decision of the U.S. Supreme Court holding racial segregation in public schools unconstitutional. The students became known as the "Little Rock Nine."

The result was a test of power between the federal and state governments. Governor Orval E. Faubus ordered the state militia to prevent blacks from entering the school, but the state was enjoined from interfering by U.S. president Dwight D. Eisenhower, who sent federal troops to the city in September to maintain order (left above, a young white segregationist is led away at bayonet point by men of the 101st Airborne; left below, Minnijean Brown, one of the Little Rock Nine, arrives at Central High School).

The army left in November, and the first black student graduated from Central High in May 1958. Within the next decade, desegregation was accomplished in all public schools. In 1998, President Bill Clinton signed legislation designating Central High School a national historic site and awarded each of the Little Rock Nine the Congressional Gold Medal.

  [6]

August 7, 1957
Actor **Oliver Hardy**—of Laurel and Hardy, the first great Hollywood motion-picture comedy team—dies in North Hollywood, California. Stan Laurel will die on February 23, 1965.

August 12, 1957
The government of **Northern Ireland** imposes a curfew in Newry and adjoining districts of counties Down and Armagh following terrorist activities by the Irish Republican Army.

August 31, 1957
The Federation of **Malaya** formally attains independence and enters the British Commonwealth of Nations as its 10th member.

September 18, 1957
Winston H. Price of Johns Hopkins University announces that he has developed a successful vaccine against a major common cold virus.

September 24, 1957
Racial desegregation takes center stage when federal troops are dispatched to **Little Rock**, Arkansas, to maintain order and enforce the right of black students to attend the local public high school.

 [7]

October 4, 1957
The Soviet Union launches into orbit the small satellite **Sputnik 1**, inaugurating the space age.

1957-1958

October 8, 1957
An accident at the **Windscale** nuclear facility in northwestern England causes a fire that burns for 16 hours and leaves 10 tons of radioactive fuel melted in the reactor core.
 [1]

October 12, 1957
About 44 percent of the world's adult population is estimated to be illiterate according to a brochure published by **UNESCO**.

October 17, 1957
Albert Camus, French novelist and playwright, is awarded the 1957 Nobel Prize in Literature.

November 3, 1957
The Soviet spacecraft **Sputnik 2** is launched, carrying the dog Laika, the first living creature to be shot into space and orbit the earth.
 [2]

November 26, 1957
U.S. president **Dwight D. Eisenhower** is revealed to have suffered what is generally called a mild stroke, but his physicians report that he is making good progress toward a complete recovery.

December 17, 1957
The United States successfully fires off, for the first time, the Atlas **intercontinental ballistic missile**.

[1] The Windscale/Calder Hall nuclear complex on the Cumbrian coast.

[9] Pelé in the air, challenging the Swedish goalkeeper.

[8] The young King Faisal II of Iraq with Crown Prince Abd al-Ilah in uniform behind him. Both will be shot in the coup.

[2] Sputnik 2 and the dog Laika ("Little Lemon") on a Russian stamp.

[11] Mamie Eisenhower, the president's wife, christens Pan American Boeing 707, "America," the first 707 to go into service.

[7] Jasper Johns away from the studio.

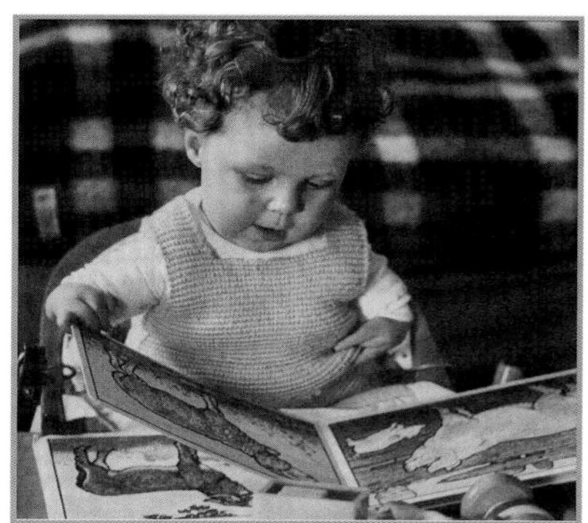
[10] A child born with stunted arms as a result of his mother taking thalidomide when pregnant.

1950-1959

 [7]
1958
An exhibition of paintings of flags and targets by American **Jasper Johns**, reintroducing representation into modern art, unsettles the art world.

 [8]
1958
Iraq's **king Faysal (Faisal) II** and several members of his family are killed in a coup led by General Abd al-Karim Qasim.

 [9]
1958
Seventeen-year-old soccer sensation **Pelé** leads Brazil to a 5-2 victory over Sweden in the World Cup final. Pelé becomes a Brazilian national hero and one of the world's best-known athletes.

 [10]
1958
Thalidomide goes on the market as a treatment for morning sickness in more than 40 countries. It is soon found to produce severe malformations in infants born of mothers who had taken the drug during early pregnancy.

1958
The **American Association of Retired Persons** is founded by Ethel Percy Andrus. Its membership will grow to some 30 million by 2000, and it will become one of the most powerful advocacy groups in the U.S.

 [11]
1958
The **Boeing 707**, the first American jetliner, goes into service.

1958
The first **laundromat** is opened by J. F. Cantrell in Fort Worth, Texas. He names it the Washateria.

1958
American **Bobby Fischer** becomes the youngest player in the world to earn the rank of chess grand master. He later becomes the first American world chess champion.

 [3]

1958
American dancer and choreographer Alvin Ailey, Jr., forms the **Alvin Ailey American Dance Theater**. The company's signature piece is *Revelations* (1960), a powerful, early work by Ailey that is set to African American spirituals.

 [4]

1958
American physicist **James Van Allen** announces discovery of the Van Allen radiation belts surrounding the earth.

1958
Beat poet **Lawrence Ferlinghetti** publishes his ingenious first book of poems, *A Coney Island of the Mind*. His City Lights bookstore becomes a center of San Francisco literary life.

 [5]

1958
Boris Pasternak wins the Nobel Prize for Literature but is forced to decline the award. His epic **Doctor Zhivago**, unpublished and criticized in the Soviet Union, is translated into 18 languages.

 [6]

[3] Bobby Fischer playing the Philippino champion Rodolfo Tan Cardoso at the Manhattan Chess Club in 1957.

[4] Alvin Ailey supporting a female dancer.

[6] Boris Pasternak at his house outside Moscow.

[5] Lawrence Ferlinghetti at a poetry reading.

[12] Backyard furnaces in China, part of the Great Leap Forward. About 600,000 are constructed, but the metal they produce is useless.

[13] Teresa Brewer, one of the most popular singers of the 1950s, shows off her skill with two hula hoops.

 [12]

1958
The Communist Party of China launches the **Great Leap Forward**, an industrialization campaign that has such a disruptive effect on Chinese agriculture that 20 million people starve between 1958 and 1960.

1958
The **integrated circuit** is independently invented by Jack Kilby at Texas Instruments and Robert Noyce at Fairchild Semiconductor.

1958
The French Fourth Republic, created in 1946, is replaced by the **Fifth Republic**, approved by 80 percent of the electorate in a September referendum.

1958
The U.S. television industry is rocked by the **Twenty-One scandal**, in which quiz-show contestants admit that they have been given answers in advance.

 [13]

1958
The Wham-O Company in California begins to manufacture its new toy, the **hula hoop**.

1958
West African author **Chinua Achebe** completes his perceptive novel *Things Fall Apart*.

1958

January 13, 1958
Linus C. Pauling, presents to U.N. Secretary General Dag Hammarskjold a petition signed by 9,235 scientists urging an immediate international agreement to **halt nuclear weapons testing**.

 [1]

January 20, 1958
The **first nuclear reactor in Latin America** goes into operation at Buenos Aires, Argentina.

January 22, 1958
The U.N. Security Council unanimously adopts a resolution calling for tighter U.N. control of the **Jerusalem** demilitarized zone between Israel and Jordan.

January 27, 1958
The **U.S. and Soviet governments** announce a compromise agreement to widen cultural, technical, educational, and sports exchanges.

January 31, 1958
The United States orbits its first satellite, **Explorer 1**, marking the country's entry into the space race.

 [2]

February 8, 1958
French aircraft raid a Tunisian village near the Algerian border, allegedly killing 68 people.

[1] Linus Pauling (center) appeals for nuclear testing to stop.

[2] American TV anchorman Walter Cronkite explains the rocketry involved in the Explorer 1 mission, with the aid of models.

[6] Rainsoaked CND members marching to Aldermaston with their new symbol.

[5] Nikita Khrushchev in Hungary. It must be doubted whether the Hungarians watching share his euphoria.

[7] Van Cliburn

March 26, 1958
The **Iraqi parliament** approves constitutional rights for women with a primary-school education and gives King Faysal the right to form a union with "one or more Arab countries."

 [5]

March 27, 1958
Nikita Khrushchev replaces Nikolay Bulganin as premier of the Soviet Union.

March 31, 1958
The Soviet Union announces a **halt in nuclear bomb tests** and calls upon the United States and Britain to take the same action.

 [6]

April 1958
The British **Campaign for Nuclear Disarmament** (CND) organizes its first Easter march to the Aldermaston Atomic Weapons Research Establishment, and the anti-nuclear symbol is introduced.

April 1, 1958
The **French economy** is paralyzed by a strike of 1,000,000 public workers.

 [7]

April 13, 1958
Van Cliburn of Texas is awarded first prize in the U.S.S.R.'s international Tchaikovsky piano competition in Moscow.

February 13, 1958
Iraq and Jordan proclaim their union as the **Arab federation**, headed by King Faysal (Faisal) II of Iraq.

February 16, 1958
U.S. airman **Donald G. Farrell** completes a seven-day simulated "trip to the moon" in an experiment at the School of Aviation Medicine in San Antonio, Texas.

February 19, 1958
Communist China and North Korea announce at **Pyongyang** that all Communist Chinese forces will be withdrawn from North Korea by the end of 1958.

 [3]

February 21, 1958
Egypt and Syria vote almost unanimously in national plebiscites for the establishment of the **United Arab Republic** with Egyptian president Gamal Abdel Nasser as its first president.

March 2, 1958
Vivian E. Fuchs and a British team complete a 2,100-mile trek across the Antarctic continent.

 [4]

March 19, 1958
The Earth Satellite panel of the U.S. National Committee for the International Geophysical Year recommends a long-range program of scientific **investigation of the moon** and planets as a prelude to manned spaceflight.

[3] Kim Il Sung and Chinese commanders are pelted with good luck rice prior to their withdrawal from Korea.

[4] Vivian Fuchs beside one of the sno-cats used on his trans-Antarctic trip.

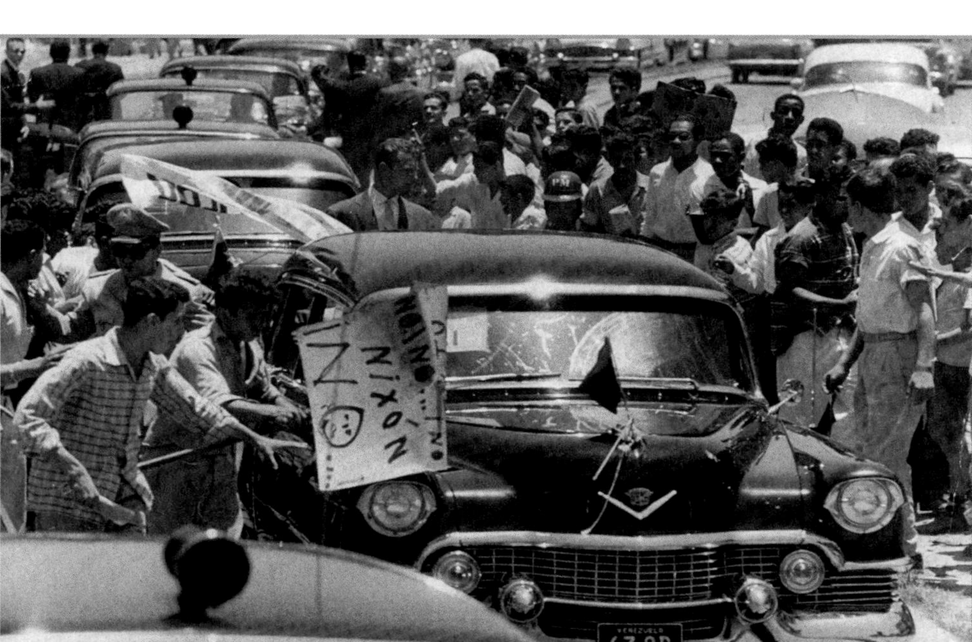

[9] Nixon's automobile is mobbed in Caracas by anti-American protesters.

[8] The Atomium, centerpiece of Brussels Exhibition, with King Baudouin's escort in the foreground, at the official opening.

[10] Dead locusts clog an automobile's air intake.

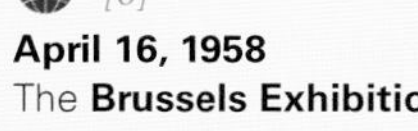 [8]

April 16, 1958
The **Brussels Exhibition** is opened in Belgium.

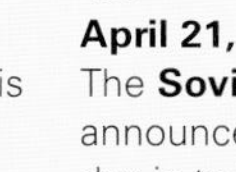

April 21, 1958
The **Soviet Union** officially announces that the working day is to be reduced to seven hours in heavy industry and to six hours for miners.

May 9, 1958
The last four **Nazi war criminals** held by the United States are revealed to have been paroled.

 [9]

May 13, 1958
Vice President Richard Nixon's car is attacked by hundreds of demonstrators upon his arrival in Caracas, Venezuela. President Dwight Eisenhower orders paratroopers and marines to Caribbean bases to guarantee Nixon's safety.

May 15, 1958
General Charles de Gaulle announces that he is ready to again assume power in France, and is helped on his way by the threat of mutiny in the French armed forces in Algeria, which only he can remove.

 [10]

June 11, 1958
President Dwight D. Eisenhower rejects requests from the governors of Colorado and Kansas to declare a state of emergency in portions of those states infested by grasshoppers.

1958-1959

June 24, 1958
The **U.S. State Department** discloses that passport applicants will no longer be required to answer questions concerning Communist Party membership.

June–July, 1958
Violence escalates in **Cyprus** between Greek and Turkish Cypriots, and British forces trying to restore order.

July 9, 1958
The **Soviet Union** renews demands for "an unequivocal [U.S.] statement" pledging the cessation of all nuclear testing as the main objective of current talks on policing a nuclear test ban.

July 20, 1958
Jordan terminates all diplomatic relations with the United Arab Republic.

July 26, 1958
Prince Charles, heir apparent to the British throne, is named Prince of Wales by his mother, Elizabeth II.
 [1]

July 29, 1958
Criticized for allowing the Soviet Union to launch the first manmade satellite to orbit earth (Sputnik 1, in 1957), U.S. president Dwight Eisenhower signs legislation that creates **NASA** (the National Aeronautics and Space Administration).

[2] The Nautilus *returns to Portland Harbor after passing beneath the North Pole.*

[1] Prince Charles in the uniform of the private boarding school that he attends.

[5] The formal photograph after the marriage of the crown prince of Japan to Princess Michiko. They are flanked by Emperor Hirohito and the empress.

[5]
November 27, 1958
The betrothal of Japanese crown prince **Akihito** to Michiko Shoda, a commoner, is announced.

November 28, 1958
Louisiana's athletic segregation law is ruled unconstitutional by a three-judge federal court in New Orleans.

December 1, 1958
Adolfo López Mateos is elected president of Mexico and proceeds to expand agrarian reform and industrial development.

December 1, 1958
Arthur S. Flemming, U.S. secretary of health, education, and welfare, reports that nearly 1,000,000 student days were lost in 1958 by the closing of public schools to avoid integration.

December 10, 1958
President Dwight Eisenhower terms "reprehensible" the refusal of **Alabama** to produce voting records for the U.S. Civil Rights Commission.

December 12, 1958
The United States, Great Britain, and the Soviet Union agree at **Geneva, Switzerland**, on the structure of an organization to police a ban on nuclear weapons tests.

August 3, 1958
The atomic submarine **Nautilus** passes beneath the thick ice cap of the North Pole, an unprecedented feat.

 [2]

September 2, 1958
Race riots erupt in the **Notting Hill** area of London, where many West Indian immigrants are living.

September 28, 1958
Madagascar votes for autonomy within the French community.

[3]

October 28, 1958
The College of Cardinals elects on the 11th ballot Angelo Giuseppe, Cardinal Roncalli, patriarch of Venice, as the 262nd supreme pontiff of the Roman Catholic Church. He will rule as **John XXIII**.

 [4]

October 28, 1958
The Soviet writers union expels **Boris Pasternak**, and the following day Pasternak, after an earlier acceptance, rejects "voluntarily" the 1958 Nobel Prize for Literature.

November 6, 1958
A court in Johannesburg, **South Africa**, fines 128 African women for demonstrating against racial pass laws.

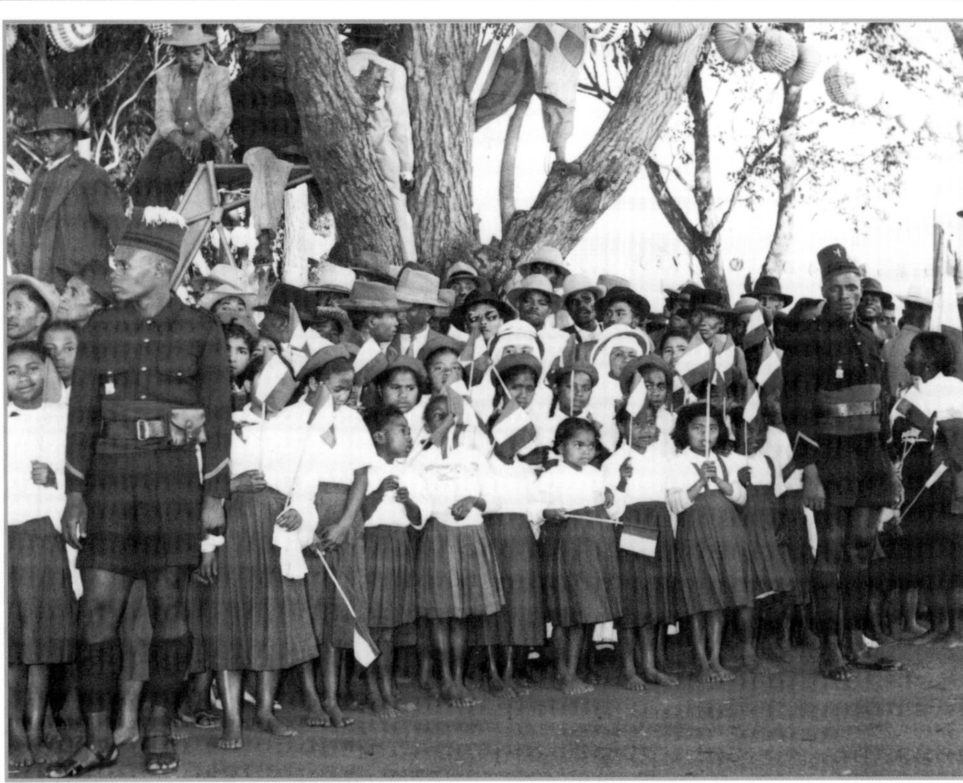

[3] *Children in Madagascar await the arrival of General de Gaulle after the vote for autonomy.*

[4] *Pope John XXIII is carried in state outside St. Peter's Basilica in Rome.*

[6] *Charles De Gaulle speaks in Algeria in October on the new constitution of the new Fifth French Republic, which will make him a very powerful president.*

[7] *Bill Russell leaps for the net past a Cincinnati Royal defender.*

 [6]

December 21, 1958
Charles De Gaulle is elected president of the new French Fifth Republic, with greatly enhanced powers.

1959
British naturalist and entomologist H. W. Bates returns from a trip to the Amazon with specimens of 14,712 species, including 8,000 new insect species. **Batesian mimicry** is named in his honor.

 [7]

1959
Center **Bill Russell** leads the Boston Celtics to the first of their eight straight National Basketball Association championships.

1959
Down's syndrome, caused by trisomy at chromosome 21, is the first chromosomal abnormality to be identified.

1959
English violinist and teacher Neville Marriner founds the **Academy of St. Martin-in-the-Fields**, in London. The chamber ensemble becomes one of the best known and most popular in the world.

1959
Fishermen in the Japanese village of **Minamata** attack the Chisso factory, which has so polluted the local bay with methyl mercury as to ruin fisheries and cause severe neurological damage and several deaths among the local population.

1959

1959
In **Two Cultures and the Scientific Revolution**, British scientist C. P. Snow argues that the worlds of science and literature are diverging, to the detriment of each.

1959
Jacques Plante is the first National Hockey League goaltender to wear a protective face mask. Other goalies soon follow suit.

 [1]

1959
Oscar Niemeyer begins work on the city plan for Brasília, Brazil. The inland capital employs the International Style to advertise Brazil's political and economic modernity.

 [2]

1959
Songwriter Berry Gordy, Jr., founds the **Motown Recording Corporation**. The label has some of the most popular musicians of the 1960s, like Diana Ross and the Supremes, Smokey Robinson and the Miracles, Stevie Wonder, and Marvin Gaye.

 [3]

1959
Swiss-born photographer Robert Frank publishes **The Americans**, in which images of ordinary small-town scenes add up to a national portrait.

1959
The **Barbie doll** makes her debut at a toy fair in New York City. Created by Ruth Handler, the doll becomes one of the best-known icons of postwar American popular culture.

 [4]

[1] Jacques Plante in his mask.

[2] The frame of Brasília's Roman Catholic cathedral, from which the cone-shaped curtain wall will be suspended.

[3] A Motown gathering: Berry Gordy at the piano, Smokey Robinson at the rear, and Stevie Wonder (second right)

[4] The Barbie doll range expands: she is joined here by her boy equivalent, Ken, and between them is a 45-rpm, seven-inch record of their songs.

CASTRO BECOMES PREMIER

Revolution in Cuba

On January 1, 1959, after three years of guerrilla warfare, 800 rebels defeated the Cuban government's 30,000-strong professional army, and dictator Fulgencio Batista fled Cuba.

In February, Fidel Castro, the undisputed leader of the revolutionaries, became commander-in-chief of the armed forces in Cuba's new provisional government, which had Manuel Urrutia, a moderate liberal, as its president. By the time Urrutia was forced to resign in July 1959, Castro was in control. The new head of the government is shown here making a speech at the microphone.

Castro began his rule promising the restoration of civil liberties and moderate reforms. But once established as Cuba's leader, he began to pursue more radical, communist policies and became openly hostile to the United States.

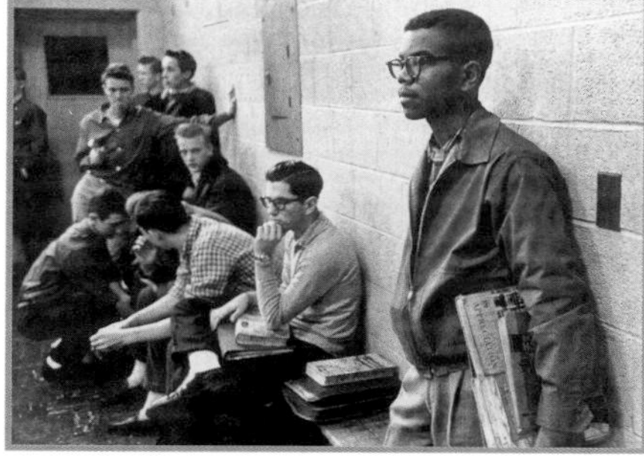

[8] A lone black student at a Norfolk, Virginia, high school.

[10] Hastings Banda. He will return as an increasingly dictatorial ruler of Malawi, as Nyasaland is rechristened.

January 19, 1959
Virginia's Supreme Court of Appeals invalidates that state's laws designed to prevent school integration.

February 1, 1959
Swiss men voters reject (2 to 1) a proposed constitutional amendment giving women the right to vote in national elections.

 [8]

February 2, 1959
African American children attend for the first time formerly all-white schools in Arlington and Norfolk, Virginia.

 [9]

February 3, 1959
Rock-and-roll innovator **Buddy Holly** is killed in a plane crash along with fellow musicians Ritchie Valens and the Big Bopper, an event remembered as the "Day the Music Died."

February 16, 1959
After defeating the forces of dictator General Fulgencio Batista, Fidel Castro becomes premier of **Cuba** and transforms the island country into the Western Hemisphere's first communist state.

 [10]

March 3, 1959
The Nyasaland government declares a state of emergency, outlaws the **Nyasaland** branch of the African National Congress, and arrests and deports the Congress's leader, Hastings Banda.

1959
The PDP-1, from the Digital Equipment Corporation, launches the **minicomputer**, created especially for use in laboratories and research institutions.

1959
The Tibetan people unsuccessfully revolt against communist Chinese forces that have occupied the region since 1950. The 14th **Dalai Lama** is forced to flee to exile in India.

1959
The **Winnipeg Blue Bombers** win the first modern Grey Cup of Canadian football.

1959
Volvo introduces the three-point seat belt. Designed by Swedish engineer Nils Bohlin, it restrains the upper and the lower body, greatly reducing the risk of injury. It becomes a standard safety device in cars worldwide.

c. 1959
Computers, previously used almost exclusively on government projects, begin to find applications in oil refining, electricity generation, and other production venues.

January 3, 1959
Alaska is admitted to the United States as the 49th state; it is the first state that is not contiguous with the others. The largest state in area, it increased the nation's size by nearly 20 percent.

[5] Tibetan monks lay down their arms, supervised by Chinese soldiers.

[6] A computer at the Standard Oil Company research laboratory in Warrenville Heights, Ohio.

[7] Anchorage, Alaska, with banners celebrating Alaska's statehood.

[11] Lorraine Hansberry (center left) at the first-night party for her play at Sardi's Restaurant, New York.

[9] Buddy Holly

[12] The Dalai Lama in Tibet, before he is forced to flee to India.

March 4, 1959
Archbishiop Makarios returns from exile to become president of the new Greco-Turkish administration in Cyprus.

March 11, 1959
Lorraine Hansberry's *A Raisin in the Sun* becomes the first play by an African American woman to be produced on Broadway.

March 23, 1959
J. Edgar Hoover, FBI director, discloses that the FBI has broken a 14-member U.S.-Canadian ring that allegedly won $45,000 by securing advance answers to newspaper word-puzzle contests.

March 28, 1959
China dissolves the rebel Tibetan local government of the **Dalai Lama** and appoints the Panchen Lama as ruler of Tibet.

April 4, 1959
In West Africa the **Mali Federation**, a short-lived union between the autonomous territories of the Sudanese Republic and Senegal, led by Léopold Senghor, is created.

April 7, 1959
Oklahoma voters decisively repeal Prohibition, leaving Mississippi the only dry state.

1959

April 20, 1959
Dame Margot Fonteyn, a British ballerina, is arrested by Panamanian authorities because of suspicions of revolutionary plotting by her husband, Roberto Arias.

 [1]

April 29, 1959
The **Warsaw Pact** countries' foreign ministers, ending a meeting in Warsaw, state in a communique that "prospects of alleviating international tension had markedly improved."

May 28, 1959
Two monkeys are recovered unhurt from the Caribbean after a 300-mile-high spaceflight in the nose cone of an **IRBM** launched by the U.S. Army from Cape Canaveral, Florida.

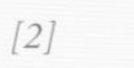 [2]

June 3, 1959
The moon is used as a reflector in transmitting recorded radio messages by President Dwight Eisenhower in Westford, Massachusetts, to Canadian prime minister Diefenbaker in Prince Albert, Saskatoon.

June 24, 1959
Peter Paul Rubens's altarpiece, *Adoration of the Magi*, is bought by an anonymous British collector for $770,000, the highest ever paid for a painting at auction to date.

July 7, 1959
The **American Lutheran Church** is formed by a merger of Evangelical Lutherans and United Evangelical Lutherans.

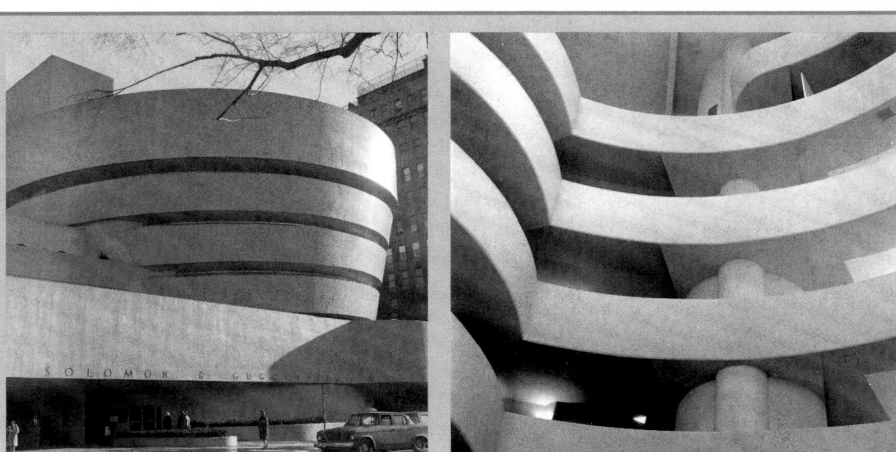

THE GUGGENHEIM IN NEW YORK

One of Frank Lloyd Wright's greatest buildings opens in Manhattan.

In 1959, the Guggenheim Museum—an art collection started by Solomon R. Guggenheim (1861–1949), the son of multimillionaire mining tycoon Meyer Guggenheim—received a permanent home on Fifth Avenue, overlooking Central Park in an innovative new building designed by Frank Lloyd Wright.

The building represented a radical departure from traditional museum design, spiraling upward and outward in smoothly sculptured coils of massive, unadorned white concrete (above left). The exhibition space consists of a spiral ramp of six "stories" (above right) encircling an open center space lit by a dome of glass. Many of the paintings are "floated" from the inclined outer wall on concealed metal arms. The Guggenheim Museum has a comprehensive collection of European paintings created throughout the 20th century and of American paintings from the second half of the century. Modern sculpture is also well represented.

[1] Margot Fonteyn with her husband, Panamanian diplomat Roberto Arias.

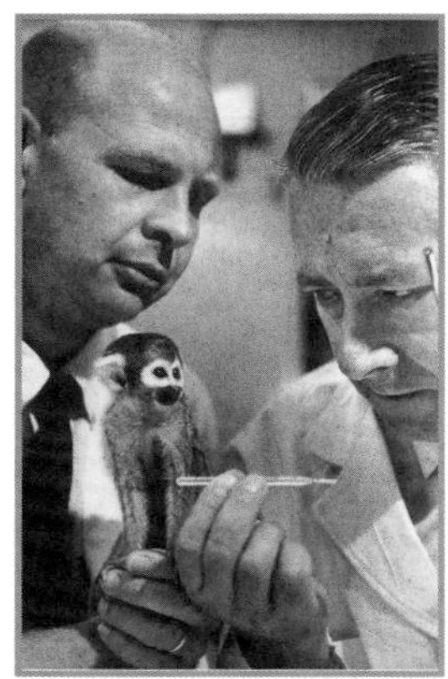

[2] One of the astronaut squirrel monkeys has its temperature taken on its return to earth.

[7] A Time *cover of the moon being orbited by Lunik III.*

September 22, 1959
A **telephone cable**, the first between North America and Europe, is placed in operation; it links Clarenville (Newfoundland) and Penmarch (France).

September 25, 1959
France's delegation walks out of a U.N. General Assembly meeting when the Saudi Arabian delegate denounces the French army in **Algeria** as "torturers."

October 21, 1959
The Guggenheim Museum, designed by Frank Lloyd Wright, opens in New York City. Its massive spiral form breaks out of the typical urban streetscape and draws the viewer in.

 [7]

October 27, 1959
The Soviet Union releases the first picture of the moon's hidden side, taken by **Lunik III**.

October 30, 1959
Antiwhite rioting mobs clash with police and troops in **Stanleyville, Belgian Congo**.

November 5, 1959
The Nobel Peace Prize for 1959 is awarded to **Philip Noel-Baker**, British statesman and author, for his work in the cause of disarmament.

July 24, 1959
Soviet Premier Nikita Khrushchev and U.S. Vice President Richard M. Nixon engage in an impromptu, profanity-filled "**kitchen debate**" at an American exhibition in Moscow.
 [3]

July 25, 1959
The first hovercraft, SRN 1, demonstrates its capabilities by crossing the English Channel.
 [4]

August 12, 1959
Little Rock, Arkansas,high schools reopen with the integration of two previously all-white schools; police and firemen quell a mob at Central High, the scene of 1957 disturbances.
 [5]

August 21, 1959
Hawaii is admitted to the United States as the 50th state; it lies more than 2,000 miles west of the mainland.
 [6]

September 12, 1959
The Soviet Union launches **Luna 2**, the first space probe to hit the moon.
 [7]

September 13, 1959
Karl Heinrich Lübke, a member of the Christian-Democratic Union, becomes president of West Germany (1959–69).

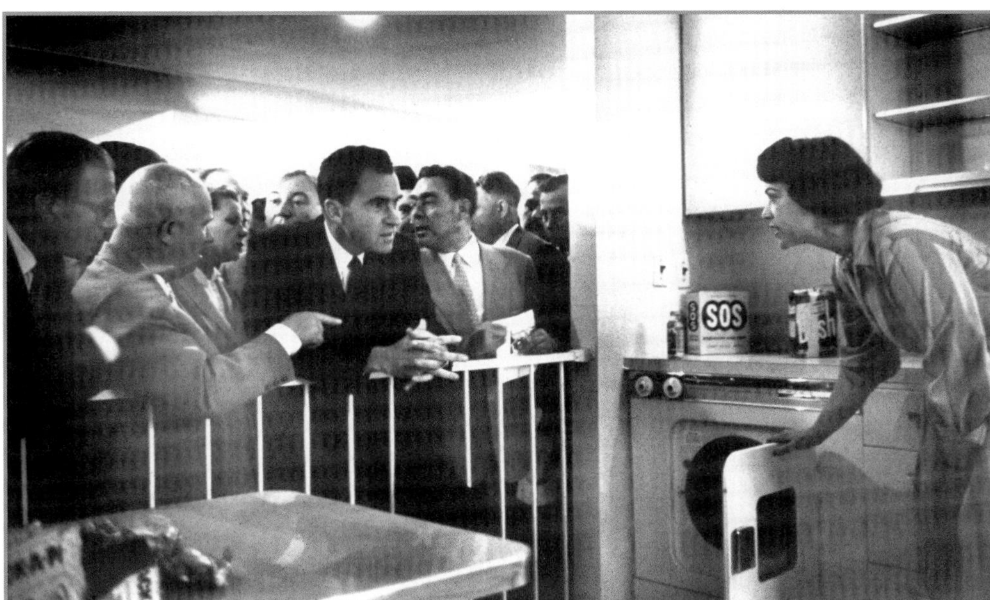

[3] *The "kitchen debate," in front of the kitchen stand at the Moscow exhibition, between Nixon and Khrushchev. Khrushchev points a finger to make a point; beyond Nixon is Leonid Brezhnev, who will succeed Khrushchev in 1964.*

[4] *The British SRN 1 prototype hovercraft, invented by Christopher Cockerell.*

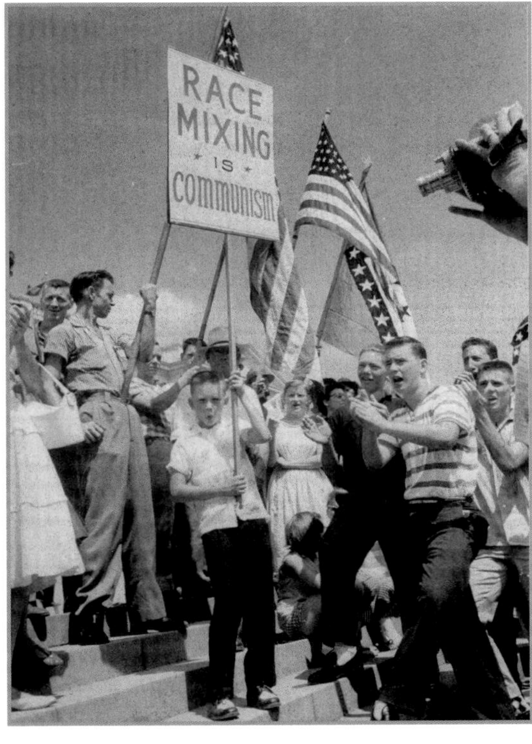

[5] *Another protest at Little Rock Central High, Arkansas.*

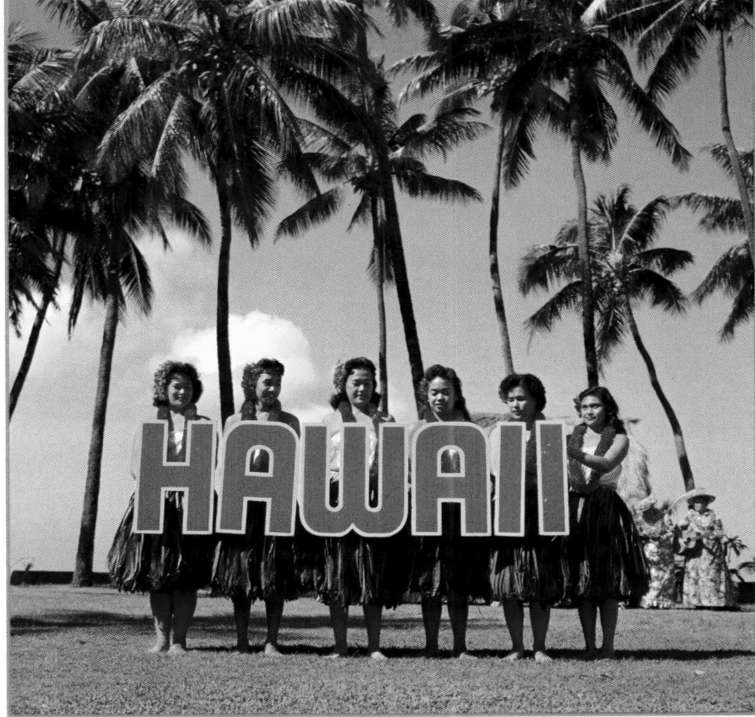

[6] *Hawaii celebrates joining the United States.*

November 17, 1959
Columbia University announces the discovery of a submarine plateau in the **Arctic Ocean**; the plateau covers an area more than twice the size of Connecticut.

December 1, 1959
Antarctica becomes a preserve for scientific research free from military activity with the signing of a 12-nation treaty in Washington, D.C.

December 4, 1959
An **age limit** of 60 for U.S. commercial aviation pilots is ordered by the Federal Aviation Administration.

December 19, 1959
Walter Williams, age 117, the last veteran of the American Civil War, dies in Houston, Texas.

65th Birthday SALE
SALE
68
Catalina

Welcomes
No Obligati
NO

1960

1960
British film director Sir Alfred Hitchcock directs the immensely popular **Psycho**. Hitchcock's greatest gift is his mastery of the technical means to build and maintain suspense.

 [1]

1960
American poet **Anne Sexton** publishes her first poetry collection, *To Bedlam and Part Way Back*. Much of her work reflects on her mental breakdowns.

 [2]

1960
At the Summer Olympics in Rome, Ethiopian **Abebe Bikila**, running in his bare feet, wins the first of his two gold medals in the marathon.

 [3]

1960
Brasília-Belém highway, a section of the transamazonian highway, opens Amazonia to rapid colonization and inaugurates an era of quick deforestation in the world's largest rainforest.

1960
COBOL (Common Business-Oriented Language), the second major higher-level programming language, is released.

1960
Harper Lee publishes her only novel, **To Kill a Mockingbird**; it is a critical and popular success, perennially at the top of lists of readers' favorite books.

 [4]

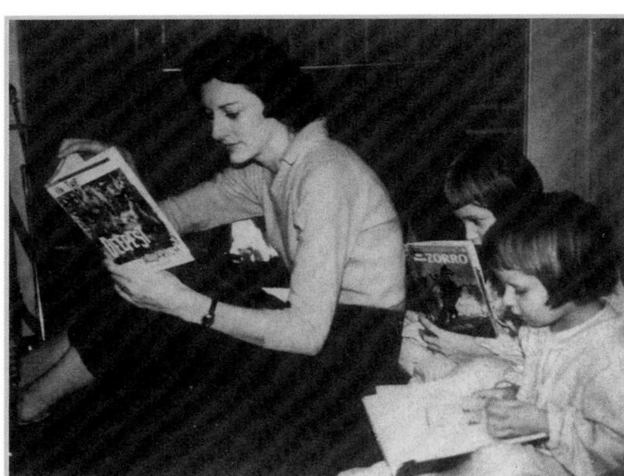

[2] *Anne Sexton with her two daughters. She has started writing poetry at the suggestion of her long-term therapist.*

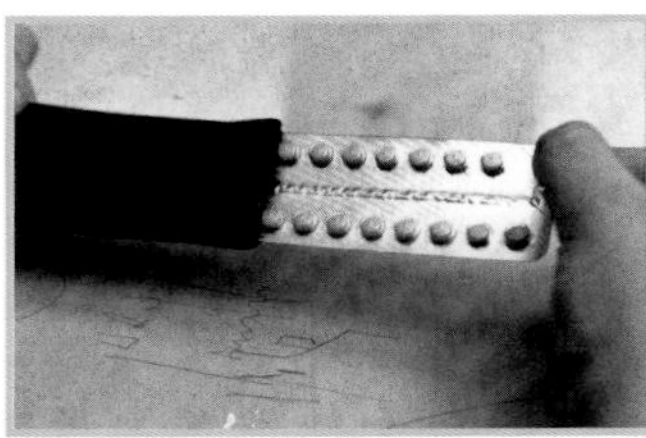

[8] *The Pill: one a day, the packaging helpfully numbered so you can check if you are up to date.*

[4] *Harper Lee in her hometown, Monroeville, Alabama. There are 30 million copies of her book in print.*

[7] *A photocopier installed for the use of the public at a London railway station: 10 pence a copy.*

[1] *Alfred Hitchcock on the set of* Psycho.

[3] *Barefooted Abebe Bikila draws away from Abdesselem Rhadi of Morocco.*

 [7]

1960
The Haloid Xerox Company markets a plain-paper **photocopier**, revolutionizing office practices and ringing the death knell for carbon paper.

1960
The **Organization of the Petroleum Exporting Countries (OPEC)** is established to coordinate the petroleum policies of its members and to provide them with technical and economic aid.

 [8]

1960
The U.S. Food and Drug Administration approves the development of "**the Pill**"—a hormone-based oral contraceptive; the availability of the pill triggers the sexual revolution of the 1960s.

1960
The **Winter Olympic Games** take place in Squaw Valley, California.

c. 1960
The number of **tractors** in Germany surpasses the number of farm horses, signaling the triumph of fossil-fuel-based agriculture in western Europe (two or three decades behind the U.S.).

c. 1960
The **water bed** is introduced as an alternative to the stuffed innerspring mattress. It becomes one of the iconic objects of the decade.

1960
Irrigation projects in Soviet Central Asia divert water from the **Aral Sea**, which soon begins to shrink in size.

1960
Joan Baez releases her first album of folk music, at the forefront of the 1960s folk-song revival. She typifies the era by her merging of music and political activism.

 [5]

1960
Kishi Nobuske, prime minister of Japan from 1957 to 1960, signs a revised **U.S.-Japan security treaty**, provoking a turbulent opposition campaign.

1960
Soviet technicians are withdrawn from China as hostility grows between the People's Republic of China and the U.S.S.R.

1960
Swiss oceanic engineer Jacques Piccard and Lieutenant Don Walsh of the U.S. Navy descend to a record 35,800 feet in the **submersible Trieste** in the Mariana Trench of the Pacific Ocean, the deepest area of the seas.

 [6]

1960
The **Echo I** communications satellite is launched. Developed by American communications engineer John Robinson Pierce, the satellite marks the beginning of efficient worldwide radio and television communication.

SIT-IN PROTESTS

The U.S. civil rights movement launches a peaceful demonstration against racial segregation.

On February 1, 1960, the sit-in movement (largely under the auspices of the newly formed Student Nonviolent Coordinating Committee, SNCC) was launched at Greensboro, North Carolina, when black students from Agricultural and Technical College of North Carolina sat down at a segregated Woolworth lunch counter (above) and waited for service.

This form of protest was not new—it was modelled on the nonviolent methods of civil disobedience used by Mohandas Gandhi, the leader of resistance to the British occupation of India. Indeed, there had been at least three previous occurrences during the civil rights movement—in Chicago, Illinois (1943), St. Louis, Missouri (1949), and Baltimore, Maryland (1953)—but none had attracted much media interest. This time, however, the sit-in was widely publicized and sparked a chain reaction. Similar protests were held, first in Nashville, Tennessee, on February 13 and then in many other cities, eventually forcing the desegregation of department stores, supermarkets, libraries, and movie theaters.

[5] *John Baez. From folk music, she will soon move into pop and rock, gospel, and country.*

[6] *Jacques Piccard's bathyscaphe* Trieste. *The cylindrical float (above) is filled with gasoline, which gives lift since it is lighter than water. Beneath is the steel ball in which the crew sits. When the crew wants to return to the surface, two tons of ballast are jettisoned.*

c. 1960
The **world's population** reaches three billion.

January 1, 1960
Cameroon's first day of independence is marked by violence.

January 24, 1960
General Maurice Challe declares a state of siege in Algiers and orders additional troops into the city to cope with rebellion by rightist European residents who fear the granting of independence.

February 2, 1960
African American college students sit quietly at store lunch counters in Greensboro, North Carolina, in the first of many **sit-in** protests against the stores' refusals to serve seated African Americans.

February 3, 1960
British prime minister Harold Macmillan, in a speech to the parliament of the Union of **South Africa**, strongly criticizes that country's racial policies.

February 13, 1960
France detonates its first atomic bomb in the Sahara desert.

1960

March 3, 1960
Elvis Presley returns home from Germany after a two-year stint in the army.

March 21, 1960
About 70 black African demonstrators are killed by police during a protest in **Sharpeville**, Gauteng province, against South Africa's pass laws.

April 1, 1960
Tiros I, the first U.S. satellite designed to provide detailed TV photos of the earth's weather, is fired into orbit from Cape Canaveral, Florida.

April 27, 1960
After several years as an autonomous republic in the French Union, the West African country of **Togo** becomes independent.

April 27, 1960
Syngman Rhee resigns as autocratic president of the First Republic of South Korea and goes into exile in Hawaii.

May 1, 1960
A U.S. **U-2 reconnaissance plane** is shot down near Sverdlovsk, in the Soviet Union, and pilot Francis Gary Powers is captured. The incident becomes known as the U-2 Affair.

[2] *Dead, dying, and wounded at the Sharpeville Massacre.*

[3] *Gary Powers. Shot down by one of the new surface-to-air missiles (the first time the U.S. is aware of their existence), he does not use the poison pin, with shellfish toxin, a standard part of his kit.*

[8] *President Makarios signs the Cyprus independence document.*

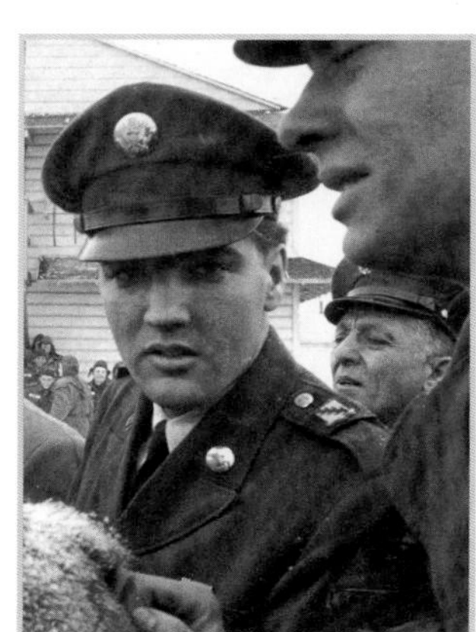

[1] *Elvis Presley on the day he is discharged from the army.*

[7] *At an independence celebration in the French Congo, a Congolese in traditional costume embraces a colonial.*

August 5, 1960
Upper Volta (now Burkina Faso, which means "Land of Incorruptible People"), a landlocked country in western Africa, proclaims its independence on this day in 1960, ending more than 60 years of French rule.

August 7, 1960
Côte d'Ivoire (the Ivory Coast) gains independence from France.

August 15, 1960
The Republic of the Congo (Congo Brazzaville) gains independence from France.

August 16, 1960
The island of **Cyprus** becomes an independent republic.

August 19, 1960
Francis Gary Powers is sentenced to 10 years' confinement by the Soviet Union for espionage following the U-2 Affair, but he is later released (1962) in exchange for the Soviet spy Rudolf Abel.

August 20, 1960
Senegal secedes from the Mali Federation, declaring its full independence.

May 22, 1960
One of the largest earthquakes on record strikes the southern coast of **Chile**, killing about 5,700 people and creating seismic sea waves that cause death and destruction in Japan and Hawaii and on the Pacific coast of the United States.

 [4]

May 23, 1960
Israeli prime minister David Ben-Gurion reports to the Knesset the capture by Israeli agents of **Adolf Eichmann**, a leader in carrying out the Nazi program for the extermination of the Jews.

 [5]

June 30, 1960
The Republic of the Congo (Congo Kinshasa) declares its independence from **Belgium** and is immediately plunged into civil war. It will change its name to **Zaire** and then to the Democratic Republic of the Congo.

July 9, 1960
The Thresher, the first of a class of U.S. nuclear-powered attack submarines, is launched, only to sink three years later in the worst submarine accident in history.

July 20, 1960
Sirimavo R. D. Bandaranaike becomes prime minister of Ceylon (modern-day Sri Lanka), making her the world's first female head of state.

 [6]

August 3, 1960
The Republic of Niger gains its independence from France.

[4] A crevasse that has been opened up in a street in Valdivia, Chile, by the earthquake.

[6] Mrs. Bandaranaike, the widow of an assassinated Ceylonese prime minister, on the campaign trail.

[9] Walter Ulbricht. In May 1945, he had been flown in from Moscow by the Russians with orders to restart German party politics, but ensuring Communists were in key positions. Now he gets his reward.

[10] Kennedy and Nixon debate before the nation, and Nixon loses out because of his five-o'clock shadow.

[11] Cassius Clay on the Olympic podium in Rome, as winner of the gold medal for light heavyweight boxing, just before turning professional.

[5] Adolf Eichmann in prison in Israel, awaiting trial, after being seized in South America.

 [9]

September 12, 1960
Walter Ulbricht, a cabinetmaker by trade and member of the Socialist Unity Party, becomes head (1960–73) of the German Democratic Republic (East Germany).

September 24, 1960
The first nuclear-powered aircraft carrier, the **Enterprise**, is launched by the United States.

 [10]

September 26, 1960
The first in a series of historic **televised debates** (seen by some 85 to 120 million viewers) between U.S. presidential candidates John F. Kennedy and Vice President Richard M. Nixon is broadcast.

October 1, 1960
Nigeria gains its independence from Britain but remains a member of the commonwealth.

October 15, 1960
All urban property in **Cuba** is nationalized.

 [11]

October 29, 1960
Cassius Clay, who will later change his name to Muhammad Ali, wins his first professional boxing match.

1960-1961

November 8, 1960
John F. Kennedy is elected president of the United States. His vice president is Lyndon Johnson.
[1]

November 28, 1960
Mauritania declares its independence and leaves the French community.

December 2, 1960
President Dwight D. Eisenhower authorizes the expenditure of up to $1,000,000 for relief of **Cuban refugees** in the United States.

December 14, 1960
The convention establishing the **Organisation for Economic Co-operation and Development** is signed by 18 European countries, the United States, and Canada.

1961
American geophysicists Harry Hess and Robert Dietz advance the theory that **mid-ocean ridges** are spreading apart and producing valleys into which hot lava from the earth's interior is rising.

1961
The ill-starred **Mohole Project**, in which scientists try to drill through the earth's crust to the mantle, begins.

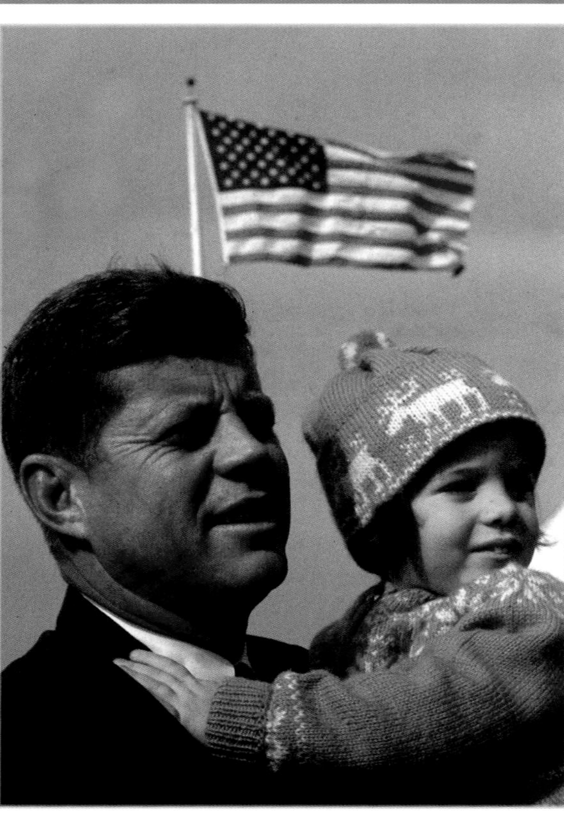

[1] JFK with his daughter, Caroline, on election day.

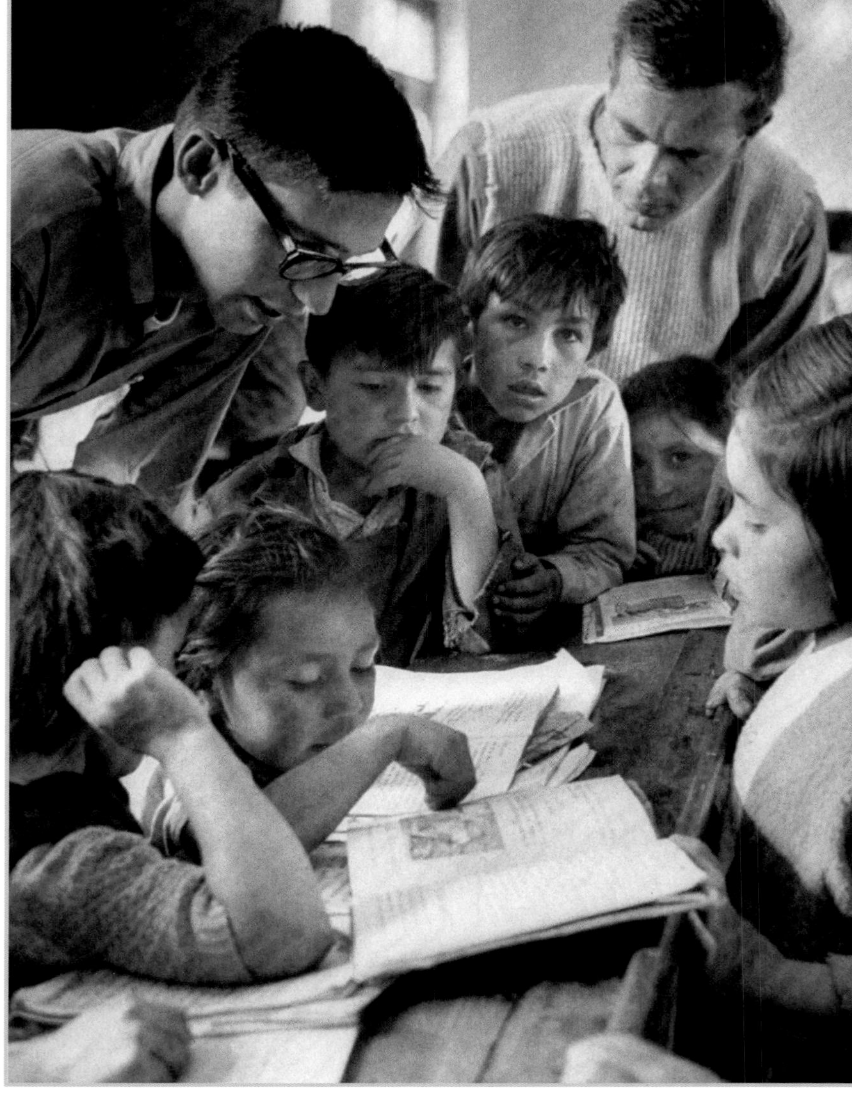

[7] Two members of the Peace Corps at work with Colombian children.

[6] Patterned pantyhose

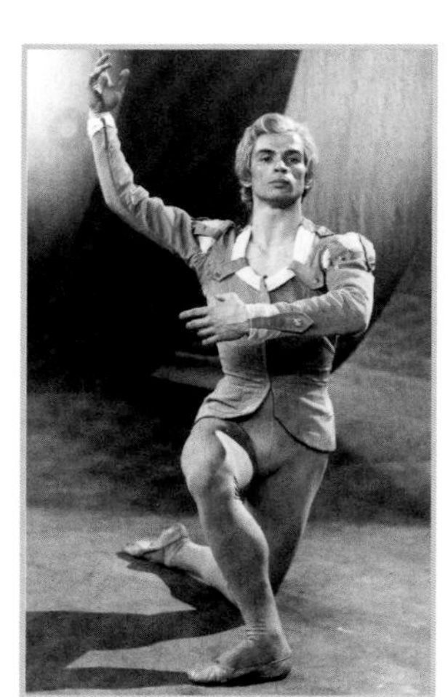

[5] Rudolf Nureyev rehearsing for an appearance on BBC television, after his defection to the West.

[10] Yuri Gagarin at a Russian exhibition at London's Earls Court.

[5]
1961
While in Paris with the Kirov Ballet in June 1961, ballet dancer **Rudolf Nureyev** eludes Soviet security men at the airport and requests asylum in France.

 [6]
1961
Women adopt **pantyhose** as a replacement for the nylon stockings that had been developed in the 1940s to supplant silk stockings.

January 7, 1961
Heads of state of Ghana, Guinea, Mali, Morocco, and the United Arab Republic meet in Casablanca and announce their intention to establish an **African organization** similar to N.A.T.O.

January 20, 1961
U.S. president John F. Kennedy, in his **inaugural address**, says, "And so, my fellow Americans: ask not what your country can do for you—ask what you can do for your country."

January 27, 1961
The Georgia legislature approves a repeal of the state's public school **segregation laws**.

February 7, 1961
President John F. Kennedy asks United States Congress to raise the **federal minimum wage** from $1.00 to $1.25 an hour and to extend coverage to more workers.

1961
In **Mapp v. Ohio** the U.S. Supreme Court finds that the Fourth Amendment prohibition of unreasonable search and seizure, and the inadmissibility of evidence obtained in violation of it, applies on the state level as well as to federal.

1961
Paraguay is the last republic in the Americas to give women the right to vote.

1961
Roger Maris breaks one of baseball's long-held records, hitting a season total of 61 home runs to beat the record of 60 set by Babe Ruth 1927.

 [2]

1961
Scottish novelist and literary critic **Muriel Spark** publishes her best-known novel, *The Prime of Miss Jean Brodie.*

 [3]

1961
The **World Wildlife Fund** is established in London, partly in response to reports of dwindling wildlife populations in East Africa, to foster conservation of endangered animals and their habitats.

1961
U Thant of Burma (now Myanmar) becomes secretary general of the U.N. He will serve until 1971.

 [4]

[8] The dogs of the Soviet Academy of Science, all prospective astronauts.

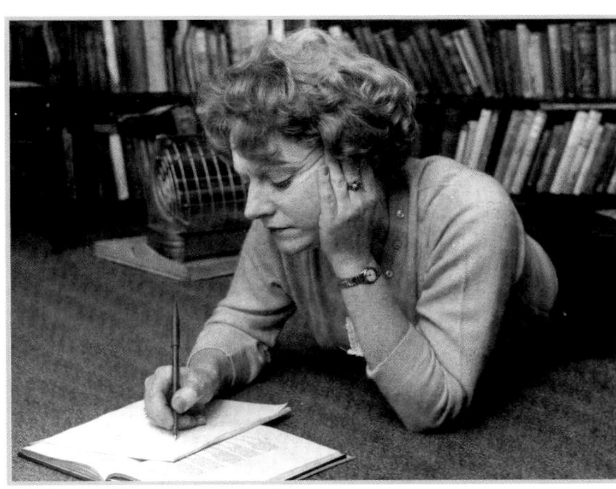

[3] Muriel Spark. Her emancipated Edinburgh schoolmistress, Jean Brodie, will be played to perfection by actress Maggie Smith in the film version of her novel.

[4] U Thant, possibly smoking a Burmese cheroot.

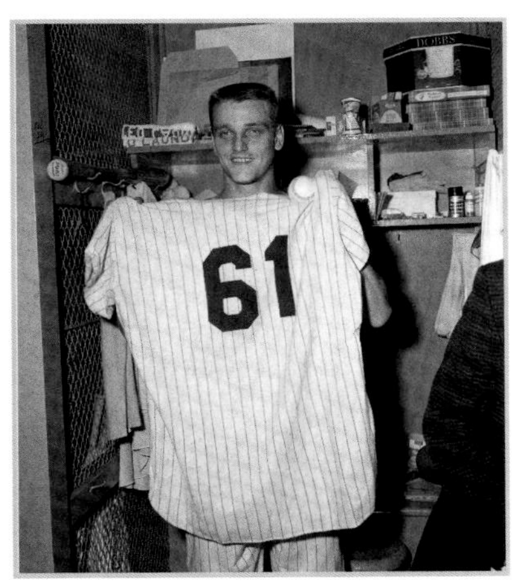

[2] Roger Maris holds up a shirt celebrating the total of his home runs.

[9] Floyd Patterson on the offensive with Ingemar Johansson.

[7]

March 1, 1961
The **Peace Corps** is established by U.S. president John F. Kennedy by means of his Peace Corps Act. It will be directed by Kennedy's brother-in-law, R. Sargent Shriver.

 [8]

March 9, 1961
Moscow radio announces that the U.S.S.R. has orbited and recovered a 10,340-pound **spaceship that carried a dog** and other live "biological specimens."

 [9]

March 13, 1961
Floyd Patterson knocks out Ingemar Johansson in the sixth round in Miami Beach, Florida, to retain the professional heavyweight championship.

March 23, 1961
The **Soviet government** abolishes prior censorship on outgoing news dispatches.

March 29, 1961
The **Twenty-third Amendment** to the U.S. Constitution, providing three electoral votes to the District of Columbia in presidential elections, is ratified.

 [10]

April 12, 1961
Soviet cosmonaut **Yuri Gagarin** becomes the first human to travel in space. His flight aboard a Vostok 1 spacecraft lasts 1 hour and 29 minutes. His spaceflight brings him immediate worldwide fame.

April 12, 1961
President John F. Kennedy pledges that United States armed forces will not intervene in **Cuba** under any conditions to bring about the overthrow of Fidel Castro.

April 12, 1961
The United States Atomic Energy commission announces the discovery of the element **lawrencium** (number 103 on the periodic table of the elements).

April 15, 1961
Three **Cuban air bases** are bombed and strafed; Cuban foreign minister Raul Roa charges that the attacks are a "prologue to large-scale invasion planned by the United States."

 [1]

April 17, 1961
Some 1,500 Cuban exiles opposed to Fidel Castro launch an abortive invasion of Cuba at the **Bay of Pigs** (Bahía de los Cochinos), on the southwestern coast. The invasion is financed and directed by the U.S. government.

April 23, 1961
French president Charles de Gaulle assumes dictatorial powers to crush the mutiny in **Algeria**.

April 27, 1961
Sierra Leone achieves independence within the British Commonwealth.

THE BAY OF PIGS

Failed invasion of Cuba directed by the U.S. Central Intelligence Agency

The invasion was intended to spark a rebellion that would topple Fidel Castro, whose Communist regime was considered a threat to U.S. interests in the region. The attack began on April 15, 1961, with the bombing of Cuban military bases; two days later a force of about 1,500—mainly Cuban exiles in Florida (left)—landed at several sites along the coast of the island, including the Bay of Pigs. The rebellion never materialized, the invasion force was quickly defeated, and more than 1,100 men were imprisoned. The result was a huge propaganda victory for Castro and a severe embarrassment for the administration of U.S. president John F. Kennedy.

[1] The remains of a plane destroyed at Santiago airport in Cuba by the air attack organized and paid for by the U.S. This attack is a precursor to the Bay of Pigs. Kennedy cancels two further air attacks because he wishes to maintain "plausible deniability."

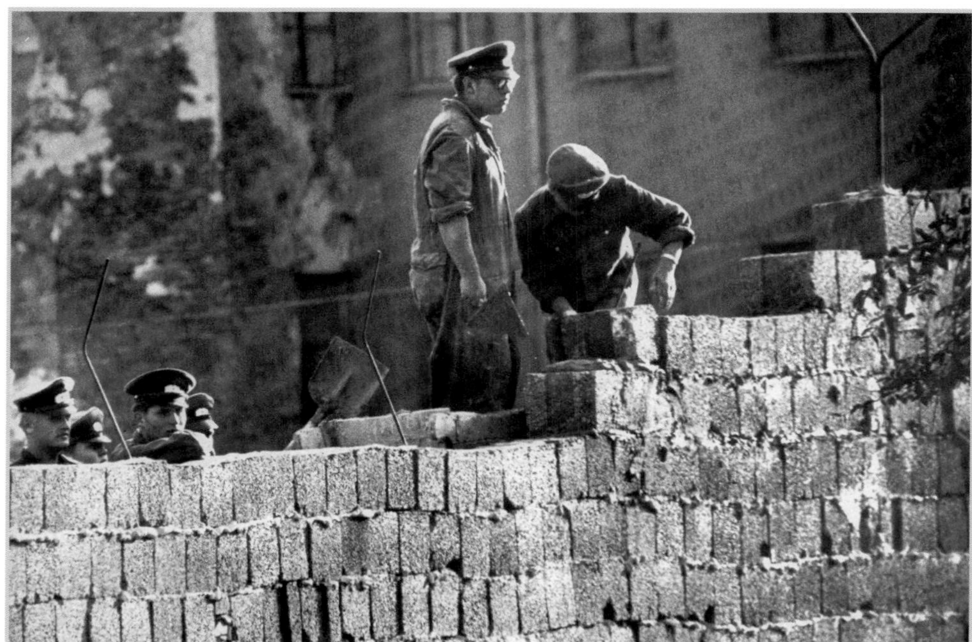

[5] The Berlin Wall is made higher and stronger. The only benefit it brings is an end to the increasingly tense confrontations of Western and Communist troops and tanks in the preceding months.

May 28, 1961
Amnesty International is founded in London. The organization is dedicated to informing public opinion about human rights and to securing the release of political prisoners. It will win the 1977 Nobel Peace Prize.

June 7, 1961
Bolivia is placed under a state of siege after the government announces it has thwarted a Communist plot to overthrow it.

June 25, 1961
Iraq lays claim to **Kuwait**, maintaining the Persian Gulf sheikhdom to be an "integral part" of Iraq. Six days earlier, Great Britain has recognized Kuwait's independence.

July 5, 1961
Eighty Muslims are slain in clashes during **Algerian nationalist demonstrations** and a general strike.

July 23, 1961
The U.S.S.R. assails as acts of espionage and aggression United States launchings of the **satellites** Tiros III (weather) and Midas III (rocket-detection).

August 1961
The **Alliance for Progress**, an international economic development program, is established by the United States and 22 Latin American countries to maintain democracy and achieve economic and social development.

May 1, 1961
Cuban prime minister **Fidel Castro**, in a speech in Havana, declares that Cuba has become a socialist nation and will no longer hold elections.

 [2]

May 1, 1961
Harper Lee is awarded the Pulitzer Prize for her novel *To Kill a Mockingbird.*

May 1, 1961
The first major **airplane hijacking** within the United States occurs when a man forces a commercial airliner en route from Miami to Key West, Florida, to detour to Cuba.

May 5, 1961
Less than one month after Yury Gagarin's flight, American astronaut **Alan B. Shepard, Jr.**, makes a 15-minute suborbital flight in the Mercury capsule Freedom 7.

 [3]

May 9, 1961
Newton N. Minow, chairman of the FCC, in a speech before the National Association of Broadcasters convention, berates the **violence and mediocrity in television programs**, calling television a "vast wasteland."

May 16, 1961
Korean general **Park Chung Hee** overthrows the Second Republic of South Korea in a bloodless coup. He will remain leader of the junta until two years later, when he wins the first of three terms as president of the Third Republic.

 [4]

[2] Fidel Castro (left) at the May Day celebrations where he abolishes elections. Ernesto Che Guevara is on the right.

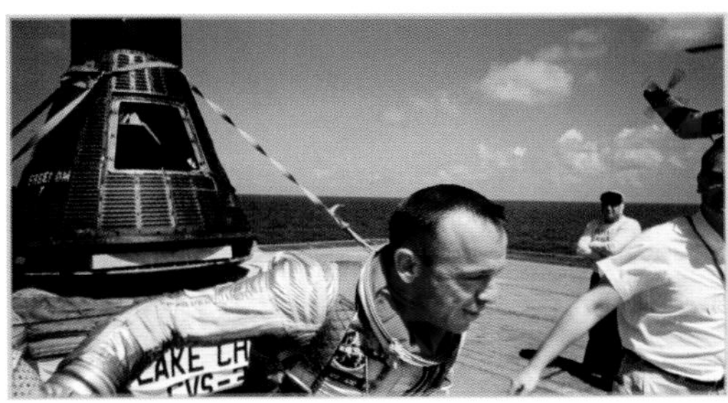

[3] Alan Shepard just after he and his capsule have been retrieved from the Atlantic.

[7] At the Russian consulate in New York, protesters against the resumption of nuclear testing don Kennedy and Khrushchev masks and diapers to indicate the leaders' childish rivalry, while holding placards with infantile rival boasts.

[6] Jomo Kenyatta (right) is greeted shortly after his release from prison in Kenya by Hastings Banda, political leader in neighboring Nyasaland (Malawi).

[4] Park Chung Hee of South Korea.

[8] Bertrand Russell during a break in his trial proceedings at Bow Street magistrates' court in London.

 [5]

August 13, 1961
East Germany begins building a wall separating Communist **East Berlin** from **West Berlin**. It is meant to stop the best and brightest East Germans abandoning their country.

 [6]

August 14, 1961
Jomo Kenyatta, imprisoned since 1953 for his part in the Mau Mau insurrection in Kenya, is released. His party has won a clear majority in elections under a new constitution, which paves the way for independence.

August 31, 1961
The **U.S.S.R.** announces that it will resume nuclear testing. The United States denounces the decision as "blackmail."

 [7]

September 5, 1961
President John F. Kennedy orders resumption of United States **nuclear tests** but specifies that they are to take place "in the laboratory and underground with no fall-out."

 [8]

September 12, 1961
Eighty-nine-year-old philosopher **Bertrand Russell** is sent to jail for inciting the public to break the law during an antinuclear demonstration in London.

September 19, 1961
The people of **Jamaica**, in a national referendum, vote in a substantial majority not to remain in the West Indies federation.

1961-1962

October 19, 1961
Georg von Bekesy of Harvard University is awarded the Nobel Prize for Medicine for his work on hearing.
 [1]

October 26, 1961
Ivo Andric of Yugoslavia is awarded the Nobel Prize in Literature. He is claimed as part of Croatian literature, Serbian literature, and Bosnian literature.
 [2]

October 27, 1961
The first **Saturn rocket** is successfully launched; years later the Saturn V will be the launch vehicle used in the Apollo moon-landing flights.
 [3]

November 15, 1961
The Rembrandt painting **Aristotle Contemplating the Bust of Homer** is purchased by the Metropolitan Museum of Art for $2,300,000, the highest auction price ever paid to date.
 [4]

November 28, 1961
Football player **Ernie Davis** of Syracuse University becomes the first African American to win the prestigious Heisman Trophy.

December 2, 1961
Cuban prime minister **Fidel Castro** announces that he has long been a Marxist and is leading Cuba into communism.

[1] Hungarian-born Georg von Bekesy (left).

[2] Ivo Andric. His most famous novel is The Bridge on the Drina.

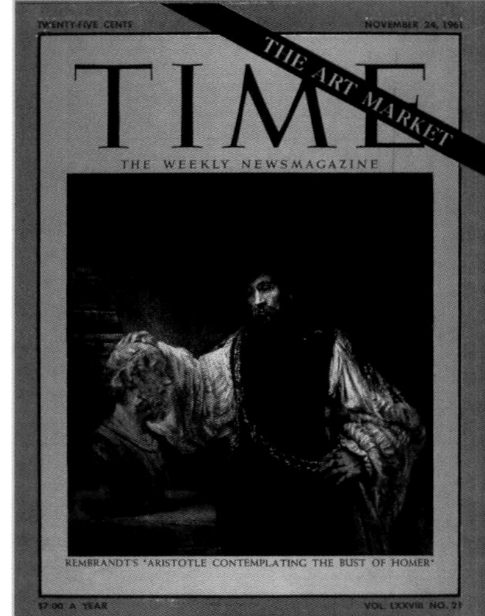

[4] The Rembrandt's price is sensational enough to attract the attention of Time *magazine.*

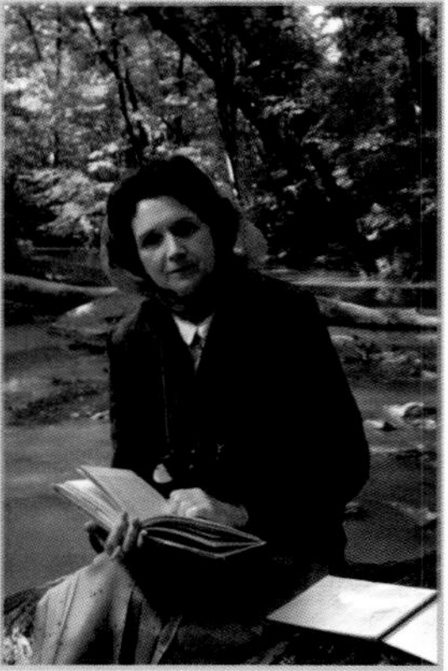

[10] Rachel Carson. Although she never called for an outright ban on DDT, she is criticized by those who believe that, used correctly, it is the best method for controling malaria, which has come back in force as a result of the ban her book prompted.

[8] John Steinbeck (bearded) at the Nobel prize ceremony, surrounded by a scientific galaxy: Maurice Williams, Francis Crick, and James Watson of DNA fame flank him. Also in the line are John Kendrew (right) and Max Perutz (second left). Their prize is for work on the structure of globular proteins.

[3] Brainerd D. Holmes, NASA director of manned space flight, with a model of the Saturn C-5 rocket.

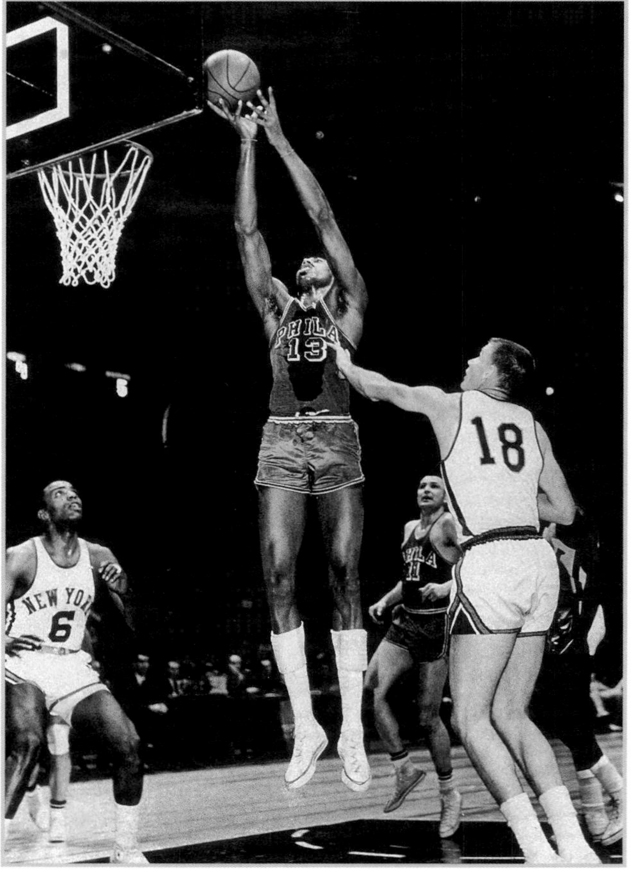

[9] Wilt Chamberlain scores in a game against the New York Knicks.

1962
In **Engel v. Vitale** the U.S. Supreme Court holds that requiring students to recite a nondenominational prayer in public schools is unconstitutional.

 [8]
1962
John Steinbeck wins the Nobel Prize for Literature for his novels, many set in the Salinas valley in California.

1962
Nick Holonyak, Jr. invents the **light-emitting diode (LED)**, a semiconductor device that emits infrared or visible light when charged with an electric current. Visible LEDs are used largely as indicator and display lamps.

 [9]
1962
Philadelphia Warriors player **Wilt Chamberlain** scores 100 points in a single game, a National Basketball Association record.

1962
Pope John XXIII convokes the **Second Vatican Council**. It reforms Catholic liturgical practice and attempts to relate the church's concept of itself and of revelation to the needs and values of contemporary culture.

 [10]
1962
Rachel Carson's **Silent Spring**, an exposé of the biological costs of chemical pesticides in wide use in the U.S., is published and helps foment a new environmental consciousness.

December 9, 1961
Tanganyika becomes independent, with Julius Nyerere as its first prime minister. In 1964 the territory will unite with the island of Zanzibar to form Tanzania.

December 15, 1961
Adolf Eichmann is sentenced to death by an Israeli court in Jerusalem after conviction of crimes against the Jewish people, crimes against humanity, and war crimes during the Nazi regime in Germany.

1962
American astronaut **John H. Glenn, Jr.**, orbits the earth three times in Friendship 7, splashing down in the Atlantic Ocean near the Bahamas.

 [5]

1962
Andy Warhol's silk-screen *Marilyn Diptych*, consisting of multiple images of actress Marilyn Monroe, draws attention to reproducibility and commodification of pop icons.

 [6]

1962
Brazil defeats Czechoslovakia in the men's **World Cup** soccer championship by a score of 3 to 1.

1962
Dr. No, the first motion picture version of an Ian Fleming spy novel, is a box-office hit. Sean Connery stars as British agent 007—James Bond—battling international crime and suavely wooing glamorous women.

[7]

[5] *John Glenn and Friendship 7 before his space shot.*

[6] *The* Marilyn Diptych *on show in the Slovak town of Medzilaborce, from which Andy Warhol's parents emigrated to the U.S. in 1913.*

[7] *A still from the first James Bond film,* Dr. No*: Sean Connery with Ursula Andress.*

[11] *Nelson Mandela at the time of his imprisonment.*

[12] *A 78-year-old AT&T stockholder looks at a scale model of Telstar.*

1962
Sam Walton opens the first **Wal-Mart** store in Rogers, Arkansas, in 1962, offering merchandise at discount prices in a no-frills setting. By his death in 1992, Wal-Mart will have become the world's largest retailer.

 [11]

1962
South African political activist **Nelson Mandela** is jailed and sentenced to five years in prison. Two years later he will be sentenced to life imprisonment for sabotage, treason, and violent conspiracy.

 [12]

1962
Telstar, the first communications satellite, is put into orbit for use by American companies.

1962
The first album by the Beatles, **Please Please Me**, is released in the United Kingdom. Led by John Lennon and Paul McCartney, the Beatles become one of the most important rock groups of all time.

1962
The new **Coventry Cathedral** is consecrated in England, replacing the one destroyed in the Blitz. It includes work by artists such as Graham Sutherland and John Piper.

1962
Unconventional Black Mountain poet **Robert Creeley** publishes his unique collection *For Love, Poems 1950–1960*.

1962

1962
Vladimir Nabokov publishes the novel *Pale Fire*, which extends and completes his mastery of unorthodox structure.

1962
West Indian poet **Derek Walcott** completes his first collection of poetry, *In a Green Night*. He will win the Nobel Prize for Literature in 1992.

c. 1962
Oil surpasses coal as a proportion of total world energy production.

January 17, 1962
Ten **television quiz show** winners, indicted in 1960 for second-degree perjury, are given suspended sentences by a special-sessions judge in New York.

February 10, 1962
U.S. airman Francis Gary Powers, captured pilot of the U-2 plane downed by the Soviet Union in 1960, is exchanged for jailed Soviet informant **Rudolf Abel**.

February 24, 1962
Chinese foreign ministry declares that a United States military build-up in **South Vietnam** is a threat to Communist China's security and demands immediate withdrawal of all United States personnel from that area.

[2] Independence celebrations in Algiers.

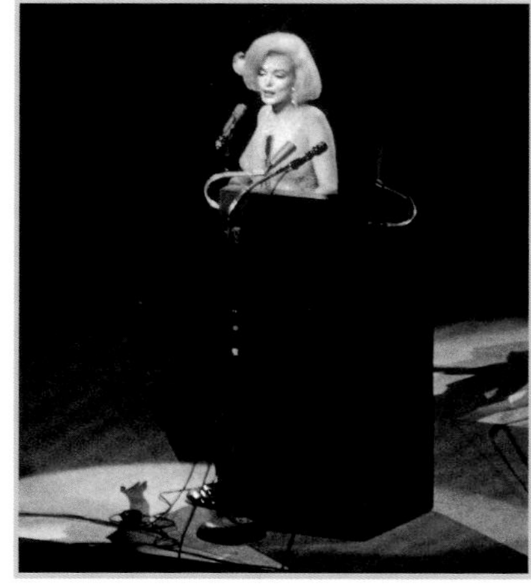

[3] Marilyn Monroe sings "Happy Birthday, Mr. President" at a Democratic fund raiser in Madison Square Garden on President Kennedy's birthday, a few months before her death.

[4] Norman Manley, the country's premier, goes to Kingston cathedral to celebrate Jamaica's independence.

[5] A West German protesting the death of Peter Fechter is carried off by West Berlin police, after a bus full of Soviet soldiers, on its way to a Soviet war memorial in West Berlin, has been stoned.

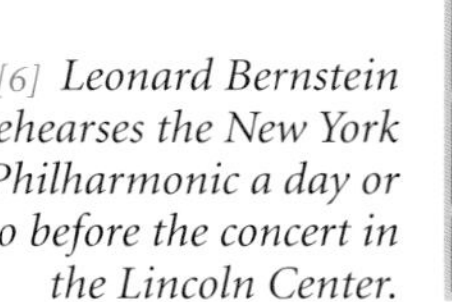

[6] Leonard Bernstein rehearses the New York Philharmonic a day or two before the concert in the Lincoln Center.

July 2, 1962
Soviet premier **Nikita Khrushchev** warns in a television speech that the U.S.S.R. will join in repelling any attack on Communist China.

 [2]

July 3, 1962
Algeria gains its independence from France.

July 13, 1962
Eugene McNeely, president of AT&T, and Jacques Marette, French minister of communications, hold the first official **transatlantic telephone conversation** via Telstar.

 [3]

August 5, 1962
American actress **Marilyn Monroe**—a cultural icon whose sex-symbol image comes from her roles in such films as *Gentlemen Prefer Blondes* (1953)—dies after taking an overdose of sleeping pills.

 [4]

August 6, 1962
After 300 years of British rule, **Jamaica** becomes an independent country within the British Commonwealth of Nations.

 [5]

August 17, 1962
The slaying of **Peter Fechter** at the Berlin Wall by East German guards incites angry demonstrations by 5,000 West Berliners; United States soldiers are booed for not assisting Fechter.

February 26, 1962
Irish Republican Army (I.R.A.) announces the end of its campaign of violence against the partition of Ireland, laying down its arms and disbanding its volunteers.

March 12, 1962
The British ministries of health and education start a drive to inform the British public of the dangers of **cigarette smoking** and its connection with lung cancer and other illnesses.

March 26, 1962
The U.S. Supreme Court forces the **Tennessee legislature** to reapportion itself on the basis of population. The case is described by Chief Justice Earl Warren as the most important one decided since his appointment to the court.

May 3, 1962
United States Air Force announces the first transmission of television pictures by means of an **orbiting satellite**.

May 31, 1962
The State of Israel hangs German official **Adolf Eichmann**, who had escaped from a prison camp in 1946 and spent some 14 years in hiding, for his part in the Nazi extermination of Jews during World War II.
 *[1]*

June 4, 1962
The first electricity to be produced by nuclear power in **Canada** is transmitted from the nuclear-power demonstration station at Rolphton, Ontario.

[1] Adolf Eichmann in a bullet-proof glass box during his trial.

[7] Sonny Liston stands over his victim, Floyd Patterson.

CUBAN MISSILE CRISIS

Major confrontation between the United States and the Soviet Union over the presence of Soviet nuclear missiles in Cuba

On October 16, 1962, a U.S. U-2 spy plane detected a ballistic missile on a launching site in Cuba. The equipment had been supplied to the island's Communist regime by the Soviet Union, and Cuba's proximity to the United States sparked fears of a third world war. The United States responded by placing a naval "quarantine" (blockade) around the island. The photograph (left above) shows the U.S. picket ship *Vesole* intercepting *Potzunov*, a missile-carrying Soviet freighter, in the waters off Havana.

When President John F. Kennedy went on television and radio on October 22, the world waited anxiously for the U.S. reaction to the crisis. The photograph (left below) shows a crowd of Americans gathered in a TV showroom to watch his address.

For several days the U.S. and the Soviet Union hovered on the brink of war. Soviet premier Nikita Khrushchev finally agreed to remove the missiles in return for a secret commitment from the U.S. to withdraw its own missiles from Turkey and to never invade Cuba.

  *[6]*
September 23, 1962
Leonard Bernstein leads the New York Philharmonic orchestra in a concert for the inauguration of **Philharmonic Hall**, the first completed building in the Lincoln Center for the Performing Arts in New York City.

 *[7]*
September 25, 1962
Sonny Liston becomes world heavyweight boxing champion with a first-round knockout of Floyd Patterson in Chicago.

October 18, 1962
Francis Crick of Cambridge, James Watson of Harvard, and H. F. Wilkins of London are awarded the **Nobel Prize for Medicine** for discovering the molecular structure of DNA, the physical basis of heredity.

October 22, 1962
President John F. Kennedy alerts Americans to the Cuban missile crisis, declaring a naval blockade to prevent further missile shipments to the island country 90 miles (145 km) off the coast of the U.S.

October 28, 1962
Soviet premier Nikita Khrushchev capitulates to U.S. demands to halt delivery of nuclear-armed missiles to Cuba, bringing an end to the **Cuban missile crisis**.

November 14, 1962
The Ethiopian parliament and Eritrean Assembly vote unanimously for the abolition of Eritrea's federal status, making **Eritrea** (today independent since 1993) a simple province of the Ethiopian empire.

1962-1963

November 20, 1962
President John F. Kennedy signs an executive order prohibiting **racial discrimination** in housing built or purchased with federal aid.

1963
American inventor Douglas Engelbart of Xerox Corporation invents the **computer mouse**.

1963
American poet and novelist **Sylvia Plath** publishes her only novel, *The Bell Jar*, under a pseudonym.

1963
Barbra Streisand releases her first solo album, which wins two Grammy Awards. She will come to be considered by many to be the greatest popular singer of her generation.

1963
Betty Friedan publishes *The Feminine Mystique*, signaling the beginning of the **women's liberation movement** of the '60s and '70s. The movement seeks equal rights and opportunities for women in their economic activities, personal lives, and politics.

1963
Boston Public Television begins broadcasting the immensely popular cookery series **The French Chef**, starring Julia Child. With her humor, exuberance, and unpretentiousness, Child becomes an unlikely star and the doyenne of American cuisine.

MARCH ON WASHINGTON

The civil rights movement reaches a dramatic climax in the U.S. capital.

In an effort to draw together the multiple forces for peaceful change and to dramatize to the United States and to the world the importance of solving the nation's racial problems, the Reverend Dr. Martin Luther King, Jr., joined other civil rights leaders in organizing the historic March on Washington for Jobs and Freedom.

The wide spectrum of the coalition is reflected in the photograph (left above), in which King (center) links arms with American Jewish leader Rabbi Joachim Prinz, Protestant churchman Eugene Carson Blake, Floyd McKissick of the NAACP and CORE, American Roman Catholic activist Matthew Ahmann, and John Lewis, president of the Student Nonviolent Coordinating Committee. They and their followers all rallied to protest racial discrimination and demonstrate support for major civil rights legislation that was pending in the U.S. Congress.

On August 28, 1963, an interracial assembly of more than 200,000 gathered peaceably in the shadow of the Lincoln Memorial to demand equal justice for all citizens under the law. Here the crowds were uplifted by the emotional strength and prophetic quality of King's famous "I Have A Dream" speech (left below), in which he emphasized his faith that all men, someday, would be brothers.

Although some black leaders, including Malcolm X, refused to participate, the March on Washington was a major contributory factor to the passage of the Civil Rights Act of 1964 and the National Voting Rights Act of 1965.

[2] Betty Friedan. Her husband, Carl, says: "She changed the course of history almost single-handedly. It took a driven, super-aggressive, egocentric, almost lunatic dynamo to rock the world the way she did."

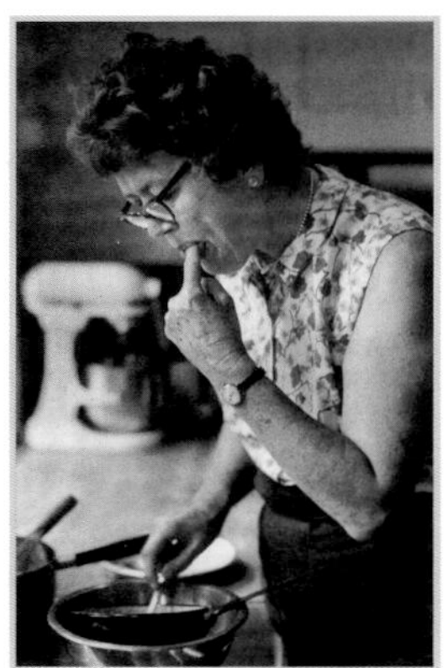

[3] Julia Child, cooking at home rather than in the studio. Her TV series follows on the very successful book, Mastering the Art of French Cooking, *which she co-wrote with Simone Beck and Louisette Bertholle.*

[6] The Rolling Stones: (left to right) Mick Jagger, Keith Richards, Brian Jones, Bill Wyman, and Charlie Watts.

1963
Russian writer **Aleksandr Solzhenitsyn's** empassioned novel *One Day in the Life of Ivan Denisovich* is removed from candidacy for the Lenin prize because of his politics.

1963
Bob Dylan makes his first appearance at the Newport Folk Festival and is virtually crowned the king of folk music. His song, "The Times They Are A-Changin'" (1964), provides an instant anthem for his generation.

1962
The Rolling Stones, led by Mick Jagger, begin to create rock music that reveals a unique vision of the dark side of post-1950s counter culture.

1963
The civil rights movement reaches a dramatic climax with a massive **march on Washington, D.C.**, where an audience of more than 200,000 hears Martin Luther King, Jr., deliver his "I Have a Dream" speech.

1963
The **liquid crystal display (LCD)**, an electronic display device that operates by applying a varying electric voltage to a layer of liquid crystal, is invented by U.S. electrical engineer George Heilmeier.

1963
The **Organization of African Unity** (later the African Union) is formed.

1963
Conservative politician **Sir Alec Douglas-Home** becomes prime minister of the United Kingdom and, in his yearlong term, gains U.S. approval for his firm anti-communism.
[4]

1963
In **Gideon v. Wainwright** the U.S. Supreme Court declares that the Sixth Amendment right to counsel applies to defendants in state as well as federal courts.

1963
Isolating and radically enlarging frames from comic strips, **Roy Lichtenstein** adopts the stylized violence of popular images in his painting *Whaam!*

1963
Japan's **Watanabe Osamu** wins his second world wrestling championship in the freestyle featherweight division. After an Olympic victory the following year, he retires undefeated with over 300 wins.

1963
Lyndon B. Johnson of the Democratic Party takes office as the 36th president of the United States. He will serve until 1969. His vice president is Hubert H. Humphrey.

1963
Robert Venturi designs the Vanna Venturi House, Chestnut Hill, Philadelphia. This house is a gentle parody of domestic architecture and one of the major buildings of postmodernism.

[5] *Roy Lichtenstein in front of one of his most famous paintings,* Whaam!, *at the Tate Gallery in London.*

[4] *Alec Douglas-Home, the former 14th Earl of Home. His emergence as prime minister from the "smoke-filled rooms" in which the Conservative Party's selection process goes on, is a surprise. R. A. Butler was expected to succeed Harold Macmillan.*

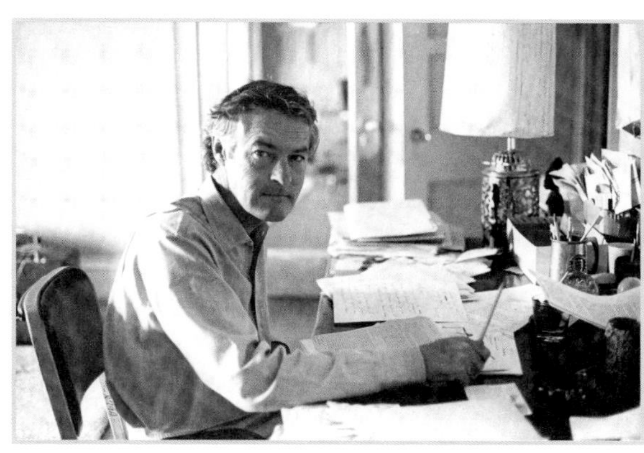

[7] *Timothy Leary. He has hopes that "acid" might have an application in the treatment of alcoholics and recidivist prisoners.*

[1] *Barbra Streisand*

c. 1963
Psychologist **Timothy Leary**, begins experimenting with LSD "acid trips" as a means of transforming personality and expanding consciousness. His admonition to "Turn on, tune in, drop out" becomes one of the catchphrases of the era.

February 4, 1963
Two British newspapermen receive prison terms for refusing to disclose the source of stories written in connection with the **Vassall spy case**.

February 5, 1963
A **federal aid program** to combat mental illness and mental retardation is proposed to Congress by President John F. Kennedy.

March 21, 1963
The U.S. federal prison on San Francisco Bay's **Alcatraz Island,** which had held some of the most dangerous civilian prisoners—including Al Capone and Robert Stroud, the "Birdman of Alcatraz"—is closed.

April 5, 1963
A House subcommittee investigating radio and TV rating services warns that the **broadcasting industry** must establish more dependable rating standards or face government action.

April 5, 1963
The Soviet Union accepts a U.S. proposal for a direct communication link between Washington, D.C., and Moscow to reduce the risk of accidental war.

April 9, 1963
An act of Congress confers honorary U.S. citizenship on **Sir Winston Churchill**.

April 12, 1963
Martin Luther King, Jr., is arrested, as racial disturbances marking antisegregation drives continue in Birmingham, Alabama.

April 18, 1963
Successful **human-nerve transplants** are reported by James B. Campbell of the New York University Medical Center.

April 22, 1963
Canadian politician and diplomat **Lester Bowles Pearson**, winner of the Nobel Peace Prize in 1957 and a member of the Liberal Party who will be known as a mediator in international disputes, becomes prime minister (1963–68).

May 15, 1963
President John F. Kennedy's science advisory committee issues a cautionary report on the use of **pesticides**.

May 22, 1963
The ministerial council of **N.A.T.O.**, meeting in Ottawa, Ontario, approves the establishment of an allied nuclear force drawn from 10 to 15 member nations.

KENNEDY ASSASSINATED

U.S. president shot dead in Dallas

John F. Kennedy toured Texas partly to show support for state governor John B. Connally, Jr. On Friday, November 22, 1963, the two men and the first lady, Jacqueline Kennedy, were in an open limousine riding slowly in a motorcade (left) through downtown Dallas. At 12:30 PM the president was struck by two rifle bullets, one at the base of his neck and one in his head. He was pronounced dead shortly after arrival at Parkland Memorial Hospital. Governor Connally, though also gravely wounded, recovered. Vice President Lyndon B. Johnson took the oath as president at 2:38 PM. Lee Harvey Oswald, a 24-year-old Dallas citizen, was accused of the slaying. Two days later Oswald was shot to death by Jack Ruby, a local nightclub owner with connections to the criminal underworld, in the basement of a Dallas police station.

[5] The locomotive pulling the mail train is stopped by the robbers by a bridge so the bags of money could easily be thrown down to waiting vehicles.

[7] The president's funeral: his son salutes him; his brothers stand either side of his widow.

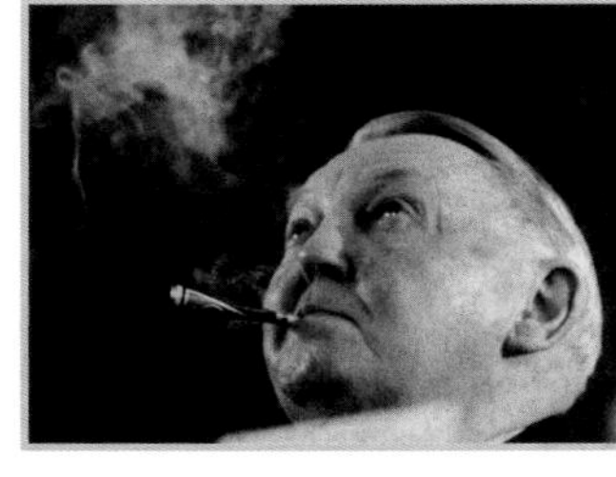

[6] Ludwig Erhard, champion of the social market economy, "capitalism with a heart."

August 5, 1963
The United States, the Soviet Union, and the United Kingdom sign the **Nuclear Test-Ban Treaty** in Moscow.

 [5]

August 8, 1963
Armed robbers steal £2.6 million from the Glasgow-London Royal Mail Train near Bridego Bridge, north of London, in the **Great Train Robbery**.

 [6]

October 16, 1963
Ludwig Wilhelm Erhard, a member of the Christian-Democratic Union who will be remembered as the chief architect of his country's post–World War II economic recovery, becomes chancellor of West Germany (1963–66).

November 2, 1963
South Vietnamese president **Ngo Dinh Diem** is assassinated. Diem's imprisoning and killing of hundreds of Buddhists, who he alleged were abetting Communist insurgents, finally persuaded the U.S. to withdraw its support.

November 22, 1963
The most notorious political murder in recent American history occurs this day, when **John F. Kennedy**, the 35th U.S. president (1961–63), is shot and killed in Dallas, Texas, while riding in an open car.

November 24, 1963
Dallas nightclub owner **Jack Ruby** fatally shoots Lee Harvey Oswald, the accused assassin of U.S. president John F. Kennedy.

June 8, 1963
The **American Heart Association** becomes the first U.S. voluntary public agency to begin a drive against cigarette smoking.

June 11, 1963
Quang Duc, a Buddhist monk, commits suicide by setting fire to himself in a Saigon street as Buddhist protests against the South Vietnamese government increase in intensity.

 [1]

June 16, 1963
Soviet cosmonaut **Valentina Tereshkova** becomes the first woman to travel in space, launched on the spacecraft Vostok 6. She returns to earth on June 19, having orbited the earth 48 times.

 [2]

June 21, 1963
Giovanni Battista Montini is elected pope of the Roman Catholic Church. He takes the name **Paul VI**.

 [3]

July 1963
British secretary of state for war **John Profumo** lies to Parliament about his affair with Christine Keeler, who was a lover of a Russian military attaché. The truth emerges, and Profumo resigns, helping topple the government of Harold Macmillan.

 [4]

July 1, 1963
The U.S. Postal Service institutes the Zone Improvement Plan Code, commonly known as the **ZIP code**.

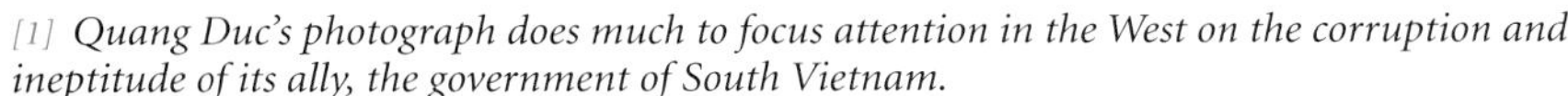

[1] Quang Duc's photograph does much to focus attention in the West on the corruption and ineptitude of its ally, the government of South Vietnam.

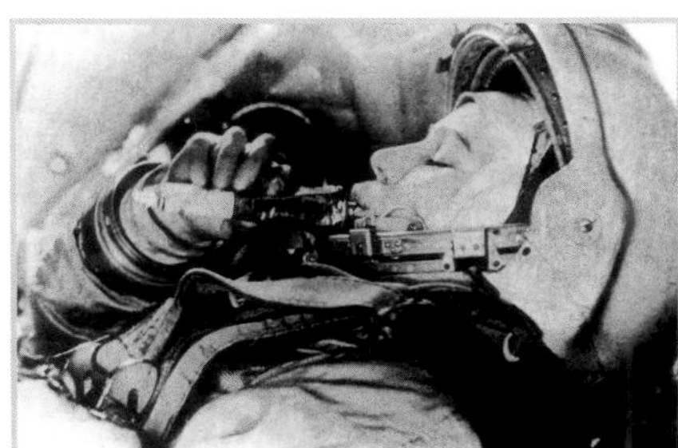

[2] Valentina Tereshkova practices feeding herself with a special device to get around the problems of lack of gravity in space.

[4] Christine Keeler (right) and showgirl Mandy Rice-Davies, after giving evidence at the trial of Stephen Ward. Both were part of Ward's circle, and he is charged with living off immoral earnings—in other words, pimping. It was Ward who introduced John Profumo to Keeler.

[3] Pope Paul VI in the Sistine Chapel after the cardinals' obeisance to him at his election.

[8] Cars wrecked by a tsunami generated by the earthquake in Alaska. They are in California, more than 1,500 miles away.

 [7]

November 25, 1963
President **John F. Kennedy is buried** with full military honors in Arlington National Cemetery.

December 9, 1963
The **Studebaker Corporation** announces that it is abandoning automobile production in the United States but will continue production in Hamilton, Ontario.

1964
American physicist **Murray Gell-Mann** introduces the concept of the quark, a particle that is the building block of electrons, protons, neutrons, and other elementary particles.

 [8]

1964
An **earthquake** of 8.5 on the Richter scale strikes Prince William Sound in Alaska, damaging Seward, Valdez, and Anchorage and unleashing a destructive tsunami.

1964
An official report to the **surgeon general** of the United States concludes that smoking tobacco is causally related to lung cancer.

1964
Ethiopian marathon runner **Abebe Bikila** becomes the first athlete to win two Olympic marathons; he set a world record while running barefoot at the 1960 Olympic Games in Rome, then bests his own record at the 1964 Olympics.

1964

1964
Italian director Sergio Leone releases the first "spaghetti western," **A Fistful of Dollars**, starring Clint Eastwood as "the man with no name."

 [1]

1964
In the Summer Olympics at Tokyo, Soviet gymnast **Larissa Latynina** wins six medals, raising her final career total to a record 18 Olympic medals.

1964
The U.S. Supreme Court holds that in **libel cases brought by public officials** "actual malice" must be demonstrated, i.e., that a falsehood has been issued with knowledge that it is false or in reckless disregard of whether it is false or not.

1964
Japanese novelist **Oe Kenzaburo** publishes his autobiographical novel *Kojinteki-na taiken* (*A Personal Matter*), about a father and his brain-damaged son. He will win the Nobel Prize for Literature in 1994.

1964
John Kemeny and Thomas Kurtz of Dartmouth College develop **BASIC** (Beginner's All-Purpose Symbolic Instruction Language).

1964
Labour Party leader **Harold Wilson** begins his first stint as prime minister of the United Kingdom (1964–70). He will be appointed to the post for a second time in 1974.

 [2]

[1] *Clint Eastwood in the first of Sergio Leone's mannered, highly stylized westerns, which inject new life into the genre.*

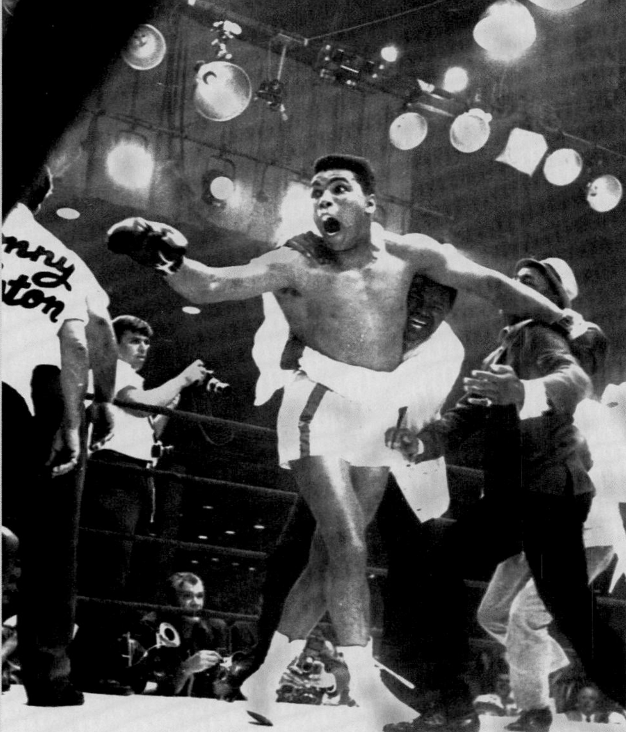

[5] *Cassius Clay becomes heavyweight world champion.*

[2] *Harold Wilson travels first class.*

[6] *Jack Ruby (center) with his defense attorney, Melvin Belli (right), and reporters at a pre-trial hearing.*

[3] *Skater Lidiya Skoblikova with her four Olympic golds. She won two in 1960.*

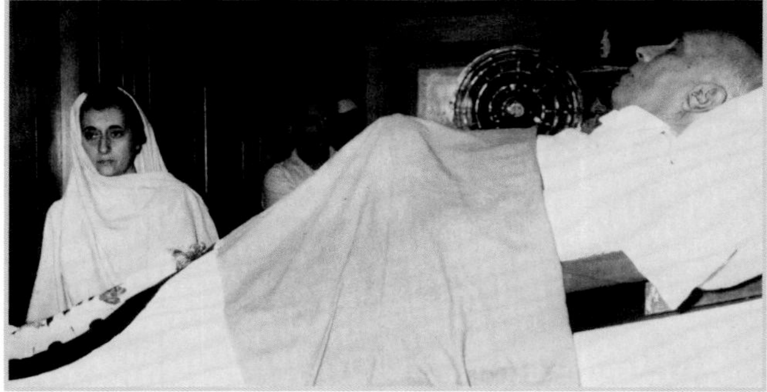

[7] *Nehru's body with his daughter, Indira Gandhi, future premier of India, behind.*

[4] *Lyndon Johnson and Martin Luther King, Jr., at the signing of the Civil Rights Act.*

January 8, 1964
President Lyndon B. Johnson, in his State of the Union message, calls for reductions in defense expenditure and for a "**war against poverty**."

February 18, 1964
The United States terminates all military and economic aid to Britain, France, and Yugoslavia and bars military assistance to Spain and Morocco because of their refusal to halt trade with **Cuba**.

 [5]

February 25, 1964
American boxer Muhammad Ali, known at the time as **Cassius Clay**, becomes the world heavyweight champion by knocking out Sonny Liston in seven rounds.

 [6]

March 14, 1964
In the first courtroom verdict to be televised in the United States, **Jack Ruby** is found guilty of the murder of Lee Harvey Oswald, assassin of U.S. president John F. Kennedy.

April 5, 1964
General **Douglas MacArthur** dies at Walter Reed Medical Center, Washington, D.C.

May 19, 1964
It is disclosed that at least 40 microphones have been found hidden in the walls of the **U.S. embassy in Moscow**.

1964
Russia's **Lidiya Skoblikova** becomes the first athlete to win four gold medals at one Winter Olympic Games when she sweeps the women's speed skating events at Innsbruck, Austria.

 [3]

1964
The **Palestine Liberation Organization** is formed at an Arab summit meeting in order to bring various Palestinian groups together under one organization. It will come to prominence after the Arab-Israeli war of June 1967, engaging in guerrilla war against Israel.

1964
The **Twenty-fourth Amendment** to the U.S. Constitution makes unconstitutional the poll tax for federal elections. Two years later this principle will be extended to state and local elections.

1964
With the release by Capitol Records of *Meet the Beatles,* full-blown **Beatlemania** is launched. Though not their first album, it is at 5.4 million copies one of the best-selling.

1964
U.S. president Lyndon Johnson signs the **Civil Rights Act** into law, giving federal law-enforcement agencies the power to prevent racial discrimination in employment, voting, and use of public facilities.

 [4]

c. 1964
In **Japan**, modern-type *juku*, or "cram schools," emerge, designed to help students study or prepare for exams. The term "juku" dates from the Tokugawa shogunate.

BEATLEMANIA

The Beatles take America by storm.

The Beatles' sensational arrival in New York City on February 7, 1964, established them as the world's top pop group and opened the gates of America to a wealth of British musical talent.

Their triumph had not been easily achieved. Although they had already had great success in the U.K. charts, they had been turned down by Capitol Records, the U.S. arm of their British label, EMI. (Their early singles had been brought out by a small Chicago company, Vee-Jay.) Few people in the record industry believed that the "mop tops'" Liverpool charm could cross the Atlantic.

Capitol executives changed their minds after the Beatles' manager, Brian Epstein, secured the group an appearance on *The Ed Sullivan Show* (left, above), rushing out "I Want To Hold Your Hand"; within 10 days of its U.S. release on December 26, 1963, the single had sold a million copies.

When the Beatles landed at Kennedy Airport, a crowd of 3,000—mainly teenagers (left below)—had gathered to welcome them. The ensuing craze—known as Beatlemania—was something new. Musicians performing in the 19th century certainly excited a frenzy—one thinks of Franz Liszt—but that was before the modern mass media created the possibility of collective frenzy.

By the summer of 1964, when the Beatles appeared in *A Hard Day's Night*, a movie that dramatized the phenomenon of Beatlemania, the band's effect was evident around the world as countless young people emulated the band members' characteristic long hair, flip humor, and whimsical displays of devil-may-care abandon.

In the wake of the Beatles, a host of British acts made it in the United States; among the first to follow were the Searchers.

 [7]

May 27, 1964
Former Indian prime minister **Jawaharlal Nehru**, a leader of the Indian independence movement of the 1930s and '40s, dies in New Delhi.

June 3, 1964
President Lyndon B. Johnson claims that U.S. military strength is stronger than that of any adversary and stronger than "the combined might of all nations in the history of the world."

July 6, 1964
Nyasaland breaks from British rule and becomes the independent country of **Malawi** within the British Commonwealth of Nations.

July 21, 1964
Race riots, which will last for three days and kill 21 people, take place between Chinese and Malays in **Singapore**.

August 1964
The **bodies of three civil rights workers**, killled by white supremacists, are found near Philadelphia, Mississippi.

August 5, 1964
U.S. president Lyndon B. Johnson puts the **Gulf of Tonkin Resolution** before Congress.

1964-1965

August 10, 1964
Pope Paul VI issues his first encyclical letter, **Ecclesiam Suam**, which makes known his readiness to mediate in international disputes.

September 27, 1964
The **Warren Commission** concludes that neither Lee Harvey Oswald nor Jack Ruby was part of any conspiracy to assassinate President John F. Kennedy.
 [1]

October 15, 1964
Nikita Khrushchev retires. Aleksey N. Kosygin takes over the premiership, and **Leonid I. Brezhnev** becomes party secretary and effective leader of the U.S.S.R.
 [2]

October 16, 1964
China, eager to join the nuclear race, successfully detonates its first atomic bomb.

November 21, 1964
The **Verrazano-Narrows Bridge**, spanning New York Harbor from Brooklyn to Staten Island, opens to traffic.
 [3]

December 10, 1964
Martin Luther King, Jr., is awarded the Nobel Peace Prize.
 [4]

[1] Chief of Justice Earl Warren presents the huge Warren Commission report to President Johnson.

[2] The new order in Russia: Kosygin on the left, Brezhnev on the right, defense minister Malinovsky in the middle. Russia wants no more of the alarms and adventures it has gone through with Khrushchev.

[4] Martin Luther King, Jr., with his Nobel Prize.

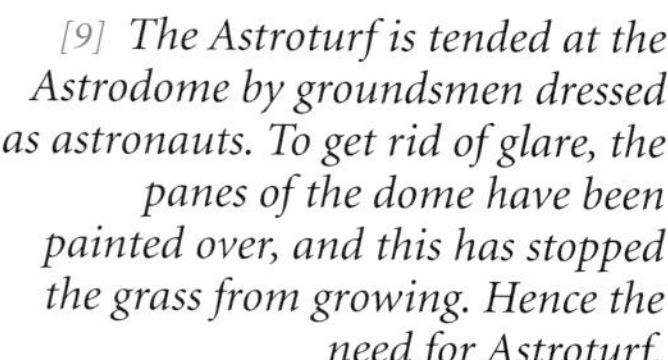

[9] The Astroturf is tended at the Astrodome by groundsmen dressed as astronauts. To get rid of glare, the panes of the dome have been painted over, and this has stopped the grass from growing. Hence the need for Astroturf.

[8] Bob Dylan goes electric with a Fender Stratocruiser at Newport.

 [8]
1965
Singer-songwriter **Bob Dylan** scandalizes the folk music establishment by playing electric instruments (and rock and roll) at the Newport Folk Festival.

 [9]
1965
Synthetic turf is invented. Because the product is installed in the Houston Astrodome, it becomes known as **Astroturf**.

1965
The U.S. Supreme Court rules that a state law prohibiting the use of **contraceptives** (including providing information, advice, or prescriptions) violates "the right of marital privacy" implied within the Bill of Rights.

1965
The **IBM 360 computer**, running OS/360, sets the standard for business machines.

1965
The **integrated circuit PDP-8** introduced.

1965
The low-calorie sweetener **aspartame** is developed in the United States by James Schlatter.

December 12, 1964
Kenya becomes a republic on the first anniversary of its independence from Britain.

 [5]

December 17, 1964
The British National Health Service announces that **prescriptions** will be issued free of charge as of February 1, 1965.

December 21, 1964
By a majority of 185, The British House of Commons votes to abolish the **death penalty**.

1965
American Southern novelist and playwright **Truman Capote** completes his journalistic "nonfiction novel," *In Cold Blood*, the story of a mass murder in rural Kansas and its perpetrators.

 [6]

1965
Construction begins on architect Richard Meier's **Smith House** in Connecticut.

 [7]

1965
Gordon Moore of Intel Corporation observes the temporal pattern for doubling computer power.

[5] *Jomo Kenyatta, with his trademark flywhisk, soaks up the applause of the Kenyan people on Independence Day in 1963.*

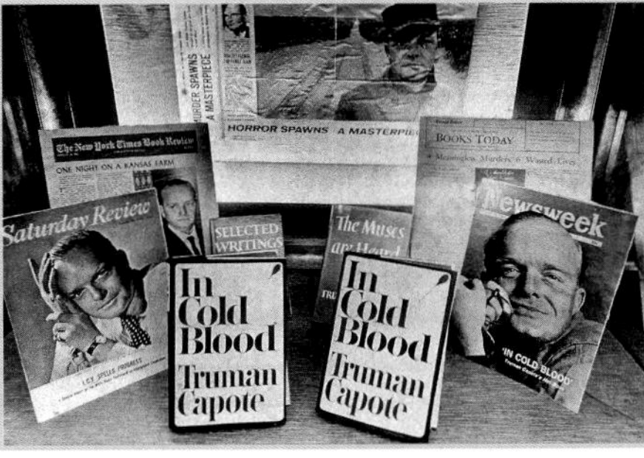

[6] *A window display at the publishers' office for* In Cold Blood, *including magazine covers featuring Truman Capote, articles, and reviews.*

[7] *Richard Meier's Smith House in Darien, Connecticut, developing from the work of the pre-war modernists, in any color as long as it is white.*

[3] *The Verrazano-Narrows Bridge*

[10] *Hare Krishna followers, who become a familiar sight on Western streets with their Eastern garb, chanting and dancing.*

1965
The **National Endowment for the Arts** is established in Washington, D.C., to support the fine arts.

1965
The U.S. and Mexico sign an agreement promoting U.S. industry in **northern Mexico**. Rapid industrialization follows and allows many U.S. firms to move their operations to the easier regulatory environment of Mexico.

1965
The U.S. Congress enacts the **Medicare** and **Medicaid** programs, providing medical insurance for the elderly and the poor.

1965
The United Nations International Children's Emergency Fund (UNICEF) receives the Nobel Peace Prize for its work in international **child welfare**.

1965
The Japanese baseball team the **Yomiuri Giants** win the first of nine consecutive Japan Series titles.

 [10]

1965
Vaishnava Hindu organization, popularly known as **Hare Krishna**, is founded in the United States by A. C. Bhaktivedanta.

1965

1965
Wu Han, Chinese historian and deputy mayor of Beijing, is attacked for his play *Hai Rui Is Dismissed From Office*, beginning the preliminary phase of the Great Proletarian **Cultural Revolution**.

January 24, 1965
Sir Winston Churchill dies at his home in London in his 91st year.

 [1]

February 21, 1965
Malcolm X, who articulated concepts of racial pride and black nationalism in the United States, is assassinated and becomes an ideological hero after the posthumous release of *The Autobiography of Malcolm X*.

 [2]

March 7, 1965
State troopers use nightsticks and tear gas to attack American civil rights activists as they cross a bridge in **Selma**, Alabama, during their first attempt to march to the state capitol in Montgomery.

March 12, 1965
U.S. Marines in **South Vietnam** engage in their first skirmish with Viet Cong forces.

March 18, 1965
Soviet cosmonaut Aleksey Arkhipovich Leonov becomes the first man to **walk in space** after passing through an air lock on the spacecraft Voskhod 2.

[2] Malcolm X. He moved away from the Nation of Islam towards traditional Islam, only to be murdered by members of the Nation.

[3] Martin Luther King, Jr.; his wife, Coretta Scott King; and other activists on the march to Montgomery.

[1] Winston Churchill lies in state in the medieval Great Hall at the Palace of Westminster, guarded by the Household Cavalry, as hundreds of thousands of ordinary people file past to pay their last respects.

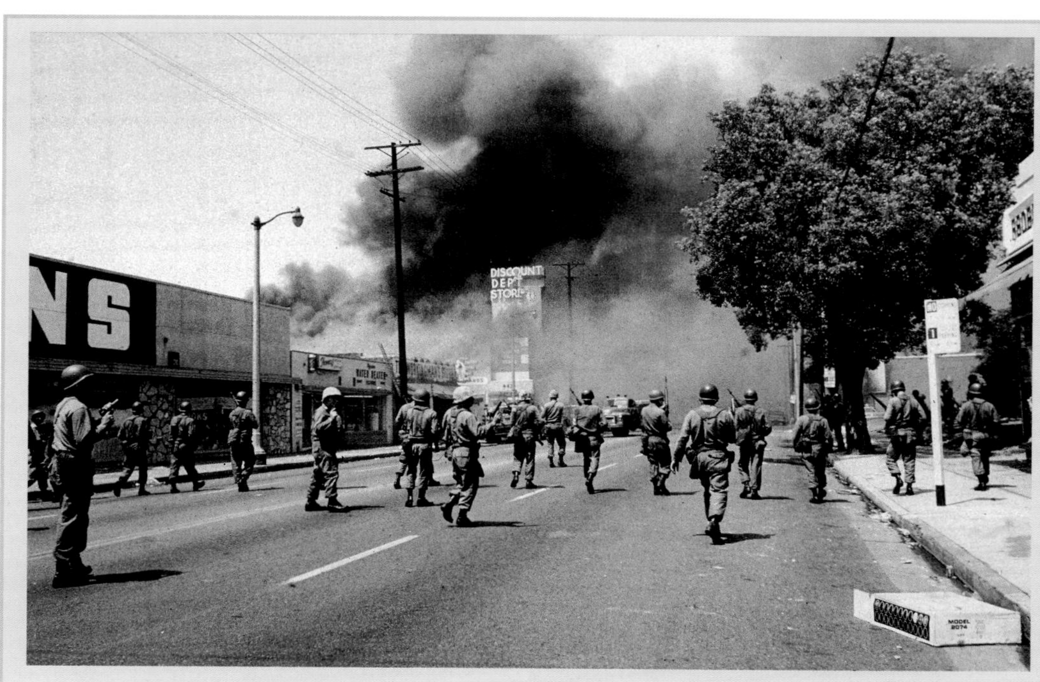

L.A. RACE RIOTS

Slow progress on civil rights drives black Americans to violent protest.

Despite the passage of the National Voting Rights Act of 1965, many blacks remained dissatisfied by the slow progress of integration. Race riots broke out in most of the nation's large cities. Some of the worst disturbances occurred in the Watts district of Los Angeles, where thousands of African Americans, angered by long-standing social injustices, rioted, burned stores, and pillaged the area from August 11 to August 16. The photograph shows National Guardsmen advancing towards burning buildings during the disturbances. Before order was restored, 34 people had been killed, nearly 4,000 arrested, and more than 1,000 injured, and hundreds of buildings had been destroyed.

July 2, 1965
Title VII of the Civil Rights Act of 1964—the first U.S. federal law prohibiting discrimination against minority groups in private employment—becomes effective.

July 13, 1965
The U.S. House of Representatives passes a compromise bill requiring a **health warning** on cigarette packages, cartons, and containers as of January 1, 1966.

July 15, 1965
Mariner 4, an unmanned space probe launched by NASA in 1964, flies by Mars and returns close-up pictures of its surface; the pictures prove that the planet's rumored canals are actually illusions.

July 26, 1965
The **Republic of Maldives** gains its independence from Britain.

August 6, 1965
The **Voting Rights Act** becomes U.S. law. It suspends literacy tests, provides for federal oversight of voter registration (primarily in the South), and challenges the use of poll taxes for state and local elections.

August 11, 1965
Race riots erupt in the Watts district of Los Angeles, resulting in the deaths of 34 people.

March 21, 1965
American civil rights activists led by Martin Luther King, Jr., begin the famous protest **march from Selma to Montgomery**, Alabama, having sought and received federal protection.

 [3]

April 6, 1965
Early Bird, the world's first commercial communications satellite, is launched from Cape Kennedy, Florida.

April 7, 1965
The British government introduces legislation designed to bar **racial discrimination** in all "places of public resort."

April 29, 1965
The U.S. Office of Education sets the fall of 1967 as the target date for complete **racial desegregation** of U.S. public schools.

May 25, 1965
Cassius Clay (later Muhammad Ali) knocks out Sonny Liston in the first round of a bout at Lewiston, Maine, to retain the world heavyweight boxing title.

June 5, 1965
Edward H. White II emerges from the orbital spacecraft Gemini 4 during its third orbit and floats in space for about 20 minutes, thus becoming the first American astronaut to walk in space.

 [4]

[4] Edward H. White, 120 miles above the Pacific.

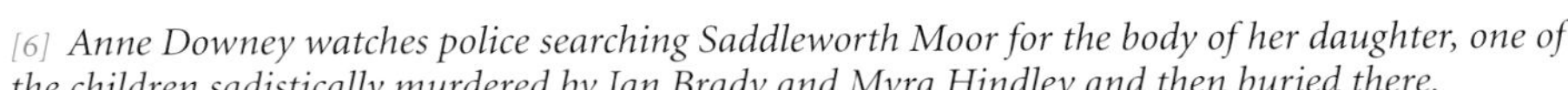

[6] Anne Downey watches police searching Saddleworth Moor for the body of her daughter, one of the children sadistically murdered by Ian Brady and Myra Hindley and then buried there.

[5] Indonesian students celebrate after the foiling of the 30th September Movement coup, blamed on the Communists, hundreds of thousands of whom are killed.

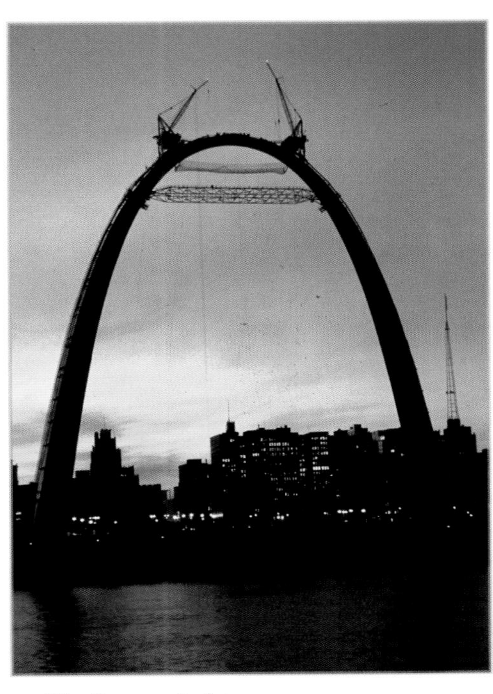

[7] The Gateway Arch in St. Louis nears completion.

August 28, 1965
A bill making killing, kidnapping, or attacking the president of the United States a federal offense is signed by **President Lyndon B. Johnson**.

September 18, 1965
Japanese astronomers Ikeya Kaoru and Seki Tsutomu discover **Comet Ikeya-Seki**.

 [5]

September 30, 1965
In Indonesia a group of army conspirators kidnap and murder six army generals. Their **30th September Movement** coup is thwarted by President Suharto.

October 3, 1965
President Lyndon B. Johnson signs a bill abolishing the **U.S. immigration quota system**; he also accepts Fidel Castro's offer to permit Cuban citizens with relatives in the United States to emigrate there.

 [6]

October 1965
The **Moors murders**, perhaps the most notorious murder case in 20th-century Britain, begins.

 [7]

October 28, 1965
The **Gateway Arch** in St. Louis, Missouri, designed by Finnish-born American architect Eero Saarinen to commemorate St. Louis's historic role as "Gateway to the West," is completed.

1965-1966

November 11, 1965
Prime Minister Ian Smith of Southern Rhodesia declares unilateral independence from Great Britain in order to maintain white minority rule.

 [1]

c. 1965
The **Green Revolution's** package of new crop breeds and fertilizers sharply increases yields of rice, wheat, and corn (maize) around the world but reduces the variety of cultivars in use.

 [2]

1966
A three-year undeclared war between Indonesia and Malaysia (aided by British forces) ends with the signing in **Jakarta** of an accord calling for referendums to determine the status of the disputed states of Sarawak and Sabah.

1966
American consumer advocate **Ralph Nader's** 1965 bestseller *Unsafe at Any Speed*, a critique of the American automobile industry, leads directly to the passage of an act letting the government enact safety standards for all cars sold in the U.S.

 [3]

1966
American engineer Stephanie Kwolek discovers a polyamide solvent that leads to the production of **Kevlar**, the primary material of bulletproof vests.

1966
American folksinger **Bob Dylan** is involved in a serious motorcycle accident and goes into a two-year period of seclusion, bringing his career of seven years and more than 10 million worldwide album sales to a sudden halt.

[1] Ian Smith in a carefully posed shot in front of the Victoria Falls, the first to be taken after issuing his country's unilateral declaration of independence (UDI).

[2] A Hungarian girl shows off one of the new strains of maize.

[4] Captain Kirk, Dr. "Bones" McCoy, and Mr. Spock, characters from Star Trek.

[3] Ralph Nader: consumers' champion, corporations' scourge, environmentalist, presidential candidate. His particular target at this time is the Chevrolet Corvair. He will successfully sue General Motors for the smear tactics they use against him.

[6] Indira Gandhi going to visit President Johnson in the White House.

[5] Bobby Moore, the English captain, kisses the World Cup trophy, flanked by George Cohen (left), Geoff Hurst, and Martin Peters.

1966
Indian prime minister Lal Bahadur Shastri and Pakistani president Muhammad Ayub Khan meet in Tashkent, U.S.S.R., at the invitation of Soviet premier Aleksey Kosygin in an effort to end their conflict over **Kashmir**.

 [6]

1966
Indira Gandhi becomes head of the Congress Party and the first female prime minister of India.

1966
Maulana Karenga, a black-studies professor at California State University at Long Beach, creates **Kwanzaa** as a nonreligious celebration of family and community.

1966
The **National Organization for Women (NOW)** is founded by Betty Friedan and other delegates to the Third National Conference of State Commissions on the Status of Women.

1966
President Lyndon B. Johnson approves a bill creating a new federal **Department of Transportation**, the 12th cabinet department.

1966
The Soviet spacecraft **Venus 3**, launched November 16, 1965, crashes on Venus, the first manmade object to touch another planet.

1966
American writer and TV and film producer Gene Roddenberry creates the popular science fiction TV series **Star Trek**, which spawns other series and a string of motion pictures.

 [4]

1966
Anton LaVey founds the **Church of Satan**, a counter-culture group promoting humanistic values.

1966
England defeats West Germany in the men's **World Cup** soccer championship by a score of 4 to 2.

 [5]

1966
France withdraws from military participation in N.A.T.O.

1966
Harold Holt of the Liberal-Country Party, who will support U.S. policies in Vietnam and sponsor the visit to Australia of Lyndon B. Johnson, the first American president-in-office to travel there, becomes prime minister of Australia.

1966
Huey Newton and Bobby Seale found the **Black Panther Party**, an American black revolutionary party, in Oakland, California.

BLACK PANTHERS

Black Power organization in the United States

The original purpose of the Black Panthers (full name: the Black Panther Party For Self-defense), founded in 1966, was to patrol black ghettoes to protect residents from acts of police brutality. However, the group eventually developed into a Marxist revolutionary group that called for the arming of all blacks, the exemption of blacks from the draft and from all sanctions of so-called white America, the release of all blacks from jail, and the payment of compensation to blacks for centuries of exploitation by white Americans.

Taken on July 22, 1968, the photograph shows Black Panthers marching to a news conference in New York City to protest the trial of one of their leaders, Huey P. Newton, convicted for the manslaughter of a policeman in Oakland, California.

[7] *Tom Stoppard at home.*

[8] *President Johnson visits U.S. forces in Vietnam.*

1966
The Beatles announce their retirement from public performing to concentrate on exploiting the full resources of the recording studio.

1966
The Latin American summit conference issues the **Declaration of Bogota**, calling for the speedy economic integration of Latin America.

 [7]

1966
Tom Stoppard's play **Rosencrantz and Guildenstern Are Dead** is performed at the Edinburgh Festival. The play displays the verbal brilliance that becomes the trademark of the Czech-born English playwright.

 [8]

January 1966
In his third State of the Union message, President Lyndon B. Johnson pledges U.S. support in **Vietnam** "until aggression has stopped" and vows to continue his Great Society programs.

January 31, 1966
The Soviets launch **Luna 9**, the first spacecraft to make a soft landing on the moon.

February 25, 1966
Leonid Brezhnev is appointed chairman of a commission to work out a new charter for **collectives**, reflecting a Soviet decision to discuss and revise the 30-year-old farming system.

1966-1967

March 25, 1966
The U.S. Supreme Court rules the **Virginia poll tax** unconstitutional as a voting requirement, thus in effect contravening all poll taxes.

May 26, 1966
Guyana, formerly a colony of the Dutch and later the British, gains its independence.

June 13, 1966
The U.S. Supreme Court rules in favor of Ernesto Miranda in **Miranda v. Arizona**, affirming that constitutional guarantees against self-incrimination include restrictions on police interrogation of an arrested suspect.

July 30, 1966
For the first time, **U.S. planes** bomb the demilitarized zone (DMZ) separating North and South Vietnam.

August 1966
Mao Zedong launches the Great Proletarian **Cultural Revolution** to renew the spirit of the revolution in China. He shuts down schools and encourages groups of youths called Red Guards to attack all traditional values and criticize party officials.

August 27, 1966
British adventurer **Sir Francis Chichester**, leaves from Plymouth, England, on an around the world solo trip, in the *Gypsy Moth IV*, sailing the 14,100 miles to Sydney in 107 days. He returns to Plymouth around Cape Horn in 119 days.

 [1]

THE CULTURAL REVOLUTION

Upheaval launched by Mao Zedong to renew the spirit of revolution in China

Mao feared urban social stratification in traditionally elitist Chinese society and believed that programs instituted to correct for the failed Great Leap Forward showed that his colleagues lacked commitment to the revolution. He organized China's urban youths into groups called the Red Guards; some of them are shown (left), brandishing copies of Mao's "Little Red Book" of political slogans, the revolutionaries' bible.

The Red Guards shut down China's schools and attacked all traditional values and "bourgeois" things. They soon splintered into zealous rival groups, and in 1968 Mao sent millions of them to the rural hinterland, bringing some order to the cities. Within the government, a coalition of Mao's associates then purged the more moderate elements.

[1] Francis Chichester aboard his yacht.

[7] A miniskirt in London.

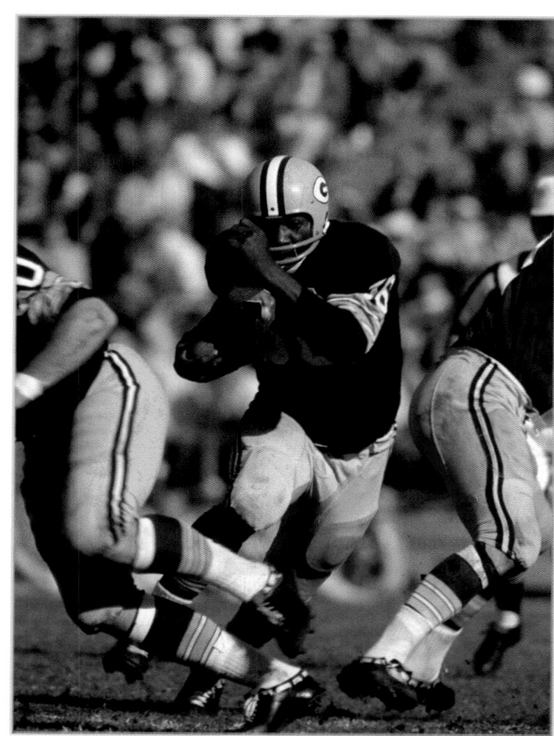

[8] The Green Bay Packers during the inaugural Super Bowl.

November 15, 1966
The U.S. **Gemini program** to prepare the way for manned flights to the moon comes to a successful conclusion with the splashdown of Gemini 12 about 700 miles southeast of Cape Kennedy, Florida.

November 30, 1966
Barbados, an island nation in the Caribbean situated about 100 miles east of the Windward Islands, achieves full independence from Britain. It had gained internal self-rule in 1961.

December 1, 1966
Conservative politician **Kurt Georg Kiesinger**, a member of the Social Democratic Party, becomes chancellor (1966–69) of the Federal Republic of Germany (West Germany).

December 19, 1966
The United Nations General Assembly endorses the **Outer Space Treaty**, an international treaty binding the parties to use outer space only for peaceful purposes.

c. 1966
The **miniskirt**, with a hemline several inches above the knee, revolutionizes women's wear and signals a new era in fashion, though more conservative observers are scandalized by its skimpiness.

1967
British radio astronomers Jocelyn Bell and Antony Hewish detect the first **pulsar**, a cosmic object that emits extremely regular pulses of radio waves.

August 31, 1966
The **Harrier** "jump-jet" fighter-bomber makes its first flight.
[2]

September 16, 1966
The **new Metropolitan Opera House** in New York City's Lincoln Center opens with the world premiere of Samuel Barber's *Antony and Cleopatra.*
 [3]

September 21, 1966
A proposed amendment to the **U.S. Constitution** that would have permitted voluntary prayers in public schools fails (49–37) to win the necessary two-thirds majority in the Senate.

September 30, 1966
Botswana (formerly the British protectorate of Bechuanaland) comes into being as an independent republic headed by Sir Seretse Khama as president.
[4]

October 21, 1966
A giant slag heap of coal-mining waste collapses onto Aberfan, a school in South Wales, killing 144, mostly children.
[5]

November 1966
Florence endures the worst floods in its history as the Arno bursts its banks. Many works of art and manuscript books are badly damaged.
[6]

[2] *An early version of what becomes the Harrier jump-jet takes off vertically.*

[3] *The new Met, full to the brim on its opening night.*

[6] *The floor of the gallery housing Michelangelo's* David *covered in a layer of mud by the Florence floods.*

[4] *Sir Seretse Khama*

[5] *Rescuers dig away at the slag heap that has swept forward to engulf part of Aberfan school, visible behind, as a result of being saturated by heavy rain.*

1967
Colombian author **Gabriel García Márquez** completes his epic novel *One Hundred Years of Solitude.* While the setting is realistic, there are fantastic episodes, a combination known as "magic realism."

 [8]
1967
Green Bay of the National Football League defeats Kansas City of the American Football League in the inaugural Super Bowl. Three years later the leagues merge into the National Football League.

1967
Heavyweight boxing champion **Muhammad Ali** refuses induction into the armed forces on religious grounds. He is subsequently convicted of violating the Selective Service Act and barred from the boxing ring.

1967
IBM introduces the **floppy disk** as a computer data storage device.

1967
In **Japan**, asthma sufferers sue the Yokkaichi petrochemical complex for damages, one of several lawsuits that quickly changes both law and environmental quality in Japan.

1967
The U.S. Supreme Court declares antimiscegenation laws (prohibitions of **interracial marriage**) have no legitimate purpose outside racial discrimination and thus violate the Fourteenth Amendment.

1967

1967
Japan enacts the Basic Law for Environmental Pollution Control, the world's first comprehensive pollution-control policy.

1967
John McEwen of the Liberal-Country Party becomes prime minister of Australia upon the death of Prime Minister Harold Holt.

1967
Kenyan anthropologist **Richard Leakey** discovers the site of Koobi Fora, the richest and most varied assemblage of early human remains found to date anywhere in the world.

1967
Private consensual sex acts between adults, including **same-sex acts**, are decriminalized in England.

1967
South African surgeon Christiaan Barnard carries out the first **human heart transplant**.

 [1]

1967
The 1967 **Montreal Expo** is dominated by the United States Pavilion, a massive geodesic dome designed by Buckminster Fuller.

 [2]

[1] Christiaan Barnard, surgeon superstar, at the launch of his autobiography.

[2] Overhead railway and geodesic dome at the Montreal Expo.

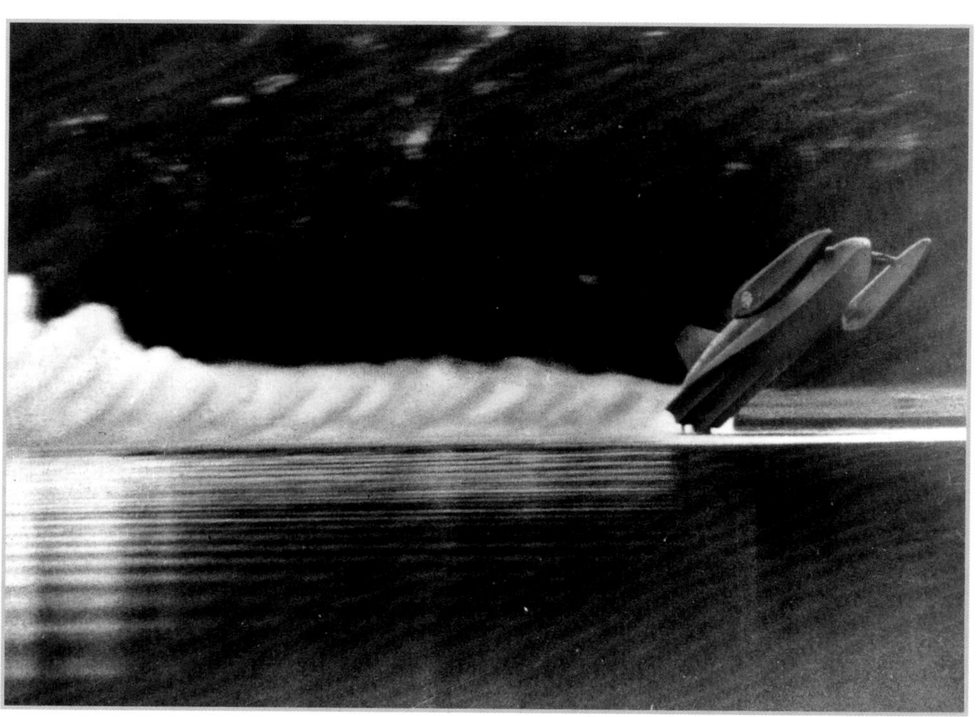

[6] Donald Campbell, who in 1964 briefly held both land and water speed records, dies in his boat Bluebird K7. *He has been traveling at well over 300 mph and on his return run hits the wash left by his first run and flips over. The boat is powered by a modified jet engine.*

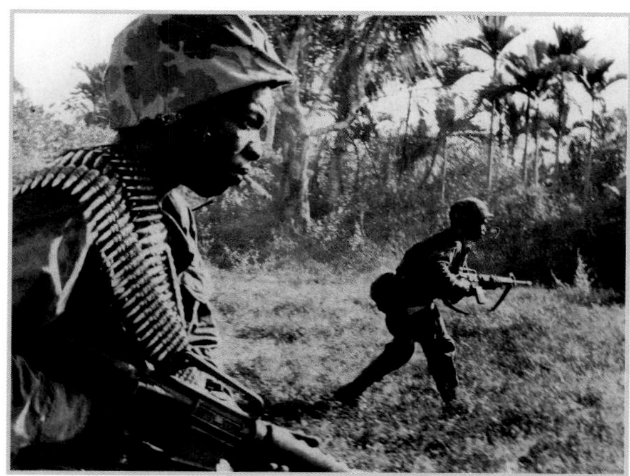

[7] GIs move over open ground against the Viet Cong.

 [6]

January 4, 1967
Donald Campbell is killed on Coniston Water in the Lake District, England, trying to break the world water speed record.

February 10, 1967
The **Twenty-fifth Amendment**, designed to clear lines of presidential succession and continuity of power in case of a president's disability, becomes part of the U.S. Constitution when it is ratified by the 38th state.

February 14, 1967
A treaty to ban nuclear weapons from Latin America is signed in **Mexico City**.

February 20, 1967
The National Gallery of Art, Washington, D.C., announces that it has purchased **Leonardo da Vinci's** painting of Ginevra dei Benci from Francis Joseph II of Liechtenstein for a reported record price of $5 to $6 million.

 [7]

February 22, 1967
A force of over 25,000 U.S. and South Vietnamese troops launch **Operation Junction City**, the largest offensive of the Vietnam War, about 70 miles north of Saigon.

February 27, 1967
Saint Kitts and Nevis (with Anguilla) become an independent state associated with the United Kingdom.

1967
The **Association of Southeast Asian Nations** is established by Indonesia, Malaysia, the Philippines, Singapore, and Thailand to accelerate economic growth, social progress, and cultural development and to promote peace and security in Southeast Asia.

1967
The BBC introduces regular TV **color broadcasts**, the first in Europe.

1967
The Beatles release their classic psychedelic concept album **Sgt. Pepper's Lonely Hearts Club Band** at the height of the "Summer of Love." [3]

1967
The first **ATM** (automated teller machine) opens at a branch of Barclays PLC bank in Enfield, a suburb of London. By 2007 there will be 1.5 million ATMs in service around the world. [4]

1967
The three crew members of **Apollo 1** are the first casualties of the U.S. space program when a flash fire sweeps their space capsule during a launch simulation. They are Command Pilot Virgil I. "Gus" Grissom, Senior Pilot Ed White, and Pilot Roger B. Chaffee.

1967
Thurgood Marshall is sworn in as the first African American member of the U.S. Supreme Court. [5]

[3] The Beatles celebrating Sgt. Pepper *at manager Brian Epstein's home. John Lennon wears a sporran as well as an Afghan coat.*

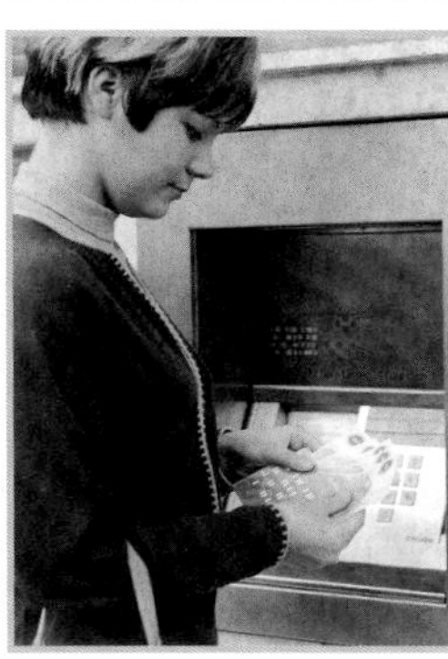

[4] The first-ever automated cashpoint.

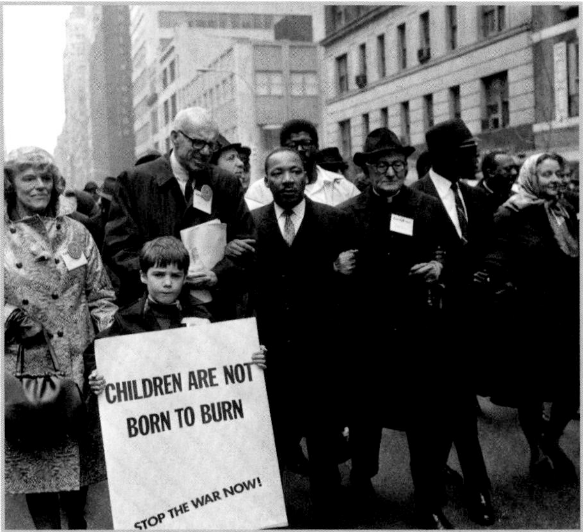

[9] Author Benjamin Spock, Martin Luther King, Jr., Father Frederick Reed, and Cleveland Robinson, a union leader, march against the Vietnam War.

[5] Thurgood Marshall in his office at the federal courthouse.

[10] Israeli half-tracks loaded with exultant troops advance towards Egypt.

[8] The Torrey Canyon *is broken apart. Her spilled cargo pollutes many miles of French and Cornish beaches, but as much, if not more, damage is done by the 10,000 tons of solvents used in the clean-up.*

March 3, 1967
The Caribbean island of **Grenada** is granted internal self-government, the latest of seven islands in the Leeward and Windward groups to achieve this status since February 27.

March 10, 1967
The **New York Stock Exchange** experiences its second greatest trading day, surpassed only by October 29, 1929.

 [8]

March 18, 1967
The supertanker **Torrey Canyon**, with 120,000 tons of crude oil on board, hits rocks between Cornwall and the Scilly Isles. It is the first such big marine oil spill.

 [9]

April 15, 1967
Peace demonstrators numbering more than 100,000, including Martin Luther King, Jr., march through the streets of New York City and assemble before the U.N. in a protest against the war in Vietnam.

April 24, 1967
Soviet cosmonaut **Vladimir Komarov** becomes the first man to die during a space mission when his spacecraft becomes entangled in its parachute when landing.

 [10]

June 5–10, 1967
Israeli forces rout all Egyptian, Jordanian, and Syrian forces in the **Six-Day War**. They seize control of the Sinai Peninsula, the West Bank, the Gaza Strip, the Golan Heights, and all of Jerusalem.

1967-1968

June 15–16, 1967
The **Monterey** (California) Pop Festival is the first commercial American music festival and features Jimi Hendrix, the Who, Janis Joplin, Jefferson Airplane, the Grateful Dead, and the Byrds.

 [1]

June 29, 1967
Arabs and Israelis mingle freely in **Jerusalem** for the first time in 19 years as the barriers that divided the city into sectors are removed.

August 15, 1967
American Nazi Party leader **George Lincoln Rockwell** is shot to death in Arlington, Virginia, by a former aide.

 [2]

September 3, 1967
Sweden successfully changes over from left-hand to right-hand traffic after four years of planning and vehicle reconstruction.

September 6, 1967
Some 160,000 employees of **the Ford Motor Company** go on strike as the company's contract with the AFL-CIO United Auto Workers expires.

October 8, 1967
A prominent communist figure in the Cuban Revolution and a South American guerrilla leader, **Che Guevara** is captured in Bolivia. He is later shot to death by the Bolivian army.

 [3]

[1] Jimi Hendrix at Monterey Pop Festival.

[2] George Lincoln Rockwell speaks, with John Patler, his later alleged assassin, beside him.

[3] The body of Che Guevara is displayed to journalists by the Bolivian army the day after he has been shot.

[6] Stanley Kubrick. Full of ambiguities, 2001 is also notable as the first film with a large special-effects content.

[7] Arthur Ashe at Wimbledon in 1968. He will become the first African American man to win there in 1975.

[8] Pot-bellied starving Biafran children. Images like this inspire freelance Western airlifts to bring in food. The civil war drags on until January 1970.

 [6]

1968
American motion-picture director Stanley Kubrick releases the hugely successful science fiction classic **2001: A Space Odyssey**, which will earn an Academy Award for special visual effects.

[7]

1968
American tennis player **Arthur Ashe** wins both the amateur and open U.S. singles championships, becoming the first African American winner of a major men's singles championship.

1968
Aurelio Peccei convenes what will become the **Club of Rome**, which publicizes pessimistic visions about resource depletion and other environmental concerns. *The Limits to Growth* (1972) summarizes this position.

 [8]

1968
Civil war in Nigeria enters its second year with the southeast region of **Biafra** having seceded under colonel Ojukwu. The people face starvation because of a blockade.

 [9]

1968
Communes become a popular living arrangement among members of the counter culture in the U.S. and Europe. Most collapse within a few years but some survive for decades.

1968
Drug testing and female gender verification are conducted for the first time at the **Summer Olympic Games** in Mexico City.

November 11, 1967
The last British troops leave **Aden**, and the city will become capital of the Peoples Republic of South Yemen.

 [4]

November 22, 1967
United Nations Resolution 242 ends the Six-Day War. It calls on Arab states to accept Israel's right to exist and for Israel to withdraw from the territories just conquered. It will continue to serve as the basis of diplomatic efforts to end Arab-Israeli conflicts.

December 1, 1967
Greece and Turkey sign an internationally mediated agreement resolving the immediate issues threatening war over **Cyprus**.

December 5, 1967
Physician Benjamin Spock and poet Allen Ginsberg are among the 264 arrested as more than 1,000 people demonstrate in an attempt to close down a New York induction center as part of a national "**Stop the Draft Week**."

December 14, 1967
Stanford University biochemists report that they have produced a synthetic version of **DNA**.

1968
American "hippie" chronicler Tom Wolfe publishes **The Electric Kool-Aid Acid Test**, examining the psychedelic drug culture of the 1960s. Wolfe is a proponent of New Journalism (the application of fiction-writing techniques to journalism).

 [5]

[9] Commune living: the family of Mystic A. Long hair—beards and beads for the men, long skirts for the women. An escape from uniformity into a kind of uniform.

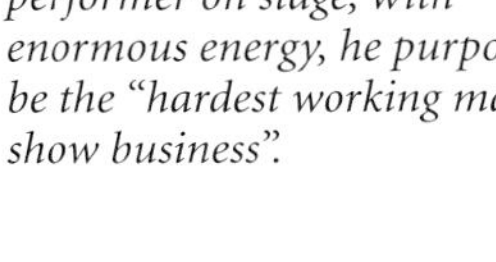

[10] James Brown. A thrilling performer on stage, with enormous energy, he purports to be the "hardest working man in show business".

[5] Tom Wolfe in his trademark white suit. He has a knack for catchy titles: The Kandy-Colored Tangerine-Flake Streamline Baby, *or* Radical Chic & Mau-Mauing the Flak Catchers.

[11] Tim Williams, chief of the Klamath River Hurok Indians of California, addresses a crowd before Alcatraz Island (in the background) is occupied.

[4] British soldiers seize a rioter in Aden a few months before the last of them leave this Red Sea outpost of the British Empire.

1968
In perhaps the greatest single feat in track and field history, American **Bob Beamon** smashes the world long-jump record by nearly two feet at the Summer Olympics in Mexico City.

 [10]

1968
James Brown, "the Godfather of Soul," celebrates the rise of African American political empowerment with the anthemic "Say It Loud—I'm Black and I'm Proud."

1968
John Gorton of the Liberal-Country Party, who will maintain a military commitment in Vietnam and expand the role of the federal government in education, science, and taxation, becomes prime minister of Australia.

 [11]

1968
The **American Indian Movement** is founded in Minneapolis, Minnesota. It will occupy Alcatraz Island (1969–71) and take over Wounded Knee in South Dakota (1973) to protest the U.S. government's Indian policy.

1968
The first **Special Olympics** are held in Chicago's Soldier Field, sponsored by the Kennedy Foundation and the Chicago Park District, to provide mentally handicapped individuals with a venue for athletic competition.

1968
The **Glomar Challenger** begins conducting deep-sea drilling voyages, collecting core samples in waters as deep as 20,000 feet and revolutionizing earth science by supporting the hypothesis of seafloor spreading.

1968

1968
The personal watercraft is developed by Canadian aircraft and rail transportation manufacturer Bombardier. Other manufacturers produce their own designs, such as the Kawasaki **Jet Ski**.

1968
The **Winter Olympic Games** take place in Grenoble, France.

1968
The year marks the apogee of large-dam (taller than 50 feet) construction in the world. More **dams** are built in 1968 than in any year before or since.

January 31, 1968
North Vietnamese forces begin the **Tet Offensive**, which will last until October. It is a military disaster for them but also effectively undermines American resolve.

 [1]

January 7, 1968
The unmanned U.S. space probe **Surveyor 7** is launched. A few days later it makes a soft landing on the moon.

February 14, 1968
Cesar Chavez begins a voluntary 25-day fast to dramatize his United Farmworkers Union's California grape boycott.

 [2]

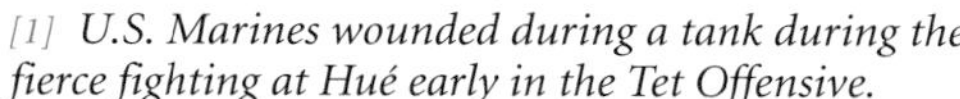

[1] U.S. Marines wounded during a tank during the fierce fighting at Hué early in the Tet Offensive.

[9] Yippies leader Jerry Rubin introduces their presidential candidate, Pigasus, during the Chicago Democratic Convention.

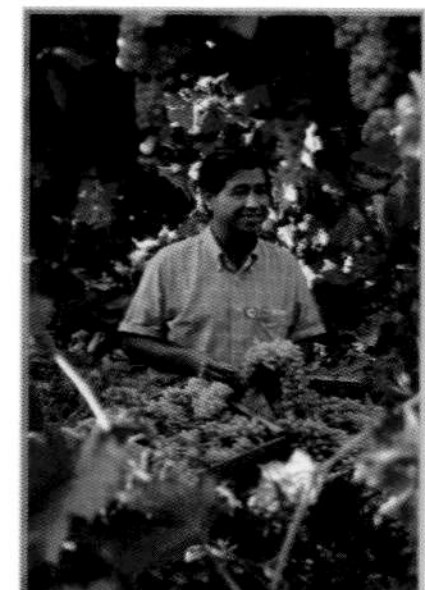

[2] Cesar Chavez standing among grapevines.

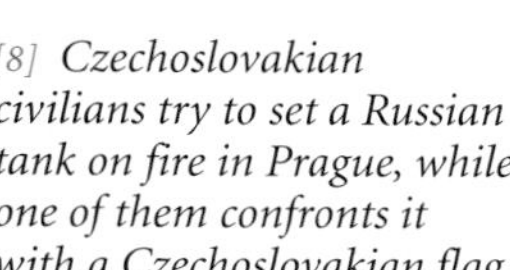

[8] Czechoslovakian civilians try to set a Russian tank on fire in Prague, while one of them confronts it with a Czechoslovakian flag.

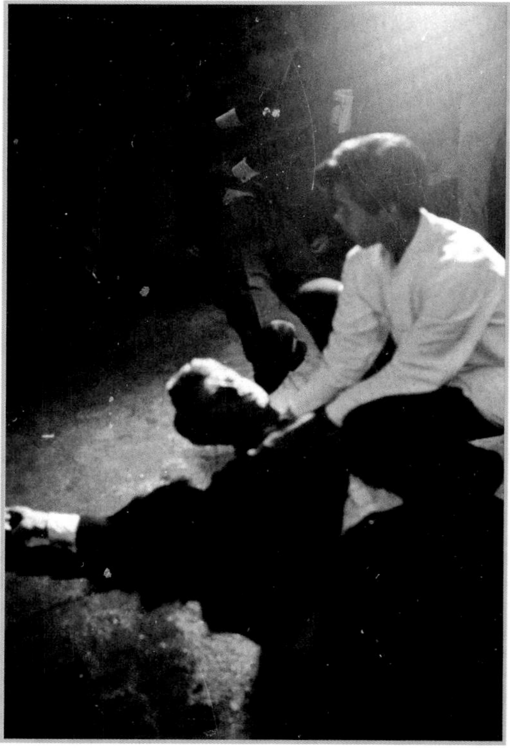

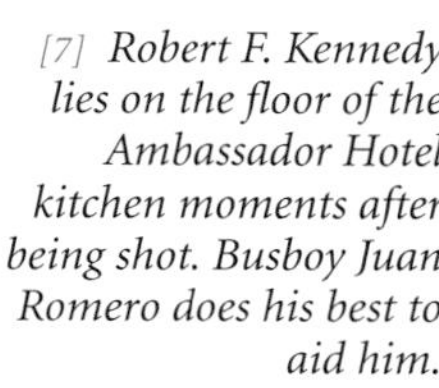

[7] Robert F. Kennedy lies on the floor of the Ambassador Hotel kitchen moments after being shot. Busboy Juan Romero does his best to aid him.

June 1, 1968
Blind and deaf American author **Helen Keller** dies in Westport, Connecticut.

 [7]

June 6, 1968
U.S. Senator **Robert F. Kennedy** dies of a bullet wound inflicted by assassin Sirhan Sirhan.

July 1, 1968
The United States, the United Kingdom, the U.S.S.R., and 59 other states sign the **Nuclear Non-proliferation Treaty** in an attempt to halt the spread of nuclear weapons.

 [8]

August 20, 1968
The Warsaw Pact nations (except Romania and Albania), led by the Soviet Union, invade Czechoslovakia to put an end to the **Prague Spring**.

 [9]

August 23, 1968
Yippies, members of the Youth International Party, and their presidential candidate, a pig, are arrested in the Chicago Civic Center.

August 24, 1968
France explodes its first **hydrogen bomb** in the South Pacific and becomes the world's fifth thermonuclear power.

February 18, 1968
The United Kingdom shifts from **Greenwich Mean Time** to the time of western Europe, one hour ahead.

March 16, 1968
During the Vietnam War, U.S. soldiers dispatched on a search-and-destroy mission kill as many as 500 unarmed villagers in the hamlet of **My Lai**, considered a stronghold of the Viet Cong.

 [3]

April 4, 1968
Civil rights leader Martin **Luther King, Jr.**, is assassinated in Memphis, Tennessee, by James Earl Ray. Over the next week riots break out in some 125 American cities.

 [4]

April 20, 1968
Pierre Elliot Trudeau of the Liberal Party becomes prime minister of Canada. He will discourage the French separatist movement, oversee the formation of a new constitution, and establish relations with China.

 [5]

May 1968
Weeks of riots and **demonstrations in Paris**, by French students and some workers, bring the country to a virtual standstill.

 [6]

June 1968
The Iraqi army overthrows the 'Arif regime with some assistance from civilian activists, paving the way for the **Ba'th Party's** rise to power.

[3] Women and children rounded up by the U.S. Army in My Lai and about to be shot.

[4] Civil rights leader Andrew Young and others point where the shot that killed Martin Luther King, Jr., came from. He lies at their feet.

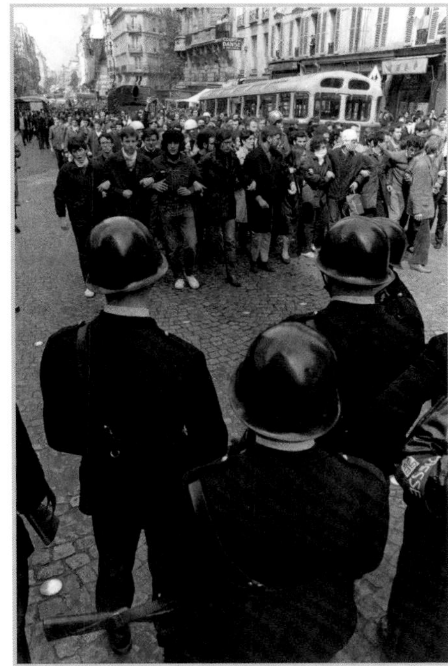

[6] French riot police confront students on a Left Bank Paris street during "Les Événements," as the May riots are called.

[5] Pierre Trudeau is congratulated after being elected prime minister.

[10] Jacqueline Kennedy with her new husband, Aristotle Onassis.

September 19, 1968
Mickey Mouse celebrates his 40th "birthday."

October 2, 1968
The bloodiest clash of troops and students in a nine-week student strike occurs in **Mexico City**.

October 3, 1968
Peruvian president Fernando Belaúnde Terry is ousted; Major General **Juan Velasco Alvarado** heads the new military government.

October 11, 1968
The U.S. spacecraft **Apollo 7**, carrying a full crew of three astronauts, achieves a 163-orbit flight. It is a major step toward placing a man on the moon.

 [10]

October 20, 1968
Former first lady **Jacqueline Kennedy** marries Greek shipping magnate Aristotle Onassis.

October 31, 1968
U.S. president Lyndon B. Johnson orders an end to American bombing in **North Vietnam**.

1968-1969

December 16, 1968
The **Spanish government** declares void a 1492 decree expelling Jews from Spain.

December 23, 1968
Eighty-two crewmen of the **USS Pueblo** are released after being held in captivity for 11 months by North Korea, which claimed the U.S. Navy intelligence ship had crossed into its waters.

c. 1968
Minimalism in painting, sculpture, and music emerges. In the visual arts, minimalism is a reaction against the subjectivity of abstract expressionism.

1969
Canada grants the French language equal status with English throughout the national government.

1969
American novelist **Kurt Vonnegut** completes his comic and satirical war novel *Slaughterhouse Five.*

 [1]

1969
ARPANET, the first component in what will become the Internet, is introduced.

[1] Kurt Vonnegut. His novel is based on his time as a prisoner-of-war in Germany in 1945, when he witnessed the Allied bombing of Dresden.

[4] Golda Meir, with her omnipresent cigarette.

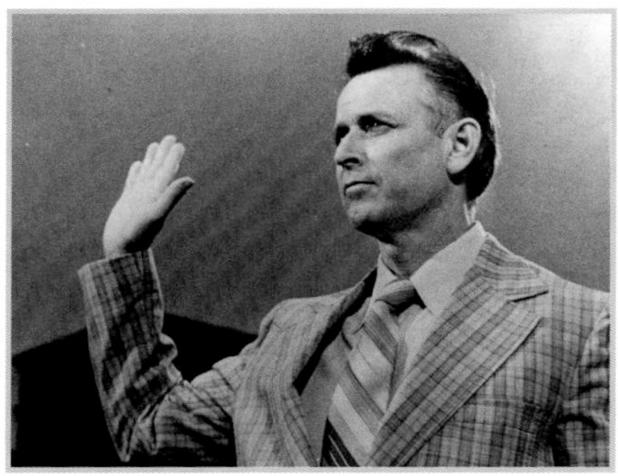

[5] James Earl Ray, an escaped convict. His guilty plea means there is no proper trial at which full facts have a chance of emerging.

[6] Thor Heyerdahl watching the vessel, in which he hopes to cross the Atlantic, being constructed from bundles of papyrus reeds, as the ancient Egyptians built their boats.

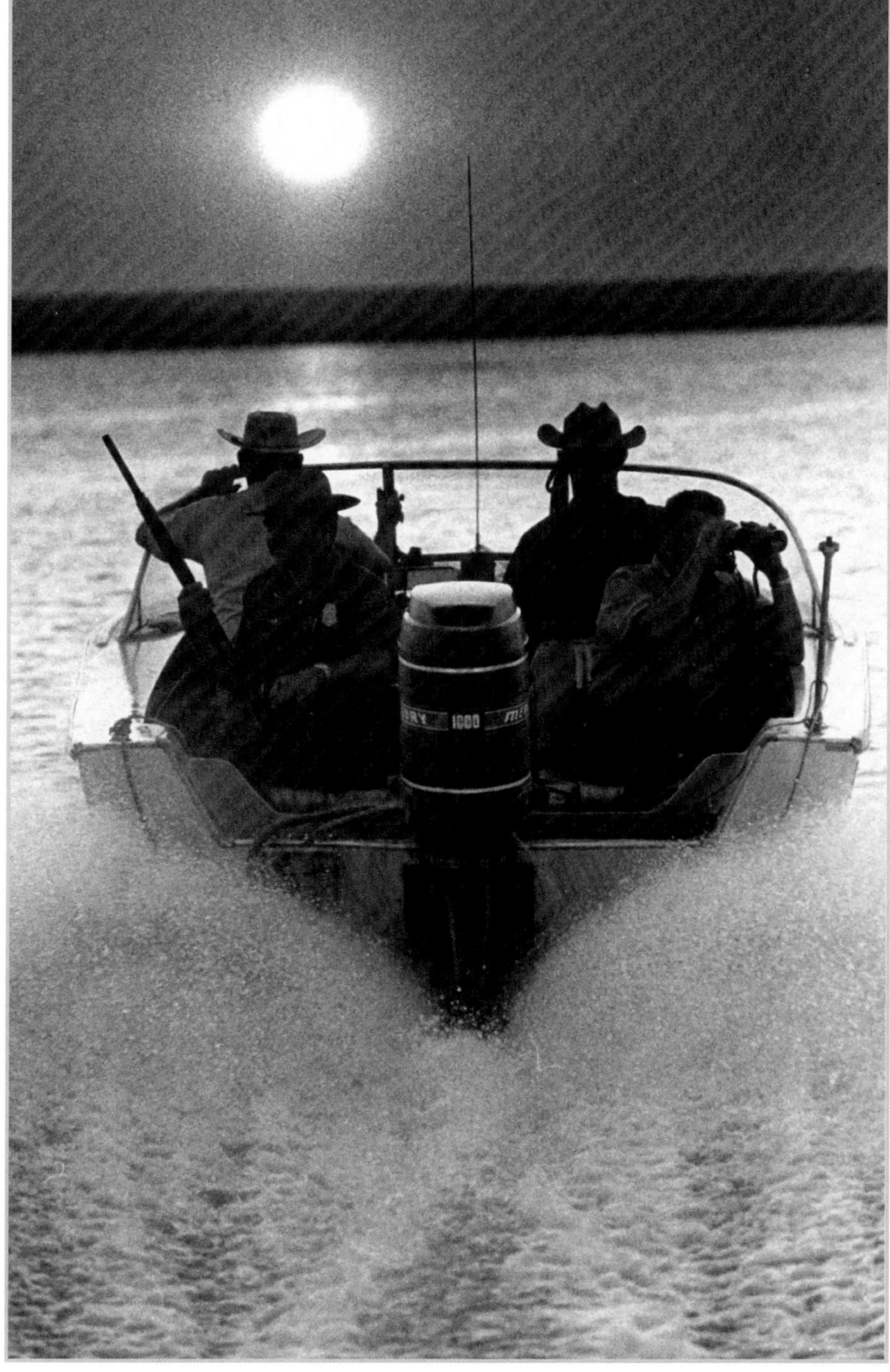

[7] U.S. officials patrol the Mexican border area in Operation Intercept.

 [4]

1969
Golda Meir becomes the first female prime minister of Israel.

1969
Intel Corporation designs the 4004, the first microprocessor; it will be used in the 1972 Pioneer 10 space probe.

 [5]

1969
James Earl Ray pleads guilty to the assassination of Martin Luther King, Jr., and is sentenced to 99 years in prison in brief court proceedings in Memphis, Tennessee.

1969
Ken Thompson of Bell Laboratories develops the **UNIX** computer operating system.

 [6]

1969
Norwegian writer-anthropologist **Thor Heyerdahl** and his crew abandon their papyrus reed boat, the *Ra*, in which they have attempted to prove that ancient Egyptians could have crossed the Atlantic Ocean.

 [7]

1969
Operation Intercept, a U.S. effort to halt the flow of drugs from Mexico, goes into effect along the U.S.-Mexico border.

1969
Bonny, a **pigtail monkey** used in a planned 30-day NASA space flight, dies 12 hours after being brought down on the ninth day.

1969
Civil rights leader **Ralph D. Abernathy** begins leading marches in Charleston, South Carolina, to support a month-old strike by non-professional hospital workers.

 [2]

1969
Currencies of 14 African nations, all former French colonies, are realigned with the devalued **franc**.

1969
Equatorial Guinea declares a state of emergency nine days after requesting a U.N. peacekeeping force to counter aggressive acts by Spanish forces.

1969
Fatah leader **Yasser Arafat** is elected chairman of the Palestine Liberation Organization.

 [3]

1969
Gary Starkweather of Xerox Corporation invents the **laser printer**.

[2] *Ralph Abernathy (center) with other Southern Christian Leadership Conference (SCLC) activists in Georgia. Jesse Jackson is on his right and Andrew Young on his left.*

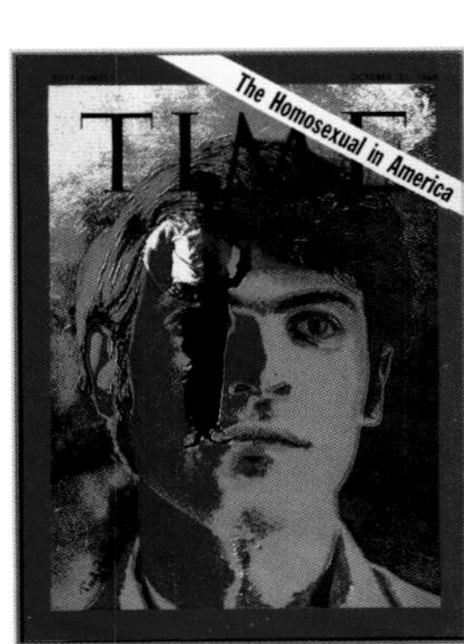

[8] Time *magazine puts the issue of homosexuality on its cover.*

[3] *Yasser Arafat, with a machine gun to act as his credentials for being a hard man, at a Palestinian Students' Congress in Amman with then Jordanian premier, Abdul Mon'er Rifai.*

[9] *President Richard M. Nixon is greeted by enthusiastic crowds on a visit to Germany.*

 [8]

1969
Patrons of the **Stonewall Inn**, a bar with a homosexual clientele in New York City, riot to protest police harassment resulting from a police raid. The event is often considered the start of the gay rights movement in the U.S.

1969
Peruvian president **Juan Velasco Alvarado** announces the seizure of all the assets of the International Petroleum Company.

1969
Plácido Domingo makes his debut at La Scala in Milan. The Spanish-born tenor is noted for his resonant and powerful voice.

 [9]

1969
Richard M. Nixon of the Republican Party becomes the 37th president of the United States. He will serve until 1974. His vice presidents are Spiro T. Agnew (1969–73) and Gerald R. Ford (1973–74).

1969
Rioting during play-offs in the World Cup soccer competition aggravates a dispute between El Salvador and Honduras, leading the former to sever diplomatic relations with the latter.

1969
Saigon comes under the heaviest and most damaging rocket attack of the current Communist offensive in the Vietnam War.

1969

1969
Spanish cabinet changes affecting 13 posts give prominence to the technocrat faction of the **Franco regime**, consisting chiefly of members of the Catholic lay organization Opus Dei.

1969
Tanzania, the first country to get U.S. Peace Corps assistance, cancels the program.

1969
The **Weatherman faction** of Students for a Democratic Society (SDS) begins four days of radical actions to "bring the war home" in Chicago with a rally in Lincoln Park, followed by a window-breaking spree through nearby streets.

1969
The battery-powered home **smoke detector** is patented by Randolph Smith and Kenneth House of the Interstate Engineering Corporation, California

1969
The Children's Television Workshop's popular television program **Sesame Street** makes its debut. Its main characters, including Big Bird and Cookie Monster, are the brainchildren of Muppet-maker Jim Henson.

1969
The first commercially successful **videocassette recorder** is introduced by the Sony. Subsequent development of the Betamax format by Sony and the VHS format by Matsushita Corporation make video recorders affordable for home use.

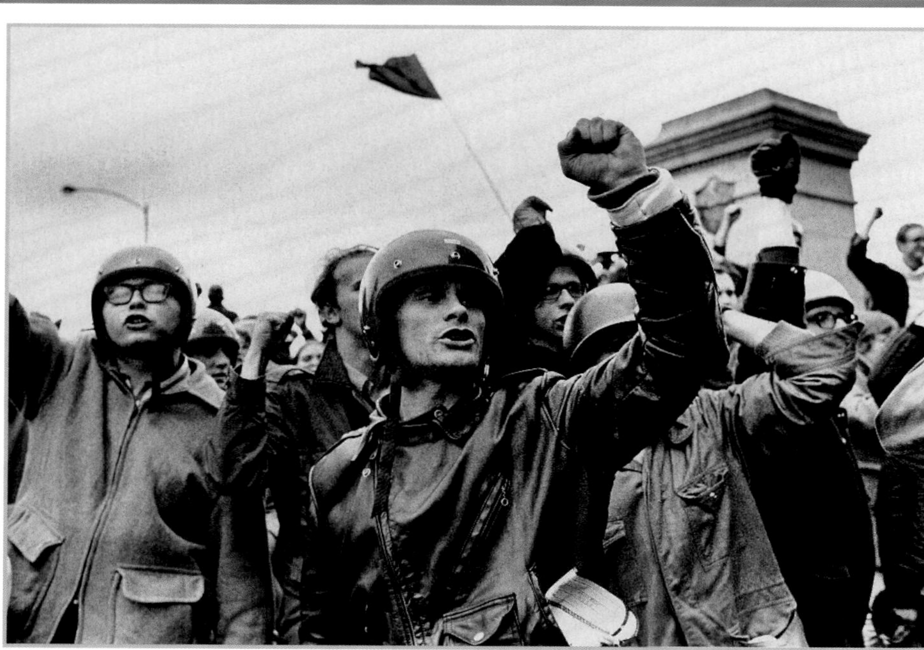

[1] Weathermen protest about the trial of the Chicago Seven, self-styled "revolutionists" from the Yippie, SDS (Students for a Democratic Society), Black Panther, and civil rights movements. Their name comes from the Bob Dylan line: "You don't need a weatherman to know which way the wind blows."

[2] Sesame Street cast members, including Big Bird, on the set.

[4] President Nixon with new and retiring chief justices of the Supreme Court: Earl Warren to the left, Warren Burger, the new chief justice, to the right.

[7] The Royal Ulster Constabulary fires tear gas during the "Battle of the Bogside," in a Roman Catholic area of Londonderry, August 12. Three days later British troops will be deployed on the streets of Belfast for the first time.

[5] Georges Pompidou: "Yes, I am in the center".

January 16, 1969
Czechoslovakian student **Jan Palach** sets fire to himself in Prague as a protest against the Soviet suppression of Czechoslovakian government reform the year before.

April 28, 1969
French leader **Charles de Gaulle**, following his defeat in a referendum, resigns, retires permanently, and resumes writing his memoirs.

May 22, 1969
Warren E. Burger is appointed 15th chief justice of the U.S. Supreme Court by President Richard Nixon. He will serve from 1969 to 1986.

June 15, 1969
French statesman, bank director, and teacher **Georges Pompidou**, who was premier of the Fifth French Republic from 1962 to 1968, is elected president.

July 1, 1969
Gustav Heinemann, a member of the Social Democratic Party of Germany, becomes president of West Germany (1969–74).

July 8, 1969
Edward Kennedy, brother of John and Robert, hurts his political career when he does not immediately report an automobile accident he is involved in on Chappaquiddick Island, near Martha's Vineyard, Massachusetts.

1969
The first **Nobel Prize in Economics** is awarded, to Ragnar Frisch of Norway and Jan Tinbergen of the Netherlands, for their work in econometrics.

1969
The Nixon administration orders an end to the use of the pesticide **DDT** within 30 days.

1969
The Saturday Evening Post, founded in 1821, announces plans to suspend publication.

1969
The TV wedding of **Tiny Tim** (Herbert Khaury) and Miss Vicky (Victoria Budinger) draws the largest audience ever recorded for a late-evening talk show.

 [3]

1969
The U.S. Food and Drug Administration reports that it has found the use of **birth-control pills** to be "safe."

January 12, 1969
American gridiron football quarterback **Joe Namath**, having "guaranteed" victory, leads the New York Jets to a 16–7 win over the favored Baltimore Colts in Super Bowl III.

MAN ON THE MOON

The United States wins the race against the Soviet Union to land a man on the moon.

On July 16, Americans Neil Armstrong, Edwin "Buzz" Aldrin, and Michael Collins set off on the Apollo 11 mission, the first lunar landing attempt. While Collins remained in lunar orbit in the command module, Armstrong brought the lunar module, nicknamed Eagle, down on a flat lava plain called the Sea of Tranquility at 4:18 PM U.S. Eastern Daylight Time on July 20. He reported to mission control, "Houston. Tranquility Base here. The Eagle has landed." Six and a half hours later, Armstrong opened the door of the lunar module and took the first human step on the surface of another celestial body. As he did so, he noted, "That's one small step for [a] man, one giant leap for mankind." (He unintentionally skipped the "a" in the statement he had prepared.) Armstrong was followed on to the lunar surface by his colleague, Aldrin (left). The two astronauts spent two and a half hours exploring and taking rock samples before blasting off and rejoining Collins for the journey home.

[6] Senator Teddy Kennedy, wearing a neck brace as a result of the accident, returns with his wife, Joan, from the funeral of Mary Jo Kopechne, who died in the same accident. The press are in attendance.

[8] A poster for Woodstock.

[9] Willy Brandt, apostle of the "New Ostpolitik"—settlement by treaty of dangerous friction points with the East.

[3] Tiny Tim, inseparable from his ukulele, and his bride, Miss Vicky.

July 20, 1969
Astronaut **Neil Armstrong** becomes the first human to set foot on the moon's surface. As he alights he says, "That's one small step for man, one giant leap for mankind." Fellow astronaut, Buzz Aldrin, joins him.

 [7]

July–August, 1969
Sectarian strife begins in **Northern Ireland**. The fighting will last for three decades and see the emergence of the Provisional IRA.

 [8]

August 15–17, 1969
The three-day **Woodstock** Art and Music Fair, one of the high points of the counter culture of the 1960s, takes place near Woodstock, New York.

October 15, 1969
President **Cabdirashiid Cali Sherma'arke** (Abdirashid Ali Shermarke) of Somalia is assassinated.

 [9]

October 21, 1969
Willy Brandt, leader of the Social Democratic Party, awarded the Nobel Peace Prize in 1971 for his efforts to achieve reconciliation between his country and those of the Soviet bloc, becomes West German chancellor.

December 6, 1969
At a music festival held at Altamont Speedway in Livermore, California, the **Hell's Angels** motorcycle gang is hired as security. As the Rolling Stones are performing, a man rushes the stage with a gun and is stabbed to death.

Mick Jagger on stage with the Rolling Stones, 1976.

1970

1970
"**Brownouts**" occur along the U.S. east coast as a prolonged heat wave taxes low power reserves.

1970
"**Women's Strike for Equality**" demonstrations mark the 50th anniversary of woman suffrage in the United States.

1970
A **jury** acquits the Chicago Seven on charges of conspiring to incite a riot during the 1968 Democratic national convention but convicts five of the seven of seeking to incite a riot through individual acts.

1970
A knife-wielding assailant dressed as a priest attempts to assassinate **Pope Paul VI** shortly after his arrival in the Philippines, the third country on his 10-day trip to Asia and the South Pacific.

1970
A noontime rally and parade around New York's City Hall in support of President Richard Nixon and his **Indochina policy** draw a crowd estimated between 60,000 and 150,000.

1970
Airbus Industrie is formed in Europe to fill a market niche for short- to medium-range, high-capacity jetliners and to compete with American manufacturers. In 2000 it will launch the development of the A380, the world's largest airliner.

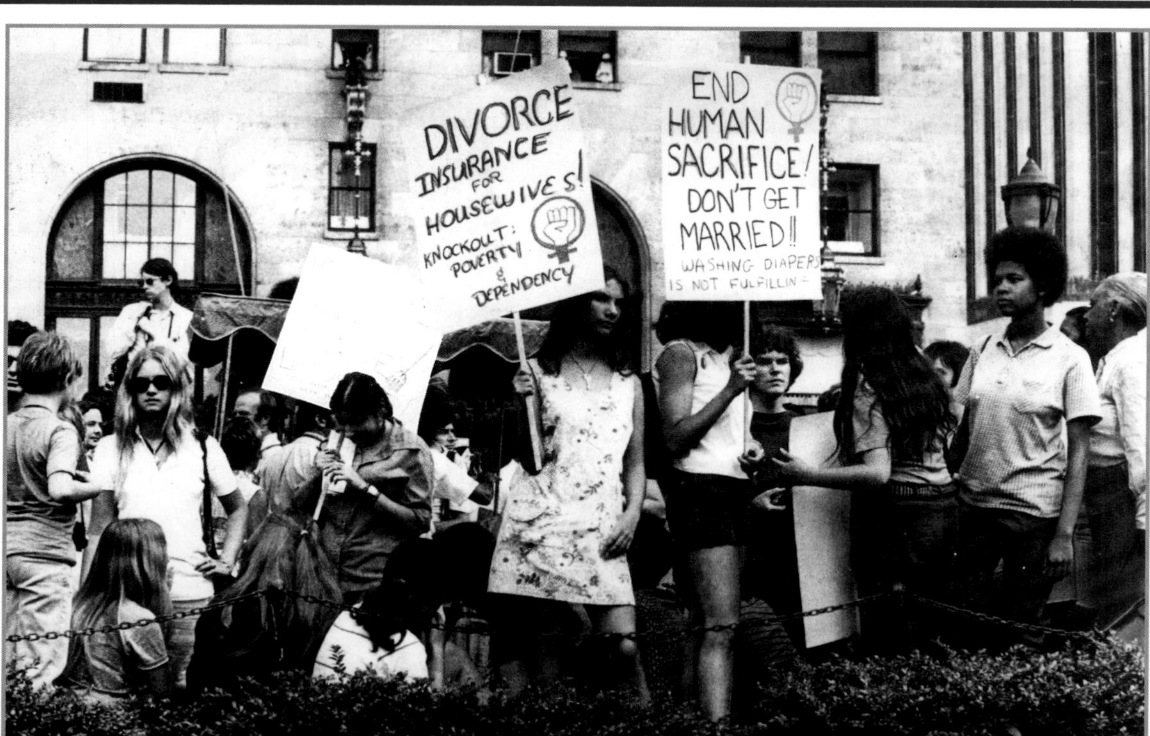

[1] A women's-liberation demonstration in New York.

[2] The Chicago Seven at a press conference during their trial: (left to right) Abbie Hoffman, John Froines, Lee Weiner, David Dellinger, Rennie Davis, Tom Hayden, and Jerry Rubin in front.

[7] The wide-body Boeing 747 with its distinctive bulging profile.

[4] The Aswan High Dam in 1967, when the waters were allowed through it for the first time.

[5] Mishima Yukio. He kills himself when, after haranguing troops about the shame of losing the Pacific War, they refuse to join his private army.

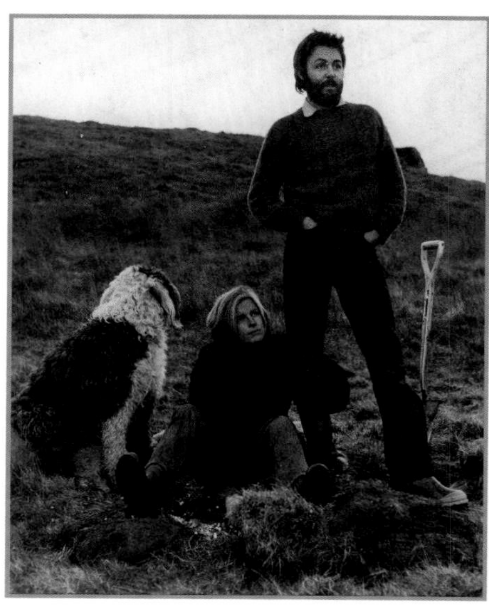

[6] Paul McCartney with his wife, Linda, in Kintyre.

 [4]

1970
Completion of the **Aswan High Dam** on the Nile River helps to protect Egypt from floods and stores water for use in droughts, but it ends a 5,000-year-old, fully sustainable irrigation agriculture system.

1970
IBM develops the **floppy disk** for storing and transporting data.

 [5]

1970
Japanese novelist **Mishima Yukio** completes his magnificent *Sea of Fertility* series. He then commits ritual suicide in a protest against Japan's "spinelessness."

1970
New York City Mayor John V. Lindsay places the city on alert as a temperature inversion along the coast sends pollution levels above the danger point; Tokyo, Sydney, and other major cities also experience **pollution crises**.

 [6]

1970
Paul McCartney announces that the Beatles have broken up.

1970
President Richard Nixon vetoes legislation limiting campaign spending on TV and radio time.

1970
American blues and rock guitarist **Jimi Hendrix** dies at age 27 of an apparently accidental overdose of barbiturates.
 [3]

1970
Amtrak is created by Congress to relieve American railroads of the burden of providing passenger service and to improve quality: the first time that passenger service has received any government financial assistance.

1970
Brazil defeats Italy in the men's **World Cup soccer** championship by a score of 4 to 1.

1970
Chilean researches develop the **contraceptive** copper-wire intrauterine device (IUD).

1970
Civil divorce is legalized in **Italy**, although it is not recognized by the dominant Roman Catholic Church.

1970
Cloning is proven possible by British molecular biologist John B. Gurdon. Gurdon transplants a mature nucleus from the cell of a tadpole into a frog's egg; it subsequently develops into an adult frog.

[3] Jimi Hendrix: for many, the greatest electric guitarist ever.

[8] A line-up of air hostesses from different airlines that hope to fly the Concorde. It flew for the first time in 1969.

CHARLES MANSON

Trial of cult leader and his followers

Charles Manson is one of America's most notorious criminals. Beginning at age nine, Manson spent much of his life in juvenile reformatories or in prison for crimes that included petty larceny, armed robbery, burglary, and auto theft. Following his release from prison in 1967, Manson moved to San Francisco, where he attracted a small but devoted group of followers from among the city's bohemian youth culture. By 1968 he had become the leader of the "Family," a communal religious cult dedicated to studying and implementing his eccentric religious teachings, which were drawn from science fiction as well as the occult and fringe psychology. He preached the coming of an apocalyptic race war that would devastate the United States and leave the Family in a position of dominant power.

Manson's hold over his followers was graphically illustrated in 1968–69, when the Family carried out several murders on Manson's orders. The most famous victim was actress Sharon Tate, wife of motion-picture director Roman Polanski, who was killed in her Los Angeles home along with three guests. The ensuing trial of Manson and his followers in 1970 attracted national attention (left, Manson with public defender Fred Schaefer). In 1971 Manson was sentenced to death, but, following the abolition of capital punishment in California in 1972, his sentence was commuted to life in prison.

1970
Rhodesia declares itself a republic, dissolving its last ties with the British crown.

1970
South Africa is expelled from the International Olympic Committee.

 [7]
1970
The **Boeing 747** is introduced into commercial service. The jumbo jet helps make transcontinental and international air travel faster, easier, and more popular.

 [8]
1970
The **Concorde** airplane reaches a speed of Mach 2.

1970
The **Gambia** is proclaimed a republic within the British Commonwealth.

1970
The trial of **Charles Manson** and three women charged with murdering Sharon Tate and her houseguests in August 1969 begins in Los Angeles.

1970

1970
The U.S. establishes the **Environmental Protection Agency (EPA)** to monitor and regulate pollution.

1970
The U.S. Internal Revenue Service announces that private schools practicing **racial discrimination** will lose their tax-exempt status.

1970
The United States implements the **Clean Air Act**, which gives the Department of Transportation the duty to reduce automobile emissions.

1970
Two days of ceremonies commemorating the centenary of Lenin's birth begin in **Moscow**.

1970
U.S. ground troops complete their withdrawal from **Cambodia**.

 [1]

1970
U.S. senator George McGovern announces the **Committee to End the War.** It seeks to bar funds for military use in Cambodia, repeal the Gulf of Tonkin Resolution, and require total U.S. troop withdrawal from South Vietnam by mid-1971.

 [2]

[1] U.S. troops in Cambodia look down from their armored personnel carrier at Viet Cong, or Cambodian, corpses on the roadside.

[5] A demonstrator in a gas mask makes her point about air quality at the first Earth Day.

[2] George McGovern

[7] Workers on an exploratory drilling rig in the Beryl field in the North Sea, working for Mobil.

[4] Prince Sihanouk toasts Premier Phan Van Dong of North Vietnam in Hanoi. It was the prince's overtures to the North Vietnamese that caused General Lon Nol to mount a coup against him.

March 5, 1970
Ratified by 45 countries, the **Nuclear Nonproliferation Treaty** of November 24, 1969, takes effect.

 [4]

March 18, 1970
Prince Norodom Sihanouk of Cambodia is overthrown in a bloodless coup, leading to the declaration of the Khmer Republic later in the year.

March 19, 1970
At Erfurt, East Germany, East and West German leaders hold their first summit since the division of **Germany**.

 [5]

April 22, 1970
The first **Earth Day** takes place in the United States.

May 1970
Iceland's volcano **Hekla** erupts and remains active for several weeks.

 [6]

May 4, 1970
Ohio National Guardsmen shoot and kill four students during antiwar protests at **Kent State University**, leading to disorder at other American universities.

1970s
Using a low-tack adhesive developed by chemist Spencer Silver, chemical engineer Arthur Fry develops the **Post-it Note**. First sold by 3M in 1980, it becomes a leading office product.

c. 1970
British and American medical researchers develop the **CAT scan**, which integrates thousands of X-ray images into a detailed picture.

c. 1970
Niklaus Wirth of Switzerland designs the computer programming language Pascal to teach structured programming.

January 12, 1970
The attempted Biafran secession from **Nigeria** ends with General Odumegwu Ojukwu's flight to the Ivory Coast.

January 16, 1970
Colonel Muammar al-Qaddafi becomes premier of Libya.

 *[3]*

February 1970
Egypt hosts a summit with Libya and Sudan in Cairo to consider military action against Israel.

[6] One of the students shot dead, or wounded, by the National Guard at Kent State University.

[8] Edward Heath at his first Conservative Party conference as prime minister, with his eventual successor as leader of the party, Margaret Thatcher.

[3] Colonel Qaddafi. He will turn out to be one of the great survivors amongst the world's dictators.

[9] Natalia Makarova in Giselle at Covent Garden.

[10] Jochen Rindt in the pits at Monza on the afternoon he is killed, when his Lotus crashes into the barriers

 *[7]*

June 1970
Oil fields are discovered in **the North Sea**.

June 4, 1970
The Kingdom of **Tonga** achieves independence within the British Commonwealth.

June 7, 1970
British novelist, essayist, and social and literary critic **E. M. Forster** dies in Coventry, Warwickshire, England.

 *[8]*

June 18, 1970
The Conservatives win the British general election and **Edward Heath** becomes prime minister.

 *[9]*

September 1970
Russian ballerina **Natalia Makarova** defects in London and receives asylum in Great Britain.

 *[10]*

September 5, 1970
Austrian racing driver **Jochen Rindt** is killed on a practice run before the Italian Grand Prix at Monza.

1970-1971

September 16, 1970
King Hussein of Jordan declares martial law following the hijacking in Amman of four international airliners by the Popular Front for the Liberation of Palestine (PFLP).

 [1]

September 25, 1970
Hostilities come to an end during **Black September**, the brief but violent civil war between the Palestine Liberation Organization and Jordan.

 [2]

October 8, 1970
Aleksandr Isayevich Solzhenitsyn is awarded the Nobel Prize for Literature.

October 10, 1970
Fiji gains independence from Great Britain.

October 10, 1970
The **Front de Libération du Québec** kidnaps Pierre Laporte, Quebec's minister of Labor. He is found murdered one week later.

October 24, 1970
Salvador Allende's election as the first Marxist president of Chile is confirmed.

 [3]

[2] Time *magazine adapts a PLO poster for the cover of its issue dealing with Black September.*

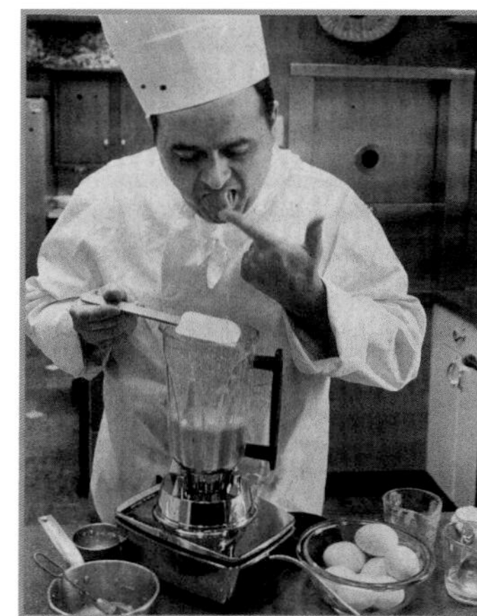

[6] *Pierre Verdon, ex–White House chef, with an early model of a liquidizer, or food processor.*

[1] *Leila Khaled, who has her moment of fame when she is one of the Palestinian terrorists released in return for the lives of the passengers from the hijacked planes at Amman. She took part in a hijacking in 1969 but was captured in an unsuccessful one aboard an El Al plane flying to London on the same day as the Amman hijackings.*

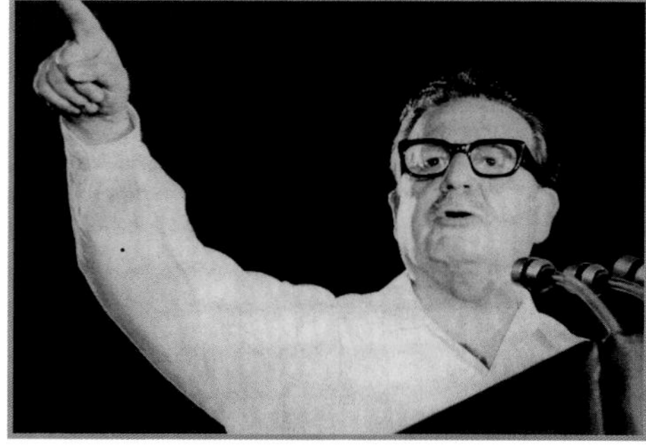

[3] *Salvador Allende addresses a Communist Party meeting in Chile. He is the first Marxist leader ever to gain office in free elections.*

[5] *Kiri Te Kanawa as the Countess in the* Marriage of Figaro. *She sings the part first at Santa Fe and then at Covent Garden. In 1981 600 million people will hear her sing at the wedding of Britain's Prince Charles and Princess Diana.*

[8] *Idi Amin takes the oath as the new head of state of Uganda.*

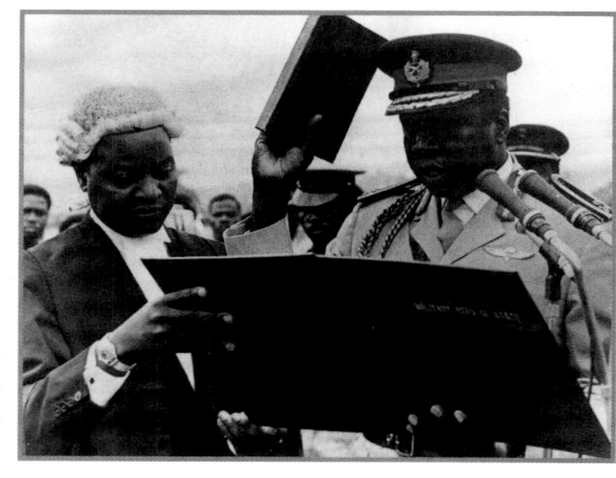

[5]

1971
New Zealand soprano **Kiri Te Kanawa** rises to international prominence as the Countess in Mozart's *Marriage of Figaro*.

1971
Pakistan wins the first World Cup of field hockey.

1971
Peruvian priest **Gustavo Gutiérrez** publishes *Teologia de la liberación*. Liberation theology, centered in Latin America, seeks to apply religion by aiding the poor and oppressed via involvement in political and civic affairs.

 [6]

1971
Pierre Verdon exhibits **Le Magi-Mix**, a compact household food processor based on his earlier model for restaurants.

1971
The "**Nixon shocks**," unilateral U.S. policy decisions leading to greater foreign policy independence for Japan, provide challenge and opportunity for Japan's government.

1971
The United Nations votes to admit the **People's Republic of China** into membership and to expel the Republic of China on Taiwan.

1971
Renzo Piano and Richard Rogers begin work on the **Centre Pompidou**, Paris. Completed in 1977, the unconventional building is at first notorious, then becomes a popular tourist attraction.
 [4]

1971
Greenpeace is founded in Vancouver, British Columbia, in response to nuclear testing in the Pacific. It soon becomes the largest direct-action environmental group, with branches in dozens of countries.

1971
South Vietnamese troops invade **Laos** with U.S. support but are driven out with heavy losses after six weeks.

1971
Intel introduces the 4004, a chip containing 2,300 transistors that is the world's first **microprocessor**.

1971
Major American **tobacco companies** agree to include warnings of the health dangers of smoking on cigarette packages and advertisements.

1971
NASDAQ, an American stock market that handles electronic securities trading around the world, begins trading.

[4] The Centre Pompidou, an iconic high-tech building, constructed inside-out with all the services—including escalators and pipework—outside, leaving big, open, uncluttered spaces within for exhibitions. The architects' demand, that half the site be left as open space to form a piazza, is, to their surprise, agreed to.

[7] William McMahon. He will be outshone by Labor opposition leader Gough Whitlam, who will win the 1972 election.

[9] The Spirit of Ecstasy: the sculptural radiator cap that is the trademark of Rolls-Royce.

1971
Thirty-four countries adopt the **Convention on Wetlands of International Importance Especially as Waterfowl Habitat**, requiring all signatories to designate at least one protected wetland area.

1971
Using the new plastic polymacon, Bausch & Lomb develops a new variety of soft, flexible **contact lenses**.

 [7]
1971
William McMahon of the Liberal-Country Party becomes prime minister of Australia.

 [8]
January 25, 1971
A coup d'état led by Major General Idi Amin deposes **Uganda's** president Milton Obote as Obote is returning from the British Commonwealth heads of state conference.

January 25, 1971
Charles Manson and three female followers are convicted of first-degree murder in the 1969 slaying of actress Sharon Tate and six others.

 [9]
February 4, 1971
Rolls-Royce is nationalized by the British government when the company goes bankrupt. The automobile business will be spun off as a separate entity from the aircraft and marine engines business in 1973.

1971

February 7, 1971
Swiss male voters approve a referendum giving women the right to vote in federal elections and to hold federal office.

February 15, 1971
The British pound sterling is officially **decimalized** into 100 new pence.

 [1]

March 8, 1971
Joe Frazier defeats Muhammad Ali in their world heavyweight title bout at Madison Square Garden in New York City.

 [2]

March 22, 1971
Argentine president **Roberto Marcelo Levingston** is deposed in a bloodless coup d'état by armed forces chiefs.

March 26, 1971
Members of the **Awami League** set up a government-in-exile in Calcutta (Kolkata) and declare Bangladesh an independent state.

March 29, 1971
U.S. Army lieutenant **William Calley** is convicted of murder charges in connection with the My Lai incident of March 1968.

 [3]

[2] Muhammad Ali nonchalantly drops his guard as he avoids Joe Frazier's left.

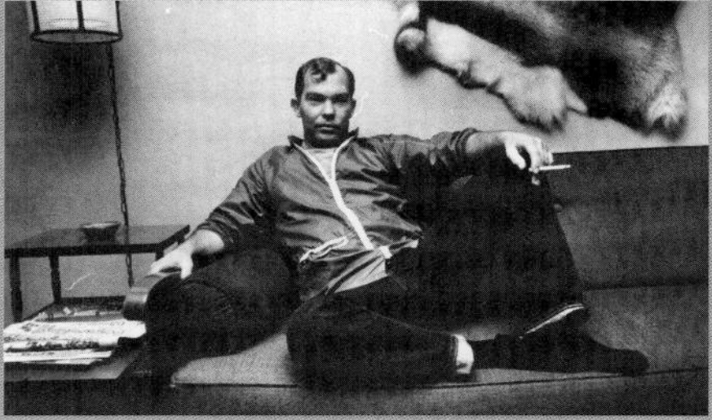

[3] William Calley at home the year before his conviction for his part in the My Lai massacre.

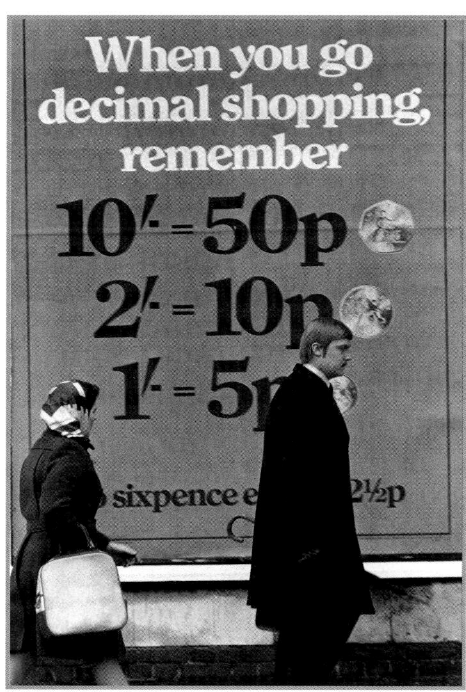

[1] A poster in London reminding shoppers what the new decimal equivalents are for ten shillings, two shillings, and one shilling.

[6] James B. Irwin salutes the U.S. flag on the moon. The Lunar Roving Vehicle can be seen on the right.

July 1, 1971
The **Twenty-sixth Amendment** to the U.S. Constitution is ratified, granting suffrage to citizens age 18 years and older.

July 26, 1971
The **Belgian parliament** passes constitutional reform bills establishing Dutch and French as its official languages.

 [6]

July 31, 1971
Apollo 15 astronauts James B. Irwin and David Scott first use the four-wheeled, battery-powered **Lunar Roving Vehicle** to extensively explore the moon's surface, in particular the Hadley-Apennine site.

 [7]

August 6, 1971
Scottish yachtsman **Chay Blyth** completes his 292-day east-to-west round-the-world voyage.

 [8]

August 9, 1971
Northern Ireland invokes emergency powers of preventative detention without trial and begins arresting suspected leaders of the outlawed Provisional Irish Republican Army (IRA); at least 12 people are killed in rioting.

August 15, 1971
Bahrain proclaims independence from Great Britain.

April 10, 1971
American journalists enter China for the first time since 1949 to cover U.S.-Chinese **table tennis** matches.
 [4]

April 20, 1971
In **Swann v. Charlotte-Mecklenburg Board of Education** the U.S. Supreme Court unanimously upholds busing programs that aimed to speed up the racial integration of public schools in the United States.

April 22, 1971
The death of Haitian president **François Duvalier** is announced; his son, Jean-Claude, is sworn in as "president for life."

May 3, 1971
Antiwar protesters in Washington, D.C., fail in their attempt to close down the U.S. government; more than 7,000 arrests are made, a record for the city.
 [5]

May 13, 1971
The New York Times begins publishing papers of a secret Pentagon study on the history of U.S. involvement in Vietnam.

July 1971
Zhou Enlai, premier and foreign minister of the People's Republic of China, meets with U.S. envoy **Henry Kissinger** in Beijing, leading to U.S. president Richard Nixon's visit to China in 1972 and Zhou's portrayal in the U.S. press as a skilled diplomat.

[4] *The U.S. table tennis team in front of the Great Wall of China. The invitation to them is the beginning of what is called "ping-pong diplomacy" between China and the U.S.*

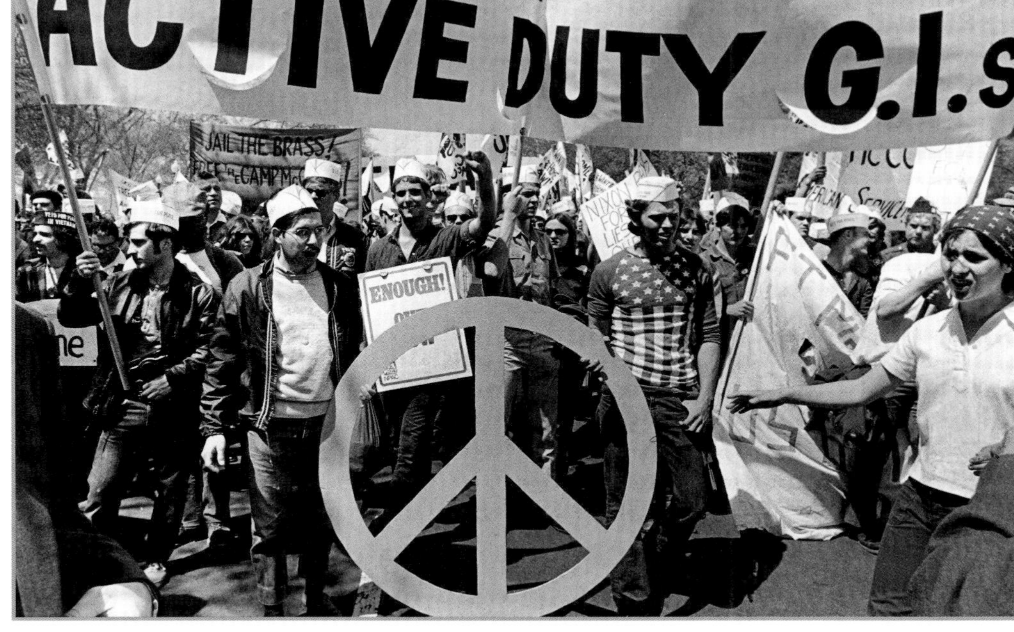

[5] *GIs out of uniform join an anti–Vietnam War protest march in Washington.*

[7] *Chay Blyth at the start of his circumnavigation.*

[9] *President Mobutu in his full finery of leopard skin hat, heraldic chain, and star.*

[8] *British soldiers in Belfast guard houses gutted in mid-August after being set on fire by IRA bombs.*

August 15, 1971
U.S. president Richard Nixon establishes a 90-day **wage and price freeze**, imposes a 10 percent import surcharge, and suspends the conversion of the dollar into gold.

September 13, 1971
Nine hostages and at least 28 prisoners are killed when about 1,500 state troopers, sheriff's deputies, and guards regain control of **Attica (New York) prison**, held for four days by 1,200 inmates.

September 25, 1971
Italian police recover more than 40 stolen works of art in a nationwide effort against gangs that had been looting churches and private collections.

September 26, 1971
Israel announces it will ignore the U.N. Security Council's call for a halt in the development of occupied Jerusalem.

October 24, 1971
South African police stage predawn searches of 115 homes of prominent persons, many critical of apartheid politics.

 [9]
October 27, 1971
Mobutu Sese Seko renames the Democratic Republic of Congo **Zaire**.

1971-1972

November 6, 1971
The U.S. Atomic Energy Commission tests a hydrogen bomb on **Amchitka Island** in the Aleutians hours after the U.S. Supreme Court denies an injunction against the test.

November 12, 1971
U.S. president Richard Nixon announces U.S. troops in **Vietnam** will be reduced by 45,000 additional men by February 1972.

November 17, 1971
Thailand's Revolutionary Party and members of the armed forces seize power in a bloodless coup.

November 28, 1971
Jordanian prime minister **Tal** is shot to death in Cairo by Palestinian guerrillas.

December 1971
The Indian army invades East Pakistan, and the Pakistani defenses surrender after 13 days. **Bangladesh** comes into being.
 [1]

December 2, 1971
Six Persian Gulf sheikdoms proclaim their independence as the **Union of Arab Emirates**.

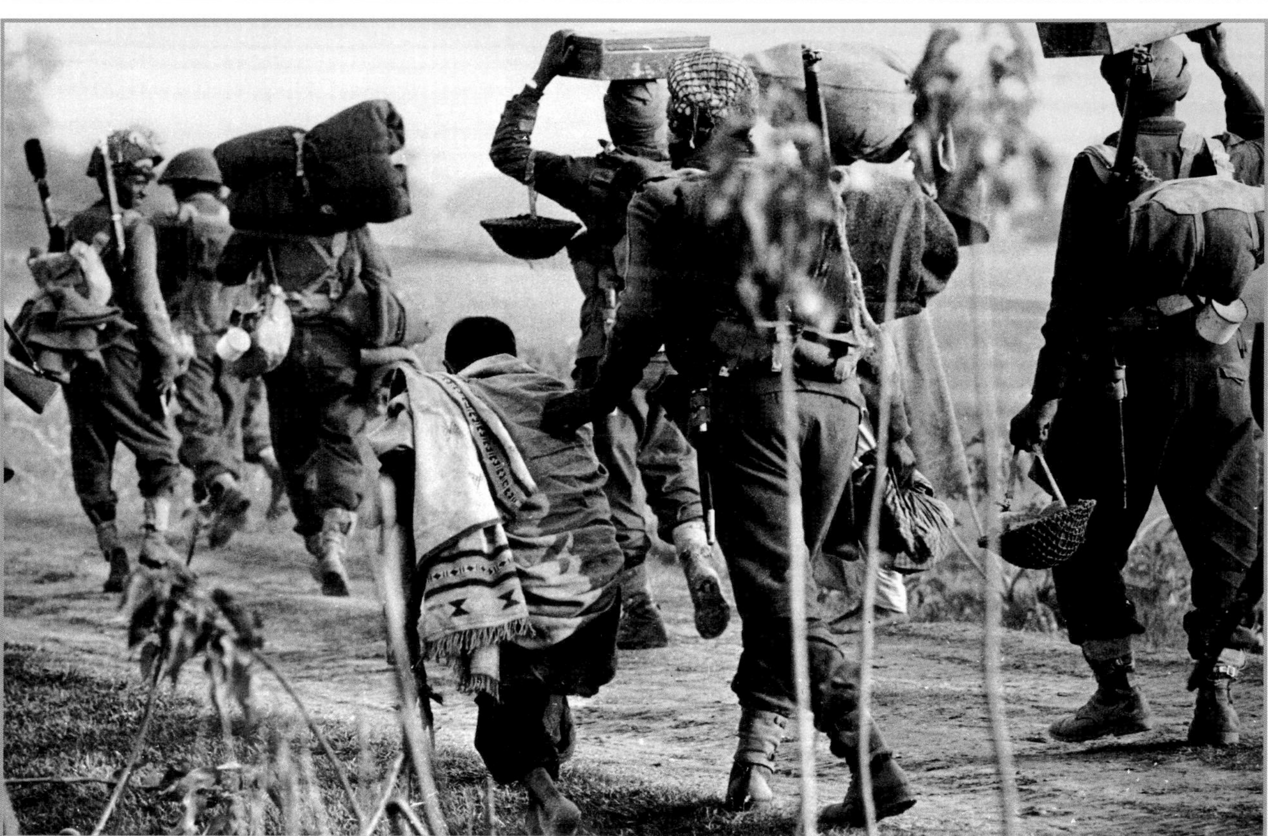

[1] *Indian soldiers advance into East Pakistan.*

[8] *Kurt Waldheim. After leaving the U.N., he will become president of Austria in 1986 despite controversy because of his war record in Yugoslavia and Greece, which he has concealed.*

[6] *Gough Whitlam and singer Little Pattie wearing T-shirts with his election slogan on them.*

[5] *The U.S. Department of Energy's Fermilab, at Batavia, Illinois: the accelerator complex and central utility building.*

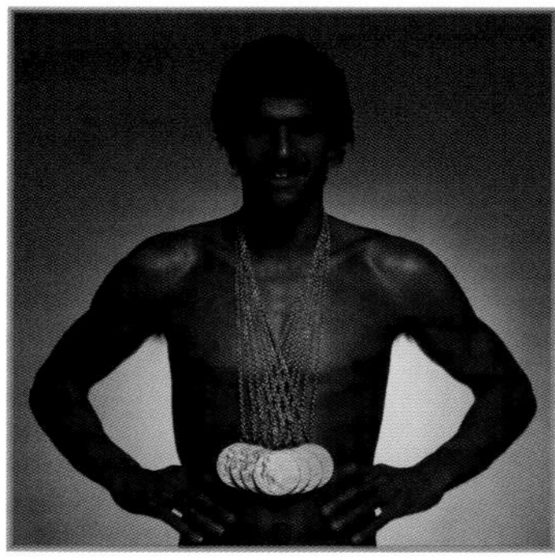

[4] *Mark Spitz with his seven gold medals.*

[7] *An Amish family in their buggy.*

[4]
1972
At the Summer Olympics in Munich, West Germany, American swimmer **Mark Spitz** becomes the first athlete to win seven gold medals in one Olympics, setting world records in all seven races.

1972
Atari Inc. introduces **Pong**, a video game, into arcades. The game's commercial success marks the beginning of an era of mass popularity for electronic games.

1972
Dennis Ritchie of Bell Laboratories develops the C programming language.

 [5]
1972
Fermilab's first **particle accelerator** begins operation. It is a proton synchrotron, a cyclic accelerator with a ring circumference of 6.3 km (3.9 miles). It can accelerate protons to 400 gigaelectron volts.

[6]
1972
Gough Whitlam of the Labor Party becomes prime minister of Australia. His unsuccessful premiership will end when he is dismissed by the governor-general in 1975.

 [7]
1972
In a case of an **Old Order Amish** community who refuses to keep its children in school past the eighth grade, the U.S. Supreme Court finds that free exercise of religion outweighs the state's interest in universal education.

December 12, 1971
Northern Ireland Unionist Party senator **John Barnhill** is killed and his home bombed.

1972
Robert Venturi, Denise Scott Brown, and Steven Izenour write **Learning from Las Vegas**, an exuberant and influential study of the architectural value of garish, commercialized Las Vegas.

1972
A United Nations conference on the environment is held in Stockholm. This is the first general international environment conference and leads to the **U.N. Environment Programme**, which is mainly concerned with pollution issues.

1972
American Black Mountain poet **Denise Levertov** revives her early sensual poetic style in one of her most popular collections, *Footprints*.

1972
American motion-picture director Francis Ford Coppola releases **The Godfather**. Sequels will follow in 1974 and 1990.

 [2]

1972
American novelist Eudora Welty publishes her quiet novel **The Optimist's Daughter**, which wins a Pulitzer Prize.

 [3]

[2] *Marlon Brando, his mouth full of cotton to alter his diction and the outline of his face, gives a masterly performance as the Mafia head-of-family, or godfather.*

[3] *Author Erica Jong sits at the feet of Eudora Welty.*

NIXON IN CHINA

U.S. president's diplomatic breakthrough

Nixon's most significant achievement in foreign affairs may have been the establishment of direct relations with the People's Republic of China after a 21-year estrangement. Following a series of low-level diplomatic contacts in 1970 and the lifting of U.S. trade and travel restrictions, the Chinese indicated that they would welcome high-level discussions, and Nixon sent his national security adviser, Henry Kissinger, to China for secret talks. Nixon's visit to China in February–March 1972, the first by an American president while in office (shown here with Premier Zhou Enlai on his right), concluded with the Shanghai Communiqué, in which the United States formally recognized the "one-China" principle—that there is only one China, and that Taiwan is a part of China. The rapprochement with China, undertaken in part to take advantage of the growing Sino-Soviet rift in the late 1960s, gave Nixon more leverage in his dealings with the Soviet Union.

 [8]

1972
Kurt Waldheim of Austria becomes secretary general of the U.N. He will serve until 1981. China vetoes a third term for Waldheim.

1972
The liner **Queen Elizabeth** is burned in Hong Kong. For over 50 years, it has been the largest passenger liner ever.

1972
The United Nations Educational, Scientific and Cultural Organization adopts the **Convention Concerning the Protection of the World Cultural and Natural Heritage**, providing a framework for international cooperation.

1972
The **Nike brand shoe** is launched and by 1979 will claim 50 percent of the U.S. running-shoe market. The company will suffer in the 1990s from revelations about conditions in its overseas factories.

1972
The **Tamil Tigers** guerrilla organization is formed in Sri Lanka. An elite unit, the "Black Tigers," will carry out suicide attacks, including (allegedly) the assassination in May 1991 of Indian prime minister Rajiv Gandhi.

1972
Texas Instruments introduces the first "**pocket**" **calculator**, which weighs 12 ounces and costs about $150.

1972

January 17, 1972
A new government designed to put **Egypt** on a war footing is formed by Aziz Sidky, who had replaced Mahmoud Fawzi as prime minister the previous day.

January 22, 1972
Britain signs a treaty of accession to join the **European Economic Community** (EEC).

January 30, 1972
In what will become known as **Bloody Sunday**, British paratroopers open fire on a demonstration in Londonderry (Derry), Northern Ireland, by Roman Catholic civil rights supporters, killing 13 and injuring 14 others (one of the injured later died).

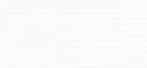

February 11, 1972
McGraw-Hill publishing company and *Life* magazine announce they have concluded that a purported biography of Howard Hughes by **Clifford Irving** is a fraud. They refuse to publish it.

February 13, 1972
The **Winter Olympic Games** close in Sapporo, Japan; U.S.S.R. leads the 35 competing nations with 16 medals.

[3]

February 18, 1972
The California Supreme Court rules the **death penalty** unconstitutional in that state, as it inflicts cruel and unusual punishment.

[2] *A British paratrooper pushes one of the demonstrators ahead of him on Bloody Sunday.*

[3] *Irina Rodnina performs a death spiral with partner Alexei Ulanov in Japan. They win gold in the pairs figure skating.*

[1] *Edward Heath signs the treaty of accession to the European Economic Community in Brussels, with Cabinet members Sir Alec Douglas-Home on his right and Geoffrey Rippon on his left.*

[6] *Zulfikar Ali Bhutto. He will meet a violent end, hanged in 1979, as will his politician daughter, Benazir, assassinated in 2007.*

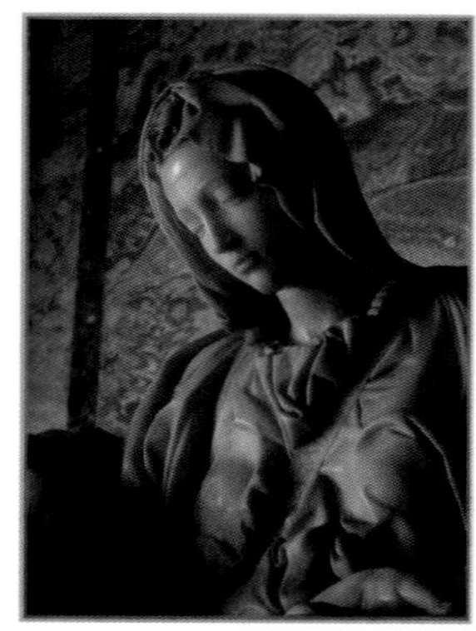

[7] *Michelangelo's* Pieta

[4] *Five of those indicted in the Harrisburg 7 trial: two of them Roman Catholic priests and one a nun. Their leader, Philip Berrigan, an antiwar activist, is not in the picture.*

April 10, 1972
The development, production, and stockpiling of biological weapons are outlawed by the **Biological Weapons Convention**, signed by more than 150 countries.

April 13, 1972
The first **players' strike** in the history of baseball ends in its 13th day, and the delayed opening of the season is scheduled for April 15.

April 16, 1972
Two **giant pandas**, given to the U.S. by China in return for a pair of musk oxen, arrive at the National Zoo in Washington, D.C.

 [6]

April 21, 1972
Zulfikar Ali Bhutto is sworn in as president of Pakistan under the new constitution he had signed the preceding day; martial law is lifted.

April 26, 1972
Yugoslav president Tito and Romanian president Nicolae Ceausescu inaugurate the **Iron Gate Dam**, Europe's largest hydroelectric powerplant on the Danube.

 [7]

May 21, 1972
Michelangelo's Pietà, a sculpture depicting the Virgin Mary supporting the body of the dead Christ, is attacked and badly damaged in St. Peter's Basilica in Rome.

February 26, 1972
An agreement ending 16 years of civil war in **the Sudan** is reached in Addis Ababa, Ethiopia.

March 1972
The U.S. Senate approves an amendment to the Constitution to prohibit discrimination on the basis of sex. **The Equal Rights Amendment** fails to gain enough state ratifications to pass.

March 12, 1972
First **national black convention**, held in Gary, Indiana, ends after adopting a political agenda and voting to set up a permanent body to provide leadership for black political and social action.

March 20, 1972
Columnist Jack Anderson begins publishing material purporting to show that the International Telephone and Telegraph Corp. (ITT), in collaboration with the CIA, had attempted to influence the 1970 presidential elections in **Chile**.

April 5, 1972
The **Harrisburg 7** jury fails to reach a verdict on charges that the defendants conspired to kidnap presidential advisor Henry Kissinger and blow up heating ducts of federal buildings. Two defendants are convicted on minor charges.

 [4]

April 7, 1972
Reputed Mafia leader **Joseph Gallo** is slain at an early morning birthday party in a New York restaurant in what authorities fear is the beginning of a crime-syndicate war.

 [5]

[5] Joeseph "Crazy Joe" Gallo on his wedding day, less than a month before he is gunned down.

[8] An Israeli security officer points to blood on the floor of Lod Airport after the massacre.

[9] The Watergate building in Washington.

BAADER-MEINHOF

Leaders of German militant left-wing group arrested

The Red Army Faction, or Baader-Meinhof gang, was a radical leftist group formed in 1968 and named after two of its early leaders, Andreas Baader and Ulrike Meinhof. From its early years, members of the terrorist group supported themselves through bank robberies and engaged in bombings and arson, especially of West German corporations and businesses and of West German and U.S. military installations in West Germany. They also kidnapped and assassinated prominent political and business figures. In 1972 several members of the group, including Baader and Meinhof (above), were captured by the German authorities.

May 22, 1972
Ceylon becomes an independent republic within the British Commonwealth, and its name changes to **Sri Lanka**.

May 26, 1972
The Soviet Union and United States sign the **Anti-Ballistic Missile Treaty**, providing that each country could have no more than two ABM deployment areas and could not establish a nationwide system of ABM defense.

 [8]

May 30, 1972
Three **Japanese gunmen** employed by Palestinian guerrillas kill 25 people and wound 76 others at Lod International Airport, Israel.

June 1972
Members of the West German urban guerrilla group known as the **Red Army Faction, or Baader-Meinhof gang**, are arrested for their role in a number of killings.

June 10, 1972
A flash flood in **Rapid City**, South Dakota, kills more than 200 people and causes $120 million in property damage.

 [9]

June 17, 1972
The **Watergate**, an office-apartment-hotel complex in Washington, D.C., and the headquarters of the Democratic National Committee, is broken into by five men who are later arrested, prompting the Watergate scandal.

1972-1973

June 25, 1972
French nuclear tests on **Mururoa Atoll** in the Pacific are reported to have begun despite protests from a number of countries.

June 29, 1972
The U.S. Supreme Court holds in *Furman v. Georgia* that the arbitrary imposition of the **death penalty** constituted cruel and unusual punishment.

July 1972
Actress **Jane Fonda**, daughter of Henry Fonda, visits Hanoi in protest at the Vietnam War.
 [1]

August 6, 1972
The death toll is reported to have reached 427 in month-long flooding on **Luzon Island**, Philippines.

August 9, 1972
Ugandan dictator **Idi Amin** gives South Asians of non-Ugandan citizenship 90 days to leave the country.
 [2]

September 1, 1972
Bobby Fischer wins the 21st game of his championship match with Boris Spassky of the U.S.S.R., thus becoming the first U.S. world chess champion.
 [3]

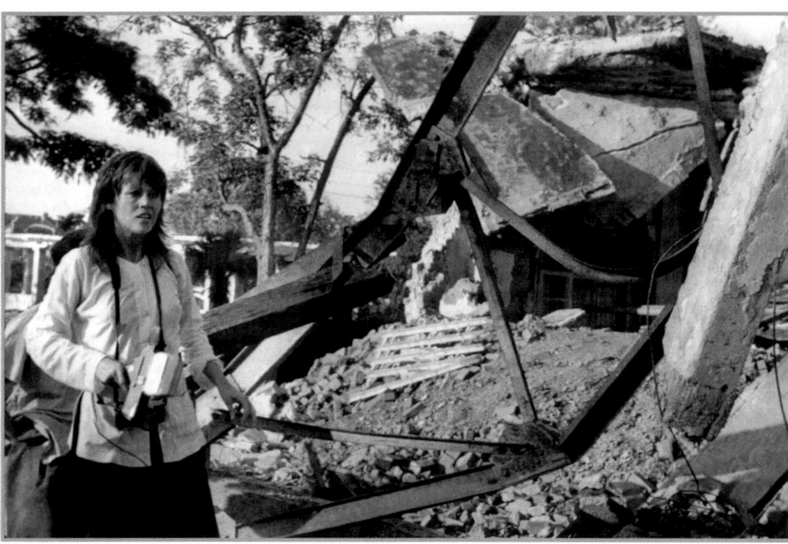
[1] Jane Fonda photographs bomb damage, the result of B-52 raids on the North Vietnamese capital.

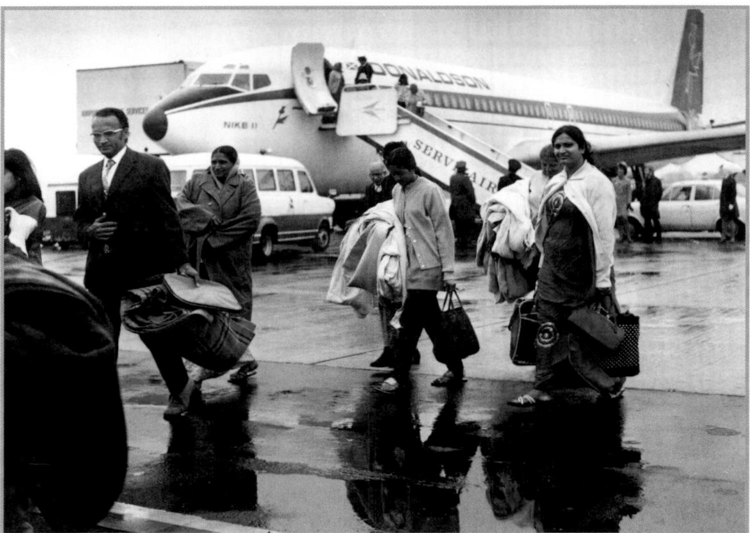
[2] Ugandan Asians landing in Britain after being expelled by Idi Amin.

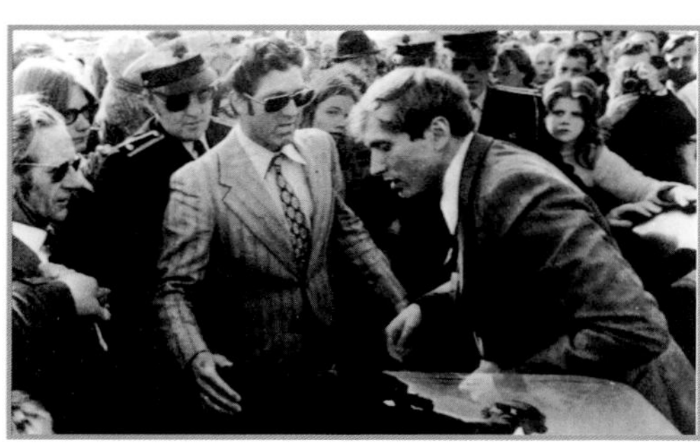
[3] Bobby Fischer arrives for his third match with Boris Spassky at Reykjavik, Iceland.

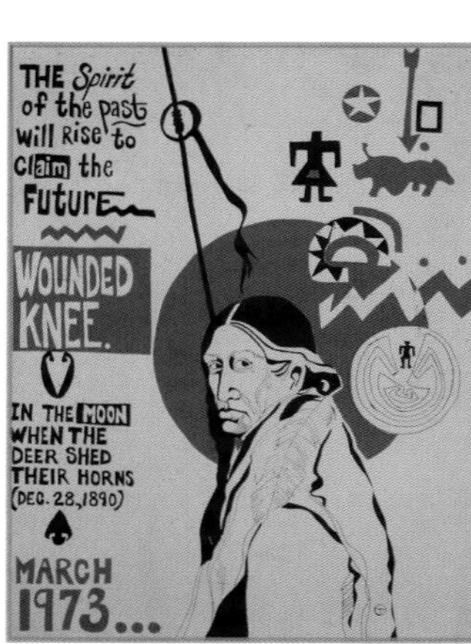

[5] A poster commemorating the siege at Wounded Knee.

[4] Roberto Clemente of the Pittsburgh Pirates.

[7] Bob Marley

December 23, 1972
Earthquakes destroy more than half of **Managua**, Nicaragua, killing 10,000 to 12,000 people.

 [4]
December 31, 1972
Baseball great **Roberto Clemente** dies in an airplane crash en route to Nicaragua with relief supplies collected for earthquake survivors.

1973
The U.S. Supreme Court establishes, in **Roe v. Wade**, a woman's right to have an abortion. The ruling in effect legalizes abortion on demand in the first three months of pregnancy.

 [5]
1973
Two hundred members of the **American Indian Movement (AIM)** take the South Dakota reservation hamlet of Wounded Knee by force on February 27. This leads to a siege that lasts until May.

1973
American postmodern novelist **Thomas Pynchon** publishes his lengthy, paranoid masterpiece *Gravity's Rainbow*.

1973
Congress passes, over a veto by President Richard Nixon, the **War Powers Resolution**, which requires, among other things, presidents to consult Congress when committing the military to hostile areas.

September 5, 1972
Palestinian terrorists attack the Israeli facility in **Munich's Olympic Village** and kill two athletes. In the ensuing rescue attempt, nine hostage-athletes, five attackers, and a West German policeman died.

September 25, 1972
Norwegians reject joining the European Economic Community by a referendum vote of more than 53 percent.

September 29, 1972
China and Japan sign an accord ending the technical state of war the countries have been in since 1937, and **Taiwan** ends diplomatic relations with Japan.

November 8, 1972
Militant Native Americans end their week-long occupation of the **Bureau of Indian Affairs headquarters** in Washington, D.C., after reaching an agreement on their demands for reforms.

November 24, 1972
Finland becomes the first Western country to recognize both West and East Germany formally and to establish diplomatic ties with both.

December 7, 1972
American astronaut **Eugene Andrew Cernan** commands the last manned flight to the moon, effectively ending the Apollo program.

TRAGEDY AT THE OLYMPICS

Palestinian terrorists take members of the Israeli team hostage.

Tragedy struck the 1972 Summer Olympics in Munich when eight Palestinian terrorists of the Black September Organization (BSO) invaded the Olympic Village on September 5 and killed two members of the Israeli team. Nine other Israelis were held hostage as the terrorists (left, a terrorist at the Olympic Village) bargained for the release of 200 Palestinian prisoners in Israel. Two helicopters took the hostages and terrorists to the nearby Fürstenfeldbrück airbase, where members of Mossad, German police, and German snipers were waiting. All the hostages, five of their captors, and a West German policeman were slain in a failed rescue attempt.

The tragedy brought the Games to a halt and cast a long shadow over what had been a memorably joyful Games. All competition was suspended for a day while a memorial service for the victims was conducted at the Olympic Stadium. International Olympic Committee president Avery Brundage's decision to continue the Games after the attack was widely criticized. In subsequent Olympics, increased security measures in the Olympic Villages and competition venues protected athletes but also diminished the festive and open atmosphere that is the heart of Olympics.

[6] Owen K. Garriott during a record seven-hour spacewalk at the Skylab space station. Garriott spends 59 days there.

[8] Sydney Opera House. Jørn Utzon disassociated himself from the project some years before its completion because of what he regarded as interference from structural engineers and others who had to turn his concepts into a feasible building.

 [6]

1973
Following the launch of the first U.S. space station **Skylab**, three teams of astronauts spend several months carrying out scientific and medical investigations in space.

1973
Genetic engineering is pioneered by American biochemists Stanley N. Cohen and Herbert W. Boyer.

 [7]

1973
Jamaican musician **Bob Marley's** album *Catch a Fire* establishes his international popularity and brings reggae music to the attention of audiences in Europe and America.

1973
Robert Metcalf of Xerox Corporation invents **Ethernet**, a high-speed communication standard for locally connecting computers and various devices.

1973
Secretariat becomes the first horse in 25 years to win the American Triple Crown; Citation had won it in 1948.

 [8]

1973
Sydney Opera House, designed by the Danish architect Jørn Utzon, is completed and soon becomes one of the most recognized buildings in the world. Its design features a series of sail-like shells.

1973

1973
The **Chipko Movement**, a popular resistance movement to logging in northern India, begins. Chipko becomes one of the major environmental movements in the less-developed world.

1973
The **Iditarod Trail Sled Dog Race** is contested for the first time at its traditional distance of 1,100 miles, between Anchorage and Nome, Alaska.

1973
The Inner London Education Authority bans **corporal punishment** in primary schools. The move signals a larger decline in the popularity of corporal punishment in Europe and America.

1973
The new **Endangered Species Act** requires that the U.S. government protect all wildlife threatened with extinction.

1973
The **OPEC** oil embargo raises world energy prices for the first time since 1945, causing brief economic dislocation but spurring energy-conservation technology and ideology.

 [1]

1973
The **push-through tab** for beverage cans is invented.

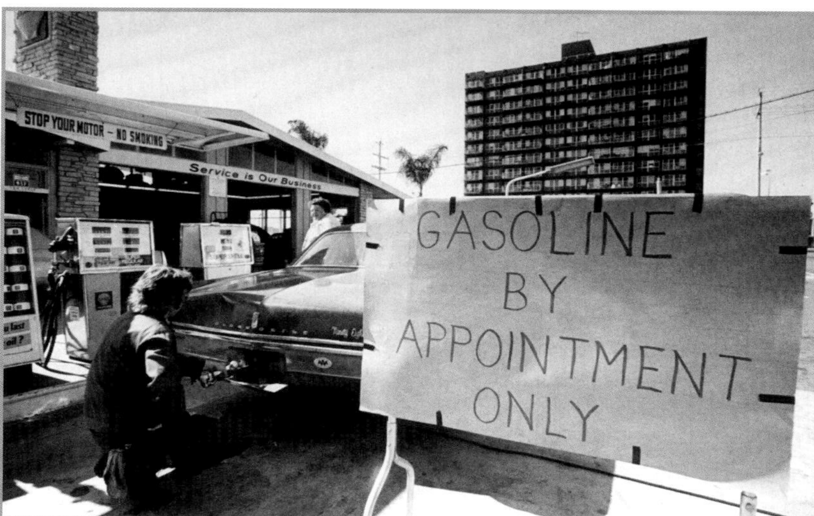

[1] A sign at a California gas station during the OPEC oil embargo.

[8] A store in Arnold, Missouri, is saved from Mississippi and Meramec floodwaters by a sandbag wall.

[7] Hector Campora (left) with Juan Perón in Rome. Perón has been in exile since 1955, but will return to Argentina in June.

[2] The Eldfell volcano in Iceland putting on a spectacular show.

[4] President Marcos of the Philippines.

March 4, 1973
Black September terrorists surrender to Sudanese authorities after having occupied the Saudi Arabian embassy in Khartoum for almost three days, during which they killed three people and held three more hostage.

 [7]

March 11, 1973
Peronista presidential candidate **Hector J. Campora** wins 49 percent of the votes in Argentina's first election since 1965. Later in 1973, Campora will resign in favor of Juan Perón's return to office.

March 17, 1973
A Cambodian air force pilot flying a stolen plane bombs the presidential palace in Phnom Penh, killing 43 and wounding 50; **President Lon Nol**, unhurt in the attack, declares a state of emergency and suspends civil liberties.

March 20, 1973
French air traffic controllers return to work after a month-long strike during which many foreign airlines had suspended service over France.

March 29, 1973
American troops evacuate **Saigon** (Ho Chi Minh City) as the United States ends its involvement in the Vietnam War.

April 14, 1973
A U.S.-owned oil installation near Saida, Lebanon, is blown up by the previously unknown **Lebanese Revolutionary Guard**.

January 20, 1973
Amilcar Cabral, leader of the African Party for the Independence of Guinea and Cape Verde, is assassinated in front of his house in Conarky, Guinea.

January 23, 1973
The **Eldfell volcano** on Heimaey Island, Iceland, dormant for thousands of years, erupts, forcing the evacuation of the town of Vestmannaeyjar.

 [2]

January 27, 1973
The **Paris Accord** ending the Vietnam War, America's longest war, is signed, providing for an exchange of prisoners and for the unilateral withdrawal of U.S. forces from South Vietnam.

 [3]

January 27, 1973
Philippine president **Ferdinand Marcos** issues a new constitution that extends his rule indefinitely. He also permanently extends martial law.

 [4]

January 30, 1973
Two former officials of President Richard Nixon's reelection campaign committee, **G. Gordon Liddy** and **James W. McCord, Jr.**, are found guilty of attempting to spy on Democratic National Committee headquarters in the Watergate building complex, Washington, D.C.

[5]

February 12, 1973
The first **U.S. prisoners-of-war** to be freed by North Vietnam are flown from Hanoi to Clark Air Force Base in the Philippines.

 [6]

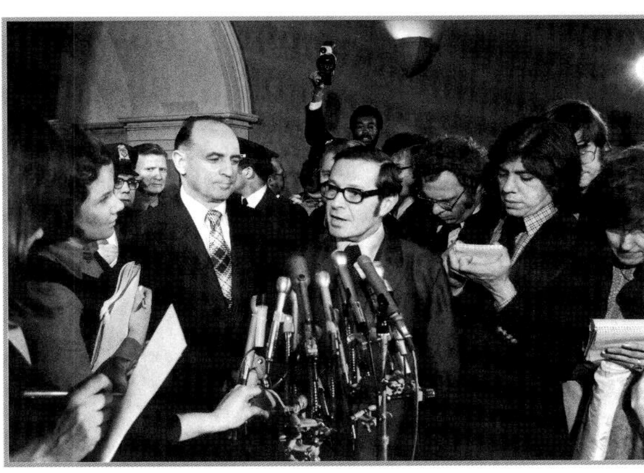

[5] James McCord stands by as his lawyer speaks to journalists, including Carl Bernstein of the Washington Post *(right). Bernstein's book,* All the President's Men, *written jointly with Bob Woodward, is the key text for the Watergate affair.*

[6] U.S. prisoners-of-war line up in Hanoi to report to U.S. representatives before being repatriated.

[3] Nguyen Duy Trinh signs the Paris peace accord for North Vietnam.

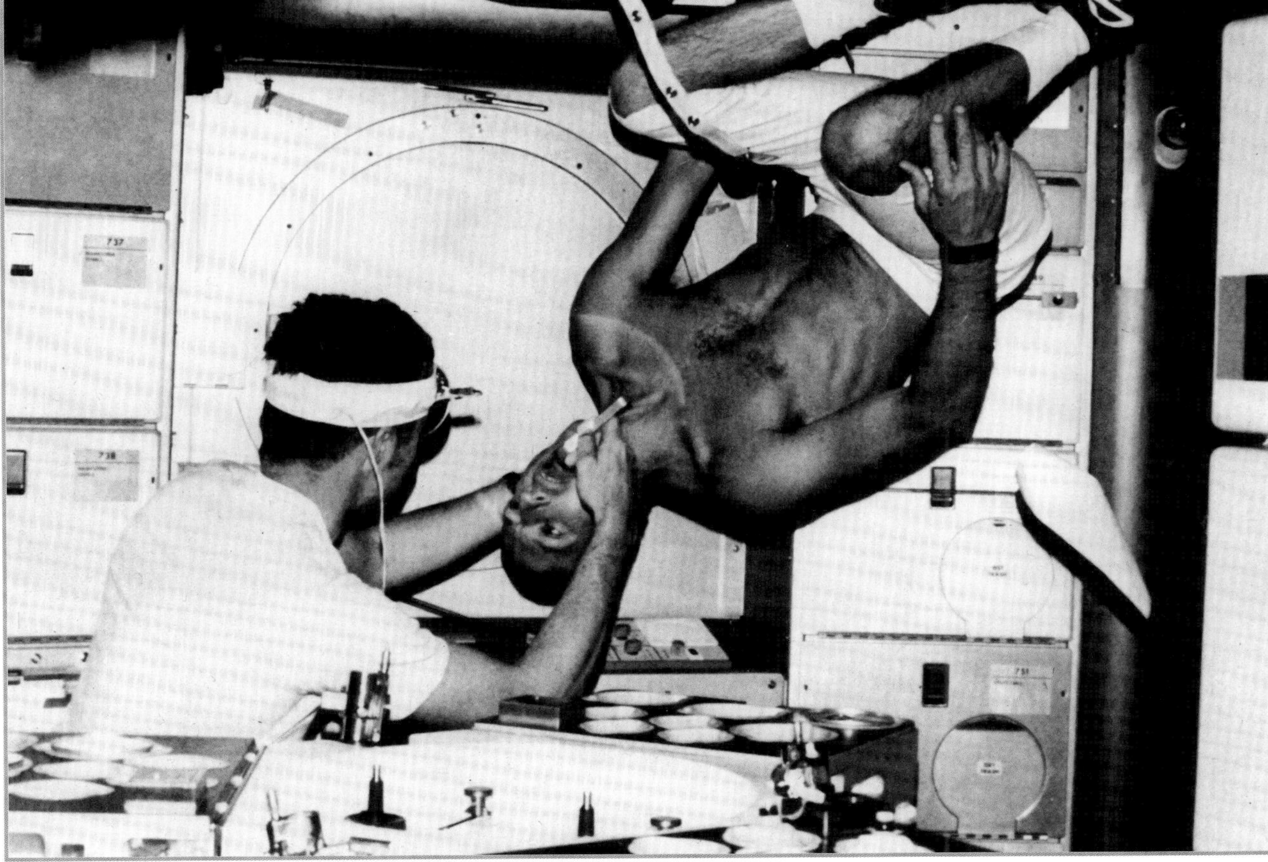

[9] Life on board Skylab: Joseph P. Kerwin examines Commander Charles Conrad's mouth as he floats weightlessly.

[8]

May 3, 1973
The **Mississippi River** and its tributaries rise to new record levels following heavy rains; damage resulting from some two months of flooding is estimated at $322 million.

May 7, 1973
Rightist demonstrators parade through **Madrid** demanding that the Spanish cabinet resign and that more power be given to the army and police.

May 17, 1973
The Argentine government ends a state of emergency triggered by the assassination of retired **rear admiral Hermes Quijada** by leftists.

June 1, 1973
Greece's military regime declares the establishment of a republic and abolition of the monarchy. Later in the summer, a referendum on a new constitution will pass by a massive margin.

 [9]

June 22, 1973
Three astronauts from the American space station **Skylab** return safely to earth after spending a record 28 days in space, during which they made two major repairs to the orbiting vehicle.

July 4, 1973
Barbados, Guyana, Jamaica, and Trinidad launch the **Caribbean Economic Community** with the Chaguaramas Treaty.

1973-1974

July 10, 1973
The **Bahamas** gain independence from Britain within the commonwealth.

August 19, 1973
Georgios Papadopoulos takes office after abolishing the monarchy and declaring himself president of Greece.

[1]

August 28, 1973
Stockholm police storm a bank vault and capture a gunman and his companion who had held four people hostage in the vault since August 23. Henceforth the reaction of hostages in becoming sympathetic to their captors is known as "**Stockholm syndrome**."

September 11, 1973
General **Augusto Pinochet** leads a coup d'état, overthrowing the government of President Salvador Allende of Chile.

[2]

September 12, 1973
Eleven black miners are killed by **South African police** at the Western Deep Levels gold mine in Carletonville during a riot over wages.

October 3, 1973
Willi Stoph, a member of the Socialist Unity Party, becomes head (1973–76) of the German Democratic Republic (East Germany).

[1] Georgios Papadopoulos, a key figure in the Regime of the Colonels in Greece, becomes president because a royalist plot in the Greek navy is feared. He shakes hands with the Greek commander-in-chief. In November there will be student riots in Athens, and he will be overthrown.

[2] Salvador Allende leaves the presidential palace with his bodyguards shortly before he is killed in the coup.

[5] The 110 floors of the Sears Tower.

[6] Some of the terra-cotta warriors, still overwhelming in their impact in spite of their weaponry having crumbled to dust and their colors having faded.

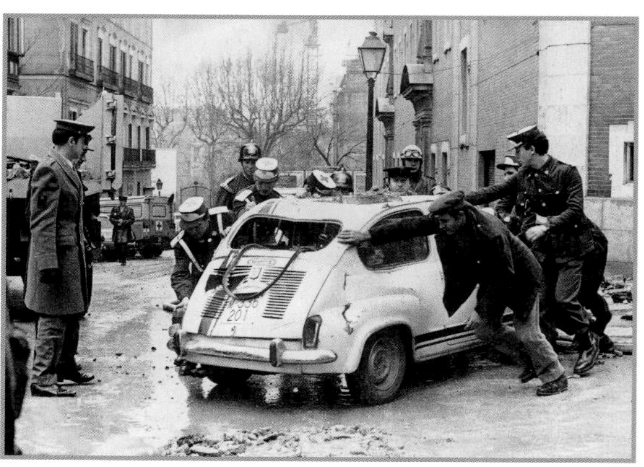

[4] Spanish police push a car damaged by the bomb that killed the prime minister.

[7] Eddy Merckx does a victory lap with the riders who came in second and third.

December 6, 1973
Gerald R. Ford is sworn in as vice president of the United States, succeeding Spiro T. Agnew.

December 20, 1973
Basque separatists assassinate Prime Minister Luis Carrera Blanco of Spain.

1974
At a height of 1,454 feet, the **Sears Tower** in Chicago stands as the world's tallest building, holding this distinction until the late 1990s.

1974
About 20 miles northeast of Xi'an, China, archaeologists begin to excavate the **tomb of Shi Huangdi**, emperor of the Qin dynasty. The site contains an army of about 6,000 exceptionally detailed, life-size terra-cotta figures arrayed in battle formation.

1974
Avant-garde German artist **Joseph Beuys's** performance art piece, *Coyote*, at a New York gallery, combines political and spiritual aims.

1974
Eddy Merckx of Belgium wins his fifth Tour de France, tying the record of Frenchman Jacques Anquetil.

October 6, 1973
On the Jewish holy day of **Yom Kippur**, Egypt and Syria attack Israel, which suffers heavy casualties. Israeli forces successfully fight back, and the war eventually ends inconclusively.

October 10, 1973
U.S. vice president **Spiro T. Agnew** resigns from office and pleads no contest to the charge of failing to report $29,500 in income while governor of Maryland.

 [3]

October 14, 1973
Prime Minister Thanom Kittikachorn is forced to leave **Thailand** following huge public demonstrations.

October 19, 1973
Lebanese police and army units storm the **Beirut** branch of the Bank of America and capture Arab guerrillas threatening to blow it up; one hostage and two gunmen are killed.

December 3, 1973
In Washington, D.C., eighty nations sign the landmark **CITES** (Convention on International Trade in Endangered Species of Wild Fauna and Flora), regulating the import and export of endangered plant and animal species.

December 4, 1973
U.S. **truck drivers** begin blocking key highways to protest the effects that rising fuel costs and lower speed limits will have on their incomes.

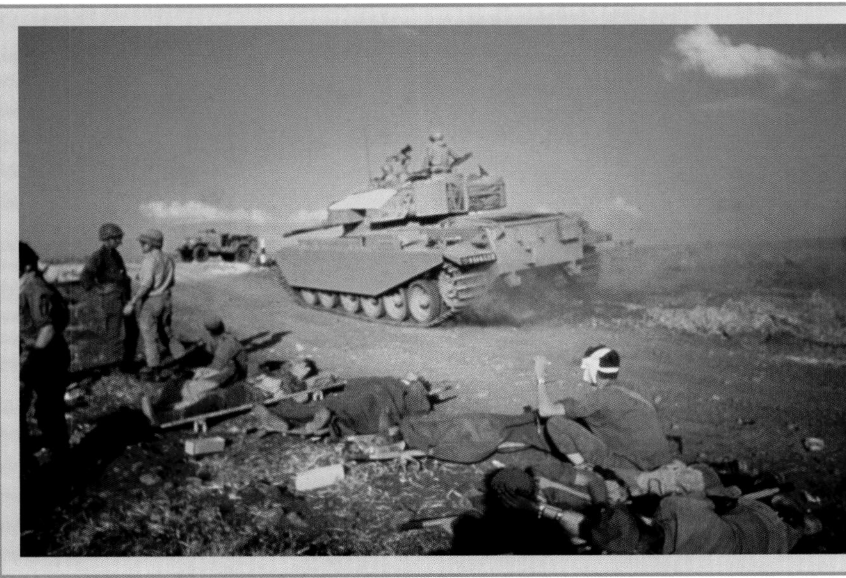

YOM KIPPUR WAR

Israel surprised by Egyptian and Syrian armies

On October 6, 1973—the Jewish Day of Atonement, Yom Kippur—Egyptian and Syrian forces staged a surprise attack on Israeli forces across the Suez Canal and the Golan Heights. The Arab armies showed greater ability than in several previous wars, and the Israeli forces suffered heavy casualties (left, Israeli tanks drive past wounded soldiers). The Israeli army, however, reversed early losses and pushed its way into Syrian territory and encircled the Egyptian Third Army by crossing the Suez Canal and establishing forces on its west bank. Israel and Egypt signed a cease-fire agreement in November and peace agreements on January 18, 1974. The accords provided for Israeli withdrawal into the Sinai west of the Mitla and Gidi passes, while Egypt was to reduce the size of its forces on the east bank of the canal.

[8] *Erno Rubik surrounded by cubes.*

[3] *Spiro Agnew*

[11] *Brian Faulkner, Unionist Party leader and chief of the Northern Ireland coalition.*

[9] *Hank Aaron hits the home run that breaks Babe Ruth's record.*

[10] *Gerd Müller of Germany fires the shot that wins the World Cup.*

 [8]

1974
Erno Rubik, a lecturer at the Academy of Applied Arts and Design in Budapest, invents and patents the **Rubik's Cube**, which will become one of the world's most popular puzzles.

 [9]

1974
Hank Aaron of the Atlanta Braves breaks Babe Ruth's major league home run record. Aaron will finish his career with 755 home runs.

1974
Sato Eisaku, former prime minister of Japan, is awarded (with Sean MacBride) the Nobel Peace Prize for his policies leading to Japan's signing of the Treaty on the Non-proliferation of Nuclear Weapons.

1974
The U.S. Congress passes the **Federal Election Campaign Act**, to provide federal financing for presidential elections, to require disclosure of contributions, and to limit individual contributions.

 [10]

1974
West Germany defeats the Netherlands in the men's **World Cup** soccer championship by a score of 2 to 1.

 [11]

January 1, 1974
A **Northern Ireland coalition**, composed of both Protestants and Roman Catholics, takes office in the beleaguered province, ending 21 months of direct rule by the British government.

1974

February 4, 1974
Patricia Hearst, the granddaughter of the late newspaper publisher William Randolph Hearst, is kidnapped by a group connected with the Symbionese Liberation Army.

 [1]

February 7, 1974
Grenada gains independence from the United Kingdom.

February 13, 1974
The Soviet Union deports dissident novelist **Aleksandr Solzhenitsyn** and issues a decree stripping him of his citizenship; it is the first forced Soviet expulsion of a major political dissident since 1929, when Joseph Stalin exiled Leon Trotsky.

 [2]

March 1, 1974
Seven former White House and Nixon campaign officials are indicted on charges including conspiracy, obstruction of justice, and making false statements to investigators by the grand jury investigating the **Watergate affair**.

 [3]

March 2, 1974
Military rule ends in **Burma** after eleven years. Under a newly ratified constitution, Burma becomes a one-party socialist republic.

March 29, 1974
Twenty-two people are reported to have been killed in **Bihar state**, India, in several days of rioting over rising food prices and political corruption.

[1] Patty Hearst sides with her kidnappers and joins in a bank robbery, armed with a submachine gun. She is caught here on a security camera.

[2] Solzhenitsyn is mobbed by the press on his arrival in Zürich. It is publication of his exposé of Russia's own system of concentration camps, The Gulag Archipelago, *that has brought about his expulsion.*

[3] John Erlichman meets the press after being sentenced. A Nixon aide, he, along with aide H. R. Haldeman and legal aide John W. Dean, are the leading figures in the Watergate case.

[6] Smoke and flames billow from the Palace of Westminster, which includes the Houses of Parliament and the medieval Westminster Hall.

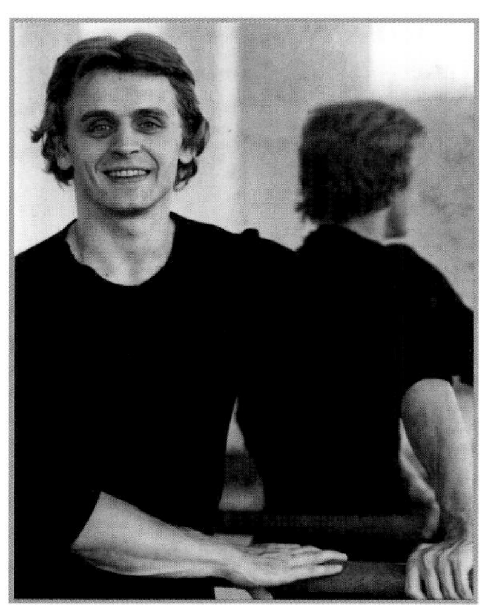

[7] Mikhail Baryshnikov limbers up before a performance with the American Ballet Theater.

May 18, 1974
In an underground test in the **Rajasthan desert**, India explodes its first nuclear device, thus becoming the sixth nuclear power; the Indian government calls it "a peaceful nuclear explosion experiment."

May 27, 1974
Valéry Giscard d'Estaing is elected president of France.

June 1974
Between 10,000 and 30,000 people are reported to have died in **India**, primarily in Bihar state, in one of the worst smallpox epidemics in recent history.

 [6]

June 17, 1974
Westminster Hall in London is damaged by a bomb explosion, leaving 11 injured. Police blame the attack on the Provisional Irish Republican Army.

$

June 26, 1974
Owing to heavy losses incurred in foreign-exchange trading, the West German **Bankhaus I.D. Herstatt KG**, one of the country's largest private banks, is ordered liquidated.

June 30, 1974
Alberta King, the mother of Martin Luther King, Jr., is assassinated as she plays the organ at Ebenezer Baptist Church in Atlanta.

April 10, 1974
Golda Meir announces her "irrevocable" decision to resign as prime minister of Israel, a post she had held since 1969.

April 25, 1974
A seven-man junta led by **General António Spínola** assumes power in Portugal after dissident army officers seize control of the government in a virtually bloodless coup.

 [4]

May 7, 1974
Walter Scheel, a member of the Free Democratic Party, becomes chancellor (1974) of the Federal Republic of Germany (West Germany).

May 9, 1974
The **House Judiciary Committee** opens formal hearings to decide whether or not to recommend that the full House impeach U.S. president Richard Nixon.

May 15, 1974
Three Palestinian guerrillas take 90 schoolchildren hostage in **Ma'alot, Israel**, demanding the release of 20 guerrillas being held by Israel. Twenty children and three guerrillas are killed when Israeli troops storm the school.

May 16, 1974
Publisher of the influential weekly *Die Zeit* **Helmut Schmidt**, a member of the Social Democratic Party, becomes chancellor (1974–82) of the Federal Republic of Germany (West Germany).

 [5]

[4] Portuguese troops out on the streets during the Spinola coup.

[9] Turkish-Cypriot prisoners taken captive during the warfare. The Turks have landed an army in northern Cyprus because of the Greek nationalist coup there against President Makarios. They soon control two-fifths of the island.

[5] Helmut Schmidt. He is more down-to-earth, less visionary than his predecessor, Willy Brandt.

[10] Nixon gives a double V for victory sign as he leaves the White House after his resignation.

[8] Isabel Perón, Juan Perón's second wife, moves from being vice president to president.

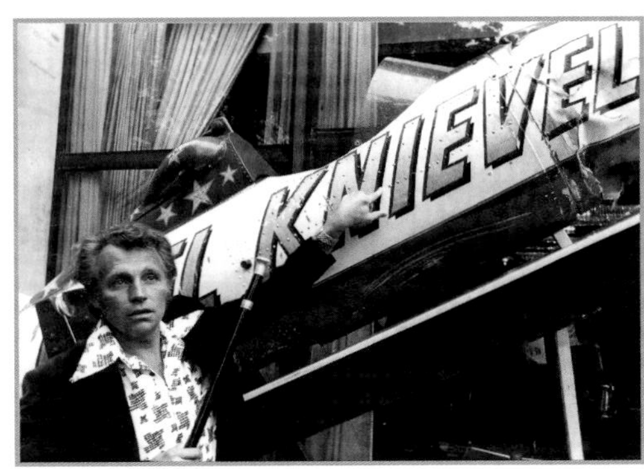

[11] Evel Knievel with his "Sky Cycle" rocket shortly after his failed attempt.

 [7]

June 30, 1974
Dancer **Mikhail Baryshnikov** defects from the Soviet Union while on tour in Canada.

 [8]

July 1, 1974
Isabel Perón becomes the first woman head of state in the Americas, succeeding Juan Perón upon his death.

July 1, 1974
Walter Scheel, a member of the Free Democratic Party, becomes president of West Germany (1974–79).

 [9]

July 20, 1974
Turkey invades **Cyprus**, claiming the need to protect Turkish islanders, which leads to the creation of the Turkish Republic of Northern Cyprus. Only Turkey recognizes the breakaway area north of the "green line."

 [10]

August 8, 1974
Three days after his admission of complicity in the Watergate cover-up, President **Richard M. Nixon** announces that he will resign the following day. On August 9, Vice President Gerald R. Ford is sworn in as president.

 [11]

September 8, 1974
Stuntman **Evel Knievel** fails in his highly publicized attempt to cross the Snake River Canyon in Idaho in a steam-propelled rocket.

1974-1975

September 8, 1974
U.S. president **Gerald R. Ford** grants a full pardon to former president Richard M. Nixon.

September 10, 1974
Guinea-Bissau gains independence from Portugal.

September 12, 1974
Emperor **Haile Selassie I** of Ethiopia is deposed by the Derg, a committee of revolutionary soldiers.

 [1]

September 19, 1974
Hurricane Fifi strikes Honduras, killing thousands and leaving millions of dollars worth of devastation in its wake.

October 1974
The U.N. General Assembly grants the **Palestine Liberation Organization (PLO)** recognition as "the representative of the Palestinian people." In November, the PLO gains observer status.

October 1, 1974
Beijing marks the 25th anniversary of Communist rule in China with widespread celebrations. Notably absent is Chairman Mao Zedong, believed to be too frail to appear on the rostrum of the Gate of Heavenly Peace.

 [2]

[1] Emperor Haile Selassie at the time of his deposition.

[2] Chinese schoolgirls perform a song-and-dance routine, which includes wooden rifles, in praise of the revolution.

[5] Darwin, northern Australia, a scene of devastation after the cyclone that destroyed nearly all the buildings there.

[6] Garfield Sobers smites the English bowling yet again.

[5]

December 25, 1974
A cyclone strikes **Darwin, Australia**, destroying 90 percent of the city and killing 47 people in what is described as the worst natural catastrophe in Australia's history.

December 30, 1974
Official reports indicate that nearly 5,000 persons were killed in an earthquake that struck a number of towns in northern **Pakistan** on December 8.

December 31, 1974
Gold bullion sales are made legal in the United States, though the widely heralded gold rush fails to materialize, as only a small number of purchases are made.

1975
Atari releases the **Pong** video game for home use. It becomes the must-have Christmas gift of 1975, sold exclusively through Sears and Roebuck.

1975
Bill Gates and Paul G. Allen, two boyhood friends from Seattle, found **Microsoft**, deriving the name from the words "microcomputer" and "software."

 [6]

1975
Cricketer **Garfield Sobers** of the West Indies is knighted. In his career, he has set test match records in runs (8,032) and centuries (26) and has come to be regarded as one of his sport's greatest performers.

October 11, 1974
The **Nuclear Regulatory Commission** (NRC) is established by President Gerald R. Ford to oversee the civilian use of nuclear materials in the United States.

October 15, 1974
Massachusetts governor Francis Sargent orders the mobilization of 50 **National Guardsmen** as racial violence ignited by court-ordered busing continues in Boston's schools.
 [3]

October 30, 1974
Muhammad Ali knocks out George Foreman in the "Rumble in the Jungle," regaining the world heavyweight boxing title.
 [4]

November 20, 1974
The Department of Justice files an **antitrust suit** in federal court in Washington, D.C., against AT&T, the world's largest privately owned corporation.

November 29, 1974
In a historic breakthrough for a predominantly Roman Catholic country, France's National Assembly votes to **legalize abortion** during the first 10 weeks of pregnancy.

December 24, 1974
Pope Paul VI taps three times on the Holy Door to St. Peter's Basilica in Rome, which had been walled up since 1950—the last Holy Year of the Roman Catholic Church—and leads a procession into the church, inaugurating the 1975 Holy Year.

[3] Children boarding school buses in Boston with a police presence in the background.

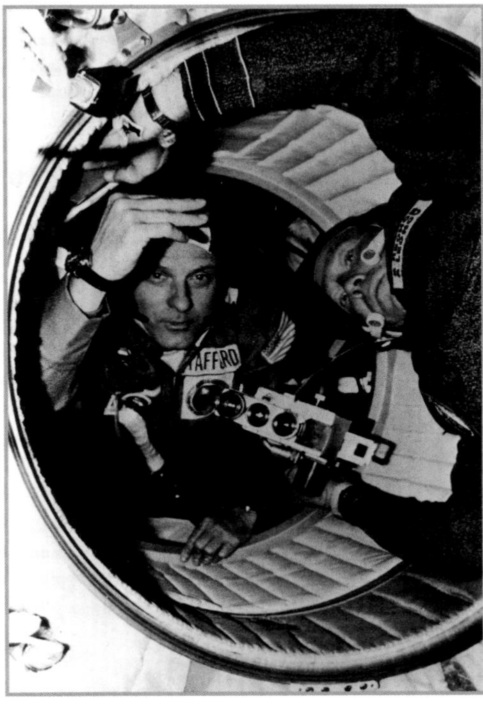

[10] Aleksey Leonov (holding camera) and Thomas P. Stafford move through the hatchway linking Apollo to Soyuz.

[4] The "Rumble in the Jungle," one of Muhammad Ali's most famous fights, in Kinshasa, capital of Zaire (Congo).

[8] Beverly Sills outside Lincoln Center in New York.

[7] Malcolm Fraser. He will stay in power until 1983, having gained it as a result of the controversial dismissal of Gough Whitlam.

[9] Richard Meier's Atheneum

1975
Eighteen nations adopt the **Mediterranean Action Plan**, an agreement designed to limit pollution of the Mediterranean Sea.

 [7]
1975
Malcolm Fraser of the Liberal Party becomes prime minister of Australia.

 [8]
1975
Playing the role of Pamira in *Le Siège de Corinthe*, at age 46, **Beverly Sills** makes her debut at the Metropolitan Opera in New York City.

1975
Polish-born mathematician Benoit B. Mandelbrot coins the term "**fractal**" for a class of complex geometric shapes that give rise to a new system of geometry.

 [9]
1975
Architect **Richard Meier** begins work on the Atheneum in New Harmony, Indiana. Firmly grounded in the principles of modernism, it nonetheless marks an evolution away from strict adherence to them.

 [10]
1975
The **Apollo-Soyuz Test Project** takes place as two spacecraft link up in orbit, featuring a "handshake in space" between Apollo commander Thomas P. Stafford and Soyuz commander Aleksey Leonov.

1975

1975
The U.S.'s "Big Three" **auto makers** initiate the practice of granting rebates to new car buyers in an attempt to lift the industry out of its worst slump since the 1940s.

1975
Through genetic engineering, Argentine researcher Cesar Milstein and colleagues discover how to produce **monoclonal antibodies** by fusing specific lymphocytes with cultured myeloma cells that reproduce indefinitely.

c. 1975
The world's population surpasses **four billion**.

c. 1975
The development of the faster and more maneuverable polyurethane wheel causes a renewed enthusiasm for **skateboarding**.

 [1]

January 2, 1975
General **Jean-Bédel Bokassa**, president of the Central African Republic, names Elisabeth Domitien as the country's first prime minister; she is the first woman to serve as prime minister of an African country.

February 11, 1975
Britain's Conservative Party elects **Margaret Thatcher** its leader.

 [2]

[1] *A skateboarder performs at a specially designed rink.*

[6] *Tabei Junko*

[2] *Margaret Thatcher just after her election.*

THE FALL OF SAIGON

The Vietnam War comes to an end.

In early March 1975, the North Vietnamese launched the first phase of what was expected to be a two-year offensive to secure South Vietnam. As it happened, the South's government and army collapsed in less than two months. Thousands of South Vietnamese troops retreated in disorder, first from the central highlands and then from Hue and Da Nang. On April 21 President Nguyen Van Thieu of the Republic of Vietnam resigned and flew to Taiwan. On April 30 what remained of the South Vietnamese government surrendered unconditionally, and North Vietnamese tank columns occupied Saigon without a struggle (left). The remaining Americans escaped in a series of frantic air- and sealifts with Vietnamese friends and coworkers. A military government was instituted, and on July 2, 1976, the country was officially united as the Socialist Republic of Vietnam with its capital in Hanoi. Saigon was renamed Ho Chi Minh City. The 30-year struggle for control over Vietnam was over.

April 22, 1975
A bloodless military coup d'etat ousts **Honduran** chief of state General Oswaldo López Arellano, who has been linked to a $1.25 million bribe from American corporation United Brands.

April 24, 1975
Terrorists attack the West German embassy in **Stockholm**, killing the military attaché and taking 12 hostages; apparently in reprisal for West German refusal to release 26 anarchists.

April 30, 1975
The South Vietnamese capital of **Saigon** (Ho Chi Minh City) falls to North Vietnamese troops without a struggle, as the remaining Americans escape in a series of frantic air- and sealifts with Vietnamese friends and coworkers.

 [6]

May 15, 1975
Tabei Junko of Japan, accompanied by Ang Tsering of Nepal, becomes the first woman to reach the summit of **Mount Everest**.

 [7]

June 5, 1975
Exactly eight years after its closure during the 1967 Arab-Israeli war, the **Suez Canal** is reopened by Egypt's president, Anwar el-Sadat.

June 25, 1975
After 470 years of colonial rule, the area that was once known as Portuguese East Africa becomes the independent **People's Republic of Mozambique**.

February 17, 1975
The municipal Gallery of Modern Art in **Milan** is robbed of 28 paintings, including works by Cézanne, Gauguin, Renoir, and Van Gogh.

March 9, 1975
Belgian novelist and poet **Marie Gevers** dies. Her works evoke Kempenland, the rural area where she spent most of her life.

March 9, 1975
Work begins on the 789-mile **Alaskan oil pipeline**, the largest private construction project in the history of the United States; construction will conclude in 1977.

 [3]

March 25, 1975
Saudi king Faisal is assassinated by a nephew and then succeeded by his brother, Crown Prince Khalid ibn Abd al-Aziz al-Saud.

 [4]

April 17, 1975
Cambodia's ruling Lon Nol government collapses, and the communist forces of the **Khmer Rouge**, led by Pol Pot, enter Phnom Penh and forcibly disperse its citizenry into rural areas.

 [5]

April 19, 1975
The **200th anniversary** of the battles that marked the beginning of the U.S. War of Independence is celebrated by more than 160,000 Americans at the scene of the first engagements at Lexington and Concord, Massachusetts.

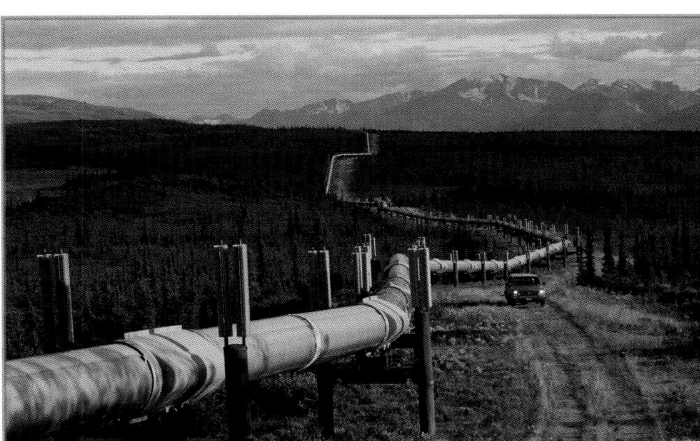

[3] The pipeline snakes across the Alaskan landscape. Much of it, as here, is elevated above the ground because of problems posed by permafrost.

[8] Jimmy Hoffa in a rearview mirror.

[5] Khmer Rouge soldiers file into Phnom Penh, capital of Cambodia.

[4] King Faisal (left). Behind him is Crown Prince Fahd who will be effective ruler of Saudi Arabia during his half-brother Khalid's reign, until he succeeds him in 1982. Prince Sultan, Saudi defense minister, is on the right.

[7] Shipping proceeds through the Suez Canal.

[9] Martina Navratilova on court number 1 at Wimbledon.

June 26, 1975
India's president **Fakruddin Ali Ahmed** declares a state of emergency and suspends many constitutional rights.

July 12, 1975
The island nation of **São Tomé** and **Príncipe** is granted independence from Portugal.

 [8]

July 30, 1975
Jimmy Hoffa, leader of the International Brotherhood of Teamsters from 1957 to 1971, disappears from a restaurant in suburban Detroit under circumstances that have never been fully determined.

August 1, 1975
The **Helsinki Accords**, an effort to reduce tension between the Soviet and Western blocs by securing their common acceptance of the post–World War II status quo in Europe, are signed.

August 26, 1975
Ethiopian emperor **Haile Selassie I**—who steered his country into the mainstream after World War II, overseeing its entrance into the League of Nations and the United Nations—dies, possibly by assassination.

 [9]

September 1975
Czech tennis player **Martina Navratilova** requests political asylum in the United States.

1975-1976

September 5, 1975
Lynette "Squeaky" Fromme attempts to assassinate U.S. president Gerald R. Ford.

September 6, 1975
An earthquake strikes along the **Anatolian fault** in eastern Turkey, killing more than 2,000 people before the tremors finally cease.

September 14, 1975
Elizabeth Ann Seton becomes the first American-born saint, when she is canonized by the Roman Catholic Church.

September 16, 1975
Papua New Guinea achieves full independence from Australia.

October 9, 1975
Andrey D. Sakharov, father of the Soviet hydrogen bomb, becomes the first Soviet citizen to win the Nobel Peace Prize.

November 11, 1975
Angola declares independence after the Portuguese withdraw.

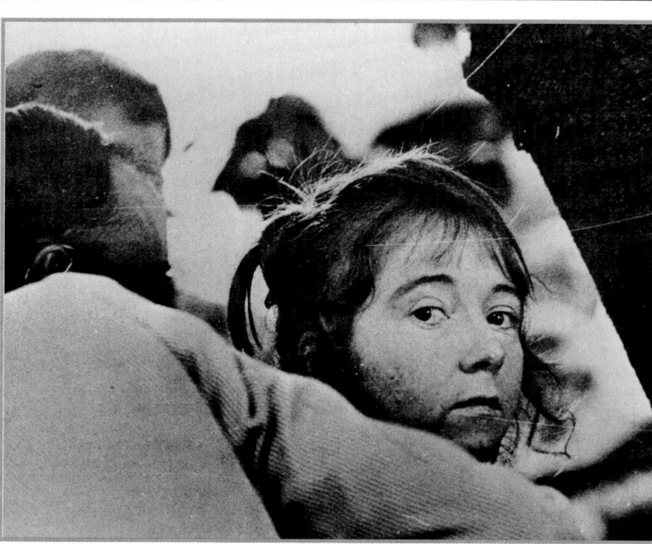

[1] Lynette "Squeaky" Fromme, an acolyte of Charles Manson, is led away after her assassination attempt.

[9] Betty Williams (left), who witnessed the death of the three children in Northern Ireland, with Mairéad Corrigan (right), who was their aunt, celebrate their establishment of the Peace People.

[6] Philip Glass

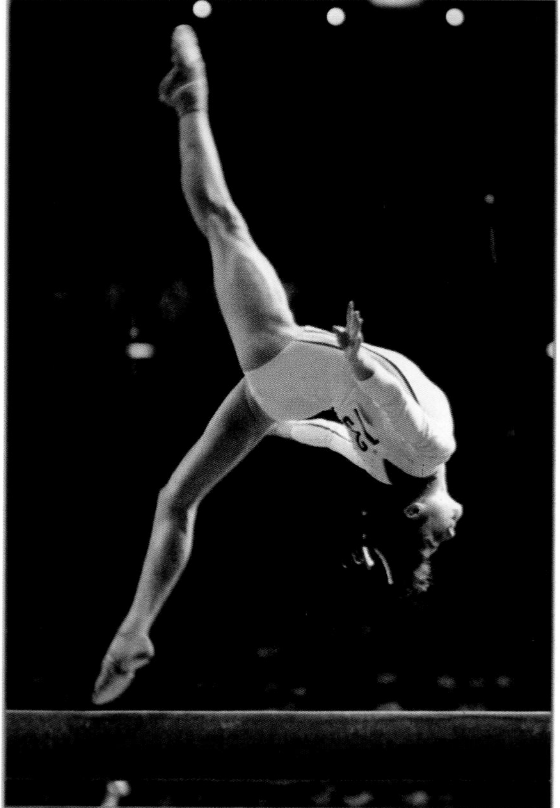

[7] Nadia Comaneci, age 14, on the beam.

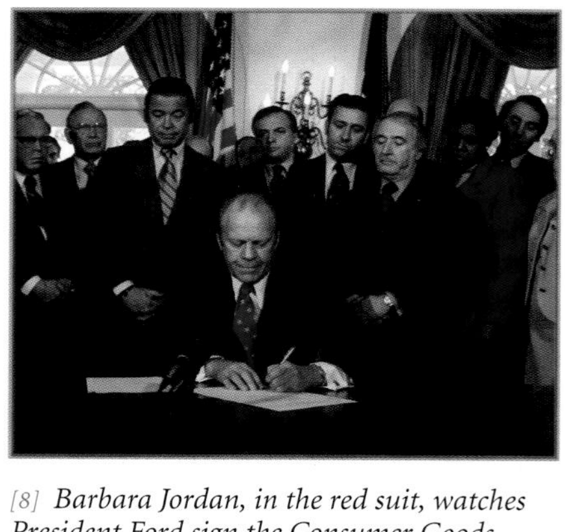

[8] Barbara Jordan, in the red suit, watches President Ford sign the Consumer Goods Pricing Act, which she has sponsored.

[10] James Callaghan

 [6]

1976
American composer **Philip Glass's** opera *Einstein on the Beach* makes its debut, winning the cerebral, minimalist Glass a wide following.

 [7]

1976
At the Summer Olympics in Montreal, Romanian gymnast **Nadia Comaneci** is the first to achieve a perfect score of 10 in an Olympic gymnastic event. She receives seven such scores during the competition.

 [8]

1976
Barbara Jordan of Texas, the first black woman elected to Congress from the Deep South, becomes the first black and the first woman to give the keynote speech at the Democratic National Convention.

 [9]

1976
Betty Williams and Mairéad Corrigan-Maguire found the **Peace People Organization**, a joint Catholic-Protestant group, after three children are killed during fighting between British soldiers and the IRA.

 [10]

1976
British foreign secretary **James Callaghan** becomes the second straight Labour prime minister upon the resignation of Harold Wilson.

1976
In three cases the U.S. Supreme Court holds that the **death penalty**, in and of itself, does not violate the Eighth Amendment if applied under certain guidelines in first-degree murder cases.

November 22, 1975
Juan Carlos becomes king of Spain, two days after the death of Francisco Franco.
[2]

December 1975
President Suleiman Kalalan Franjieh of **Lebanon** accuses the PLO of encouraging the civil war wrecking Beirut. Palestinian refugees kicked out of Jordan are siding with the Druze against Maronite Christians.
[3]

December 6, 1975
The **Balcombe Street siege** begins. Four IRA gunmen, after murdering a man and attacking a restaurant, take two people hostage in a London house. The police surround it, and the gunmen surrender on December 12.
[4]

December 7, 1975
Shortly after declaring its independence, **East Timor** is invaded and occupied by Indonesian forces.

December 29, 1975
A **bomb** explodes in New York City, killing 11 people and injured 75 in a crowded locker area in the main terminal of La Guardia Airport.

1976
The **Aboriginal Land Rights Act** recognizes Australian Aborigine land rights, especially over territory with particular religious significance.
[5]

[3] *Palestinian refugees with a Christian militiaman, in Beirut.*

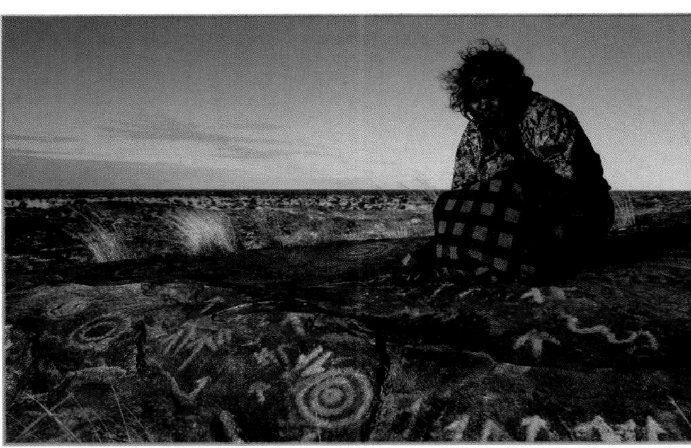

[5] *An Aborigine by some ancient markings on the Corroboree Rock in the Simpson Desert in Australia's Northern Territory.*

[2] *King Juan Carlos speaks during his proclamation as king of Spain. His wife, Queen Sophia, looks on.*

[4] *Police maneuver around the besieged IRA gunmen at Balcombe Street.*

1976
Labour minister **Tina Anselmi** is the first woman in the Italian Cabinet.

1976
A Polynesian crew led by anthropologist Ben Finney uses traditional navigational methods to sail a 62-foot **ocean double canoe** called *Hokulea* from Hawaii south to Tahiti to answer questions about inter-island voyaging.

1976
The **Apple I** personal computer is introduced.

1976
The first known outbreak of the **Ebola virus**, in Zaire (Democratic Republic of the Congo), causes hundreds of deaths through severe hemorrhaging. Fatality rates range from 50 to 90 percent.

1976
The Grameen (Bengali: "Rural") model of banking is devised by economist **Muhammad Yunus** as a means of providing small loans to poor individuals. In 2006 Grameen and Yunus will be awarded the Nobel Peace Prize.

1976
The **International Lesbian and Gay Association** is founded in Coventry, England. It lobbies for human rights and fights discrimination against lesbian, gay, bisexual, and transgendered persons.

1976

1976
The **Winter Olympic Games** take place in Innsbruck, Austria.

January 21, 1976
The **Concorde**, a supersonic commercial aircraft built with funding from the British and French governments, begins regular service.

 [1]

February 4, 1976
An **earthquake** kills 23,000 people and injures more than 75,000 in Guatemala.

 [2]

February 24, 1976
The regime of **Fidel Castro** adopts the constitution of Cuba, which mandates the operation of only one political party—the Communist Party of Cuba.

February 26, 1976
Spain relinquishes the **Western Sahara**.

March 8, 1976
More than 100 stony **meteorites** fall near Kirin in northeastern China, representing perhaps the largest stony meteorite fall in recorded history; the largest fragment weighs an estimated 3,900 pounds.

[1] The Concorde: the routes it can fly are restricted by its sonic boom. Many countries are not prepared to have that in their airspace.

[2] The aftermath of the earthquake in Guatemala.

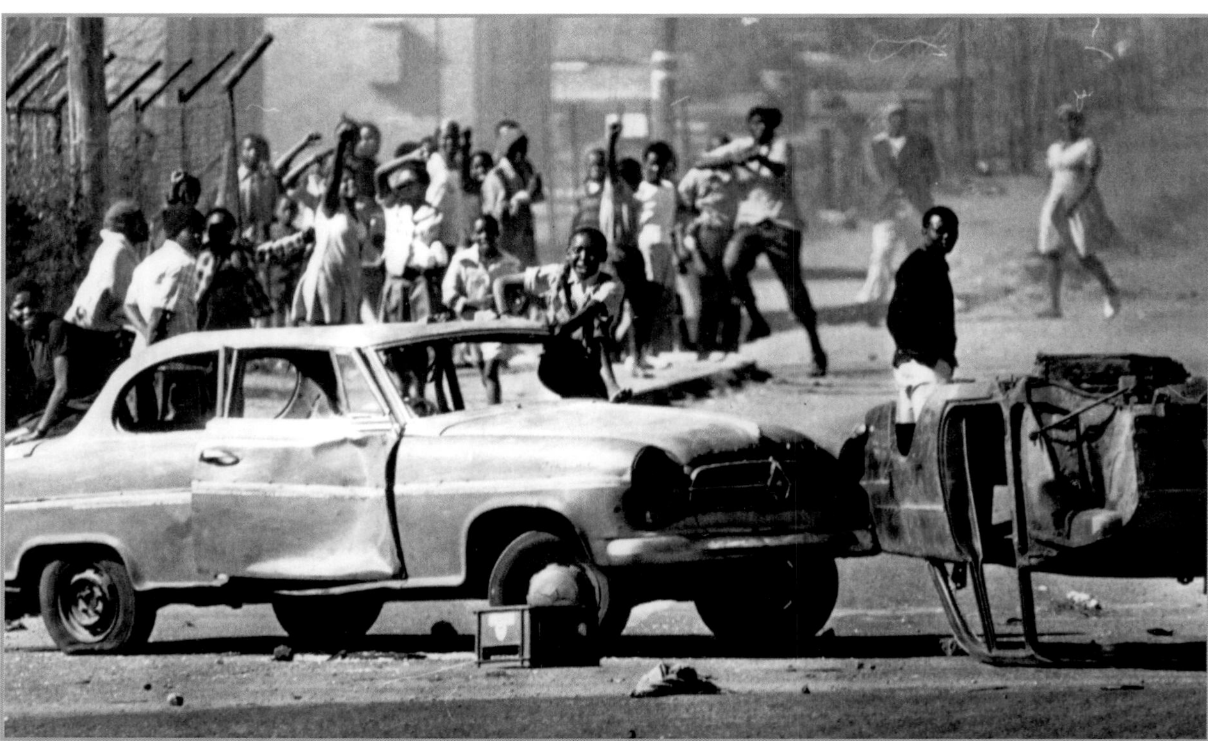

[5] A street barricade in Soweto, South Africa. The rioting, which goes on for five days, began with a protest against school instruction having to be in the Afrikaans language.

[7] The CN Tower in Toronto.

June 3, 1976
About 5,000 **Quebec dairy farmers** riot on Parliament Hill in Ottawa, protesting against reductions in milk quotas and other farm subsidies.

June 5, 1976
A new **dam** on the Teton River in Idaho bursts, resulting in a flood that kills one person and leaves 30,000 homeless.

June 18, 1976
U.S. baseball commissioner **Bowie Kuhn** orders the New York Yankees and the Boston Red Sox to return three star players they had bought from Charles Finley, owner of the Oakland Athletics, for $3.5 million.

[7]

June 26, 1976
CN Tower, built by the Canadian National Railway Company at a cost of $63 million (Canadian), opens to the public in Toronto. At 1,815 feet it is the world's tallest freestanding structure.

July 2, 1976
South Vietnam and **North Vietnam** are reunited and leaders proclaim a socialist republic

July 4, 1976
The **United States** celebrates its bicentennial with pageantry, prayer, games, parades, picnics, and fireworks.

March 23, 1976
The **International Covenant on Civil and Political Rights** enters into force, incorporating almost all the international human rights proclaimed in the Universal Declaration of Human Rights of 1948.

March 24, 1976
María Estela (Isabel) Martínez de Perón, president of Argentina since July 1974, is deposed and arrested by the commanders of three branches of Argentina's armed forces.

 [3]

April 1976
Hua Guofeng is named premier of the People's Republic of China.

 [4]

May 28, 1976
The United States and the Soviet Union sign a five-year treaty limiting the size of **underground nuclear explosions** for peaceful purposes and providing for U.S. on-site inspection of Soviet tests.

June 1976
A demonstration by 10,000 black students in **Soweto**, near Johannesburg, South Africa, turns into a riot that spreads to a number of black townships and to two universities, leaving at least 175 people dead and more than 1,000 injured.

 [5]

June–July 1976
Palestinian terrorists hijack an Air France plane and land it at **Entebbe**, Uganda. After the hijackers free the crew and all the passengers who do not appear Israeli, Israeli commandos rescue nearly all the hostages.

 [6]

[3] General Jorge Videla, who becomes president of Argentina, after Isabel Perón is deposed. During the rule of the military junta that he heads until 1981, up to 30,000 Argentinians will disappear, probably murdered. After democracy is restored in 1983, he will spend five years in prison.

[4] Hua Guofeng is a little-known politician from Chairman Mao's home province of Hunan, but he has carefully followed the correct Maoist line.

[6] Israeli defense minister Shimon Peres (left) congratulates Israeli paratroopers, and their commander Major Dan Shomron, on their successful Entebbe raid.

[8] A photograph of the surface of Mars, where Viking 1 has taken a sample of soil.

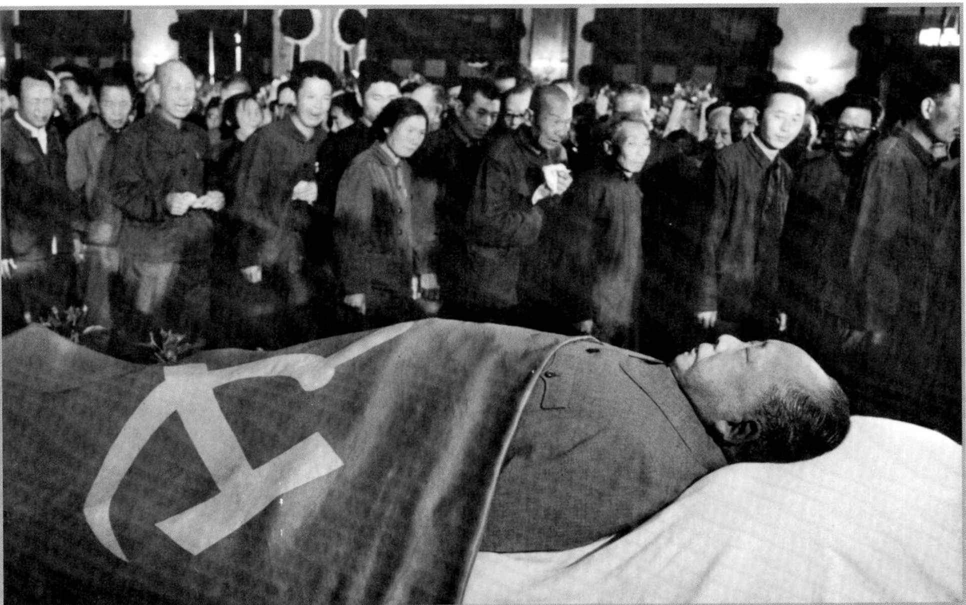

[9] Mao Zedong lies in state. "Peasants from Beijing's outskirts, with boundless profound proletarian feelings, paying respect to the remains of the most esteemed and beloved leader," says the picture's official caption.

 [8]

July 20, 1976
After a nearly yearlong journey, NASA's robotic spacecraft **Viking 1** lands on Mars and begins relaying information about the planet's atmosphere and soil, as well as color photographs of the rocky surface.

July 28, 1976
An earthquake in the industrial city of **Tangshan, China**, kills more than 240,000 people.

August 1976
Tanaka Kakuei, prime minister of Japan from 1972 to 1974, is indicted for having accepted, while prime minister, about $2,000,000 in bribes from the Lockheed Aircraft Corporation to influence All Nippon Airways to buy Lockheed jet airliners.

 [9]

September 9, 1976
Mao Zedong dies; he emerged as the undisputed Chinese Communist Party leader following the Long March (1934–35) and dominated China in the period after the Communist takeover in 1949.

September 10, 1976
The worst **midair disaster** to date occurs when a Yugoslav DC-9 and a British Airways Trident collide over northern Yugoslavia, killing all 176 people on board.

September 16, 1976
The **Episcopal Church** approves the ordination of women as priests and bishops.

1976-1977

September 30, 1976
California becomes the first U.S. state to give terminally ill persons the right to authorize the withdrawal of life-sustaining procedures when death is perceived to be imminent.

October 11, 1976
In China the **Gang of Four**, having lost their influence with the death of Mao Zedong, are arrested.

October 12, 1976
China's premier **Hua Guofeng** is chosen to succeed Mao Zedong as chairman of the Chinese Communist Party.

October 13, 1976
Scientists at the University of Michigan announce that, through a skull X-ray and hair samples, they have identified the mummy of King Tutankhamen's grandmother, **Queen Tiy**, who lived from about 1400 to 1360 BC.

October 21, 1976
Americans win five **Nobel prizes**: Saul Bellow for literature; Baruch S. Blumberg and D. Carleton Gajdusek for medicine; Milton Friedman for economics; Burton Richter and Samuel C. C. Ting for physics; and William N. Lipscomb for chemistry.

 [1]

October 29, 1976
Erich Honecker, a member of the Socialist Unity Party, becomes head (1976–89) of the German Democratic Republic (East Germany).

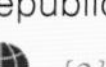 [2]

[1] Milton Friedman, Nobel prizewinner, who has developed the theory of monetarism that has great influence in the later decades of the 20th century.

[7] Star Wars*: (left to right) , Mark Hamill (as Luke Skywalker) Carrie Fisher (as Princess Leia), and Harrison Ford (as Han Solo).*

[2] Erich Honecker in a highly symbolic Russian bear hug from Leonid Brezhnev. Honecker will remain in control of the Democratic Republic until Russia releases its grip under Gorbachev and the East German Communists are left to fend for themselves.

[6] The Sex Pistols. John Lydon (Johnny Rotten) opens a can of lager, which sprays the camera.

[8] Reggie Jackson

 [6]

1977
British punk rockers the **Sex Pistols** release the anarchic single "God Save the Queen" to coincide with the 25th anniversary of Queen Elizabeth II's ascension to the throne.

 [7]

1977
George Lucas's **Star Wars**—an intergalactic swashbuckler with colorful characters, realistic extraterrestrial settings, and an array of breathtaking special effects—is released.

1977
In her "Untitled Film Stills" series (completed in 1980), American photographer **Cindy Sherman**, serving as her own model, creates film-noir-style images that question stereotypes and identity.

 [8]

1977
In the greatest hitting feat of baseball's World Series, **Reggie Jackson** of the New York Yankees hits three home runs in one game—in three consecutive at-bats, on three consecutive pitches.

1977
Le Centre National d'Art et de la Culture Georges Pompidou opens in **Paris**.

1977
Scientists on the deep-sea submersible *Alvin* discover clams, crabs, and worms living alongside hot, sulfuric vents in the depths of the **Mid-Atlantic Ridge**.

November 2, 1976
Jimmy Carter, former Democratic governor of Georgia and future recipient of the Nobel Peace Prize in 2002, is elected 39th president of the United States, narrowly defeating Gerald R. Ford. His vice president is Walter Mondale.
[3]

December 1, 1976
José López Portillo becomes president of Mexico and proceeds to exploit natural gas and oil reserves through the state-owned Mexican oil agency Petróleos Mexicanos (Pemex).
 [4]

December 5, 1976
President Jean-Bédel Bokassa of the Central African Republic proclaims himself **Emperor Bokassa I** of the Central African Empire. He will be deposed in 1979.

December 20, 1976
A treasure chest of **19th-century literary papers**, including manuscripts by Lord Byron and Percy Bysshe Shelley, is discovered in a bank vault in London.

December 21, 1976
The Liberian-registered tanker **Argo Merchant** splits in half after running aground near Nantucket Island and releases 7.5 million gallons of crude oil into the North Atlantic.

1977
The **Apple II**, the first mass-produced practical home computer, is developed by Steven P. Jobs and Stephen G. Wozniak; the IBM PC will follow in 1981.
 [5]

[3] *Jimmy Carter and Walter Mondale at the Democratic National Convention. Rosalynn Carter and daughter Amy are on the left.*

[4] *President Portillo of Mexico.*

[5] *Steve Jobs with an Apple II computer. It has a chess game on its screen.*

[9] *The cover of the soundtrack album of* Saturday Night Fever *with the Australian group the Bee Gees and star John Travolta striking a pose on a disco dance floor.*

[10] *Toni Morrison.*

[11] *Walter Payton playing in a snowstorm against the New York Giants.*

 [9]
1977
The Bee Gees provide the soundtrack for the movie **Saturday Night Fever** and the explosion of the disco phenomenon.

1977
The **National Council of Women of Kenya** organizes the Green Belt Movement, which is dedicated to afforestation and is led by Wangari Maathai. For her efforts she will win the 2004 Nobel Peace Prize.

 [10]
1977
Toni Morrison, noted for her examination of black experience (particularly of women) within the black community, publishes her third novel, *Song of Solomon.*

1977
U.S. interplanetary probes Voyager 1 and 2 begin their travels. Before leaving the solar system, the two **probes** collect a wealth of information about the outer planets and make a variety of discoveries.

 [11]
1977
Walter Payton of the Chicago Bears rushes for an NFL record 275 yards in one game. He will end his career with a record total of 16,726 yards rushing.

January 1, 1977
The **Episcopal Church** confers priestly ordination on a woman from Indianapolis, Indiana, and another 40 women are scheduled to enter the priesthood in the coming months.

1977

January 17, 1977
Gary Gilmore becomes the first person executed in the U.S. in ten years, after the Supreme Court's ruling that the death penalty does not violate the Eighth Amendment.

 [1]

January 19, 1977
In one of his last official acts as president, Gerald Ford pardons Iva Toguri D'Aquino, known as "**Tokyo Rose**," who had been convicted on charges of treason during World War II.

January 19, 1977
Radio astronomers at the **Max Planck Institute** in Bonn, West Germany, report finding water molecules in a nebula about 2.2 million light years away from earth.

January 31, 1977
Intellectual discontent erupts in Czechoslovakia when prominent intellectuals sign a petition, known as **Charter 77**, which airs their grievances against the Communist regime.

 [2]

February 8 1977
Larry C. Flynt, publisher of *Hustler* magazine, is convicted by a court in Cincinnati, Ohio, for pandering obscenity and engaging in organized crime.

February 1977
NASA begins test flights of its **space shuttle** Orbiter 1.

 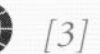 [3]

[1] Gary Gilmore, executed for the murder of two students.

[6] New York workers walk home through darkened streets.

[3] The first space shuttle gets a ride on a 747.

[5] The Orient Express on its last journey.

 [5]

May 22, 1977
After 94 years of service, the famed **Orient Express** completes its last 1,900-mile run between Paris and Istanbul, Turkey.

July 8, 1977
A double explosion and fire at Pump Station No. 8 on the **trans-Alaska pipeline**, opened in the previous month, kills one technician, injures five workers, and necessitates an immediate shut down.

 [6]

July 13, 1977
New York City is plunged into darkness from a **power blackout** that lasts 23 hours. Many are trapped on the upper stories of buildings; looting and arson result in 4,000 arrests and $350 million in damages.

July 22, 1977
After falling from favor during the Cultural Revolution (1966–76), **Deng Xiaoping** returns to power after the Chinese Communist Party reinstates him in all his former high posts, including that of vice premier.

 [7]

September 1977
Black activist **Steve Biko** is killed while in police custody in South Africa. His funeral is attended by 15,000 people, including many Western diplomats.

 [8]

September 16, 1977
American operatic soprano **Maria Callas** dies. During her career she revived classical coloratura roles with her lyrical and dramatic versatility and inspired a cult-like following.

February 24, 1977
British scientists report they have discovered the complete genetic structure of a living organism, a **virus**. The research disproves the belief that each gene carries a code for reproduction of only one type of protein molecule.

March 9, 1977
Members of the **Hanafi Muslim sect** seize control of three buildings in Washington, D.C. One person is killed and nearly 20 injured as the terrorists secure the Islamic Center and Mosque, the headquarters of B'nai B'rith, and the city hall.

March 16, 1977
An Italian mechanic, seeking custody of two young daughters, commandeers a Boeing 727. He manages to pick up one daughter and collect a $140,000 ransom before Swiss police end the 44-hour ordeal at the **Zürich airport**.

March 27, 1977
Two airplanes, a Pan Am 747 and a KLM 747, collide on a runway in the **Canary Islands**, killing 582.

 [4]

March 28, 1977
Major Marien Ngouabi, the 38-year-old president of the Congo, is shot and killed at his official residence in Brazzaville.

April 9, 1977
Amid some sharp dissension, especially from the military, the **Spanish government** legalizes the Communist Party after a 38-year ban imposed by the late, long-reigning chief of state Francisco Franco.

[2] *Václav Havel, leading figure of the Charter 77 group and future president of the Czech Republic.*

[10] *Anwar el-Sadat (right) and President Menachim Begin of Israel in front of the Israeli Knesset.*

[8] *Maria Callas. During her last years, she has lived a reclusive life in Paris.*

[4] *Wreckage at Santa Cruz airport, Tenerife, after the worst-ever plane disaster.*

[7] *Steve Biko's body in a mirror-lined coffin.*

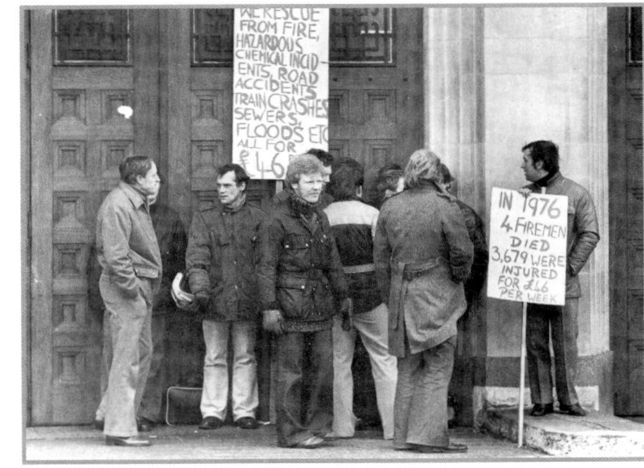

[9] *British firemen on strike, for the first time ever.*

October 3, 1977
Eleven members of the **Japanese Red Army**, a left-wing terrorist group, surrender to authorities in Algiers, ending a five-day ordeal that began on September 28 with the hijacking of a Japan Air Lines DC-8 over India.

October 10, 1977
A brigadier general of the Philippine army and 33 other military personnel are killed by insurgents upon arriving at a market on Jolo Island to discuss amnesty with a leader of the **Moro National Liberation Front**.

October 13, 1977
Palestinians hijack a **Lufthansa airliner** to Somalia and demand the release of imprisoned Red Army Faction members.

November 4, 1977
Richard Helms, former director of the CIA, pleads "no contest" when charged with failing to testify "fully, completely, and accurately" before a Senate committee investigating **CIA activity in Chile**.

 [9]

November 14, 1977
Some 30,000 British firemen begin a **national strike** to back up their demand for a 30 percent increase in pay; army troops are assigned to fire-fighting duty but are forced to use outdated trucks.

 [10]

November 19, 1977
After the Arab-Israeli war of 1973–74, Egyptian president **Anwar el-Sadat** began to work toward peace, and on this day he begins his historic visit to Israel, during which he offers a peace plan to its parliament.

1977-1978

December 4, 1977
Just one year after declaring the Central African Republic to be an empire, the former Jean-Bédel Bokassa crowns himself emperor and becomes **Imperial Majesty Bokassa I**.

 [1]

December 6, 1977
The South African government officially grants independence to **Bophuthatswana**, a black homeland consisting of six separate districts.

December 10, 1977
Thousands of **farmers** drive tractors and trucks into Washington, D.C., and into some 30 state capitals to focus national attention on the financial difficulties they face because of low prices for their commodities.

December 25, 1977
Silent-film comedian, producer, writer, and director **Charlie Chaplin** dies at the age of 88. A giant of the silent-film era, he was creator of the beloved Little Tramp character.

 [2]

1978
Argentina defeats the Netherlands in the men's **World Cup** soccer championship by a score of 3 to 1.

1978
At **Jonestown** in northwestern Guyana, Peoples Temple cult leader Jim Jones leads his congregation in a mass suicide in which 913 people die.

[1] Emperor Bokassa, remembered today for the diamonds he supposedly offered President Giscard d'Estaing and claims that he kept body parts of murdered members of his cabinet in his freezer.

[2] Charlie Chaplin's widow, Oona, and other family members at his funeral near Geneva.

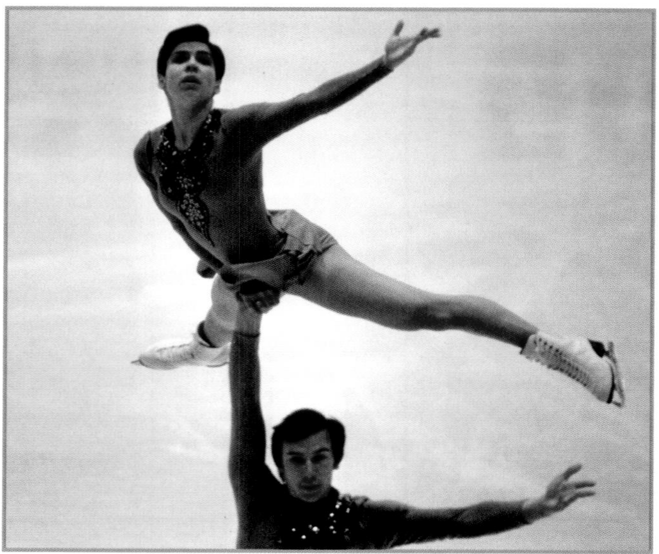

[3] Irina Rodnina and Aleksandr Zaytsev in action.

[6] The Amoco Cadiz *aground off Brittany. It was carrying 230,000 tons of crude oil when its steering gear failed and its captain delayed asking for assistance.*

[7] Prime Minister Ian Smith of Southern Rhodesia (in a trilby hat) pretends the situation is normal by using traditional British military trappings, as seen at this parade.

1978
The **Entertainment and Sports Programming Network (ESPN)** is founded in Bristol, Connecticut. By 1996, it will be the largest U.S. cable network, carried to nearly 70 million homes.

 [6]

1978
The oil tanker **Amoco Cadiz** spills its contents on the coasts of Brittany, in the Atlantic Ocean, covering about 180 miles of shoreline in oil.

1978
The U.S. Supreme Court hears the **reverse discrimination** case of Allan Bakke, who alleges that racial quotas designed to help minorities have prevented his acceptance at the University of California. He wins.

 [7]

1978
The endgame begins for Ian Smith's white regime in **Rhodesia**. Under guerrilla attack from two sides, Smith begins the process of transferring power to black leaders.

$

c. 1978
Citicorp builds a network of automated teller machines. In the ensuing years, ATMs will become immensely popular for conducting basic banking transactions.

January 6, 1978
U.S. secretary of state Cyrus Vance turns over to Hungarian officials the jeweled **crown of St. Stephen**. U.S. military personnel were given the crown in 1945 to prevent it from falling into Soviet hands.

1978
At **Love Canal** near Niagara Falls, New York, officials announce that hazardous chemicals dumped over previous decades are a health hazard to residents. Toxic waste becomes a hot political issue.

1978
British anthropologist **Mary Leakey** discovers footprints at Olduvai Gorge, Tanzania, made by early hominins 3.5 million years ago.

1978
Irina (Konstantinovna) Rodnina of the Soviet Union wins her 10th consecutive world championship in pairs figure skating (first with Alexey Ulanov and later with Aleksandr Zaytsev).

 [3]

1978
Polish cardinal Karol Wojtyla is elected pope and takes the name **John Paul II**. He is the first non-Italian pope in 455 years and the first from a Slavic country.

 [4]

1978
Polish-born American novelist **Isaac Bashevis Singer**, chronicler of Jewish life in Poland and the U.S. and the century's most acclaimed Yiddish writer, wins the Nobel Prize for Literature.

 [5]

1978
Soviet superheavyweight weightlifter **Vasily Alekseyev** sets the last of his 80 world records in weightlifting.

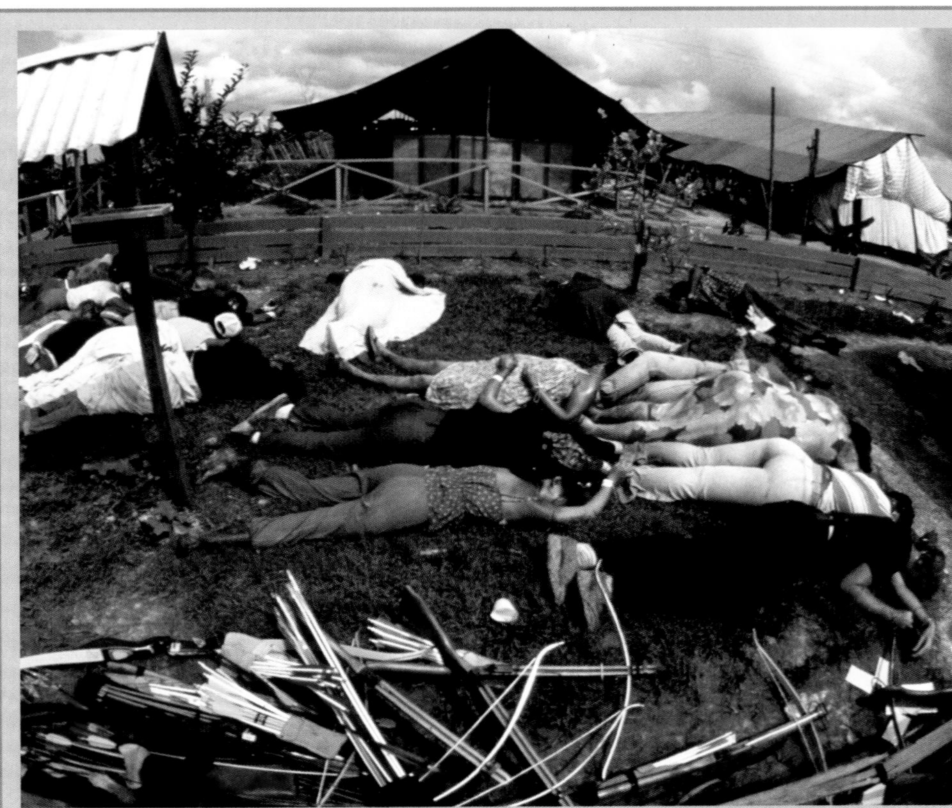

JONESTOWN

Mass suicide of cult members in Guyana

In 1977 an American charismatic churchman and cult leader, James Warren Jones, and hundreds of his followers emigrated to Guyana and set up an agricultural commune called Jonestown. As ruler of the sect, Jones confiscated passports and millions of dollars and manipulated his followers with threats of blackmail, beatings, and death. He also staged bizarre rehearsals for a ritual mass suicide.

On November 14, 1978, U.S. Representative Leo Ryan of California arrived in Guyana with a group of newsmen and relatives of cultists to conduct an unofficial investigation of alleged abuses. Four days later, as Ryan's party and 14 defectors from the cult prepared to leave from an airstrip near Jonestown, Jones ordered the group assassinated. When he learned that only Ryan and four others (including three newsmen) had been killed and that those that had escaped might bring in authorities, Jones activated his suicide plan. On November 18, he commanded his followers to drink cyanide-adulterated punch, an order that the vast majority of them passively and inexplicably obeyed (above). Jones himself died of a gunshot wound in the head, possibly self-inflicted. Guyanese troops reached Jonestown the next day, and the death toll of cultists was eventually placed at 913 (including 276 children).

[4] *Pope John Paul II*

[5] *Isaac Bashevis Singer*

[8] *Aldo Moro, forced to pose in front of a Red Brigade flag by his kidnappers. His bullet-riddled body will be found in the trunk of a car in Rome on May 9.*

February 4, 1978
A dangerously radioactive fragment of **Cosmos 954**, the Soviet satellite that disintegrated over Canada on January 24, is recovered from the ice on Great Slave Lake in northern Canada.

February 9, 1978
The Canadian minister of external affairs announces in Parliament that 11 Soviet diplomats are being expelled from **Canada** for operating a highly sophisticated spy ring.

February 15, 1978
Leon Spinks defeats Muhammad Ali to become the heavyweight boxing champion of the world.

February 19, 1978
In an attack on a hijacked plane at **Larnaca Airport** in Cyprus, 15 of 74 Egyptian commandos are killed. The affair began in Nicosia on February 18 when two Palestinians assassinated the editor of Cairo's daily *Al-Ahram*.

March 6, 1978
The **repatriation** of U.S. and Mexican prisoners that began in December 1977 ends when 48 Americans and 36 Mexicans are returned to their respective countries.

 [8]

March 16, 1978
Former Italian premier **Aldo Moro**, president of the ruling Christian Democrat Party and one of the country's most respected politicians, is kidnapped in Rome by left-wing terrorists.

1978-1979

March 26, 1978
The official opening of Japan's newest international airport at **Narita** is postponed after demonstrations, mainly by environmentalists and farmers.

April 6, 1978
President Jimmy Carter signs into law a bill raising the national mandatory retirement age, giving most employees the option of retiring at 70 rather than 65.
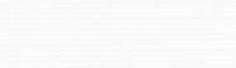

April 7, 1978
A copy of the **Gutenberg Bible** sells for $2.2 million at Christie's in New York.
 [1]

April 20, 1978
A **South Korean Boeing 707** carrying 100 people on a flight from Paris to Seoul strays far off course into Soviet territory, where it crash-lands, killing 2 and injuring 13, after a Soviet jet allegedly fires on it.

May 20, 1978
Agents of the U.S. Federal Bureau of Investigation arrest two Soviet citizens, both employees of the U.N., on charges of **espionage**.

June 6, 1978
California voters overwhelmingly endorse a state constitutional amendment to reduce property taxes by 57 percent. The outcome is seen as the beginning of a national tax revolt against recent tax increases.

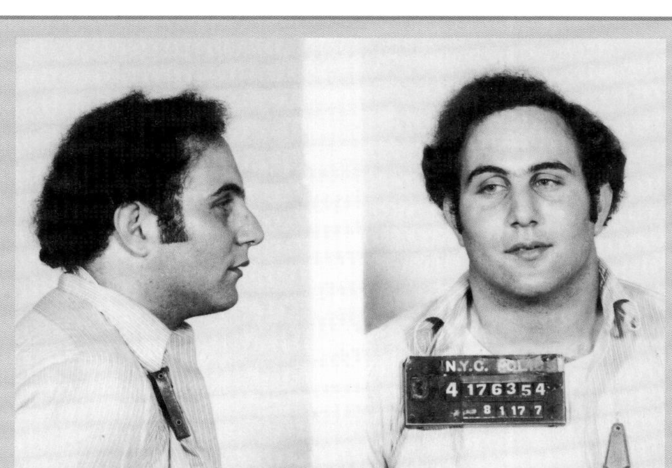

SON OF SAM

Serial killer sentenced to life imprisonment

David Berkowitz (above, in police custody) was a multiple murderer who terrorized New York City in 1976 and 1977 and inspired one of the biggest manhunts in U.S. history. Originally an arsonist—he claimed to have started 1,500 fires in the mid-1970s—he first attempted to kill a woman in December 1975, but she survived several stab wounds. He then murdered a woman in July 1976, and over the next year he attacked several couples, claiming five more victims. During his killing spree, he sent letters to New York newspapers, signing them "Son of Sam," a reference to a demon he believed lived inside the black Labrador retriever owned by a neighbor.

Berkowitz was arrested on August 10, 1977, 11 days after committing his last murder. He soon confessed, was convicted in 1978, and finally sentenced to 315 years in jail.

[5] *The Double Eagle II over the Dorset coast, accompanied by an RAF Hunter fighter.*

[7] *President Jimmy Carter smiles on the handshake exchanged by Anwar el-Sadat of Egypt (left) and Menachim Begin of Israel at Camp David, Maryland.*

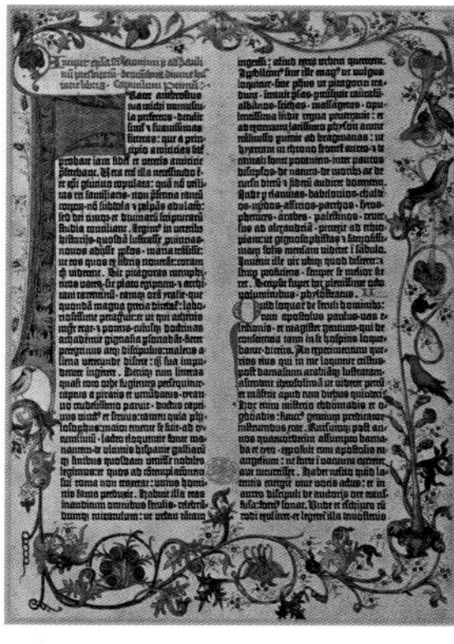

[1] *A page of the Gutenberg Bible, printed in the 1450s but with colored decorations (illuminations) of birds and foliage added by hand.*

[8] *Anatoly Karpov*

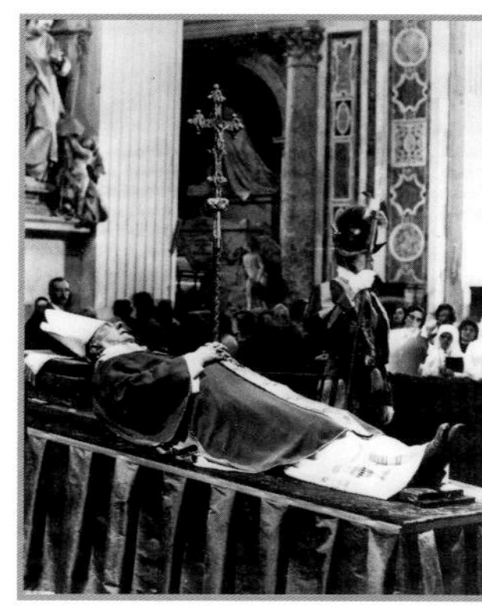

[4] *Pope Paul VI's body lies in state in St. Peter's in Rome, watched over by a Swiss Guard.*

 [4]
August 6, 1978
Pope Paul VI, spiritual leader of the Roman Catholic Church, dies of a heart attack at the age of 80 at his summer residence at Castel Gandolfo.

 [5]
August 17, 1978
Ben L. Abruzzo, Maxie Anderson, and Larry Newman complete the first transatlantic balloon flight, in the **Double Eagle II**.

August 19, 1978
Arsonists reportedly pour gasoline on the floor of a crowded movie theater in **Abadan, Iran**, then lock the theater doors and set the building on fire with bombs. The conflagration claims the lives of 430 people.

 [6]
August 22, 1978
Rebel **Sandinistas** occupy the National Palace in Managua, Nicaragua, holding more than 1,000 hostages for two days, in opposition to the Somoza government.

August 26, 1978
Cardinal Albino Luciani is elected pope as **John Paul I**, but he dies of a heart attack 33 days later.

 [7]
September 1978
U.S. president Jimmy Carter hosts peace talks between Egyptian president Anwar el-Sadat and Israeli prime minister Menachem Begin that result in the **Camp David Accords**.

June 22, 1978
James W. Christy and Robert S. Harrington discover **Charon**, Pluto's only known satellite.

June 25, 1978
Argentina defeats the Netherlands 3 to 1 in overtime to capture its first **World Cup** soccer championship at River Plate Stadium in Buenos Aires.

June 26, 1978
The south wing of the historic 17th-century **Palace of Versailles** is severely damaged by a powerful bomb planted by French radicals. Three of the 14 ground-floor rooms, all containing priceless works of art, are virtually destroyed.

July 7, 1978
The Solomon Islands become an independent nation.

July 14, 1978
Soviet dissident **Anatoly B. Sharansky**, after being convicted in a Moscow court of treason, espionage, and anti-Soviet agitation, is sentenced to three years in prison and another 10 years in a labor camp.
 [2]

July 25, 1978
Louise Joy Brown, the first human child conceived through *in vitro* fertilization, is born in Great Britain. The technique is pioneered by British doctors Patrick Steptoe and R. G. Edwards.
 [3]

[6] Sandinistas manning a barricade made out of paving stones in Nicaragua.

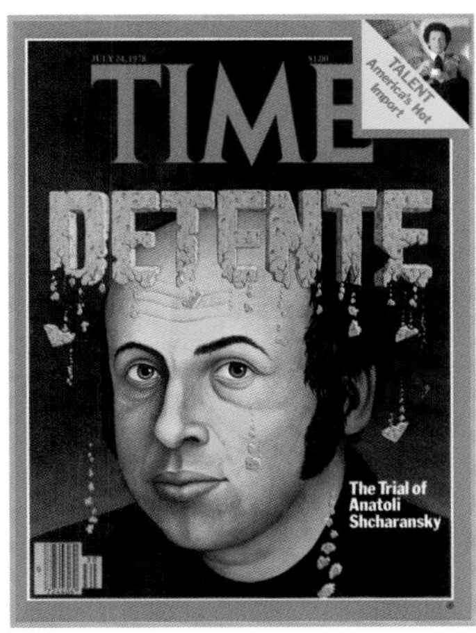

[2] Anatoly Sharansky on the cover of Time *magazine, his prosecution not a good augury for détente between East and West.*

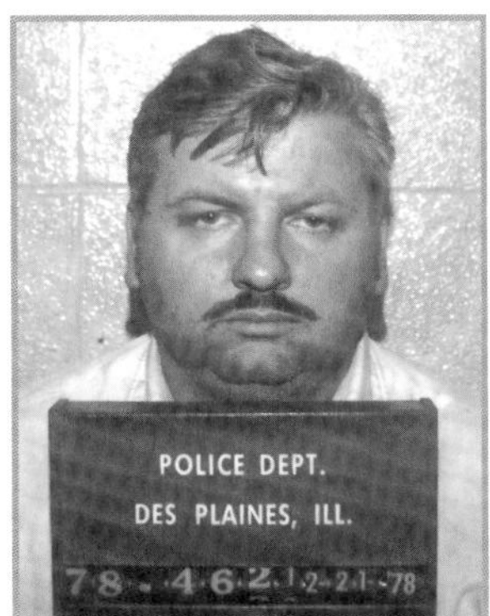

[9] Mug shot of mass murderer John Wayne Gacy, who will be executed for the rape and murder of 33 boys and men.

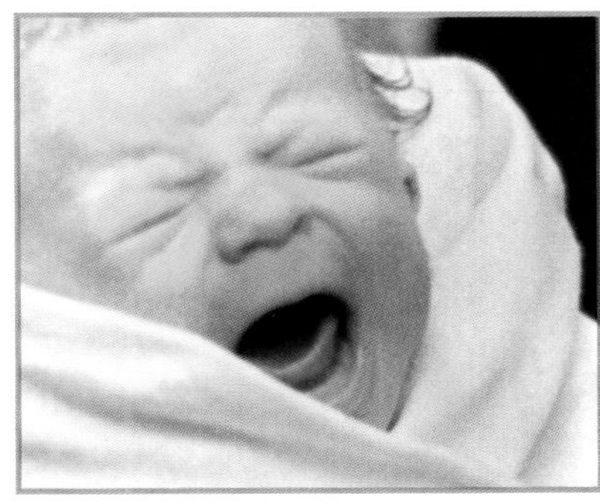

[3] Louise Joy Brown, the first in vitro *baby.*

September 15, 1978
Muhammad Ali wins the world heavyweight boxing championship for the third time, against Leon Spinks.

 [8]
October 17, 1978
World chess champion **Anatoly Karpov** of the Soviet Union successfully defends his title against challenger Viktor Korchnoi.

November 3, 1978
Dominica achieves full independence, with Patrick Roland John as its first prime minister.

November 6, 1978
After an **88-day strike**, the *New York Times* and the *Daily News* resume publication. Striking workers settle the dispute for a weekly pay increase of $68 over a three-year period.

 [9]
December 31, 1978
Police investigate suspected mass murderer **John Wayne Gacy**, whom they believe to be connected with the sex murders of teenaged boys. Twenty-six bodies have already been recovered from his house.

1979
American cowboy **Tom R. Ferguson** becomes the first man to win the Professional Rodeo Cowboys Association's all-around title six times in a row.

1979

1979
China passes its first environmental protection law. Many more follow, but enforcement remains lax; China's urban air and water quality are quickly worsening.

1979
China promulgates its **one-child per family policy** in an effort to slow population growth. The Chinese population approaches one billion.

 [1]

1979
Deng Xiaoping announces the **Four Modernizations**, the Chinese Communist Party's plan for economic recovery following the Cultural Revolution.

1979
Britain suffers its **Winter of Discontent** as public sector workers, from garbage collectors to grave diggers, go on strike.

 [2]

1979
Frank Gehry designs the Gehry House, Santa Monica, California. Using mundane and unglamorous materials and broken forms, Gehry almost single-handedly invents "deconstructivist" architecture.

 [3]

1979
Hip-hop music first comes to national prominence in the United States with the release of the Sugarhill Gang's song "Rapper's Delight."

 [4]

[1] A billboard in China promotes the one-child family.

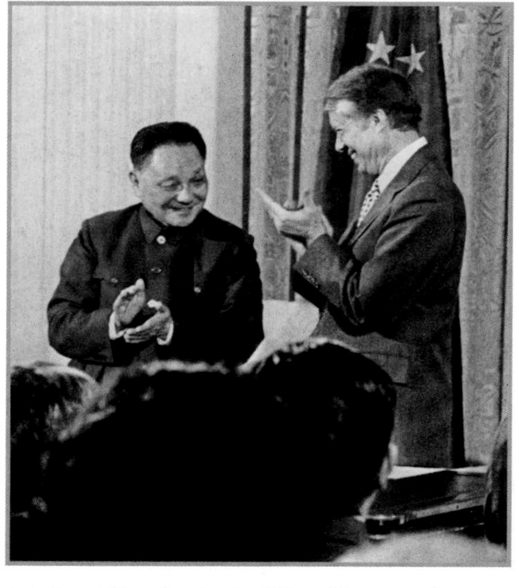

[7] Deng Xiaoping in the White House with Jimmy Carter at the end of January.

[8] Pol Pot: 1.7 million Cambodians die under his regime.

[2] Piles of uncollected rubbish on the streets of central London.

[10] Sid Vicious with his American girlfriend, Nancy Spungen.

1979
Scientists announce that **smallpox** has been eradicated.

 [7]

January 1, 1979
The People's Republic of China and the United States formally establish full **diplomatic relations** as had been promised in a surprise announcement made in both Beijing and Washington, D.C., on December 15, 1978.

January 1, 1979
Sweden bans **aerosol sprays**, becoming the first country to do so.

 [8]

January 7, 1979
The Cambodian capital falls to the Vietnamese, bringing an end to the regime of the murderous **Pol Pot**.

 [9]

February 1, 1979
The spacecraft **Voyager 1** photographs Jupiter from a distance of 20.3 million miles (32.7 million km).

 [10]

February 2, 1979
Sid Vicious of the Sex Pistols, early proponents of British punk rock, dies of a drug overdose in New York City.

1979
Iran's **Shah Reza Pahlavi** goes into exile in January after months of civil unrest. Ayatollah Ruhollah Khomeini returns from exile in February, and an Islamic republic is established by popular vote in March.

1979
Macedonian missionary **Mother Teresa**, founder of the Order of the Missionaries of Charity—a Roman Catholic congregation of women dedicated to helping the poor—is awarded the Nobel Peace Prize.

 [5]

1979
Stock-car driver **Richard Petty** wins his seventh and final Winston Cup racing championship. Known as "the King," Petty is the first driver to win more than three such titles.

1979
The Conservative Party's **Margaret Thatcher** becomes the first female prime minister of Great Britain.

 [6]

1979
The partial meltdown of an atomic reactor at **Three Mile Island** in Pennsylvania shatters the prestige of the nuclear energy industry in the U.S.

1979
The **Pritzker Architectural Prize** is founded. It is among the highest awards in the field.

[5] Mother Teresa gets her Nobel Prize.

[3] Frank Gehry in front of his house in Santa Monica, California.

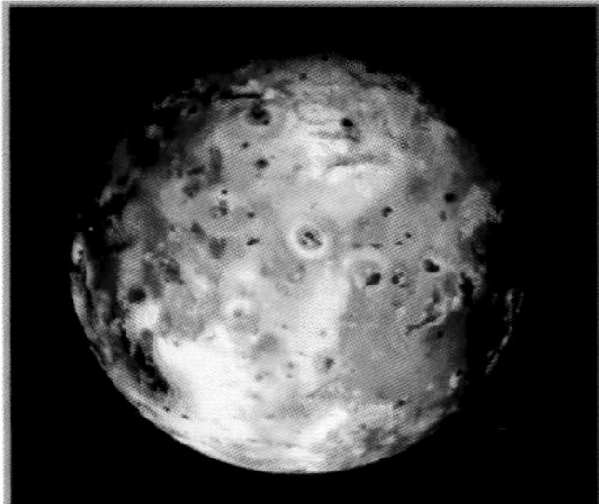

[9] Jupiter's satellite moon Io is photographed by Voyager 1.

[6] Margaret Thatcher, with her husband, Denis, celebrates her win.

[11] Ayatollah Khomeini is greeted on his return to Tehran from exile in France.

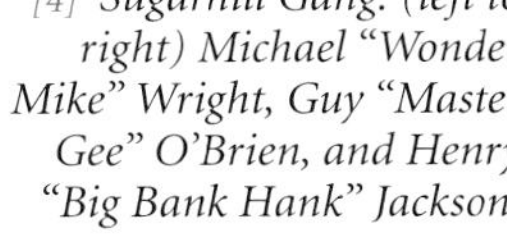

[4] Sugarhill Gang: (left to right) Michael "Wonder Mike" Wright, Guy "Master Gee" O'Brien, and Henry "Big Bank Hank" Jackson.

February 11, 1979
After several days of intense violence in Iran, supporters of **Ayatollah Ruhollah Khomeini** are assured of victory when the army declares its neutrality, and prime minister Shahpur Bakhtiar resigns.

February 14, 1979
The U.S. ambassador to Afghanistan, **Adolph Dubs**, is shot and killed after being kidnapped in Kabul by Muslim extremists.

February 17, 1979
After the Vietnam War, **Vietnam** bolsters its ties with the Soviet Union rather than with China, and, following a series of anti-Chinese, pro-Soviet maneuvers by Vietnam, China invades its southern neighbor.

 [9]

March 5, 1979
The U.S. space probe Voyager 1 flies by **Io**, the innermost of Jupiter's satellites, and observes nine active volcanoes on its surface.

March 26, 1979
The historic **peace accord between Israel and Egypt**, agreed to by Menachem Begin and Anwar el-Sadat and negotiated by U.S. president Jimmy Carter at Camp David, Maryland, in September 1978, is signed.

April 4, 1979
Pakistan's former president **Zulfikar Ali Bhutto** is hanged after being convicted on charges of conspiracy to murder.

1979

April 11, 1979
Ugandan dictator **Idi Amin** is deposed.

April 14, 1979
In **Monrovia**, the capital of Liberia, a demonstration to protest a substantial increase in the price of rice turns into a violent confrontation with the military; hundreds are reported injured and more than 40 killed.

April 27, 1979
Five leading **Soviet dissidents** are expected at Kennedy International Airport in New York City in exchange for two Soviet citizens convicted in October 1978 of espionage in the United States.

May 25, 1979
All 272 persons aboard an **American Airlines DC-10** jetliner are instantly killed as the plane loses an engine during takeoff and crashes moments later at Chicago's O'Hare International Airport.

June 4, 1979
Joseph Clark, a Progressive Conservative, becomes prime minister of Canada (1979–80).

June 18, 1979
The **SALT** (Strategic Arms Limitation Talks) II treaty is signed by U.S. president Jimmy Carter and Soviet leader Leonid Brezhnev.

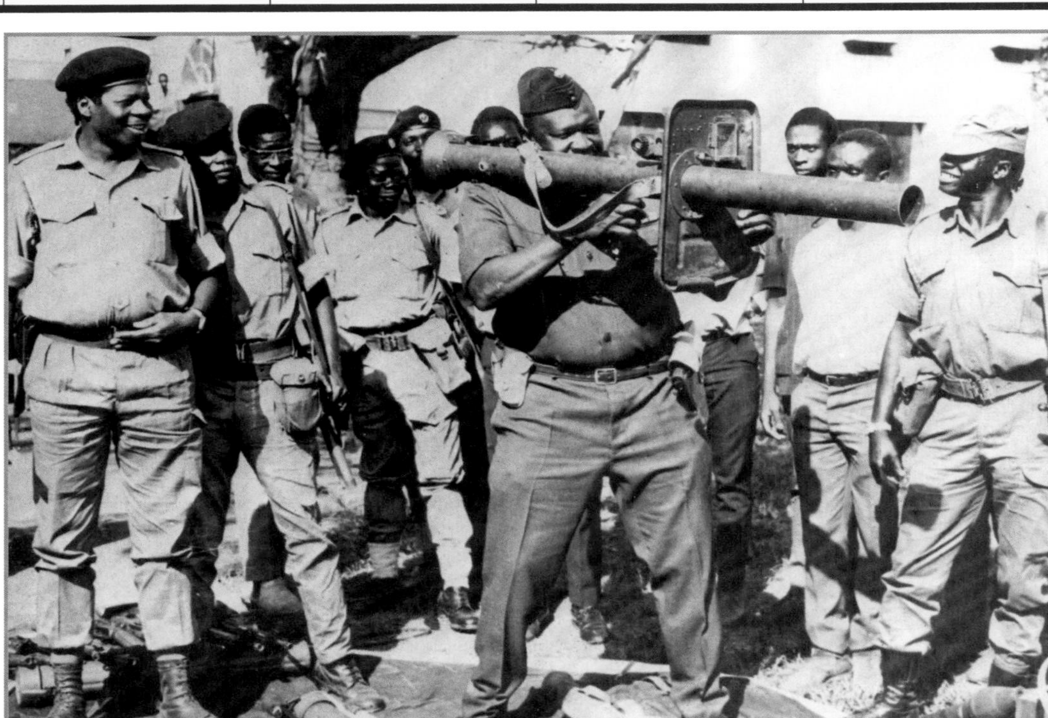

[1] Idi Amin, just before his fall from power, tries out a rocket launcher with troops still loyal to him.

[5] Lord Mountbatten, a month before his assassination, with his great-nephew Prince Charles, at Smith's Lawn, the polo ground in Windsor Great Park.

[6] Robert Mugabe and Joshua Nkomo, the two Patriotic Front leaders, at the Lancaster House Conference. Mugabe will win the first Zimbabwe elections, which have been agreed to at the conference, and thereafter rule the country in an increasingly despotic fashion.

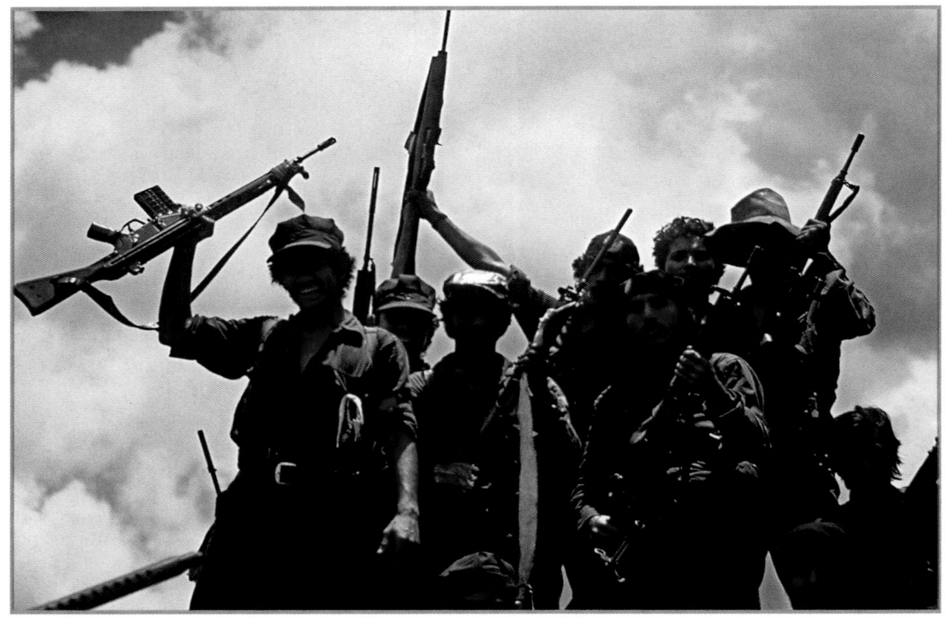

[3] Jubilant Sandinista guerrillas, having ousted the Somoza family and taken over Nicaragua.

[4] Aleksandr Godunov

August 21, 1979
Nicaragua's **Sandinista** junta issues a provisional bill of rights guaranteeing basic rights and promising new social programs, especially in the areas of health care and education.

August 23, 1979
Aleksandr Godunov, a 30-year-old principal dancer with the Bolshoi Ballet, is granted political asylum in the United States after defecting during the Bolshoi's New York engagement.

August 27, 1979
British statesman **Lord Mountbatten**, a veteran of World War II and last viceroy of India, is assassinated by the Provisional Irish Republican Army.

September, 1979
The **Lancaster House Conference** is held in London to decide the future of Rhodesia (Zimbabwe). It is attended by the Patriotic Front leaders, the moderate Bishop Abel Muzorewa, and Ian Smith.

October 1, 1979
After 76 years of U.S. administration, Panama assumes control of the **Panama Canal**.

October 26, 1979
Park Chung Hee, president of the Third Republic of South Korea, is assassinated by his lifelong friend Kim Jae Kyu, head of the Korean CIA.

July 1, 1979
German politician **Karl Carstens**, a member of the Christian-Democratic Union who will help shape his country's place in postwar Europe, becomes president of West Germany (1979–84).

July 2, 1979
The United States issues the **Susan B. Anthony** dollar coin.

July 3, 1979
West Germany's **Bundestag** (lower house of parliament), after a bitter debate, votes 255 to 222 to remove the statute of limitations on murder, allowing for the further prosecution of Nazi war crimes.

July 11, 1979
During its annual meeting in London, the **International Whaling Commission** bans for at least 10 years all whale hunting in the Red Sea, Arabian Sea, and most of the Indian Ocean.

July 11, 1979
The U.S. space station **Skylab**, while orbiting the Earth for the 4,981st time since its launching in 1973, enters the atmosphere and disintegrates over Australia and the Indian Ocean.

July 16, 1979
Saddam Hussein becomes president of Iraq after Ahmad Hassan al-Bakr resigns from office because of poor health.

 *[2]*

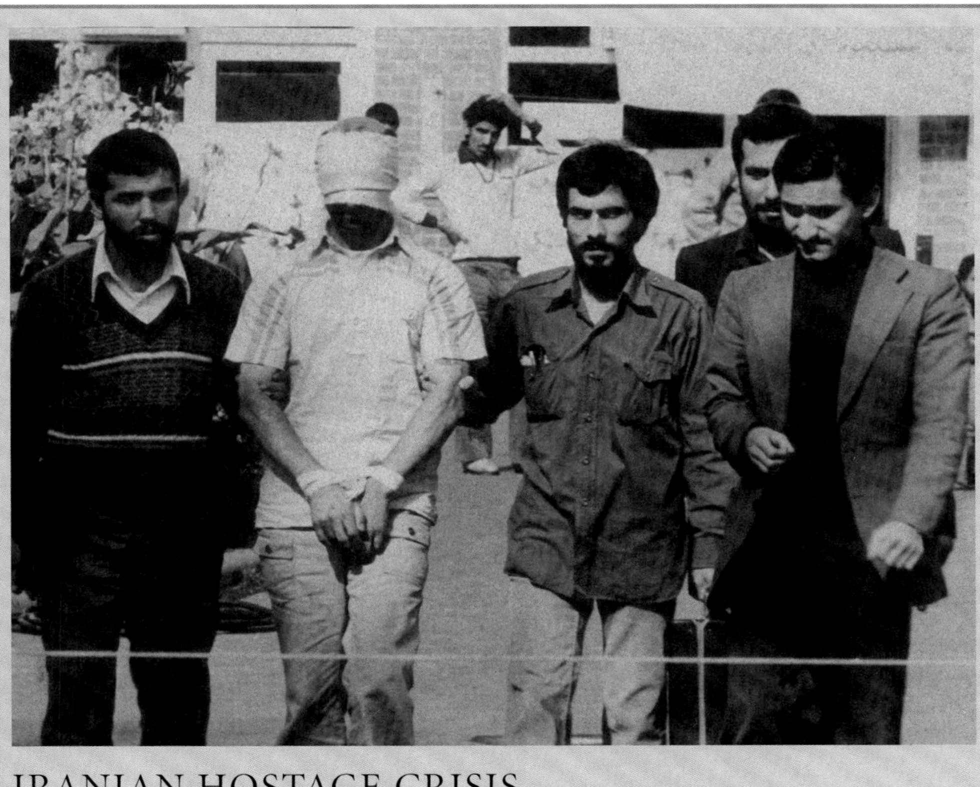

IRANIAN HOSTAGE CRISIS

The American embassy in Tehran is seized by revolutionary students.

In October 1979, the U.S. State Department was informed that the deposed Iranian monarch, the Shah of Iran, required medical treatment that his aides claimed was available only in the United States; U.S. authorities, in turn, informed the Iranian prime minister, Mehdi Bazargan, of the shah's impending arrival on American soil. The shah arrived in New York City on October 22. The initial public response in Iran was moderate, but on November 4 the U.S. embassy in Tehran was attacked by a mob of perhaps 3,000, some of whom were armed and who, after a short siege, took 63 American men and women hostage (above, an American hostage is paraded before the press by his Iranian captors). Within the next few days, representatives of U.S. president Jimmy Carter and Tehran-based diplomats from other countries attempted but failed to free the hostages. An American delegation headed by former U.S. attorney general Ramsey Clark was refused admission to Iran.

The hostage drama dragged on for nearly 15 months. When diplomacy failed to free the hostages in Tehran, Carter resorted in April 1980 to a military rescue mission, hoping to repeat the success of a brilliant Israeli commando raid that had freed 103 airline passengers at Entebbe, Uganda, in 1976. But the operation was a humiliating failure. Only in January 1981, after Carter was overwhelmingy defeated in his reelection bid, were the hostages released.

[2] Saddam Hussein, new ruler of Iraq.

[7] Sir Anthony Blunt, Marxist, director of the Courtauld Institute of Art at the University of London, surveyor of the queen's pictures, and, with Burgess, Maclean, and Philby, the "Fourth Man" in a Russian spy ring.

[8] Typical Afghan Mujaheddin fighters, who will eventually force the Russians to withdraw from their country.

October 27, 1979
Saint Vincent and the Grenadines, an island nation lying within the Lesser Antilles in the eastern Caribbean Sea, achieves its independence.

November 4, 1979
The **hostage crisis in Iran** begins as the U.S. embassy in Tehran is seized by Iranian militants in a move sanctioned by Ayatollah Ruhollah Khomeini.

 *[7]*

November 15, 1979
British prime minister Margaret Thatcher reveals that **Sir Anthony Blunt**, the highly respected art historian who has served as an adviser to the queen, had been a spy for the Soviet Union during World War II.

December 3, 1979
Iranians overwhelmingly approve a new constitution that establishes Shi'ite Islam as the state religion and makes **Ayatollah Khomeini** the country's political and religious leader for life.

December 3, 1979
Puerto Rican terrorists, armed with automatic rifles, ambush a U.S. Navy bus carrying 18 passengers near San Juan, killing two and injuring 10 others.

 *[8]*

December 24, 1979
The Soviet Union invades **Afghanistan** to support a Marxist regime.

Chipping off a souvenir from the Berlin Wall, November1989.

1980

1980
Darién National Park is established in Panama. Acting as a barrier between Central and South America, it is home to diverse wildlife and also halts the northern spread of certain infectious diseases.

1980
Japan becomes the world's largest car manufacturer.

1980
Kenya establishes a department of the environment to coordinate, administer, and enforce environmental policy. By this date, scores of countries have departments or ministries of the environment.

1980
Architect Michael Graves designs the Portland Public Service Building in Portland, Oregon. Bright colors, oversized art deco, and Egyptian ornaments mark this building as the epitome of the **postmodern style**.

1980
Polish poet **Czeslaw Milosz** wins the Nobel Prize for Literature. Milosz is known for both his poetry and essays in which he deals with philosophical and political issues.

 *[1]*

1980
South African writer **Nadine Gordimer** publishes her monumental short-story collection *A Soldier's Embrace*. She will win the Nobel Prize for Literature in 1991.

[9] Ted Turner is interviewed on CNN in June.

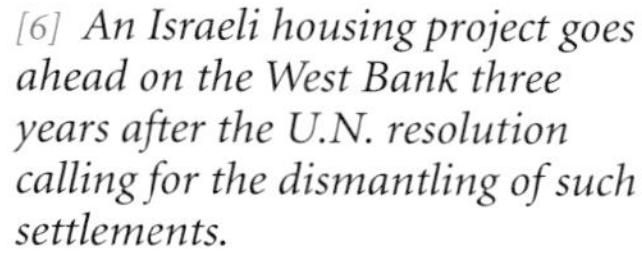

[6] An Israeli housing project goes ahead on the West Bank three years after the U.N. resolution calling for the dismantling of such settlements.

[7] Queen Beatrix and her husband, Claus.

[4] Eric Heiden poised at the start of one of his Olympic races at Lake Placid.

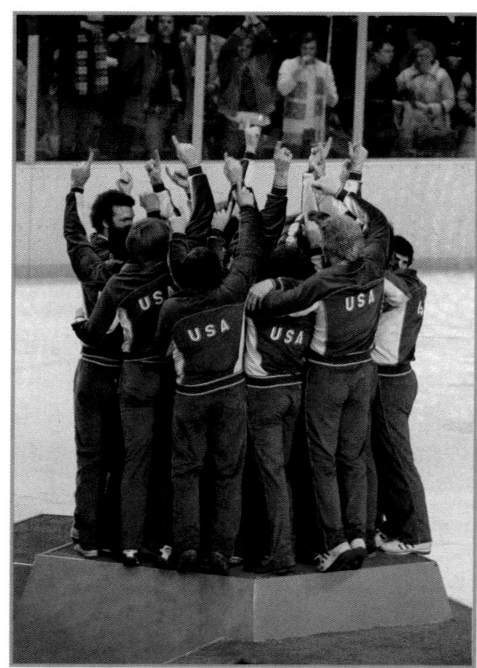

[5] The U.S. ice hockey team on the podium after receiving their Olympic gold medals at Lake Placid. In a match called the "Miracle on Ice" they defeated the Russian team two days earlier, before defeating the Finns in the final.

[1] Czeslaw Milosz. He has had political asylum, first in France and then in the U.S. since 1951.

 *[4]*

1980
American **Eric Heiden** wins all five speed-skating gold medals in the Winter Olympics at Lake Placid, New York.

 *[5]*

February 22, 1980
During the Winter Olympics, against the backdrop of the Cold War, the American **ice hockey** team defeats the heavily favored Soviet team in one of the greatest upsets in the history of the Olympic Games.

 *[6]*

March 1, 1980
All 15 members of the U.N. Security Council, including the United States, approve a resolution calling on Israel to dismantle its settlements in the **West Bank** and Gaza Strip.

March 17, 1980
President Jimmy Carter signs into law the **Refugee Act of 1980**, extending the definition of refugees to include persons from every part of the world and increasing the number of refugees and immigrants allowed to enter the U.S.

April 7, 1980
The U.S. government formally severs diplomatic relations with **Iran** and orders all Iranian diplomats to leave the United States by midnight the following day.

April 18, 1980
Zimbabwe achieves its independence from the United Kingdom.

1980
The United States and approximately 60 other countries **boycott** the Summer Olympic Games in Moscow to protest the Soviet invasion of Afghanistan.

1980
The United States creates the Superfund to pay for the cleanup of **hazardous-waste** dump sites and spills. By the beginning of the 21st century, cleanups at more than 750 sites will have been completed.

1980
Zhao Ziyang is appointed premier of China after his economic-development policies while party secretary in Sichuan province prove successful. His policies become the guiding principles for China's future economic development.

 [2]

c. 1980
Researchers in the United Kingdom introduce magnetic resonance imaging (**MRI**), based on the 1946 discovery of nuclear magnetic resonance, into medical practice.

 [3]

c. 1980
The **compact disc** begins to appear in record stores. Within a decade the small, digital discs will all but replace phonograph records and radically improve the quality of music recording.

January 11, 1980
Cuban president **Fidel Castro** assumes personal control of the ministries of defense, interior, public health, and culture.

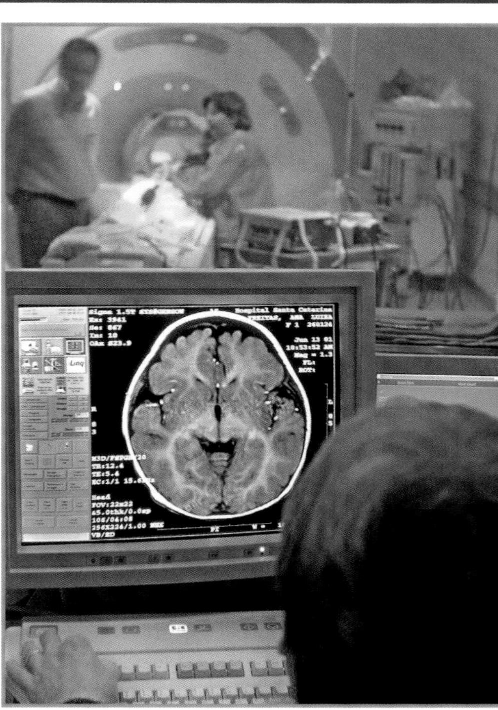

[3] A MRI scanner (behind) and what it is capable of (on screen, foreground), 20 or so years after its introduction.

[2] Zhao Ziyang (right) with his predecessor, Hua Guofeng. Zhao Ziyang forms an effective team with Deng Xiaoping, releasing China's economic potential.

[8] Mount St. Helens erupts.

 [7]

April 30, 1980
Queen Beatrix ascends the throne of the Netherlands. Her marriage to a German diplomat caused a national furor because of his past membership in the Hitler Youth and the German army, but hostility dies down.

May 1980
An armed uprising of students and other citizens in the South Korean city of **Kwangju**, calling for the restoration of democracy, is suppressed. Martial law is extended, all political activity is again banned, and universities are closed.

May 16, 1980
The **Japanese government** falls when 69 members of Prime Minister Masayoshi Ohira's factious Liberal-Democratic Party abstain in a vote of no confidence.

 [8]

May 18, 1980
Mount St. Helens in the Cascade Range erupts in one of the greatest volcanic explosions ever recorded in North America. Thousands of animals are killed, and 10 million trees of are blown down by the lateral air blast.

May 20, 1980
Voters in **Quebec** reject a referendum that would have allowed the Quebec government the opportunity to negotiate with the national government for sovereignty-association status.

 [9]

June 1, 1980
Ted Turner's Cable News Network (CNN), headquartered in Atlanta, begins **24-hour live news broadcasts**. It will gain worldwide attention in 1991 for its around-the-clock coverage of the Persian Gulf War.

1980-1981

July 28, 1980
Peru returns to democracy when the presidential inauguration of Fernando Terry ends 12 years of military rule.

July 30, 1980
The Israeli **Knesset** (parliament) passes a law formally making all of Jerusalem the nation's capital.

August 11, 1980
The Central Committee of the Chinese Communist Party publishes a directive calling for the removal of most public portraits, statues, slogans, and poems of the late chairman **Mao Zedong**.

August 20, 1980
The United States reveals that it has developed an airplane that can avoid detection by radar; the so-called **stealth aircraft** is reportedly coated with a special material that diffuses radar waves.
 [1]

August 27, 1980
Chun Doo Hwan is elected president of the Republic of South Korea. In late 1980 he will push through a new constitution allowing him to rule with a firm hand, but ultimately he will serve only one seven-year term under it.

August 31, 1980
Polish labor activist **Lech Walesa** and **Mieczyslaw Jagielski**, Poland's first deputy premier, sign an agreement that concedes to workers the right to organize freely and independently.

[1] The stealth bomber

[4] Jiang Qing, on trial as one of the Gang of Four, hardline advocates of the Cultural Revolution, who were maneuvering for the overthrow of Hua Guofeng. This one-time actress will have her death sentence commuted to life imprisonment.

[5] Hu Yaobang: he will be dismissed in 1987, a scapegoat for the stirrings of student unrest. His death in 1989 will spark the Tiananmen Square occupation. Deng Xiaoping stands on his right.

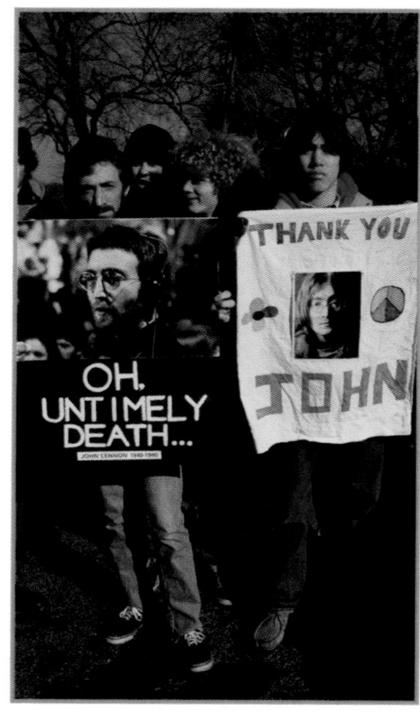

[3] Mourners gather in Central Park, in New York City, after the killing of John Lennon.

[6] The Louvre pyramid

 [3]
December 8, 1980
Former Beatle **John Lennon** is murdered in New York City by a demented fan, prompting an international outpouring of grief.

 [4]
1981
The Gang of Four, the four most powerful members of a radical political elite that includes Mao Zedong's third wife, Jiang Qing, are convicted for their role in implementing the harsh policies of Mao during the Cultural Revolution.

1981
Cesar Pelli begins work on the World Financial Center and World Financial Center Plaza, New York City. The complex shows Pelli's mastery of urban form and the return to publicly oriented spaces.

1981
Chariots of Fire is nominated for seven Academy Awards and is awarded five, including the award for best picture of the year.

 [5]
1981
Hu Yaobang, general secretary of the Chinese Communist Party, is elevated to party chairman, a position he will help abolish in 1982 to prevent any future domination of the party by one person.

 [6]
1981
I. M. Pei begins designing his glass pyramid addition to the Louvre Museum, Paris. Originally a source of much controversy, the pyramid becomes as beloved as the surrounding building.

September 12, 1980
The senior command of the Turkish army, led by **General Kenan Evren**, carries out a bloodless coup in their homeland.

September 22, 1980
Solidarity, the Polish trade union and political party that becomes a hotbed of resistance to Soviet control, is founded this day in 1980 when delegates of 36 unions meet and unite under the leadership of Lech Walesa.

September 22, 1980
The **Iran-Iraq War** begins when Iraqi armed forces invade western Iran along the countries' joint border.

 [2]

October 23, 1980
Some 60,000 members of the Screen Actors Guild and the American Federation of Television and Radio Artists end their 94-day **strike** by accepting a 32.5 percent increase in minimum salaries over a three-year period.

November 12, 1980
The U.S. space probe **Voyager 1** reaches the planet Saturn.

December 4, 1980
UNESCO issues a report stating that one-third of the world's population can neither read nor write.

SOLIDARITY

Union speeds the decline of communism in Poland.

A workers' strike in 1980 at the Lenin Shipyards in Gdansk inspired other labor strikes in Poland and compelled the government to agree to demands for independent unions. A trade union named Solidarity was founded to bring together the regional workers' groups, and Lech Walesa (left, with supporters in Warsaw) was elected chairman. The movement won economic reforms and free elections before pressure from the Soviet Union forced the Polish government to suppress the union in 1981. The focus of worldwide attention, Solidarity continued as an underground organization until 1989, when the government was forced to recognize its legality. In the free elections of 1989, Solidarity candidates won most of the contested seats in the assembly and formed a coalition government.

[2] Iraqi forces at Khorramshahr on the Shatt al-Arab waterway near the border with Iran.

[8] Ronald and Nancy Reagan after his swearing-in.

[9] Sandra Day O'Connor

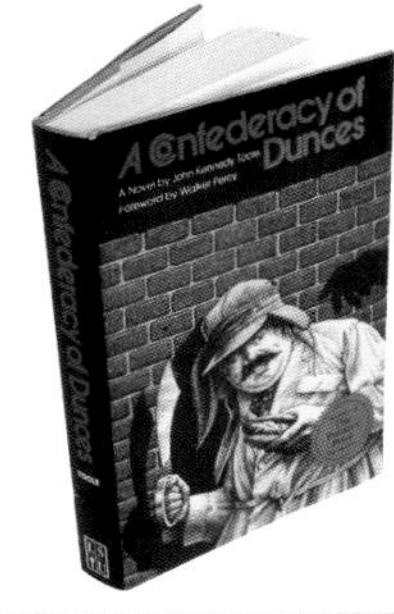

[7] A Confederacy of Dunces, *New Orleans' very own novel, appears eleven years after the author's suicide.*

1981
IBM releases **personal computers** with the MS-DOS operating system by Microsoft.

 [7]

1981
John Kennedy Toole is awarded the Pulitzer Prize posthumously for his eccentric novel, *A Confederacy of Dunces*.

 [8]

1981
Ronald Reagan of the Republican Party becomes the 40th president of the United States. He will serve until 1989. His vice president is George H. W. Bush.

 [9]

1981
Sandra Day O'Connor becomes the first woman on the United States Supreme Court, nominated by President Ronald Reagan.

1981
The first cases of **acquired immune deficiency syndrome (AIDS)** appear in California and New York.

1981
Israeli planes bomb **Iraq's one nuclear reactor** to prevent development of nuclear weaponry.

1981

1981
The U.S. inaugurates its **space shuttle** program featuring the reusable space vehicles *Columbia*, *Challenger*, *Discovery*, and *Atlantis*, which are designed to glide to a terrestrial landing.
 [1]

1981
Inner city **riots** erupt in England, first in Brixton, South London, in April, then in Southall, West London, and Toxteth, Liverpool, in July.
 [2]

1981
The **Office of the United Nations High Commissioner for Refugees** (UNHCR), an international relief organization founded by the U.N. in 1951, is awarded the Nobel Peace Prize.

1981
The **MTV** channel appears on cable television, its "veejays" presenting music videos, commentary, and music news. Its rapid pace and the sophisticated techniques in the music videos have a noticeable effect on films, commercials, and TV.

January 1981
Heavy rains ravage the area of **Mindanao**, Philippines, severely damaging roads and bridges and killing nearly 200 people while leaving some 300,000 others homeless.

January 16, 1981
Leon Spinks, the former heavyweight boxing champion (1978), is mugged outside his home in Detroit; his assailants escape with his removable gold teeth and blue fox coat.

[1] *The* Columbia *space shuttle lands, escorted by a fighter.*

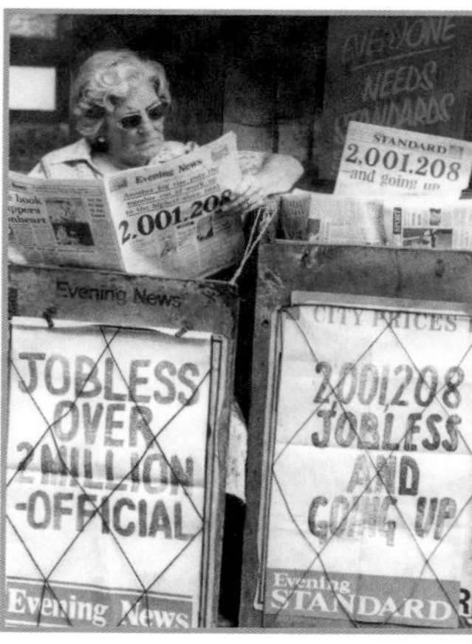

[8] *Another way of expressing British unemployment.*

[2] *Brixton, London on the second of three days of violence. Firemen stand by a burned-out building.*

[6] *François Mitterrand at a press conference in London with Margaret Thatcher, who listens to the simultaneous translation.*

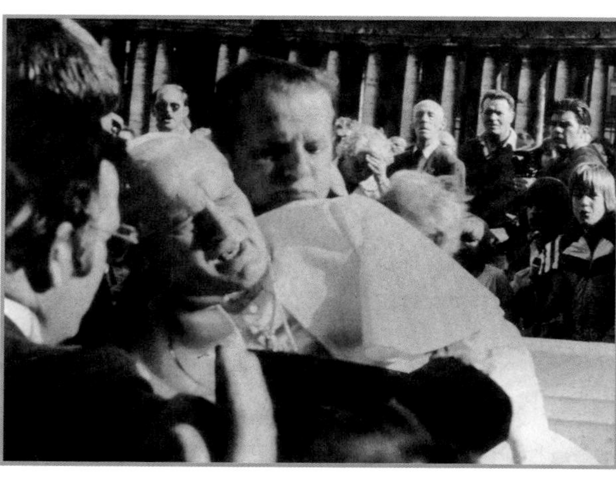
[7] *Pope John Paul II is in agony after being shot in St. Peter's Square.*

[5] *Secret servicemen surround the wounded president and hold down the would-be assassin.*

 [5]
March 30, 1981
In Washington, D.C., barely two months after his inauguration as the 40th president of the United States, **Ronald Reagan** is shot and seriously wounded by would-be assassin John W. Hinckley, Jr.

 [6]
May 10, 1981
François Mitterrand, the first socialist to hold the office, is elected president of France, leading his country to closer political and economic integration with western Europe.

May 12, 1981
President Ronald Reagan proposes fundamental changes in Social Security legislation to restore the system to a sound financial basis.

 [7]
May 13, 1981
Pope John Paul II survives an assassination attempt in Vatican City, in which he is shot and seriously wounded in St. Peter's Square by Mehmet Ali Agca, a Turkish national.

May 21, 1981
The **World Health Organization (WHO)** votes overwhelmingly that the use of baby formula be discouraged in Third World countries, with the United States casting the only dissenting vote.

 [8]
June 23, 1981
The British government announces that the country's **unemployment** rate has climbed to 11.1 percent, the highest it has been in half a century.

January 20, 1981
The **Iran hostage crisis** ends when Ayatollah Ruhollah Khomeini releases 52 Americans held hostage for 15 months.

 [3]

January 28, 1981
William J. Casey is named the 13th director of the Central Intelligence Agency (CIA), replacing Admiral Stansfield Turner.

February 7, 1981
A fire sweeps through the main tent of the Venus Circus near the conclusion of a three-hour matinee attended by 4,000 persons in **Bangalore**, India; of the 66 persons killed, most are trampled to death.

February 23, 1981
An attempted coup by right-wing army elements fails in Spain after **King Juan Carlos** takes a firm stand.

 [4]

March 6, 1981
Klaus Grabowski, a convicted child molester, is shot and killed in Lubeck, Germany, by the mother of the girl he strangled and molested; Grabowski had previously agreed to castration to avoid a life sentence.

March 6, 1981
Walter Cronkite signs off for the final time after 20 years as anchor of the *CBS Evening News*.

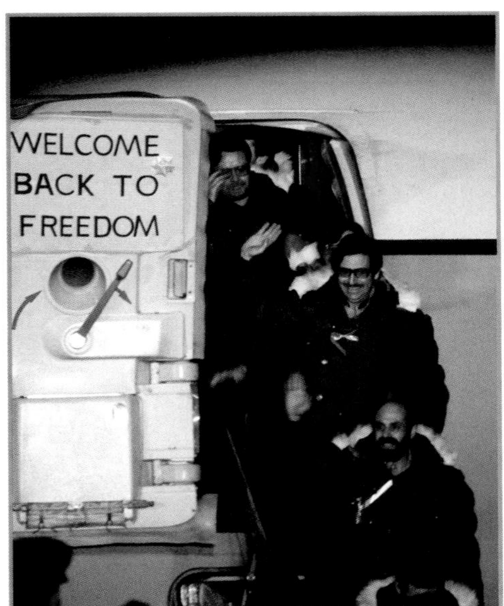

[3] Tehran hostages after their release.

[9] Prince Charles and Princess Diana on the Buckingham Palace balcony after their wedding.

[4] Lieutenant Colonel Tejero Molina holds up the Spanish Cortes (parliament) at gunpoint with 300 Civil Guardsmen at the start of the attempted military coup.

[10] Muslim fundamentalist assassins fire into the reviewing stand where Sadat had been watching a military parade.

 [9]

July 29, 1981
Prince Charles and **Lady Diana Spencer** are married in St. Paul's Cathedral in London. Their globally televised wedding ceremony is watched by about 500 million people.

August 1981
A **poisonous cooking oil**, sold illegally door-to-door in Spain, kills an estimated 200 people from early May to late August and affects at least 11,000 others.

September 1981
Pablo Picasso's **Guernica** is moved to Spain's Prado Museum after spending over 40 years in New York's Museum of Modern Art (MOMA); the artist's will stated that the painting was not to return to Spain until democracy was restored.

September 6, 1981
A police helicopter carrying a cabinet minister and five members of Parliament disappears during a storm over the northern section of **Thailand**; all 11 occupants are presumed dead.

September 26, 1981
The twin-engine **Boeing 767-200** makes its maiden flight in Everett, Washington

[10]

October 6, 1981
Anwar el-Sadat is assassinated by members of the radical fringe of the Muslim opposition in Egypt.

1981-1982

November 1, 1981
Antigua and Barbuda achieve independence from the United Kingdom, with Vere Bird serving as the first prime minister.

November 30, 1981
Representatives of the United States and the Soviet Union hold their first talks in Geneva on the reduction of medium-range **nuclear weapons** in Europe.

1982
Italy wins its first **World Cup** in 44 years. Its third victory comes in a 3–1 match against fellow national powerhouse and regular World Cup finalist West Germany.

1982
Michael Jackson releases *Thriller*, one of the most successful albums ever produced. Its sales are helped by Jackson's music videos for MTV cable television.

 [1]

1982
American motion-picture director and producer **Steven Spielberg** releases two back-to-back box office successes: *Poltergeist* and *E.T.: The Extra-Terrestrial.*

 [2]

1982
American writer Alice Walker, wins the Pulitzer Prize for her novel **The Color Purple**, depicting the growing up and self-realization of an African American woman in Georgia.

 [3]

[1] *The cover for Michael Jackson's* Thriller *album.*

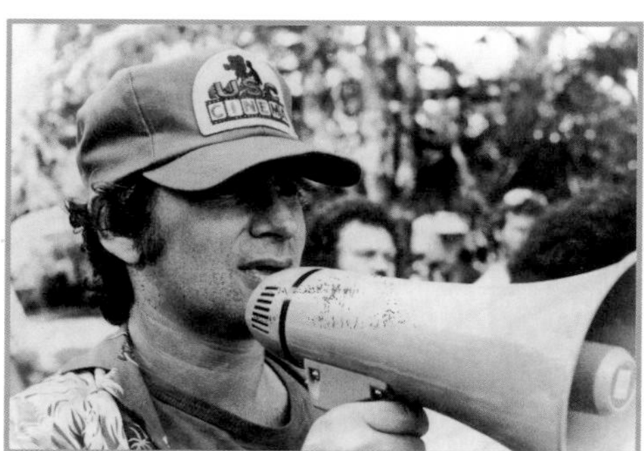

[2] *Steven Spielberg directing* E.T.

[8] *John Belushi*

[3] *Alice Walker. Steven Spielberg will direct the film version of her novel.*

[9] *Smoke pours out of West Beirut as a result of Israeli shelling.*

1982
The **camcorder**, a hand-held video recording device, is developed by the Sony Corporation in Japan.

February 1982
First Lady Nancy Reagan begins her "**Just Say No**" antidrug campaign by traveling to Florida and Texas, where she visits various facilities to draw attention to the problem of drug abuse.

 [8]

March 5, 1982
U.S. comic actor **John Belushi**, most famous for his roles in *National Lampoon's Animal House* and *The Blues Brothers* dies from a drug overdose of heroin and cocaine.

March 10, 1982
The Reagan administration places an embargo on oil imported from **Libya** and on exports to Libya of certain high technology. The announcement follows a long series of warnings to Libya to cease its support for international terrorism.

March 19, 1982
Argentine forces mobilize after a dispute between Argentine workers and British scientists on British-controlled South Georgia island, leading to Argentina's invasion of the Falklands two weeks later.

April 17, 1982
The Canada Act, also known as the Constitution Act, takes effect, establishing certain individual rights, preserving parliamentary supremacy, and making Canada a wholly independent, fully sovereign state.

1982
An **artificial heart** designed by American physician Robert K. Jarvik is implanted into a patient. This first recipient survives 112 days and dies as a result of various physical complications caused by the implant.
 [4]

1982
At the World Aquatic Championships, American diver **Greg Louganis** becomes the first in his sport to earn a perfect score of 10 from all the judges.
 [5]

1982
Grace Kelly, American actress and princess of Monaco, dies in a car accident in France.
 [6]

1982
Italy defeats West Germany in the men's **World Cup** soccer championship by a score of 3 to 1.

1982
Javier Pérez de Cuéllar of Peru becomes the Secretary General of the U.N. He will serve until 1991.

1982
Architect Philip Johnson's **AT&T Building** opens in New York City. Featuring a top that looks like a Chippendale cabinet, the building announces Johnson's turn to postmodernism.
 [7]

[4] *Dr. Robert Jarvik holding an artificial heart.*

[5] *Greg Louganis. The moment from his career that most people remember comes at the Seoul Olympics in 1988, when he hits his head on a lower board while performing a tricky dive. But he goes on to win.*

[6] *Princess Grace arriving at the Monte Carlo Opera with her husband, Prince Rainier, on National Day.*

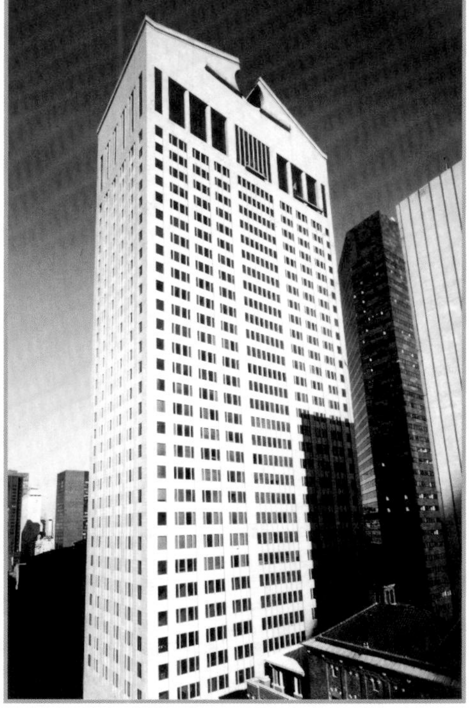

[7] *The AT&T Building in New York, finished off with a postmodern broken pediment.*

FALKLANDS WAR

Brief but fierce war over ownership of islands in the South Atlantic Ocean

Both Argentina and Great Britain had long claimed sovereignty over the Falklands, and there had been protracted talks between them over the future of the remote islands.

On April 2, 1982, Argentina's military government, impatient with the lack of diplomatic progress, occupied the islands with some 10,000 troops. British prime minister Margaret Thatcher responded by sending a shipborne task force to the region. Within three months British forces had defeated the Argentines and reoccupied the islands. Britain lost about 250 men—some of them on board HMS *Antelope* (left)—and Argentina about 700. Argentina's defeat discredited its military government and helped lead to the restoration of civilian rule in 1983.

April 26, 1982
The U.S. Immigration and Naturalization Service begins a week-long roundup of **illegal aliens** working in big cities including New York, Chicago, and Los Angeles. In all, 5,635 people are taken into custody.

May 11, 1982
Lee Chul Hi and his wife, Chang Yong Ja, are arrested in **South Korea** for alleged fraudulent transactions on Seoul's unregulated curb (over-the-counter) market, uncovering a huge loan swindle.

 [9]
June 6, 1982
Israel invades **Lebanon** and subsequently defeats the Palestine Liberation Organization (PLO), the Syrian armed forces, and assorted leftist Lebanese groups.

June 7, 1982
After two years of civil war, rebel forces under the command of former premier Hissen Habré capture N'Djamena, the capital of **Chad**, and topple the government of President Goukouni Oueddei.

June 14, 1982
The surrender of the large Argentine garrison at Port Stanley to the British military concludes the **Falklands War**.

June 15, 1982
The U.S. Supreme Court, in a 5–4 vote, strikes down a **Texas law** permitting local school districts to either bar children of illegal aliens from public schools or charge them tuition.

June 21, 1982
Buckingham Palace announces that a son has been born to Prince Charles and Princess Diana. **Prince William** of Wales will be second in line to the British throne.
 [1]

June 21, 1982
John Hinckley, Jr., is ruled to be innocent by reason of insanity in his shooting of U.S. president Ronald Reagan.
 [2]

June 22, 1982
The U.S. Department of Justice charges 18 Japanese with conspiring to steal **industrial secrets** from IBM, the world corporate leader in the computer industry.

September 1, 1982
Mexican president **José López Portillo** closes all the country's private banks so they can be "incorporated directly into the service of the nation."

September 1, 1982
Some 60 percent of all the farms in **Australia** are being harshly affected by one of the worst droughts in the nation's history.
 [3]

September 15, 1982
The Gannett Company begins publishing **USA Today**, the United States' first national, general-interest newspaper.

[1] Princess Diana holds Prince William while his father looks on.

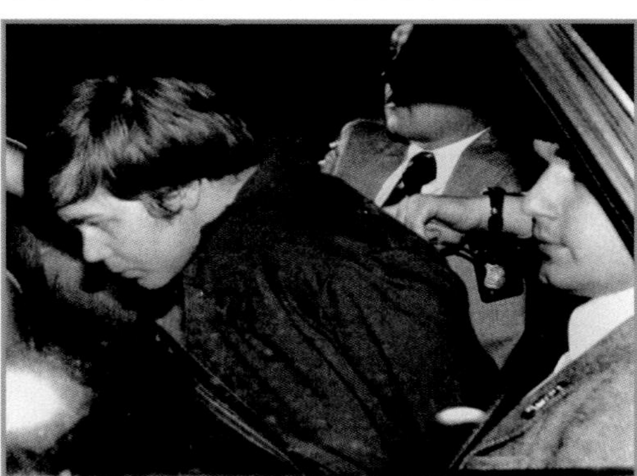

[2] John Hinckley, Jr.

[5] A boy traces a name on the Vietnam Veterans Memorial.

[7] Alan Alda (middle, second left) on set with other lead players in M*A*S*H.

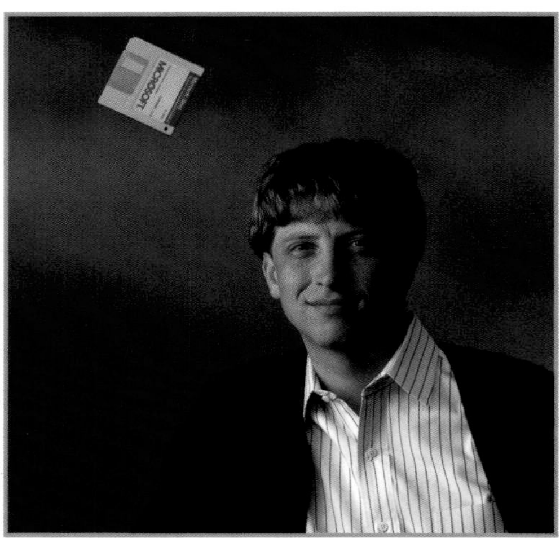

[6] Bill Gates with not a halo, but a floppy disk hovering by his head.

 [5]
November 10, 1982
The **Vietnam Veterans Memorial**, designed by Maya Lin, is dedicated in Washington, D.C.

November 12, 1982
Former head of the KGB **Yury Vladimirovich Andropov** takes the position of general secretary of the Communist Party of the U.S.S.R.

December 1, 1982
Miguel de la Madrid, a political conservative and friend of the business community, takes office as president of Mexico and promises to combat government corruption

December 10, 1982
A treaty codifying the **Law of the Sea** is signed by 117 countries.

1983
The **Internet** is established to link computer users worldwide and enable them to share all manner of data; e-mail is one primary use.

 [6]
1983
The Microsoft Corporation releases the **Windows operating system**, a sequel to its popular MS-DOS; software developer Bill Gates will eventually become the richest man in the world.

September 21, 1982
Players belonging to the professional **National Football League (NFL)** go on strike against all the league's 28 teams. It is the first in-season strike in the 63-year history of the NFL.

October 1982
A book of cartoonist Jim Davis's **Garfield** comic strips knocks *The Joy of Sex* off the paperback bestseller list.

October 1, 1982
Helmut Kohl becomes chancellor of the Federal Republic of Germany (West Germany). He is a member of the Christian-Democratic Union. Kohl will preside over the integration of East and West Germany in 1990.

 *[4]*

October 1, 1982
Congress establishes the **U.S. Claims Court** (now the U.S. Court of Federal Claims) to handle cases in which the United States is a defendant.

October 7, 1982
The **New York Stock Exchange** sets a one-day record when 147,070,000 shares change hands. The rally continues the following week, which registers the highest weekly total on record with 592,460,000 shares traded.

October 11, 1982
A group of **Sikhs** besiege India's House of Parliament in New Delhi, killing four and injuring scores of others.

[3] An Australian farmer stands by a weakened sheep during the drought.

[10] Bob Hawke, a pragmatic Labor Party prime minister who attributes much of his popularity to holding the Guinness Book of Records best time for sinking a "yard of ale"—about three pints: eleven seconds.

[8] Henry Kissinger in El Salvador, back doing what he does best, brokering diplomatic deals.

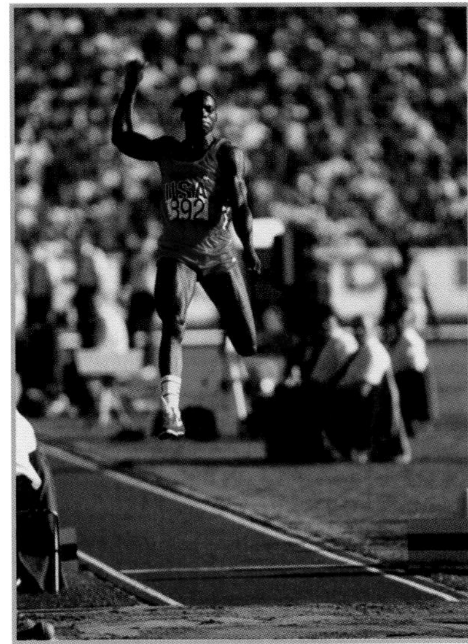

[9] Carl Lewis in mid-jump.

[4] Helmut Kohl. He will oversee the reunification of his country.

1983
A California condor born at the **San Diego Zoo** is the first of the endangered species ever hatched in captivity.

 *[7]*

1983
After 11 years and 251 episodes, U.S. TV's **M*A*S*H** goes off the air.

[8]

1983
After a hiatus of more than six years, former national security adviser and secretary of state **Henry Kissinger** is appointed to head a national commission on Central America by President Ronald Reagan.

1983
American researchers studying Duchenne's **muscular dystrophy** discover that it is caused by a defect on the 23rd chromosome. This is the first discovery of a specific marker for a genetic disease.

 *[9]*

1983
At the Athletics Conference (TAC), American athlete **Carl Lewis** becomes the first man since 1886 to win the 100-meter and 200-meter dashes and the long jump in a national outdoor championship.

 *[10]*

1983
Bob Hawke of the Labor Party becomes prime minister of Australia. He will be noted for achieving greater industrial harmony by instituting a unified wage accord among Australia's fractious labor unions and lowering the rate of inflation.

1983
British actor **Ben Kingsley** plays the title role in Sir Richard Attenborough's *Gandhi*, which wins eight Oscars at the 1983 Academy Awards.
 [1]

1983
Brunei achieves independence from the United Kingdom.

1983
Compaq introduces the first portable IBM PC-clone.

1983
German Neo-Expressionist **Anselm Kiefer**, struggling with the legacy of Nazism, paints *To the Unknown Painter*, in which haunting images emerge from encrusted paint and straw.

1983
Guion Bluford, Jr., a member of the crew of the space shuttle *Challenger*, becomes the **first African American in space**.
 [2]

1983
In **Iran**, women are now required to wear the *chador* (a full-length cloak covering the head and body); the sentence for appearing unveiled is prison for 1 to 12 months.
 [3]

[1] Ben Kingsley with his best-actor Oscar.

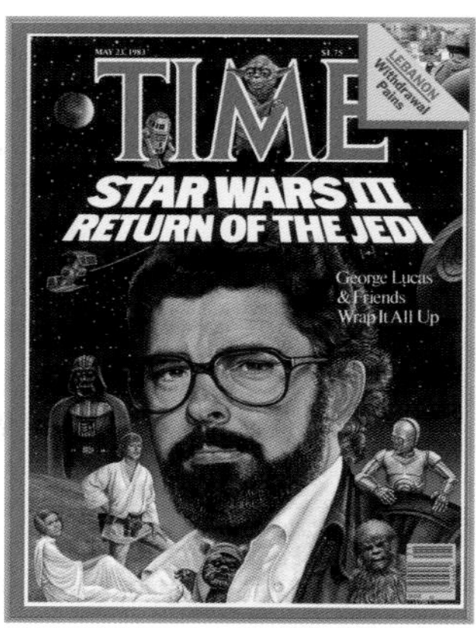

[7] George Lucas surrounded by Star Wars *characters on the cover of* Time.

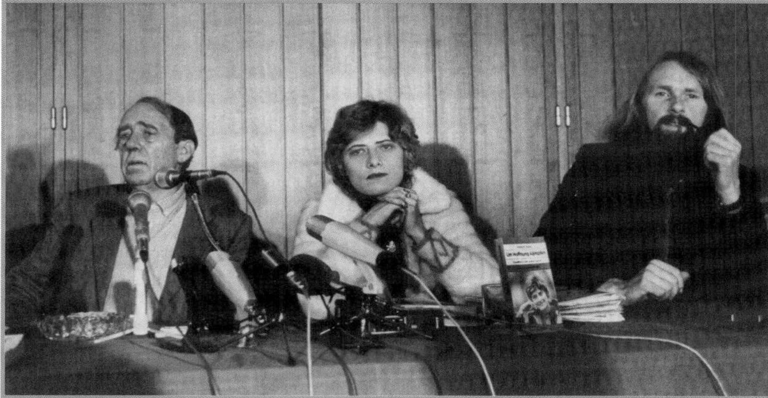

[6] The German Green Party: Petra Kelly, center, with novelist Heinrich Böll to the right and Lukas Beckmann, Green Party leader from 1984 to 1987, to the left. By 1990 they will not have the votes needed for a presence in parliament.

[2] Guion Bluford on an exercise machine aboard the Challenger.

[5] Joan Miró in front of one of his paintings at a one-man show in London.

 [5]
1983
Spanish Surrealist painter **Joan Miró**, last survivor of the group of writers and painters whose work in Paris during the early part of the century revolutionized Western literature and art, dies.

1983
A federal commission recommends that the U.S. government pay $20,000 to each of the estimated 60,000 surviving **Japanese Americans** placed in detention camps during World War II.

 [6]
1983
The Green Party enters the West German parliament with 27 members and an environmentalist agenda. It is the first new party in the Bundestag (Federal Diet) in three decades.

1983
The Sandinista National Liberation Front government of **Nicaragua** officially announces that almost all citizens who left the country in recent years can return without fear of punishment.

 [7]
1983
The third installment of the American **Star Wars** saga, *Return of the Jedi*, is released.

1983
The **U.S. embassy in Beirut**, Lebanon, is virtually destroyed a car bomb. Among the fatalities are 17 Americans.

1983
In the United Kingdom, front-seat occupants of motor vehicles are required by law to wear **seat belts**.

1983
Lech Walesa, founder of Solidarity, the now-outlawed Polish federation of labor unions, wins the Nobel Peace Prize.

1983
Malaysian cabinet minister **Datuk Mokhtar bin Haji Hashim** is sentenced to death for killing the speaker of the Negri Sembilan state assembly.

1983
Menachem Begin informs the Israeli cabinet that he will formally resign within a few days as prime minister and as leader of the Herut Party.

 [4]

1983
President Ronald Reagan signs legislation reforming the U.S. Social Security system to help ensure its short- and long-term solvency.

1983
Roy L. Williams, president of the International Brotherhood of Teamsters, is sentenced to 55 years in prison on 11 counts of fraud and conspiracy.

BEIRUT BOMBING

U.S. embassy attacked by suicide bomber

A 2,000-lb bomb was brought into the embassy compound in a delivery van at lunchtime on April 18. It was detonated by the driver, who was one of more than 60 people killed in the explosion; some of the devastation to the embassy building is shown above. Suicide attacks later became widespread, especially in the Middle East.

The Beirut attack came in the wake of U.S. intervention in the Lebanese Civil War and the massacre of Palestinians at the Sabra and Shatila refugee camps by Lebanese Christian militiamen. Responsibility for the atrocity was later claimed by Islamic Jihad, an Iranian-backed organization whose stated aim was to expel all Americans from Lebanon.

[3] Iranian women in chadors, ironically at a U.N. Decade for Women conference in Nairobi, Kenya, in 1985.

[8] Klaus Barbie during his days in France in 1943.

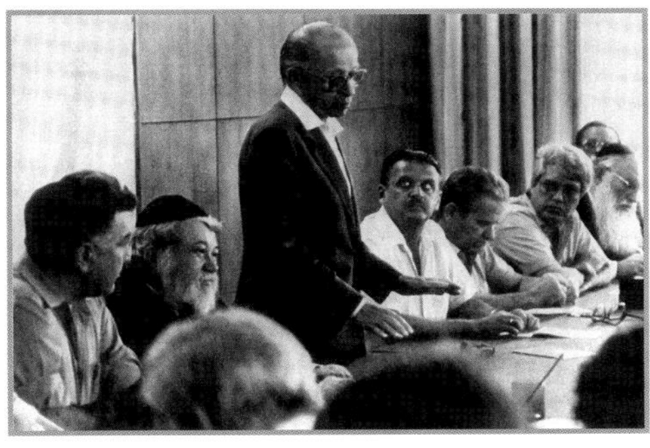

[4] An ailing Menachem Begin makes his announcement that he is retiring.

1983
The U.S. government names acquired immune deficiency syndrome (**AIDS**) the government's top medical priority.

1983
The West German magazine *Stern* announces that it has acquired 60 volumes of **Adolf Hitler's diaries**, later proved to be forgeries by the West German government.

1983
Harold Washington is elected the first black mayor of Chicago.

1983
Work begins on the **Great Man-Made River** (GMR) in Libya. One of the world's largest water-transmission projects, it is designed to carry fresh water from under the Sahara to the Libyan coast.

January 17, 1983
Nigeria's minister of internal affairs orders all illegal aliens to leave the country by the end of the month. The edict affects an estimated two million people.

 [8]

January 25, 1983
Klaus Barbie, a Nazi war criminal, is arrested in Bolivia. He will be extradited to France, where he had been tried in absentia in 1954 and sentenced to death for crimes he committed as head of the Gestapo in Lyon during World War II.

1983-1984

March 23, 1983
U.S. president Ronald Reagan announces the **Strategic Defense Initiative**, popularly known as Star Wars, a proposed system against potential nuclear attacks.
 [1]

June 9, 1983
British Conservative prime minister **Margaret Thatcher**, buoyed by victory in the Falklands War and by deep divisions within the Labour Party, is easily reelected to a second term.
 [2]

June 18, 1983
The first American woman to fly into outer space, **Sally Ride**, is launched with four other astronauts aboard the space shuttle *Challenger*.
 [3]

June 27, 1983
The **U.S. stock market collapses**, following which 74 railroads go bankrupt, 15,000 businesses fail, and 600 banks close over the next four years.

July 21, 1983
The world's lowest recorded temperature, minus 128.6°F, is measured at **Vostok Station**, Antarctica.

August 17, 1983
Lyricist **Ira Gershwin** dies in Beverly Hills, California. He has written the words to dozens of popular songs, working with composers Moss Hart, Kurt Weill, Jerome Kern, Harry Warren, and Harold Arlen in addition to his brother, George.

[1] An artist's impression of a space-based Star Wars interceptor missile on collision course with a nuclear intercontinental ballistic missile (ICBM).

[2] Margaret Thatcher on the last day of the election campaign, in front of the doors of a factory on the Isle of Wight where the British-invented Hovercraft is built.

[7] Steve Jobs of Apple Corporation with the new Apple Macintosh computer.

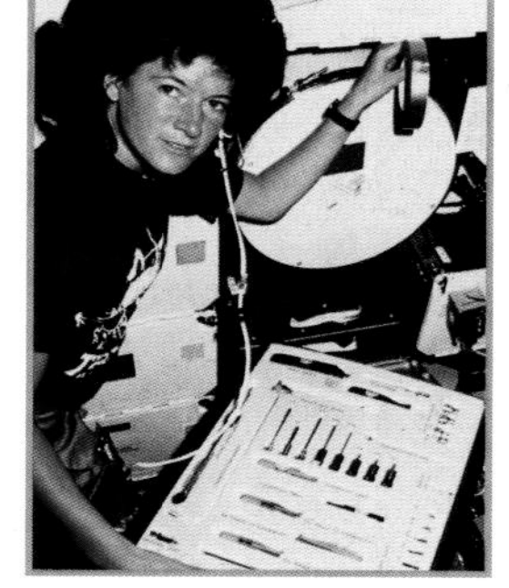

[3] Sally Ride, with a toolkit aboard the Challenger.

[10] Linda Hunt with her Oscar for portraying the male Chinese-Australian dwarf Billy Kwan.

[8] Ted Hughes, in his office as poet laureate, unveils a floor plaque in Poet's Corner, Westminster Abbey, in memory of Britain's World War I poets, including Wilfred Owen, Siegfried Sassoon, and Ivor Gurney.

[9] Alec Jeffreys holds up a DNA "fingerprint."

[7]
1984
Apple introduces the **Macintosh** and popularizes the graphical user interface (GUI).

1984
At the Summer Olympics in Los Angeles, American **Carl Lewis** repeats the feat of Jesse Owens, winning gold medals in the same four events that Owens won at the 1936 Berlin Games.

[8]
1984
British poet **Ted Hughes** is appointed Britain's poet laureate for his years of prolific poetic genius.

[9]
1984
DNA fingerprinting, based on scientific analysis of individuals' genetic makeup, is developed by British geneticist Alec Jeffreys.

1984
Geraldine Ferraro is named Walter Mondale's vice presidential running mate on the Democratic ticket. This is the first time a major American political party has nominated a woman for the vice presidency.

[10]
1984
Linda Hunt becomes the first performer to win an Oscar for portraying a character of the opposite gender, in *The Year of Living Dangerously*.

October 23, 1983
A terrorist bent on suicide drives a truckload of high explosives through a series of barricades and into the U.S. Marine Corps headquarters at the **Beirut** airport in Lebanon, killing 241 U.S. servicemen.
 [4]

October 25, 1983
The U.S. military invades the tiny island country of **Grenada**.
 [5]

November 2, 1983
U.S. President Ronald Reagan signs a bill designating the third Monday in January a national holiday in memory of **Martin Luther King, Jr**.

1984
Black South African Anglican archbishop **Desmond Tutu** is awarded the Nobel Peace Prize for his work in opposition to apartheid.
 [6]

1984
The Indian army attacks **Sikh separatists** in the Harimandir (Golden Temple) at Amritsar, one of the holiest sites in the Sikh religion.

1984
American researcher Robert Gallo and French researcher Luc Montagnier announce independent discoveries of the virus, later named **the human immunodeficiency virus (HIV)**, that causes AIDS.

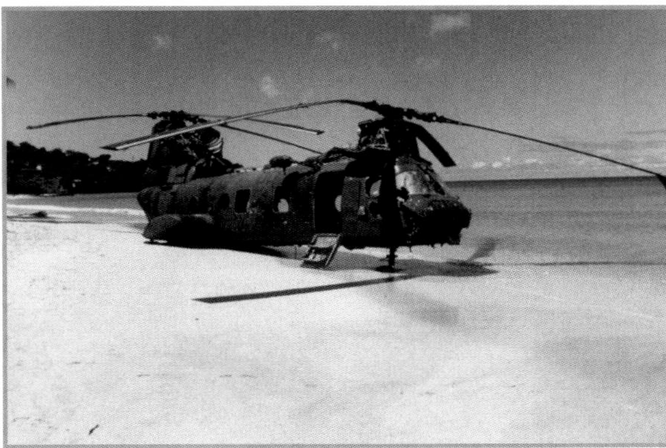

[5] An American Sea Knight helicopter shot down during the invasion of Grenada.

[6] Archbishop Desmond Tutu, a year after receiving his Nobel Prize, trying to calm a crowd attacking a suspected police informer at the funeral of four black victims of a hand-grenade attack.

[4] A Marine survivor is carried on a stretcher from the wreckage in Lebanon.

[11] British skaters Jayne Torvill and Christopher Dean, winning their ice-dancing gold in Sarajevo. Their dramatic interpretations take ice dancing to a whole new level of artistry, and they receive perfect scores from all twelve judges.

[12] Kareem Abdul-Jabbar

 [11]
1984
The **Winter Olympic Games** take place in Sarajevo, Yugoslavia.

1984
Between 600,000 and one million people die in **Ethiopia** from drought-induced famine. A massive international relief effort is mounted.

January 5, 1984
Four **Colombians** accused of international drug trafficking and money laundering are flown to the U.S. to face federal charges in the first extradition of Colombian citizens to the U.S.

February 9, 1984
Soviet premier **Yury Andropov** dies 15 months after succeeding Leonid Brezhnev. He is replaced by Konstantin Chernenko.

April 1, 1984
American entertainer **Marvin Gaye** is shot and killed by his father in Los Angeles.

 [12]
April 5, 1984
Kareem Abdul-Jabbar surpasses Wilt Chamberlain as the all-time leading scorer in the National Basketball Association.

1984-1985

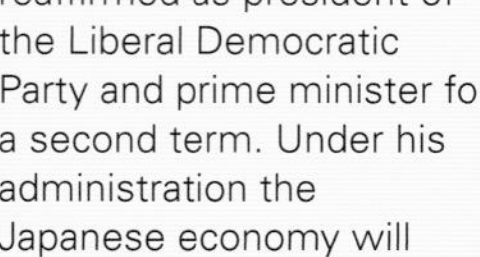

June 27, 1984
Jean Casimir-Périer is elected president of France.

September 17, 1984
Martin Brian Mulroney, leader of the Progressive Conservative Party of Canada, becomes prime minister. He will oversee strong economic growth and the control of inflation.

October 1984
Yasuhiro Nakasone is reaffirmed as president of the Liberal Democratic Party and prime minister for a second term. Under his administration the Japanese economy will continue its growth and become the world's largest creditor nation.

October 12, 1984
An IRA bomb explodes in the **Grand Hotel**, **Brighton**, England, where the Conservative Party conference is being held. Five are killed, thirty injured. Margaret Thatcher insists the conference goes on. [1]

October 31, 1984
Indira Gandhi, the Indian prime minister, is killed by Sikh members of her bodyguard, in revenge for her having ordered troops into the Golden Temple in Amritsar, the Sikh holy of holies. [2]

November 6, 1984
U.S. president **Ronald Reagan** wins reelection in a landslide victory over Democratic candidate Walter F. Mondale. [3]

[1] *The front of the Grand Hotel in Brighton after the IRA bomb has exploded.*

[2] *Indira Gandhi's body is burned after her assassination, watched by her son, Rajiv, the new prime minister, in a white cap, with his daughter, Priyanka, and his wife, Sonia, beyond.*

[6] *Rows of china dishes from the kitchen of the* Titanic *sitting on the ocean bed two-and-a-half miles below the surface.*

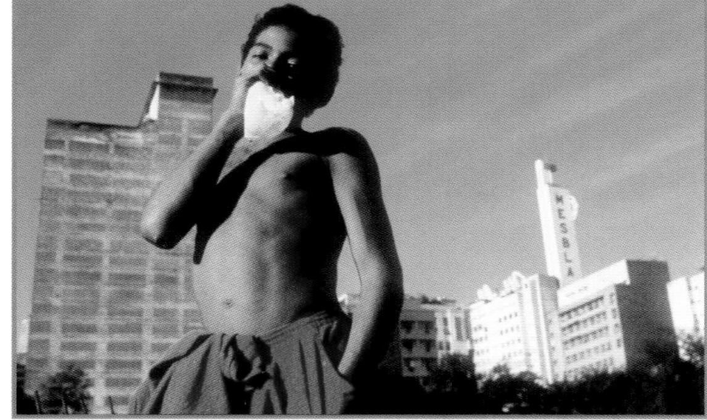

[7] *A child who lives on the streets of Rio in Brazil.*

[8] *Daniel Ortega, Sandinista leader and now president of Nicaragua.*

1985
The Canadian avant garde circus **Cirque du Soleil** begins touring. By 2007 Cirque du Soleil will have over nine shows in production, including resident shows in Orlando, Las Vegas, and New York.

1985
The first **CD encyclopedia** is introduced. Within a decade, electronic encyclopedias become hugely popular: more CDs are given away in the 1990s than print sets sold in the previous 200 years.

[6]
1985
The wreckage of the **RMS Titanic** is discovered at a depth of about 13,000 feet by a team of oceanographers led by Robert Ballard. The ship had sunk in 1912.

[7]
c. 1985
Brazilian street children organize the National Movement for Street Boys and Girls, an advocacy group that helps craft new child-protection laws. Previously street children had been targets of torture and murder.

c.1985
The **zebra mussel** arrives in the North American Great Lakes, probably from the U.S.S.R. It reproduces prolifically, clogging water intakes of factories and city water systems.

[8]
January 10, 1985
In a ceremony attended by only one foreign head of state, Cuban president Fidel Castro, Daniel Ortega Saavedra takes the oath of office as president of **Nicaragua**.

December 3, 1984
In **Bhopal**, India, the worst industrial accident in history occurs, when about 45 tons of gas escape from an insecticide plant. The death toll is between 15,000 and 20,000, and some half million are left with serious health problems from exposure to the toxic gas.

 [4]

1985
Bernard Hinault of France becomes the third cyclist to win the Tour de France five times.

1985
British scientists detect sharp seasonal reductions in the Earth's stratospheric **ozone layer**, which protects life from harmful ultraviolet radiation.

1985
The **first registered internet domain name**, symbolic.com, is issued.

1985
Pete Rose of the Cincinnati Reds surpasses Ty Cobb's record of hits in a career (4,191) to become baseball's all-time hits leader.

 [5]

1985
The Chinese-language Concise **Encyclopaedia Britannica** is announced in Beijing. The 10-volume set is the first joint project between the People's Republic of China and a Western publishing house.

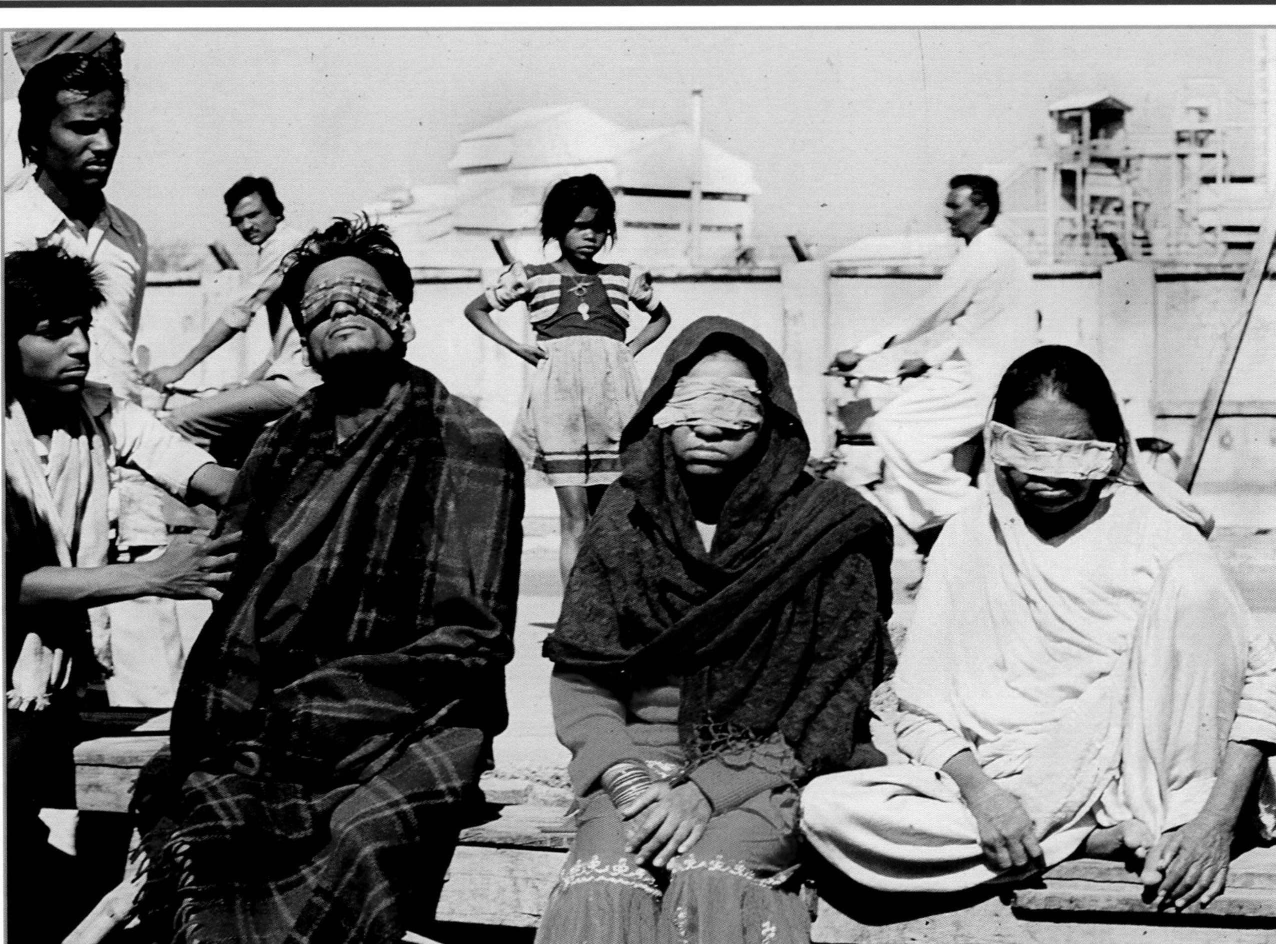

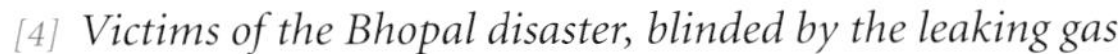

[4] *Victims of the Bhopal disaster, blinded by the leaking gas.*

[3] *Ronald Reagan campaigning for reelection.*

[9] *The Rock of Gibraltar, dominating the entry to the Mediterranean.*

[5] *Pete Rose*

[10] *Mikhail Gorbachev, with his distinctive birthmark.*

January 14, 1985
Sixteen persons, including a Presbyterian minister and Roman Catholic priests and nuns, are indicted on charges of **smuggling Central American aliens** into the U.S. or giving them refuge.

 [9]

February 5, 1985
Spain officially removes all restrictions on travel to and from **Gilbraltar**, the tiny British enclave on the southern tip of Spain whose land border had been closed a decade and a half earlier.

February 10, 1985
Nelson Mandela, the leader of South Africa's banned African National Congress, refuses a government offer of freedom even though he has already been jailed for 20 years. Mandela refuses to renounce violence, the condition for his release.

February 26, 1985
Nine men are accused of belonging to a crime commission that ruled five **Cosa Nostra** families in New York City. The indictments represent the first time that the Mafia organization, rather than individuals, is the focus of federal court attention.

 [10]

March 11, 1985
Mikhail Gorbachev succeeds Konstantin Chernenko as leader of the Soviet Union.

March 18, 1985
The American Broadcasting Corporation (ABC) acknowledges an offer from Capital Cities Communications to buy ABC in a $3.5 billion deal, the largest business acquisition in the U.S. outside the oil industry.

1985-1986

May 1985
Within three weeks there are two tragedies in soccer stadiums. On May 11 a fire at **Bradford City** ground in Yorkshire kills 56, then on May 29 at the **Heysel** stadium in Belgium, 41 die.

 [1]

April 17, 1985
The antidiscrimination section of **Canada's** three-year-old federal constitution becomes the law of the land even though many local laws have yet to be rewritten to conform to the principles laid down.

May 5, 1985
President Ronald Reagan, ignoring the protests of Jewish organizations, U.S. veterans' groups, and numerous U.S. congressmen, pays a brief visit to a military cemetery in West Germany.

May 17, 1985
The **Japanese Diet** approves a bill that opens up new job opportunities for women by removing certain restrictions on the time of day and number of hours they can work.

May 25, 1985
As many as 40,000 drown in **Bangladesh** as a killer cyclone sweeps across the Bay of Bengal and drives a one-story-high wall of water across small inhabited islands in the delta of the Ganges River.

 [2]

June 10, 1985
Israel completes its three-stage withdrawal of combat troops from **Lebanon** but leaves an unannounced number of patrols, advisors, and observers in the "security zone" it has established in Lebanon along Israel's northern border.

 [3]

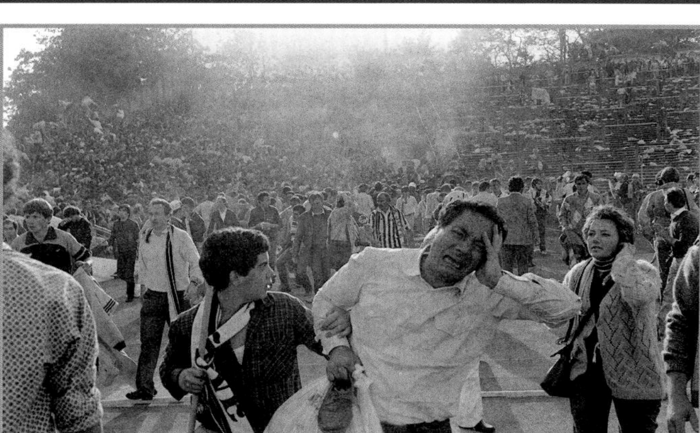

[1] Spectators flee the stand at the Heysel Stadium in Belgium after the wall has collapsed, as the result of rioting. It crushes many to death.

[2] Bangladeshis who have lost their homes in the cyclone sit in lines waiting for food to be distributed.

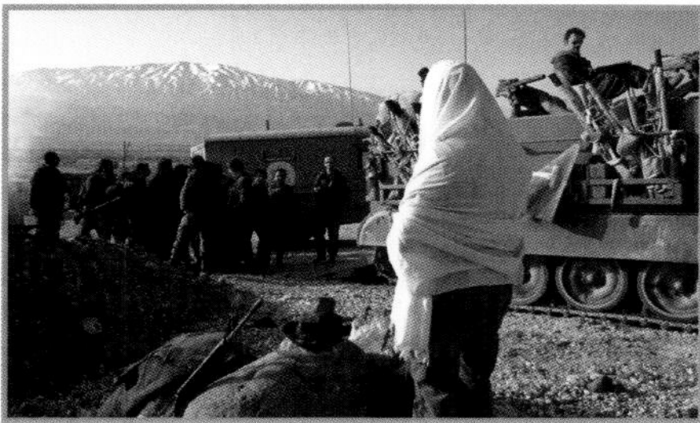

[3] An Israeli soldier, his head covered by his prayer shawl, says his devotions, as the Israeli army withdraws from Lebanon.

[5] The Rainbow Warrior *half submerged after the bombs planted by the French secret service have gone off. It was trying to prevent French nuclear testing in the Pacific.*

[8] The remains of a hotel in Mexico City after the earthquakes.

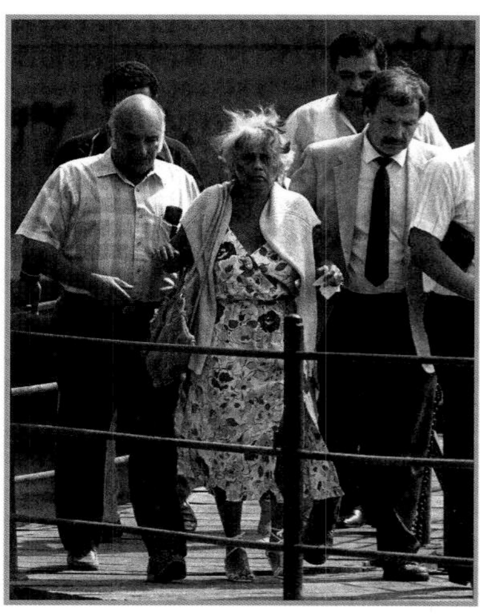

[9] Marilyn Klinghoffer disembarks from the Achille Lauro *in Egypt. During the three-day hijacking, her husband, Leon, 69, has been killed and thrown overboard. His death will become the subject of an opera.*

September 9, 1985
Both white and black youths begin rampaging through the Handsworth area of **Birmingham, England**. Looting and arson continue into the following day and are directed especially against Asians.

 [8]

September 19, 1985
The first of two powerful **earthquakes** hits Mexico, toppling buildings in Mexico City. A massive rescue effort ensues for those trapped in the rubble, but it will later be estimated that more than 20,000 people had died.

 [9]

October 7, 1985
Members of the Palestine Liberation Front, a small faction headed by Abu Abbas within the Palestine Liberation Organization (PLO), hijack an Italian cruise ship, the **Achille Lauro**.

October 11, 1985
The 1985 **Nobel Peace Prize** is awarded to the International Physicians for the Prevention of Nuclear War, a five-year-old Boston-based organization with 135,000 members in 41 countries.

October 25, 1985
Argentine **president Raúl Alfonsín** imposes a 60-day state of siege to combat violence believed to be instigated by right-wing advocates of amnesty for the former military leaders on trial for murder, torture, and kidnapping.

November 6, 1985
Poland's newly formed Sejm (parliament) elects **General Wojciech Jaruzelski** chairman of the Council of State (president); he replaces Henryk Jablonski, who had held the post since 1972.

July 7, 1985
Boris Becker, age 17, becomes the youngest person to date to win the Wimbledon men's singles title.
 [4]

June 14, 1985
Argentina discards the peso and replaces it with the austral, which has a fixed value of $1.25, approximately 1,000 times more than the peso.

July 10, 1985
The Greenpeace ship **Rainbow Warrior** is sunk by two bomb explosions while berthed in Auckland Harbor, New Zealand.
 [5]

July 13, 1985
Live Aid concerts raise funds to aid famine victims in Ethiopia. The concerts are performed simultaneously in several venues around the world.
 [6]

July 15, 1985
A 12-day women's conference opens in Nairobi, **Kenya**, to mark the end of the United Nations Decade for Women. The meeting is called to assess the achievements and failures of the past 10 years and set goals for the next 15.

August 12, 1985
In the worst single-plane disaster to date, a **Japan Air Lines jumbo jet** crashes in central Japan when the pilot loses control of the disabled aircraft. Only 4 of the 524 passengers will be found alive.
 [7]

[4] *Boris Becker on his way to his first Wimbledon title.*

[11] *Diego Maradona of Argentina with the World Cup trophy. In the quarter final against England he has scored what is called "the goal of the century."*

[10] *Rescuers try, unsuccessfully, to save the life of a girl trapped for more than 60 hours in the wreckage of the town of Armero.*

[7] *A scarred hillside and part of a wing from the Japan Airlines 747 crash.*

[6] *Mick Jagger performs with Tina Turner at the Live Aid concert held at the JFK Stadium in Philadelphia.*

[10]
November 13, 1985
Mount Ruiz in the Cordillera Central of the Andes, in west-central Colombia, erupts twice, burying the town of Armero on the Lagunilla River and killing an estimated 25,000 people.

1986
American golfer **Jack Nicklaus** wins a record sixth Masters Tournament. In his career, Nicklaus is named the Professional Golfers' Association player of the year five times.

[11]
1986
Argentina defeats West Germany in the men's **World Cup** soccer championship by a score of 3 to 2.

1986
Japanese architect **Isozaki Arata's** Los Angeles Museum of Contemporary Art exhibit establishes him as one of the world's foremost designers.

1986
Nigerian playwright, poet, and novelist **Wole Soyinka** is awarded the Nobel Prize for Literature. He writes of modern West Africa in a satiric style and with a tragic sense of the obstacles to progress.

1986
The core module (base block) of the Soviet modular space station **Mir** is launched into earth orbit. Over the next decade additional modules will be attached to it, creating a versatile space laboratory.

1986

1986
The first **genetically engineered vaccine**, which protects against hepatitis B infection, is approved for sale in the United States.

1986
The International Whaling Commission institutes a trial **moratorium on commercial whaling**. The agreement reduces hunting pressure on whales, permitting some recovery in populations of most species.

1986
Lead as a gasoline additive is banned in the United States. Subsequently, the mean blood-lead level of the American population declines more than 75 percent.

1986
The **Oprah Winfrey Show** is nationally syndicated in the U.S. Winfrey's compassion and honesty attract a wide audience and the talk show becomes a leader of the genre.

 [1]

1986
The **Iran-Contra** investigation reveals that the U.S. National Security Council has secretly been selling armaments to Iran and funneling some of the proceeds to the *contras,* the U.S.-backed rebels fighting the Sandinista government of Nicaragua.

 [2]

January 6, 1986
General Samuel K. Doe, Liberian head of state since he seized power in 1980, is sworn in as president of a new civilian government.

 [3]

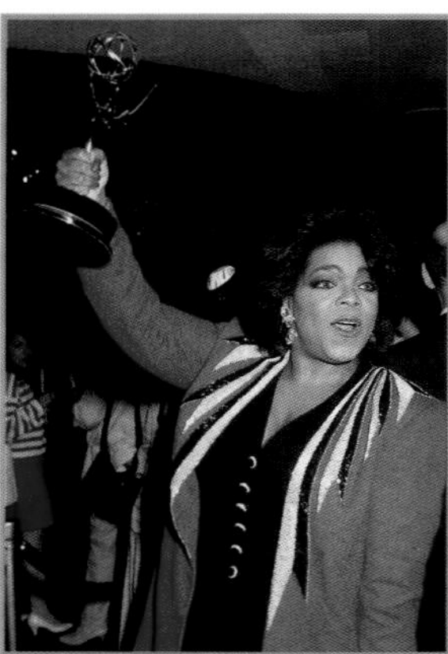

[1] *Oprah Winfrey with her Daytime Emmy trophy.*

[2] *Colonel Oliver North sworn in before the House Foreign Affairs Committee investigating "Irangate," as it is called. Known as President Reagan's "swashbuckler-in-chief," he has been at the center of this affair.*

[3] *Samuel Doe, center, the first ruler of native African descent, not American-Liberian. His regime is marked by increasing paranoia and corruption.*

[6] *Olof Palme. A small-time criminal and drug addict named Christer Pettersson is convicted of his killing two years later, but the conviction is quashed on appeal.*

[4] *The huge smoke trail left by the explosion of the* Challenger *space shuttle 73 seconds after liftoff.*

[7] *Halley's Comet streaking across a backdrop of stars.*

[5] *Imelda Marcos rewards her husband, President Ferdinand Marcos, with a kiss for "winning" the election, a few days before they flee the Philippines.*

March 13, 1986
Soviet cosmonauts Leonid Kizim and Vladimir Solovyev are sent aloft aboard a Soyuz spacecraft to rendezvous with the space station Mir and become its first occupants.

March 15, 1986
The judicial council of the **American Medical Association** declares that it would be ethical for doctors to withhold all means of life-prolonging medical treatment from any patient who is beyond doubt in an irreversible coma.

 [7]

April 11, 1986
Halley's Comet reaches its perigee (point nearest the earth) during its most recent passage near the planet.

April 14, 1986
A force of U.S. warplanes based in Britain bomb several sites in **Libya**, killing or wounding several of Muammar al-Qaddafi's children and narrowly missing Qaddafi himself.

April 25–26, 1986
In **Chernobyl**, **Ukraine**, a nuclear power station releases large amounts of radioactive material, which spreads over Belarus, Russia, and Ukraine and as far west as France and Italy.

May 8, 1986
Oscar Arias Sanchez is sworn in as president of Costa Rica.

January 20, 1986
The United States observes the first **federal holiday** in honor of civil rights activist Martin Luther King, Jr.

January 26, 1986
The U.S. space shuttle **Challenger** explodes shortly after liftoff, killing all aboard, including six astronauts and a private citizen, schoolteacher Christa McAuliffe.

 [4]

February 7, 1986
In the wake of political unrest, Haitian president **Jean-Claude Duvalier** flees his country, with U.S. assistance, for France.

February 19, 1986
The United States Senate approves the U.N. Convention on the Prevention and Punishment of the Crime of Genocide, that defines **genocide** as an international crime and obliges the signatories to punish anyone found guilty of it.

February 25, 1986
Philippine president **Ferdinand E. Marcos**, under pressure from the United States, flees his country for Hawaii after a fraudulent electoral victory over Corazon Aquino, who replaces him as president.

February 28, 1986
Olof Palme, the internationally prominent prime minister of Sweden (1969–76, 1982–86) whose strong pacifist beliefs included opposition to the Vietnam War, is assassinated in Stockholm.

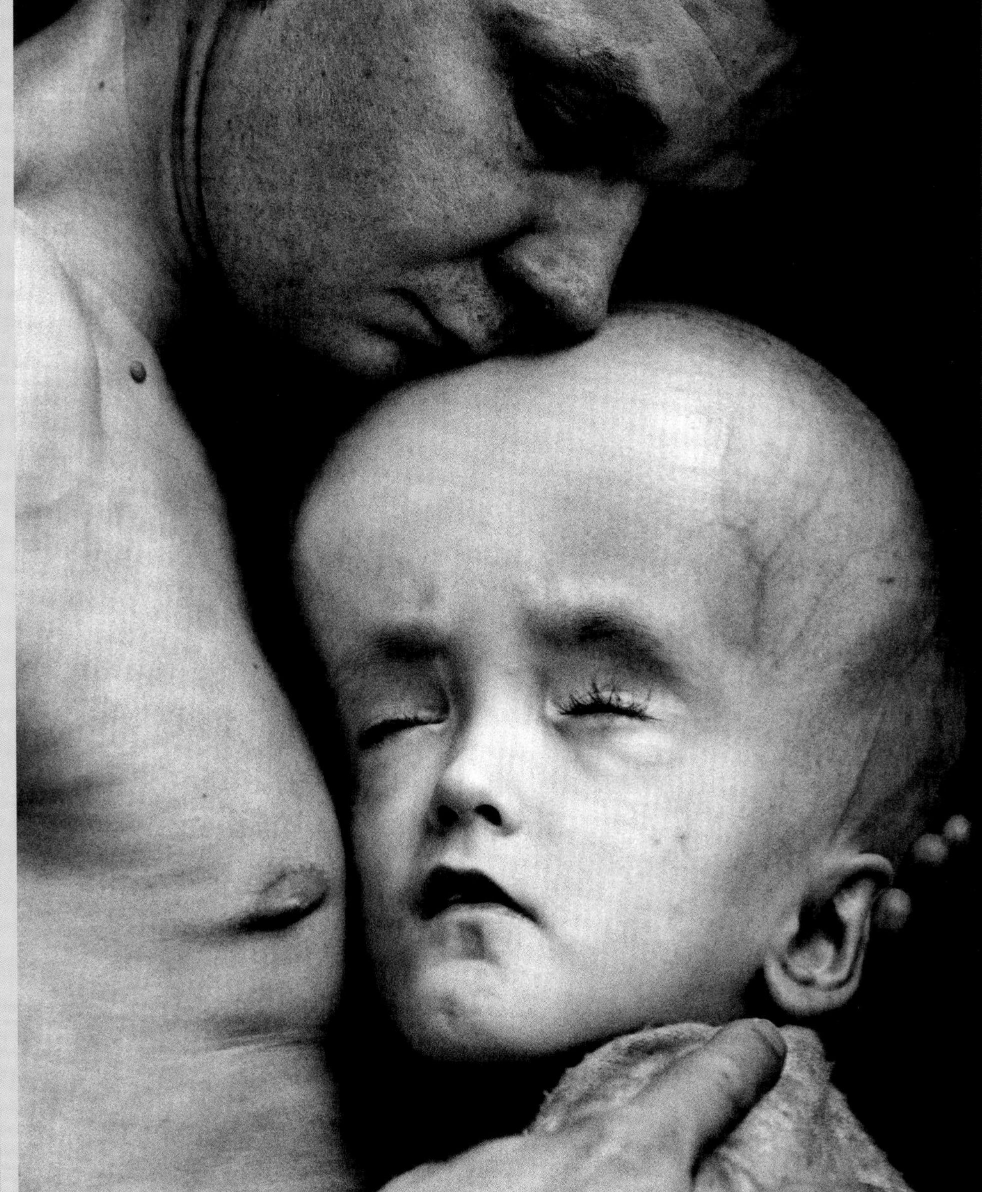

CHERNOBYL DISASTER

Explosion at a Soviet power station causes the worst nuclear accident in history

On April 25 and 26, technicians at the Chernobyl nuclear power plant, 65 miles north of Kiev, attempted a poorly designed experiment. Workers shut down the reactor's power-regulating system and its emergency safety systems and withdrew most of the control rods from its core while allowing the reactor to continue running at 7 percent power. These mistakes were compounded by others, and at 1:23 AM on April 26 the chain reaction in the core went out of control. Several explosions triggered a large fireball and blew off the heavy steel and concrete lid of the reactor. This and the ensuing fire in the graphite reactor core released large amounts of radioactive material into the atmosphere, where it was carried great distances by air currents.

On April 27 the 30,000 inhabitants of the nearby town of Pryp'yat began to be evacuated. A cover-up was attempted, but on April 28 Swedish monitoring stations reported abnormally high levels of wind-transported radioactivity. The Soviet government was then forced to admit that there had been an accident.

By May 4 both the heat and the radioactivity leaking from the reactor core were being contained. Radioactive debris was buried at some 800 temporary sites, and later in the year the highly radioactive reactor core was enclosed in a concrete-and-steel sarcophagus.

Initially the Chernobyl accident caused the deaths of 32 people. Dozens more contracted serious radiation sickness; some of these people later died. The amount of radioactivity that was carried on the winds across Europe was several times more than that created by the atomic bombs dropped on Hiroshima and Nagasaki, Japan. In the photograph, taken in Belarus in 2006, a father holds his daughter who is suffering from hydrocephalus (fluid on the brain) caused by radioactive fallout from Chernobyl.

May 16, 1986
Joaquin Balaguer, the 78-year-old former president of the Dominican Republic, regains the presidency with a narrow victory.

June 1986
William H. Rehnquist is appointed 16th chief justice of the U.S. Supreme Court by President Ronald Reagan. He will serve from 1986 to 2005.

June 1, 1986
The General Assembly of the **United Nations** approves a Program of Action for African Economic Recovery and Development; it is the first time the U.N. takes the initiative to solve economic problems in a specific region of the world.

July 14, 1986
Former FBI agent **Richard W. Miller** is sentenced to two life sentences and to 50 years in prison, all to be served concurrently, for spying for the Soviet Union; Miller is the first FBI agent ever convicted of espionage.

July 25, 1986
Drought devastates the United States; farm experts estimate that the drought in eight mid-Atlantic and southern states will result in the loss of about $2 billion in crops and livestock.

August 21, 1986
An estimated 1,700 sleeping villagers in a remote village of northwest **Cameroon** are killed by toxic gases that erupt from a crater lake.

1986-1987

September 6, 1986
Two terrorists enter the **Neve Shalom synagogue in Istanbul**, seal the doors with iron bars, and fire submachine guns and hurl grenades; seven rabbis and 14 others are killed.

October 2, 1986
The United States Senate votes to override President Ronald Reagan's veto of sanctions against **South Africa** because it has steadfastly refused to abandon apartheid.

 [1]

October 22, 1986
President Ronald Reagan signs into law a revolutionary tax-reform bill.

October 27, 1986
Prominent leaders of 12 different religious groups join **Pope John Paul II in Assisi**, Italy, for a World Day of Prayer for Peace.

 [2]

December 23, 1986
Dick Rutan and Jeana Yeager make aviation history when they land their **Voyager** aircraft at Edwards Air Force Base in California after a nine-day nonstop flight around the world without refueling either on the ground or in the air.

1987
The term **"virtual reality" (VR)** is coined in 1987 by Jaron Lanier, an American computer scientist and artist whose research and engineering contributes a number of products to the nascent VR industry.

[2] The Dalai Lama with other religious leaders in Assisi, home of St. Francis. A Franciscan monk on the right has a basket of white doves, with one dove on his outstretched arm and two on his shoulder.

[1] Protesters outside the South African embassy in Washington.

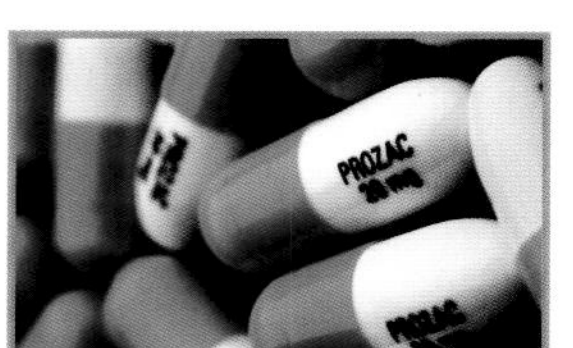

[5] Prozac pills

[6] John Whitney Payson, former owner, stands by the painting at Sotheby's. It is now in the Getty Center, Los Angeles.

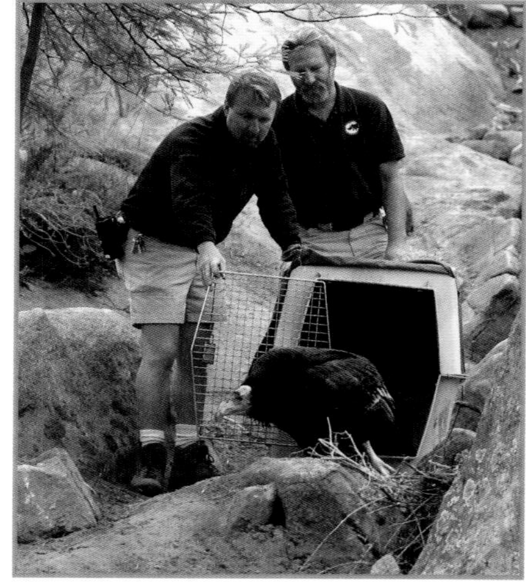

[7] A California condor released in the San Diego Wild Animal Park in 2000. By this year California has 150 of them, with more than 50 flying free in the wild.

 [5]

1987
Prozac is first prescribed in the United States, revolutionizing the treatment of depression. It is the first of the class of antidepressant medications called selective serotonin reuptake inhibitors (SSRIs).

1987
Pulitzer Prize–winning African American author **Toni Morrison** publishes her most critically acclaimed novel, *Beloved.* In 1993 she will become the first African American woman to win the Nobel Prize for Literature.

 [6]

1987
Vincent Van Gogh's painting **Irises** is sold at Sotheby's in New York for $49 million, making it the most expensive painting sold to date.

1987
The **Intermediate-Range Nuclear Forces Treaty** is concluded by the United States and the Soviet Union, the first agreement to abolish an entire category of weapon: intermediate-range and shorter-range land-based missiles.

 [7]

1987
The last California free wild **condor** is captured and placed in the San Diego Wild Animal Park (California) along with 13 others, bringing the world population to 27.

1987
The Legend of Zelda is released for the **Nintendo** Entertainment System in North America. The game interface features new elements, such as screens that are activated to manage the hero's items or abilities.

1987
Construction begins on the **Channel Tunnel**, a rail tunnel under the English Channel between England and France that will connect the road and rail networks of Britain and the Continent. Work will be completed in 1991, and the "Chunnel" will open in 1994.

1987
Alan Greenspan becomes chairman of the Board of Governors of the Federal Reserve System. He will serve until 2006 and receive a share of the credit for the longest official economic expansion in U.S. history (March 1991–February 2000).

 [3]

1987
Christian Lacroix, who will become one of the leading fashion designers of his time, presents his first haute couture collection, which brings mid-thigh "pouf" skirts and huge hats with bowl-like brims filled with flowers to the forefront of high fashion.

 [4]

1987
Computer programmer Larry Wall releases **Perl**, a comprehensive practical programming language that will become one of the most important foundations for the rapid development of personal computer programming.

1987
Les Miserables is awarded eight Tony awards, including Best Score and Best Musical.

1987
Our Common Future, published by the World Commission on Environment and Development, greatly influences the design and application of modern environmental law.

[3] *Alan Greenspan*

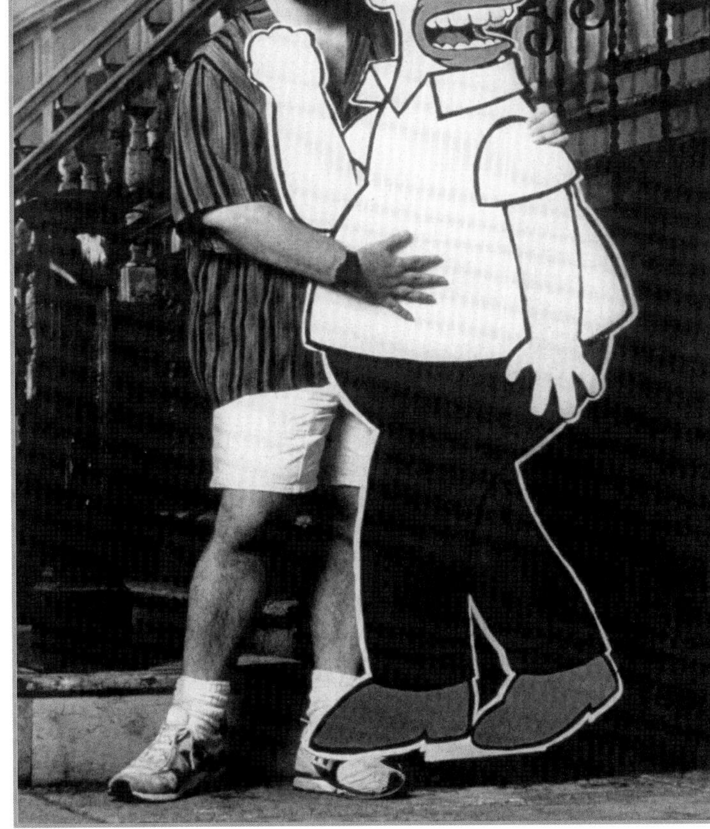

[8] *Matt Groening with one of his creations, Homer Simpson.*

[4] *A stunning Christian Lacroix creation, on a Spanish theme, with a tight black embroidered jacket and a Castilian hat, as well as one of his signature "pouf" skirts.*

[9] *Terry Waite in Beirut surrounded by armed guards shortly before his kidnapping.*

[10] *Corazon Aquino at a rally in support of the new constitution for her country.*

1987
The **Montreal Protocol on Substances That Deplete the Ozone Layer** is signed by 24 nations of the world, which agree to limit production of chlorofluorocarbons, so slowing the deterioration of stratospheric ozone.

 [8]

1987
The Simpsons, created by cartoonist Matt Groening, appears as a series of 30-second spots on *The Tracey Ullman Show*. The cartoon, expanded to half-hour episodes, will become the longest-running animated television series.

 [9]

January 1987
British hostage-release negotiator and sometime envoy of the Archbishop of Canterbury **Terry Waite** is himself taken hostage in Beirut. He will not be released until November 1991.

February 4, 1987
Colombian soldiers capture and extradite **Carlos Enrique Lehder Rivas**, a former state senator and reputed billionaire drug dealer, to the U.S. under the 1979 extradition treaty.

 [10]

February 18, 1987
Philippine voters vote to approve the new constitution proposed by **President Corazon Aquino**.

March 1987
Jonathan Jay Pollard, a civilian navy intelligence analyst, is sentenced to life in prison for selling secret U.S. documents to Israel.

1987-1988

March 3, 1987
Italian prime minister **Bettino Craxi**, a Socialist, resigns as head of the ruling five-party coalition.

March 6, 1987
The ferry **Herald of Free Enterprise** sinks outside Zeebrugge, Belgium, when the bow doors are left open.

 [1]

March 7, 1987
American boxer **Mike Tyson** becomes the youngest heavyweight to acquire the World Boxing Association (WBA) championship belt when he defeats James Smith in 12 rounds.

 [2]

March 19, 1987
Assemblies of God television evangelist **Jim Bakker** resigns his ministry in the wake of accusations that he is guilty of sexual misconduct and has paid blackmail money to keep the matter secret.

 [3]

March 20, 1987
AZT (azidothymidine) becomes the first drug to be approved by the U.S. Food and Drug Administration for the treatment of AIDS.

April 13, 1987
Portuguese prime minister Anibal Cavaco Silva and Chinese prime minister Zhao Ziyang sign a declaration in Beijing, China, that will restore the Portuguese overseas territory of **Macau** to Chinese sovereignty on December 20, 1999.

[1] *The capsized British roll-on roll-off ferry* Herald of Free Enterprise *resting on a sand bank. One hundred and eighty-four people have died in this disaster.*

[2] *The formidable physique of Mike Tyson.*

[3] *A carefully composed shot of Jim Bakker and his wife, Tammy Faye. Accusations of accounting fraud will follow those of sexual misconduct, and he will go to prison and get divorced.*

[8] *The cage for prisoners within the specially constructed courtroom in a Palermo prison, built for the big Mafia trial. Mafia boss Giuseppe Caló, "the Cashier," looks on.*

[6] *The floor of the New York Stock Exchange on the day the Dow Jones drops 500 points.*

[7] *Govan Mbeki is greeted by Winnie Mandela on his release from Robben Island. Mandela's husband, Nelson, is still in prison there. Mbeki is the father of Thabo Mbeki, who will become president of South Africa.*

October 15, 1987
A military coup in **Burkina Faso** overthrows head-of-state Thomas Sankara, killing him and eight others.

 [6]

October 19, 1987
The **Dow Jones** Industrial Average plummets nearly 23 percent, the largest one-day drop in the stock market's history.

 [7]

November 5, 1987
The former leader of the African National Congress, 77-year-old **Govan Mbeki**, is released by the South African government. Mbeki had been convicted in 1964 of plotting the violent overthrow of South Africa's white rulers.

November 29, 1987
Haiti's first presidential election in 30 years is halted as weeks of violence reach a new intensity as voters go to the polls. It will be two months before elections resume.

December 8, 1987
An uprising of **Palestinians**, called the *intifada*, begins in the territories occupied by Israel.

December 15, 1987
The **Association of Southeast Asian Nations** (ASEAN) concludes a two-day meeting in Manila that is only the third in the 20-year history of the organization.

April 30, 1987
The **Evangelical Lutheran Church in America** comes into existence after the American Lutheran Church, the Lutheran Church in America, and the Association of Evangelical Lutheran Churches formally merge.

May 28, 1987
West German teenager **Mathias Rust** exposes Soviet air defenses to ridicule by flying to Moscow and landing his light aircraft in Red Square without being detected.
 [4]

June 1, 1987
Lebanese prime minister **Rashid Karami** is killed when a bomb explodes aboard the military helicopter carrying him from Tripoli to Beirut.

June 3, 1987
Margaret "**the Iron Lady**" Thatcher wins her third consecutive five-year term as Britain's prime minister.

July 4, 1987
Klaus Barbie, the head of the Gestapo in Lyon, France, during World War II, is convicted of crimes against humanity and sentenced to life in prison.
[5]

September 3, 1987
The president of **Burundi**, Jean-Baptiste Bagaza, is overthrown by military leaders.

[4] Mathias Rust on trial in Moscow after landing his plane on Red Square. He gets a prison sentence.

[5] Klaus Barbie during his trial.

[9] Part of Andy Warhol's collection of 137 china cookie jars. Businessman Gedalio Grindberg, seen here, buys them all for $200,000.

INTIFADA

Palestinian protests against Israeli occupation take a new form.

In December 1987, Israeli soldiers in the Gaza Strip killed an Arab youth engaged in a protest. Widespread unrest soon spread throughout the Israeli-occupied territories, leading to 21 deaths in two weeks. This was the start of the the first *intifada* ("shaking"), a wave of Palestinian protests that took several forms—civil disobedience, demonstrations (left), strikes, boycotts of Israeli produce, graffiti, and the erection of barricades.

Israeli armed forces then clamped down hard on opposition in the West Bank and East Jerusalem. In response, the Fatah faction of the Palestine Liberation Organization (PLO) stepped up its attacks on Israel from bases in Lebanon. As a result, Middle East peace talks acquired a new urgency.

 [8]
December 16, 1987
The longest and most significant trial of **Mafia** leaders in Italian history concludes in Palermo, Sicily, with the convictions of 338 of 452 defendants.

December 20, 1987
Off the coast of **Mindoro, Philippines**, a ferry believed to be packed with over 2,900 passengers and crewmen collides with an oil tanker with a crew of 13; both vessels explode and sink, and only 26 badly burned persons survive.

December 29, 1987
Soviet cosmonaut **Yuri Romaneko** returns to earth in a Soyuz TM-3 after establishing an endurance record of 326 days aboard the Mir space station.

 [9]
1988
A year after artist **Andy Warhol's death**, a 10-day auction of his paintings and personal collections at Sotheby's in New York raises $20 million for his foundation. Among the fine art and antique furniture are more than 130 cookie jars.

1988
After becoming partially paralyzed, American painter **Chuck Close** changes his technique to a grid of tiles daubed with colorful elliptical and ovoid shapes. From a distance, the tiles come together as dynamic deconstructed faces.

1988
African American **Matthew Robert Henson**, who accompanied Robert E. Peary on his voyages to the North Pole and died in 1955, is reburied in Arlington National Cemetery.

1988

1988
After extensive and costly renovations, **Union Station** reopens in Washington, D.C., with stores, restaurants, and theaters.

1988
American **Florence Griffith Joyner** becomes the fastest woman in the world with her record-setting times in the 100-meter sprint (10.49 seconds) and the 200-meter sprint (21.34 seconds).

 [1]

1988
American short-story writer **Raymond Carver**, known for his honest portrayals of working-class people, publishes his last collection, *Where I'm Calling From.*

 [2]

1988
Anglo-Indian novelist Salman Rushdie publishes his controversial novel **The Satanic Verses**. After being condemned to death by Iranian Muslim clerics, he has to go into hiding.

 [3]

1988
At the 24th Olympics in Seoul, South Korea, swimmer **Kristin Otto** of East Germany becomes the first woman to win six gold medals in one Olympic Games.

 [4]

1988
At the **Winter Olympics** in Calgary, Alberta, ice skater Brian Boitano and speed skater Bonnie Blair are the only two Americans to win gold medals.

[3] *Salman Rushdie*

[2] *Raymond Carver. He dies in August.*

[4] *Kristin Otto with her six gold medals. East Germany is later accused of widespread use of performance-enhancing drugs in sport.*

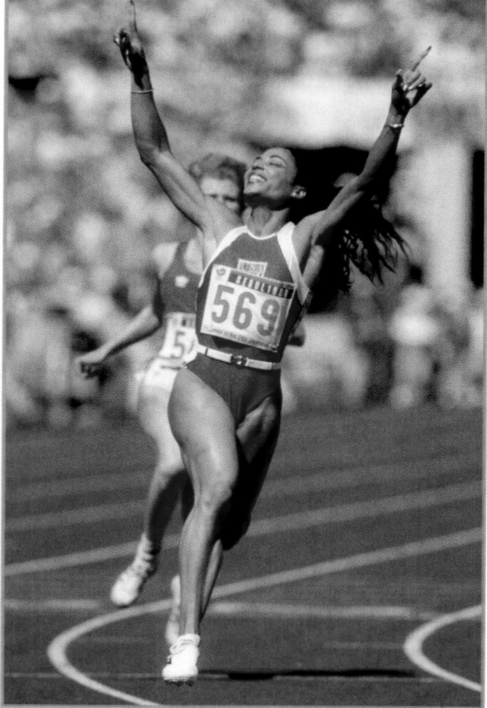

[1] *Florence Griffith Joyner celebrates winning the 100 meters at the Seoul Olympics.*

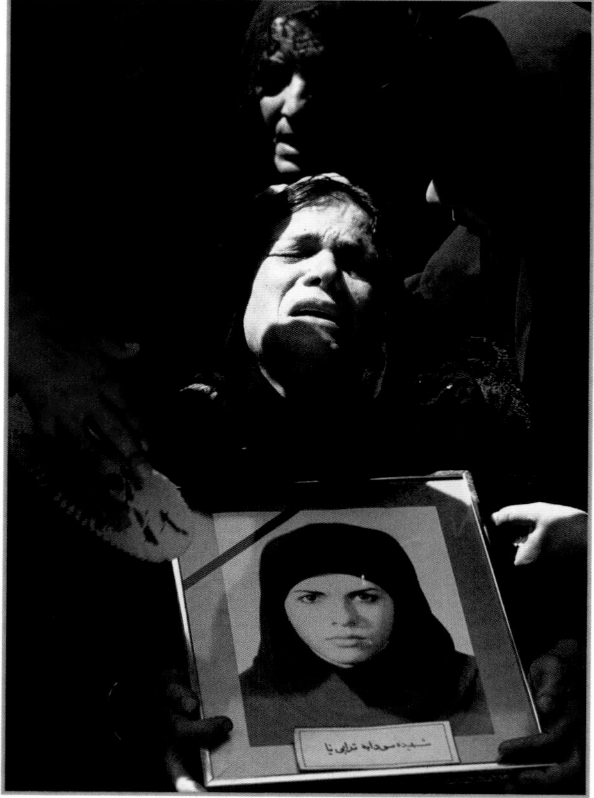

[8] *The photograph of a girl killed in the* Vincennes *incident is held by her mother.*

[9] *Burning the Brazilian rain forest to clear it for crops.*

1988
Many agricultural communities in the United States are burdened by one of the driest growing seasons since the Dust Bowl. Many wonder if it should be attributed to **global warming**, now beginning to be discussed.

1988
Romanian president **Nicolae Ceausescu** announces plans to bulldoze thousands of his country's villages and move their residents into new apartment buildings.

 [8]

1988
U.S.-Iranian relations reach new lows after U.S. warship **Vincennes** shoots down an Iranian Airbus by mistake in the Persian Gulf.

 [9]

1988
The deforestation rate in Brazil's **Amazonia** region peaks and attracts increased international concern.

1988
The Liberal Democrats form in Britain as a merger of the Liberal Party and the **Social Democratic Party**. They will occupy a center-left, libertarian position.

1988
The economy of **Namibia**, in southwestern Africa, continues to worsen, causing South Africa to consider abandoning its hold. Namibia will gain independence from South Africa within the next two years.

1988
Carnegie Hall celebrates the 100th birthday of American songwriter Irving Berlin, who wrote the scores for 18 motion pictures, with a concert in his honor.
 [5]

1988
Evan Mecham, the governor of Arizona, is impeached and removed from office for charges of misconduct, including lending state money to his auto dealership.

1988
Fast-food chain **McDonald's** makes plans to open several of its restaurants in the Soviet Union.
 [6]

1988
Hip-hop group **Public Enemy**, whose Chuck D famously characterized rap as the "black CNN," releases the politically charged *It Takes a Nation of Millions to Hold Us Back.*
 [7]

1988
Intifada violence between Israelis and Palestinians continues in Israel.

1988
Left-wing **Rodrigo Borja Cevallos** is elected president of Ecuador. His presidency will be marked by native uprisings and protests for land rights.

[5] *Singer Nell Carter at Irving Berlin's birthday tribute.*

[6] *A McDonald's supply truck in Moscow, with the slogan "Big Mac" in Cyrillic script on the side.*

[7] *Flavor Flav (right) and Chuck D of Public Enemy.*

[10] *The Parade of Sails, part of Australia's bicentennial celebrations, goes past the Sydney Opera House.*

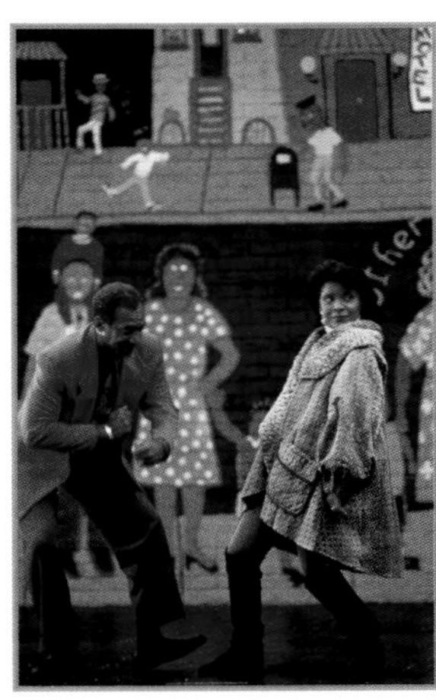

[11] *Bill Cosby and Phylicia Rashad on the set of* The Cosby Show.

1988
Violence associated with **Northern Ireland** continues. Alleged IRA bombers are shot by members of the SAS in Gibraltar. Weeks later two British soldiers are lynched at an IRA funeral.

 [10]
1988
Australia celebrates the bicentenary of the arrival of the first European settlers there.

1988
U.S. singer **Bobby McFerrin** releases his album *Simple Pleasures*, which includes the song "Don't Worry, Be Happy."

 [11]
c. 1988
Appearing on NBC, **The Cosby Show**, which depicts a stable, prosperous African American family, continues its run as one of the most popular shows on TV.

c. 1988
Sales of VCRs and video cassettes continue to boom, although stores that rent **video cassettes** are starting to share in the profit.

c. 1988
The so-called **baby boomers** born after World War II are producing babies in record numbers, with the U.S. government reporting the most live births in a quarter of a century.

1988-1989

February 25, 1988
Roh Tae Woo becomes president of the Republic of South Korea after the two major opposition candidates split the opposition vote in the November 1987 elections.

March 1988
Lieutenant Colonel Oliver North is indicted on charges extending from the Iran-Contra Affair.

March 1988
Saddam Hussein authorizes Iraqi forces to use chemical weapons against the Kurdish village of Halabja, killing 5,000 people.

 [1]

April 10, 1988
The **Seto Great Bridge**, spanning the Inland Sea in Japan, is opened to traffic.

 [2]

August 1988
Iran's deteriorating economy and recent Iraqi gains on the battlefield lead Iran to accept a U.N.-mediated cease-fire that it had previously resisted.

 [3]

September 10, 1988
By winning the U.S. Open, **Steffi Graf** completes the grand slam of tennis; she is the first woman to accomplish the feat since Margaret Court in 1970.

 [4]

[1] *A dead mother and baby in Halabja after the Iraqi chemical attack.*

[4] *Steffi Graf on her way to winning Wimbledon and her grand slam. She also wins an Olympic singles gold this year.*

[3] *Iranian prisoners-of-war captured during Iran's Faith in God offensive.*

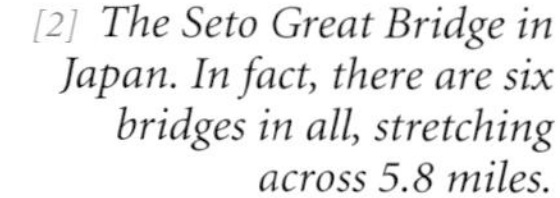

[2] *The Seto Great Bridge in Japan. In fact, there are six bridges in all, stretching across 5.8 miles.*

LOCKERBIE

A bomb planted aboard a 747 causes the airliner to crash near Lockerbie, Scotland.

On December 21, Pan Am Flight 103 blew up in midair on its way from London Heathrow to New York's Kennedy Airport; the remains landed in and around the town of Lockerbie (left), killing all 259 people on board and 11 on the ground.

Investigators discovered that the crash had been caused by one pound (450g) of plastic explosive planted in the cargo hold. It was probably hidden in luggage transferred from a connecting flight from Frankfurt, Germany. In 2001, a Scottish court, sitting for security reasons in the Netherlands, found a Libyan, 'Abd al-Baset al-Megrahi, guilty of murder. A second Libyan charged with him was acquitted.

December 21, 1988
The Pan Am 747 Clipper Maid of the Seas explodes over **Lockerbie, Scotland**. Victims and debris are scattered by a 100-knot wind over 845 square miles. Britain's largest criminal inquiry is launched.

1989
A court in **Warsaw** officially restores the legal status of Solidarity, the Polish federation of trade unions that was declared illegal under martial law in October 1982.

1989
African American social activist **Barbara Harris**, despite the opposition of the archbishop of Canterbury and others, is consecrated suffragan bishop of Massachusetts. She is the first woman to hold this office.

1989
American physicist **Norman Ramsey** shares the Nobel Prize for Physics for his development of the atomic clock, the most precise timepiece in the world.

1989
An estimated 200,000 Latvians stage the largest **anti-Russian demonstration** in the Soviet republic's history, as they seek to establish Latvian as the dominant language of the republic.

1989
Ayatollah Ruhollah Khomeini, who became Iran's supreme spiritual leader and unchallenged political authority after the 1979 overthrow of Shah Mohammad Reza Pahlavi, dies in Tehran.

October 13, 1988
The archbishop of Turin, Italy, announces that carbon-14 dating indicates that the **Shroud of Turin** dates only to the Middle Ages, though the origins of the shroud remain controversial.

 [5]

November 1988
Democratic candidate **Michael Dukakis**, the governor of Massachusetts, loses the presidential election to Republican George H. W. Bush.

November 15, 1988
Meeting at Algiers, the **Palestine National Council**, at the urging of PLO chairman Yasser 'Arafat, issues a declaration of independence for a state of Palestine in the West Bank and Gaza Strip.

November 16, 1988
Benazir Bhutto is elected prime minister of Pakistan, becoming the first woman in modern history to lead a Muslim country. She will serve as prime minister from 1988 to 1990 and again from 1993 to 1996.

 [6]

December 1, 1988
Carlos Salinas de Gortari, a member of the Partido Revolucionario Institucional (Institutional Revolutionary Party), becomes president of Mexico after a close election. He will go on to co-negotiate the North American Free Trade Agreement (NAFTA).

December 7, 1988
An earthquake in **Armenia** kills between 50,000 and 100,000.

[5] *The Shroud of Turin with the face, supposed to be that of Christ, computer-enhanced.*

[9] *A Statue of Liberty put up in Tiananmen Square by art students during the pro-democracy demonstration there.*

[6] *Benazir Bhutto holds a press conference after her election.*

[8] *President George Bush and his wife, Barbara, at the inaugural ball.*

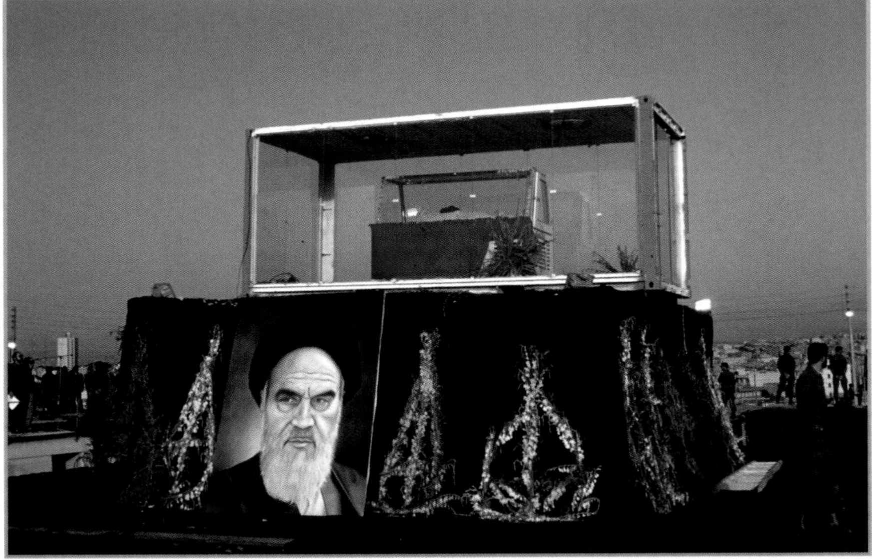

[7] *The body of Ayatollah Khomeini lies in state.*

[10] *Kenyan wildlife director and anthropologist Richard Leakey in front of three million dollars worth of poached ivory about to be burned.*

1989
Chinese American novelist **Amy Tan** publishes *The Joy Luck Club*, the story of four Chinese mothers and their Chinese American daughters.

1989
Denmark becomes the first country to establish registered partnerships for same-sex couples.

 [8]

1989
George H. W. Bush of the Republican Party becomes the 41st president of the United States. His vice president is Dan Quayle.

1989
In the first national election since the 1917 October Revolution, **Soviet citizens** go to the polls to elect the Congress of People's Deputies.

 [9]

1989
Jiang Zemin succeeds Zhao Ziyang as general secretary of the Chinese Communist Party after massive student demonstrations in Tiananmen Square. In 1997, Jiang becomes paramount leader of China.

 [10]

1989
Kenyan president **Daniel arap Moi** incinerates a 12-ton pile of elephant tusks during a gathering of environmentalists, government officials, and reporters in Nairobi National Park.

1989

1989
Romanian president **Nicolae Ceausescu**, the most brutal and fanatical communist leader in Eastern Europe, flees Bucharest as large crowds fight to take over large areas of the capital.
 [1]

1989
Scientists at CERN, a physics research facility in Switzerland, begin work on the **World Wide Web**, a network to speed the circulation of scientific preprints and research reports.

1989
The 12 nations constituting the European Communities agree to eliminate, by the end of the century, the production and use of chemicals that harm the **ozone layer** protecting the earth from harmful ultraviolet radiation.

1989
The 14th **Dalai Lama** is awarded the Nobel Peace Prize for his nonviolent efforts to liberate Tibet from Chinese rule.

1989
The gene responsible for **cystic fibrosis** is isolated, leading to the development of a genetic test for the inherited metabolic disorder that causes premature death in those affected.

1989
The U.S. Congress approves $49.7 million in aid to **Nicaraguan Contras** fighting the Sandinista government of President Daniel Ortega.

THE FALL OF THE BERLIN WALL

Notorious barrier between East and West dismantled after 28 years

The wall was erected by the East Germans to stem the tide of refugees to the West. By the night of August 12–13, 1961, when it first went up, some 2.5 million people had fled the Communist regime.

The Berlin Wall eventually became a system of walls up to 15 feet high (4.6 m), topped with barbed wire and guarded with watchtowers, gun emplacements, and mines. In addition there were electrified fences and other fortifications. The system stretched for 28 miles through the city, dividing it into two parts, and extended a further 75 miles around West Berlin, separating it from the rest of East Germany.

The Berlin Wall came to symbolize the Cold War's division of both Germany and Europe. About 5,000 East Germans managed to cross the Berlin Wall (by various means) and reach West Berlin safely, while another 5,000 were captured by East German authorities in the attempt and 191 more were killed during the actual crossing of the wall.

East Germany's hard-line Communist leadership was forced from power in October 1989 during the wave of democratization that swept through Eastern Europe. On November 9 the East German government opened the country's borders with West Germany (including West Berlin), and openings were made in the Berlin Wall through which East Germans could travel freely to the West. The photographs show East German border guards looking on as a man on top of the wall waves a German flag (left above) and civilians on the western side of the wall starting to dismantle it (left below). East and West Germany were soon reunited into a single country.

[5] *Soviet armor withdrawing from Afghanistan.*

[6] *A lone student confronts a tank at the entrance to Tiananmen Square the day after the shooting of the demonstrators there.*

1989
Yasser 'Arafat, chairman of the Palestine Liberation Organization (PLO), is nominated by its executive committee to the post of president of the newly proclaimed Palestinian state.

 [4]
January 7, 1989
Emperor Hirohito, who had been enthroned in 1926 and ruled during World War II and in democratic postwar Japan, dies. His death marks the end of an era, as he was the longest-reigning monarch in Japanese history.

 [5]
February 15, 1989
Under president **Mikhail Gorbachev**, the Soviet Union withdraws its last troops from Afghanistan after occupying the country since 1979.

 [6]
June 4, 1989
Massive student demonstrations in Beijing's **Tiananmen Square** are forcibly ended by Chinese authorities with the loss of hundreds of lives.

September 4, 1989
The National Aeronautics and Space Administration (NASA) and the U.S. Air Force launch the last **Titan III rocket**.

 [7]
October 17, 1989
An earthquake strikes **San Francisco**, California, killing more than 60, causing severe damage to the Marina District and to some freeways and even more devastation to surrounding areas. Modern office towers are largely unaffected.

1989
The **Society for Ecological Restoration (SER)** holds its first annual conference in Madison, Wisconsin. By the end of the 20th century the practice of healing damaged lands and waters will take on a new urgency.

1989
The oil tanker **Exxon Valdez** runs aground in Prince William Sound, Alaska. Strong winds and waves disperse its cargo, polluting thousands of miles of shoreline. The spill kills up to 500,000 birds, 2,800 to 5,000 sea otters, 300 harbor seals, and 250 bald eagles.
 [2]

1989
The U.S. Senate votes 92 to 0 to confirm the nomination of **Dick Cheney**, a Republican member of the House of Representatives, as secretary of defense.

1989
The U.S. Supreme Court, in a 5–4 decision, rules in effect that the **First Amendment** to the Constitution, which guarantees free speech, invalidates any laws prohibiting peaceful political activists from burning the U.S. flag in protest.

1989
The **United Nations Convention on the Rights of the Child** is passed by the General Assembly. One of the most popular human rights conventions, by 1995 it is ratified by 180 nations.

1989
Wayne Gretzky breaks Gordie Howe's National Hockey League all-time scoring record (1,850 points). He will finish his career in 1999 with 2,857 points.
 [3]

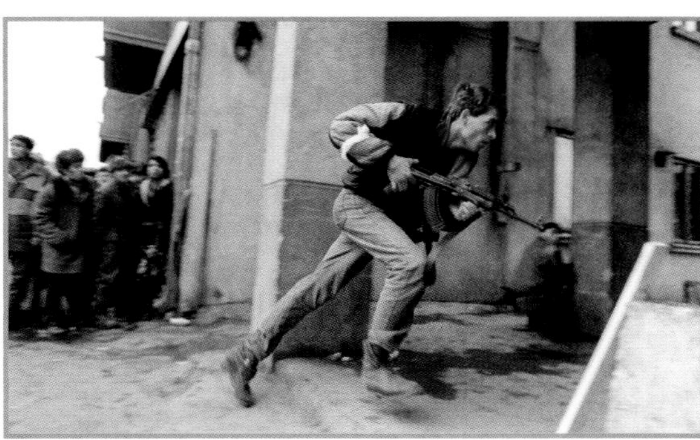

[1] *A freedom fighter pursues Securitate secret police in Bucharest on December 24, the day before Nicolae Ceausescu and his wife, Elena, are put before a firing squad.*

[2] *Skimming an oil slick from the* Exxon Valdez *in Prince William Sound, Alaska—part of its cargo of 11 million gallons of crude oil.*

[3] *Wayne Gretzky*

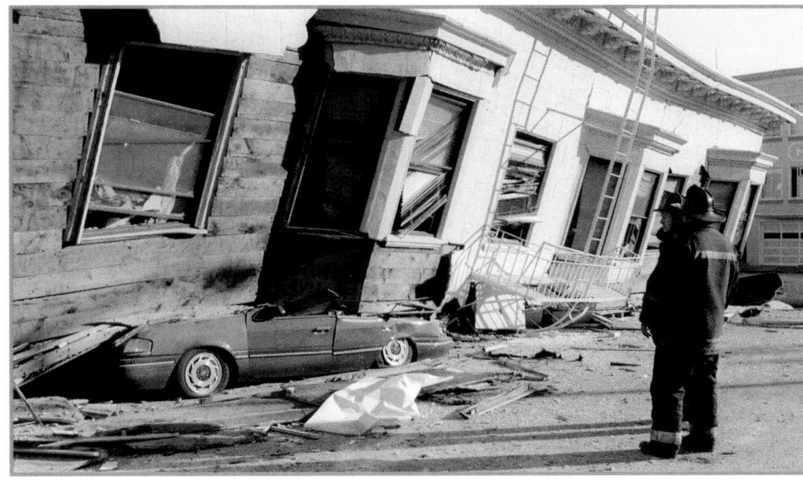

[7] *A scene reminiscent of the great San Francisco earthquake of 1906: a car crushed by a collapsed house there in 1989.*

[8] *Douglas Wilder in the garden of his residence.*

[9] *Czechoslovakian crowds celebrating the fall of the Communist regime in Wenceslaus Square, Prague.*

[4] *The new empress, Michiko, in deepest mourning, after meditating before the coffin of her father-in-law, Emperor Hirohito.*

 [8]
November 8, 1989
Douglas Wilder is elected governor of Virginia. He is the first African American to win a U.S. gubernatorial election. He will serve until 1994 and later be elected mayor of Richmond.

November 9, 1989
Long a symbol of the Cold War, the **Berlin Wall** is opened by the East German government.

 [9]
November 17, 1989
Massive antigovernment demonstrations in **Czechoslovakia** are set off by police brutality at a demonstration commemorating the 50th anniversary of a student demonstration in German-occupied Prague.

December 15, 1989
Antigovernment demonstrations erupt in Timisoara, **Romania**, beginning the revolution that topples the Communist leader Nicolae Ceausescu from power a few days afterward.

December 20, 1989
The United States launch **Operation Just Cause**, a military invasion of Panama, the initial attack focusing primarily on the Panama City headquarters of leader Manuel Noriega.

December 22, 1989
The **Brandenburg Gate** in Berlin is reopened, signifying the reunion of

East and West Germany.

A Chinese gymnast trains, 1993.

1990-1991

 [1]

1990
Conservative politician **John Major** becomes prime minister of the United Kingdom following the resignation of Margaret Thatcher.

 [2]

1990
British computer scientist Tim Berners-Lee develops the protocol for sharing information over the Internet that will become the **World Wide Web** (WWW) in 1991.

1990
An exhibit of the work of American photographer **Robert Mapplethorpe** draws criticism because of its sadomasochistic and homoerotic themes. It sparks a debate about government (National Endowment for the Arts) subsidies of "obscene" art.

1990
Kim Young Sam merges his Reunification Democratic Party in Korea with the ruling Democratic Justice Party of President Roh Tae Woo. As the candidate of this ruling Democratic Liberal Party, Kim will win election to the presidency in December 1992.

1990
Microsoft releases **Windows 3.0**, the first version that successfully supplants DOS.

 [3]

1990
The **Hubble** space telescope, a highly sophisticated optical observatory, is placed into orbit above the earth via the space shuttle *Discovery*. Unfortunately, a serious design flaw and several malfunctions are soon apparent.

[1] John Major and his wife, Norma, outside No. 10 Downing Street.

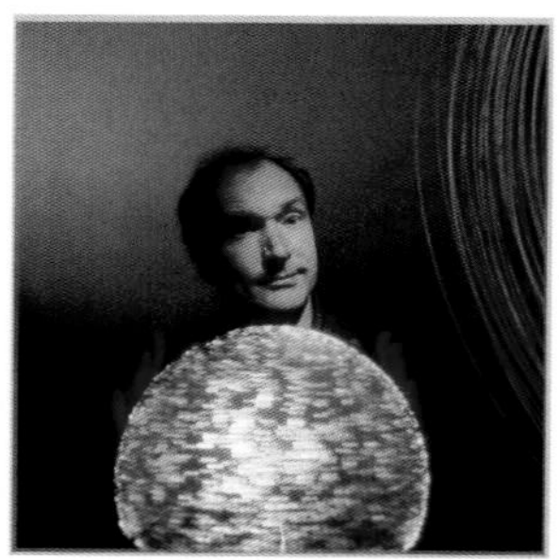

[2] Tim Berners-Lee, a physicist working at the European Nuclear Physics Centre, CERN, when he starts designing the World Wide Web.

[5] President Violeta Chamorro receives an AK-47 from a Contra guerrilla to symbolize an end to the fighting between Contras and Sandinistas in Nicaragua.

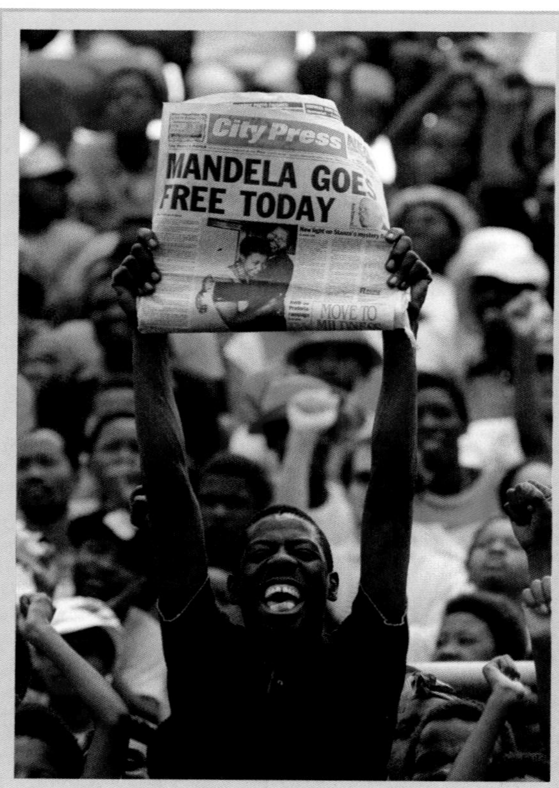

MANDELA RELEASED FROM PRISON

The release of the black nationalist leader heralds the end of apartheid in South Africa.

Nelson Mandela had originally been imprisoned in 1962 for advocating sabotage against the apartheid regime in South Africa. On June 12, 1964, while still in jail, he was sentenced to a life term for sabotage, treason, and violent conspiracy.

From 1964 to 1982 Mandela was incarcerated at Robben Island Prison, off Cape Town. He was subsequently kept at the maximum-security Pollsmoor Prison until 1988, at which time he was hospitalized for tuberculosis. Throughout his long confinement Mandela retained wide support among South Africa's black population, and his imprisonment became a cause célèbre among the international community that condemned apartheid.

Under mounting pressure from the international community, the South African government under President F. W. de Klerk released Mandela from prison on February 11, 1990. The joy of the black community was widespread and public (left). On March 2 Mandela was chosen as deputy president of the African National Council (ANC), and he replaced Oliver Tambo as president in July 1991. Mandela and de Klerk worked to end apartheid and bring about a peaceful transition to nonracial democracy in South Africa. In 1993 they were awarded the Nobel Peace Prize.

1990
West Germany defeats Argentina in the men's **World Cup** soccer championship by a score of 1 to 0.

1990
The world's total use of inanimate energy surpasses 80 billion megawatts, reflecting the spread of **high-energy societies** beyond Europe and North America.

c. 1990
Japan's "bubble" economy, based on easy credit and speculation, bursts, leading to years of economic **recession in Japan**.

c. 1990
The **world's population** surpasses five billion.

February 2, 1990
South African president **F. W. de Klerk** lifts the 30-year ban on the African National Congress, resulting in the release from prison of Nelson Mandela and marking the beginning of the end of apartheid.

 [5]

February 25, 1990
In Nicaragua, **Violeta Barrios de Chamorro** of the U.S.-financed National Opposition Union achieves an upset victory over the incumbent president, Daniel Ortega of the Sandinista National Liberation Front.

1990
The **Human Genome Project**, to map the location of all the genes on every chromosome in human beings, begins under the sponsorship of the U.S. Department of Energy and the National Institutes of Health.

1990
The National Institutes of Health's Recombinant DNA Advisory Committee approves the first **gene therapy** for humans, to treat adenosine deaminase deficiency and severe combined immunodeficiency.

1990
The U.S. Supreme Court finds that, in the absence of "clear and convincing evidence" of a person's desire to refuse **medical treatment** or not to live on life support, a state can require that such treatment continue.

1990
The United States passes the **Americans with Disabilities Act**, forbidding discrimination in employment and requiring "reasonable accommodation" in public facilities.

1990
The **video game industry**, only 20 years old, exceeds annual revenues of $10 billion.

1990
Three renowned operatic **tenors**—Luciano Pavarotti, José Carreras, and Plácido Domingo—give a concert in Rome on the eve of the World Cup final, with Zubin Mehta conducting. Their rousing success leads to a series of recordings and further concerts.

 [4]

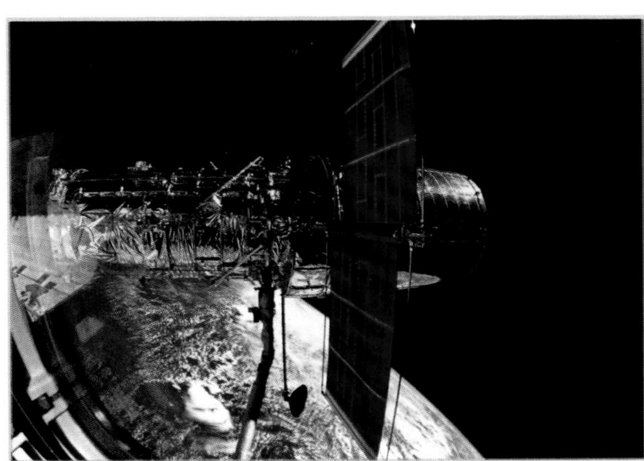

[3] *The Hubble space telescope still connected to* Discovery *by its remote manipulator system. Earth can be seen in the background.*

[8] *Lech Walesa roaring with laughter at a European Council press conference in Strasbourg.*

[4] *The Three Tenors rehearse for their concert in the Baths of Caracalla in Rome: (left to right) Placido Domingo, José Carreras, and Luciano Pavarotti.*

[6] *U.S. marines try out their chemical warfare protective clothing a few days after arriving in Saudi Arabia. The threat of Saddam Hussein using chemical weaponry is taken seriously.*

[7] *Emperor Akihito walks to a Shinto sanctuary within the Imperial Palace to report his enthronement to his ancestors.*

[9] *Mia Hamm. She does much to increase the popularity of U.S. women's soccer, playing for the National Team from 1987 until 2004.*

 [6]

August 2, 1990
Iraq invades Kuwait, and Saddam Hussein's subsequent refusal to withdraw his troops sparks the first Persian Gulf War. An international force led by the United States takes up position in Saudi Arabia.

October 3, 1990
Germany is reunified after four decades of Cold War division.

 [7]

November 12, 1990
Japanese **Emperor Akihito**—according to tradition, the 125th direct descendant of Jimmu, Japan's legendary first emperor—is formally enthroned, nearly two years after the death of his father, Hirohito.

 [8]

December 9, 1990
Lech Walesa—who led Solidarity, Poland's first independent trade union, and received the Nobel Peace Prize in 1983—wins Poland's first direct presidential election by a landslide.

1991
In **Rust v. Sullivan** the U.S. Supreme Court rules that Congress may not prohibit recipients of family-planning funds from providing or discussing abortion as a family-planning option.

 [9]

1991
Led by star forward Mia Hamm, the United States wins the first **women's soccer World Cup**.

1991
Paul Keating of the Labor Party becomes prime minister of Australia.

1991
Robert Venturi's **Sainsbury Wing** of the National Gallery, London, opens. Venturi's addition is respectful of the original building and bears the mark of the architect's unique style.

1991
Seattle-based rock band **Pearl Jam** releases its debut CD, *Ten.* The band's success marks the growing popularity of grunge rock, developed in Seattle in the 1980s.

 [1]

1991
The Nobel Peace Prize is awarded to Burmese opposition leader **Aung San Suu Kyi**, daughter of assassinated Burmese nationalist Aung San.

 [2]

1991
The **Strategic Arms Reduction Talks** call for the Soviets to reduce their arsenal of nuclear warheads and bombs by 25 percent and for the United States to reduce theirs by 15 percent.

1991
The United States defeats Norway in the **women's World Cup** soccer championship by a score of 2 to 1.

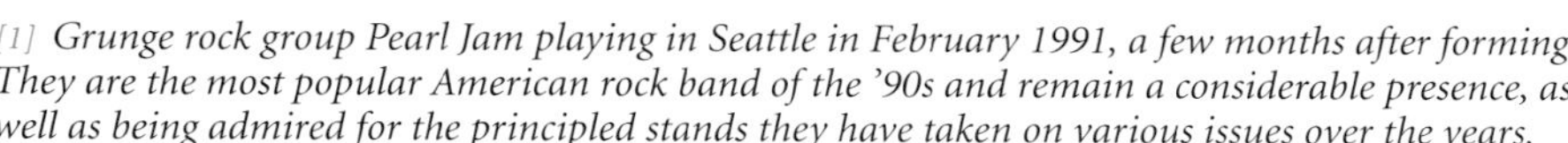

[1] Grunge rock group Pearl Jam playing in Seattle in February 1991, a few months after forming. They are the most popular American rock band of the '90s and remain a considerable presence, as well as being admired for the principled stands they have taken on various issues over the years.

[7] French Prime Minister Edith Cresson.

[2] Aung San Suu Kyi addresses supporters on her fourth day of freedom in July 1995 after nearly six years of house arrest.

[5] The Shining Path winds on. A Peruvian policeman stands by a bomb crater, one of several that the Shining Path exploded in Lima in May 1992. The windows of the building behind have been blown in.

[6] Chittagong, Bangladesh, in the aftermath of the cyclone, in which winds reached 143 mph.

March 31, 1991
For the first time since 1923, **Albanians** go to the polls to cast ballots in a free, multiparty election.

 [5]

April 5, 1991
Members of **Sendero Luminoso (Shining Path)**, a Peruvian Maoist guerilla group, attack a wide variety of targets in the capital city of Lima and cut off electricity to about half of the country's population.

April 24, 1991
Angola moves to end its civil war. Angolan president Jose Eduardo dos Santos voids his Popular Liberation Movement of Angola (MPLA) party's allegiance to Marxism-Leninism.

 [6]

April 30, 1991
A cyclone of terrifying proportions batters **Bangladesh** for some eight hours, leaving an estimated 138,000 people dead and millions of others homeless.

May 3, 1991
The **Swiss Federal Banking Commission** announces that by September 1992 most of the country's notorious secret bank accounts will be eliminated.

May 12, 1991
The Kingdom of **Nepal**, functioning under a new constitution that imposes unprecedented limits on the monarchy, holds its first multiparty election since 1959.

January 16, 1991
The **Persian Gulf War**, triggered by Iraq's occupation of Kuwait in August 1990, begins with a U.S.-led air offensive against Iraq that continues until a cease-fire is declared on February 28.

 [3]

February 24, 1991
U.S. ground operations begin in the Persian Gulf War, more than a month after an air war is launched against Iraq to free Iraqi-occupied **Kuwait**.

 [4]

March 15, 1991
The French government announces that Western nations have agreed to write off about 50 percent of the $33 billion owed to them by **Poland**.

March 18, 1991
Mexican president Carlos Salinas orders an immediate shutdown of the largest oil refinery in **Mexico City** to eliminate one of the worst sources of pollution in the capital.

March 19, 1991
Ethnic Kurds living in northern Iraq report the capture of **Kirkuk**, the country's fourth largest city and the site of a major oil facility. However, this Kurdish uprising and the Shia one in the South are brutally attacked by Saddam Hussein.

March 22, 1991
General Moussa Traore, president of Mali since 1968, declares a state of emergency in an effort to stifle the worst antigovernment riots in the West African nation's history.

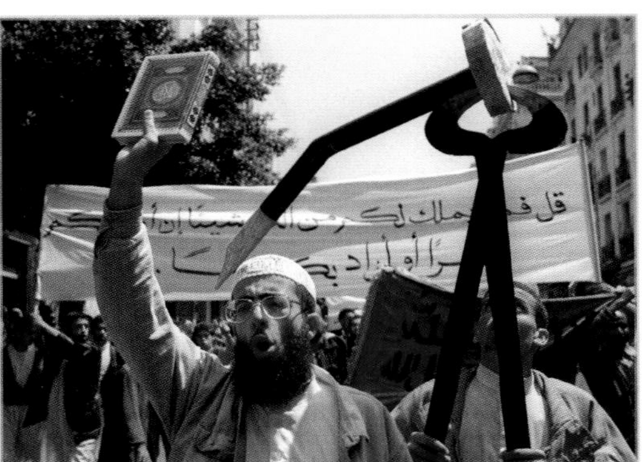

[10] An Islamic Salvation Front member brandishes the Koran during a demonstration in Algiers. The pliers hold a bent nail, which presumably symbolizes the Algerian government that must be forcibly removed.

[4] A dug-in Iraqi tank burns as U.S. forces drive by.

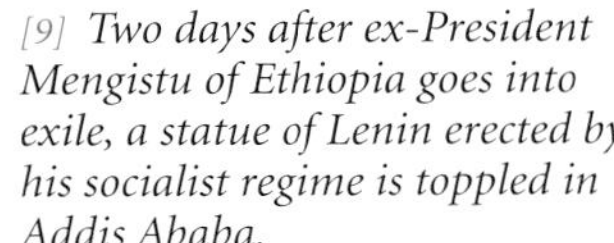

[9] Two days after ex-President Mengistu of Ethiopia goes into exile, a statue of Lenin erected by his socialist regime is toppled in Addis Ababa.

[8] Rajiv Gandhi campaigning in the 1991 Indian elections five days before he is assassinated by a Sri Lankan Tamil in southern India, in revenge for Indian forces having aided the Sri Lankan army against the Tamil Tigers.

[3] An attack bomber on the aircraft carrier USS John Kennedy *about to be launched by catapult for a mission against Iraqi targets.*

 [7]

May 15, 1991
Edith Cresson of the Socialist Party becomes the first female premier of France, but she will lose the office because of rising unemployment and declining support from within her party.

 [8]

May 21, 1991
During the most violent political campaign in India's history, **Rajiv Gandhi**, who is seeking to become prime minister for a second time, is assassinated.

 [9]

May 21, 1991
Lieutenant Colonel **Mengistu Haile Mariam**, president of Ethiopia, announces his resignation and then flees by plane to Zimbabwe.

May 31, 1991
Angolan president Jose Eduardo dos Santos and Jonas Savimbi, head of the insurgent National Union for the Total Independence of Angola **(UNITA)**, sign a peace agreement to end the 16-year-old civil war.

June 3, 1991
France announces that it has decided to add its name to a 1968 treaty banning the proliferation of nuclear weapons.

 [10]

June 5, 1991
Algerian president **Chadi Bendjedid**, reacting to 12 consecutive days of rioting by Islamic fundamentalists in Algiers, the nation's capital, declares a state of emergency and postpones elections.

1991

June 12, 1991
Boris Yeltsin is easily elected president of Russia in the republic's first direct, popular elections. He will remain president of independent Russia after the breakup of the Soviet Union.

 [1]

June 12, 1991
Mount Pinatubo, a volcano situated about 55 miles northwest of Manila, begins to erupt after being dormant for more than 600 years.

 [2]

June 17, 1991
South Africa's all-white House of Assembly, in a historic vote, voids the 41-year-old **Population Registration Act**, which had classified South Africans by race.

June 20, 1991
The Bundestag (parliament), in a major political decision, votes 337 to 320 to make **Berlin** the federal capital of reunited Germany.

 [3]

June 25, 1991
Slovenia and **Croatia** declare their independence from Yugoslavia. After a few days' fighting with the Yugoslav army, Slovenia is left alone but a bitter conflict begins in Croatia.

 [4]

July 7, 1991
King Hussein of Jordan restores most of the freedoms that had been curtailed when he declared martial law during the 1967 Arab-Israeli war: freedom of speech, freedom of the press, and the right of public assembly.

[1] Russian democracy. Boris Yeltsin and his wife on their way to cast their votes in the election that will make him Russian president.

[3] The German flag flies over the restored Reichstag building in Berlin, home of the German Parliament after reunification and the move from Bonn. "The German People" is proclaimed under the pediment.

[2] A spectacular cloud of volcanic ash and smoke towers up over Mount Pinatubo, seen from the U.S.'s Clark Air Base.

[4] Serbian artillery shells Croatian targets.

[7] Gorbachev speaks on August 24 at the funeral of three killed in the coup that tried to topple him. On the same day, he resigns as head of the Soviet Communist Party.

September 23, 1991
Some 3,000 **Zairian paratroopers** go on a two-day looting and arson spree in the capital city of Kinshasa.

September 25, 1991
During a meeting in New York, presided over by the U.N. Secretary-General, President Alfredo Cristiani of **El Salvador** and five guerrilla commanders approve a blueprint for the country's political and economic future.

 [8]

October 15, 1991
After controversial hearings, the U.S. Senate narrowly votes 52 to 48 to confirm **Clarence Thomas's nomination** to the U.S. Supreme Court. Thomas is the second African American to serve on the court.

October 23, 1991
Representatives of the four factions that have been waging war for years over control of **Cambodia** move closer to a final resolution of their differences by signing a formal peace treaty in Paris.

October 27, 1991
Japan's ruling Liberal-Democratic Party (LDP) chooses 72-year-old **Kiichi Miyazawa** to be the nation's new prime minister.

 [9]

October 29, 1991
Great Britain and Vietnam, after months of negotiations, sign an agreement that sanctions the forcible repatriation of tens of thousands of **Vietnamese refugees** being held in detention centers in Hong Kong.

July 10, 1991
President George H. W. Bush announces that he is lifting the **economic sanctions** that the U.S. imposed on South Africa in 1986.

August 8, 1991
John McCarthy, a 34-year old British television journalist, is set free in Lebanon after being held hostage for more than five years by Islamic Jihad, a pro-Iranian group of terrorists.

 [5]

August 19, 1991
Hard-liners among top-ranking Soviet officials attempt to overthrow Soviet president Mikhail Gorbachev while he is vacationing in the Crimea. He returns to **Moscow** the following day, badly shaken but determined to punish those who conspire to overthrow him.

 [6]

August 24, 1991
Mikhail Gorbachev resigns as general secretary of the Communist Party. Although he does not call for the abolition of the party or cancel his own party membership, he deliberately inflicts irreparable damage on it.

 [7]

August 28, 1991
Thirteen former high-ranking Soviet officials are charged with high treason for their actual or suspected involvement in the **failed coup** against President Mikhail Gorbachev.

September 19, 1991
The U.N. Security Council votes 13 to 1 to allow **Iraq** to sell up to $1.6 billion worth of oil over a six-month period.

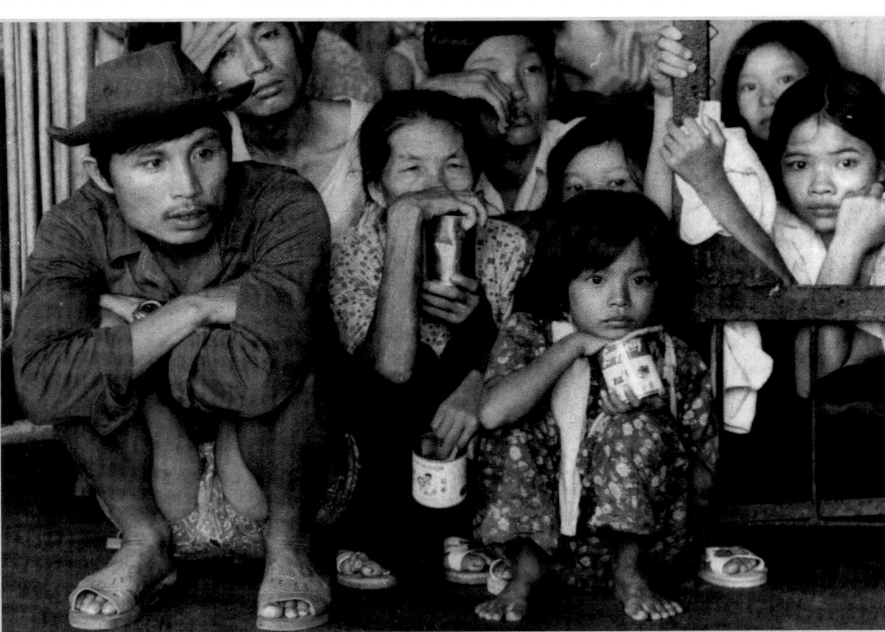

[9] Vietnamese "boat people" held at the government dockyard in Hong Kong.

[6] A defiant Yeltsin rallies Russia behind him, speaking from the top of a tank in front of the Russian Federation building in Moscow after the military coup launched against President Gorbachev on August 19, 1991.

[8] Clarence Thomas gives the thumbs up while President George H. W. Bush applauds after Thomas is sworn in as a justice of the Supreme Court.

[11] Kenneth Kaunda speaking in Angola in 1990, the year before he ceases to be president of Zambia.

[10] Hannah Ashrawi, member of the Palestinian delegation to the Madrid talks and for many years a familiar face on Western TV news programs speaking for Palestinians.

[5] A happy return. Released hostage John McCarthy, his father beside him, waves from the steps of the plane that has brought him back from Beirut to England.

[12] Terry Anderson makes it onto the cover of Time *magazine after being held captive for over six and a half years in Lebanon.*

 [10]

October 30, 1991
Representatives of Israel, the Arab nations, and the Palestinians sit down together in Spain's Royal Palace in Madrid to begin **Middle East peace talks**.

 [11]

October 31, 1991
Kenneth Kaunda, who has been Zambia's only ruler since it gained independence from Britain in 1964, loses the presidency by a wide margin to Frederic Chiluba.

November 5, 1991
An estimated three million to four million black workers in **South Africa** end a two-day strike called by the African National Congress (ANC) and the Congress of South African Trade Unions (COSATU).

November 9, 1991
A team of European scientists at the Joint European Toru laboratory in Oxfordshire, England, produce a record amount of energy from a controlled **nuclear-fusion** reaction.

November 27, 1991
Khieu Samphan, Cambodia's head of state during the Khmer Rouge reign of terror, is severely beaten by a mob just after he returns as a Khmer Rouge representative on the new Supreme National Council.

 [12]

December 4, 1991
Associated Press correspondent **Terry Anderson**, a U.S. hostage held by Muslim terrorists in Lebanon, is set free by Islamic Jihad after 2,455 days in captivity.

1991-1992

December 16, 1991
The **United Nations** General Assembly votes 111 to 25 in favor of a U.S.-sponsored proposal to repeal its November 1975 resolution that specifically identified Zionism as a form of racism and racial discrimination.

December 18, 1991
Mexico's Chamber of Deputies overwhelmingly approves constitutional changes that will end more than 70 years of official government hostility towards the Roman Catholic Church.

December 25, 1991
Mikhail Gorbachev resigns the presidency of the Soviet Union.

December 31, 1991
The Soviet Union legally ceases to exist, **Russia** and other former Soviet republics having declared themselves independent and having founded the Commonwealth of Independent States on December 21, 1991.

December 31, 1991
Prolonged efforts to end the 12-year-old civil war in **El Salvador** succeed at the U.N. headquarters in New York City when President Alfredo Cristiani and the leaders of the five leftist armies reach a peace agreement.

1992
After 151 years, the British satirical magazine **Punch** stops publication.

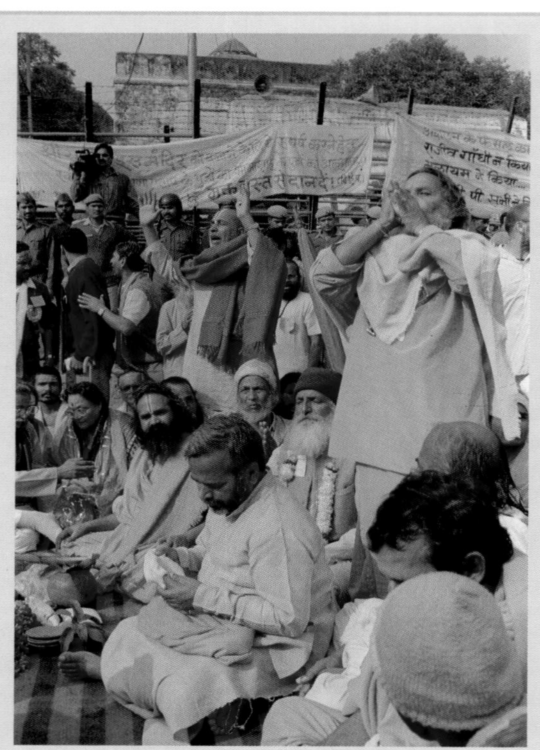

HINDU-MUSLIM RIOTS

Tensions between India's two main religious groups erupt in violence.

The 16th-century Babri Mosjid (Mosque of Babur) at Ayodhya, in the northern Indian state of Uttar Pradesh, had long been a source of resentment by Hindus, who claimed that the Muslims had built it after razing a temple.

After demonstrations outside the building (above), a mob of militant Hindus tore down the mosque; the subsequent rioting spread throughout the country and led to the deaths of more than 1,000 people.

Although there was real religious fervor associated with the belief that the site of the mosque was the birthplace of the Hindu god Rama, the attack was above all a reflection of the Hindu nationalists' belief in the essentially Hindu character of India and their perception of Muslims as inherently alien.

[5] Fireworks over Sleeping Beauty's Castle at Euro Disney.

[2] Edward O. Wilson. His ideas on the sociological basis of behavior are derived from his systematic study of ants.

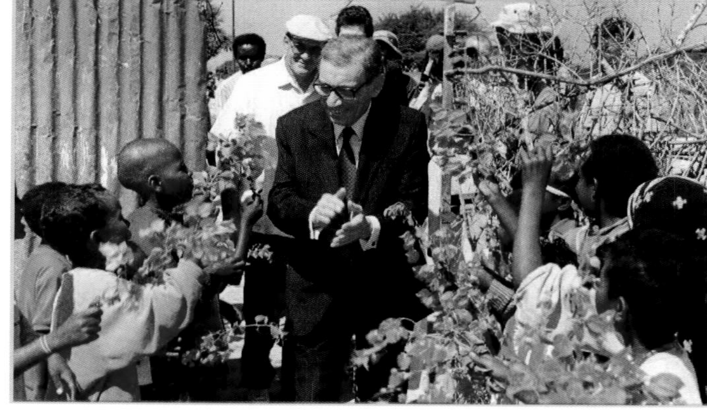

[4] Boutros Boutros-Ghali welcomed by Somali children near Mogadishu.

1992
Continued globalization of the **automobile industry** leads to opening of Japanese manufacturing plants in the United Kingdom and the United States and restructuring among European firms.

1992
Disneyland Paris opens and will become Europe's busiest attraction.

1992
FBI agents shoot and kill the wife of white supremacist Randy Weaver and wound several others who have holed up in a cabin in **Ruby Ridge**, Idaho. Weaver's son and a deputy U.S. marshal have already been killed in a shootout.

1992
France **bans smoking** in selected public places, but the law is largely ignored.

1992
Gary S. Becker becomes the third University of Chicago professor to win the Nobel Prize in Economics.

1992
Hindu nationalists attack a Muslim mosque in **Ayodhya**, India, sparking Hindu-Muslim riots throughout much of India, Pakistan, and Bangladesh.

1992
The **Mall of America**, the largest shopping mall in the world, opens in Bloomington, Minnesota, near Minneapolis. Its approximately 400 stores attract shoppers from around the world.

1992
American biologist Edward O. Wilson's **The Diversity of Life** is published. He traces how the world's living species became diverse and examines the massive species extinctions caused by human activities in the 20th century.

 [2]

1992
Tony Kushner's **Angels in America** opens in Los Angeles. The play addresses controversial themes of homosexuality, AIDS, and politics during the conservative Reagan era. It will win Tony Awards and be produced for television.

1992
Jockey **Angel Cordero, Jr.**, retires. The Puerto Rico–born 49-year-old has ridden more than 7,000 races, won each of the Triple Crown races at least once, and has become one of the greatest jockeys in U.S. horse-racing history.

 [3]

1992
Both **Canada** and **Australia** move to restrict immigration in the face of high domestic unemployment.

1992
Boutros Boutros-Ghali of Egypt becomes the secretary general of the U.N. He will serve until 1996.

 [4]

[3] Angel Cordero waves as he walks beside trainer D. Wayne Lukas.

[8] President George H. W. Bush (left) and Fidel Castro, forced into each other's company, even if they studiously avoid recognizing each other, at the Rio Earth Summit.

[6] Gary S. Becker. His Nobel lecture is titled "The Economic Way of Looking at Behavior."

[1] A Russian crowd makes it plain that the Soviet era is over: no red flags, but the new Russian tricolor instead, and the cancelled-out portrait of Gorbachev, the last Soviet president.

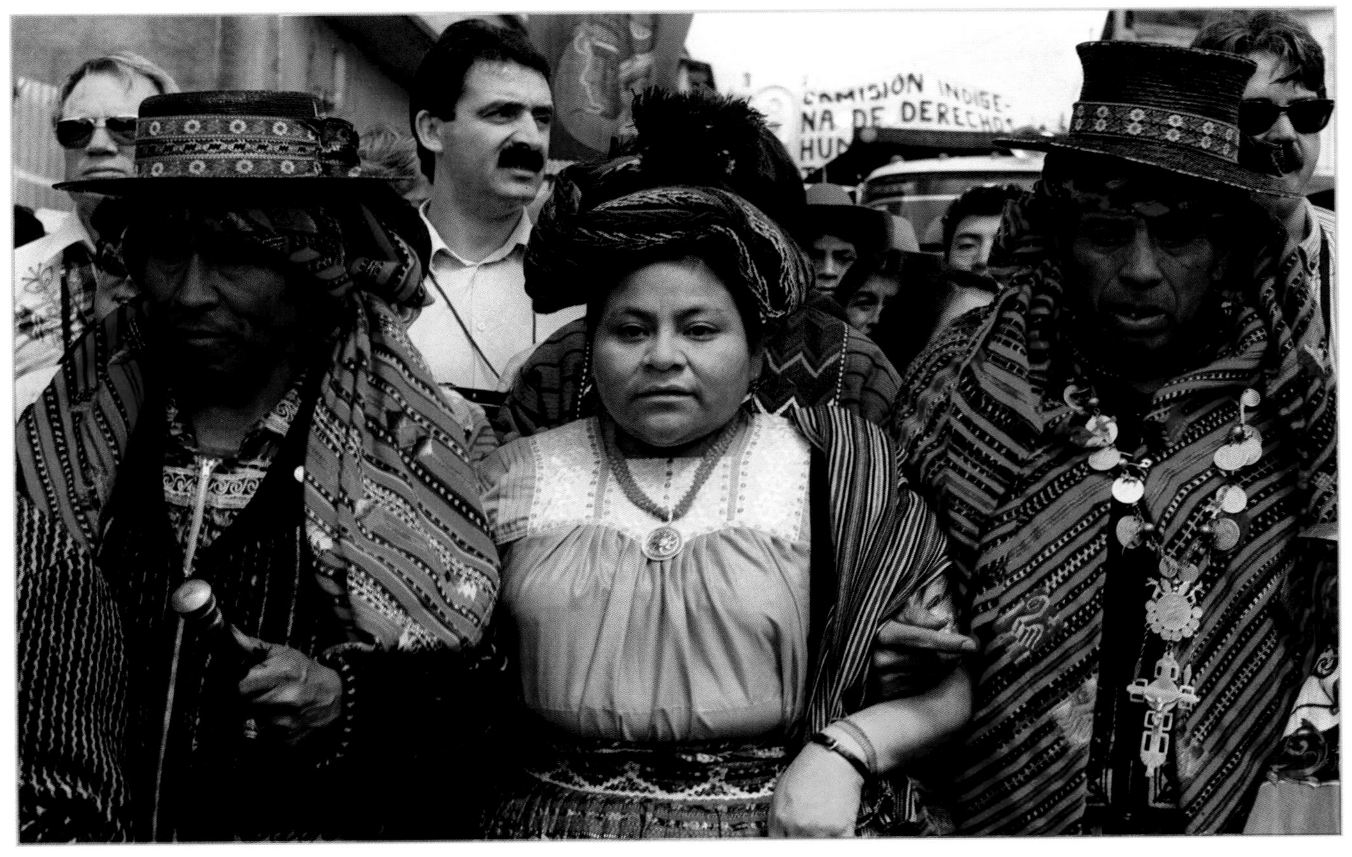

[7] Rigoberta Menchú (center) demonstrates with Guatemalan Indians.

1992
The U.S. Supreme Court finds that some **state regulation of abortion** prior to fetal viability, including a 24-hour waiting period, mandatory counseling, and a parental-consent requirement for minors, is permissible.

1992
The **North American Free Trade Agreement (NAFTA)** is signed. It will gradually eliminate most tariffs and other trade barriers on products and services passing between the United States, Canada, and Mexico.

 [7]

1992
Rigoberta Menchú, a Guatemalan Indian-rights activist, wins the Nobel Peace Prize. She continues to campaign for indigenous rights worldwide, although her credibility will be challenged.

 [8]

1992
Rio de Janeiro hosts the U.N. Conference on Environment and Development (UNCED), popularly known as the **Earth Summit**, to reconcile economic development with protection of the environment.

1992
Tadao Ando's Japan Pavilion opens in Expo '92, Seville, Spain. It showcases Ando's ability to meld Western and Japanese architectural ideas and his fascination with space and light.

1992
The ambitious 106-mile **Europa Canal** opens, linking the Danube and Main rivers, allowing barges to move from the North Sea to the Black Sea. Its 16 locks, south of Nuremberg, raise boats 1,332 feet.

1992-1993

1992
The **Summer Olympic Games** take place in Barcelona, Spain. They are the first Summer Games since 1972 unaffected by a political boycott.

 [1]

1992
The Pequot Indians open the **Foxwoods Casino** in Connecticut. Within a few years Indian-owned casinos will challenge Las Vegas and Atlantic City as casino gambling snowballs in the U.S.

1992
The British rock quintet **Radiohead** releases the album *Creep*. The group's trademark experimentation with rock's sonic possibilities will begin in earnest on its masterpiece album *OK Computer* (1997).

1992
The U.S. Department of Agriculture introduces its controversial **food pyramid**. This innovative graphic approach to nutrition education is widely copied and imitated. Critics will detect the hand of agribusiness in the details.

1992
The **Winter Olympic Games** take place in Albertville, France.

1992
West Indian poet, playwright, journalist, and painter **Derek Walcott** wins the Nobel Prize for Literature.

[1] *A diver at the Olympic park, with Barcelona forming the background.*

[2] *Radiohead: singer Thom Yorke in front with (left to right) Phil Selway, Ed O'Brian, Colin Greenwood, and Johnny Greenwood.*

[3] *Derek Walcott*

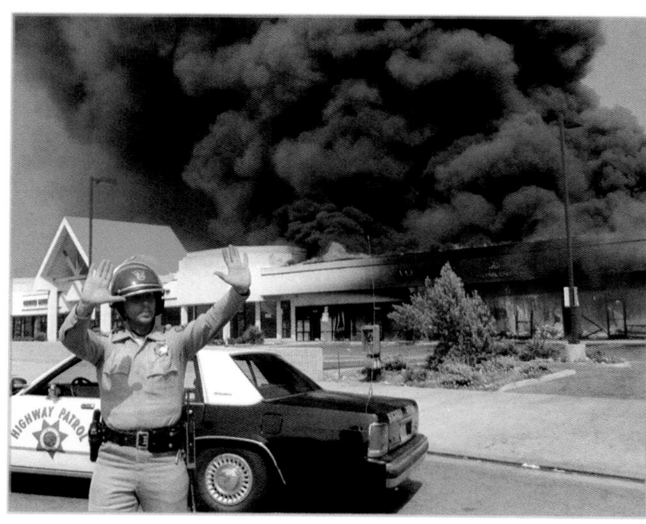

[6] *A California highway patrolman diverts traffic around a burning shopping center in Los Angeles.*

[9] *A "forex"—foreign-exchange dealer—in the city of London shouts orders to buy or sell on Black Wednesday.*

[7] *A Miami apartment block with its front ripped off by Hurricane Andrew.*

 [6]

April 29, 1992
A suburban jury acquits four Los Angeles policemen on charges connected with the beating of **Rodney King**, a black motorist they arrested. Within hours riots erupt in Los Angeles.

May 18, 1992
The **Twenty-seventh Amendment** to the U.S. Constitution, stipulating that Congress may not increase its pay without an intervening election, is ratified.

June 20, 1992
A new constitution goes into effect in **Paraguay**, signaling the end of military rule established in the 1950s by Alfredo Stroessner.

 [7]

August 1992
Hurricane Andrew strikes the Bahamas and South Florida, leaving 250,000 homeless and causing record-breaking property damage.

August 24, 1992
South Korea and China agree in Beijing to establish diplomatic relations. Korea's existing ties with **Taiwan** are immediately severed.

  [8]

August 28, 1992
A fleet of U.S. military cargo planes begins delivering supplies to 1.5 million **Somalis** facing starvation after internal conflicts. More than 1,000 people a day are dying. In December 28,000 U.S. troops arrive in Somalia.

January 1992
R.H. Macy Company files for bankruptcy. The company will merge with Federated Department Stores in 1994.

February 1, 1992
U.S. president George H. W. Bush and Russian president Boris Yeltsin sign a statement of general principles that bring an end to the **Cold War**. The leaders agree to "work to remove any remnants of Cold War hostility."

March 3, 1992
Bosnia and Herzegovina declares its independence, and the focus of the Balkan War switches from Croatia, one third of which is now under Serbian control. The siege of Sarajevo begins, as does "ethnic cleansing" by the Serbs.

March 17, 1992
Nearly 69 percent of white **South African voters** back F. W. de Klerk's reforms—which include the repeal of racially discriminatory laws—and effectively endorse the dismantling of apartheid.

March 26, 1992
Heavyweight boxing champion **Mike Tyson** is sentenced to six years in prison following a rape conviction in Indianapolis, Indiana.

April 5, 1992
A **pro-choice rally** sponsored by the National Organization for Women brings an estimated 750,000 people to Washington, D.C., to resist antiabortion regulation.

WAR IN BOSNIA

A new phase in the dissolution of Yugoslavia

After declaring independence from Yugoslavia, Bosnia and Herzegovina faced growing tensions between its three main groups: Bosniacs (44% of the population); Serbs (33%); and Croats (18%). The world's leading nations proposed various solutions to the mounting crisis, but none was acceptable to all parties. Finally, the Bosnian government rejected the idea of "safe havens" for Bosniacs within the Serbian and Croatian territories and launched an offensive against Croat troops. The Bosniacs made considerable headway against the Croats, although the latter managed to hold on to the strategic city of Mostar, where Croatian shelling destroyed the 16th-century bridge that had connected the Bosniac and Croat parts of the city. The Serbs, meanwhile, besieged Sarajevo. The photograph (left) shows a Bosnian soldier in the city returning Serbian sniper fire; moments later, the soldier was killed.

[4] Presidents Bush (right) and Yeltsin in Washington when the latter is on an official visit in June 1992.

[5] Mike Tyson leaves the courtroom during his trial.

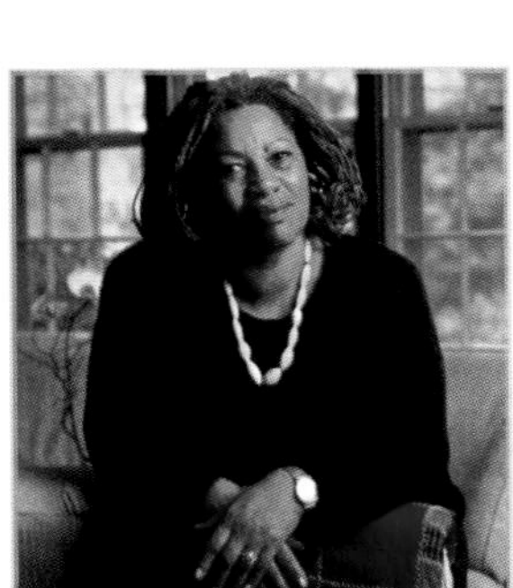

[10] Toni Morrison

[8] Starving Somali children.

September 3, 1992
The **Chemical Weapons Convention**, banning the use of chemical weapons in war and also prohibiting all development, production, acquisition, stockpiling, or transfer of such weapons, is adopted by the United Nations.

September 16, 1992
John Major withdraws Britain from the European exchange-rate mechanism and devalues the pound on what is dubbed "**Black Wednesday**."

1993
The European community removes further trade barriers to create the **European Single Market**.

1993
Melchior Ndadaye, president of Burundi, is slain in a coup.

1993
A U.S. Senate committee issues its final report on the fate of hundreds of U.S. servicemen listed as **missing in action** during the Vietnam War. The report indicates that there is no strong evidence that any are still being held captive.

1993
American novelist **Toni Morrison** wins the Nobel Prize for Literature for "breaking the male domination of Black American literature."

1993

1993
An exhibit of **Lucian Freud's** work opens at New York City's Metropolitan Museum of Art, generating controversy for its realistic and intense nudes.

1993
Computer programmer Marc Andreessen develops the first **browser** for displaying text and images over the Internet.

1993
William J. Clinton of the Democratic Party becomes the 42nd president of the United States. His vice president is Albert Gore, Jr.

 [1]

1993
Construction begins on the **Three Gorges Dam**, to be the world's largest hydroelectric project, on the Yangtze River in China, after nearly 40 years of planning and controversy.

 [2]

1993
Serbian tropps attack a U.N. safe area of Gorazde, and there is much fighting around Mostar during the ongoing civil war in **Bosnia and Herzegovina**.

 [3]

1993
Hosokawa Morihiro becomes Japan's first non–Liberal Democratic Party prime minister since 1955.

[2] The Three Gorges Dam, scheduled to be fully operational in 2011. It involves the displacement of 1.5 million people, and there are major concerns about silt accumulation at the foot of the dam.

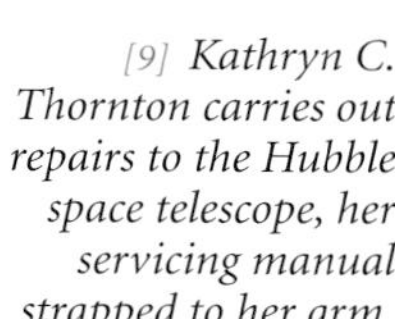

[9] Kathryn C. Thornton carries out repairs to the Hubble space telescope, her servicing manual strapped to her arm.

[3] A mosque in central Bosnia, near Vitez, destroyed in fighting between Bosnian Croat and Bosnian Muslim forces, with a French-manned United Nations vehicle in front. It is only in 1994 that the U.S. brokers peace between these two forces, and they unite against Bosnian Serbs.

 [7]

1993
Sears, Roebuck and Company ends publication of its mail-order catalog, "**the big book**," after 97 years.

1993
President Bill Clinton signs the **Brady Handgun Violence Protection Act**. The new law establishes a five-day waiting period before anyone can purchase a handgun.

1993
President Bill Clinton proposes a "**don't ask, don't tell**" policy, allowing gay men and lesbians to serve in the military so long as they refrain from any open expressions of their sexual orientation.

1993
Several developers introduce versions of the **PDA**, or personal digital assistant. This palm-size computer is notable for having no keyboard. Instead, users write on its plastic screen with a special pen, and software then converts the handwriting to type.

1993
Steven Spielberg's **Jurassic Park** replaces his *E.T.: The Extraterrestrial* as the highest-grossing motion picture of all time.

1993
Czechoslovakia is dissolved. The Czech Republic and Slovakia take its place. Vaclav Havel, the former president of Czechoslovakia, becomes president of the Czech Republic, while Michal Kovac becomes president of Slovakia.

1993
Tansu Ciller becomes the first woman prime minister of Turkey.

 *[4]*

1993
Kim Campbell becomes the first woman prime minister of Canada.

 *[5]*

1993
Mathematician Andrew Wiles announces a proof of **Fermat's last theorem**, one of the oldest puzzles in mathematics. Two years later, Wiles publishes a stronger, definitive version of the proof.

1993
Microsoft's operating system Windows 3.0 and its subsequent versions are selling at a rate of one million copies per month, and nearly 90 percent of the world's PCs run on a **Microsoft** operating system.

1993
Motion-picture director **Federico Fellini** dies. He is remembered for his many films, including *La Strada* (1954; *The Road*), *Le notti di Cabiria* (1957; *The Nights of Cabiria*), and *La Dolce Vita* (1960; *The Sweet Life*).

 *[6]*

1993
Paraguay holds the first democratic elections in the country's history. The ruling Colorado Party wins, but opposition candidates collectively win almost 60 percent of the vote.

[1] Bill Clinton plays the sax at an inaugural week ball.

[4] Tansu Ciller with President Clinton.

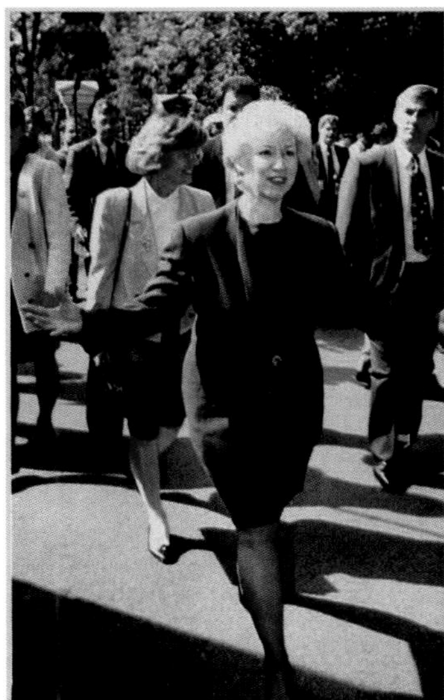

[5] Kim Campbell, prime minister of Canada.

[7] The cover of the 1942 Sears, Roebuck catalog.

[6] Federico Fellini

[8] H. Ty Warner, the entrepreneur responsible for Beanie Babies, holds the product.

 *[8]*

1993
The first **Beanie Baby** is sold at a toy fair. The animal-shaped beanbags create a frenzy among collectors around the world, and in 1996 an estimated 100 million will be sold.

1993
Ireland and Britain sign the **Downing Street Declaration**. They pledge to seek mutually agreeable political structures in Northern Ireland and between the two islands. The IRA declares a cease-fire in 1994.

1993
The United States and Russia sign the **Strategic Arms Reduction Treaty** (START II), calling for total elimination of land-based multiple-warhead missiles and a two-thirds reduction in long-range nuclear weapons.

1993
The **Vitra** furniture factory complex opens in Weil am Rhein, Germany. Its many notable buildings include a fire station designed by Iraqi-born deconstructivist architect Zaha Hadid.

 *[9]*

1993
U.S. astronauts repair the **Hubble space telescope**, which was launched in 1990 but has not worked as well as planned since that time.

1993
Vice President **Al Gore** dedicates a bronze sculpture in Washington, D.C., in honor of the 11,500 women who served their country during the Vietnam War.

1993

1993
Voters in **Puerto Rico** choose to keep the territory's status as a U.S. commonwealth rather than become the 51st state.

1993
At least 12 U.S. soldiers are killed and at least 75 are wounded in a 15-hour battle with the rebel forces of Somali warlord General Muhammad Farah Aydid. The losses lead to a promise by President Bill Clinton to pull U.S. troops out of **Somalia**.

 [1]

c. 1993
Saudi-born **Osama bin Laden** forms a terrorist network known as al-Qaeda (Arabic: "the Base"), which consists largely of militant Muslims bin Laden has met in Afghanistan, where he has gone to fight against the Soviet occupation.

 [2]

February 11, 1993
Janet Reno is nominated by President Bill Clinton to head the Department of Justice as U.S. attorney general. She becomes the first woman to head the nation's highest law-enforcement agency.

 [3]

February 26, 1993
The **World Trade Center** in New York City is bombed; Islamic radicals are later convicted for the crime.

March 1993
President **Boris Yeltsin** of Russia escapes being impeached when his opponents are unable to get a two-thirds vote. Later in the year his opponents take over the Parliament building after Yeltsin dissolves the Parliament.

[4]

[1] A Somali woman carrying a rocket-propelled grenade launcher to the forces of warlord Muhammad Farah Aydid in Mogadishu.

[10] Michael Jordan goes up for two.

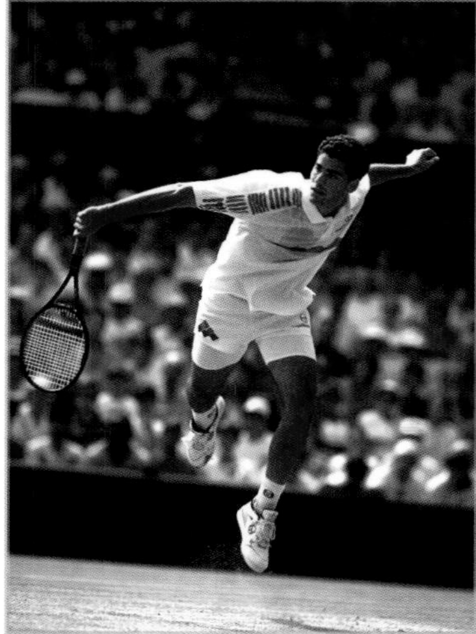

[6] Pete Sampras—the dominant figure in men's tennis.

[2] Osama bin Laden

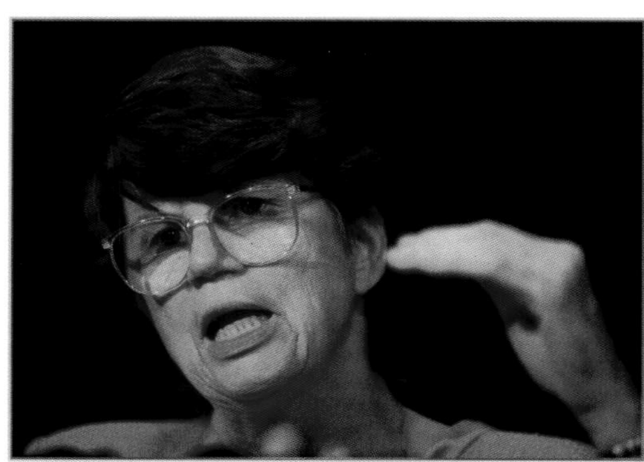

[3] Janet Reno

[4] The Parliament Building, the White House, in Moscow with the tanks called up by President Yeltsin to bombard his opponents inside into submission. Evidence of the shelling can be seen as smoke pours from some windows.

May 1, 1993
Sri Lankan president **Ranasinghe Premadasa** is killed along with most of his bodyguards and several aides when a man detonates explosives strapped to his body. Suspicion quickly falls on the Tamil Tigers.

May 27, 1993
A terrorist bomb goes off in **Florence**, damaging a wing of the famous Uffizi Gallery.

June 1993
Kiichi Miyazawa resigns as Liberal Democratic Party leader and prime minister of Japan, and in the ensuing general elections the LDP will lose control of the Diet for the first time in its 38-year history.

 [8]

June 9, 1993
Japan's crown prince Naruhito marries **Masako Owada**, a commoner who gave up a career in Japan's Foreign Ministry to marry the prince.

August 3, 1993
The U.S. Senate confirms (96–3) Bill Clinton's nomination of **Ruth Bader Ginsburg** to the U.S. Supreme Court. She is only the second woman to serve on the nation's highest court.

August 4, 1993
Rwandan president **Juvenal Habyarimana** and two leaders of the rebel Rwandan Patriotic Front sign a peace accord in Tanzania designed to end three years of civil conflict between the majority Hutu tribe and the Tutsi.

March 12, 1993
A series of bombings in western **India** destroys many buildings, including several floors of the Bombay Stock Exchange. More than 300 people are killed and 2,000 injured in what is called the worst wave of criminal violence in India's history.
 [5]

April 12, 1993
Pete Sampras becomes the top-ranked tennis player in the world. Later this year he will set men's tennis tour records with 1,011 aces (unreachable first serves), earnings of $3,648,075, and a margin of 683 points ahead of second-ranked Michael Stich.
 [6]

April 15, 1993
The **Allen Guttmacher Institute** publishes a survey finding that males who describe themselves as exclusively homosexual make up 1 percent of the population. For decades the 10 percent figure from the1948 Kinsey Report was assumed relatively accurate.

April 19, 1993
Some 80 members of the **Branch Davidians**, an apocalyptic cult led by David Koresh, are killed in a confrontation with the FBI near Waco, Texas.

April 23, 1993
After a long history of foreign rule and decades of war, the small East African country of **Eritrea** begins three days of voting on a referendum to make official its independence from Ethiopia.
 [7]

May 1993
To prevent further acts of **ethnic cleansing** and to restore peace and security to the Balkan region, the U.N. Security Council establishes a criminal tribunal to prosecute persons responsible for serious violations of international humanitarian law.

[5] Outside the Air India offices in Bombay after the bombings. They are thought to have been organized by a conjunction of Islamic militants and Bombay gangsters in revenge for the destruction in 1992 of the Ayodhya mosque and subsequent rioting.

[8] The crown prince of Japan with his bride.

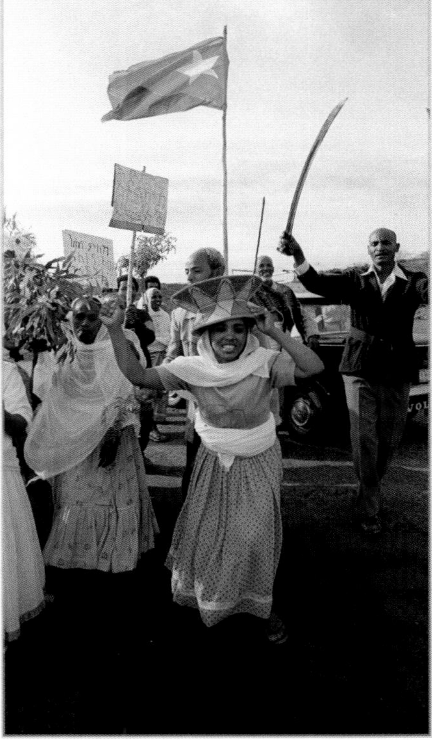

[7] Eritreans celebrate the independence referendum result in Massawa. An Italian colony, Eritrea was administered by the British until 1952 and had been part of Ethiopia since then.

[9] Yitzhak Rabin (left) and Yasser Arafat shake hands, encouraged by Bill Clinton. Arafat has formally renounced violence and terrorism; Israel has recognized the PLO and vice

THE WACO SIEGE

Bloodbath after federal agents attempt to storm the headquarters of a religious sect

On February 28, the headquarters of the Branch Davidians (an offshoot of the Seventh-day Adventists), near Waco, Texas, was raided by the U.S. Bureau of Alcohol, Tobacco and Firearms (ATF) after its leader, David Koresh, launched a gun retail business. Four federal agents were killed in the assault. A lengthy standoff between the group and government agents then followed. It ended on April 19, after some 80 members of the group, including Koresh, died when the Mount Carmel complex was burned to the ground (left) following an attempted entrance by Federal Bureau of Investigation (FBI) agents.

Following the incident, several agents were disciplined for improper actions. A few survivors of the raid were tried in court. They were found not guilty of the murder of the ATF agents but were jailed for their actions during and after the raid.

August 9, 1993
Prince Albert is sworn in as Belgium's king, succeeding his brother, King Baudouin I.

 [9]
September 13, 1993
Israeli prime minister Yitzhak Rabin and Palestine Liberation Organization (PLO) chairman Yasser Arafat sign a basic agreement on **Palestinian self-government** in the West Bank and Gaza Strip.

September 24, 1993
Norodom Sihanouk is crowned king of Cambodia for the second time.

 [10]
October 6, 1993
Michael Jordan retires from professional basketball, saying "I don't have anything else to prove," only to return in March 1995.

November 1, 1993
The **Maastricht Treaty** establishing the European Union enters into force. It provides for EU citizenship and for the introduction of a central banking system, paving the way for the introduction of the euro in 2002.

November 4, 1993
Jean Chrétien, becomes prime minister of Canada. He will experience a tense relationship with the United States, which will be underscored by his refusal to commit Canadian troops to the U.S.-led war against Iraq in 2003.

1993-1994

December 30, 1993
The **Vatican City State** and Israel sign an agreement in Jerusalem to establish diplomatic relations and initiate a new era of understanding and cooperation.

1994
A **baseball strike** in the United States causes the cancellation of the World Series for the first time in 90 years.

 [1]

1994
A team of American researchers headed by geneticist Mark H. Skolnick discovers the **BRCA1 gene**, mutations in which are believed to cause 5 to 10 percent of breast cancers.

1994
Brazil defeats Italy in the men's **World Cup** soccer championship by a score of 0 to 0 (3–2; penalty kick shoot-out).

1994
Following the death of John Smith, **Tony Blair** is elected leader of the British Labour Party. He will lead the party to a landslide election victory in 1997.

 [2]

1994
Frank Gehry's American Center opens in Paris. The center, with its complex layout and references to traditional French architecture, establishes Gehry as one of the major architects of his generation.

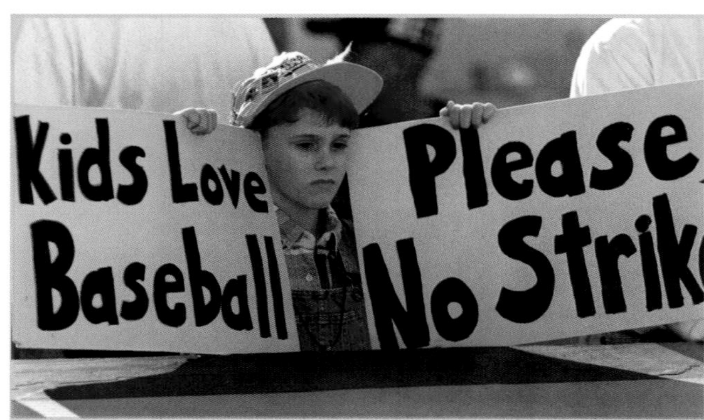

[1] A young girl makes clear her feelings about the baseball strike.

[2] Tony Blair and his wife, Cherie, with the red rose symbol of New Labour, on the day he becomes Labour Party leader.

[4] The Mighty Morphin Power Rangers stand in cement at Mann's Chinese Theater in Hollywood, so that they will leave their footprints behind for posterity.

[5] Cathy Turner takes a corner in the 500-meter race in Lillehammer, on her way to winning gold.

[9] Nelson Mandela at an election rally in March.

 [4]

1994
The Mighty Morphin **Power Rangers**, created by Japanese company Bandai, become an international hit, leveraged into toys, television shows, and movies.

1994
The Pan American Health Organization declares that **paralytic poliomyelitis (polio)** has been eradicated in North and South America and in the Caribbean.

1994
The white **Pentecostal Fellowship** of North America reverses segregationist policies and unites with black churches to form the Pentecostal/Charismatic Churches of North America.

 [5]

1994
The **Winter Olympic Games** take place in Lillehammer, Norway.

1994
Yemen plunges into civil war because of a dispute over the sharing of power between the north and south, which were two separate republics before agreeing to unite in 1990.

 [6]

March 22, 1994
Aldrich Ames, a former member of the Soviet counterintelligence unit of the CIA, is arrested and charged with spying for Moscow, both before and after the breakup of the Soviet Union.

1994
Japanese novelist **Kenzaburo Oe** becomes the second Japanese author to win the Nobel Prize for Literature.

1994
John F. Nash of Princeton University, John C. Harsanyi of the University of California at Berkeley, and Reinhard Selten of the University of Bonn, Germany, share the 1994 Nobel Prize in Economics for their work on **game theory**.

1994
Kim Jong Il becomes North Korea's leader when his father, Kim Il-sung, dies. He will be named chairman of the Korean Workers Party in October 1997, and in September 1998 he will formally assume the nation's highest post.

1994
The Church of England (Anglican Church) ordains 32 **women priests**. The controversial step highlights the international debate over the place of women in church hierarchies.

 [3]

1994
The cleaning of the artwork in the **Sistine Chapel** is completed, restoring Michelangelo's famous frescoes to their original vividness and brightness.

1994
The **Council of Europe** establishes as a condition of membership the requirement that prospective member countries suspend executions and commit themselves to its abolition. The European Union will adopt a similar rule in 1998.

THE SISTINE CHAPEL RESTORATION

A 15-year cleanup operation recaptures the former glory of some of the Vatican's greatest works of art.

Completed in 1989, a 10-year-long restoration project removed several centuries' accumulation of dirt, smoke, and varnish from the frescoes on the ceiling of the Sistine Chapel. These works had been commissioned by Pope Julius II in 1508 and were painted by Michelangelo in the years from 1508 to 1512.

The Last Judgment—a fresco on the west wall of the chapel also painted by Michelangelo, this time for Pope Paul III in the period from 1534 to 1541—took longer to restore. The photograph (left) shows Pope John Paul II (in yellow robes) celebrating Mass in front of the newly renovated masterpiece on April 8.

[6] Aldrich Ames in shackles.

[3] Two of the 32 newly ordained Church of England women priests in Bristol Cathedral after the service of ordination.

[7] Kurt Cobain

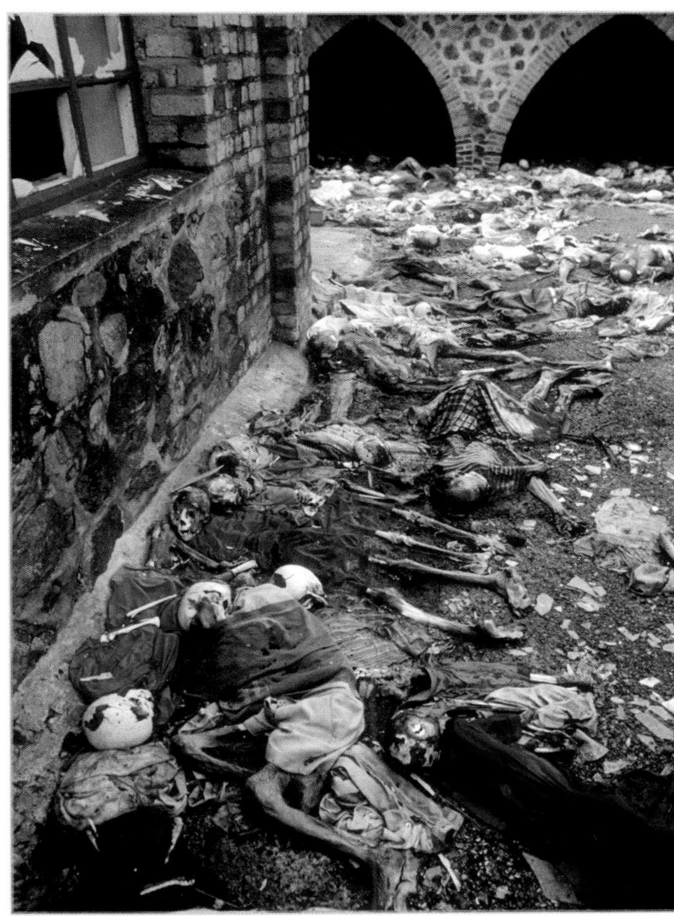

[8] The scene at Nyarubuye Church in Rwanda, where 4,000 civilians were murdered by Hutu militia on May 25.

March 30, 1994
French prime minister **Edouard Balladur** yields to student demands and revokes a government decree that would have allowed employers to hire young people at less than the minimum wage.

 [7]

April 5, 1994
Alternative rocker **Kurt Cobain** of Nirvana, the tortured voice of Generation X, commits suicide.

April 6, 1994
Cyprien Ntaryamira and Juvenal Habyarimana, the presidents of **Burundi** and **Rwanda**, respectively, are killed when their plane crashes as it lands in Kigali, Rwanda's capital.

 [8]

April 7, 1994
Violence between **Hutu** extremists and Tutsis in **Rwanda** begins. The violence will turn into genocide as some 800,000 people, mostly Tutsis, are killed in the next three months.

 [9]

May 10, 1994
Nelson Mandela, whose struggle to end apartheid led to his imprisonment (1962–90), becomes president of South Africa, following the first-ever multiracial elections there.

May 25, 1994
Holland Ford of Johns Hopkins University, Baltimore, Maryland, announces that the Hubble space telescope has provided "conclusive evidence of a **supermassive black hole**" in the center of galaxy M87 in the constellation Virgo.

May 27, 1994
Exiled from the Soviet Union since February 13, 1974, for writing *The Gulag Archipelago*, **Aleksandr Solzhenitsyn** returns to Russia.

June 17, 1994
American football hero **O. J. Simpson** is charged with the murders of his ex-wife, Nicole Simpson, and her friend, Ronald Goldman, though he will be acquitted the following year.

July 31, 1994
A U.N. Security Council resolution authorizes the use of "all necessary means" to restore democracy to **Haiti**.

August 11, 1994
Cuban president **Fidel Castro** indicates in a speech that his government is lifting restrictions on those wishing to leave the country, leading thousands of Cubans to set sail for Florida on homemade boats and makeshift rafts.

[1]

August 31, 1994
The **IRA** announces a cease-fire in Northern Ireland. The Protestant loyalist paramilitary groups will follow suit in October.

September 21, 1994
Timothy D. White, a paleontologist at the University of California at Berkeley, announces the discovery in Ethiopia of ancient fossils belonging to apelike creatures that were the ancestors of modern humans.

O. J. SIMPSON ON TRIAL

Former football star acquitted of double murder charges

On June 12, 1994, Nicole Brown Simpson and her friend, Ronald Goldman, were stabbed to death outside her home in Los Angeles. Her ex-husband, former football player O. J. Simpson (above right, with attorney Robert Shapiro), was arrested and charged with the two murders on June 17; he pleaded not guilty and hired a team of prominent lawyers to handle his defense. His lengthy, nationally televised trial became the focus of unprecedented media scrutiny. A jury acquitted Simpson of the murder charges on October 3, 1995.

In a separate civil trial decision in 1997, Simpson was found liable for the deaths of his ex-wife and Goldman and was ordered to pay $33.5 million in damages to the families. Simpson later collaborated (with Pablo F. Fenjves) on *If I Did It*, a book in which he hypothesized about how he would have committed the murders. Public outrage prevented its initial publication in 2006, but a bankruptcy court subsequently awarded the book's rights to the Goldman family, who released the work in 2007.

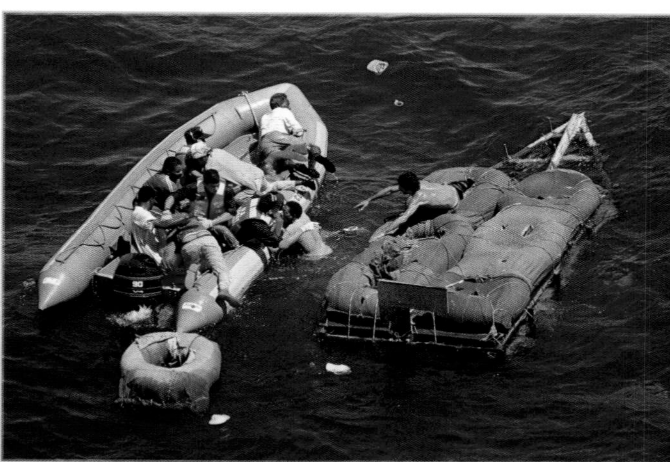

[1] The U.S. Coast Guard rescues Cuban refugees after their raft has capsized 25 miles off the Cuban coast.

[9] Miguel Indurain wearing the yellow jersey.

[5] Shoko Asahara, head of the Aum Supreme Truth sect.

[4] A collapsed building blocks the main street in central Kobe.

1995
A variety of studies show that **Eastern European** nations are among the most polluted in the world. Eighty-two percent of Poland's forests are damaged by acid rain.

1995
American scientists succeed in producing the **Bose-Einstein condensate**, a form of matter predicted in 1924–25 by Albert Einstein and the Indian physicist Satyendra Bose.

 [4]

1995
An earthquake hits **Kobe**, Japan, killing about 5,100 and causing great damage and widespread fires in the city.

 [5]

1995
Aum Shinrikyo ("Supreme Truth"), a Japanese Buddhist sect, releases the nerve gas sarin into the Tokyo subway system, killing 12 and injuring thousands.

 [6]

1995
Bulgarian-born environmental sculptor **Christo** (famous for wrapping large objects, including islands) and his wife, Jeanne-Claude, wrap the Berlin Reichstag in silver fabric.

 [7]

1995
Continued debate over **global warming** dominates environmental news, as climatologists announce evidence of long-term warming trends.

October 14, 1994
Naguib Mahfouz, the 82-year-old novelist and 1988 winner of the Nobel Prize for Literature, is stabbed by Islamic militants in Cairo.
[2]

October 15, 1994
Three years after a coup forced him to flee, President **Jean-Bertrand Aristide**, Haiti's first freely elected president, returns to Haiti urging reconciliation.

November 1, 1994
The National Aeronautics and Space Administration (NASA) launches its **Wind spacecraft** on a mission that would include a "halo orbit" between the sun and earth to explore the space environment there.

November 10, 1994
The **Iraqi parliament** agrees to recognize Kuwait's sovereignty and the existing border as delineated by the U.N.

November 22, 1994
Mount Merapi, on the island of Java, erupts, killing 64 people.

December 11, 1994
Russian troops invade **Chechnya** in an effort to suppress a rebel Chechen government led by Dzhokhar Dudayev.
 [3]

[8] *Seamus Heaney*

[2] *Naguib Mahfouz*

[7] *Ice from the Twitcher Glacier on South Georgia in the South Atlantic breaking off into the sea.*

[10] *Buzz Lightyear, a major character in* Toy Story.

[3] *Russian T-72 tanks advancing towards Grozny, the Chechen capital. The one on the right has a mine-clearing system mounted on it.*

[6] *The Reichstag wrapped by Christo.*

1995
Dominique Perrault's Bibliotheque Nationale de France (National Library of France) is completed. It is one of many architecturally significant libraries built in the 1990s and one of the most controversial.

 [8]
1995
Irish poet **Seamus Heaney** is awarded the Nobel Prize for Literature.

 [9]
1995
Miguel Indurain of Spain becomes the first to win the Tour de France five consecutive times.

1995
Norway defeats Germany in the **women's World Cup** soccer championship by a score of 2 to 0.

1995
Online auction site **eBay**, founded by Pierre Omidyar, is launched.

 [10]
1995
Pixar releases **Toy Story**, the first fully computer-animated feature film; it is hugely successful, the highest-grossing feature film of 1995 worldwide. It wins two Oscars and numerous other awards.

1995

1995
Pope John Paul II leads programs aimed at easing doctrinal or theological divisions between the Roman Catholic Church and the Eastern Orthodox Church.

1995
Sun Microsystems introduces the **Java programming** language.

1995
The death of guitarist **Jerry Garcia** marks the end of the Grateful Dead, one of the longest lived and iconoclastic groups in psychedelic rock music.

 [1]

1995
The **Requiem of Reconciliation** commemorates the 50th anniversary of the end of World War II. It presents the Roman Catholic mass for the dead in fourteen sections, each written by a different composer from a country involved in the war.

1995
The **Rock and Roll Hall of Fame** opens in Cleveland, Ohio, honoring performers, producers, songwriters, and disc jockeys.

 [2]

1995
The U.S. space shuttle *Atlantis* docks with the Russian space station **Mir**, opening a new period of international collaboration in space research and exploration.

[4] *A bas-relief carving of Osiris, god of the dead, on the wall of the royal mausoleum.*

[1] *Jerry Garcia performing in 1994.*

[2] *The opening ceremony at the Rock and Roll Hall of Fame.*

[5] *Jacques Chirac (left) with the outgoing President, François Mitterrand.*

OKLAHOMA CITY BOMBING

The worst act of domestic terrorism in U.S. history.

On April 19, a massive homemade bomb concealed in a rental truck exploded, heavily damaging the Alfred P. Murrah Federal Building (left). A total of 168 people were killed, including 19 children, and more than 500 were injured.

Police soon arrested two men: Timothy McVeigh and Terry Nichols. Both were former U.S. Army soldiers and were associated with the extreme right-wing and militant Patriot movement. Their crime was thought to have been in response to the U.S. government's handling of the Waco siege. McVeigh was convicted on 11 counts of murder, conspiracy, and using a weapon of mass destruction. He was executed in 2001—the first person executed for a federal crime in the United States since 1963. Nichols was sentenced to life in prison.

May 11, 1995
After more than three weeks of debate at U.N. headquarters in New York City, representatives from 174 nations agree to extend the **Nuclear Non-proliferation Treaty** indefinitely.

 [4]

May 15, 1995
Kent R. Weeks, Egyptologist at the American University in Cairo, reports on an enormous royal mausoleum recently explored in the **Valley of the Kings** and believed to contain the tomb of the sons of Ramses II.

 [5]

May 17, 1995
Jacques Chirac, who served as the country's prime minister (1974–76, 1986–88), is elected president of France.

May 25, 1995
The legislature in **Australia's** Northern Territory votes in favor of a bill on the rights of the terminally ill, granting patients the right to request that they be put to death if they are suffering.

May 30, 1995
The World Health Organization (WHO) announces that according to the latest statistics, 153 persons have died in **Zaire** after being infected with the Ebola virus.

June 12, 1995
In **Adarand Constructors v. Pena** the U.S. Supreme Court rules that federal affirmative-action programs are unconstitutional unless they fulfill a "compelling governmental interest."

January 1, 1995
The **World Trade Organization**, established to supervise and liberalize world trade, begins operations.

January 3, 1995
The World Health Organization (WHO) announces that the number of **AIDS** reported cases has officially passed the one million mark.

 [3]

January 18, 1995
French minister of Culture and Francophone Affairs Jacques Toubon confirms that **cave paintings** and engravings believed to be 17,000 to 20,000 years old have been discovered in southern France.

February 1, 1995
The United States' annual report on the observance of **human rights** is released, denouncing the "flagrant and systematic abuses of basic human rights" in Cuba, Iran, Iraq, North Korea, and Myanmar (Burma).

March 2, 1995
Two teams of particle physicists at the Fermi National Laboratory in Batavia, Illinois, announce the discovery of the **top quark**, the last of six quarks that are believed to be the building blocks of all matter.

April 19, 1995
A massive homemade bomb concealed in a rental truck explodes in **Oklahoma City**.

[3] A poster in Hanoi, Vietnam, warns that prostitution and drug addiction can lead to AIDS.

[7] Bosnian-Serb soldiers in a deserted Srebrenica, a week after they have occupied this United Nations "safe area." The massacre of its male inhabitants is the worst atrocity perpetrated in Europe since 1945.

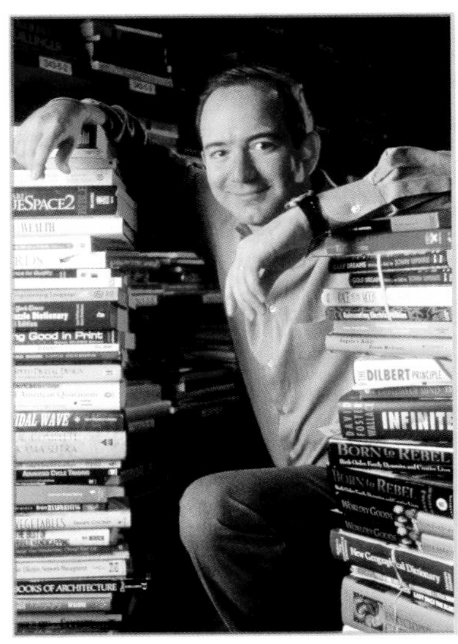

[6] Jeff Bezos with some of Amazon's stock.

[8] A Korean woman protests nuclear testing at the World Conference on Women.

[9] Yitzhak Rabin (right) with Foreign Minister Shimon Peres an hour or so before Rabin is killed.

 [6]

July 1995
Amazon.com, founded by Jeff Bezos, sells its first book.

 [7]

July 1995
The Bosnian Serb army under General Ratko Mladic carries out the **Srebrenica** Massacre, killing 8,000 Bosnian Muslim men and boys.

July 27, 1995
With the approval of the United States Food and Drug Administration, researchers at Duke University Medical Center announce that they are preparing to test the viability of **mixed-species organs** in human beings.

 [8]

September 4, 1995
Women from 185 countries convene in Beijing for the **Fourth World Conference on Women**. The assembly will agree on a "platform for action" at the close of the conference on September 15.

 [9]

November 4, 1995
Israeli prime minister **Yitzhak Rabin**, corecipient with Shimon Peres and Yasser Arafat of the Nobel Peace Prize in 1994, is assassinated by a Jewish extremist while attending a peace rally.

December 23, 1995
Aleksander Kwasniewski, formerly an apparatchik of Poland's ruling communist party, is sworn in as the country's president, having narrowly defeated Lech Walesa, Poland's first postcommunist president.

1996

1996
The Prince of Wales and Princess Diana are divorced after several years of separation.

1996
A report sponsored by the U.S. Agency for International Development on female **genital mutilation** (FGM) urges international action to end the ritual that has been performed on more than 85 million women worldwide.

1996
British oarsman **Steve Redgrave** wins the coxless pairs gold medal in the Summer Olympics at Atlanta, Georgia, and becomes the first endurance-event champion in four different Olympics.

[1]

1996
Geologists announce that they have discovered evidence of organic matter in a 4.5-billion-year-old **Martian meteorite**, suggesting that life existed on Mars. The finding is controversial.

1996
In **Romer v. Evans** the U.S. Supreme Court invalidates a Colorado referendum passed by popular vote that had prohibited conferral of protected status on the basis of sexual orientation.

1996
John Howard of the Labor Party becomes prime minister of Australia. He will introduce several controversial labor-relations reforms, including the abolition of unfair dismissal laws in workplaces.

[2]

[1] Steve Redgrave. He wins his medal with Matthew Pinsent, with whom he also won at Barcelona in 1992. In 2000 he will win a fifth gold, as a member of Britain's coxless four.

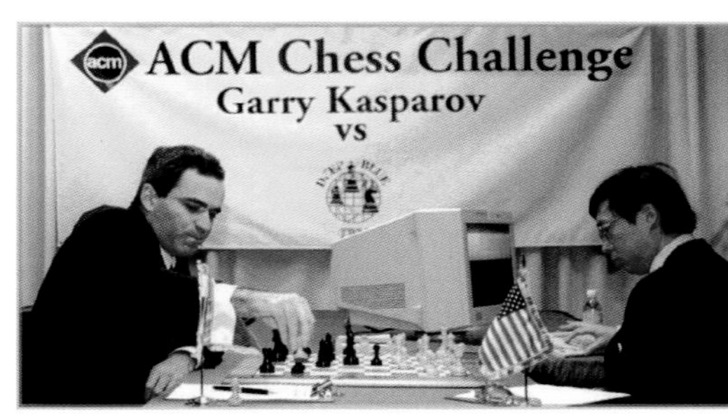

[5] Garry Kasparov takes one of the IBM Deep Blue pawns at the start of the six-game, six-day contest. Feng-hsiung Hsu, principal designer of Deep Blue, keys his move into the computer.

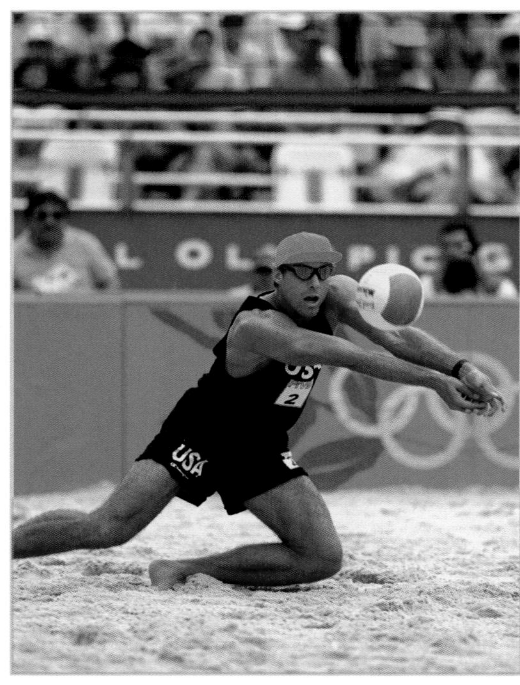

[6] Karch Kiraly playing at the Atlanta Olympics.

[7] The spectacular roof of the Tokyo International Forum.

[4] Bishop Belo and fellow East Timor independence activist José Ramos-Horta with their Nobel medals. Ramos-Horta will become president of East Timor in 2001.

1996
The **Palm Pilot** is introduced, the first truly successful personal digital assistant (PDA).

[6]

1996
The first Olympic **beach volleyball** competition is won by Kent Steffes and Karch Kiraly of the United States. For Kiraly, arguably volleyball's greatest player, it is his third Olympic gold medal.

1996
The **Comprehensive Nuclear-Test-Ban Treaty**, to prohibit all forms of nuclear explosive testing, fails to enter into force because some of the 44 states whose signatures were required choose not to sign.

[7]

1996
The Tokyo International Forum, designed by Uruguayan-born U.S. architect **Rafael Viñoly**, is completed. Its enormous, self-supporting Glass Hall (about 200 meters long) is both a technological and aesthetic tour de force.

1996
U.S. television host **Oprah Winfrey** adds a book-club segment to her popular show, creating a literary sensation as her selections become instant best sellers.

[8]

January 20, 1996
Palestinian voters in the Gaza Strip and West Bank overwhelmingly support Yasser Arafat's bid to become president of the self-ruling Palestinian National Authority.

1996
The **Petronas Twin Towers** in Kuala Lumpur, Malaysia, designed by Argentine-born American architect Cesar Pelli, are completed. They are among the world's tallest buildings, beating the Sears Tower in Chicago by 29 feet.

 [3]

1996
Polish lyric poet **Wislawa Szymborska** wins the Nobel Prize for Literature.

1996
Protease inhibitors provide a new treatment for **AIDS**, which dramatically improves rates of survival.

1996
Roman Catholic bishop and East Timorese activist **Carlos Filipe Ximenes Belo** is awarded the 1996 Nobel Peace Prize. Belo is one of many Third World religious figures who campaign for human rights.

 [4]

1996
Sweden hosts the first World Congress Against Commercial Sexual Exploitation of Children.

1996
The chess-playing computer **Deep Blue** raises new questions about artificial intelligence after defeating Garry Kasparov, the game's best human player.

 [5]

[3] *The Petronas Twin Towers. They are largely constructed from super-high-strength reinforced concrete because of a shortage of steel in this period.*

[2] *John Howard. He will be reelected in 1998, 2001, and 2004, leading Australia through a period of considerable prosperity.*

[9] *The burned-out shell of the stage of Teatro La Fenice opera house in Venice.*

[8] *Yasser Arafat casts his vote.*

[10] *The last Cuban from the Guantanamo Bay camp. At its height it held 46,000 refugees, including 20,000 Haitian "boat people."*

January 21, 1996
Cleanup of 1.8 million gallons (6.8 million liters) of oil begins near **Block Island National Wildlife Refuge**, Rhode Island, two days after the barge *North Cape* runs aground and creates a 12-mile (19-km) oil slick.

January 27, 1996
Colonel **Ibrahim Baré Maïnassara** leads a successful military coup in Niger against the democratically elected government of President Mahamane Ousmane.

 [9]

January 29, 1996
One of Venice's most glorious monuments, the 204-year-old **Teatro La Fenice** opera house, is almost totally destroyed by a fire that rages for nine hours before it is extinguished.

 [10]

January 31, 1996
Some 125 Cubans, the last of numerous refugees who had been housed at the U.S. **Guantanamo Bay** naval base in Cuba, are flown to Florida. The camps are then officially closed.

February 9, 1996
German physicist **Peter Armbruster** synthesizes the chemical element 112, a heavy, transuranium element.

February 17, 1996
An **earthquake** and an accompanying tsunami in Indonesia leave 108 people dead, 423 injured, and 58 missing.

1996

February 18, 1996
An **IRA bomb** blows up on a London bus, less than 10 days after a previous IRA bomb exploded in London's Docklands, ending the 17-month cease-fire. [1]

March 19, 1996
For the first time since 1992, **Sarajevo** and five suburbs are united under the authority of the Muslim-dominated government of Bosnia and Herzegovina. [2]

March 19, 1996
One of the worst fires in the history of the Philippines sweeps through a **Manila discotheque**, killing 159 of the 400 people in the nightclub, which was intended to hold no more than 35.

March 23, 1996
In the first direct presidential election in Chinese history, **Lee Teng-hui** wins a second five-year term as president of the Republic of China on Taiwan.

March 27, 1996
The European Union (EU) announces a worldwide ban on the export of **British beef** products amid fears that bovine spongiform encephalopathy ("mad cow disease") is linked to a similar disease that affects humans. [3]

April 3, 1996
U.S. federal agents in Montana apprehend Theodore J. Kaczynski, who they believe is the serial killer known as the "**Unabomber**."

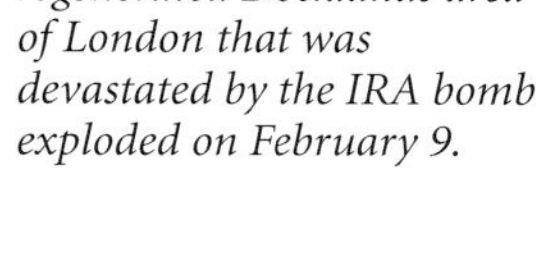

[1] A new office block in the regenerated Docklands area of London that was devastated by the IRA bomb exploded on February 9.

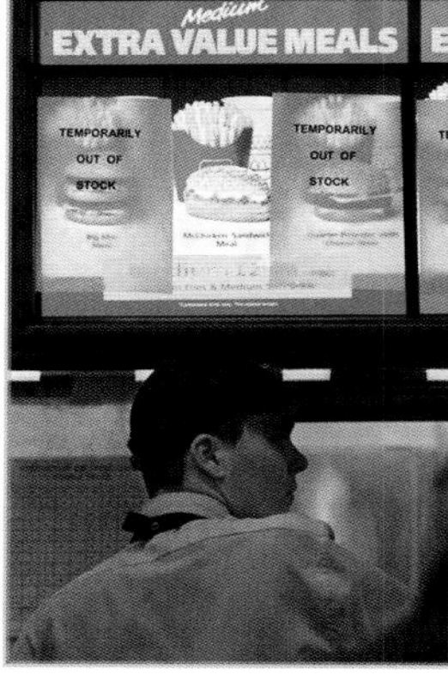

[3] McDonald's takes British beef off the menu in response to the "mad cow disease" scare.

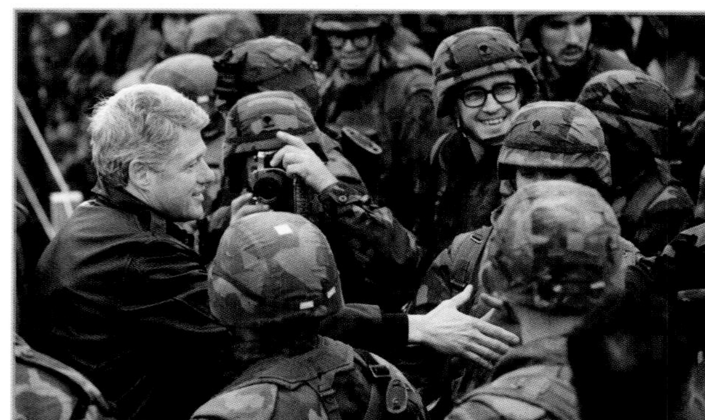

[2] President Clinton visits U.S. peacekeeping troops in Bosnia.

[7] An American F-18 fighter taking off from the carrier Carl Vinson *to carry out a strike in retaliation for Iraqi incursions into the Kurdish safe zone in northern Iraq.*

May 10, 1996
Following the massacre in **Tasmania** of 35 people in late April, the national, state, and territorial governments of Australia agree to outlaw the sale and possession of all automatic and semiautomatic weapons.

June 10, 1996
The Daily Show, a television program that will become well known for its comedic political commentary, premieres on Comedy Central.

July 27, 1996
A **pipe bomb** explodes in Olympic Centennial Park in Atlanta, Georgia, killing 1 person and injuring 111 in the first terrorist attack at the Olympics since the 1972 Games in Munich, West Germany.

August 1996
Chun Doo Hwan and Roh Tae Woo, former **South Korean presidents**, are sentenced to death for their involvement in a 1979 coup and the uprising in Kwangju in 1980 and for accepting bribes. Both will receive pardons in December 1997.

August 16, 1996
The youngest person ever elected president of the Dominican Republic, **Leonel Fernández Reyna** is sworn in and soon institutes measures to end corruption and to improve the country's economy.

 [7]

September 9, 1996
For the second straight day, U.S. Navy ships and Air Force planes fire cruise missiles at **Iraqi military** and command targets south of the 32nd parallel in punishment for Iraqi movement northward along the 36th parallel.

April 18, 1996
More than 100 civilians are killed and numerous others are injured when Israeli soldiers fire artillery shells into a U.N. camp at **Qana, Lebanon**, that houses Lebanese refugees.

April 20, 1996
President Bill Clinton's veto of a bill that would have outlawed "**partial-birth**" abortions is denounced, as expected, by pro-life groups.

May 3, 1996
At the first formal review of the 1980 **Geneva Convention** on Inhumane Weapons, the signatories agree to curtail the use of land mines over the next decade.

May 4, 1996
José María Aznar of the conservative Popular Party becomes prime minister of Spain and will serve until 2004, overseeing an improving economy while facing growing terrorism by Islamic terrorists and the Basque separatist movement known as ETA.

May 7, 1996
The U.S. House of Representatives supports (418–0) an amendment to a 1994 federal anticrime bill requiring state officials to notify communities when a convicted **sex offender** moves into their area.

May 9, 1996
Canada's House of Commons passes (153–76) an amendment to the Federal Human Rights Act that prohibits discrimination against homosexuals who work for the federal government or in institutions regulated by the government.

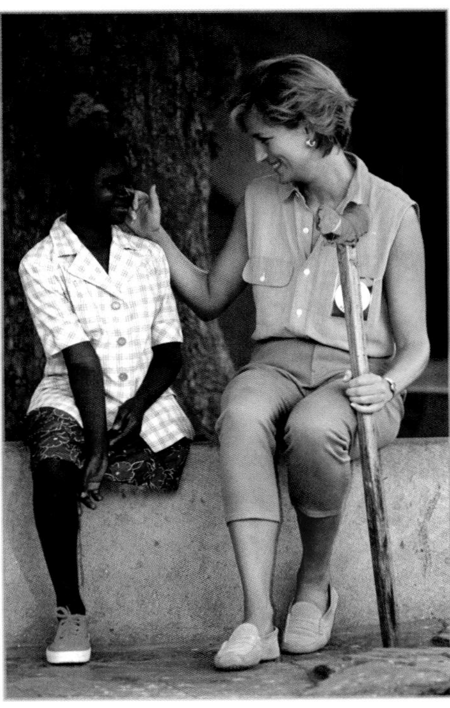

[5] Princess Diana, who makes the campaign against land mines a personal crusade, seen with a land-mine victim in Angola.

[6] José María Aznar

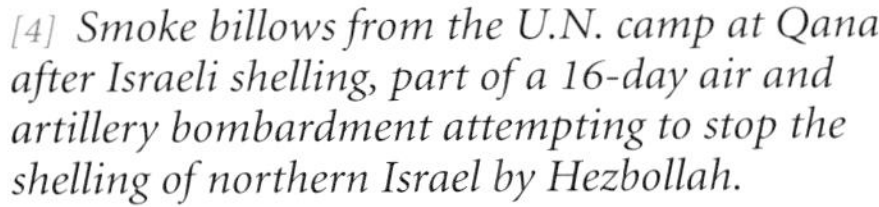

[4] Smoke billows from the U.N. camp at Qana after Israeli shelling, part of a 16-day air and artillery bombardment attempting to stop the shelling of northern Israel by Hezbollah.

KABUL UNDER THE TALIBAN

Extremist militia takes control of the Afghan capital

The Taliban—an ultraconservative political and religious faction—emerged as a force for social order in 1994 in the southern Afghan province of Kandahar. Most were students trained in Islamic religious schools. They quickly subdued the local warlords who controlled the southern part of the country. By late 1996 popular support for the Taliban among Afghanistan's southern Pashtun ethnic group, as well as assistance from conservative Islamic elements abroad, enabled the faction to consolidate its power. The photograph (left) shows Taliban gunners 19 miles north of Kabul. The capital fell to the Taliban by the end of the year, and it gained effective control of Afghanistan.

September 27, 1996
Taliban leaders seize the capital city of Kabul, declaring all of Afghanistan an Islamic state.

November 5, 1996
After a political campaign that many Americans considered far too long and much too expensive, Democrat **Bill Clinton** is reelected U.S. president with 379 electoral votes.

November 9, 1996
Evander Holyfield scores a technical knockout against Mike Tyson to win the heavyweight boxing championship for a third time.

November 30, 1996
A block of gray sandstone known as the **Stone of Scone** is returned to Scotland, 700 years after it had been taken to England as war booty by King Edward I.

December 3, 1996
Gay unions become an issue in the U.S.; a circuit court judge in Honolulu rules that a state ban on same-sex marriages is unconstitutional and orders the state to issue licenses for such unions.

December 10, 1996
South African president **Nelson Mandela** signs a new constitution that completes a transition from a long period of white-minority rule (apartheid) to full-fledged democracy.

1996-1997

December 19, 1996
Responding to demands that television programs be rated for their violence, profanity, and sexual content, the television industry proposes a **rating system** keyed to the age of viewers.

1997
As many as 1.5 million revelers crowd the streets of Berlin for the **Love Parade**, an annual celebration of peace, joy, and techno music.

 [1]

1997
Author **Philip Roth** wins a Pulitzer Prize for his novel *American Pastoral.*

 [2]

1997
Boxer **Mike Tyson** is disqualified for biting off a portion of Evander Holyfield's ear during a World Boxing Association heavyweight title match.

 [3]

1997
Digital video (or versatile) disc (DVD) is introduced to U.S. consumers as a viewing alternative to videocassettes.

1997
Displaying "Girl Power," the **Spice Girls** make history in England as their first four singles hit number one on the British charts.

 [4]

[1] Berlin's annual Love Parade.

[3] Evander Holyfield's ear is examined by the ringside doctor as blood runs down his arm and chest. Mike Tyson is disqualified, so Holyfield wins the bout.

[8] A jug for use at the table, from around 100 BC, rescued from the depths of the Mediterranean.

[2] Philip Roth

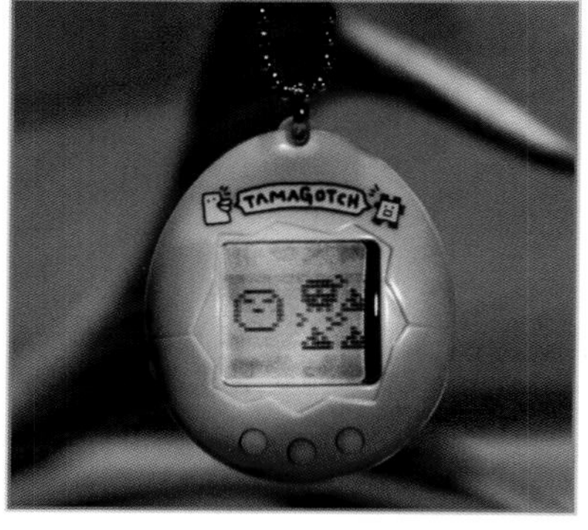

[9] A Tamagotchi. The virtual pet grows from a chick to an adult on-screen in ten days, if the owner looks after it by pressing the right buttons.

THE FIRST ANIMAL CLONE

The birth of an artificially conceived sheep delights scientists but has alarming moral implications.

The announcement in February 1997 of the birth of Dolly the sheep (left), the first clone of an adult mammal, by a group of scientists at a research laboratory in Edinburgh, Scotland, attracted international attention because of the new medical and agricultural opportunities and the new ethical concerns raised by the breakthrough. The term "cloning" (derived from the Greek word *klon,* meaning "twig") strictly indicates the taking of a cutting, as in plant breeding, but it has also come to be used to describe the production, by means of a process known as nuclear transfer, of genetically identical animals. Nuclear transfer involves removing the chromosomes from an unfertilized egg and replacing them with a nucleus from a donor cell. As it is the transferred nucleus that determines almost all of the characteristics of the resulting offspring, a clone will resemble its "parent," the animal from which the donor cell was taken.

In response to the announcement of Dolly's birth Italy banned the cloning of any mammal, whereas a number of groups in other countries welcomed the technique. Dolly lived to the age of six.

 [8]

1997
Oceanographer **Robert Ballard** discovers eight ancient ships 2,500 feet underneath an old trade route. The finding gives rise to deep-sea archaeology.

1997
Scottish researchers announce they have produced the first cloned mammal—**Dolly**, a sheep.

1997
Seven months after being launched, *Mars Pathfinder* arrives on the surface of **Mars** and begins transmitting data. It marks a renaissance in NASA interplanetary missions.

1997
Singer Sarah McLachlan founds **Lilith Fair**, a traveling summer concert tour of female performers. Its phenomenal success proves the marketability of female artists.

 [9]

1997
Tamagotchi "virtual pets," introduced in Japan in 1996, reach the United States. Other new electronic toys include ActiMates Barney, a version of the popular purple dinosaur.

 [10]

1997
The billion-dollar **Getty Center**, designed by Richard Meier, opens in Los Angeles. The hilltop museum complex includes a garden designed by the conceptual artist Robert Irwin.

1997
Frank Gehry's **Guggenheim Museum** in Bilbao, Spain, opens. The much-discussed building features curved exterior surfaces sheathed in gleaming titanium and cavernous interior spaces.

 [5]

1997
In an unprecedented move, the **Liggett Group**, a tobacco company in the United States, acknowledges the health risks of smoking when its CEO admits that cigarettes are addictive and can cause cancer.

1997
Tony Blair becomes prime minister of the United Kingdom. He is the youngest prime minister since 1812 and, upon his resignation in 2007, the longest-serving Labour prime minister.

 [6]

1997
In New Labour's first major initiative—and perhaps its boldest—Chancellor of Exchequer Gordon Brown grants the **Bank of England** the power to determine interest rates without government consultation.

1997
J. K. Rowling publishes **Harry Potter and the Philosopher's Stone** (1997; U.S. title *Harry Potter and the Sorcerer's Stone*). It is an immediate success, appealing to both children (its intended audience) and adults.

 [7]

1997
Kofi Annan of Ghana becomes secretary general of the U.N. He will serve until 2006.

[4] The Spice Girls at the MTV Music Awards in New York. Posh Spice, in black on the left, will go on to further celebrity as Victoria Beckham, wife of the English footballer.

[10] The Getty Center

[6] Tony Blair is greeted in Downing Street the day after his election.

[7] J. K. Rowling signing a copy of her book for an American fan in Washington, D.C.

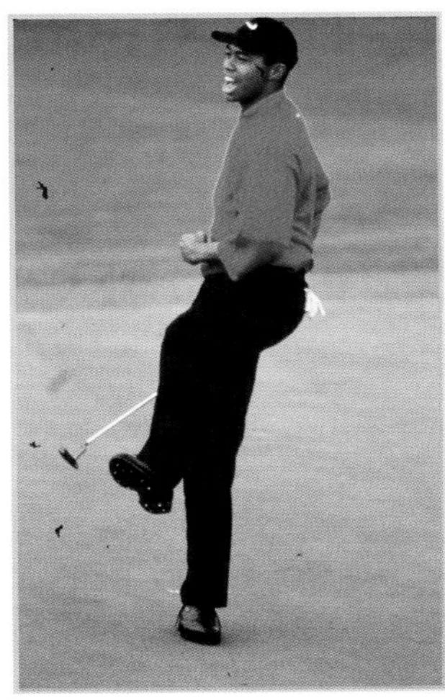

[11] Tiger Woods kicks the air on the 18th green at Augusta with such joy and vigor after winning his first Masters, that lumps of grass fly off his spiked shoes.

[5] The Guggenheim Museum in Bilbao: an example of the building-as-sculpture, the structure of the museum displacing its contents in importance.

1997
The collective suicide of 39 members of the **Heaven's Gate** group in southern California raises concerns about millenarian apocalyptic groups.

 [11]

1997
Tiger Woods shoots a 270 over 72 holes at the Masters Tournament to become the first person of African descent, as well as the first person of Asian descent, to win a major professional golf title.

1997
U.S. **gambling** revenues hit $47.6 billion. The 1980s and '90s have seen a vast growth in the number of casinos in the United States and in the popularity and social acceptability of gambling.

1997
Woolworth Corporation closes its last five-and-dime stores in the United States.

1997
World music is firmly established as a niche in popular music, spurred by marketing developments, technological advances, and collaboration among musicians in the West, Africa, and Asia.

January 8, 1997
The principality of **Monaco** begins a yearlong celebration in honor of the 700th anniversary of the rule of the Grimaldi family, who seized power in 1297 and gained firm possession of Monaco in 1419.

1997-1998

January 13, 1997
President **Abdala Bucaram** of Ecuador visits President Alberto Fujimori of Peru, the first official visit to Peru by an Ecuadoran president in 150 years.

January 14, 1997
Greek archaeologists announce that they have discovered an ancient site in **Athens** that may have been Aristotle's Lyceum.

January 23, 1997
Madeleine Albright, who had earlier served as U.S. ambassador to the U.N., assumes under President Bill Clinton the office of secretary of state, becoming the first woman to hold that cabinet post.

 [1]

January 23, 1997
The **Age of Aquarius** dawns, some astrologers believe, because for the first time since 1475 a number of planets, the sun, and the moon are aligned in a perfect six-pointed star in the first degrees of Aquarius.

February 13, 1997
The **Dow Jones** Industrial Average first eclipses the 7,000 mark, then closes at 7,022.44.

March 19, 1997
Dutch-born American painter **Willem de Kooning** dies; he was a major exponent of abstract expressionism and action painting whose series *Woman I–VI* caused a stir with its violent images and impulsive technique.

 [2]

[1] Madeleine Albright (right) with Hillary Clinton.

[10] Astronaut and senator John Glenn about to board the space shuttle.

[9] A mass Moonie wedding in Washington: Mr. and Mrs. Moon receive bouquets.

[2] Willem de Kooning

[8] Prince Charles with his sons, William and Harry, inspect the flowers on the railings at Kensington Palace before Princess Diana's funeral.

September 11, 1997
Voters in Scotland overwhelmingly approve the creation of a **Scottish Parliament** with tax-raising authority. The legislature begins sittings two years later.

October 9, 1997
Italian playwright **Dario Fo** is awarded the Nobel Prize for Literature.

 [9]

November 29, 1997
In a ceremony that is broadcast around the world by satellite, some 28,000 couples gather at RFK Stadium in Washington, D.C., for a "wedding" conducted by **Sun Myung Moon**, leader of the Unification Church.

December 15, 1997
Janet Rosenberg Jagan is elected president of Guyana, becoming the first elected female president in South America and the first white president of Guyana.

December 15, 1997
The U.S. Department of Defense orders that all 1.4 million Americans in its service be inoculated against **anthrax**, a potential weapon of biological warfare.

December 18, 1997
Kim Dae Jung is elected president of South Korea, the first opposition leader in that country's history to win that position.

April 5, 1997
American poet **Allen Ginsberg**, whose 1956 poem *Howl* is revered as an American masterpiece, dies in New York City.
[3]

June 1, 1997
A jury in Denver, Colorado, finds the right-wing sociopath **Timothy McVeigh** of the militia movement guilty of murder and conspiracy in the deaths of 168 people in the 1995 Oklahoma City bombing.
[4]

July 1, 1997
Hong Kong, parts of which became a British colony in 1842, is returned to the People's Republic of China by Great Britain.
[5]

July 23, 1997
Slobodan Milosevic becomes president of the Federal Republic of Yugoslavia (comprising Serbia and Montenegro) after serving as president of Serbia from 1989. He will die in prison in 2006 while on trial on charges of genocide.
[6]

July 25, 1997
In Cambodia leaders of the Khmer Rouge revolutionary movement hold a "people's tribunal" for the movement's long-time leader, **Pol Pot**, and sentence him to life imprisonment; he disappears shortly thereafter.
[7]

August 31, 1997
Britain's **Princess Diana** is killed in an automobile accident in Paris along with her escort, Dodi Fayed. Her death and funeral produce unprecedented expressions of public mourning, testifying to her enormous hold on the British national psyche.
[8]

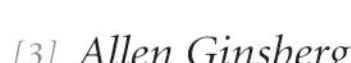

[3] *Allen Ginsberg*

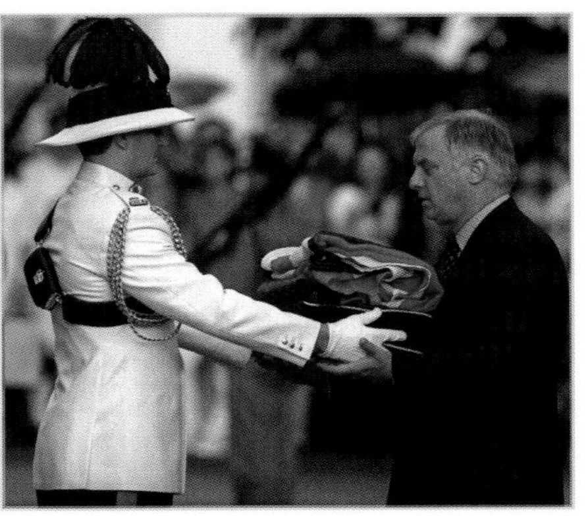

[5] *Governor Chris Patten receives the Union Jack after it has been lowered for the last time at Government House in Hong Kong.*

[6] *Slobodan Milosevic and his powerful wife, Mirjana Markovic, after he has been sworn in as president.*

[4] *Timothy McVeigh. He will later request that all judicial appeals on his behalf be halted and that he be executed.*

[7] *A map of Cambodia constructed out of different colored skulls at the former school in Phnom Penh that became a holding prison for those later executed by the Khmer Rouge in the Killing Fields. The school is now a museum.*

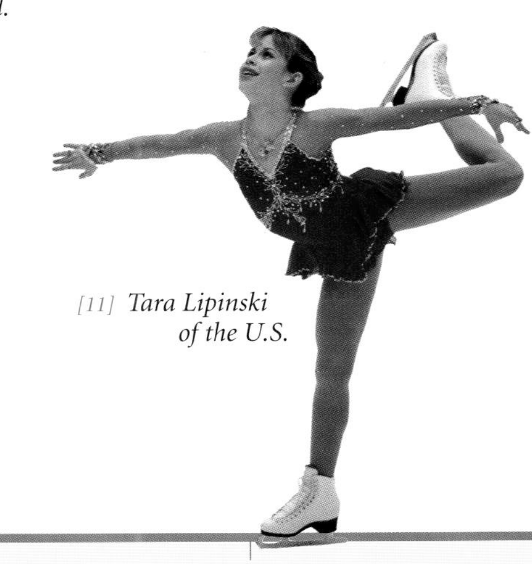

[11] *Tara Lipinski of the U.S.*

1998
A team of researchers in Hawaii, led by Ryuzo Yanagimachi, produce the world's first **cloned mouse**, from which several other clones are created.

[10]
1998
American astronaut **John Glenn** returns to space after a 36-year hiatus. At age 77, he is the oldest human to travel in space.

1998
British writer **Ian McEwan's** novel *Amsterdam* wins the Booker Prize.

1998
Cal Ripken, Jr., sits out a Major League Baseball game, ending his record of most consecutive games played at 2,632.

[11]
1998
Fifteen-year-old figure skater **Tara Lipinski** becomes the youngest female athlete to win a gold medal in an individual event at the Winter Olympic Games, in Nagano, Japan.

1998
France defeats Brazil in the men's **World Cup** soccer championship by a score of 3 to 0.

1998

1998
Keizo Obuchi of the LDP becomes prime minister of Japan; he will suffer a stroke in 2000 and be replaced by Yoshiro Mori.

1998
In **Oncale v. Sundowner Offshore Services, Inc., et al.**, the U.S. Supreme Court finds that Title VII's prohibition of workplace sexual discrimination applies equally in cases when the harasser and victim are of the same sex.

1998
Fighting between **Serbian forces** and the **Kosovo Liberation Army** escalates. NATO intervention brings a cease-fire and partial withdrawal of Serbian troops from the province of Kosovo.

 [1]

1998
Genetic analyses positively identify the remains of **Tsar Nicholas II, Alexandra**, three of their daughters (probably Anastasia, Tatiana, and Olga), and four servants. The remains are given a state funeral and reburied in St. Petersburg.

1998
Novelist **José Saramago** becomes the first Portuguese writer to win the Nobel Prize for Literature.

1998
One of the largest enclosed public spaces in the world, the new **Hong Kong International Airport** opens on the artificial island Chek Lap Kok.

 [2]

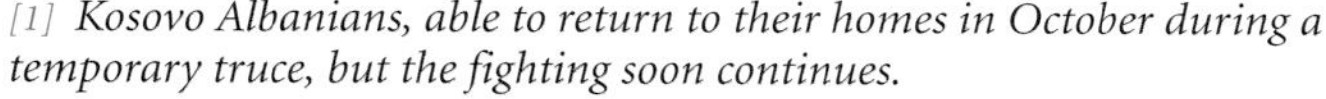

[1] *Kosovo Albanians, able to return to their homes in October during a temporary truce, but the fighting soon continues.*

[4] *Karine Ruby of France, winner of the women's snowboard.*

[2] *Hong Kong International Airport, seeming to stretch out of sight.*

[5] *President Daniel arap Moi of Kenya. His regime is being seen outside Africa as increasingly repressive and corrupt.*

[3] *Sergey Brin and Larry Page*

[6] *Bono of the Irish rock band U2 holds up the hands of David Trimble of the Ulster Unionists (left) and John Hume of the Social Democratic Labor Party (SDLP) at a Belfast rally to promote a "yes" vote in the referendum.*

1998
The **Vatican** issues a statement apologizing for the Roman Catholic Church's failure to act to save Jews and other victims of Nazis persecution during the Holocaust.

 [5]

January 5, 1998
Daniel arap Moi is sworn in as president of Kenya for his fifth consecutive term.

January 22, 1998
One of the most notorious domestic terrorists in U.S. history, **Theodore Kaczynski**, the so-called Unabomber, who killed three people and injured 22 in 16 attacks between 1979 and 1995, is sentenced to life without parole.

 [6]

May 22, 1998
In a referendum in Ireland and Northern Ireland—the first all-Ireland vote since 1918—the **Belfast Agreement** is approved. It provides for a Northern Ireland Assembly and for cross-border cooperation.

July 17, 1998
The United Nations completes the statute establishing the **International Criminal Court**, which begins sittings four years later.

 [7]

August 7, 1998
Islamist terrorists bomb **U.S. embassies in Kenya and Tanzania**, killing 268, 12 of them Americans, and wounding thousands.

1998
Sergey Brin and Larry Page of Stanford University deploy the **Google** search engine.

 [3]

1998
Snowboarding and curling are contested for the first time at the **Olympics**, in the Winter Games at Nagano, Japan.

 [4]

1998
The Brazilian government announces that it will set aside 25 million hectares (62 million acres) of the **Amazon rain forest** for conservation.

1998
The first U.S. television station begins broadcasting in **digital high-definition** television (HDTV). Enabling sharper and brighter pictures, HDTV is scheduled to replace nondigital signals.

1998
The Internet Corporation for Assigned Names and Numbers is established. It promulgates a Uniform-Domain-Name-Dispute-Resolution Policy to resolve **domain-name** controversies and licenses several arbitration services to interpret and enforce it.

1998
The U.S. Food and Drug Administration approves **Viagra** (sildenafil), the first oral drug treatment for male impotence.

THE LEWINSKY AFFAIR

A sex scandal rocks the United States and almost brings down the president.

In 1998 President Bill Clinton faced several charges of personal impropriety. He was forced to testify in an ongoing case of sexual harassment brought against him by Paula Corbin Jones, a state employee when Clinton was governor of Arkansas. The case was later dismissed, but in November Clinton agreed to an $850,000 payment to Jones.

Following the Jones trial, Clinton faced additional charges, this time involving his personal relationship with a White House intern, Monica Lewinsky (left, with the president). He denied the accusations before a grand jury but ultimately acknowledged "improper relations" in a televised address. At the end of the year Clinton became only the second president in history to be impeached. Charged with perjury and obstruction of justice, he was acquitted by the Senate in 1999.

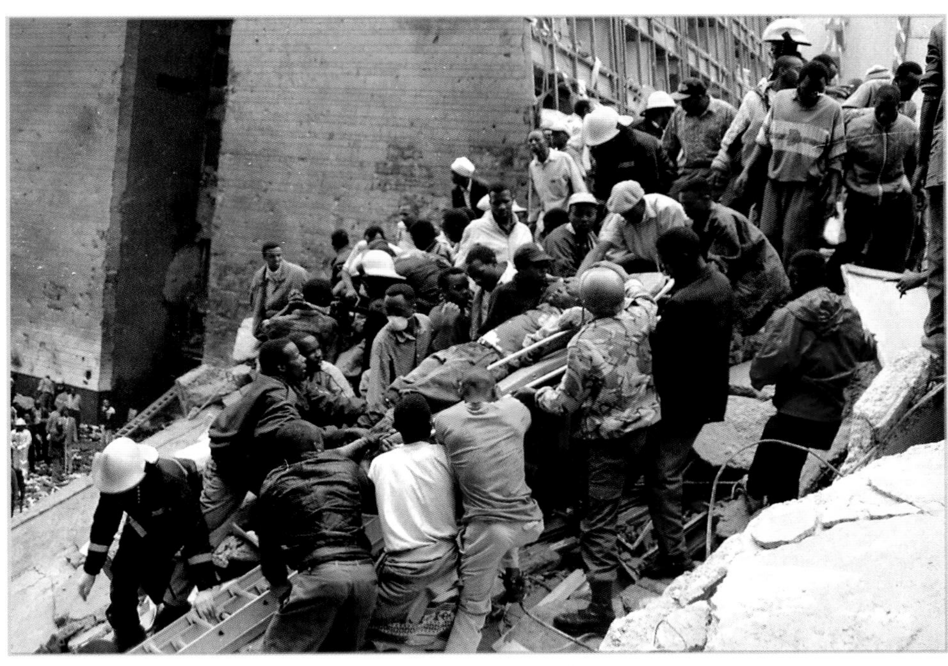

[7] *Dead and injured are carried from the remains of the U.S. Embassy in Nairobi.*

[8] *Graffiti in Bilbao demanding an amnesty for imprisoned ETA terrorists after the cease-fire has been announced.*

[9] *Gerhard Schröder. He will become unpopular for trying to introduce cuts in the social welfare system.*

September 8, 1998
Mark McGwire of the St. Louis Cardinals breaks Roger Maris's 1961 record for most home runs in a regular professional baseball season by hitting his 62nd of the season (he will finish the season with 70 home runs).

September 9, 1998
Special prosecutor **Kenneth W. Starr** sends to Congress the report on his investigation into the actions of U.S. president Bill Clinton in the Whitewater affair and with Monica Lewinsky.

 [8]

September 16, 1998
The Basque separatist organization **ETA** announces an indefinite cease-fire after 30 years of terrorist guerrilla attacks in Spain that are blamed for 800 deaths; the peace lasts 14 months.

October 19, 1998
The antitrust trial against **Microsoft Corporation**, brought by the U.S. government, opens in Washington, D.C.

 [9]

October 27, 1998
Gerhard Schröder of the Social Democratic Party, who will concern himself with reducing high unemployment, with limiting nuclear energy, and with economic reconstruction, becomes chancellor of Germany.

November 3, 1998
Scientists announce the discovery in the Hui Autonomous Region of Ningxia of a previously unknown 15.5-mile segment of the **Great Wall of China**, which runs in toto about 4,500 miles.

1998-1999

November 5, 1998
The journal **Nature** publishes a report that DNA testing has confirmed (still disputed by some) that Thomas Jefferson fathered at least one child by his slave Sally Hemings.

November 20, 1998
American **tobacco companies** agree with 46 U.S. states to reimburse Medicaid funds spent treating smoking-related illnesses.

November 24, 1998
British Parliament announces that the right of hereditary peers to vote in the House of Lords will end, though compromise legislation later allows 92 **hereditary peers** to remain in the Lords.

December 9, 1998
The United Nations General Assembly declares **anti-Semitism** a form of racism.

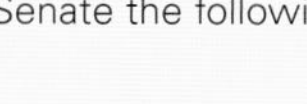

December 19, 1998
The U.S. House of Representatives **impeaches** President Bill Clinton, charging him with perjury and obstruction of justice. He will be acquitted by the Senate the following month.

[1]

1999
Argentina and the **Falkland Islands** resume air links that have been broken since the war of 1982.

[1] Protests at the House impeachment of the president. "Big Brother" is the author of the report that has led to the impeachment, Kenneth Starr. The rally is organized by the Rev. Jesse Jackson.

[5] The Millennium Dome, designed by the Richard Rogers Partnership, is the largest cable-net-supported structure in the world.

[4] Lauryn Hill

[6] The dome added to the top of the Reichstag (Parliament) in Berlin. A ramp inside spirals up to the public viewing platform around an inverted cone of mirrors that deflect daylight into the debating chamber below.

1999
Lennox Lewis defeats Evander Holyfield to become the only British boxer in the 20th century to hold the undisputed world heavyweight title.

1999
Michael Jordan, the greatest player in basketball history, announces his second retirement. He has won two Olympic gold medals and 10 league scoring titles, and he has led the Chicago Bulls to six national titles.

[5]

1999
The Millennium Dome opens in London. Built to house an exhibition for the opening of the 21st century, it is the largest dome in the world.

1999
Mireya Moscoso becomes the first female president of Panama and in December oversees the U.S. handover of the Panama Canal.

[6]

1999
Sir Norman Foster finishes the renovation and redesign of the **Reichstag**. A study of line and light, the historic German building is topped by a magnificent glass dome.

1999
The **AIDS** epidemic worsens in Africa as reports indicate that some 9,400 people on the continent are infected with the fatal disease every day.

1999
As the **world population** passes the six billion mark, a study is issued that projects a serious crisis in 2100 if the current rate of growth is not slowed.

1999
At **Columbine High School** in Littleton, Colorado, two students kill 12 fellow students and a teacher and wound more than 20 others before taking their own lives.

1999
English ballooning instructor Brian Jones and Swiss psychiatrist Bertrand Piccard are the first to circumnavigate the earth nonstop in a **hot-air balloon**. The trip is made in just under 20 days.

1999
French golfer **Jean Van de Velde** approaches the final hole of the Open Championship at Carnoustie, Scotland, with a three-stroke lead, only to score a remarkable triple bogey in one of the most spectacular collapses in golf history.

1999
Hugo Chávez becomes president of Venezuela. He will have tense relations with the United States and domestic opponents and will be ousted in a coup in April 2002, only to win a recall election in 2004 and then be reelected in December 2006.

1999
Lauryn Hill wins five Grammy Awards for her groundbreaking solo album, *The Miseducation of Lauryn Hill*, credited with establishing rap music firmly in the mainstream.

COLUMBINE MASSACRE

Thirteen killed as disaffected teenagers go on killing spree in a middle-class American high school

On April 20, in Littleton, Colorado, two students cloaked in black trench coats and armed with guns and bombs opened fire at Columbine High School, killing 13 people and wounding more than 20 before taking their own lives. The killers were identified as 18-year-old Eric Harris and Dylan Klebold, aged 17 (shown above on CCTV). Both were said to have been members of an outcast group of about a dozen high-school students known as the Trench Coat Mafia, the members of which often wore trench coats and had German slogans and swastikas emblazoned on their clothes.

One female eyewitness told police she was in the library when one of the boys burst in and began firing shots. "He said he would kill everyone who had been mean to him and his friends over the last year," she said. Other witnesses said the gunmen were targeting popular athletes and students from ethnic minorities.

After the shootings, as FBI agents and specialist firearms teams carefully picked their way through the carnage, a bomb set on a timing device exploded. At least 12 further bombs were found in other parts of the school.

The Columbine tragedy, which followed closely a number of similar deadly incidents of school violence, prompted renewed debate in the United States about gun control and the need to make schools weapon-free zones.

[2] *Jean Van de Velde in the Barry Burn on the final hole at Carnoustie, where he will squander his lead.*

[3] *Hugo Chávez and his wife, Marisabel, outside the tomb of the great South American liberator Simón Bolívar. Chávez is drawing Bolívar's sword from its scabbard.*

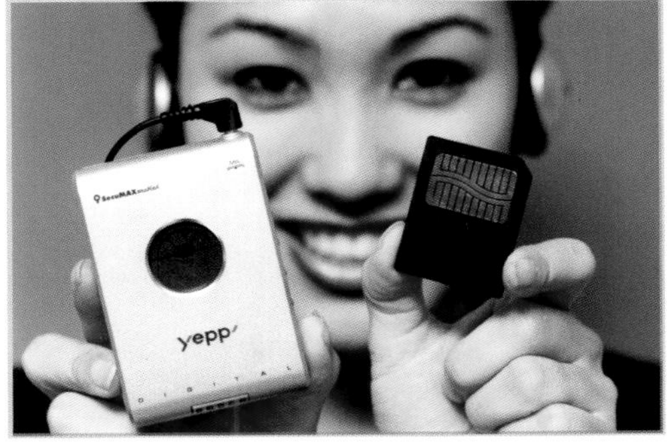

[7] *An early MP3 player and the chip that makes it possible. In the next few years the capacity of such players will go up by leaps and bounds.*

1999
The **bald eagle**, the national bird of the U.S., is removed from the endangered species list.

1999
The final film of legendary director **Stanley Kubrick**, *Eyes Wide Shut*, which stars Tom Cruise and Nicole Kidman, is released in the U.S.

1999
The Melissa and Chernobyl **computer viruses** sweep across the world, crippling computer networks and drawing attention to the problem of cyber crime.

1999
The music compression technology **MP3** becomes widely popular with the advent of portable music players that are compatible with the format.

1999
The National Gallery of Art, Washington, D.C., kicks off a multiyear presentation of the largest and most complete collection of **Alfred Stieglitz's** work. Many of the prints have never been published.

1999
The number of **Roman Catholics** in the world passes the one billion mark.

1999

1999
The U.S. **Lunar Prospector** is deliberately crashed into the moon as telescopes watch for spectral signatures unique to water. None are seen, but other data indicates that water is present.

 [1]

1999
The United States defeats China in the **Women's World Cup** soccer championship after a draw decided by a penalty shootout.

 [2]

1999
The World Conservation Union announces that a quarter of the world's **coniferous tree species** are under threat of extinction.

1999
The **Vermont Supreme Court** declares that same-sex couples are entitled under the state constitution to the same legal rights as married heterosexual couples. Shortly thereafter the state legislature enacts a law creating "civil unions."

1999
The world's longest cable-stayed bridge, the **Tatara Ohashi**, opens, connecting Honshu and Shikoku in Japan.

[3]

March 12, 1999
The formerly Communist-controlled countries of Poland, Hungary, and the Czech Republic become members of the **North Atlantic Treaty Organization (NATO)** shortly before the group's 50th anniversary.

 [4]

[1] The Lunar Prospector sits on top of the Trans-Lunar Injection stage of its rocket.

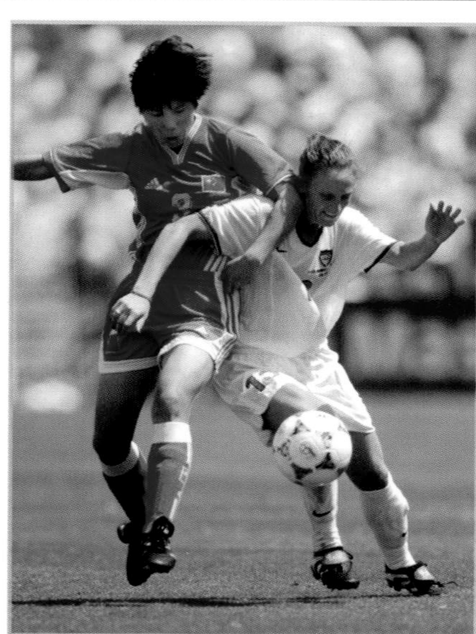

[2] China and the U.S. battle for the Women's World Cup.

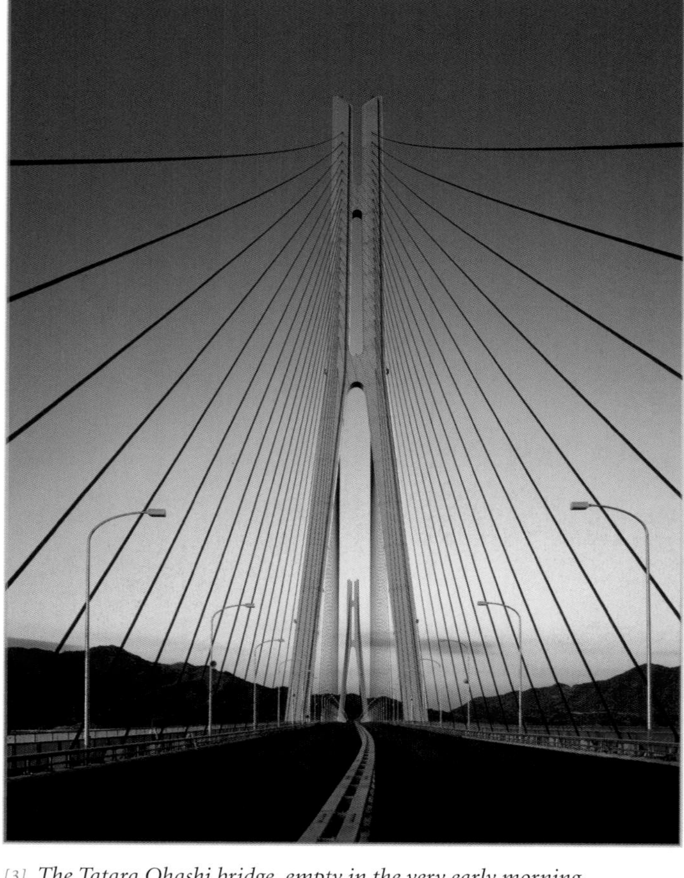

[3] The Tatara Ohashi bridge, empty in the very early morning.

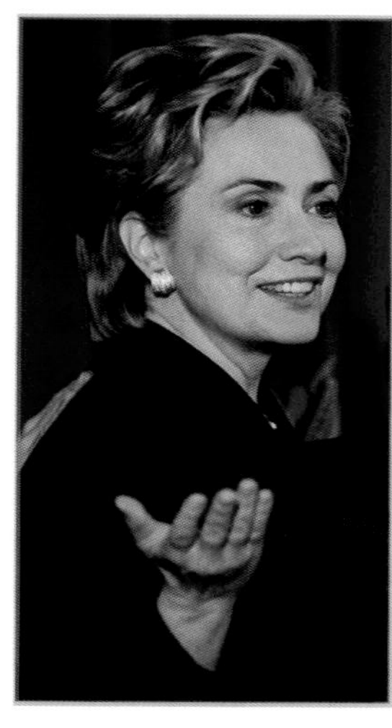

[7] Hillary Clinton talks to reporters just after she has announced that she will run for the Senate.

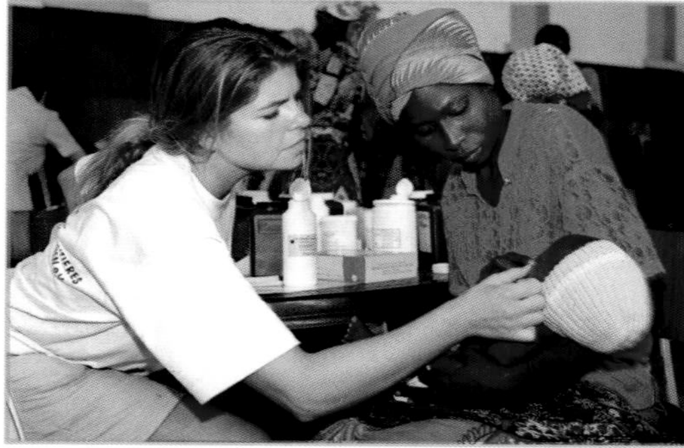

[8] A German Médecins Sans Frontières doctor helps during floods in Mozambique.

[4] NATO's 50th anniversary gathering of the leaders of its 19 member states: Tony Blair shakes hands with Bill Clinton.

July 16, 1999
John F. Kennedy, Jr., his wife, Carolyn, and her sister, Lauren Bessette, are killed when their plane, piloted by Kennedy, falls into the Atlantic Ocean off the coast of Massachusetts.

 [7]

November 23, 1999
Ending months of speculation, **Hillary Rodham Clinton**, wife of former U.S. president Bill Clinton, confirms that she will be a Democratic candidate for the U.S. Senate in New York in 2000.

 [8]

December 1999
The Nobel Peace Prize is awarded to **Médicins Sans Frontières** (Doctors Without Borders), a privately funded, independent humanitarian organization based in Paris.

 [9]

December 20, 1999
Macau is returned by the Portuguese to China. This ends 422 years of Portugese rule.

December 31, 1999
Boris Yeltsin resigns as president of Russia and appoints as acting president Russian intelligence officer and politician Vladimir Putin, who will go on to win the March 2000 elections easily.

December 31, 1999
Control of the **Panama Canal** is passed to Panama from the United States. Administration of the canal is the responsibility of the Panama Canal Authority, which answers solely to the government of Panama.

April 1, 1999
The Canadian territory of **Nunavut** is created out of a vast region of Canada's Northwest Territories. It stretches across much of the Canadian Arctic and encompasses the traditional lands of the Inuit.

 [5]

May 1, 1999
The **Treaty of Amsterdam**, enters into force in the European Union. It expands protection for employment and working conditions, and gives the Council of Ministers the power to penalize members for violations of human rights.

May 10, 1999
American poet **Shel Silverstein**, the author of many popular children's books, dies in Key West, Florida.

June 1999
The appointment of **James Hormel** as U.S. ambassador to Luxembourg, which had been stalled in the U.S. Senate for almost two years because he is openly gay, receives approval.

June 12, 1999
NATO decides the Serbs must be forced to withdraw from **Kosovo** to avoid atrocities on civilians. NATO planes fly 38,000 combat missions in March to June, and then NATO's multinational units (KFOR) move into Kosovo on June 12.

 [6]

July 1, 1999
Politician **Johannes Rau**, a member of the Social Democratic Party who will promote closer ties with Israel and greater acceptance of foreign immigrants, becomes president of Germany (1999–2004).

[6] A Humvee of the U.S. forces forming part of NATO's KFOR is greeted by Kosovo Albanians and welcoming graffiti on the wall behind.

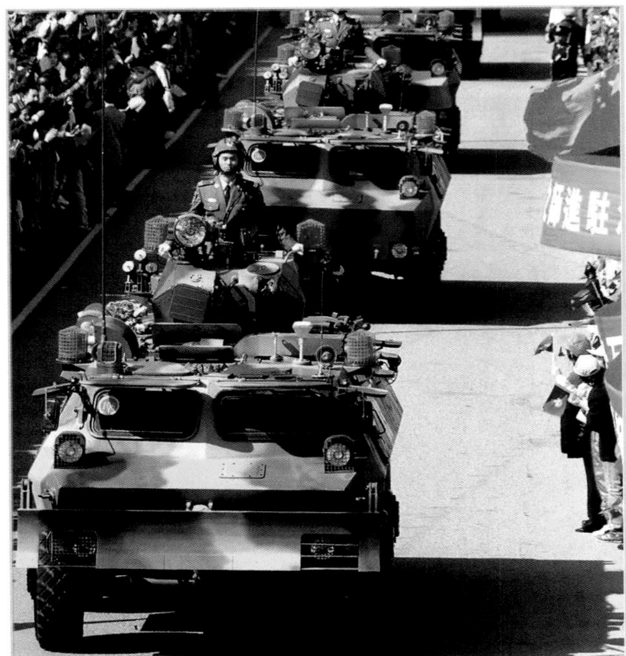

[9] China's PLA puts on a show of strength at the handover of Macau. This contrasts with the handover of Hong Kong to China in 1997, when the armed forces were kept very much in the background.

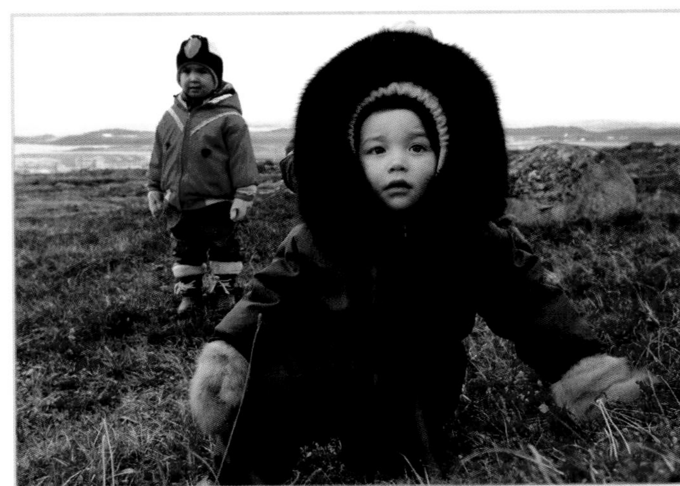

[5] Two Inuit children near Iqaluit, the capital of the newly created Nunavut territory.

A jubilant Liberian soldier during the civil war.

2000

2000
An e-mail virus known as the **Love Bug** sweeps through much of the world, causing many businesses to shut down their e-mail systems.

2000
Yugoslav president **Slobodan Milosevic** is forced from office.

 [1]

2000
As head of the **Human Genome Project**, American geneticist Francis Collins announces that the entire human genome has been sequenced. It is believed that the achievement will revolutionize medicine.

 [2]

2000
At the **World Education Forum**, it is reported that some 113 million children, most of which are girls, do not have access to primary education.

2000
Author **Jorge Edwards** becomes the first Chilean to win the Cervantes Prize for literature in Spanish. The lifetime achievement award recognizes his realistic work, which often focused on his country's politics.

2000
The last **Peanuts** comic strip is published, following the death of its creator, Charles Schulz.

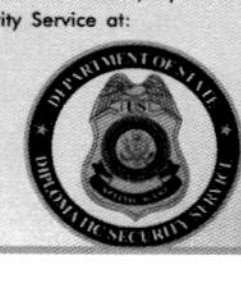

[1] A wanted poster, issued by the U.S. State Department, for Slobodan Milosevic (top), Bosnian Serb leader Radovan Karadzic (left), and Bosnian Serb military commander Ratko Mladic, indicted for crimes against humanity in the Balkan wars by the U.N. International Criminal Tribunal.

[6] A genetically modified cocoa plant being treated with respect.

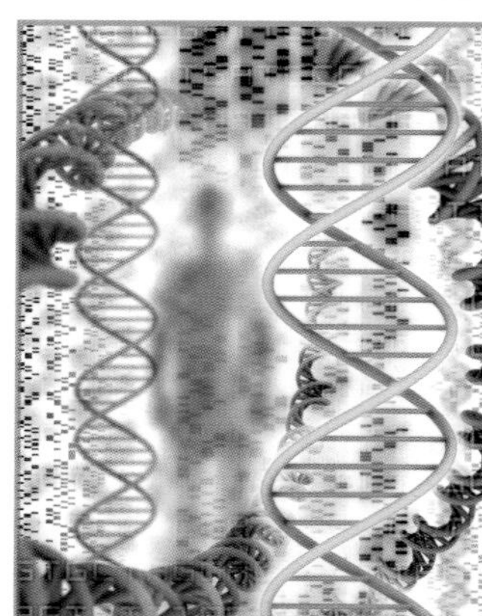

[2] A striking image formed out of a DNA sequence and helix models.

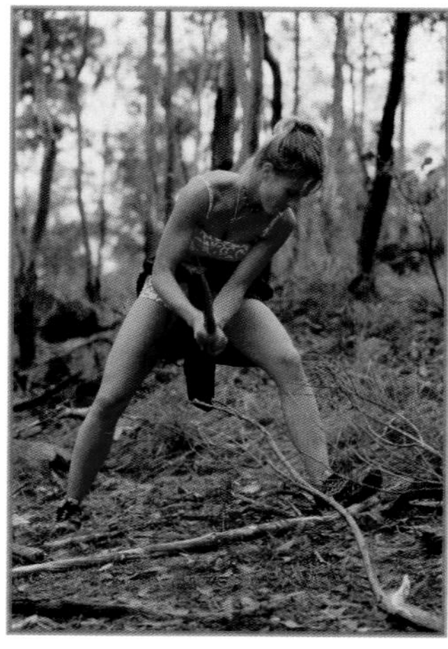

[4] An American contestant chopping wood in Survivor.

[5] Part of the Öresund Link joining Denmark to Sweden.

[4]
2000
Survivor, a television series in which two teams struggle for their existence in a remote, challenging locale with only minimal equipment, sets off a craze for "reality TV."

2000
The first-ever analysis of the **world's health care** systems is conducted, with France's being found the best in the world.

 [5]
2000
The **Öresund Link**, a bridge and tunnel system connecting Malmö, Sweden, and Copenhagen, Denmark, is opened over one of the busiest sea lanes in the world.

 [6]
2000
The rise of **genetically modified plants** draws heated debates over possible dangers to humans and animals that consume them, as well to ecosystems in general.

 [7]
2000
The **Russian Orthodox Church** canonizes Tsar Nicholas II and his family, designating them "passion bearers" (the lowest rank of sainthood) because of the piety they showed during their final days.

 [8]
2000
Fears about the computer system problems to be caused by the rollover to the year 2000—so-called "**Y2K Bug**"—emerge as unfounded in the early days of January.

2000
Cigarette companies are ordered by a Miami court to pay almost $145 billion dollars in punitive damages to Floridians who have been harmed by cigarette smoking. A long court battle ensues, and in 2006 Florida Supreme Court will throw out the award.

2000
Gao Xingjian, Chinese émigré novelist, playwright, and critic, is the first Chinese-language writer awarded the Nobel Prize for Literature "for an oeuvre of universal validity, bitter insights and linguistic ingenuity."

2000
Green Architecture, a movement to construct buildings that are environment friendly, continues to gain in popularity around the world, especially in Europe.

2000
Jamaican cricketer **Courtney Walsh** becomes the highest wicket taker (435) in Test history.

 [3]

2000
Publishing books in electronic format, known as **e-publishing**, grows in popularity as several publishing houses announce plans to enter the field.

2000
Reports indicate that some 27 million people are **enslaved**—more than ever before.

[7] Tsar Nicholas II with his family, in a photograph taken in 1905.

[10] Tate Modern, a converted electricity power station on the South Bank of the Thames. Its most interesting feature is the vast Turbine Hall for which a series of installations and huge sculptures are commissioned. Norman Foster's Millennium Bridge for pedestrians is on the left.

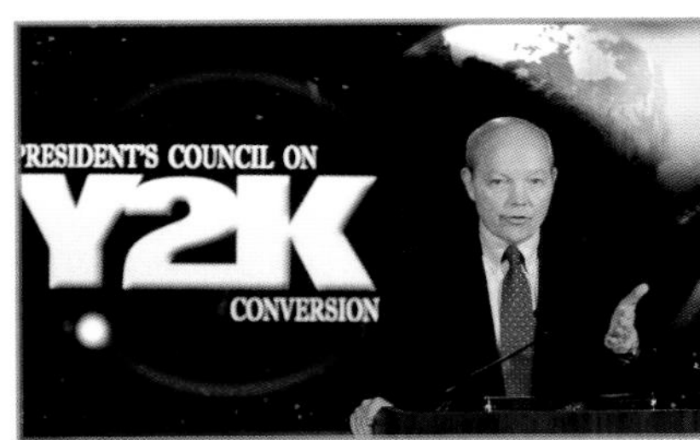

[8] An unnecessary precaution: a press conference called on February 29, 2000, Leap Day, by the portentously named President's Council on Y2K Conversion, to confirm that even this tricky date has given no real problems.

[9] The Sony Center in Potzdamer Platz, Berlin.

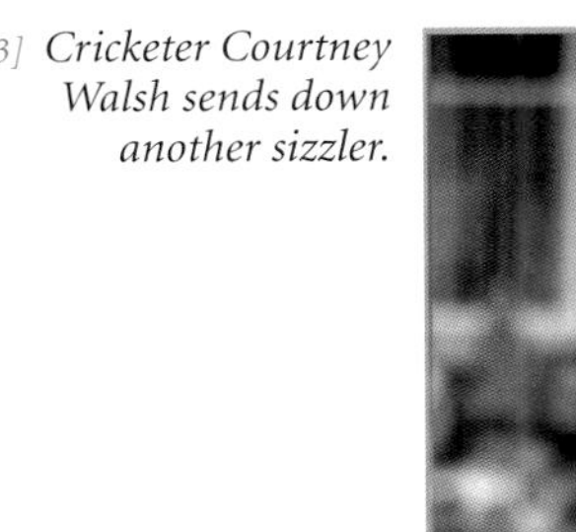

[3] Cricketer Courtney Walsh sends down another sizzler.

[9]
2000
The **Sony Center** opens in Berlin. The building's transparent feel epitomizes German architect Helmut Jahn's use of steel and glass.

2000
The **Summer Olympic Games** take place in Sydney, Australia.

[10]
2000
The **Tate Modern**, a new art museum in London, opens. All significant movements are accounted for: cubism, futurism, abstract expressionism, Dada, surrealism, and pop art.

2000
The U.S. Supreme Court rules that a state law criminalizing the performance of dilation and extraction—or late-term—**abortions** violates the Constitution because it allows no consideration of the health of the woman.

2000
The U.S. Supreme Court rules that the **Boy Scouts**, because it is a private organization, was within its rights when it dismissed a scoutmaster expressly because of his avowed homosexuality.

2000
The **Vatican** reveals the long-awaited subject of the third prophecy of the Virgin Mary (revealed in 1917 to peasant children in Fatima) is the 1981 assassination attempt on Pope John Paul II.

2000-2001

2000
The Whitney Museum of American Art holds the first comprehensive exhibition of painter **Alice Neel's** work, which includes her portraits, noted for their poignant record of the human condition.

2000
With his win at the British Open, American golfer **Tiger Woods** becomes the youngest player to win the sport's four major championships.

 [1]

2000
AIDS reaches epidemic proportions in Africa, with nearly 40 percent of the population in some countries HIV-positive.

January 31, 2000
British doctor **Harold Shipman** is sentenced to life imprisonment. He is suspected of having killed between 260 and 360 people. He will kill himself in 2004.

March 18, 2000
Chen Shui-bian, a leader of the pro-independence movement seeking statehood for the Republic of China (Taiwan), is elected president of Taiwan, breaking the Nationalist Party's 55-year rule.

 [2]

April 4, 2000
The government of **South Korea** orders some 85 percent of the country's livestock markets closed in an attempt to end an outbreak of foot-and-mouth disease that had struck Asian livestock.

 [3]

2000-2007

[1] *Tiger Woods kisses the claret jug trophy after winning the British Open at St. Andrews.*

[2] *Chen Shui-bian, a new face for Taiwan in place of the old Kuomintang nationalist leaders. He will win a second term in 2004.*

[3] *A South Korean stall carries on selling steamed pork regardless of the foot-and-mouth epidemic raging there.*

[5] *Damage to the destroyer USS Cole is clearly visible. Islamic extremsts, probably al-Qaeda, are to blame.*

[6] *Vicente Fox*

 [5]

October 12, 2000
An explosion triggered by suicide bombers causes the deaths of 17 sailors aboard a U.S. naval ship, the **USS Cole**, in the Yemeni port of Aden.

October 27, 2000
At a concert near Tel Aviv, the music of German composer **Richard Wagner**, which many associate with the Nazi regime, is played for the first time in public in Israel.

November 21, 2000
The **United Farm Workers** call off the boycott of California table grapes begun in 1984 by union organizer Cesar Chavez, saying the goals of the strike have been met.

November 28, 2000
The parliament of **The Netherlands** passes a bill permitting euthanasia under specified conditions.

 [6]

December 1, 2000
Vicente Fox, a member of the National Action Party, becomes president of Mexico. His election marks the end of 71 years of uninterrupted rule by the Partido Revolucionario Institucional (Institutional Revolutionary Party).

 [7]

December 12, 2000
In the disputed U.S. presidential election the U.S. Supreme Court stops the **manual recounts**, underway in certain Florida counties, as a violation of the Fourteenth Amendment's equal protection clause.

April 15, 2000
U.S. president Bill Clinton establishes the **Giant Sequoia National Monument**, a preserve near Sequoia National Park covering more than 500 square miles (1,300 square km) of Sequoia National Forest in the Sierra Nevada of California.

June 13, 2000
South Korean president **Kim Dae Jung** meets North Korean leader **Kim Jong Il** in a summit that marks the first meeting between heads of the two countries. They reach an agreement to pursue reunification.

 [4]

July 27, 2000
An Air France **Concorde** crashes shortly after take-off in Paris, killing 109 on board and 4 on the ground. It had hit debris left on the runway by another plane.

September 6, 2000
Tuvalu, a group of nine coral islands in the west-central Pacific with a population of about 10,000, becomes the 189th member of the United Nations.

October 6, 2000
Near Sakaiminato, Japan, an **earthquake** of magnitude 7.3 strikes, the most powerful since the devastating Great Hanshin Earthquake in 1995, but damage and casualties are relatively low because the epicenter was in a sparsely inhabited area.

October 11, 2000
In a ceremony in London, the International Women of the Year Association awards the title Greatest Woman Achiever of the Century to Russian cosmonaut **Valentina V. Tereshkova**, the first woman in space.

[4] South (right) and North Korean presidents embrace—or at least wearers of their masks do.

[9] Barry Bonds follows the trajectory of his 73rd and record-breaking home run.

[8] Protective clothing and breathing apparatuses are worn outside the National Enquirer *offices in Florida, one of several news-media offices to be sent anthrax letters.*

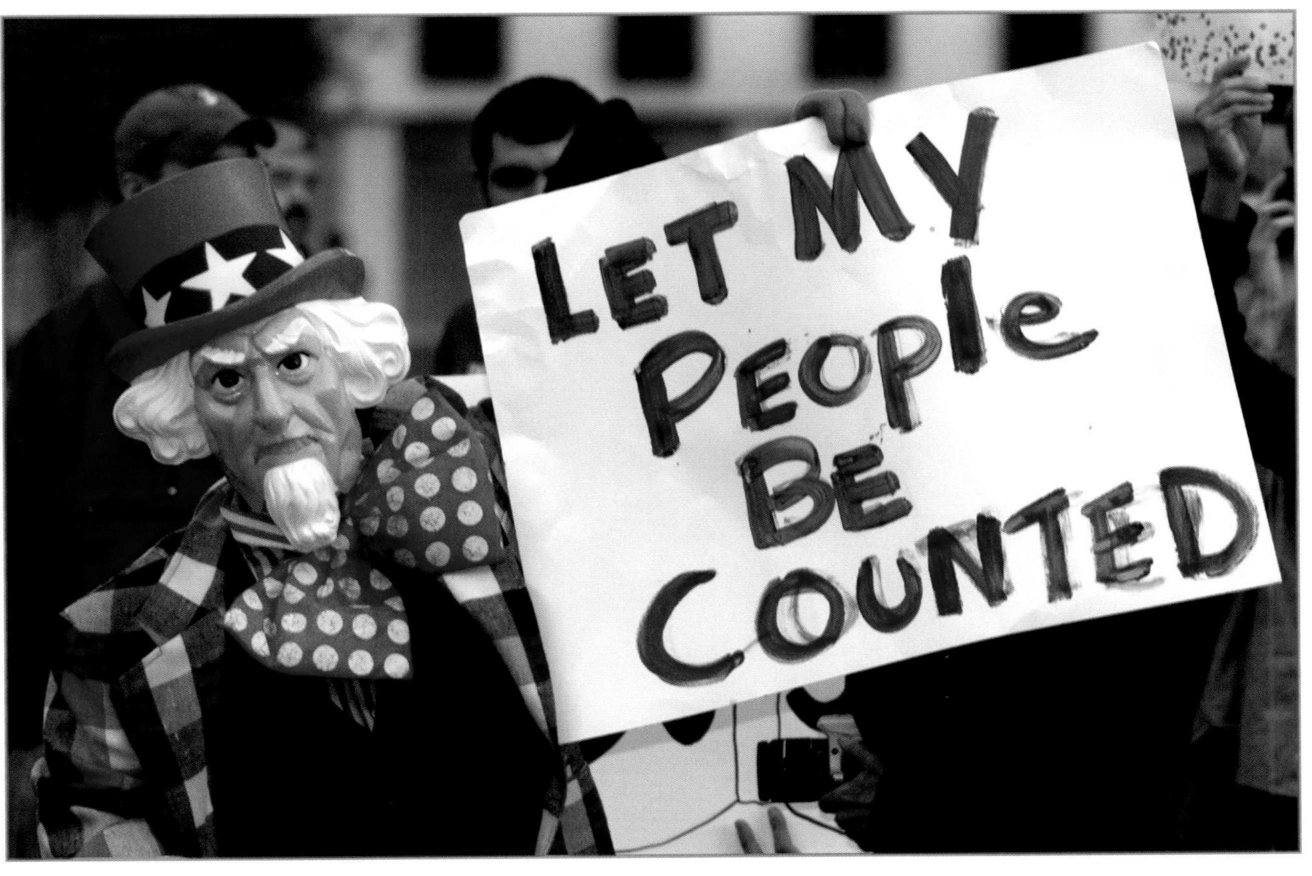

[7] Uncle Sam makes his views clear outside the Florida state capitol building.

2001
A Moscow judge rules that **Jehovah's Witnesses** have not violated a law banning religious sects that incite violence and thus can practice their religion in Russia. The case is seen as a test of religious freedom in the country.

2001
An environmental battle over the Arctic National Wildlife Refuge in **Alaska** erupts as the U.S. government begins talks to consider opening the refuge for oil drilling.

 [8]

2001
Anthrax-laced letters are mailed to U.S. media and political figures, resulting in several deaths. The U.S. government reassesses its vaccines against anthrax and smallpox.

2001
Apple begins selling the **iPod**, a portable MP3 player, which quickly becomes the market leader. "Podcasting," combining iPod and broadcasting, is coined to refer to audio or video material downloaded for playback.

2001
Apple introduces its new operating system, **OS X**.

 [9]

2001
Baseball outfielder **Barry Bonds** of the San Francisco Giants hits 73 home runs to break Mark McGwire's single-season home run record.

2001

2001
George W. Bush of the Republican Party becomes the 43rd president of the United States by a 5–4 decision of the U.S. Supreme Court. His vice president is Richard B. Cheney.

 [1]

2001
Despite worldwide protests and pleas, Afghani troops begin destroying all of the country's statues, including two huge fifth-century rock-cut Buddhas, after the ruling **Taliban** claims they are offensive to Islam.

 [2]

2001
Debates concerning the medicinal use of **marijuana** continue. The U.S. Supreme Court rules that under federal law there is no acceptable medical use for marijuana, but several months later Canada approves the drug in certain medical cases.

2001
Hillary Clinton is sworn in as a New York senator, becoming the first First Lady to win elected office.

 [3]

2001
Jacques Rogge succeeds Juan Antonio Samaranch, whose tenure had been plague by controversy and allegations of corruption, as head of the International Olympic Committee.

2001
Penn State football coach **Joe Paterno** wins his 324th game to break Bear Bryant's career record as the "winningest" football coach in major college history; Paterno finishes the season with 327 victories.

 [4]

[1] George W. Bush and Dick Cheney

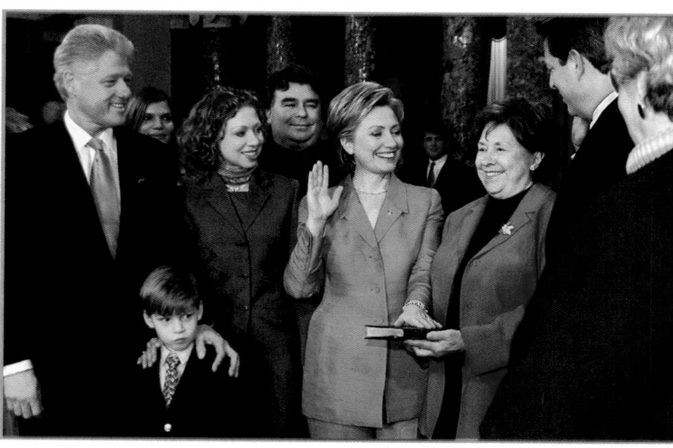

[3] The first step back to the White House? The Clinton and Rodham families reenact Hillary Clinton's oath-taking as senator for New York. Her mother holds the Bible, Al Gore is on the right, and Hillary's brother, Hugh Rodham, is behind her.

[4] Joe Paterno is carried on the shoulders of his team.

[9] The Mir space station with the Spektr module projecting from it. This module was damaged when it was hit by an unmanned supply ship in 1997.

[2] A Taliban militiaman stands proudly by his, or his comrades', handiwork, an empty niche—all that's left after the destruction of its statue of the Buddha.

2001
The Netherlands parliament legalizes physician-assisted suicide if certain criteria of due care have been fulfilled.

 [9]

2001
The Russian space station **Mir** is abandoned and falls into the Pacific Ocean. It had been in service for more than 14 years.

2001
The Texas-based energy giant **Enron Corporation** files for Chapter 11 bankruptcy protection. The Department of Justice begins a criminal investigation of the company for potential accounting fraud.

 [10]

2001
Trinidadian-born writer **Sir V. S. Naipaul** is awarded the Nobel Prize for Literature. He is best known for his pessimistic novels set in Third World countries, such as *A Bend in the River* (1979).

January 7, 2001
John Kufuor is inaugurated as president of Ghana in that country's first peaceful transition from one elected government to another.

January 9, 2001
Australian scientists say that analysis of DNA taken from 60,000-year-old local human remains show no links with human ancestors from Africa, suggesting that Africa was not the only site of the genesis of the human species.

2001
Scientists report findings that suggest the earth was struck by an **asteroid** some 250 million years ago, triggering volcanic eruptions that caused the worst mass extinction in the planet's history.

 [5]

2001
Southern Cross II, a U.S. Global Hawk spy plane, becomes the first unmanned aircraft to fly across the Pacific Ocean.

2001
The **Coalition to Stop the Use of Child Soldiers** reports that at least 300,000 children under the age of 18 are fighting as soldiers in 41 countries.

 [6]

2001
The **Eden Project**, the world's largest greenhouse complex, opens in Cornwall, England.

 [7]

2001
The **Leaning Tower of Pisa** opens for the first time since 1990 after engineers reduce its tilt in an effort to save the building from collapse.

 [8]

2001
The Netherlands becomes the first country to legalize **same-sex marriages**. Two years later it is followed by Belgium and Canada.

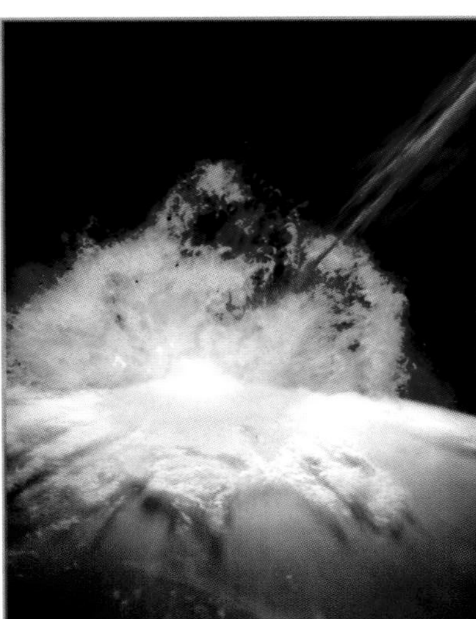

[5] *A simulation of an asteroid hitting the earth.*

[7] *The Eden Project, with geodesic domes inside which tropical and semitropical habitats can be simulated. The domes are built within a disused china-clay quarry.*

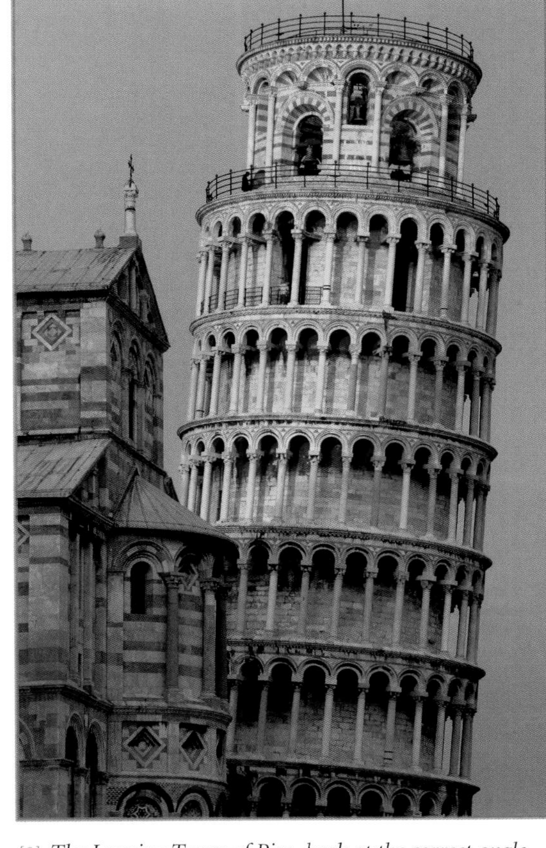

[8] *The Leaning Tower of Pisa, back at the correct angle.*

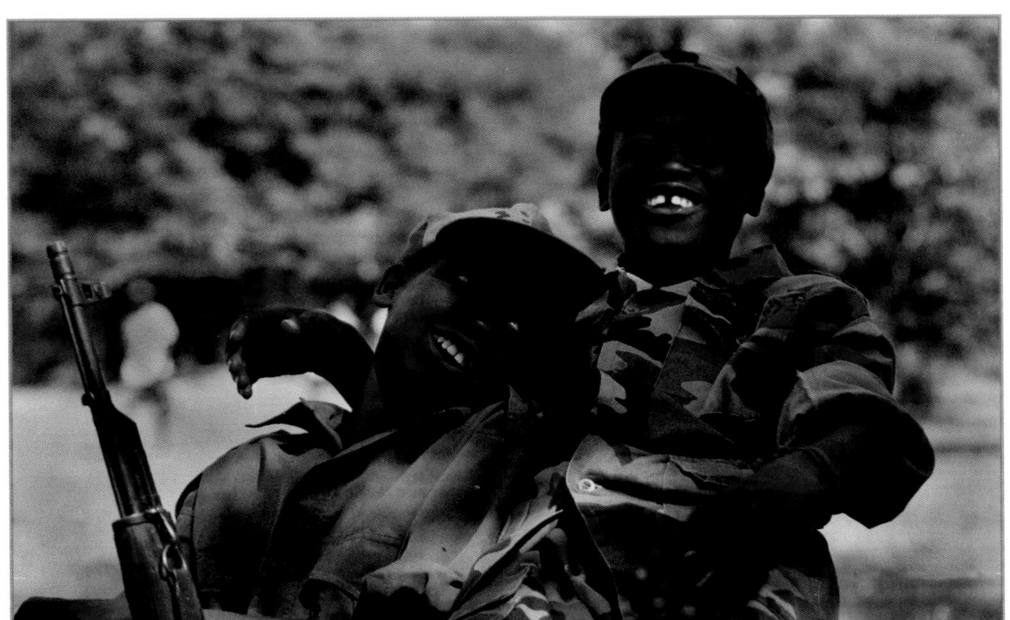

[6] *Child soldiers of the Sudan People's Liberation Army, which has been fighting the Islamist Sudanese government in the south of the country.*

[10] *V. S. Naipaul*

January 11, 2001
The U.S. Federal Communications Commission approves the biggest merger in history, and **AOL Time Warner** (since shortened to Time Warner) stock begins trading the next morning.

February 18, 2001
Veteran American **stock-car racer Dale Earnhardt**, Sr., dies from injuries suffered during a crash in the final lap of the Daytona 500.

April 2001
Junichiro Koizumi becomes prime minister of Japan in the first election in which prefecture-level party members, as well as members of the Diet, can vote.

April 1, 2001
The **midair collision** of a U.S. spy plane and a Chinese fighter over the South China Sea results in the death of the Chinese pilot and the landing of the damaged American plane on Hainan Island, where its crew is detained.

April 9, 2001
American Airlines officially completes its acquisition of **Trans World Airlines** and becomes the world's largest airline.

June 11, 2001
Timothy McVeigh, convicted of the bombing of a federal building in Oklahoma City on April 19, 1995, which killed 168 people in what was then the worst terrorist attack in the U.S., is executed.

2001-2002

June 27, 2001
American actor **Jack Lemmon** dies. He was adept at both comedy and drama, and in a career that spanned more than 50 years, he won two Academy Awards.

September 5, 2001
At a scientific conference in Washington, D.C., scientists describe an observation of energy flares that provides strong evidence of the theorized **black hole** at the center of the Milky Way Galaxy.

September 11, 2001
Terrorists hijack four commercial airplanes. Two of the planes are flown into the **World Trade Center** in New York City, one into the Pentagon, and one crashes in rural Pennsylvania.

September 18, 2001
For the second straight day, **Typhoon Nari** pounds Taiwan with record rainfalls, causing massive flooding and killing 79 people.

September 21, 2001
In **stock market** trading in the United States, the Dow Jones industrial average posts its largest weekly loss (14.3 percent) since the Great Depression.

October 8, 2001
In Italy's worst civilian air disaster in nearly 30 years, a Cessna takes a wrong turn on a taxiway at **Linate Airport** in Milan and crashes into an SAS airliner about to take off, which explodes, killing 118 people, including 4 airport workers.

9/11

A series of airline hijackings and suicide attacks against U.S. targets

The attacks, perpetrated by 19 militants associated with the Islamic extremist group al-Qaeda, were planned well in advance. The militants—most of whom were from Saudi Arabia—traveled to the United States, where a number received commercial flight training. Working in small groups, the hijackers boarded four domestic airliners on September 11, and took control of the planes soon after takeoff. At 8:46 AM (local time), the terrorists piloted the first plane into the north tower of the World Trade Center in New York City (above). A second plane struck the south tower some 15 minutes later. Both structures erupted in flames and, badly damaged, soon collapsed. A third plane struck the southwest side of the Pentagon near Washington, D.C., at 9:40 AM, and within the next hour the fourth crashed in Pennsylvania after its passengers—aware of events via cellular telephones—attempted to overpower their assailants. Some 2,750 people were killed in New York, 184 at the Pentagon, and 40 in Pennsylvania. All 19 terrorists died.

After 9/11, President George W. Bush declared a war on terrorism, which became the focus of U.S. foreign policy.

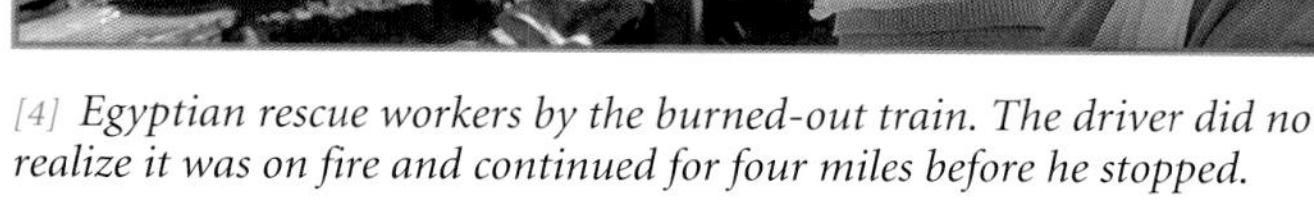

[4] Egyptian rescue workers by the burned-out train. The driver did not realize it was on fire and continued for four miles before he stopped.

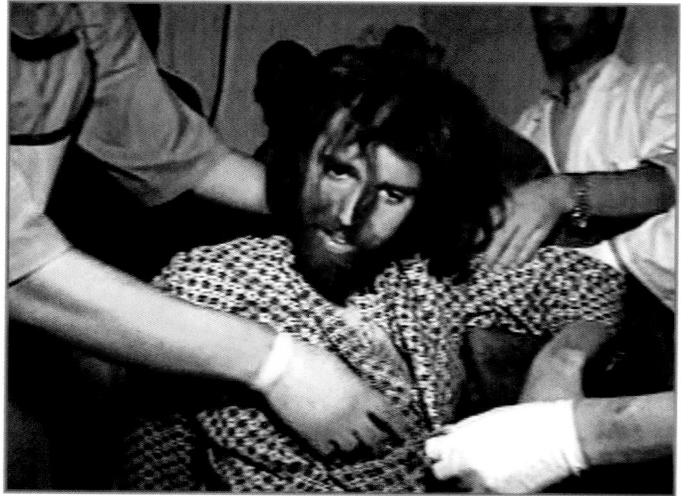

[3] John Walker-Lindh, the American Taliban, is patched up. After pleading guilty at his trial in 2002, he is expected to serve 20 years.

December 2001
Crown Prince Naruhito and Crown Princess Masako of **Japan** have their first child, a girl, who is ineligible to succeed to the throne.

 [3]

December 3, 2001
The U.S. military announces that one of the Taliban prisoners who surrendered after the November uprising at a prison in Mazar-e Sharif, Afghanistan, is a U.S. citizen, **John Walker-Lindh**.

December 23, 2001
Argentina announces the suspension of payments on its external debt—the biggest debt default in history to date.

 [4]

2002
A train fire south of **Cairo** kills over 370 passengers.

2002
Chinese airlines have three major accidents during the year. In April 128 are killed and in May 103, followed by 225.

 [5]

2002
American adventurer **Steve Fossett** becomes the first balloonist to circumnavigate the world alone.

October 9, 2001
The United Service Organizations (USO) appoints entertainer **Wayne Newton** as its official celebrity front man, replacing Bob Hope, who had served in that capacity since the early 1950s.

October 12, 2001
The centennial Nobel Peace Prize is awarded to **Kofi Annan**, secretary general of the United Nations, and to the United Nations.

November 10, 2001
After 15 years of negotiations, China's membership in the **World Trade Organization (WTO)** is approved; Taiwan's membership is approved the following day.

 [1]

November 13, 2001
On the heels of the U.S.-led invasion of **Afghanistan**, prompted by the deadly terrorist attacks of 9/11, the army of the anti-Taliban Northern Alliance captures the capital city of Kabul.

 [2]

November 24, 2001
The Grand National Assembly of **Turkey** ratifies changes to the country's legal code that makes women equal to men before the law and no longer subject to their husbands.

November 29, 2001
George Harrison, formerly of the Beatles, dies of cancer at the home of a friend in Los Angeles.

[1] China's foreign trade minister, Shi Guangsheng, toasts his country's accession to the WTO in Qatar. Many feel China's human rights record should stand in the way of its admittance, but its economic clout speaks too loudly.

[6] Queen Elizabeth meeting schoolchildren on her Golden Jubilee tour of Britain.

[2] Northern Alliance forces drive triumphantly into Kabul.

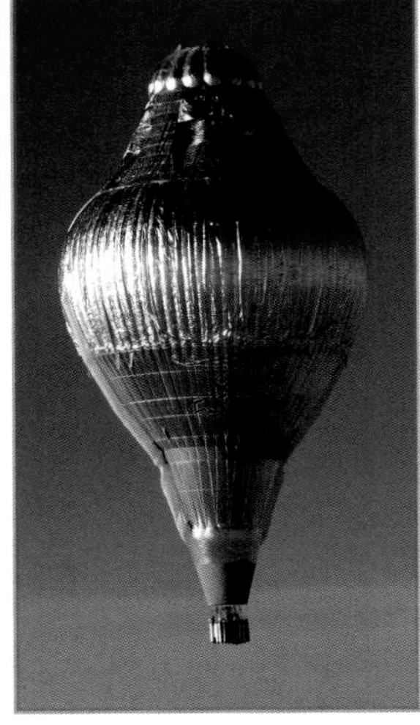

[5] Steve Fossett's balloon, Spirit of Freedom, at 21,000 feet off the coast of Chile.

[7] Russian security forces carry hostage victims out of the Moscow theater. It seems that the gas they used in their assault was the cause of most of the fatalities.

2002
Bahrain becomes a constitutional monarchy; for the first time, women may run for public office.

2002
Brazil defeats Germany in the men's **World Cup** soccer championship by a score of 2 to 0.

 [6]

2002
Britain's **Queen Elizabeth** celebrates her Golden Jubilee, marking 50 years on the throne.

2002
Controversy engulfs the **Roman Catholic Church** after revelations of widespread sexual abuse by clergy and cover-ups by church hierarchy. U.S. dioceses alone will pay out settlements of more than $1.5 billion.

 [7]

2002
Chechen rebels attempt to force Russia out of their country by targeting civilians. Among other actions, they take 800 theatergoers hostage in Moscow; 120 hostages and most of the rebels die in the subsequent rescue attempt.

2002
Eritrea and Ethiopia agree to adopt the common border suggested by an independent commission. However, both sides immediately claim the town of **Badme**.

2002

2002
Foreign peacekeeping forces arrive in Afghanistan to support the interim government of **Hamid Karzai**.

2002
Former shoeshine boy **Inacio Lula da Silva** wins the Brazilian presidency; he will lead the country's first left-wing government in more than four decades.

 [1]

2002
Hindus and Muslims riot in India in response to a train fire in **Godhra**, Gujarat, that killed 59 Hindu pilgrims. More than 1,000 people, mainly Muslims, die.

2002
Hu Jintao succeeds Jiang Zemin as general secretary of the Chinese Communist Party.

2002
In **Atkins v. Virginia** the U.S. Supreme Court rules that the death penalty, when applied to mentally retarded individuals, constitutes a "cruel and unusual punishment" prohibited by the Eighth Amendment.

2002
In their largest joint venture ever, Jordan and Israel agree to work together to pipe water to the shrinking **Dead Sea**.

 [2]

AFGHANISTAN'S NEW GOVERNMENT

Progress toward political stability

Warlordism and ethnic rivalry were prominent in Afghanistan throughout 2002, yet important steps were taken toward building a stable, democratic social structure based on traditional Afghan values. Hamid Karzai (left below), picked to head an Interim Authority in Afghanistan by a UN-sponsored international conference in Bonn, Germany, in December 2001, sought to maintain balance among the country's ethnic and tribal groups while laying a foundation for national institutions. Although Karzai was a Pashtun tribal leader, he had no armed group of his own. Security in Kabul was maintained by an International Security Assistance Force (ISAF) of 4,000 to 5,000 troops whose command was rotated among various participating countries. The photograph (left above) shows British ISAF soldiers patrolling among friendly Afghans.

In April the country's former king, Mohammed Zahir Shah, returned to Kabul after an exile of 29 years. Many hoped that he would reestablish Afghanistan's Pashtun monarchy, but he himself ruled this out. In June Zahir Shah officially opened an emergency Loya Jirga, as prescribed by the Bonn agreement. An assembly of the most important leaders from across Afghanistan, the Loya Jirga embodied supreme authority in Afghanistan's political life. Its most important task was to choose a president of the Transitional Authority that, according to the Bonn agreement, should replace the Interim Authority. Karzai was expected to be elected, and challenges from former president Burhaneddin Rabbani, a Tajik, and from supporters of the former king were avoided when both men withdrew in a demonstration of national unity. The Loya Jirga then approved Karzai and 13 members of his cabinet.

[1] *President Lula da Silva and his wife after his inauguration.*

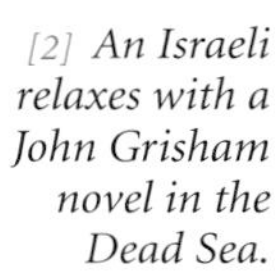

[2] *An Israeli relaxes with a John Grisham novel in the Dead Sea.*

2002
Scientists decode the **malaria genome**. The discovery is expected to aid in the development of vaccines and drugs to combat the disease.

 [5]

2002
Scientists in **Texas** clone a domestic cat. Other cloned animals now include sheep, pigs, mice, and goats.

2002
Stem cell research is at the center of an international debate. While scientists support stem cell use for its possible health advances, others oppose the use of human fetal cells on religious or ethical grounds.

2002
The 100th anniversary of the first publication of **The Times Literary Supplement,** considered one of the finest literary reviews in the English language, is celebrated in London.

 [6]

2002
The **Bibliotheca Alexandrina** formally opens in Egypt. Costing more than $120 million, it is named in honor of the original Library of Alexandria, which was the most renowned of antiquity.

2002
The **Caribbean Community** (Caricom) trade bloc accepts Haiti as a full member.

2002
India successfully tests a ballistic missile, the Agni. The missile is nuclear-capable.

 [3]

2002
Kim Jong Il apologizes to Japanese prime minister Junichiro Koizumi for North Korea's abduction of Japanese citizens during the 1970s and '80s

 [4]

2002
Pakistan successfully tests three Ghauri missiles, nuclear-capable surface-to-surface weapons.

2002
Pope John Paul II visits Azerbaijan for the first time, where he advocates putting all religious wars to an end.

2002
Russia and the United States reach agreement on the **reduction of nuclear weapons**: both will reduce their stocks to about 2,000 each in the next decade, a significant drop from the 6,000 missiles each currently owns.

2002
Scientists announce that they have found a gene that increases the risk of developing **Type 2 diabetes**, a form of the disease once limited to adolescents and adults but that is becoming increasingly common in children.

[4] A Japanese father holds up pictures of his daughter at time of her kidnapping (left) and in 2002. She and others were seized by the North Koreans to teach Japanese language and customs in spy schools.

[3] India shows off an Agni II missile during the 2002 Republic Day parade in New Delhi.

[7] Various denominations of euro currency. The 500 euro note is very popular with money launderers because of its high denomination and is also a natural target for forgers.

[5] Copycat, the first cloned cat, as a seven-week-old kitten, with her surrogate mother.

[8] A farmer in Cumbria, England, watches as some of his healthy lambs are taken for slaughter. The British government's policy of dealing with foot-and-mouth by a preemptive cull of 11 million animals, rather than vaccination as recommended by the world's leading veterinary experts, is heavily criticized.

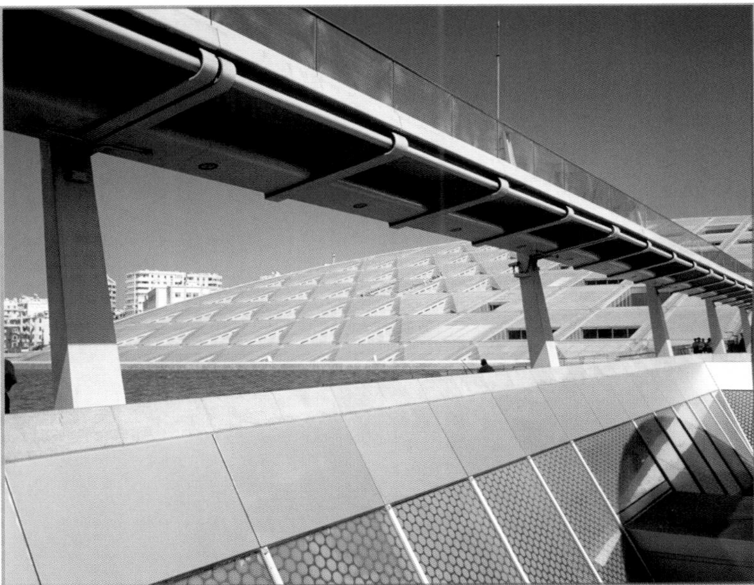

[6] The new Bibliotheca Alexandrina at Alexandria in Egypt. The original library there was one of the Seven Wonders of the Ancient World.

$ [7]

2002
The **euro** becomes the sole currency in 12 European countries, and such monetary units as the mark and lira cease to be legal tender.

[8]

2002
The **foot-and-mouth epidemic** that devastated England's cattle and sheep farmers ends after the British government announces that the country is officially free of the highly contagious viral disease.

$

2002
The lawsuit between record companies and **Napster**, an Internet site where users swap music files, raises issues of copyright infringement and misuse and underlines the major shift in the public's acquisition of music.

2002
The **Winter Olympic Games** take place in Salt Lake City, Utah.

2002
Turkey's Islamist **Justice and Development Party** wins a landslide election by promising to adhere to the secular principles of the country's constitution.

2002
With more than one billion worldwide, **cell phones** are at the forefront of a wireless revolution. No longer just used for making calls, the new mobile phones can take photographs and record home movies.

2002-2003

January 23, 2002
American journalist **Daniel Pearl** is kidnapped in Karachi, Pakistan. His death will be confirmed after American officials receive a videotape showing his execution.

 [1]

January 29, 2002
U.S. president **George W. Bush** delivers his State of the Union address, describing Iraq, Iran, and North Korea as an "**axis of evil**" for their attempts to develop nuclear, chemical, or biological weaponry.

February 12, 2002
Slobodan Milosevic, president of Yugoslavia from 1997 to 2000, goes on trial for war crimes in The Hague, at the International Criminal Tribunal for the Former Yugoslavia.

February 13, 2002
The **Scottish Parliament** passes the Protection of Wild Mammals Bill, which makes it illegal to hunt wild mammals with dogs, effectively outlawing foxhunting in Scotland.

March 24, 2002
Film stars Denzel Washington and Halle Berry become the second and third African Americans to win **Academy Awards** for performances in leading roles.

 [2]

March 30, 2002
Elizabeth, **the Queen Mother**, dies in her sleep at Windsor Castle at age 101. She was queen consort of the United Kingdom of Great Britain and Ireland from 1936 to 1952.

  [3]

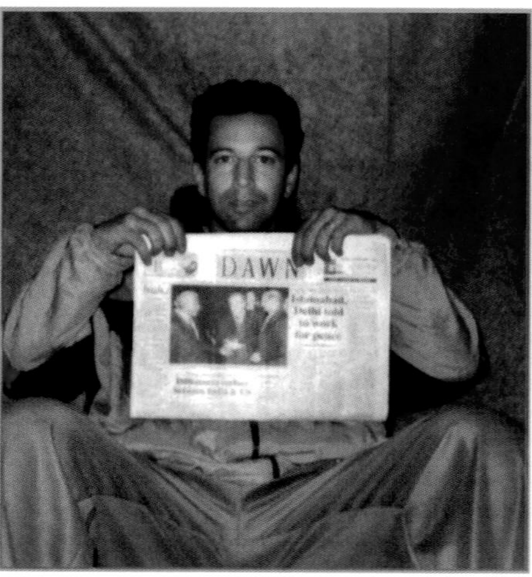

[1] *Daniel Pearl in a photograph sent to news media by his captors. He holds a current newspaper to prove the authenticity of the picture.*

[2] *Denzel Washington and Halle Berry with their awards, backstage at the Oscars.*

[3] *Prince Charles, in his admiral's uniform, stands vigil by his grandmother's coffin, which is draped with her personal standard, in Westminster Hall.*

[5] *The remains of the Bali bar blown up by al-Qaeda. Most of the victims are young Australian holidaymakers.*

[6] *Nancy Pelosi, with Dick Gephardt, whom she succeeds as leader of the Democratic Party in the House of Representatives.*

October 20, 2002
Blue Stream, the deepest underwater pipeline in the world, opens in Turkey and is put in use for the transport of natural gas.

November 2, 2002
In Norwegian-brokered peace negotiations held in Thailand, the government of **Sri Lanka** and the Liberation Tigers of Tamil Eelam agree to set up a panel to discuss ways to share power.

 [6]

November 14, 2002
Chosen as leader of the Democratic Party in the U.S. House of Representatives, **Nancy Pelosi** of California becomes the first woman to be named leader of either party in either house of Congress.

November 8, 2002
The U.N. Security Council unanimously approves **Resolution 1441**, forcing Saddam Hussein to disarm or face "serious consequences."

November 21, 2002
A **North Atlantic Treaty Organization (NATO)** summit meeting in Prague extends Bulgaria, Estonia, Latvia, Lithuania, Romania, Slovakia, and Slovenia an official invitation to become new alliance members.

November 25, 2002
In London the Agatha Christie play **The Mousetrap** celebrates its 50th anniversary with a royal gala. It opened on November 25, 1952, and the performance on November 25, 2002, is its 20,807th.

April 13, 2002
The military coup that a day before had installed businessman Pedro Carmona Estanga as interim president of **Venezuela** collapses this day, and the following morning Hugo Chávez is restored to the presidency.

April 18, 2002
After 29 years in exile, the former king of Afghanistan, **Mohammad Zahir Shah**, returns to the capital city of Kabul in the aftermath of the U.S. invasion of the country and toppling of the Taliban government.

July 9, 2002
Fearing that there would not be enough eligible players to continue, Major League Baseball commissioner **Bud Selig** stops the annual All-Star Game in the 11th inning with the score tied at 7–7.

September 22, 2002
Hundreds of thousands of rural protesters converge on London to demonstrate in favor of **foxhunting**, which two years later the House of Commons will ban in England and Wales.

 [4]

October 11, 2002
The U.S. Congress passes a bill, by a wide margin, granting U.S. president George W. Bush broad authority to use force against **Iraq**.

October 12, 2002
A terrorist bombing on the island of Bali linked to **al-Qaeda** kills some 200 people.

 [5]

[4] The Countryside Alliance March in London against the proposed ban on foxhunting.

[8] Chechen women pass a Russian armored personnel carrier.

[7] Kashmiri Muslim boys at an anti-India demonstration in Karachi, Pakistan.

 [7]

2003
After months of serious tension between the two countries, India and Pakistan agree to a cease-fire in **Kashmir**.

2003
An **earthquake** near Bingol, Turkey, kills more than 160 people.

2003
As the child sexual abuse scandal continues, the Roman Catholic **Boston Archdiocese** agrees to sell more than $100 million in real estate to fund reparations to more than 500 victims.

2003
Cambodia is seriously affronted by assertions that Angkor Wat, an ancient temple complex, was stolen from Thailand. The Thai embassy in Phnom Penh is attacked by crowds, causing Thailand to evacuate Thai nationals.

 [8]

2003
Chechen separatists attempt to drive Russia out of their country by suicide bombings of government buildings, military encampments, rock concerts, hospitals, buses, and trains, leaving more than 200 dead.

2003
For the first time, **Oman** allows all citizens over age 21 to vote for candidates to the Consultative Council.

2003

2003
England beats Australia to win the **Rugby World Cup** in Sydney.
 [1]

2003
Germany defeats Sweden in the women's **World Cup** soccer championship by a score of 2 to 1.

2003
Hu Jintao is elected president of China by the National People's Congress.
 [2]

2003
The U.S. Supreme Court upholds a 1998 federal statute that granted a 20-year **extension to all existing copyrights**.

2003
In its first operation outside Europe, NATO deploys security forces to Kabul, **Afghanistan**.

2003
The U.S. Supreme Court declares that **gay men and lesbians** are "entitled to respect for their private lives" under the due process clause of the Fourteenth Amendment.

2000-2007

[1] Johnny Wilkinson kicking the drop goal that wins England the Rugby World Cup in the last seconds of the final.

[2] Jiang Zemin congratulates his successor, Hu Jintao.

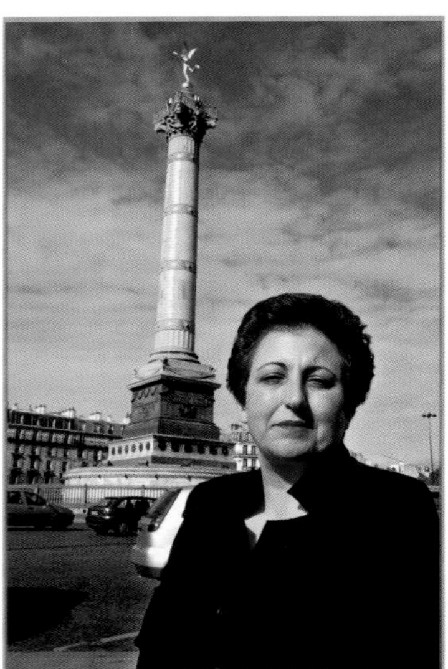
[3] Shirin Ebadi in the Place de la Bastille in Paris.

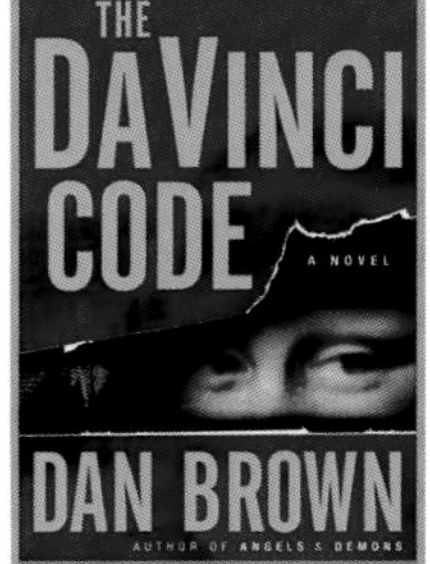

[8] The cover of the original hardback edition of The Da Vinci Code.

[5] Rowan Williams after being formally received as archbishop at Canterbury Cathedral.

[7] The Swiss yacht Alinghi *leads Team New Zealand at Auckland.* Alinghi *wins all five America's Cup races.*

2003
Social networking site **MySpace** goes online. By 2007 it will be one of the most popular Web sites and will have nearly 200 million members.

2003
Spam (unsolicited e-mail) is a growing problem; some experts predict it will soon overtake the volume of legitimate e-mail.

 [7]
2003
Switzerland wins its first **America's Cup**, sailing's premier prize.

 [8]
2003
The Da Vinci Code by Dan Brown is released and becomes one of the fastest-selling books of all time. The work of fiction generates real controversy over its theories concerning Christianity's origins.

2003
The **Turkish parliament** refuses to allow the staging of U.S. forces in the country preparatory to attacks on Iraq but does allow the United States the use of Turkish air space.

2003
The U.S. **Department of Homeland Security** becomes fully operational. Created in response to the terrorist attacks on September 11, 2001, its primary responsibility is to protect the country from future attacks.

2003
The U.S. Supreme Court holds that state governments may be sued by their employees for failing to honor the federally guaranteed right to take **time off from work** for family emergencies.

2003
The Supreme Court upholds the **Children's Internet Protection Act**, which conditions access to federal grants and subsidies upon the installation of antipornography filters on all Internet-connected computers.

2003
Iranian lawyer and activist **Shirin Ebadi** becomes the first Muslim woman to be awarded the Nobel Peace Prize. She is honored for her work promoting democracy and human rights.

 [3]

2003
Polish-born architect **Daniel Libeskind** is selected to rebuild the World Trade Center site in New York City. His plans include a tower that will stand 1,776 feet, which would be the tallest building in the world.

 [4]

2003
Rowan Williams is enthroned as the 104th archbishop of Canterbury. The questions of homosexuals in the church and the appointment of female bishops will be major concerns for him.

 [5]

2003
Six years after the end of British rule there, a demonstration protesting a controversial anti-subversion law is mounted by half a million in **Hong Kong**. The law is abandoned.

 [6]

[4] Libeskind's winning design for the Word Trade Center site. His plan has been changed so much that he now does not even acknowledge it as his own. The separate buildings are meant to be the responsibility of a range of architects, including Frank Gehry, Norman Foster, and Richard Rogers.

[6] A seething mass of demonstrators in the Central district of Hong Kong has brought the trams to a standstill.

[9] The crew of the Columbia *who are all killed when it breaks up returning from space.*

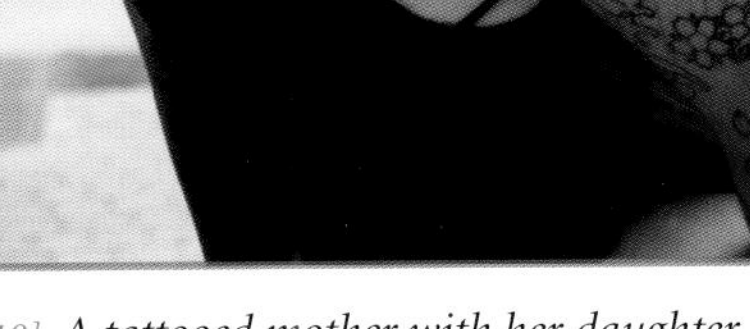

[10] A tattooed mother with her daughter.

 [9]

2003
The U.S. space shuttle **Columbia** breaks up catastrophically as it returns from a mission. All seven crew members, including an Israeli astronaut, are killed.

 [10]

c. 2003
Tattoos become increasingly popular. A 2003 Harris Poll finds that 16 percent of all American adults have at least one tattoo and the proportion rises to 36 percent among ages 25 to 29 years.

January 2003
Despite international protest, **Libya** becomes chair of the United Nations Human Rights Commission.

January 7, 2003
By presidential decree, Christmas—this day on the Coptic Orthodox calendar—is celebrated for the first time as a national holiday in **Egypt**, an almost entirely Muslim country.

February 1, 2003
The **Treaty of Nice**, negotiated in preparation for the admission of new members to the European Union from eastern Europe, enters into force.

February 4, 2003
Yugoslavia officially changes its name to **Serbia and Montenegro**.

February 5, 2003
U.S. secretary of state **Colin Powell** appears before the United Nations Security Council to present evidence that Iraq possesses proscribed weapons of mass destruction.
 [1]

March 12, 2003
The World Health Organization (WHO) issues a worldwide health alert about **severe acute respiratory syndrome (SARS)** that has struck hundreds of people in China, Hong Kong, and Vietnam.
 [2]

March 19, 2003
U.S. president George W. Bush orders air strikes against **Baghdad**, the capital of Iraq, thus launching the Iraq War to oust Iraqi dictator Saddam Hussein.
 [3]

March 30, 2003
A law banning **cigarette smoking** in all places of employment, including restaurants and bars, goes into effect in New York City.

April 10, 2003
Haiti officially recognizes Vodou as a religion.

April 15, 2003
U.S. president George W. Bush declares that the government of Saddam Hussein in Iraq had fallen as a result of the **Iraq War** and the following day asks the United Nations to lift sanctions against Iraq.

[1] Colin Powell holds up a vial of powder to demonstrate the amount of anthrax it took to close the Senate the year before. This is a prop in his argument for the danger posed by Saddam Hussein's weapons of mass destruction.

[2] Masks are worn in Hong Kong in an attempt to avoid infection by SARS.

[8] Arnold Schwarzenegger takes a question at his first press conference as governor.

[3] The Presidential Palace in Baghdad is hit.

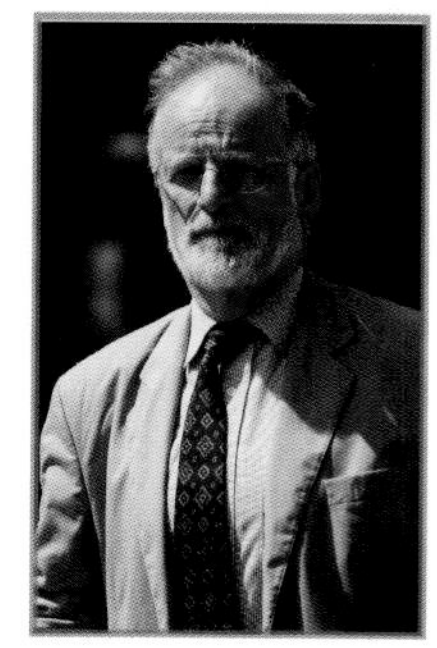

[7] Dr. David Kelly. The inquest finds that he took his own life.

 [7]
July 18, 2003
Dr. David Kelly, a scientific adviser to the British government and a "whistle blower" about overinflated claims in the government's dossier about Saddam Hussein's weapons of mass destruction, is found dead.

August 2003
Libya takes responsibility for the 1988 Lockerbie airline bombing and agrees to provide $2.7 billion in compensation to the families of the victims. In September 2003 the U.N. Security Council will lift its sanctions against Libya.

October 15, 2003
China launches its first manned spacecraft, **Shenzhou 5**, becoming the third country after the Soviet Union and the United States, to do so.

 [8]
November 17, 2003
Republican **Arnold Schwarzenegger**, an Austrian-born American bodybuilder and film actor, is inaugurated as the governor of California following a recall election that ousted the sitting governor.

December 12, 2003
Paul Martin, Jr., a member of the Liberal Party, becomes prime minister of Canada. He will pursue major reforms of his country's health care system and secure passage of legislation that legalizes same-sex marriage.

 [9]
December 13, 2003
Saddam Hussein is captured while he is hiding in a secret underground bunker near Tikrit, his hometown, in Iraq.

April 17, 2003
Anneli Jäätteenmäki is sworn in as prime minister of Finland, which thereby becomes the second country (after New Zealand) to install a woman as head of both state and government.

April 24, 2003
Officials of **North Korea** inform U.S. diplomats that it has nuclear weapons and is making bomb-grade plutonium.

May 1, 2003
President George W. Bush makes a now notorious speech aboard the aircraft carrier *Abraham Lincoln* saying "**Mission Acomplished**" in Iraq.

 [4]

May 11, 2003
Benvenuto Cellini's priceless gold salt cellar is stolen from the Kunsthistorishe Museum in Vienna, while it is covered in scaffolding.

 [5]

June 4, 2003
American entrepreneur and domestic lifestyle innovator **Martha Stewart** is indicted on criminal charges in relation to a stock sale, and in 2004 she is convicted and sentenced to five months in prison.

 [6]

July 2003
The **Canadian Supreme Court** recognizes the legality of same-sex marriage.

THE FALL OF SADDAM

Iraqi dictator toppled by the United States and its allies

On March 20, three days after U.S. president George W. Bush ordered Saddam Hussein to step down from office, U.S. and allied forces launched an attack on Iraq. Baghdad fell to U.S. soldiers on April 9. Monuments that symbolized Saddam's 24-year rule, such as the great statue of him in Baghdad (above), were pulled down by the troops and Iraqi citizens.

During the round-up that followed, Saddam's sons, Uday and Qusay, were cornered and killed in Mosul on July 22. The former dictator himself remained in hiding until December.

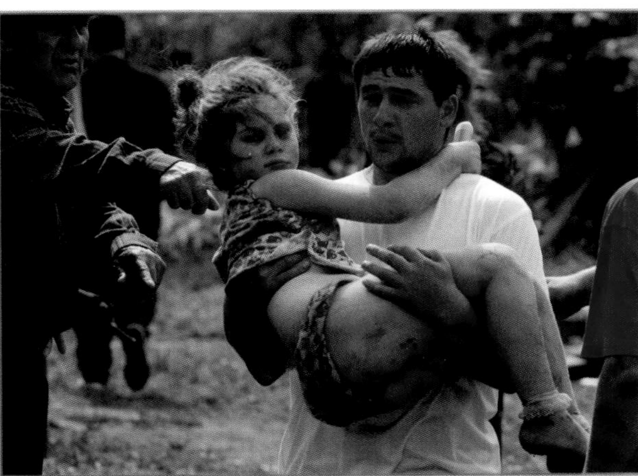

[10] A child is carried out of Bezlan school in North Ossetia after it has been stormed by Russian special forces.

[5] Cellini's salt cellar, perhaps the most famous piece of precious metalwork in the world. It will be recovered in 2006, having been buried in a lead box in an Austrian forest.

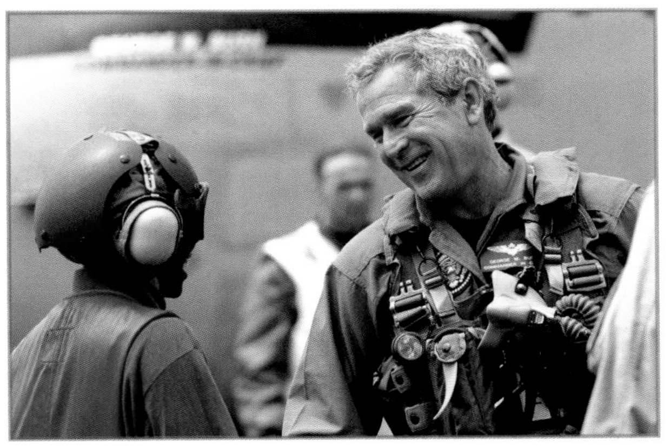

[4] George W. Bush just after landing in a Navy S-3B Viking jet on the aircraft carrier Abraham Lincoln *off San Diego, to announce "mission accomplished."*

[9] Saddam Hussein, bearded and dishevelled, the day after his capture.

[6] Martha Stewart leaves court.

2004
AIDS has become one of the worst epidemics in history. According to the United Nations 2004 report on AIDS, some 38 million people are living with HIV, 5 million become infected annually, and about 3 million die each year.

2004
Brazil, Germany, India, and Japan apply for permanent membership on the **U.N. Security Council**.

2004
Californian Don Beld begins the nationwide **Home of the Brave Project**. Quilts, made by volunteers and modeled on those made for soldiers in the Civil War, are presented to the families of all soldiers killed in Iraq and Afghanistan.

 [10]

2004
Chechen separatists sieze a school in North Ossetia. More than 330 people, mostly children, die in the subsequent gun battle.

2004
Due to an owners' lockout, the entire 2004–05 **National Hockey League season** is cancelled. It is the first time a North American professional sports league has called off an entire season.

2004
Facebook joins MySpace in dominating social networking traffic on the Internet; the two sites are both among the most visited sites on the Web.

2004

2004
Illinois Democrat **Barack Obama, Jr.**, defeats Republican Alan Keyes in the first U.S. Senate race in which the two main candidates are African Americans.

 [1]

2004
In **Saudi Arabia**, Muslim pilgrims stampede, leaving 251 dead.

 [2]

2004
The U.S. Supreme Court holds that the Washington state system permitting judges to make independent findings that **increase a convicted defendant's sentence** beyond the ordinary range for the crime violates the Sixth Amendment.

2004
In compensation for its involvement in human rights abuses, **Guatemala** pays $3.5 million to the victims of its civil war.

2004
In a pair of decisions involving enemy combatants in U.S. custody, the **U.S. Supreme Court** declares that "a state of war is not a blank check for the president when it comes to the rights of the nation's citizens."

2004
Iraqi-born British architect **Zaha Hadid**, noted for her radical deconstructivist designs, becomes the first woman to be awarded the Pritzker Architecture Prize.

[3]

DARFUR GENOCIDE

State-sponsored mass murder creates an unprecedented humanitarian crisis in the Sudan and neighboring Chad.

Ethnic tensions, long simmering between nomadic Arab herders and sedentary Fur and other agriculturalists in the Darfur region of Sudan, began erupting into armed conflict in the late 1980s. The violence, although bloody, generally was sporadic until 2003, when rebels from among the agriculturalists attacked government installations to protest what they contended was the Sudanese government's disregard for the western region and its non-Arab population. The government in Khartoum responded by creating the Janjaweed, an Arab militia that began attacking the sedentary groups in Darfur. One of the Janjaweed's numerous atrocities was the destruction of the village of Tuadubai, the burned-out remains of which are shown in the photograph above.

Within a year, an estimated 50,000 people (primarily Fur and other agriculturalists) had been killed, and 1.2 million had been displaced and left homeless. Many fled westward to refugee camps in neighboring Chad; others remained internally displaced.

Latest estimates point to the death toll having reached between 450,000 and 500,000, with two million driven from their homes. Warfare has spread into Chad. Efforts to persuade China, a major trading partner of the Sudan, to stop selling arms to the Sudanese government and instead bring pressure to bear on it, are meeting with little success.

[2] The great mosque in Mecca on the final day of the 2004 Hajj pilgrimage, during which the stampede took place.

[3] Zaha Hadid

[1] Barack Obama shakes hands with his Republican opponent, Alan Keyes, after a debate in Chicago during the election.

[7] Michael Schumacher celebrates winning the German Grand Prix in July.

[5] A Cape Town citizen celebrates South Africa winning the right to host the 2010 Soccer World Cup.

2004
Since its creation in 1988, the **Global Polio Eradication Initiative**, the largest public-health campaign ever undertaken, has vaccinated at least two billion children against the highly infectious virus.

[5]

2004
South Africa is selected by FIFA (Fédération Internationale de Football Association) to host the 2010 World Cup, the first time an African country will host the world's biggest sporting event.

2004
The international community officially recognizes that the campaign of repression, executions, rapes, and forced relocations in the **Darfur** region of the Sudan is of sufficient scale to be designated genocide.

2004
The **sultan of Oman** appoints the country's first female minister, Rawya bint Saud al-Bousaidi, who becomes the minister of higher education.

 [6]

2004
The **Summer Olympic Games** take place in Athens, Greece.

2004
The **Turkish parliament** introduces measures to prevent torture and violence against women and drops a proposal to criminalize adultery.

2004
Ireland becomes the first country to ban smoking in enclosed workplaces.

2004
Libya agrees to pay $35 million in compensation to victims and their families for the bombing of a German nightclub in 1986.

2004
Libya agrees to compensate victims' families for the bombing of a French aircraft in 1989.

2004
Millennium Park opens in downtown Chicago and quickly becomes a tourist attraction; it includes fountains, eye-catching sculptures, extensive gardens and an outdoor ice skating rink.

 [4]

2004
Nanotechnology, which enables the manufacture of materials and devices at an extremely small scale, moves to the forefront as researchers look to develop new products such as implants that will identify cancer cells in the human body.

2004
Nicaragua receives debt relief that is unprecedented outside of war time, as the World Bank discharges 80 percent of the country's total debt; Russia also discharges a significant proportion of the debt taken on under the Soviet regime.

[4] The pavilion designed by Frank Gehry for outdoor concerts at Chicago's Millennium Park.

[8] French Muslim girls demonstrate in Paris, demanding a choice, "un choix," as to whether they wear a head scarf to school or not.

[9] The Palestinian women walking beside it indicate the scale of Israel's West Bank security wall.

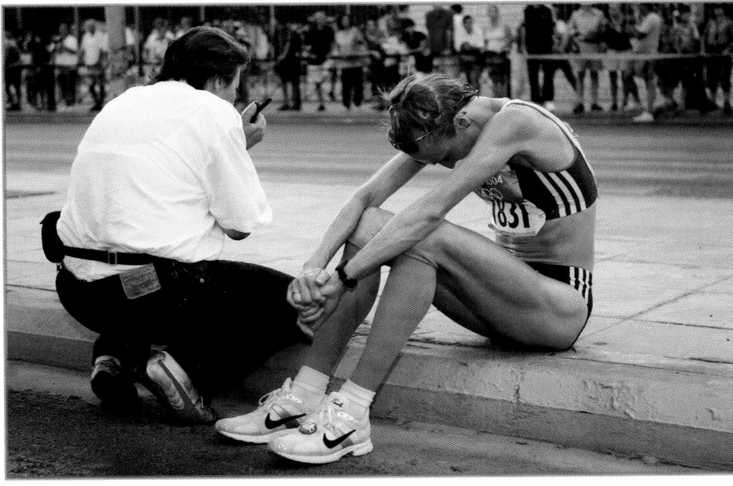

[6] Paula Radcliffe of Great Britain sits on the curb in Athens after having to pull out of the marathon because of an upset stomach. She will win the London Marathon in 2005 and the New York Marathon in 2007.

[7]
2004
Michael Schumacher wins a record seventh World Formula One motor racing championship. He won the first two driving for Benetton and the rest for Ferrari. The previous record was five championships, held by Juan Fangio.

2004
The U.S. Senate fails to pass a bill calling for a constitutional amendment banning **same-sex marriage**.

2004
The U.S. spacecraft **Cassini** becomes the first to enter into orbit around Saturn. Its mission, scheduled to last four years, is to study the planet and its ring system and numerous moons.

 [8]
2004
The wearing of religious symbols, including head scarves by Muslim women and girls, is banned in **French public schools**. The country is noted for its strict secularism.

2004
Turkey bans the death penalty, an important step in gaining European Union membership.

 [9]
2004
Israel continues the construction of the **security wall** to divide it from the West Bank. The wall may not be completed until 2010.

2004-2005

January 2004
Haiti celebrates 200 years of independence but is so rife with civil unrest that President Jean-Bertrand Aristide flees the country.

January 24, 2004
Launched in mid-2003, the six-wheeled robotic rover **Opportunity** lands on Mars and—like its twin rover, Spirit, which landed on January 3—analyzes rocks and soils and relays pictures back to earth.

March 11, 2004
Bombs explode on four commuter trains near central **Madrid**. The government, which initially blames Basque separatists, is ousted in elections on March 14.

 [1]

March 14, 2004
Vladimir Putin, the intelligence officer and politician who became president of Russia in 1999 upon the resignation of Boris Yeltsin, is overwhelmingly reelected to a second term as president.

March 20, 2004
The U.S. Army announces that charges are being brought against six American soldiers in connection with the reported abuse of Iraqi prisoners-of-war being held in **Abu Ghraib prison** in Iraq during the Iraq War.

April 14, 2004
Bartholomew I, ecumenical patriarch of the Eastern Orthodox church, formally accepts the apology offered by Pope John Paul II in 2001 for the **sacking of Constantinople** (now Istanbul) by Crusader armies in the early 13th century.

2000-2007

TSUNAMI

The biggest tidal waves in recorded history

On December 26, at 7:59 AM local time, an undersea earthquake with a magnitude of 9.0 on the Richter Scale struck off the coast of the Indonesian island of Sumatra. Over the next seven hours, a tsunami—a series of immense ocean waves (above)—triggered by the quake reached out across the Indian Ocean, devastating coastal areas as far away as East Africa. Some locations reported that the waves had reached a height of 9 m (30 ft) or more when they hit the shoreline. At least 225,000 people were killed across a dozen countries, with Indonesia, Sri Lanka, India, Maldives, and Thailand sustaining massive damage. Indonesian officials estimated that the death toll there could exceed 200,000. Tens of thousands were reported dead or missing in Sri Lanka and India, a large number of them from the Indian Andaman and Nicobar islands. The low-lying island nation of Maldives reported more than a hundred casualties and economic damage that could exceed the country's gross domestic product.

[1] *Blankets cover bodies in a wrecked commuter train in Madrid. It is Spain's worst terrorist attack ever, and al-Qaeda is to blame. More than 190 die and 1,500 are injured.*

[3] *The Millau Viaduct in 2003, with the Tour de France passing beneath it.*

[4] *Lance Armstrong heads for the Champs Elysées and victory on the last stage of the Tour de France.*

November 18, 2004
Chile becomes one of the last countries in the West to legalize divorce.

December 16, 2004
The breathtaking **Millau Viaduct** over the valley of the River Tarn in southern France is opened to traffic. Designed by Norman Foster it is the world's tallest vehicular bridge.

December 26, 2004
A large earthquake shakes the Indian Ocean floor west of the island of Sumatra, triggering a devastating **tsunami** that swamps coastal areas from Thailand to Africa and kills more than 200,000 people.

2005
American cyclist **Lance Armstrong**, who overcame cancer in the late 1990s, wins a record seventh Tour de France and subsequently retires from racing.

[5]

2005
An **earthquake** measuring 7.6 on the Richter scale strikes Pakistan, Afghanistan, and India, killing some 80,000 people.

2005
Apple unveils its newest iPod, a version that also plays video. Introduced in 2001, the pocket-sized portable music player has become a phenomenon, with more than 42 million sold.

April 28, 2004
American television network CBS broadcasts photographs depicting harsh treatment of Iraqi inmates at the **Abu Ghraib prison** in U.S.-occupied Iraq. A national debate on torture and the Geneva Convention begins.

 [2]

May 1, 2004
The **European Union** is enlarged to include the new member states of Cyprus, the Czech Republic, Estonia, Hungary, Latvia, Lithuania, Malta, Poland, Slovakia, and Slovenia.

May 17, 2004
Massachusetts begins issuing marriage licenses to same-sex couples.

June 2004
The U.S.-led coalition forces occupying **Iraq** turn over sovereignty to an interim Iraqi government.

July 1, 2004
Banker and economist **Horst Köhler**, a member of the Christian-Democratic Union, becomes president of Germany.

October 9, 2004
For the first time in Afghanistan's history, voters go to the polls to choose a president, selecting **Hamid Karzai**, who has served as the interim president after the fall of the Taliban regime in 2001.

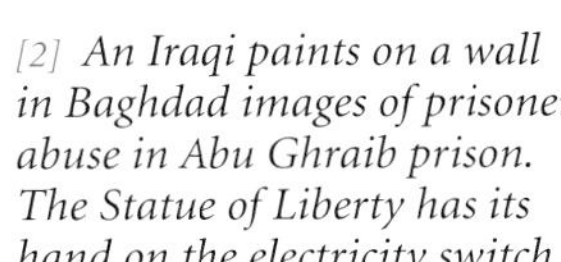

[2] An Iraqi paints on a wall in Baghdad images of prisoner abuse in Abu Ghraib prison. The Statue of Liberty has its hand on the electricity switch.

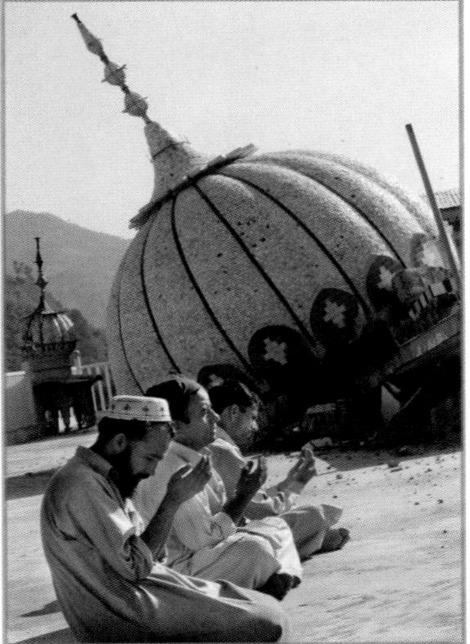

[5] Pakistani Muslims pray outside a Muzaffarabad mosque destroyed by the earthquake of October 8, 2005.

[6] A dragon-and-lion dance is performed at Shanghai airport to celebrate nonstop flights starting between Taiwan and the mainland.

KATRINA

A hurricane brings massive destruction to the southern United States.

On August 28, Hurricane Katrina hit the southern coast of the United States, causing an estimated 1,800 deaths and more than $81 billion worth of damage. The worst-hit states were Louisiana and Mississippi. In the aftermath there was a temporary breakdown in law and order; the photograph above shows the response by the owners of one devastated house in Biloxi, Mississippi, to the threat of looting.

The disaster raised concerns about the adequacy of hurricane-protection measures, especially the flood protection around low-lying New Orleans, and sparked a debate about whether the damaged buildings should be reconstructed in traditional styles or replaced with more contemporary designs. There was also the question of whether rebuilding would be undertaken by a few big developers appointed by the government or carried out in a slower, piecemeal manner. The failure to resolve these matters by the year's end caused much ill feeling.

2005
August Wilson's **Radio Golf** is produced; it is the final play in his cycle of plays about black American life. Each play is set in a different decade of the 20th century.

 [6]

2005
China and Taiwan reach an agreement to allow charter flights between the mainland and **Taiwan** to fly nonstop during the Chinese New Year holidays; they are the first nonstop flights between the two entities since 1949.

2005
Ecuador's National Congress dismisses the country's Supreme Court, claiming that the judges have too-close ties to the opposition Social Christian Party, the largest group in Congress.

2005
English playwright **Harold Pinter**, author of ambivalent yet powerful dramas, receives the Nobel Prize for Literature.

2005
Hurricane Katrina devastates the U.S. Gulf Coast area, destroying much of New Orleans. The lack of preparation and inadequate initial government response draws much criticism.

2005
North Korea announces that it posesses nuclear weapons.

2005

2005
South Africa becomes the first African country to legalize same-sex marriage.

2005
Researchers announce that the **ivory-billed woodpecker**, believed to be extinct, has been spotted in Arkansas.

2005
In the mountains of Swabia in southwestern Germany, archaeologists unearth what is believed to be the **world's oldest musical instruments**, a 35,000-year-old flute fashioned out of a wooly mammoth tusk and two smaller flutes made of swan bones.

2005
The most deadly variety of **bird flu** infects poultry in Asia and Russia. Hundreds of millions of birds die from the disease or are killed in attempts to control the epidemic. More than 100 cases in humans have also occurred, with about 50 fatalities.

2005
The complete genetic code of a **chimpanzee** is sequenced and is found to be more than 96 percent identical to that of a human. This discovery adds to the growing debate over evolution and intelligent design.

2005
The first **human face transplant** is performed in France on a woman who had been attacked by a dog. Doctors debate the ethical ramifications of the procedure.

 [1]

[1] *Isabelle Dinoire's partially transplanted face.*

[3] *Members of a Japanese environmental group demonstrating in Kyoto.*

[5] *Mahmoud Abbas (right) with former president Jimmy Carter.*

[2] *The Turning Torso building in Malmö, Sweden.*

[7] *Condoleezza Rice in Germany ten days after becoming secretary of state, at a press conference with the German chancellor, Gerhard Schröder.*

[6] *Viktor Yushchenko, his face bearing the scars left by his poisoning at the hands of the pro-Russian party within Ukraine, during the election campaign.*

2005
Venezuelan president **Hugo Chavez** announces the formation of an energy alliance of 15 Caribbean countries (Petrocaribe), in which Venezuela offers members oil at low prices.

2005
Voters in **Saudi Arabia** take part in the country's first-ever elections; but only at the municipal level. Only men are allowed to vote or run for office.

2005
W. Mark Felt, the number two official at the FBI in the 1970s, is identified as **Deep Throat**, the source for *Washington Post* reporters Bob Woodward and Carl Bernstein, who broke the Watergate scandal story in 1972.

2005
YouTube, a video-sharing Web site, is launched and becomes an immediate hit despite recurring problems with copyright holders.

 [5]

January 9, 2005
Mahmoud Abbas, who was a founder of Fatah in the 1950s and had served briefly as prime minister of the Palestinian Authority (PA) in 2003 under Yasser Arafat, is elected president of the PA.

 [6]

January 23, 2005
Following a tumultuous political battle in what becomes known as the **Orange Revolution**, Viktor Yushchenko is inaugurated as the new president of Ukraine. He declares that Ukraine's future is in the European Union.

2005
The first tenants move into Turning Torso, Spanish architect **Santiago Calatrava's** mixed-use residential tower in Malmö, Sweden. Fifty-four stories high, it is the tallest building in Scandinavia.

 [2]

2005
The **Kyoto Protocol**, designed to reduce the emission of greenhouse gases, comes into effect. Ratified by 141 countries, it is hailed as a landmark, although critics question its modest goals and the U.S.'s refusal to sign.

 [3]

2005
The Nobel Peace Prize is awarded to the International Atomic Energy Agency and its director general, **Mohamed ElBaradei**.

2005
The U.S. National Trust for Historic Preservation estimates that more than 38,000 historic structures in New Orleans were affected by **Hurricane Katrina** and many are beyond saving.

2005
U.S. president George W. Bush admits that he instructed the National Security Agency to conduct **electronic eavesdropping** within the United States without warrant.

2005
Uganda-born **John Sentamu** is enthroned as the first black archbishop in the Church of England, becoming the 97th archbishop of York, the church's second highest position.

 [4]

[8] Yulia Tymoshenko

[11] Prince Charles and the Duchess of Cornwall leave St. George's Chapel, Windsor.

[4] Archbishop John Sentamu after his enthronement at York.

[9] A Lebanese youth chants anti-Syrian slogans amidst a sea of Lebanese flags at the big demonstration following Rafik Hariri's assassination.

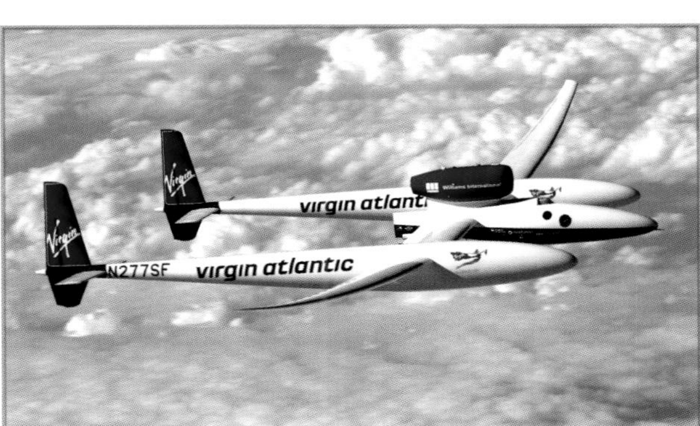

[10] Steve Fossett's plane, the Virgin Atlantic Global Flyer.

 [7]

January 26, 2005
Condoleezza Rice is confirmed as U.S. secretary of state.

 [8]

February 4, 2005
Yulia Tymoshenko, a major figure in the Orange Revolution, becomes prime minister of Ukraine.

[9]

February 14, 2005
Rafik Hariri, prime minister of Lebanon, is killed along with 15 others in a massive explosion. One month later one million people demonstrate in Beirut, accusing Syria of being responsible for the killings.

 [10]

March 3, 2005
American adventurer **Steve Fossett** becomes the first person to complete a solo nonstop circumnavigation of the globe without refueling when he lands his plane in Kansas after more than 67 hours in flight.

April 2, 2005
Millions worldwide mourn the death of **John Paul II**, one of the most beloved of modern popes.

 [11]

April 9, 2005
Prince Charles marries Camilla Parker Bowles at Windsor. She is to be known as the **Duchess of Cornwall**.

2005-2006

April 19, 2005
German cardinal **Joseph Ratzinger** is elected pope and takes the name Benedict XVI.
 [1]

April 27, 2005
The Airbus **Superjumbo A380** makes its first flight at Toulouse in France.
[2]

May 5, 2005
The **Labour Party** wins a third term at the British general election, but with a substantially reduced majority.

July 7, 2005
Islamist suicide bombers, all British citizens, cause explosions on three Underground trains and a bus in London, killing 56 and injuring 700. Two weeks later a copycat attack is launched, but the bombs fail to go off.
 [3]

July 19, 2005
John G. Roberts, Jr., is nominated as 17th chief justice of the U.S. Supreme Court by President George W. Bush. The nomination will be confirmed by Congress on September 29.

July 28, 2005
A formal statement is issued by the IRA that its armed campaign in **Northern Ireland** is ended and its members are instructed to dump their arms.

[1] Benedict XVI in St. Peter's Square after saying his first mass as pope.

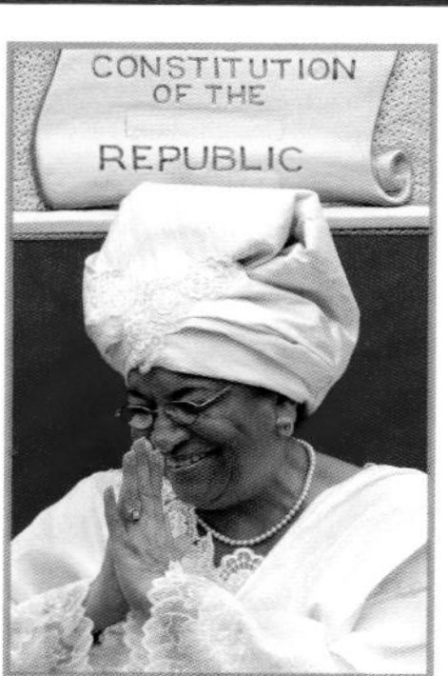

[7] Ellen Johnson-Sirleaf, president of Liberia.

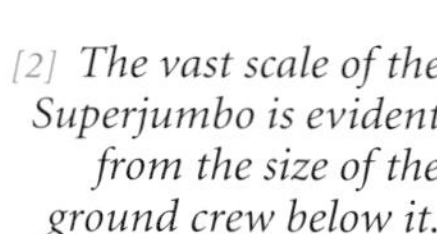

[2] The vast scale of the Superjumbo is evident from the size of the ground crew below it.

[5] Angela Merkel

[3] A victim of one of the bombs that exploded on the London Underground is helped to safety.

2006
Argentina pays off its remaining debt to the International Monetary Fund and terminates its relationship with the organization.

 [7]
2006
Ellen Johnson-Sirleaf is sworn in as president of **Liberia**, becoming the first woman elected to head an African country.

 [8]
2006
A Danish newspaper prints **cartoons depicting the Prophet Muhammad**, including some that link him to terrorism, which are then reprinted in other papers. Muslims stage violent protests.

2006
Google acquires YouTube.

2006
Italy defeats France in the men's **World Cup** soccer championship by a score of 5 to 3.

2006
Japan wins the first **World Baseball Classic**. The 16-team tournament had been in jeopardy until the U.S. allowed Cuba to participate.

September 2005
Israel competes the evacuation of all its citizens and associated security personnel from the **Gaza Strip** and four West Bank settlements, under its unilateral disengagement plan.

 [4]

November 22, 2005
Angela Merkel, a member of the Christian-Democratic Union, becomes the first female chancellor of Germany.

 [5]

December 20, 2005
In **Kitzmiller v. Dover Area School District**, a federal court rules that intelligent design is not clearly distinct from creationism and therefore should be excluded from the educational curriculum.

2006
A 1,700-year-old codex containing a **Gospel of Judas**, which portrays Jesus's betrayer as a friend who acted out of loyalty, is made public by the National Geographic Society in Washington, D.C.

2006
A new tomb in Egypt's **Valley of the Kings** is found, containing sarcophagi and five mummies believed to date from the 18th pharaonic dynasty at the beginning of the New Kingdom (1539–1292 BC).

 [6]

2006
Al-Jazeera English, a television news channel in English, begins broadcasts from Doha, Qatar.

[4] An Israeli woman cries as she is about to be evicted, with her children, from her West Bank house, by Israeli forces.

[9] The first Episcopal woman bishop, Katherine Jefferts Schori.

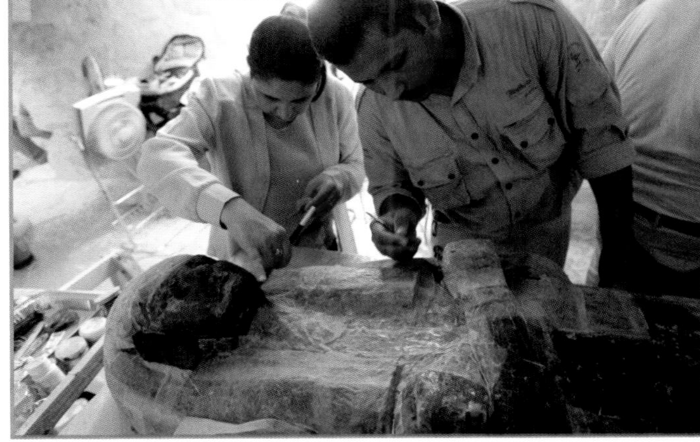

[6] Archaeologists brush one of the sarcophagi, from the first tomb to be found in the Valley of the Kings since Tutankhamun's in 1922.

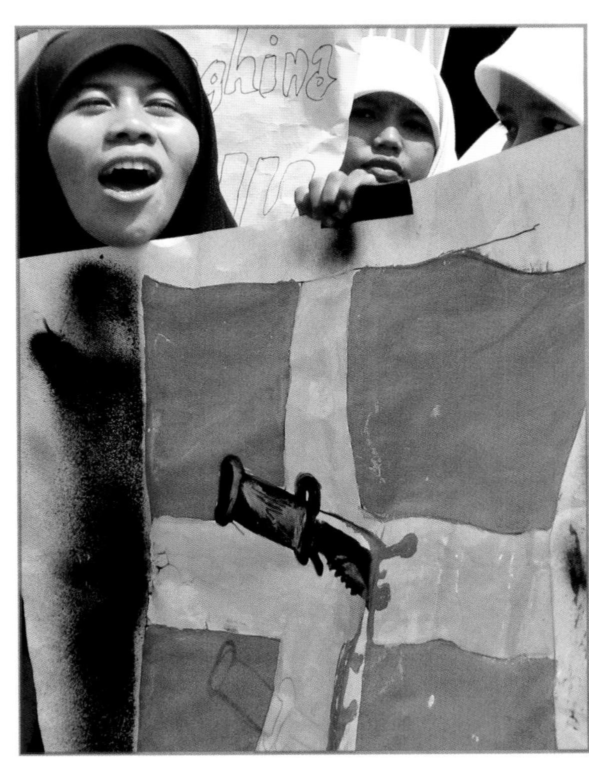

[8] Indonesian women protest a Danish newspaper's cartoons by holding up a crude Danish flag with a dagger depicted stabbing it in the middle.

[10] Players enjoy a game of tennis using Nintendo's Wii.

[12] Jamaica's first woman prime minister, Portia Simpson Miller.

[11] Orham Pamuk dances with his daughter at the Nobel banquet in Stockholm.

 [9]

2006
Katharine Jefferts Schori of Nevada becomes the first woman to serve as presiding bishop of the Episcopal Church.

2006
New Jersey becomes the third U.S. state to allow same-sex couples to form civil unions.

 [10]

2006
Nintendo releases **Wii**, an innovative video game console featuring a wireless remote that users move to replicate the motions of such items as a tennis racket or baseball bat. Wii quickly becomes a leader in the industry.

 [11]

2006
Orhan Pamuk wins the Nobel Prize for Literature, becoming the first Turk to receive a Nobel Prize.

 [12]

2006
Portia Simpson Miller is sworn in as Jamaica's first woman prime minister.

2006
President **Fidel Castro** of Cuba announces that while he recovers from surgery, he is temporarily turning power over to his brother, Defense Minister Raul Castro.

2006

2006
The International Astronomical Union removes **Pluto** from the list of planets and gives it the new classification of dwarf planet.

2006
Television host Oprah Winfrey publicly excoriates James Frey, author of Winfrey's book club selection **A Million Little Pieces**, a memoir that was found to be fictional in significant sections.

2006
The first **sudoku** world championship is held in Lucca, Italy. An international phenomenon, the puzzle game requires players to use logic in order to fill in each cell on a nine-by-nine grid with numbers.

2006
Responding to **obesity** among schoolchildren, the three largest U.S. soft drink companies announce that they will remove sweetened drinks from cafeterias and vending machines in schools, replacing them with water, milk, and fruit juice. *[1]*

2006
The number of people living with **HIV** has risen from about 8 million in 1990 to nearly 40 million. About 63 percent of people living with HIV are in sub-Saharan Africa.

2006
The **Phantom of the Opera** becomes the longest-running Broadway musical, surpassing *Cats*. Both musicals are the work of British composer Andrew Lloyd Webber. *[2]*

[1] A Chicago schoolgirl eats her lunch at school in front of a bank of vending machines selling sweetened drinks.

[5] Young supporters in the refugee camp of Khan Yunes in Gaza celebrate the Hamas victory. Green Hamas flags fly behind.

[2] A curtain call for the Phantom on the night the show becomes the longest-running. The title character receives congratulations from one of the dancers in Cats.

[4] Somali women cheer the restoration of the Transitional Federal Government in Mogadishu with the backing of Ethiopian troops, in place of the Islamist regime there, at the end of 2006.

2006
U.S. president George W. Bush vetoes a bill passed by Congress that would expand research into medical uses of **embryonic stem cells**.

2006
Ethiopia becomes involved in civil war–torn Somalia, taking the side of the Transitional Federal Government against the Islamic Court Union. *[4]*

2006
With the soaring popularity of **digital photography**, Nikon and Konica Minolta announce that they will cease producing most or all of their film cameras.

2006
Suicide bombings, executions, and other terrorist attacks become a nearly daily occurrence in **Iraq**, as sectarian violence intensifies. Estimates of civilian casualties vary widely but have at a minimum surpassed 60,000 by July.

January 2006
In legislative elections for the **Palestinian Authority**, 74 of 132 seats are won by Hamas (Islamic Resistance Movement), ending four decades of Fatah domination. *[5]*

February 6, 2006
Stephen Harper, a member of the Conservative Party of Canada, becomes prime minister.

2006
The U.S. Food and Drug Administration approves the first vaccine against **cervical cancer**. Designed for females between the ages of 9 and 26, Gardasil proves controversial as some believe it will encourage teenage sex.

2006
The U.S. Food and Drug Administration approves the over-the-counter sale of the morning-after contraceptive pill known as **Plan B** to women 18 years of age or older.

2006
The U.S. Supreme Court upholds an **Oregon law** that allows physician-assisted suicide for people who are terminally ill.

2006
The **Winter Olympic Games** take place in Turin, Italy.

 [3]

2006
The total value of merchandise sold on **eBay** for the full year 2006 is more than $52 billion. The Web site has more than 233 million registered users worldwide in 37 markets.

2006
U.S. president George W. Bush makes a surprise visit to **Afghanistan**; it is the first visit to the country by a U.S. president since Dwight D. Eisenhower visited in 1959.

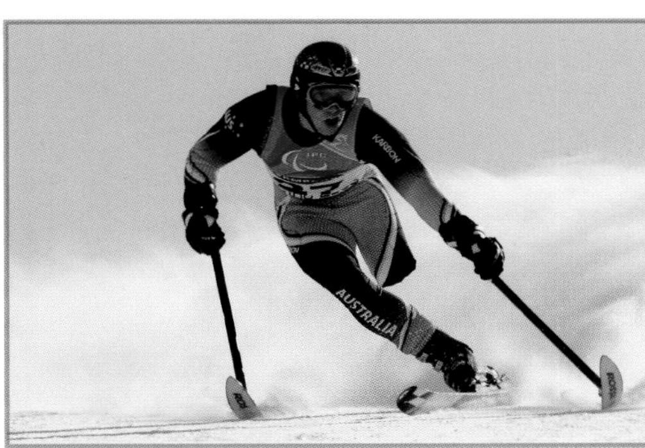

[3] Cameron Rahles of Australia competes in the Paralympics in Turin.

[7] Donald Rumsfeld shortly after his resignation.

[6] Debris filling the streets of Beirut after Israeli air raids.

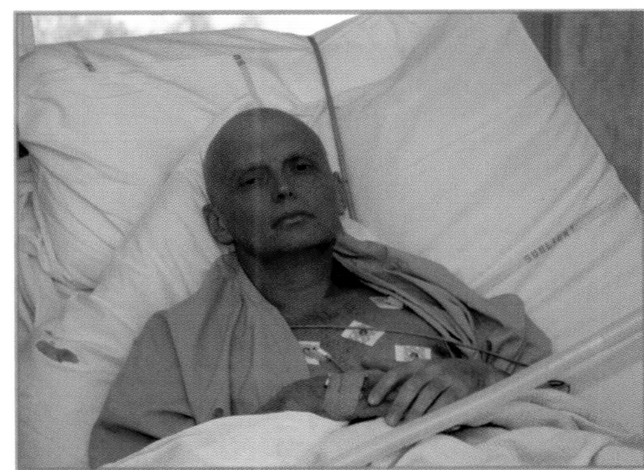

[9] Alexander Litvinenko on his deathbed in a London hospital. Russia will refuse to extradite Andrei Lugovoi, the chief suspect in the case, although there is much compelling evidence pointing towards him.

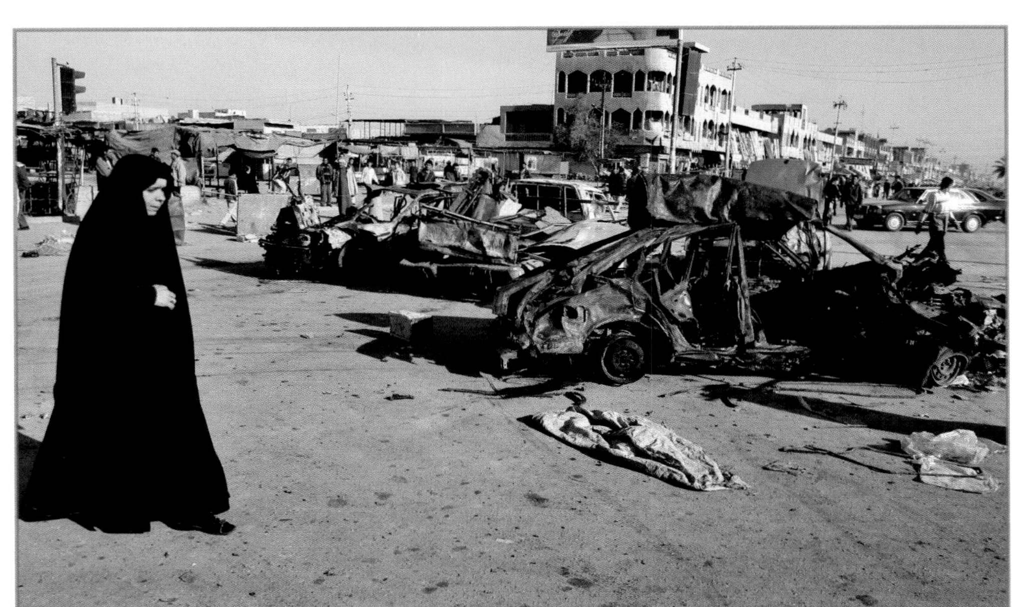

[8] The day after at the scene of one of five car bombings in Sadr City, Baghdad, that killed over 200 in this Shi'ite stronghold on November 23.

July 11, 2006
The White House issues a statement that all suspected terrorists, including members of al-Qaeda and the Taliban, have the protection granted by the **Geneva Convention**, contrary to an executive order issued on February 2, 2002.

 [6]

August 5, 2006
Israel assails **Lebanon** with some 250 air raids and 4,000 shells in an effort to create a security zone along Lebanon's border with Israel.

October 2006
North Korea successfully tests a small nuclear weapon, with a detonation in the mountains above Kilju.

 [7]

November 8, 2006
U.S. defense secretary **Donald Rumsfeld** resigns. Much of the blame for the chaos and bloodshed in Iraq after 2003 is laid at his door.

 [8]

November 23, 2006
In **Baghdad**, Sunni insurgents besiege the Shi'ite-run Health Ministry from all directions for two hours; five car bombs and mortar shells kill more than 200 people in the Shi'ite Sadr City neighborhood.

 [9]

November 23, 2006
Alexander Litvinenko, a former lieutenant colonel in the KGB/FSB, now an associate of Vladimir Putin's sworn enemy, the expatriate multimillionaire Boris Beresovsky, is poisoned with radioactive Polonium 210.

2006-2007

December 2006
The **Japanese Diet** approves creation of the first ministry of defense since World War II.

December 1, 2006
National Action Party member Felipe Calderón becomes president of **Mexico** after winning the election by just 0.56 percent of the vote.

December 6, 2006
The **Iraq Study Group**, an independent, bipartisan U.S. panel, issues a report that finds the situation in Iraq to be "grave and deteriorating."

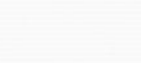

December 30, 2006
Former Iraqi president **Saddam Hussein** is hanged.

[1]

2007
Alberto Contador of Spain wins the Tour de France by a narrow margin in a competition marred by drug scandals and the departure of several competitors and even entire teams.

2007
Apple announces that more than two billion songs have been purchased from **iTunes**. The world's most popular online music store, iTunes allows users to download songs to their computers and MP3 players.

[1] Raghad Hussein, daughter of Saddam Hussein, at a demonstration in Amman, Jordan, two days after his execution.

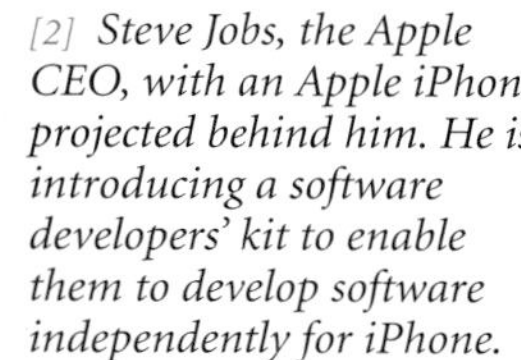

[2] Steve Jobs, the Apple CEO, with an Apple iPhone projected behind him. He is introducing a software developers' kit to enable them to develop software independently for iPhone.

[3] Bobby Knight acknowledges the crowd after his 880th win.

[6] Nancy Pelosi, surrounded by grandsons, takes the oath as speaker in the U.S. Capitol.

[7] Ian Paisley (left) and Gerry Adams at a press conference on March 26.

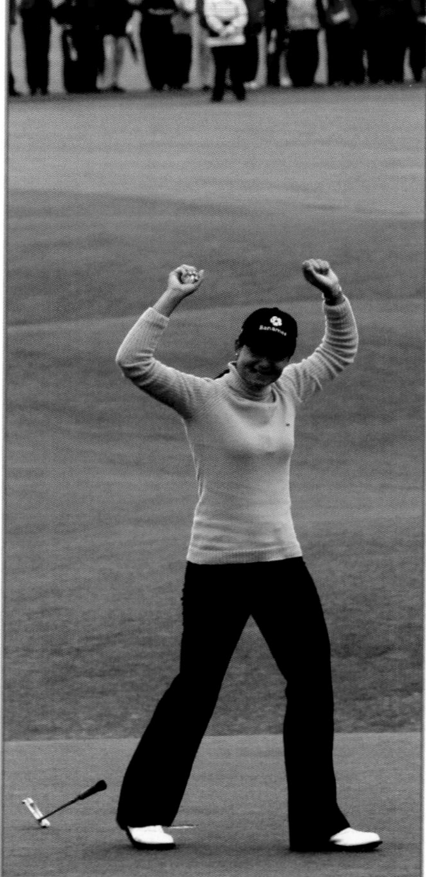

[9] Lorena Ochoa of Mexico wins the first Women's British Open golf tournament held at St. Andrews.

2007
The **Democratic Party** takes control of the U.S. Congress after more than 12 years of Republican rule. The Democratic gains are credited in part to voters' growing opposition to the Iraq War.

[6]

2007
Representative **Nancy Pelosi** of California becomes the first woman to serve as speaker of the U.S. House of Representatives.

2007
The oldest continuously published weekly paper in the world, Sweden's **Post-och Inrikes Tidningar**, which was first published in 1645, adopts an Internet-only format.

2007
The United Nation's Intergovernmental Panel on Climate Change releases a report that calls evidence of **global warming** "unequivocal" and cites human activity as the leading cause.

[7]

March 26, 2007
Sinn Féin's **Gerry Adams** and the Democratic Unionist Party's Ian Paisley reach a historic agreement to form a power-sharing government in Northern Ireland.

April 18, 2007
The U.S. Supreme Court rules in **Gonzales v. Carhart** that the Partial-Birth Abortion Ban Act is constitutional.

2007
Apple introduces the **iPhone**, a combination cellular telephone, MP3 player, and Internet-access device.

 [2]

2007
Ban Ki-moon becomes the secretary general of the United Nations.

2007
Bobby Knight records his 880th career win to become the most successful coach in U.S. men's college basketball.

 [3]

2007
Gordon Brown, the longest continuously serving chancellor of the Exchequer since the 1820s, becomes prime minister of the United Kingdom following the resignation of Tony Blair.

 [4]

2007
J. K. Rowling, the richest woman in Great Britain, completes the last book in the Harry Potter series, *Harry Potter and the Deathly Hallows*. The book sells a staggering 8.3 million copies in its first 24 hours on sale in the United States.

 [5]

2007
Microsoft introduces its new operating system, **Vista**, the successor to Windows.

[4] Gordon Brown arrives in Downing Street for the first time as prime minister, accompanied by his wife, Sarah.

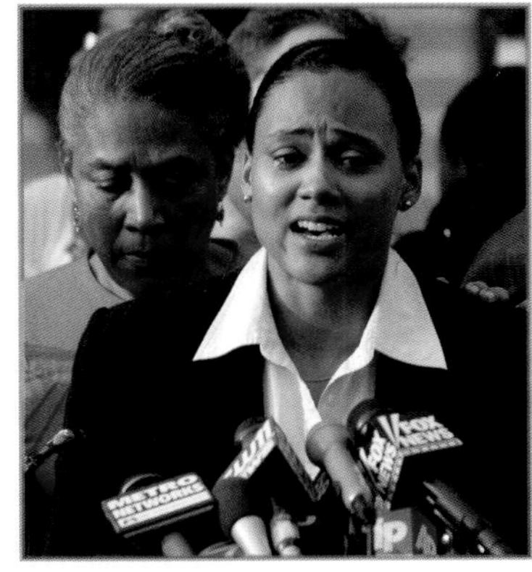

[10] Marion Jones, her mother behind her, speaks to the media outside the federal court after pleading guilty.

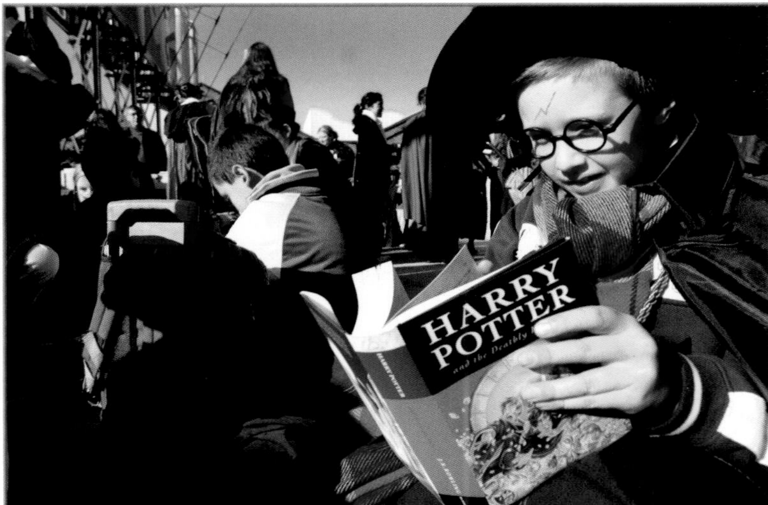

[5] A young Harry Potter fan in a wizard's hat and cloak starts to devour the last book in the series early on its publication day in Sydney, Australia.

[8] Nicolas Sarkozy receives the embrace of an elegant supporter as he arrives to cast his vote in the second round of the French presidential election.

[11] A photo taken on a mobile phone of Benazir Bhutto electioneering in Rawalpindi seconds before she is shot in the back of the neck.

 [8]

May 6, 2007
Nicolas Sarkozy is elected president of France.

June 28, 2007
The **U.S. Supreme Court** rejects plans by Seattle, Washington, and Louisville, Kentucky, to integrate their public schools, with Chief Justice John Roberts arguing "The way to stop discrimination on the basis of race is to stop discriminating on the basis of race."

July 24, 2007
Six medical workers are released after being held prisoner in **Libya** for more than eight years on charges that they deliberately infected hundreds of children with the AIDS virus. Libya reached an agreement with the European Union that allowed them to be released.

 [9]

August 2007
The **Women's British Open** is held on the Old Course at St. Andrews, Scotland, for the first time. The tournament also marks the first time that women are allowed to play at the club, one of the world's oldest and most prestigious.

 [10]

October 2007
Marion Jones, the track athlete, admits to lying about her use of performance-enhancing drugs. This revelation will result in her losing the five gold medals she won at the Sydney Olympics in 2000.

 [11]

December, 2007
Pakistan's former primer minister **Benazir Bhutto** is assassinated at an election rally in Rawalpindi, shortly after her return to the country from exile.

The new Hayden Planetarium at the American Museum of Natural History in New York, 2000.

INDEX

C

D

E

F

G

J

K

L

M

N

O

P

Q

R

S

T

U

V

W

X

Y

T

PHOTO CREDITS

All images courtesy of Getty Images including the following which have additional attributions:

Agence France Presse: 9, 31(4), 132(8), 180(7), 184(1), 187(10), 188(7), 209(4), 213(6), 220(3), 228(Spotlight), 228(2), 232(3), 236(3), 247(8), 305(8), 306(1), 308(6), 310(2), 311(6 & 9), 312(1 & 2), 314(3), 315(9), 322(5), 325(4), 327(4), 329(5), 330(5), 331(6), 338(4), 340(2), 341(3), 347(12), 350(1), 353(5), 361(4), 365(2), 367(11), 370(Spotlight), 374(3 & 7), 376(4), 382(Spotlight), 385(9), 386(3 & 6), 388(8), 396(4), 398(5), 399(3), 400(1 & 3), 406(3 & 6), 407(8), 408(1), 409(8), 412(7), 413(10), 414(1), 417(4), 418(Spotlight), 419(4 & 5), 420(7), 421(2), 423(4 & 9), 424(2), 427(2), 428(1 & 3), 430(7), 432(7), 433(11), 434(3), 435(8), 438(7), 439(3), 440(4 & 5), 443(10), 444(9), 446(2), 449(4), 452(2), 453(4), 454(1, 5, 8 & 9), 455(7,10 &11), 456(2 & 5), 459(4), 460(6, 7 & 8), 461(4, 5 & Spotlight), 464(1), 465(9), 467(1, 2 & 7), 470(5 & Spotlight), 471(6, 7 & 8), 472(2,5,6 & 7), 473(8,9 &10), 474(1,2,4 & 7), 475(5,6 &10), 476(4,5 &Spotlight), 477(6,7, & 8), 478(3,6,7 & 9), 479(4 & Spotlight), 480(2 & 3), 481(1,5,6, & Spotlight), 482(2 & 4), 483(5,8,9 & 10), 484(5 & 10), 485(3,7, & Spotlight), 486(1,4,5 & Spotlight), 487(3 & 6), 488(2,5 & Spotlight), 489(3,7,8 & 9), 490(4 & 5), 491(8,9 & 10), 492(1 & 3), 493(4,6 & Spotlight), 494(1,3 & 8), 495(5,6 & 7), 496(1,9 & 10), 497(4,5,6 & 7), 498(3,5 & 6), 499(7 & 8), 501(3 & 7), 502(1,2 & 7), 503(5 & 9), 506(1), 508(2 & 6), 509(9), 510(1,2 & 3), 511(10), 513(1,2 & 7), 514(1), 515(8), 516(3 & 5), 517(8), 518(2,3 & 8), 519(6), 520(3 & 8), 521(4 & 5), 522(2,3,5 & Spotlight), 523(9), 524(Spotlight), 526(1,3 & 6), 527(8 &9), 528(2,3,5 & 7), 529(6,8,10,11 & 12), 530(4 & 5), 531(8), 532(7 & 9); **American Stock:** 85(9), 122(1), 144(1),148(2), 151(4), 173(4), 177(Spotlight), 181(4), 261(8); **Anne Frank House, Amsterdam:** 290(3); **Augusta National:** 495(11); **Alan Band:** 412(5); **B.Bennett:** 164(1), 210(8), 304(6); **Blank Archives:** 249(10), 306(4), 346(2), 393(8), 425(9); **Alex Bowie:** 420(9); **Tim Boyle:** 431(9); **Bridgeman Art Library:** 26(2)/Musee de l'Air, Bourg-en-Bresse, France; 52(1)/Ashmolean Museum, University of Oxford, UK; 57(Spotlight) Musee d'Orsay, Paris; 76(3)/Private Collection; 89(7)/Museu Calouste Gulbenkian,Lisbon,Portugal; 89(8)/Private Collection; 92(2)/Private Collection; 128(2)/Musee Marmottan, Paris; 167(2)/Musee Marmottan, Paris; 176(8)/Osterreichische Galerie Belvedere, Vienna; 209(5)/Haags Gemeentemuseum, The Hague, Netherlands; 214(1)/Sergei Vasil'evich Chekhonin/Stapleton Collection, London; 222(Spotlight)/Tretyakov Gallery,Moscow; 229(3)/British Museum,London; **CBS Photo Archive:** 320(7), 332(3), 336(6), 344(1), 348(2), 371(1), 446(7), 506(4); **CNN:** 466(6), 512(3), 516(1); **John Cohen:** 343(3); **Consolidated News:** 380(6), 392(4), 414(3), 420(1), 426(3); **DAJ:** 502(3); **de Agostini:** 255(6); **Francis Dean:** 506(5); **Georges De Keerle:** 500(1); **Diamond Images:** 363(2); **Richard Ellis:** 499(9); **Daniel Farson:** 330(3); **David Fenton:** 392(1), 396(2), 403(5); **John Filo:** 399(7); **Fine Art Photographic:** 207(5); **Focus on Sport:** 382(8); **Frank Driggs Collection:** 150(1), 236(11), 238(1), 249(9), 333(6); **George Eastman House:** 22(5), 38(2),43(5), 46(4), 54(2), 78(Spotlight), 79(3), 83(3),116(6), 122(3), 158(5),161(5),172(5), 180(1),182(1), 182(Spotlight), 188(2); **John Jonas Gruen:** 346(7); **Ernst Haas:** 6, 356; **Hirz:** 147(4), 241(6); **Historic Photo Archive:** 115(2); **isifa:** 367(6); **Imagno:** 20(7), 30(1), 37(9), 48(1), 64(2), 68(2), 74(6), 79(9), 80(2), 84(4), 86(2), 87(9), 91(4), 93(4), 101(5), 106(5), 118(4), 119(8), 131(10), 135(2), 143(4), 147(Spotlight), 147(Spotlight), 152(1), 165(10), 172(1), 175(3), 176(7), 178(4), 182(4), 183(8), 186(1), 202(1), 211(11), 223(5), 233(9), 235(3), 256(Spotlight), 257(7), 262(7), 262(Spotlight), 263(6), 265(8), 276(2), 307(7), 319(3), 393(9), 404(8); **John Kobal Foundation:** 7,145(Spotlight), 218; **Tom Keller:** 427(10); **David Hume Kennerly:** 429(Spotlight), 441(9); **V. Kinelovsky:** 295(4); **Laski Diffusion:** 288(4); **Gene Lester:** 291(1); **David Levenson:** 446(1); **Liaison:** 431(6), 438(9), 445(4), 447(8),450(7), 452(6 & 7), 454(2), 458(5 & 6), 461(9),462(6 & 9), 464(Spotlight), 465(7), 466(5 & Spotlight), 470(2), 475(11), 479(8), 485(9), 498(1), 501(Spotlight), 502(8), 507(8), 511(6); **Library of Congress:** 118(9), 137(4); **Victor Malafronte:** 495(4); **Joe McNally:** 446(6), 463(11); **Metronome:** 277(8); **MLB/National Baseball Hall of Fame:** 86(5), 172(6), 214(5), 227(5); **Ronald C.Modra:** 424(8), 453(5); **Leon Morris:** 462(2); **Tim Mosenfelder:** 463(7), 488(1); **Museum of the City of New York:** 32(3), 92(1), 93(6), 100(2), 124(7), 126(2),130(2), 147(5),160(8), 164(8), 190(5), 268(6); **NASA/Science Faction:** endpapers; **NBAE:** 451(12); **NFL/Pro Football Hall of Fame:** 260(6); **National Geographic Society:** 183(2), 200(1), 419(3), 421(5), 438(6), 465(5); **Newsmakers:** 509(4); **New York Times:** 210(7), 256(6), 385(5), 314(6), 332(7), 347(3), 366(9), 377(6),390(1); **Nordic Photos:** 410(2); **Terry O'Neill:** 404(4); **OnlineUSA:** 454(10); **Franco Origlia:** 471(4); **Paramount Pictures:** 405(2); **Scott Peterson:** 531(6); **John Pineda:** 374(5); **Popperfoto:** 7, 123,156(1), 159(4), 167(6), 173(10),178(3)/Bob Thomas, 191(Spotlight), 275(8), 279(7), 293(8), 303(6), 353(9), 402(1), 406(1), 410(8), 442(6); **Steve Pyke:** 478(2),487(8); **RDA:** 239(10), 290(2); **Red Cover:** 250(1); **Robert Riger:** 351(7), 376(9), 425(11), 438(5); **Robert Harding:** 225(10); **Roger Viollet:** 15(10), 17(3), 19(5), 26(6), 41(4), 43(9), 61(Spotlight), 63(3), 71(7), 74(Spotlight), 104(3), 108(1), 108(6), 110(5), 117(8), 120(Spotlight), 127(4), 138(2), 140(9), 143(8), 149(11), 160(1), 164(7), 168(8), 171(5), 172(8), 173(3), 187(8 & 9), 195(5 & 7), 198(3), 207(4), 212(9), 217(Spotlight), 227(6), 248(1), 309(4), 325(5), 364(1), 421(3), 441(2); **Paul Rogers:** 500(5); **George Rose:** 433(3); **Eric Ryan:** 445(6); **Herb Scharfman:** 408(4), 413(9): **Science Faction:** 404(5), 491(3); **Sean Sexton:** 88(Spotlight), 98(3), 111(7), 163(6), 216(2), 223(11); **Slava Katamidze Collection:** 224(1); **Chris Smith:** 460(2); **Sean Smith:** 521(Spotlight); **Paul Souders:** 489(6); **Stock Montage:** 71(5), 91(6), 109(11), 112(5), 133(10), 187(11); **Tom Stoddart:** 7, 436, 457(Spotlight), 466(Spotlight), 468, 470(1); **Tim Graham Photo Library:** 109(3), 434(5), 443(9), 493(5), 513(6); **Time and Life Pictures:** 7,13(1), 14(4 & 7), 15(8 & 9), 20(1), 21(6), 24(4), 27(4), 30(2), 37(8), 40(6), 41(8), 42(6), 44(8), 47(8), 50 (3), 53(Spotlight), 56(1 & 6), 57(8), 58(3 & 5), 60(3 & 6), 63(1 & 7), 64(5), 72(7), 73(5), 75(8 & 9), 76(1), 85(8), 86(7), 87(3), 100(8), 101(13), 107(10), 111(Spotlight), 113(8), 115(4), 116(3), 118(5), 119(3 & 10), 121(3), 122(4), 126(6), 130(3), 131(6), 134(3), 136(2), 137(3), 138(1 & 4), 139(8), 140(3), 149(4), 151(5), 154(6), 155(10), 156(2), 156(3), 160(2, 7 & 9), 161(3), 162(1,7 & 8), 166(Spotlights), 170(1 & 6), 172(7), 176(2), 178(5), 179(7), 180(6), 181(3 & 11), 183(9), 185,190(1 & 3), 193(10), 195(1), 196(1), 199(4 & Spotlight), 200(9), 202(3,5 & 8), 204(3), 205(9), 206(3), 210(2,6 & 9), 212(8), 213(4), 215(2), 222(1), 226(10), 227(Spotlight), 229(4 & 8), 231(6), 236(1,7 & 9), 237(8).240(2 & Spotlight), 242(6 & Spotlight), 243(4,8,9 & 10), 246(2), 247(6), 250(5), 254(2 & Spotlight), 255(7), 257(4), 258(6 & 7), 259(5), 260(5), 263(5 & 9), 264(5), 265(3), 268(1,7 & 7), 269(12), 270(6), 271(2), 273(4 & Spotlight), 274(5), 275(10), 276(1), 278(6), 279(8), 280(1 & Spotlight), 282(2), 283(6,8 & 10), 284(3), 285(9), 286(5), 289(8), 291(9 & 10), 292(2 & 6), 293(4), 294(2 & 8), 295(7 & 9), 296(1,5 & 7), 297(Spotlight), 298(1 & 9), 299(5 & 12), 300(Spotlight), 301(6), 302(2 & 8), 303(3,7 & 9), 305(2,3,4 & 9), 306(3), 307(6), 308(3), 309(8), 310(5), 311(1,3,7 & 8), 312(5), 313(3 & Spotlight), 314(1 & 2), 315(4 & 10), 316(2), 318(8 & 9), 319(4,5 & 7), 320(1,2 & Spotlight), 321(3,5 & 8), 322(6 & 7), 323(3,4 & 9), 324(1 & 8), 325(Spotlight), 326(2,3 & 6), 327(8,9 & Spotlight), 328(1), 329(6), 330(4), 331(7 & Spotlight), 332(4,8 & 9), 333(5 & 11), 334(1,2 & 3), 336(3,4 & 5), 337(7), 338(3 & 7), 339(6 & 9), 341(Spotlight), 342(1,6 & 7), 343(4 & 5), 344(2 & 3), 345(4,5 & Spotlight), 346(8,10 & 11), 347(5,6 & 13), 348(1,5 & 7), 349(9), 351(6), 352(1,2,3,8 & 10), 353(6,7 & 11), 354(2 & 7), 355(3 & 5), 358(2 &4), 359(Spotlight), 360(1,3,7 &8), 361(9 & 10), 362(1 & 7), 363(4,8 & 9), 364(5 & Spotlight), 366(3,4 & 10), 367(12), 368(3 & 6), 369(7 & Spotlights), 370(2,3 & Spotlight), 372(6), 373(3 & 8), 374(6), 376(1), 377(3), 378(2), 379(4 & 7), 380(2), 381(8), 383(3 & 6), 386(2), 387(1,5 & 9), 388(1,2,7 &9), 389(3,4 &5), 390(4 & 7), 391(2,8 & 9), 393(3 & Spotlight), 396(5), 397(Spotlight), 398(2), 400(3 & 6), 402(2,3 & 6), 403(4), 405(3 & Spotlight), 406(4 & 7), 410(1), 411(5), 413(Spotlight), 415(10), 417(3 & 8), 419(7 & 8), 420(6 & 8), 422(2), 423(8), 425(5), 428(7), 430(1), 431(2), 432(1 & 8), 433(9), 434(4), 439(8), 440(1), 441(7 & 8), 442(5), 443(3), 444(1), 445(7), 446(3), 447(4), 448(1,6 & 7), 449(3 & Spotlight), 450(1,2 & 9), 451(4,5 & 6), 452(8), 453(3 & 10), 456(1,3,4 & 6), 458(1 & 2), 459(3,8,9 & 10), 460(3), 462(3 & 8), 463(5,6 & 10), 464(3), 465(6, 8 & 10)), 467(4,8 & 9), 471(3 & 9), 473(3 & 4), 475(8 & 12), 476(2), 477(1), 479(10), 480(7 & 10), 481(8), 482(1 & 3), 483(Spotlight), 487(2 & 10), 488(4), 492(7), 494(2 & 9), 496(8), 497(3), 509(8);534; **Transcendental Graphics:** 7, 58(1), 71(8), 118(1), 144(7), 153, 163(12), 216(4), 220(2), 279(5), 286(2); **Vintage Images:** 122(2); **Ami Vitale:** 503(6); **Armin T. Wegner:** 203(Spotlight), 515(3); **Natasja Weitsz:** 531(9); **WireImage:** 393(3); **Georgi Zelma:** 293(Spotlight).